WAYNE WILLE
3-19-13

21st Century Land Development Code

21st Century Land Development Code

Robert H. Freilich and S. Mark White

with

Kate F. Murray

AMERICAN PLANNING ASSOCIATION
Chicago, Illinois
Washington, D.C.

Copyright 2008 by the American Planning Association
122 S. Michigan Ave., Suite 1600, Chicago, IL 60603

ISBN (paperback): 1-932364-17-x and 978-1-932364-17-0
ISBN (hardcover): 1-932364-18-8 and 978-1-932364-18-7
Library of Congress Control Number: 2007936593
Printed in the United States of America
All rights reserved

Copyediting, interior design and layout, and CD-ROM preparation by Joanne Shwed, Backspace Ink

Cover by Michael Sonnenfeld

Contents

Acknowledgements	xv
List of Figures	xvii
List of Tables	xix
Acronyms and Abbreviations	xxiii

Introduction 1
The Substantive Law of Planning; Zoning;
    Subdivision Regulation; State, Regional, and
    Federal Controls; Growth Management; Smart
    Growth; Environmental Review; Sustainability;
    and New Urbanism That Underlies This Land
    Development Code 1
Historical Background 1
Advent of Planning 2
Nuisance and Restrictive Covenants 2
Zoning 3
State, Regional, and Federal Controls 3
Growth Management and Smart Growth 4
Subdivision Regulations 5
New Urbanism 8
Sustainability 13
Conclusion 14
The Land Development Code:
    Instructions for Use 14
Unified Development Ordinance 14
Objectives of the Land Development Code 14
What Is a Code? 15
Certainty 16
Process 16
Incentives, Conditions, and Overlays 16
Multijurisdictional and Intergovernmental
    Approaches 16
Nonbinding Options 16
Binding Options 17
Content of the Land Development Code 17

1. General Provisions 31
1.0 Purpose and Findings 31
1.1 Citation 32
1.2 Authority 32
1.3 Applicability 32
1.4 Consistency with Comprehensive Plan 32
1.5 Coordination with Other Regulations 32
    1.5.1 Generally 32
    1.5.2 Zoning 32
    1.5.3 Rules of Construction 32
1.6 Development Approvals 32
Commentary 33

2. Use Patterns 39
2.0 Purpose and Findings 39
2.1 Applicability 39
2.2 Conservation Subdivision 39
    2.2.1 Applicability 40
    2.2.2 Processing Procedures 40
    2.2.3 Size and Location of Site 40
    2.2.4 Uses 41
    2.2.5 Lot and Block Design 41
    2.2.6 Transportation 41
    2.2.7 Stormwater Management 42
    2.2.8 Utilities 42
    2.2.9 Conservation Areas 42
    2.2.10 Environmental Protection 43
    2.2.11 Landscaping and Screening 43
    2.2.12 Parking 43
2.3 Neighborhood Center 43
    2.3.1 Applicability 43
    2.3.2 Processing Procedures 43
    2.3.3 Size and Location of Site 43
    2.3.4 Uses and Dimensional Standards 44
    2.3.5 Lot Layout 44
    2.3.6 Parks and Open Space 44
    2.3.7 Landscaping and Screening 44
    2.3.8 Parking 44
    2.3.9 Open Space 44
2.4 Campus 45
    2.4.1 Applicability 45
    2.4.2 Processing Procedures 45
    2.4.3 Size and Location of Site 45
    2.4.4 Uses 45
    2.4.5 Lot Layout 45

- 2.4.6 Building Design ... 46
- 2.4.7 Street Design and Transportation ... 46
- 2.4.8 Parks and Open Space ... 46
- 2.4.9 Landscaping and Screening ... 46
- 2.4.10 Parking ... 46
- 2.5 Commercial Retrofit ... 46
  - 2.5.1 Applicability ... 47
  - 2.5.2 Processing Procedures ... 47
  - 2.5.3 Site Design and Building Disposition ... 47
  - 2.5.4 Adequate Public Facilities ... 47
  - 2.5.5 Lot Layout ... 47
  - 2.5.6 Transportation ... 47
  - 2.5.7 Stormwater Management ... 47
  - 2.5.8 Utilities ... 48
  - 2.5.9 Parks and Open Space ... 48
  - 2.5.10 Environmental Protection ... 48
  - 2.5.11 Landscaping, Screening, and Tree Preservation ... 48
  - 2.5.12 Parking ... 48
- 2.6 Traditional Neighborhood Development ... 48
  - 2.6.1 Applicability ... 48
  - 2.6.2 Processing Procedures ... 49
  - 2.6.3 Size and Location of Site ... 49
  - 2.6.4 Uses and Density ... 49
  - 2.6.5 Adequate Public Facilities ... 50
  - 2.6.6 Lot Arrangement ... 50
  - 2.6.7 Building Design ... 51
  - 2.6.8 Transportation ... 51
  - 2.6.9 Parks and Open Space ... 51
  - 2.6.10 Landscaping and Screening ... 52
  - 2.6.11 Parking ... 52
- 2.7 Transit-oriented Development ... 52
  - 2.7.1 Applicability ... 52
  - 2.7.2 Processing Procedures ... 52
  - 2.7.3 Size and Location of Site ... 52
  - 2.7.4 Uses and Density ... 53
  - 2.7.5 Lot Arrangement and Dimensions ... 53
  - 2.7.6 Building Design ... 53
  - 2.7.7 Adequate Public Facilities ... 54
  - 2.7.8 Transportation ... 54
  - 2.7.9 Parks and Open Space ... 54
  - 2.7.10 Environmental Protection ... 54
  - 2.7.11 Landscaping and Screening ... 54
  - 2.7.12 Parking ... 54

Commentary ... 55

3. Zoning ... 67
3.0 Purpose and Findings ... 67

Division 1: Introduction ... 67
- 3.1 General Requirements ... 68
- 3.2 Establishment of Districts ... 68
  - 3.2.1 Tier System ... 68
  - 3.2.2 Base Zoning Districts ... 69
  - 3.2.3 Overlay Zoning Districts ... 69
  - 3.2.4 Conditional Zoning Districts ... 69
  - 3.2.5 Floating Zones ... 69
  - 3.2.6 Zoning Districts (Additional) ... 69
- 3.3 Official Zoning Map ... 69
- 3.4 Zoning District Boundaries ... 69
- 3.5 Newly Annexed Territory ... 70
  - 3.5.1 Master Planned Developments ... 70
  - 3.5.2 Development Agreements ... 70
  - 3.5.3 Specific Plan ... 70

Division 2: Base Zoning Districts ... 70
- 3.10 Generally ... 70
- 3.11 Use Regulations ... 70
  - 3.11.1 Generally ... 70
  - 3.11.2 Uses Not Mentioned ... 70
  - 3.11.3 Uses Preempted By State Statute ... 70
  - 3.11.4 Interpretation—Materially Similar Uses ... 70
- 3.12 Dimensional Regulations ... 81
- 3.13 "RP" (Resource Protection) ... 81
  - 3.13.1 Permitted Uses ... 81
  - 3.13.2 Dimensional Standards ... 81
- 3.14 "RE" (Residential Estate) ... 81
  - 3.14.1 Permitted Uses ... 82
  - 3.14.2 Dimensional Standards ... 82
- 3.15 "NS" (Neighborhood Suburban) ... 82
  - 3.15.1 Permitted Uses ... 82
  - 3.15.2 Dimensional Standards ... 82
- 3.16 "NU" (Neighborhood Urban) ... 82
  - 3.16.1 Permitted Uses ... 83
  - 3.16.2 Dimensional Standards ... 83
- 3.17 "O" (Office) ... 83
  - 3.17.1 Permitted Uses ... 84
  - 3.17.2 Dimensional Standards ... 84
  - 3.17.3 Scale ... 84
  - 3.17.4 Outdoor Display/Sales ... 84
  - 3.17.5 Design ... 84
- 3.18 "CN" (Commercial Neighborhood) ... 84
  - 3.18.1 Permitted Uses ... 85
  - 3.18.2 Dimensional Standards ... 85
  - 3.18.3 Scale ... 85
  - 3.18.4 Design ... 85
  - 3.18.5 Service Entrances/Service Yards ... 85
- 3.19 "CG" (Commercial General) ... 85
  - 3.19.1 Permitted Uses ... 86
  - 3.19.2 Dimensional Standards ... 86
  - 3.19.3 Scale ... 86
  - 3.19.4 Outdoor Storage or Display ... 86
- 3.20 "CL" (Commercial Large-Scale) ... 86
  - 3.20.1 Permitted Uses ... 87
  - 3.20.2 Dimensional Standards ... 87
  - 3.20.3 Scale ... 87
  - 3.20.4 Outdoor Storage or Display ... 87
- 3.21 "D" (Downtown) ... 87
  - 3.21.1 Permitted Uses ... 88
  - 3.21.2 Dimensional Standards ... 88
  - 3.21.3 Design ... 88
- 3.22 "IL" (Industrial Light) ... 88
  - 3.22.1 Permitted Uses ... 88

3.22.2 Dimensional Standards 88
3.22.3 General Provisions 88
3.23 "IH" (Industrial Heavy) 88
   3.23.1 Permitted Uses 89
   3.23.2 Dimensional Standards 89
   3.23.3 General Provisions 89
3.24 "PD" (Planned Development) 89
   3.24.1 Evaluation Criteria 90
   3.24.2 Minimum Size 90
   3.24.3 Permitted Uses and Density 90
   3.24.4 Height and Yard Requirements 90
   3.24.5 Infrastructure Requirements 91
   3.24.6 Parks/Open Space 91
   3.24.7 Parking Requirements 91
   3.24.8 Common Areas and Facilities 91
   3.24.9 Master Site Plan 92
3.25 "MX" (Mixed Use) 92
   3.25.1 Locational Criteria 92
   3.25.2 Use Regulations 92
   3.25.3 Lot and Building Specifications 92

Division 3: Overlay Zoning Districts 92
3.40 "NP" (Neighborhood Preservation) 92
   3.40.1 Designation Criteria 93
   3.40.2 Zoning Authority 93
   3.40.3 Neighborhood Preservation District 93
   3.40.4 Designation Procedures 93
   3.40.5 Design Standards 93
3.41 "AO" (Airport Overlay) 94
   3.41.1 Airport Zones Established and Defined 94
   3.41.2 Height Limitations 94
   3.41.3 Use Restrictions 94
   3.41.4 Regulations to Be Considered
      in Review of Zoning Development
      Approval Applications 94
   3.41.5 Conditions on Variances 94
   3.41.6 Application of Regulations to
      Preexisting Structures and Uses 94
   3.41.7 Exemption of Utility Structures 96

Division 4: Flexible Zoning 96
3.50 Density Bonus 96
   3.50.1 Applicability 96
   3.50.2 Bonus Criteria 96
3.51 Transfer of Development Rights 97
   3.51.1 Sending Areas Created 97
   3.51.2 Receiving Districts Designated 99
   3.51.3 Timing 99
   3.51.4 Right-of-Way Dedication 99

Commentary 100

4. Procedures 119
4.0 Purpose and Findings 119

Division 1: General 119
4.1 Procedural Requirements 119
   4.1.1 Generally 119
   4.1.2 Appeals 119
4.2 Categories of Development Approvals 120
   4.2.1 Legislative Development Approvals 120
   4.2.2 Quasi-judicial Development Approval 120
   4.2.3 Ministerial Development Approvals 120
4.3 Completeness Review 120
   4.3.1 Preapplication Conference 121
   4.3.2 Application Materials 121
   4.3.3 Review Procedures 121
   4.3.4 Jurisdiction 121
   4.3.5 Time Limits by Complete Application 121
   4.3.6 Review by [PLANNING OFFICIAL] 121
   4.3.7 Time Limits 121
   4.3.8 Limitation on Further
      Information Requests 122
   4.3.9 Traffic Impact Reports or Analyses 122
4.4 Notice Provisions 126
   4.4.1 Generally 126
   4.4.2 Contents of Notice 126
   4.4.3 Action to Be Consistent with Notice 126
   4.4.4 Minor Amendments
      Not Requiring Renotification 126
4.5 Public Hearing 127
   4.5.1 Applicability 127
   4.5.2 Meetings 127
   4.5.3 Records 127
   4.5.4 Legislative Body 127

Division 2: Quasi-judicial and Legislative Approvals 127
4.6 Quasi-judicial Public Hearings 127
   4.6.1 Generally 127
   4.6.2 Conduct of Hearing 127
   4.6.3 Hearing Officer 128
4.7 Legislative Hearings 128
   4.7.1 Generally 128
   4.7.2 Conduct of Hearing 128
   4.7.3 Record of Proceedings 128
   4.7.4 Appeals 128
4.8 Revocation of a
   Development Approval 128
   4.8.1 Initiation 128
   4.8.2 Grounds for Revocation 128
   4.8.3 Notice and Public Hearing 129
   4.8.4 Decision and Notice 129
   4.8.5 Appeals 129
   4.8.6 Right Cumulative 129
4.9 Neighborhood Registration 129
   4.9.1 Applicability 129
   4.9.2 Contents 129
   4.9.3 Effect of Neighborhood Registry 129
4.10 Neighborhood Participation Meeting 129
   4.10.1 Applicability 130
   4.10.2 Recommended Procedures 130

Division 3: Ministerial Development Approvals 131
4.11 Development Approval 131
4.12 Grading and Land Disturbance 131

- 4.12.1 Grading Development Approval ... 131
- 4.12.2 Land Disturbance Activity ... 131
- 4.13 Zoning Certificates ... 131
  - 4.13.1 Initiation ... 131
  - 4.13.2 Completeness Review ... 131
  - 4.13.3 Decision ... 131
  - 4.13.4 Approval Criteria ... 131
  - 4.13.5 Amendments ... 131
  - 4.13.6 Scope of Approval ... 131
  - 4.13.7 Recording Procedures ... 131
- 4.14 Certificate of Occupancy ... 132
  - 4.14.1 Requirement ... 132
  - 4.14.2 Records ... 132

Division 4: Zoning Procedures ... 132
- 4.20 Plans and Plan Amendments ... 132
  - 4.20.1 Applicability ... 132
  - 4.20.2 Initiation ... 132
  - 4.20.3 Completeness Review ... 133
  - 4.20.4 Decision ... 133
  - 4.20.5 Criteria ... 133
  - 4.20.6 Scope of Approval ... 133
- 4.21 Code Amendments ... 133
  - 4.21.1 Applicability ... 133
  - 4.21.2 Initiation ... 133
  - 4.21.3 Completeness Review ... 133
  - 4.21.4 Decision ... 133
  - 4.21.5 Approval Criteria ... 134
  - 4.21.6 Subsequent Applications ... 134
  - 4.21.7 Amendments ... 135
  - 4.21.8 Scope of Approval ... 135
  - 4.21.9 Recording Procedures ... 135
- 4.22 Conditional Zoning ... 135
  - 4.22.1 Applicability ... 135
  - 4.22.2 Initiation ... 135
  - 4.22.3 Completeness Review ... 135
  - 4.22.4 Decision ... 135
  - 4.22.5 Criteria ... 135
  - 4.22.6 Subsequent Applications ... 136
  - 4.22.7 Amendments ... 136
  - 4.22.8 Scope of Approval ... 136
  - 4.22.9 Recording Procedures ... 137
- 4.23 Conditional Use Permits ... 137
  - 4.23.1 Conditional Applicability ... 137
  - 4.23.2 Initiation ... 137
  - 4.23.3 Completeness Review ... 137
  - 4.23.4 Approval ... 138
  - 4.23.5 Approval Criteria ... 138
  - 4.23.6 Subsequent Applications ... 138
  - 4.23.7 Amendments ... 139
  - 4.23.8 Scope of Approval ... 139
  - 4.23.9 Recording Procedures ... 139
- 4.24 Site Plans ... 140
  - 4.24.1 Applicability ... 140
  - 4.24.2 Initiation ... 140
  - 4.24.3 Completeness Review ... 140
  - 4.24.4 Decision ... 140
  - 4.24.5 Appeal ... 140
  - 4.24.6 Approval Criteria ... 140
  - 4.24.7 Subsequent Applications ... 140
  - 4.24.8 Amendments ... 140
  - 4.24.9 Scope of Approval ... 141
  - 4.24.10 Recording Procedures ... 141

Division 5: Subdivisions ... 141
- 4.30 Applicability and General Rules ... 141
  - 4.30.1 Subdivisions Subject to This Section ... 141
  - 4.30.2 Exemptions ... 142
  - 4.30.3 Recordation of Unapproved Plat Prohibited ... 142
  - 4.30.4 Sale or Lease ... 142
  - 4.30.5 Development Approval ... 142
- 4.31 Classification of Subdivisions ... 142
- 4.32 Sketch Plat Procedures ... 142
- 4.33 Preliminary Plat Procedures ... 143
  - 4.33.1 Applicability ... 143
  - 4.33.2 Initiation ... 143
  - 4.33.3 Completeness Review for Plat Approval ... 143
  - 4.33.4 Decision ... 143
  - 4.33.5 Criteria ... 143
  - 4.33.6 Subsequent Applications ... 144
  - 4.33.7 Amendments ... 144
  - 4.33.8 Major Amendments ... 145
  - 4.33.9 Scope of Approval ... 145
  - 4.33.10 Recording Procedures ... 145
- 4.34 Final Plat Procedures ... 145
  - 4.34.1 Applicability ... 145
  - 4.34.2 Initiation ... 145
  - 4.34.3 Completeness Review for Plat Approval ... 145
  - 4.34.4 Decision ... 145
  - 4.34.5 Criteria ... 146
  - 4.34.6 Subsequent Applications ... 146
  - 4.34.7 Amendments ... 146
  - 4.34.8 Scope of Approval ... 146
  - 4.34.9 Recording Procedures ... 147
- 4.35 Construction Plans ... 147
  - 4.35.1 Applicability ... 147
  - 4.35.2 Public Agency Reviews ... 147
  - 4.35.3 Timing of Improvements ... 147
  - 4.35.4 Modification of Construction Plans ... 147
  - 4.35.5 As-Built Drawings ... 147
  - 4.35.6 Inspection and Acceptance of Improvements ... 148
- 4.36 Subdivision Improvement Agreements ... 149
  - 4.36.1 Applicability ... 149
  - 4.36.2 Covenants to Run with the Land ... 149
  - 4.36.3 Base Course to Be Installed ... 149
  - 4.36.4 Performance Security ... 149
  - 4.36.5 Type of Security ... 149
  - 4.36.6 Guarantees ... 150
  - 4.36.7 Reimbursement ... 150
  - 4.36.8 Maintenance Bond ... 150
  - 4.36.9 Temporary Improvements ... 150
- 4.37 Subdivision Variances ... 150

4.37.1 Applicability 150
4.37.2 Initiation 150
4.37.3 Completeness Review 150
4.37.4 Decision 150
4.37.5 Approval Criteria 151
4.38 Dedication (Acceptance) 151
4.39 Plat Vacation 151
 4.39.1 Applicability 151
 4.39.2 Initiation 151
 4.39.3 Completeness Review 151
 4.39.4 Decision 151
 4.39.5 Approval Criteria 151
 4.39.6 Scope of Approval 151
 4.39.7 Recording Procedures 151
4.40 Plats (Amending) 151
 4.40.1 Applicability 152
 4.40.2 Initiation 152
 4.40.3 Completeness Review 152
 4.40.4 Decision 152
 4.40.5 Approval Criteria 152
 4.40.6 Recording Procedures 152

Division 6: Variances and Appeals 152
4.51 Generally 152
 4.51.1 Powers and Duties of Hearing Officer 152
 4.51.2 Stay of Development Approvals 153
4.52 Appeals to Hearing Officer 153
 4.52.1 Applicability 153
 4.52.2 Initiation 153
 4.52.3 Stay of Proceedings 153
 4.52.4 Decision 153
 4.52.5 Appeals Involving Constitutional or Statutory Claims 153
4.53 Variances 154
 4.53.1 Applicability 154
 4.53.2 Initiation 154
 4.53.3 Decision 154
 4.53.4 Approval Criteria 155

Division 7: Miscellaneous Development Orders 155
4.55 Development Agreements 155
 4.55.1 Applicability 155
 4.55.2 Criteria for Entering into Development Agreements 155
 4.55.3 Initiation 156
 4.55.4 Contents of Development Agreement 156
 4.55.5 Completeness Review 156
 4.55.6 Decision 157
 4.55.7 Recordation 157
 4.55.8 Coordination of Development Agreement Application with Other Discretionary Approvals 157
 4.55.9 Existing and Subsequently Adopted Rules, Regulations, Ordinances, Laws, and Policies 158
 4.55.10 Subsequently Adopted State and Federal Laws 158

 4.55.11 Periodic Review, Termination, or Modification 158
 4.55.12 Amendment or Cancellation of Agreement 158
 4.55.13 Annexation 158
 4.55.14 Enforcement 158

Division 8: Enforcement, Violations, and Penalties 159
4.61 Types of Violations 159
4.62 Civil Enforcement 159
 4.62.1 Enforcement Actions 159
 4.62.2 Penalties 159
4.63 Violation of Conditions 159
 4.63.1 Penalty 159
 4.63.2 Revocation of Development Approval 159
 4.63.3 Civil Action 159
4.64 Completion of Improvements 159
 4.64.1 Liability 159
 4.64.2 Remedy 159
 4.64.3 Exemptions 160

Commentary 161

5. Development Standards 177

Division 1: Generally 177
5.1 Applicability 177
5.2 Administrative Exceptions 177
 5.2.1 Applicability 177
 5.2.2 Standards for Administrative Exceptions 177
5.3 Variances 177
5.4 Standard Specifications 177
 5.4.1 Generally 177
 5.4.2 Sampling and Testing 177
5.5 Americans with Disabilities Act 178
 5.5.1 Infrastructure 178
 5.5.2 Multifamily Housing 178
5.6 Operation and Maintenance 178
 5.6.1 Dedication of Land 178
 5.6.2 Homeowners' Association 178
 5.6.3 Condominiums 179
 5.6.4 Dedication of Easements 179
 5.6.5 Transfer of Easements 179
 5.6.6 Improvement or Special Assessment Districts 179

Division 2: Design Standards 179
5.10 Lots 179
 5.10.1 Buildings to Be on a Lot 179
 5.10.2 Compliance with Zoning District Regulations 179
 5.10.3 Frontage 179
 5.10.4 Front and Side Setbacks 180
 5.10.5 Corner Lots 180
 5.10.6 Double Frontage Lots 180
 5.10.7 Setback Encroachments 180

5.10.8 Vehicle and Pedestrian Areas for Single-Family, Duplex, Triplex, and Quadraplex Lots 180
5.10.9 Flag Lots 182
5.10.10 Reduction of Lot Size by Governmental Action 183
5.11 Blocks 183
    5.11.1 Lots to Be Contiguous 183
    5.11.2 Block Width 183
    5.11.3 Length 183
5.12 Building Height 183
    5.12.1 Generally 183
    5.12.2 Measurement 183
    5.12.3 Height Exceptions 183
5.13 Building Design 183
    5.13.1 Single-Family Residential Dwellings 184
    5.13.2 Duplexes, Triplexes, and Quadraplexes 186
    5.13.3 Manufactured Homes 186
    5.13.4 Multifamily Dwellings 187
    5.13.5 Commercial Buildings 187
    5.13.6 Civic Buildings 189
5.14 Fences and Walls 190
    5.14.1 Design 190
    5.14.2 Height 190
    5.14.3 Residential Subdivisions 190
5.15 Lighting 191
    5.15.1 Applicability 191
    5.15.2 Shielding and Filtration 191
    5.15.3 Illumination 192
    5.15.4 Control of Glare— Luminaire Design Factors 192
    5.15.5 Prohibitions 192
    5.15.6 Recreational Facilities 193
    5.15.7 Outdoor Display Lots 193
    5.15.8 Measurement 193
5.16 Homeland Security Site-Specific Vulnerability Assessment 194
5.17 Sustainability 194

Division 3: Infrastructure Standards 194
5.21 Parks/Open Space 194
    5.21.1 Applicability 194
    5.21.2 Required Parks/Open Space 199
    5.21.3 Categories of Parks/Open Space 199
    5.21.4 Fee in Lieu of Park Development (Optional) 199
    5.21.5 Park and Open Space Characteristics 203
    5.21.6 Designation of Parks/Open Space 204
    5.21.7 Development Phasing 204
    5.21.8 Connectivity 205
5.22 Stormwater Management 205
    5.22.1 Applicability 205
    5.22.2 Regional Stormwater Management Program 205
    5.22.3 Options 205
    5.22.4 Timing of Payment 206
    5.22.5 System Criteria 206
    5.22.6 Level of Service 206
    5.22.7 Method of Computing Run-off 206
    5.22.8 Drainage Easements/Rights-of-Way 209
    5.22.9 Site Design and Grading 210
    5.22.10 Low-Impact Stormwater Management Design 210
    5.22.11 Stormwater Detention 214
    5.22.12 Multiuse Facilities 214
    5.22.13 Location of Detention Facilities 214
    5.22.14 Streets for Stormwater Drainage 215
    5.22.15 Drainage Channels and Watercourses 215
    5.22.16 Concrete Channels 217
    5.22.17 Storm Sewers 217
    5.22.18 Inlets and Openings 217
5.23 Street Design and Transportation 218
    5.23.1 Applicability 218
    5.23.2 Classification 218
    5.23.3 Geometric Design 218
    5.23.4 Connectivity 222
    5.23.5 Cul-de-Sacs 224
    5.23.6 Street Intersections 224
    5.23.7 Street Names and Signage 224
    5.23.8 Street Lights 225
    5.23.9 Private Streets 225
    5.23.10 Pavement Design 225
    5.23.11 Sidewalks 226
    5.23.12 Access and Driveways 226
    5.23.13 Gated Subdivision Streets 227
    5.23.14 Traffic Calming 228
5.24 Utilities 228
    5.24.1 Applicability 228
    5.24.2 Generally 230
    5.24.3 Central Water and Sewer Required 230
    5.24.4 Private Water System 230
    5.24.5 Private Wastewater System 230
    5.24.6 Easements 230

Division 4: Greenspace (Landscaping, Tree Preservation, Screening, and Environmental Protection) Standards 231
5.30 Greenspace Areas, Generally 231
    5.30.1 Applicability 231
    5.30.2 Interpretation of Terms 232
    5.30.3 Greenspace Plan 232
    5.30.4 Acceptable Landscape Materials 232
    5.30.5 Protection of Plant Areas 233
5.31 Buffers and Screening 233
    5.31.1 Applicability 233
    5.31.2 Required Buffer Yards 233
    5.31.3 Natural Buffer Yards 234
    5.31.4 Location of Buffer Yard 234
    5.31.5 Permitted Uses Within the Buffer Yard 234
    5.31.6 Size and Type of Plant Materials 234
    5.31.7 Fences and Walls 236
    5.31.8 Berms 236
    5.31.9 Screening 236
    5.31.10 Utilities 236
5.32 Streetscape Landscaping 236

Contents xi

    5.32.1 Applicability 236
    5.32.2 Street Trees 236
5.33 Building Landscaping 237
    5.33.1 Applicability 237
    5.33.2 Standards 237
5.34 Parking Lot Landscaping 237
    5.34.1 Applicability 237
    5.34.2 Calculation of Shaded Area 237
    5.34.3 Design 237
5.35 Entrance Landscaping 237
    5.35.1 Applicability 237
    5.35.2 Standards 238
5.36 House-Lot Landscaping 238
    5.36.1 Applicability 238
    5.36.2 Generally 238
    5.36.3 Installation Standards 238
    5.36.4 Greenspace Plan Not Required 238
5.37 Tree Preservation and Tree Save Areas 238
    5.37.1 Applicability 238
    5.37.2 Tree Protection Zone 239
    5.37.3 Protected Trees 239
    5.37.4 Preservation Standards 239
    5.37.5 Tree Survey Required 239

Division 5: Environmental Protection of Critical Areas ... 240
5.40 Riparian Buffers 240
    5.40.1 Applicability 240
    5.40.2 Riparian Corridors 240
    5.40.3 Permitted Uses and
         Activities in Riparian Buffers 240
    5.40.4 Dimensional Regulations 240
    5.40.5 Development Standards
         in Riparian Buffers 240
5.41 Steep Slopes 242
    5.41.1 Applicability 242
    5.41.2 Measurement of Slope 242
    5.41.3 Contents of Application 242
    5.41.4 Construction Techniques 243
5.42 Wetlands 243
    5.42.1 Applicability 243
    5.42.2 Generally 243
    5.42.3 Exemption 243
    5.42.4 Standards 243

Division 6: Parking and Storage Standards 244
5.50 Outdoor Storage 244
    5.50.1 Applicability 244
    5.50.2 Standards 245
5.51 Parking 245
    5.51.1 Parking Ratios 245
    5.51.2 Shared Parking 246
    5.51.3 Dimensions 256
    5.51.4 Location 256
    5.51.5 Construction and Maintenance 257
    5.51.6 Bicycle Parking 257
5.52 Loading 258
    5.52.1 General Requirements 258

    5.52.2 Responsibility 258
    5.52.3 Types and Location 258
    5.52.4 Location 258
    5.52.5 Construction and Maintenance 258
    5.52.6 Minimum Requirements and Area 259
    5.52.7 Waiver 259
5.53 Sustainability 259
    5.53.1 Generally 259
    5.53.2 Site Design 259
    5.53.3 Building Design 259
Commentary 260

6. Adequate Public Facilities 285
6.0 Purpose and Findings 285
6.1 Adequate Public Facilities 286
6.2 Applicability 286
6.3 Procedures for the Processing of
    Applications for Development Approval 286
    6.3.1 Determination 286
    6.3.2 Comprehensive Plan
        and Zoning Amendments 286
6.4 Determination of Adequacy
    of Public Facilities 287
    6.4.1 Scope 287
    6.4.2 Duration 287
6.5 Advancement of Capacity 287
    6.5.1 Advancement of Public Facilities 287
    6.5.2 Standards 287
    6.5.3 Construction Commitment 288
    6.5.4 Partial Construction or Funding 288
6.6 Methodology 288
    6.6.1 Generally 288
    6.6.2 Level of Service Standards 288
    6.6.3 Adequacy of Public Facilities 288
    6.6.4 Transportation Analysis 288
    6.6.5 Fire, Police, and Emergency Services 289
    6.6.6 Water 289
    6.6.7 Sewer 289
    6.6.8 Community Parks 289
6.7 Capital Improvements Program 289
    6.7.1 Capital Improvements
        Data Requirements 290
    6.7.2 Capital Improvements
        Analysis Requirements 290
    6.7.3 Requirements for Capital
        Improvements Implementation 290
Commentary 293

7. Supplemental Use Regulations 307
7.0 Purpose and Findings 307
7.1 Generally 307
    7.1.1 Compliance Mandatory 307
    7.1.2 Regulations Supplement
        Other Code Regulations 307

7.2 Accessory Uses and Structures 307
    7.2.1 Applicability 307
    7.2.2 Establishment 307
    7.2.3 Dimensional and Density Standards.............. 308
    7.2.4 General Requirements....................................... 308
    7.2.5 Height 308
7.3 Accessory Dwelling Units 308
    7.3.1 Accessory Dwelling Units
         in Detached Buildings.. 309
    7.3.2 Accessory Apartments 310
7.4 Auto-oriented Development 310
    7.4.1 Applicability 310
    7.4.2 Permitted Uses 310
    7.4.3 General Standards.. 310
    7.4.4 Automobile Service and Repair 311
    7.4.5 Car Washes 311
    7.4.6 Service Stations, Gas Stations,
         and Related Uses 311
7.5 Commercial Buildings... 313
    7.5.1 Applicability 313
    7.5.2 Big-Box Development.. 313
    7.5.3 Building Structure 313
    7.5.4 Ground-Floor Design 314
    7.5.5 Street Wall Standards 314
    7.5.6 Windows and Entryways 314
    7.5.7 Pedestrian-oriented Uses 314
    7.5.8 Mechanical Equipment..................................... 314
7.20 Extractive Use.. 314
    7.20.1 Applicability 315
    7.20.2 Development Approvals and Orders............ 317
    7.20.3 Separation Distances....................................... 318
    7.20.4 Quarries 319
    7.20.5 Sand or Gravel Excavation 320
    7.20.6 Land Alteration 321
    7.20.7 Reclamation Standards................................... 322
    7.20.8 Financial Assurances 324
    7.20.9 Inspection and Monitoring 324
7.21 Group Homes 324
    7.21.1 Applicability 324
    7.21.2 Fair Housing Act Protections 325
    7.21.3 Location 325
    7.21.4 Standards.. 325
7.30 Home Occupations 325
    7.30.1 Applicability 325
    7.30.2 Exempt Home Occupations........................... 325
    7.30.3 Permitted Home Occupations....................... 325
    7.30.4 Prohibited Home Occupations...................... 326
    7.30.5 Performance Standards 326
    7.30.6 Rural Home Occupations............................... 326
    7.30.7 Unsafe Home Occupations............................ 327
7.31 Housing Facilities for Older Persons 328
    7.31.1 Applicability 328
    7.31.2 Uses 328
    7.31.3 Federal Restrictions 328
    7.31.4 "NS" (Neighborhood Suburban)
         Districts 328

7.32 Inclusionary Zoning/
      Affordable Dwelling Units................................... 328
    7.32.1 Applicability 328
    7.32.2 Architectural Design and Character 328
    7.32.3 Density Bonus and
         Set-Aside Requirements 328
    7.32.4 Project Phasing 329
    7.32.5 Enforcement.. 329
    7.32.6 Administration 329
7.40 Junkyards and Automobile Graveyards 329
    7.40.1 Applicability 329
    7.40.2 Conditional Use Permit 330
    7.40.3 Standards for Conditional Use Permit......... 330
7.50 Manufactured Home
      Land-Lease Communities 330
    7.50.1 Applicability 330
    7.50.2 Density... 331
    7.50.3 Standards 331
    7.50.4 Streets.. 331
    7.50.5 Infrastructure and Utilities............................. 331
7.51 Mixed-Use Buildings
      and Live-Work Units 332
    7.51.1 Location of Uses and Density 332
    7.51.2 Mix of Uses 332
    7.51.3 Parking 332
7.60 Outdoor Display Areas... 333
    7.60.1 Applicability 333
    7.60.2 Permitted.. 333
7.61 Outdoor Storage 334
    7.61.1 Applicability 334
    7.61.2 Standards 334
7.70 Residential Dwelling Units 334
    7.70.1 Applicability 335
    7.70.2 General Criteria 335
    7.70.3 Single-Family Dwelling Units....................... 337
    7.70.4 Attached Dwellings, Generally..................... 337
    7.70.5 Two-Family Dwellings (Duplexes) 337
    7.70.6 Townhouses or Row Houses......................... 338
    7.70.7 Multifamily Housing.. 339
    7.70.8 Manufactured Homes 340
    7.70.9 Cottage Housing Developments 341
    7.70.10 Zero Lot Line 341
7.80 Satellite Dish Antennas... 342
    7.80.1 Applicability 342
    7.80.2 Location.. 342
    7.80.3 Zoning Certificate 342
    7.80.4 Screening 342
    7.80.5 Height.. 342
7.81 Self-storage Facility 343
    7.81.1 Applicability 343
    7.81.2 Procedures 343
    7.81.3 Standards 343
7.82 Solid Waste Facilities 343
    7.82.1 Applicability 343
    7.82.2 Standards for Sanitary Landfills.................... 344
    7.82.3 Submittal Requirements 344
7.90 Temporary Uses.. 344

Contents   xiii

- 7.90.1 Applicability 344
- 7.90.2 Construction Dumpsters 344
- 7.90.3 Construction-Related Uses 344
- 7.90.4 Public Assembly 344
- 7.90.5 Yard/Garage Sales 345
- 7.91 Utilities 345
  - 7.91.1 Applicability 345
  - 7.91.2 Utility Stations and Plants 346
- 7.92 Wireless Communications Facilities 346
  - 7.92.1 Applicability 346
  - 7.92.2 Development Review and Permitted Uses 347
  - 7.92.3 Development Review Process 347
  - 7.92.4 Submission Requirements............................. 349
  - 7.92.5 Standards... 349
  - 7.92.6 Antenna Supporting Structures 349
  - 7.92.7 Collocations... 352
  - 7.92.8 Roof-Mounted Antenna Supporting Structure 352
  - 7.92.9 Surface-Mounted Antennas.......................... 352
  - 7.92.10 Stealth Wireless Communications Facilities 352
  - 7.92.11 Expert Review... 353
  - 7.92.12 Discontinuance 353
  - 7.92.13 Nonconforming Antenna Supporting Structures.......................... 353
  - 7.92.14 Variances—Additional Criteria 353
  - 7.92.15 Signs 354
  - 7.92.16 Satellite Antennas... 354
  - 7.92.17 Adult-oriented Uses..................................... 354
  - 7.92.18 Flood Controls 354
  - 7.92.19 Affordable Dwelling Units/ Inclusionary Zoning 354

Commentary 355

8. Nonconforming Uses/Vested Rights 367

Division 1: Nonconformities.. 367

- 8.10 Generally 367
  - 8.10.1 Applicability 367
  - 8.10.2 Continuation 367
  - 8.10.3 Abandonment 367
- 8.11 Nonconforming Uses.. 367
  - 8.11.1 Applicability 367
  - 8.11.2 Continuance 367
  - 8.11.3 Enlargement 368
  - 8.11.4 Conditions 368
  - 8.11.5 Change of Use Regulations........................... 368
- 8.12 Nonconforming Sites 369
  - 8.12.1 Applicability 369
  - 8.12.2 Authority to Continue 369
  - 8.12.3 Nonconforming Site Categories 369
  - 8.12.4 Extension 369
  - 8.12.5 Relocations 369
  - 8.12.6 Change in Use 369
  - 8.12.7 Abandonment 369

- 8.12.8 Exception for Repairs Pursuant to Public Order........................... 369
- 8.13 Nonconforming Structures..................................... 370
  - 8.13.1 Applicability 370
  - 8.13.2 Continuance of Nonconforming Structures 370
  - 8.13.3 Enlargement 370
  - 8.13.4 Termination of Nonconforming Structures 370
- 8.14 Nonconforming Lots 370
  - 8.14.1 Applicability 370
  - 8.14.2 Generally 370
  - 8.14.3 Newly Annexed Territory 370
  - 8.14.4 Incomplete Construction 370
  - 8.14.5 Proposed Construction 370
- 8.15 Certificate of Nonconforming Use 371
  - 8.15.1 Applicability 371
  - 8.15.2 Contents... 371
  - 8.15.3 Denial of Registration 371
  - 8.15.4 Amendment 371
- 8.16 Termination of Nonconformities.......................... 371
  - 8.16.1 Violation of Chapter 371
  - 8.16.2 Specific Acts of Termination 371
  - 8.16.3 Notice 371
  - 8.16.4 Action of the Board of Adjustment 371
  - 8.16.5 Destruction or Damage of Structure 372
- 8.17 Expansion of Nonconformity................................ 372
  - 8.17.1 Applicability 372
  - 8.17.2 Criteria for Conditional Use Permit 372
  - 8.17.3 Conditions Applicable 372

Division 2: Vested Rights.. 372

- 8.20 Common Law, Statutory, and Consent Agreement Rights 372
  - 8.20.1 Applicability 372
- 8.21 Vested Rights Determination 372
  - 8.21.1 Generally 372
  - 8.21.2 Consent Agreement 373
  - 8.21.3 Terms and Conditions 373
  - 8.21.4 Failure to Comply with Consent Agreement 373
- 8.22 Vested Rights Determination Process.................. 373
  - 8.22.1 Initiation 373
  - 8.22.2 Review and Approval 373
  - 8.22.3 Variance... 373
  - 8.22.4 Recordation 374

Commentary 375

9. Administrative Agencies... 383

- 9.1 Authority... 383
  - 9.1.1 Generally 383
  - 9.1.2 Specific Power 383
- 9.2 Planning Commission 383
  - 9.2.1 Duties of Planning Commission 383
  - 9.2.2 Quorum, Majority Vote.................................. 383
  - 9.2.3 Conflict of Interest 384

9.2.4 Recommendations 384
9.2.5 Robert's Rules of Order 384
9.3 Planning Department and Administration 384
9.4 Hearing Officer (Optional Provision) 384
    9.4.1 Establishment 384
    9.4.2 Appointment and Removal 384
    9.4.3 Qualifications 384
    9.4.4 Compensation 384
    9.4.5 Powers and Duties 384

Commentary 385

10. Legal Status 387
10.1 Severability 387
10.2 Conflict with Other Laws 387
10.3 Repeal of Existing Zoning Regulations 387
10.4 Effective Date 387

Commentary 388

Appendix A.
Definitions and Rules of Interpretation 389
A-1 Rules of Interpretation 389
A-2 Definitions 389

Appendix B.
Specifications for Documents to Be Submitted 417
B-1 Generally 417
    B-1.1 General Requirements 417
    B-1.2 Forms 417
    B-1.3 Information Required 417
    B-1.4 Certifications 417
    B-1.5 Digital Plat Requirements 417
    B-1.6 Control Points and Monumentation Guidelines 422
    B-1.7 Digital Requirements for Street and Drainage Construction Plan Submittals 422
B-2 Citizen Participation Plan 422
B-3 Conditional Use Permit 422
    B-3.1 Number of Copies 422
    B-3.2 Format 422
    B-3.3 Contents 423
B-4 Land Alteration Development Approval 423
    B-4.1 Required Plans 423
    B-4.2 Assessment of Existing/Prealteration Conditions 423
    B-4.3 Grading Plan 423
    B-4.4 Operations Plan 424
    B-4.5 Reclamation Plan 424
B-5 Landscape Plans 425
    B-5.1 Number of Copies 425
    B-5.2 Format 425
    B-5.3 Contents 425
    B-5.4 Certification 426
B-9 Nonconforming Use Certification 426
    B-9.1 Number of Copies 426
    B-9.2 Format 426
    B-9.3 Contents 426
B-10 Plat Vacation and Resubdivision 426
    B-10.1 Number of Copies 426
    B-10.2 Format 426
    B-10.3 Contents 426
    B-10.4 Certification 426
B-11 Rezoning 426
B-12 Stormwater Management Plan 427
    B-12.1 Number of Copies 427
    B-12.2 Format 427
    B-12.3 Contents 427
    B-12.4 Report 427
    B-12.5 HEC-2 Submittal Checklist 428
B-13 Street Plans 429
    B-13.1 Number of Copies 429
    B-13.2 Format 429
    B-13.3 Contents 429
B-14 Subdivision Plat Applications 429
    B-14.1 Number of Copies 429
    B-14.2 Format 429
    B-14.3 Contents 429
B-15 Traffic Impact Analysis 430
    B-15.1 Applicability 430
    B-15.2 Contents 430
B-16 Tree Preservation Plan 431
    B-16.1 Number of Copies 431
    B-16.2 Format 431
    B-16.3 Contents 431
B-17 Vested Rights Determination 431
B-18 Site Plan Checklist 432

Table of Cases 433

Subject Index 439

Bibliography 451

About the Authors 456

Acknowledgements

ROBERT H. FREILICH

This monumental work is an outgrowth of two sets of *Model Subdivision Regulations*—the first edition (with Peter S. Levi), which I published with the American Society of Planning Officials in 1975, and the second edition (with Michael M. Shultz), which I published with the American Planning Association in 1995.

I wish first of all to thank my current firm of Miller Barondess, LLP, Los Angeles, and especially Skip Miller. I am indebted to Peter Levi and Michael Shultz for their earlier work on the *Model Subdivision Regulations*. Secondly, I owe the greatest debt of gratitude to my former partner and colleague Mark White for his brilliant collaboration. I also wish to thank Elisa Paster for her editing and contributions to substantive portions of the work; and Seth Mennillo, for helping to write the sections on big boxes and sustainability, as well as helping with the editing. Both Mark and I owe thanks to Kate Murray, a former student at the University of Missouri-Kansas City School of Law and a law clerk at Freilich, Leitner & Carlisle, who worked for an entire year in helping to organize code provisions and commentaries. I am also indebted to my secretary Dianne Fowler for typing manuscript and providing suggestions for format. Both Mark and I wish to thank our editor, Joanne Shwed of Backspace Ink, for her dedication to this project over several years with insight, perseverance, and extraordinary skill.

Thanks go to my wife Carole who has endured 35 years of my writing and practice and who is a constant source of encouragement for my work.

Substantial credit goes to the over 250 cities, counties, and states with which I have worked (a number with my partner Mark White during our 15 years together at Freilich, Leitner & Carlisle) for providing the laboratories in which this code has been fashioned, from the many comprehensive and growth management plans, development codes, and the over 100 cases litigated in the United States Supreme Court; state supreme, appeals, and trial courts; and federal district and appellate courts on every aspect of land-use regulation involving public and private clients.

S. MARK WHITE

Developing a comprehensive, written work requires the sacrifice of many people. First and foremost, I am very fortunate to have a family—my wife, Marla, and my daughters, Rachelle and Maryn—who are willing to tolerate the long hours required to produce this work. My wife is both an inspiration to me and is able to keep my theories grounded. My hope is that my daughters will benefit from a better built environment produced by smarter growth in the years ahead.

Many people assisted in the production of this volume. My secretary, Sharon Henderson, spent long hours translating the authors' handwriting and instructions into written form. Her patience and skills contributed greatly to this work. Kate Murray (a law student at the University of Missouri-Kansas City School of Law), Chris Brown (a law student at the University of Cincinnati), Zeb Curtin (a law student at the University of Iowa), and Chad Lamer (at the University of Kansas) assisted in compiling research, writing, and editing. Kristen Phillips (a student at the Kansas City Art Institute) contributed the excellent illustrations of the use patterns in Chapter 2, Use Patterns, of the LDC.

Finally, the authors are deeply grateful to the colleagues, clients, and community stakeholders with whom they have worked over the years. Many of the ideas expressed in this book are the shared contributions of people who were willing to nurture a creative, and often politically courageous, idea in their communities. Your contributions have made the world a better place in which to live.

List of Figures

Readers will find that some of the graphics have greater clarity on the CD-ROM accompanying this book. The graphics are not to scale and do not represent actual physical dimensions. If there is a conflict between a graphic and the text, the text governs.

Figure I-1 2
Laws of the Indies—Plan of San Antonio

Figure 2-1 40
Conservation Subdivisions

Figure 2-2 43
Conventional Commercial Centers

Figure 2-3 44
Illustration of Neighborhood Center Dimensional Standards

Figure 2-4 45
Rear Parking with Buildings Aligned at the Street

Figure 2-5 45
Campus-Style Development

Figure 2-6 47
Retrofitting Conventional Centers

Figure 2-7 48
Separate Versus Joint Access

Figure 2-8 48
Traditional Neighborhood Development

Figure 2-9 51
Variable Block Lengths

Figure 2-10 52
Transit-oriented Development

Figure 2-11 56
Small-Scale Commercial Sites in Residential Neighborhoods

Figure 2-12 56
Small-Scale Commercial Uses in Residential Neighborhoods

Figure 2-13 60
Pedestrian Pathways

Figure 2-14 61
Inappropriate Front Yard Parking

Figure 2-15 61
Front-Facing Buildings

Figure 2-16 61
Appropriate Rear Yard Parking

Figure 2-17 62
Greyfield Redevelopment

Figure 2-18 63
Transit-Supportive Development

Figure 3-1 81
Dimensional Standards—"RP" (Resource Protection)

Figure 3-2 82
Dimensional Standards—"RE" (Residential Estate)

Figure 3-3 83
Dimensional Standards—"NS" (Neighborhood Suburban)

Figure 3-4 83
Dimensional Standards—"NU" (Neighborhood Urban)

Figure 3-5 84
Zero Lot Line Commercial

Figure 3-6 85
Dimensional Standards—"CN" (Commercial Neighborhood)

Figure 3-7 86
Dimensional Standards—"CG" (Commercial General)

Figure 3-8 87
Dimensional Standards—"CL" (Commercial Large-Scale)

Figure 3-9 88
Dimensional Standards—"D" (Downtown)

Figure 3-10 89
Dimensional Standards—"IL" (Industrial Light)

Figure 3-11 90
Dimensional Standards—"IH" (Industrial Heavy)

Figure 3-12 102
Columbia Pike Special Revitalization District Form-Based Code (Excerpt)

Figure 3-13 108
Conventional Suburban Corridors

xvii

Figure 3-14 109
Shallow Setback Streets

Figure 3-15 110
Maximizing Floor Area Ratio

Figure 3-16 110
Clustered Courtyard Buildings

Figure 3-17 110
Traditional Courtyard

Figure 3-18 111
Transfers of Development Rights

Figure 4-1 120
Development Approval Application Flow Chart

Figure 4-2 137
Legislative Discretionary Development Approval

Figure 4-3 139
Administrative Discretionary Development Approval

Figure 5-1 183
Block Tier Standards

Figure 5-2 188
Commercial Design Elements

Figure 5-3 189
Form-Based Zoning

Figure 5-4 190
Fence Height

Figure 5-5 193
Lighting Intensity

Figure 5-6 211
Grading

Figure 5-7 212
LID Manuals

Figure 5-8 214
Bioretention Facility

Figure 5-9 215
Sustainable Open Space

Figure 5-10 223
Subdivision Connectivity

Figure 5-11 225
Cul-de-sac Landscaping

Figure 5-12 227
Cross Access

Figure 5-13 240
Riparian Buffers

Figure 5-14 256
Parking Space and Stall Dimensions

Figure 5-15 257
Utilizing Effective Parking

Figure 5-16 261
Fenestration

Figure 5-17 262
Snout-Featured Housing

Figure 5-18 270
Surface Parking

Figure 5-19 270
Rear Parking

Figure 5-20 272
Effective Use of Open Space

Figure 5-21 273
Sustainable Water Retention

Figure 5-22 274
Narrowing Streets

Figure 5-23 274
Adaptable Fire Service Delivery

Figure 5-24 275
Loop Lanes

Figure 5-25 276
Eyebrow Road Configurations

Figure 6-1 294
Synchronizing Growth with Adequate Public Facilities

Figure 7-1 309
Accessory Dwelling Units

Figure 7-2 310
Architectural Design

Figure 7-3 312
Form-Based Zoning

Figure 7-4 332
Vertical Mixed Use

Figure 7-5 337
Window Treatments

Figure 7-6 338
Human Versus Auto Design

Figure 7-7 339
Townhouses

Figure 7-8 339
Multifamily Transitional Standards

Figure 7-9 340
Compatible Multifamily and Single-Family Massing

Figure 7-10 341
Cottages

Figure 7-11 342
Smaller Homes Promote Usable Open Space

Figure 7-12 355
Design Standards

Figure 7-13 360
Jobs-Housing Balance

List of Tables

Table I-1 12
Neighborhood Design Comparison Chart

Table 1-1 34
Eschewing Obfuscation

Table 1-2 36
Code Language Found Void for Vagueness

Table 1-3 37
Code Language Upheld
Against Vagueness Challenges

Table 2-1 40
Lot Arrangement for Conservation Subdivisions

Table 2-2 44
Neighborhood Center Location Standards

Table 2-3 44
Neighborhood Center Dimensional Standards

Table 2-4 47
Height Bonus for Greyfield Redevelopment

Table 2-5 50
Traditional Neighborhood Development Density
and Intensity Standards

Table 2-6 50
Traditional Neighborhood Development Use
Location

Table 2-7 51
Setback for Principal Buildings

Table 2-8 53
Transit-oriented Development Dimensional
Standards

Table 2-9 54
Transit-oriented Development
Parking Requirements

Table 2-10 57
Comparison of New Urbanism
and Conventional Subdivisions

Table 2-11 60
Connectivity Alternatives

Table 2-12 63
Greyfield Redevelopment Alternatives

Table 3-1 68
Tier, Plan, and Zoning District Correspondence

Table 3-2 69
Overlay Zoning Districts

Table 3-3 69
Floating Zones

Table 3-4 71
Use Matrix

Table 3-5 80
Permitted Use Terminology

Table 3-6 80
Dimensional Standards

Table 3-7 81
Dimensional Standards—"RP"
(Resource Protection)

Table 3-8 82
Dimensional Standards—"RE"
(Residential Estate)

Table 3-9 83
Dimensional Standards—"NS"
(Neighborhood Suburban)

Table 3-10 83
Dimensional Standards—"NU"
(Neighborhood Urban)

Table 3-11 84
Dimensional Standards—"O" (Office)

Table 3-12 85
Dimensional Standards—"CN"
(Commercial Neighborhood)

Table 3-13 86
Dimensional Standards—"CG"
(Commercial General)

Table 3-14 86
Building Scale Restrictions in "CG"
(Commercial General) Districts

xix

Table 3-15 87	Table 5-5 184
Dimensional Standards—"CL" (Commercial Large-Scale)	Applicability of Single-Family Design Regulations
Table 3-16 87	Table 5-6 192
Building Scale Restrictions in "CL" (Commercial Large-Scale) Districts	Shielding Requirements
Table 3-17 88	Table 5-7 192
Dimensional Standards—"D" (Downtown)	Illumination Standards
Table 3-18 89	Table 5-8 195
Dimensional Standards—"IL" (Industrial Light)	Building Practices
Table 3-19 89	Table 5-9 199
Dimensional Standards—"IH" (Industrial Heavy)	Required Parks
Table 3-20 91	Table 5-10 200
"PD" (Planned Development) District Parks and Open Space	Park and Open Space Categories
Table 3-21 95	Table 5-11 204
Airport Overlay Zones and Height Restrictions	Development Phasing for Parks and Open Space
Table 3-22 96	Table 5-12 206
Incentive Zoning Bonus	Stormwater Management Design Conditions
Table 3-23 97	Table 5-13 207
Adjusted Lot Sizes, Incentive Zoning	Design Rainfall Values (Inches)
Table 3-24 98	Table 5-14 207
Bonus Density Chart	Time-of-Concentration Calculation Methods
Table 3-25 104	Table 5-15 208
Land-Based Classification Standards	Run-off Coefficients (C)—Percentage
Table 3-26 109	Table 5-16 208
Rationale for Setbacks	Run-off Coefficients (C)—Percentage (Areas That Will Not Be Developed)
Table 3-27 113	Table 5-17 208
Performance Zoning Measurements	Soil Conservation Service Curve Number by Soil Type
Table 3-28 114	Table 5-18 209
Land-Use Intensity Ratios	Percent Impervious Cover by Land Use
Table 3-29 115	Table 5-19 209
Building Volume Ratio	Channel Routing
Table 4-1 126	Table 5-20 209
Notice Requirements	Manning's Roughness Coefficient
Table 4-2 142	Table 5-21 213
Subdivision Procedures	Integrated Management Practices
Table 4-3 159	Table 5-22 214
Penalties for Code Violations	Bioretention Design Components
Table 4-4 162	Table 5-23 216
Elements of Procedure	Storm Drainage, Street Velocities, and Capacities
Table 5-1 181	Table 5-24 217
Accessory Uses and Structures	Stormwater Management Capacity by Street Classification
Table 5-2 182	Table 5-25 217
Driveway Restrictions	Velocity Control
Table 5-3 182	Table 5-26 219
Maximum Number of Flag Lots	Functional Street Classification System
Table 5-4 183	
Maximum Block Length	

List of Tables xxi

Table	Title	Page
Table 5-27	Street Geometric Design	220
Table 5-28	Bike Lane Geometric Design Criteria	223
Table 5-29	Cul-de-sac Length (Maximum)	224
Table 5-30	Minimum Driveway Throat Lengths	228
Table 5-31	Approved Traffic Control Devices and Description	229
Table 5-32	Applicability of General Standards	232
Table 5-33	Minimum Greenspace Planting Specifications	232
Table 5-34	Required Buffer Yards	234
Table 5-35	Minimum Plant Materials Required for Each Buffer Yard Type	235
Table 5-36	Buffer Yard Density	236
Table 5-37	Parking Lot Shading	237
Table 5-38	Entrance Landscaping Standards	238
Table 5-39	Preservation Ratios	239
Table 5-40	Definition of Stream Corridor Zones	240
Table 5-41	Permitted Uses Within Riparian Buffer Corridor Zones	241
Table 5-42	Dimensional Regulations in Riparian Buffer Zones	241
Table 5-43	Slope Construction Restrictions	242
Table 5-44	Outdoor Storage Categories	244
Table 5-45	Outdoor Storage Standards	245
Table 5-46	Parking Ratios	247
Table 5-47	Shared Parking Standards	256
Table 5-48	Minimum Stall Length and Aisle Width (Feet)	256
Table 5-49	Minimum Truck Loading Spaces	259
Table 5-50	LEED® Building Rating System Maximum and Required Points	259
Table 5-51	10 Questions for a Local Government to Consider When Creating a Parking Policy	269
Table 5-52	Street-Drainage Elements	276
Table 6-1	Adopted Level of Service Standards	287
Table 6-2	Equivalent Residential Units for Transportation (Per Day)	291
Table 6-3	Equivalent Residential Units for Law Enforcement or Parks/Open Space	292
Table 7-1	Accessory Uses	308
Table 7-2	Permitted Uses for "AOD" (Auto-oriented District)	311
Table 7-3	Height Accessory Structures	312
Table 7-4	Quarry, Sand, and Gravel Excavation and Land Alteration Separation Distances	316
Table 7-5	Home Occupation Performance Standards By Zoning District	327
Table 7-6	Affordable Dwelling Unit Set-Aside Requirements	328
Table 7-7	Mixed-Use Buildings and Live-Work Units	332
Table 7-8	Mixed-Use Buildings—Ratio of Uses	333
Table 7-9	Mixed-Use Buildings—Parking Adjustments	333
Table 7-10	Applicability of Design Regulations	335
Table 7-11	Private Open Space	339
Table 7-12	Attached Dwelling Unit Dimensional Standards	341
Table 7-13	Temporary Uses	345
Table 7-14	Telecommunications Facility Height and Procedures	347
Table 7-15	Telecommunications Facility Submittal Requirements	348

Table 7-16 359
Senior Housing

Table 7-17 360
Live-Work Regulatory Options

Table 8-1 368
Nonconformities

Table 8-2 368
Change of Use

Table 8-3 369
Nonconforming Site Categories

Table A-1 397
Equivalent Dwelling Units

Table B-1 418
Summary of Application Requirements

Table B-2 421
Layer and Level Element Types

Table B-3 421
Digital Plat Submittal

Table B-4 422
Horizontal Control Points

Acronyms and Abbreviations

ADA	Americans with Disabilities Act
ALI Code	American Law Institute's Model Land Development Code
"AO"	Airport Overlay [overlay zoning district]
"AOD"	Auto-oriented District [zoning district]
APA	American Planning Association
APFO	adequate public facilities ordinance
ASHRAE/IESNA	American Society of Heating, Refrigerating and Air-Conditioning Engineers, Inc./ Illuminating Engineering Society of North America
BOC	back of the curb
BVR	building volume ratio
CC&Rs	covenants, conditions, and restrictions
CFC	chlorofluorocarbon
C.F.R.	Code of Federal Regulations
"CG"	Commercial General [zoning district]
CHD	cottage housing development
CIP	capital improvements program
"CL"	Commercial Large-Scale [zoning district]
"CN"	Commercial Neighborhood [zoning district]
CUP	conditional use permit
CWP	Center for Watershed Protection
"D"	Downtown [zoning district]
DBH	diameter breast height
DVD	digital video disc
ECHO	elder cottage housing opportunities
EPU	equivalent planting unit
"EU"	Extractive Use [zoning district]
FAA	Federal Aviation Administration
FAR	floor area ratio
FCC	Federal Communications Commission
FEMA	Federal Emergency Management Agency
FHA	Fair Housing Act
FIRM	Flood Insurance Rate Map
GFA	gross floor area
GLA	gross land area
HEC	[United States Army Corps of Engineers] Hydrologic Engineering Center
HFOP	Housing Facility for Older Persons
HOA	homeowners' association
HUD	[United States Department of] Housing and Urban Development
HVAC	heating, ventilation, and air-conditioning
HVAC&R	heating, ventilation, air conditioning, and refrigeration
IDA	International Dark-Sky Association
IGA	intergovernmental agreement
"IH"	Industrial Heavy [zoning district]
"IL"	Industrial Light [zoning district]
IMP	integrated management practice
ISO	International Standards Organization

xxiii

ITE	Institute of Transportation Engineers
JPA	joint planning area
LBCS	[American Planning Association's] Land-Based Classification Standards
LDC	Land Development Code
LDR	land development regulation
LEED®	Leadership in Energy and Environmental Design
LID	low-impact design
LOS	level of service
LSR	livability space ratio
LUI	[United States Federal Housing Administration's] land-use intensity [system]
MOU	Memoranda of Understanding
MUTCD	[United States Department of Transportation, Federal Highway Administration's] *Manual on Uniform Traffic Control Devices*
"MX"	Mixed Use [zoning district]
NAHB	National Association of Home Builders
NAICS	North American Industry Classification System
NEC	National Electrical Code
NFPA	National Fire Protection Agency
NIMBY	Not In My Back Yard
"NP"	Neighborhood Preservation [overlay zoning district]
"NS"	Neighborhood Suburban [zoning district]
"NU"	Neighborhood Urban [zoning district]
"O"	Office [zoning district]
OILSR	Office of Interstate Land Sales Registration
OSR	open space ratio
"PD"	Planned Development [zoning district]
PI	plasticity index
PUD	planned unit development
RCD	resource conservation district
"RE"	Residential Estate [zoning district]
RLUIPA	Religious Land Use and Institutionalized Persons Act
"RP"	Resource Protection [zoning district]
RSR	recreation space ratio
RSWF	regional stormwater facility
RSWMP	regional stormwater management program
SCPEA	Standard City Planning Enabling Act
SIC	Standard Industrial Classification
"SSF"	Self-storage Facility [zoning district]
SPEA	Standard City Planning Enabling Act
SRI	Solar Reflective Index
SZEA	Standard State Zoning Enabling Act
TCA	Telecommunications Act
TCR	total car ratio
TDM	Transportation Demand Management
TDR	transfer of development rights
TIA	traffic impact analysis
TND	traditional neighborhood development
TOD	transit-oriented development
TOD-C	transit-oriented development core
TOD-P	transit-oriented development periphery
"TOZ"	Transit Overlay Zone
UCCC	Uniform Consumer Credit Code
UDO	unified development ordinance
UPS	United Parcel Service
U.S.C.	United States Code
U.S.C.A.	United States Code Annotated
USDA	United States Department of Agriculture
US EPA	United States Environmental Protection Agency
USGBC	United States Green Building Council
USGS	United States Geological Survey
V/C	volume-to-capacity [ratio]
VMT	vehicle miles travelled
ZLL	zero lot line

Introduction

THE SUBSTANTIVE LAW OF PLANNING; ZONING; SUBDIVISION REGULATION; STATE, REGIONAL, AND FEDERAL CONTROLS; GROWTH MANAGEMENT; SMART GROWTH; ENVIRONMENTAL REVIEW; SUSTAINABILITY; AND NEW URBANISM THAT UNDERLIES THIS LAND DEVELOPMENT CODE

The Land Development Code (LDC) is a good place to start local code reform efforts. The LDC is not intended to be cut and pasted wholesale as a new code, nor does it attempt to resolve every issue facing local governments today.[1] Instead, it provides the basis for a local code update in your jurisdiction. Many local practitioners have problems with "cut-and-paste" codes. Those concerns can be resolved by:

- Undertaking a strong public participation process to "vet" the code provisions with key stakeholders;
- Using local data to adapt dimensional and other standards to physical topology and the built environment of the local community; and
- Conducting an audit of your state's zoning and land-use enabling legislation and court decisions in order to determine what can be used in your state and how it can be adapted to fit the requirements of your particular state law.

This book addresses three different major categories of land use control in use today:

(1) *Conventional, "Euclidean" zoning:* Many communities either lack the staff resources to undertake more innovative code reforms, or are comfortable with the development approval process that occurs under their conventional systems. These communities will want to focus on Chapter 3, Zoning, and Chapter 7, Supplemental Use Regulations, of the LDC.

(2) *Growth management:* In communities facing rapid growth, the cost of providing infrastructure or the capacity of infrastructure to accommodate development is a major issue. If this is an important issue in your community, you will want to focus on Chapter 6, Adequate Public Facilities, of the LDC. Chapter 6 establishes the timing and sequencing of capital improvements programs (CIPs) and phasing of development based upon level of service standards adopted by the local government. It also establishes the mitigation standards for impact fees and development exactions.

(3) *New urbanism:* The LDC also builds on the concepts of "new urbanism" and "sustainability"—two of the most important planning movements in the past two decades. Chapter 2, Use Patterns, of the LDC regulates design from the building, lot, block, and neighborhood levels. Unlike conventional zoning, it is highly concerned with the appearance and functional relationships of development. New urbanism is not a substitute for zoning or growth management approaches. Local governments using this approach should focus on Chapter 2.

Each community should use all three approaches. Some communities overlay growth management and new urbanism onto the conventional zoning platform. This approach is often the only politically acceptable alternative for communities that wish to advance a smart growth agenda or to improve the design quality of development. Others will use the full palette of LDC code provisions.

The following is a summary of the major developments in land-use regulations over the past two decades, which undergirds the substantive provisions and direction of the LDC.

HISTORICAL BACKGROUND

The American landscape is constantly shaped and reshaped by human settlement. From the earliest mound-building societies in the Ohio and Mississippi River Basins to modern sprawl, environmental degradation, and urban congestion, humans build and shape the land to meet their needs. Regulations and rules guiding these developments have an equally long history. From the earliest fiats laid down by kings across the ocean to modern-day planning, zoning, environmental, subdivision, and development codes, these rules shape societies just as communities shape the landscape.

One of the earliest development ordinances known in America is the Laws of the Indies (see Figure I-1), pro-

Figure I-1
Laws of the Indies—Plan of San Antonio

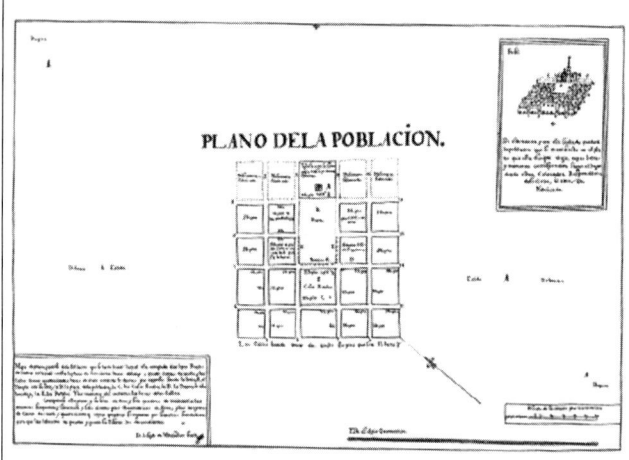

The Spanish Laws of the Indies established a system for laying out uses and structures in early North American settlements.

mulgated by the Spanish Emperor Phillip II in 1573. These laws regulated the spatial development of Spanish settlements in their American colonies.[2] The laws set forth the requirements and prescribed the placement of churches, public buildings, shops, slaughterhouses, and other uses. Specifically, they created the street patterns serving the new towns and cities of the Spanish colonies, expanding from a central plaza in an orthogonal grid with adequate width to allow for sufficient pedestrian and cart traffic. The laws required that buildings be set back from the street to allow for sidewalks and eventual street-widening projects, similar to today's official street maps reserving future right-of-way and zoning setback provisions.[3]

Based upon the architectural tradition established by the Roman scholar Vitruvius in his *The Ten Books on Architecture*,[4] the Laws of the Indies established that churches and other public structures were set in places where their adornment and decoration would be most prominent. Public buildings were placed in the large forum or plaza, which became the center of the new community. The Laws of the Indies guided much of Spanish colonial development and became the foundation for several southwestern cities, such as San Antonio, Texas, and Santa Fe, New Mexico.

Almost 400 years passed before development regulations on a nationwide scale came into effect in the U.S. During the 17th and 18th centuries—as the English, French, and Germans settled North America—development patterns were reminiscent of the towns and villages found in England[5] and Germany.[6] Except for a few cities, such as Philadelphia, Boston, and Savannah,[7] few public planning rules shaped the nature of colonial development. As America emerged from the American Revolution and began to settle the West, speculative profit instead of planning and regulations set the urban form.[8] Settlements were laid out on a grid to allow for a larger number of more valuable corner lots.

ADVENT OF PLANNING

Prior to the widespread adoption of zoning, the public interest in land development arose from a series of planning events leading up to and following the Civil War. In the 19th century, a creative landscape architect devised the plan for Central Park in New York. Frederick Law Olmstead went on to found the "city beautiful" movement in the United States (Buffalo, New York; Cincinnati, Ohio; Kansas City, Missouri; and Minneapolis, Minnesota), creating cities with open space, boulevards, statues, fountains, and parks, which improved property values and neighborhoods. The brilliant 1893 Columbian Exposition in Chicago brought to the forefront the "city beautiful" movement and the work of great architects like Louis Sullivan, inventor of the skyscraper, and Daniel Burnham, one of the founders of modern city planning, whose famous statement "make no small plans" electrified the nation.[9] At the turn of the century, the Beaux Arts movement added further glamour to planning and architecture. During and after World War I, major planning organizations, such as New York's Regional Plan Association, organized to more formally address the need for zoning legislation and land development regulation.

NUISANCE AND RESTRICTIVE COVENANTS

At the beginning of the 20th century, those who could afford it used nuisance law and restrictive covenants to control the placement of land-use and development patterns. A system of public enforcement of private land-use control still exists in a few cities, such as Houston (where restrictive covenant enforcement by the city replaces zoning), but has increasingly dominated the development of urban, suburban, and retirement common interest communities through condominiums; cooperatives; and planned, walled, or gated communities using homeowners' association restrictive covenants.[10]

Equally as important as the restrictive covenant in the early days of regulation was the use of private and public nuisance laws and litigation where, in the absence of land development regulations, adjacent owners could obtain injunctions and damages where a land use constituted an unreasonable interference with the use or enjoyment of land.[11] Application of nuisance law is a form of zoning limited to ad hoc specific cases without overall community planning or consideration.[12] Cases under nuisance law alternatively prohibit or permit a greater mix of industrial and housing uses without any consistency[13] while focusing more heavily on "antisocial values" uses, such as halfway houses, soup kitchens, and pig farms (concentrated animal feeding operations).[14]

Nuisance law slowly keeps up with changing times.[15] Funeral parlors and cemeteries in residential areas are often classified as nuisances, yet they were not so regarded a century ago.[16]

The whole subject of nuisance law has been reinvigorated in the past decade by the United States Supreme Court decision in *Lucas v. South Carolina Coastal Council*, 505 U.S. 1003 (1992), where the Court made nuisance law a factor in deciding whether a local government or state, regulating land use to prevent serious public harm, must compensate a property owner who is deprived of economically viable use and value of land. Note the following question raised in *Lucas*[17]:

"There is no property right to conduct a nuisance so that prohibiting such conduct cannot constitute an injury to constitutional property rights. As we gain new insight into the effects of human conduct on the environment, the capacity of nuisance law to change becomes critically important. A century ago filling wetlands, typically denominated swamps, was considered a beneficial action. Today we know that filling wetlands results in increased flooding, depletes groundwater and destroys fish spawning grounds. Could the act of filling wetlands once considered beneficial, be a nuisance today?"

ZONING

Zoning officially arose with the first comprehensive zoning law, the New York City Zoning Resolution in 1916. A number of other cities followed during the decade of 1916 to 1926. Some state courts approved zoning as constitutional[18] while others rejected it.[19] Some utilized, as Kansas City and Minneapolis did, zoning with compensation, by condemning certain residential uses out of industrial zones and vice versa to establish segregated uses.[20]

Herbert Hoover, as secretary of commerce under the Harding administration, issued a draft Standard State Zoning Enabling Act (SZEA) in 1922. The concept was so popular that, by the time of its final release in 1926, 43 states had enacted it and 22 million people lived in 200 zoned cities—40 percent of the urban population of the United States.[21]

Major principles of the SZEA enunciated the creation of districts for the separation of incompatible uses and used a set of broad purposes which stated that "such regulations be made in accordance with a comprehensive plan."[22]

Zoning has both lived up to and failed its promise. Segregation of use in cities destroyed the essence of mixed-use, vibrant neighborhoods.[23] It was most successful in the new, burgeoning suburbs where multiple-family housing was excluded from single-family housing districts. While acknowledging that zoning has led to a great rise in housing values, some critics have complained since the 1920s that zoning is exclusionary and, rather than segregating uses, it has separated the poor from the rich and the black from the white.[24] Others have asserted that it has prevented the development community from building affordable housing. In a number of states, regional general welfare cases since the 1970s have invalidated municipal parochial actions under state substantive due process under the theory that the state, when delegating authority to zone to local government, did not grant the right to act without regard to adjacent communities or the interests of the state in creating affordable housing or protecting the environment as measured by the region concerned.[25]

Other objections to zoning relate to the failure of the courts to enforce the "in accordance with a comprehensive plan" requirement, allowing instead the zoning ordinance itself to constitute the plan[26] with the resultant inability to think of development as occurring over the build-out life of the community[27] disregard of: (1) state and regional interests, and federal and state environmental laws; (2) the cost, availability, and adequacy of infrastructure; (3) the loss of agricultural and environmentally sensitive land due to urban sprawl; (4) the mounting decline of existing built-up areas; and (5) the enormous energy crisis.[28]

STATE, REGIONAL, AND FEDERAL CONTROLS

To deal with these problems,[29] a number of states since the 1970s have revised the SZEA[30] together with the Standard City Planning Enabling Act (SPEA) to incorporate a greater state and regional role in overseeing local interests.[31] A well-established line of New Jersey cases from the 1940s through the 1960s established that zoning in one community must take into consideration the character of neighboring communities to be considered a legitimate exercise of the police power.[32] These state acts were called a quiet revolution in land use control, creating a new frontier of local-state-regional controls.[33]

Four states—Hawaii (1961), Vermont (1970), Florida (1972), and Oregon (1973)—adopted systems that supersede in some fashion local land use regulatory powers and focus on three principal areas:

(1) Preservation of identified, critical natural resources and environmentally sensitive lands;

(2) Growth management controls dealing with traffic congestion, unplanned sprawl development patterns, and adequate public facilities; and

(3) Control of developments and zoning regulations with regional impacts.[34]

In 1985, Florida became the first state to require mandatory concurrency or adequate public facilities provisions, "assuring that public facilities and services needed to support development shall be concurrent with the impacts of such development."[35] Today, a second wave of state legislation has expanded the role of state government influence in states as diverse as Georgia, Maine, Colorado, Maryland, South Carolina, Rhode Island, New Jersey, and Washington.[36]

Other states, including California and New York, have adopted wide-sweeping environmental quality acts that require comprehensive environmental review of all public and private projects, including mandatory review of "cumulative impacts" that necessarily bring the surrounding regions into consideration.[37]

Finally, a number of states now require local governments to adopt and implement comprehensive plans in order to carry out zoning and subdivision controls emulating the Ramapo Plan's incorporation of a four-volume master plan as the foundation of the 18-year timing and sequence controls based upon the adequacy of public facilities measured by three six-year capital improvements plans.[38] Additional legislation incorporates federal guidelines into state coastal management acts.[39]

Federal regulation of land use has also moved into overdrive. While a national federal planning law has never been enacted,[40] the enactment of dozens of federal laws affecting state, regional, and local land use amounts to a major de facto national system. Among these laws are the:

• Civil Rights Act of 1964 (Title VI), 42 U.S.C.A. §§ 2000(d)-2000(d.7) (prohibiting discrimination by local governments in federally financed programs)
• Clean Water Act of 1977, 33 U.S.C.A. §§ 1251-1387 (especially the sections dealing with wetlands)
• Coastal Zone Management Act of 1972, 16 U.S.C.A. §§ 1451 et seq.
• Comprehensive Environmental Response, Compensation, and Liability Act of 1980, 42 U.S.C.A. §§ 9601-9675
• Emergency Planning and Community Right-to-Know Act of 1986, 42 U.S.C.A. §§ 11,001-11,050
• Endangered Species Act of 1973, 16 U.S.C.A. §§ 1531-1544
• Energy Policy and Conservation Act of 1975, 42 U.S.C.A. § 6201 et seq.
• Fair Housing Act (Title VIII of the Civil Rights Act of 1968), 42 U.S.C.A. § 3601 et seq.
• Federal Highway Beautification Act of 1965, 23 U.S.C.A. §§ 131-135 (highway signs)
• Federal Land Policy and Management Act of 1976, 43 U.S.C.A. §§ 1701-1784 (incorporating Bureau of Land Management to oversee all federal lands)
• Federal Securities Act of 1934, 15 U.S.C.A. §§ 77a et seq. (regulating subdivision purchases and hotel-condominium sales and other sales of security interests in land)
• Federal Trade Commission Act of 1914, 15 U.S.C.A. §§ 41 et seq.
• Federal Uniform Relocation Assistance and Real Property Acquisitions Act of 1970, 42 U.S.C.A. Chap. 61

• General Mining Act of 1872, 30 U.S.C.A. § 26
• Housing and Community Development Act of 1974, 42 U.S.C.A. § 1451(c) (e.g., housing subsidies, housing and building codes, redevelopment, community and development, and block grants)
• Interstate Land Sales Full Disclosure Act of 1968, 15 U.S.C.A. §§ 1701 et seq.
• Local Government Antitrust Act of 1984, 5 U.S.C.A. §§ 34-36
• National Environmental Policy Act of 1969, 42 U.S.C.A. §§ 4321-4370(f)
• National Historic Preservation Act of 1966, 16 U.S.C.A. §§ 470 et seq.
• Postal Reorganization Act of 1969, 39 U.S.C.A. §§ 3005 et seq.
• Religious Land Use and Institutional Property Act of 2000, 42 U.S.C.A. §§ 2000 cc et seq.
• Resource Conservation and Recovery Act of 1976, 42 U.S.C.A. §§ 6901-6992(k)
• Safe Drinking Water Act of 1974, 42 U.S.C.A. §§ 300f-300j-26
• Telecommunications Act of 1996, 47 U.S.C.A. § 332 (prohibiting local governments from interfering with site locations for towers)
• Toxic Substances Control Act of 1976, 15 U.S.C.A. §§ 2601-2692
• Transportation Equity Act for the 21st Century of 1998, Pub. L. No. 105-178
• Truth in Lending Act of 1968, 15 U.S.C. § 1601 et seq.

GROWTH MANAGEMENT AND SMART GROWTH

Simultaneous with the new state legislation, cities and counties across the nation began to adopt growth management systems (later termed "smart growth")[41] without waiting for new legislative authority. Florida's "concurrency" system adopted in 1985 had its genesis in the father of growth management systems—the Ramapo Plan—authored and defended in the courts by Dr. Freilich. In 1972, the New York Court of Appeals[42] upheld the constitutionality of the Ramapo Plan, a seminal decision establishing the legality of timing and phasing controls linking development approval with the availability of adequate off-site public facilities (e.g., schools, roads, police, fire, parks, and drainage) over an 18-year period.

As one commentator put it:

"The *Ramapo* decision shifted the balance of power from the developer to the public land use agencies. The developer no longer has an absolute right to proceed with development, irrespective of whether public facilities can reasonably accommodate growth. Instead, the developer can be made to wait a reasonable period to allow public facilities to catch up or be forced to expend funds to ripen the land for development. At the same time, the *Ramapo* case has expanded the judicial view of just what incidental public costs affiliated with development may be shifted to the developer."[43]

The judicial sanction of the Ramapo Plan has had a tremendous influence on infrastructure planning in this country. Following the *Ramapo* decision, local adequate public facility requirements proliferated throughout the nation, particularly in high-growth areas.[44] A 1992 survey revealed that 30 percent of California's cities had adopted adequate public facility growth management systems[45]; the same was true for other high-growth areas in Nevada, Arizona, Colorado, and Florida.[46]

In 1985, Florida became the first state to adopt Ramapo's mandatory concurrency or adequate public facilities legislation, "assuring that public facilities and services needed to support development shall be concurrent with the impacts of such development."[47]

Ramapo's 18-year capital improvements programming has provided the basis for most city-, county-, regional-, and state-level growth management programs. In 1976, the eight-county Metropolitan Council in the Minneapolis-St. Paul region utilized Ramapo to create a four-tier, 20-year growth management development framework:
- Tier I (Minneapolis and St. Paul);
- Tier II (existing built-up suburbs);
- Tier III (a 20-year timed and sequenced new-growth Ramapo tier); and
- Tier IV (permanent rural and agricultural area).[48]

Ramapo led to the San Diego General Plan Growth Management System in 1979, which utilized three growth tiers (urbanized, planned urbanizing (a 20-year Ramapo tier), and future urbanizing). By charging impact fees only in the planned urbanizing tier, and timing and sequencing its growth over the 20-year CIP, San Diego changed its growth pattern from 90 percent in Tier II and 10 percent in Tier I in 1979 to 50 percent in Tier II and 50 percent in Tier I (1985-2007) while increasing its annual growth rate from 9,000 development approvals annually to 16,000. The phenomenal growth in downtown and infill neighborhoods has totally revived the city.[49]

Growth management systems grew from urban service area lines (Portland, Ventura, and Lexington, marking the boundaries of Tier II) to sophisticated transportation corridor and centers plans[50] (Los Angeles, San Diego, and the Seattle-Tacoma four-county region), enabling the creation of transit-oriented development (TOD) around corridor centers, the backbone of new urbanism[51] and smart growth.[52]

Maryland's state government initiated the term "smart growth" as a euphemism for growth management that would sell better to developers because it implied growth rather than restrictions on growth.[53] The Maryland program focuses primarily on containing sprawl by channeling state funds to cities and state construction programs in "priority funding areas" identified by local governments within state-mandated standards.[54] Similar to the Ramapo system, the smart growth legislation allows Maryland to provide incentives for locating urban growth in areas where adequate public facilities are available.[55]

Other states have joined the march towards state growth management systems. In 1999, Wisconsin enacted its "smart growth" adequate public facilities legislation.[56] Tennessee in 1998 enacted a new law incorporating many smart growth boundaries and planned growth areas.[57] Georgia, Maine, New Jersey, Rhode Island, and Vermont have joined the earlier states of Florida, Oregon, Hawaii, and Washington in enacting smart growth legislation.[58]

SUBDIVISION REGULATIONS

A new subdivision of land is not an isolated experience involving only the buyer and seller. The pattern of a subdivision becomes the pattern of a community, which in turn may influence the character of an entire city.[59] If growth is to be orderly and rational, control over land development must be exercised.

In the past, the line of urbanization moved south and westerly. Uncontrolled subdivision of land left many communities without adequate streets, water mains, or sewers. Governments often extended their facilities to many more people than the facilities were designed to serve. Urban areas became characterized by "sprawl," disorderly and chaotic growth, followed by depressed economic values.[60]

Today, subdivision regulations are a tool for fashioning development in defined ways and by prescribed methods, regulating the use of private land in the public interest.[61] However, prior to 1928, the purpose behind subdivision regulations was to provide a more efficient method for selling land, permitting a seller to record a plat of land by dividing it into blocks and lots, laid out and sequentially numbered. During this first period of subdivision regulation, plats or maps of a subdivision showed the location of individual lots, public areas, and streets, and were recorded in the office of the county clerk or recorder of deeds. Sales of land could then be made by reference to this recorded plat, rather than by a more cumbersome description in metes and bounds. The platting of land reduced costs and prevented conflicting deeds. Uniformity was established in survey methods and boundary and monument descriptions.[62] Real property taxes became easier to assess and collect.

A second period of subdivision regulation commenced in 1928 when it was officially recognized that subdivision regulation could be used to control urban development, particularly through requirements for onsite subdivision improvements. The SPEA, published by the United States Department of Commerce, was offered in that year as a partial answer to the problems created by land speculation and premature subdivision.

The SPEA shifted the concept of subdivision regulation away from a procedure exclusively for recording land to one providing a means to implement a comprehensive community plan. Emphasis on requiring internal improvements for the subdivision was added to the convenient method for transferring lots by plat reference. The new enabling act included provisions dealing with the "arrangement of streets in relation to other existing or planned streets and to the master plan, for adequate and convenient open spaces of traffic, utilities, access of fire fighting apparatus, recreation, light, and air, and for avoidance of congestion of population, including minimum width and area of lots."[63] Following state adoption of enabling acts patterned on the SPEA, decisions from state courts across the country indicated acceptance of the use of subdivision regulations as a substantive land-use control device.[64]

The SPEA, however, did not gain uniform acceptance in state legislatures. In this area of land-use regulation, states have tended to go their separate ways, adopting varied legislation representing each state's attempt to balance private property rights with the public's interest in regulating new development.[65]

This second period of subdivision regulation continued through World War II and was marked by the passage of state subdivision enabling acts influenced by the SPEA, "designed to enact comprehensive regulatory standards which would facilitate orderly future growth along preconceived lines; in short, a planned community growth."[66] Legislation of this period reveals the change in emphasis of subdivision regulation from merely a recording device designed "to provide a method for filing maps officially so that future conveyancing instruments refer to a parcel of real estate by lot numbers . . . and to set forth sound engineering standards for maps so filed so as to avoid surveying errors"[67] to a tool to shape the growth of the entire community, but primarily emphasizing on-site subdivision improvements.[68]

After World War II, the concern in subdivision regulation shifted into a third phase. Communities felt the increasing demand that subdivision activity, particularly in the suburbs, was placing on inadequate municipal facilities and services located away from the site of the subdivision. Concern focused on the needs of new subdivision residents for public open space, parks and recreation facilities, and adequate street systems serving the subdivision. Governments added new provisions to their subdivision regulations concerning the mandatory dedication of roads, parks, school sites, and open space.[69] New devices for collecting money in lieu of land dedication were also added to state acts and local regulations to develop schools and parks in the vicinity of the subdivision; the courts generally upheld these provisions.[70]

The new regulations, however, were hardly adequate to stem the tide of sprawl that typified urban America. Major governmental reports in the late 1960s and early 1970s emphasized the need to control urban sprawl as the number one priority in land-use planning. The problems attendant to sprawl are numerous: wasteful and inefficient use of the land coupled with increased utility and municipal capital, maintenance and service costs, rising tax rates, environmental degradation, poor quality of services, and racial and socioeconomic exclusion.[71]

The National Commission on Urban Problems (the Douglas Commission) was directed by President Johnson to study the problems that urban areas were facing. The commission surveyed the problems of suburban development, urban sprawl, and premature subdivision. After two years of deliberation, five volumes of testimony, and 19 separate technical reports, the commission recommended to President Johnson and Congress:

> "At the metropolitan scale, the present techniques of development guidance have not effectively controlled the timing and location of development. Under traditional zoning, jurisdictions are theoretically called upon to determine in advance the sites needed for various types of development. . . . In doing so, however, they have continued to rely on techniques which were never designed as timing devices and which do not function well in controlling timing. The attempt to use large lot zoning, for example, to control timing has all too often resulted in scattered development on large lots, prematurely establishing the character of much later development—the very effect sought to be avoided. *New types of controls are needed if the basic metropolitan scale problems are to be solved.*"[72]

In response to the increasing call for control of urban sprawl, new subdivision regulation techniques began to emerge that went far beyond regulating the design of the subdivision and its immediate impact on the community. Communities denied subdivision approval where development could cause serious off-site flooding or environmental degradation, or worsen the problem of inadequate off-site municipal facilities, such as roads and sewers.[73]

Ultimately, in the landmark decision of *Golden v. Planning Board of the Town of Ramapo*, the New York high court upheld the constitutionality of timing and sequential controls of residential subdivision activity for the life of a comprehensive plan (18 years).[74] This marked the emergence of growth management, a fourth phase of subdivision regulation in the 1970s. This new phase resulted in a linking of the police power controls of zoning with environmental and subdivision regulations to assure that development did not impose unreasonable negative impacts on the community.[75]

In the fourth period of subdivision regulation, subdivision controls were related to the external environment and the community's comprehensive plan. Subdivision regulations were allowed to help pace the development of the community.[76]

The subdivision of land did not, however, present problems only for urban areas. The premature subdivision of land that plagued the eastern United States during the first period of subdivision development has also struck the Sunbelt states and many of the Rocky Mountain states, commencing with the Arab oil embargo and energy crisis in 1973.[77]

The federal Office of Interstate Land Sales Registration (OILSR), which administers the registration requirements of the Interstate Land Sales Full Disclosure Act,[78] reported that more than nine million undeveloped lots were registered for sale or lease since the inception of the act. The vast majority of those lots are in a handful of states. Specifically, 61 percent of all subdivisions registered with the OILSR are found in five states, while 77 percent are located in 10 states.[79] Large-scale lot-sale subdivisions (those with 1,000 or more acres) are similarly concentrated. For example, 17 counties in the United States have between 5 and 15 percent of their land area devoted to large-scale lot-sale subdivisions. The majority of these counties are in Florida, Texas, California, Arizona, New Mexico, and Colorado.[80]

The most fundamental consequence of the premature subdivision of land is the premature commitment of the land to residential development. Premature subdivision reserves a tract of real property for residences before any need for building exists. Thus, the location, layout, and density of the subdivision are established long before any substantial building occurs. By the time a need to build exists, the subdivision may be obsolete because the design standards used at the time of platting are no longer considered appropriate.[81]

Premature subdivision also contributes to environmental degradation. Even when there is no building within a subdivision, the clearing and grading of land may have substantial impact on the natural environment, contributing to erosion and drainage problems.[82] Environmental consequences increase dramatically when building occurs. Often, premature subdivisions lack central water and wastewater treatment systems. Individual lot purchasers must drill wells and install septic tanks or other individual sewage disposal systems. These systems may pollute wells within the subdivision and contribute to pollution of neighboring streams and lakes.

During the fourth phase of subdivision regulation, many local governments adopted provisions that brought unregulated subdivision activity to a halt.[83] As a result, the challenge for these governments now is to deal with subdivisions created before substantive regulations were in place.[84] Some local governments have failed, however, to deal with premature subdivision[85] and will undoubtedly have to confront the problems at some point in the future.

Planning commissions and legislative bodies have assumed the responsibility for protecting the public and future owners and occupants of property in a subdivision by imposing reasonable conditions on development.[86] These conditions are designed to mitigate the impact of development on the entire community as well as to assure quality development within the subdivision itself. As early as 1952, a subdivision application was denied on the grounds that no adequate water supply was provided for the residents.[87]

Today, several other conditions are considered before subdivision approval is granted. A prime example is imposing restrictions to control development in areas where replacing natural vegetation—which would normally absorb rain run-off—with artificial concrete, asphalt, and steel construction would lead to increased flooding problems. Planning boards have been given authority under some statutes to require "that the land shown on such plats be of such a character that it can be used safely for building purposes without danger to health or peril from fire, flood, or other menace."[88] This should help prevent the alteration of natural streams by residential and commercial building, which would lead to increased flooding damage from smaller amounts of rainfall.

Courts have upheld the denial of subdivision approval when off-site roads leading to the subdivision site are inadequate in surface and width to handle the volume of traffic that would be generated by the proposed subdivision.[89] This is a new extension of the requirement that the subdivision's internal roads must be adequate and provide appropriate access to the lots.[90]

The potential for water pollution in off-site areas furnishes another justification for establishing stringent subdivision regulations. The New York Court of Appeals has held that the threat of pollution to local wells and to a community's entire water basin warranted the enactment of a zoning ordinance increasing lots sizes. That reduced the number of septic tanks, thereby decreasing the likelihood that effluent from the subdivision would seep into the community's water sources.

Similarly, to protect navigable waters from deterioration or degradation due to uncontrolled shoreland development, the Wisconsin Supreme Court upheld as constitutional and nonconfiscatory an ordinance preventing development that would alter the natural character of land within 1,000 feet of a navigable lake and within 300 feet of a navigable river. The court held that the public trust duty of the state to protect waters for navigation—as well as for fishing, recreation, and scenic beauty—justified the stringent development control.[91] The requirement that a developer contribute toward improvement of an off-site drainage basin was upheld by the New Jersey Supreme Court under a local government's implied authority to require off-site improvements in the protection of the public interest.[92] Exactions, dedications of land, and impact fees are used for on- and off-site facilities the need for which are generated by development for roads, sewer, water, storm drainage, schools, parks, and libraries and affordable workforce housing.[93]

There also is an increasing emphasis on public-private joint ventures in real estate development.[94] Rather than the government acting only as a regulator of development, it becomes involved in the development process, permitting the development of public facilities in conjunction with the commercial or residential structures being constructed. These joint ventures often result when the government is interested in acquiring property for a public use and the property owner proposes a project that will benefit both the government and the owner.[95]

The final trend that can be identified is a move to simplify the presently complex and time-consuming land-use approval process.[96] Developers often must obtain discretionary approvals from federal, state, and local officials, and may even need approval from a regional planning body. At the local government level, the developer may need to obtain a variety of development approvals.[97] This process takes time, is costly, and may often doom worthwhile projects. Related to this procedural complexity is the difficulty that a developer may have in demonstrating a vested right to finish a project once it has commenced. Case law and state statutes appear to be developing sympathy for the property owner.[98]

This brief review of the history of subdivision regulation reveals the evolution of subdivision controls from a convenient mapping method to a complete process of community planning and protection. Subdivision development does more than create lots for sale or development; it establishes a virtually permanent pattern of community growth and leaves a legacy for future generations. Subdivision code regulation must be up to the challenge presented by the subdivision process. The LDC deals with all of these subdivision regulation challenges.

NEW URBANISM

Traditional Neighborhood Development

Traditional neighborhood development (TND) is one of several new urbanism concepts that have been embraced over the past 15 years as an alternative to the conventional development patterns that defined growth in the United States starting in the 1920s. Conventional subdivision design is characterized by auto-dependent design and segregated land uses, resulting in suburban sprawl. Conventional "sprawl" development consists of five main components, including:

(1) Housing subdivisions;
(2) Shopping centers, composed of single-use retail buildings, usually a single story with exclusive parking areas;
(3) Office/business parks, also single use and served by exclusive parking areas;
(4) Civic institutions, such as churches, schools and libraries, generally large and separated from other uses and served by exclusive parking areas; and
(5) Roadways, connecting these separated land uses and designed exclusively for the use of automobiles.[99]

Conventional subdivision design is based on a hierarchical street pattern that channels local traffic onto collector roads in order to reach almost all destination points, increasing congestion and impeding nonauto access to typical daily destinations.[100] In conventional suburban development, "adjacency" and "accessibility" have been defined as distinct concepts and, while typical daily destinations are oftentimes adjacent to one another, suburban design makes these destinations difficult to access directly and makes walking an inefficient form of transportation.[101]

TND responds to this inefficient and costly separation of uses and auto-dependency as a development alternative that promotes "mixed-use, pedestrian-friendly communities of varied population, either standing free as villages or grouped into towns and cities."[102]

There are a number of alternative development forms similar to TND that have become prominent in recent years, including neotraditional development, new urbanism, pedestrian-oriented development, and TOD. Many of these development forms share certain characteristics, although there are differences among them. Brief summaries of each of these development types are included below.

TND is based on historical development patterns that defined development in the United States through World War II.[103] The TND pattern is based on each neighborhood containing a clear center for commerce, culture, and civic activity; compact development within a 5-minute walk of the center; a street network based on small, connected blocks, generally in a grid layout; narrow, versatile streets; mixed uses; and special sites for civic structures and buildings.[104] Historically, places for living, working, and shopping were designed and built in close proximity simply because this was the most economic and convenient way to build. In times when transportation options were expensive, dangerous, dirty, and sometimes unavailable, supplying daily needs within walking distance made sense to developers and consumers.

TND employs physical design concepts to achieve social objectives. The physical conventions include the following[105]:

• The neighborhood area is limited in size, with clear edges and a focused center.

- Shops, workplaces, schools, and residences for all income groups are located in close proximity.
- Streets are sized and detailed to equitably serve the needs of the automobile and the pedestrian.
- Building size and character are regulated to spatially define streets and squares.
- Squares and parks are distributed and designed as specialized places for social activity and recreation.
- Well-placed civic buildings act as symbols of the community identity and provide places for purposeful assembly.

The social objectives promoted through these concepts include the following[106]:
- Compact form reduces requirements for energy, infrastructure, and automobile use; lessens pollution; and facilitates public transit.
- A full range of housing types and workplaces integrates age groups and economic classes.
- Provision of comfortable public places allows residents to know each other and watch over their collective security.
- Provision of a majority of daily life's necessities within walking distance allows the elderly and the young to gain independence of movement.
- Suitable civic buildings are intended to encourage democratic initiatives.

Transit-oriented Development

Proponents of new urbanism consider the major alternative to urban sprawl to be a return to mixed-use villages and centers that promote pedestrian and transit travel. TOD challenges both cities and suburbs to employ new concepts of transportation corridors and centers.[107] These new planning concepts champion:
- Increased density along transit corridors;
- The location of residences, jobs, and retail destinations close to public transit facilities;
- The provision of mixed-use development within walking distance of residential areas;
- The development of a multimodal, interconnected transportation network; and
- The development of urban design guidelines that encourage a more pedestrian and walkable community.

By establishing transportation corridors and concentrated urban centers, new urbanism:
- Encourages residents and workers to walk, ride bicycles, or utilize public transit rather than the automobile as a means of transportation;
- Lowers congestion on surrounding roadways and reduces detrimental effects on air quality; and
- Balances the distribution of land uses to concentrate development around transportation nodes within developed areas, thus preserving rural, open space, agricultural, and environmental lands.

TOD promotes design principles as one means for addressing growth management issues, including "the balance of jobs and housing, school size and placement, and the equitable distribution of resources."[108]

TOD is defined as a mixed-use community located within an average 2,000 feet walking distance of a transit stop and core commercial area. The goal of TODs is to create a mixed-use, pedestrian-friendly environment with access to a variety of transportation options, including walking, biking, transit, or car. TODs can be located in a variety of settings, from newly urbanizing areas to infill sites, but they must have convenient (existing or planned) transit access and "their uses and configuration must relate to existing surrounding neighborhoods."[109] TODs must include core commercial areas adjacent to the transit stop; residential areas within 2,000 feet (a 10-minute walk) of the transit stop; and civic and public uses, such as parks, schools, libraries, and other related public facilities.[110]

A brief overview of the guiding principles of TOD includes the following[111]:
- The site must be located on an existing or planned transit line, and land-use patterns should lead transit service planning.
- The site must be mixed use and must contain a minimum amount of public, core commercial, and residential uses.
- The site must provide a mix of residential densities, housing types, ownership patterns, and prices.
- The street system should be simple, connected, and pedestrian friendly.
- Buildings should be oriented to the street, with parking to the rear, and should be accessible on foot.
- The site should meet minimum size requirements to provide a mix of uses.
- The project should adhere to a single "specific area plan."

According to Peter Calthorpe, TOD provides a wide array of benefits and efficiencies to residents and local governments:

"TOD not only promotes alternatives to auto use, but can be a formula for affordable communities—affordable in many senses. Communities are affordable to the environment when they efficiently use land, help to preserve open space, and reduce air pollution; they are affordable for diverse households when a variety of housing types, at various costs and densities, are encouraged in convenient locations."[112]

Transit-supportive planning and development rethinks land-use and development patterns so that communities may be effectively served by a balanced transportation system. According to the Mid-America Regional Council (the metropolitan planning organization for the Kansas City area), transit-supportive development enables citizens to choose an alternative to the automobile for at least one or more of their daily trips between home, work, shopping, school, or services.

This is accomplished primarily by designing communities so that walking, cycling, riding transit, and driving a car can work together to create a balanced transportation system. Transit-supportive planning elements are included within modern transportation corridor plans. Communities that include transit-supportive elements in their plans and design, even if they are not currently served by public transportation, are referred to as "transit-ready." These communities are designed to accommodate transit service in the future. Transit-ready communities may pass through various stages of transit service over a period of many years, from conventional bus service to bus rapid transit, and finally rail service.[113] Transit-supportive design elements include:[114]

Travel Connections
- Convenient and direct pedestrian connections
- Pedestrian-scale blocks
- Interconnected street network
- Bicycle circulation and parking

Building Scale and Orientation
- Human-scale architecture
- Buildings and entrances oriented along the street

Public Spaces
- Pedestrian-friendly streets
- Parks and plazas as community gathering spaces
- Quality facilities for transit users

Parking
- Pedestrian-friendly parking facilities
- Structured and shared parking

Land Use
- Mixed-use buildings and neighborhoods
- Increased density in neighborhood centers

Design

New urbanism has garnered national attention in communities across the country in recent years as demographic shifts and environmental and fiscal concerns have come to the fore of community planning concerns.[115]

Similar to smart growth and growth management, the issues addressed by new urbanism include:
- Community quality of life
- Design
- Economics
- Environment
- Health
- Housing
- Transportation

Implementation of new urbanism concepts requires actions to[116]:
- Mix land uses
- Utilize compact building design
- Establish a range of housing opportunities and choices
- Create walkable neighborhoods
- Foster distinctive, attractive communities with a strong sense of place
- Preserve open space, farmland, natural beauty, and critical environmental areas
- Strengthen and direct development towards existing built-up areas and downtowns
- Provide a variety of transportation choices
- Make development decisions predictable, prompt, fair, and cost effective
- Encourage community and stakeholder collaboration
- Utilize sustainable development practices

Hybrid Development Types

A pseudo new urbanist movement has spurred several hybrid-type development classifications that use selective elements of new urbanism while adhering to a principally conventional development pattern. For instance, a community might be designed with the design elements of TND (e.g., front porches, narrow streets, and pedestrian orientation) but built at typical conventional densities with no mixed uses. While this might be preferable to pure conventional subdivision design, this type of development does not truly meet the objectives nor provide the social, environmental, and economic benefits of new urbanism.

The heart of new urbanism discussed above, including TND and TOD, is in the design of development.[117] The following discussion of design principles utilizes the literature available on these related development forms, as characterized by the elements discussed below.

Size

A traditional neighborhood district consists of an area of not less than approximately 40 contiguous acres and not more than approximately 250 contiguous acres. The majority of dwelling units are located within a 5-minute walk of the neighborhood center, which is roughly 2,000 feet.

Traditional Neighborhood Districts

The neighborhood is divided into at least two types of areas, and each type of area has different land-use and site development regulations. A traditional neighborhood district must have one neighborhood center area and at least one mixed residential area. The neighborhood may also have a neighborhood edge area, a workshop area, or an employment area.[118] Within each neighborhood district, there should be shops and offices that can supply the basic weekly needs of a household.

Neighborhood Center Area

The neighborhood center area serves as a focal point for the traditional neighborhood district, containing retail, commercial, civic, and public services to meet the daily needs of community residents. A neighborhood center area is pedestrian oriented and designed to encourage pedestrian movement between a mixed residential area and a neighborhood center area. A square is required with retail and commercial uses generally located adjacent to the square. Neighborhood center uses include retail shops, restaurants, offices, banks, hotels, post offices, government offices, churches, community centers, and attached residential dwellings. A transit stop should be located at the center.

Mixed Residential Areas

Mixed residential areas include a variety of residential land uses, including single-family residential, duplex, townhouse, and multifamily. The objective is to provide appropriate living spaces so that younger and older people, singles and families, and the poor and the wealthy may find places to live within the neighborhood.

Residential-scale retail and commercial uses are permitted within a mixed residential area with strict architectural and land-use controls. Accessory use buildings are permitted in backyard areas to be used as a rental unit or a place to work (e.g., an office or a craft workshop).

Neighborhood Edge Area

The neighborhood edge area is the least dense portion of the traditional neighborhood district, with larger lots and greater setbacks than the rest of the neighborhood, with only single family residential dwellings permitted.

Employment Center Areas

Employment center areas are utilized for commercial and light industrial uses and workshops that are not appropriate for the aforementioned areas but which serve the local residents.

Civic Uses

Civic uses are essential components of the social and physical fabric of the traditional neighborhood district. Special attention should be paid to the location of libraries, government offices, museums, schools, and other prominent public buildings to create focal points and landmarks for the community.[119] An elementary school is close enough so that most children can walk from their home.

Open Spaces

Open spaces are vital aspects for the traditional neighborhood district as they serve as areas for community gatherings, as landmarks, and as organizing elements for the neighborhood.[120] There are small playgrounds within 1/10 of a mile of most residential units, and larger open spaces within the neighborhood for more intense recreation uses, such as sports fields and pools.

Streets and Alleys

A traditional neighborhood district is designed to be pedestrian oriented. To accomplish this goal, street pattern and design are used to reduce vehicle travel speeds and encourage pedestrian activity.[121] The streets are narrow and form an interconnected network that connects the neighborhood to surrounding communities. Homes and buildings are located close to the street to define the public space, and parking areas and garages are not oriented to the street but are located to the side or rear of buildings, usually accessed by alleys. Importantly, "new street networks connect whenever possible to existing streets, to become part of a regional network."[122]

The underlying goal for development codes is to require new development to adapt to many features of the emerging concept of new urbanism and TND, including the following principles[123]:

- *Mixing of land uses:* While suburban dwellers must drive from one single use to the next (i.e., from residential to commercial areas), neotraditionalists make it possible to live, work, walk, and shop in the same vicinity.
- *Increased density:* Increased density is another attribute common to neotraditional communities. By increasing the density of a community, it is likely that people will begin to walk, carpool, or rely on public transit to meet their transportation needs.
- *Walkability:* Neotraditionalists strive to make the communities they develop walkable by linking the community with a network of paths, trails, and sidewalks. To achieve walkability, efforts are made to ensure that 1/4 mile is the furthest distance between uses.
- *Distinct architectural design features:* Neotraditional communities are oftentimes easy to spot due to defining design features. Such places often reinvent their cities by modeling architectural design standards on historical and regional tastes.

Research shows that better interconnectivity of streets in lieu of cul-de-sacs, proximity to light rail, new traditional design including porches and rear garages, and pedestrian accessibility to shops and other commercial uses have created a class of buyers willing to pay more to live in a new urbanist community.[124]

In order to encourage walkability and to replicate the traditional urbanism of new towns and older cities, most "greenfield"[125] new urbanism projects feature short blocks with few cul-de-sacs. Few developments include all of the design features desired by new urbanist practitioners. In many of the new "hybrid" projects, such as Otay Ranch in Chula Vista, nonurban

Table I-1
Neighborhood Design Comparison Chart

Conventional Development	Traditional Neighborhood Development
Orientation	
• Designed to emphasize privacy • Homes and buildings set back from the street at minimum distances • Designed as an independent "pod," without true linkages to surrounding development • Private orientation, with indoor and outdoor living areas located to the rear of the home	• Designed to offer opportunities for community interaction • Build-to lines that move homes and buildings closer to the street and create a more defined streetscape • Designed to enhance community and to be a long-term asset, connected to surrounding development • Public orientation, with porches and living areas located at the front of the home
Land Uses	
• Separation of uses, no neighborhood-based commercial or employment opportunities within walking or biking distance • Maximum densities that do not support transit as a viable option • Does not efficiently use infrastructure • Does not create any jobs/housing balance	• Mixed uses, including neighborhood-based commercial uses and live-work options • Minimum densities that support transit and nearby commercial uses • Designed to efficiently use infrastructure • Provides employment opportunities and strives to create jobs/housing balance
Street Network and Parking	
• Street standards designed for cars, with wide lanes and minimal streetscape standards • Curvilinear and cul-de-sac streets, with poor connections to adjacent neighborhoods and commercial areas • Minimum parking requirements, with garages and parking areas located at the front of the homes • Shared parking not an option • Auto-dependent	• Street standards designed for all users, including bikes and pedestrians, with narrow lanes and defined streetscape standards • Interconnected street network with good connections to adjacent neighborhoods and commercial areas • Maximum allowable parking areas, with garages and parking areas located to the side or rear of the homes, sometimes along alleys • Shared parking encouraged, especially among commercial uses with different peak parking demands • Supports a variety of transportation options, including cars, mass transit, walking, and biking
Environment	
• Privately owned and maintained open space and yards, fewer opportunities for public gathering spaces • Minimum parking requirements, with garages and parking areas located at the front of the homes • Regional environmental concerns not as important	• Shared open space and parks generally maintained by a property owner's association, open space designed for active and passive uses • Maximum allowable parking areas, with garages and parking areas located to the side or rear of the homes, sometimes along alleys • Supports regional environmental initiatives
Housing	
• Homes are of similar form, size, and selling price, encouraging residents of similar demographic characteristics • Larger building lots	• Homes are of a variety of sizes, forms, and prices, including affordable/attainable housing options, in order to encourage residents of varying backgrounds • Smaller building lots

See S. Mark White, "Neotraditional Development: A Legal Analysis," 49 Land Use Law & Zoning Digest, No. 8 at 3 (August 1997), and S. Mark White, "The Zoning and Real Estate Implications of Transit-Oriented Development," Transportation Research Board Project J-5 (January 1999); Joel Hirschord and Paul Souza, New Community Design to the Rescue: Fulfilling Another American Dream (Washington, DC: National Governors Association, 2001), 33.

features such as gates, six-lane arterial roads, and cul-de-sacs coexist with mixed uses and generous pedestrian infrastructure.[126]

The most successful and renowned greenfield new urbanist projects have been satellite communities similar to new towns, rather than infill projects. Examples include: Seaside, Florida; Celebration (Orlando, Florida); Laguna West (Sacramento, California); The Kentlands (Gaithersburg, Maryland); Carpenter Village (Cary, North Carolina); and Southern Village (Chapel Hill, North Carolina). These experiences demonstrate that satellite locations can promote smart growth and good urbanism while providing housing, jobs, and walkable streets.

Development code standards should differentiate smart growth and new urbanism patterns and design from sprawl by requiring answers to the following questions[127]:

- Is it located in an already developed area?
- Is there a mix of housing, office space, schools, retail shopping, outdoor recreation, and civic open spaces?
- Does the housing include multiple types, from single-family detached to multifamily condos, and does it have a range of prices from luxury to affordable?
- Does the project convert prime agricultural land or environmentally sensitive land, or does its density consume less agricultural and environmental land than the average sprawl development?
- Does the project use energy-efficient, water-captive, and green building methods?
- Is there access to public transit?
- Does the design and layout of buildings and streets promote real neighborhood interaction and compatible style?
- Has the local government adopted zoning codes that give as much support for mixed-use communities as it does for segregated, single-use Euclidean zoning?[128]

SUSTAINABILITY

Many communities are also requiring developers to abide by "sustainable" environmental and energy design. Sustainable development requires that buildings and land forms be designed with an eye toward reducing long-term operational costs and minimizing adverse effects on the environment, energy utilization, public works infrastructure, and employee health and productivity.[129] Developers of "sustainable subdivisions" and "green" buildings strive to meet these goals by using "key resources like energy, water, materials, and land much more efficiently than buildings that are simply built to code."[130]

The sustainable development movement had a halting beginning, primarily due to developers and their clients viewing green building practices as aspirational, serving the greater community's interests at the expense of the builder's bottom line.[131] That view has proven to be a myth, however, in light of recent data demonstrating how various intrinsic benefits of green building far outweigh additional up-front costs.

One oft-cited and particularly exhaustive study was conducted in 2003 on behalf of California's Sustainable Building Task Force. The study projected that incorporating green features into a building's design would generate a 10-fold return on investment over the life of the building.[132] That estimate was derived from a comparison of a few dozen green buildings and their conventional counterparts.[133] The findings were substantial: the green buildings consumed 30 percent less energy,[134] used 30 to 50 percent less water,[135] and produced 50 to 75 percent less construction waste.[136] The valuation included increases in the health and productivity of employees working in green buildings.

While admitting that "[m]easuring the exact financial impact of healthier, more comfortable and greener buildings is difficult," the study pointed to data showing that green building features increase "indoor environmental and air quality," resulting in increased productivity, reduced absenteeism, and reduced unemployment and medical insurance costs. Other commentators emphasize the importance of indoor environmental and air quality in the "war for talent," noting that "top employees" will actively seek out "a high-quality workplace."[137]

Proponents of sustainable development have latched onto these benefits[138] in an effort to persuade developers and architects that sustainable development is in their clients' best financial interest.[139] By most accounts, their campaign has been remarkably successful. Membership in the United States Green Building Council (USGBC), consisting of corporations, nonprofits, and governmental agencies, has grown by more than 1,000 percent since 2000.[140]

In ever-increasing numbers, developers are seeking USGBC Leadership in Energy and Environmental Design (LEED®) project certification (discussed below) to satisfy local green building requirements or to qualify for land-use incentives rewarding sustainable development. The LDC provides for mandatory minimum LEED-sustainability criteria. Any local government can change that to an incentive system by authorizing alternative bonuses for density or floor area ratio. By 2000, only 12 projects had been LEED certified[141]; as of January 2006, that number had grown to 461 projects, with an additional 3,261 projects registered and seeking certification.[142]

The trend has not been limited to commercial development. The National Association of Home Builders has issued a set of guidelines designed to "[h]ighlight the ways a mainstream home builder can effectively weave environmental solutions holistically into a new home."[143] The City of Scottsdale, Arizona, recently announced that one-third of all new single-family homes satisfy the city's voluntary green building standards.[144]

Notably, the indoor and outdoor environmental benefits of sustainable development provides a legal basis for local governments seeking to mandate green building practices for private developers. A 2003 Calabasas, California, ordinance cited USGBC statistics in comparing the effects of traditional and sustainable development on natural resources consumption, waste production, and the health and productivity of workers.[145] In order to "minimize local ecological degradation (habitat, air, soil, and water)" and ensure "healthy interiors," the city required all new and remodeled nonresidential buildings over 500 square feet to meet the minimum requirements for LEED certification, and those over 5,000 square feet to achieve a LEED Silver rating.[146]

In addition to building design and layout, the LDC (§ 5.17 Sustainability in Chapter 5, Development Standards, of the LDC) provides for regulations and incentives for important sustainable building practices relating to provision of (1) alternative energy (particularly solar)[147] and (2) sustainable water techniques and technologies (vegetated swales, rain gardens, rain capture through barrels and cisterns, permeable paving); house features (dishwashers, washing machines, showers, faucets, toilets); gray water landscape irrigation; irrigation automated systems; and rainfall harvesting.[148]

CONCLUSION

We have traced through most of the new developments in land-use regulation. The LDC is designed to integrate these new trends into a cohesive, usable, and comprehensive code that will fit the needs of every city, county, town, village, and borough in the United States, and will provide the planning and legal support to sustain the code provisions upon judicial challenge.

THE LAND DEVELOPMENT CODE: INSTRUCTIONS FOR USE

UNIFIED DEVELOPMENT ORDINANCE

Many communities have sought to unify their zoning and subdivision regulations. In the 1980s, unified development ordinances (UDOs) reached a peak in popularity.[149] The purpose of UDOs was to:

- Achieve flexibility in regulating new development;
- Improve administrative efficiency in processing; and
- Consolidate and integrate zoning, subdivision, official maps, signs, floodplains, and design standards into one manageable code.

Unfortunately, most UDOs ended up being "three-ring binders" that simply gathered all of the community's ordinances land brought them into a single book, with each having its own code chapter. Since most of the rigid use and bulk regulations were simply repackaged, the objectives of flexibility and integration were never attained.

The LDC utilizes the UDO approach but goes far beyond compilation to advance true implementation of the comprehensive plan into regulations. Flexibility, sustainability, design, usability, efficiency, balanced growth, fiscal impact analysis, infrastructure finance, infill, housing mix and affordability, and revitalization of existing areas have been integrated into a seamless web.

OBJECTIVES OF THE LAND DEVELOPMENT CODE

The LDC provides a user-friendly, readable code format for use by local governments. The LDC is designed to incorporate a number of objectives that are missing in many model codes or limited codes. These include the following:

- *Comprehensiveness:* The LDC is not limited to zoning, subdivision, or urban design as are other model or "unified" development codes. In that case, language from both codes may be combined as needed to meet local objectives. The LDC, on the other hand, is a comprehensive "land development regulation" or "LDR" that embraces most of the topics faced by local planning officials. Florida, for example, has passed a comprehensive growth management statutory system that requires all city and county governments to adopt LDRs. The LDRs include zoning, subdivision, official mapping of future rights-of-way, building, health, housing and safety codes, environmental regulations, and financing of infrastructure.[150]

- *Consistency:* Internally between elements of the comprehensive plan; and externally between regulations, development approvals, and the comprehensive plan.

- *Clarity:* The LDC is user friendly, organized logically, and written in accordance with sound technical writing principles. While special terminology is sometimes needed for legal reasons (e.g., nonconforming uses), this terminology is explained and defined in Appendix A, Definitions and Rules of Interpretation, of the LDC. This provides a usable format for all code users, including administrators, applicants, and the general public.

- *Usability:* The LDC is not targeted to large or small planning staffs. Instead, it is usable by any level of local government.

- *Enforceability:* The LDC is designed to be legally enforceable from a broad constitutional sense. However, the LDC is not adapted to all 50 states, and any attempt to do so would be futile. Local governments are advised to carefully review their state planning legislation and to adapt the LDC accordingly.

- *Adaptability:* The LDC is designed to be changed over time. Instead of having to tack new issues onto the LDC in a piecemeal fashion, local governments can add new sections to the existing body of the LDC as needed to address new situations.

WHAT IS A CODE?

A code has the following elements:

• *Land-use policies:* A development code in many states remains the principal document for establishing fundamental land-use policies. In some states (such as California, Florida, Georgia, Oregon, and Washington), a separate, written comprehensive plan is required in order to establish land-use policies, and the code of land development regulations follows. However, in "unitary view" states, the zoning ordinance itself provides the "comprehensive plan." In addition, even in "plan-as-law" states, codes established many policies at the "micro" level, such as how individual development approvals are handled, which are not resolved by the more global policies established in the plan.

• *Instruction manual:* A code is an instruction manual for the development of land. This creates an important tension because the instruction manual applies both to infrequent and frequent users of the code. The types of users read the code differently. A major push of the planning profession today is to write codes in a manner that is readily understandable by the general public. However, people who use the code on a day-to-day basis (such as zoning administrators, engineering and architectural consultants, home builders, and planning commissioners) must also find the code usable. The LDC resolves this tension by combining graphics, clear technical writing, and "purpose and findings" statements for use by the general public, with terminology that is generally accepted in the planning profession and building industries.

• *Law:* A code is a legal document and separates a development code from a comprehensive plan, or even an informal handbook. The code is legally binding, and compliance or noncompliance with the code carries significant legal consequences. It is essential that the code be written in a legally enforceable manner, and avoids creating significant litigation costs or risk of liability for the public and private sectors.[151]

• *Mediator:* A code mediates the preferences of many diverse stakeholder groups. Ideally, the code is the product of a lengthy and an involved public participation process that involves various groups with an interest in the development approval process. These include planning staff, home buyers, developers, economic development groups, neighborhoods, environmentalists, and public officials at different levels of government. Normally, all of these groups will have different ideas about how the code should be written, administered, and enforced. Each group has several legitimate interests, which often conflict. During this process, reasonable compromises need to be forged between each group. Compromise needs to be clearly written into the ordinance; otherwise, the code could be enforced in a manner that reflects the ideals of a single group, which do not reflect the compromises that were reached during the public participation process.

• *Dictionary:* A development code is used to define terms and concepts, many of which are not clearly understood by the general public. The code needs to clearly state what these concepts are and establish clear rules for compliance.

Readability

Zoning and development regulations are often criticized for their wordiness, obtuse language, and poor organizational structure. A development code is, in essence, a legal document. It is a jurisdiction's authority to require development to occur in a certain manner or to prescribe conditions. As with contracts or other legal documents, a code must contain some boilerplate language and be written with sufficient particularity to be legally enforceable.

However, a legal document does not have to be obtuse, wordy, or dry. Many techniques can be used to enhance the readability of a code, including a more logical organizational structure, punchier formatting, and illustrations or diagrams that embellish the legal text. These modifications can make the document understandable to a layperson as well as preserve the enforceability of the ordinance.

It is important to recognize that the relative strictness of an ordinance does not increase with its length. Short ordinances with vague, discretionary standards are often confusing to both staff and the development community because they leave key questions unanswered and provide virtually unfettered discretion for development approval decision-makers.

Discretionary standards should be minimized while avoiding excessive regulations. Adding detail and length to the code can actually streamline regulations (single, integrated hearings) by minimizing unanticipated conditions. Codes should provide a good list of objective standards.

Development codes can be simplified by following a logical order, adding graphics, and providing an executive summary of its contents. Because a development code is a complete set of standards and procedures for all development within a jurisdiction, it can never be designed to be read from cover to cover. A state-of-the-art organizational format includes introductory and substantive chapters near the beginning of the document, and definitions and technical materials in appendices or later chapters. An index can assist the reader in locating information.

In addition, the page design can be organized with chapter headings, section borders, and other features to enhance layout. The use of columns and matrices can organize standards by category, which in turn can be tied to graphics in the ordinance.[152] Columns can be provided to more efficiently utilize space. Using an 11 x 17-inch page format can improve the integration of text and graphics and provide more information per page; however, it is difficult to copy and read in tight spaces, such as in airplane seats.

CERTAINTY

Land development codes are often unclear and subject to interpretation. This creates an aura of uncertainty that can discourage development and drive up costs. While planners and developers may disagree on the issue of whether permitting is sufficiently streamlined, both groups usually agree that clarity in the standards is needed. Builder and real estate interests sometimes make this their top priority during a code revision process.

PROCESS

The process of obtaining approval can also create an atmosphere of uncertainty for developers and neighborhoods. Developers often report that there is considerable uncertainty about the likelihood of some types of development approval, and that neighborhood opposition and NIMBY (Not In My Back Yard) politics can derail discretionary development approvals. Certainly, neighborhood input is a valuable part of the development approval process; however, codes should provide ways for decisions to reflect agreed-upon land-use policies and to avoid unnecessary procedural hurdles where an application satisfies those policies.[153]

The development community often faces uncodified staff directives that are not supported by adopted ordinances. Items that are not required by ordinance are often requested during the development approval process. This exposes jurisdictions to expensive litigation, which could be avoided by using standards that are carefully thought out and comprehensive.

INCENTIVES, CONDITIONS, AND OVERLAYS

Development incentives are an important tool in obtaining public amenities, design concessions, and other benefits that may not be available under state or federal laws. Incentives can also be used to build support for code revisions with the development community. While they often require additional staffing and potential neighborhood conflicts, they can encourage the type of development that a jurisdiction wants (e.g., infill and TND).

Incentives can take the form of substantive relief, such as through increases in density and reductions in improvement standards, or procedural relief through development approval streamlining. Particular incentives are discussed in the specific topical areas (e.g., affordable housing in Chapter 3, Zoning, of the LDC). Examples of incentives that may be administered through a code include:

- Density bonuses, mandatory cluster (tiers), and transfer of development rights (TDRs)
- Reductions in improvement standards, such as street pavement widths and parking requirements
- Fast-track one-stop permitting
- Federal and state growth
- Minimum/maximum density and area requirements (i.e., commercial from 10 to 40 percent and residential from 60 to 90 percent, to allow flexibility by the developer to meet market conditions)

Other incentives (such as tax abatement, insurance, tax increment financing, predevelopment loans, and risk sharing) are typically not part of a regulatory code but may be found elsewhere in the local code of ordinances.

MULTIJURISDICTIONAL AND INTERGOVERNMENTAL APPROACHES

Local governments are increasingly engaging in multijurisdictional development codes, which apply the same, or similar, development standards and procedures across several jurisdictions. This has many distinct benefits, such as:

- Minimizing "forum shopping" by developers seeking to use lower standards;
- Allowing regions to more effectively control sprawl by regulating the extraterritorial impacts and adapting critical regional environmental, infrastructure, and housing standards across jurisdictional lines;
- More efficiently using public resources by sharing staff and enforcement on a regional basis; and
- Enhancing predictability for the private sector within metropolitan areas by providing a single-code format or standard, as opposed to different formats and standards for each jurisdiction.

A multijurisdictional code could be optional or binding on the participating jurisdictions. Nonbinding options include model ordinances, referral, and cross acceptance. Binding options include joint planning commission and/or development review committees, joint planning areas (JPAs), interlocal agreement, or consolidated planning commissions and/or planning departments. These options are described in greater detail below.

NONBINDING OPTIONS

Model Ordinance

The model ordinance approach simply involves the voluntary adoption and separate administration of the code by each jurisdiction. No jurisdiction would be obligated to adopt the code, and the code could be adopted in its entirety or in parts. This approach preserves local autonomy but raises the potential for individual jurisdictions to undermine regional development policies. It also raises the spectre of each jurisdiction adopting slightly different versions of the code, thereby undermining the objective of coordinating and simplifying the development codes. It is similar to the approach adopted by the American Planning Association's *Growing Smart™ Legislative Guidebook*.[154]

There are several options for implementing a model ordinance:

• A designated lead agency, such as a city or county, could adopt the ordinance with other jurisdictions permitting the ordinance to apply where permitted by state law.[155] Designated lead agencies would also be utilized in reviewing and certifying environmental impact statements.[156]

• A nonbinding memorandum of understanding could be adopted that expresses each jurisdiction's intent to adopt and to implement the standards of the code.

• A formal intergovernmental agreement (IGA) can be adopted that binds all participating governments and agencies.

Referral

A referral procedure involves an agreement among the jurisdictions whereby applications for development approval within designated areas of influence will be referred to designated jurisdictions. Those jurisdictions would then have an opportunity to comment on the development applications. However, the agency within which the application was submitted would retain final approval authority.

Cross-acceptance

Cross-acceptance, which was used by New Jersey to implement its State Development and Redevelopment Plan, involves a formal mechanism for ensuring consistency between neighboring jurisdiction's zoning and subdivision ordinances. Cross-acceptance would be effectuated by means of an IGA among the jurisdictions (see "Intergovernmental Agreements," below).

BINDING OPTIONS

Binding intergovernmental planning options provide a legal commitment for all of the local governments to commit, at some level, to the implementation of the code. These include joint or consolidated planning commissions and/or development review committees, joint powers agreements, interlocal agreements, and interstate compacts.

Joint or Consolidated Planning Commissions

Joint or consolidated planning commissions involve the administration of a unified ordinance by a single agency. This mechanism potentially provides the most powerful and effective mechanism for accomplishing interjurisdictional land-use objectives, while at the same time surrendering local autonomy to a certain degree.

The difference between the two approaches is that:

• A joint commission approach would include representatives from the planning commissions of each jurisdiction, with some matters remaining within the exclusive jurisdiction of each agency.

• A consolidated commission approach would disband the separate planning commissions and/or planning departments for each jurisdiction, combining all land-use authority into one agency. For example, the City of Charlotte and Mecklenburg County, North Carolina, have a joint planning department and have established a joint planning commission pursuant to a 1988 Interlocal Cooperation Agreement. However, the local governments retain their own zoning ordinances. Several major policy decisions under this approach include the development of procedures for appointment of the planning commission members and the delegation of authority to the planning commission. The planning commission may have final review authority on designated matters or may simply submit a nonbinding recommendation for final review by the local government.

Joint Planning Areas

A JPA uses any of the institutional approaches discussed above on a discrete, geographic basis. A JPA could be designated for areas subject to the extraterritorial jurisdiction of cities as provided in many state statutes. An example is Chapel Hill and Orange County, North Carolina, which jointly process applications for development approval in a "rural buffer" area established pursuant to a 1986 Joint Planning Agreement.

Intergovernmental Agreements

An IGA or Memoranda of Understanding (MOU) is a flexible approach whereby each jurisdiction would contractually adopt the code, parts of the code, or common development standards. Alternative approaches for structuring an IGA or MOU include the following:

• The IGA/MOU could contractually bind each jurisdiction to the adoption and implementation of the code.

• The IGA/MOU could establish minimum standards throughout the area, with each jurisdiction retaining the authority to adopt stricter standards for all or parts of the ordinance. A similar approach is followed in the "critical areas" or "development of regional impact" legislation of some states, such as Florida and Colorado, in which state and local governments share approval authority over large-scale development approvals or in environmentally constrained areas.[157]

CONTENT OF THE LAND DEVELOPMENT CODE

The LDC establishes standards and procedures for new development. It is designed to be read either from cover to cover or for readers to look up only the parts they need. A list of chapters and divisions in the Contents shows the main topics and overall organization of the LDC. There are many other ways to use the LDC, depending on the reader's objectives.

A major purpose of the LDC is to implement the comprehensive plan. It is designed to provide clear rules about what is expected of applicants in order to gain approval to develop land in a city. It is also designed to streamline the development approval process, removing unnecessary delay and confusing or vague standards from the process.

Numbering and Cross-referencing

The format of the LDC is consistent with many local codification practices. The chapter, division, and section numbers use a uniform numbering system. Some of the chapters are divided into divisions, and the divisions are divided into sections.

Outside the Chapter

When a cross-reference refers to text outside of the chapter, it includes the section number, the other chapter number, and the chapter title (e.g., "see § 1.1 Citation in Chapter 1, General Provisions, of the LDC," if the cross-reference is outside of Chapter 1). At the end of the cross-reference, "of the LDC" is used if it refers to the entire code.

Within the Chapter or Section

When a cross-reference refers to text within the same chapter, it includes the section number and ends with "of this chapter" (e.g., "see § 1.1 Citation of this chapter," if the cross-reference is within Chapter 1). Cross-references within the same section include the appropriate subsection letter (e.g., "see subsection (B)(2)"), which refers to the second numbered paragraph of subsection (B) of the same chapter and section of the LDC.

"Purpose and Findings" Statements

The beginning of many chapters, divisions, and sections includes a "purpose and findings" statement, which summarizes the comprehensive plan policies that the section is designed to implement, other relevant public policies, and factual findings governing the section. These "purpose and findings" statements provide the basis for the development standards but are not standards. In other words, an application for approval of a development cannot be denied because of a conflict with the "purpose and findings" statement; however, an application will be denied where it conflicts with the standards.

Chapter 1, General Provisions, of the LDC contains some basic information on the legal framework of the LDC and a guide on how to use it.

Use Patterns

Chapter 2, Use Patterns, of the LDC consolidates the regulations applicable to particular forms of development into a single package. These use patterns reflect either the majority of anticipated permitting activity or patterns, such as TND, TOD, a master planned community, corridor centers, or specified infill that the local government may want to encourage. Each section in Chapter 2 describes the use pattern, the procedure for approval, and the standards relating to approval, with cross-references to other parts of the LDC where needed. The intent is to present a visual, user-friendly overview of the regulations that apply to those types of uses or development styles. The use patterns established in Chapter 2 are not zoning districts or overlay zones. Instead, they are forms of development that are authorized in the various zoning districts established by Chapter 2 and other relevant zoning district regulations.

Zoning

Chapter 3, Zoning, of the LDC contains regulations for the base, overlay, flexible, and special zoning districts. These regulations establish the uses that are permitted in each zone.
- *Division 1: Introduction*
- *Division 2: Base Zoning Districts*
- *Division 3: Overlay Zoning Districts*
- *Division 4: Flexible Zoning*

A summary schedule showing the permitted and conditional uses in all districts is presented in Table 3-4, Use Matrix. Uses may be permitted as of right or as a conditional use. Uses permitted as of right need only obtain a zoning certificate and development approval before starting construction. Conditional uses require special review by the planning commission.

Base zoning districts are the general districts in which nearly all parcels are divided: residential, commercial, and industrial. Development standards for each base zoning district are included. These standards include limits on the maximum height, required setbacks, and (for several districts) building size. A schedule of these standards is shown in Table 3-6, Dimensional Standards, which summarizes the particular standards established in each district.

Chapter 3 includes overlay, special, and incentive zoning districts. Overlay zoning districts consist of regulations that address unusual subjects, such as requirements for historic districts and landmarks, floodplains, airports, and environmentally sensitive areas (habitat, wetlands, and steep slopes). Regulations for protection of environmentally sensitive lands (wetlands, riparian buffers, and steep slopes) are contained in § 5.40 Riparian Buffers through § 5.42.4 Standards in Chapter 5, Development Standards, of the LDC. Satellite antennas and wireless communications facilities (see § 7.80 Satellite Dish Antennas and § 7.92 Wireless

Communications Facilities in Chapter 7, Supplemental Use Regulations, of the LDC) and sustainability (see § 5.53 Sustainability in Chapter 5, Development Standards, of the LDC) are covered.

Special districts consist of regulations that have been tailored to a specific geographic area or a specific type of development. Flexible zoning allows a range of densities and area provisions as of right (i.e., single-family residential from three to eight units per acre and setbacks from 35 to 50 feet).

One form of special district—the "PD" (Planned Development) district—allows flexibility in development standards for large parcels under unified control. It may contain an overall cap of population or floor area, or dwelling units, which allow for conversions from residential to commercial, or vice versa, based on equivalent dwelling units measured by a common standard (e.g., trip generation or numbers of persons per dwelling unit). The official zoning map will identify overlay zoning districts, "PD" districts, flexible, and special districts as well as the base zoning districts.

Flexible zoning allows density bonuses where an applicant provides special amenities or provides special amenities, such as enhanced open space, redevelopment, public art, or affordable housing. TDRs are permitted between properties in order to encourage the protection of open space.

This chapter also contains regulations for specific uses and development types that apply in all base zoning districts. Examples include accessory dwellings, home occupations, and wireless towers. These uses may or may not be permitted as of right or as a conditional use, depending on how they are listed in the particular district under Table 3-4, Use Matrix. The standards are designed to address particular issues that are raised by the particular use.

Procedures

Chapter 4, Procedures, of the LDC tells the applicant how to obtain development orders and describes what happens if the LDC is violated. This chapter provides information on the city's administrative framework and procedures that relate to land-use and development standards.

- *Division 1: General* provides general information about the application process, public hearings, and notification.
- *Division 2: Quasi-judicial and Legislative Approvals*
- *Division 3: Ministerial Development Approvals* describes how to obtain site plan approval. Master site plans are large-scale development orders requiring discretionary approval, while minor site plans are nondiscretionary development orders required for particular types of uses (regardless of size or scale).
- *Division 4: Zoning Procedures* describes the procedures for obtaining development approval, including rezoning, conditional zoning, conditional uses, and "ministerial" development orders for particular uses, which do not require a public hearing. In addition, this division establishes procedures for registering neighborhood associations and establishing neighborhood plans.
- *Division 5: Subdivisions* describes how to divide property into lots and provides a description of the process for constructing and dedicating site infrastructure.
- *Division 6: Variances and Appeals* establishes procedures for variances and appeals, including procedures for zoning variances and subdivision variances. A separate division contains both administrative and other legal remedies available to enforce the LDC.
- *Division 7: Miscellaneous Development Orders*
- *Division 8: Enforcement, Violations, and Penalties*

The procedures established in Chapter 4 should be read in conjunction with Appendix B, Specifications for Documents to Be Submitted, of the LDC. This establishes a convenient checklist of information so that the reviewing agencies and the local government can determine whether an application is complete.

Development Standards

The standards for land development are consolidated in Chapter 5, Development Standards, of the LDC. Infrastructure standards include standards for parks and open space, stormwater management, street design and access management, and utilities. Landscaping requirements include grading, site landscaping, buffering, and street tree planting requirements.

- *Division 1: Generally*
- *Division 2: Design Standards* establishes standards for lot layout, explains how to measure setbacks, and describes building height. (Remember that the individual districts establish the setbacks and height restrictions within each zoning district.)
- *Division 3: Infrastructure Standards*
- *Division 4: Greenspace (Landscaping, Tree Preservation, Screening, and Environmental Protection) Standards*
- *Division 5: Environmental Protection of Critical Areas* establishes natural resource protection requirements for the floodplains and tree preservation.
- *Division 6: Parking and Storage Standards* includes the schedule of minimum and maximum number of parking spaces for each land use.

Adequate Public Facilities

Standards for measuring the capacity of off-site public facilities to serve new development are established in Chapter 6, Adequate Public Facilities, of the LDC.

Supplemental Use Regulations

By reason of size considerations, the supplemental use regulations in Chapter 7, Supplemental Use Regulations, of the LDC does not contain provisions for flood control, signs, or adult uses. These provisions are extremely lengthy and numerous models exist. We have made room in the LDC for insertion of these provisions in Chapter 7, and have provided references to specific model ordinances for these subjects.

Nonconforming Uses and Vested Rights

Chapter 8, Nonconforming Uses/Vested Rights, of the LDC protects existing development lawfully in existence from new regulations. In addition, the rights of landowners with applications in progress are also protected as required by state law in all states.
- *Division 1: Nonconformities*
- *Division 2: Vested Rights*

Administrative Agencies and Appendices

Chapter 9, Administrative Agencies, of the LDC formally establishes or recognizes the agencies involved in the development approval process. These include the planning commission, the board of adjustment, and administrative staff.

Chapter 10, Legal Status, and the appendices (Appendix A, Definitions and Rules of Interpretation, and Appendix B, Specifications for Documents to Be Submitted) of the LDC conclude with legal usage, definitions, and specifications for application submissions.

Determining the Regulations for a Specific Site

To determine the regulations of the LDC applicable to a site, the user must first find the site on the official zoning map. The appropriate map will show the base zoning district that is applied to the site. It will also show if the site is subject to any overlay zoning and flexible and special districts (e.g., if the site contains an historic landmark).

The user should then look up all the corresponding regulations. Start with the base zoning districts (see *Division 2: Base Zoning Districts* in Chapter 3, Zoning, of the LDC). The base zoning districts state whether a use is allowed as of right, allowed as a conditional use, or prohibited. The zoning district regulations contain the setback and building height standards, which apply to the uses that are allowed. In addition, the user should consult Chapter 7, Supplemental Use Regulations, of the LDC to see if additional requirements apply to the use they are contemplating.

Determining Location of Specific Uses

To determine in what base zoning district a specific use may be located, the user must first determine the land-use category. Use the definitions in the use matrix (see Table 3-4, Use Matrix, in Chapter 3, Zoning, of the LDC) to look up a specific use. These are listed by category (e.g., retail sales or heavy industry) rather than types of business. If there is a question as to how the use is defined, the Land-Based Classification Standard (LBCS), published by the American Planning Association, should be consulted. The LBCS is a comprehensive classification system for land uses, which is cross-referenced in the LDC.

Table 3-4 enables any code user easy access to the status of the particular land use. Land-use categories may be allowed as of right, allowed with special limitations, allowed only as a special exception (with additional conditions possible), or prohibited. The user should also check base zoning district regulations for supplemental use regulations because some uses are subject to special standards.

Finally, although a base zoning district may allow a use, a specific site may be subject to additional regulations from an overlay, flexible, or special zoning district. The regulations of the overlay, flexible, or special district are applicable in addition to the regulations of the base zoning district and may affect or limit uses allowed and conditions required in the base regulations, so those regulations should also be consulted.

Determining Which Procedures Apply

Each section of Chapter 4, Procedures, of the LDC that contains a development approval process includes a subsection entitled "Applicability." This subsection describes the situations where a particular process is needed. If the section applies, the user should then consult the following subsections, which describe how an application is initiated, how an application is processed, the criteria for review, and cross-references to other parts of the LDC.

In addition, most sections have a subsection entitled "Scope of Approval," which describes the rights granted to an applicant by the development approval. Keep in mind that not all development approvals entitle an applicant to begin construction. In fact, many only authorize an applicant to proceed to the next step in the development approval process.

NOTES

1. In the United States, state law typically assigns the authority to implement land-use controls to local governments. A local government typically includes cities, counties, townships, or other local entities with general police powers. In this book, the term "local government" refers generally to any that adopts land-use regulations governing development approvals. In the text of the LDC, the placemarker "[LOCAL GOVERNMENT]" refers to the name of the adopting entity.
2. John W. Reps, *Town Planning in Frontier America* (Columbia: University of Missouri Press, 1980), at 27-31.
3. *Palm Beach County v. Wright*, 641 So.2d 50 (Fla. 1994) (upholding Official Thoroughfare Right-Of-Way Protection Map, protecting the future right-of-way of the county's identified transportation corridors from per se takings' challenges).

4. Vitruvius, *The Ten Books on Architecture* (New York: Dover Publications, 1960).
5. See 31 Eliz. I C.7 (Statutes at Large Vol. 6 at 409) where English cottages and homes were required to have at least 4 acres of land to avoid urban filth and congestion. Indeed, after the great fire of 1666, Parliament's "Act for the Rebuilding of London" divided all housing into four classes with separate regulations for each. Sir William S. Holdsworth, *A History of English Law*, Vol. 4 (London: Methuen & Co., Ltd. and Sweet & Maxwell, 1964-2004), at 132-3.
6. See Thomas H. Logan, "The Americanization of German Zoning," 42 *J. Am. Inst. Planners* 377 (1966).
7. Philadelphia 2, Pennsylvania Stat. § 66, Ch. 53 (planting of shade trees); Boston, Massachusetts, Laws 1672 at 269 (building laws and regulations); Savannah, Georgia (planned city squares); Eric Freyfogle, "Land Use and the Study of Early American History," 94 *Yale L. J.* 717 (1985); see also David L. Callies, Robert H. Freilich, and Thomas E. Roberts, *Cases and Materials on Land Use*, 4th ed., "Introduction & Historical Overview" (Eagan, MN: West, 2004).
8. Robert H. Freilich and Michael M. Schultz, *Model Subdivision Regulations: Planning and Law*, 2d ed. (Chicago: American Planning Association, 1995). Land speculation often resulted in economically depressing situations. One of the more famous personalities to fall victim to the rainbow of land speculation was Charles Dickens. In 1840, Dickens succumbed to the economic temptations of Cairo City, Illinois, located at the junction of the Mississippi and Ohio Rivers. He invested more than he could afford, not knowing that the prime land was generally submerged most of the year. His realization and bitterness prompted the novel *Martin Chuzzlewitt*, which reflected Dickens' temperament following his visit to the United States in 1842. Dickens' comment following his trip is a summation of the results of premature land speculations: "A dismal swamp on which the half-built houses rot away; cleared here and there for the space of a few yards, and teeming with rank unwholesome vegetation, in whose baleful shade the wretched wanderers who are tempted hither, droop and die, and lay their bones; the hateful Mississippi circling and eddying before it, and off upon its southern course, a shiny monster hideous to behold; a hotbed of disease, an ugly sepulchre, a grave uncheered by any gleam of promise; a place without one single quality, in earth or air or water, to command it, such is this dismal Cairo."

    See E. Rachlis and J. Marqusee, *The Landlords* (New York: Random House, 1963), 37-40. Speculation brought orators of unusual distinction to the American scene. One of the most exotic stories is about El Camino Real, a street 219 feet wide to accommodate 20 lanes, yet only 1/2 mile long, leading to the storied city of Boca Raton, Florida. High-pressure sales (by orators no less famous than William Jennings Bryan) resulted in skyrocketing prices of the lots until the bottom dropped out during the infamous Florida land bust of the 1920s. The gimmick was "vision"—"Can you imagine a city not being there?"—and the result was pathos. See Alva Johnston, *The Legendary Mizners* (New York: Farrar, Straus and Young, 1953), 235, 238, 242, 274, 276-7.
9. See Donald L. Miller, *City of the Century: The Epic of Chicago and the Making of America (Illinois)* (New York: Simon & Schuster, 1997).
10. For the significant issues confronting gated communities and restrictive covenant governance, see the Association of American Law held on January 7, 2005, and published in the summer issue of *The Urban Lawyer*, containing the following articles:
    • David L. Callies, "Common Interest Communities: An Introduction," 37 *Urb. Law.* 325 (2005);
    • Michael A. Heller, "Common Interest Developments at the Crossroads of Legal Theory," 37 *Urb. Law.* 329 (2005);
    • Paula A. Franzese, "Privatization and Its Discontents: Common Interest Communities and the Rise of Government for the 'Nice,'" 37 *Urb. Law.* 335 (2005) (noting that more than 50 million Americans live in a condominium, a cooperative, or a planned, walled, or gated community); and
    • Susan F. French, "Making Common Interest Communities Work: The Next Step," 37 *Urb. Law.* 359 (2005) (noting that, while common interest communities may create additional value of shared amenity resources, these communities, by having the developer transfer the cost of maintaining public infrastructure of streets, sewers, drainage, schools, and parks to the community instead of to the public sector, pay double taxes and see greater deficiencies and lack of service).

    See also Edward J. Blakely and Mary Gail Snyder, *Fortress America: Gated Communities in the United States* (Washington, DC: Brookings Institution Press, 1997) (a sociological examination of Americans retreating from communities into gated subdivisions with like-minded people, the affluent, the retired, and the fearful) and Neil Shouse, "The Bifurcation: Class Polarization and Housing Segregation in the Twenty-First Century Megalopolis," 30 *Urb. Law.* 145 (1998).
11. See Restatement (Second) of Torts §§ 827 and 828, which is a frequently cited source for determining whether a nuisance exists.
12. See Jacob H. Beuscher and Jerry W. Morrison, "Judicial Zoning Through Recent Nuisance Cases," 1955 *Wis. L. Rev.* 440.
13. *Bove v. Donna-Hanna Coke Corporation*, 258 N.Y.S. 229 (App. Div. 4th Dep't.) (1932) (permitting); *Hadacheck v. Sebastian*, 239 U.S. 394 (1915) (prohibiting brick manufacturing in residential areas).
14. *Pendoley v. Ferreira*, 187 N.E.2d 142 (Mass. 1963) (hog farm); *Armory Park Neighborhood Association v. Episcopal Community Services in Arizona*, 712 P.2d 914 (Ariz. 1985) (soup kitchen is nuisance); *Smith v. Gill*, 310 So.2d 1214 (Ala. 1976) (halfway house for mental patients is a nuisance).
15. Note in the United States Supreme Court decision upholding the constitutionality of zoning, through analogy to nuisance law, the Court actively stated: "Building zone laws are of modern origin—regulations the wisdom, necessity and validity of which as applied to existing conditions, are so apparent that they are now uniformly sustained, a century ago, or even a half

century ago, probably would have been rejected as arbitrary and oppressive." *Village of Euclid, Ohio v. Amber Realty Co.*, 272 U.S. 365 (1926). The Court analogized land development regulations to nuisance abatement powers for helpful clues. "A regulatory zoning ordinance which would be clearly valid as applied to the great cities might be clearly invalid as applied to rural communities. In solving doubts, the common law of nuisances ordinarily will furnish a fairly helpful clue."

16. Compare *Powell v. Taylor*, 263 S.W.2d 906 (Ark. 1954) (nuisance) with *Westcott v. Middleton*, 11 A. 490 (N.J. 1887) (no nuisance).
17. See David L. Callies, Robert H. Freilich, and Thomas E. Roberts, *Cases and Materials on Land Use*, 4th ed., "Chapter One: Setting The Stage, The Un-Planned Environment, Sec. B, Nuisance As A Land Use Control Device" (Eagan, MN: West, 2004), at 11.
18. See *Lincoln Trust Co. v. Williams Bldg. Corp.*, 128 N.E. 209 (N.Y. 1920).
19. See *Goldman v. Crowther*, 128 A. 50, 53 (Md. 1925) ("[zoning] at a stroke arrests that process of natural evolution and growth . . .").
20. See Julian C. Juergensmeyer and Thomas E. Roberts, *Land Use Planning and Development Regulation Law* (St. Paul, MN: West Group, 2003).
21. Alfred Bettman, "Constitutionality of Zoning," 37 *Harv. L. Rev.* 834, 835 (1924).
22. A Standard State Zoning Enabling Act Under Which Municipalities May Adopt Zoning Regulations, § 3 Purposes in View (recommended by the United States Department of Commerce) (1925).
23. See Jane Jacobs, *The Death and Life of Great American Cities* (New York: Random House and Vintage Books, 1961).
24. Martha A. Lees, "Preserving Property Values? Preserving Proper Homes? Preserving Privilege? The Pre-Euclid Debate Over Zoning For Exclusively Private Residential Areas, 1916-1926," 56 *U. Pitt. L. Rev.* 364 (1994).
25. Charles M. Haar, *Suburbs under Siege: Race, Space, and Audacious Judges* (Princeton, NJ: Princeton University Press, 1996); *Southern Burlington County N.A.A.C.P. v. Township of Mount Laurel*, 336 A.2d 713 (N.J. 1975) (regional general welfare—housing) and *S.A.V.E. v. City of Bothell*, 576 P.2d 401 (Wash. 1976) (regional general welfare—the environment). See Richard F. Babcock and David L. Callies, "Ecology and Housing: Virtues in Conflict," in Marion Clawson, ed., *Modernizing Urban Land Policy* (Baltimore: Resource for the Future, 1973).
26. See the oft-quoted language of Justice Weintraub in *Kozesnik v. Township of Montgomery*, 131 A.2d 1, 7-8 (N.J. 1957): "No doubt good housekeeping would be served if a zoning ordinance followed and implemented a master plan . . . but the history of the subject dictated another course . . . a plan may be revealed readily in an end product—here a zoning ordinance—and no more is required by statute." See contra, *Udell v. Haas*, 235 N.E.2d 897 (N.Y. 1967): "Zoning is not just an expansion of the common law of nuisance . . . underlying the entire concept of zoning is the assumption that zoning can be a vital tool for maintaining a civilized form of existence only if we employ the insights and learning of . . . the city planner, the economist, sociologist, the public health expert and all the other professions concerned with urban problems."
27. See "Building The American City," report of the National Commission on Urban Problems (the Douglas Commission) (1968), 245.
28. See Robert H. Freilich, *From Sprawl to Smart Growth: Successful Legal, Planning, and Environmental Systems* (Chicago: American Bar Association, 1999).
29. As the Douglas Commission, Note 27, supra, at 245, pointed out in 1968, "Today a basic problem results because of the delegation of the zoning power from states to local governments of any size. This often results in a type of Balkanization which is intolerable in large urban areas where local government boundaries rarely reflect the true economic and social watersheds. The present indiscriminate distribution of zoning authority leads to incompatible uses along municipal borders, duplication of public facilities and attempted exclusion of regional facilities."
30. Standard State Zoning Enabling Act (United States Department of Commerce, 1926); Standard City Planning Enabling Act (United States Department of Commerce, 1928).
31. In *Hunter v. City of Pittsburgh*, 207 U.S. 161 (1907), the United States Supreme Court held that local governments (counties and cities) are merely "creatures" of the state, which may modify their powers, boundaries, and assets or even abolish them without consent of the local governments or its citizens.
32. See *Duffcon Concrete Products, Inc. v. Borough of Cresskill*, 64 A.2d 347 (N.J. 1949) ("the [police power] is not limited by the boundaries of any particular zoning district nor even by the boundaries of the municipality adopting the ordinance").
33. See Fred P. Bosselman and David L. Callies, *The Quiet Revolution in Land Use Controls* (Washington, DC: Council on Environmental Quality, 1972); John M. DeGrove and Deborah A. Miness, *The New Frontier For Land Policy: Planning and Growth Management in the States* (Cambridge, MA: Lincoln Institute of Land Policy, 1992). See Stuart Meck, FAICP, "Notes on Planning Statute Reform in the United States: Guideposts for the Road Ahead," in *Planning Reform in the New Century*, Daniel R. Mandelker, ed. (Chicago: American Planning Association, 2005). For a comprehensive review of state land-use legislation divided into the critical three periods, Meck defines them as:
    • 1920s—Standard State Zoning Enabling Act (1926) and Standard City Planning Enabling Act (1928) (creating the establishment of planning commissions, development of master plans, master street plans (official maps), and the modern control of land subdivision based upon comprehensive planning;
    • 1970s—the quiet revolution in land-use control; and
    • The second generation of state legislation in growth management.
34. Florida, in particular, became the only state to directly adopt the American Law Institute's Model Land Development Code, Article 7, calling for "areas of critical state concern" and "developments of regional

impacts." See *Askew v. Cross Key Waterways*, 372 So.2d 913 (Fla. 1978) (upholding constitutionality of statute regulating "developments of regional impact").

35. Florida's Local Government Comprehensive Planning Act, West's Fla. Stat. Ann., Ch. 163, specifically incorporated the adequate public facility timed and sequenced growth management techniques upheld in *Golden v. Planning Board of the Town of Ramapo*, 285 N.E.2d 291 (N.Y. 1972), *app. dismissed*, 409 U.S. 1003 (1972); see Thomas G. Pelham, "From the Ramapo Plan to Florida's Statewide Concurrency System: Ramapo's Influence On Infrastructure Planning," 35 *Urb. Law.* 113 (2003). See Note 47 (GMA), infra.

36. Peter Buchsbaum and Larry Smith, *State & Regional Comprehensive Planning: Implementing New Methods for Growth Management* (Chicago: American Bar Association, 1993).

37. "Guidelines for California Environmental Quality Act," Cal. Code of Regulations, Title 14, Ch. 3, § 15130 (2006).

38. See the comprehensive review of state legislation in Edward J. Sullivan and Matthew J. Michel, "Ramapo Plus Thirty: The Changing Role of the Plan in Land Use Regulation," 35 *Urb. Law.* 75 (2003), and Daniel R. Mandelker, ed., *Planning Reform in the New Century* (Chicago: American Planning Association, 2005).

39. See, e.g., California Coastal Commission Act, Cal. Pub. Res. Code § 3060 et seq. The federal act is the national Coastal Zone Management Act of 1972, which enjoins Federal Emergency Management Agency federal flood insurance from being issued in Listed Endangered Species Habitats; see *Florida Key Deer et al. v. Brown et al.*, 364 F.Supp.2d 1345 (So. Dist. Fla. 2005); Endangered Species Act, 16 U.S.C. § 1536.

40. Shelby D. Green, "The Search For A National Land Use Policy: For The Cities' Sake," 26 *Fordham Urb. L.J.* 69 (1998) (describing the failure of Senator Henry "Scoop" Jackson to obtain passage in the 1960s of a National Planning Act).

41. "Golden and its Emanations: The Surprising Origins of Smart Growth," 35 *Urb. Law.* 15 (2003).

42. *Golden v. Planning Board of the Town of Ramapo*, 285 N.E.2d 291 (N.Y. 1972); *appeal denied*, 403 U.S. 1009 (1972).

43. Patrick J. Rohan, 1 *Zoning and Land Use Controls* (New York: M. Bender, 2003), § 4.05.

44. Thomas G. Pelham, "From the Ramapo Plan To Florida's Statewide Concurrency Systems: Ramapo's Influence on Infrastructure Planning," 35 *Urb. Law.* 113, 114 (2003).

45. Madelyn Glickfeld and Ned Levine, *Regional Growth: Local Reaction: The Enactment and Effects of Local Growth Control and Management Measures in California* (Cambridge, MA: Lincoln Institute of Land Policy, 1992).

46. Douglas R. Porter, "The APF Epidemic," *Urban Land* 36 (November 1990).

47. See Washington's 1990 Growth Management Act mandating concurrency in the state's Puget Sound region consisting of four counties including the cities of Seattle, Tacoma, and Olympia. See Note 35 (LGCPA), supra.

48. See Robert H. Freilich and John Ragsdale, "Timing and Sequential Controls, The Essential Basis For Effective Regional Planning in the Minneapolis-St. Paul Region," 58 *Minn. L. Rev.* 1009 (1974).

49. See Note 28 (Freilich), supra (describing Baltimore County, San Diego, Palm Beach County, Miami-Dade County, Broward-Ft. Lauderdale County, Orange County-Orlando, Seattle-King County, Tacoma-Pierce County, Clark-Las Vegas County, Lexington-Fayette County, Monterey County, Ventura County (CA); Los Angeles transportation corridor center system; Salt Lake-Summit County; San Antonio; New Orleans; among over 200 city-county systems developed by the coauthors).

50. Robert H. Freilich and Stephen I. Chinn, "Transportation Corridors: Shaping and Financing Urbanization Through Integration of Eminent Domain, Zoning and Growth Management Techniques," 55 *UMKC L. Rev.* 153 (1987).

51. Michael S. Bernick and Amy E. Freilich, "Transit Villages and Transit Based Development: The Rules Are More Flexible: How Government Can Work With The Private Sector To Make It Happen," 30 *Urb. Law.* 1 (1998).

52. Robert H. Freilich and S. Mark White, "The Interaction of Land Use Planning and Transportation Management: Lessons from the American Experience," *Transport Policy*, 101-115 (1994).

53. See Chapter 759, Md. Code Ann. (1997); David L. Winstead, "Smart Growth, Smart Transportation: A New Program to Manage Growth in Maryland," 30 *Urb. Law.* 537 (1998).

54. MD Code Ann. State Fin. & Proc. §§ 5-7B to 10.

55. John Frece and Andrea Leahy-Fucheck, "Smart Growth and Neighborhood Conservation," 13 *Nat. Res. & Env't*. 319 (1998).

56. 1999 Wisconsin Act 9.

57. Public Act 1101 (1998); S.B. 3278/H.B. 3295.

58. Patricia Salkin, "Smart Growth at Century's End: The State of the States," 31 *Urb. Law.* 601 (1989). Recently, Oregon adopted Measure 37, which requires that local governments compensate property owners for reductions in land value traced to regulatory land-use measures. Florida has also adopted a statutory compensation scheme to compensate landowners for "inordinate burden," a standard less than that earned for a regulatory Fifth Amendment taking under *Penn-Central Transportation Company v. City of New York*, 438 U.S. 104 (1978), approved as constitutional. *Brevard County v. Stack*, 932 So.2d 1258 (Fla. App. 2006).

59. Norman Williams, Jr., *American Land Planning Law* § 156.01 (2005).

60. The Interstate Land Sales Full Disclosure Act of 1968, 15 U.S.C. 1702 (1968), now requires that interstate sale of unimproved lots in subdivisions of 25 or more units be registered with the United States Secretary of Housing and Urban Development and a detailed "report" of the land be made available to prospective purchasers of lots.

Other federal acts offering consumer protection in real estate transactions involving subdivision lot sales are: the Truth In Lending Act, 15 U.S.C. §§ 1601 et seq. (including Regulation Z, 12 C.F.R. §§ 226 et seq., the administrative guidelines for the act); the Federal Trade Commission Act, 15 U.S.C. §§ 41 et seq. (under the act the FTC, upon complaint and hearing, may issue a cease-and-desist order to a land subdivider misrepresenting the product); and the Postal Reorganization Act, 39 U.S.C. § 3005 (providing for criminal prosecutions of persons conducting schemes or devices for obtaining money or property through the mails by use of false or fraudulent pretenses, representations, or promises).

See David L. Callies, Robert H. Freilich, and Thomas E. Roberts, *Cases and Materials on Land Use*, 4th ed. (Eagan, MN: West, 2004), 278-282. Similarly, states have enacted Blue Sky laws made applicable to land subdivision sales (*Florida Realty, Inc. v. Kirkpatrick*, 509 S.W.2d 114 (Mo.Sup. 1974); have adopted the Uniform Consumer Credit Code (UCCC) providing disclosure protections and penalties (UCCC § 5-203(1)(a)); and there remains common law judicial protection through the erosion of the doctrine of caveat emptor by use of judicial theories of fraud, express and implied warranty, negligence, and strict liability to provide injunctive relief or compensation for the unwary home buyer. (See, e.g., *Foxcroft Townhome Owners Association v. Hoffman Rossner Corp.*, 435 N.E.2d 210 (Ill. App. 1982); *Crowder v. Vandendeale*, 564 S.W.2d 879 (Mo. 1978).)

61. *Marx v. Zoning Bd. of Appeals of Vil. of Mill Neck*, 137 A.D.2d 333, 529 N.Y.S.2d 330 (App. Div. 2d Dept. 1988), "Subdivision control is aimed at protecting the community from an uneconomical development of land and assuring persons living in the area where the subdivision is sought that there will be adequate streets, sewers, water supply and other essential services."

62. See Paul W. Gates, "History of Public Land Development," 3 *American Law of Property* § 12.102 (A. Casner, ed.) (1952).

63. Standard City Planning Enabling Act 14 (1928). At this point, a caveat should be mentioned. Just as the zoning requirement contained in the Standard State Zoning Enabling Act that zoning "be in accordance with a comprehensive plan" was never at first interpreted under these enabling acts to require that a master plan precede adoption of a zoning ordinance (Charles M. Haar, "In Accordance With a Comprehensive Plan," 68 *Harv. L. Rev.* 1154 (1954)), it was generally held that a master plan is not required in order to adopt valid subdivision regulations. Grant Nelson, "The Master Plan and Subdivision Control," 16 *Me. L. Rev.* 107 (1964).

Nevertheless, denial of subdivision approval may be based upon failure to comply with provisions of an adopted master plan. See *Board of County Comm'rs v. Gaster*, 401 A.2d 666 (Md. 1979) (although the subdivision plat met all zoning requirements, the county legislative body could properly disapprove the application because it failed to comply with the master plan's density provision and its projected impact on roads and school districts); *Save Centennial Valley Ass'n., Inc. v. Schultz*, 284 N.W.2d 452 (S.D. 1979) (the approval of a subdivision in an agricultural area authorized by zoning was ruled void by the court because the commission, in approving it, disregarded the clear interest of the comprehensive plan).

See also *Schultheis v. Board of Supervisors of Upper Bern Township*, 727 A.2d 145 (Pa. Cmwlth. 1999); *Board of County Commmissioners of Larimer County v. Conder & Sommervold*, 927 P.2d 1339 (Colo. 1996); *Samperi v. Planning & Zoning Commission*, 674 A.2d 432 (Conn. App. 1996)—all holding that denial of a subdivision for inconsistency with the comprehensive plan is appropriate even though the zoning regulations authorize the use at that location.

64. Typical of this was a 1938 decision of the New Jersey Supreme Court: "[I]t is essential to adequate planning that there be provision for future community needs reasonably to be anticipated. We are surrounded with the problems of planless growth. The baneful consequences of haphazard development are everywhere apparent, there are evils affecting the health, safety, and prosperity of our citizens that are well-nigh insurmountable because of the prohibitive corrective cost. To challenge the power to give proper direction to community growth and development in the particulars mentioned is to deny the vitality of a principle that has brought men together in organized society for their mutual advantage. A sound economy to advance the selective in local affairs is the primary aim of local government." *Mansfield & Swett, Inc. v. West Orange*, 198 A. 225, 229 (N.J. 1938).

65. Note, "Analysis of Subdivision Control Legislation," 28 *Ind. L.J.* 544 (1952); Robert M. Anderson and Bruce B. Roswig, *Planning, Zoning, and Subdivision: A Summary of Statutory Law in the Fifty States* (New York: New York State Federation of Official Planning Organizations, 1966), 228 (Standard City Planning Enabling Act). Two other model acts of the same vintage—Bassett and Williams' Municipal Planning Enabling Act and Bettman's Municipal Subdivision Act—are reprinted in Bassett. Edward M. Bassett, Frank B. Williams, Alfred Bettman, and Robert Whitten, *Model Laws for Planning Cities, Counties, and States* (Cambridge: Harvard University Press, 1935).

66. *Miller v. City of Port Angeles*, 691 P.2d 229 (Wash. App. 1984) (subdivision concerns adequate off-site public facilities); *Serpa v. County of Washoe*, 901 P.2d 690 (Nev. 1995) (subdivision concerns inadequate off-site water resources).

67. *Lake Intervale Homes, Inc. v. Parsippany-Troy Hills*, 147 A.2d 28, 33 (N.J. 1958).

68. See *Brous v. Smith*, 106 N.E.2d 503 (N.Y. 1952) (the leading case for establishing the validity of on-site requirements that a road giving access to the proposed structures be "suitably improved" before a development approval may be issued. However, four problems with "on-site" regulations must be carefully addressed:

• The requirements must be related to the health, safety, and general welfare of the subdivision itself. Unreasonable requirements external to needs created by the subdivision will be found to be unlawful action. *Parks v. Watson*, 716 F.2d 646 (9th Cir. 1983) (refusal of a city to vacate a street unless the developer dedicates wholly extraneous geothermal wells); *New Jersey Builders Assn. v. Bernards Township*, 511 A.2d 740 (N.J. Super. 1985) (relationship between the development and the need for improvements must be clear, direct, and substantial) but reasonable regulations for design (*Wolf Pen Preservation Association, Inc. v. Louisville and Jefferson County Planning Commission and Canfield-Knopf*

Properties, Inc., 942 S.W.2d 310 (Ky. App. 1997)) and environmental regulation (*In re McDonald's Corp.*, 505 A.2d 1202 (Ut. 1984) and *Goodman v. Board of Commissioners of the Township of Whitehall*, 411 A.2d 838 (Pa. Cmwlth. 1980)) will be upheld.

- The requirements must be expressly contained in the regulations. *Southern Coop. Dev. Fund v. Driggers*, 696 F.2d 1347 (11th Cir. 1983) (improper to deny plat approval on grounds not explicit in the subdivision regulations).

- "Oversized facilities" built by a developer should allow for proper equitable redistribution to other sharing developments through reimbursement techniques. See Donald G. Hagman and Dean J. Misczynski, *Windfalls for Wipeouts: Land Value Capture and Compensation* (Chicago: American Society Planning Association, 1978).

- Excessive on-site requirements should be scrutinized to avoid unnecessary inflation of housing costs. See Robert Burchell and David Listokin, "The Impact of Local Government Regulations on Housing Costs and Potential Avenues for State Meliorative Measures," in George Sternlieb and James W. Hughes, *America's Housing: Prospects and Problems* (New Brunswick, NJ: Center for Urban Policy Research, Rutgers University, 1980); David Listokin and Carole Walker, *The Subdivision and Site Plan Handbook* (New Brunswick, NJ: Center for Urban Policy Research, Rutgers University, 1989).

69. See Heyman and Gilhool, "The Constitutionality of Imposing Increased Community Costs on New Suburban Residents Through Subdivision Exactions," 73 *Yale L.J.* 1119, 1121 (1964); *Ayres v. City of Los Angeles*, 338 P.2d 498 (Cal. 1949) (dedication of perimeter streets bordering subdivision); *Rosen v. Village of Downers Grove*, 167 N.E.2d 230 (Ill. 1960) (dedication of public school site); *Kamhi v. Yorktown*, 547 N.E.2d 346 (N.Y. 1989); *River Birch Assoc. v. City of Raleigh*, 388 S.E.2d 538 (N.C. 1990); *Nunziato v. Planning Bd. of Edgewater*, 541 A.2d 1105 (N.J. Super. 1988); *Sudarsky v. City of New York*, 779 F. Supp. 287 (S.D.N.Y. 1991).

70. *Coulter v. City of Rawlins*, 662 P.2d 888 (Wyo. 1983); *Krughoff v. City of Naperville*, 354 N.E.2d 489 (Ill. App. Ct. 1976); *City of College Station v. Turtle Rock Corp.*, 680 S.W.2d 802 (Tex. 1984); *Black v. City of Waukesha*, 371 N.W.2d 389 (Wis. Ct. App. 1985); *Jenad, Inc. v. Village of Scarsdale*, 218 N.E.2d 673 (N.Y. 1966); *Associated Home Builders of Greater East Bay, Inc. v. City of Walnut Creek*, 484 P.2d 606 (Cal. 1971).

71. See the National Commission on Urban Problems (the Douglas Commission), "Alternatives to Urban Sprawl," at 45, Research Report No. 15 (1968); New York State Planning Law Revision Study Document No. 4 (Feb. 1970) (see proposed Land Use and Development Planning Law 2-106, Feb. 1970); American Law Institute, "A Model Land Development Code," Tent. Draft No. 1 2-101, 2-201, 2-206 (1970); Frederick H. Bair, Jr., "Toward a Regulatory System: For Use, Development, Occupancy, and Construction," Planning Advisory Service Report No. 243 (Chicago: American Planning Association, 1969).

72. "Building The American City," report of the National Commission on Urban Problems (the Douglas Commission) (1968), 245 (emphasis added).

73. *Eschete v. City of New Orleans*, 245 So.2d 383 (La. 1971) (drainage); *Pearson Kent Corp. v. Bear*, 271 N.E.2d 218 (N.Y. 1971) (inadequate off-site roads); *Salamar Builders, Inc. v. Tuttle*, 29 N.Y.2d 221, 275 N.E.2d 585 (1971) (environmental protection of off-site water resources); *Rouse/Chamberlain, Inc. v. Board of Supervisors of Charlestown Township*, 504 A.2d 375 (Pa. Commw. Ct. 1986) (ecological considerations); *Canter v. Planning Bd. of Westborough*, 390 N.E.2d 1128 (Mass. App. Ct. 1979) (streets and stormwater drainage); *Hrenchuk v. Planning Bd. of Walpole*, 397 N.E.2d 1292 (Mass. App. Ct. 1979) (inadequate street access); *North Landers Corp. v. Planning Bd.*, 400 N.E.2d 273 (Mass. App. Ct. 1980) (inadequate off-site roads); *Wright Dev., Inc. v. City of Wellsville*, 608 P.2d 232 (Utah 1980) (water mains); *Land County v. Oregon Bldgs., Inc.*, 606 P.2d 676 (Or. Ct. App. 1980) (sidewalks); *Garipay v. Town of Hanover*, 351 A.2d 64 (N.H. 1976) (inadequate access via off-site roads); *Just v. Marinette County*, 201 N.W.2d 761 (Wis. 1972) (shoreland zoning). See generally N. Williams, *American Land Planning Law* 156.04-156.05 (1985).

74. *Golden v. Planning Board of the Town of Ramapo*, 285 N.E.2d 291 (N.Y. 1972).

75. Note 28 (Freilich), supra. Prevention of deterioration or overburdening of the infrastructure is the primary rationale for the use of sequential timing as a legitimate exercise of the police power. *Contractors & Builders Association of Pinellas County v. City of Dunedin*, 329 So.2d 314 (Fla. 1976); *Coulter v. City of Rawlins*, 662 P.2d 888 (Wyo. 1983); *Hollywood, Inc. v. Broward County*, 431 So.2d 606 (Fla. Dist. Ct. App. 1983).

76. In *Golden v. Planning Board of the Town of Ramapo*, 285 N.E.2d 291 (N.Y. 1972), a zoning ordinance was upheld whereby developers would not be permitted to subdivide and develop their land for periods of up to 18 years until the town completed scheduled capital improvements necessary to assure the adequacy of public facilities for subdivision residents. The court held that if a comprehensive plan is reasonable and not exclusionary, there is no reason why it should not be time-related. See also *Diversified Properties, Inc. v. Town of Hopkinton Planning Bd.*, 480 A.2d 194 (N.H. 1984); but see *Robinson v. City of Boulder*, 547 P.2d 228 (Colo. 1976) (en banc) (authorizing timing controls through subdivision regulation but not through extraterritorial utility extension).

For a complete update of the *Ramapo* decision 30 years later, see John R. Nolon, "Golden and Its Emanations: The Surprising Origins of Smart Growth in Symposium, The 30th Anniversary of Golden v. Ramapo: A Tribute to Robert H. Freilich," 35 *Urb. Law.* 15 (2003). See generally David L. Callies, Robert H. Freilich, and Thomas E. Roberts, *Cases and Materials on Land Use*, 4th ed. (Eagan, MN: West, 2004), 692-746.

77. Many of the states experiencing the greatest population increases from 1970 to 1980 were in the western United States. For example, Colorado's population increased 30.7 percent, Wyoming's 41.6 percent, Arizona's 53.1 percent, and Nevada's 83.5 percent. See Robert Ellickson

and A. Dan Tarlock, *Land-Use Controls*, Figure 1-2 (Boston: Little, Brown & Co., 1981).

78. 15 U.S.C. § 1704 (1982).

79. See *Diamond Multimedia Systems, Inc. v. Superior Court*, 968 P.2d 539 (Cal. 1999) (out-of-state purchases are securities under both federal and state law). For a comprehensive review, see Thomas Lee Hazen, *Treatise on the Law of Securities Regulation*, 3d. ed. (St. Paul,. MN: West Pub. Co., 1995), § 8.1 at 490-95.

   Consequently, unless the developer is eligible for an exemption (see 15 U.S.C. § 1702 (1982)), it must satisfy complex and comprehensive registration and disclosure requirements. Specifically, it is unlawful for a developer to sell or lease a lot in a subdivision unless a statement of record is in effect, thereby registering the land with United States Department of Housing and Urban Development and the purchaser or lessee has received a property report. Id. at 1703(a); 24 C.F.R. § 1700.1 (1987). Failure to comply with the property report requirement enables the purchaser or lessee to revoke the contract within two years from the date of signing. 15 U.S.C. § 1703(c) (1982). While the statute appears to require two separate documents—a statement of record and property report—the regulations have made the property report a part of the statement of record, thereby combining the two documents. 24 C.F.R. § 1710.100(a) (1987).

   For the information that a developer must include in the statement of record and property report, see id. at 1705; 24 C.F.R. §§ 1710.20, .101-.219 (1987). See also Paul Barron, *Federal Regulation of Real Estate*, revised ed., ¶ 3.02[5], at 3-24 to 3-25 (New York: Warren Gorham & Lamont, 1983). For the procedure for filing a statement of record or amendments, see 15 U.S.C. 1706 (1982); 24 C.F.R. 1710.20, .23 (1987). See also Barron, supra, 3.02[5][c], at 3-25 to 3-28. For a discussion of the two-year rescission remedy, see Steven I. Peretz, "Rescission Under the Interstate Land Sales Full Disclosure Act," 58 *Fla. B.J.* 297 (1984).

80. Susan Stroud, "The Magnitude of Large Lot-Sales Subdivisions in the United States," 3 *The Platted Lands Press: A Journal of Land Readjustment Studies*, 1, 2 (January 1986). As Stroud notes, "[i]f all HUD listings are included, the total exceeds 19,000 interstate land sales operations in the United States with over 700 subdivisions exceeding 1,000 acres in size." Id.

81. Under the antifraud provisions of the Interstate Land Sales Full Disclosure Act, a developer or agent may not represent that the developer will provide roads, sewers, water, gas, electric service, or recreational amenities without stipulating in the contract for the provision of these amenities. 15 U.S.C. § 1703(2)(d). In addition, the statute prohibits the use of the property report for any promotional purposes before the effective date of the statement of record, and then requires the use of the property report in its entirety. Id. at 1707(b).

   See also 24 C.F.R. § 1715.20 (1987) (sets forth list of promotional activities that constitute an unlawful sales practice); id. at § 1715.25 (sets forth advertising representations that are regarded as misleading unless developer provides specific safeguards to guarantee the accuracy of the representation); id. at § 1715.50 (requires the display of a disclaimer statement on all written material in connection with the sale of a lot for which a statement of record is in effect); id. at § 1710.9, .12, .13 (requires contracts to contain safeguard provisions in order for the sale or lease of a lot in a subdivision to be exempt from the entire act or from the act's registration and disclosure paragraphs). For a discussion of unlawful and misleading sales practices, see Note 79 (Barron), supra, ¶ 3.02[7] at 3-31 to 3-32. Violations of subdivision regulations can bring heavy fines and injunctive relief. See *Ojavan v. California Coastal Comm'n*, 62 Cal.Rptr. 2d 803, 54 Cal. App. 4th 373 (Cal. App. 1997).

82. Residential development, under traditional revenue-raising schemes, simply does not pay for the full cost of services provided to the new development. See Robert W. Burchell, "The Economic and Fiscal Costs of Sprawl," 29 *Urb. Law.* 159 (1997); James E. Frank, *The Costs of Alternative Development Patterns* (Washington, DC: The Urban Land Institute, 1989); Kevin Kasowski, "The Costs of Sprawl Revisited in Development," *National Growth Management Project Newsletter* (September 1992). For environmental impact of subdivision, see *Godorov v. Board of Comm'rs*, 475 A.2d 964 (Pa. Commw. Ct. 1984).

83. *Jordan v. Village of Menomonee Falls*, 317 N.W.2d 442 (Wis. 1966) (dedication of land or fee-in-lieu for recreational purposes upheld); *Norsco Enters. v. City of Fremont*, 126 Cal.Rptr. 659 (Cal. Ct. App. 1976) (park fees as a condition of condo conversion upheld).

84. See generally, Michael M. Shultz and Jeffrey B. Groy, *The Premature Subdivision of Land in Colorado* (Cambridge, MA: Lincoln Institute of Land Policy, 1986).

85. The local government committee of the Colorado Bar Association is in the process of drafting state laws to address the problem of premature subdivision. Premature subdivisions have been called the "sleeping giant" of Florida's growth management problems. Frank Schnidman, "Resolving Platted Lands Problems: The Florida Experience," 1 *Land Assembly & Development* 27 (1987).

86. *Noble v. Chairman of Menahem Township*, 219 A.2d 335, 340 (N.J. Super. Ct. App. Div. 1966); *City of College Station v. Turtle Rock Corp.*, 680 S.W.2d 802 (Tex. 1984).

87. *Shorb v. Barkley*, 240 P.2d 337 (Cal. Dist. Ct. App. 1952).

88. *Kessler v. Town of Shelter Island Planning Bd.*, 338 N.Y.S.2d 778, 780 (App. Div. 1972). See also *Durant v. Town of Dunbarton*, 430 A.2d 140 (N.H. 1981); *E. Grossman & Sons, Inc. v. Rocha*, 272 A.2d 496 (R.I. 1977).

89. *Diversified Properties, Inc. v. Town of Hopkinton Planning Bd.*, 480 A.2d 194 (N.H. 1984); *Pearson Kent Corp. v. Bear*, 271 N.E.2d 218 (N.Y. 1971); *Smith v. Township Comm.*, 244 A.2d 145 (N.J. Super. Ct. App. Div. 1968); *Isabelle v. Town of Newbury*, 321 A.2d 570 (N.H. 1974); *Traymore Associates v. Board of Supervisors of Northampton*, 357 A.2d 729 (Pa. Commw. Ct. 1976); *Salamar Builders Corp. v. Tuttle*, 275 N.E.2d 585 (N.Y. 1971).

90. *New Jersey Builders Ass'n v. Mayor*, 511 A.2d 740 (N.J. Super. Ct. Law Div. 1985) (township's off-tract improvement ordinance would have been valid had a "clear, direct and substantial" relationship between the development and improvement been shown).

91. *Just v. Marinette County*, 201 N.W.2d 761 (Wis. 1972); *Town of Salem v. Kenosha County*, 204 N.W.2d 467 (Wis. 1973).
92. *Divan Builders, Inc. v. Planning Bd. of the Township of Wayne*, 334 A.2d 30 (N.J. 1975).
93. *Homebuilders Assoc. of Northern California*, 108 Cal.Rptr. 2d 60 (Cal. App. 2001); *Commercial Builders v. City of Sacramento*, 941 F.2d 872 (9th Cir. 1991).
94. *Miller v. City of Port Angeles*, 691 P.2d 229 (Wash. Ct. App. 1984); *Fasano v. Washington County Comm'n*, 507 P.2d 23 (Ore. 1973).
95. See Robert H. Freilich and Brenda L. Nichols, "Public-Private Partnership in Joint Development: The Legal and Financial Anatomy of Large-Scale Urban Development Projects" 7 *Mun. Fin. J.* 1 (Winter 1986); Robert H. Freilich and Stephen P. Chinn, "Transportation Corridors: Shaping and Financing Urbanization Through Integration of Eminent Domain, Zoning and Growth Management Techniques," 55 *UMKC L. Rev.* 153 (1987).
96. See David Listokin and Carole Walker, *The Subdivision and Site Plan Handbook* (New Brunswick, NJ: Center for Urban Policy Research, Rutgers University, 1989).
97. *In re Belgrade Shores, Inc.*, 371 A.2d 413 (Me. 1977) (environmental board permit); *Hale v. First Nat'l Bank of Mt. Prospect*, 372 N.E.2d 959 (Ill. App. Ct. 1978) (approval of zoning board of appeals).
98. *Howard County v. JJM, Inc.*, 482 A.2d 908 (Md. App. 1984); *Norco Constr., Inc. v. King County*, 649 P.2d 103 (Wash. 1982). State law in Pennsylvania grants the developer a vested right to develop his property according to an approved development plan, irrespective of any intervening zoning regulation. Pa. Stat. Ann. tit. 53, 10508(4) (Purdon Supp. 1987).
99. See Andres Duany, Elizabeth Plater-Zyberk, and Jeff Speck, *Suburban Nation: The Rise of Sprawl and the Decline of the American Dream* (Union Square West, NY: North Point Press, 2000), 5-7.
100. Kenneth B. Hall, Jr. and Gerald A. Porterfield, *Community by Design: New Urbanism for Suburbs and Small Communities* (New York: McGraw-Hill, 2001), 254.
101. Note 99 (Duany), supra, 25.
102. Note 99 (Duany), supra, 4.
103. Note 99 (Duany), supra, 3-4.
104. Note 99 (Duany), supra, 15-17.
105. William Lennertz, "Codes," in Andres Duany and Elizabeth Plater-Zyberk, *Towns and Town-making Principles* (New York: Rizzoli, and Cambridge, MA: Harvard University Graduate School of Design, 1991), 102.
106. Ibid., see Robert H. Freilich and Bruce G. Peshoff, "The Social Costs of Sprawl," 29 *Urb. Law.* 183, 185 (1997).
107. Peter Calthorpe, *The Next American Metropolis: Ecology, Community, and the American Dream* (New York: Princeton Architectural Press, 1993); Peter Katz, *The New Urbanism: Toward An Architecture of Community* (New York: McGraw-Hill, 1994).
108. William Lennertz, "Town-Making Fundamentals," in Andres Duany and Elizabeth Plater-Zyberk, *Towns and Town-making Principles* (New York: Rizzoli, and Cambridge, MA: Harvard University Graduate School of Design, 1991), 23.
109. Id.
110. See Robert H. Freilich and Stephen A. Chinn, "Transportation Corridors: Shaping and Financing Urbanization Through Integration of Eminent Domain, Zoning & Growth Management," 55 *UMKC L. Rev.* 153 (1987); Amy E. Freilich and Michael S. Bernick, "Transit Villages and Transit Based Development: The Rules Are Flexible: How Government Can Work With The Private Sector To Make It Happen," 30 *Urb. Law.* 1 (1998); Robert H. Freilich and S. Mark White, "The Interaction of Land Use Planning and Transportation Management: Lessons From The American Experience," *Transport Policy* 101-115 (1994).
111. Ibid., 62-65.
112. Note 107 (Calthorpe), supra, 43.
113. *Principles of Transit Supportive Development* (Kansas City, MO: Mid-America Regional Council, 2000); Robert H. Freilich and S. Mark White, "Transportation Congestion and Growth Management: Comprehensive Approaches To Resolving America's Major Quality of Life Crisis," 24 *Loyola L.A. L. Rev.* 915 (1991).
114. Ibid.
115. Note 28 (Freilich), supra; Smart Growth Network, "About Smart Growth," available on-line at www.smartgrowth.org/about/default.asp.
116. Smart Growth Network. "Principles of Smart Growth," available on-line at www.smartgrowth.org/about/principles/default.asp
117. Town planners Andres Duany and Elizabeth Plater-Zyberk, two of the founders of the Congress for the New Urbanism, define 13 elements of new urbanism. *New Urban News*, "About New Urbanism," available on-line at www.newurbannews.com/AboutNewUrbanism.html.
118. See Linde B. Altman, "Picket Fences," *Builder* (February 1994), at 94-96; Lloyd W. Bookout, "Neotraditional Town Planning: Bucking Conventional Codes and Standards," *Urban Land* (April 1992), at 18-25.
119. See Charles Lockwood, "The New Urbanism's Call to Arms," *Urban Land* (February 1994), at 10-12.
120. See Jerry Adler, "15 Ways to Fix the Suburbs," *Newsweek* (May 15, 1995).
121. See John M. Fernandez, "Boulder Bring Back the Neighborhood Street," *Planning* (June 1994), at 21-26.
122. Note 105 (Lennertz), supra, 22.
123. S. Mark White and Dawn Jourdan, "The New Urbanism and Neotraditional Development: A Legal Analysis," *Land Use L. & Zoning Dig.* (August 1997), at 3.
124. "New Urbanism and House Values," National Center For Smart Growth Research For Education, University of Maryland (2002).
125. A "greenfield" project refers to a new subdivision in an undeveloped area, as opposed to an infill project in an existing neighborhood.
126. Timothy Egan, "A Development Fuels a Debate on Urbanism," *The New York Times* (June 14, 2002), at A20.
127. Joel Hirschhorn and Paul Souza, "Report to the National Governors' Association: New Community Design to the Rescue" (2001).
128. See, e.g., Wellington, Colorado, which won the 2002 award for smart growth achievement from the United States Environmental Protection Agency (US EPA) and is cited as one of 10 examples of good planning

decisions by the Colorado Sprawl Action Center. US EPA, 2002 National Award for Smart Growth Achievement, available on-line at www.epa.gov/smartgrowth; Colorado Sprawl Action Center, Smart Growth Hall of Fame, 2001.

129. See Kevin J. Krizek and Joe Power, "A Planner's Guide to Sustainable Development," Planning Advisory Service Report No. 467 (Chicago: American Planning Association, 1996); Gwendolyn Hallsmith, *The Key to Sustainable Cities* (Gabriola Island, BC, Canada: New Society Publishers, 2003); Adrian Pitts, *Planning and Design Strategies for Sustainability and Profit* (Burlington, MA: Architectural Press (Elsevier Inc.), 2004).

130. Capital E et al., "The Costs and Financial Benefits of Green Buildings: A Report to California's Sustainable Building Task Force" (October 2003), available on-line at www.cap-e.com/ewebeditpro/items/O59F3259.pdf.

131. See id. at 12; Anne Frej, "Green Buildings and Sustainable Development: Making the Business Case" (Washington, DC: Urban Land Institute, 2003), 2, available on-line at www.uli.org/AM/TemplateRedirect.cfm?template=/CM/ContentDisplay.cfm&ContentID=11028.

132. Note 130 (Capital E), supra, n. 1, at ii, 15 (calculating the average "cost premium for green buildings" to be 2 percent).

133. Id. at 14.

134. Id. at 19.

135. Id. at 40.

136. Id. at 47-48.

137. Id. at 55-56.

138. Note 131 (Frej), supra, at 6.

139. See generally id.

140. *Green Building Fact Sheet: March 2006* (Washington, DC: United States Green Building Council, 2006), 1, available on-line at www.usgbc.org/FileHandling/show_general_file.asp?DocumentID=871.

141. Jason Scully, *Sustainable Development and Green Building* (Washington, DC: Urban Land Institute, 2004), 3, available on-line at www.uli.org/AM/Template.cfm?Section=Home&CONTENTID=11057&TEMPLATE=/CM/ContentDisplay.cfm.

142. Note 140 (USGBC), supra, at 1.

143. *Model Green Home Building Guidelines* (Washington, DC: National Association of Home Builders, 2005), available on-line at www.nahbrc.org/greenguidelines.

144. *One out of Three Scottsdale Homes are Going Green* (Jan. 12, 2006), available on-line at www.scottsdaleaz.gov/news/2006/January/01-12-06.asp.

145. Calabasas, California, Ordinance 2003-185 (Jan. 7, 2004), available on-line at www.cityofcalabasas.com/pdf/green-building-ordinance.pdf.

146. Id.; see also City Council of the City of Pleasanton, California, Ordinance 1873 (Dec. 3, 2002), available on-line at www.ci.pleasanton.ca.us/pdf/greenbldg.pdf ("The green building practices referenced in this Chapter are designed . . . to encourage resource conservation; to reduce the waste generated by construction projects; to increase energy efficiency; and to promote the health and productivity of residents, workers, and visitors to the city.").

147. See Southern California Edison's solar incentives (www.sce.com/rebatesandsavings/californiasolarinitiative).

148. For an interesting and comprehensive review of techniques for water conservation, see Punam Prahalad, Matthew P. Clagett, and N. Theresa Hoagland, "Beyond Water Quality: Can the Clean Water Act Be Used to Reduce the Quantity of Stormwater Runoff?," 39 *Urb. Law.* 85 (2007).

149. See Barry Hogue, "Unified Development Ordinances: A Coordinated Approach to Development Regulations," *Zoning News* (Chicago: American Planning Association, December 2002).

150. See, e.g., Fla. Stat. ch. 380 (1972); Fla. Stat. ch. 23 (State Comprehensive Planning Act) (1990); Fla. Stat. ch. 163 (State and Local Government Planning Act) (1990); for a detailed analysis of Florida's system, see Robert H. Freilich, *From Sprawl to Smart Growth: Successful Legal, Planning, and Environmental Systems* (Chicago: American Bar Association, 1999), Chapter 6, "Smart Growth in the States," at 234-236; Thomas G. Pelham, "The Florida Experience: Creating a State, Regional and Local Comprehensive Planning Process," in Peter A. Buchsbaum and Larry J. Smith, eds., *State and Regional Comprehensive Planning: Implementing New Methods for Growth Management*, at 102-110 (Chicago: American Bar Association, 1993).

151. Statutory or code ambiguity may weigh against a city's argument that appeal is directly to the courts rather than an administrative agency. *City of Olympia v. Bd. of Comm'rs*, 125 P.3d 997 (Wash. App. 2005); ambiguity as to whether provision allows citywide or individualized impact fee assessments, *City of Olympia v. Drebick*, 126 P.3d 802 (Wash. 2006); court had to decide whether planned unit development (PUD) districts could be formed with resort hotels—ordinance was ambiguous, *In re 232511 Investments, Ltd.*, 898 A.2d 109 (Vt. 2006); PUD ordinance is not void for vagueness even though ordinance fails to define critical terms, *Palm Beach Polo, Inc. v. Village of Wellington*, 918 So.2d 988 (Fla. App. 2006). In all of these recent state cases, additional attorney's fees and litigation ensued over ambiguous terms that could have been avoided with careful analysis of the terms of an ordinance or statute that were ill defined. In federal constitutional cases, the void-for-vagueness requirement comes under a substantive due process standard, *Seventh Street LLC v. Baldwin County Planning and Zoning Commission*, 2006 WL 531446 (11th Cir. 2006) (regulations must be so vague that there is no standard at all).

152. Dover, Kohl & Partners, "Alternative Methods of Land Development Regulation," prepared for the Town of Fort Myers Beach, Florida, by Victor Dover, AICP (Sept. 2, 1996), available on-line at www.spikowski.com/victor_dover.htm.

153. In many cases, these problems are avoided in the LDC through provision of standards for buffers, landscaping, alternative traffic access, and quantitative provisions for limiting the number of infill dwelling units or projects so that communities do not face the quandary of whether a project is the first of one or the first of a hundred. In other cases where irrational fear of loss of

property values drives opposition, the use of insurance to maintain values can be utilized. *Clayton v. Village of Oak Park*, 453 N.E.2d 937 (Ill. App. 1st Dist. 1983).

154. Stuart Meck, FAICP, gen. ed., *Growing Smart™ Legislative Guidebook: Model Statutes for Planning and the Management of Change* (Chicago: American Planning Association, 2002).

155. See, e.g., N.C.G.S. § 153A-122. Under the North Carolina statutes, this permission could be withdrawn by providing notice to the county.

156. See the California Environmental Quality Act, Public Resources Code §§ 21000 et seq. (2006).

157. See Nicholas Panos, "History of the Colorado Land Use Commission's Intervention," 24 *Colo. Law.* 303 (1995); see also the North Carolina Land Policy Act of 1974, N.C.G.S. § 113A-150 et seq. (providing for designation of areas of environmental concern), Coastal Area Management Act of 1974, N.C.G.S. § 113A-100 et seq., and Mountain Ridge Protection Act of 1983, N.C.G.S. § 113A-205 et seq.

CHAPTER

1

General Provisions

1.0 PURPOSE AND FINDINGS

The Land Development Code (LDC) is designed to implement and be consistent with the goals, objectives, policies, and strategies of the adopted comprehensive plan through complete, integrated, effective, and concise land development regulations. In some states, the words "general plan" or "master plan" are substituted for "comprehensive plan." Since the majority of states use the term "comprehensive plan," the LDC will always refer to "comprehensive plan." It is extremely useful to preface the comprehensive plan goals, objectives, policies, and strategies with a "vision" statement setting forth the community's views of how it should prioritize its values for its unique urban form.

If the local government has not adopted a comprehensive plan, use the following substitute provision: The LDC is designed to implement the goals, objectives, policies, and strategies of the local government as reflected in all adopted ordinances, resolutions, development approvals, intergovernmental agreements, reports, and studies. Interpretation of the goals, objectives, policies, and strategies should not be solely confined or restricted to the language of the LDC itself where the additional sources clarify ambiguous language, changed circumstances, or errors, or reflect longstanding historical and policy decisions.

- The zoning and land use regulations set forth in Chapter 2, Use Patterns, and Chapter 3, Zoning, of the LDC promote the public health, safety, morals, or general welfare of the state, the region, and the local government, and protect and preserve places and areas of historical, cultural, architectural, or environmental importance and significance.
- The subdivision regulations set forth in Chapter 4, Procedures, and Chapter 5, Development Standards, of the LDC promote the health, safety, morals, or general welfare of the local government and the safe, orderly, and healthful development of the local government, taking into account all factors both on and off the site of the subdivision. The processing procedures set forth in Chapter 4 consolidate regulations governing the processing of approvals for the development of land. They ensure that notification and procedures comply with state law, provide ample opportunity for public participation in the land development process, provide for the efficient and timely processing of development approvals, and promote the readability of the document for the general public and for applicants requesting development approvals. The development standards in Chapter 5 consolidate the substantive standards relating to the issuance of development approvals for zoning and subdivision approval in order to provide clarity and certainty in the development approval process.
- Chapter 6, Adequate Public Facilities, of the LDC ties development approval to designated infrastructure level of service standards as set forth in the comprehensive plan, master utility plans, regional and area-wide standards, state statutes, or other applicable documents or policies.
- Chapter 7, Supplemental Use Regulations, of the LDC provides specific development standards for designated uses. These establish supplemental conditions that protect the public while establishing predictable standards for the applicant.

- Chapter 8, Nonconforming Uses/Vested Rights, of the LDC protects legal nonconforming uses and vested rights in accordance with state and federal decisional and statutory law.
- Chapter 9, Administrative Agencies, of the LDC establishes various administrative agencies involved in the development approval process, as well as the role of administrative and legislative bodies.
- Definitions are established in Appendix A, Definitions and Rules of Interpretation, of the LDC, which includes a glossary to provide a common understanding of the meaning of particular terms. Placing the definitions in an appendix reserves the balance of the LDC for substantive standards.
- Application submittal requirements are established in Appendix B, Specifications for Documents to Be Submitted, of the LDC to provide guidance to applicants in the submittal of development approval applications, to avoid the unnecessary expenditure of public resources for the processing of incomplete applications, and to avoid unnecessary delay in the approval of applications for development approval.

1.1 CITATION

This [INSERT REFERENCE TO "CHAPTER," "ARTICLE," OR OTHER HEADING OF LOCAL GOVERNMENT CODE] shall be known and may be cited as the Land Development Code of [LOCAL GOVERNMENT].

1.2 AUTHORITY

The LDC is authorized by the following: [LIST APPLICABLE STATUTORY AND/OR CHARTER CITATIONS].

1.3 APPLICABILITY

This chapter applies to all buildings, structures, lands, and uses over which the [LOCAL GOVERNMENT] has jurisdiction under the constitution and law(s) of the State of [INSERT STATE] and of the United States.

1.4 CONSISTENCY WITH COMPREHENSIVE PLAN

The LDC is consistent with the adopted comprehensive plan. Any amendments to this chapter, including, but not limited to, rezoning approval pursuant to Chapter 4, Procedures, of the LDC, and all development approvals, shall be consistent with the following:

 (A) The adopted comprehensive plan, as it may be amended from time to time, in effect at the time of the request for amendment; and

 (B) Any neighborhood, area, or specific plan adopted pursuant to Chapter 4, Procedures, of the LDC.

   An amendment to the text of the LDC is consistent and in accordance with the comprehensive plan if it complies with the goals, objectives, policies, and strategies and any vision statement contained in the comprehensive plan.

1.5 COORDINATION WITH OTHER REGULATIONS

1.5.1 Generally

The use of buildings and land within the [LOCAL GOVERNMENT] is subject to all other regulations as well as the LDC, whether or not such other provisions are specifically referenced in the LDC. References to other regulations or provisions of the LDC are for the convenience of the reader. The lack of a cross-reference does not exempt a land, building, structure, or use from other regulations.

1.5.2 Zoning

If a regulation adopted by the LDC requires a greater width or size of a yard, court, or other open space; requires a lower building height or fewer number of stories for a building; requires a greater percentage of lot to be left unoccupied; or otherwise imposes higher standards than those required under another statute or local ordinance or regulation, the regulation adopted under the LDC controls. If the other statute or local ordinance or regulation imposes higher standards, that statute, ordinance, or regulation controls.

1.5.3 Rules of Construction

 (A) Interpretation and application of the LDC are the basic and minimum requirements for the protection of public health, safety, comfort, morals, convenience, prosperity, and welfare. The LDC shall be liberally interpreted in order to further its underlying purposes. The meaning of any and all words, terms, or phrases in the LDC shall be construed in accordance with Appendix A, Definitions and Rules of Interpretation, of the LDC, which is incorporated by reference.

 (B) The LDC contains numerous graphics, pictures, illustrations, and drawings in order to assist the reader in understanding and applying the LDC. However, to the extent that there is any inconsistency between the text of the LDC and any such graphic, picture, illustration, or drawing, the text controls unless otherwise provided in the specific section.

1.6 DEVELOPMENT APPROVALS

No development activity shall occur on any property within the jurisdiction of the LDC until an applicable development approval for the activity has been granted (refer to Chapter 4, Procedures, of the LDC).

COMMENTARY

This chapter establishes the purpose of the LDC and describes its applicability and jurisdiction. The LDC provides a broad assertion of authority over development or land use within the territorial boundaries of the local government. Other sections of the LDC may limit its applicability.

The major purpose of the LDC is to implement the jurisdiction's comprehensive plan. Known in some states as a "master plan" or "general plan," the comprehensive plan establishes the local government's basic land-use policies. Many states follow the so-called "unitary view," prevalent after the promulgation of the Standard State Zoning Enabling Act, that the zoning ordinance itself is the comprehensive plan. In other words, no separate, written plan is required and the plan is found in the zoning scheme established by the zoning.

GENERAL PRINCIPLES

Some basic principles for good technical writing[1] as it relates to code drafting are as follows:

- Planning commissioners, neighborhood groups, developers, and other code users are often not professionals. Most people want codes that are well organized, readable, and understandable.[2]
- An ordinance should function like a "technical manual," effectively organizing a system or group of related systems to allow the code user easy access to information.
- Codes should implement goals, objectives, policies, and strategies. Extraneous provisions should be eliminated.
- Similar subjects should be arranged together by chapter (e.g., procedures, improvement standards, or nonconformities) rather than scattered throughout the ordinance.
- The most interesting and/or commonly used parts of the ordinance should be placed up front. Technical matters should be relegated to appendices, including application submittal requirements.
- Short codes are not better unless the jurisdiction is willing to let the courts interpret the codes for them. User friendliness is typically perceived to be a function of the length of the ordinance (i.e., the notion that shorter is more user friendly). This may make the ordinance easier to review but not useful for development review. A longer ordinance should answer many of the questions that inevitably arise during development review. A shorter ordinance typically leaves questions unanswered, leading to frustration for the applicant and the reviewer, and greater judicial review. Avoid the temptation to use vague, "sound-bite" language that is not legally enforceable. If the length of the ordinance is a concern, the ordinance can be trimmed by using the following alternatives:

  ○ *Consolidate repetitive lists of standards into matrices.* Older ordinances typically repeat for each district "laundry lists" of permitted, conditional, and accessory uses; and area, floor area ratios, yard, buffer, parking, and dimensional standards. The alternative is a matrix of permitted uses and/or dimensional standards.

  ○ *Graphics should be used to illustrate the text language.* Some users believe that graphics can substitute for and shorten text. A graphic alone does not explain how a standard is applied, who renders the determination, and what the key regulatory requirements are. Photo-editing technology can use local examples to illustrate how a design standard works or what a particular use looks like. Graphics add to the length of the ordinance for those concerned about shortcuts over comprehensiveness.

  ○ *Remove provisions dealing with unique situations, technical criteria that are not related to planning issues, or situations that are not part of the normal development review process.* For example, signage, flood protection, or state-mandated sedimentation controls could be placed as separate, stand-alone ordinances.

  ○ *Streamline standards by focusing on critical issues.* This reduces volume, budget, and staffing needs.

  ○ *Increase cross-references to avoid repeating standards, reducing text length, and minimizing the potential for inconsistencies when the code is amended.* See "Consolidating and Cross-referencing," below.

CONSOLIDATING AND CROSS-REFERENCING

Cross-referencing minimizes the need to repeat standards throughout the ordinance, but requires readers to look in different places for information. To address this issue, information about specific items can be placed together. However, this lengthens the text in each section, requires most readers to wade through material in which they are not interested (e.g., submittal requirements), and requires information to be repeated. Options to eliminate cross-referencing include:

- *Eliminate references to statutes and put the statutory language in the ordinance.* Many codes repeat standards or procedures from state law in their ordinances. This has the advantage of placing the standards in front of the reader without having to look up the statute. The disadvantages are that a change in the statute will require a change in the ordinance and it adds to the length of the ordinance. A "commentary" could repeat or summarize the statute, but this still adds to the length of the ordinance. This issue could also be resolved through pamphlets or manuals available at the permitting office.
- *Remove separate use matrices and dimensional matrices from each zoning district, and repeat the list of uses and*

dimensional requirements in each zoning district regulation. This has the obvious disadvantage of repeating uses in several districts, which adds to ordinance length. Using smaller fonts, tables, or columns can help. Prepare a separate use matrix that can be distributed to readers who prefer this format.

- *Place definitions in the sections to which they primarily relate.* A cross-reference could be added to the definitions (Appendix A, Definitions and Rules of Interpretation, of the LDC) in order to provide indexing. The disadvantage is the potential for discrepancies between terms used in different places of the ordinance. This can be minimized by the indexing procedure, with a notation or a more general definition of more general use. Of course, some definitions will be used throughout the ordinance rather than in only one section.

- *Determine page size.* How large should the pages be? Should they be in landscape or portrait format? Most ordinances place the regulations in portrait format with 8-1/2 x 11-inch pages. Some codes use a larger page format, squeezing more standards onto one page and providing more flexibility for integrating graphics and text. The downside of this approach is that most word processors are not familiar with working in these formats, which creates challenges when amendments are made. In addition, its sheer size can be difficult to manage.

- *Definitions should be placed in the rear of the ordinance.* Avoid duplicates and definitions for terms that are not used in the code.

- *Use attention grabbers.* Use subject headings and titles, with bold print, italics, icons, or other attention grabbers. The writer can also use icons to denote similar things, such as "purpose and findings" statements.

- *Avoid "legalese."* Legal documents do not require "legalese," unnecessary language, and archaic terminology.[3] Write in a clear, concise, and direct manner. Break long sentences into shorter, choppy sentences. Some phrases that unnecessarily clutter and prolong an ordinance, and suggested rewrites, are provided in Table 1-1.

- *Eliminate unnecessary words and phrases.* These include "herewith," "therewith," "herein," "therein," "hereby," "thereto," "thereof," "thereon," "heretofore," "theretofore," "hereafter," "thereafter," "hereunder," "in furtherance of," "deemed to be," "said to be," and "on account of."[4] Replace "shall be required to" and "shall be responsible for" with "shall" or "must." Rewrite all "woulds" and "shoulds" and similar phrases to "shall." Use the word "and" (not "or") when the meaning is that both terms shall apply. Use short, declarative sentences rather than long sentences separated by commas or semicolons.[5] Avoid double negatives (e.g., use "shall be consistent with" rather than "shall not be considered inconsistent with").

- *Use "purpose and findings" statements.* Insert "purpose and findings" statements (goals, objectives, policies, and strategies) at the beginning of sections so that the intent is clear. The code writer can highlight "purpose and findings" statements with an icon and/or italics.

- *Avoid using antiquated language from older ordinances.* Such terms often require construction in expensive litigation.[6] Ambiguous language may be construed against the zoning authority and in favor of the property owner.[7]

- *Eliminate provisions that have outlived their usefulness.* Many code standards are carried forward from past years. The desire to condense or to eliminate code provisions in an attempt to make a code more readable can offend neighborhood or business constituencies that championed those provisions. The LDC cannot be all things to all people or interest groups. The LDC cannot be held to a reasonable length if it attempts to address every conceivable undesirable situation. Instead, reasonable choices must be made to implement the city's planning policies while respecting the rights of landowners, businesses, and neighborhood groups. The use of focus groups during the LDC adoption period will help to openly resolve these differences as they appear.

Table 1-1
Eschewing Obfuscation

Legalese or Archaic Language	Suggested Rewrite
"The applicant shall be required to . . ."	"The applicant shall . . ." or "the applicant will . . ."†
". . . herein"	". . . in this section"
". . . provided, however, that . . ."	". However, . . ."
"The provisions of this section shall not apply to . . ."	"This section does not apply to . . ."
". . . shall not be subject to . . ."	". . . is not subject to . . ."
"The provisions of this section are designed to permit . . ."	"This section permits . . ."
"The provisions of this section apply . . ."	"This section applies . . ."

† *Some drafters suggest using the term "will" rather than "shall" for mandatory language. The problem with this approach is that the term "will" is technically incorrect (i.e., "will" is a prediction, while "shall" is a command). Courts routinely interpret "shall" as mandatory language, and using "will" as an alternative could produce the unintended result of having the language become optional and unforceable. If "will" is used, the definitions section should clearly indicated that the term is mandatory.*

- *Integrate all amendments from past years and integrate into the LDC.* Local governments tend to amend development codes in a piecemeal fashion. This results in inconsistent standards, outdated cross-references, and requirements that do not fulfill—or that contradict—new planning policies. The code drafter needs to find the appropriate place for these amendments in the new code, and ensure that they reflect current development policies.

- *Write clear parameters that reflect the community's land-use policies, rather than providing a comprehensive list of forbidden situations.* Ambiguous language will be construed against the zoning authority.[8]

- *Eliminate provisions that are not needed to implement the community's land-use policies.* The most important principle in drafting the LDC is to affirmatively establish clear parameters that reflect the community's positive planning policies, rather than providing a comprehensive list of forbidden situations. This may require trimming standards or restrictions that have been issued for specific situations, which will now be integrated within the overall land-use policies. If the goals, objectives, policies, and strategies are produced with city neighborhood and specific interest group involvement, individualized regulations will be unnecessary. Eliminating marginally necessary standards reduces the code's volume as well as reducing budget and staffing needs.

CONFLICT AND DUPLICATION OF PROVISIONS

Avoid conflict between the LDC provisions and statutory sections. While state statutes are binding, home rule local governments may regulate matters that are not preempted or precluded by statute.[9] A local government may have some leeway, however, in defining concepts that are contained in the state's enabling act.[10] Local governments, unless preempted, may often adopt stricter standards than the state.[11] Ordinarily, building, housing, environmental codes, and zoning ordinances should be read together and harmonized wherever possible.[12]

INCLUDED AND EXCLUDED USES

One of the thorniest problems in the drafting of use district regulations is how to differentiate between included and excluded uses.[13] Clarity is always desirable. Failing to define uses clearly can lead to surprising results. For example, "motels" have been determined not to be included within the term "inns."[14] Ten college students were able to convince a court that they were a "facility."[15] Even where the local government has the authority to regulate or exclude a particular use, it must make sure that it has incorporated such a regulation into its code.[16]

DESIGN REGULATIONS

Defining good design creates unique drafting difficulties. In addition, court cases on vagueness have had widely inconsistent results. In terms of providing guidance to applicants, see Table 1-2 and Table 1-3 for the differences in code language.

Attorneys should carefully research case law in their state to determine how appropriate code language should be written. Several of the examples that were upheld in the language in Table 1-3 were taken from California, which has one of the most permissive rules in the nation. As was stated by the California Court of Appeals in *Novi v. City of Pacifica*: "California courts permit vague standards because they are sensitive to the need of government in large urban areas to delegate broad discretionary power to administrative bodies if the community's zoning business is to be done without paralyzing the legislative process."[17]

Most states do not provide this amount of leniency in code drafting. Our suggestion is to make sure that the code is either written or checked by an attorney to determine these types of issues. Note that, in the case of design, aesthetic considerations and definitions will play a major role.[18] Stringent height limitations will be upheld on aesthetic grounds if there are views of mountains or other vistas deserving of protection.[19] Definitions should find support in the comprehensive plan goals, objectives, policies, and strategies, especially when based on sensory (i.e., design and aesthetics) as opposed to geometric standards.[20]

LEGISLATIVE USES AS OF RIGHT AND QUASI-JUDICIAL SPECIAL OR CONDITIONAL USES

Speedy processing of development applications and one-stop approvals and the use of "ombudsmen" have been legitimately suggested as a means to make the development approval process more efficient.[21] Local governments, on the other hand, have to be aware of the distinctions between uses as of right and special or conditional uses. Distinctions in uses must be clearly drawn to avoid due process violations with regard to quasi-judicial development approvals depriving property owners of their rights to a full hearing.[22] Procedures for intensive uses that are as of right have been criticized for resolving important land-use issues without neighborhood input.[23] They are, however, a useful tool for streamlining development approvals for mixed uses and infill development that the community has agreed is necessary in order to avoid long delays in multiple hearings.

An important case in point involved Baltimore County. The county received an inquiry from United Parcel Service (UPS) that it wished to build a new $13 million facility in the county. The county code has a provision for special use permits for "trucking facilities." UPS, because of urgent time needs, urged the

Table 1-2
Code Language Found Void for Vagueness

• "The Board of Zoning Appeals may grant or deny the application as the Board sees fit, being guided in its decision by its opinion as to whether or not the proposed use would be desirable or advantageous to the neighborhood or the community or the county at large."[a]
• "conservation of natural beauty"[b]
• "Monotony of design in single or multiple building projects shall be avoided. Efforts should be made to create an interesting project by use of complimentary details, functional orientation of buildings, parking and access provisions and relating the development to the site. In multiple building projects, variable siting of individual buildings, heights of buildings, or other methods shall be used to prevent a monotonous design." • "Evaluation of a project shall be based on quality of its design and relationship to the natural setting of the valley and surrounding mountains." • "Building components, such as windows, doors, eaves and parapets, shall have appropriate proportions and relationship to each other, expressing themselves as a part of the overall design." • "Colors shall be harmonious, with bright or brilliant colors used only for minimal accent." • "Design attention shall be given to screening from public view all mechanical equipment, including refuse enclosures, electrical transformer pads and vaults, communication equipment, and other utility hardware on roofs, grounds or buildings." • "Exterior lighting shall be part of the architectural concept. Fixtures, standards and all exposed accessories shall be harmonious with the building design."[c]
• "Preservation of Landscape. The landscape shall be preserved in its natural state, insofar as practicable, and where desirable by minimizing tree and soil removal, and any grade changes shall be in keeping with the general appearance of neighboring developed areas. Landscape treatment that is appropriate to the area and the terrain and which will enhance the overall appearance of the site shall be employed." • "Relation of Proposed Buildings to Environment. Proposed structures shall be related harmoniously to the terrain and to existing buildings in the vicinity that have a visual relationship to the proposed buildings. Such relationship shall be achieved by: (2.1) Architectural design which is harmonious with the character of existing development. (2.2) The use of exterior colors, façade or roof materials or the combination of colors and materials that are harmonious. (2.3) The relationship of design features, such as height and mass, building proportions, roof lines, building projections and ornamental features that will create a coordinated and harmonious appearance." • "Similarity and Dissimilarity of Design. Excessive similarity of appearance and the repetitiveness of features resulting in displeasing monotony of design should not permitted. Proposed building construction whose architectural design is inconsistent with established architectural character in any neighborhood, shall be avoided." • "Open Space, Circulation and Parking. Open spaces, access driveways and the location and design of parking areas shall be in scale with the project as a whole. Special attention shall be given to location and number of access points to the public streets, width of interior drives and access points, general interior circulation, separation of pedestrian and vehicular traffic, and arrangement of parking areas that are safe and convenient and, insofar as practicable, do not distract from the design of proposed buildings and structures and the neighboring properties." • "Special Features. Exposed storage areas, exposed machinery installations including roof installations, service areas, truck loading areas, utility buildings and structures, and similar accessory areas and structures shall be so located and screened with plantings or by other methods to prevent their being incongruous with the existing or contemplated environment and the surrounding properties." • "Advertising Features and Fences. The size, location, design, color, lighting, texture and materials of signs, outdoor advertising structures or features as well as fences or other man-made visual barriers shall not detract from the design and appearance of existing or proposed structures and the surrounding area, nor create confusion with traffic or any other signs."[d]

[a] Andrews v. Board of Sup'rs of Loudoun County, *200 Va. 637, 107 S.E.2d 445 (Va. 1959)*.
[b] Kosalka v. Town of Georgetown, *752 A.2d 183 (Me. 2003)*.
[c] Anderson v. City of Issaquah, *70 Wash. App. 64, 851 P.2d 744 (Wash. App. Div. 1, May 24, 1993)*.
[d] Morristown Road Associates v. Mayor and Common Council and Planning Bd. of Borough of Bernardsville, *163 N.J. Super. 58, 394 A.2d 157 (N.J. Super. 1978)*.

**Table 1-3
Code Language Upheld
Against Vagueness Challenges**

• Prohibits uses that would "be detrimental to the health, safety, morals, comfort, and general welfare of the persons residing or working in the neighborhood of such proposed use or be injurious or detrimental to property and improvements in the neighborhood or to the general welfare of the city."[a]
• Development Guidance System involving "compatibility assessment," which is an informal compatibility meeting of the applicant, surrounding property owners, and the commission's staff to discuss the proposed development. If no consensus is reached, a public hearing is held, following which the commission decides whether to reject the proposal as incompatible or place conditions on the project in order to make it compatible.[b]
• "not unreasonably interfere with existing scenic uses"[c]
• "variety in the design of the structure and grounds to avoid monotony in the external appearance."[d]
• Architectural Review Board to determine "whether the proposed structure will conform to proper architectural standards in appearance and design, and will be in general conformity with the style and design of surrounding structures and conducive to the proper architectural development of the City" and to "disapprove the application if it determines that the proposed structure will constitute an unsightly, grotesque or unsuitable structure in appearance, detrimental to the welfare of surrounding property or residents . . ."[e]

[a] Novi v. City of Pacifica, *169 Cal. App. 3d 678, 215 Cal.Rptr. 439 (Cal. App. 1 Dist. June 25, 1985).*
[b] Hardin County v. Jost, *897 S.W.2d 592 (Ky. App. 1995).*
[c] Uliano v. Maine Board of Environmental Practice, *2003 WL 1667733 (Me. Super. 2003).*
[d] Note a (Novi), *supra.*
[e] State ex rel. Stoyanoff v. Berkeley, *458 S.W.2d 305 (Mo. 1970).*

county zoning administrator to treat its large semis and small brown trucks as a permitted industrial use—subject to obtaining a ministerial development approval as of right—rather than a trucking facility requiring a special use permit with its attendant public hearing, public notice, and potential public opposition. After the facility was erected, the neighbors, who had no notice of the issuance of the development approval, petitioned the board of adjustment to order that the building be subject to a full hearing and possible demolition if the board were to subsequently deny the special development approval after holding a hearing.[24] An illegally issued development approval could have resulted in demolition of the facility and municipal liability. The issue was not resolved until it reached Maryland's highest court.[25]

NOTES

1. "Untechnical writing: how to write about technical subjects and products so anyone can understand," *The Fine Art of Technical Writing: Key Points to Help You Think Your Way through Writing Scientific or Technical Publications and Business Reports* (Hillsboro, OR: Blue Heron Publishing, 1991); Charles H. Sides, *How to Write and Present Technical Information* (Phoenix: Oryx Press, 1999); Elizabeth Slatkin, *How to Write a Manual* (Berkeley: Ten Speed Press, 1991). Organizational formats include chronological, spatial, climactic, and task oriented. Phillip Rubens, ed., *Science and Technical Writing: A Manual of Style* (New York: Henry Holt, 1992), at 9. Climactic formats organize progress from the least to the greatest impact, with the most interesting or forceful concepts, which are most often used in the brochure, appearing at the end. Rubens, supra, at 15. Task-oriented formats are used where readers use the information to do something. Rubens, supra, at 15-16. The LDC is a combination of climactic and task-oriented formats.
2. See Rodney C. Nanney, "Is It Time for a New Zoning Ordinance?" *Florida Planning* (December 2001), at 7.
3. *Coots v. J.A. Tobin Construction Co.,* 634 S.W.2d 249 (Mo. App. 1982).
4. Id.
5. Id.
6. Id.
7. *Cunningham v. Board of Aldermen of City of Overland,* 691 S.W.2d 464 (Mo. App. 1985).
8. Id.
9. *City of Kansas City v. Taylor,* 689 S.W.2d 645 (Mo. App. 1985).
10. *Rumson Estates, Inc. v. Mayor and Council of the Borough of Fair Haven,* 828 A.2d 317 (N.J. 2003). A local government may be bound to a narrower interpretation than that of the state if its regulation is inadvertently drawn narrower or an antiquated charter provision is not amended or removed; *Bussieve v. Roberge,* 714 A.2d 894 (N.H. 1998). However, in some states, the code's definitions must conform exactly to the enabling act definitions. *Pennobscot v. Board of County Commissioners,* 642 P.2d 915 (Colo. 1982) See Laurie Reynolds, "Local Subdivision Regulation: Formulaic Constraints In An Age of Discretion," 24 *Ga. L. Rev.* 525 (1990).
11. *Burnt Fork Citizen's Coalition v. Ravalli County BCC,* 951 P.2d 1020 (Mont. 1997); *Ronning v. Thompson,* 483 N.Y.S.2d 949 (1985).
12. *Fleming v. Moore Bros. Realty Co.,* 251 S.W.2d 8 (Mo. 1952).
13. *Amcare 2 Partners v. Zoning Hearing Board,* 609 A.2d 887, 891 (Pa. Commw. 1992) ("in construing a zoning ordinance, the permissive widest use of land is the rule and not the exception, unless specifically restrained in the reasonable exercise of the police power").

14. *Von Der Heide v. Zoning Board of Appeals*, 123 N.Y.S.2d 726 (1953); see also *Pierro v. Baxendale*, 118 A.2d 401 (N.J. 1955).
15. *Borough of Glassboro v. Vallorosi*, 568 P.2d 888 (N.J. 1990); for problems with the definition of "family," see *Village of Belle Terre v. Boraas*, 416 U.S. 1 (1974).
16. *Akin v. South Middleton Township Zoning Hearing Board*, 547 A.2d 883 (Pa. Commw. 1988).
17. *Novi v. City of Pacifica*, 169 Cal. App. 3d 678, 215 Cal.Rptr. 439 (Cal. App. 1 Dist. 1985).
18. *Manalapan Realty, L.P. v. Township Committee of the Township of Manalapan*, 639 A.2d 318 (N.J. 1999) ("a municipality can reasonably decide what types of stores it will permit to operate [in the C-1 regional commercial district] to protect the 'retail' character of the C-1 zone as well as on 'aesthetic grounds,' to zone out stores with outdoor sales of materials").
19. *Landmark Land Co. v. City and County of Denver*, 728 P.2d 1281 (Colo. 1986).
20. *A-S-P Associates v. City of Raleigh*, 258 S.E.2d 444 (N.C. 1979).
21. Fred P. Bosselman, Duane A. Feurer, and Charles L. Siemon, *The Permit Explosion: Coordination of the Proliferation* (Washington, DC: Urban Land Institute, 1976).
22. Animus and misconduct by planning staff and municipal officials can lead to damages for violation of procedural due process. *L.A. Ray Realty v. Town of Cumberland*, 698 A.2d 202 (R.I. 1997).
23. See Tom Angotti, "'As-of-Right' Development: An Invitation to Ethical Breaches?," *Gotham Gazette* (Jun. 19, 2003).
24. "Mandatory injunctions for demolition are, of course, permitted as an appropriate remedy for zoning violations." *AVCO Community Developers v. South Coast Regional Comm'n*, 5553 P.2d 546 (Cal. 1976); *Parkview Assoc. v. City of New York*, 519 N.E.2d 1372 (N.Y. 1988) (ordering demolition of the top 12 stories of 31-story building); *City of Chicago v. Handler*, 288 N.E.2d 714 (Ill. App. 1972).
25. The Maryland Court of Special Appeals affirmed a decision by the board of appeals that it had jurisdiction to review the legality of the development approval. *United Parcel Service v. People's Counsel for Baltimore County*, 611 A.2d 993 (Md. App. 1992). The Maryland Court of Appeals (the highest court of the state) by a 4-3 decision reversed the decision by rejecting the Special Court of Appeal's use of the "discovery" rule and instead applying the 30-day statute of limitations for appeal of the issuance of the development approval even though the neighbors had no notice of its issuance. *United Parcel Service v. People's Counsel for Baltimore County*, 650 A.2d 226 (Md. 1994).

CHAPTER

2

Use Patterns

2.0 PURPOSE AND FINDINGS

This chapter establishes design templates for certain types of development. The procedures for permitting such activities are also described. The purpose is to consolidate the various aspects of the Land Development Code (LDC) applicable to these activities in order to improve the readability of the LDC and, in some cases, to encourage certain types of development. Each section in this chapter describes the use pattern, the procedure for approval, and the standards relating to approval, with cross-references to other parts of this chapter where needed. The intent is to present a visual, user-friendly overview of the regulations that apply to those types of uses or development styles.

The use patterns established in this chapter are not zoning districts, overlay zoning districts, or special zoning districts. Instead, they are forms of development that may be permitted in the various zoning districts established by the LDC. The use patterns typically involve multiple uses on the same property. They are described here and in the base zoning district regulations (Table 3-4, Use Matrix, in Chapter 3, Zoning of the LDC) as a land-use activity in order to trigger the appropriate development approval process. Some multiple-use developments, such as "PD" (Planned Development) districts (see § 3.4 Zoning District Boundaries in Chapter 3, Zoning, of the LDC), are permitted through a special or overlay zoning district. However, a planned development is not a land-use activity but rather a procedure for providing design flexibility. By contrast, the use patterns are specific land-use activities involving land-use and design controls that produce a distinct pattern of development.

2.1 APPLICABILITY

This section applies to any application where the applicant chooses to develop pursuant to the standards and procedures of a use pattern described in this chapter.

2.2 CONSERVATION SUBDIVISION

Purpose and findings: The purpose of this section is to provide flexibility in site design in order to allow developers to preserve common open space and natural resources. The specific purposes of this section are to:
• Protect the public health, safety, and general welfare by avoiding surface and groundwater pollution, contaminated run-off, air quality contamination, and urban heat islands that result from pavement and the clearing of natural vegetation;
• Protect and preserve natural resources, such as wetlands, streams, lakes, steep slopes, woodlands, and water recharge areas;
• Reduce infrastructure and housing costs by reducing the engineering and construction costs produced by conventional subdivision design, which requires more pavement, wetland crossings, grading of trees and natural areas, and maintenance from lawn and landscaping maintenance;
• Protect property values by allowing open space design features that enhance the marketability of development;
• Provide design flexibility; and

Table 2-1
Lot Arrangement for Conservation Subdivisions

(A) Lot Form	(B) Definition
Single-family detached homes	This is a single-family dwelling that is not attached to any other dwelling by any means and is surrounded by open space or yards.
Detached eyebrow homes	As an alternative to the cul-de-sac scheme, this configuration groups homes around a common green area with two access points.
Attached eyebrow homes	An eyebrow street includes dwellings fronting a street that surrounds a close. The eyebrow street configuration may be used for duplexes or triplexes. The close shall include a landscaped island or a natural area that contains the same planting density as a Type N buffer (see § 5.31 Buffers and Screening in Chapter 5, Development Standards, of the LDC).
Detached homes with shared driveways	This pattern permits the grouping of up to four homes on a shared driveway. The driveway is limited to 50 feet in length.
Detached homes with shared courtyards	A courtyard is an open area adjacent to, or part of, a group of residential buildings. Courtyards function as gathering places and may incorporate a variety of nonpermanent activities, such as vendors and display stands. See § 5.21 Parks/Open Space in Chapter 5, Development Standards, of the LDC for standards applicable to courtyards.
Detached homes with commons	This approach to clustering emphasizes open space by orienting the front doors of houses to a formal common area. The common area may include a greenway, close, playground, green, park, or parkway as set forth in § 5.21 Parks/Open Space in Chapter 5, Development Standards, of the LDC. Cottage homes are small homes built around common, private open space, typically on smaller tracts. Cottage homes must conform to the requirements of § 7.70.9 Cottage Housing Developments, in Chapter 7, Supplemental Use Regulations, of the LDC.
Detached patio homes	A patio home or garden home is a single-family residential structure of one or two stories, which is constructed in such a manner that one, but not both, of the side exterior walls is constructed along one of the side property lines of each lot. The side setback shall be waived on one side of the property line.
Detached "Z" lot homes	Detached "Z" lot homes are aligned along the diagonal axis of the lot, either perpendicular to the street or at an angle. The minimum side setback requirements shall not apply.

Figure 2-1
Conservation Subdivisions

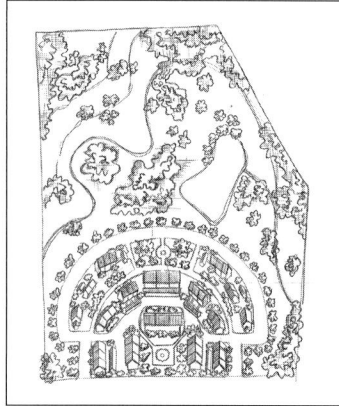

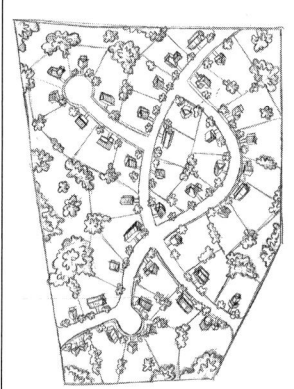

Conservation subdivisions (left) feature smaller lots with a high percentage of open space. Conventional subdivisions (right) feature large lots with little common open space. A conventional subdivision is subject to all of the base zoning district standards, such as minimum lot size, front setbacks, landscaping, and adequacy of public facilities.

- Promote development on soils that are most suitable for urban densities while preserving soils that are primarily adaptable to other uses, such as woodlands, wildlife habitat, and agriculture.

2.2.1 Applicability

A conservation subdivision (see Figure 2-1) is permitted in any zoning district excluding the following: "D" (Downtown), "IL" (Industrial Light), "IH" (Industrial Heavy), or "MX" (Mixed Use).

2.2.2 Processing Procedures

Conservation subdivisions are processed in accordance with the subdivision procedures (see *Division 5: Subdivisions*, in Chapter 4, Procedures, of the LDC).

2.2.3 Size and Location of Site

There is no minimum or maximum size for a conservation subdivision. However, the minimum open space

Table 2-1 (cont.)
Lot Arrangement for Conservation Subdivisions

(A) Lot Form	(B) Definition
Detached wide-shallow lot homes	A wide-shallow lot has a frontage and lot width that exceeds its depth. The rear setback shall be waived for wide-shallow lot configurations.
Attached homes with private parking courts	This configuration involves townhouse groups with up to eight units in a row.
Attached homes with automobile courtyards, park circle, or private parking courts	This pattern is similar to the private courtyard scheme in that it provides a turnaround circle with a small park or open space area. The common area for the automobile-courtyard configuration contains parking.
Stacked quadrangle homes	Quadrangles are multifamily dwellings with at least two stories arranged in a continuous, rectangular form with an inner courtyard.
Stacked and attached homes with parking courts	Angled stacked and attached homes are multifamily dwellings with at least two stories in height and aligned with a horizontal curve or "L" configuration. The dwellings shall contain porches facing a walkway, courtyard with parking, or common open space.
Single-family attached and multifamily stacked homes with park square	This configuration involves a combination of single-family dwellings, duplexes, row houses, or multifamily dwellings facing a square, green, or plaza.
Single-family attached homes with midrise cluster	This configuration includes a mix of townhouses with not more than one apartment per block. The apartment frontage shall not exceed 200 feet.
Single-family detached and attached homes in a traditional block	This option includes a mix of single-family detached dwellings and townhouses or row houses fronting local streets with a connectivity ratio (see § 5.23.4 Connectivity in Chapter 5, Development Standards, of the LDC) of at least 1.8. Access shall be from a rear alley.
Traditional neighborhood cluster street	This option includes a mix of single-family detached dwellings and townhouses or row houses fronting local streets with a connectivity ratio (see § 5.23.4 Connectivity in Chapter 5, Development Standards, of the LDC) of at least 1.8. At least 50 percent of the blocks shall contain an eyebrow street with a close. The close shall include a landscaped island or a natural area that contains the same planting density as a Type N buffer (see § 5.31 Buffers and Screening in Chapter 5, Development Standards, of the LDC).

Adapted from Frederick D. Jarvis, Site Planning and Design for Great Neighborhoods (Washington, DC: Home Builder Press, National Association of Home Builders, 1993).

requirements may limit the availability of this option for some landowners.

2.2.4 Uses

Permitted uses are governed by the applicable zoning district regulations.

2.2.5 Lot and Block Design

2.2.5.1 Lot Configurations

(A) A conservation subdivision shall comply with the lot standards (§ 5.10 Lots, in Chapter 5, Development Standards, of the LDC), except as provided in subsections (B), (C), (D), and (E), below.

(B) Lots within a conservation subdivision are not subject to the minimum lot size, minimum frontage, or minimum lot width requirements of the zoning district.

(C) In order to provide undivided open space for direct views and access, at least 40 percent of the lots within a conservation subdivision shall abut a conservation area. Direct pedestrian access to the open space from all lots not adjoining the open space shall be provided through a continuous system of sidewalks and trails. This subsection does not apply to prime farmland, as it is vulnerable to trampling damage and disturbance.

(D) Lots within 100 feet of a primary or secondary conservation area shall front on a conservation access street. Lots shall not front on a collector or higher-order street.

(E) Lots may be arranged in any of the patterns set forth in Table 2-1.

2.2.6 Transportation

(A) A conservation subdivision shall comply with the street design standards (§ 5.23 Street Design and Transportation in Chapter 5, Development Standards, of the LDC), unless otherwise provided, and of this subsection.

(B) The design of local streets shall comply with the standards for conservation access streets, as set forth in § 5.23 Street Design and Transportation in Chapter 5, Development Standards, of the LDC.

(C) The connectivity ratio for streets (§ 5.23.4 Connectivity in Chapter 5, Development Standards, of the LDC) does not apply to local streets within a conservation subdivision, except for that portion of the street network that includes the following lot configurations:

(1) Single-family detached and attached homes in traditional neighborhood; and

(2) Traditional neighborhood cluster street.

(D) The conservation subdivision shall include a pedestrian circulation system. All sidewalks shall connect to other sidewalks or with trail sidewalks, and trails shall connect to potential areas qualifying as conservation areas on the development parcel, adjoining undeveloped parcels, or with existing parks and open space on adjoining developed parcels.

(E) Streets shall not cross wetlands or existing slopes exceeding 15 percent.

2.2.7 Stormwater Management

See the stormwater management standards (§ 5.22 Stormwater Management in Chapter 5, Development Standards, of the LDC). Stormwater management ponds or basins may be included as part of the minimum required conservation areas.

2.2.8 Utilities

(A) A conservation subdivision shall comply with the utilities standards (§ 5.24 Utilities in Chapter 5, Development Standards, of the LDC), except as provided in subsection (B), below.

(B) Land within the rights-of-way for underground pipelines may be included as part of the required conservation areas. Land within the rights-of-way of high-tension power lines shall not be included as part of the minimum required conservation area.

(C) Where permitted by [HEALTH DEPARTMENT OR AGENCY THAT APPROVES SEPTIC SYSTEMS], a conservation subdivision may use a shared septic drainfield system, as defined in [STATE REGULATIONS], to dispose of on-site wastewater. The drainfield or absorption area for the shared septic system may be located in a conservation area if the location is permitted by the [HEALTH DEPARTMENT OR AGENCY THAT APPROVES SEPTIC SYSTEMS] and complies with the following to the extent permitted by state law and the applicable [LOCAL GOVERNMENT] regulations:

(1) The absorption field is an underground drainage field or an absorption field for spray irrigation purposes for a land treatment disposal system; or

(2) The absorption field is a mound system [STATE REGULATIONS] that is limited to not more than 10 percent of the required minimum open space.

2.2.9 Conservation Areas

2.2.9.1 Generally

(A) This section establishes the standards for conservation areas. Conservation areas are the parks, natural features, and passive open space that distinguish this use pattern from other types of development.

(B) Conservation areas shall be designated as permanent open space, not to be further subdivided, and protected through a conservation easement held by the [LOCAL GOVERNMENT] or by a land trust or conservancy.

(C) The conservation easement shall prohibit further development in the conservation areas and may establish other standards safeguarding the site's special resources from negative changes.

(D) The parks and open space standards relating to maintenance (§ 5.21 Parks/Open Space in Chapter 5, Development Standards, of the LDC) apply to a conservation subdivision. No other requirements of the parks and open space standards apply to a conservation subdivision.

2.2.9.2 Set-Aside and Allocation of Conservation Areas

A minimum of 60 percent of the total tract area shall be designated as conservation areas. The following areas shall be designated as conservation areas:

(A) Wetlands;

(B) Woodlands;

(C) Sensitive aquifer recharge features;

(D) All of the floodway and flood fringe within the 100-year floodplain, as shown on the official Federal Emergency Management Agency (FEMA) maps;

(E) All areas within 100 feet of the edge of the 100-year floodplain, as delineated on the FEMA maps, and any Letter of Map Revision;

(F) All areas within 100 feet of the banks of any stream shown as a blue line on the U.S. Geological Survey 1:24,000 (7.5 minute) scale topographic maps for [LOCAL GOVERNMENT];

(G) Steep slopes (slopes exceeding 25 percent);

(H) Soils subject to slumping, as indicated on the medium-intensity maps contained in the county soil survey, published by the U.S. Department of Agriculture Natural Resources Conservation Service;

(I) Significant wildlife habitat areas;

(J) Areas with highly permeable (excessively drained) soil;

(K) Significant wildlife habitat areas not designated as a conservation area;

(L) Prime farmland;

(M) Historic, archaeological, or cultural features listed (or eligible to be listed) on national, state, or [LOCAL GOVERNMENT] registers or inventories; or

(N) Scenic views into the property from existing public roads.

**Figure 2-2
Conventional Commercial Centers**

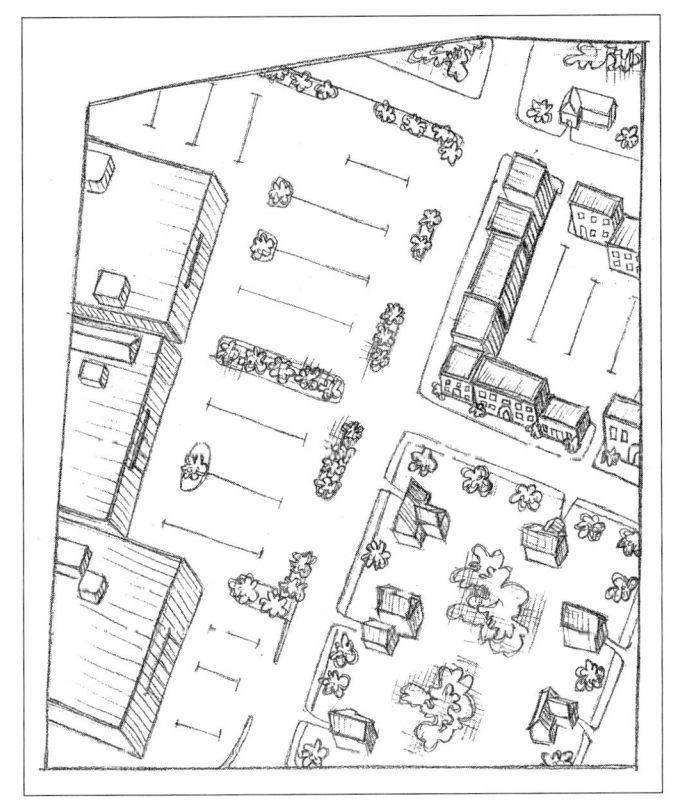

Conventional commercial centers (left side of street) feature front-loaded parking, long blocks, and a lack of architectural detailing. Neighborhood centers (right side of street) feature buildings that align the street, short blocks, and a pedestrian scale.

2.2.9.3 *Connectivity*

Conservation areas shall abut existing conservation areas, parks, open space, or farmland on adjacent parcels.

2.2.10 Environmental Protection

A conservation subdivision shall comply with the environmental protection standards of this chapter. In addition, the conservation subdivision shall comply with the following standards:

(A) No conservation area shall be cleared, graded, filled, or subject to construction. However, rights-of-way for trails (see § 5.23 Street Design and Transportation in Chapter 5, Development Standards, of the LDC); any streets needed to provide access to the proposed subdivision; and water, sewer, electric, or cable lines may be cleared. The width of rights-of-way for streets or trails shall be restricted to the minimum as designated in § 5.23 Street Design and Transportation; and

(B) No lot may be located on highly erodible soils with slopes exceeding 10 percent.

2.2.11 Landscaping and Screening

See the landscaping and screening standards (*Division 4: Greenspace (Landscaping, Tree Preservation, Screening, and Environmental Protection) Standards* in Chapter 5, Development Standards, of the LDC).

2.2.12 Parking

In order to encourage design flexibility, to preserve open space, and to minimize impervious surfaces, a conservation subdivision is not subject to the minimum parking requirements of the parking standards (§ 5.51 Parking in Chapter 5, Development Standards, of the LDC). A conservation subdivision is subject to the maximum parking requirements of the parking standards of this chapter.

2.3 NEIGHBORHOOD CENTER

Purpose and findings: A neighborhood center:
• Provides shopping, service, and employment opportunities within walking or driving distance of residential areas;
• Is spatially defined and concentrated in a nodal pattern, as opposed to conventional strip shopping centers; and
• Features urban design guidelines, such as zero setbacks and streetscapes with windows and entryways.

This section permits neighborhood centers in a wider variety of districts and situations, subject to strict design standards that prohibit strip development and encourage walkable streetscapes. Free-standing commercial uses that do not meet the standards of this section shall be located in the "CN" (Commercial Neighborhood) zoning district.

2.3.1 Applicability

This section applies to any application meeting the requirements of this section and which is designated a "neighborhood center" by the applicant (see Figure 2-2).

2.3.2 Processing Procedures

A neighborhood center requires approval of a site plan and zoning certificate. A neighborhood center may also be approved as part of a master site plan or planned development.

2.3.3 Size and Location of Site

(A) A neighborhood center may be located at the intersection of any of the street classifications and within the zoning districts as set forth in Table 2-2.

(B) A neighborhood center shall not exceed 150 feet of frontage. No neighborhood center shall be approved in locations where the combined lineal frontage, including the proposed development, exceeds 660 feet.

(C) The establishment of a neighborhood center shall not establish a precedent for higher-density zoning between the nodes or intersections where the neighborhood centers are established.

2.3.4 Uses and Dimensional Standards

In order to stimulate pedestrian activity, the first floor (street level) of any new building abutting an arterial or collector street shall devote at least 50 percent of the net first-floor area to retail uses.

Residential dwellings shall be permitted above or below the first floor of any building with commercial and/or retail uses.

A neighborhood center may include any of the uses permitted in the "CN" (Commercial Neighborhood), "CG" (Commercial General), or "O" (Office) districts. Dimensional requirements shall conform to Table 2-3 (see Figure 2-3).

2.3.5 Lot Layout

Buildings shall conform to the commercial building standards (§ 5.13.5 Commercial Buildings in Chapter 5, Development Standards, of the LDC).

2.3.6 Parks and Open Space

A neighborhood center may incorporate plazas, courtyards, or forecourts consistent with the parks and open space standards (§ 5.21 Parks/Open Space in Chapter 5, Development Standards, of the LDC). If the proposed development includes at least [NUMBER BASED ON LOCAL STUDIES] square feet, at least [NUMBER BASED ON LOCAL STUDIES] square feet of parks/open space shall be provided per equivalent dwelling unit. No other provisions of the parks and open space standards apply to a neighborhood center.

2.3.7 Landscaping and Screening

See landscaping and screening standards (*Division 4: Greenspace (Landscaping, Tree Preservation, Screening, and Environmental Protection) Standards* in Chapter 5, Development Standards, of the LDC). A neighborhood center is not subject to the tree preservation standards of this chapter.

2.3.8 Parking

See parking standards (§ 5.51 Parking in Chapter 5, Development Standards, of the LDC). Parking shall be located to the rear of any principal building or in a midblock location (see Figure 2-4).

2.3.9 Open Space

At least 1 linear foot of seating shall be provided for each 50 square feet of open space. Seating dimensions shall comply with the requirements of the Americans with Disabilities Act.

At least two of the following amenities shall be provided in an open space area:

Table 2-2
Neighborhood Center Location Standards

(A) Street Classification	(B) RP, RE	(C) RP, NS, NU	(D) CN, O, CG, D	(E) MX
Arterial—Arterial	C	P	P	P
Arterial—Collector	C	P	P	P
Arterial—Local	—	P	P	P
Collector—Collector	—	P	P	P
Local—Collector	—	C	P	P
Local—Local	—	—	—	—

RP = Resource Protection; RE = Residential Estate; NS = Neighborhood Suburban; NU = Neighborhood Urban; CN = Commercial Neighborhood; O = Office; CG = Commercial General; D = Downtown; MX = Mixed Use; C = a neighborhood center may be permitted only upon approval of a conditional use permit; and P = a neighborhood center may be established as of right at the intersection of the street classifications listed in Columns (B) through (E). A dash ("—") means that the neighborhood center is not permitted at that location.

Figure 2-3
Illustration of Neighborhood Center Dimensional Standards

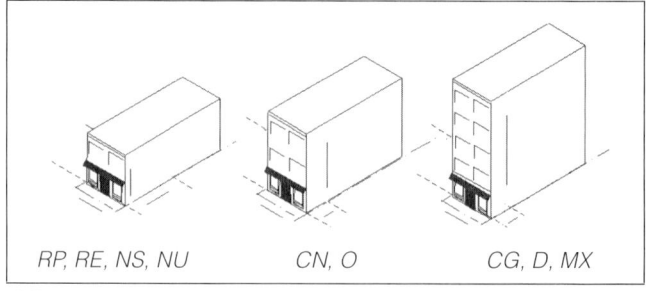

RP, RE, NS, NU   CN, O   CG, D, MX

RP = Resource Protection; RE = Residential Estate; NS = Neighborhood Suburban; NU = Neighborhood Urban; CN = Commercial Neighborhood; O = Office; CG = Commercial General; D = Downtown; and MX = Mixed Use.

Table 2-3
Neighborhood Center Dimensional Standards

(A) Category	(B) RP, RE, NS, NU	(C) CN, O	(D) MX
Minimum frontage	20	20	20
Maximum height (stories)	2	3	5
Minimum front setback	0	0	0
Maximum front setback (arterial)	30	15	15
Maximum front setback (collector, local)	5	5	5
Minimum rear setback	30	30	30

RP = Resource Protection; RE = Residential Estate; NS = Neighborhood Suburban; NU = Neighborhood Urban; CN = Commercial Neighborhood; O = Office; and MX = Mixed Use.

**Figure 2-4
Rear Parking with Buildings Aligned at the Street**

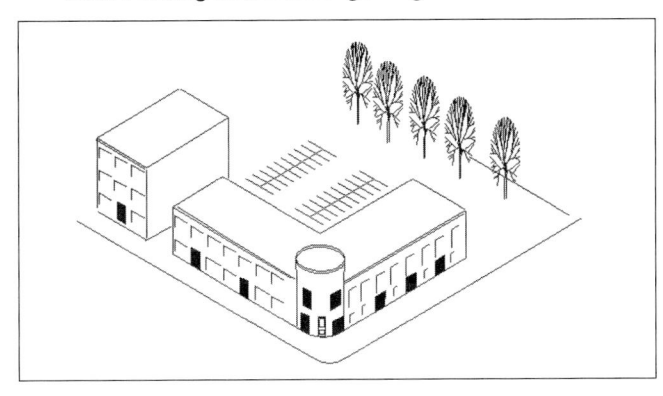

(A) Ornamental fountains;
(B) Ornamental lamp posts;
(C) Stairways;
(D) Waterfalls;
(E) Sculptures;
(F) Arbors;
(G) Trellises;
(H) Planted beds;
(I) Drinking fountains;
(J) Clock pedestals;
(K) Awnings; or
(L) Canopies.

2.4 CAMPUS

Purpose and findings: An office or institutional campus ("campus") provides employment, civic, and/or residential uses interspersed with open space areas and pedestrian walkways. A campus may be established as part of a larger mixed-use development or as a self-contained development or community.

**Figure 2-5
Campus-Style Development**

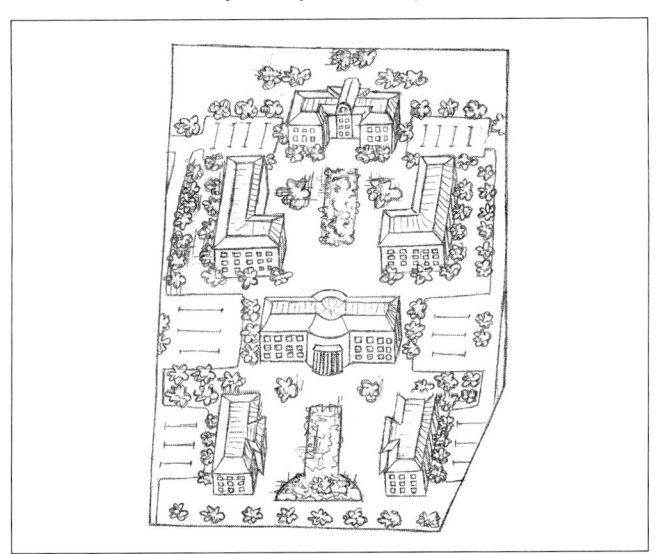

2.4.1 Applicability

This section applies to any application meeting the requirements of this section and which is designated a "campus" by the applicant (see Figure 2-5).

2.4.2 Processing Procedures

A campus requires approval of a site plan and zoning certificate. A campus may also be approved as part of a master site plan or planned development.

2.4.3 Size and Location of Site

A campus shall be located in the "O" (Office), "CG" (Commercial General), "CL" (Commercial Large-Scale), or "IL" (Industrial Light) districts.

2.4.4 Uses

2.4.4.1 Generally

Any use permitted in the "IL" (Industrial Light) or "O" (Office) districts are permitted in a campus. Uses permitted in the "NU" (Neighborhood Urban) districts are also permitted so long as at least 60 percent of the building floor area is devoted to uses permitted in the "IL" or "O" districts.

2.4.4.2 Accessory Uses

Accessory uses may include:

(A) Personal services, such as cafeteria, restaurant, barber/beauty shop, newsstand, laundry/dry cleaning pickup station, sundries store, or child day care center, provided that such facilities shall have no advertising display other than directional or informational signs;

(B) Retail incidental to or in support of any of the principal permitted uses;

(C) Recreational facilities, industrial health clinics and first-aid stations, technical libraries, auditoriums, employee training facilities, and meeting and display rooms;

(D) Outdoor storage, provided that the requirements for screening are met, and that not more than 10 percent of each lot is so used;

(E) Temporary buildings, trailers, and vehicles for uses incidental to construction work; and

(F) Other accessory uses and structures customarily incidental to any permitted principal use.

2.4.5 Lot Layout

See lot layout standards (§ 5.10 Lots and § 5.11 Blocks in Chapter 5, Development Standards, of the LDC) and as outlined in § 2.4.5.1 Area and § 2.4.5.2 Setbacks of this chapter.

2.4.5.1 Area

The ground-level square footage of all buildings and improvements shall not exceed 60 percent of the development parcel.

2.4.5.2 Setbacks

No building or other structure, except streets, walks, and parking facilities, shall be erected within the following setback lines measured along the perimeter of the development parcel:

(A) 45 feet from any perimeter abutting a developed residential area; and

(B) 25 feet from any perimeter abutting an undeveloped or nonresidential area.

2.4.6 Building Design

2.4.6.1 Height

The height of buildings and other improvements shall not exceed 30 feet within a distance of 100 feet from any perimeter abutting a developed residential area. The height of buildings and other improvements may be increased 2 feet for each 1 foot they are set back beyond the 100-foot distance.

2.4.6.2 Orientation

Buildings shall be oriented to streets, parks, and open space, or pedestrian ways. Buildings shall not be oriented to parking areas.

2.4.7 Street Design and Transportation

See street design and transportation standards (§ 5.23 Street Design and Transportation in Chapter 5, Development Standards, of the LDC) and § 2.4.7.1 Access and § 2.4.7.2 Streets of this chapter.

2.4.7.1 Access

(A) *Vehicular access:* Vehicular access to a campus is permitted only from major thoroughfares. The classification of any street as a major thoroughfare shall be determined by the major thoroughfare plan.

(B) *Pedestrian access:* Sidewalks shall be provided on public and private streets in accordance with the street design and transportation standards (§ 5.23 Street Design and Transportation in Chapter 5, Development Standards, of the LDC).

2.4.7.2 Streets

Streets within a campus may be public or private. Private streets shall comply with the specifications and design standards set forth in the street design and transportation standards (§ 5.23 Street Design and Transportation in Chapter 5, Development Standards, of the LDC).

2.4.8 Parks and Open Space

See parks and open space standards (§ 5.21 Parks/Open Space in Chapter 5, Development Standards, of the LDC). In lieu of the set-aside requirements of § 5.21.2 Required Parks/Open Space in Chapter 5, Development Standards, of the LDC, at least 50 percent of the development parcel shall be reserved for parks and open space. Parks and open space provided pursuant to this section shall be maintained in private ownership. The [CITY/COUNTY] may accept dedication of all or part of the parks and open space if it finds that the dedication serves a predominantly public purpose.

2.4.9 Landscaping and Screening

See landscaping and screening standards (*Division 4: Greenspace (Landscaping, Tree Preservation, Screening, and Environmental Protection) Standards* in Chapter 5, Development Standards, of the LDC) and § 2.4.9.1 Screening through § 2.4.9.2 Buffers of this chapter.

2.4.9.1 Screening

Structures other than buildings that are visible from view outside of the campus development shall be screened by plantings, landscaping, and/or a solid wall/fence at least 6 feet in height. The use of a wall or fence is in addition to, and does not replace, the requirements for landscaping or trees as set forth in § 5.31 Buffers and Screening in Chapter 5, Development Standards, of the LDC.

2.4.9.2 Buffers

A buffer yard, as defined in § 5.31 Buffers and Screening in Chapter 5, Development Standards, of the LDC, shall be installed and maintained along the perimeters of the campus that abut developed residential areas. Along the perimeters of a business park district abutting undeveloped or nonresidential areas, a Type B buffer yard shall be installed and maintained.

2.4.10 Parking

Parking shall be located to the rear of any principal building or in a midblock location. Structured parking that has a retail use at the ground floor may be located at the street frontage.

2.5 COMMERCIAL RETROFIT

Purpose and findings: This section encourages the redevelopment of existing shopping centers, big-box retail sites, and other sites characterized by large expanses of surface parking into a development pattern that is pedestrian friendly, is compatible with surrounding development, provides a visually attractive site design, and which reduces reliance on the automobile for vehicular trips.

**Figure 2-6
Retrofitting Conventional Centers**

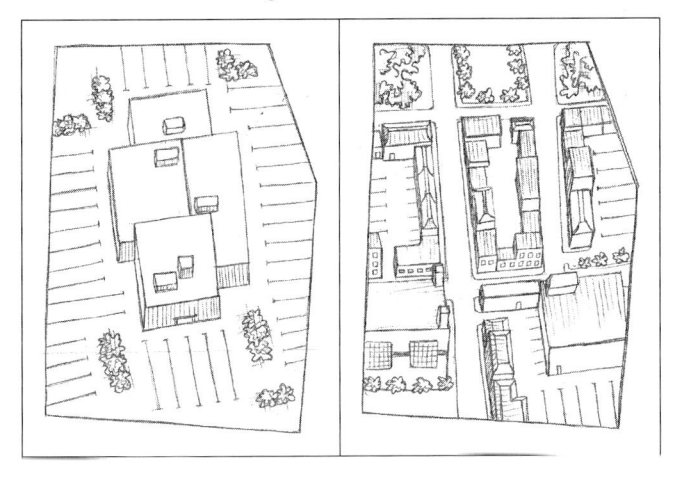

2.5.1 Applicability

Existing parking lots adjoining the frontage of any site located within the "CG" (Commercial General) or "CL" (Commercial Large-Scale) zoning districts may be replaced with buildings. A density bonus may be permitted to encourage such activities pursuant to Chapter 3, Zoning, of the LDC (see Figure 2-6).

2.5.2 Processing Procedures

A commercial retrofit requires site plan and development approval.

**Table 2-4
Height Bonus for Greyfield Redevelopment**

Zoning District	Existing Number of Stories	Additional Stories of Apartment Use Permitted
"CN" (Commercial Neighborhood), "O" (Office)	1	2
	2	1
	3 or more	0
"CG" (Commercial General)	1	2
	2	2
	3 or more	1
"CL" (Commercial Large-Scale)	1	3
	2	3
	3	3
	4	3
	5 or more	3
Other district	1	2
	2	2
	3 or more	2

2.5.3 Site Design and Building Disposition

Development may consist of the following activities:

(A) Additional buildings shall be constructed between a collector street right-of-way and the existing buildings. The façades of the additional buildings shall face the public right-of-way and the existing buildings. The additional building façades that are oriented to a street, a driveway, or existing buildings shall conform to the commercial urban design standards (§ 5.13 Building Design in Chapter 5, Development Standards, of the LDC).

(B) Apartments may be placed above new or existing office or retail uses. The floor area devoted to apartments shall not exceed what is shown in Table 2-4.

(C) In order to stimulate pedestrian activity, the first floor (street level) of any new building abutting a major arterial roadway, minor arterial roadway, or major collector roadway shall devote at least 50 percent of the net first-floor area to retail uses.

(D) The additional buildings shall occupy at least 70 percent of the site frontage.

2.5.4 Adequate Public Facilities

The adequate public facilities standards (Chapter 6, Adequate Public Facilities, of the LDC) do not apply to a commercial retrofit.

2.5.5 Lot Layout

The additional buildings shall have a façade oriented to the principal buildings and a façade facing the frontage line. The façades facing the principal buildings shall conform to the commercial building standards (§ 5.13.5 Commercial Buildings in Chapter 5, Development Standards, of the LDC).

2.5.6 Transportation

Development parcels of at least 2 acres shall add at least one through street that complies with the street design and transportation standards (§ 5.23 Street Design and Transportation in Chapter 5, Development Standards, of the LDC). Development parcels with at least 5 acres shall include at least one block designated as a main street.

2.5.7 Stormwater Management

A commercial retrofit shall comply with the stormwater management standards (see § 5.22 Stormwater Management in Chapter 5, Development Standards, of the LDC) unless no additional impervious surface will be added. If no additional impervious surface is added, a commercial retrofit is exempt from the stormwater management standards. For purposes of this section, "additional impervious surface" means a net addition to the total impervious surface existing on the development parcel or the extension of impervious surface to a new location.

**Figure 2-7
Separate Versus Joint Access**

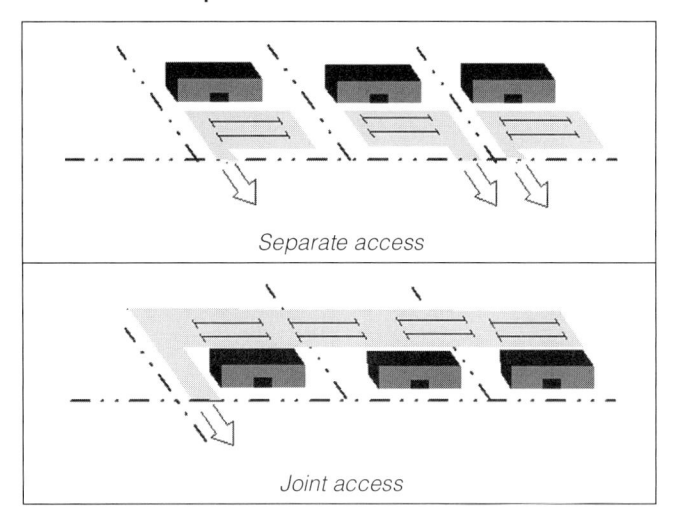

Separate access

Joint access

**Figure 2-8
Traditional Neighborhood Development**

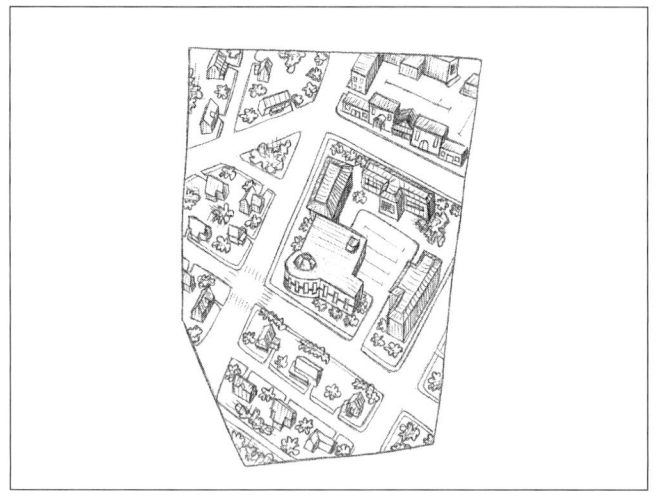

2.5.8 Utilities

See the utilities standards (§ 5.24 Utilities in Chapter 5, Development Standards, of the LDC).

2.5.9 Parks and Open Space

A commercial retrofit shall include plazas, courtyards, and/or forecourts consistent with the parks and open space standards (see § 5.21 Parks/Open Space in Chapter 5, Development Standards, of the LDC).

2.5.10 Environmental Protection

The environmental protection standards (*Division 5: Environmental Protection of Critical Areas* in Chapter 5, Development Standards, of the LDC) do not apply to a commercial retrofit.

2.5.11 Landscaping, Screening, and Tree Preservation

See the landscaping and screening standards (*Division 4: Greenspace (Landscaping, Tree Preservation, Screening, and Environmental Protection) Standards* in Chapter 5, Development Standards, of the LDC). The tree preservation standards (§ 5.37 Tree Preservation and Tree Save Areas in Chapter 5) do not apply to a commercial retrofit.

2.5.12 Parking

(A) Additional parking may be placed to the rear of the principal buildings so long as the number of spaces for the entire site does not exceed the maximum parking requirements of the LDC.

(B) Parking areas may be connected to rear parking lots on adjoining properties in order to allow customers to drive to other locations without reentering the major roadway network and adding to traffic volumes (see Figure 2-7).

(C) Service entrances and service yards shall be located only in the rear or side yard. Service yards shall be screened from adjacent residentially zoned or used property by the installation of a Type B buffer yard as set forth in the buffer standards (§ 5.31 Buffers and Screening in Chapter 5, Development Standards, of the LDC).

(D) No more than four continuous rows of parking may be placed or maintained between the existing buildings and the additional buildings.

2.6 TRADITIONAL NEIGHBORHOOD DEVELOPMENT

Purpose and findings: The traditional neighborhood development (TND) option (see Figure 2-8) is designed to permit the development of land in a manner consistent with the historic and timeless principles of [LOCAL GOVERNMENT]'s existing neighborhoods. A TND combines a variety of housing types with commercial and civic uses in a compact, walkable neighborhood setting. TNDs feature a highly interconnected street network and setbacks appropriate to create a public realm built on a human scale. The street network should recognize a site's topography and other natural features. A TND may not be appropriate where severe environmental constraints, such as steep slopes, wetlands, or streams, preclude street interconnections and high-impervious surface coverage.

2.6.1 Applicability

A TND may be approved in any of the following zoning districts: "NS" (Neighborhood Suburban), "NU" (Neighborhood Urban), "O" (Office), "CN" (Commercial Neighborhood), "CG" (Commercial General), "CL" (Commercial Large-Scale) or "MX" (Mixed Use).

2.6.2 Processing Procedures

2.6.2.1 *Generally*

There are two procedures for approval of a TND:

(A) The TND may be approved administratively with a combined subdivision plat and master site plan.

(B) Where the existing zoning classification does not permit a TND, the applicant may request a rezoning to an "MX" (Mixed Use) zoning district.

2.6.2.2 *Combined Subdivision Plats and Site Plans*

Applications for subdivision approval in any of the districts in which a TND is permitted may file a combined subdivision plat and master site plan that complies with the standards of this section and other applicable provisions of the LDC. Such applications shall be labeled "TND Subdivision" and may be processed and approved in accordance with the master site plan procedures and the subdivision plat procedures set forth in Chapter 4, Procedures, of the LDC.

2.6.2.3 *Neighborhood Meetings*

A neighborhood participation meeting (§ 4.10 Neighborhood Participation Meeting in Chapter 4, Procedures, of the LDC) is mandatory for a TND.

2.6.3 Size and Location of Site

2.6.3.1 *Location*

(A) A TND may be located adjacent to, but shall not be bisected by, a secondary arterial or primary arterial street unless the street is designed to conform to the requirements of an avenue or main street (see § 5.23 Street Design and Transportation in Chapter 5, Development Standards, of the LDC).

(B) If the TND is located adjacent to a collector or higher-classification street, and the street is not designed to conform to the standards of an avenue or main street, the following criteria shall apply:

(1) The internal streets providing access to the TND shall be aligned perpendicular to the collector or higher-order street; and

(2) The buildings or structures that take access from the internal streets shall face the internal streets and not the collector or higher order streets.

2.6.3.2 *Subareas*

The site shall be divided into the following subareas:

(A) *A center consisting of civic, retail, service, and multifamily uses:* The size of the center is based on the size of the entire site, as provided in § 2.6.3.3 Centers of this chapter.

(B) *A neighborhood or series of neighborhoods consisting of multifamily and single-family uses, small-scale retail and service uses, and public outdoor gathering places:* It is the intent of this chapter that all areas within a neighborhood are within a 5-minute walking distance from edge to edge. A neighborhood shall be at least 10 and no more than 40 acres in size. This land area does not include greenbelts.

(C) *Parks and open space, including a plaza and a greenbelt:* The plaza provides a community focal point and public gathering place, while the greenbelt provides a clear edge to the community, open space for community residents, and natural areas for stormwater management (see § 5.21 Parks/Open Space in Chapter 5, Development Standards, of the LDC).

2.6.3.3 *Centers*

The center shall have a minimum area of 30,000 square feet. For a TND exceeding 250 dwelling units, the TND shall have a minimum area of 120 square feet per dwelling unit.

(A) A center shall only be located on a main street (see § 5.23 Street Design and Transportation in Chapter 5, Development Standards, of the LDC).

(B) The center may face or surround the plaza or square.

(C) A continuous system of sidewalks shall connect the center with streets and lanes that provide access to dwelling units (e.g., a proposed TND has 600 dwelling units; the minimum square footage for the center is 600 x 120, or 72,000 square feet).

2.6.4 Uses and Density

2.6.4.1 *Density*

The requested densities, in terms of number of units per gross residential acre and total number of dwelling units, shall be set forth in the subdivision and/or master site plan application. The subdivision plat or master site plan for a TND shall comply with Table 2.5.

2.6.4.2 *Abutting Uses*

Uses may abut at side or rear lot lines, or face across streets or parks. This applies regardless of whether they are in the same or a different land-use category.

2.6.4.3 *Vistas*

Prominent sites shall be reserved for the following building types:

(A) Civic buildings, including government offices, libraries, museums, schools, or churches;

(B) Hotels; or

(C) Office buildings.

Buildings located on a prominent site shall be at least two stories in height, and shall conform to the commercial building standards (§ 5.13 Building Design in Chapter 5, Development Standards, of the LDC). A "prominent site" may include a location along a main street, or the termination of a vista running from a

Table 2-5
Traditional Neighborhood Development Density and Intensity Standards

(A) Land-Use Category	(B) Minimum Land Allocation	(C) Maximum Land Allocation	(D) Minimum Density	(E) Maximum Density—Base	(F) Maximum Density—TDR	(G) Minimum FAR	(H) Maximum FAR—Base	(I) Maximum FAR—TDR
Parks and open space	5% or 5 acres, whichever is greater	—	—	—	—	—	—	—
Civic uses	2%	20%	—	—	—	2.0	6.0	10.0
Retail or service uses	5%	20%	—	—	—	1.5	6.0	10.0
Multifamily uses	10%	40%	5	30	50	1.5	6.0	10.0
Single-family uses	15%	75%	4	10	15	—	—	—

TDR = transfer of development rights; FAR = floor area ratio. A dash ("—") means that the standard is not applicable. The applicable land-use categories are set forth in Column (A). The minimum land area that shall be devoted to the land use is shown in Column (B) and the maximum land area that shall be devoted to the land use is shown in Column (C). Minimum land area is stated as the percentage of gross land area. The density for the particular use shall be at least the amount set forth in Column (D) for residential uses, and shall not exceed the amount shown in Column (E). The density may exceed the amount prescribed in Column (E), up to the amount prescribed in Column (F), if development rights are transferred pursuant to § 3.51 Transfer of Development Rights in Chapter 3, Zoning, of the LDC. The FAR for the particular use shall be at least the amount set forth in Column (G) and shall not exceed the amount shown in Column (H). The FAR may exceed the amount prescribed in Column (H), up to the amount prescribed in Column (I), if development rights are transferred pursuant to Chapter 3. The density may exceed the amount prescribed in Column (E), up to the amount prescribed in Column (F), if development rights are transferred pursuant to Chapter 3.

main street, boulevard, or avenue and its intersection with an equal or lower-order street.

2.6.4.4 Location of Uses

The location of uses shall be governed by street frontage as shown in Table 2-6.

2.6.4.5 Accessory Dwelling

Accessory dwellings are permitted on any lot designated for single-family detached dwellings.

Table 2-6
Traditional Neighborhood Development Use Location

(A) Street	(B) Civic Uses	(C) Retail or Service Uses	(D) Multifamily Uses	(E) Single-Family Uses
Parkways	✓	—	—	—
Boulevard	✓	✓	✓	—
Main street	✓	✓	✓	—
Avenue	✓	✓	✓	—
Local	—	—	✓	✓
Lanes	—	—	—	✓

✓ = the use or building type is permitted. A dash ("—") means that the use or building type is not permitted.

2.6.5 Adequate Public Facilities

The [LOCAL GOVERNMENT] finds that the proximity of jobs and retail uses to housing in a TND development can achieve significant trip reductions produced by the internal capture of home-work and home-retail trips. The [LOCAL GOVERNMENT] further finds and determines that there is a compelling public interest to encourage new development to occur in accordance with the criteria set forth in this section. Accordingly, a TND subdivision plat or master site plan are not required to file a traffic impact analysis (TIA) pursuant to the adequate public facilities standards (Chapter 6, Adequate Public Facilities, of the LDC).

2.6.6 Lot Arrangement

(A) All lots shall include frontage abutting a street or plaza. For a proposed TND not exceeding 80 acres in size, at least 90 percent of the dwelling units shall be located within a 5-minute walk (1,320 feet) from the perimeter of a plaza. For a proposed TND that is at least 80 acres in size, at least 50 percent of the dwelling units shall be located within a 5-minute walk (1,320 feet) from the perimeter of a plaza.

(B) Blocks shall not exceed the dimensions as shown in Figure 2-9.

(C) The setback for principal buildings shall be as set forth in Table 2-7. Setbacks for accessory structures or

Table 2-7
Setback for Principal Buildings

(A) Location	(B) Minimum Frontage	(C) Maximum Average Frontage	(E) Minimum Front Setback	(F) Maximum Front Setback	(G) Minimum Side Setback	(H) Maximum Side Setback	(I) Minimum Rear Setback
Parkways	100 feet	—	10 feet	20 feet	5 feet	—	40 feet
Boulevard	40 feet	80 feet	5 feet	20 feet	5 feet	20 feet	20 feet
Main street	—	40 feet	—	5 feet	—	5 feet	5 feet
Avenue	20 feet	40 feet	5 feet	20 feet	5 feet	—	20 feet
Local	20 feet	70 feet	5 feet	30 feet	5 feet	—	20 feet
Lanes	20 feet	70 feet	5 feet	30 feet	5 feet	—	20 feet

A dash ("—") means "not applicable."

accessory dwellings shall comply with § 7.2 Accessory Uses and Structures in Chapter 7, Supplemental Use Regulations, of the LDC. The frontage and setback requirements shall not apply to parks and open space. In order to allow for variations for unique uses, such as anchor retail tenants or auditoriums, the maximum frontage requirements in Column (C) shall be computed as an average.

2.6.7 Building Design

2.6.7.1 Generally

Building design shall conform to § 5.13 Building Design in Chapter 5, Development Standards, of the LDC and this section. The principal entrance of all buildings shall open to a street (excluding outbuildings).

2.6.7.2 Building Orientation

All principal buildings shall be oriented to parks and open space or to a street. Loading areas shall not be oriented to a street. Buildings that abut both a street and parks or open space shall be oriented to both features.

2.6.7.3 Front Porches

Front porches shall be provided on at least 50 percent of all dwelling units within the single-family land-use allocation. Porches shall be constructed of masonry or wood materials. Architectural metal may be used if it is consistent with the exterior or roofing materials of the primary building. The seating area shall have a minimum width of 9 feet and a minimum depth of 5 feet.

2.6.7.4 Retail and Service Buildings

Retail and service buildings shall comply with the commercial building standard (§ 5.36 House-Lot Landscapings in Chapter 5, Development Standards, of the LDC). Retail and service uses may designate the entire building area above the ground floor or the second floor for residential use. The applicant shall submit floor plans identifying the use of each room.

2.6.8 Transportation

See street design and transportation standards (§ 5.23 Street Design and Transportation in Chapter 5, Development Standards, of the LDC). The connectivity ratio (see § 5.23.4 Connectivity in Chapter 5, Development Standards, of the LDC) shall be at least 1.8.

2.6.9 Parks and Open Space

Open space shall comply with the standards of § 5.21 Parks/Open Space in Chapter 5, Development Standards, of the LDC. The amount of land for each park or open space classification set forth in Column (A) of Table

**Figure 2-9
Variable Block Lengths**

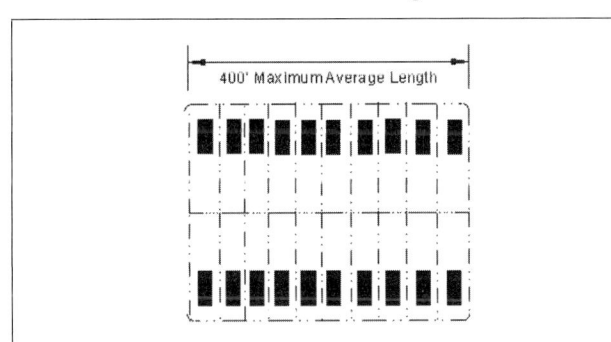

Blocks shall have an average length not exceeding 400 feet, with no block exceeding 1,000 feet in length.

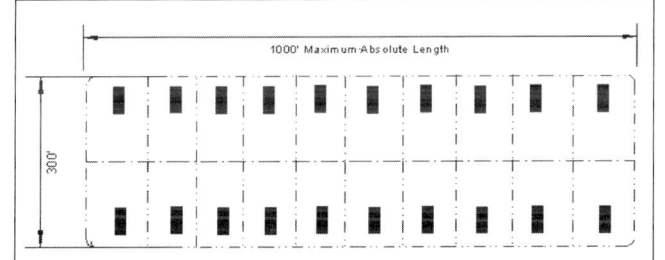

Blocks shall have an average perimeter not exceeding 1,200 feet, with no perimeter block exceeding 1,600 feet.

2-7 shall not be less than that prescribed in Column (B), and not more than that prescribed in Column (C). TND parks and open space shall comply with the parks and open space standards (§ 5.21 Parks/Open Space).

2.6.10 Landscaping and Screening

(A) The following standards do not apply to a TND:
(1) § 5.31 Buffers and Screening in Chapter 5, Development Standards, of the LDC;
(2) § 5.33 Building Landscaping in Chapter 5, Development Standards, of the LDC;
(3) § 5.35 Entrance Landscaping in Chapter 5, Development Standards, of the LDC; and
(4) § 5.37 Tree Preservation and Tree Save Areas in Chapter 5, Development Standards, of the LDC.
(B) The following standards do apply to a TND:
(1) § 5.32 Streetscape Landscaping in Chapter 5, Development Standards, of the LDC;
(2) § 5.34 Parking Lot Landscaping in Chapter 5, Development Standards, of the LDC; and
(3) § 5.36 House-Lot Landscaping in Chapter 5, Development Standards, of the LDC.
(C) In order to provide a continuous pedestrian transition for residential neighborhoods and commercial areas, retail, service, or civic land uses shall not be separated from multifamily or single-family land uses within the TND by berms or buffers unless a trail or sidewalk is established that provides a direct connection between the uses.

2.6.11 Parking

(A) Except as otherwise provided by this section, parking requirements for all uses shall comply with the parking standards (§ 5.51 Parking in Chapter 5, Development Standards, of the LDC).
(B) The minimum parking space requirements of the parking standards shall not apply to a TND.
(C) Parking lots shall be located at the rear of principal buildings or in midblock locations.
(D) Parking lots and parking garages shall not:
(1) Abut street intersections or civic use lots;
(2) Be located adjacent to parks or open space; or
(3) Occupy lots that terminate a street vista.
(E) Parking lots shall be located in the interior of a block or shall take access from an alley.
(F) Loading areas shall adjoin alleys or parking areas to the rear of the principal building. On-street metered and structured parking is encouraged.

2.7 TRANSIT-ORIENTED DEVELOPMENT

Purpose and findings: The transit-oriented development (TOD) zone encourages a mixture of residential, commercial, and employment opportunities within identified light rail station areas or other high-capacity transit areas. The use pattern is intended to encourage a mixture of residential, commercial, and employment opportunities within transit corridors or areas served by transit. This district is intended to promote transit-supportive development, to ensure access to transit, and to limit conflicts between vehicles and pedestrians and transit operations. The zone allows for a more intense and efficient use of land at increased densities for the mutual reinforcement of public investments and private development. Uses and development are regulated to create a more intense built-up environment that is oriented to pedestrians and to provide a density and intensity that is transit supportive.

The development standards of the zone are also designed to encourage a safe and pleasant pedestrian environment near transit stations by encouraging an intensive area of shops and activities; by encouraging amenities, such as benches, kiosks, and outdoor cafés; and by limiting conflicts between vehicles and pedestrians. It is the intent of this section that a TOD district be restricted to areas within 1/2 mile of a transit station, which is equivalent to a 10-minute walking distance.

2.7.1 Applicability

The provisions of this section apply to any use or development located within a TOD (see Figure 2-10).

2.7.2 Processing Procedures

Development consistent with this section may occur as of right in any "MX" (Mixed Use) district.

2.7.3 Size and Location of Site

2.7.3.1 Generally

The TOD shall be divided into two subdistricts known as the TOD core (TOD-C) and the TOD periphery (TOD-P), which shall be considered separate zoning districts subject to the requirements set forth in this sec-

**Figure 2-10
Transit-oriented Development**

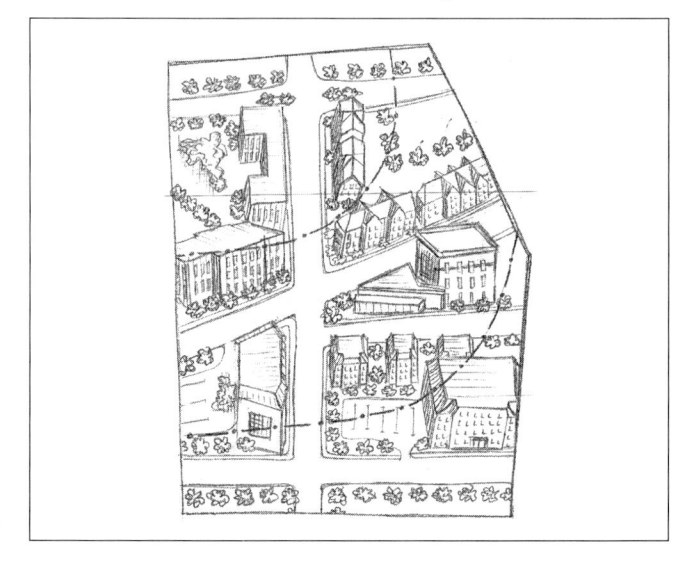

Table 2-8
Transit-oriented Development Dimensional Standards

(A) Location/Size	(B) Minimum Density	(C) Maximum Density	(D) Maximum Density with TDR	(E) Minimum FAR	(F) Maximum FAR	(G) Maximum FAR with TDR
TOD-C						
Less than 2 acres	16	40	80	2.5	6.0	12.0
2 acres or more	12	36	72	2.0	4.0	6.0
TOD-P						
Less than 2 acres	12	36	70	1.5	4.0	6.0
2 acres or more	8	32	60	1.0	2.0	4.0

TDR = transfer of development rights; FAR = floor area ratio. The applicable land-use categories are set forth in Column (A). The minimum land area that shall be devoted to the land use is shown in Column (B), and the maximum land area that shall be devoted to the land use is shown in Column (C). Minimum land area is stated as the percentage of gross land area. The density for the particular use shall be at least the amount set forth in Column (B) for residential uses, and shall not exceed the amount shown in Column (C). The density may exceed the amount prescribed in Column (C), up to the amount prescribed in Column (D), if development rights are transferred pursuant to § 3.51 Transfer of Development Rights in Chapter 3, Zoning, of the LDC. The FAR for the particular use shall be at least the amount set forth in Column (E) and shall not exceed the amount shown in Column (F). The FAR may exceed the amount prescribed in Column (F), up to the amount prescribed in Column (G), if development rights are transferred pursuant to Chapter 3. Density or FAR may exceed the maximum density prescribed in this table if development rights are purchased in accordance with Chapter 3.

tion. The requirements of this section shall apply to both the TOD-C and TOD-P subdistricts, unless otherwise provided. Following any rezoning to an "MX" (Mixed Use) district, the official zoning map shall be amended to denote the subdistricts as defined in § 2.7.3.2 Locational Criteria of this chapter.

2.7.3.2 Locational Criteria

(A) All areas within 1/4 mile of a transit station or major bus boarding location shall be classified as TOD-C.

(B) All areas between 1/4 mile and 1/2 mile from a transit station or major bus boarding location shall be classified as TOD-P. No land area shall be zoned TOD-P unless it adjoins an area zoned TOD-C.

2.7.4 Uses and Density

Because most transit users will walk only 1/4 to 1/2 mile to a transit facility, transit influence areas require high densities on small areas of land. The [LOCAL GOVERNMENT] finds that uses inconsistent with transit will undermine the most efficient use of limited land areas within a TOD, and may render the transit system unworkable. Accordingly, the uses permitted within the TOD zoning districts are those that are dependent upon, or which may generate, a relatively high level of transit usage. Uses that interfere with transit usage and that generate few transit trips are not permitted. Further, the [LOCAL GOVERNMENT] finds and determines that minimum levels of density as set forth in this section are required to support transit ridership, and that lower levels of density will not support transit ridership and will create unacceptable levels of vehicular congestion.

Permitted, conditional, and prohibited uses shall comply with the use matrix (Table 3-4, Use Matrix, in Chapter 3, Zoning, of the LDC). The requested densities, in terms of number of units per gross residential acre and total number of dwelling units, shall be set forth in the application. The application shall comply with Table 2-8.

2.7.5 Lot Arrangement and Dimensions

The front setback shall be established as follows:

(A) *Minimum front setback:* 0 feet from the edge of the sidewalk. A minimum setback of 5 feet from the property line shall be required where streetscape planting is required pursuant to § 5.32 Streetscape Landscaping in Chapter 5, Development Standards, of the LDC.

(B) *Maximum front setback:* 15 feet.

2.7.6 Building Design

2.7.6.1 *Generally*

All buildings and sites shall orient their interior and on-site circulation to the closest adjacent transit station or bus shelter.

2.7.6.2 *Pedestrian Access*

New retail, office, and institutional buildings within the TOD-C district shall provide for convenient pedestrian access to transit through the measures listed in subsections (A), (B), and (C), below:

(A) Pedestrian connections to adjoining properties shall be provided except where such a connection is impracticable due to unique topography.

(B) Pedestrian connections shall connect the on-site circulation system to existing or proposed streets, walkways, and driveways that abut the property. Where adjacent properties are undeveloped, streets, accessways, and walkways on site shall be aligned or stubbed to allow for extension to the adjoining property.

(C) A direct pedestrian connection shall be provided between the transit stop and building entrances on the site.

2.7.6.3 Parking Structures

Parking structures, where allowed, shall have retail or residential uses along the first-floor building area that abuts the sidewalk.

2.7.7 Adequate Public Facilities

A TOD is not subject to the adequate public facilities standards (Chapter 6, Adequate Public Facilities, of the LDC).

2.7.8 Transportation

For a proposed TOD that involves a subdivision, the street design standards shall conform to the traditional street design standards (§ 5.23 Street Design and Transportation in Chapter 5, Development Standards, of the LDC).

2.7.9 Parks and Open Space

The parks and open space standards (§ 5.21 Parks/Open Space in Chapter 5, Development Standards, of the LDC) do not apply to a TOD.

2.7.10 Environmental Protection

Environmental protection standards (*Division 5: Environmental Protection of Critical Areas* in Chapter 5, Development Standards, of the LDC) do not apply to a TOD.

2.7.11 Landscaping and Screening

(A) The following standards do not apply to a TOD:

(1) § 5.31 Buffers and Screening in Chapter 5, Development Standards, of the LDC;

(2) § 5.33 Building Landscaping in Chapter 5, Development Standards, of the LDC;

(3) § 5.35 Entrance Landscaping in Chapter 5, Development Standards, of the LDC; and

(4) § 5.37 Tree Preservation and Tree Save Areas in Chapter 5, Development Standards, of the LDC.

(B) The following standards do apply to a TOD:

(1) § 5.32 Streetscape Landscaping in Chapter 5, Development Standards, of the LDC;

(2) § 5.34 Parking Lot Landscaping in Chapter 5, Development Standards, of the LDC; and

(3) § 5.36 House-Lot Landscaping in Chapter 5, Development Standards, of the LDC.

(C) In order to provide a continuous pedestrian transition for residential neighborhoods and commercial areas, retail, service, or civic land uses shall not be separated from multifamily or single-family land uses within the TOD by berms or buffers unless a trail or sidewalk is established that provides a direct connection between the uses.

2.7.12 Parking

(A) The minimum parking requirements within the TOD-C and TOD-P districts are described in Table 2-9.

(B) The maximum number of parking spaces shall not exceed the amount set forth in the parking standards (§ 5.51 Parking in Chapter 5, Development Standards, of the LDC).

(C) Existing development is allowed to redevelop up to 75 percent of existing parking areas for transit-oriented uses, including bus stops and pullouts, bus shelters, park-and-ride stations, TODs, and similar facilities, where appropriate.

(D) All other provisions of the parking standards shall apply to a TOD.

**Table 2-9
Transit-oriented Development
Parking Requirements**

Area	Minimum Parking Requirement
TOD-C, within 500 feet of a light rail alignment	None
TOD-C, balance of area	50% of the parking spaces required by the parking standards (§ 5.51 Parking in Chapter 5, Development Standards, of the LDC)
TOD-P	75% of the parking spaces required by the parking standards

COMMENTARY

Encouraging better development patterns is one of the central challenges of drafting development codes. Ironically, in many jurisdictions the desired development patterns are discouraged or banned by the development codes. For example, while many communities want to encourage "smart growth" with compact, pedestrian-friendly development, the zoning districts require large lots, large front setbacks, large minimum frontages and lot widths, surface parking areas, and generous landscaped buffering.[1] The result is a postwar, suburban-style development pattern scaled to automobiles rather than to pedestrians. While it provides privacy and a sense of security, it might not provide the development pattern reflected in local comprehensive plans or state planning policies.

Most codes do not provide clear direction as to how the development standards affect the shape and form of development. Zoning district classifications often provide little clue about the locational context of each district. While most districts contain a statement about the character of development internal to the district, there is no linkage to the context of the district where, how, and why it may be applied. The concept of use patterns is intended to provide this linkage.

Developers who want to incorporate smart growth into their projects have two avenues for relief under conventional zoning. One avenue is to seek multiple variances from the use and dimensional standards of the ordinance. This is an expensive and unpredictable alternative. More importantly, the legal standards for variances typically do not allow for this type of relief. Most statutes require undue hardship in order to justify a variance and many states do not permit use variances.[2] A leading zoning treatise predicts that true judicial supervision would result in invalidation of at least 90 percent of all variances.[3] The variance is not a tool that is appropriate to the creation of mixed-use communities.

A second avenue of relief are planned developments, which were originally conceived in 1965 to allow the development of mixed-use neighborhoods that do not correspond to the rigorous use, density, bulk, and setback regulations of conventional zoning.[4] In practice, however, most planned developments have developed with master site plans that divide the neighborhoods into single-use "pods" with no functional relationship to each other. The pods are often segregated by buffers, collector or arterial roads, fences, or other obstacles to pedestrian mobility. Furthermore, planned developments do not typically address other barriers to compact development that may be found in the community's street design, stormwater management, and other site improvement standards. The LDC uses a more streamlined and flexible process in the "PD" (Planned Development) district.

Excessive or inappropriate improvement standards can also produce inappropriate development standards. For example, the impact of excessively wide streets is a hotly debated and well-documented topic (see the commentary at the end of Chapter 5, Development Standards, of the LDC). Integrating infrastructure with the use and dimensional standards of zoning closes a gap in many mixed-use zoning regulations and ensures a proper relationship between buildings and streets.

Ideally, a development code makes plan implementation easy. Many development codes make development that is consistent with the plan difficult. Patterns that are consistent with plan policies face inappropriate standards and an unpredictable and lengthy development approval process. In addition, conventional zoning ordinances and development codes fail to illustrate the outcome of the ordinance standards. Standards that lead to compact development or affordable housing in one part of the ordinance are truncated by excessive improvement standards in other parts of the code. Further, these standards are often administered by separate agencies that have little understanding of comprehensive plan policies.

The concept of use patterns resolves these dilemmas by consolidating the development standards for development patterns in one part of the development code. Use patterns are the development archetypes that a jurisdiction wants to encourage (e.g., compact, pedestrian-friendly corridors in the traditional neighborhoods and nicely landscaped and appropriately buffered corridors in suburban neighborhoods). Consistent with the "purpose and findings" statements in Chapter 1, General Provisions, of the LDC, this chapter describes an approach to implementing the overall vision for urban form.

Many urban plans create a framework for urban form, but few zoning regulations have any meaningful relationship to urban form. A use pattern is a design archetype for new development or land use that closes this gap. The design archetypes can be combined with location standards, such as a "tier" system, to illustrate where the use patterns are appropriate. As with conventional planned developments, use patterns can be implemented in several ways:

- A separate chapter of the code can pull together the various standards into design packages for development as described here. Under this concept, the chapter would cross-reference different parts of the code that apply to the use pattern and illustrate how they apply to that particular project category. Because this alternative may be applied within multiple zoning districts, it has the potential disadvantage of creating a new set of rules to administer. This may be modified by eliminating or consolidating districts. However, the task of

Figure 2-11
Small-Scale Commercial Sites in Residential Neighborhoods

Small-scale commercial sites in residential neighborhoods sometimes have difficulty surviving, in part due to zoning nonconformities, inappropriate building sizes, and lack of convenient parking.

Figure 2-12
Small-Scale Commercial Uses in Residential Neighborhoods

Small-scale commercial uses can blend into residential neighborhoods and operate successfully.

remapping all property into a completely new set of districts could create an even larger burden on staff time.

• The use patterns could replace a jurisdiction's zoning districts, combining use and dimensional restrictions with improvement, landscaping, and environmental standards. This has the advantage of creating a single, new set of streamlined district regulations. However, the remapping process could prove time-consuming and controversial.

• The use patterns could be written as separate zoning districts, thereby requiring a rezoning to incorporate the principles set out in the regulations. These districts should include strong "purpose and findings" statements that guide their permissible location and geographic extent. This alternative has the weakest relationship to a jurisdiction's desired urban form because it requires a discretionary land-use decision. Moreover, it leaves staff with two separate zoning district regimes to administer.

• The use patterns could be adopted as supplementary regulations for particular uses and be located in Chapter 3, Zoning, of the LDC or a separate chapter relating to supplemental use regulations. This makes the concept more readily understandable to zoning staff but may de-emphasize design concepts that are an important feature of a plan.

NEIGHBORHOOD CENTERS

Many zoning regulations do not permit retail or commercial uses in residential zoning districts, while permitting civic uses, such as churches and community centers,[5] thus compelling mixed uses and places for shopping, entertainment, or personal services to obtain a rezoning. The neighborhood center use pattern allows nonresidential uses that accommodate mixed-use policies to be established without a full rezoning, thereby streamlining the development approval process and establishing more predictable standards. In addition, it permits local governments to treat commercial uses uniformly, thereby avoiding potential legal pitfalls with the emerging body of case law relating to churches and similar uses (see Figure 2-11 and Figure 2-12).[6]

NEW URBANISM AND TRADITIONAL NEIGHBORHOOD DEVELOPMENT

"New urbanism" (also known as neotraditional development or TND) is a concept that attempts to replicate the development patterns of traditional towns and villages in newly developing areas.[7] A TND generally emphasizes street and pedestrian activity, a mixed-use core or center within walking distance of neighborhoods, interconnected neighborhoods, and the mixing of income and age groups.[8] A comparison of neotradi-

**Table 2-10
Comparison of New Urbanism
and Conventional Subdivisions**

New Urbanism	Conventional Subdivisions
Rectilinear street grid	Curvilinear streets
Narrow streets	Wide streets
Sidewalks at curb	Meandering sidewalks/ off-street paths
On-street parking/ structured parking	Off-street surface parking
Alleys behind buildings	Street access only
Semienclosed spaces	Open spaces
Shallow setbacks	Deep setbacks
Street-level shopping	Enclosed malls/strip centers
Mixed-use neighborhoods	Single-use neighborhoods

tional and conventional planning concepts is described in Table 2-10.[9]

New urbanism embraces TND and village development practices and the use of TOD, which is used by many jurisdictions on the west coast, including Portland, Oregon; Sacramento County, California; and San Diego, California.[10] As with TND, TOD ordinances provide for mixed uses, higher densities, and pedestrian-oriented infrastructure in the vicinity of transit facilities. While many of the concepts in TND and TOD are the same, TND has more of an urban design focus and is less concerned with the types of densities and uses permitted in a district. Where appropriate, components of TOD ordinances that are related to TND are examined and discussed in the LDC.

While TND is not a complete solution to urban sprawl, it has been proposed as an alternative to conventional suburban development patterns. The goal of TND is to channel growth into higher-density, mixed-use development patterns that are conducive to pedestrian activity, public transportation, and a sense of community. TND will accommodate more growth than low-density, suburban development patterns while providing those densities needed to support transit ridership, economic growth in village and town employment and retail centers, and destinations that do not require automobile use.[11]

Some jurisdictions throughout the country use planned development for mixed-use development, urban design, and pedestrian districts containing elements of a TND ordinance. Unfortunately, many of these elements are inadequate. First, there is substantial resistance in the marketplace to using new urbanist principles in many regions of the country. Without substantial incentives, such as approving new urbanist developments as of right, these communities will not be built. Second, most of these ordinance provisions are limited to zoning standards, such as uses, setbacks, height, and other dimensional standards. These standards do not address infrastructure requirements, such as street widths, the location of utilities, and other "sustainability" features that can have a profound impact on the shape and form of development. Accordingly, the "use patterns" approach suggested in the LDC both permits new urbanist approaches as of right and consolidates all of the standards—zoning and infrastructure—that are needed to successfully implement this approach.

In order to facilitate new urbanism, the LDC also includes revisions to TIA requirements, the adoption of an adequate public facilities ordinance (APFO), and the use of low-density agricultural zoning and purchases of development rights in areas that are permanently unsuitable for urbanization. Urban growth boundaries and transfers of development rights can be used to strategically guide growth into areas that are suitable for urbanization at the scale envisioned by an urban or suburban approach to new urbanism. The transportation level of service standards in the APFO should account for the reduced trip generation and vehicle miles travelled (VMT) of a TND.

PERMISSIBLE USES OR BUILDING FORMS

TND ordinances should specify the uses, or range of uses, that are permitted. Effective TND ordinances prescribe a minimum and maximum percentage of the development that must be devoted to certain uses. The purpose is to ensure that the permitted uses promote a sense of community, pedestrian activity, and alternatives to automobile travel. Under a "form-based" zoning approach, districts are divided into permitted structural types rather than uses. The LDC uses a hybrid approach because neighborhoods will continue to have legitimate concerns about uses, particularly noise, loss of property values, and environmental and safety impacts that can be created by the wrong use in an appropriate building type. Ground-floor retail uses are required in the centers and other commercial or retail areas of a TND in order to stimulate pedestrian activity.[12]

Mixing uses provides for the "internal capture" of automobile trips and greater opportunities for pedestrian travel. The mixing of residential, employment, and retail uses has been estimated to reduce vehicle trips by as much as 18 to 25 percent in some instances.[13] TND generally permits residential uses over ground-level commercial or retail uses, and prescribes minimum and maximum land-use allocations for residential, civic, commercial, retail, light industrial, and/or parks and open space.

In urban areas, a wide range of residential and non-residential uses are permitted. In addition, accessory dwelling units are often permitted in order to provide affordable housing. In a rural or suburban TND, the permitted uses are smaller in scale and intensity than those found in an urban or redevelopment TND. However, rural TNDs generally permit a variety of small-scale retail and office uses focused around a town center, with residential uses permitted above street-level retail in order to encourage pedestrian activity. Residential uses are typically located within a reasonable walking distance of the town center, which is generally 1/4 mile.

PROCEDURES

Procedures for approval of a TND range from the use of a planned development or floating zone procedure to optional standards under which development may be permitted as of right. In some instances, TND uses may be permitted as a conditional use. Generally, the local legislative body (city council or county commission) is required to approve a rezoning. Therefore, the legislative body is the approving agency where the planned development or floating zone approach is used. However, uses permitted as of right in a TND district can assign more approval responsibility to the administrative level and thereby expedite the development approval process.

In infill and redeveloping areas, some uses may be designated as of right as a TND option or to continue an existing pattern of development. The floating zone option is more appropriate in newly developing (rural or suburban) areas. In order to encourage the use of TND, the local government can premap areas that may develop under TND standards where certain uses conducive to TND (e.g., a central retail core) have developed.

LOCATION AND LAND AREA (MINIMUM-MAXIMUM) ZONING

New urbanist codes typically require a minimum and a maximum land area for different use classifications. The reason for minimum and maximum land areas is to ensure that the proposed community does not evolve into a monoculture but instead has the range of uses expected in an urban neighborhood. This not only protects the character of the neighborhood but also creates opportunities for the internal capture of traffic, elimination of traffic by substituting pedestrian for vehicular trips, and the provision of affordable housing by including a range of housing types.

Some ordinances distinguish between the land area required for the entire development and the land area required for individual neighborhoods within each development. As is common with planned development ordinances, many TND ordinances require a minimum land area (typically 40 acres) in order to use the TND approach. This ensures that there is sufficient land area to include the variety of uses required by the TND. However, it also limits the availability of TND on sites where the uses can be creatively adapted to smaller sites. The draft code rejects the minimum land area requirement but requires all of the uses to be included. New urbanist design can be applied to smaller sites with a more limited range of uses by using a "pedestrian-oriented development" approach instead of the TND approach. This approach will be written into future versions of the LDC.

The TND ordinance may restrict the TND option exclusively to certain districts as designated in the ordinance. Districts that are mapped exclusively in urban areas may be eligible for TND, while districts located in agricultural or suburban areas may be eligible for a rural or hamlet TND. The LDC does not permit a TND in the "RP" (Resource Protection) or "RE" (Residential Estate) districts.

Many TND ordinances prescribe a minimum and maximum size for neighborhoods within the development. This ensures that the entire neighborhood is accessible by foot. As with minimum sizes for the development, it can also provide a limit on the usability of this concept.

WALKABILITY

Walkable neighborhoods have become more popular in recent years because of the increased health concerns associated with urban sprawl.[14] Americans spend little time on foot. Even in places where pedestrians should be common, such as in shopping centers and office parks, it is not unusual to see people driving from one point in the parking lot to another to avoid the inherent danger of walking in these parking lots.[15] Cities are now attempting to counteract the health-related problems of air pollution from greater VMT, suburban traffic fatalities exceeding inner-city crime per capita, and obesity from lack of exercise.[16] The Urban Land Institute estimates that 5 to 15 percent of new development now follows the principles of "walkable neighborhoods" and "mixed-use centers."[17]

HEALTH CONSIDERATIONS

Recent national studies show a clear adverse relationship between people living in sprawl development and personal health. People living in unincorporated county areas marked by sprawl development walk less and weigh more than people living in compact urban communities.[18] The study shows that people living in sprawling counties are likely to have:

- Higher weight and greater obesity;
- Greater hypertension and high blood pressure; and
- Less opportunity to walk, bike, climb stairs, or get physical activity.[19]

Other public health reports document that people in sprawling communities drive three to four times more than those who live in efficient, well-planned areas, increasing vehicle emissions that contribute to asthma and other respiratory diseases.[20]

A recent Cornell University study found that children whose families relocated to areas with more public greenspace experience an increase in cognitive functioning.[21] It is estimated that for each additional 10 minutes of driving time, there are increases in rates of mental and physical disabilities.[22] In 2001, 4,882 pedestrians were killed by vehicles and 78,000 were injured.[23] Over 55 percent of all pedestrian deaths occur in neighborhoods that are designed with a bias toward automobile travel in which there are no sidewalks or otherwise inadequate pedestrian accommodations.[24] For walkable communities to prosper, a public health approach will be more acceptable than a lecture to citizens on the virtues of smart growth and the vices of sprawl.[25]

DENSITY

Density requirements are designed to maintain neighborhood character while permitting an adequate concentration of population to support neighborhood businesses, public transportation, and pedestrian activity. Some TOD ordinances require a minimum density in order to encourage transit ridership.

CENTER

The center provides the nexus of retail, civic, and employment activity in the TND. It includes a wide range of services within walking distance of residences, thereby capturing automobile trips and promoting pedestrian activity. A neighborhood center is generally provided within a 5-minute walking distance (1/4 mile) for a majority of neighborhood residents.[26]

PERIMETER BUFFER/GREENBELT

A perimeter buffer is normally required around a TND and/or neighborhoods within a TND in order to provide a definable edge between the TND and other neighborhoods. This prevents development from "spilling" into the periphery, thereby eliminating the distinctions between neighborhoods, and creates a greenbelt of open space around the community. Perimeter buffers might be waived or may not be required in infill areas in order to preserve the continuity of existing neighborhoods. Perimeter buffers might be required in newly developing areas in order to define neighborhood edges and to protect agricultural uses.

BUILDING DESIGN

Design standards in a TND are generally designed to de-emphasize the automobile, to enhance pedestrian activity in a street orientation for buildings, and to enhance the character of the community. The most common stereotype of new urbanist communities is the use of front porches. Front porches may be required in order to enhance the traditional feel of the community and to provide a sense of community between neighbors. Front porches are not essential so long as an adequate relationship can be maintained between the building and the street, and should not be required if they are inconsistent with the traditional design vernacular of the region. For residential neighborhoods, however, front porches are the clearest and most established mechanism to provide street-building relationships.

Colonnades, canopies, and other overhead materials can be used to shelter pedestrians, orient buildings to the street, and create an inviting streetscape. Wall materials, roofs, and other architectural elements of buildings are often regulated in order to add to the traditional character of the community. Examples of urban design features that may be regulated or required include:
- Balconies;
- Canopies/colonnades;
- Front porches;
- Roof shapes;
- Street trees;
- Wall materials; and
- Windows on the ground floor.

BUILDING ORIENTATION

Building orientation in a TND is generally toward the street. Ordinances may require that main entrances open onto a front sidewalk, street, or square (except outbuildings). Principal entrances in the center may also front on sidewalks, plazas, or town greens.

STREETS AND BLOCKS

TND ordinances eliminate the traditional street hierarchy of local, collector, and arterial streets.[27] Instead, street widths and posted speeds vary by surrounding land use. Alley access permits automobiles to park in the rear, thus de-emphasizing the automobile and permitting the front areas to be devoted to pedestrian activity. Alleys can either be required or permitted as an optional design standard. While alleys are a common new urbanist stereotype, they are not essential as long as driveways are narrow or other measures are taken to avoid storing vehicles in areas between principal buildings and the street.

Street design for TNDs typically permits a narrower street section. Wider streets generate higher traffic volumes and speeds and lower pedestrian activity, while smaller lane widths can accommodate larger traffic volumes without discouraging pedestrian activity.[28] TNDs generally provide for a maximum of two travel lanes plus on-street parking, or about 20 to 40 feet for two travel lanes and 12 to 14 feet for one-way streets.[29] A standard of 1 foot vertical to 6 feet horizontal,[30] or a width not exceeding three times the defining wall or edges,[31] can provide a sense of enclosure along the streets.

TND street design reduces clearance between the street and fixed objects, such as trees and street furni-

**Table 2-11
Connectivity Alternatives**

Standard	Discussion
Prohibit cul-de-sacs.	This prevents conventional subdivisions with front porches from packaging themselves as new urbanist communities. This may be excessive. The limited use of cul-de-sacs will not destroy the integrity of the new urbanist community, but they should be used only in certain situations.
Restrict cul-de-sacs or dead-end streets by number, acreage, or percent of street nodes.	These approaches curtail cul-de-sacs without the inflexible approach of simply banning them. It keeps cul-de-sacs from overwhelming or setting the character of a neighborhood, while providing design flexibility.
Establish a high connectivity index.	

**Figure 2-13
Pedestrian Pathways**

Pedestrian pathways (Kentlands, Gaithersburg, Maryland).

ture. Curb radii are reduced to 8 to 10 feet or less in order to reduce vehicle turning speeds and to minimize pedestrian walking distances. Curb radii are generally 8 to 10 feet, with radii of 20 to 30 feet found in some jurisdictions.[32]

The interconnected street pattern of TNDs reduce VMT and take better advantage of street capacities.[33] Curvilinear streets are thought to open more connections between destinations and to decrease the distance between destinations.[34] A common stereotype of new urbanism is that it requires a gridiron street. While the gridiron is an effective way to achieve connectivity, it is not the only way. The important concept is to connect streets and to ensure that blocks are small in order to provide walkability and openness. Alternative standards are discussed in Table 2-11.

Requiring short blocks is key to achieving new urbanist design. A small block perimeter conforms to the pedestrian scale, provides alternative paths for vehicle traffic, and accommodates on-street parking. Block perimeters are generally 1,200 feet, which yields a 300-foot intersection spacing with a 200-foot minimum.[35]

Arterials are generally limited to the periphery of a TND or are permitted to bisect the TND. This restriction is designed to permit a linkage and interconnection with other communities while maintaining the grid street pattern, which does not have a street hierarchy. Care must also be taken to ensure that large volumes of vehicular traffic at high travel speeds do not create a barrier to pedestrian activity. While it is important to ensure that high-volume, conventional streets do not destroy the character of the new urbanist community, the requirement should not be so restrictive that it chokes off the economic potential of the center and other commercial areas of the community. Older TND ordinances typically required the center to be located in the geographic center of the community. The LDC resolves this issue by allowing the center to access higher-order streets in a perpendicular fashion or directly onto higher-order streets if they are redesigned to conform to the TND street design standards.

PEDESTRIAN ACCESS

Pedestrian access in the form of accessible entryways and the elimination of barriers are required in order to stimulate foot traffic. Pedestrian access may be required to all lots or to a main entrance on the street. Planting strips may be required between vehicular travel lanes and pedestrian areas. Public access easements may also be required. A continuous system of sidewalks is normally required in order to accommodate and to encourage pedestrian activity, as well as to replicate the feel of a traditional town or village (see Figure 2-13).

LOTTING STANDARDS

The zoning ordinance should permit a reduction in lot sizes for TND options in order to increase densities and to provide for framing and massing of the streetscape. The front setback for TND ordinances are smaller than those required by conventional zoning ordinances in order to bring homes closer to the street, thereby encouraging a sense of community. The setback is either relaxed or mandatory. A mandatory front setback may include a maximum setback or "build-to" line as opposed to a deep minimum setback from the street (see Figure 2-14).

The front setback should be reasonable in its application to particular uses. For example, the application of a build-to line to a gas station was invalidated in *Dallen v. City of Kansas City*.[36] The court's rationale in

**Figure 2-14
Inappropriate Front Yard Parking**

The parking lot facing the street is the dominant feature.

**Figure 2-15
Front-Facing Buildings**

Front-facing buildings with mixed-use retail on the ground floor and residential/offices above.

the *Dallen* case emphasized that there were no built examples of gasoline stations with their pumps to the rear of the property. Accordingly, the court felt that it would be impossible to establish a gasoline station, which was permitted by the underlying zoning district, if pumps are required to be located to the rear of the principal building. However, the *Dallen* case involved a mandatory zoning overlay rather than an optional TND. In addition, there are now built examples of "gas-backwards" gasoline stations in new urbanist communities, such as the Kentlands in Maryland (see Figure 2-16).

Lot coverage in a TND generally varies by use. Coverage requirements should be sufficiently low to permit open space and high enough to provide adequate densities in urban and infill access. Coverage may also increase with a cluster option (see Figure 2-15)

REAR PARKING

Requiring parking at the rear of retail, office, or commercial buildings facilitates pedestrian access from transit and bus facilities to the primary building, provides a visual barrier to the parking lot, and moves active uses closer to the sidewalk and other pedestrian-related facilities. Bicycle parking shall be provided as required by § 5.51.6 Bicycle Parking in Chapter 5, Development Standards, of the LDC.

Blank walls are ordinarily discouraged, and windows and other visual articulations are ordinarily required, to create an interesting streetscape, which encourages pedestrian activity. TND can require ground-level retail or a designated percentage (e.g., 70 percent) of block frontage to be ground-floor retail, or it can rely on fenestration requirements coupled with market demands.

**Figure 2-16
Appropriate Rear Yard Parking**

This Kentlands, Maryland, gasoline station features pumps located to the rear of the building and connected to an adjoining parking area.

INFILL

Regulatory incentives to encourage infill development include development approval streamlining and appropriate development standards in infill areas. Revising setback requirements and regulating by density or average lot size can permit the development of small lots and decaying buildings while protecting neighborhoods. At the very least, revising excessive lot area dimensions that preclude infill development would be a good first step to encourage the reutilization of underutilized sites and buildings.[37]

Communities need to be prepared to utilize a host of incentives, techniques, and new programs other than zoning to encourage infill, including:

- Tax abatement[38];
- Tax increment finance[39];
- Joint public-private partnerships[40];
- Empowerment and enterprise zones[41];
- Federal community development block grants[42];
- Business improvement districts[43];
- Brownfield revitalization[44];
- Land banking and assembly[45]; and
- Urban property insurance.[46]
- Housing code enforcement and receiverships[47]; and
- Residential rehabilitation long-term loans and bonds.[48]

An effective method to encourage infill is a coordinated program to control the urbanization of undeveloped and agricultural areas at the periphery of a jurisdiction.[49] By controlling growth at the periphery of a jurisdiction, or in areas not served by infrastructure, areas in a jurisdiction that are appropriate for development become more attractive for development.[50] Regulatory controls on the outside are sometimes far more effective than all of the incentives used to buy growth back into our existing built-up areas.

GREYFIELD REDEVELOPMENT

Many commercial corridors have numerous commercial sites with large surface parking areas, typically located between the street and the primary structure. Throughout the nation, many obsolete regional malls and strip centers are being redeveloped as town centers as their owners struggle to find new uses for the sites.[51] Redevelopment of these "greyfield" malls can provide a "win-win" situation for a jurisdiction by:

- Converting underutilized parking areas into pedestrian- and transit-friendly streets;
- Providing new uses for landowners holding economically struggling retail sites;
- Allowing landowners to charge economic rents in lieu of free parking; and
- Eliminating the "urban heat island" and stormwater run-off issues created by large surface parking areas.

**Figure 2-17
Greyfield Redevelopment**

"Winter Park Village replaced one of the nation's first air-conditioned malls with a mixed-use community in this suburb of Orlando."

Source: Photo by Mark White. "Makeovers bring new life to old malls," USA Today (April 23, 2003).

Robert Gibbs, a leading expert on new urbanist retail design, suggests three patterns of development that can accommodate big-box retail on urban sites[52]:

(1) An "urban vestibule," with a large anchor providing street frontage and parking to the rear of the site. This permits a single entrance and exit into the center, which many retailers prefer for security reasons;

(2) A "vestibule and liner," which divides the big-box store into separate compartments with street frontage along a portion of a block. The anchor is located internal to the block and can be accessed from the stores; and

(3) The "T model," with an anchor internal to the block and separate retail shops lining the street (see Figure 2-17).

The alternatives shown in Table 2-12 should be considered when writing regulations to encourage greyfield redevelopment. However, local governments need to understand that regulations alone will not typically suffice to encourage corridor redevelopment. Public-private partnerships and public financing incentives may be needed in order to provide an incentive for reconfiguration of conventional commercial sites. This will obviously depend on the particular market situation as well as perceptions in the local development community.

TRANSIT-ORIENTED DEVELOPMENT

The TOD or "transit village" concept has many similarities to TND and new urbanism; however, there are several important differences. First, the TOD concept establishes minimum density and floor area (intensity)

Table 2-12
Greyfield Redevelopment Alternatives

Regulatory Alternative	Advantages	Disadvantages
Allow greyfield development as of right subject to design controls.	Most streamlined approach to encourage development of greyfield parcels.	Additional intensity could be resisted by some neighborhood groups.
Establish greyfield redevelopment overlay or "PD" (Planned Development) district.	Provides discretionary review of greyfield proposals.	Provides discretionary review of greyfield proposals.
Abolish minimum parking requirements in commercial districts.	Frees empty parking spaces for new uses.	Does not ensure that more parking than what is needed will be provided.
Establish maximum parking ratios.	Restricts parking to actual needs. Minimizes adverse effects of oversized parking areas (e.g., traffic congestion, streets hostile to pedestrians, stormwater run-off, and urban heat islands).	Typically resisted by development community. Lenders in some areas require more parking than is required by zoning.

requirements in order to encourage the use of public transportation in lieu of vehicular travel. By contrast, the minimum density and steel requirements of the TND regulations are designed to encourage an appropriate relationship between buildings and streets. While this concept is also important to TND, minimum restrictions are more critical for transit-supportive uses in order to insure that the densities are coordinated with transit facilities (see Figure 2-18).

Second, restrictions on the amount of parking are critical for TOD. With TND, parking should be relegated to the rear of a site in order to avoid disruption of the street and building relationship. With TOD, the supply of parking is also important. An oversupply of parking will discourage the use of transit but defeat the purpose of the regulations.

Finally, use restrictions are more important for TOD than for TND. TND is oriented to neighborhoods while TOD must develop in concert with high, intense, mixed-use development that is dependent on transit movement. Restrictions on uses that do not generate transit ridership are important in order to ensure that transit facilities are used.

NOTES

1. Emily Talen and Gerrit Knaap, *The Implementation of Smart Growth Principles: An Empirical Study of Land Use Regulations in Illinois*. Paper presented at the Annual Conference of the Association of Collegiate Schools of Planning, Atlanta, GA (November 2000).

2. Even where use variances are permitted by state law, applicants are still confronted with the rigorous,

Figure 2-18
Transit-Supportive Development

Transit-supportive development includes high-density office uses adjacent to transit facilities, as in downtowns (left) and traditional transit villages with a variety of uses at modest densities (right).

unnecessary hardship standard. *Simplex Technologies v. Town of Newington*, 145 N.H. 727, 766 A.2d 713 (2001); *Matthew v. Smith*, 707 S.W.2d 411 (Mo. banc 1996).
3. Donald G. Hagman and Julian Conrad Juergensmeyer, *Urban Planning and Land Development Control Law*, 2d ed. (St. Paul, MN: West Publishing Co., 1986), § 6.5, at 173.
4. Note 3 (Hagman/Juergensmeyer), supra, § 7.15.
5. Peter Smirniotopoulos, "University Town Centers Can Fuel Local Economies," *Urban Land* 90, 91 (Washington, DC: Urban Land Institute, October 2003); A.J. Van Arsdale, "Revitalizing Older Commercial Areas," *Urban Land* (Washington, DC: Urban Land Institute, October 2003), at 38.
6. See Douglas R. Porter, "Business-Oriented Neighborhoods: Their Time Has Come," *Planning* 30 (Chicago: American Planning Association, January 2004).
7. S. Mark White and Dawn Jourdan, "Neotraditional Development: A Legal Analysis," 49 *Land Use Law & Zoning Digest* 3 (August 1997).
8. Farhad Atash, "Redesigning Suburbia for Walking and Transit: Emerging Concepts," 120 *Journal of Urban Planning and Development* 48, 49-50 (March 1994).
9. Lloyd W. Bookout, "Neotraditional Town Planning: A New Vision for the Suburbs?" *Urban Land* (January 1992), 20-26; Reid Ewing, *Developing Successful New Communities* (Washington, DC: Urban Land Institute, 1991).
10. S. Mark White, *The Zoning and Real Estate Implications of Transit-Oriented Development*, TCRP J-5, Topic 3-03 (Washington, DC: National Research Council, Transportation Research Board, 1998).
11. See Hank Dittmar and Shelley Poticha, "Reconnecting America's Centers for Transit-Oriented Development," in *Platform: Building the New Transit Town* (Oakland, CA: Reconnecting America, Winter 2003), 31; Robert Steuteville, "Developer Fascination with Urban Centers Grows," *New Urban News* (October/November 2003).
12. A Brookings Institute study reveals that new urbanist neighborhoods actually increase the supply of housing and generate more affordable housing than traditional suburban subdivisions. See Arthur C. Nelson et al., *The Link Between Growth Management and Housing Affordability: The Academic Evidence*. Discussion paper prepared for The Brookings Institution Center on Urban and Metropolitan Policy (Washington, DC: The Brookings Institution, February 2002).
13. Robert Cervero, *America's Suburban Centers: A Study of the Land Use Transportation Link* (Washington, DC: United States Department of Transportation, 1988), at 431; Colorado/Wyoming Technical Committee, "Trip Generation for Mixed Use Developments," *ITE Journal* 57, 2 (1987): 27-32.
14. Martha T. Moore, "City, suburban designs could be bad for your health," *USA Today* (April 22, 2003).
15. Mark Brodeur, "Ten Tips for Designing a Consumer Friendly Downtown," *Planning* 24-27 (April 2003).
16. Howard Frumkin, "Urban Sprawl and Public Health," 117 *Public Health Reports* 201 (May-June 2002).
17. David L. Callies, Robert H. Freilich, and Thomas E. Roberts, *Cases and Materials on Land Use*, 4th ed. (Eagan, MN: West, 2004), 193.
18. The findings presented appear in the article by Reid Ewing, Tom Schmid, Richard Killingsworth, Amy Zlot, and Stephen Raudenbush, "Relationship Between Urban Sprawl and Physical Activity, Obesity, and Morbidity," *American Journal of Health Promotion* (September 2003).
19. See Barbara A. McCann and Reid Ewing, "Measuring the Health Effects of Sprawl: A National Analysis of Physical Activity, Obesity, and Chronic Disease," Smart Growth America (Washington, DC: Surface Transportation Policy Project, September 2003), reporting on American attitudes involving walkable communities. See also www.transact.org/report.asp?id=205.
20. Fact Sheet, National Association of City & County Health Officers (Washington, DC: National Association of Local Boards of Health, May 28, 2004). Between 1980 and 1994, asthma rates rose by 75 percent.
21. Id., at note 42c, 1.
22. Note 16 (Frumkin), supra.
23. National Highway Transportation Safety Administration Traffic Safety Facts (Washington, DC: United States Department of Transportation, 2001).
24. "Mean Streets, Pedestrian Safety and Reform of the Nation's Transportation Law," The Environmental Working Group/The Tides Center (Washington, DC: Surface Transportation Policy Project and The Environmental Working Group, 1997).
25. Note 14 (Moore), supra.
26. E. Lerner-Lam, Stephen P. Celniker, Chester "Rick" Chellman, Gary W. Halbert, and Sherry Ryan, "Neo-Traditional Neighborhood Design and Its Implications for Traffic Engineering," *ITE Journal* (January 1992).
27. Walter Kulash, Joe Anglin, and David Marks, "Traditional Neighborhood Development: Will the Traffic Work?" *Development* (July/August 1990), 21-23.
28. Richard K. Untermann, "Why you can't walk there: strategies for improving the pedestrian environment in the United States," Chapter 11 in *The Greening of Urban Transport: Planning for Walking and Cycling in Western Cities*, Rodney Tolley, ed. (London: Belhaven Press, 1990).
29. Walter Kulash et al., "Traditional Neighborhood Development: Will the Traffic Work?" Paper presented at the American Society of Civil Engineers Conference on Successful Land Development (March 1990); Frank Spielberg, "The Traditional Neighborhood Development: How Will Traffic Engineers Respond?" *ITE Journal* (1989).
30. Andres Duany, Elizabeth Plater Zyberk, and Richard Shearer, "Zoning for Traditional Neighborhoods," *Land Development* (Fall 1992), 20-26.
31. Randall Arendt, *Rural by Design* (Chicago: American Planning Association, 1994), at 10.
32. Note 29 (Kulash), supra; Note 29 (Spielberg), supra.
33. Note 8 (Atash), supra; Lloyd W. Bookout, "Neotraditional Town Planning: Cars, Pedestrians, and Transit," *Urban Land* (February 1992), at 10-15.
34. Note 33 (Bookout), supra.
35. Note 29 (Spielberg), supra.
36. *Dallen v. City of Kansas City*, 822 S.W.2d 429 (Mo. App. 1991).
37. "The Principles of Smart Development," Planning Advisory Service Report No. 479 (Chicago: American Planning Association, 1998), 20.
38. Robert L. Zoeckler, "The Tax Abatement Program for Historic Properties in Georgia," 28 *Ga. St. Bar J.* 129 (1992); Marco Menzes and Lawrence Morgan, "Michigan's Industrial Property Tax Abatement Law: Fortuity or

Futility," 7 *Cooley L. Rev.* 139 (1990); *Annbar Assocs. v. Westside Redevelopment Corp.*, 397 S.W.2d 635 (Mo. 1965); *D.S. Alamo Assocs. v. Commissioner of Finance*, 525 N.Y.S.2d 823 (1988); John Martinez & Michael Libonati, *Local Government Law* (St. Paul, MN: Thomson/West, 2006), Vol. 3, §§ 16:19, 16.56; 1AP Matthews Municipal Ordinances (St. Paul, MN: Thomson/West, 2003 & Supp. 2005), Vol. 1A, § 33:67.

39. Gary P. Winter, "Tax Increment Financing: A Potential Redevelopment Financing Mechanism for New York Municipalities," 18 *Fordham Urb. L.J.* 655 (1991); Robert Denlow, "Tax Increment Finance from the Property Owner's View," ABA Section of State and Local Government newsletter (October 1999).

40. Robert H. Freilich and Brenda L. Nichols, "Public-Private Partnerships in Joint Development: The Legal and Financial Anatomy of Large-Scale Urban Development Projects," 7 *Municipal Finance J.* 5 (1986); Michael S. Bernick and Amy E. Freilich, "Transit Villages and Transit-Based Development: The Rules are Becoming More Flexible—How Government Can Work with the Private Sector to Make It Happen," 30 *Urb. Law.* 1 (1998); Richard Babcock, "City As Entrepreneur: Fiscal Wisdom or Folly," 29 *Santa Clara L. Rev.* 931 (1989); Judith Welch Wegner, "Utopian Visions: Cooperation Without Conflicts in Public-Private Ventures," 31 *Santa Clara L. Rev.* 313 (1991).

41. David Williams II, "The Enterprise Zone Concept at the Federal Level: Are Proposed Tax Incentives the Needed Ingredient?," 9 *Va. Tax Rev.* 711 (1990); Scott A. Tschirgi, "Aiming the Tax Code at the Distressed Areas: An Examination and Evaluation of Current Enterprise Zone Proposals," 43 *Fla. L. Rev.* 991 (1991); Marilyn M. Rubin and Edward J. Trawinski, "New Jersey's Urban Enterprise Zones: A Program That Works," 23 *Urb. Law.* 461 (1991).

42. Peter W. Salsich, Jr., "A Decent Home for Every American: Can the 1949 Goal Be Met?," 71 *N.C. L. Rev.* 1619 (1993); the legislation now requires that 70 percent of community development block grant funds be used for the benefit of persons of low and moderate income. 42 U.S.C.A. § 5301(c). Recent legislation also permits grants for economic development characterized as "microenterprises," consisting of businesses with five or fewer employees. Salsich, 71 *N.C. L. Rev.*, at 1644-45.

43. Mark S. Davies, "Business Improvement Districts," 52 *Wash. U. J. Urb. & Contemp. L.* 187 (1997).

44. Todd S. Davis and Kevin D. Margolis, eds., *Brownfields: A Comprehensive Guide to Redeveloping Contaminated Property* (Chicago: American Bar Association, 1997); Andrea Wortzel, "Greening the Inner Cities: Can Federal Tax Incentives Solve the Brownfields Problem?," 29 *Urb. Law.* 309 (1997); Mark Johnson, "Brownfields are Looking Greener," *Planning*, at 14 (November 2002).

45. See Norman Krumholz and Byron Lloyd, "Land Banking and Neighborhood Revitalization in Cleveland," *Planners' Casebook* (Chicago: American Institute of Certified Planners, Summer 2002).

46. *Clayton v. Village of Oak Park*, 453 NE.2d 937 (Ill. App. 1983) (village has authority to insure homeowners of present value of property to prevent abandonment).

47. Otto Hetzel, "The Search for Effective and Cost-Efficient Housing Strategies: Enforcing Housing Condition Standards Through Code Inspections at Time of Sale or Transfer," 36 *J. Urb. & Contemp. L.* 25 (1989); Sanford Wool, "Initiation of Receiverships in Housing Code Enforcement," 1 *Urb. L. Ann.* 157n (1968).

48. See *City and County of San Francisco v. Municipal Court*, 213 Cal.Rptr. 477 (Cal. App. 1985) (discussing California's long-term loan and bond program, Health and Safety Code § 37910 for residential rehabilitation).

49. Many jurisdictions have coordinated programs to control the urbanization of undeveloped and agricultural areas at the periphery of a jurisdiction. There is an ongoing dispute about the need to protect farmland in the U.S. The 1997 National Resources Inventory of the United States Department of Agriculture (USDA) asserts that nationally nearly 16 million acres of forest, cropland, and open space were converted to urban and other uses from 1992 to 1997. Texas led the nation with 1,219,500 acres developed and a conversion rate of 243,900 acres per year. In a 1999 press release, Vice President Al Gore announced that nearly 16 million acres of forest, cropland, and open space were converted to urban and other uses from 1992 to 1997, based on statistics provided by the 1997 National Resources Inventory of the USDA. "Press Release on VP Releases New Figures on Loss of Farmland to Development" at Clinton Foundation, available on-line at www.clintonfoundation.org/legacy/120699-press-release-on-vp-releases-new-figures-on-loss-of-farmland-to-development.htm. The National Association of Home Builders (NAHB) has responded with an estimate that only 3 million acres of the land converted nationally were used for residential growth, or about 1/10 of 1 percent of the nation's total land mass of 2.4 billion acres. "One-Tenth of One Percent of Total U.S. Land Used By Housing, Study Shows," remarks of Charles Ruma, President of NAHB, *Smart Growth: Building Better Places to Live, Work and Play* (1999), at 8, available on-line at www.smartgrowth.org/pdf/smart.pdf; see also NAHB, "Cancel the Crisis: Farmland is Not Disappearing" (1999), at 8-9.

50. San Diego achieved a reversal of 90 percent growth in outlying areas and only 10 percent growth in the 167-square-mile existing built-up city, to 50 percent and 50 percent, respectively, by utilizing impact fees and adequate public facilities in outlying areas and waiving those requirements in the infill areas. See Robert H. Freilich, *From Sprawl to Smart Growth: Successful Legal, Planning, and Environmental Systems* (Chicago: American Bar Association, 1999), Chapter IV, at 120-121.

51. Richard Bailey, "Mall over: a retail hybrid helps to revitalize an inner suburban ring in Chattanooga, Tennessee," *Urban Land* (July 1998: 46-49, 84-85); Robert Gibbs, "Main Street Retail," in *New Urbanism: Comprehensive Report and Best Practices Guide*, 2d ed. (Ithica, NY: New Urban Publications, Inc., 2001).

52. See Note 51 (Gibbs), supra.

CHAPTER

3

Zoning

3.0 PURPOSE AND FINDINGS

This chapter establishes zoning districts and describes the use and design regulations that apply to each district. Several types of zoning districts are established:

- *Division 2: Base Zoning Districts* establishes districts that divide the local government into various residential, commercial, and industrial zones. Each district establishes uses that are permitted "as of right" and as a conditional use. A use permitted as of right is compatible with the other uses within the purpose of the district and therefore requires only administrative approval. Conditional uses require a public hearing to assess whether conditions are needed in order to make the use compatible with other uses in the district.
- *Division 3: Overlay Zoning Districts* establishes districts within which the standards of both the base and overlay zoning districts apply. These districts address special situations that require additional regulations to protect the public health, safety, and general welfare.
- *Division 4: Flexible Zoning* establishes incentives in the form of additional density and other regulatory measures in order to encourage the provision of affordable housing, the preservation of environmental resources, the dedication of rights-of-way for arterial streets, and the redevelopment of underutilized sites. Landowners are permitted through rezoning to transfer densities from sites that are inappropriate for development to sites that are suitable for increases in density.
- The "supplemental use regulations" in Chapter 7, Supplemental Use Regulations, of the Land Development Code (LDC) establish regulations for some uses that are permitted in a zoning district but raise special concerns that require additional uniform regulations. The regulations set forth apply regardless of whether the use is permitted as of right or as a conditional use within the district.

DIVISION 1: INTRODUCTION

Pursuant to [ENABLING LEGISLATION], the purpose of this section is to promote the public health, safety, morals, or general welfare, and to protect and preserve places and areas of historical, cultural, or architectural importance and significance. These regulations are adopted in accordance with the comprehensive plan and are designed to:

- Lessen congestion in the streets;
- Secure safety from fire, panic, and other dangers;
- Promote health and general welfare;
- Provide adequate light and air;
- Prevent the overcrowding of land;
- Avoid an undue concentration of population; or
- Facilitate the adequate provision of transportation, water, sewers, schools, parks, and other public requirements.

Consistent with the goals and objectives listed in the comprehensive plan, these regulations are designed to foster the following subsidiary purposes:

- Distribute land uses to meet the physical, social, cultural, economic, and energy needs of present and future populations;

- Ensure that new development is compatible with surrounding development in use, character, and size;
- Provide for land uses that serve important public needs, such as affordable housing and employment generators;
- Promote mixed-use buildings and mixed-use neighborhoods;
- Promote infill housing and downtown retail and residential development;
- Integrate civic uses into neighborhoods;
- Protect natural resources; and
- Encourage retail development in urban, neighborhood, and regional centers, including the historic downtown and "main street."

In accordance with the foregoing purposes, this section establishes regulations governing the following:

- The height, number of stories, and size of buildings and other structures;
- The percentage of a lot that may be occupied;
- The size of yards, courts, and other open spaces;
- Population density; and
- The location and use of buildings, other structures, and land for business, industrial, residential, or other purposes.

3.1 GENERAL REQUIREMENTS

No land shall be used or occupied and no structures shall be designed, erected, altered, used, or occupied except in conformity with all of the regulations, compliance with all design standards, and upon performance of all conditions attached to any special or conditional use permit (CUP), variance, appeal, conditional rezoning, planned development rezoning, or master site plan approved pursuant to this chapter.

No person, firm, or corporation and no officer or employee (either as owner or as participating principal, agent, servant, or employee of such owner) shall sell, rent, or lease, or offer or attempt to sell, rent, or lease, any land or structure upon the representation, falsely made and known to be false, that such land or structure may be used or occupied in a manner or for a use prohibited by this chapter.

3.2 ESTABLISHMENT OF DISTRICTS

3.2.1 Tier System

The [LOCAL GOVERNMENT] finds that its rural, suburban, and urban areas have substantially different physical, geographic, and functional characteristics that require alternative regulatory treatment. Rural areas are largely undeveloped and are characterized by woodlands, agricultural lands, horse farms, and scattered residential and commercial uses at very low densities. Suburban areas are automobile oriented, with auto-medium densities, front-loaded garages, and separate commercial areas. Residents of suburban neighborhoods desire a living environment that favors the values of security and privacy. Urban neighborhoods are more compact and pedestrian friendly, reflecting traditional community character and architecture. Residents of urban neighborhoods prefer a strong sense of community and a mixed-use living environment.

A rural tier, a suburban tier, and a traditional tier are established by this section in order to provide a framework for assigning land-use categories, zoning districts, and development standards. The tiers are shown on the official zoning map.

Table 3-1
Tier, Plan, and Zoning District Correspondence

Zoning District	Comprehensive Plan Land-Use Category	Tier
"RP" (Resource Protection)	[THE COMMUNITY SHOULD INSERT ITS CORRESPONDING LAND-USE CATEGORIES FROM THE COMPREHENSIVE PLAN.]	Rural
"RE" (Residential Estate)		Rural or suburban
"NS" (Neighborhood Suburban)		Suburban
"NU" (Neighborhood Urban)		Traditional
"O" (Office)		Traditional or suburban
"CN" (Commercial Neighborhood)		Traditional or suburban
"CG" (Commercial General)		Traditional or suburban
"CL" (Commercial Large-Scale)		Suburban
"D" (Downtown)		Traditional
"IL" (Industrial Light)		Suburban
"IH" (Industrial Heavy)		Traditional or suburban
"PD" (Planned Development)		Suburban
"MX" (Mixed Use)		Traditional or suburban

Table 3-2
Overlay Zoning Districts

District Name
"NP" (Neighborhood Preservation)
"AO" (Airport Overlay)

3.2.2 Base Zoning Districts

The [LOCAL GOVERNMENT] is divided into the zoning districts shown in Table 3-1.

3.2.3 Overlay Zoning Districts

The [LOCAL GOVERNMENT] establishes the overlay zoning districts set out in Table 3-2. These impose additional requirements on certain properties within one or more underlying base or conditional zoning districts.

3.2.4 Conditional Zoning Districts

See § 4.22 Conditional Zoning in Chapter 4, Procedures, of the LDC.

3.2.5 Floating Zones

Floating zones are established in Table 3-3 in order to establish a process and standards for the siting of uses that have unique neighborhood, environmental, or design impacts, and have not been previously identified on the official zoning map, and that require individual, legislative approval in order to establish appropriate standards. The sections of Chapter 7, Supplemental Use Regulations, of the LDC referenced in Table 3-3 establish the permitted uses within the applicable floating zone, and constitute the standards for the district.

3.2.6 Zoning Districts (Additional)

Additional zoning districts may be added from time to time upon the recommendation of the planning commission to the [GOVERNING ENTITY] pursuant to § 4.21 Code Amendments in Chapter 4, Procedures, of the LDC.

3.3 OFFICIAL ZONING MAP

The maps delineating the boundaries of the various zoning districts, together with all matters and things shown on such maps, are adopted and approved, and collectively constitute the "official zoning map." The official zoning map is incorporated by reference and made a part of the LDC. These maps are on file in the office of the [PLANNING OFFICIAL] and in the office of the clerk or recorder of the [LOCAL GOVERNMENT]. All amendments to the official zoning map shall be listed in the order adopted in a separate register maintained in and kept current by the [PLANNING OFFICIAL]. The official zoning map carries the zoning district designations established in this chapter.

3.4 ZONING DISTRICT BOUNDARIES

When definite distances in feet are not shown on the zoning map, the following rules apply:

(A) Boundaries indicated as approximately following the right-of-way or centerlines of streets, highways, or alleys shall be construed to follow such right-of-way or centerlines;

(B) Boundaries indicated as approximately following platted lot lines shall be construed as following such lot lines;

(C) Boundaries indicated as approximately following [MUNICIPAL] limits shall be construed as following [MUNICIPAL] limits;

(D) Boundaries indicated as following railroad lines shall be construed to be midway between the main tracks;

(E) Boundaries indicated as approximately following the centerlines of streams, rivers, canals, lakes, or other bodies of water shall be construed to follow such centerlines;

(F) Whenever any street, alley, or other public way not subject to zoning regulations is vacated by official action of the [LOCAL GOVERNMENT], or whenever such area is franchised for building purposes, the zoning district line adjoining each side of such street, alley, or other public way shall be automatically extended to the center of such vacation, and all areas so involved

Table 3-3
Floating Zones

Zoning District	Comprehensive Plan Land-Use Category	Tier	Reference
"EU" (Extractive Use)	[THE COMMUNITY SHOULD INSERT ITS CORRESPONDING LAND-USE CATEGORIES FROM THE COMPREHENSIVE PLAN.]	Rural	§ 7.20 Extractive Use in Chapter 7, Supplemental Use Regulations, of the LDC
"SSF" (Self-storage Facility)		Rural or suburban	§ 7.81 Self-storage Facility in Chapter 7, Supplemental Use Regulations, of the LDC
"AOD" (Auto-oriented District)		Any	§ 7.4 Auto-oriented Development in Chapter 7, Supplemental Use Regulations, of the LDC

shall then be subject to all regulations of the extended districts; and

(G) Where physical or cultural features existing on the ground vary from those shown on the official zoning maps, or in other circumstances where the zoning boundary is unclear, the [PLANNING OFFICIAL] shall interpret the district boundaries with appeal to the board of adjustment.

3.5 NEWLY ANNEXED TERRITORY

From the date of annexation until the property is zoned to a permanent zoning classification, annexed property will be zoned as an interim "RE" (Residential Estate) district except as otherwise provided in this section.

3.5.1 Master Planned Developments

For any master planned development approved as a "PD" (Planned Development) or an "MX" (Mixed Use) district, the [LOCAL GOVERNMENT] may incorporate the terms of the approved master site plan into a zoning ordinance following annexation of a property.

3.5.2 Development Agreements

Property that is subject to a development agreement may be designated in accordance with any zoning district classification set forth in the development agreement, and shall be regulated by the development agreement. The zoning classifications shall be applied upon the revision of the official zoning map (see § 4.22 Conditional Zoning in Chapter 4, Procedures, of the LDC).

3.5.3 Specific Plan

The [LOCAL GOVERNMENT] may prepare a specific plan pursuant to § 4.20 Plans and Plan Amendments in Chapter 4, Procedures, of the LDC. The owner(s) of property may apply for rezoning to a classification consistent with the specific plan in lieu of a temporary zoning classification.

DIVISION 2: BASE ZONING DISTRICTS

This division implements the land-use policies of the comprehensive plan. Each subsection describes the relationship between the various zoning district and the comprehensive plan, and prescribes the design regulations for the district.

3.10 GENERALLY

No development approval shall be issued unless the proposed development conforms to the design regulations prescribed within the applicable zoning district. Rules for interpreting the design regulations are included in the lot layout, height, and density/intensity standards (see *Division 2: Design Standards* in Chapter 5, Development Standards, of the LDC).

3.11 USE REGULATIONS

3.11.1 Generally

No use is permitted unless it is listed as a permitted or conditional use in this section. Those uses permitted as principal uses or buildings within each zoning district are those uses listed in the use matrix (Table 3-4). (Permitted accessory uses are set forth in the accessory use regulations in *Division 3: Overlay Zoning Districts* of this chapter.)

3.11.2 Uses Not Mentioned

A use not specifically mentioned or described by category in the use matrix (Table 3-4) is prohibited. Evaluation of these uses shall be as set forth in § 3.11.4 Interpretation—Materially Similar Uses of this chapter.

3.11.3 Uses Preempted By State Statute

Notwithstanding any provision of this section to the contrary, uses that are required to be permitted in any zoning district by state statute may be permitted in accordance with state law whether or not the use is included in the use matrix (Table 3-4).

3.11.4 Interpretation—Materially Similar Uses

The [PLANNING OFFICIAL] shall determine if a use not mentioned can reasonably be interpreted to fit into a use category where similar uses are described. Interpretations may be ratified by the [GOVERNING ENTITY] upon recommendation by the planning commission at a regularly scheduled meeting. It is the intent of this chapter to group similar or compatible land uses into specific zoning districts, either as permitted uses or as uses authorized by a CUP. Uses not listed as a permitted use or CUP are presumed to be prohibited from the applicable zoning district. In the event that a particular use is not listed in the use matrix (Table 3-4), and such use is not listed as a prohibited use and is not otherwise prohibited by law, the [PLANNING OFFICIAL] shall determine whether a materially similar use exists in this section.

Should the [PLANNING OFFICIAL] determine that a materially similar use does exist, the regulations governing that use shall apply to the particular use not listed, and the [PLANNING OFFICIAL]'s decision shall be recorded in writing. Should the [PLANNING OFFICIAL] determine that a materially similar use does not exist, the matter may be referred to the planning commission for consideration for amendment to the LDC to establish a specific listing for the use in question. Unless an appeal is timely filed pursuant to § 4.52 Appeals to Hearing Officer in Chapter 4, Zoning, of the LDC, the [PLANNING OFFICIAL]'s decision is valid. If, when seeking periodic ratification of interpretations, the [PLANNING OFFICIAL]'s interpretation is reversed,

Table 3-4
Use Matrix

Use/Activity	RP	RE, NS	NU	CN	O	CG	CL	D	IL	IH	Variable	Code
Residential buildings											Structure	1000
Single-family detached dwellings	P	P	P	—	—	—	—	P	—	—	Structure	1110
Single-family attached dwellings	—	—	P	—	—	—	—	P	—	—	Structure	1120
Duplex structures	—	—	P	—	—	—	—	P	—	—	Structure	1121
Zero lot line or row houses	—	—	P	—	—	—	—	P	—	—	Structure	1122
Accessory dwelling units	—	P	P	—	—	—	—	P	—	—	Structure	1130
Accessory apartments	—	P	P	—	—	—	—	P	—	—	Structure	1130
Townhouses	—	—	P	—	—	—	—	P	—	—	Structure	1140
Manufactured housing, residential design	—	—	P	—	—	—	—	—	—	—	Structure	1150
Manufactured housing, other	P	—	—	—	—	—	—	—	—	—	Structure	1150
Multifamily dwellings	—	—	P	—	—	—	—	P	—	—	Structure	1202-99
Retirement housing services	C	—	P	—	—	—	—	P	—	—	Function	1210
Congregate living services	C	—	P	—	—	—	—	P	—	—	Function	1220
Assisted living services	C	—	P	—	—	—	—	P			Function	1230
Life care or continuing care services	C	—	P	—	—	—	—	P	—	—	Function	1240
Skilled nursing services	C	—	P	—	—	—	—	P	—	—	Function	1250
Community home	P	P	P	P	—	—	—	P	—	—	NAICS	623210
Barracks	—	—	—	—	—	—	—	—	—	—	Structure	1310
College fraternities	—	—	P	—	—	—	—	P	—	—	Structure	1320
Dormitories	—	—	P	—	—	—	—	P	—	—	Structure	1320
Single-room occupancy units	—	—	—	—	—	—	—	P	—	—	Structure	1340
Temporary structures, tents, etc., for shelter	C	—	C	—	C	C	—	P	—	—	Structure	1350
Other structurally converted buildings	—	—	—	—	—	—	—	P	—	—	Structure	1360
Hotels, motels, or other accommodation services											Function	1300
Bed-and-breakfast inn	—	—	C	P	P	P	P	P	—	—	Function	1310
Rooming and boarding house	—	—	C	P	—	C	C	P	—	—	Function	1320
Hotel, motel, or tourist court	—	—	—	P	—	P	P	P	P	—	Function	1330
Commercial buildings											Structure	2000
Commercial center	C	P	P	P	—	P	P	P	P	P	Structure	2200
Shop or store building with drive-through facility	—	—	—	—	—	P	P	P	—	—	Structure	2210
Restaurant, with incidental consumption of alcoholic beverages	—	—	—	—	—	—	P	P	P	—	Structure	2220

Table 3-4 (cont.)
Use Matrix

Use/Activity	RP	RE, NS	NU	CN	O	CG	CL	D	IL	IH	Variable	Code
Restaurant, with no consumption of alcoholic beverages permitted	—	—	—	P	—	P	P	P	P	—	Structure	2220
Stand-alone store or shop building	—	—	—	P	—	P	P	P	—	—	Structure	2230
Department store building	—	—	—	P	—	P	P	P	—	—	Structure	2240
Warehouse discount store/superstore	—	—	—	—	—	P	P	P	—	—	Structure	2250
											Function	2124
Market shops, including open markets	—	—	—	P	—	P	P	P	—	—	Structure	2260
Gasoline station	—	—	—	—	—	—	—	—	—	P	Structure	2270
Automobile repair and service structures	—	—	—	—	—	—	—	—	—	P	Structure	2280
Car dealer	—	—	—	—	—	—	—	—	—	—	Function	2111
Bus, truck, mobile home, or large vehicle dealers	—	—	—	—	—	—	—	—	—	P	Function	2112
Bicycle, motorcycle, all-terrain vehicle dealers	—	—	—	—	—	P	P	P	—	—	Function	2113
Boat or marine craft dealer	—	—	—	—	—	—	—	—	—	—	Function	2114
Parts, accessories, or tires	—	—	—	C	—	P	P	P	—	—	Function	2115
Gasoline service	—	—	—	—	—	—	—	—	—	P	Function	2116
Lumberyard and building materials	—	—	—	—	—	P	P	C	P	P	Function	2126
Outdoor resale business	—	—	—	—	—	P	P	P	P	P	Function	2145
Pawnshops	—	—	—	—	—	P	P	—	—	—	NAICS	522298
Beer, wine, and liquor store (off-premises consumption of alcohol)	—	—	—	—	—	—	P	P	—	—	Function	2155
Shopping center	—	—	—	P	—	P	P	P	—	—	Structure	2510-2580
Convenience stores or centers	—	—	—	P	—	P	P	P	—	—	Structure	2591
Car care center	—	—	—	—	—	—	—	—	—	P	Structure	2593
Car washes	—	—	—	—	—	—	—	—	—	P	NAICS	811192
Office or bank building, stand-alone (without drive-through facility)	—	—	—	P	P	P	P	P	—	—	Structure	2100
Office building (with drive-through facility)	—	—	—	—	P	P	P	P	—	—	Structure	2110
Office or store building with residence on top	—	—	—	P	P	P	P	P	—	—	Structure	2300
Office building over storefronts	—	—	—	P	P	P	P	P	—	—	Structure	2400

Table 3-4 (cont.)
Use Matrix

Use/Activity	RP	RE, NS	NU	CN	O	CG	CL	D	IL	IH	Variable	Code
Research-and-development services (scientific, medical, and technology)	—	—	—	C	P	P	P	P	P	P	Function	2416
Car rental and leasing	—	—	—	—	—	—	—	—	—	P	Function	2331
Leasing trucks, trailers, recreational vehicles, etc.	—	—	—	—	—	—	—	—	—	P	Function	2332
Services to buildings and dwellings (pest control, janitorial, landscaping, carpet/upholstery cleaning, parking, and crating)	—	—	—	—	—	P	P	P	P	P	Function	2450
Bars, taverns, and nightclubs	—	—	—	—	—	—	P	P	—	—		
Camps, camping, and related establishments	P	C	—	—	—	P	P	—	—	—	Function	5400
Tattoo parlors	—	—	—	—	—	P	P	P	—	—		
Industrial buildings and structures											Structure	2600
Light industrial structures and facilities (not enumerated in Codes 2611-2615, below)	—	—	—	—	C	—	—	—	P	P	Structure	2610
Loft building	—	—	—	—	P	—	—	P	P	P	Structure	2611
Mill-type factory structures	—	—	—	—	—	—	—	—	C	P	Structure	2612
Manufacturing plants	—	—	—	—	—	—	—	—	—	P	Structure	2613
Industrial parks	—	—	—	—	P	—	—	—	P	P	Structure	2614
Laboratory or specialized industrial facility	—	—	—	—	P	—	—	P	P	P	Structure	2615
Assembly and construction-type plants			—	—	—	—	—	—	—	P	Structure	2621
											Function	3000
Process plants (metals, chemicals, etc.)	—	—	—	—	—	—	—	—	—	P	Structure	2622
											Function	3000
Construction-related businesses	—	—	—	—	—	—	—	—	C	P	Function	7000
Automotive wrecking and graveyards, salvage yards, and junkyards	—	—	—	—	—	—	—	—	—	P		
Demolition business	—	—	—	—	—	—	—	—	—	P		
Recycling business	—	—	—	—	—	—	—	—	—	P		
Warehouse or storage facility											Structure	2700
Mini-warehouse	—	—	—	—	—	P	P	C	P	P	Structure	2710
High-rise mini-warehouse	—	—	—	—	—	—	—	—	C	P	Structure	2720
Warehouse structure	—	—	—	—	—	—	—	—	C	P	Structure	2730
Produce warehouse	—	—	—	—	—	—	—	—	C	P	Structure	2740

Table 3-4 (cont.)
Use Matrix

Use/Activity	RP	RE, NS	NU	CN	O	CG	CL	D	IL	IH	Variable	Code
Refrigerated warehouse or cold storage	—	—	—	—	—	—	—	—	C	P	Structure	2750
Large area distribution or transit warehouse	—	—	—	—	—	—	—	—	C	P	Structure	2760
Wholesale trade—durable goods	—	—	—	—	—	—	—	—	C	P	Function	3510
Wholesale trade—nondurable goods	—	—	—	—	—	—	—	—	C	P	Function	3520
Warehouse and storage services	—	—	—	—	—	—	—	—	C	P	Function	3600
Tank farms	—	—	—	—	—	—	—	—	C	P	Structure	2780
Public assembly structures											Structure	3000
Performance theater	—	—	—	P	—	P	P	P	—	—	Structure	3110
Movie theater	—	—	—	P	—	P	P	P	—	—	Structure	3120
Amphitheater	—	—	—	P	—	P	P	P	—	—	Structure	3130
Drive-in theaters	—	—	—	P	—	P	P	P	—	—	Structure	3140
Indoor games facility	—	—	—	P	—	P	P	P	—	—	Structure	3200
Amusement, sports, or recreation establishment (not specifically enumerated)	—	—	—	P	—	P	P	P	—	—	Function	5300
Amusement or theme park	—	—	—	—	—	P	P	—	—	—	Function	5310
Arcade	—	—	—	P	—	P	P	P	—	—	Function	5320
Miniature golf establishment	C	—	—	C	—	P	P	C	P	P	Function	5340
Fitness, recreational sports, gym, or athletic club	—	—	—	P	—	P	P	P	P	P	Function	5370
Bowling, billiards, pool, etc.	—	—	—	P	—	P	P	P	—	—	Function	5380
Skating rinks	—	—	—	P	—	P	P	P	—	—	Function	5390
Sports stadium or arena	—	—	—	—	—	P	P	P	P	P	Structure	3300
Racetrack	—	—	—	—	—	P	P	—	—	—	Function	5130
Exhibition, convention, or conference structure	—	—	—	P	—	P	P	P	—	—	Structure	3400
Churches, temples, synagogues, mosques, and other religious facilities	P	P	P	P	P	P	P	P	P	P	Structure	3500
Covered or partially covered atriums and public enclosures	—	—	—	P	P	P	P	P	P	P	Structure	3700
Passenger terminal, mixed mode	—	—	—	P	P	P	P	P	P	P	Structure	3810
Active open space/athletic fields/golf courses	P	P	P	P	P	P	P	P	P	P	Function	6340
											Site Development	6100 & 6200

Table 3-4 (cont.)
Use Matrix

Use/Activity	RP	RE, NS	NU	CN	O	CG	CL	D	IL	IH	Variable	Code
Passive open space	P	P	P	P	P	P	P	P	P	P	Function	6340
											Site Development	6100 & 6200
Institutional or community facilities											Structure	4000
Hospital building	—	—	—	—	—	P	P	P	P	P	Structure	4110
Medical clinic building	—	—	—	P	—	P	P	P	P	P	Structure	4120
Social assistance, welfare, and charitable services (not otherwise enumerated)	—	—	—	P	—	P	P	P	—	—	Function	6560
Child and youth services	—	—	—	P	—	P	P	P	—	—	Function	6561
Child care institution (basic)	P	P	P	P	P	P	P	P	P	P	Function	6562
Child care institution (specialized)	—	—	—	P	P	P	P	P	P	P	Function	6562
Day care center	C	C	C	P	P	P	P	P	P	P	Function	6562
Community food services	—	—	—	C	—	P	P	P	—	—	Function	6563
Emergency and relief services	—	—	—	C	—	P	P	P	—	—	Function	6564
Other family services	—	—	—	C	—	P	P	P	—	—	Function	6565
Services for elderly and disabled	—	—	—	P	—	P	P	P	—	—	Function	6566
Animal hospitals	P	C	C	P	—	P	P	P	P	—	Function	6730
School or university buildings (privately owned)	—	—	—	C	P	P	P	P	P	—	Structure	4200
Grade school (privately owned)				P	P	P	P	P	—	—	Structure	4210
College or university facility (privately owned)	—	—	—	P	P	P	P	P	—	—	Structure	4220
Trade or specialty school facility (privately owned)	—	—	—	P	P	P	P	P	—	—	Structure	4230
Library building	—	—	—	P	—	P	P	P	—	—	Structure	4300
Museum, exhibition, or similar facility	—	—	—	P	—	P	P	P	—	—	Structure	4400
Exhibitions and art galleries		—	—	P	—	P	P	P	—	—	Structure	4410
Planetarium	—	—	—	P	—	P	P	P	—	—	Structure	4420
Aquarium	—	—	—	P	—	P	P	P	—	—	Structure	4430
Outdoor facility, no major structure	—	—	—	—	—	P	P	P	—	—	Structure	4440
Zoological parks	—	—	—	—	—	P	P	P	—	—	Structure	4450
Public safety-related facility	—	—	—	P	P	P	P	P	—	—	Structure	4500
Fire and rescue station	—	—	—	P	P	P	P	P	—	—	Structure	4510
Police station	—	—	—	P	P	P	P	P	—	—	Structure	4520

Table 3-4 (cont.)
Use Matrix

Use/Activity	RP	RE, NS	NU	CN	O	CG	CL	D	IL	IH	Variable	Code
Emergency operation center	—	—	—	P	P	P	P	P	—	—	Structure	4530
Correctional or rehabilitation facility	—	—	—	—	—	—	—	—	—	P	Structure	4600
Cemetery, monument, tombstone, or mausoleum	P	C	C	C	C	C	C	C	C	C	Structure	4700
Funeral homes				C	—	P	P	P	—	—	Structure	4800
Cremation facilities	—	—	—	—	—	—	—	—	—	P	Structure	4800
Public administration	—	—	—	P	P	P	P	P	P	P	Structure	6200
Post offices	—	—	—	P	P	P	P	P	P	P	Structure	6310
Space research and technology	—	—	—	—	P	—	—	P	P	—	Function	6330
Clubs or lodges	—	—	—	—	—	P	P	P	—	—		
Transportation-related facilities											Structure	5000
Automobile parking facilities	—	—	—	—	—	—	—	P	—	—	Structure	5200
Surface parking, open	—	—	—	—	—	C	C	P	C	P	Structure	5210
Surface parking, covered	—	—	—	C	C	C	C	C	C	P	Structure	5220
Multistoried parking structure with ramps	—	—	—	—	C	C	C	C	P	P	Structure	5230
Underground parking structure with ramps	—	—	—	—	C	C	C	C	P	P	Structure	5240
Rooftop parking facility	—	—	—	—	P	P	P	P	P	P	Structure	5250
Bus terminal	P	P	P	P	P	P	P	P	P	P	Structure	3830
Bus stop shelter	P	P	P	P	P	P	P	P	P	P	Structure	5300
Bus or truck maintenance facility	—	—	—	—	—	—	—	—	C	P	Structure	5400
Truck and freight transportation services	—	—	—	—	—	—	—	—	C	P	Function	4140
Road, ground passenger, and transit transportation	P	P	P	P	P	P	P	P	P	P	Function	4150
Local transit systems—includes mixed mode	P	P	P	P	P	P	P	P	P	P	Function	4151
Local transit systems—commuter rail	P	P	P	P	P	P	P	P	P	P	Function	4152
Local transit systems—bus, special needs, and other motor vehicles	P	P	P	P	P	P	P	P	P	P	Function	4153
Interurban, charter bus, and other similar establishments	P	P	P	P	P	P	P	P	P	P	Function	4154
Taxi and limousine service	—	—	—	P	P	P	P	P	P	P	Function	4155
School and employee bus transportation	P	P	P	P	P	P	P	P	P	P	Function	4156
Towing and other road services	—	—	—	—	P	P	P	P	P	P	Function	4157

Table 3-4 (cont.)
Use Matrix

Use/Activity	RP	RE, NS	NU	CN	O	CG	CL	D	IL	IH	Variable	Code
Space transportation	—	—	—	—	—	—	—	—	C	P	Function	4160
Pipeline transportation	—	—	—	—	—	—	—	—	C	P	Function	4170
Postal transportation services	—	—	—	—	P	P	P	P	P	P	Function	4180
Courier and messenger services	—	—	—	P	P	P	P	P	P	P	Function	4190
Air and space transportation facility	—	—	—	—	—	—	—	—	C	P	Structure	5600
Airport terminal	—	—	—	—	—	—	—	—	—	P	Structure	3820
Runway	—	—	—	—	—	—	—	—	—	P	Structure	5610
Airport maintenance and hangar facility	—	—	—	—	—	—	—	—	—	P	Structure	5620
Airport control tower	—	—	—	—	—	—	—	—	—	P	Structure	5630
Heliport facility	—	—	—	—	—	—	—	—	—	P	Structure	5640
Glideport, seaport, stolport, ultralight, or baloonport facility	—	—	—	—	—	—	—	—	—	P	Structure	5650
Railroad facility	—	—	—	—	—	—	—	—	—	P	Structure	5700
Utility and other nonbuilding structures											Structure	6000
Utility structures on right of way	P	P	P	P	P	P	P	P	P	P	Structure	6100
Water supply-related facility	—	—	—	—	—	—	—	—	—	—	Structure	6200
Water supply pump station	P	P	P	P	P	P	P	P	P	P	Structure	6210
Dam	P	P	P	P	P	P	P	P	P	P	Structure	6220
Levee	P	P	P	P	P	P	P	P	P	P	Structure	6230
Culvert	P	P	P	P	P	P	P	P	P	P	Structure	6240
Water tank (elevated, at grade, underground)	P	P	P	P	P	P	P	P	P	P	Structure	6250
Wells	P	P	P	P	P	P	P	P	P	P	Structure	6260
Water treatment and purification facility	C			P	P	P	—	P	P		Structure	6270
Water reservoir	C	—	—	—	P	P	P	—	P	P	Structure	6280
Irrigation facilities	P	P	P	P	P	P	P	P	P	P	Structure	6290
Wastewater storage or pumping station facility; lift stations	P	—	—	—	—	—	—	—	P	P	Structure	6310
Solid waste landfill facility									P	P	Structure	6320
											Function	4345
Incinerator, composting, or similar facility	—	—	—	—	—	—	—	—	—	P	Structure	6330
Hazardous waste collection	—	—	—	—	—	—	—	—	—	P	Function	4341
Hazardous waste treatment and disposal	—	—	—	—	—	—	—	—	—	P	Function	4342
Solid waste collection	—	—	—	—	—	—	—	—	—	P	Function	4343

Table 3-4 (cont.)
Use Matrix

Use/Activity	RP	RE, NS	NU	CN	O	CG	CL	D	IL	IH	Variable	Code
Solid waste combustor or incinerator	—	—	—	—	—	—	—	—	—	P	Function	4344
Waste treatment and disposal	—	—	—	—	—	—	—	—	—	P	Function	4346
Septic tank and related services	—	—	—	—	—	—	—	—	—	P	Function	4347
Hazardous waste storage facility	—	—	—	—	—	—	—	—	—	P	Structure	6340
Sewer treatment plant	—	—	—	—	—	—	—	—	—	P	Structure	6350
Gas or electric power generation facility	P	—	—	—	—	—	—	—	—	P	Structure	6400
Communication towers	C	—	—	—	—	—	—	—	—	P	Structure	6500
Radio, television, or wireless transmitter	P	P	P	P	P	P	P	P	P	P	Structure	6510
Weather stations or transmitters	C	—	—	—	—	—	—	—	—	P	Structure	6520
Environmental monitoring station (air, soil, etc.)	—	—	—	—	—	—	—	—	—	P	Structure	6600
Sign, free-standing (must comply with Article ___ of [LOCAL GOVERNMENT] code)	A	A	A	A	A	A	A	A	A	A	Structure	6700
Billboard (must comply with Article ___ of [LOCAL GOVERNMENT] code)	—	—	—	—	—	—	—	—	—	—	Structure	6700
Highway rest stops and welcome centers	P	P	P	P	P	P	P	P	P	P	Structure	6910
Roadside stand, pushcarts, etc.	P	P	P	P	P	P	P	P	P	P	Structure	6920
Kiosks	P	P	P	P	P	P	P	P	P	P	Structure	6930
Playground equipment	P	P	P	P	P	P	P	P	P	P	Structure	6940
Fountain, sculpture, or other aesthetic structure	P	P	P	P	P	P	P	P	P	P	Structure	6950
Outdoor stage, bandstand, or similar structure	P	—	—	C	P	P	P	P	P	P	Structure	6960
Agriculture, forestry, fishing, and hunting											Structure	8000
Grain silos and other storage structure for grains and agricultural products	P	P	P	P	P	P	P	P	P	P	Structure	8100
Animal production, including slaughter	P	—	—	—	—	—	—	—	—	P	Function	9200
Livestock pens or hog houses	P	—	—	—	—	—	—	—	—	P	Structure	8200

Table 3-4 (cont.)
Use Matrix

Use/Activity	RP	RE, NS	NU	CN	O	CG	CL	D	IL	IH	Variable	Code
Hatcheries and poultry houses	P	—	—	—	—	—	—	—	—	P	Structure	8300
Greenhouses/nurseries	P	—	—	—	—	—	—	—	—	P	Structure	8400
Stables and other equine-related facilities	P	—	—	—	—	—	—	—	—	P	Structure	8500
Kennels and other canine-related facilities	P	—	—	—	—	—	—	—	—	—	Structure	8600
Apiary and other related structures	P	P	P	P	P	P	P	P	P	P	Structure	8700
Crop production	P	P	P	P	P	P	P	P	P	P	Function	9100
Forestry and logging	P	—	—	—	—	—	—	—	—	—	Function	9300
Fishing, hunting, and trapping, including game preserves and retreats	P	P	P	P	P	P	P	P	P	P	Function	9400
Support functions for agriculture and forestry	P	—	—	P	P	P	P	P	P	P	Function	9500
Mining and extraction establishments											Function	8000
Oil and natural gas	—	—	—	—	—	—	—	—	—	P	Function	8100
Metals (iron, copper, etc.)	—	—	—	—	—	—	—	—	—	P	Function	8200
Coal	—	—	—	—	—	—	—	—	—	P	Function	8300
Nonmetallic mining	—	—	—	—	—	—	—	—	—	P	Function	8400
Quarrying and stone cutting	—	—	—	—	—	—	—	—	—	C	Function	8500

RP = Resource Protection; RE = Residential Estate; NS = Neighborhood Suburban; NU = Neighborhood Urban; CN = Commercial Neighborhood; O = Office; CG = Commercial General; CL = Commercial Large-Scale; D = Downtown; IL = Industrial Light; IH = Industrial Heavy; P = permitted uses; C = conditional uses; A = accessory uses; and NAICS = North American Industry Classification System. A dash ("—") indicates prohibited uses.

then decisions made in reliance on the [PLANNING OFFICIAL]'s interpretation are in violation of the LDC.

3.11.4.1 Rules of Construction

The [PLANNING OFFICIAL] may determine that a use is materially similar if:

(A) The use is listed as within the same structure or function classification as the use specifically enumerated in the use matrix (Table 3-4), as determined by the Land-Based Classification Standards (LBCS) of the American Planning Association (APA). The [PLANNING OFFICIAL] shall refer to the following documents in making this determination, which documents are incorporated by reference and are maintained on file in the office of the planning department:

(1) LBCS Structure Dimension with Detail Descriptions (September 13, 1999);

(2) LBCS Function Dimension with Detail Descriptions (September 13, 1999); and

(3) LBCS Tables (September 13, 1999).

The use shall be considered materially similar if it falls within the same LBCS classification.

(B) If the use cannot be located within one of the APA's LBCS classifications pursuant to subsection (A), above, the [PLANNING OFFICIAL] shall refer to the *1997 NAICS Manual*.[1] The use shall be considered materially similar if it falls within the same industry classification of the *1997 NAICS Manual* (Table 3-5).

(C) In order to assist in interpretation of the use matrix (Table 3-4), the LBCS and North American Industry Classification System (NAICS) numbers precede each use in the use matrix. In interpreting the use matrix, the following rules of construction apply:

(1) If a use is listed for a specific classification, while a more general classification within the same industry classification is also listed for another use, the specific classification governs. The specific use is not permitted in all districts where the uses coded to the general classification are permitted simply because they share a similar LBCS or NAICS code number. The numbers increase as the classifications get more specific.

**Table 3-5
Permitted Use Terminology**

The letter …	Has the following meaning …
P	*Permitted uses:* The letter "P" indicates that the listed use is permitted by right within the zoning district. Permitted uses are subject to all other applicable standards of this chapter.
C	*Conditional uses:* The letter "C" indicates that the listed use is permitted within the respective zoning district only after review and approval of a conditional use permit, in accordance with the review procedures of § 4.23 Conditional Use Permits in Chapter 4, Procedures, of the LDC.
A	*Accessory uses:* The letter "A" indicates that the listed use is permitted only where it is accessory to another use that is permitted in the district on the same lot.
—	*Prohibited uses:* A dash indicates that the use is not permitted in the district.

**Table 3-6
Dimensional Standards**

Zoning District	RP	RE	NS	NU	O	CN	CG	CL	D	IL	IH
Lot size (minimum, square feet)	10 acres	43,560	20,000	5,000	—	—	—	—	—	—	—
Density (maximum, dwelling units per gross acre)	0.1	1	2	9	—	—	—	—	—	—	—
Frontage (minimum, feet)	—	100	65	30	50	10-150	40	50	—	50	50
Lot width (minimum, feet)	—	100	65	45	50	—	—	—	—	50	50
Lot width (maximum, feet)	—	—	—	150	—	—	—	—	—	—	—
Height (maximum, feet)	35	35	35	35	48	35	48	48	150	50	50
Stories (maximum)	2½	2½	2½	2½	4	2½	4	4	15	5	5
Front setback (minimum, feet)	30	30	20	10	0	0	5	20	0	20	20
Maximum front setback (maximum, feet)	—	—	—	35	35	15	100	—	10	—	—
Side setback (minimum, feet)	15	15	5	5	20	10	—	—	—	20	20
Rear setback (minimum, feet)	—	30	20	20	30	30	30	30	—	30	30
Lot coverage (percent)	5-15	15	15	10	50	70	80	70	—	70	80
Maximum front building façade (individual)	—	—	—	—	3,000	2,000	—	—	—	—	—
Maximum building size (aggregate)	—	—	—	—	30,000	20,000	—	—	—	—	—

RP = Resource Protection; RE = Residential Estate; NS = Neighborhood Suburban; NU = Neighborhood Urban; O = Office; CN = Commercial Neighborhood; CG = Commercial General; CL = Commercial Large-Scale; D = Downtown; IL = Industrial Light; and IH = Industrial Heavy. A dash ("—") means that the standard does not apply.

**Table 3-7
Dimensional Standards—"RP"
(Resource Protection)**

Zoning District	"RP"
Lot size (minimum, square feet)	435,600
Density (maximum, dwelling units per gross acre)	0.1
Frontage (minimum, feet)	—
Lot width (minimum, feet)	—
Lot width (maximum, feet)	—
Height (maximum, feet)	35
Stories (maximum)	2½
Front setback (minimum, feet)	30
Side setback (minimum, feet)	15
Rear setback (minimum, feet)	—
Lot coverage (maximum, percent) — lot less than 10 acres (nonconforming) — lot 10 acres or greater	15 5

A dash ("—") means "not applicable."

(2) Some uses are listed separately but fall within the same LBCS or NAICS classification. The uses within one such classification are not permitted in all of the zoning districts as the others simply because they fall within the same LBCS or NAICS classification. For example, NAICS 5413 ("Architectural Engineering, and Related Services") is coded under "Office, General." Assume that the use matrix (Table 3-4) sets out a classification for "Laboratories, Testing," which is NAICS 54138 ("Testing Laboratories," a subheading of 54183). The latter five-digit number (i.e., 54183) is more specific than the four-digit code (i.e., 5413). Accordingly, "Testing Laboratories" is not included within the same classification as "General Offices." However, if "Testing Laboratories" had not been separately listed, it would be permitted in all districts where "General Offices" is permitted.

**Figure 3-1
Dimensional Standards—"RP"
(Resource Protection)**

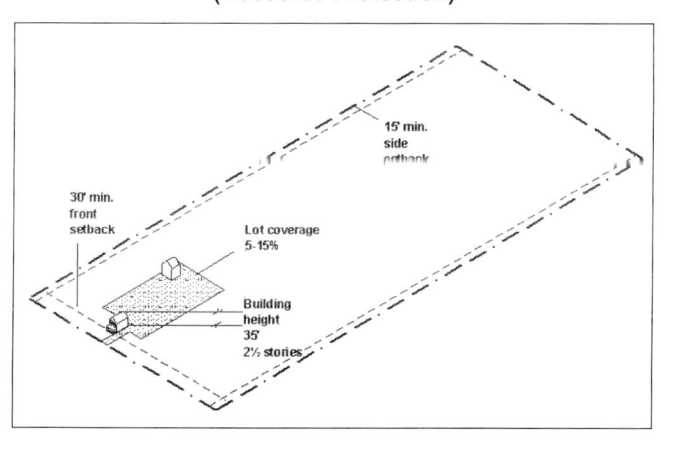

3.12 DIMENSIONAL REGULATIONS

The lot design (frontage, setback, and coverage) and building design (height) requirements are established in each zoning district regulation below. Each district includes an illustration of the design regulations. To the extent that there is any inconsistency between the illustration and written regulations in each district, the written regulations govern. Specific rules of interpretation and exceptions to the zoning district design regulations are as set forth in the design standards (*Division 2: Design Standards* in Chapter 5, Development Standards, of the LDC). A summary of the dimensional regulations is provided in Table 3-6 for the convenience of the reader. To the extent of any inconsistency between the summary provided in Table 3-6 and the zoning district regulations, the zoning district regulations control.

3.13 "RP" (RESOURCE PROTECTION)

Purpose and findings: "RP" (Resource Protection) districts provide areas for agricultural operations and natural resource industries. These districts are composed mainly of unsubdivided lands that are vacant or are in agricultural uses with some dwellings and some accessory uses. "RP" zoning:

• Protects and preserves valuable agricultural areas;
• Implements agricultural and natural resource protection;
• Establishes performance standards for rural businesses;
• Preserves rural areas;
• Preserves pasture land and agriculture; and
• Identifies areas appropriate for agricultural preservation.

The "RP" (Resource Protection) district may be used to establish a buffer of low-intensity uses along streams, floodplains, and similar environmentally sensitive areas. The "RP" district is suitable for areas with large tracts of open space, agricultural areas, woodlands, or fields. The "RP" district is not suitable for areas with central water and sewer, or where collector or higher-order streets are spaced closer than 1 mile apart.

3.13.1 Permitted Uses

See § 3.11 Use Regulations of this chapter.

3.13.2 Dimensional Standards

The dimensional standards within the "RP" (Resource Protection) district are outlined in Table 3-7 (see Figure 3-1).

3.14 "RE" (RESIDENTIAL ESTATE)

Purpose and findings: "RE" (Residential Estate) districts are the designation for a low-density residential use on a lot that is a minimum of 1 acre. "RE" districts implement the following policies by:

• Ensuring that proposed land uses and development are compatible in their use, character, and size to the site and the surrounding areas;

• Based on a comprehensive land-use plan, encouraging more intensive development in and near neighborhood centers with less intensive development between neighborhood centers, and implementing these changes through zoning; and

• Encouraging patterns of urban development that provide a full range of housing choices and promoting a sense of community, urban vitality, and the efficient provision of infrastructure.

3.14.1 Permitted Uses

See § 3.11 Use Regulations of this chapter.

3.14.2 Dimensional Standards

The dimensional standards within the "RE" (Residential Estate) district are outlined in Table 3-8 (see Figure 3-2).

3.15 "NS" (NEIGHBORHOOD SUBURBAN)

Purpose and findings: "NS" (Neighborhood Suburban) districts provide areas for low-density, single-family uses that provide a buffer between the agricultural and "RE" (Residential Estate) classifications and higher density. Minimum lot size requirements are provided in order to allow for market and design flexibility while preserving neighborhood character. "NS" districts encourage more intensive development in and near neighborhood centers with less intensive development between neighborhood centers. They provide a full range of housing choices and promote a sense of community, urban vitality, and the efficient provision of infrastructure.

3.15.1 Permitted Uses

See § 3.11 Use Regulations of this chapter.

3.15.2 Dimensional Standards

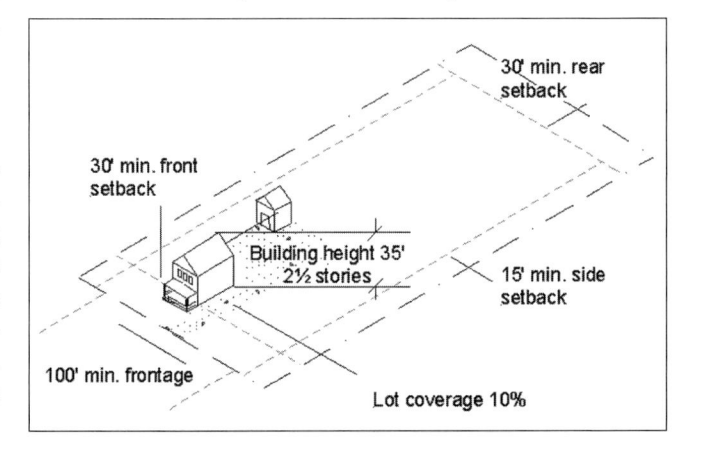

The dimensional standards within the "NS" (Neighborhood Suburban) district are outlined in Table 3-9 (see Figure 3-3).

3.16 "NU" (NEIGHBORHOOD URBAN)

Purpose and findings: "NU" (Neighborhood Urban) districts provide areas for medium to high-density, single-family residential uses mixed with a variety of housing types where adequate public facilities and services exist with capacity to serve development. These districts are composed mainly of areas containing a mixture of single-family, two-family, and multifamily dwellings, and open space where similar residential development seems likely to occur.

**Table 3-8
Dimensional Standards—"RE"
(Residential Estate)**

Zoning District	"RE"
Lot size (minimum, square feet)	43,560
Density (maximum, dwelling units per gross acre)	1
Frontage (minimum, feet)	100
Lot width (minimum, feet)	100
Lot width (maximum, feet)	—
Height (maximum, feet)	35
Stories (maximum)	2½
Front setback (minimum, feet)	30
Maximum front setback (maximum, feet)	—
Side setback (minimum, feet)	15
Rear setback (minimum, feet)	30
Lot coverage (maximum, percent)	10

A dash ("—") means "not applicable."

The district regulations are designed to encourage a suitable neighborhood environment for family life by including among the permitted uses such facilities as schools and churches, and to preserve the openness of the area by requiring certain minimum yard and area standards. Mixed residential districts provide flexible minimum lot size and density requirements in order to allow for market and design flexibility while preserving the neighborhood character and permitting applicants to cluster development in order to preserve environmentally sensitive and agricultural land areas. These districts encourage more intensive development in and near neighborhood centers with less intensive development between neighborhood centers. They provide a full range of housing choices and promote a sense of community, urban vitality, and the efficient provision of infrastructure.

**Figure 3-2
Dimensional Standards—"RE"
(Residential Estate)**

Table 3-9
Dimensional Standards—"NS"
(Neighborhood Suburban)

Zoning District	"NS"
Lot size (minimum, square feet)	20,000
Density (maximum, dwelling units per gross acre)	2
Frontage (minimum, feet)	65
Lot width (minimum, feet)	65
Lot width (maximum, feet)	—
Height (maximum, feet)	35
Stories (maximum)	2½
Front setback (minimum, feet)	20
Maximum front setback (maximum, feet)	—
Side setback (minimum, feet)	5
Rear setback (minimum, feet)	20
Lot coverage (maximum, percent)	15
Maximum building size (individual)	—
Maximum building size (aggregate)	—

A dash ("—") means "not applicable."

Figure 3-3
Dimensional Standards—"NS"
(Neighborhood Suburban)

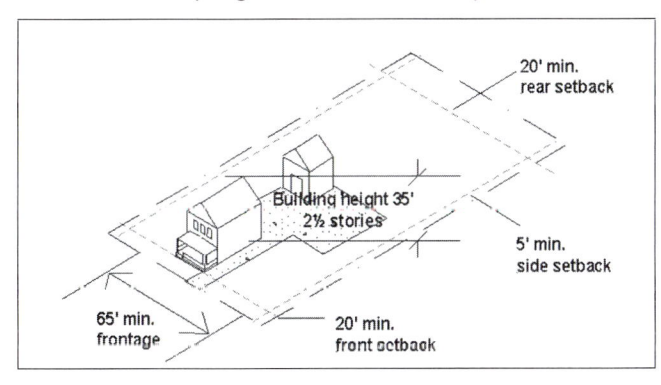

Figure 3-4
Dimensional Standards—"NU"
(Neighborhood Urban)

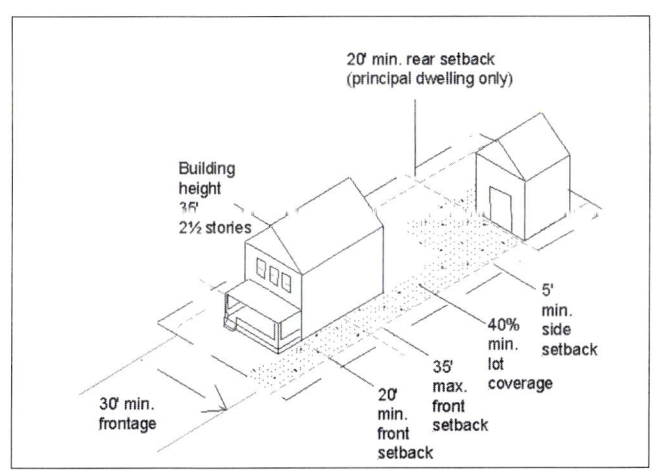

Table 3-10
Dimensional Standards—"NU"
(Neighborhood Urban)

Zoning District	"NU"
Lot size (minimum, square feet)	5,000
Density (maximum, dwelling units per gross acre)	9
Frontage (minimum, feet)	30
Lot width (minimum, feet)	45
Lot width (maximum, feet)	150
Height (maximum, feet)	35
Stories (maximum)	2½
Front setback (minimum, feet)	10
Maximum front setback (maximum, feet)	35
Side setback (minimum, feet)	5
Rear setback (minimum, feet)	20
Lot coverage (maximum, percent)	40
Maximum building size (individual)	—
Maximum building size (aggregate)	—

A dash ("—") means "not applicable."

3.16.1 Permitted Uses

See § 3.11 Use Regulations of this chapter.

3.16.2 Dimensional Standards

The dimensional standards within the "NU" (Neighborhood Urban) district are outlined in Table 3-10 (see Figure 3-4).

3.17 "O" (OFFICE)

Purpose and findings: "O" (Office) districts permit institutional, indoor retail, service, and office uses requiring arterial or collector street access and business and commercial development along urban arterials. The purpose of "O" districts is to accommodate well-designed development sites that provide excellent transportation access, make the most efficient use of existing infrastructure, and provide for orderly transitions and buffers between uses.

"O" (Office) districts facilitate the development and expansion of targeted industries, including manufacturing and assembly, research, high technology, aviation and regional distribution, and business incubator facilities. These districts encourage economic development activities that will:

• Strengthen neighborhoods and communities;
• Provide educational, training, and employment opportunities;
• Provide necessary support services; and
• Promote and encourage economic participation for all citizens.

They restrict uses primarily to offices and ancillary uses that do not have peak weeknight or weekend usage

Table 3-11
Dimensional Standards—"O" (Office)

Zoning District	"O"
Lot size (minimum, square feet)	—
Density (maximum, dwelling units per gross acre)	—
Frontage (minimum, feet)	50
Lot width (minimum, feet)	50
Lot width (maximum, feet)	—
Height (maximum, feet)	48
Stories (maximum)	4
Front setback (minimum, feet)	0
Maximum front setback (maximum, feet)	35
Side setback (minimum, feet)	20
Rear setback (minimum, feet)	30
Lot coverage (maximum, percent)	50
Maximum front building façade (individual)	3,000
Maximum building size (aggregate)	30,000

A dash ("—") means "not applicable."

in order to provide a buffer between residential areas and more intensive uses.

3.17.1 Permitted Uses

See § 3.11 Use Regulations of this chapter.

3.17.2 Dimensional Standards

(A) The dimensional standards within the "O" (Office) district are outlined in Table 3-11 (see Figure 3-5).

(B) The aggregate square footage under "Maximum building size (aggregate)" in Table 3-11 refers only to nonresidential square footage. Square footage devoted to residential uses does not count toward the maximum square footage.

3.17.3 Scale

Buildings within 100 feet of a neighborhood district shall conform to the following building envelope requirements:

- *Primary height:* 24 feet
- *Secondary height:* 36 feet
- *Building coverage:* 4,000 square feet
- *Floor area (individual buildings):* 10,000 gross square feet

3.17.4 Outdoor Display/Sales

The outdoor display or sale of merchandise is prohibited in the "O" (Office) district.

3.17.5 Design

(A) Parking shall be located to the rear of the principal use or principal building, provided that up to two rows of parking may be located to the front, or to the side abutting a residential use, of the principal use or principal building.

(B) Buildings shall contain ground-level fenestration (e.g., transparent windows and openings at street level) consistent with the commercial building design standards (§ 5.13.6 Civic Buildings in Chapter 5, Development Standards, of the LDC).

(C) Buildings shall be articulated so that façades, which face public streets and exceed 50 feet in horizontal length, shall include vertical piers or other vertical visual elements to break the plane of the façade. Such vertical piers or any other vertical visual elements shall be between 15 and 40 feet apart along the façade. This provision does not apply to the conversion of a residential building to a commercial use.

3.18 "CN" (COMMERCIAL NEIGHBORHOOD)

Purpose and findings: "CN" (Commercial Neighborhood) districts provide small areas for offices, professional services, service, and shopfront retail uses—all designed in scale with surrounding residential uses. The district regulations are designed to protect and encourage the transitional character of the districts by permitting a limited group of uses of a commercial nature, and to protect the abutting and surrounding residential areas by requiring certain minimum yard and area standards, which are comparable to those called for in the residential districts. These districts are also intended to reduce auto trips by permitting a limited group of commercial uses to be located in close proximity to residential areas.

These districts provide a balance of residential and nonresidential land-use opportunities, reflecting the economic needs of residents and business owners. "CN" (Commercial Neighborhood) districts implement the following policies by:

Figure 3-5
Zero Lot Line Commercial

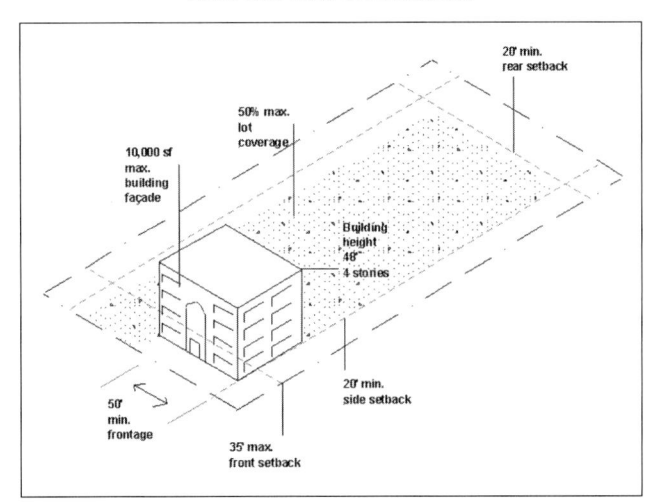

Moving buildings to the front and the side of streets without setback allows greater open space and rear setbacks.

Table 3-12
Dimensional Standards—"CN"
(Commercial Neighborhood)

Zoning District	"CN"
Lot size (minimum, square feet)	—
Density (maximum, dwelling units per gross acre)	—
Frontage (minimum, feet)	10
Lot width (minimum, feet)	—
Lot width (maximum, feet)	—
Height (maximum, feet)	35
Stories (maximum)	2½
Front setback (minimum, feet)	5
Maximum front setback (maximum, feet)	20
Side setback (minimum, feet)	0
Rear setback (minimum, feet)	30
Lot coverage (maximum, percent)	70
Maximum building size (individual)	2,000
Maximum building size (aggregate)	20,000
Minimum frontage built-out (percent)	65

A dash ("—") means "not applicable."

- Based on a comprehensive land-use plan, encouraging more intensive development in and near neighborhood centers with less intensive development between neighborhood centers, and implementing these changes through zoning; and
- Encouraging resident and employment growth within walking distance of the downtown area and neighborhood centers in order to support an intermodal transportation system.

"CN" (Commercial Neighborhood) districts are limited to:

- The intersection of arterial/collector, collector/collector, and collector/local street intersections, except where an existing commercial area has been established prior to the adoption of this chapter; or

Figure 3-6
Dimensional Standards—"CN"
(Commercial Neighborhood)

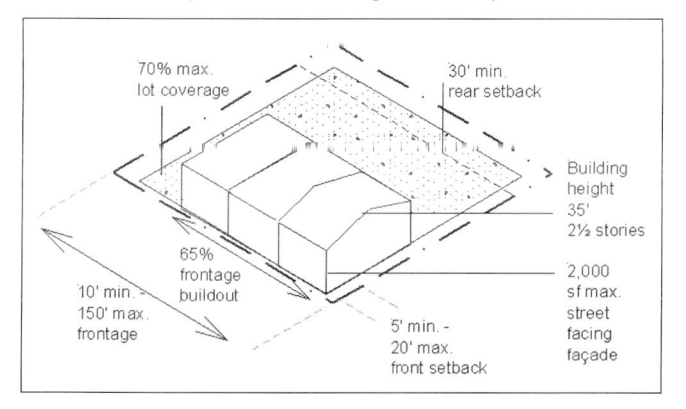

- The interior of a block along an arterial or collector street that lies parallel to an existing commercial area.

3.18.1 Permitted Uses

See § 3.11 Use Regulations of this chapter.

3.18.2 Dimensional Standards

The dimensional standards within the "CN" (Commercial Neighborhood) district are outlined in Table 3-12 (see Figure 3-6).

3.18.3 Scale

In addition to the provisions set forth below, the following restrictions shall apply to the scale of buildings in each "CN" (Commercial Neighborhood) district. Individual buildings shall not exceed the following.

(A) 3,000 square feet of gross floor area for a single-use building; or

(B) 3,000-square-foot building footprint for a mixed-use building or a live-work unit, so long as the building does not exceed two stories.

3.18.4 Design

(A) Parking areas for new buildings or structures shall be located in the rear of the principal use or principal building. This subsection shall not apply to buildings that exist at the time of a rezoning to "CN" (Commercial Neighborhood).

(B) Buildings shall contain ground-level fenestration (e.g., transparent windows and openings at street level) and shall conform to the commercial building design standards (§ 5.13.5 Commercial Buildings in Chapter 5, Development Standards, of the LDC).

(C) Buildings shall be articulated so that façades which face public streets and exceed 50 feet in horizontal length shall include vertical piers or other vertical visual elements to break the plane of the façade. Such vertical piers or any other vertical visual elements shall be between 15 and 40 feet apart along the façade. This provision does not apply to the conversion of a residential building to a commercial use.

3.18.5 Service Entrances/Service Yards

Service entrances and service yards shall be located only in the rear or side yard of the business use. Service yards shall be screened from adjacent residential zones or uses by the installation and maintenance of a solid wall or fence having a height of at least 4 feet or greater than 6 feet, or vegetation having a minimum height of 4 feet. Refuse enclosures shall be located at the rear of the site and screened with a wall and a gate.

3.19 "CG" (COMMERCIAL GENERAL)

"CG" (Commercial General) districts permit general commercial activities, such as repair shops, wholesale

**Table 3-13
Dimensional Standards—"CG"
(Commercial General)**

Zoning District	"CG"
Lot size (minimum, square feet)	—
Density (maximum, dwelling units per gross acre)	—
Frontage (minimum, feet)	40
Lot width (minimum, feet)	—
Lot width (maximum, feet)	—
Height (maximum, feet)	48
Stories (maximum)	4
Front setback (minimum, feet)	5
Maximum front setback (maximum, feet)	100
Side setback (minimum, feet)	0
Rear setback (minimum, feet)	30
Lot coverage (maximum, percent)	80
Minimum frontage built-out (percent)	65

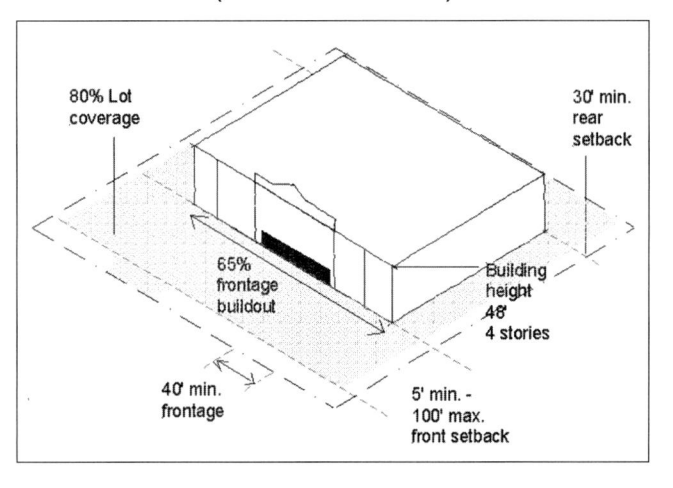

A dash ("—") means "not applicable."

**Table 3-14
Building Scale Restrictions in "CG"
(Commercial General) Districts**

(A) Maximum Building Size (Square Feet) (Individual)	(B) Maximum Building Size (Square Feet) (Aggregate)	(C) Design Standards
15,000 or more	60,000 or more	RP, F
5,000 to 15,000	30,000	F
Less than 5,000	Less than 30,000	N

Aggregate = the total square footage located within a contiguous district; RP = parking shall be located in the rear of the principal use or principal building; F = buildings shall contain ground-level fenestration (e.g., transparent windows and opening at street level), which conforms to the commercial building design standards (§ 5.13.5 Commercial Buildings in Chapter 5, Development Standards, of the LDC); and N = specific standards are not required but may be imposed as a condition of granting a conditional use permit consistent with the criteria established in § 4.23 Conditional Use Permits in Chapter 4, Procedures, of the LDC.

businesses, warehousing, and limited retail sales with some outdoor display of goods. These districts promote a broad range of commercial operations and services necessary for large regions, providing community balance. "CG" districts ensure that proposed land uses and development are compatible in their use, character, and size to the site and the surrounding areas. They support diversification of the economic base and neighborhood services, including schools, libraries, stores, transit centers, and community service facilities in accessible, pedestrian-friendly environments.

3.19.1 Permitted Uses

See § 3.11 Use Regulations of this chapter.

**Figure 3-7
Dimensional Standards—"CG"
(Commercial General)**

[Diagram showing: 80% Lot coverage; 30' min. rear setback; 65% frontage buildout; Building height 48' 4 stories; 40' min. frontage; 5' min. - 100' max. front setback]

3.19.2 Dimensional Standards

The dimensional standards within the "CG" (Commercial General) district are outlined in Table 3-13 (see Figure 3-7).

3.19.3 Scale

Purpose and findings: In addition to the provisions set forth below, the following restrictions shall apply to the scale of buildings in each commercial district. Individual buildings shall not exceed the maximum square footage established in Column (A) of Table 3-14. Buildings on lots adjoining on the same side of a blockface shall not exceed the maximum square footage established in Column (B) of Table 3-14. Buildings shall conform to the design standards established in Column (C) of Table 3-14.

3.19.4 Outdoor Storage or Display

No outdoor storage or display of goods is permitted except for outdoor dining.

3.20 "CL" (COMMERCIAL LARGE-SCALE)

Purpose and findings: "CL" (Commercial Large-Scale) districts permit general commercial activities designed to serve the community, such as repair shops, wholesale businesses, warehousing, and limited retail sales with some outdoor display of goods. These districts promote a broad range of commercial operations and services necessary for large regions, providing community balance. The "CL" districts ensure that proposed land uses and development are compatible in their use, character, and size to the site and the surrounding areas. They

Table 3-15
Dimensional Standards—"CL"
(Commercial Large-Scale)

Zoning District	"CL"
Lot size (minimum, square feet)	—
Density (maximum, dwelling units per gross acre)	—
Frontage (minimum, feet)	50
Lot width (minimum, feet)	—
Lot width (maximum, feet)	—
Height (maximum, feet)	48
Stories (maximum)	4
Front setback (minimum, feet)	20
Maximum front setback (maximum, feet)	—
Side setback (minimum, feet)	—
Rear setback (minimum, feet)	30
Lot coverage (maximum, percent)	70
Maximum building size (individual)	—
Maximum building size (aggregate)	—

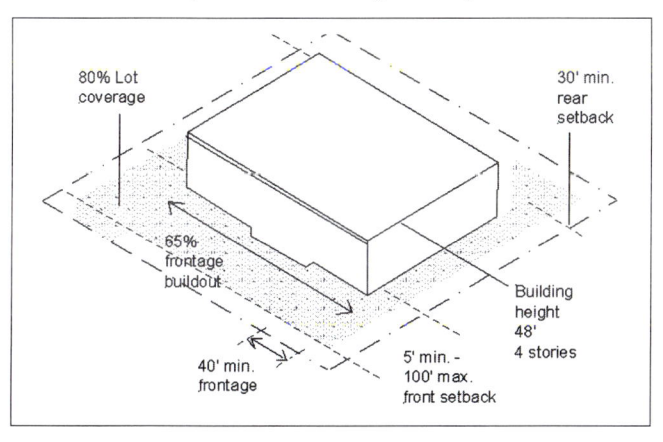

A dash ("—") means "not applicable."

Table 3-16
Building Scale Restrictions in "CL"
(Commercial Large-Scale) Districts

(A) Maximum Building Size (Square Feet) (Individual)	(B) Maximum Building Size (Square Feet) (Aggregate)	(C) Design Standards
100,000 or more	500,000	F
Less than 100,000	Less than 500,000	N

Aggregate = the total square footage located within a contiguous district; F = buildings shall contain ground-level fenestration (e.g., transparent windows and opening at street level), which conforms to the commercial building design standards (§ 5.13.5 Commercial Buildings in Chapter 5, Development Standards, of the LDC; and N = specific standards are not required but may be imposed as a condition of granting a conditional use permit consistent with the criteria established in § 4.23 Conditional Use Permits in Chapter 4, Procedures, of the LDC.

support diversification of the economic base and neighborhood services, including schools, libraries, stores, transit centers, and community service facilities in accessible, pedestrian-friendly environments.

"CL" (Commercial Large-Scale) districts provide for more intensive commercial uses than those located within the "CN" (Commercial Neighborhood) or "CG" (Commercial General) zoning districts. "CL" district uses are typically characterized as community and regional shopping centers, power centers, and/or assembly of similar uses into a single complex under either single ownership or the structure of a property owner or condominium-styled organization. Development in "CL" districts incorporates shared internal circulation and limited curb cuts to arterial streets.

Figure 3-8
Dimensional Standards—"CL"
(Commercial Large-Scale)

3.20.1 Permitted Uses

See § 3.11 Use Regulations of this chapter.

3.20.2 Dimensional Standards

The dimensional standards within the "CL" (Commercial Large-Scale) district are outlined in Table 3-15 (see Figure 3-8).

3.20.3 Scale

In addition to the provisions set forth below, the following restrictions shall apply to the scale of buildings in each commercial district. Individual buildings shall not exceed the maximum square footage established in Column (A) of Table 3-16. Buildings on lots adjoining on the same side of a blockface shall not exceed the maximum square footage established in Column (B) of Table 3-16. Buildings shall conform to the design standards established in Column (C) of Table 3-16.

3.20.4 Outdoor Storage or Display

No outdoor storage or display of goods is permitted except for outdoor dining.

3.21 "D" (DOWNTOWN)

Purpose and findings: "D" (Downtown) districts provide concentrated downtown retail, service, office, and mixed uses in the existing central business districts. Major/regional shopping centers are permitted, but urban design standards are required in order to maintain a neighborhood commercial scale, to promote pedestrian activity, and to maintain the unique charac-

Table 3-17
Dimensional Standards—"D" (Downtown)

Zoning District	"D"
Lot size (minimum, square feet)	—
Density (maximum, dwelling units per gross acre)	—
Frontage (minimum, feet)	—
Lot width (minimum, feet)	—
Lot width (maximum, feet)	—
Height (maximum, feet)	—
Stories (maximum)	—
Front setback (minimum, feet)	0
Maximum front setback (maximum, feet)	20
Side setback (minimum, feet)	—
Rear setback (minimum, feet)	—
Lot coverage (maximum, percent)	—
Maximum building size (individual)	—
Maximum building size (aggregate)	—
Minimum frontage built-out (percent)	80

A dash ("—") means "not applicable."

ter of the center. Pedestrian circulation is required as are common parking areas.

"D" (Downtown) districts:

• Promote the long-term vitality of the central business district;

• Encourage development of the downtown area as a complete neighborhood to enhance its image to both visitors and residents;

• Accommodate a broad range of housing stock, including single-occupancy hotels; low-, moderate-, and upper-income housing; and housing for elderly persons; and

Figure 3-9
Dimensional Standards—"D" (Downtown)

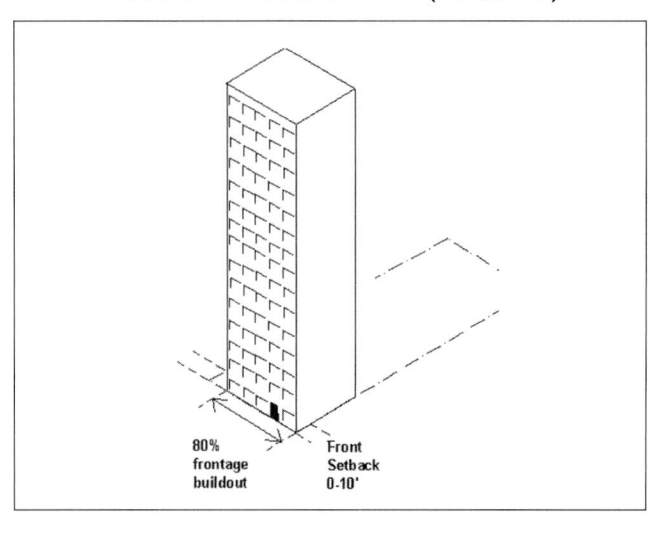

• Give priority to existing buildings, particularly vacant upper floors in existing buildings, for meeting housing needs.

3.21.1 Permitted Uses

See § 3.11 Use Regulations of this chapter.

3.21.2 Dimensional Standards

The dimensional standards within the "D" (Downtown) district are outlined in Table 3-17 (see Figure 3-9).

3.21.3 Design

Ground-level fenestration (e.g., transparent windows and opening at street level) shall conform to the commercial building design standards (§ 5.13.5 Commercial Buildings in Chapter 5, Development Standards, of the LDC).

3.22 "IL" (INDUSTRIAL LIGHT)

Purpose and findings: "IL" (Industrial Light) districts provide for a mix of light manufacturing, office park, flex space, and limited retail and service uses that service the industrial uses with proper screening and buffering—all compatible with adjoining uses.

3.22.1 Permitted Uses

See § 3.11 Use Regulations of this chapter.

3.22.2 Dimensional Standards

The dimensional standards within the "IL" (Industrial Light) district are outlined in Table 3-18 (see Figure 3-10).

3.22.3 General Provisions

Uses in the "IL" (Industrial Light) district shall comply with the following and other applicable sections of this chapter:

(A) Principal vehicle access to and from the site shall be from a primary driveway.

(B) All loading shall be from the rear or side of the building and shall be completely screened from view at the street. These loading standards apply to new structures only, and existing buildings with loading docks facing the street may continue to be used, restored, or enlarged without being subject to the side or rear loading requirement of this section. Loading docks may be located in the rear yard, or a side yard facing a street that is internal to an "IL" (Industrial Light) or "IH" (Industrial Heavy) zoning district.

3.23 "IH" (INDUSTRIAL HEAVY)

Purpose and findings: "IH" (Industrial Heavy) districts accommodate areas of heavy and concentrated fabrication, manufacturing, and industrial uses that are suitable based upon adjacent land uses, access to transportation, and the availability of public services

Table 3-18
Dimensional Standards—"IL" (Industrial Light)

Zoning District	"IL"
Lot size (minimum, square feet)	—
Density (maximum, dwelling units per gross acre)	—
Frontage (minimum, feet)	50
Lot width (minimum, feet)	—
Lot width (maximum, feet)	—
Height (maximum, feet)	50
Stories (maximum)	5
Front setback (minimum, feet)	20
Maximum front setback (maximum, feet)	—
Side setback (minimum, feet)	30
Rear setback (minimum, feet)	30
Lot coverage (maximum, percent)	70
Maximum building size (individual)	—
Maximum building size (aggregate)	—

A dash ("—") means "not applicable."

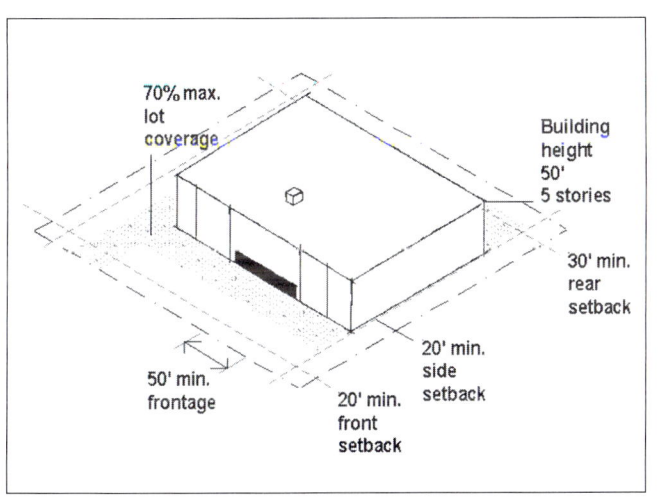

Table 3-19
Dimensional Standards—"IH" (Industrial Heavy)

Zoning District	"IH"
Lot size (minimum, square feet)	—
Density (maximum, dwelling units per gross acre)	—
Frontage (minimum, feet)	100
Lot width (minimum, feet)	100
Lot width (maximum, feet)	—
Height (maximum, feet)	60
Stories (maximum)	5
Front setback (minimum, feet)	30
Maximum front setback (maximum, feet)	—
Side setback (minimum, feet)	50
Rear setback (minimum, feet)	50
Lot coverage (maximum, percent)	80
Maximum building size (individual)	—
Maximum building size (aggregate)	—

A dash ("—") means "not applicable."

and facilities. It is the intent of these districts to provide an environment for industries that is unencumbered by nearby residential or commercial development.

"IH" (Industrial Heavy) districts:

• Must be located in areas where conflicts with other uses can be minimized to promote orderly transitions and buffers between uses;

• Are located for convenient access for existing and future arterial thoroughfares and railway lines; and

• Support efforts to diversify the economic base, promote the safe storage of hazardous materials in locations that do not endanger neighborhoods, and establish appropriate locations and standards for heavy industrial activities, such as the storage of hazardous and toxic materials.

3.23.1 Permitted Uses

See § 3.11 Use Regulations of this chapter.

3.23.2 Dimensional Standards

The dimensional standards within the "IH" district are outlined in Table 3-19 (see Figure 3-11).

3.23.3 General Provisions

(A) All driveways, parking areas, and pedestrian ways shall be surfaced with an all-weather surface. Curb and gutter shall be provided where required by the street design standards (§ 5.23 Street Design and Transportation in Chapter 5, Development Standards, of the LDC).

(B) All delivery and freight handling areas shall be screened from the boundary of any property not zoned "IL" (Industrial Light) or "IH" (Industrial Heavy).

(C) Sites shall not be accessed from residential streets.

3.24 "PD" (PLANNED DEVELOPMENT)

Purpose and findings: "PD" (Planned Development) districts are established to:

• Provide flexibility in the planning and construction of development projects by allowing a combination of uses developed in accordance with an approved plan that protects adjacent properties;

• Provide an environment within the layout of a site that contributes to a sense of community and a coherent living style;

Figure 3-10
Dimensional Standards—"IL" (Industrial Light)

70% max. lot coverage
Building height 50' 5 stories
30' min. rear setback
20' min. side setback
50' min. frontage
20' min. front setback

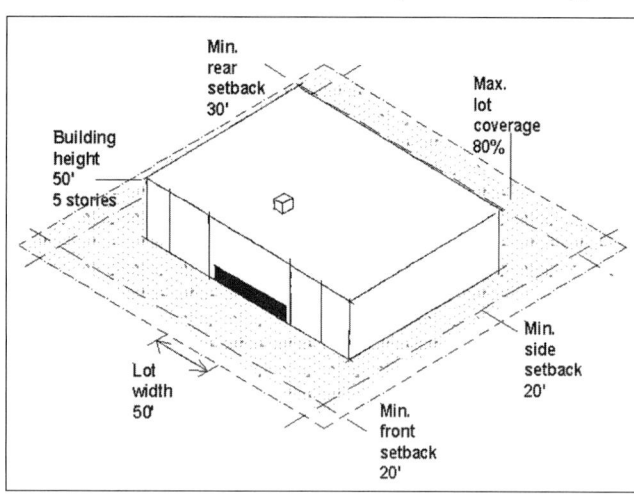

**Figure 3-11
Dimensional Standards—"IH" (Industrial Heavy)**

- Min. rear setback 30'
- Max. lot coverage 80%
- Building height 50' 5 stories
- Lot width 50'
- Min. side setback 20'
- Min. front setback 20'

• Encourage the preservation and enhancement of natural amenities and cultural resources; to protect the natural features of a site that relate to its topography, shape, and size; and to provide for a minimum amount of open space;

• Provide for a more efficient arrangement of land uses, buildings, circulation systems, and infrastructure; and

• Encourage infill projects and the development of sites made difficult for conventionally designed development because of shape, size, abutting development, poor accessibility, or topography.

3.24.1 Evaluation Criteria

(A) In order to foster the attractiveness of a "PD" (Planned Development) district and its surrounding neighborhoods, preserve property values, provide an efficient road and utility network, ensure the movement of traffic, implement comprehensive planning, and better serve the public health, safety, and general welfare, the following criteria apply to master site plans. These criteria shall neither be regarded as inflexible requirements nor are they intended to discourage creativity or innovation.

(B) Insofar as practicable, the landscape shall be preserved in its natural state by minimizing tree and soil removal.

(C) Proposed buildings shall be sited harmoniously to the terrain and to other buildings in the vicinity that have a visual relationship to the proposed buildings.

(D) With respect to vehicular and pedestrian circulation and parking, special attention shall be given to the location and number of access points to public streets, width of interior drives and access points, general interior circulation, separation of pedestrian and vehicular traffic, and the arrangement of parking areas that are safe and convenient and, insofar as practicable, do not detract from the design of proposed structures and neighboring properties.

(E) Private streets and gates may be approved as part of the application but are not required. They shall conform to Chapter 5, Development Standards, of the LDC.

3.24.2 Minimum Size

There is no minimum size for a "PD" (Planned Development) district.

3.24.3 Permitted Uses and Density

3.24.3.1 Uses

A "PD" (Planned Development) district may include residential, commercial, and industrial uses; cluster housing; common areas; unusual arrangements of structures on site; or other combinations of structures and uses that depart from standard development. The uses permitted in a "PD" district are those designated in the approved master site plan. Density limits are used to determine the maximum number of permitted dwelling units.

3.24.3.2 Density Table

The master site plan shall divide the "PD" (Planned Development) district into land-use categories and shall indicate the uses permitted in each category.

3.24.3.3 Attached Dwelling Units

Dwelling units may be attached in all "PD" (Planned Development) districts except for land-use categories designated "RE" (Residential Estate) and "NS" (Neighborhood Suburban) districts.

3.24.3.4 Lots

There is no minimum area requirement for lots, and lots do not need to front onto a street. Lot boundaries may coincide with structure boundaries except where perimeter lot setbacks are required.

3.24.4 Height and Yard Requirements

3.24.4.1 Height Limitation

The maximum height of structures shall be as prescribed for each land-use category or category of uses.

3.24.4.2 Required Setbacks

Setbacks shall be governed by the "PD" (Planned Development) district plan. Lots located on the perimeter of a "PD" district shall adhere to the minimum and maximum setback requirements of the base zoning district unless a lesser setback is approved in the master site plan. There are no setbacks for interior lots, provided that the requirements of the Uniform Building Code are met.

If access to a garage or carport is provided from the front or side of a lot, then the garage/carport shall maintain a 20-foot setback from the back of the sidewalk, or curb if there is no sidewalk, as measured along the centerline of the driveway.

3.24.5 Infrastructure Requirements

3.24.5.1 Streets and Sidewalks

Streets within a "PD" (Planned Development) district may be public or private. However, the planning commission may require dedication and construction of public streets through or into a "PD" district. Public or private streets shall conform to the transportation standards (see § 5.23 Street Design and Transportation in Chapter 5, Development Standards, of the LDC).

3.24.5.2 Utilities

All utility systems shall comply with the utilities standards (see § 5.24 Utilities in Chapter 5, Development Standards, of the LDC). Water and sanitary sewer systems within a "PD" (Planned Development) district may be publicly or privately owned; however, the maintenance of private systems shall be the responsibility of the proposed development's community association. Public utility systems shall be approved by the applicable agency or [LOCAL GOVERNMENT].

3.24.5.3 Easements

Publicly owned and/or maintained utilities shall be placed in public streets or easements that are a minimum of 16 feet in width unless a narrower width is approved by the applicable utility. Dead-end easements shall not be permitted unless a [LOCAL GOVERNMENT]-approved vehicular turnaround is provided at the end of each such easement.

3.24.5.4 Garbage Collection

If, in the opinion of the [PUBLIC WORKS OFFICIAL], private streets in a "PD" (Planned Development) district are arranged so that garbage may be collected without creating a safety hazard, the [LOCAL GOVERNMENT] will collect the garbage, provided that proper indemnification is received from the community association or individual property owners. Garbage collection locations shall be subject to the approval of the [PUBLIC WORKS OFFICIAL]. In the event the [LOCAL GOVERNMENT] does not collect garbage within a "PD" district, all units within the "PD" district may be exempted from payment of garbage fees upon furnishing of evidence, ensuring acceptable removal of all garbage and refuse by private means. To receive such exemption, written application must be submitted to and approved by the [FINANCE OFFICER].

Table 3-20
"PD" (Planned Development) District
Parks and Open Space

Land-Use Category	Required Parks/Open Space
Residential	2,500 square feet per dwelling unit
Nonresidential	200 square feet per 1,000 square feet of floor area, and 250 square feet per 1,000 square feet of parking and loading area

3.24.6 Parks/Open Space

Each master site plan shall provide for a minimum amount of parks/open space as required by § 5.21 Parks/Open Space in Chapter 5, Development Standards, of the LDC.

3.24.6.1 Parks/Open Space Percentages

The minimum open space percentage requirements are as indicated in Table 3-20. They are calculated by dividing the total open space within a "PD" (Planned Development) district by the gross site area. The land-use category shall be determined by the base zoning district. For "PD" districts that include both residential and nonresidential uses, the required open space shall be calculated by multiplying the open space percentage by the area of each use and adding the products thus obtained.

3.24.6.2 Reduction in Parks/Open Space

At its discretion, the planning commission may approve a decrease in the amount of required parks/open space when the master site plan includes unique design features or amenities that achieve an especially attractive and desirable development such as, but not limited to, terraces, sculptures, water features, preservation and enhancement of unusual natural features, or landscape sculpture (i.e., areas that are intensely landscaped).

3.24.7 Parking Requirements

Off-street parking and truck loading facilities shall be provided in accordance with the parking standards (§ 5.51 Parking in Chapter 5, Development Standards, of the LDC). Parking shall be prohibited on any private street less than 28 feet in width; if utilized on streets 28 feet or wider, the parking must be clearly distinguishable from the movement lanes.

3.24.8 Common Areas and Facilities

Adequate provision shall be made for a community association or other legal entity with direct responsibility to, and control by, the property owners involved to provide for the operation and maintenance of all common areas and facilities, including private streets and sidewalks, which are a part of the "PD" (Planned Development) district.

The applicant shall submit a legal instrument establishing a plan for the use and permanent maintenance of the common areas/facilities and demonstrating that the community association is self-perpetuating and adequately funded to accomplish its purposes, and providing the [LOCAL GOVERNMENT] with written permission for access at any time without liability when on official business, and further, to permit the [LOCAL GOVERNMENT] to remove obstructions if necessary for emergency vehicle access and assess the cost of removal to the owner of the obstruction. The instrument must be approved by the [LOCAL GOVERNMENT] as to legal form prior to any plat recordation and shall be recorded at the same time as the plat.

3.24.9 Master Site Plan

After the "PD" (Planned Development) district zoning is granted, a master site plan shall be submitted to and approved by the planning commission prior to approval of any plats or the issuance of any development approvals or certificates of occupancy. The master site plan shall incorporate any conditions imposed with the granting of the "PD" district zoning.

3.25 "MX" (MIXED USE)

Purpose and findings: "MX" (Mixed Use) districts allow the emergence of complete neighborhoods with a complete mix of residential, retail, service, and office activities. These districts de-emphasize land-use regulations, and instead permit any use to be established subject to design standards established in the use patterns (Chapter 2, Use Patterns, of the LDC). Urban design standards are required in order to maintain a neighborhood commercial scale, to promote pedestrian activity, and to maintain the unique character of the center. Pedestrian circulation and common parking areas are required.

3.25.1 Locational Criteria

An "MX" (Mixed Use) district may be designated for areas:

 (A) With an existing mix of retail, office, service, and residential uses located within a radius of 1/4 mile, or

 (B) On a tract or parcel for which a traditional neighborhood development (TND) use pattern is proposed.

3.25.2 Use Regulations

 (A) No development approval shall be issued unless the requested use conforms to:

  (1) A site plan that is approved as part of a rezoning to an "MX" (Mixed Use) district; or

  (2) The regulations that apply to the use pattern that is requested (see § 2.6 Traditional Neighborhood Development and § 2.7 Transit-oriented Development in Chapter 2, Use Patterns, of the LDC).

 (B) A TND (§ 2.6 Traditional Neighborhood Development in Chapter 2, Use Patterns, of the LDC) or transit-oriented development (TOD) (§ 2.7 Transit-oriented Development in Chapter 2, Use Patterns, of the LDC) is permitted in an "MX" (Mixed Use) district as of right.

3.25.3 Lot and Building Specifications

See § 2.6 Traditional Neighborhood Development or § 2.7 Transit-oriented Development in Chapter 2, Use Patterns, of the LDC.

DIVISION 3: OVERLAY ZONING DISTRICTS

The overlay zoning districts address special siting, use, and compatibility issues that require use and development regulations in addition to those found in the underlying zoning districts. If any regulation in an overlay zoning district requires lower densities, greater setbacks, or otherwise imposes greater standards than those required by the base zoning district, the more restrictive standard applies.

The zoning designation of property located within an overlay zoning district shall consist of the regular zone acronym and the overlay zoning district symbol as a suffix. For example, if a parcel is zoned "NS" (Neighborhood Suburban) and is also located within an "NP" (Neighborhood Preservation) overlay zoning district, the zoning designation of the property is "NS(NP)." In effect, the designation of property as being within the "NP" district places such property in a new zoning district classification and all procedures and requirements for zoning and rezoning must be followed.

3.40 "NP" (NEIGHBORHOOD PRESERVATION)

Purpose and findings: The [LOCAL GOVERNMENT] has many unique and distinctive residential neighborhoods or commercial districts that contribute significantly to the overall character and identity of the community. They are worthy of preservation and protection but may lack sufficient historical, architectural, or cultural significance at the present time to be designated as historic districts. As a matter of public policy, the [LOCAL GOVERNMENT] aims to preserve, protect, enhance, and perpetuate the value of these residential neighborhoods or commercial districts through the establishment of "NP" (Neighborhood Preservation) districts.

The purposes of an "NP" (Neighborhood Preservation) district in residential neighborhoods or commercial districts are to:

• Protect and strengthen desirable and unique physical features, design characteristics, and recognized identity and charm;

• Promote and provide for economic revitalization;

• Protect and enhance the livability of the community;

• Reduce conflict and prevent blighting caused by incompatible and insensitive development, and promote new compatible development;

- Stabilize property values;
- Provide residents and property owners with a planning tool for future development;
- Promote and retain affordable housing;
- Encourage and strengthen civic pride; and
- Ensure the harmonious, orderly, and efficient growth and redevelopment of the city.

The "NP" (Neighborhood Preservation) district planning tool implements:

- The creation and adoption of urban design guidelines and standards that will enhance the quality of life and encourage the preservation and enhancement of the community's important historic and cultural characteristics, including architectural styles and historic districts as well as existing residential and commercial districts and neighborhood centers; and
- Neighborhood involvement in developing neighborhood-specific plans that define the character and pattern of development for their neighborhood and that establish infill development guidelines.

3.40.1 Designation Criteria

To be designated as an "NP" (Neighborhood Preservation) district, the area must meet the following criteria:

(A) It must contain a minimum of one blockface (all the lots on one side of a block);

(B) At least 75 percent of the land area in the proposed district was improved at least 25 years ago, and is presently improved; and

(C) It must possess one or more of the following distinctive features that create a cohesive, identifiable setting, character, or association:

(1) Scale, size, type of construction, or distinctive building materials;

(2) Spatial relationships between buildings;

(3) Lot layouts, setbacks, street layouts, alleys, or sidewalks;

(4) Special natural or streetscape characteristics, such as creek beds, parks, greenbelts, gardens, or street landscaping and use patterns, including mixed or unique uses or activities; or

(5) Abutments or links to designated historic landmarks and/or districts.

3.40.2 Zoning Authority

Separate ordinances are required to designate each "NP" (Neighborhood Preservation) district. Ordinances designating each district shall identify the designated boundaries, applicable designation criteria, and design standards for that district and shall be consistent with any existing neighborhood and/or community plans.

3.40.3 Neighborhood Preservation District

"NP" (Neighborhood Preservation) districts are overlay zoning districts. Property designated within these districts must also be designated as being within one or more of the base zoning classifications. Authorized uses must be permitted in both the regular zoning district and the overlay zoning district. In the event of a conflict between the provisions of a specific "NP" district ordinance and the base zoning district regulations, the provisions of the "NP" district ordinance apply.

3.40.4 Designation Procedures

3.40.4.1 Initiation

A zoning change application for designation as an "NP" (Neighborhood Preservation) district shall be initiated at the direction of the:

(A) Request of owners representing 51 percent of the land area within the proposed district;

(B) Request of 51 percent of property owners within the proposed district; or

(C) The [PLANNING OFFICIAL], pursuant to a neighborhood plan adopted by [LOCAL GOVERNMENT] or community revitalization program.

3.40.4.2 Neighborhood Preservation Plan

Following initiation for designation of an "NP" (Neighborhood Preservation) district, the planning department shall develop a neighborhood preservation plan for the proposed district, which includes:

(A) Maps indicating boundaries, age of structures, and existing land use within the proposed district;

(B) Maps and other graphic and written materials identifying and describing the distinctive neighborhood and building characteristics of the proposed district;

(C) A list of all property owners (with legal addresses), neighborhood associations, and/or other organizations representing the interests of property owners in the proposed district; and

(D) Design standards.

3.40.5 Design Standards

(A) The conservation plan approved as part of the zoning ordinance creating an "NP" (Neighborhood Preservation) district shall include design standards for new construction of any building or structure or the relocation or rehabilitation to the street façade of an existing building or structure.

(B) The neighborhood preservation plan and requisite design standards shall not apply to those activities that constitute ordinary repair and maintenance (i.e., using the same or similar material and design).

(C) The design standards for the "NP" (Neighborhood Preservation) district must include at a minimum (or note the inapplicability) the following elements governing the physical characteristics and features of all property (public or private) within the proposed district:

(1) Building height, number of stories;

(2) Building size, massing;

(3) Principal elevation features;

(4) Lot size, coverage;
(5) Front and side yard setbacks;
(6) Off-street parking and loading requirements;
(7) Roof line and pitch; and
(8) Paving, hardscape covering.

In addition, the design standards may include, but shall not be limited to, the following elements:
(1) Building orientation;
(2) General site planning (primary, ancillary structures);
(3) Density;
(4) Floor area ratio (FAR);
(5) Signage;
(6) Architectural style and details;
(7) Building materials;
(8) Garage entrance location;
(9) Window/dormer size and location;
(10) Landscaping;
(11) Fences and walls;
(12) Entrance lighting;
(13) Driveways, curbs, and sidewalks;
(14) Utility boxes, trash receptacles;
(15) Street furniture;
(16) Building relocation; and
(17) Right-of-way (exceeding public works standards).

3.41 "AO" (AIRPORT OVERLAY)

Purpose and findings: The intent of this section is to regulate and restrict the height of structures and objects of natural growth and otherwise regulate the use of property in the vicinity of the [LOCAL GOVERNMENT] airport by creating certain airport zones within the zoned districts, and to define their boundaries by adopting and referring to the [LOCAL GOVERNMENT] airport zoning map.

This section implements the following plan policies:
• Land use adjacent to the airport should be reserved for commercial and industrial development related to air transportation or those businesses needing easy access to airport facilities;
• Airport-related uses will be encouraged in the areas near the airport; and
• Residential land uses will be discouraged in the areas where noise exceeds recommended land-use standards.

3.41.1 Airport Zones Established and Defined

(A) There is created within the [CITY/COUNTY] certain zones that include all of the land lying within instrument approach zones, noninstrument approach zones, transition zones, horizontal zones, and conical zones, as defined in this section. Such area and zones are shown on a map entitled "Zoning Overlay Map," consisting of one sheet, attached as part of the "Airport Master Plan" [INCLUDE DATE]. This map is adopted and made a part of this section by reference. This map shall be filed and kept as a part of the official zoning map of the city.

(B) Airport zones, as shown on the [LOCAL GOVERNMENT] "Airport Zoning Map," are established and defined in Table 3-21.

3.41.2 Height Limitations

Except as otherwise provided in this section, no structure or tree shall be erected, altered, or allowed to grow or be maintained in any zone created by this division to a height in excess of the height limit established for that zone. Such height limitations are established for each of the zones in Table 3-21. Where an area is covered by more than one height limitation, the more restrictive limitation shall prevail.

3.41.3 Use Restrictions

No use may be made of land within any zone established by this division in such a manner as to:
• Create electrical interference with radio communication between the airport and aircraft;
• Make it difficult for flyers to distinguish between airport lights and other lights;
• Result in glare in the eyes of flyers using the airport;
• Impair visibility in the vicinity of the airport; or
• Otherwise endanger the landing, taking off, or maneuvering of aircraft.

3.41.4 Regulations to Be Considered in Review of Zoning Development Approval Applications

This section in its entirety shall be considered by the zoning administrator when reviewing applications for zoning development approvals. The applicant for a zoning development approval shall include and submit adequate information and detail necessary to ensure that the limitations of this division shall not be exceeded. Such information shall include, at a minimum, a completed Federal Aviation Administration (FAA) Form 7460-1, along with the comments submitted on the completed Form 7460-1 by the FAA.

3.41.5 Conditions on Variances

Except as provided in § 3.41.6 Application of Regulations to Preexisting Structures and Uses of this chapter, any variance authorized to this division shall be so conditioned as to require the owner of the structure or tree in question, at his/her own expense, to install, operate, and maintain such markers and lights as may be deemed necessary by the Board of Zoning Appeals, acting with the advice and recommendation of the FAA or the airport manager.

3.41.6 Application of Regulations to Preexisting Structures and Uses

(A) Except as provided in subsection (B), below, the regulations prescribed by this section shall not be con-

Table 3-21
Airport Overlay Zones and Height Restrictions

Zone	Definition	Height
Instrument approach zone	An instrument approach zone at each end of the instrument runways for instrument landings and take-offs. The instrument approach zones shall have a width of 1,000 feet at a distance of 200 feet beyond each end of the runway, widening uniformly to a width of 16,000 feet at a distance of 50,200 feet beyond each end of the runway, its centerline being the continuation of the centerline of the runway.	1 foot in height for each 50 feet in horizontal distance, beginning at a point 200 feet from and at the centerline elevation of the end of the instrument runway and extending to a distance of 10,200 feet from the end of the runway; thence, 1 foot in height for each 40 feet in horizontal distance to a point 50,200 feet from the end of the runway.
Noninstrument approach zone	A noninstrument approach zone at each end of all noninstrument runways for noninstrument landings and take-offs. The noninstrument approach zone shall have a width of 500 feet at a distance of 200 feet beyond each end of the runway, widening uniformly to a width of 2,500 feet at a distance of 10,200 feet beyond each end of the runway, its centerline being the continuation of the centerline of the runway.	1 foot in height for each 40 feet in horizontal distance, beginning at a point 200 feet from and at the centerline elevation of the end of the noninstrument runway and extending to a point 10,200 feet from the end of the runway.
Transition zones	Transition zones are adjacent to each instrument and noninstrument runway and approach zone, as indicated on the Airport Zoning Map. Transition zones symmetrically located on either side of runways have variable widths as shown on the Airport Zoning Map. Transition zones extend outward from a line 250 feet on either side of the centerline of the noninstrument runway, for the length of such runway, plus 200 feet on each end; and 500 feet on either side of the centerline of the instrument runway, for the length of such runway, plus 200 feet on each end, and are parallel and level at such runway centerlines. The transition zones along such runways slope upward and outward 1 foot vertically for each 7 feet horizontally to the point where they intersect the surface of the horizontal zone. Further, transition zones shall be adjacent to both instrument and noninstrument approach zones for the entire length of the approach zones. These transition zones have variable widths, as shown on the Airport Zoning Map. Such transition zones flare symmetrically with either side of the runway approach zones from the base of such zones and slope upward and outward at the rate of 1 foot vertically for each 7 feet horizontally to the points where they intersect the surfaces of the horizontal and conical zones. Furthermore, transition zones shall be adjacent to the instrument approach zone where it projects through and beyond the limits of the conical zone, extending a distance of 5,000 feet, measured horizontally from the edge of the instrument approach zones at right angles to the continuation of the centerline of the runway.	1 foot in height for each 7 feet in horizontal distance, beginning at any point 250 feet normal to and at the elevation of the centerline of noninstrument runways, extending 200 feet beyond each end, and 500 feet normal to and at the elevation of the centerline of the instrument runway, extending 200 feet beyond each end, extending to a height of 150 feet above the airport elevation, which is 1,175 feet above mean sea level. In addition to the foregoing, there shall be height limits of 1 foot vertical height for each 7 feet horizontal distance, measured from the edges of all approach zones for the entire length of the approach zones and extending upward and outward to the points where they intersect the horizontal or conical surfaces. Further, where the instrument approach zone projects through and beyond the conical zone, a height limit of 1 foot for each 7 feet of horizontal distance shall be maintained beginning at the edge of the instrument approach zone and extending a distance of 5,000 feet from the edge of the instrument approach zone measured normal to the centerline of the runway extended.
Horizontal zone	A horizontal zone shall be the area within a circle with its center at the airport reference point and having a radius of 7,000 feet. The horizontal zone does not include the instrument and noninstrument approach zones and the transition zones.	150 feet above the airport elevation or a height of 1,175 feet above mean sea level.
Conical zone	A conical zone shall be the area that commences at the periphery of the horizontal zone and extends outward therefrom a distance of 5,000 feet. The conical zone does not include the instrument approach zones and transition zones.	1 foot in height for each 20 feet of horizontal distance beginning at the periphery of the horizontal zone, extending to a height of 400 feet above the airport elevation.

strued to require the removal, lowering, or other changes or alterations of any structure or tree not conforming to the regulations as of [DATE OF ORIGINAL ADOPTION], or where applicable, as of the effective date of any subsequent amendment to these regulations. Nothing contained in this section shall require any change in the construction, alteration, or intended use of any structure, the construction or alteration of which was begun prior to [DATE], or where applicable, prior to the effective date of any subsequent amendment, and is diligently prosecuted.

(B) The owner of any structure, tree, natural growth, or use that existed prior to [DATE], or where applicable prior to the effective date of any subsequent amendment to this section, and which is inconsistent with or in violation of this section or an amendment, shall be required, as a condition of the continued maintenance of such structure, tree, or use, to permit the installation, operation, and maintenance of such markers and lights as deemed necessary by the FAA or the [CITY/COUNTY]'s airport manager, in order to indicate the presence of such object or hazardous use to operators of aircraft in the vicinity of the airport. Such markers and lights shall be installed, operated, and maintained at the expense of the [LOCAL GOVERNMENT] and not of such owner.

3.41.7 Exemption of Utility Structures

Structures of public utilities shall be excluded from the requirements of this division, provided that plans for such structures have been first reviewed and determined by the FAA to have no adverse affect on air navigation as provided in Part 77 of the FAA's regulations.

DIVISION 4: FLEXIBLE ZONING

3.50 DENSITY BONUS

Purpose and findings: There are instances where it is in the best interests of the private landowner and the [LOCAL GOVERNMENT] to exceed the minimum requirements of this chapter. In such instances, the city's interests in restricting density or imposing certain regulatory requirements can be offset by increases in open space, natural resources, or the provision of affordable housing or certain amenities. Further, the system provides incentives to landowners while preserving the overall integrity of the comprehensive plan by providing uniform rules of general application for density increases. This system provides regulatory incentives while ensuring that regulatory modifications are not made solely and exclusively for the private benefit of the landowner.

This division implements the following provisions:

• Develop ordinance revisions and development proposals that conserve energy and water, enhance the attractiveness of the area, and protect valuable natural and cultural resources;

• Create a land exchange mechanism to acquire land for public purposes;

• Encourage a balance of new development and redevelopment; and

• Promote the provision of sound and affordable housing to all [LOCAL GOVERNMENT] residents.

Table 3-22
Incentive Zoning Bonus

	(A) Active Open Space	(B) Passive Open Space	(C) Affordable Housing	(D) Percent to Total Permitted Dwelling Units
A	✓			120%
B		✓		120%
C	✓	✓		130%
D	✓		✓	130%
E		✓	✓	130%
F	✓	✓	✓	130%

✓ = Applicable incentive item. For example, under Row (C), if the application includes additional Active Open Space and Passive Open Space but not Affordable Housing, a 30% density bonus applies. See Table 3-24 for an interpretation of this table.

3.50.1 Applicability

This subsection applies to density and intensity on the parcel subject to an application for development approval. Density bonuses will be granted as of right if the applicant complies with the criteria established in § 3.50.2 Bonus Criteria, subsection (B), of this chapter. Applicants requesting a density bonus for a residential subdivision may also reduce lot sizes through approval of a conservation subdivision (see § 2.2 Conservation Subdivision in Chapter 2, Use Patterns, of the LDC).

3.50.2 Bonus Criteria

(A) An applicant may be granted a density bonus by establishing any of the incentive items as described in Column (A) of Table 3-22 consistent with the standards described in Columns (B) and (C) of Table 3-22. The total permissible dwelling units shall be calculated in accordance with Column (C) of Table 3-24. In no event shall the cumulative total permissible dwelling units for public parks or open space in Table 3-22 exceed that which is described in Table 3-22.

(B) In no event shall minimum lot sizes be less than that shown in Table 3-23.

Table 3-23
Adjusted Lot Sizes, Incentive Zoning

Zoning District	Minimum Adjusted Lot Size
"RP" (Resource Protection)	304,920 square feet
"RE" (Residential Estate)	30,000 square feet
"NS" (Neighborhood Suburban)	7,000 square feet
"NU" (Neighborhood Urban)	3,500 square feet

3.51 TRANSFER OF DEVELOPMENT RIGHTS

Purpose and findings: It is the policy of the [LOCAL GOVERNMENT] that landowners subject to development restrictions in the sending zones, or as the result of regulations protecting critical areas, should have regulatory incentives to permanently restrict such lands from urbanization. The state zoning enabling legislation [CITATION] authorizes the [LOCAL GOVERNMENT] to control the density of population through zoning.

While such regulations may be legally imposed where they further a legitimate public purpose and are reasonable, the transfer of development rights (TDR) provides a vehicle to enable the private market to allocate economic benefits to landowners in the restricted areas. This enhances the viability of businesses in the sending areas and avoids potential legal disputes between the private landowners and the [LOCAL GOVERNMENT]. This section establishes procedures for transferring densities from sending to receiving parcels. At the voluntary request of the landowners in the sending areas and the receiving areas, the [LOCAL GOVERNMENT] may increase densities in the receiving areas and reduce densities in the sending areas.

The TDR system is based on the theory of carrying capacity of the [LOCAL GOVERNMENT]. In other words, a finite amount of development is permitted in the areas within the sending and receiving zones. The [LOCAL GOVERNMENT] is indifferent as to who does the development. Instead, it lets the market decide the price. A purchase of TDR does not increase the total amount of development possible in these areas. Accordingly, the accumulation of transfer rights is related to the overall purpose of preserving resources in the area.

3.51.1 Sending Areas Created

(A) Severable development rights are created in the sending areas designated below. Sending areas may be located in [INSERT REFERENCE TO OTHER LOCAL GOVERNMENTS THAT CAN SEND DEVELOPMENT RIGHTS] if the landowner has recorded a conservation easement, or reserved rights-of-way, in accordance with the provisions of this section. All sending areas are assigned development rights at the following ratios:

(1) *Critical areas:* 50 percent of the development potential of critical areas, as defined in subsection (C), below, may be transferred.

(2) *Agricultural preservation:* 100 percent of the development potential of agricultural areas, as defined in subsection (D), below, may be transferred.

(3) *Transportation corridors:* Any land area within a designated right-of-way.

(4) *Historic district:* 50 percent of the development potential of historic districts, as defined in [REFERENCE TO ANY HISTORIC DISTRICT REGULATIONS], may be transferred.

(B) For purposes of this section, "development potential" means:

(1) For areas within the incorporated boundaries of the [LOCAL GOVERNMENT], the density permitted by the underlying zoning district;

(2) For areas within the extraterritorial jurisdiction of the [LOCAL GOVERNMENT], one dwelling unit per 5 gross acres; and

(3) For areas within the unincorporated areas of _____ County, one dwelling unit per 10 acres.

(C) For purposes of this subsection, a "critical area" means any natural resource or environmentally sensitive area that is:

(1) Subject to the standards set forth in *Division 4: Greenspace (Landscaping, Tree Preservation, Screening, and Environmental Protection) Standards* in Chapter 5, Development Standards, of the LDC, in order to protect the public health, safety, and general welfare;

(2) Protected by a conservation easement; and

(3) Physically developable at the development potential described in subsection (B), above, as certified by a professional engineer.

(D) For purposes of this subsection, an "agricultural area" means any tract or parcel:

(1) That has a valid, unexpired agricultural appraisal;

(2) Is protected by a conservation easement; and

(3) Is not used as a Concentrated Animal Feeding Operation, as defined in 40 C.F.R. Part 122, which contains more than 1,000 animal units.

(E) For purposes of this subsection, a "transportation corridor" means any proposed right-of-way for an arterial street, thoroughfare, or light rail line as designated in the thoroughfare plan, and which is dedicated to and accepted by the [LOCAL GOVERNMENT], state department of transportation, or [TRANSIT AGENCY].

(F) Documentation of compliance with the requirements for eligibility as a sending area shall be submitted with the application for development approval requesting an increase in density in the receiving area provided; however, the proposed development in the sending area may be approved subject to completion of such requirements, including, but not limited to, recordation of a conservation easement or approval of an agricultural or open space land tax appraisal, as a condition of development approval.

Table 3-24
Bonus Density Chart

(A) Incentive Item	(B) Criteria	(C) Bonus Calculation
Parks and open space	Establishment of active or passive open space in excess of the minimum acreage requirements of the parks and open space standards (§ 5.21 Parks/Open Space in Chapter 5, Development Standards, of the LDC). The area dedicated to open space shall comprise at least 1 acre and shall comply with parks and open space standards to receive bonus credit.	• For conventional subdivisions: BD = [(NA ÷ MLS) + (AOS x 4)] < [(NA ÷ MLS) x C] where: BD = total permissible dwelling units with bonus; NA = net acreage (adjusted for right-of-way but not open space); MLS = minimum lot size; AOS = additional open space (in acres) multiplied by maximum permitted density; and C = cap on density from Table 3-23. • For conservation subdivisions: BD = [(GA x MD) + (AOS x 4)] < [(GA x MD) x C] where: BD = total permissible dwelling units with bonus; GA = gross acres; MD = maximum density of base district; AOS = additional open space (in acres) multiplied by maximum permitted density; and C = cap on density from Table 3-23.
Redevelopment	Redevelopment of existing strip centers in accordance with the provisions of the commercial retrofit standards (§ 2.5 Commercial Retrofit in Chapter 2, Use Patterns, of the LDC).	For each 100 spaces of surface parking converted to structured parking on an area not exceeding 20% of the site area, an additional 20,000 feet of nonresidential space may be constructed.
Retail site design	Superstores, shopping centers, or other retail uses located in zoning districts "CG" (Commercial General) or "CL" (Commercial Large-Scale) may obtain a density bonus pursuant to Column (C) where the proposed development complies with the neighborhood center design criteria (§ 2.3 Neighborhood Center in Chapter 2, Use Patterns, of the LDC).	A 30% increase in permitted height (permitted height x 1.3) may be granted.
Affordable housing: very low income	At least 5% of all dwelling units must be restricted as very low-income housing through a deed restriction or an enforceable contract with a public housing authority or community development corporation.	BD = TD x Y where: BD = total permitted dwelling units, with bonus density; TD = maximum number of dwelling units permitted by applying the maximum density of the base zoning district (see § 3.12 Dimensional Regulations of this chapter); and Y = 1.20. The factor "Y" shall increase by 0.05 for every additional 15% of units restricted as very low-income housing, up to the maximum set forth in this section.

Table 3-24 (cont.)
Bonus Density Chart

(A) Incentive Item	(B) Criteria	(C) Bonus Calculation
Affordable housing: low income	At least 15% of all dwelling units must be restricted as low-income housing through a deed restriction or an enforceable contract with a public housing authority or community development corporation.	BD = TD x Y where: BD = total permitted dwelling units, with bonus density; TD = base calculation of total permitted dwelling units; and Y = 1.10. The factor "Y" shall increase by 0.05 for every additional 5% of units restricted as low-income housing, up to the maximum set forth in this section.

3.51.2 Receiving Districts Designated

No severable development rights shall be exercised in conjunction with the development of subdivision of any parcel of land that is not located in a receiving district. A parcel of land that receives developments rights pursuant to this section shall be referred to as a "receiver site." The following districts are designated receiving districts for purposes of transferring severable development rights: "D" (Downtown) and "MX" (Mixed Use) that are restricted by a conditional rezoning to a TOD use pattern.

3.51.3 Timing

Development rights allotted to a sending area may be transferred to any person at any time and shall be deemed, for taxation and all other purposes, to be appurtenant to the land from which the rights are transferred until a development order is issued authorizing use of the development rights at a receiver site, at which time they shall attach to the receiver site for all purposes.

3.51.4 Right-of-Way Dedication

3.51.4.1 Evidence of Restriction Required for Development Approval

A developer of a receiver site must submit, in conjunction with his/her application for development approval, evidence that the transferor parcel has been restricted to nondevelopment uses and that a boundary plat has been recorded in accordance with the above provisions. No plat for a subdivision in conjunction with which severable development rights are exercised shall be recorded by the register of deeds, and no new building, or part of a building, or addition to or enlargement of an existing building that is part of a development project in conjunction with which severable development rights are exercised, shall be occupied until documents have been recorded in the office of the register of deeds transferring title from the owner of the severable development rights to the [LOCAL GOVERNMENT] and providing for their subsequent extinguishments.

3.51.1.2 Severable Development Treated Interest in Real Property

Once a deed for severable development rights has been transferred by a [LOCAL GOVERNMENT] to the dedicator and recorded, the severable development rights shall vest and become freely alienable.

3.51.4.3 Notice and Hearing Requirements

Any proposed TDR from the sending property or to the receiving property shall be subject to the notice and hearing requirements of § 4.21 Code Amendments in Chapter 4, Procedures, of the LDC (rezonings).

3.51.4.4 Preceding Transfer of Development Rights

Prior to any TDR, the [LOCAL GOVERNMENT] shall adopt an ordinance providing for:

(A) The issuance and recordation of the instruments necessary to sever development rights from the sending property and to affix development rights to the receiving property. These instruments shall be executed by the affected property owners and lienholders;

(B) The preservation of the character of the sending property and assurance that the prohibitions against the use and development of the sending property shall bind the landowner and every successor in interest to the landowner;

(C) The severance of transferable development rights from the sending property and the delayed TDR to a receiving property;

(D) The purchase, sale, exchange, or other conveyance of transferable development rights prior to the rights being affixed to a receiving property;

(E) A system for monitoring the severance, ownership, assignment, and TDRs; and

(F) The right of the [LOCAL GOVERNMENT] to purchase development rights and to hold them for resale.

COMMENTARY

Zoning plays one of the most critical roles in shaping urban development. Much of the landscape constructed in the 20th century is the direct result of underlying zoning codes and ordinances. From sprawl to neighborhood disinvestment, many problems and solutions can be traced to the zoning code. The zoning portion of the LDC addresses many of the criticisms of zoning and conventional zoning ordinances while introducing various concepts and principles that allow local communities to use zoning for positive growth, development, and the creation of neighborhoods and communities.

The LDC, like other zoning ordinances, has four basic parts:

(1) General provisions;
(2) Base district regulations;
(3) Overlays and special zones; and
(4) Regulations for specific use types.

Zoning involves the division of land uses by district. At its core, the basic purposes of zoning are to protect residential uses from encroachment by nonresidential or high-density residential uses, and to restrict the density and intensity of development. Most codes include basic residential, business/commercial, and industrial zoning districts, as well as overlay zoning districts or specialized districts for particular areas or situations. Most development would occur under the basic zoning districts, with the overlay zoning districts reserved for special purposes.

In theory, zoning is designed to protect land uses, such as single-family residential uses, from incompatible uses that are not harmonious with the character of those uses, and that could have adverse impacts on property values and public health, safety, and welfare. As they are written and administered, conventional zoning ordinances have several key objectives that are thought to promote "compatibility." First, the tendency is to keep densities low in order to control human activity. Second, most zoning ordinances are written and administered in a fashion that establishes a clear separation between residential and nonresidential uses. Conventional wisdom says that this will protect the property values of residential neighborhoods and promote "compatibility."

The conventional wisdom of use segregation is coming under increasing attack from the planning, architectural, and building professions. By segregating uses at low densities, development is spread over a wider amount of territory, which lengthens trips, increases infrastructure costs, and minimizes opportunities for pedestrian interaction. Accordingly, most state-of-the-art comprehensive plans encourage "mixed-use" development patterns, which allow residential and nonresidential uses to locate in close proximity. This creates a fine grain of uses similar to those found in traditional neighborhoods.

A common issue—particularly with older, mature zoning ordinances—is that there are too many zoning districts. This tends to complicate the ordinance, with many districts written to resolve individual, particularized issues that have long vanished from the public consciousness. However, if districts are too broad and permit too wide a range of activities, neighborhoods may face "speculative zoning," whereby landowners obtain rezonings without present plans for use of the property.

This situation illustrates a further weakness in zoning as a tool to protect compatibility. Landowners in most communities may use their property for any use permitted by the zoning district. This situation creates fear and consternation from neighborhoods that feel that not all of the uses permitted in their zoning district are appropriate. At the same time, it inhibits economic development by creating resistance to rezonings where the landowner has only one intended use for the property.

Before discussing the LDC, it may be helpful to include a brief discussion on zoning law. A local government's authority to regulate land uses and building forms is found in the police powers. Generally, the police power of a local government allows it to regulate for the health, safety, and welfare of its citizens. In the landmark case of *Village of Euclid v. Ambler Realty*,[2] the Supreme Court held that zoning by segregating uses and density was a legitimate exercise of the police power. Most states now have encoded this police power into state zoning enabling statutes that establish many of the basic goals of zoning, including the facilitation of water, sewer, and emergency services, and protecting/providing adequate light and air.

The authority for zoning has been extended to include the authority to designate local historic districts and landmarks; assess impact fees toward the development of infrastructure benefiting new development; and create environmental programs, such as open space regulations, cluster developments, wetland preservation, and the authority to regulate building and sign design. This authority allows local governments to play an active role in shaping their built environment. The LDC incorporates many of the development regulatory powers given to local governments through the zoning enabling and other statutes.

GENERAL CONCEPTS

The general provisions section is the road map listing what the zoning portion of the LDC seeks to accomplish and the framework for its administration. The zoning portion of the LDC, like most zoning ordinances, begins with a "purpose and findings" statement. This section integrates the major elements and policy provisions of a zoning portion while providing for internal consistency. Often drawing from the language of the comprehensive plan or the state zoning enabling statute, the "purpose and findings" statement explicitly lists what and how the zoning ordinance accomplishes the goals, objectives, and vision of the community. Communities often base these goals and objectives on the comprehensive plan and the design standards a community wishes to achieve through its zoning ordinance. However, "purpose and findings" statements are more than just a soundboard for a community's vision; they may also provide a legal defense against takings and other land-use suits.[3] While the LDC provides for a standard "purpose and findings" statement, communities should, as part of their adoption process, look at their unique comprehensive plan and create their own "purpose and findings" statement reflecting the goals and objectives tailored for the local community.

DISTRICTS

Types of Districts

Zoning involves the division of land uses and dimensional standards by district. There are several different types of zoning districts:

- *General districts or base districts:* These are the basic residential, business/commercial, and industrial zoning districts in which most land is typically classified.
- *Overlay zones:* These are districts in which additional requirements are imposed on certain properties within one or more underlying general or special use districts.[4] Some overlay zoning districts do not change the use and dimensional regulations of the general districts but instead impose additional requirements. Others change just one or more general district requirements, either by not allowing some uses that are otherwise permitted or by allowing additional density or uses if certain standards are complied with.
- *"PD" (Planned Development) districts:* These are districts in which a tract is developed as a single entity and which includes various housing types, commercial uses, and sometimes industrial uses.[5] A "PD" district frees the developer from the "inherent limitations of the lot by lot approach and thereby promote[s] the creation of well planned communities."[6] To create flexibility, a "PD" district may diverge from zoning the regulations of the general districts. Unlike an overlay zoning district, many conditions of approval are negotiated as part of the development approval process. A "PD" district can be established either as a floating zone or a conditional use.
- *Floating zones:* These are created by the text but are not mapped. "PD" (Planned Development) districts are usually established as floating zones.
- *Special use or conditional use districts:* These are districts in which uses are permitted only upon the issuance of a special use permit or a CUP.[7] Property may be placed in a special use district or a conditional use district only in response to a petition by the owners of all the property to be included.

Number of Zoning Districts

Reducing the number of zoning districts is often cited as a way to streamline and to simplify a zoning ordinance. Many ordinances have a number of districts that has outlived its usefulness or that has never been applied. Many districts have few meaningful distinctions. However, larger jurisdictions typically require a number of districts in order to recognize the distinctions between different neighborhood types.

Spot Zoning Versus Nodal Zoning

Spot zoning is illegal in most states. Unfortunately, the law of spot zoning is often misconstrued to require conventional zoning patterns, characterized by large, unbroken expanses of single-use zoning. This misunderstanding flows from statements in cases that say "[l]ots that are rezoned in a way that is substantially inconsistent with the zoning of the surrounding area, whether more or less restrictive, are likely to be invalid."[8]

By contrast, nodal zoning for small, neighborhood serving uses (e.g., bakeries and small restaurants) is a legitimate public purpose. Nodal zoning contemplates uses that purposely differ from surrounding uses but that benefit surrounding uses by providing a functional, mixed-use environment. For example, in *Marshall v. Salt Lake City*,[9] the city had established small "utility zones" for neighborhood serving groceries, drugstores, and gasoline stations at each corner of the intersections of main thoroughfares. Utility zones were established within residential zoning districts. The court rejected a spot zoning challenge, with the following prescient (albeit somewhat politically incorrect) statement:

> "Here the general zoning plan of the city set within a reasonable walking distance of all homes in Residential 'A' districts the possibilities of such homes securing daily family conveniences and necessities, such as groceries, drugs, and gasoline for the family car, with free air for the tires and water for the radiator, so the wife and mother can maintain in harmonious operation the family home, without calling Dad from his work to run errands."[10]

Other, more modern cases have recognized that spot zoning principles do not require single-use zoning and that the law accommodates a finer mix of uses.[11] As an alternative to nodal zoning, neighborhood centers

**Figure 3-12
Columbia Pike Special Revitalization
District Form-Based Code (Excerpt)**

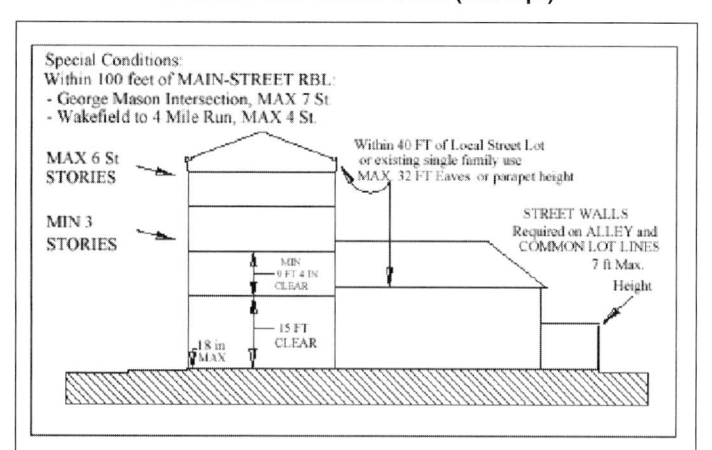

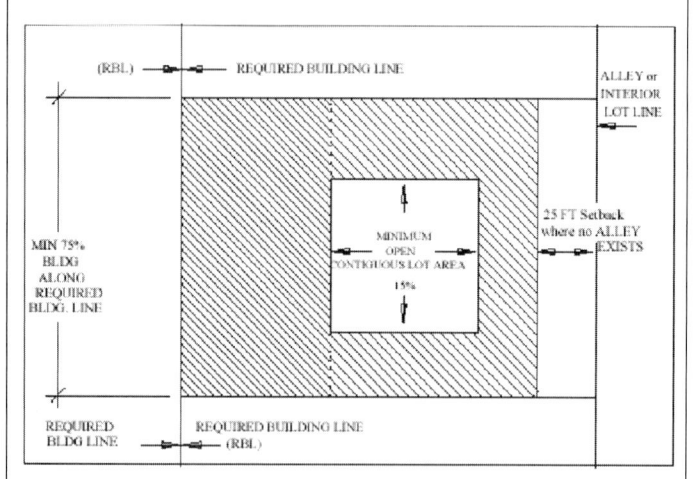

Competing methods of districting: Columbia Pike form-based code (Arlington County, Virginia), prepared by Geoffrey Farrell and Associates, regulates building envelope by districts (top two images). An excerpt of the list of permitted uses, from the C-2 Service Commercial—Community Business Districts, is shown at the bottom.

Source: Municipal Code Corporation (www.municode.com).

could be defined as uses permitted by right, subject to strict standards governing scale, design, and parking location. In addition, neighborhood centers may be permitted only in special zoning districts. This provides the flexibility of a discretionary hearing but can discourage applicants from using this approach. Spacing standards could be established to ensure that the neighborhood centers are dispersed and compact, avoiding the precedent-setting impact of commercial zoning, which can lead to the formation of commercial strips. The spacing standards can be stated as a standard (for by-right uses) or as a guideline in a "purpose and findings" statement if a special zoning classification is used. A distance of 1/4 to 1/2 mile could be used to allow for a 5- to 10-minute walk from residential blocks.

CONVENTIONAL VERSUS FORM-BASED ZONING

Form-based zoning (see Figure 3-12) uses scale and design to resolve compatibility issues. Transitional densities can be required between the heart of residential neighborhoods and the heart of corridors. This may include primary, secondary, and tertiary densities or building envelope standards, which can be accomplished in several ways:

- Establish variable density and FAR limitations for areas interior to corridors and on the edge of corridors (exterior). Under this option or under any of the options discussed below, the neighborhoods interior to the corridors provide the tertiary densities.

- Provide "neighborhood edge" and "corridor edge" standards for commercial corridors. The neighborhood edge criteria would permit garage apartments and smaller scale retail and service uses along the edge of the corridor abutting residential neighborhoods. The corridor edge would permit higher densities along with appropriate architectural restrictions and, in suburban corridors, buffering.

- Establish transitional zoning districts, and identify in "purpose and findings" statements the districts or areas that a designated district may abut.

- Establish and refine locational standards for parking, landscaping, and detention/retention facilities to buffer commercial uses and neighborhoods. In traditional neighborhoods, midblock locations and other solutions should be permitted in order to retain the walkable scale of the neighborhood. Landscaped buffer requirements should be minimized in traditional neighborhoods. In suburban neighborhoods, landscaped buffers are a viable solution.

FLEXIBLE ZONING

The LDC also has provisions for flexible zoning. Flexible zoning allows local governments to grant bonuses, usually in the form of density or FAR, in exchange for developer-provided amenities not normally obtainable via zoning regulations. For example, landowners can be allowed to build at a higher density than permitted in the zone if they agree to sequence development over a defined time period. Thus, growth is timed in accordance with the provision of necessary public facilities, while the developer obtains a financial benefit in the form of increased density.[12]

It is anticipated that the advantage given to the developer will be sufficient to persuade him or her to provide an amenity not otherwise required. For example, a developer may be allowed to exceed the established height restrictions in a zoning district in exchange for providing additional open space around the structure. In most instances, the use of bonus and incentive zoning must be tied to a site plan approval process to assure that the granting of the bonus does not have an adverse effect on adjacent properties in the zoning district.

Development bonuses are often used in urban areas to achieve public benefits related to urban design objectives. However, they also have great potential for achieving broad environmental and social benefits, such as a greater variety of housing types, ecological area preservation, and provision of open space. Bonuses can also be used to encourage high-density development at specified locations where such density is desirable, such as transportation corridors.[13]

The LDC lists some of the basic amenities associated with flexible zoning. A community may wish to expand the amenities available for flexible zoning in order to better serve the local needs, goals, objectives, or visions. In addition, the LDC provides the formula to calculate the bonuses associated with each amenity. A community should review and modify the formula to achieve the desired goals and objectives of the flexible zoning program.

A planned development or similar process is useful for good projects that do not fit into the mold established by the standards. No set of standards could possibly anticipate every type of project that has merit. The objective of this process is to codify the general rules that produce a positive outcome in the land-use decision-making process. However, the local government may retain the right to approve, and applicants may be given the right to advance, a proposal that has merit but is not contemplated by the code. The process should be a discretionary one because such situations are not the norm. It should be noted that these projects typically involve large-scale or otherwise visible projects that should not become the norm but which might have merit in very particularized settings.

USES

Most older zoning ordinances provide a separate list of uses for each zoning district. This creates some duplication because individual uses must be repeated in each district regulation. Most modern ordinances have consolidated use regulations into a single matrix of uses. A "use matrix" allows the location of uses to be compared across districts, and abridges the ordinance by avoiding the need to repeat use listings. A possible disadvantage is that all of the regulations pertaining to a specific district are not consolidated in one place, requiring the reader to look in two different places for the district regulations and use regulations.

The modern trend in zoning regulations is to list the uses permitted in each zoning district in a consolidated matrix. This avoids repetition and thereby minimizes the length of the ordinance. It also permits the reader to compare permitted uses across the various zoning districts.[14]

An important consideration in use regulations is between cumulative and noncumulative zoning districts. Many older zoning ordinances are cumulative where uses permitted in residential districts are also permitted in nonresidential districts. Most modern zoning ordinances are not cumulative (i.e., uses permitted in "higher," typically residential districts are not permitted in the "lower" districts).

The advantage of a cumulative system is flexibility and, from the landowner's perspective, the broader range of uses permitted. It also creates an opportunity for mixed-used development. However, it destroys the concept of zoning because nonresidential districts could build out as residential areas.[15] This creates a mismatch between the zoning map and actual land uses. Further, it does not allow a jurisdiction to reserve areas for economic development or employment-generating uses. If a jurisdiction wishes to retain zoning, the districts should be noncumulative. Better urban design standards and criteria for locating high-density residential and commercial uses in and near neighborhoods may be used to encourage mixed uses.

Zoning district use regulations typically require several modifications. First, zoning districts can be under-inclusive in that numerous types of uses seen are not listed. The most common reason for this is that uses, which are common today, were not known when the regulations were drafted. While it is impossible to contemplate every possible use in existence either today or in the future, it is possible to develop a comprehensive list of uses. This can be accomplished by using several national classification systems for uses or industries, such as the NAICS and the APA's LBCS.

The NAICS is a comprehensive industry classification system that replaces the Standard Industrial Classification system. It is thorough, but the classifications do not always make sense for zoning purposes (e.g., tattoo parlors are in the same industry classification as personal services). The LBCS (see Table 3-25) consists of five classification systems:

(1) Activity;
(2) Function;
(3) Structure;

Table 3-25
Land-Based Classification Standards

Category	Description
Activity	"Activity" refers to the actual use of land based on its observable characteristics. It describes what actually takes place in physical or observable terms (e.g., farming, shopping, manufacturing, and vehicular movement). An office activity, for example, refers only to the physical activity on the premises, which could apply equally to a law firm, a nonprofit institution, a courthouse, a corporate office, or any other office use. Similarly, residential uses in single-family dwellings, multifamily structures, manufactured houses, or any other type of building would all be classified as residential activity.
Function	"Function" refers to the economic function or type of establishment using the land. Every land use can be characterized by the type of establishment it serves. Land-use terms (e.g., agricultural, commercial, or industrial) relate to establishments. The type of economic function served by the land use gets classified in this dimension, independent of actual activity on the land. Establishments can have a variety of activities on their premises yet serve a single function. For example, two parcels are said to be in the same functional category if they serve the same establishment, even if one is an office building and the other is a factory.
Structure	"Structure" refers to the type of structure or building on the land. Land-use terms embody a structural or building characteristic, which indicates the utility of the space (in a building) or land (when there is no building). Land-use terms (e.g., single-family house, office building, warehouse, hospital building, or highway) also describe structural characteristics. Although many activities and functions are closely associated with certain structures, it is not always so. Many buildings are often adapted for uses other than their original use. For instance, a single-family residential structure may be used as an office.
Site Development Character	"Site Development Character" refers to the overall physical development character of the land. It describes "what is on the land" in general physical terms. For most land uses, it is simply expressed in terms of whether the site is developed or not. However, not all sites without observable development can be treated as undeveloped. Land uses, such as parks and open spaces, which often have a complex mix of activities, functions, and structures on them, need categories independent of other dimensions. This dimension uses categories that describe the overall site development characteristics.
Ownership	"Ownership" refers to the relationship between the use and its land rights. Since the function of most land uses is either public or private, and not both, distinguishing ownership characteristics seems obvious. However, relying solely on the functional character may obscure such uses as private parks, public theaters, private stadiums, private prisons, and mixed public and private ownership. Moreover, easements and similar legal devices also limit or constrain land-use activities and functions. This dimension allows classifying such ownership characteristics more accurately.

Source: S. Mark White, "Land Use Classification," Zoning Practice, Issue 9 (September 2005), at 5.

(4) Site Development Character; and
(5) Ownership.

The Function classification works as an industry classification, although at a much less detailed scale than the NAICS. The Structure classification is best for design-based codes in communities or situations where the concern is more about the form and massing of buildings rather than on how they are used. In practice, most communities in which we have worked prefer a combination of the Function and Structure classifications. The Activity, Site Development Character, and Ownership classifications tend to be more adaptable to mapping than to zoning regulation. Most states prohibit regulation of forms of ownership through zoning, eliminating this classification for zoning.

A second issue is overinclusiveness. Many zoning regulations rigidly separate uses because they are different rather than basing them on any real (or even perceived) problems with locating the uses in the same neighborhood. This can present a hardship to landowners as well as thwart planning policies that foster more compact, pedestrian-friendly neighborhoods. This can create sprawling development patterns with uses separated beyond walking distance because of the need to locate in different districts. This issue can be resolved by focusing more on building types than on uses in the regulations. When a jurisdiction does not seem prepared to completely abandon use controls, a greater emphasis on building design and a de-emphasis on use can permit the evolution of mixed-use, complete neighborhoods. The Structure classification in the APA's LBCS can be built into the matrix to substitute for some use restrictions.

Finally, all zoning ordinances with comprehensive use listings fail to define all of the listed uses. Developing a complete list of definitions would take years and consume hundreds of pages. Fortunately, the use classification systems described above contain definitions of uses and industry classifications. Specific definitions should be provided where state or federal law, local policies, or other factors require a unique definition.

A design-based code could use a reference to building form, rather than simply to uses, in each zoning district. This focuses more on how buildings are designed in each district rather than on the type of business occupying the building. One example is the Hillsborough County, Florida, TND code. The LDC divides new "PD" (Planned Development) districts into four subareas:

(1) Greenspace;

(2) Residential Neighborhoods;

(3) Commercial; and

(4) Core areas.

Within each subarea, a zoning matrix, using the APA's LBCS structure, controls building form.

DISCRETIONARY USES

Most zoning ordinances establish two types of uses:

(1) Uses permitted by right; and

(2) Uses permitted by special or CUP (also referred to as "discretionary uses").

A conditional or special use is a use that is expressly permitted by a zoning ordinance, subject discretionary review, and conditions. A special or CUP allows property to be used in a manner conditionally permitted by the ordinance.[16] Uses permitted by right are those deemed to be compatible with the other uses in the district and require only staff approval (e.g., a certificate of zoning compliance). By contrast, conditional or special uses require a public hearing, usually before the planning commission and the local government. Older ordinances may require special exception approval by the board of adjustment. The minor differences between conditional/special uses and special exceptions are discussed in Chapter 4, Procedures, of the LDC.

CONTRACT AND CONDITIONAL ZONING

Older state court decisions prohibited contract zoning. While a rezoning permits a landowner to use its property for any of the uses permitted in the underlying zoning district, these court decisions equated contract zoning with conditional zoning, and prohibited landowners from proffering restrictions on the use of their property in order to address the concerns of local governments and neighbors.[17] Rezoning to a district in which the desired use is permitted as a conditional use is not considered a viable option for most landowners because it requires a subsequent set of hearings in order to procure a CUP—a time-consuming and expensive procedure. Most states have approved the use of conditional use districts in which a property owner may request a rezoning to a parallel district subject to special conditions.[18]

DISTRICTS

BASE DISTRICTS

Base district regulations form the heart of a zoning ordinance. In fact, the term "zoning" derives from the districting of a community based on use and intensity. The current debate and criticism of zoning revolves around the way in which a community is districted, the uses permitted in each district, and the density for each district.

Historically, zoning developed as a means to modify and regulate the ill effects caused by the rapid industrialization and urbanization of the U.S. Early zoning sought to segregate those uses, which might adversely affect residential property (and, more importantly, residential property values). The codes and ordinances strictly segregated areas for working, shopping, and living, which contributed toward much of the urban sprawl and loss of community associated with modern development. The LDC recognizes that while not every use is compatible with one another, many uses, through proper design and siting, should be allowed to mingle and combine to form a more appealing built environment.

The LDC zoning districts have two main components, which shape much of the built environment:

(1) A list of permitted, conditional, and prohibited uses; and

(2) The height, setback, and bulk requirements for each district.

The traditional role and the primary goal of zoning are to separate uses that may be incompatible with one another. Historically, this resulted in the strict separation of residential from nonresidential, commercial and industrial from other commercial, and office from retail, because the uses are different rather than being based on any real (or even perceived) problems with locating the uses in the same neighborhood. This strict separation made many places (e.g., historic Charlestown, South Carolina; Country Club Plaza in Kansas City, Missouri; Mariemont, Ohio; and Telegraph Hill in San Francisco, California) nonconforming with conventional zoning requirements.

The strict separation of uses broke up the finely integrated neighborhood structures, causing many communities to cease functioning. This led to abandonment of nonconforming properties within neighborhoods and the loss of residents in commercial and office zones. In the undeveloped portions of a metropolitan area, the result was suburban sprawl with large tracts of housing separated by miles from the nearest grocery store or shopping area. The result has been an increase in traffic, the loss of open space and farmland, and a general sense of disconnectivity toward built places.

This strict segregation can present a hardship to landowners and can thwart the comprehensive plan's goals and objectives of community-based design and compact development of a community. Modern land-use scholars and planners now advocate for a more fine-grained use pattern where different uses are mixed together as appropriate. The LDC recognizes that certain uses should mix (e.g., residential uses near schools, day care centers, coffee shops, and other retail uses) while recognizing that some uses should still remain segregated (e.g., residential uses should be kept away from industrial uses).

To determine which mix of uses should be permitted in each district, a community should look at the underlying purpose of the zoning district and the comprehensive plan. For instance, the purpose of an "RE" (Residential Estate) district is for low-density residential uses on larger lots. The uses for the "RE" district reflect those that conform to the stated purpose of the zone. A single-family home, stable, or truck garden would more likely conform to this purpose than would an apartment building, retail shop, or shopping center. These types of uses are more appropriate in community centers, downtowns, or neighborhood centers. The uses chosen, or left out, will impact not only the level of intensity of a district but how far occupants of that district must travel to meet their needs, the type of transportation they employ, and the urban form of a community. The LDC addresses this issue by focusing on building and development types rather than use regulations. The Structure classification in the APA's LBCS can be built into the matrix to substitute for some use restrictions.

The LDC also addresses the problem of keeping the uses listed in the ordinance current. Zoning ordinances are often underinclusive and address uses commonly known today but unknown or uncommon at the time the ordinances were adopted. Without flexibility within the code, uses, such as Internet providers and cyber cafés, would be prohibited within a community while mechanical/pinball arcades would be permitted. While it is impossible for the LDC to contemplate every possible use in existence today or in the future, the code uses the LBCS, which ties uses to their general characteristics. For instance, many modern uses, such as cyber cafés, are usually not specifically listed in a zoning ordinance; however, their impact and form classify them as commercial entertainment. By classifying uses in the broadest terms and impacts, the new use will be able to integrate within the zoning ordinance.

In addition to addressing the broader issues of strict separation versus integration, the LDC addresses the problem of readability of zoning codes. Zoning ordinances often provide detailed lists of uses for each zoning district. This lengthens the ordinance by repeating uses throughout the document, and does not allow the reader to compare the districts where a given use is allowed. The LDC provides its list of uses in a table format, which is easier to read, easier to reference, and easier to use than those ordinances that provide a list for each district.

While the debate over the segregation and integration of uses continues, a community should base its distribution of uses on the comprehensive plan, community goals, objects, and visions. Some communities may wish to provide for more integration of uses; others may wish to maintain a certain character and limit the mixing of uses to reflect that character.

Whatever the use classification, the key goal of zoning is to designate the uses appropriate or inappropriate for each zoning district. The use matrix (Table 3-4) lists four types of use classifications:

(1) Uses permitted by right;
(2) Uses permitted by special exception;
(3) Prohibited uses; and
(4) Uses allowed only as part of a planned development.

Those uses designated as permitted uses are compatible with the purpose of the district and would cause no adverse affects on other property owners within the district. Special exception uses are those that may be compatible after meeting certain specified conditions placed on the use by the local planning commission or zoning board of appeals. These uses may cause adverse impacts to adjoining property unless certain requirements are met. In addition, these uses require a hearing before the board of adjustment and allow local property owners to voice any concern or favor toward the proposed use.

Prohibited uses are those uses that would be incompatible with the purpose of the zoning district and with the other uses permitted within the zoning district, and would have adverse impacts on the property owners. A community should thoroughly review their comprehensive plan, zoning "purpose and findings" statements, and their community's goals and vision before completely prohibiting a use in a zoning district. Uses permitted only within a planned development are those that may be incompatible when designed on a property-by-property basis but, when brought together through a unified development, may be designed to lessen their impact on adjoining uses and property owners. This type of use classification is common when apartments and single-family residents are brought together in a housing development, cluster development, or TND.

While the separation of uses has an impact in shaping the landscape of the entire community, height, lot, and bulk requirements shape the larger community as well as the form of the individual zoning districts. Setback, lot, and bulk requirements were historically often larger than necessary and led to the suburban strip and the large subdivisions devouring open space and agricultural land. Primarily, the reasons for the large dimensional requirements were the goal of maximizing the light and air along streets in order to avoid the "canyon effect" associated with large buildings constructed close to a sidewalk, and the belief that high density was bad.

Large setbacks also facilitated road-widening projects caused by the increased traffic associated with wide setbacks. In addition, the front yard setbacks provided a convenient place for parking and allowed suburban strip malls and shopping plazas to indicate the existence of ample parking for its customers. These wide setbacks and large lot requirements, however, encouraged sprawl by prohibiting the concentration of uses or the clustering of development in order to save natural features and open space. They also use infrastructure much less efficiently and do not sufficiently accommodate increases in population. The wide setbacks also required the removal of buildings away from the street, making the parking lot the prime visual element of a development. As buildings became more spread out, walking became less and less of an alternative for making local trips. The wide setbacks also decreased the appeal of the walking environment.

To address the many problems associated with inappropriate dimensional requirements, the LDC relies on minimum/maximum lot sizes, lot width, frontage, lot depth, front setbacks, side setbacks, rear setbacks, height, and on-lot open space regulations. Maximum density or intensity is the basic and traditional application of zoning techniques. It establishes a maximum number of dwelling units per acre (density), or a maximum ratio of nonresidential square footage per land area (FAR—a measure of "intensity"). Minimum lot size regulations also restrict density and intensity. For example, a minimum lot size of 1 acre does not permit development of more than one dwelling unit per acre.[19]

The LDC dimensional requirements are kept small and allow for small lots and shallow setbacks. In addition, most of the zoning districts have maximum setbacks in order to provide a consistent street wall or build line. This follows the code's underlying concept that density linked to a good design may have positive instead of negative impacts on a community. In addition, minimum density requirements are required to encourage transportation corridors, transit centers, nodes, and mixed-use centers.

These minimum densities within corridors and centers increase potential transit ridership, reduce auto dependency, reduce energy consumption, conserve land, attract economic development, encourage infill development, and create opportunities for recipient zones for TDRs from agricultural and environmentally sensitive lands. The setbacks and density requirements reflect the trend of slowing the negative environmental impacts of sprawl by reducing the amount of land needed for new development and, in return, by creating communities that provide greater mobility options and a more traditional atmosphere focused on towns, neighborhoods, and villages.

In addition, unlike traditional zoning codes, the LDC uses graphics to visually represent these requirements. This representation allows for developers and lay people to understand the relationship between setbacks and the visual appearance of the built environment. The graphics also allow users to visualize how the regulations will impact the design of their project. While these setbacks provide a model, communities are encouraged to review the setback requirements based on their own urban form. Communities may wish to further reduce the dimensional requirements where appropriate.

OVERLAY ZONES

While zoning is meant to apply to all areas of a community, certain areas are unique either in their environmental or their built characteristics. These unique areas often require special regulations tailored to each place. The requirements of the overlay zone are in addition to the zoning requirements for the underlying district. Often, the overlay zone modifies dimensional and use requirements of the underlying zone so new development can be consistent with the context of the additional standards.

While overlay zones provide flexibility for special areas, a community's reliance on overlay zones may be misplaced. When a community finds itself dependent on overlay zones to achieve its objectives, they may wish to reevaluate the underlying zoning to see if it is consistent with the community's goals and visions.

There are many different types of overlay zones. Whether an overlay zone is needed depends on the unique physical, institutional, political, legal, and other considerations of the local government. The LDC makes no attempt to categorize and explain every conceivable type of overlay zone.

The corridor overlay zone provides pedestrian-friendly design by establishing maximum setbacks, building design, and connectivity standards. This approach requires a conscious policy decision to mandate a change in retail and industrial site design practices. It is appropriate for mixed-use corridors, roads with lower vehicular traffic volumes, and roads with narrower rights-of-way (collector or lower-order classifications) where pedestrian access is a feasible alternative. This approach has also been applied to arterial roads, typically with a concerted public capital investment effort to humanize roads by adding medians, pedestrian refuges, sidewalks, and traffic calming.

Both approaches could be applied. For example, areas already built with intrinsically auto-dependent development (e.g., car dealers and big-box stores) could receive a conventional corridor overlay designation. Areas with narrower roads could receive a pedestrian corridor overlay designation. The "A" street and "B" street classification applied in older cities provides an

**Figure 3-13
Conventional Suburban Corridors**

Conventional suburban corridors feature front-loaded parking, pole signs, and little landscaping (left). Corridors can be redesigned to include monument signs and landscaping to humanize their scale (right).

example of this approach. An adaptation of this approach would involve "A" streets carrying pedestrian-oriented design standards and "B" streets using conventional corridor zoning. The Providence, Rhode Island, zoning ordinance uses this approach in its downtown area. A possible third approach could involve a gateway zoning overlay designation, with enhanced conventional corridor overlay techniques, such as restricting signage to monument signs and stricter landscaping requirements (see Figure 3-13).

Most corridor zoning districts are overlay zoning districts (i.e., the uses permitted in the underlying districts are permitted subject to the corridor standards). A separate approach would involve separate corridor overlay zoning districts with independent use restrictions. The use pattern concept could establish corridor use patterns as the general rule for development rather than the unique situations for which overlay zoning districts are typically reserved.

"PD" (PLANNED DEVELOPMENT) DISTRICTS

Planned developments (sometimes referred to as "planned unit developments" in statutes, cases, and literature) are a mechanism for preserving design flexibility, mixing uses, and eliminating the rigidity of "straight" zoning classifications and dimensional requirements by providing for the creation of an overlay "PD" (Planned Development) district. The planned development concept emerged as a "floating zone" to permit the orderly development of large-scale projects that do not fit the typical zoning prototype. A planned development permits a developer to obtain site-specific approval and to negotiate specific conditions. A planned development requires establishment of a "PD" zoning district that is designated on the official zoning map and is applied on a case-by-case basis following an application by a landowner.[20] A planned development releases the landowner from many of the restrictions of the underlying zoning districts as a trade-off for better design amenities, infrastructure provision, and mixed use. It also encourages more creative development patterns.

The lack of certainty is a disadvantage of the planned development technique. Because planned development is a negotiated process, private developers and neighborhoods face uncertainty in the zoning process. In addition, planned development regulations typically fail to address infrastructure standards necessary to achieve flexible and innovative development design. Accordingly, a successful planned development rezoning could be a Pyrrhic victory for developers seeking to build new urbanist communities, infill subdivisions, or other design patterns that depend upon narrower streets, smaller buffers, and other infrastructure concessions to produce a more compact form of mixed-use or residential development.

The LDC includes a generalized "PD" zoning district, which is required to be established prior to planned development approval. It can be refined to fit local needs and considerations.

DIMENSIONAL REGULATIONS

The following bulk and density controls are typically established by zoning ordinances:

- Minimum lot size;
- Frontage;
- Lot coverage; and
- Minimum front, side, and rear setbacks.

Design controls are often criticized as being inflexible, stalling creative development options, and driving up development costs.

LOT STANDARDS (LOT SIZE AND SETBACKS)

Conventional zoning ordinances typically prohibit certain structures within the front, side, and rear areas of a lot. Setbacks can also be established for other features, such as from riparian corridors, wetlands, floodplains, or view corridors. Setback and yard requirements have long been upheld as a legitimate exercise of local police powers.[21] The rationale for setback requirements are described in Table 3-26.[22]

A typical problem in urban communities is excessive setback requirements that do not conform to existing development patterns of existing neighborhoods. For example, apartments and commercial buildings in many urban neighborhoods are built to the sidewalk or within 10 to 15 feet of the front property line, while the front setback may range from 20 to 30 feet. This imposes a suburban paradigm onto traditional lot and building patterns, which has the effect of discouraging (or, at times, prohibiting) the redevelopment or adaptive reuse of property and delaying development in infill locations by requiring variance applications for development that is sensitive to existing neighborhood design patterns. Accordingly, the local government

Table 3-26
Rationale for Setbacks

Rationale	Front	Side	Rear	Other
Provide light and air.	✓	✓	✓	
Protect privacy.	✓	✓	✓	
Provide room for lawns and trees.	✓	✓	✓	
Protect dwelling units from traffic, noise, dust, and similar situations.	✓	✓	✓	✓
Avoid conflicts between the expansion of road surfaces within the right-of-way and structures.	✓			
Provide areas for recreation.	✓	✓	✓	
Improve the attractiveness of residential areas.	✓	✓	✓	✓
Provide access for fire protection.	✓	✓		✓
Provide fire separation between structures.	✓	✓		✓
Provide sight distances at street intersections.	✓	✓		✓
Ensure adequate space for accessory structures or uses.			✓	✓
Ensure adequate space for off-street parking and loading.		✓	✓	✓
Ensure adequate space for landscaping and buffers.			✓	✓
Provide adequate space for underground utilities.	✓	✓	✓	✓
Protect community character.	✓	✓	✓	✓
Protect sensitive environmental features.				✓
Protect viewsheds.				✓
Minimize stormwater discharges.				✓

Figure 3-14
Shallow Setback Streets

A 1:1 enclosure ratio and shallow setbacks create an "outdoor room" effect.

should consider smaller or lighter setbacks that match existing urban neighborhoods.

Of course, simply establishing small setbacks does not insure that buildings will fit the existing neighborhood context. Buildings sited too far away from the front or side property can also be inconsistent with neighborhood character. In addition, they can create a scattered, sprawling development pattern that conflicts with comprehensive plan policies, which require more compact, pedestrian friendly development patterns. Accordingly, many jurisdictions now require maximum front or side setbacks, or "build-to" lines, that pull buildings closer to the street or to other buildings, in order to create a "street wall."

In lieu of maximum setbacks, local governments could establish an "enclosure ratio." The enclosure ratio refers to the ratio of building height to spaces in front of the building. Ratios not exceeding 1:4 are considered optimal, while a 1:6 height-to-width ratio is the absolute minimum required for appropriate urban spatial definition.[23] An appropriate average ratio is 1:3.

For example, a building (Building A), which is 15 feet in height, faces a building (Building B), which is 24 feet in height, across a street with a 40-foot right-of-way. Building A is located 15 feet and Building B is located 20 feet from the edge of the right-of-way, producing a building-to-building space of 75 feet. The enclosure ratio is 1:5 (15:75 or 1:5) (see Figure 3-14).

INTENSITY

FARs are a more contemporary method of measuring nonresidential bulk. Some jurisdictions use a measurement of square footage per acre rather than FAR. This measurement is consistent with a FAR, although it is not always clear whether developers may concentrate development on nonsensitive portions of their projects in order to preserve open space while maintaining profitable levels of development.

FAR is a measure of building intensity that divides floor area by site area. Accordingly, smaller sites require smaller buildings, while building volume can increase on larger sites. While FAR is a flexible concept and is widely accepted, it is an imperfect control of scale. Some jurisdictions using the "form-based" zoning concept now use building envelope standards in lieu of FAR. FAR measures the total floor area to site area, while a building envelope measures the exterior dimensions of a building. Buildings with similar building envelopes can have widely different FAR measurements because of variable floor sizes (see Figure 3-15). Building envelope standards are more

**Figure 3-15
Maximizing Floor Area Ratio**

The building on the left only has one story, while the building on the right has two stories. The two buildings have nearly the same size building footprint. The building on the left is slightly taller than the building on the right; however, it has only half the floor area ratio because it has only one floor.

**Figure 3-16
Clustered Courtyard Buildings**

Building frontages clustered on a courtyard.

complicated but provide a closer fit with most urban design policies.

DENSITY

The traditional measures of development density are the use of dwelling units per acre for residential uses and height limits for nonresidential uses. A jurisdiction could consider zoning by density rather than by minimum lot size. Zoning by density has the advantage of design flexibility. This approach permits subdividers to plat smaller lots and to reserve larger areas for common open space. Eliminating minimum lot size could also encourage redevelopment. A potential downside to this approach is neighborhood resistance. In most cities, the perception is that larger lot sizes protect property values. However, some of the most valuable and desirable neighborhoods are those with small lots and historic homes.

As a corollary to policies that encourage compact, pedestrian-friendly development, many comprehensive plans call for higher densities and a richer blend of uses. However, public pressure inevitably leads to lower densities in individual zoning cases. One approach is to zone by density rather than by minimum lot size. The practice of permitting developers to cluster lots on smaller portions of a tract, so that the remainder may be devoted to open space, is known as "cluster" or "conservation" design.

Large lots are considered one of the primary contributors to sprawl because they require large amounts of land for yards, driveways, and streets. Conversely, in urban settings, some neighborhoods want to preserve large lots that are consistent with the existing development patterns. However, most neighborhoods will support higher density with character, which provides pedestrian, transit, and shopping opportunities, such as historic courthouse-style apartments (see Figure 3-16 and Figure 3-17).

TRANSFER OF DEVELOPMENT RIGHTS

A TDR program permits landowners to shift densities from one site to another through a negotiated transaction. Under this approach, a landowner in a "sending" area could sell development rights to a landowner in a

**Figure 3-17
Traditional Courtyard**

Courthouse-style apartments.

**Figure 3-18
Transfers of Development Rights**

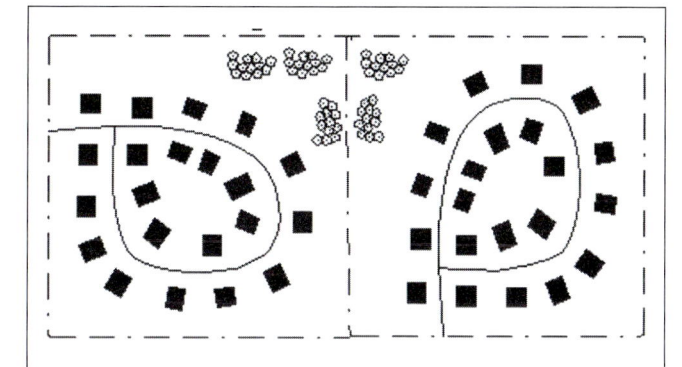

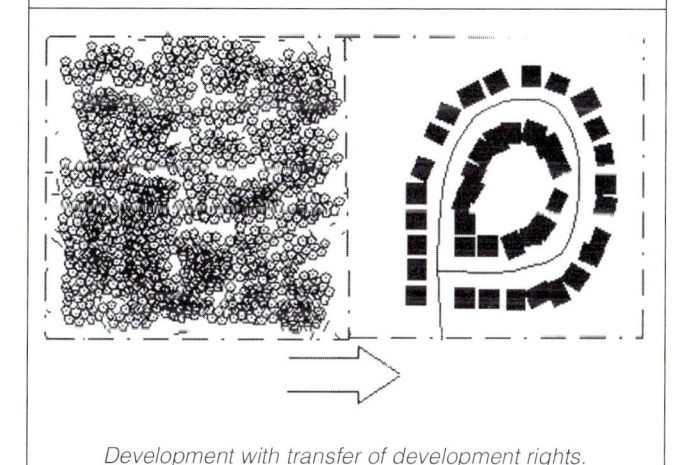

Development without transfer of development rights.

Development with transfer of development rights.

"receiving" area. The receiving area landowner would receive a density bonus in exchange for purchasing development rights in the sending areas. The sending area landowner would be required to record a conservation easement to restrict the use of the property for open space or agricultural uses. The advantage of TDRs is that landowners can use the free market to protect environmentally sensitive lands while providing for increased densities in appropriate areas. The disadvantage is the additional staffing needed to administer the process (see Figure 3-18).

The LDC provides for TDR. Zoning ordinances allocate a development potential to each parcel of land. Development rights transfer permits the transfer of unused development rights from one parcel to another (generally within a defined district) through purchase and resale by a development rights bank or through direct purchase/resale between property owners. TDR systems authorize owners of land in areas that the community desires to preserve or in areas in which development opportunities are to be limited, such as land designated for open space,[24] prime agricultural land,[25] environmentally sensitive land, or land on which historic buildings are located (sending zones) to sell their unused development rights to property owners in designated areas where higher densities can be accommodated (receiving zones).[26]

The concept of TDRs is simple and straightforward, although the legal, practical, and administrative issues associated with its use tend to be complex and difficult. Ownership of land carries with it a bundle of rights, including the right to construct improvements on the land (i.e., the ability to develop the land).[27] Although local governments, through their police and zoning powers, have the right to restrict the use of land to protect public health, safety, or general welfare, regulation that goes too far may constitute a taking without just compensation in violation of the Fifth Amendment to the U.S. Constitution or similar state constitutional provisions.[28]

A primary purpose of a TDR program is to ameliorate the harshness of governmental regulation, such as permanent, low-density zoning or downzoning of land.[29] Development rights represent a form of noncash compensation to property owners. Accordingly, even severely regulated property owners are left with a reasonable return on their property and investment. Transferability of development rights "undoubtedly mitigates whatever financial burden the law has imposed . . . and are to be taken into account in considering the impact of regulation."[30]

The major attraction of TDRs is its role in offsetting economic hardships incurred by private landowners. Fundamental to TDRs is the premise that the resource owner's confiscation objection to regulation will be blunted by the benefits that the resource owner is enabled to receive, either by selling his/her package of development rights to owners of transferee parcels or, should the resource owner also be the owner of the transferee site, by retailing the market value of the additional development potential that the rights represent.[31]

A TDR program also offers a means for providing equity and fairness to landowners whose land is subject to restriction even when those restrictions cannot be said to be confiscatory. In such a case, the technique can be viewed as a means of balancing the burdens and benefits of land-use regulation in the context of a comprehensive plan in which areas containing agricultural land, open space, and environmentally sensitive lands are designated for preservation, while other areas are designated for growth and development.[32]

A TDR program can enhance planning and growth management, especially when the program is integrated with and implements the city's general, community, area, and specific plans. By providing compensation and mitigation to owners of restricted lands designated for preservation because of their agricultural, historical, environmental, or even aesthetic values, and by providing incentives of increased densities to owners of land in areas designated for redevelopment and growth, the TDR program facilitates traditional growth management goals and objectives. The result is a better urban form through preservation of open space and the shifting of growth into areas targeted for higher density (e.g., urban centers and designated nodes or transportation corridors). The improved urban form achieves efficiencies in the utilization and development of infrastructure, promotes energy savings by reducing sprawl, concentrates mixed development in centers creating enhanced employment opportunities, and stimulates infill in underdeveloped areas.

TDR programs can be used to assist in the prevention of harm to the environment by mitigating the economic impact of restrictions on a landowner's use of property. If the landowner is restrained through regulation from developing steep hillsides, wetlands, and other environmentally sensitive areas, which, if developed, would have adverse environmental consequences, the landowner may be compensated for all or a portion of such regulatory restraints by compensation from the TDR. When governmental action is in the nature of harm prevention, the government has significantly more latitude in the imposition of a regulation.[33]

There are two basic operational alternatives for transferring development rights from the sending zone to the receiving zone. The first is an open market scheme allowing rights to be sold as a commodity among private individuals without government involvement. In this system, the development rights become another facet of the real estate business. The value of the development rights is determined by the value that a willing buyer will pay to a willing seller in the free market. Several successful programs in the U.S. have used this technique. However, open markets are effective only if there is an active demand for such rights in the receiving zone. If there is not, the alternative is for the government to become involved in the creation of a market for the development rights.

The second alternative is a bank system.[34] This type of system was proposed for environmental lands in Puerto Rico[35] and implemented in New Jersey.[36] It allows a sending zone landowner, in the absence of a private purchaser, to sell rights to the government. The government retains these rights in a development bank until a receiving zone landowner wishes to purchase them in order to gain additional density on a property.

Proposals have been made for the government to issue a certain number of development rights for an initial deposit in the bank. Judicial review of TDR programs has involved analysis of the ease with which a landowner in the sending zone can actually sell the rights. If the rights are not reasonably saleable, the TDR program may be invalidated.[37] In order for the local government to have a successful program, it may need to create a government-run bank if the receiving zone property owners are unable or unwilling to purchase the development rights. However, government involvement may be at considerable administrative and financial cost because it may become the unwilling owner of unmarketable development rights.

Once the basic mechanism is selected to transfer the rights, certain other questions concerning land titles in the sending zone can be resolved. For example, restrictive covenants should be placed on the preserved land. In the case of a development rights bank, the local government may wish to become a party to those agreements. Further, the title to preserved land may be retained by the owner or may be dedicated to the city. The local government may require this latter option in the case of a development bank.

Several courts have upheld TDR systems using open markets.[38] This option is preferred by the courts and eliminates the need for governmental involvement in the marketplace. If a market for increased density is unavailable, an option is the creation of a public development rights bank. This option is potentially riskier since the courts are less familiar with this approach and because it creates a financial risk for the local government.

Several court cases have commented favorably on the extent and type of planning documentation necessary to appropriately support the selection of sending and receiving areas in a successful TDR program.[39] In terms of judicial approval of TDRs, the more information that can be gathered, the better the chances for a successful program. Therefore, the local government should undertake comprehensive planning studies and analyses to select appropriate criteria for identifying sending and receiving zones. These planning studies are insurance against the potentially greater time and effort necessary to defend the selection of sending and receiving zones if litigation ensues.

The LDC program creates three types of sending areas from where development rights can be transferred or sold. Critical areas reflect those lands that are environmentally sensitive or important, including hillsides, wetlands, shorelines, or habitats for endangered animals. Agriculture preserves reflect the desire to preserve active farmland in order to mitigate the encroachment of new, incompatible development into rural areas and to preserve agriculturally productive land. Transportation corridors are rights-of-way for future transportation areas. A community, in connection with its comprehensive plan, may further add other land-use categories or districts as sending areas. This may include local historic districts, landmarks, viewsheds, or other areas where development should be minimal.

From those areas designated as sending areas, development rights may be transferred to increase the allowable density in the receiving areas. The LDC has two receiving areas: TOD and TND. These areas are appropriate for high-density developments created with the additional development rights. In addition, a TDR program encourages new developments within these

Table 3-27
Performance Zoning Measurements

Intensity	Description
	÷ gross/net site area
Impervious surface ratio	Impervious surface (acres) ÷ gross/net site area
Floor area ratio	Ratio of total floor area to the total land area, or net land area excluding environmentally sensitive lands or other undevelopable areas
Livability space ratio	Landscaped open space as a ratio of gross or net land area
Recreation space ratio	Total recreation space as a ratio of gross or net land area
Building volume ratio	Total building volume by site area, measured as follows: ((VB + VP + VL + VE) ÷ 10) ÷ gross/net site area where: VB = building volume (exterior walls); VP = parking area x 5; VL = loading area x truck heights; and VE = exterior storage x stack heights.

Sources: Porter, 1988; Kendig, 1980; Kendig, 1987.

zones. A community may add other zones, including downtown or urban redevelopment zones.

PERFORMANCE ZONING

Performance zoning regulates land-use intensity through a series of ratios or other numeric standards rather than by minimum lot size and setbacks. Sample intensity ratios are in Table 3-27.

Performance standards have the advantage of releasing the applicant from the rigidity of minimum lot sizes. The disadvantage of performance zoning is the difficulty of administering the standards and devising a system that is understandable to the public. Performance zoning codes are more difficult to interpret and to apply than traditional zoning standards, such as minimum lot size.

LAND-USE INTENSITY RATIOS AND PERFORMANCE STANDARDS

Performance standards have arisen primarily as a response to the rigidity of traditional, "Euclidean" zoning, which inhibits creative site design and does not always square with the specific goals, objectives, and policies of the community.[40] Performance standards are designed to achieve the following objectives:

• *Increase the precision of measuring development scale and impact on community resources.* While traditional zoning ordinances attempt to match community objectives with new development through use and density standards, the calibration is imprecise. For example, while density limits might limit the aggregate level of population and stormwater run-off into environmentally sensitive areas, such as wetlands, low-density zoning results in inefficient development patterns and may in fact result in the placement of buildings directly on the affected areas.[41]

• *Minimize discretion in the administration of ordinances.* Traditional, "Euclidean" zoning was designed to be a ministerial process. Landowners could simply look at the zoning map and determine what development was permitted by reference to the density and use regulations in the zoning ordinance. However, as discretionary approval procedures, such as CUPs, have gained popularity, developers are often subject to vague and imprecise standards, and the standards that will ultimately be applied to a particular parcel of land are difficult to decipher from the terms of the ordinance. Aside from the legal issues raised by such standards, their use inhibits sound, predictable planning and is unfair to developers. Performance standards seek to remedy this deficiency by quantifying the applicable standards while allowing ample room for flexibility and creativity.

• *Enhance flexibility for new development by eliminating rigid standards.* The use of rigid setback, density, and infrastructure requirements inhibit creative site design. For example, many developers are able to successfully preserve open space and environmentally sensitive areas by clustering development on small portions of the property, thereby avoiding the need to build in sensitive areas and reducing unit costs for roads, sewers, and other facilities. However, the application of rigid standards would result in a net loss of density and increase the spacing between buildings, which increases the amount of impervious surface coverage needed for roads and the length of piping needed for water and sewer. Many communities eliminate minimum lot size and site area requirements in these situations and simply prescribe the permissible net density. This standard allows the site designer to creatively utilize space, thereby achieving the community's goals and objectives while allowing the market to operate.

Flexible zoning standards easily fit within most zoning statutes that authorize regulation of building height, building size, percentage of lots that may be occupied, size of yards, courts and open spaces, and population density. In addition, performance standards can be viewed as nothing more than a mechanism to regulate density, which is expressly authorized as a zoning technique. The use of performance zoning was approved in Pennsylvania—a state that follows "Dillon's Rule" (a rule of narrow construction of local authority)—by a lower court decision.[42]

A disadvantage of performance zoning is the difficulty of administering the standards and devising a system that is understandable to the public. Performance zon-

Table 3-28
Land-Use Intensity Ratios

Standard	Explanation	Relationship to Other Ratios
Floor area ratio (FAR)	Ratio of total floor area to the total land area, or net land area excluding environmentally sensitive lands or other undevelopable areas.	Independent of other ratios. The combined FAR and OSR can exceed 1:0, since developers may compensate by increasing the number of stories instead of spreading the buildings over the parcel.
Open space ratio (OSR)	Total open space (in square footage) in relation to gross or net land area.	Independent of other ratios (see above). Includes LSR.
Livability space ratio (LSR)	Landscaped open space as a ratio of gross or net land area.	Included in OSR.
Recreation space ratio (RSR)	Total recreation space as a ratio of gross or net land area.	Part is included in OSR, although some recreation areas may be enclosed. LSR plus RSR may exceed OSR.
Total car ratio (TCR)	Minimum amount of parking space required per living unit.	OSR-LSR.
Occupant-car ratio	Minimum parking space required for each occupant of a building without time limits.	TCR-parking provided for visitors/tradesmen.

Sources: Bair, Jr., 1976; Hanke, 1965.

ing codes are more difficult to interpret and to apply than traditional zoning standards, such as minimum lot size. Examples of performance standards include open space ratios, impervious surface ratios, building volume ratios, landscaping ratios, and revised buffer and setback requirements. Performance standards could also go beyond mere site design to encompass the aesthetic qualities of the buildings themselves. Courts have also upheld the use of "specific design plans" regulating exterior construction and other development characteristics affecting community character.[43]

Where the community wants to protect environmental resources or infrastructure capacity, performance standards can be used to establish a carrying capacity ceiling for a particular area or resource based upon quantifiable standards. "Carrying capacity" is defined as the maximum amount of development that may occur in a given location given the assimilative capacity of certain resources affected by that development. Carrying capacity analysis, as a planning tool, studies the effects of growth (e.g., amount, type, location, and quality) on the natural and man-made environment in order to identify critical thresholds beyond which public health, safety, or welfare will be threatened by serious environmental problems unless changes are made in public investment, governmental regulation, or human behavior.[44]

Where the carrying capacity of a particular area (e.g., a defined "critical area") has been identified, the applicable performance standards can be calculated and applied. The carrying capacity analysis would assess the effects that the proposed development would have on the resource or area with each given standard. The zoning agency could then determine the appropriate, quantifiable standard for future application.

A problem with traditional measures of density is that the total building volume estimate is somewhat imprecise. For example, a large, single-family dwelling unit situated on a 1-acre parcel could consume as much space as a small apartment building while appearing less dense under conventional measurements. In order to obtain a more precise measurement system while permitting creativity in site design, the U.S. Federal Housing Administration developed a land-use intensity (LUI) system in the 1960s for mortgage guarantee purposes. The LUI ratios are described in Table 3-28.

Some communities apply FARs to residential as well as nonresidential developments. In addition, residential densities can be calculated on the basis of floor areas in order to create design flexibility. For example, Boulder, Colorado, eliminates the application of minimum lot size and site area to dwelling unit ratios in "developing" and "redeveloping districts," and computes the permissible number of dwelling units as follows[45]:

n = (f x a) ÷ ([f x os] + [f x p] + u)

where:

n = number of dwelling units permitted;

f = number of floors;

a = site area;

os = required minimum open space per dwelling unit;

p = required minimum parking area; and

u = average size of dwelling units and common areas.

This formulation allows the developer to increase the permissible number of dwelling units in a number of ways, such as by increasing building height (which

Table 3-29
Building Volume Ratio

Building volume ratio	((VB + VP + VL + VE) ÷ 10) ÷ gross/net site area where: VB = building volume (exterior walls); VP = parking area x 5; VL = loading area x truck heights; and VE = exterior storage x stack heights.

increases the numerator) or by installing parking facilities underground (which reduces the denominator).

Since their introduction in the 1960s, some observers have suggested revisions to the use of performance standards. FAR measurements often fail to take into consideration parking, loading, and exterior storage areas, which can render a project that meets the minimum requirements of the zoning ordinance out of scale with its environs and is destructive of critical natural resources. The building volume ratio (BVR) described in a recent APA report provides a measure of the true bulk of all land uses on the site.[46] BVR adds the bulk of all buildings on the site to parking and loading-area volumes, including anticipated volumes added by cars and trucks, and divides the sum by 10 in order to equate a ratio of one to a building covering the entire site to a height of 10 feet.[47] The result is a fairly accurate measurement of total project scale and bulk on full occupancy and use (see Table 3-29).

Performance standards can provide an accurate and flexible mechanism for linking the goals and policies of the comprehensive plan with new development. Performance standards can also serve a wide range of public purposes, such as protecting the environment, preventing public facilities congestion, preserving community scale and character, and providing a variety of housing and nonresidential choices. Performance zoning also allows for creative site design and market flexibility while establishing enforceable rules.

As the discussion above illustrates, performance standards and LUI ratios can become quite complicated. In addition, the numeric standards, while precise, do not always relate well to the appearance of a building or its relation to the public realm. For this reason, performance standards in the LDC are restricted to areas characterized by environmentally sensitive lands, such as riparian buffers, floodplains, steep slopes, and similar areas.

BUILDING ENVELOPE

Restrictions on building envelope include regulations governing height, floor area, and lot coverage. These controls are expressly or implicitly authorized in every state.[48]

Many zoning ordinances establish fairly low permitted building heights in order to maintain neighborhood character. Buildings, such as towers and steeples, which form vistas, may be exempt from height requirements.

Many new urbanist codes control height by setting a maximum number of stories rather than a uniform height requirement. The rationale for this requirement has never been clearly articulated, although it seems to be based on an assumption that this allows more careful control of building design. Regulation by a number of stories is thought to permit more design discretion than is permitted by traditional 24- to 35-foot heights permitted in residential and lower-intensity commercial zones.[49] If height is controlled by stories, a minimum and maximum floor-to-ceiling height should be required for each story. Excessive floor-to-ceiling heights can create a "big-box" appearance, while smaller heights may permit more intensity than is intended by the code.[50] For residential zones and transitional commercial areas, a primary and secondary height is established in order to control scale, require façade articulation, and maintain the flexibility to provide necessary building intensities.

NOTES

1. *North American Industry Classification System-United States* ("*1997 NAICS Manual*") (Washington, DC: Executive Office of the President, Office of Management and Budget, 1997).
2. *Village of Euclid v. Ambler Realty*, 272 U.S. 365 (1926).
3. *Kosinski v. Lawlor*, 418 A.2d 66, 68, 177 Conn. 420, 423 (1979) (The canons of statutory construction require that the regulations be construed as a whole, since particular words or sections, and especially the "purpose and findings" statements, when considered separately, may be insufficient to provide reasonably precise standards. Thus, the commission may base its denial on the "purpose and findings" statement only in conjunction with, and not as an alternative to, the substantive standards set forth in the applicable zoning regulations). Also, *Hock v. Board of Sup'rs of Mount Pleasant Township*, 622 A.2d 431 (Pa. Commw. 1993) (a significant factor in determining the reasonableness of a land-use restriction is whether the restriction is consistent with the stated purpose of the particular zoning district).
4. See, e.g., N.C.G.S. § 153A-342.
5. *Woodhouse v. Board of Commissioners of Town of Nag's Head*, 299 N.C. 211, 261 S.E.2d 882 (1980).
6. Note 5 (*Woodhouse*), supra.
7. Note 4 (N.C.G.S.), supra.
8. *City of Pharr v. Tippitt*, 616 S.W.2d 173, 177 (Tex. 1981).
9. 105 Utah 111, 141 P.2d 704, 149 A.L.R. 282 (1943).
10. Id.
11. *Purser v. Mecklenburg County*, 127 N.C. App. 63, 488 S.E.2d 277 (1997); *Giger v. City of Omaha*, 232 Neb. 676, 442 N.W.2d 182 (1989).
12. Robert H. Freilich, "Awakening the Sleeping Giant: New Trends and Development in Environmental and Land Use

Controls," in *Institute on Planning, Zoning, and Eminent Domain* (Dayton, OH: LexisNexis Matthew Bender, 1974), 1.
13. Comment, "Bonus or Incentive Zoning Legal Implications," 21 *Syracuse L. Rev.* 895 (1970).
14. The disadvantage is that the reader must consult two different places in the ordinance to read all of the regulations applicable to the district. This issue can be resolved with administrative handbooks for specific districts.
15. This is not to imply that the concept of use segregation is ideal. There is a constituency in a jurisdiction to eliminate the use segregation standards of the zoning districts.
16. *Cyclone Sand & Gravel v. ZBA of the City of Ames*, 351 N.W.2d 778 (Iowa, 1984). See also Edward H. Ziegler, Jr., *Rathkopf's The Law of Zoning and Planning*, 4th ed. (St. Paul, MN: Thomson West, 2004), § 41:4 (the purpose of a conditional use is to permit uses that are necessary, desirable, or convenient, but which may have negative externalities); Kenneth H. Young, *Anderson's American Law of Zoning*, 4th ed. (Deerfield, IL: Clark Boardman Callaghan, 1996), § 21.01 (special development approvals involve uses that are permitted rather than proscribed; the purpose is to reduce the impact on surrounding areas and control "troublesome uses").
17. *Blades v. City of Raleigh*, 280 N.C. 531, 187 S.E.2d 35 (1972); *American Nat'l Bank & Trust Co. v. Arlington Heights*, 450 N.E.2nd 898 (Ill. App. 1983).
18. *Chrismon v. Guilford County*, 322 N.C.611, 370 S.E.2d 579 (1988); *Scrutton v. County of Sacramento*, 79 Cal.Rptr. 872 (Cal. App. 1969); Judith W. Wegner, "Moving Toward the Bargaining Table: Contract Zoning Development Agreements and the Theoretical Foundations of Government Land Use Deals," 65 *N.C. L. Rev.* 957, 983-84 (1987). The conditional use district's procedure is also expressly authorized by city and county zoning enabling legislation. N.C.G.S. §§ 153A-342 and 160A-382.
19. It is typically estimated that 15 to 30 percent of developed land is devoted to streets and rights-of-way, environmentally restricted areas, or other undeveloped areas. Accordingly, development potential is actually restricted more than what is suggested as a simple division of minimum lot size into gross land area.
20. See, e.g., John Mixon, James L. Dougherty, Jr., and Brenda McDonald, *Texas Municipal Zoning Law*, 3d ed. (Carlsbad, CA: Michie Publications, 1999), § 7.101.
21. *Gorieb v. Fox*, 274 U.S. 603 (1927).
22. For an excellent summary, with case citations, see Edward H. Ziegler, Jr., et al., *Rathkopf's The Law of Zoning and Planning, Vol. 3* (St. Paul, MN: Thomson West, 2004), § 53:2.
23. See Paul Craighead, ed., *The Hidden Design in Land Use Ordinances* (Portland: University of Southern Maine, 1991), at 45; Randall Arendt, *Rural by Design* (Chicago: American Planning Association, 1994), at 10-11.
24. Rick Pruetz, "Transfer of Development Rights Update," in Proceedings of the 1999 American Planning Association National Conference, available on-line at www.asu.edu/caed/proceedings99/PRUETZ/PRUETZ.HTM.
25. *Appeal of Buckingham Developers*, 61 Pa. Commw. 408, 433 A.2d 931 (1981); *West Montgomery County Citizens Association v. Maryland National Capital Park & Planning Comm'n*, 309 Md. 183, 522 A.2d 1328 (1987) (invalidating transfer of development rights ordinance under doctrine of improper delegation of authority, but noting that the ordinance could be remedied by changes to zoning text).
26. Donald G. Hagman and Dean J. Miscynski, *Windfalls for Wipeouts: Land Value Capture and Compensation* (Chicago: American Society Planning Association, 1978); John J. Costonis, "Development Rights Transfer: An Exploratory Essay," 83 *Yale L. J.* 75 (1983); Dwight H. Merriam, "Making TDR Work," 56 *N.C. L. Rev.* 77 (1978).
27. Robert H. Freilich and Michael Quinn, "Effectiveness of Flexible and Conditional Zoning Techniques—What They Can and What They Cannot Do For Our Cities," in *Institute on Planning, Zoning, and Eminent Domain* (Dayton, OH: LexisNexis Matthew Bender, 1979), 167, 231-39; Richard J. Roddewig and Cheryl A. Inghram, "Transferable Development Rights Programs: TDRs and the Real Estate Marketplace," Planning Advisory Service Report No. 401 (Chicago: American Planning Association, 1987).
28. *Pennsylvania Coal Co. v. Mahon*, 260 U.S. 293 (1922).
29. Robert Freilich and Wayne Senville, "Takings, TDRs, and Environmental Preservation: 'Fairness' and the Hollywood North Beach Case," 35 *Land Use L. & Zon. Dig.* 9, at 4 (1983); Note, "Transfer of the Relevant Right: A Remedy for Prior Excessive Subdivision," 10 *U.C. Davis J. Int'l L. & Pol'y* 1 (1977); Note, "Transfer of Development Rights as Reasonable Beneficial Use of Property," 10 *U.C. Davis J. Int'l L. & Pol'y* 23 (1977).
30. *Penn Central Transportation Co. v. New York City*, 438 U.S. 104, 137 (1978).
31. John J. Costonis, "'Fair' Compensation and the Accommodation Power: Antidotes for the Taking Impasse in Land Use Controversies," 75 *Colum. L. Rev.* 1021, 1062 (1975).
32. See *City of Hollywood v. Hollywood, Inc.*, 432 So.2d 1332 (Fla. App. 1983) (environmentally sensitive lands); *Matlack v. Burlington County Freeholders Board*, 191 N.J. Super. 236, 466 A.2d 83 (1982) aff'd., 194 N.J. Super. 359, 476 A.2d 1262 (1984) (open space); and *Appeal of Buckingham Developers Inc.*, 61 Pa. Commw. 408, 433 A.2d 931 (1981).
33. See *Keystone Bituminous Coal Assoc. v. DeBenedictus*, 107 S.Ct. 1232 (1987).
34. Note 27 (Roddewig/Inghram), supra, 26-27.
35. Franklin J. James and Dennis E. Gale, *Zoning For Sale: A Critical Analysis of Transfer Development Rights Programs* (Washington, DC: Urban Institute, Land Use Series, 1997).
36. N.J. Stat. Ann. §§ 13:18A-30 to 13:18A-49 (West Supp. 1989).
37. See *Fred F. French Inv. Co. v. City of New York*, 39 N.Y.2d 587, 597, 350 N.E.2d 381, 388, *diss'd.*, 429 U.S. 990 (1976).
38. See *DuFour v. Montgomery County*, Law Nos. 56964, 56968, 56969, 56970, and 56983 (Montgomery County, Maryland, Circuit Court, January 20, 1983). While the transfer of development rights (TDR) program provided for the creation of a bank, no bank had been established at the time of the lawsuit. The court held that the downzoning did not amount to a taking in itself, and that the absence of a bank did not change that result because TDRs are, in effect, an "unnecessary optional bonus." John J. Delaney, William Kominers, and Larry A. Gordon, "TDR Redux: A Second Generation of Practical Legal Concerns," 15 *Urb. Law.* 593, 605 (1983).

39. Appropriate data and information include existing land use (*Appeal of Buckingham Developers, Inc.*, 61 Pa. Commw. 408, 433 A.2d 931 (1981)); existing densities in sending and receiving zones (*City of Hollywood v. Hollywood, Inc.*, 432 So.2d 1332 (Fla. Dist. Ct. App. 1983) and *Appeal of Buckingham Developers*, supra); traffic (*City of Hollywood*, supra); water and sewer capacity (*City of Hollywood*, supra); fire and police protection (*City of Hollywood*, supra, and *A Local & Regional Monitor v. City of Los Angeles*, 16 Cal.Rptr.2d 358 (Cal. App. 1993)); open space protection (*Appeal of Buckingham Developers*, supra, and *Matlock v. Burlington County Freeholders Board*, 191 N.J. Super. 236, 466 A.2d 83 (1982)); aesthetics (*Penn Central Transportation Co. v. New York City*, 438 U.S. 104 (1978)); recent development activity (*Penn Central*, supra); and potential land use as evidenced by adopted plans and market demand (*Matlock*, supra).

40. Douglas R. Porter, P. Phillips, and T. Lassar, *Flexible Zoning: How it Works* (Washington, DC: Urban Land Institute, 1988); Lane Kendig et al., *Performance Zoning* (Chicago: American Planning Association, 1980).

41. See, e.g., *Ginsburg Development Corp. v. Town Bd. of Town of Cortlandt*, 565 N.Y.S.2d 371 (N.Y.Sup. 1990).

42. *Jones v. Zoning Hearing Board of Town of McCandless*, 134 Pa. Commw. 435, 578 A.2d 1369 (1990).

43. *Coscan Washington, Inc. v. Maryland-National Capital Park & Planning Comm'n*, 87 Md. App. 602, 590 A.2d 1080 (1991).

44. Devon M. Schneider, David R. Godschalk, and Norman Axler, "The Carrying Capacity Concept as a Planning Tool," Planning Advisory Service Report No. 338 (Chicago: American Planning Association, December 1978).

45. Boulder, Colorado, Rev. Code, Title 9, App. "B" (1981).

46. Lane Kendig, "New Standards for Nonresidential Uses," Planning Advisory Service Report No. 405 (Chicago: American Planning Association, 1987), at 9.

47. Id., at 8-9.

48. Note 22 (Ziegler), supra, § 54:3.

49. See Fenno Hoffman, posted to Pro-Urb listserve at www.listserv.uga.edu (Nov. 6, 2003).

50. Note 22 (Ziegler), supra, § 54:2, note 6.

CHAPTER

4

Procedures

4.0 PURPOSE AND FINDINGS

The purpose of this chapter is to consolidate the procedures for filing and processing applications for development approval. The format is designed to allow users to quickly and efficiently ascertain the various steps involved in obtaining development approval—from the initiation and filing of an application, the administrative completeness review, the review for compliance with substantive standards, through the public hearings.

- *Division 1: General*
- *Division 3: Ministerial Development Approvals*
- *Division 4: Zoning Procedures*
- *Division 5: Subdivisions*
- *Division 6: Variances and Appeals*
- *Division 7: Miscellaneous Development Orders*
- *Division 8: Enforcement, Violations, and Penalties*

The provisions of this chapter are designed to implement the comprehensive plan elements (i.e., land use, administrative circulating, natural resources, housing, implementation, economic development, agricultural, environmental, and all subarea (specific neighborhood) and functional (transportation, redevelopment, utility, and downtown) plans).

DIVISION 1: GENERAL

4.1 PROCEDURAL REQUIREMENTS

4.1.1 Generally

No development or development activity is permitted unless all development approvals applicable to the proposed development are issued in accordance with this chapter. Development approvals are required for all development, unless otherwise excepted, to ensure compliance with the various adopted codes, standards, and laws, and to ensure consistency with the comprehensive plan and policies of the city. This division describes procedural elements common to all applications. The specific procedures followed in reviewing various applications for development approval differ. Reference shall be made to the appropriate section in this chapter, which addresses the procedures and requirements of a particular application. Generally, the procedures for all applications have five common elements:

(1) Submittal of a complete application, including required fee payments and appropriate information and studies;

(2) Review of the submittal by appropriate staff, agencies, and boards;

(3) A decision to approve, approve with conditions, or deny together with the description of the actions authorized and the time period for exercising rights;

(4) If necessary, amending or appealing the decision; and

(5) Recording the decision.

Figure 4-1 is a flow chart illustrating the general review process.

4.1.2 Appeals

This division describes procedural elements common to all applications. *Division 3: Ministerial Development Approvals* through *Division 8: Enforcement, Violations, and Penalties* describe the procedures for processing certain types of

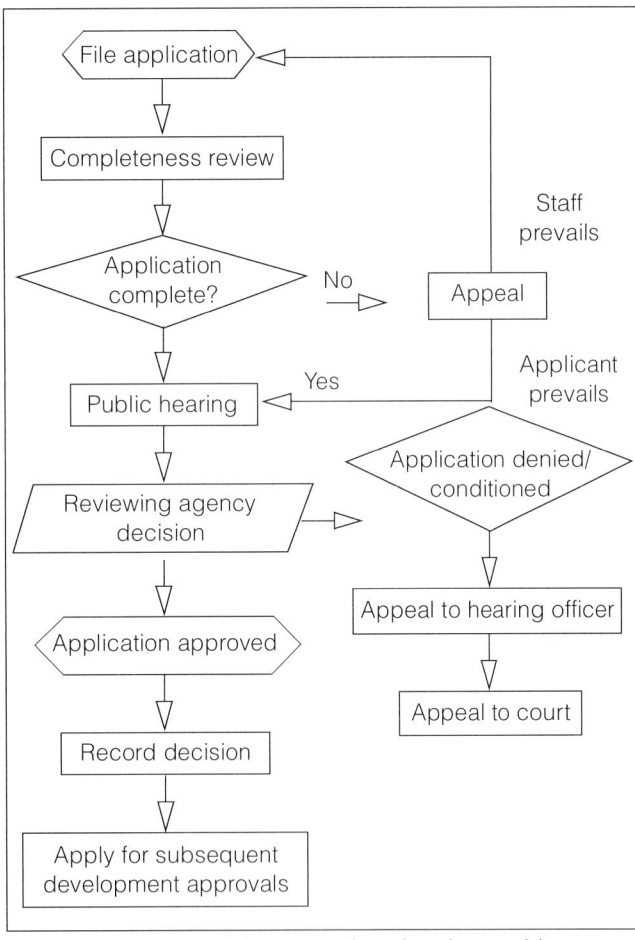

**Figure 4-1
Development Approval Application Flow Chart**

Flow charts in permitting manuals or brochures aid applicants in understanding the process.

applications. Each division or section relating to procedure provides the following information:

(A) *Initiation:* This describes how the application for the development approval is filed.

(B) *Preapplication procedures:* This describes the procedure for discussions with appropriate staff as to requirements for application submittal and compliance with the Land Development Code (LDC).

(C) *Completeness review:* This describes the process for determining whether sufficient information has been submitted in order to process an application, which includes the required fee payment and appropriate information. A determination that an application is complete or incomplete does not constitute a determination as to whether the application complies with the standards for approval of the application.

(D) *Decision:* This describes the procedures for review of the submittal by appropriate staff, agencies, and boards, and for reaching a determination as to whether the application for development approval is approved, denied, or approved with conditions.

(E) *Approval criteria:* This lists the criteria for approval of the particular application. These criteria supplement and do not displace any other criteria required by this chapter for approval of the application.

(F) *Subsequent applications:* This provides time periods for processing of renewal applications.

(G) *Scope of approval:* This indicates the rights that an applicant obtains from approval or conditional approval of an application, what actions the development approval authorizes, and the time period for exercising rights under the order or development approval.

(H) *Recording procedures:* This describes how the decision on the application is recorded or filed in the public records.

4.2 CATEGORIES OF DEVELOPMENT APPROVALS

There are three basic categories of development approvals pursuant to this chapter, defined in § 4.2.1 Legislative Development Approvals, § 4.2.2 Quasi-judicial Development Approval, and § 4.2.3 Ministerial Development Approvals.

4.2.1 Legislative Development Approvals

Legislative development approvals involve a change in land-use policy. A public hearing is required but the procedural requirements of a quasi-judicial hearing do not apply. Legislative development approvals include any change in the comprehensive or specific plan, any change to the text of the LDC, any rezoning, and any creation of a "PD" (Planned Development) district or floating zone.

4.2.2 Quasi-judicial Development Approval

A quasi-judicial development approval involves the application of a discretionary standard required by this chapter to an application. It requires a public hearing. Procedural due process requirements apply as established in § 4.4 Notice Provisions of this chapter. Examples include master development approvals, conditional use permits (CUPs), variances, and administrative appeals.

4.2.3 Ministerial Development Approvals

Ministerial development approvals involve the application of the standards of the LDC to an application by an administrative official or agency. A public hearing is not required. A ministerial development approval typically occurs late in the development approval process. Examples include building permits and certificates of occupancy.

4.3 COMPLETENESS REVIEW

This section applies to any application, unless otherwise provided in the regulations for the specific application.

4.3.1 Preapplication Conference

Before any application is filed with the [PLANNING OFFICIAL], any applicant for a legislative or quasi-judicial development approval shall attend a preapplication meeting with the [PLANNING OFFICIAL]. The purpose of the preapplication meeting is to discuss, in general, the procedures and substantive requirements for the application.

4.3.2 Application Materials

No application is complete unless all of the information required by Appendix B, Specifications for Documents to Be Submitted, of the LDC is included and all filing fees have been paid. An application that includes such information is deemed complete. Current application materials shall be made available in the planning department. Such applications shall be filed in advance of any public hearing neighborhood meeting or public meeting required pursuant to the LDC or statute.

4.3.3 Review Procedures

These procedures shall be used to review any application for completeness unless a different procedure is established elsewhere in this chapter.

4.3.4 Jurisdiction

Unless the provisions pertaining to a particular application prescribe otherwise:

(A) All applications shall be reviewed by the [PLANNING OFFICIAL] for completeness; and

(B) The final determination of the [PLANNING OFFICIAL] on completeness of an application constitutes a final development order and is appealable.

4.3.5 Time Limits by Complete Application

Whenever this chapter establishes a time period for processing an application, such time period does not commence until the [PLANNING OFFICIAL] has reviewed such application for completeness in order to determine whether the application has been properly submitted, the applicant has corrected all deficiencies in the application, and the [PLANNING OFFICIAL] has issued a certificate of completeness. Review for completeness of application forms is solely for the purpose of determining whether preliminary information required for submission with the application is sufficient to allow further processing, and shall not constitute a decision as to whether application complies with the provisions of the LDC.

4.3.6 Review by [PLANNING OFFICIAL]

(A) Unless a different procedure is described in this chapter, this section applies to the review of an application for completeness.

(B) Not later than 15 working days after the [PLANNING OFFICIAL] has received an application, the [PLANNING OFFICIAL] shall determine in writing whether the application is complete and shall immediately transmit the determination to the applicant. Unless the application requires review by any other local or special district, or regional, state, or federal agency or entity, the [PLANNING OFFICIAL] shall within five workings days transmit the application to such agency or entity requesting written comments within 15 working days. In such case, the [PLANNING OFFICIAL] shall have 30 days to render his/her decision. If the written determination is not made within the 15- or 30-day period, whichever is applicable, after receipt of the application, the application shall be deemed complete for purposes of this chapter. Upon receipt of any resubmittal of the application, a new five-day period shall begin, during which period the [PLANNING OFFICIAL] shall determine the completeness of the application. If the application is determined not to be complete, the [PLANNING OFFICIAL]'s determination shall specify those parts of the application that are incomplete and shall indicate the manner in which they can be made complete, including a list and thorough description of the specific information needed to complete the application. The applicant shall submit materials to the [PLANNING OFFICIAL] in response to the list and description.

(C) If the application, together with the submitted materials, are determined not to be complete, the [PLANNING OFFICIAL] shall specify in writing the information required and the applicant may resubmit the application with the information required by the [PLANNING OFFICIAL] or may appeal that decision in writing to the appellate agency as follows:

(1) *Legislative development applications:* to the planning commission; and

(2) *Quasi-judicial development applications:* to the board of appeals.

(D) The appellate agency shall render a final written determination on the appeal not later than the next available meeting after receipt of the applicant's written appeal. Notwithstanding a decision by the [PLANNING OFFICIAL] that the application and submitted materials are incomplete, if the final written determination on the appeal is not made within 30 working days after the appellate agency's initial meeting, the application with the submitted materials shall be deemed complete for the purposes of this chapter.

(E) Nothing in this section precludes an applicant and the [PLANNING OFFICIAL] from mutually agreeing to an extension of any time limit provided by this section.

4.3.7 Time Limits

If the reviewing agency fails to act within the time period required for completeness review, the application is deemed complete.

4.3.8 Limitation on Further Information Requests

After the [PLANNING OFFICIAL] or the appellate agency accepts a development application as complete, the [PLANNING OFFICIAL] or the reviewing agency may, in the course of processing the application, request the applicant to clarify, amplify, correct, or otherwise supplement the information required for the application, if such would be required by the agency to render a final determination on the merits.

4.3.9 Traffic Impact Reports or Analyses

4.3.9.1 General

The intent of this section is to provide the information necessary to allow decision-makers to assess the transportation implications of site-generated traffic associated with a proposed development. The goal is to address the transportation-related issues associated with development proposals that may be of concern to neighboring residents, business owners, and property owners, and to provide a basis for negotiation regarding improvements and funding participation in conjunction with an application for development.

The isolated and cumulative impact of the proposed development needs to be understood in relation to the existing and proposed capacity of the street system, and to ensure that traffic congestion will be maintained at reasonable levels so as not to hinder the passage of public safety vehicles, degrade the quality of life, or contribute to hazardous traffic conditions. This section establishes requirements for the analysis and evaluation of transportation impacts associated with proposed developments.

4.3.9.2 Purpose

Purpose and findings: The purpose of the traffic impact report is to identify the impacts on capacity, level of service (LOS), and safety, which are likely to be created by a proposed development. A traffic impact report should identify the improvements needed to:

(A) Ensure safe ingress to and egress from a site;

(B) Maintain adequate street capacity on adjacent public streets;

(C) Ensure safe and reasonable traffic operating conditions on streets and at intersections in the vicinity of a proposed development;

(D) Avoid creation of or mitigate existing hazardous traffic conditions;

(E) Minimize the impact of nonresidential traffic on residential neighborhoods in the community; and

(F) Protect the substantial public investment in the existing street system.

4.3.9.3 Types of Studies

Traffic impact studies may be required at several stages in the development process. No application for development will be accepted without an appropriate traffic impact report. The types of traffic impact reports required under the ordinance are as follows:

(A) A traffic impact report will be required for any application for a development order for any change in the comprehensive or specific plan, any change to the text of the LDC, any rezoning, or any creation of a proposed development or floating zone. The purpose of such study will be to evaluate whether adequate transportation capacity exists or will be available within a reasonable time period to safely and conveniently accommodate proposed uses permitted under the requested land-use or zoning classification.

(B) A traffic impact report will also be required for certain permitted and conditional uses and major subdivisions exceeding specific trip generation thresholds. The purpose of a traffic impact report will be to:

(1) Evaluate traffic operations and impacts at site access points under projected traffic loads;

(2) Evaluate the impact of site-generated traffic on affected intersections in the vicinity of the development site;

(3) Evaluate the impact of site-generated traffic on the quality of traffic flow on public streets located in the vicinity of the site;

(4) Evaluate the impact of the proposed development on residential streets in the vicinity of the site;

(5) Ensure that site access and other improvements needed to mitigate the traffic impact of the development meet commonly accepted engineering design standards and access management criteria; and

(6) Ensure that adequate facilities for pedestrians, transit users, and bicyclists have been provided.

(C) All land subdivisions that do not require a traffic impact report will be required to complete a traffic design analysis. The purpose of a traffic design analysis will be to:

(1) Ensure that the proposed street layout is consistent with the public roadway design standards;

(2) Ensure the proper design and spacing of site access points and identify where limitations on access should be established;

(3) Ensure that potential safety problems have been properly evaluated and addressed;

(4) Ensure that internal circulation patterns will not interfere with traffic flow on existing public streets; and

(5) Ensure that appropriate facilities for pedestrians, transit users, and bicyclists have been provided in plans for the development.

4.3.9.4 Applicability

(A) A traffic impact report shall also be required for any major subdivision, CUP, or site plan under the following described conditions:

(1) A proposed rezoning that could generate 150 or more directional trips during the peak hour or at least 1,000 more trips per day than the most intensive use that could be developed under existing zoning;

(2) A project on a site located along, or which has the potential to take access within 500 feet of, a corridor identified as a freeway or expressway on the thoroughfare plan; or

(3) A proposed development for a 3.5-acre or larger site.

(B) Where a traffic impact report is required, the acceptance of the application for the purposes of beginning the mandatory 60-day time limit applicable to action shall not commence until the traffic impact report has been reviewed for completeness and has been accepted by the [PLANNING OFFICIAL] as meeting the content requirements of the LDC. The applicant shall be notified within 10 days if the traffic impact report is found to be inadequate.

(C) Traffic design analysis shall be required for any subdivision or general development plan for which a traffic impact report is not required. Traffic design analyses completed at an early stage of development may need to be updated to include more detail as development plans become more specific or approval actions result in the reformulation of plans. As part of the review for determining whether a development application is complete, proposals for which an earlier traffic design analysis or traffic impact report has been completed will be reviewed to insure consistency with previous approvals or to identify the need for revision or refinement of previously completed analyses or reports.

4.3.9.5 Waiver

The requirements of this section for a traffic impact report may be waived by the [LOCAL GOVERNMENT] engineer upon a determination that such report is not necessary to determine needed road improvements or that no unsafe or hazardous conditions will be created by the development as proposed. Developments in the central development core district that are not required to provide on-site, off-street parking are exempt from the requirements of this section.

4.3.9.6 Preparation

The applicant may choose to have a traffic impact report prepared by a qualified professional with experience in the preparation of such analysis, or may choose to have the [PLANNING OFFICIAL] prepare a report once the development application is submitted. Where the applicant chooses to have the [PLANNING OFFICIAL] prepare the report, the time frame for the [PLANNING OFFICIAL] to render a decision shall be extended by 45 days to permit time to prepare the report. The applicant shall be responsible for the costs of preparation of the traffic study incurred by the [PLANNING OFFICIAL].

4.3.9.7 Traffic Service Standards

The standards for traffic service that shall be used to evaluate the findings of traffic impact reports or analyses are as follows:

(A) *Capacity:* A volume-to-capacity (V/C) ratio of 0.80 shall not be consistently exceeded on any freeway or expressway as designated on the thoroughfare plan, and a V/C ratio of 0.90 shall not be consistently exceeded on any arterial or collector street as designated on the thoroughfare plan. "Consistently" means that the V/C ratios are exceeded based on average daily peak-hour traffic counts, projections, or estimates.

(B) *Level of service:* For corridors, including mainline, merging areas, and ramp junctions, an LOS C shall be maintained on any expressway, freeway, or arterial, and an LOS D on any other designated nonlocal street on the thoroughfare plan. At all intersections, an LOS C shall be maintained on any arterial or higher-order street and an LOS D on any other nonresidential street. Where the existing LOS is below these standards, the traffic impact report shall identify those improvements or transportation demand management techniques needed to maintain the existing LOS, and what additional improvements would be needed to raise the LOS to the standards indicated.

(C) *Number of access points:* The number of access points provided shall be the minimum needed to provide adequate access capacity for the site. Evidence of LOS D operations for individual public street movements at access locations is a primary indication of the need for additional access points. However, the spacing and geometric design of all access points shall be consistent with the access management criteria of the LDC.

(D) *Residential street impact:* Average daily traffic on residential streets shall be within the ranges spelled out in the thoroughfare plan for the class of street involved. No nonresidential development shall increase the traffic on a residential street with at least 300 average daily trips by more than 25 percent, and shall contribute no more than 20 percent of the traffic on any street segment providing residential access.

(E) *Traffic flow and progression:* The location of new traffic signals or proposed changes to cycle lengths or timing patterns of existing signals to meet LOS standards shall not interfere with the goal of achieving adequate traffic progression on major public streets in the vicinity of the development.

(F) *Vehicle storage:* The capacity of storage bays and auxiliary lanes for turning traffic shall be adequate to insure that turning traffic will not interfere with through traffic flows on any public street.

(G) *Internal circulation:* On-site vehicle circulation and parking patterns shall be designed so as not to interfere with the flow of traffic on any public street and shall accommodate all anticipated types of site traffic.

(H) *Safety:* Access points shall be designed to provide for adequate sight distance and appropriate facilities to accommodate acceleration and deceleration of site traffic. Where traffic from the proposed development will impact any location with an incidence of high accident frequency (defined as one of the five to 10 highest accident locations in the area), the accident history should be evaluated and a determination made that the proposed site access or additional site traffic will not further aggravate the situation. It is understood that the correction of an existing off-site safety deficiency is not typically the responsibility of the developer.

4.3.9.8 Contents

A traffic impact report shall contain information addressing the factors listed in subsections (A) through (I), below:

(A) *Site description:* The traffic impact report shall contain illustrations and narratives that describe the characteristics of the site and adjacent land uses as well as expected development in the vicinity that will influence future traffic conditions. A description of potential uses and traffic generation to be evaluated shall be provided. A description of the proposed development, including access plans, staging plans, and an indication of land use and intensity, shall be provided.

(B) *Study area:* The traffic impact report shall identify the geographic area under study and identify the roadway segments, critical intersections, and access points to be analyzed. The focus shall be on intersections and access points adjacent to the site. Roadways or intersections within 1/2 mile of the site, where at least 5 percent of the existing peak-hour capacity will be composed of trips generated by the proposed development, shall be included in the analysis.

(C) *Existing traffic conditions:* The traffic impact report shall contain a summary of the data utilized in the study and an analysis of existing traffic conditions, including:

(1) Traffic count and turning movement information, including the source of and date when traffic count information was collected;

(2) Correction factors that were used to convert collected traffic data into representative design-hour traffic volumes;

(3) Roadway characteristics, including the design configuration of existing or proposed roadways, existing traffic control measures (e.g., speed limits and traffic signals), and existing driveways and turning movement conflicts in the vicinity of the site; and

(4) Identification of the existing LOS for roadways and intersections without project development traffic using methods documented in the *Highway Capacity Manual 2000*[1] or comparable accepted methods of evaluation. LOS should be calculated for the weekday peak hour and, in the case of uses generating high levels of weekend traffic, the Saturday peak hour.

(D) *Horizon year(s) and background traffic growth:* The traffic impact report shall identify the horizon year(s) that were analyzed in the study, the background traffic growth factors for each horizon year, and the method and assumptions used to develop the background traffic growth. Unless otherwise approved by the [PLANNING OFFICIAL], the impact of development shall be analyzed for the year after the development is completed and 10 years after the development is completed.

(E) *Time periods to be analyzed:* For each defined horizon year, specific time periods are to be analyzed. For most land uses, this time period will be the weekday peak hours. However, certain uses (e.g., major retail centers, schools, or recreational uses) will have characteristic peak hours different than that found for adjacent streets, and these unique peak hours may need to be analyzed to determine factors, such as proper site access and turn lane storage requirements. The [PLANNING OFFICIAL] shall be consulted for determination of the peak hours to be studied.

(F) *Trip generation, reduction, and distribution:* The traffic impact report shall summarize the projected peak hour and average daily trip generation for the proposed development and illustrate the projected trip distribution of trips to and from the site, and should identify the basis of the trip generation, reduction, and distribution factors used in the study.

(G) *Traffic assignment:* The traffic impact report shall identify projected design-hour traffic volumes for roadway segments, intersections, or driveways in the study area, with and without the proposed development, for the horizon year(s) of the study.

(H) *Impact analysis:* The traffic impact report shall address the impact of traffic volumes of the projected horizon year(s) relative to each of the applicable traffic service standards and shall identify the methodology utilized to evaluate the impact. The weekday peak-hour impact shall be evaluated as well as the Saturday peak hour for those uses exhibiting high levels of weekend traffic generation.

(I) *Mitigation/alternatives:* In situations where the traffic LOS standards are exceeded, the traffic impact report shall evaluate each of the following alternatives for achieving the traffic service standards by:

(1) Identifying where additional rights-of-way are needed to implement mitigation strategies;

(2) Identifying suggested phasing of improvements where needed to maintain compliance with traffic service standards; and

(3) Identifying the anticipated cost of recommended improvements.

4.3.9.9 Process for the Review and Preparation of a Traffic Impact Report

This section provides an outline of the steps to be included in the preparation and review of a traffic impact report.

(A) The city engineer and zoning administrator shall be consulted for assistance in determining whether a traffic impact report needs to be prepared for a proposed development application.

(B) The city engineer and zoning administrator shall meet with applicants to identify study issues, assumptions, horizon years, and time periods to be analyzed; analysis procedures; available sources of data; past and related studies; report requirements; and other topics relevant to study requirements.

(C) Following initial completion of a traffic impact report, it shall be submitted to the zoning administrator for distribution to the staff of all roadway jurisdictions involved in the construction and maintenance of public roadways serving the development.

(D) Within 10 working days, staff shall complete an initial review to determine the completeness of the study and shall provide a written summary to the applicant outlining the need for any supplemental analysis to adequately address the traffic service standards. A meeting to discuss the contents and findings of the traffic impact report and the need for additional analyses may be requested by the applicant.

(E) Following a determination that the technical analysis is complete, staff shall prepare a report outlining recommendations that have been developed to address the findings and conclusions included in the study regarding the proposed development's access needs and impacts on the transportation system. Depending on the type of traffic study, presentation of recommendations to the planning commission and/or city council may proceed as follows:

(1) For a traffic rezoning analysis, staff recommendations will be presented as part of the staff report to the planning commission and city council as part of the proceedings on a rezoning or land-use plan application;

(2) For a traffic impact report, a separate report will be forwarded to the city council for consideration of the recommendations; and

(3) For a traffic design analysis, staff recommendations will be presented as part of the staff report to the planning commission or city council for any land subdivision or general development plan.

(F) Negotiations based on the conclusions and findings resulting from the traffic impact report or analysis shall be held with the city council. A development agreement, detailing the applicant's responsibilities and the city's responsibilities for implementing identified mitigation measures, shall be prepared following the negotiations for action by both parties.

4.3.9.10 Report Findings

(A) If staff finds that the proposed development will not meet applicable service-level standards, staff shall recommend one or more of the following actions by the public or the applicant:

(1) Reduce the size, scale, scope, or density of the development to reduce traffic generation;

(2) Divide the project into phases and authorize only one phase at a time until traffic capacity is adequate for the next phase of development;

(3) Dedicate a right-of-way for street improvements;

(4) Construct new streets;

(5) Expand the capacity of existing streets;

(6) Redesign ingress and egress to the project to reduce traffic conflicts;

(7) Alter the use and type of development to reduce peak-hour traffic;

(8) Reduce background (existing) traffic;

(9) Eliminate the potential for additional traffic generation from undeveloped properties in the vicinity of the proposed development;

(10) Integrate design components (e.g., pedestrian and bicycle paths or transit improvements) to reduce vehicular trip generation;

(11) Implement traffic demand management strategies (e.g., carpool or vanpool programs, flex time, staggered work hours, and telecommuting) to reduce vehicular trip generation; and

(12) Recommend denial of the application for development for which the traffic study is submitted.

(B) The planning commission may recommend, and the governing board may adopt, a statement of principle partially or fully exempting a project from meeting the traffic service standards where it finds that the social and/or economic benefits of the project outweigh the adverse impacts of the project. The city council may temporarily exempt certain street locations from some or all of the traffic service standards, owing to special circumstances that make it undesirable or unfeasible to provide further capacity improvements at these locations.

These special circumstances may include a finding that there would be significant negative fiscal, economic, social, or environmental impact from further construction, or that a significant portion of the traffic is generated by development outside the control of the [LOCAL GOVERNMENT]. However, where these conditions exist, the governing board will make every effort to design alternate improvements, and development projects affecting these areas may be required to implement traffic demand management programs and other measures to reduce the impact on these locations as much as possible.

4.4 NOTICE PROVISIONS

4.4.1 Generally

The notice requirements for each type of application are prescribed in the individual subsections of this chapter and/or the state statute. The notice requirements for certain types of public hearings are established in Table 4-1 provided, however, that to the extent of any inconsistency between the provisions of this section and any state statute, the state statute governs.

4.4.2 Contents of Notice

The notice shall state the time, date, and place of hearing, and a description of the property subject to the application that includes, at a minimum:

(A) The street address or, if the street address is unavailable, the legal description by metes and bounds;
(B) The current zoning classification, if any;
(C) The category of development approval requested and a brief description of the proposed development, including density or building intensity, revised zoning classification (if any), and uses requested; and
(D) The real property tax assessment roll parcel number.

4.4.3 Action to Be Consistent with Notice

The reviewing body may take any action on the application that is consistent with the notice given, including approval of the application, conditional approval (if applicable) of the application, or denial of the application.

4.4.4 Minor Amendments Not Requiring Renotification

This section governs to the extent consistent with provisions relating to minor amendments for a specific type of application. The reviewing body may allow minor amendments to the application without resubmittal of the entire application. For purposes of this section, "minor amendments" are amendments that do not:

(A) Increase the number of dwelling units, floor area, height, impervious surface development, or any additional land-use disturbance;
(B) Introduce different land uses than that requested in the application;

Table 4-1
Notice Requirements

(A) Type of Notice	(B) Amendments to Comprehensive Plan or to the Text of This Chapter	(C) Rezoning (Involving Amendments to the Zoning Maps)	(D) Master Site Plan	(E) Appeals to Hearing Officer	(F) Variances from Hearing Officer	(G) Subdivision Plat, Major	(H) Subdivision Plat, Minor	(I) Ministerial Development Approvals, Orders
Publication: Publication in an official newspaper of general circulation must occur before the 15th day before the date of the hearing.	✓	✓	—	✓	✓	✓	—	✓
Mail: Before the 10th day before the hearing date, written notice of the public hearing shall be sent.	—	✓b,c	✓b,c	✓	✓	✓d	—	✓
Internet: A copy of the notice on the city's Web site must be posted until the proceeding has been completed.	✓	✓	✓	✓	✓	✓	✓	✓
Signage: A sign must be posted on the property subject to the application signs to be installed and provided by the [LOCAL GOVERNMENT].a	—	✓	—	—	—	—	—	—

a The sign shall measure at least 4 feet x 4 feet with a caption stating, "Site of Proposed Rezoning," as applicable. The letters shall be at least 8 inches in height and 2 inches in width. The sign must state, "Required by § 4.4.2 Contents of Notice," subsection (B), of this chapter."
b Notice shall be sent to registered neighborhood associations within 200 feet of the project.
c Notice shall be sent to each owner, as indicated by the most recently approved real property assessment tax roll, of real property within 200 feet of the property.
d Notice shall be sent prior to the 15th day before the date of the public hearing. Notice shall be sent only if a plat requires a public hearing with required notice.

✓ = the type of notice prescribed in Column (A) is required for the category of development order prescribed in Columns (B) through (F). A dash ("—") means that the notice is not required.

(C) Request larger land area than indicated in the original application;

(D) Request greater variance than that requested in the application;

(E) Allow any diminution in buffer or transition areas, reduction in landscaping, reduction of required yards, or any change in the design characteristics or materials used in construction of the structures; or

(F) Reduce or eliminate conditions attached to a legislative or quasi-judicial development order unless a new notice is provided.

4.5 PUBLIC HEARING

4.5.1 Applicability

This section applies to any application involving a legislative development order.

4.5.2 Meetings

The planning commission shall hold regularly scheduled public hearings to receive and review public input on all legislative processes required by this chapter. The planning commission shall recommend that the [LOCAL GOVERNMENT] approve, approve with conditions, or deny applications. If a comprehensive area, an LDC amendment, a floating zone, or a rezoning requiring final approval of the [GOVERNING ENTITY] has been duly submitted to the planning commission, and the planning commission has failed to convene a quorum or to make a recommendation approving or denying such action at two consecutive meetings, such action, at the option of the applicant, shall be deemed to be a negative recommendation. The [PLANNING OFFICIAL] shall then submit the application to the [GOVERNING ENTITY] for its consideration.

4.5.3 Records

The [PLANNING OFFICIAL] shall provide for minutes to be written, shall retain the evidence submitted within the hearing time allotted for the item being considered, and shall include a summary of the considerations and the action of the planning commission.

4.5.4 Legislative Body

The [GOVERNING ENTITY] shall hold regularly scheduled public hearings to act upon all items required by this chapter to be considered by the [GOVERNING ENTITY]. The [GOVERNING ENTITY] shall decide whether or not to approve, approve with conditions (if applicable), or deny such applications.

DIVISION 2: QUASI-JUDICIAL AND LEGISLATIVE APPROVALS

4.6 QUASI-JUDICIAL PUBLIC HEARINGS

4.6.1 Generally

This section applies to any application for a master development approval, CUP, variance, appeal, preliminary subdivision plat, or any other action pursuant to this chapter that is considered quasi-judicial under state law. In making quasi-judicial decisions, decision-makers must investigate facts or ascertain the existence of facts, hold hearings, weigh evidence, and draw conclusions from them, as a basis for their official action, and exercise discretion of a judicial nature. In the land-use context, these quasi-judicial decisions involve the application of land-use policies to individual properties as opposed to the creation of policy.

These decisions involve two key elements:

(1) The finding of facts regarding the specific proposal, and

(2) The exercise of discretion in applying the standards of the ordinance.

Due process requirements for quasi-judicial decisions mandate that all fair trial standards be observed when these decisions are made. This includes an evidentiary hearing with the right of the parties to offer evidence; cross-examine adverse witnesses; inspect documents; have sworn testimony; and have written findings of fact supported by competent, substantial, and material evidence.

4.6.2 Conduct of Hearing

Any person or persons may appear at a public hearing and submit evidence, either individually or as a representative. Each person who appears at a public hearing shall take a proper oath and state, for the record, his/her name, address, and, if appearing on behalf of an organization or group, the name and mailing address of the organization or group. The hearing shall be conducted in accordance with the procedures set forth in this subsection. At any point, members of the agency conducting the hearing may ask questions of the applicant, staff, or public, or of any witness, or require cross-examination to be conducted through questions submitted to the chairperson of the agency who will direct the questions to the witness. The order of proceedings is as follows:

(A) The [PLANNING OFFICIAL] or designees shall present a description of the proposed development and the relevant sections of plans and ordinances involved, and set forth the legal or factual issues to be determined. A written or oral recommendation may be given at the opening of the hearing or, in complex cases, may be reserved by the [PLANNING OFFICIAL] or designee until the close of the hearing in order to review the testimonial and document any evidence. The recommendation shall address each factor required by the LDC to be considered prior to development approval;

(B) The applicant shall present such information or evidence that the applicant deems appropriate, subject to reasonable time limits established by the agency;

(C) Public testimony, including expert or lay witnesses on the applicant's behalf, and relevant evidence shall be received;

(D) The [PLANNING OFFICIAL] or other staff member shall not respond to any statement made by the applicant or any public comment during the hearing, but may respond to questions from the agency concerning any statements or evidence received during the deliberations of the agency;

(E) The applicant may reply to any testimony or evidence presented by staff or the public; and

(F) The agency conducting the hearing shall close the public portion of the hearing and conduct deliberations.

4.6.3 Hearing Officer

An agency conducting a quasi-judicial hearing may appoint a hearing officer to conduct the public hearing, make findings of fact and conclusions of law, and file a report with such findings and conclusions to the agency for final action.

4.7 LEGISLATIVE HEARINGS

4.7.1 Generally

Purpose and findings: The purpose of a legislative hearing is to provide the public with an opportunity to be heard consistent with procedures provided by statute. Unlike quasi-judicial hearings, a legislative proceeding does not require due process protections, such as the right of the parties to offer evidence, cross-examination, sworn testimony, or written findings of fact. Similar to quasi-judicial hearings, legislative hearings are public hearings preceded by notice to interested parties. Public hearings are required for legislative review hearings, such as amendments to a comprehensive plan, amendments to this chapter (including zoning provisions of this chapter and the zoning map), and applications for a proposed development.

4.7.2 Conduct of Hearing

The order of the proceedings for a legislative hearing shall be as set forth in § 4.6 Quasi-judicial Public Hearings of this chapter. Testimony may be presented by the applicant, and any member of the public, but need not be submitted under oath or affirmation. The planning commission or [LOCAL GOVERNMENT] may establish a time limit for testimony and may limit testimony where it is repetitive. Each appellate agency may adopt administrative regulations and procedures governing the practice of that agency.

4.7.3 Record of Proceedings

The agency conducting the hearing shall record the minutes of the proceedings by any appropriate means as prescribed by rule and consistent with state law. Such record shall be provided at the request of any person upon application to the [PLANNING OFFICIAL] and payment of a fee set by the [GOVERNING ENTITY] to cover the cost of duplication of the transcribed record.

4.7.4 Appeals

4.7.4.1 Applicability

Any person, including any officer or agency of the [LOCAL GOVERNMENT], aggrieved by a final development order relating to an application for development approval by the [PLANNING OFFICIAL] or other final decision-maker, may appeal such development order to the appellate body designated by this chapter in the manner provided in this section.

4.7.4.2 Notice of Appeal

A notice of appeal shall be filed with the appellate body within 30 days after the development order is filed. The appeal shall contain a written statement of the reasons for which the appellant claims the final decision is erroneous. The appeal shall be accompanied by the fee established by the [GOVERNING ENTITY].

4.7.4.3 Time Limit

The appellate body shall hear and decide the appeal within at least 60 days after the filing of the appeal.

4.8 REVOCATION OF A DEVELOPMENT APPROVAL

4.8.1 Initiation

The [PLANNING OFFICIAL] shall investigate alleged violations of imposed condition or conditions. The [PLANNING OFFICIAL] shall determine whether or not to terminate or suspend a development approval. If the [PLANNING OFFICIAL] determines that a termination, or suspension, of a development approval is appropriate, a recommendation, including the reason or reasons for their determination, shall be made to the agency who shall conduct a public hearing on the matter.

4.8.2 Grounds for Revocation

The following are grounds for revocation of a development approval:

(A) The intentional provision of materially misleading information by the applicant (the provision of information is considered "intentional" where the applicant was aware of the inaccuracies or could have discovered the inaccuracies with reasonable diligence); and

(B) The failure to comply with any condition of a development approval.

4.8.3 Notice and Public Hearing

Notice of the hearing shall be provided to the development approval holder at least 10 working days prior to the hearing. Said notice shall be in writing and delivered by personal service or certified mail and shall advise of the [PLANNING OFFICIAL]'s recommendation as well as the date and location of the hearing before the agency.

4.8.4 Decision and Notice

The agency shall prepare a development order approving, approving with conditions, or denying the [PLANNING OFFICIAL]'s recommendation. The development order shall contain findings that address the basis for the decision. The development order shall state the condition or conditions that have been violated and the harm such violation has caused. In the case of a suspension of the use, the development order shall state the length of time such violation can be cured. In the case of a termination, the development order shall state the reason such violation cannot be cured.

4.8.5 Appeals

An aggrieved party may appeal the agency's decision to a court of competent jurisdiction. The appeal shall be presented within the period of time authorized by state statute.

4.8.6 Right Cumulative

The right to revoke a development approval, as provided in this section, is cumulative to any other remedy allowed by law.

4.9 NEIGHBORHOOD REGISTRATION

4.9.1 Applicability

Purpose and findings: Neighborhood registration is established in order to provide notification of neighborhoods involving legislative or quasi-judicial development orders, as provided in other sections of this chapter. The purpose of this section is to establish procedures for the registration of neighborhoods and interested nonprofit associations.

4.9.2 Contents

(A) A neighborhood registry shall be maintained by the planning department.

(B) In order to be included within the neighborhood registry, the neighborhood association shall provide the following information:

(1) A map or written description of the neighborhood boundaries;

(2) A list of the officers in the association, including their addresses and phone numbers;

(3) A signed copy of the adopted by-laws;

(4) A regular meeting location and a regular meeting date;

(5) The date the association was founded;

(6) The number of association members;

(7) The approximate number of housing units in the area; and

(8) The approximate population of the neighborhood.

(C) The neighborhood association shall contact the planning department in the event of a change in the above-referenced information. An applicant shall be entitled to rely on the above-referenced information for purposes of preparing any notices or otherwise contacting neighborhood associations where required by this chapter.

4.9.3 Effect of Neighborhood Registry

Upon a neighborhood association registration as provided herein, the planning department shall notify the neighborhood association of any application for rezoning or master site plan approval filed within the boundaries of a registered neighborhood association. Individual citizens who reside outside of the 200-foot notice area required by this chapter, but within the boundaries of a registered neighborhood association, are considered notified when any such notification is sent to the neighborhood association within 200 feet of the subject site. This notice is a courtesy, and hearings may proceed despite claims of a lack of notice.

4.10 NEIGHBORHOOD PARTICIPATION MEETING

Purpose and findings: The purpose of citizen participation is to:

• Encourage applicants to pursue early and effective communication with the affected public in conjunction with applications, giving the applicant an opportunity to understand and attempt to mitigate any documentable adverse impact of the proposed project on the adjoining community and to educate and inform the public;

• Provide citizens and property owners of affected areas with an opportunity to learn about applications and to work with applicants to resolve concerns at an early stage of the process; and

• Facilitate ongoing communication between the applicants, interested citizens, property owners, [LOCAL GOVERNMENT] staff, boards and commissions, and elected officials throughout the application review process.

4.10.1 Applicability

It is the policy of the [LOCAL GOVERNMENT] to encourage applicants to meet with surrounding neighborhoods prior to filing an application for a development approval requiring review and a public hearing. Neighborhood review is mandatory for any application for a legislative or quasi-judicial development order. The applicant at their option may elect to include citizen participation as a preparatory step in the development process for ministerial development orders. Inclusion of citizen participation prior to required public hearings will be noted by the reviewing agency when considering the need for a continuance. This section requires neighborhood meetings prior to submission of an application and documentation of efforts that have been made to resolve any potential concerns prior to the formal application process.

4.10.2 Recommended Procedures

4.10.2.1 Meetings

The applicant shall facilitate at least one meeting with surrounding neighborhoods before formally filing an application.

4.10.2.2 Target Area

The target area shall include the following:

(A) Property owners within the public hearing notice area required by statute; and

(B) A neighborhood association that includes the subject property and/or is within 200 feet of the subject property, and is registered with the planning department in accordance with the requirements of § 4.9 Neighborhood Registration of this chapter.

4.10.2.3 Citizen Participation Documentation

Citizen participation shall include the following information as required in B-2 Citizen Participation Plan in Appendix B, Specifications for Documents to Be Submitted, of the LDC.

4.10.2.4 Report on Implementation of Citizen Participation

The applicant shall provide a written report on the results of its citizen participation efforts with the filing of the application. The report shall be forwarded to the reviewing agency. At a minimum, the citizen participation report shall include details of techniques the applicant used to involve the public, including:

(A) Dates and locations of all meetings where citizens were invited to discuss the applicant's proposal;

(B) Content, dates mailed, and numbers of mailings, including letters, meeting notices, newsletters, and other publications;

(C) Where residents, property owners, and interested parties receiving notices, newsletters, or other written materials are located;

(D) The number of people who participated in the process;

(E) A summary of concerns, issues, and problems expressed during the process;

(F) How the applicant has addressed or intends to address concerns, issues, and problems expressed during the process; and

(G) Concerns, issues, and problems the applicant is unable to address, including reasons why the concerns cannot or should not be addressed.

4.10.2.5 Signature or Affidavit of Compliance

If the applicant prepares a citizen participation report, the report shall include a list of persons contacted, a list of persons invited to any neighborhood meeting, and one of the following:

(A) The signature of the president or vice president of any neighborhood association required to be contacted, certifying that the neighborhood meeting was conducted, provided, however, that the signature need not certify agreement with the applicant as to any issues raised at the neighborhood meeting;

(B) If the president or vice president of the neighborhood association was unavailable or refused to sign such certification, a statement as to the efforts to contact them and, in the event of unavailability, the reasons as to why they were unable to sign the certification; or

(C) A statement that there are no registered neighborhood associations within the required notification area.

4.10.2.6 Restrictions on Continuances

It is the intent of this chapter to encourage applicants to involve neighborhoods in the development approval process while, at the same time, streamlining the development approval process through the discouragement of continuances and frivolous appeals by neighbors or neighborhood associations. Accordingly, any person who received notice of a neighborhood meeting and who failed to participate in a neighborhood meeting shall not be permitted:

(A) A continuance of any hearing relating to a development approval application requiring a public hearing; or

(B) To file an administrative appeal from any development order approving the application on any issue that was resolved at a neighborhood meeting.

For the purpose of this section, persons will be considered to have "received notice" if their names appear on the invitation list.

DIVISION 3: MINISTERIAL DEVELOPMENT APPROVALS

4.11 DEVELOPMENT APPROVAL

A development approval is a ministerial development approval, including a building permit, that authorizes construction of a structure or improvement or disturbance of land. No land shall be disturbed and no building or structure shall be erected, added to, or structurally altered within the zoning jurisdiction until a development approval has been issued by the [PLANNING OFFICIAL]. All development approvals shall comply with the requirements of the LDC. No grading approval, building permit, certificate of appropriateness, or certificate of occupancy shall be issued for any building or structure or for any land disturbance where said construction, addition, alteration, or use violates any provision of the LDC, except upon written order of the board of appeals.

4.12 GRADING AND LAND DISTURBANCE

4.12.1 Grading Development Approval

Separate grading development approval is required for disturbances of land that require the removal of more than 10 cubic feet of soil and less than 100 cubic feet of soil prior to the issuance of any development approval.

4.12.2 Land Disturbance Activity

Any disturbance of land greater than 100 cubic feet of soil requires a development approval pursuant to § 7.20.1.2 Substantial Land Alteration, subsection (B), in Chapter 7, Supplemental Use Regulations, of the LDC.

4.13 ZONING CERTIFICATES

Purpose and findings: The purpose of this section is to prescribe procedures for development approvals that do not require quasi-judicial or legislative notice or a public hearing. A public hearing is not required for development approvals set forth in this section for one or more of the following reasons:

- If required, public hearings have already been conducted relating to the development approval application, and the development approval application procedure is designed to ensure that the proposed use complies with a previously approved subdivision plat, site plan, specific plan, comprehensive plan amendment, or conditional rezoning (e.g., development approval or certificate of occupancy);
- The proposed use is permitted as of right in the applicable zoning district (e.g., development approval or certificate of occupancy); and
- The proposed use is subject to expedited review in order to avoid an unconstitutional prior restraint on speech (e.g., sexually oriented businesses or signs) or because of federal law (e.g., telecommunications development approval).

4.13.1 Initiation

The applicant shall file a complete application for a zoning certificate with the [PLANNING OFFICIAL]. If site plan review is required in accordance with § 4.10 Neighborhood Participation Meeting of this chapter, the approved site plan shall be submitted with the application. An application is available from the planning department. If the proposed development or development activity is not subject to site plan review, the application shall include the information required by Appendix B, Specifications for Documents to Be Submitted, of the LDC.

4.13.2 Completeness Review

The [PLANNING OFFICIAL] shall review an application for completeness within two working days. The appellate agency for purposes of completeness review is the hearing officer.

4.13.3 Decision

The [PLANNING OFFICIAL] shall review the application for conformance with the LDC. Within 15 working days of receipt of a complete application, the [PLANNING OFFICIAL] shall approve, approve with conditions, or deny the application for a zoning certificate. Applications that are denied shall have the reasons for denial, in writing, attached to the application. If the [PLANNING OFFICIAL] fails to render a decision relating to the application within this time period, the application shall be deemed approved. The applicant and the [LOCAL GOVERNMENT] may agree to extend the response time contained in this section.

4.13.4 Approval Criteria

The zoning certificate shall be issued by the [PLANNING OFFICIAL] only if the application complies with all applicable provisions of the LDC and any approved CUP, conditional rezoning, or site plan.

4.13.5 Amendments

Any revision to an application for a zoning certificate shall be processed in the same manner as the original application.

4.13.6 Scope of Approval

The zoning certificate shall be valid for a period of 180 days.

4.13.7 Recording Procedures

An application for a zoning certificate shall be maintained in the files of the planning department. The applicant shall maintain an original signed copy of the approved zoning certificate.

4.14 CERTIFICATE OF OCCUPANCY

4.14.1 Requirement

All uses, including nonconforming uses, shall obtain a certificate of occupancy where required by the Uniform Building Code or other applicable national building code, state law, and this chapter. All of the requirements and conditions contained in any development approvals applicable to the property, including zoning, site plan, and subdivision final plat approval, that have not been met at the time of the issuance of the development approval, shall be required to have been met before the issuance of any certificate of occupancy.

4.14.2 Records

The [PLANNING OFFICIAL] shall maintain a record of all ministerial development orders. Copies shall be furnished, upon request, to any person upon the payment of a fee established by the [PLANNING OFFICIAL].

DIVISION 4: ZONING PROCEDURES

4.20 PLANS AND PLAN AMENDMENTS

This section establishes uniform procedures for the preparation or amendment of the comprehensive plan. Where the existing comprehensive plan does not provide sufficient densities, or where the goals and objectives do not support a proposed development, these procedures may be used to apply for an amendment to the comprehensive plan.

4.20.1 Applicability

4.20.1.1 Generally

This section applies to any amendment to the comprehensive plan or to the preparation or amendment of a specific plan or neighborhood plan.

4.20.1.2 Specific Plans

A specific plan accompanying the development of specific property or properties provides a bridge between the comprehensive, area, and neighborhood plan policies, and specific regulations, and which may be approved to permit mixed-use and planned development.

A specific plan is considered an amendment to, and a part of, the comprehensive plan. A specific plan shall include text and a diagram or diagrams that specify all of the following in detail:

(A) The distribution, location, and extent of the uses of land, including open space, within the area covered by the specific plan or any applicable area plan;

(B) The proposed distribution, location, and extent and intensity of major components of public and private transportation, sewage, water, drainage, solid waste disposal, energy, and other essential facilities proposed to be located within the area covered by the specific plan and needed to support the land uses described in the specific plan;

(C) Standards and criteria by which development will proceed, and standards for the conservation, development, and utilization of natural resources, where applicable;

(D) A program of implementation measures, including zoning, land development regulations, programs, public works projects, financing measures, development agreements, and conditions, covenants, and regulations necessary to carry out subsections (A), (B), and (C), above; and

(E) A statement of the relationship of the specific plan to the comprehensive plan.

4.20.1.3 Area Plans

An area plan is a plan that provides specific planning, design, and implementation, for a defined geographic area of the [LOCAL GOVERNMENT] to guide specific development applications, governmental facilities, official maps, utility and infrastructure plans, annexations, and creation of special districts.

4.20.1.4 Neighborhood Plans

A "neighborhood plan" means a plan that guides the platting or development of remaining vacant parcels in a partially built-up neighborhood in order to make reasonable use of all land, correlate street patterns, and achieve the best possible land-use relationships. A neighborhood plan is considered an amendment to, and a part of, the comprehensive plan. A neighborhood plan may provide more detailed guidance about applying the future land-use map of the comprehensive plan to a specific neighborhood.

4.20.2 Initiation

(A) A property owner or his/her designated representative may initiate a comprehensive area, specific, or neighborhood plan amendment. The applicant may combine an application for an amendment to the comprehensive plan with an application for approval of a rezoning, and said applications may be processed concurrently.

(B) Before any application is made, the applicant shall schedule a preapplication conference with the [PLANNING OFFICIAL] to discuss, in general, the procedures and requirements for a comprehensive plan amendment request pursuant to these regulations.

(C) An application for a comprehensive area, specific, or neighborhood plan amendment shall be filed with the [PLANNING OFFICIAL] and shall contain the information set forth in Appendix B, Specifications for Documents to Be Submitted, of the LDC.

(D) The planning commission, the [LOCAL GOVERNMENT], the [PLANNING OFFICIAL], a property owner, a neighborhood association, or the owner of any business located in the [LOCAL GOVERNMENT] may initiate a request for an amendment to the future land-use maps of the comprehensive plan. The application for amendment of the future land-use map may be accompanied by an application for a zoning district map amendment. By resolution, the [GOVERNING ENTITY] may establish a schedule prescribing when and how frequently comprehensive plan text amendments will be considered.

4.20.3 Completeness Review

The [PLANNING OFFICIAL] shall review the comprehensive plan amendment application and shall determine if the application is complete pursuant to this section. The [PLANNING OFFICIAL] shall inform the applicant of the status of the completeness of the application. If the [PLANNING OFFICIAL] determines that the application is incomplete, the application shall be returned to the applicant along with the requisite fees. The applicant shall be instructed as to the reasons for the incompleteness of the application and informed of the schedule for the next application period.

4.20.4 Decision

The planning commission shall hold a legislative public hearing and shall render its decision in accordance with the procedures set forth in § 4.5 Public Hearing of this chapter. The [LOCAL GOVERNMENT] shall hold a public hearing and shall render its decision in accordance with the procedures set forth in § 4.5 Public Hearing.

4.20.5 Criteria

In determining whether the proposed amendment shall be approved, the planning commission and [LOCAL GOVERNMENT] shall consider the factors set forth in [STATE LAW]. No specific plan or neighborhood plan will be approved unless it is consistent with the comprehensive plan.

4.20.6 Scope of Approval

The approval of an amendment to the comprehensive plan does not authorize the use, occupancy, or development of property. The approval of a plan amendment shall require the applicant to apply for zoning changes and/or subdivision or site plan approval consistent with the goals, objectives, and policies of the comprehensive plan.

4.21 CODE AMENDMENTS

This section provides uniform procedures for the amendment of the LDC or the official zoning map by the [LOCAL GOVERNMENT] whenever the public necessity, convenience, general welfare, or good planning practice so requires.

4.21.1 Applicability

The provisions of this section apply to any application to:
(A) Revise the text of the LDC; or
(B) Reclassify a tract, parcel, or land area from one zoning district to another.

4.21.2 Initiation

(A) All petitions, applications, recommendations, or proposals for changes in the zoning district classification of property (referred to as a "rezoning") or for changes in the text of the LDC shall be filed with the [PLANNING OFFICIAL].
(B) Text amendments may be proposed by any person.
(C) A proposed rezoning may be initiated by:
(1) The [GOVERNING ENTITY] or planning commission by resolution; or
(2) An application properly signed and filed by the owner or, with the owner's specific written consent, a contract purchaser or owner's agent of a property included within the boundaries of a proposed rezoning, unless otherwise provided by the LDC. The applicant may file an application for subdivision plat approval concurrent with an application for a rezoning.

4.21.3 Completeness Review

The [PLANNING OFFICIAL] shall conduct a completeness review as set forth in § 4.2 Categories of Development Approvals of this chapter within two working days of application submittal. The appellate agency for purposes of completeness review is the planning commission.

4.21.4 Decision

Upon certification by the [PLANNING OFFICIAL] that the application is complete and required fees have been paid, the application shall be deemed complete and referred to the planning commission for its review and recommendation.

4.21.4.1 Type of Hearing

The public hearings before the planning commission and [GOVERNING ENTITY] shall be conducted as legislative hearings.

4.21.4.2 Planning Commission

The planning commission shall hold at least one public hearing on such application, and as a result thereof shall transmit its final report to the [GOVERNING

ENTITY]. All applications for a change in zoning that have been considered by the planning commission shall be presented by the applicant to the [GOVERNING ENTITY] within six months from the date of the planning commission's final consideration.

4.21.4.3 [GOVERNING ENTITY]

After receipt of the final report of the planning commission, the [GOVERNING ENTITY] shall approve or deny the rezoning or text amendment. If the proposed rezoning is inconsistent with the comprehensive plan, a specific plan, or a neighborhood plan, an application for an amendment to the comprehensive plan, specific plan, or neighborhood plan shall be submitted by the applicant. Amendments to the official zoning map and the comprehensive plan, specific plan, or neighborhood plan may be considered concurrently.

4.21.5 Approval Criteria

In its review of an application for rezoning, the [GOVERNING ENTITY] shall consider the criteria as defined in § 4.21.5.1 Consistency through § 4.21.5.7 Other Factors of this chapter. No single factor is controlling; instead, each must be weighed in relation to the other standards.

4.21.5.1 Consistency

Rezoning shall be consistent with the adopted comprehensive plan.

4.21.5.2 Adverse Impacts on Neighboring Lands

The [GOVERNING ENTITY] shall consider the nature and degree of an adverse impact upon neighboring lands. Lots shall not be rezoned in a way that is substantially inconsistent with the uses of the surrounding area, whether more or less restrictive. Further, the [LOCAL GOVERNMENT] finds and determines that vast acreages of single-use zoning produces uniformity with adverse consequences, such as traffic congestion, air pollution, and social alienation. Accordingly, rezonings may promote mixed uses subject to a high degree of design control.

4.21.5.3 Suitability as Presently Zoned

The [GOVERNING ENTITY] shall consider the suitability or unsuitability of the tract for its use as presently zoned. This factor, like the others, must often be weighed in relation to the other standards, and instances can exist in which the use for which land is zoned may be rezoned upon proof of a real public need, substantially changed conditions in the neighborhood, or to effectuate important goals, objectives, policies, and strategies of the comprehensive plan, specification, or LDC.

4.21.5.4 Health, Safety, and Welfare

The amendatory ordinance must bear a substantial relationship to the public health, safety, morals, or general welfare, or protect and preserve historical and cultural places and areas. The rezoning ordinance may be justified, however, if a substantial public need or purpose exists, and this is so even if the private owner of the tract will also benefit.

4.21.5.5 Public Policy

Certain public policies in favor of the rezoning may be considered. Examples include a need for affordable housing, economic development, mixed-use development, or sustainable environmental features, which are consistent with neighborhood, area, or specific plans.

4.21.5.6 Size of Tract

The [GOVERNING ENTITY] shall consider the size, shape, and characteristics of the tract in relation to the affected neighboring lands. Amendatory ordinances shall not rezone a single lot when there have been no intervening changes or other saving characteristics. Proof that a small tract is unsuitable for use as zoned, or that there have been substantial changes in the immediate area, may justify an amendatory ordinance.

4.21.5.7 Other Factors

The [GOVERNING ENTITY] may consider any other factors relevant to a rezoning application under state law.

4.21.6 Subsequent Applications

4.21.6.1 Applicability

The provisions of this subsection do not apply to any application for a rezoning that is initiated by the [GOVERNING ENTITY].

4.21.6.2 Withdrawal After Planning Commission Hearing

No rezoning application shall be received or filed with the planning commission if, during the previous six months, an application was received or filed and withdrawn after a full, fair, complete, and final hearing occurred on the rezoning before the planning commission. However, if the applicant certifies with a sworn affidavit that the evidence is new, relevant, and substantial, and could not have been secured at the time set for the original hearing, the planning commission may hear and consider the application.

4.21.6.3 Denial of Rezoning

No application for rezoning shall be received or filed with the planning commission within one year after the

[GOVERNING ENTITY] has denied an application for rezoning of the same property.

4.21.7 Amendments

Any subsequent rezoning requires a new application and shall be processed as set forth in § 4.21.1 Applicability through § 4.21.6 Subsequent Applications of this chapter.

4.21.8 Scope of Approval

An amendment to the LDC or a rezoning does not authorize the development of land. An amendment authorizes the applicant to apply for development approval consisting of a development approval, in the case of uses permitted as of right; a CUP, in the case of uses designated as conditional uses within the applicable zoning district; or to proceed with site plan or subdivision plat approval. An amendment does not supersede any requirement for site plan or subdivision plat approval by the LDC.

4.21.9 Recording Procedures

When the amendment involves changes to the existing zoning district boundaries, the form of the amending ordinance shall contain a narrative description of the land to be reclassified or reference to an accompanying plat of such land showing the new zoning classifications and indicating their boundaries. The [PLANNING OFFICIAL] shall refer to the attested ordinance as a record of the current zoning status until such time as the zoning map can be changed.

4.22 CONDITIONAL ZONING

The conditional zoning procedure is designed to provide for a land use within an area that is not permitted by the established zoning district but, due to individual site considerations or unique development requirements, would be compatible with adjacent land uses under given conditions. The granting of a conditional zoning classification shall not be for all of the uses permitted in a given district but only for the specific use named in the ordinance approving the conditional zoning district.

4.22.1 Applicability

This section applies to any application for reclassification of a tract, parcel, or land area to a conditional zoning district. A conditional zoning district may also be applied as an overlay zoning district to any base zoning district.

4.22.2 Initiation

(A) A proceeding for approval of a conditional zoning district shall be initiated by filing an application with the [PLANNING OFFICIAL]. The application shall be signed and filed by the owner or, with the owner's specific written consent, a contract purchaser or owner's agent of a property included within the boundaries of a proposed conditional rezoning. The application for a conditional use district shall be the same as that for a change in the base zoning district. If the requested use or uses is listed as a conditional use within the conditional zoning district, the approval of a conditional zoning district shall constitute approval of the conditional use.

(B) A conditional zoning district may be granted as an amendment to an ongoing rezoning case before the planning commission or [GOVERNING ENTITY]. Before granting the amendment, the [GOVERNING ENTITY] may issue a courtesy notice to affected parties of the proposed conditional zoning district and will not require the applicant to submit a new application or pay additional fees other than for the difference (if any) between a conventional case and a conditional zoning case. Such amendment shall then be considered at the next regularly scheduled planning commission meeting or, in the case of the [GOVERNING ENTITY], at the next regularly scheduled meeting at which zoning cases will be considered. All costs associated with issuance of the courtesy notice shall be borne by the city.

4.22.3 Completeness Review

The [PLANNING OFFICIAL] shall conduct a completeness review as set forth in § 4.3 Completeness Review of this chapter. The appellate agency for purposes of a completeness review is the planning commission.

4.22.4 Decision

The procedure for approving a conditional zoning classification is the same as is required for a rezoning and as further provided in this section. In approving the conditional zoning classification, the [GOVERNING ENTITY] may impose such requirements and safeguards as indicated by § 4.22.5 Criteria of this chapter and may specifically authorize the location of uses, subject to the requirements set forth.

4.22.5 Criteria

4.22.5.1 Generally

Notwithstanding any provisions of this chapter to the contrary, a conditional zoning district may be permitted as provided in this section so long as the criteria for approval of a rezoning are met.

4.22.5.2 Development Constraints (Generally)

In considering a request for a conditional zoning classification, the planning commission shall make a recommendation to the [GOVERNING ENTITY] with reference to the use and development conditions that insure compatibility with surrounding properties and environmental conditions. "Compatibility" means the compatibility of the proposed use with surrounding uses, including building character, construction material, or architectural design of the proposed structures.

The following development constraints may be attached as conditions to the rezoning:

(A) Range of allowable uses;

(B) Protective screening and/or buffering of property perimeter;

(C) Protective screening/location of dumpsters, mechanical systems, and loading docks;

(D) Landscaping relative to screening, buffering, and ingress/egress control and not solely for beautification purposes;

(E) Lighting;

(F) Height limitations;

(G) Setbacks;

(H) Parking (the location of parking and, in some instances, reduction in the amount of parking to be allowed);

(I) Ingress/egress;

(J) Hours of operation for conditional uses permitted in, or adjacent to, residential zoning districts;

(K) Signage;

(L) Performance standards relative to air pollution, noise, glare and heat, vibration, noxious odors, toxic and liquid wastes, fire and explosion, radioactivity, and electromagnetic radiation;

(M) Protection of environmentally sensitive areas, including but not limited to steep slopes, wetlands, habitats, riparian areas, and geological formations; and

(N) The proposed uses to the maximum extent feasible, which utilize sustainability features authorized by the LDC.

4.22.5.3 Development Constraints in Residential Districts

The following conditions apply to the operation of nonresidential conditional uses permitted within any residential district, unless otherwise approved by the [GOVERNING ENTITY]:

(A) There shall be no exterior display or sign with the exception that a nameplate, not exceeding 3 square feet in area, may be permitted when attached to the front of the main structure.

(B) No construction features shall place the structure out of character with the surrounding neighborhood.

(C) Business or office hours of operations shall not be permitted before 7:00 PM or after 6:00 PM.

4.22.5.4 Variances Prohibited

A variance shall not be granted to any development constraint specified in this section or to any condition imposed by the [GOVERNING ENTITY].

4.22.6 Subsequent Applications

4.22.6.1 Applicability

The provisions of this subsection do not apply to any application for a rezoning that is initiated by the [GOVERNING ENTITY].

4.22.6.2 Withdrawal After Planning Commission Hearing

No rezoning application shall be received or filed with the planning commission if, during the previous six months, an application was received or filed and withdrawn after a full, fair, complete, and final hearing occurred on the rezoning before the planning commission. However, if the applicant certifies with a sworn affidavit that the evidence is new, relevant, and substantial, and could not have been secured at the time set for the original hearing, the planning commission may hear and consider the application.

4.22.7 Amendments

4.22.7.1 New or Different Uses

An amendment to a conditional zoning district to authorize a new or different use shall require a new application for a rezoning to a conditional zoning district.

4.22.7.2 Expansion

Expansion of the building area, land area, or intensity of the conditional zoning classification for a property granted a conditional zoning classification is not permitted unless authorized by the [GOVERNING ENTITY] after consideration of an application for a new conditional zoning classification.

4.22.8 Scope of Approval

4.22.8.1 Compliance with Development Constraints

The [GOVERNING ENTITY] may grant a conditional zoning classification subject to such development constraints as the [GOVERNING ENTITY] deems necessary to protect the public health, safety, or welfare. The [GOVERNING ENTITY] may specify that compliance with certain conditions must be achieved prior to the issuance of a certificate of occupancy. Violation of any condition, subsequent to the issuance of a certificate of occupancy, may result in initiation of a rezoning of the property to its base zoning classification and judicial and/or administrative action by the city.

4.22.8.2 Time Period

A conditional zoning classification shall run with the land until such time that the zoning is changed or the conditional use granted has been discontinued on the property for a period of 12 months. However, the [GOVERNING ENTITY] may impose a time limitation on a conditional zoning classification granted in a single-family residential district. Failure to renew the conditional zoning classification prior to the date of its expiration may cause the conditional use to expire and the conditional use to terminate on that date. The [PLANNING OFFICIAL] may then initiate proceedings to rezone the property to its former zoning classification.

4.22.8.3 Base Zoning District Regulations Apply

A conditional zoning classification does not permit the applicant to use the subject property for uses other than those requested in the application for a conditional zoning classification. The granting of a conditional zoning classification does not waive the regulations of the underlying zoning district.

4.22.9 Recording Procedures

A conditional zoning classification shall be recorded in the same manner as a rezoning. The conditional zoning classification shall be indicated by the symbols "CD" following the zoning district designation of, for example, "O-CD." A flow chart of the conditional zoning district process is shown in Figure 4-2.

4.23 CONDITIONAL USE PERMITS

Purpose and findings: This section provides for certain uses that, because of unique characteristics or potential impacts on adjacent land uses, are not permitted in zoning districts as a matter of right but which may, under appropriate standards and factors set forth in the LDC, be approved. These uses shall be permitted through the issuance of a CUP within a site plan adopted by the planning commission after ensuring that the use can be appropriately accommodated on the specific property; that it will conform to the comprehensive plan; that it can be constructed and operated in a manner that is compatible with the surrounding land uses and overall character of the community; and that the public interest, health, safety, and general welfare will be promoted.

No inherent right exists to receive a CUP. Such authorization must be approved under a specific set of circumstances and conditions. Each application and situation is unique. Every CUP amendment or application shall at a minimum be required to comply with every requirement contained in each chapter of the LDC. Mere compliance with the generally applicable requirements however may not be sufficient, and additional measures and conditions may be necessary to mitigate the impact of the proposed development.

4.23.1 Conditional Applicability

The provisions of this section apply to any application for approval of a CUP. Conditional uses are those uses that are generally compatible with the land uses permitted by right in a zoning district but that require individual review of their location, design, and configuration, and the imposition of conditions or mitigations in order to ensure the appropriateness of the use at a particular location within a given zoning district. Only those uses that are enumerated as conditional uses in a zoning district, as set forth in the zoning regulations, shall be authorized by the planning commission. A CUP is not required for a use permitted by right in a given zoning district.

4.23.2 Initiation

An owner of real property, or that owner's authorized representative, may apply for a CUP for that property by filing an application with the [PLANNING OFFICIAL]. The application shall include the material required in Appendix B, Specifications for Documents to Be Submitted, of the LDC.

4.23.3 Completeness Review

The [PLANNING OFFICIAL] shall review the application for the CUP for completeness in accordance with

**Figure 4-2
Legislative Discretionary Development Approval**

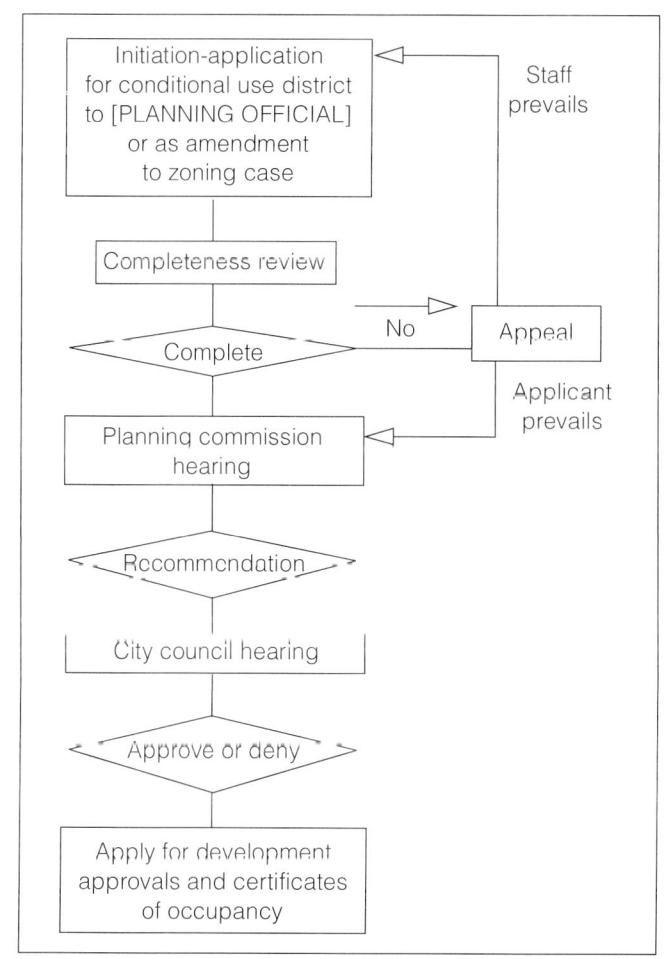

Flow chart aids applicant in understanding the process of legislative discretionary review.

§ 4.2 Categories of Development Approvals of this chapter. The review agency for purposes of completeness review (see § 4.2.3 Ministerial Development Approvals of this chapter) shall be the planning commission.

4.23.4 Approval

When the [PLANNING OFFICIAL] has certified that the application is complete, it shall be deemed received and shall be referred to the planning commission for its review and decision. The planning commission, after public notice in accordance with applicable state laws, shall hold at least one public hearing on the application. The planning commission may concurrently process and review a rezoning site plan, subdivision approval, and CUP.

4.23.4.1 Type of Hearing

The public hearing before the planning commission and [GOVERNING ENTITY] shall be conducted as a quasi-judicial hearing.

4.23.4.2 Conditions

In approving any CUP, the planning commission may:
 (A) Impose such reasonable standards, conditions, or requirements, in addition to or that supersede any standard specified in the LDC, as it may deem necessary to protect the public interest and welfare. Such additional standards may include, but need not be limited to:
  (1) Financing and availability of adequate public facilities or services;
  (2) Dedication of land;
  (3) Reservation of land;
  (4) Payment of exactions;
  (5) Impact fees;
  (6) Creation of special assessment districts;
  (7) Creation of restrictive covenants or easements;
  (8) Special setbacks;
  (9) Yard requirements;
  (10) Increased screening or landscaping requirements;
  (11) Area requirements;
  (12) Development phasing; and
  (13) Standards pertaining to traffic, circulation, noise, lighting, hours of operation, protection of environmentally sensitive areas, and similar characteristics;
  (14) Provision of sustainable features, solar or other renewable energy source, rain water capture, storage and treatment or other sustainability requirement in § 5.53 Sustainability in Chapter 5, Development Standards, of the LDC;
 (B) Require that a performance guarantee—acceptable in form, content, and amount to the [LOCAL GOVERNMENT] attorney—be posted by the applicant to ensure continued compliance with all conditions and requirements as may be specified; and
 (C) Require that a development agreement be entered into by the applicant.

4.23.5 Approval Criteria

A conditional use is permitted only if the applicant demonstrates that:
 (A) The proposed conditional use shall comply with all regulations of the applicable zoning district; Chapter 5, Development Standards, of the LDC; and any applicable supplemental use regulations as set forth in Chapter 6, Adequate Public Facilities, of the LDC.
 (B) The proposed conditional use shall conform to the character of the neighborhood within the same zoning district in which it is located. The proposal as submitted or modified shall have no more adverse effects on health, safety, or comfort of persons living or working in the neighborhood, or shall be no more injurious to property or improvements in the neighborhood than would any other use generally permitted in the same district. In making such a determination, consideration shall be given to:
  (1) The location, type, and height of buildings or structures;
  (2) The type and extent of landscaping and screening on the site; and
  (3) Whether the proposed use is consistent with any policy of the comprehensive plan that encourages mixed uses and/or densities.
 (C) Adequate utilities shall be provided as set forth in Chapter 5, Development Standards, of the LDC.
 (D) Adequate measures shall be taken to provide ingress and egress so designed as to minimize traffic hazards and to minimize traffic congestion on the public roads.
 (E) The proposed use shall not be noxious or offensive by reason of vibration, noise, odor, dust, smoke, or gas.
 (F) The proposed use shall not injure the use and enjoyment of the property in the immediate vicinity for the purposes already permitted nor substantially diminish or impair the property values within the neighborhood.
 (G) The proposed use shall not impede the orderly development and improvement of surrounding property for uses permitted within the zoning district.
 (H) The establishment, maintenance, or operation of the proposed use shall not be detrimental to or endanger the public health, safety, morals, comfort, or general welfare.
 (I) The public interest and welfare supporting the proposed use shall be sufficient to outweigh the individual interests that are adversely affected by the establishment of the proposed use.
 (J) The proposed uses and structures comply with the sustainability requirements of the LDC.

4.23.6 Subsequent Applications

An application for a CUP may be withdrawn at any time. If the application has been advertised in compliance with state law, an application requesting substantially the same use on all or part of the same described land shall not be reconsidered within one year of withdrawal. No application for a CUP for any lot or parcel that requests the same use and same conditions shall be considered within one year of a final decision denying the application.

4.23.7 Amendments

4.23.7.1 Minor Amendments

An amendment is a request for any enlargement, expansion, increase in intensity, relocation, or modification of any condition of a previously approved and currently valid CUP. Amendments shall be processed as follows: shifts in on-site location and changes in size, shape, intensity, or configuration of less than 5 percent, or a 5 percent or less increase in either impervious surface or floor area over what was originally approved, may be authorized by the [PLANNING OFFICIAL], provided that such minor changes comply with the following criteria:

(A) No previous minor modification has been granted pursuant to this section;

(B) There will be no detrimental impact on any adjacent property caused by significant change in the appearance or use of the property or any other contributing factor;

(C) Nothing in the currently valid CUP precludes or otherwise limits such expansion or enlargement; and

(D) The proposal conforms to the LDC and is in keeping with the spirit and intent of any adopted comprehensive plan.

4.23.7.2 Major Amendments

Any proposed amendment other than those provided for in § 4.23.7.1 Minor Amendments of this chapter are considered a major amendment and shall be approved in the same manner and under the same procedures as are applicable to the issuance of the original development approval.

4.23.7.3 Nonconforming Uses

For an existing and currently valid conditional use that is no longer allowed as a conditional use in the zoning district in which it is located, the [GOVERNING ENTITY], upon receipt of an application, may review and approve an amendment to said development approval, provided that such amendment does not allow the use to be enlarged, expanded, increased in intensity, relocated, or continued beyond any limitation specified in the existing use development approval or established in Chapter 8, Nonconforming Uses/Vested Rights, of the LDC.

4.23.8 Scope of Approval

Once a CUP is granted, such use may be enlarged, extended, increased in intensity, or relocated only in accordance with this section unless the [GOVERNING ENTITY], in approving the initial development approval, has specifically established alternative procedures for consideration of future expansion or enlargement. The provisions of Chapter 8, Nonconforming Uses/Vested Rights, of the LDC, relative to expansion of nonconforming uses, do not supersede this requirement unless the conditionally permitted use for which the development approval was initially granted is no longer a use permitted as of right or as a conditional use in the zoning district in which it is located.

4.23.9 Recording Procedures

A certified copy of all resolutions authorizing a conditional use pursuant to this section shall be recorded at the expense of the applicant in the name of the property owner as grantor in the office of the county clerk. A flow chart of the CUP process is shown in Figure 4-3.

**Figure 4-3
Administrative Discretionary Development Approval**

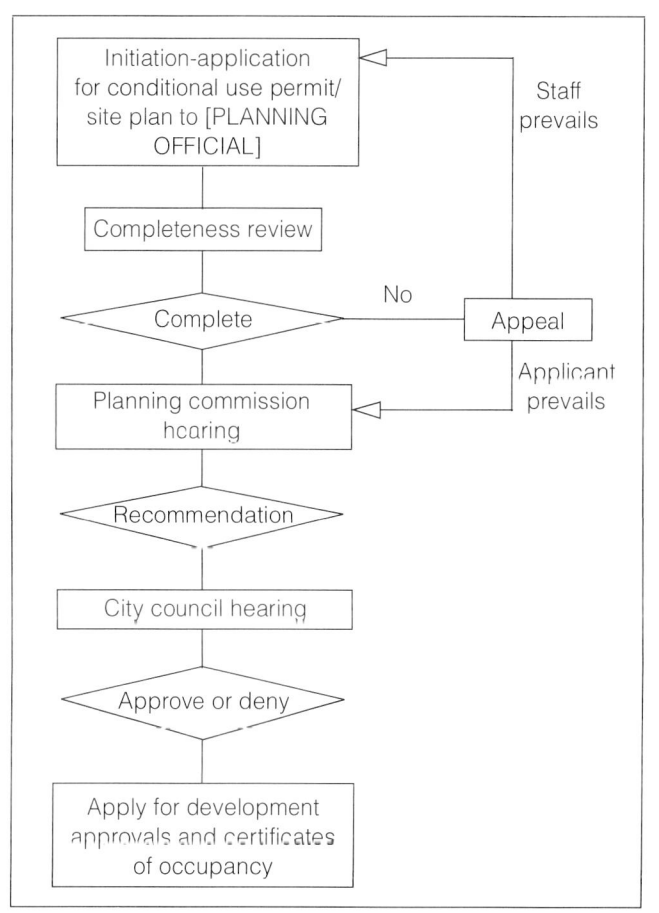

Flow chart aids applicant in understanding a conditional use permit, a site plan, or other administrative discretionary approval.

4.24 SITE PLANS

Purpose and findings: This section enables the [LOCAL GOVERNMENT] and the developer to collaborate in the processing of certain development approvals in order to enhance planning and timely, integrated processing and review. The site plan is intended to provide an overview of the applicant's projected land development. In this context, the site plan will be used to determine if the proposed development is in compliance with current statutes, ordinances, regulations, the [LOCAL GOVERNMENT] comprehensive plan, the LDC, and specific or neighborhood plans, and other applicable local, regional, state, and federal requirements.

4.24.1 Applicability

4.24.1.1 Mandatory Site Plan

A site plan is required where:
  (A) The application proposes three or more residential dwelling units;
  (B) The application will generate (upon build-out) more than 30 vehicle trips per day;
  (C) The application contains land designated for non-residential use;
  (D) The application requests rezoning or approval of a floating zone, "PD" (Planned Development) district, or a plan amendment;
  (E) The application requires a CUP;
  (F) The application requires regional, state, or federal review of approval or is subject to state or federal law; and
  (G) The land is located within an historic, agricultural, environmentally sensitive, or transportation corridor district.

4.24.2 Initiation

A site plan shall be submitted concurrently with an application for a rezoning (see § 4.12 Grading and Land Disturbance of this chapter) for a specific plan amendment, subdivision plat approval, CUP approval, or any other discretionary development approval. Applicants for a site plan shall incorporate citizen participation pursuant to § 4.10 Neighborhood Participation Meeting of this chapter and submit documentation of such efforts at the earliest feasible time in the process.

4.24.3 Completeness Review

Completeness review shall be governed by this section and § 4.2 Categories of Development Approvals of this chapter, to the extent consistent with this section. The [PLANNING OFFICIAL] shall provide a written response within 15 working days after submittal indicating whether or not the site plan is complete. The applicant shall file a written response to any staff comments or resolve outstanding issues prior to final approval. This response shall occur within 30 days of the mailing date of staff comments unless a time extension is requested and granted in writing. The maximum limit on an extension is six months from the original staff comment date. The appellate agency for purposes of completeness review (see § 4.3 Completeness Review of this chapter) is the planning commission.

4.24.4 Decision

Within 60 days after certification that the application is complete, the planning commission shall, after a duly noticed public hearing, render a determination approving, approving with conditions, or denying the site plan.

4.24.5 Appeal

(A) The hearing officer may consider an appeal by an applicant, and affirm or reverse, in whole or in part, the decision of the [PLANNING OFFICIAL] based on any error in an order, requirement, decision, or determination made by the [PLANNING OFFICIAL] in approving, denying, or attaching a condition to the site plan.
(B) A notice of appeal shall be submitted within 30 working days following receipt of a written denial by the planning commission. A notice of appeal shall be in writing and shall provide a chronological listing of the dates and meetings held during the course of consideration of the site plan. In addition, the notice must outline in writing the specific justifications supporting the appeal.

4.24.6 Approval Criteria

No site plan shall be approved unless it conforms to all applicable requirements of each chapter of the LDC including criteria for sustainable development set out in § 5.53 Sustainability in Chapter 5, Development Standards, of the LDC. The planning commission must approve a site plan that is required to be prepared under this section and that satisfies all applicable regulations.

4.24.7 Subsequent Applications

If the site plan is denied, a new site plan proposing the same development for the same property shall not be filed within six months after a final decision.

4.24.8 Amendments

4.24.8.1 Classification

Amendments to a previously approved plan shall be classified as a minor or major revision. Minor amendments may be administratively accepted by the [PLANNING OFFICIAL] and will not be subject to review by the legislative body, planning commission, or other [LOCAL GOVERNMENT] agencies and departments. Within 20 working days after filing of the proposed amendments, required items, and information, the [PLANNING OFFICIAL] shall provide a written response indicating whether or not the revised master site plan has been accepted as a minor or major amendment.

4.24.8.2 Minor Amendments

Minor amendments include the following:

(A) Changes to the timing or phasing of the proposed development, provided that the use and overall geographic land area remains the same;

(B) Adjustment of unit boundaries within tracts or parcels adjoining the outer boundaries of the site plan, provided that the use and overall geographic land area remains the same;

(C) A reduction in the number of proposed platted lots, provided that the use and overall geographic land area remains the same;

(D) A decrease in overall residential density;

(E) Updating of ownership or consultant information;

(F) A decrease in the overall land area, provided that the initial design is maintained;

(G) Site plan or subdivision plat name change; and

(H) Change in internal street circulation pattern not increasing the number of lots or lowering the connectivity ratio.

4.24.8.3 Major Amendments

All other revisions shall be classified as major amendments and shall be processed in the same manner as the initial site plan submittal.

4.24.9 Scope of Approval

(A) The site plan expires unless a final plat is approved within 18 months from the approval of the site plan that plats at least 20 acres or 8 percent of the net area of the site plan area.

(B) The site plan expires unless 50 percent of the net area within the approved site plan is the subject of final plats or other development approval within 10 years from the date of approval of the site plan. The remaining 50 percent must obtain final plat or development approval and commence substantial construction within 10 years after the initial 50 percent of the net area within the site plan has been platted or developed.

(C) Development activities subject to this section shall conform to the approved site plan and any conditions or restrictions. Any deviation from the approved site plan, unless approved in advance and in writing by the [PLANNING OFFICIAL], is deemed a violation of the LDC.

4.24.10 Recording Procedures

The site plan shall be maintained in the permanent files of the [PLANNING OFFICIAL] and shall be recorded with the county recorder of deeds or clerk.

DIVISION 5: SUBDIVISIONS

This section establishes the general rules and regulations governing plats, the subdivision of land, and the procedures for the extension of the city's streets, major thoroughfares, and public utilities.

4.30 APPLICABILITY AND GENERAL RULES

4.30.1 Subdivisions Subject to This Section

(A) The owner or proprietor of any tract of land who desires to subdivide land (i.e., to create a "subdivision") shall submit a plat of such subdivision to the [PLANNING OFFICIAL]. No person shall subdivide land without making and recording a plat and complying fully with this chapter. No person shall sell or transfer ownership of any lot or parcel of land by reference to a plat of a subdivision before such plat has been duly recorded with the register of deeds, unless such subdivision was created prior to the adoption of this chapter. No development approval or certificate of occupancy shall be issued for any plat, map, or plan that was created prior to subdivision approval under the LDC, or for any parcel or plat of land that was created by subdivision after the effective date of the LDC, and no excavation of land or construction of any public or private improvements shall be commenced, except in conformity with the requirements of the LDC.

(B) A final subdivision plat shall be approved by the [PLANNING OFFICIAL] before the subdivision of a parcel may be recorded. No land may be subdivided through the use of any legal description other than with reference to a plat approved by the [PLANNING OFFICIAL] in accordance with these regulations.

(C) The [PLANNING OFFICIAL] may review and approve, conditionally approve, or disapprove the sale, lease, or development of lands subdivided prior to or following the effective date of these regulations where:

(1) The applicant proposes to combine or to recombine previously subdivided and recorded lots, and the total number of lots will increase or does not meet the standards of the LDC; or

(2) The original subdivider or their successor failed to complete subdivision improvement requirements pursuant to a subdivision improvement agreement entered into when the plat for the subdivided land was approved, and the plat contains contiguous lots in common ownership where one or more of the contiguous lots are undeveloped. This subsection applies whether the lots are owned by the original subdivider or an immediate or remote grantee from the original subdivider. This subsection does not apply if the [LOCAL GOVERNMENT] has obtained possession of sufficient funds from security provided by the subdivider with which to complete construction of improvements in the subdivision.

Table 4-2
Subdivision Procedures

Classification	Definition	Sketch Plat	Preliminary Plat	Final Plat
Minor subdivision	Any subdivision: • Involving three or fewer lots; • Fronting on an existing street; • Not involving the creation of any new street; • Not involving the extension of municipal utilities; • Not involving the creation of public improvements; • Not adversely affecting the remainder of the parcel or adjoining the property; and • Not in conflict with the comprehensive plan, official map, or zoning regulations. A series of related minor subdivisions or contiguous land cumulatively totaling four or more lots shall be construed to create a major subdivision.	O		✓
Major subdivision	Any subdivision not exempted by the Land Development Code or state law, other than a minor subdivision.	✓	✓	✓

O = optional process and ✓ = mandatory process.

4.30.2 Exemptions

A subdivision plat is not required for any of the following:

(A) The combination or recombination of portions of previously subdivided and recorded lots where the total number of lots is not increased and the resultant lots are equal to or exceed the standards of the [LOCAL GOVERNMENT];

(B) The public acquisition by purchase of strips of land for the widening or opening of streets; and

(C) If a court orders the partition of land by dividing the same among the owners, provided that the [LOCAL GOVERNMENT] is made a party defendant to said action and gives its consent.

4.30.3 Recordation of Unapproved Plat Prohibited

The county clerk or register of deeds shall not file or record any subdivision plat required by the LDC until the plat is approved in accordance with the regulations set forth in this chapter.

4.30.4 Sale or Lease

No land described in this section shall be subdivided, sold, leased, transferred, or developed until each of the following conditions has occurred in accordance with these regulations:

(A) The subdivider or their agent has obtained approval of the preliminary plat (when required) and a final plat as provided in this chapter; and

(B) The subdivider or their agent files the approved plats with the county clerk or register of deeds.

4.30.5 Development Approval

No development approval, including land-use alteration, building permit, certificate of zoning compliance, or certificate of occupancy shall be issued for any parcel or plat of land created by subdivision unless the approvals conform to a previously approved and lawful subdivision plat or site plan.

4.31 CLASSIFICATION OF SUBDIVISIONS

Major and minor subdivisions are subject to the criteria for approval of subdivision plats, unless a specific provision indicates that it does not apply to minor subdivisions. Different time limits are prescribed for the review and processing of major and minor subdivisions in order to reflect the level of complexity involved in review of the applications. Subdivisions shall be classified as set forth in Table 4-2, which summarizes the procedures for the plat classifications.

4.32 SKETCH PLAT PROCEDURES

The applicant may file a sketch plat with the [PLANNING OFFICIAL]. The [PLANNING OFFICIAL] may meet with the applicant to discuss the procedures for processing a subdivision plat. A sketch plat shall not be formally approved or denied and is not binding on either the applicant or the [LOCAL GOVERNMENT].

4.33 PRELIMINARY PLAT PROCEDURES

The preliminary plat serves as a guide to the density, intensity, land uses, pedestrian and bicycle ways, trails, parks, open space, and future lot, street, and drainage patterns established for a site in the platting process. It is the intent of the preliminary plat requirement to insure that a landowner investigates the broad effects that development of property will have on the site itself as well as on adjacent properties and public infrastructure systems. Approval of a preliminary plat shall constitute acceptance of the land-use mix, development intensity, general street patterns, drainage patterns, lot patterns, parks and open space lands, and the general layout of pedestrian and bicycle trails, provided that these may be modified in conjunction with subsequent approvals if additional information reveals development constraints that are not evident during preliminary plat review.

4.33.1 Applicability

Approval of a preliminary plat is required for any site where the eventual platting of the property involves a major subdivision. No final plat shall be approved until a preliminary plat for the property has been approved, unless the application is for a minor subdivision.

4.33.2 Initiation

A preliminary plat shall be filed with the [PLANNING OFFICIAL] and shall contain the information required by Appendix B, Specifications for Documents to Be Submitted, of the LDC.

4.33.3 Completeness Review for Plat Approval

The [PLANNING OFFICIAL] shall notify the applicant within 10 days whether the application is complete.

4.33.4 Decision

4.33.4.1 Reviewing Agency

The reviewing agency for preliminary plats is the planning commission. All preliminary plats shall be processed through a quasi-judicial procedure. Upon final approval, a preliminary plat shall be made a matter of record as follows:

(A) The reasons for approval, disapproval, or approval with conditions shall be maintained on file with the [PLANNING OFFICIAL]; and

(B) The approved plat shall be indexed and filed by the [PLANNING OFFICIAL].

4.33.4.2 Time Limit for Approval

The reviewing agency shall act on a plat within 30 days after the date the plat is filed. Plats shall not be deemed filed unless and until it is determined that complete information has been provided, as set forth in § 4.33.4.3 Withdrawal of Application of this chapter. A plat is deemed approved unless it is approved or disapproved within the 30-day period.

4.33.4.3 Withdrawal of Application

Once filed with the reviewing agency, a plat may be withdrawn, provided that a written notice of withdrawal stating the reasons for the request is submitted to the [PLANNING OFFICIAL]. The 30-day time limitation shall cease on the date that the notice is received by the [PLANNING OFFICIAL]; however, the [PLANNING OFFICIAL] may elect to present a withdrawal request to the planning commission for consideration.

4.33.5 Criteria

(A) The planning commission shall not approve a plat unless it complies with the standards of this chapter. The plat shall be approved unless it is inconsistent with any of the criteria set forth in Chapter 5, Development Standards, of the LDC. The plat shall not be approved if it does not comply with any of the criteria set forth in Chapter 5. The decision-making entity shall not approve a plat if it fails to conform to:

(1) The comprehensive plan and future streets, alleys, parks, playgrounds, and public utility facilities;

(2) The transportation plan and major thoroughfare plan (or official map) for the extension of major thoroughfares, streets, and public highways, taking into account access to and extension of sewer and water mains and the instrumentalities of public utilities;

(3) Any applicable watershed drainage plan adopted by the city; and

(4) The rules and regulations contained within Chapter 5, Development Standards, of the LDC.

(B) It is the intent of the LDC that land to be subdivided shall be of a character that can be used safely for building purposes without danger to health or peril from fire, flood, or other menace; furthers environmentally sensitive area protection and sustainability; and that land shall not be subdivided until adequate public facilities and improvements exist or proper provision has been made for drainage, water, sewerage, and capital improvements, such as schools, parks, recreational facilities, transportation facilities, and improvements. Accordingly, the [PLANNING OFFICIAL] or planning commission shall not approve a subdivision plat unless all of the following findings with respect to the proposed development are made:

(1) The proposed land uses are in accord with the adopted comprehensive plan, specific plan, and the official zoning map, or that the means for reconciling any differences have been addressed. A preliminary plat may be processed concurrently with a rezoning request.

(2) The proposed subdivision conforms to all relevant requirements of the LDC and variances have been granted to permit any nonconformance. The plat shall:

(a) Meet all requirements with respect to lot size and area of Chapter 3, Zoning, of the LDC;

(b) Meet all provisions of this chapter;

(c) Meet all development standards of Chapter 5, Development Standards, of the LDC;

(d) Meet the criteria for sustainable development set out in § 5.53 Sustainability in Chapter 5, Development Standards, of the LDC;

(e) Meet any supplemental regulations pertaining to the proposed use or uses as set forth in Chapter 7, Supplemental Use Regulations, of the LDC; and

(e) In no way create a violation of any applicable current ordinances, statutes, or regulations.

(3) The proposed development, including its lot sizes, density, access, and circulation, is compatible with the existing and/or permissible future use of adjacent property.

(4) The proposed public facilities are adequate to serve the normal and emergency demands of the proposed development, and to provide for the efficient and timely extension to serve future development as defined in Chapter 6, Adequate Public Facilities, of the LDC.

(5) The proposed subdivision complies with the Chapter 5, *Division 4: Greenspace (Landscaping, Tree Preservation, Screening, and Environmental Protection) Standards*, of the LDC); and the vehicular and pedestrian system is consistent with adopted transportation plans, including the thoroughfare plans and the collector street plan, and the street layout standards set forth in the street design and transportation standards (§ 5.23 Street Design and Transportation in Chapter 5, Development Standards, of the LDC).

(6) The lot, block, and street layout conform to the requirements of the design standards (§ 5.10 Lots through § 5.11 Blocks in Chapter 5, Development Standards, of the LDC).

(7) Rights-of-way and easements of adequate size and dimension are provided for the purpose of constructing the street, utility, and drainage facilities needed to serve the development as provided in the utilities standards (§ 5.24 Utilities in Chapter 5, Development Standards, of the LDC).

(8) The proposed subdivision provides the appropriate land and improvements necessary to satisfy the requirements of the park and open space standards (§ 5.21 Parks/Open Space in Chapter 5, Development Standards, of the LDC).

(9) The proposed subdivision includes any parking facilities in conformance with the parking standards (§ 5.51 Parking in Chapter 5, Development Standards, of the LDC).

(10) Any outdoor storage facilities comply with the outdoor storage standards (§ 5.50 Outdoor Storage in Chapter 5, Development Standards, of the LDC).

(11) The proposed subdivision provides adequate pedestrian access to parks; open space; and commercial, employment, and retail destinations as set forth in the street improvement standards (§ 5.23 Street Design and Transportation in Chapter 5, Development Standards, of the LDC).

(12) The proposed subdivision will not have detrimental impacts on the safety or viability of permitted uses on adjacent properties.

(13) The soils, topography, and water tables have been adequately studied to ensure that all lots are developable for their designated purposes.

(14) Any land located within Zone A, as shown on the currently adopted flood boundary and floodway maps of the flood insurance study, is determined to be suitable for its intended use, and the proposed subdivision adequately mitigates the risks of flooding, inadequate drainage, soil and rock formations with severe limitations for development, severe erosion potential, or any other floodplain-related risks to the health, safety, or welfare of the future residents of the proposed subdivision in a manner consistent with the LDC.

4.33.5.1 Subdivision Name

The proposed name of a subdivision shall not use a word that is the same as, similar to, or pronounced the same as a word in the name of any other subdivision in the [LOCAL GOVERNMENT] except for the words "court," "addition," "place," "heights," "hills," and similar words, unless the land platted is contiguous to and platted by the same applicant who platted the existing subdivision bearing the name, or the applicant has obtained the written consent of the party who platted the subdivision bearing that name, or the [PLANNING OFFICIAL] requires the use of the same name for purposes of clear identification.

4.33.5.2 Conditions on Approvals

In considering an application for a subdivision plat, the planning commission shall consider and may impose modifications or conditions to the extent that such modifications or conditions are necessary to insure compliance with the criteria in § 4.33.5 Criteria of this chapter.

4.33.6 Subsequent Applications

There is no restriction on reapplication for subdivision approval.

4.33.7 Amendments

Amendments to a subdivision plat shall be approved in the same manner as the original plat, except as otherwise provided for amending plats or replats herein. Amendments to preliminary plats may be initiated by the owner of property within the preliminary plat area subject to the following:

(A) Minor amendments may be approved by the [PLANNING OFFICIAL] without filing a new preliminary plat. Minor amendments include the following:

(1) Changes in the internal alignment of streets that do not affect external properties or the connectivity index;

(2) Changes in internal parcel boundaries that do not abut external property lines;

(3) Changes in setbacks along internal property lines;

(4) Changes in the routing of trails and pedestrian ways; or

(5) Changes in the orientation of buildings on internal parcels.

(B) No minor change authorized by this section may cause any of the following:

(1) Change in the permitted uses;

(2) Increased intensity of use as measured by the number of dwelling units or square feet of nonresidential building area;

(3) Increased trip generation or demand for public utilities;

(4) Decreased public or private open space area; or

(5) Increased volume or velocity of stormwater runoff from the development.

4.33.8 Major Amendments

All other changes to an approved preliminary plat require the filing and approval of a new preliminary plat.

4.33.9 Scope of Approval

(A) The preliminary plat governs the preparation of the final subdivision plat, which must be submitted for final approval and recordation upon fulfillment of the requirements of this chapter.

(B) The approval is valid so long as the applicant receives and maintains a valid subsequent development approval or initiates construction within two years of the preliminary plat approval. If development has not been initiated within two years of preliminary plat approval, any changes in development standards shall apply to the development proposed by the preliminary plat.

(C) If a final plat is not submitted within 12 months after approval of the preliminary plat, or within such extended period as may be allowed, the preliminary plat approval shall be void. The planning commission may approve a staging plan extending the effective period of the preliminary plat approval up to five years where it is the intent of the landowners to proceed to final plats covering only a portion of the site at any one time. Beyond two years or, in the case of staged development, five years, the applicant shall resubmit a preliminary plat to the [PLANNING OFFICIAL] for review by staff and the referral agencies to insure that the application is still in compliance with the LDC and any requirements of other agencies.

(D) After the expiration of two years following approval of a preliminary plat, changes to the final plat may be required where a change in the comprehensive plan or the LDC has occurred that affects compliance of the application with the ordinance. The applicant may make the necessary changes and then proceed to a final plat, or they may choose to resubmit the preliminary plat for review through the normal development approval review process.

4.33.10 Recording Procedures

A copy of the preliminary plat shall be maintained by the applicant and kept in the planning department offices.

4.34 FINAL PLAT PROCEDURES

4.34.1 Applicability

There shall be a final plat for each subdivision that received preliminary plat approval. No final subdivision plat shall be recorded until a final plat has been approved as provided in this section.

4.34.2 Initiation

The materials required by Appendix B, Specifications for Documents to Be Submitted, of the LDC shall be submitted to the [PLANNING OFFICIAL] for a determination as to whether it complies with the approved preliminary plat. The subdivider may submit final plat copies for only that portion of the approved preliminary plat that they propose to record and develop at that time, if such portion conforms to all requirements of this chapter. The final plat shall conform to the approved preliminary plat. Any deviation from the approved preliminary plat that does not constitute a minor amendment requires additional review and approval by the planning commission.

4.34.3 Completeness Review for Plat Approval

Upon submittal of the copies of the final plat and other required materials, the [PLANNING OFFICIAL] shall review the application for completeness, and shall initiate and coordinate review by the affected [LOCAL GOVERNMENT] and state agencies in order to determine substantial compliance with the approved preliminary plat and general compliance with the provisions of the ordinance set forth herein and other applicable laws and regulations.

4.34.4 Decision

The final plat and related materials shall be approved or disapproved by the [PLANNING OFFICIAL] within 30 days after a complete application is filed. Approval shall be in the form of a written letter to the subdivider advising that the final plat and engineering plans, as required, meet all local and state requirements, and that the original of the final plat may be submitted to the [PLANNING OFFICIAL].

The [PLANNING OFFICIAL] shall execute the plat. The action of the [PLANNING OFFICIAL] shall be noted on all copies of the final plat to be retained as required for records or further action of the department or other affected agencies of the [LOCAL GOVERNMENT] or state. Following execution of the final plat, the applicant shall record it with the register of deeds.

The [PLANNING OFFICIAL] may introduce conditions not applied to previous applications only upon finding that new information reveals conditions that directly affect the subdivision's ability to satisfy the criteria established in § 4.35.5 As-Built Drawings of this chapter.

4.34.5 Criteria

4.34.5.1 Compliance with Preliminary Plat Required

The final subdivision plat shall comply in all respects with the preliminary plat, as approved.

4.34.5.2 Completion of Improvements

(A) Except as provided in § 4.36 Subdivision Improvement Agreements of this chapter, all applicants shall complete all street, sanitary, and other public improvements of the subdivision as required by the LDC before the final plat is recorded.

(B) No person shall subdivide any tract of land unless it conforms to all applicable provisions of the LDC. The plat shall be approved unless it is inconsistent with any of the criteria set forth in Chapter 5, Development Standards, of the LDC. The plat shall not be approved if it does not comply with any of the criteria set forth in Chapter 5.

(C) The final subdivision plat application shall be accompanied by formal, irrevocable offers of dedication to the public of all streets, [LOCAL GOVERNMENT] uses, utilities, parks, and easements, in a form approved by the [CITY/COUNTY] attorney, and the subdivision plat shall be marked with a notation indicating the formal offers of dedication as follows:

The owner, or his/her representative, hereby irrevocably offers for dedication to the [LOCAL GOVERNMENT] all the streets, uses, easements, parks, and required utilities shown on the subdivision plat and construction plans in accordance with an irrevocable offer of dedication dated _____, and recorded in the register of deeds.

By_____
    Owner or Representative

Date_____

(D) The applicant shall deliver a full covenant and warranty deed to all dedicated lands and improvements in proper form for recording.

(E) The [PLANNING OFFICIAL] shall not approve a final plat unless and until satisfactory evidence is filed that the final plat is in a form acceptable for recording with the register of deeds, and that all subdivision improvement agreements have been signed by the applicant. The subdivider will also be required to submit a final subdivision plat fee, payment of all design costs for improvements, and appropriate performance surety.

(F) The final plat shall comply with any staging or sequence plan set forth in the preliminary plat.

4.34.5.3 Monuments

The applicant shall place reference monuments in the subdivision as required by [STATUTE].

4.34.6 Subsequent Applications

There is no restriction on reapplication for subdivision approval.

4.34.7 Amendments

Amendments to a subdivision plat shall be approved in the same manner as the original plat, except as otherwise provided for amending plats or replats herein.

4.34.8 Scope of Approval

(A) Approval of the final plat for a subdivision or section thereof shall not be deemed to be accepted by the [LOCAL OR STATE GOVERNMENT] of any street, alley, public space, utility, or other physical improvements shown on the final plat and engineering plans for the maintenance, repair, or operation.

(B) No development approval or certificate of occupancy shall be issued or approved until the expiration of two weeks after a final plat has been recorded. The purpose of this time period is to permit the assignment of addresses and personal identification numbers in the land records.

(C) An application for plat approval shall expire, and shall be void for all purposes, if a plat is not approved in accordance with this chapter within two years from the date that the plat was formally submitted. Upon expiration of the plat application, a new plat number, application, and fee shall be required if plat approval is still sought.

(D) If a plat is not recorded within three years from the date of plat approval or upon expiration of any time extension thereto, approval of such plat shall expire. Thereafter, should the applicant desire to record the plat, a new application shall be required in the same manner as for a previously unsubmitted plat.

4.34.9 Recording Procedures

Within 12 months after final plat approval, the applicant shall file the plat with the register of deeds as provided by law. The final plat approval shall expire within the above-referenced time period, unless the [GOVERNING ENTITY] has granted an extension. The [PLANNING OFFICIAL] may grant up to two extensions of final plat approval, each up to six months. Failure to record the final plat within the time frame noted shall cause the final plat approval to be void.

4.35 CONSTRUCTION PLANS

4.35.1 Applicability

Following approval of the preliminary plat, the applicant shall have prepared, by a professional engineer registered in [STATE], construction plans consisting of complete construction drawings and specifications of all easements, streets, traffic control devices, street lights, sanitary sewers, stormwater facilities, water system facilities, sidewalks, and other improvements required by this chapter. Construction plans shall be submitted to the [PLANNING OFFICIAL] for review and approval as a ministerial development approval. All improvements required pursuant to these regulations shall be constructed in accordance with the applicable requirements of Chapter 5, Development Standards, of the LDC and, where applicable, the requirements and authorization of the appropriate state agency, utility company, or local franchisee.

4.35.2 Public Agency Reviews

The [PLANNING OFFICIAL] shall review and act on all construction plan applications in consultation with the [ENGINEERING OFFICIAL].

4.35.3 Timing of Improvements

Except upon the written approval of the [PLANNING OFFICIAL], no grading, removal of trees or other vegetation, land filling, construction of improvements, or other material change, except for purposes of aiding in preparation of final engineering drawings or plans, shall commence on the subject property until the applicant has:
 (A) Received the approval of the construction plans and all necessary development approvals from the [PLANNING OFFICIAL]; or
 (B) Entered into a subdivision improvement agreement with the [LOCAL GOVERNMENT] or otherwise arranged for completion of all required improvements.

4.35.4 Modification of Construction Plans

All installations of improvements and all construction shall conform to the approved construction plans. If the applicant chooses to make minor modifications in design and/or specifications during construction, such changes shall be made at the applicant's own risk, but only with the written approval of the [PLANNING OFFICIAL]. It shall be the responsibility of the applicant to notify the [PLANNING OFFICIAL] in advance of any changes to be made from the approved drawings. In the event that actual construction work deviates from that shown on the approved construction plans, and such deviation was not approved in advance by the [PLANNING OFFICIAL], the applicant may be required to correct the installed improvements to conform to the approved construction plans. In addition, the [PLANNING OFFICIAL] may take such other actions as may be deemed appropriate, including, but not limited to, revocation of development approvals already issued and/or withholding of future approvals and development approvals.

4.35.5 As-Built Drawings

4.35.5.1 Submittal

Prior to final inspection of the required improvements, the applicant shall submit to the [PLANNING OFFICIAL] one reproducible copy and two prints of as-built engineering drawings for each of the required improvements that have been completed. Each set of drawings shall be recertified by the applicant's professional engineer, indicating the date when the as-built survey was made.

4.35.5.2 Sewer and Storm Drainage

As-built drawings shall show the constructed vertical elevation, horizontal location and size of all sanitary and storm sewers, manholes, inlets, junction boxes, detention basins, and other appurtenances or elements of the sewerage and storm drainage systems constructed to serve the subdivision. The subdivider shall cause all grading, excavations, open cutting, and similar land surface disturbances to be mulched, seeded, sodded, or otherwise protected. No work shall be initiated relative to the preparation of land or the installation of general improvements until such time as all aspects of the subdivider's engineering plans and sedimentation control proposals have received approval.

4.35.5.3 Water

As-built drawings shall depict water lines, valves, fire hydrants, and other appurtenances or elements of the water distribution system constructed to serve the project. Such information shall include the horizontal location and size of water lines and the location and description of valves with dimensional ties.

4.35.5.4 Sidewalks

As-built drawings shall depict the location with respect to the street right-of-way, width, and vertical elevation.

4.35.5.5 Control Points

As-built drawings shall show all control points and monumentation.

4.35.6 Inspection and Acceptance of Improvements

4.35.6.1 Inspection Required

During the preparation of land and the installation of general improvements, periodic inspections shall be made to ensure conformity with the approved plans, specifications, and standards. Appropriate agencies of the [STATE AND LOCAL GOVERNMENT] may make inspections at any time during the progress of work. All improvements required by these regulations shall be inspected prior to acceptance by the [LOCAL GOVERNMENT]. Where inspections are made by individuals or agencies, other than the [PLANNING OFFICIAL], the applicant shall provide the [PLANNING OFFICIAL] with written reports of each final inspection.

4.35.6.2 Inspection Schedule

The applicant shall notify the [PLANNING OFFICIAL] of the commencement of construction of improvements 24 hours prior thereto. Inspections are required at each of the following stages of construction or as otherwise determined through an owner contract or development improvement agreement:

(A) Site grading/erosion control completion;
(B) Underground utility installation;
(C) Subgrade preparation prior to aggregate base installation;
(D) Aggregate base compaction;
(E) Concrete curb and gutter installation;
(F) Bituminous binder placing; and
(G) Final surfacing prior to seal coat.

4.35.6.3 Compliance with Standards

The applicant or the bonded construction contractor shall bear full and final responsibility for the installation and construction of all required improvements according to the provisions of these regulations and the standards and specifications of other public agencies.

4.35.6.4 Acceptance

(A) Approval of the installation and construction of improvements by the [PLANNING OFFICIAL] shall not constitute acceptance by the [LOCAL GOVERNMENT] of the improvement for dedication purposes. The installation of improvements in any subdivision shall in no case serve to bind the [LOCAL GOVERNMENT] to accept such improvements for maintenance, repair, or operation thereof. Such acceptance shall be subject to the existing regulations concerning the acceptance of each type of improvement.

(B) The [LOCAL GOVERNMENT] shall not have any responsibility with respect to any street or other improvement, notwithstanding the use of same by the public, unless the street or other improvements have been accepted.

(C) When improvements have been constructed in accordance with the requirements and conditions of these regulations and the specifications of this chapter, and the applicant has submitted as-built reproducibles to the [PLANNING OFFICIAL], the [PLANNING OFFICIAL] shall accept the improvements for maintenance by the [LOCAL GOVERNMENT], except that this shall not apply to improvements maintained by another entity.

(D) The provisions shall not relieve the subdivider or the subdivider's agent or contractor of any responsibility in notifying any agency for the [LOCAL GOVERNMENT] of completed work and formal request for inspection of same. The approving authorities having jurisdiction shall inspect and approve all completed work prior to the release of any applied performance sureties.

4.35.6.5 Site Cleanup

The applicant shall be responsible for removal of all equipment, material, and general construction debris from the subdivision and from any lot, street, public way, or property therein or adjacent thereto. Dumping of such debris into sewers, onto adjacent property, or onto other land in the [LOCAL GOVERNMENT] is prohibited.

4.35.6.6 Failure to Complete Improvements

If a subdivision improvement agreement has been executed, and security has been posted and required public improvements are not installed pursuant to the terms of the agreement, the [PLANNING OFFICIAL] may:

(A) Declare the agreement to be in default and require that all public improvements be installed regardless of the extent of completion of the development at the time the agreement is declared to be in default;

(B) Obtain funds pursuant to the surety and complete the public improvements by themselves or through a third party;

(C) Assign its right to receive funds pursuant to the surety in whole or in part to any third party, including a subsequent owner of the subdivision or addition for whom the public improvements were not constructed, in exchange for the subsequent owner's agreement to complete the required public improvements; and/or

(D) Exercise any other rights available under the law.

4.36 SUBDIVISION IMPROVEMENT AGREEMENTS

4.36.1 Applicability

The [PLANNING OFFICIAL] may waive the requirement for the completion of required improvements if the applicant enters into a subdivision improvement agreement by which the applicant covenants and agrees to complete all required on- and off-site public improvements no later than one year following the date upon which the final plat is recorded. Such period may be extended for up to an additional six months upon its expiration at the discretion of the [PLANNING OFFICIAL].

The [PLANNING OFFICIAL] may require the applicant to complete and dedicate some required public improvements prior to approval of the final plat and to enter into a subdivision improvement agreement for completion of the remainder of the required improvements during such one-year period. The applicant shall bear the responsibility to prepare a subdivision improvement agreement. The [CITY/COUNTY] attorney shall approve any subdivision improvement agreement as to form.

4.36.2 Covenants to Run with the Land

The subdivision improvement agreement shall provide that the covenants contained therein shall run with the land and bind all successors, heirs, and assignees of the applicant. The subdivision improvement agreement shall be recorded with the register of deeds. All existing lienholders shall be required to subordinate their liens to the covenants contained in the subdivision improvement agreement.

4.36.3 Base Course to Be Installed

In order to provide for emergency access, no subdivision improvement agreement shall be approved, and no performance guarantee shall be accepted, until the base course for the streets within the applicable phase for which a final plat is proposed has been installed.

4.36.4 Performance Security

Whenever the [PLANNING OFFICIAL] permits an applicant to enter into a subdivision improvement agreement, the applicant shall be required to provide sufficient security to ensure completion of the required public improvements. The performance security shall be in an amount approved by the [ENGINEERING OFFICIAL] as reflecting 125 percent of the cost of the improvements in the approved construction plan, and shall be sufficient to cover all promises and conditions contained in the subdivision improvement agreement. In addition to all other security, when the [LOCAL GOVERNMENT] participates in the cost of an improvement, the applicant shall provide a performance bond from the contractor, with the [LOCAL GOVERNMENT] as a co-obligee. The issuer of any surety bond shall be subject to the approval of the [CITY/COUNTY] attorney.

4.36.5 Type of Security

The security shall be in the form of a performance bond, a trust agreement, a letter of credit, cash escrow, or a surety bond. The guarantees shall conform to the standards described in § 4.36.5.1 Performance Bond through § 4.36.5.5 Cash Escrow or Surety Bond of this chapter.

4.36.5.1 Performance Bond

A performance bond shall be executed by a surety company licensed to do business in the state in an amount equal to the cost estimate, as approved by the [ENGINEERING OFFICIAL], of all uncompleted and unaccepted improvements required by these regulations (other than gas and electric lines), with the condition that the subdivider shall complete such improvements and have them accepted by the [LOCAL GOVERNMENT] within three years from the date of plat approval. The [ENGINEERING OFFICIAL] may sign the bond instrument on behalf of the [LOCAL GOVERNMENT], and the [CITY/COUNTY] attorney shall approve same as to form.

4.36.5.2 Trust Agreement

The subdivider shall cause to be placed in a trust account on deposit in a bank or trust company or with a qualified escrow agent selected by the subdivider and approved by the [ENGINEERING OFFICIAL] a sum of money equal to the cost estimate, as approved by the [ENGINEERING OFFICIAL], of all uncompleted and unaccepted site improvements (other than gas and electric lines) required by these regulations. The [ENGINEERING OFFICIAL] is authorized to sign the agreement on behalf of the [LOCAL GOVERNMENT], and the [CITY/COUNTY] attorney shall approve same as to form.

4.36.5.3 Letter of Credit

The subdivider shall provide an irrevocable letter of credit in an amount equal to the cost estimate, as approved by the [ENGINEERING OFFICIAL], of all uncompleted and unaccepted site improvements (other than gas and electric lines) required by these regulations. The [ENGINEERING OFFICIAL] is authorized to sign the agreement on behalf of the [LOCAL GOVERNMENT], and the [CITY/COUNTY] attorney shall approve same as to form.

4.36.5.4 Cash or Cashier's Check

The subdivider shall provide to the [LOCAL GOVERNMENT] cash or a cashier's check in an amount equal to the cost estimate as approved by the [ENGINEERING OFFICIAL] of all uncompleted and unacceptable site improvements (other than gas and electric lines) required by these regulations. Upon completion of the required site improvements and their acceptance by the [ENGINEERING OFFICIAL], the amount will be refunded to the subdivider by the city.

4.36.5.5 Cash Escrow or Surety Bond

If security is provided in the form of a cash escrow, the applicant shall deposit with the [PLANNING OFFICIAL] a cash amount or certified check endorsed to the escrow agent for a face value in an amount of at least the amount specified by the [ENGINEERING OFFICIAL]. A surety bond or cash escrow account shall accrue to the [LOCAL GOVERNMENT] for administering the construction, operation, and maintenance of the improvements.

4.36.6 Guarantees

When a subdivider has given security in any of the forms provided in § 4.36.5 Type of Security of this chapter, and when 50 percent of the required site improvements has been completed and accepted by the [ENGINEERING OFFICIAL], or whenever any segment or segments of the required site improvements have been completed and accepted by the [ENGINEERING OFFICIAL], the subdivider may substitute for the original guarantee a new guarantee in an amount equal to the cost of the remaining site improvements. The cost estimate shall be approved by the [ENGINEERING OFFICIAL]. Such new guarantee need not be in the same form as the original guarantee so long as such guarantee is one that is listed in § 4.36.5 Type of Security of this chapter. However, in no event shall the substitution of one security for another in any way change or modify the terms and conditions of the performance agreement or the obligation of the subdivider as specified in the performance agreement.

4.36.7 Reimbursement

Where oversized facilities are required, the [PLANNING OFFICIAL] and applicant shall specify a reimbursement procedure in the subdivision improvement agreement.

4.36.8 Maintenance Bond

The applicant shall guarantee the improvements against defects in workmanship and materials for a period of five years from the date of acceptance of such improvements. In exceptional situations, where undue hardship would otherwise result and the shorter term would be consistent with the purposes of the LDC, the [PLANNING OFFICIAL] may recommend and the planning commission may approve a shorter-term maintenance guarantee. The maintenance guarantee shall be secured by a surety bond or cash escrow in an amount reflecting 50 percent of the cost of the completed improvements.[2]

If the applicant has entered into a subdivision improvement agreement for the completion of required improvements, an appropriate percentage of the performance bond or cash escrow may be retained by the [LOCAL GOVERNMENT] in lieu of a maintenance bond.

If the applicant has not entered into a subdivision improvement agreement, the applicant shall guarantee the improvements as required by this section. A surety bond or cash escrow totaling 50 percent of the costs of the completed improvements shall be provided by the applicant.

4.36.9 Temporary Improvements

The applicant shall construct and pay for all costs of temporary improvements required by the [PLANNING OFFICIAL] and shall maintain said temporary improvements for the period specified.

4.37 SUBDIVISION VARIANCES

4.37.1 Applicability

The [LOCAL GOVERNMENT] hereby finds and determines that some standards of the LDC may be impracticable in some situations due to exceptional circumstances, such as difficult terrain and unique topographical conditions. The [LOCAL GOVERNMENT] finds and determines that the granting of such exceptions is in the public interest, but that administrative review is needed in order to ensure that the spirit and intent of the LDC is preserved. Accordingly, these procedures permit administrative exceptions to be granted as part of the subdivision plat approval process without the need for a variance. Applicants who are denied an administrative exception may then seek a variance in accordance with *Division 6: Variances and Appeals* of this chapter.

4.37.2 Initiation

An exception shall be requested as part of the application for a subdivision plat approval. The exception shall be specifically labeled in the application with a specific reference to this section of the ordinance, along with any supporting documentation justifying the need for an exception.

4.37.3 Completeness Review

The application for an exception shall be reviewed for completeness concurrent with the completeness review for the subdivision plat or development plat.

4.37.4 Decision

The exception shall be approved, denied, or approved with conditions as part of the decision approving, denying, or approving with conditions the application for approval of a subdivision plat or development plat.

4.37.5 Approval Criteria

The exception shall be granted if the reviewing agency finds and determines that:

(A) The exception will not be contrary to the spirit and intent of the LDC and the specific regulations from which an exception is requested;

(B) The applicant has taken all practicable measures to minimize any adverse impacts on the public health, safety, and public welfare;

(C) Under the circumstances, the public interest underlying the proposed exception outweighs the public interest underlying the particular regulation for which the exception is granted; and

(D) The proposed exception complies with all other applicable standards of the LDC to the extent practicable.

4.38 DEDICATION (ACCEPTANCE)

The approval of a plat shall not be considered an acceptance of any proposed dedication and does not impose on the [LOCAL GOVERNMENT] any duty regarding the maintenance or improvement of any dedicated parts until the appropriate [LOCAL GOVERNMENT] authorities make an actual appropriation of the dedicated parts by entry, use, or improvement. The disapproval of a plat shall be considered a refusal by the [LOCAL GOVERNMENT] of the offered dedication indicated on the plat.

4.39 PLAT VACATION

4.39.1 Applicability

The provisions of this section establish a process for approving the elimination of a plat, in whole or in part. The record owners of the tract covered by a plat may vacate the plat at any time before any lot in the plat is sold. The plat is vacated when a signed, acknowledged instrument declaring the plat vacated is approved and recorded in the manner prescribed for the original plat. If lots in the plat have been sold, the plat, or any part of the plat, may be vacated on the application of all the owners of lots in the plat with approval obtained in the manner prescribed for the original plat.

4.39.2 Initiation

The owner or owners of lots in any approved subdivision, including the developer, shall initiate a plat vacation by filing a petition and declaration with the [PLANNING OFFICIAL] to vacate the plat with respect to their properties. The petition shall conform to the requirements of Appendix B, Specifications for Documents to Be Submitted, of the LDC. If the subdivider so desires, the vacating declaration and an application requesting resubdivision of the plat may be filed and processed simultaneously. The filing fee shall not be required if the vacating declaration is filed and processed simultaneously with a resubdivision plat.

4.39.3 Completeness Review

The [PLANNING OFFICIAL] shall review an application for a plat vacation as provided in § 4.3 Completeness Review of this chapter. The appellate agency for purposes of completeness review is the planning commission.

4.39.4 Decision

The petition may be approved, conditionally approved, or disapproved at a regular public meeting of the planning commission subject to the criteria in § 4.39.5 Approval Criteria of this chapter.

4.39.5 Approval Criteria

The planning commission shall approve the petition for vacation on such terms and conditions as are reasonable to protect public health, safety, and welfare. The planning commission shall not approve a petition for vacation if:

(A) It will materially injure the rights of any nonconsenting property owner or any public rights in public improvements, unless expressly agreed to by the agency with jurisdiction over the improvements; or

(B) The plat vacation would cause block lengths to exceed the maximum established by Chapter 5, Development Standards, of the LDC.

4.39.6 Scope of Approval

On the execution and recording of the vacating instrument, the vacated plat has no effect. A plat may be resubdivided upon vacation of the original plat. The resubdivision of the land covered by a plat that is vacated shall be platted in the same manner as is prescribed by this chapter for an original plat. In addition, a copy of the vacating declaration form shall be submitted with the resubdivision plat.

4.39.7 Recording Procedures

The recorder of deeds shall write legibly on the vacated plat the word "vacated," and shall enter on the plat a reference to the volume and page at which the vacating instrument is recorded.

4.40 PLATS (AMENDING)

Purpose and findings: This section provides a streamlined and efficient process for the combination of parcels or the replat of parcels. The [LOCAL GOVERNMENT] does not require extensive platting for every division of land otherwise within the scope of the state subdivision enabling legislation.

4.40.1 Applicability

A plat may be amended, and the [PLANNING OFFICIAL] may issue an amending plat, if the amending plat is signed by the applicants only and is solely for one or more of the following purposes:

(A) To correct an error in a course or distance shown on the preceding plat;

(B) To add a course or distance that was omitted on the preceding plat;

(C) To correct an error in a real property description shown on the preceding plat;

(D) To indicate monuments set after the death, disability, or retirement from practice of the professional engineer or surveyor responsible for setting monuments;

(E) To show the location or character of a monument that has been changed in location or character or that is shown incorrectly as to location or character on the preceding plat;

(F) To correct any other type of scrivener or clerical error or omission previously approved by the municipal authority responsible for approving plats, including lot numbers, acreage, street names, and identification of adjacent recorded plats;

(G) To correct an error in courses and distances of lot lines between two adjacent lots if:

(1) Both lot owners join in the application for amending the plat;

(2) Neither lot is abolished;

(3) The amendment does not attempt to remove recorded covenants or restrictions; and

(4) The amendment does not have a material adverse effect on the property rights of the other owners in the plat;

(H) To relocate a lot line to eliminate an inadvertent encroachment of a building or other improvement on a lot line or easement;

(I) To relocate one or more lot lines between one or more adjacent lots if:

(1) The owners of all those lots join in the application for amending the plat;

(2) The amendment does not attempt to remove recorded covenants or restrictions; and

(3) The amendment does not increase the number of lots.

4.40.2 Initiation

A subdivider wishing to amend an approved plat shall file with the planning department the amending plat, together with a copy of the plat being amended and a statement detailing the amendments being proposed. The [PLANNING OFFICIAL] will determine the extent to which the amending plat will require review by the various departments and agencies of the city. If the plat being amended has been recorded, the additional recordation fee shall be deposited with the [LOCAL GOVERNMENT] at the time of plat filing.

4.40.3 Completeness Review

The [PLANNING OFFICIAL] shall review an application for an amending plat in accordance with § 4.3 Completeness Review of this chapter. The appellate agency for purposes of completeness review is the planning commission.

4.40.4 Decision

Notice, a hearing, and the approval of other lot owners are not required for the approval and issuance of an amending plat. The amending plat shall be processed by the [PLANNING OFFICIAL] in the same manner as a minor plat. If the plat being amended has been recorded, the amending plat shall be clearly marked as follows:

Amending plat of (_____ [PLAT NUMBER] and _____ [NAME]). This plat amends the plat previously recorded in the plat and deed records of _____ County, Volume _____, Page _____.

The amending plat shall then be recorded if all requirements have been met. If the plat being amended has not been recorded, the amending plat may be approved by the [PLANNING OFFICIAL]. Upon approval by the [PLANNING OFFICIAL], the amending plat shall be annotated with the following statement:

This plat includes amendments approved by the [PLANNING OFFICIAL].

4.40.5 Approval Criteria

The amending plat shall be approved unless it is inconsistent with any of the criteria set forth in Chapter 5, Development Standards, of the LDC. The amending plat shall not be approved if it does not comply with any of the criteria set forth in Chapter 5.

4.40.6 Recording Procedures

The amending plat may be recorded as provided in § 4.34.7 Amendments of this chapter. Once recorded, the amending plat is controlling over the preceding plat without vacation of that plat.

DIVISION 6: VARIANCES AND APPEALS

4.51 GENERALLY

4.51.1 Powers and Duties of Hearing Officer

(A) The hearing officer shall consider and decide all applications for variances and appeals, except as otherwise provided in the LDC, and take testimony and evidence as provided in the LDC.

(B) Failure to comply with or maintain compliance with any conditions imposed by the hearing officer or the [PLANNING OFFICIAL] on an application shall constitute a violation of the LDC.

4.51.2 Stay of Development Approvals

The building inspector shall not issue a development approval until the appeal period in the division has expired and any appeal or protest has been determined.

4.52 APPEALS TO HEARING OFFICER

4.52.1 Applicability

(A) The hearing officer shall hear and decide appeals where it is alleged that there is an error in any written order, requirement, decision, interpretation, or determination made by the [PLANNING OFFICIAL] in the enforcement of this chapter and other chapters that specifically provide for appeal to the hearing officer. Appeals to the hearing officer may be taken by any person aggrieved by or affected by any written decision of the [PLANNING OFFICIAL].

(B) An aggrieved or adversely affected party may appeal the issuance of a development order or development approval pursuant to this chapter. For purposes of this subsection, an "aggrieved or adversely affected party" means any person or [LOCAL GOVERNMENT] that will suffer an adverse effect to an interest protected or furthered by the comprehensive plan, including interests related to health and safety, police and fire protection service systems, densities or intensities of development, transportation facilities, health care facilities, equipment or services, and environmental or natural resources. The adverse interest may be shared in common with other members of the community at large but must exceed in degree the general interest in community good shared by all persons. The term includes the owner, developer, or applicant for a development order.

4.52.2 Initiation

An application for a variance shall be filed with the [CITY/COUNTY CLERK].

4.52.3 Stay of Proceedings

When an appeal is filed to the hearing officer, all proceedings in furtherance of the action affected by the decision being appealed shall be stayed, unless:

(A) The [PLANNING OFFICIAL] certifies to the hearing officer, after the notice of appeal has been filed with the [PLANNING OFFICIAL], that by reason of facts stated in the certificate, a stay would cause imminent peril to life or property; or

(B) The appellant is not diligently pursuing the appeal.

4.52.4 Decision

(A) The hearing officer shall give public notice of the hearing as provided in this chapter, shall hold the hearing, and shall decide the appeal within a reasonable time after such hearing.

(B) Any party may appear before the hearing officer at any hearing, in person, or by agent or attorney.

(C) The hearing officer may:

(1) Reverse or affirm, wholly or partly, or may modify the order, requirement, decision, or determination appealed;

(2) Make such order, requirement, decision, or determination as ought to be made; and

(3) Exercise all the powers of the officer or agency from whom the appeal is taken.

4.52.5 Appeals Involving Constitutional or Statutory Claims

4.52.5.1 Exemption from This Chapter

(A) The hearing officer may approve an exemption from any of the requirements of this chapter, to the extent necessary to comply with or conform to federal or state law, or to avoid or resolve any alleged violation of the freedom of religion based rights afforded to any person under federal or state law caused by the enforcement of any regulation imposed by this chapter.

(B) Any person desiring such an exemption shall file a written petition with the [PLANNING OFFICIAL], who shall forward the petition to the hearing officer for purposes of conducting a public hearing on the petition and issuing a final determination. The petition shall include separate statements that:

(1) Advise to which particular regulation of the [LOCAL GOVERNMENT] the requested exemption relates;

(2) Explain how the regulation is not in conformance with federal or state law, or how it allegedly violates the person's freedom of religion-based rights afforded under federal or state law, the Telecommunications Act of 1996, the Fair Housing Act, or other rights;

(3) Describe how granting the exemption would be in the public interest and not be contrary to health, safety, and welfare considerations; and

(4) Describe the intended use of land or activity for which the exemption is being sought.

(C) The petitioner shall submit any additional information requested by the hearing officer and shall appear before the hearing officer at the public hearing to explain the request and to answer any questions relative to the petition.

(D) In considering an exemption from the requirements of this chapter, the hearing officer may approve the exemption, provided that it makes findings, based on the evidence presented, regarding at least one of the following criteria:

(1) The exemption is in the public interest and is not contrary to health, safety, and welfare considerations;

(2) The exemption is necessary for the petitioner or the [LOCAL GOVERNMENT] to comply with or conform to federal or state law;

(3) If the claim is based on First Amendment rights of the U.S. Constitution or freedom of religion that the [LOCAL GOVERNMENT] regulation does not constitute or further a compelling governmental interest in need of protection and is not the least restrictive alternative for satisfying or achieving the governmental interest;

(4) The exemption is necessary to avoid or resolve any alleged violation of rights afforded to any person under federal or state law caused by the enforcement of any regulation of the LDC; and

(5) The [LOCAL GOVERNMENT] regulation does not constitute or further a compelling governmental interest in need of protection and is not the least restrictive alternative for satisfying or achieving the governmental interest.

(E) The hearing officer shall either grant or deny the exemption within 30 days of the conclusion of the public hearing at which it considered the exemption. The hearing officer may request additional information from the petitioner, may continue the hearing from time to time in order to fully consider the petition and all pertinent information, and may grant the exemption in full or in part by waiving compliance with certain aspects of this chapter. The hearing officer may grant the exemption in full or in part, subject to conditions that are related to the public health, safety, and welfare. If the hearing officer grants the exemption in full or in part, it shall prepare a written order that approves the exemption. If appropriate, the order may contain conditions relating to the exemption. If the hearing officer denies the exemption, it shall issue a written decision that identifies the reasons for the denial and shall provide a copy of the decision to the petitioner.

4.52.5.2 Temporary Certificate of Compliance

The petitioner may file a written request with the hearing officer for a temporary certificate of compliance to allow the use or activity during the pendency of the exemption petition process pursuant to this chapter.

4.52.5.3 [LOCAL GOVERNMENT] Policy or Practice

In regard to an exemption from any [LOCAL GOVERNMENT] policy or practice, the same procedures and criteria under § 4.52.5.1 Exemption from This Chapter shall apply, except that there shall be no public hearing before the hearing officer. The [PLANNING OFFICIAL] shall forward the petition to the hearing officer who shall consider the exemption petition at an open public meeting, which shall be attended by the petitioner. The public meeting shall be scheduled within 30 days of receipt of the petition and the hearing officer may request additional information from the petitioner.

The hearing officer shall grant or deny the exemption within 30 days of the conclusion of the last public meeting at which it considers the information relative to the exemption. The hearing officer may grant the exemption in full or in part, subject to conditions that are related to the public health, safety, and welfare. If the hearing officer grants the exemption in full or in part, it shall prepare a written order that approves the exemption. If appropriate, the order may contain conditions relating to the exemption. If the hearing officer denies the exemption, it shall issue a written decision that identifies the reasons for the denial and shall provide a copy of the decision to the petitioner.

4.53 VARIANCES

4.53.1 Applicability

The hearing officer may authorize a variance from the provisions of this chapter that comply with the requirements of this section. No nonconforming use of neighboring lands, buildings, or other structures, legal or illegal, in the same district, and no permitted use of lands, buildings, or other structures in adjacent districts, shall be considered as grounds for issuance of a variance permitting similar uses.

4.53.2 Initiation

A variance application shall be filed with the [PLANNING OFFICIAL]. The application shall state fully the special conditions and circumstances applying to the building or other structure or land for which such variance is sought. The application shall demonstrate that the existing conditions and circumstances are such that the strict application of the provisions of the LDC provisions would deprive the applicant of reasonable use of said land, building, or structure, equivalent to the use made of lands, buildings, or structures in the same district and permitted under the terms of this provision and that the peculiar conditions and circumstances are not the result of the actions of the applicant.

4.53.3 Decision

The hearing officer shall hold a public hearing. Notice shall be provided as set forth in this chapter. The [PLANNING OFFICIAL] shall submit a report to the hearing officer and the applicant who evaluates the application based on the criteria required by this section. The hearing officer shall render a decision and deny, approve, or approve with conditions the variance after considering the evidence presented at this hearing or agreed on by the parties.

4.53.4 Approval Criteria

The hearing officer shall not approve a variance unless it finds that special circumstances or conditions exist that are peculiar to the land, buildings, or other structures for which the variance is sought and do not apply generally to lands, buildings, or other structures in the same district. Special circumstances or conditions to be considered for variances shall include, but not be limited to, the circumstances as described in § 4.53.4.1 Redevelopment through § 4.53.4.7 Public Facilities of this chapter.

4.53.4.1 Redevelopment

The proposed project involves the redevelopment or utilization of an existing developed or partially developed site.

4.53.4.2 Substandard Lot(s)

The proposed project involves the utilization of an existing legal nonconforming lot(s).

4.53.4.3 Preservation Area

The proposed project site contains a designated preservation area.

4.53.4.4 Historic Resources

The proposed project site contains historical significance.

4.53.4.5 Significant Vegetation or Natural Features

The proposed project site contains significant vegetation or other natural features.

4.53.4.6 Neighborhood Character

The proposed project promotes the established historic or traditional development pattern of a blockface, including setbacks, building height, and other dimensional requirements.

4.53.4.7 Public Facilities

The proposed project involves the development of public parks; public facilities; nongovernmental or public educational facilities, colleges, private schools, and universities; and public utilities or hospitals.

  (A) Strict application of the provisions of the chapter would provide the applicant with no means for reasonable use of the land, buildings, or other structures.
  (B) The peculiar conditions and existing circumstances are not the result of the actions of the applicant.
  (C) The reasons set forth in the application justify the granting of a variance.
  (D) The variance proposed to be granted is the minimum variance that will make possible the reasonable use of the land, building, or other structure.
  (E) The variance will be in harmony with the general purpose and intent of this chapter.
  (F) The variance will not injure the neighborhood or otherwise be detrimental to the public welfare.

DIVISION 7: MISCELLANEOUS DEVELOPMENT ORDERS

4.55 DEVELOPMENT AGREEMENTS

Purpose and findings: This section promotes and facilitates orderly and planned growth and development through the provision of certainty in the development approval process by the [LOCAL GOVERNMENT] and through corresponding assurances by developers. This section:

• Eliminates uncertainty in the development approval process, which results in a waste of resources that contributes to escalating costs of development and which, in turn, discourages investment and produces higher prices for consumers;

• Assures applicants that, upon approval of their project, they may proceed in accordance with existing policies, rules, and regulations;

• Encourages the achievement of growth management goals and objectives, including assurances of adequate public facilities at the time of development, proper timing and sequencing of development, effective capital improvements programming, and appropriate development incentives in accordance with existing policies, rules, and regulations;

• Strengthens the public planning process, encourages private participation in comprehensive planning, and reduces the economic costs of government;

• Provides a mechanism for allowing exemptions from ordinances or regulations in order to promote flexibility and to respond more selectively to specific development proposals; and

• Encourages plan implementation through a more flexible development procedure.

4.55.1 Applicability

This section applies to any development agreement entered into between an applicant and the [LOCAL GOVERNMENT] in order to:
  (A) Enforce a condition of development approval;
  (B) Recognize the existence of vested rights;
  (C) Provide for the provision of infrastructure, design amenities, or other conditions; and/or
  (D) Resolve potential legal disputes.

4.55.2 Criteria for Entering into Development Agreements

The [GOVERNING ENTITY] may enter into a development agreement pursuant to this section only if it finds that:
  (A) The development agreement has been duly adopted in accordance with the provisions of this section;

(B) The development to which the development agreement pertains is consistent with the comprehensive plan and capital improvements program, zoning regulations, impact fee regulations, and other applicable requirements; and the development subject to the agreement contains outstanding features that advance the policies, goals, and objectives of the comprehensive plan or growth management plan beyond mere conformity, in accordance with the criteria established in the zoning regulations; or the property owner agrees to make contributions of capital improvements for community-related facilities for one or more types of public improvements, which are in excess of the development's proportionate share of the costs of the facilities needed to serve the development and which thereby advance provision of such facilities to serve the community.

4.55.3 Initiation

4.55.3.1 Generally

An application for a development agreement may be made to the [PLANNING OFFICIAL]. Application may be made by any person having a legal or equitable interest in the subject real property. If made by the holder of an equitable interest, the application shall be accompanied by a verified title report and by a notarized statement of consent to proceed with the proposed development agreement executed by the holder of the legal interest.

4.55.3.2 Contents of the Application

The application shall be on a form prescribed by the [PLANNING OFFICIAL] and shall be accompanied by a proposed ordinance and development agreement.

4.55.4 Contents of Development Agreement

4.55.4.1 Mandatory Provisions

The development agreement shall include, at a minimum, provisions pertaining to the following:
 (A) The land that is the subject of the agreement;
 (B) The duration of the agreement;
 (C) The permitted land use or uses and density/intensity for the proposed development project and any conditions attached thereto;
 (D) The maximum height and size of the proposed buildings; and
 (E) Any provisions for the dedication of any portion of the land for public use.

4.55.4.2 Optional Provisions

If agreed to by the applicant and approved by the [GOVERNING ENTITY], the development agreement may include, without limitation, provisions pertaining to the following:

 (A) The phasing of the proposed development project in coordination with the provision of public facilities, including, but not limited to, roads, water, sewer, drainage, parks, municipal, and other facilities, required to accommodate the impacts of the proposed development project on such facilities at the [LOCAL GOVERNMENT]'s adopted LOS standards;
 (B) The identification of public facilities to be dedicated, constructed, or financed by the developer pursuant to the development agreement and the designation of such facilities as project improvements, system improvements, or subsystem improvements;
 (C) The determination of the development project's proportionate share of the total system and subsystem improvement costs required to be dedicated, constructed, or financed by the developer of the development project;
 (D) The determination of offsets to impact fees otherwise due from the dedication, construction, or financing of system or subsystem improvements;
 (E) The [LOCAL GOVERNMENT]'s share of the costs of system and subsystem improvements to be dedicated, constructed, or financed pursuant to the development agreement;
 (F) Reimbursements, as applicable, to the owner of the subject property for the amount of any contributions for system or subsystem improvements in excess of the proportionate share of the benefit derived from such facility by the subject property;
 (G) The rules, regulations, ordinances, laws, plans, and official policies of the [LOCAL GOVERNMENT] governing development applicable to the subject property; and
 (H) If the property to which the development agreement relates is located outside the incorporated area of the [LOCAL GOVERNMENT], the period of time within which each property shall be annexed to the [LOCAL GOVERNMENT].

4.55.5 Completeness Review

Upon submission of an application for a development agreement, the [PLANNING OFFICIAL] shall review the application and accompanying documentation for legal sufficiency, compliance with technical requirements, consistency with the adopted comprehensive plan for the [LOCAL GOVERNMENT], and applicable specific plans and applicable [LOCAL GOVERNMENT] rules, regulations, and policies. Upon satisfactory completion of such review, the [PLANNING OFFICIAL] shall place the matter on the agenda of the planning commission for public hearing at the next regularly scheduled planning commission meeting. If the application for development agreement is incomplete or legally insufficient, the [PLANNING OFFICIAL] shall notify the applicant by certified U.S. mail, return receipt requested, within 14 days after the date of submission of such application. Said notifications shall detail the specific grounds for rejection of the application. The applicant may resubmit at any time.

4.55.6 Decision

4.55.6.1 Notice of Planning Commission Public Hearing

Notice of the planning commission public hearing shall be provided in the manner required by § 4.4 Notice Provisions of this chapter.

4.55.6.2 Planning Commission Recommendation

The planning commission shall conduct a legislative public hearing and shall make a report and recommendation to the [GOVERNING ENTITY] by the affirmative vote of at least a majority of its voting members, as follows:

 (A) That the development agreement be adopted as proposed;

 (B) That the development agreement be adopted with modifications, as proposed by the planning commission; or

 (C) That the development agreement be denied.

 Any action taken by the planning commission shall be by resolution.

4.55.6.3 Failure of Planning Commission to Approve

If the planning commission fails to recommend approval or approval with modifications of the requested development agreement, no further action shall be taken on the application unless, within 10 days of the public hearing on the matter by the planning commission, the applicant files with the planning commission a request for consideration of the matter by the [GOVERNING ENTITY]. If such a request is timely filed with the planning commission, the request shall be forwarded to the [LOCAL GOVERNMENT] clerk for placement of the item on the [GOVERNING ENTITY] agenda of the next regularly scheduled meeting for a public hearing.

4.55.6.4 City Council Public Hearing

Upon receipt of the notice of action by the planning commission or request for a public hearing by the applicant, the [LOCAL GOVERNMENT] clerk shall thereupon set the matter for a public hearing before the [GOVERNING ENTITY], giving notice of the time, place, and purpose of such hearing in the same manner and in the same terms as provided in § 4.4 Notice Provisions of this chapter. The [GOVERNING ENTITY] shall consider the proposed development agreement at the public hearing on the date set for said hearing or on the date or dates to which such hearing may be continued from time to time by the [GOVERNING ENTITY].

 The [GOVERNING ENTITY] may:

 (A) Approve the development agreement as recommended by the planning commission;

 (B) Approve the development agreement with modifications; or

 (C) Reject the development agreement as recommended by the planning commission, in whole or in part, and take such further action as it deems to be in the public interest.

 Any such action shall be taken by the affirmative vote of at least a majority of the voting members of the [GOVERNING ENTITY].

4.55.6.5 Ordinance

The [GOVERNING ENTITY] may approve such agreement by ordinance. The [GOVERNING ENTITY]'s action shall be final and conclusive.

4.55.6.6 Execution of Development Agreement

If approved by the [GOVERNING ENTITY], the development agreement shall become effective upon execution by the [GOVERNING ENTITY], acting by and through the [MAYOR/CHIEF EXECUTIVE], by the applicant, and by any other parties to the development agreement.

4.55.7 Recordation

4.55.7.1 Notice

Within 10 days following rejection of a development agreement, the [CITY/COUNTY CLERK] shall give notice of such action to the applicant at the address shown on the application and to the planning commission through the [PLANNING OFFICIAL].

4.55.7.2 Recordation of Agreement

Within 10 days following complete execution of a development agreement, the [CITY/COUNTY CLERK] shall record with the recorder of deeds a fully executed copy of the development agreement and ordinance, which shall describe the land subject thereto. The agreement shall be binding upon, and the benefits of the agreement shall inure to the parties and all successors in interest to, the parties of the development agreement.

4.55.8 Coordination of Development Agreement Application with Other Discretionary Approvals

It is the intent of these regulations that the application for a development agreement will be made and be considered simultaneously with the review of other necessary applications, including, but not limited to: rezoning; subdivision and plat approval; planned commercial, residential, or industrial development; and CUPs. If combined with an application for rezoning, subdivision, plat approval, planned development, or CUP, the application for a development agreement shall be submitted with said application and shall be processed, to the maximum extent possible, jointly to avoid duplication of hearings and repetition of information. A development agreement is not a substitute for, nor an alternative to, any other required development approval, and the applicant must comply with all other required procedures for development approval.

4.55.9 Existing and Subsequently Adopted Rules, Regulations, Ordinances, Laws, and Policies

(A) Unless otherwise provided by the development agreement, rules, regulations, ordinances, laws, general or specific plans, and official policies of the [LOCAL GOVERNMENT] governing permitted uses, development, density and intensity of use, permitted uses of the land, growth management, adequacy of public facilities, environmental considerations, and governing design, improvement, and construction standards and specifications applicable to the subject property shall be those in force and effect at the time of commencement of the term of the development agreement.

(B) The adoption of a development agreement, however, shall not prevent the [LOCAL GOVERNMENT], in subsequent actions applicable to the property or to the [LOCAL GOVERNMENT] in general, from applying such newer, modified rules, regulations, ordinances, laws, general or specific plans, and official policies that do not conflict with those applicable to the property at the time of commencement of the development agreement and that do not prevent the development of the land as set forth in the development agreement. The existence of the development agreement shall not prevent the [LOCAL GOVERNMENT] from denying or conditionally approving any subsequent project development application not expressly addressed in said agreement on the basis of such existing or new rules, regulations, and policies.

(C) Application, processing and inspection fees, development fees, improvement standards as set forth in the [LOCAL GOVERNMENT] subdivision regulations and construction standards, and specifications that are revised during the term of a development agreement shall apply to the property, provided that:

(1) Such fees, standards, and specifications apply to public works within the [LOCAL GOVERNMENT]; and

(2) Their application to the subject property is prospective only as to applications for building and other development approvals or approvals of tentative subdivision maps not yet accepted for processing.

4.55.10 Subsequently Adopted State and Federal Laws

In the event that state or federal laws or regulations are enacted following approval of a development agreement that prevent or preclude compliance with one or more provisions of the development agreement, the provisions of the agreement shall be modified or suspended as may be necessary to comply with such state or federal laws or regulations, and every such development agreement shall so provide.

4.55.11 Periodic Review, Termination, or Modification

An adopted development agreement shall be reviewed at least every 24 months, at which time the owner or owners of the property subject to the development agreement shall be required to demonstrate good faith compliance with the terms of the development agreement. If, as a result of such review, the [GOVERNING ENTITY] finds and determines, on the basis of substantial evidence, that the owner or owners have not complied in good faith with the conditions of the development agreement, the [GOVERNING ENTITY] may unilaterally terminate or modify the agreement. Such action shall be taken by the [GOVERNING ENTITY] at a regular or special meeting, provided that the developer is notified at least 10 days in advance of such meeting.

4.55.12 Amendment or Cancellation of Agreement

A development agreement may be amended or canceled, in whole or in part, by mutual consent of the parties to the development agreement or their successors in interest. The procedure for amendment or cancellation shall be the same as that for adoption as provided in § 4.55.9 Existing and Subsequently Adopted Rules, Regulations, Ordinances, Laws, and Policies of this chapter. Notice of intent to amend or cancel any portion of the development agreement shall be given in the manner provided in § 4.4 Notice Provisions of this chapter.

4.55.13 Annexation

If a development agreement relates to property located outside the incorporated area of the [LOCAL GOVERNMENT], the development agreement does not become operative unless annexation proceedings to annex the property to the [LOCAL GOVERNMENT] are completed within the period of time specified by the development agreement or any extension of such time. Any development agreement relating to such property shall specify a time period within which such property shall be annexed to the [LOCAL GOVERNMENT].

4.55.14 Enforcement

A development agreement shall be enforceable by any party to the agreement, even if there is a change in any applicable rule, regulation, ordinance, law, plan, or official policy of the [LOCAL GOVERNMENT] that alters or amends the rules, regulations, ordinances,

**Table 4-3
Penalties for Code Violations**

Chapter Section	Minimum Fine	Maximum Fine
Subdivision	$200	$1,000
Zoning		

laws, plans, or official policies specified in the agreement as provided in § 4.55.4.2 Optional Provisions of this chapter, or in the development agreement itself, except insofar as new plans or regulations are made applicable to the development by the terms of this chapter or by provisions of the development agreement. The remedies specified herein and in the development agreement are not exclusive, and any party to the agreement may pursue any other available remedies at law or in equity.

DIVISION 8: ENFORCEMENT, VIOLATIONS, AND PENALTIES

4.61 TYPES OF VIOLATIONS

Any act of commission or omission contrary to the commands or directives of this chapter, or any breach of any duty imposed by this chapter, is a violation of this chapter.

4.62 CIVIL ENFORCEMENT

4.62.1 Enforcement Actions

The [PLANNING OFFICIAL] or any proper person may institute any appropriate civil action or proceedings to prevent violations or threatened violations of these regulations. In particular, but without limitation, in case any building or structure is erected, constructed, reconstructed, altered, repaired, converted, or maintained, or any building, structure, or land is used in violation of this chapter, the [PLANNING OFFICIAL] or any proper person may institute any appropriate action or proceedings to:

(A) Prevent such unlawful acts and restrain, correct, or abrogate such violation;

(B) Prevent the occupancy of the building, structure, or land; or

(C) Prevent any illegal act, conduct, business, or use in or about such premises, including, but not limited to, all remedies provided in [ZONING AND SUBDIVISION ENABLING LEGISLATION].

The imposition of any penalty does not preclude the [LOCAL GOVERNMENT] or any proper person from instituting any appropriate action or proceedings to require compliance with the provisions of the LDC and with administrative orders and determinations made under the LDC.

4.62.2 Penalties

The penalty for violating any section or other part of the LDC is shown in Table 4-3. Each day a violation is permitted to exist constitutes a separate offense.

4.63 VIOLATION OF CONDITIONS

4.63.1 Penalty

The violation of any condition imposed pursuant to a development order or a development approval pursuant to this chapter, including, but not limited to, a CUP or conditional zoning district is a violation of this chapter and may be prosecuted in municipal court regardless of whether civil or administrative action is taken against the development approval holder.

4.63.2 Revocation of Development Approval

The [PLANNING OFFICIAL] is authorized to issue any administrative order necessary to terminate or suspend a use found, as a result of the administrative process noted in § 4.2.2 Quasi-judicial Development Approval of this chapter, to be in violation of a condition.

4.63.3 Civil Action

The [PLANNING OFFICIAL] may request the [LOCAL GOVERNMENT] attorney to institute a civil action as prescribed in this chapter regardless of whether a criminal or administrative action is taken against the development approval holder.

4.64 COMPLETION OF IMPROVEMENTS

4.64.1 Liability

A subdivider shall be held liable to the [LOCAL GOVERNMENT] for the completion of all site improvements required by these regulations until such time as the improvements shall have been actually completed and accepted by the [LOCAL GOVERNMENT].

4.64.2 Remedy

If the construction of site improvements has been guaranteed by a form of security described in § 4.36 Subdivision Improvement Agreements of this chapter, and such improvements have not been completed and accepted by the [LOCAL GOVERNMENT] within the time period prescribed by these regulations, the [ENGINEERING OFFICIAL], after written notification has been given to the subdivider, shall take such action as may be required to cause payment to be made to the [LOCAL GOVERNMENT] of the amounts of money secured by a guarantee of performance. Such amounts of money shall be used by the [ENGINEERING OFFICIAL] to finance the completion of the required improvements. In the event that the amounts of money referred to above are insufficient to finance the completion of the required improvements, the [ENGINEERING OFFICIAL] shall so notify the subdivider in writing and shall require the subdivider either to complete the improvements without delay or to make available to the [LOCAL GOVERNMENT] the amount of money required to finance their completion.

Should the subdivider fail to do either of the above and such failure is not due to strikes, riots, acts of God, acts of a public enemy, injunction, or other court action, or any other cause similar to those enumerated beyond the subdivider's control, the [ENGINEERING OFFICIAL] shall refer the matter to the [CITY/COUNTY] attorney for such action as the [CITY/COUNTY] attorney may deem appropriate to compel the subdivider to comply with the provisions of the improvement agreement entered into by the subdivider as a condition precedent to the approval of the plat, or to pursue any other remedy that may be available to the city. Until such time as the required site improvements have been completed and accepted by the city, the [ENGINEERING OFFICIAL] shall refuse to accept from such subdivider a performance guarantee under any form that is related to the plat of a subdivision, in which such subdivider has a principal or subsidiary interest.

4.64.3 Exemptions

This section does not apply if a subdivider is prevented from completing and having accepted such required site improvements within the prescribed time by reason of strikes, riots, acts of God, acts of a public enemy, injunction, or other cause similar to those enumerated beyond the subdivider's reasonable control. The subdivider shall be entitled to an extension of time equal to the time of such delay that shall be fixed by written certificate made by the [ENGINEERING OFFICIAL]. It is expressly declared that no such allowance of time will be made unless claimed by the subdivider and allowed and certified in writing by the [ENGINEERING OFFICIAL] at the end of each period of such delay.

COMMENTARY

This chapter consolidates application processing procedures of the LDC with submission requirements attached as Appendix B, Specifications for Documents to Be Submitted. The process of making land-use decisions is extremely important to plan implementation. Appropriate guidelines must be established to protect applicants' due process rights, guide decision-makers in their consideration of applications, and allocate staff resources.

Procedures can also have a profound impact on the shape and form of development. Those that are slow and unpredictable can discourage the type of development that a jurisdiction desires; those that are streamlined, along with clear standards, can save money and create predictability. With these goals in mind, this chapter provides a set of guidelines for streamlining local land-use decision-making processes.

Procedural sections should be designed to accomplish the following objectives:
- Provide for quasi-judicial hearings for individual parcel rezonings as an option for the local government;
- Implement the comprehensive plan;
- Provide an efficient allocation of staff resources;
- Avoid unnecessary delay in processing applications;
- Assign the appropriate agency to various permitting functions;
- Ensure that approval standards are clearly understood;
- Comply with state land-use enabling legislation;
- Respect applicants' due process rights;
- Provide for effective public participation;
- Provide alternatives for the resolution of disputes between applicants and neighborhoods;
- Establish avenues for appeals and variances;
- Provide mechanisms for recording the outcome of the permitting decision; and
- Clearly establish the scope of the permitting decision.

Development code updates often focus on improving the efficiency of land-use approval processes.[3] Poorly drafted regulations waste valuable resources—time and money—for the public and private sectors. Such regulations include those that lack cohesive organization and precise language, those that create unduly complicated and cumbersome approval procedures, and those that have been amended without any thought of integrating the amendments into the existing process. Development regulations, like any regulatory scheme, must be reviewed periodically to ensure that substantive provisions are not obsolete and to conform the written regulations with the actual application review process. The regulations should attempt to strike a proper balance between the need for the careful analysis of applications and the need for regulatory efficiency.[4]

While adequate procedures are needed in order to ensure that development complies with a jurisdiction's land-use policies, unduly cumbersome policies can discourage the type of development that a jurisdiction desires. A good example of this dilemma are policies that encourage mixed-use developments. Mixed-use developments can result from a master plan development on a large, undeveloped site (commonly known as a "greenfield" development) or through the evolution of mixed uses in established residential neighborhoods. Under most codes, the developer has three options.

First, the developer could request multiple rezonings for the tract. Rezonings to individual commercial or business districts can also occur adjacent to residential districts. However, the landowner is confronted with the political, legal, and procedural hurdles created by the rezoning process.

Second, the developer could seek variances for uses that are not permitted in the zoning district. Both of these techniques are highly complex and fraught with uncertainty. In addition, most variance applications filed for this reason do not meet the hardship tests established by state law.

Third, the developer may file an application for a proposed development, which may consist of multiple uses. While this permits a developer to package a development consisting of residential and nonresidential uses into one application for development approval, it still requires a rezoning. Rezonings are a difficult and uncertain approval process because a jurisdiction retains broad discretion to deny a rezoning. Accordingly, developers who propose master planned, mixed-use communities can have projects derailed by citizen and neighborhood opposition, even at late stages in the development approval process. Accordingly, many developers simply opt to build single-use residential subdivisions that are permitted by the base zoning districts. This produces monotonous "sprawl" of residential units.

Addressing these issues thoroughly requires a detailed and complete explanation in the code text. Too many ordinances fail to address these issues because of ignorance or because the code drafters want to keep the ordinance short and "user friendly." However, omitting discussion of these issues creates significant problems behind the permit counter. The LDC is designed to provide a complete explanation of how permitting decisions are handled in the context of legal and institutional realities while avoiding unnecessary complexity.

The following techniques can be used to provide clarity while ensuring that statutory authority, due process, and institutional issues are thoroughly addressed:

Table 4-4
Elements of Procedure

Subsection	Description
Applicability	This subsection describes the situations to which the development approval applies. It obligates landowners to seek permission before commencing construction or taking some other action with respect to the property.
Initiation	This subsection indicates who receives the application and what the application should contain. This typically includes a cross-reference to Appendix B, Specifications for Documents to Be Submitted, of the LDC (submittal requirements), although there may be other conditions. For example, there may be a requirement that the application be certified by a professional engineer, if there are highly technical engineering considerations.
Completeness review	This subsection requires staff to ascertain whether or not the application is sufficiently complete to be processed. If not, the application is returned to the applicant and the process terminates. If the application is complete, the local government has an obligation to process it. This subsection provides the applicant with assurance that complete filings will not be delayed or subjected to endless requests for information. At the same time, the decision-making agencies are given enough information to make an intelligent decision.
Decision	This subsection establishes the procedures for rendering a formal decision. It may or may not require a noticed public hearing, depending upon state law and whether or not the decision is legislative, quasi-judicial, or ministerial.
Approval criteria	This subsection describes any standards that are specific to the development approval situation. All applications are subject to the requirements of Chapter 3, Zoning, and Chapter 5, Development Standards, of the LDC. However, some applications (such as conditional use permits) are subject to additional discretionary standards.
Appeals	This subsection indicates whether an appeal is available and to whom the appeal is filed. Appeals are not available from legislative decisions, such as rezonings. However, ministerial decisions can be appealed to a hearing officer—in most states, the board of zoning adjustment.
Subsequent applications	If the application was denied, this subsection establishes a waiting period before subsequent applications can be filed.
Amendments	This subsection allows the application to be amended without going back through the entire process. Minor amendments may be processed by staff; major amendments may require reapplication or some sort of discretionary review.
Scope of approval	This subsection states what rights are conferred by the application. Some development approvals do not authorize development but simply authorize the applicant to proceed to the next stage of the permitting process (e.g., preliminary plats). It is important to clearly define the scope of the development approval so that applicants are not misled about what they can do with their property.
Recording procedures	This subsection describes how the application is recorded. Applications that are not properly recorded may be subject to termination.

- *Maintain a consistent style for each code section.* The LDC establishes subsections for each type of permitting decision as described in Table 4-4.
- *Use flow charts and other graphics to explain how the processes work.* Flow charts graphically illustrate how the processes work together. This provides an easy-to-use format for many users. However, flow charts should not supplant the text but instead should support and reinforce it.
- *Establish administrative guidelines for the appropriate agencies.* These guidelines can be written in less formal language than the adopted code and can typically be revised without a public hearing. Guidelines are beyond the scope of this publication but should be considered by local agencies that administer the code.

GENERAL ISSUES

COMPREHENSIVE PLANNING

The procedures should facilitate the local government's comprehensive planning policies. Development patterns that the plan encourages should have an easy road to approval; those discouraged by the plan should receive more careful consideration. For example, many local comprehensive policies encourage "compact, pedestrian-friendly development."

However, the zoning ordinances in these communities often divide the jurisdiction into single-use zoning districts, with mixed-use developments on smaller lots requiring a lengthy, discretionary, planned development approval process. It is no wonder that developers often choose to build sprawling, low-density communities that are permitted as of right in the zoning districts instead of subjecting themselves to lengthy, unpredictable processes to achieve the development patterns espoused in the comprehensive plan. Procedures that streamline approvals for compact development forms can encourage the type of development that these communities want.

As discussed above, oftentimes "greenfield" developments suffer the most by these procedural defects. Although these mixed-use developments further comprehensive planning goals by promoting walkability and avoiding sprawl, they are discouraged in practice by the complexity and uncertainty inherent in the process of obtaining rezonings or variances.

Rezonings to individual commercial or business districts can also occur adjacent to residential districts. Again, however, the landowner is confronted with the political, legal, and procedural hurdles created by the rezoning process. Further, the height restriction in many zoning districts ranges from 25 to 35 feet, coupled with 25-foot front and 10-foot side setback restrictions. Even if the proper zoning exists, these restrictions often discourage infill development on small lots in urban core locations and in nodes adjacent to residential areas.

The achievement of mixed-use development patterns is contingent primarily upon the decisions of individual developers, landowners, and investors. Cumbersome and unpredictable processes discourage this type of development. Mixed-use development with traditional neighborhood design patterns can be difficult to finance, although lenders are showing an increased interest in the concept.[5] Unless procedures are streamlined, and appropriate standards are available in the code, these types of development patterns are unlikely to emerge.

CLASSIFYING THE PROCESS: LEGISLATIVE, QUASI-JUDICIAL, AND ADMINISTRATIVE FUNCTIONS

The regulations should clearly distinguish between legislative, quasi-judicial, and administrative functions. This is critical to assigning the appropriate decision-maker to the application process, establishing decision-making processes, and assigning development criteria. The wrong choice here could result in constitutional violations and expensive litigation.

DEVELOPMENT APPROVAL STREAMLINING

One of the most controversial aspects of the development approval process is the time needed to gain development approval. Development codes should provide adequate time for staff and agency review of applications. Larger, more complex applications will take longer to review than smaller, ministerial ones. However, the carrying costs incurred while a project awaits approval can be significant. Unreasonable permitting delays can drive up development costs, discourage the production of affordable housing, and inhibit economic development. It is in the best interest of both local governments and developers to seek efficient approval processes, which balance the local government's interest in adequate review with the need for speedy permitting decisions.

The LDC uses a variety of tools to streamline land-use approvals:

• *In order to enhance certainty in the development approval process, the code emphasizes bright-line, quantitative standards, as opposed to discretionary standards.* This limits the discretion of reviewing agencies to impose unanticipated standards, provides advance notice to applicants of clear expectations, and allows neighborhoods to anticipate how surrounding parcels can be developed.

• *Because standards are clear and predicable, land-use decisions can be made administratively rather than on a case-by-case basis.* This requires a concomitant improvement in the design and development standards for all development.

• *A checklist of items that the developer must provide is consolidated as an appendix to the code.* This assures the applicant that additional expenses associated with preparing the application will not be required, while providing staff the authority to return applications that do not provide sufficient information for review.

• *Procedural delays are minimized in a variety of ways.* Just cause is required for a continuance. The party requesting a continuance must file a sworn affidavit that provides the reasons for seeking. No similar procedure is provided for in *Robert's Rules of Order*,[6] which is the typical standard for administrative hearings, yet similar requirements are frequently used in administrative and judicial proceedings and should help to prevent abuse of the system by parties who seek to merely delay projects. At the same time, allowing for a showing of just cause recognizes that there are circumstances in which continuances are appropriate.

• *Public hearing processes are minimized and used only where discretion is required by the nature of the application.* Public hearings require considerable time of applicants, neighborhood groups, staff, and paid consultants. Public hearings are a useful tool for resolving exceptional issues, such as variances and uses whose impacts will vary widely, depending on their setting. In most cases, the development community does a better job if they know the standards in advance of making financial commitments.

• *Most uses are permitted as of right rather than by conditional use.*

• *Applicants can self-certify compliance with technical standards.* For technical issues, this certification can be performed by a professional engineer, an architect, or a similar professional, and submitted to staff. This does not relieve the applicant from compliance with the standards. Instead, it allows the applicant to proceed with construction without the delays associated with the development approval process. Professional consultants might be reluctant to use this procedure due to liability concerns.

• *A development review committee process is used in lieu of separate reviews by each local department.* The lack of formal coordination between departments can create delay and erode confidence in the process where a single permitting official is forced to delay or deny a development approval because of regulations he/she is administering. A formal development review committee process allows each department to better understand each other's functions, thereby allowing planning staff to notify the applicant of potential problems early in the process. This process can be established internally, rather than formally by the code. Internal regulations provide flexibility in the event that the process proves unworkable. However, formally established regulations would ensure support from each agency involved in development approval review.

• *A completeness review process establishes time limits for staff to certify that an application is complete, as well as authority to return incomplete applications without processing them.* This avoids wasted review time on applications that lack the information needed to make an informed decision. In addition, it protects applicants from delays based on unexpected requests for information. However, it is an additional step in the review process, and additional ordinance text is required to explain it.

• *Standards are established for standing to appeal, and clear grounds are required for appeal.* The applicant must always have an opportunity to appeal, while affected neighbors may be given standing as well. Affected neighbors can be abutting neighbors, those within a given distance from the proposed project, or those uniquely impacted as defined in the ordinance. Neighborhood or environmental organizations could be given standing as well, but this is rarely found in local land-use regulations. In addition, many administrative regulations require that the appellant participate in the hearing or development approval process from which an appeal was filed and provide a limited period of time for filing the appeal. If this is done, due process typically requires that such parties be given adequate notice of the proceedings.

• *A sunset period is established for development approvals and land-use decisions.* Each section relating to a development approval or land-use decision establishes the scope of the decision. The scoping sections explain what the land-use decision permits the applicant to do and explains how long the applicant has to take further action before the development approval expires. This establishes a clear road map to avoid misunderstandings and vested rights litigation.

• *The code institutionalizes procedures for mediating disputes with neighborhood associations.* Applicants should have the right to rely on clear standards established in the ordinance. However, at least for discretionary hearings, the code could either mandate or encourage pre-meetings with citizen groups in order to avoid disputes during the hearing process. Neighborhood meetings occur prior to the formal submission of a rezoning application, subdivision plat application, or variance request. While this might delay the processing of the application somewhat, it has the potential of resolving issues before they become adversarial.

• *A planned development process is available in Chapter 3, Zoning, of the LDC for exceptional projects that do not fit into the mold established by the standards.* No set of standards could possibly anticipate every type of project that has merit. The objective of this process is to codify the general rules that produce a positive outcome in the land-use decision-making process. However, a jurisdiction may retain the right to approve, and applicants may be given the right to advance, a proposal that has merit but is not contemplated by the code. The process should be discretionary because such situations are not the norm. It should be noted that these projects typically involve large-scale or otherwise visible projects that should not become the norm but that might have merit in very particularized settings.

There are also a number of other streamlining mechanisms that need not be reflected in the development code, including:

• Using one-stop development approval processing as a procedural reform, which has become a popular technique implemented in a variety of ways[7];

• Reshuffling offices to locate all development approval functions in one geographic area;

• Establishing a central information center where staff members provide materials and explain procedures to developers;

• Assigning to one department or office the primary responsibility for accepting and processing all applications and maintaining files. This central department coordinates all reviews, schedules hearings, and serves as the sole contact for the developer; and

• Expediting the staff review phase of the development approval process by using development approval expeditors and joint review committees, outsourcing site plan reviews, using deadlines, and implementing fast-track processing.

These procedures can be established in internal processing guidelines or informal guidelines.

Public Hearings

Public hearings can significantly add to the time consumed in processing development approvals. The amount of time needed to hear public comment creates delay, often requiring public hearings to be continued indefinitely. Furthermore, they devolve into a forum for opposing development approval. While public hearings are typically required for discretionary review (see the section entitled, "Discretionary Review," below), the public hearing process can be minimized.

Self-certification

A somewhat risky streamlining technique is to allow applicants to self-certify compliance with technical standards. For technical issues, this certification can be performed by a professional engineer, an architect, or a similar professional, and submitted to staff. This does not relieve the applicant from compliance with the standards. Instead, it allows the applicant to proceed with construction without the delays associated with the development approval process. However, some professionals are reluctant to use self-certification due to liability concerns. In addition, many communities are reluctant to release the public or staff oversight that results from self-certification.

Interdepartmental Coordination

Interdepartmental coordination may be used to streamline development approvals as well as develop more coherent land-use policies. Development approval applications are often reviewed separately by various departments and agencies, such as planning, engineering, fire protection, and schools. There is often no formal coordination between the departments. This can create delays and a lack of confidence in the process where a single permitting official is forced to delay or deny a development approval because of regulations he/she is administering.

A formal development review committee process allows each department to better understand each other's functions, thereby allowing planning staff to notify the applicant of potential problems early in the process. This process can be established internally, rather than formally by the code. Internal regulations provide flexibility in the event that the process proves unworkable. However, formally established regulations would ensure support from each agency involved in development approval review.

DISCRETIONARY REVIEW

Discretionary public hearing processes are used extensively in many communities for a variety of reasons. Discretionary review is useful:
• Where the public does not trust the LDC (a discretionary approval process is seen as a way to fill regulatory gaps not addressed by the code, or to obtain regulatory concessions that the code does not require);
• Where there is a high level of trust between applicants, reviewing agencies, and the public (discretionary review can provide a flexible, informal method of development approval); or
• For unique uses or situations where comprehensive, uniform standards are impracticable.

These situations are exceptional. Discretionary review is unpredictable and always creates opportunities for arbitrary decision-making. The lack of predictability creates risks for the private sector that can drive up development costs. In addition, it creates uncertainty for neighborhoods. Finally, discretionary processes are normally longer and more expensive than ministerial procedures. Accordingly, the LDC minimizes, but does not eliminate, the use of discretionary review.

Discretionary review can be minimized by allowing more uses to be permitted as of right, writing clear standards for uses or structures, and assigning decision-making authority to staff. This permits land-use decisions to be made administratively rather than on a case-by-case basis. It also requires a concomitant improvement in the design and development standards for all development.

NEIGHBORHOOD PARTICIPATION

The suggested procedures balance competing interests in public participation and development approval streamlining. There is increasing interest in encouraging public participation in land-use decisions. For example, the "charrette" process is a central theme of new urbanism. A charrette introduces neighborhoods to the concepts of new urbanism and allows them to participate in designing the project through a hands-on, interactive process. Several cities have adopted procedures for neighborhood preapplication meetings.[8] Hillsborough County, Florida, has established a "Neighborhood Bill of Rights" with special notification and hearing requirements for applications that affect registered neighborhoods.[9] Public participation is a noble objective but can significantly delay development proposals. This conflict can be resolved by using fair and equitable procedures for expediting development approvals while focusing on public participation early in the process.

Most developers attempt to meet with neighborhoods before filing applications for development approval as a matter of practice. Addressing neighborhood issues early in the development approval process can avoid subsequent surprises and delays. However, many developers resist mandatory neighborhood premeeting requirements, which they see as an additional step in the development approval process. In addition, most state enabling legislation is silent about neighborhood premeetings. While optional or mandatory neighborhood meetings might be an acceptable option to developers, they should be tied to:

• *More effective communication between the applicant, staff, and decision-makers, and implementation of procedures to ensure that new issues are not raised late in the development approval process:* Developers who make good faith efforts to address reasonable neighborhood issues should be rewarded with prompt permitting decisions and enhanced certainty.

• *Ensuring that those who had an opportunity to participate (but chose not to) are not able to derail the approval after critical decisions have already been made:* Allowing those who choose not to participate in premeetings to delay development approval decisions undermines the integrity of the process and signals to the development community that the process does not work. Conversely, relatively speedy approvals create a strong incentive for developers to reach out to neighborhoods.

The LDC's neighborhood participation procedures are designed to maximize the opportunity for citizen participation and minimize delay. Citizens express their views early in the process in a neutral setting. This allows citizens the opportunity to influence the outcome of a development proposal before an application is filed. Developers hear about issues and can respond to them before committing substantial resources to project approval. To induce developers to use this process, continuance requests and other mechanisms to delay project approval are restricted or eliminated.

In addition to premeeting procedures, there should be a formal process for registering neighborhoods. Registration tells applicants whom they need to contact and who speaks for the neighborhood. It also creates an incentive for neighborhoods to organize and develop clear, substantive policies relating to community development. This minimizes ad-hoc, visceral reactions to development proposals and creates an incentive for proactive planning. The registration procedure is codified in a separate section from neighborhood premeetings because it is also used for a variety of other purposes, including the development of neighborhood plans.

PROJECT PHASING

The general concept of a preliminary plat or site plan is to prepare an overall plan of the property with the layout of lots and streets. The preliminary plat allows for early review of the project and ties together the initial stage of subdivision approval and future phases into a single document that forms the basis for development exactions, environmental mitigation, roadway access, and master utility planning, including the sizing and location of utility lines.[10] However, providing such detailed information early in the process requires significant time and monetary commitments, often before the specific use has been approved. Accordingly, a procedure for reviewing and tentatively approving the overall project uses, site configuration, and infrastructure issues, while providing certainty for private developers, is needed.[11]

COMMON PROCEDURAL ELEMENTS

APPLICABILITY

Each section should describe the situation to which the development approval applies. This creates a legal obligation to engage the development approval process before starting development.

INITIATION

Development codes should be clear about who receives applications, what the applications must include, and any other requirements that must be fulfilled before the application is filed. In the LDC, the planning official receives the application and acts as a central agency for coordinating the procedures.

In order to expedite the development approval process, a combined site plan (zoning) and subdivision plat procedure may be adopted to expedite development approval. The submission requirements may be combined, with certification of approval on the application forms, when the appropriate procedures have been completed.

COMPLETENESS REVIEW

In the context of plat approval, most state statutes or ordinances provide time limits for responses from the reviewing agencies. However, applications may be delayed by claiming that they are incomplete. Local governments may consider a separate completeness review and compliance review for purposes of processing plats and other development approval applications. Completeness review establishes a process with time limits for staff to certify an application as complete, as well as authority to return incomplete applications without processing them. This process avoids wasted review time on applications that lack the information needed to make an informed decision. In addition, it protects the applicant from delays based on unexpected requests for information. However, it is an additional step in the review process, and additional ordinance text is required to explain it.

If an application is not certified as complete, the applicant may file an appeal and move the application forward. In order to make the process meaningful, completeness review appeals could be given priority on the hearing officer's or reviewing agent's docket.

DECISION

This section explains the process for reaching a decision. For the purpose of identifying due process rights, it also establishes whether the decision is legislative, quasi-judicial, or ministerial. The procedures should clearly assign development approval authority to the agencies involved in the development approval process.

APPROVAL CRITERIA

This section establishes the criteria for development approval. While developers typically press for standards that are clear and predictable, some developers like the flexibility of discretionary standards. This allows developers and neighborhoods to negotiate approval in a flexible, and sometimes creative, manner. This works well where neighborhoods, developers, and governments enjoy an open, trusting relationship. Unfortunately, many communities do not have this type of cooperative relationship among development stakeholders.

Legislative decisions are always subject to discretionary considerations. For example, most state courts have established a number of discretionary factors applicable to rezoning cases. The LDC establishes a representative set of factors to guide planning commissions and local governing bodies in considering selling cases.

Uses or situations that require individualized, case-by-case determinations can be subject to discretionary criteria. Conditional or special use permits are often required for uses with significant, localized neighborhood or environmental impacts. However, public hearings that involve discretionary decision-making (i.e., general standards that are applied on a case-by-case basis) have the following disadvantages:

• If there is overreliance on discretionary review, only projects that have positive outcomes from the community's perspective will be approved.

• The development community does not know the rules in advance, which can inhibit financing and drive up costs.

• Public hearings can require considerable time of applicants, neighborhood groups, staff, and paid consultants.

Discretionary review can be a useful tool for resolving exceptional issues, such as variances and uses whose impacts will vary widely depending on their setting. In most cases, the development community will do a better job if they know the standards in advance of making financial commitments.

APPEALS

For zoning approvals, most states assign appeals functions to the board of adjustment. The board of adjustment typically consists of laypersons appointed by the local government. The LDC uses a hearing officer as an alternative to a lay board of adjustment for appeals and variances. This has the advantage of replacing lay experience with professional expertise, which is more appropriate for resolving such matters. However, in some states, the use of a hearing officer could not supplant the jurisdiction of the board of adjustment without special legislative authority.

The LDC defines who has standing to appeal and on what grounds. The applicant must always have an opportunity to appeal, while affected neighbors may be given standing as well. Affected neighbors can be abutting neighbors, those within a given distance from the proposed project, or those uniquely impacted as defined in the ordinance. Neighborhood or environmental organizations could be given standing as well, but this is rarely found in local land-use regulations. In addition, many administrative regulations require that the appellant participate in the hearing or development approval process from which an appeal was filed and provide a limited period of time for filing the appeal. If this is done, due process typically requires that such parties be given adequate notice of the proceedings.

SCOPE OF APPROVAL

Each section relating to a development approval or land-use decision should establish the scope of the decision. The scoping sections should explain what the land-use decision permits the applicant to do, and explain how long the applicant has to take further action before the development approval expires. Sunset periods for development approvals and land-use decisions establish a clear road map to avoid misunderstandings and vested rights litigation.

ZONING PROCEDURES

DISCRETIONARY REVIEW: SPECIAL EXCEPTIONS AND CONDITIONAL OR SPECIAL USE PERMITS

Most older, conventional zoning ordinances have procedures for designated uses requiring a special exception by the board of adjustment. More modern codes may require conditional or special use permits. The major difference between special exceptions and conditional uses is that the former are issued by the board of adjustment while the latter may be approved by a planning commission or local government.[12] Most zoning statutes expressly establish special exceptions as part of the board of adjustment's powers.[13] Another difference is that many codes permit special exceptions in any zoning district, whereas conditional or special uses are permitted only in designated districts.

In reviewing an application for a CUP, courts typically require the reviewing authority to issue findings of fact and conclusions of law. Findings of fact establish the factual basis, and conclusions of law establish the legal principles, that the board uses to reach its decision and assure more careful administrative consideration.[14]

REZONINGS

In most states, rezoning is considered a legislative decision. This means that due process protections and written criteria are not required. However, the procedures for rezoning are normally prescribed by statute. Procedures such as automatic approval are usually unavailable for legislative decisions. In a minority of states, rezoning is considered administrative or quasi-judicial. In these states, procedural due process protections apply to rezoning decisions. This requires a written record, an opportunity to confront adverse witnesses, and compliance with judicially imposed standards for rezoning.

SUBDIVISION PROCEDURES

Zoning and subdivision regulations typically have distinct processing procedures. The process for obtaining development approval begins with securing the proper zoning designation; filing a site plan or development plan for discretionary approvals, such as a conditional or special use; obtaining a development approval for construction; and obtaining an occupancy permit prior to sale. Some jurisdictions also require a certificate of zoning compliance for uses permitted as of right. Any variances needed are typically processed by the board of adjustment.

DEFINITION OF SUBDIVISION

In order for a local government's subdivision controls to be activated, a "subdivision" of land must be contemplated by an owner or developer. The definition of "subdivision" is, therefore, crucial. Unfortunately, but not surprisingly, there is no simple or single definition. In some states, the legislature provides a specific definition that the local government must incorporate into its subdivision regulations without additions, changes, or deletions[15]:

"Subdivision: Any land, vacant or improved, which is divided, or proposed to be divided, into two or more lots, parcels, sites, units, condominium units, tracts, plots, or interests for the purpose of offer, sale, lease, or development, whether immediate or future, either on the installment plan or upon any and all other plans, terms, and conditions. Subdivision includes the division or development of residential and nonresidential zoned land, whether by deed, partition, devise, intestacy, lease, map, plat, or any other recorded instrument. Subdivision includes resubdivision, approval of antiquated plats, condominium, cooperative, or time-share creation or conversion, judicial partition, or division into lots, parcels, or unit through probate, equitable proceedings, or any other judicial proceeding."

This definition eliminates the following problems that have plagued many communities:

• Division into lots does not include division into parcels since the former implies "building lots"[16];

• Leases are excluded from subdivision regulations unless defined (e.g., trailer parks)[17];

• Resubdivision may be excluded unless specifically defined[18];

• Nonresidential subdivisions may be excluded[19];

• Partition may not be resolved before a planning commission but must be resolved in the courts[20]; and

• Testamentary (devise) or intestate divisions of property may be excluded.[21]

In 1991, Utah adopted a version along the lines of the LDC model approach.[22] Some statutes and local subdivision regulations continue to define subdivision as being the division of land into more than two parcels.[23] Some statutes exempt from municipal review those subdivisions that do not involve the creation of new streets or public improvements.[24] The LDC treats these as "minor" subdivisions if they also have less than four lots.

States and local governments have allowed these types of exemptions avoiding regulating the simple lot split, where there is no need for public improvements, or the division of agricultural or rural land. Theoretically, the exemption has the salutary purpose of protecting farmers from onerous bureaucratic regulations and excluding minor divisions of land because of the relatively small impact they are likely to make on patterns of land development. However, these exemptions create potential legal problems for subsequent purchasers of lots divided without subdivision approval.

A few states exempt large parcels from subdivision control in urban counties.[25] This practice negates many of the theories behind the need for subdivision regulations, such as creating new streets; shaping the future of municipal utility services, parks, and open spaces; and having a recorded system of plats on file. For example, huge valleys of Colorado are divided into 35-acre "ranchettes," promoting irrational urban sprawl and disturbing open space for wildlife that could be managed under planned development, cluster zoning, or minor subdivision approval.[26]

The LDC provides an alternative that meets the need that subdivision regulation was designed to fulfill and also lessens the rigors of plat approval for smaller subdivisions. For maximum effectiveness, a "tight" definition of subdivision is provided; however, a classification of subdivision into "major" or "minor" provides for a variation in the review and appeal process to accommodate the differences in detail necessitated by complex versus simple subdivisions. Thus, at the time of sketch plat approval, a subdivision may be classified as "major" or "minor" as follows:

• *Major subdivision:* All subdivisions not classified as minor subdivisions, including, but not limited to, subdivisions of four or more lots, or any size subdivision requiring any new street or extension of the local government facilities or the creation of any public improvements.

• *Minor subdivision:* Any subdivision containing not more than three lots fronting on an existing street; not involving any new street, the extension of municipal facilities, or the creation of any public improvements;

not adversely affecting the remainder of the parcel of adjoining property; and not in conflict with any provision or portion of the comprehensive plan, official map, or zoning ordinance. A series of related minor subdivisions on contiguous land cumulatively totaling four or more lots shall be construed to create a major subdivision.[27]

The advantage of being classified as a minor subdivision is that the development approval process is abbreviated. Only two steps are required—sketch plat and final approval—but the plat is still reviewed and must be properly recorded. This classification and abbreviated technique has been successfully utilized.[28] The less significant impacts of a minor subdivision should generally minimize the need for extensive review of the proposal, but local governments must take care that developers are not using the process to avoid the more substantial procedures of the major subdivision.[29]

The conversion of apartments to condominiums and cooperatives has been especially problematic to local governments. The change of existing (and approved) multifamily apartment buildings into cooperatives and condominiums should come under the requirements of subdivision regulations.[30]

Some states have amended the planning enabling act to expressly allow local governments to treat condominium projects as subdivisions.[31] In Alabama, the attorney general recently opined that condominiums may be regulated as subdivisions so long as the planning commission also regulates similar physical structures, such as multifamily rental units, as subdivisions.[32] A few states have adhered to the traditional rule. The Supreme Court of Vermont held that neither a subdivision nor a zoning development approval was necessary to convert rental property to condominium ownership.[33]

SUBDIVISION PROCESS

Most subdivision regulations establish a two-step process involving preliminary subdivision plat approval and final plat approval. Some regulations permit a sketch plat to be submitted prior to a preliminary plat in order to resolve potential discrepancies. The application and review procedure outlined in the *Model Subdivision Regulations*[34] involves a two-step process for minor subdivisions and a three-step process for major subdivisions. The procedures are designed to achieve maximum coordination between the developer and the planning commission with the least amount of administrative delay.

As the developer proceeds from initial preapplication conference with the administrative assistant and submission of the sketch plat to the more detailed preliminary and final plats, an agreement is reached on the overall concept and best design for the subdivision and the conditions that are necessary to mitigate the impact of the development on the community. This methodology assures the developer that there is always one official (the administrative assistant) with whom all papers are filed and from whom all information is received about the progress of the application, especially when the application must be reviewed by numerous departments of the local government and outside federal, state, regional, and local officials and governments. This prevents undue expense to the developer and unneeded time delays occasioned by the review of agencies outside of the planning department and planning commission.

To obtain subdivision approval, the usual procedure includes filing a sketch plat with the planning staff, obtaining preliminary plat approval, filing construction plans for the subdivision improvements, and securing final plat approval. Most jurisdictions now require site plans for discretionary zoning approvals. Site plans often contain much of the same information required for subdivision plats.

SUBDIVISION REGULATIONS AND THE COMPREHENSIVE PLAN

Subdivision regulations control the conversion of raw land into building sites. Apart from zoning, subdivision regulations are the most commonly used development control technique.[35] The traditional concepts—that zoning and platting are mutually exclusive and that "use" of land relates only to zoning—are slowly being swept away. Modern courts treat zoning as presuming that the needs of the community have become sufficiently crystallized to permit the enactment of specific regulations, while subdivision control establishes general standards aligned with the comprehensive plan in order to ensure that overall changes in use will not be detrimental to the community.[36]

As the parameters of the police power have expanded, the subdivision regulation has increasingly involved denial of applications for inconsistency with the comprehensive plan, even though the zoning regulations authorize the use.[37]

The courts have also recognized denial of subdivision approval based upon improper design,[38] adverse environmental impact,[39] and lack of adequate off-site public facilities.[40] Subdivision regulations require a developer to comply with a set of defined improvements, public facilities, a lot layout, and other design standards before approval of the proposed subdivision plat. Subdivision approval may be delayed or denied where there is a fair and substantial showing that the subdivision will cause serious off-site flooding or environmental degradation, or increase the burden of inadequate municipal facilities, such as roads and sewers. Subdivision regulations may require the provision of both on- and off-site public improvements that are made necessary by the subdivision. Facility requirements are enforced by requiring developers to post performance bonds.

MINOR AMENDMENTS

The realignment of lot lines not creating an increase in density or intensity, or impacts that exceed the permitted density or intensity, should be treated as an administrative process. Applicants will benefit from having a jurisdiction certify plat approval for such changes in order to secure financing.

JUDICIAL REVIEW OF SUBDIVISION DETERMINATIONS

Courts will go to great lengths before intervening a subdivision dispute if a property owner has not exhausted all administrative remedies available. In *Hensler v. City of Glendale*,[41] the California Supreme Court rejected an inverse condemnation claim by a property owner several years after the city approved the subdivision with a 65 percent open space dedication requirement. The court reasoned that:

• The property owner was required to raise the constitutional issues at subdivision review before bringing an action for inverse condemnation; and

• The property owner's action was governed by the California Subdivision Map Act's 90-day limitations period for actions attacking decisions concerning subdivisions.[42]

DEEMED-APPROVED STATUTES

Many states have statutes requiring the reviewing agency to make a decision within a specific time frame after the filing of the application for subdivision approval and other nonlegislative development approvals, such as special use permits and site plans. The failure of the reviewing agency to act within the statutory time frame results in a forfeiture of the right to deny the application, and the plat will be deemed approved.[43] The deemed-approved status is not gained until the developer submits an application that is complete, containing all of the requirements specified in the preliminary plat regulations.[44] The city should not accept an incomplete application; it usually has 20 days to determine such noncompliance. The *Model Subdivision Regulations* provide for a "notice to proceed" within 20 days.[45]

Nevertheless, the city must process the application in accordance with existing city plans and regulations, and cannot rely on a state recommendation for a moratorium on processing because the state has not made a hazardous waste determination.[46] The deemed-approved statutes do not apply when the city rejects a developer's plans as premature. In *Miles v. Foley*,[47] the city rejected the developer's subdivision plans as having been submitted prematurely. The developer brought a mandamus action to compel the city to approve the subdivision plans, claiming that the rejection as premature was "action" as required by the statute. The developer claimed that the city's failure to take an approved statutory action was equivalent to no action. The court disagreed and held that the rejection of the plans as premature constituted an approval, conditional approval, or disapproval as required by the statute.

Since these statutes are for the protection of developers, only developers are entitled to waive the statutory time-frame requirements.[48] Additionally, where delay is caused by the subdivider, the developer may be deemed to have implicitly agreed to extend the time limit.[49]

In *Turnpike Woods, Inc. v. Town of Stony Point*,[50] an action was brought to compel the issuance of a certificate giving final plat approval to a proposed subdivision. The Court of Appeals held that the town's local law, which purported to suspend for six months, under an emergency moratorium, its duty to act on an application for a subdivision's final plat approval, was ineffective to supersede the state's Town Law, which required that the planning board act on applications for final plat approval within a 45-day period, and was therefore invalid.

VESTED RIGHTS AND SUBDIVISION APPROVAL

The *Youngblood* case[51] establishes the principle that a preliminary plat approval vests the subdivision through to final approval and recordation.[52] No new conditions can be added when the plat is submitted for final approval.[53] Thus, preliminary plat approval is the most important step since it is the only "discretionary" process.[54]

While the landowner is protected from future subdivision regulatory change, no vested right to zoning use or density will occur without the issuance of a valid development approval after subdivision recording with substantial construction.[55] This common law rule has been changed in a number of states under the recent flurry of property rights legislation. Some Atlantic coast states have early on provided that a recorded subdivision is exempt from zoning change for a period of two to eight years.[56] The State of Washington generally follows an early vested rights rule requiring the ordinances and regulations in effect at the time of the initial application to govern throughout the review process.[57] Kitsap County argued in this action that a subsequently submitted planned development application should not be part of the previous subdivision application process because it opens the door to a lengthy negotiated review process. The court disagreed and concluded that when a planned development application is joined with a preliminary plat approval request, the vested right attached to the entire project, including the proposed development.

ADMINISTRATIVE COSTS

A significant area of subdivision regulation is the requirement that the developer pay for the administrative cost incurred in reviewing subdivision applications. Reasonable fees imposed for examination to determine proper design and improvement, and other necessary inspections, are properly chargeable to the developer under the theory that "regulatory fees" are properly assessable under the police power, provided they are proportional to the actual costs of the review. A fee is deemed reasonable if it covers the cost of administering the subdivision regulation.

In *Prudential Co-op. Realty Co. v. City of Youngstown*,[58] a challenge was made that an examining fee of $5.00 for the first lot and $3.00 for each additional lot was in excess of actual costs incurred by the planning commission. In upholding the fees, the court stated, "it is not to be expected that fees can be charged which will exactly balance the cost and expense, and a reasonable excess will not operate to invalidate the ordinance."[59] This holding seems to mirror U.S. Supreme Court requirements in *Dolan v. City of Tigard*[60] that regulatory impact fees must be roughly proportional to the need generated by the development and need not be mathematically precise.[61]

OVERSIZED FACILITIES

The need for "oversized facilities" to handle future growth creates a particular problem. The first development in a planning area or a drainage or sewerage basin may be required to provide a larger-sized facility or excess capacity to serve future development in the area. Without providing for equitable distribution of improvement costs, one developer will sustain a "wipe out," while later developers will accrue a "windfall."[62] Such requirements, where they involve dedication of land or monetary exactions, will be measured by the constitutional test of rough proportionality.[63] A major issue in recent years deals with excessive regulatory costs associated with various stages of development (e.g., zoning, growth controls, building codes, subdivision requirements, and title costs).[64]

Evidence of the need for such facilities must be contained in the record by the local government in order to sustain a decision denying development based on inadequate water quality and quantity.[65]

PAYMENT, PERFORMANCE, AND MAINTENANCE BONDS

A local government might consider requiring both a performance bond and a payment bond.[66] The distinction between the two is substantial. The former only ensures that the actual work called for is completed. There is no assurance that all labor and material costs have been fully paid for the work performed. Under most state statutes, such persons may file a mechanic's or materialman's lien on the improvement, and if the local government accepts dedication of the improvement, it may find itself liable for such payment in the event of developer insolvency.[67] The local government may avoid this prior to final plat approval by obtaining and recording an offer of irrevocable dedication with a title search to ensure that there are no prior liens. A provision in the bond that requires dedication of the improvements after construction, free and clear of all liens and encumbrances, makes it a payment bond as well as a performance bond. A few jurisdictions have refused to extend the bond to include a guarantee of all labor and materials furnished.[68]

Another tool available to ensure full performance by the developer is the maintenance bond, which is a device used to cover the cost of maintaining improvements until they are accepted by the city or county through dedication. Maintenance bonds have been upheld as an extension of the requirement of guaranteeing performance.[69]

ANTIQUATED SUBDIVISIONS

Often referred to as "paper subdivisions," antiquated subdivisions create difficult problems for regulating authorities. The problem of premature subdivision is particularly acute in some Sunbelt states and vacation areas, such as Arizona, Colorado, Texas, Florida, New Mexico, and California.[70] Resolution of this problem requires some degree of retroactive application of police power controls. Retroactive application of subdivision regulations in order to eliminate or change property lines, or assemble parcels without the consent of the property owners, may be subject to strict nullifying statutory interpretation,[71] and may run afoul of due process requirements[72] or the takings clause.[73] The problems of antiquated subdivisions extend to European and Asian nations[74]:

> "§ 1.5.3: The Planning Commission shall have authority to review ... the sale ... of lands: (a) [where] the plat contains contiguous lots in common ownership where one or more of the lots are undeveloped, whether the lots are owned by the original subdivider or an immediate or remote grantee ..."

Many developers, in the absence of statutory protection, sell off lots through "checkerboarding" to prevent merger application. Such merger provisions might constitute a "taking" of property. In *Fulling v. Palumbo*,[75] the court held that merger provisions, applying 1-acre minimum zoning to a previously 1/2 acre zoned and recorded subdivision, would constitute an "as-applied" taking to an unbuilt lot owned by a father who had purchased two half-acre lots—one on which he built his own house and one adjoining lot which he reserved for his daughter.

Antimerger Legislation

Antimerger provisions[76] are designed to prevent new zoning regulations that increase the lot size of subdivision lots from applying to prior approved subdivisions. Without such legislation, contiguous lots under the same ownership and meeting zoning standards at the time of the subdivision would be required to merge if subsequent zoning provisions increased lot sizes.[77]

Land Readjustment Techniques

Techniques for dealing with undersized lots without sewer or water vary dramatically by:
• Offering zoning bonuses for the voluntary merger of lots, which was used successfully in creating the Miami Beach/South Beach Art Deco District.[78] The city used an ascending scale of zoning bonuses for small lot owners to assemble their parcels into usable sizes;
• Encouraging lot owners to pool lots to create a large, usable parcel in which each lot owner receives an equitable share in the capital investment and profits[79];
• Authorizing condemnation of antiquated subdivision through redevelopment blight statutes[80];
• Permitting landowners within antiquated subdivisions to vacate the plat ("reversions to acreage") against dissenting landowners[81]; and
• Creating equity corporations of landowners who develop or sell the unified property, remitting proceeds to individual lot owners by percentage of ownership.[82]

Plat Vacation

Most states provide for governmental vacation, altering, or amendment of plats only if neither the public nor any person is unilaterally injured by the governmental action.[83] Oregon prohibits government-initiated vacation when one or more lots has been sold.[84] Plat vacation and resubdivision will be approved upon initiation and consent of the property owners, but the property owners may be subject to new design and improvement requirements[85] or zoning regulations unless vested rights or estoppel are applicable.

VARIANCES AND APPEALS

Variances are designed to allow the board of adjustment to relax zoning requirements where the regulations will produce unnecessary hardships. They are reserved for unusual situations. Use variances—or variances to permitted use restrictions as opposed to setback and dimensional requirements—are not permitted in many states. In most states, variances and zoning appeals are delegated to the board of adjustment, and attempts to delegate these powers to other boards are null and void.

A few states, such as Florida, do not have conventional zoning variance legislation, but variances are usually included in order to minimize potential takings claims. Without some type of variance procedure, takings claims could expose a jurisdiction to financial liability in the form of landowner compensation. Florida's Private Property Rights Protection Act[86] now requires compensation for "inordinate burdens" on land uses that would not be compensable under normal takings law. While there is no reported Florida case that construes this language as applied to particular land-use controls, a jurisdiction should retain some mechanism to negotiate potential land-use disputes at the local level in order to avoid potential liability.

Even with a variance or appeals mechanism, there are ways to avoid or to minimize unwarranted variances, including:
• *Replacing the board of adjustment with a professional hearing officer:* A hearing officer is typically an attorney, urban planner, or other professional person well versed in land-use law and procedure. While no procedure can eliminate outcomes that fail to please all parties, professionals are often seen as less likely to make decisions that are politically motivated or responsive only to one stakeholder group.
• *Adjusting standards that create the need for unwarranted variances:* These include items, such as setbacks for small lots and other regulations, that have proven unworkable because of a jurisdiction's built form and lotting patterns.
• *Enhancing the "purpose and findings" statements and findings for development regulations:* Some state takings statutes require a compensation settlement to protect the public interest served by the regulations. Strong "purpose and findings" statements provide a basis for negotiating a better outcome for the community when variances have to be granted.

NOTES

1. Transportation Research Board, *Highway Capacity Manual 2000* (Washington, DC: TRB, 2000).
2. See *R.J.P. Builders, Inc. v. Township of Woolwich*, 61 N.J. Super. 207, 824 A.2d 1114 (App. Div. 2003) (approving condition of two-year maintenance guarantees to survive recordation of the plat).
3. Annette Kolis, "Thirteen Perspectives on Regulatory Simplification," Research Report No. 29 (Washington, DC: Urban Land Institute, 1979); John Vranicar, Welford Sanders, and David Mosena, *Streamlining Land Use Regulation: A Guidebook for Local Governments* (Chicago: American Planning Association, November 1980); Carolyn Garmise and Stuart S. Hershey, *Streamlining Local Regulations—A Handbook for Reducing Housing and Development Costs* (Washington, DC: United States Department of Housing and Urban Development, Joint Venture for Affordable Housing, May 1983), No. 11.
4. Fred Bosselman, "Time and the Regulatory Process: Recent Decisions," Vol. 1, Land Use Institute Planning, Regulation, Litigation, Eminent Domain, and Compensation (Washington, DC: ALI-ABA Course of Study Materials, 1986).
5. Robert Chapman, "New Urbanist Projects Attract Investments," 4 *New Urban News* (January/February 1999). The Congress for the New Urbanism reports that six "new urbanist" projects in the State of Texas are under construction, although others are underway.

"Nationwide Survey, Growth in TND Steady, but Slower; Neotraditional Home Sales Strong," 4 *New Urban News* (September/October 1999).

6. Henry M. Robert III et al., *Robert's Rules of Order*, 10th ed. (Cambridge, MA: Perseus Publishing, 2000).
7. Note 3 (Kolis), supra, at 36; see Fred P. Bosselman, Duane A. Feurer, and Charles L. Siemon, *The Permit Explosion: Coordination of the Proliferation* (Washington, DC: Urban Land Institute, 1976) (discussing at length the need for expedited development approval processing).
8. Gary Fulk, *The Citizen Participation Ordinance, Glendale Arizona*, 1999 Proceedings of the American Planning Association National Conference, available on-line at www.asu.edu/caed/proceedings99/FULK/FULK.HTM; Code of Ords. Glendale, Arizona, available on-line at www.municode.com/resources/gateway.asp?pid=13944&sid=3 (navigate to "Appendix A Zoning" § 3.304 "Citizen Participation Plan"); "Enhancing Citizen Participation," 5 *Populace*, No. 1, at 1 (Spring 2003); San Antonio, Texas, Unified Development Code § 35-409.
9. Hillsborough County Land Development Code § 10.03.02.
10. Robert H. Freilich and Michael M. Schultz, *Model Subdivision Regulations: Planning and Law*, 2d ed. (Chicago: American Planning Association, 1995), at 89-91.
11. Note 10 (Freilich/Schultz), supra, at 91-92.
12. John Mixon, James L. Dougherty, Jr., and Brenda McDonald, *Texas Municipal Zoning Law*, 3d ed. (Carlsbad, CA: Michie Publications, 1999), § 6.215.
13. See, e.g., Texas Local Government Code §§ 211.008(a) and 211.009(a)(3).
14. *Citizens Against Lewis & Clark Landfill v. Pottawattamie County Bd. of Adj.*, 277 N.W.2d 921, 925 (Ia. 1979). See *PSI Energy, Inc. v. Indiana Office of Utility Consumer Counsel*, 764 N.E.2d 769, 773 (Ind. App. 2002) ("Requiring an agency to set forth basic findings also assists the agency 'in avoiding arbitrary or ill considered action.'").
15. See, e.g., *Pennobscot, Inc. v. Board of County Commissioners*, 642 P.2d 915 (Colo. 1982) (although the powers conferred on the county were quite broad, the State Land Use Act did not confer the authority to adopt a definition of subdivision that is contrary to the express statutory definition found in the county planning statute). In other states, a local government granted general power under a state planning enabling act can adopt its own definition of a subdivision. See *Ronning v. Thompson*, 483 N.Y.S.2d 949 (1985). The LDC recommends a definition to be adopted by a local government that closes off many loopholes.
16. See, e.g., *Wall v. Ayrshire Corp.*, 352 S.W.2d 496 (Tex. Civ. App. 1961); *Bloom v. Planning Board of Brookline*, 191 N.E.2d 684 (Mass. 1963); *Goldstein v. Planning Board of Lincoln Park*, 144 A.2d 724 (N.J. Super. App. Div. 1958).
17. *Higdon v. Campbell County Fiscal Court*, 374 S.W.2d 511 (Ky. 1964).
18. See, e.g., *Vinyard v. St. Louis County*, 399 S.W.2d 99 (Mo. 1966); Note, "Substandard Lots and the Exception Clause: 'Checkerboarding' As a Means of Circumvention," 16 *Syracuse L. Rev.* 612 (1965).
19. See, e.g., *Clark v. Sunset Hills Memorial Park*, 273 P.2d 645 (Wash. 1954) (cemetery); *Green v. Bourbon County Joint Planning Comm'n*, 637 S.W.2d 626 (Ky. 1982) (agricultural use).
20. *Borough of Braddock v. Allegheny County Planning Dept.*, 687 A.2d 407 (Pa. Commw. 1996) (railroads sought judicial partition for lands no longer dedicated to railroad purposes); *Hoepker v. City of Madison Plan Commission*, 209 Wis.2d 633, 563 N.W.2d 145 (Wis. 1997); but see *Town of Windham v. Lawrence Savings Bank*, 776 A.2d 730 (N.H. 2001) (judicial foreclosure cannot bypass planning commission subdivision approval).
21. See, e.g., *Kiska v. Skrensky*, 138 A.2d 523 (Conn. 1958); *Metzdorf v. Borough of Rumson*, 170 A.2d 249 (N.J. Super. App. Div. 1961); *In re Estate of Sayewich*, 413 A.2d 581 (N.H. 1980) (testamentary devise of real property as four separate parcels to four children not invalid for failure to receive subdivision approval).
22. Utah Code Ann. § 10-9-103(1)(q).
23. See, e.g., Wis. Stat. Ann. § 236.02(12)(a), § 236.45(2)(a) (five or more parcels constitute a subdivision, but a local government with a planning agency may provide more restrictive provisions); Mass. Gen. Laws Ann. c. 41, § 81(L) (two or more lots but not including a subdivision in which each lot fronts on an existing way); but see *Pasaro Builders, Inc. v. Township of Piscataway*, 446 A.2d 187 (N.J. Super. App. Div. 1982) (conveyance of one lot out of more than 20 contiguous lots was not exempt from subdivision approval).
24. See, e.g., *Dube v. Senter*, 219 A.2d 456 (N.H. 1966); *Town of Cherry Hills Village v. Shafroth*, 349 P.2d 368 (Colo. 1960).
25. See, e.g., West's Colo. Rev. Stat. Ann. § 30-28-101(10)(a) and (b) (subdivision is defined as "any parcel of land . . . which is to be used for . . . multiple-dwelling units . . . or which is divided into two or more parcels, separate interests, or interests in common . . ." but this definition "shall not apply to any division of land which creates parcels of land each of which comprises 35 or more acres of land and none of which is intended for use by multiple owners.").
26. See *Board of County Commissioners v. O'Dell*, 920 P.2d 48 (Colo. 1996) (court upheld commissioners' disapproval of minor subdivision request to divide a 41-acre parcel into two smaller parcels because of concerns about the impact of increased development on wildlife and problems of fire suppression due to lack of water).
27. Note 10 (Freilich/Schultz), supra, at 217-18.
28. See *Graves v. Bloomfield Planning Board*, 235 A.2d 51 (N.J. Super. Law Div. 1967). *Kass v. Lewin*, 104 S.2d 572 (Fla. 1958) (minor subdivision regulation held unconstitutional as not germane to subdivision control, traffic planning, and as an unreasonable restraint). However, the board could condition minor subdivision plat approval on removal of uses that violate the zoning ordinance. *Olivieri v. Planning Board*, 645 N.Y.S.2d 545 (A.D. 1996).
29. For strict control of evasion, see *Orrin Dressler, Inc. v. Burr Ridge*, 527 N.E.2d 1063 (Ill. App. 1988) and *Corcoran v. Planning Bd. of Sudbury*, 530 N.E.2d 357 (Mass. App. 1988). A related sequence of conveyances and subdivisions constructed to use plat exemptions to create an 18-parcel plat was held to be an illegal effort to circumvent the purposes of the platting ordinance. *Gerard v. San Juan County*, 715 P.2d 149 (Wash. App. 1986).
30. See, e.g., *Pennobscot, Inc. v. Board of County Commissioners*, 642 P.2d 915 (Colo. 1982) (although the powers conferred

on the county were quite broad, the State Land Use Act did not confer the authority to adopt a definition of subdivision that is contrary to the express statutory definition found in the county planning statute). In other states, a local government granted general power under a state planning enabling act can adopt its own definition of a subdivision. See *Ronning v. Thompson*, 483 N.Y.S.2d 949 (1985). California's Map Act, West's Ann. Cal. Govt. Code § 66424, specifically defines condominium and cooperative projects as subdivisions. California courts have held that a local government may adopt supplementary development and design standards pursuant to the Subdivision Map Act, covering condominium conversions that reasonably relate to purposes of the act. *Griffin Development Co. v. City of Oxnard*, 703 P.2d 339 (1985); *Norsco Enterprises v. City of Fremont*, 54 Cal. App. 3d 488 (1976); *Soderling v. City of Santa Monica*, 191 Cal.Rptr. 140 (Cal. App. 1983). See also *Shelter Creek Development Corp. v. City of Oxnard*, 669 P.2d 948 (Cal. 1983); *Cf. City of West Hollywood v. Beverly Towers, Inc.*, 805 P.2d 329 (Cal. 1991) (local government could not enforce condominium conversion regulations enacted after real estate developer secured final subdivision map approval and permission from the Department of Real Estate to sell individual apartments as condominium units).

31. Minnesota Uniform Condominium Act, Ch. 582; New Hampshire Rev. Stat. Ann. 36.1 VIII: Colorado Rev. Stat. 30-20-101; N.Y. Real Prop. Law § 339f(2). A number of other states have now judicially recognized that condominium development is specifically covered by subdivision approval. *Cohen v. Town of Henniker*, 134 N.H. 425, 593 A.2d 1145 (1991); *Stillwater Condominium Association v. Town of Salem*, 668 A.2d 38 (N.H. 1995); *Maplewood Village Tenants Ass'n v. Maplewood Village*, 282 A.2d 428 (N.J. Super Ch. 1971); *Ronning v. Thompson*, 130 Misc.2d 107, 483 N.Y.S.2d 949 (1985).

32. Op. Attorney General Solomon, Alabama (Oct. 27, 1997), citing Ala. Code § 11-52-30 and § 25-8A-106 ("Because it involves the division of land into two or more parcels, technically a condominium involves a subdivision of real estate.") The opinion extends the authority to commercial and recreational condominiums. Alabama specifically recognizes subdivision regulation of "sale or building development." Ala. Code § 11-52-1(6).

33. See *In re Lowe*, 666 A.2d 1178 (Vt. 1995); *cf. P.O.K. RSA, Inc. v. Village of New Paltz*, 555 N.Y.S.2d 476 (App. Div. 1990) (finding that law which regulated conversion of property ownership that did not involve alteration in use of property as distinguished from "ownership" was *ultra vires* and void); *Ohio Mall Contractors, Inc. v. Dickinson*, 585 N.E.2d 506 (Ohio App. 1990) (laws pertaining to subdivisions are inapposite and inapplicable to condominiums); *Young v. Flathead County*, 757 P.2d 772 (Mont. 1988) (county was not liable to condominium developers for damages sustained in failed condominium venture based on alleged reliance upon county's representations that regulations applicable to subdivision development did not apply to condominium project).

34. Robert H. Freilich and Michael M. Schultz, *Model Subdivision Regulations: Planning and Law*, 2d ed. (Chicago: American Planning Association, 1995).

35. Some states permit rejection of a subdivision application based upon considerations of underlying use. See *Wood v. City of Madison*, 659 N.W.2d 31 (Wis. 2003).

36. *Wood v. City of Madison*, 659 N.W.2d 31 (Wis. 2003); *Town of Sun Prairie v. Storms*, 327 N.W.2d 642 (Wis. 1983); in *Lake City Corp. v. City of Mequon*, 207 Wis.2d 155, 558 N.W.2d 100 (Wis. 1997), the court stated that the subdivision enabling statute providing that subdivision regulations "shall be made . . . for encouraging the most appropriate use of land throughout the municipality, town or county" (Wis. Stat. § 236.45(1)), which means that "the authority of the agency assigned to plat review may not be limited by zoning regulations." *Lake City*, 207 Wis.2d at 173.

37. *Schultheis v. Board of Supervisors*, 727 A.2d 145 (Pa. Commw. 1999); *Board of County Commissioners v. Sommerudd*, 927 P.2d 1339 (Colo. 1996); *Samperi v. Planning and Zoning Commission*, 674 A.2d 432 (Conn. App. 1996); *Coffey v. Maryland National Capital Park and Planning Comm'n*, 441 A.2d 1041 (Md. 1982); *Giuliano v. Town of Edgertown*, 531 F.Supp. 1076 (D. Mass. 1982); *Save Centennial Valley Ass'n v. Schultz*, 284 N.W.2d 542 (S.D. 1979) (approval of a subdivision in an agricultural area ruled void because the planning commission disregarded the clear intent of the comprehensive plan).

38. *Wolf Pen Preservation Association v. Louisville and Jefferson County Planning Commission*, 942 S.W.2d 310 (Ky. App. 1997).

39. *In re McDonald's Corp.*, 505 A.2d 1202 (Vt. 1985); *Goodman v. Board of Commissioners*, 411 A.2d 838 (Pa. Commw. 1980); *Miller v. City of Port Angeles*, 691 P.2d 229 (Wash. App. 1984).

40. *Serpa v. County of Washoe*, 901 P.2d 690 (Nev. 1995); *Garipay v. Town of Hanover*, 351 A.2d 64 (N.H. 1976).

41. 876 P.2d 1043 (Cal. 1994).

42. See also *Petrone v. Town of Foster*, 769 A.2d 591 (R.I. 2001) (claim by property owners, who subdivided their land without approval from the town planning board, that the town's refusal to authorize owners to construct buildings on land not approved for subdivision deprived them of a beneficial use of their land was not ripe, as property owners failed to exhaust their administrative remedies in seeking approval of their proposed use of land).

43. *Bensalem Township v. Blank*, 539 A.2d 948 (Pa. Commw. 1988) (final application deemed approved 90 days after the regular meeting of the reviewing agency); *Paladac Realty Trust v. Rockland Planning Comm'n*, 541 A.2d 919 (Me. 1988) (if ordinance does not specify time frame, hearing must be held within a reasonable time).

44. *Frankland v. City of Lake Oswego*, 517 P.2d 1042, 1048, 1051 (Ore. 1973).

45. Note 10 (Freilich/Schultz), supra, § 3.2(b), 67.

46. *Beck Development Co., Inc. v. Southern Pacific Transportation Co.*, 52 Cal.Rptr.2d 518 (Cal. App. 1996).

47. 752 A.2d 503 (Conn. 2000).

48. *Carmel Valley View, Ltd. v. Maggini*, 155 Cal.Rptr. 208 (Cal. App. 1979) (where developer consented to an extension of time, 50-day time limit for subdivision plat approval not violated).

49. *Metropolitan Homes, Inc. v. Town Plan & Zoning Commission*, 202 A.2d 241 (Conn. 1964) (holding that a subdivider's willingness to wait for an extension of sewers by the town will be interpreted to constitute a

consent to a time extension within which the commission could act on the plat application).
50. 514 N.E.2d 380 (N.Y. 1987).
51. *Youngblood v. Board of Supervisors of San Diego County*, 586 P.2d 556 (Cal. 1978).
52. See David L. Callies, "Vested Rights," Chapter 52D, in Patrick J. Rohan, *Zoning and Land Use Controls* (New York: M. Bender, 2003), at 52D.03[2]b.
53. *Board of Supervisors v. West Chestnut Realty Corp.*, 532 A.2d 942 (Pa. Commw. 1987).
54. *Commonwealth Properties, Inc. v. Washington County*, 582 P.2d 1384, 1389 (Or. App. 1978).
55. See Chapter 2, Section G, "Vested Rights," *Avco Community Developers, Inc. v. South Coast Regional Commission*, 553 P.2d 546 (Cal. 1976); *State ex rel. Mar-Well, Inc. v. Dodge*, 177 N.E.2d 515 (Ohio App. 1960).
56. N.Y. Gen. City Law § 83-a (three years); Conn. Gen. Stat. § 8-26a; N.J.S.A. 40.55 D-49 (three years); Mass. Gen. L. Ch. 40A, § 6 (eight years) (enforced in *Heritage Park Development Corp. v. Town of Southbridge*, 674 N.E.2d 233 (Mass. 1997)).
57. *Association of Rural Residents v. Kitsap County*, 4 P.3d 115 (Wash. 2000).
58. 160 N.E. 695 (Ohio 1928).
59. Id. at 699.
60. 512 U.S. 374, 114 S.Ct. 2309, 129 L.Ed.2d 304 (1994).
61. See *Teter v. Clark County*, 704 P.2d 1171 (Wash. 1985) and *S&P Enterprises v. City of Memphis*, 672 S.W.2d 213 (Tenn. App. 1983) (upholding fees as reasonable); *West Park Ave., Inc. v. Ocean Township*, 224 A.2d 1 (N.J. 1966) (excessive fees will be stricken as an illegal tax); but see *National Realty Corp. v. City of Virginia Beach*, 163 S.E.2d 154 (Va. 1968) (holding fee ordinance invalid in absence of statute). Where a fee is in reality a revenue device, courts will strike it down as an invalid excise tax. See, e.g., *Sussex Woodlands, Inc. v. Mayor and Council of West Milford*, 263 A.2d 502 (N.J. Super. 1970) (held ordinance purporting to condition subdivision approval on payment of real estate taxes invalid).
62. See Donald Hagman and Dean Misczynski, *Windfalls for Wipeouts: Land Value Capture and Compensation* (Chicago: American Planning Association, 1978).
63. *Benchmark Land Company v. City of Battle Ground*, 972 P.2d 944 (Wash. App. 1999).
64. For an interesting article, see Robert Burchell and David Listokin, "The Impact of Local Government Regulations on Housing Costs and Potential Avenues for State Meliorative Measures," in George Sternlieb and James W. Hughes, *America's Housing: Prospects and Problems* (New Brunswick, NJ: Center for Urban Policy Research, Rutgers University, 1980).
65. *Hurrle v. County of Sherburne*, 594 N.W.2d 246 (Minn. App. 1999) (local government offered no evidence to countermand developer's expert witness testimony and decision to deny plat approval was overturned).
66. Note 10 (Freilich/Schultz), supra, 1 6.
67. *Tanner Cos. v. Insurance Marketing Services, Inc.*, 743 P.2d 951 (Ariz. App. 1987).
68. *W.S. Dickey Clay Mfg. Co. v. Ferguson Investment Co.*, 388 P.2d 300 (Okl. 1963).
69. *Legion Manor, Inc. v. Township of Wayne*, 231 A.2d 201 (N.J. 1967) (approving a maintenance bond equal to 10 percent of the performance bond for all defects in material and workmanship within three years). See Michael M. Schultz and Richard Kelly, "'. . . Or Other Security': Using, Structuring, and Managing the Standby Letter of Credit to Ensure the Completion of Subdivision Improvements," 19 *Urb. Law.* 39 (1987).
70. See Michael M. Schultz and Jeffrey B. Groy, "The Failure of Subdivision Control in the Western States: A Blueprint for Local Government Action," *Utah L. Rev.* 569 (1988); Frank Schnidman and R. Lisle Baker, "Planning for Platted Lands: Land Use Remedies for Lot Sale Subdivisions," 11 *Fla. St. U. L. Rev.* 505 (1983).
71. *Maselli v. Orange County*, 488 So.2d 904 (Fla. App. 1986).
72. *Usery v. Turner Elkhorn Mining Co.*, 428 U.S. 1, 96 S.Ct. 2882, 49 L.Ed.2d 752 (1976).
73. *City of Annapolis v. Waterman*, 745 A.2d 1000 (Md. 2000).
74. See Nishiyama, "Land Readjustment: A Japanese Land Development Technique," 1 *Land Assembly & Dev.* 1 (Spring 1987); Kuppers, Nishiyama, and Nakamura, "Selected European Land Readjustment Experiences in Land Readjustment," *The Japanese System* 33 (1986) (commenting on German land readjustment resulting from feudal patterns incompatible with rapid urbanization).
75. 233 N.E.2d 272 (N.Y. 1967).
76. See, e.g., California Government Code § 66451.10(a).
77. *Sherman-Colonial Realty Corp. v. Goldsmith*, 230 A2d 568, 572 (Conn. 1967); *Toothaker v. Planning Board of Billerica*, 193 N.E.2d 582, 584 (Mass. 1963). See Note 34 (Freilich/Schultz), supra.
78. See Robert H. Freilich, "Inducing Replatting Through Performance Zoning," 2 *Platted Lands Press* 5 (Jan. 1985).
79. See Johnson, "Neighborhood Pooling—An Overview," 3 *Platted Lands Press* 1 (Feb. 1986); B. Berns and Y. Chandler, "Neighborhood Buyouts: Balancing Conflicting Interests (Research Atlanta, 1986). Public or private condemnation may also be authorized. *Annbar Assocs. v. West Side Redevelopment Corp.*, 397 S.W.2d 635 (Mo. 1965).
80. See Mo. Rev. Stat. § 353.130 (2003) (permitting private urban redevelopment corporations to exercise governmental condemnation powers); Shultz and Sapp, "Urban Redevelopment and the Elimination of Blight," 37 *J. Urb. & Contemp. Law* 3 (1990).
81. See Cal. Govt. Code § 66499.12; Ore. Rev. Stat. §§ 92.040, .234; Va. Code Ann. §§ 15.10482(2) and (b); Utah Code Ann. § 57-5-7.1.
82. See Northrop, "The Farmer's Market District," *Urban Land* 19 (1984) (discussing commercial redevelopment in Dallas).
83. Utah Code Ann. § 57-5-8; Nev. Rev. Stat. §§ 270.160, 270.170; N.M. Stat. Ann § 47-6-7(c).
84. Ore. Rev. Stat. § 92.225(2)(e).
85. *Lumpton v. Plnaire*, 610 S.W.2d 915, 921-22 (Ky. App. 1980).
86. F.S. § 70.001.

CHAPTER

5

Development Standards

DIVISION 1: GENERALLY

5.1 APPLICABILITY

This chapter applies to any application for development approval, except as otherwise provided.

5.2 ADMINISTRATIVE EXCEPTIONS

5.2.1 Applicability

To facilitate flexibility in design while maintaining the safety, health, and welfare of the public, the [PLANNING OFFICIAL] may grant administrative exceptions to the following technical design requirements found in the following sections of this chapter:

- *Stormwater management* (§ 5.22 Stormwater Management of this chapter)
- *Design homeland security and sustainability* (§ 5.10 Lots through § 5.17 Sustainability of this chapter)
- *Infrastructure standards* (§ 5.21 Parks/Open Space through § 5.22 Stormwater Management of this chapter)
- *Street design and transportation* (§ 5.23 Street Design and Transportation of this chapter)
- *Utilities* (§ 5.24 Utilities of this chapter)
- *Parking and loading standards* (§ 5.51 Parking and § 5.52 Loading of this chapter)

5.2.2 Standards for Administrative Exceptions

No administrative exception shall be granted unless:

(A) The [PLANNING OFFICIAL] certifies that the proposed exception does not conflict with the goals and policies of the comprehensive plan; and

(B) The applicant demonstrates, through documentation and/or studies based on generally accepted engineering principles, that the proposed exception would not pose a threat to health and safety.

5.3 VARIANCES

Where an administrative exception is not granted, or where an administrative exception is not permitted (as in the case of street connectivity, maximum parking requirements, and other items not enumerated in § 5.2.2 Standards for Administrative Exceptions, subsection (B), of this chapter), the applicant may seek a variance from the planning commission pursuant to § 4.37 Subdivision Variances in Chapter 4, Procedures, of the Land Development Code (LDC) in the case of subdivision plats, or an appeal or variance pursuant to § 4.52 Appeals to Hearing Officer through § 4.53 Variances in Chapter 4 in the case of zoning development approvals.

5.4 STANDARD SPECIFICATIONS

5.4.1 Generally

All construction shall conform to [LOCAL GOVERNMENT STANDARD SPECIFICATIONS] to the extent consistent with this chapter.

5.4.2 Sampling and Testing

Sampling and testing of materials, and laboratory inspection of materials and processes, shall be performed at the expense of the developer. Firms providing construction materials testing services must have an established in-house laboratory whose tests meet the standards of the American Society for Testing and Materials requirements.

5.5 AMERICANS WITH DISABILITIES ACT

5.5.1 Infrastructure

Infrastructure construction and improvements of facilities shall comply with the Americans with Disabilities Act (ADA) of 1990.[1] Applicants shall consult both the Title III *Technical Assistance Manual*[2] and the Title II *Technical Assistance Manual*.[3]

5.5.2 Multifamily Housing

Multifamily housing and condominium development shall comply with § 804(f)(5)(C) of the Fair Housing Act of 1988 and the implementing regulations codified at 24 C.F.R. 100.205. Applicants shall consult the *Fair Housing Accessibility Guidelines*.[4]

5.6 OPERATION AND MAINTENANCE

All improvements required by this chapter shall be operated and maintained as required by this section. The instruments creating the dedication, homeowners' association (HOA), condominium association, easement, transfer, or improvement district shall be attached to the application for subdivision plat approval.

5.6.1 Dedication of Land

Dedication of the improvement to the [LOCAL GOVERNMENT] satisfies the requirements of this section. Dedication shall take the form of a fee simple ownership. The [LOCAL GOVERNMENT] may accept the improvement if:

(A) Such land is accessible to the residents of the [LOCAL GOVERNMENT];

(B) There is no cost of acquisition other than any costs incidental to the transfer of ownership, such as title insurance; and

(C) The improvement conforms to the applicable standards of this chapter.

5.6.2 Homeowners' Association

(A) Improvements that are owned in common by all owners of lots or units in the subdivision or condominium are required by this chapter to be operated and maintained by an HOA established in the covenants, conditions, and restrictions (CC&Rs) adopted as a condition of development approval. The CC&Rs shall provide that, in the event that the association fails to maintain the improvements according to the standards of this chapter, the [LOCAL GOVERNMENT] may, following reasonable notice and demand that deficiency of operation or maintenance be corrected, enter the land area to repair, operate, or maintain the improvement. The cost of such maintenance shall be the responsibility of the HOA, which shall be required by the CC&Rs to levy an assessment to be charged to all owners.

(B) The HOA shall be formed and operated under the following provisions:

(1) The developer shall provide a description of the HOA, including its bylaws and methods for operating and maintaining the improvement.

(2) The HOA shall be organized by the developer, and shall be operated with a financial subsidy from the developer, before the sale of any lots or units within the development or condominium.

(3) Membership in the HOA is mandatory for all purchasers of homes and their successors. The conditions and timing of transferring control of the HOA from developer to homeowners shall be identified.

(4) The HOA shall be responsible for maintenance of insurance and taxes on undivided improvement, enforceable by liens placed by the [LOCAL GOVERNMENT] on the HOA. The HOA shall be authorized under its bylaws to place liens on the property of residents who fall delinquent in payment of such dues or assessments. Such liens may require the imposition of penalty interest charges. Should any bill or bills for maintenance of undivided improvement by the [LOCAL GOVERNMENT] be unpaid by November 1 of each year, a late fee of 15 percent shall be added to such bills and a lien shall be filed against the premises in the same manner as other municipal claims.

(5) A proposed operations budget and plan for long-term capital repair and replacement of the improvement shall be submitted with the final plat. The members of the HOA shall share the costs of maintaining and developing such undivided improvement. Shares shall be defined within the HOA bylaws. The operations and budget plan shall provide for construction of any improvements relating to the improvement within three years following recordation of the plat.

(6) In the event of a proposed transfer, within the methods here permitted, of undivided improvement land by the HOA, notice of such action shall be given to all property owners within the development.

(7) The HOA shall have or hire staff to administer common facilities and properly and continually maintain the undivided improvement.

(8) The HOA may lease improvement lands to any other qualified person, or corporation, for operation and maintenance of park and/or open space lands, but such a lease agreement shall provide that:

(a) The residents of the development shall at all times have access to the reserved park and/or open space lands;

(b) The undivided improvement to be leased shall be maintained for the purposes set forth in this chapter; and

(c) The operation of improvement facilities may be for the benefit of the residents only, or may be open to the residents of the [LOCAL GOVERNMENT], at the election of the developer and/or HOA, as the case may be. The lease shall be subject to the approval of the board, and any transfer or assignment of the lease shall be further subject to the approval of the board. Lease agreements so entered upon shall be recorded with the register of deeds within 30 days of their execution and a copy of the recorded lease shall be filed with the [LOCAL GOVERNMENT].

(9) Failure to adequately maintain undivided improvements in reasonable order and condition constitutes a violation of this chapter. The [LOCAL GOVERNMENT] is authorized to give notice, by personal service or by U.S. mail, to the owner or occupant, as the case may be, of any violation, directly to the owner to remedy same within 30 days.

5.6.3 Condominiums

The undivided improvement and associated facilities may be controlled through the use of permanent condominium agreements, approved by the [LOCAL GOVERNMENT]. All undivided improvement land shall be held as a common element. A proposed operations budget and plan for long-term capital repair and replacement shall be submitted with the application.

5.6.4 Dedication of Easements

The [LOCAL GOVERNMENT] may, but is not required to, accept easements for public use of any portion or portions of undivided improvement land, the title of which is to remain in ownership by the condominium or HOA, provided that:

(A) Such land is accessible to [LOCAL GOVERNMENT] residents;

(B) There is no cost of acquisition other than any costs incidental to the transfer of ownership, such as title insurance; and

(C) A satisfactory maintenance agreement is reached between the developer, the condominium, the HOA, and the [LOCAL GOVERNMENT].

Land dedicated as a natural area, greenway, or greenbelt (§ 5.21 Parks/Open Space of this chapter) shall be subject to a duly executed conservation easement meeting the requirements of and enforceable in accordance with state statute, which easement shall be unlimited in duration.

5.6.5 Transfer of Easements

For parks and open space only, an owner may transfer perpetual easements to a private, nonprofit organization, among whose purposes it is to conserve improvement and/or natural resources (such as a land conservancy), provided that:

(A) The organization is a bona fide conservation organization with perpetual existence;

(B) The organization is financially capable of maintaining such improvement;

(C) The conveyance contains legally enforceable provisions for proper reverter or retransfer in the event that the organization becomes unwilling or unable to continue carrying out its functions;

(D) The organization shall provide a proposed operations budget and plan for long-term capital repair and replacement; and

(E) A maintenance agreement is entered into by the developer and the organization.

5.6.6 Improvement or Special Assessment Districts

This section includes an improvement or special assessment district established pursuant to statute with authority to levy taxes, fees, charges, exactions, land dedications, or special assessments to provide, operate, and maintain parks and open space lands and facilities.

DIVISION 2: DESIGN STANDARDS

This division provides for lots, blocks, buildings, and structures that provide a pedestrian scale, offer alternative paths for vehicular traffic, and accommodate on-street parking. Standards are provided to ensure that lots have adequate access and conform to the zoning provisions of the LDC. The [LOCAL GOVERNMENT] finds and determines that long blocks lined with homes and other buildings reduce street connectivity and impair the efficiency of public and safety services while increasing distances between residences and nonresidential destinations or public gathering places. Exceptions to these standards are made for nonurban districts and zoning districts that require greater flexibility in order to encourage environmental protection or economic development.

5.10 LOTS

5.10.1 Buildings to Be on a Lot

Except as permitted in the "PD" (Planned Development) district, every building shall be located on a lot. In the neighborhood zoning districts, no more than one principal building is permitted on a lot unless otherwise provided in the applicable zoning district regulations.

5.10.2 Compliance with Zoning District Regulations

The size, width, depth, shape, and orientation of lots shall comply with the applicable zoning district regulations.

5.10.3 Frontage

All lots shall front on a public or private street and shall have a minimum frontage width as indicated in the zoning district regulations. On irregularly shaped lots, a minimum street frontage of 15 feet is required. Residential lots shall not front on a collector street, arterial street, or parkway. An "irregularly shaped lot" includes any lot located on a cul-de-sac or abutting a curved section of a roadway with a centerline radius of less than 200 feet.

5.10.4 Front and Side Setbacks

5.10.4.1 Designation

Front and side setbacks adjacent to streets shall be shown on all plats as required by Chapter 3, Zoning, of the LDC. A subdivider may elect to impose greater setbacks through restrictive covenants. The [LOCAL GOVERNMENT] shall only enforce the setbacks required by Chapter 3.

5.10.4.2 Side Yard Building Line

The building line for an existing residence having a side yard of 3 or more feet may be maintained on any addition to the residence, but in no instance shall the side yard be less than 3 feet.

5.10.4.3 Yards Adjacent to Rights-of-Way and Easements

On lots that abut a public alley, railroad right-of-way, or a utility/drainage right-of-way or easement that is not part of a platted lot, one-half of such alley, right-of-way, or easement, up to a maximum of 15 feet, may be considered as part of the minimum required rear or side yard.

5.10.4.4 Variation in Front Yard

In any block in which 70 percent of the lots have front yards that are less than required by the existing zoning regulations, construction on any remaining vacant lots is permitted to the average yard of the existing improved lots.

5.10.4.5 Rear Yards on Irregular Lots

For lots fronting on cul-de-sacs, eyebrows, or elbows, and other irregularly shaped lots, a rear yard of 15 feet is permitted based on the mean horizontal distance of the principal structure from the rear lot line, provided that no part of the structure is closer than 10 feet to the lot line. The mean horizontal distance shall be calculated by adding the products of the width of each segment of the principal structure multiplied by its average distance from the property line and then dividing this sum by the total width of the structure.

5.10.4.6 Dwelling on Small Lot

A platted lot within a residential district that contains less than the minimum area for the district may be used for a single-family dwelling, provided that the lot is held in separate and different ownership from any immediately abutting lot, has a minimum area of 3,500 square feet, and has a minimum street frontage of 20 feet.

5.10.5 Corner Lots

(A) Corner lots shall have two front setbacks and two side setbacks.

(B) For corner lots, the side having the shortest street frontage is considered the front for setback purposes. The [PLANNING OFFICIAL] may waive this requirement and determine the front yard to be on the street front that is in line with the prevailing pattern of front yards on the street in order to be consistent with the established pattern of the street.

5.10.6 Double Frontage Lots

Double frontage or through lots are prohibited except in commercial or industrial districts.

5.10.7 Setback Encroachments

The features designated in Table 5-1 may encroach into a required yard as indicated in the table. The accessory structures shown in Table 5-1 are permitted in the locations indicated.

5.10.8 Vehicle and Pedestrian Areas for Single-Family, Duplex, Triplex, and Quadraplex Lots

Restrictions on driveway areas are designed to avoid the domination of front yards by large expanses of impervious surfaces, which deaden the streetscape and discourage pedestrian activity. Reducing the width of driveways can reduce total site imperviousness.

5.10.8.1 Applicability

This section applies to any subdivision plat, site plan, or development approval authorizing a single-family, duplex, triplex, or quadraplex structure.

5.10.8.2 Alleys

If the site is served by an alley, access for motor vehicles must be from the alley and not from a street frontage.

5.10.8.3 Location

Parking areas may not be located in the front setback. Parking may be provided in the rear yard, and access may be provided through alleys where the front yard is insufficient to accommodate a driveway.

5.10.8.4 Vehicle Areas Between the Porch and the Street

Vehicle areas may not be located between the building's porch or porches and an adjacent street.

Table 5-1
Accessory Uses and Structures

(A) Structure	(B) Maximum Number	(C) Permitted Location (Yards)	(D) Setback (Feet)	(E) Setback Encroachment (Feet)	(F) Maximum Size (Square Feet)	(G) Maximum Height (Feet)
Arbor	1	Any	0	—	80	12
Basketball goal	1	Any	0	—	—	15
Berms	—	Any	0	—	—	—
Bird houses	—	Any	0	—	—	—
Clothes line with no more than two poles	—	Rear or side	0	—	—	—
Covered decks or covered patios	—	Rear	10	—	—	—
Driveways	—	Any	0	—	—	—
Equipment, ancillary In nonresidential districts	—	Interior side or rear	4	—	—	—
	—	Interior side or rear	4	—	—	—
Fences, subject to § 5.14 Fences and Walls of this chapter	—	Any	0	—	—	—
Fire escapes, fire towers, storm enclosures, or handicap ramps where required by the building code	—	Any	0	—	—	—
Flagpole	—	Any	0	—	—	—
Garages, attached or detached and loaded from an alley	2	Rear	5	—	—	24
Gates	—	Any	0	—	—	—
Heating and cooling units	—	Rear or side	0	3	—	—
Light pole	1	Any	0	—	—	15
Low-voltage patio lights and 110 voltage lights	—	Any	0	—	—	3
Mailboxes installed in conformance with U.S. postal regulations, if not permitted on the residential structure by the U.S. Postal Service	—	Any	0	—	—	—
Open pools, screened or enclosed pools, spas, and uncovered decks or patios (except in waterfront yards), not closer than 20 feet from a dwelling unit on an abutting lot	—	Rear or side	0	—		
Overhanging roofs, eaves, bay windows, balconies, gutters, cornices, buttresses, piers, awnings, steps, stoops, windowsills, chimneys, structural overhangs, or projections enclosing habitable living space, or similar architectural features and awnings	—	Any	—	3	—	—
Parking areas	—	Rear unless otherwise indicated in the zoning district standards	0	—	—	—
Porch (unenclosed), stoop, awning, or roof overhang	—	Front	5	8	—	—
Projecting overhangs on the ground floor not listed above	—	Any	0	3	—	—
Protective hoods or overhangs over a doorway	—	Any	0	3	—	—
Ramps for citizens with impairments	—	Any	0	—	—	—
Retaining walls	—	Any	0	—	—	—

Table 5-1 (cont.)
Accessory Uses and Structures

(A) Structure	(B) Maximum Number	(C) Permitted Location (Yards)	(D) Setback (Feet)	(E) Setback Encroachment (Feet)	(F) Maximum Size (Square Feet)	(G) Maximum Height (Feet)
Sidewalks	—	Any	0	—	—	—
Signs, free-standing, subject to [LOCAL GOVERNMENT CODE]	3	Any	15	—	—	—
Stormwater detention or retention facilities or ditches, unless the [PLANNING OFFICIAL] finds that underground stormwater management facilities are not currently available	—	Rear	0	—	—	—

A dash ("—") means that no restriction applies. Where a setback and a setback encroachment is indicated, the stricter standard applies.

5.10.8.5 Walkways

A walkway shall extend from the sidewalk or street to the main entrance. The walkway shall be at least 2 feet but not more than 5 feet in width.

5.10.8.6 Driveways

(A) Driveways and other impervious surfaces shall not comprise more than the percentage of the front yard as specified in Column (B) of Table 5-2 for the zoning districts or use patterns designated in Column (A) of the same table. Driveways shall not exceed the width established in Column (C) of Table 5-2. Parking may be provided in the rear yard, and access may be provided through alleys where the front yard is insufficient to accommodate a driveway. Table 5-2 does not apply to irregularly shaped lots as defined by § 5.30 Greenspace Areas, Generally of this chapter.

(B) In order to reduce run-off and increase stormwater travel times, alternative materials for driveway surfaces, such as pervious pavers or gravel, is permitted in any residential zoning district.

5.10.9 Flag Lots

(A) No more than the number of flag lots shown in Table 5-3 may be authorized, allowing for the more efficient use of irregularly shaped parcels of land, sites with physical limitations, or where the integrated nature of multiple buildings on a site dictates the need for such lots. Flag lots are not permitted where they will increase the number of lots accessing collector or arterial streets.

(B) The minimum driveway width for a flag lot is 9 feet.

(C) The minimum frontage at the right-of-way line for any flag lot shall be equal to the minimum required driveway width plus 4 feet. The flagpole portion of the lot shall not be considered in determining the area of the lot.

Table 5-2
Driveway Restrictions

(A) Zoning District or Use Pattern	(B) Maximum Percent of Front Yard (Percent)	(C) Maximum Width (Feet)
"RP" (Resource Protection) "RE" (Residential Estate) "IL" (Industrial Light) "IH" (Industrial Heavy)	25	24
"NS" (Neighborhood Suburban) "NU" (Neighborhood Urban) "NP" (Neighborhood Preservation)	25	18
"MX" (Mixed Use) "CN" (Commercial Neighborhood) "D" (Downtown) "TOZ" (Transit Overlay Zone) Traditional neighborhood development or transit-oriented development use patterns	—	12
"O" (Office) "CG" (Commercial General) "CL" (Commercial Large-Scale)	—	—
"IL" (Industrial Light) "IH" (Industrial Heavy)	—	—

Table 5-3
Maximum Number of Flag Lots

Size of Subdivision	Maximum Number or Percentage of Flag Lots
	20%
51 or more	20%

**Figure 5-1
Block Tier Standards**

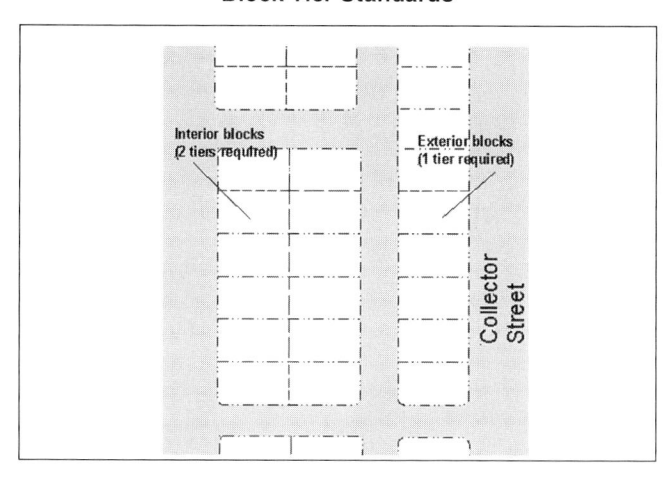

5.10.10 Reduction of Lot Size by Governmental Action

Where the owner of a legally platted lot or successor in title has a lot reduced in size as a result of governmental action, and does not own sufficient land to enable the lot to conform to the dimensional requirements of this chapter, such lot may be used as a building site for a single-family residence or other nonresidential use permitted in the district in which the lot is located, provided that:

(A) Where the lot area or mean lot width is reduced by governmental action by less than 20 percent of the minimum specified in this chapter, the [PLANNING OFFICIAL] shall issue a development approval or certificate of occupancy; and

(B) In those cases where the lot area or mean lot width is reduced by governmental action by more than 20 percent, the [PLANNING OFFICIAL] may approve as a building site a dimension that conforms as closely as possible to the required dimensions of this chapter, provided that the combined area of the principal building and accessory buildings shall not cover more than 40 percent of the lot area remaining after governmental action.

5.11 BLOCKS

5.11.1 Lots to Be Contiguous

Lots shall be arranged in a contiguous pattern within blocks or abutting a cul-de-sac. For minor subdivisions, all lots shall be contiguous, and any new lots subdivided from a tract that has been previously subdivided shall adjoin the existing lots.

5.11.2 Block Width

Blocks to the interior of the subdivision shall have sufficient width to provide for two tiers of lots. One tier of required block width is permitted in blocks adjacent to collector or arterial streets or waterways. Not more

**Table 5-4
Maximum Block Length**

(A) Zoning District(s) or Use Pattern	Max. Length (Feet)	
	(B) Any Block	(C) Average
"RP" (Resource Protection) "RE" (Residential Estate) "IL" (Industrial Light) "IH" (Industrial Heavy)	Not applicable	
"NS" (Neighborhood Suburban) "NU" (Neighborhood Urban) "NP" (Neighborhood Preservation)	600	400
"MX" (Mixed Use) "CN" (Commercial Neighborhood) "D" (Downtown) Traditional neighborhood development or transit-oriented development use patterns	300	200
"O" (Office) "CG" (Commercial General) "CL" (Commercial Large-Scale)	600	300

than two tiers of lots shall be provided for any block. This section does not apply to flag lots (Figure 5-1).

5.11.3 Length

Maximum block length for each zoning district or use pattern is illustrated in Table 5-4.

5.12 BUILDING HEIGHT

5.12.1 Generally

Building height shall conform to the requirements of the applicable zoning district regulations (Chapter 3, Zoning, of the LDC).

5.12.2 Measurement

Building height shall be measured as provided in the Uniform Building Code.

5.12.3 Height Exceptions

The height limits for the various districts do not apply to church spires, belfries, cupolas, or domes not used for human habitation, nor to chimneys, ventilators, skylights, parapet walls, cornices, solar energy systems, or necessary mechanical appurtenances usually located on the roof level, provided that such features are limited to the height necessary for their proper functioning and do not exceed the limitations of the airport hazard zoning regulations.

5.13 BUILDING DESIGN

Purpose and findings: The purpose of these regulations is to provide specific criteria so that new buildings blend into the historic architectural framework of the [LOCAL GOVERNMENT]. These criteria are not intended to restrict imagination, innovation, or variety, but rather to assist in focusing design principles, which can result in creative solutions that will develop a satisfactory visual appearance within the [LOCAL GOVERNMENT]; preserve taxable values; and promote the public health, safety, and general welfare.

These standards:

- Provide a physical and visual connection between the living area of the residence and the street;
- Enhance public safety by allowing people to survey their neighborhood from inside their residences, places of work, or shopping areas;
- Provide a more pleasant pedestrian environment by preventing large expanses of blank façades along streets;
- Ensure that the location and amount of the living area of the residence, as seen from the street, is more prominent than the garage;
- Prevent garages from obscuring the main entrance from the street and ensure that the main entrance for pedestrians, rather than automobiles, is the prominent entrance;
- Provide for a more pleasant pedestrian environment by preventing garages and vehicle areas from dominating the views of the neighborhood from the sidewalk;
- Enhance public safety by preventing garages from blocking views of the street from inside the residence;
- Supplement the zoning regulations applied to site-built, modular, and manufactured homes, with additional standards and procedures that will promote a satisfactory living environment for residents of single-family homes and that will permit a mix of homes and other types of housing within the [LOCAL GOVERNMENT];
- Permit greater diversity in the types of housing communities;
- Ensure that all new single-family dwellings are compatible with other forms of housing; and
- Ensure the provision of single-family housing opportunities for persons or families of low or moderate income by providing for design standards that ensure compatibility among various types of housing units as an alternative to exclusionary zoning.

5.13.1 Single-Family Residential Dwellings

5.13.1.1 Applicability

(A) *Types of dwelling units:* Unless otherwise specified in this ordinance, this section applies to:

(1) Any single-family dwelling unit;

(2) Any duplex; and

(3) Any triplex.

(B) *Design elements required:* The combination of design elements, as shown in Table 5-5, is required for any dwelling unit subject to this section.

5.13.1.2 Size Limitations

No single-family dwelling unit, duplex, or triplex shall exceed 8,000 square feet in size, nor exceed a floor area ratio (FAR) of .60. The total area of all dwellings and accessory structures shall not exceed a FAR of .75.

5.13.1.3 Main Entrance

(A) *Location of main entrance:* The main entrance of each primary structure must face the street. On corner lots, the main entrance may face either of the streets or be oriented to the corner. With buildings that have more than one main entrance, only one entrance must meet this requirement. A building must include a front porch or stoop at all main entrances that face a street. The porch or stoop shall adjoin the main entrance and the main entrance shall be accessible from the porch.

(B) *Porches*

(1) Porches shall be covered by a solid roof. The roof shall not be located more than 12 feet above the floor of the porch. If the roof of a required porch is developed as a deck or balcony, it may be flat.

(2) The porch shall have minimum dimensions of 6 feet by 6 feet. For single-family dwellings, the covered area provided by the porch must be at least 48 square feet and a minimum of 8 feet wide. If the main entrance is for more than one dwelling unit, the covered area

**Table 5-5
Applicability of Single-Family Design Regulations**

Standard	Zoning District or Use		
	RE, RP	NS, NU	D, TND, PD
§ 5.13.1.3 Main Entrance of this chapter	M	M	M
§ 5.13.1.4 Garages of this chapter	O	M	M
§ 5.13.1.5 Roofs of this chapter	O	O	O
§ 5.13.1.6 Foundation of this chapter	O	O	O
§ 5.13.1.7 Exterior Finish Materials of this chapter	O	O	O
§ 5.13.1.8 Windows and Entryways of this chapter	O	O	M

RE = Residential Estate; RP = Resource Protection; NS = Neighborhood Suburban; NU = Neighborhood Urban; D = Downtown; TND = traditional neighborhood development; PD = Planned Development; M = the standard is mandatory; and O = the standard is optional. Single-family dwellings subject to this section must comply with at least two of the optional standards.

provided by the porch must be at least 63 square feet and a minimum of 9 feet wide.

(C) *Covered balconies:* The covered area provided by the balcony must be at least 48 square feet, a minimum of 8 feet wide, and no more than 15 feet above grade. The covered balcony must be accessible from the interior living space of the house.

(D) *Openings between porch floor and ground:* Openings of more than 1 foot between the porch floor and the ground must be covered with a solid material or lattice.

5.13.1.4 Garages

(A) *Generally:* Garages shall either be detached or shall be facing the side or rear lot line. A garage wall may not be closer to the street lot line than the front of the porch.

(B) *Detached garages.* These standards encourage detached garages as an alternative to front-loaded attached garages.

(1) Detached garages are permitted in any zoning district. Detached garages shall be located in the rear yard. The footprint for the garage structure shall not exceed 24 by 24 feet. The garage walls shall not exceed 15 feet in height or the height of the principal structure, whichever is less.

(2) A detached garage that is nonconforming due to its location in a setback may be rebuilt on its existing foundation if it was originally constructed legally. An addition may be made to these types of garages if the addition complies with the standards of this section, or if the combined size of the existing foundation and any additions are no larger than 12 feet wide by 18 feet deep. The garage walls shall not exceed 10 feet in height.

(C) *Street-facing garage walls*

(1) *Applicability:* This section applies to garages that are accessory to single-family dwelling units, manufactured homes, duplexes, or triplexes. Where a proposal is for an alteration or addition to existing development, the standard applies only to the portion being altered or added. Garages that are accessory to attached houses, development on flag lots, or development on lots that slope up or down from the street with an average slope of 20 percent or more, are exempt from this standard.

(2) *Maximum length and size:* The length of that portion of a garage wall facing the street shall not exceed 30 percent of the length of the street-facing building façade. Garage doors may not exceed 75 square feet in area. There may be no more than two individual garage doors. On corner lots, only one street-facing garage wall must meet this standard. Where the street-facing façade of the building is less than 24 feet long, the garage wall facing the street may be up to 12 feet long if there is one of the following:

(a) Interior living area above the garage; or

(b) A covered balcony above the garage that is at least the same length as the street-facing garage wall, at least 6 feet deep, and accessible from the interior living area of the dwelling unit.

(D) *Street lot line setbacks:* A garage wall that faces a street shall be located at least 20 feet behind the plane of the front façade. A street-facing garage wall may adjoin the front façade or be located within the area described above, where:

(1) The street-facing garage wall does not exceed 30 percent of the length of the building facade; and

(2) The interior living area is located above the garage. The living area must be set back no more than 4 feet from the street-facing garage wall, or shall include a covered balcony above the garage that is at least the same length as the street-facing garage wall, at least 6 feet deep, and accessible from the interior living area of the dwelling unit.

(E) *Street-facing garage walls prohibited in "D" (Downtown) district or traditional neighborhood development (TND):* Garage walls facing the street or extending beyond the front elevation of a dwelling unit are prohibited in the "D" district or a TND use pattern or district.

5.13.1.5 Roofs

(A) *Slope:* Principal structures must have a roof that is sloped, with a pitch that is no flatter than six units of horizontal run to 12 units of horizontal rise.

(B) *Architectural features:* The roof of a principal structure shall include the following architectural details:

(1) At least one dormer facing the street. If only one dormer is included, it shall be at least 5 feet wide and shall be centered horizontally between each end of the front elevation. If more than one dormer is provided, a dormer at least 4 feet wide must be provided on each side of the front elevation; or

(2) A gable end, or gabled end of a roof projection, facing the street.

(C) *Roof eaves:* Roof eaves must project from the building wall at least 12 inches, measured horizontally, on at least the front and side elevations.

5.13.1.6 Foundation

The ground level of the first floor, including the lowest elevation of any point of the front façade, shall be elevated at least 3 feet from the horizontal surface of the street or sidewalk. Plain concrete block or plain concrete may be used as foundation material if the foundation material is not visible by more than 3 feet above the finished grade level adjacent to the foundation wall.

5.13.1.7 Exterior Finish Materials

(A) Plain concrete block, plain concrete, corrugated metal, plywood, and sheet pressboard are not allowed as exterior finish material. Composite boards manufactured from wood or other products, such as hardboard or hardiplank, may be used when the board product is less than 6 inches wide.

(B) Where wood products are used for siding, the siding must be shingles or horizontal siding and not shakes.

(C) Where horizontal siding is used, it must be shiplap or clapboard siding composed of boards with a reveal of 3 to 6 inches, or vinyl or aluminum siding that is in a clapboard or shiplap pattern where the boards in the pattern are 6 inches or less in width.

5.13.1.8 Windows and Entryways

(A) At least 15 percent of the area of a street-facing façade must include windows or main entryways.

(B) Street-facing windows shall comply with the following requirements:

(1) Each window must be square or vertical—at least as tall as it is wide; or

(2) A horizontal window opening may be created subject to the following standards:

(a) Two or more vertical windows are grouped together to provide a horizontal opening, and they are either all the same size or no more than two sizes are used. Where two sizes of windows are used in a group, the smaller window size must be on the outer edges of the grouping. The windows on the outer edges of the grouping must be vertical; the center window or windows may be vertical, square, or horizontal;

(b) There is a band of individual lights across the top of the horizontal window. These small lights must be vertical and must cover at least 20 percent of the total height of the window; or

(c) Windows in rooms with a finished floor height 4 feet or more below grade are exempt from this standard.

5.13.2 Duplexes, Triplexes, and Quadraplexes

5.13.2.1 Generally

Duplexes shall include at least two of the following architectural elements, as described in § 5.13.2 Duplexes, Triplexes, and Quadraplexes of this chapter:

(A) Dormers;
(B) Front porches;
(C) Bay windows; and
(D) Balconies.

5.13.2.2 Covered Balconies

Duplexes or triplexes may provide a covered balcony on the same façade as the main entrance instead of a front porch.

5.13.2.3 Windows

Windows shall have a vertical-to-horizontal ratio of at least 1.5:1 and less than 3:1, which are recessed into the face of the building and broken up with smaller panes of glass.

5.13.2.4 Roofs

The roof of each attached unit must be distinct from the other through either separation of roof pitches or direction, or other variation in roof design.

5.13.3 Manufactured Homes

Manufactured homes shall conform to the requirements of § 5.13.1 Single-Family Residential Dwellings of this chapter and to the standards and criteria shown in § 5.13.3.1 Zoning Standards through § 5.13.3.3 Orientation of this chapter.

5.13.3.1 Zoning Standards

Any manufactured home on an individual lot shall conform to the same building setback standards, side and rear yard requirements, standards for enclosures, access, vehicle parking, and square-footage standards and requirements that would be applicable to a conventional, single-family residential dwelling on the same lot.

5.13.3.2 Foundation

The dwelling shall be attached to a permanent foundation system in compliance with the [INSTALLATION STANDARD REFERENCE][5] as may be amended, and the following requirements:

(A) All wheels, hitches, axles, transporting lights, and removable towing apparatus shall be permanently removed prior to installation of the dwelling unit;

(B) The foundation shall be excavated and shall have continuous skirting or backfill leaving no uncovered open areas excepting vents and crawl spaces. The foundation shall either not be located above grade or shall include masonry skirting; and

(C) All manufactured homes shall be anchored to the ground by means of anchors attached both to the frame and with straps extending over the top and completely surrounding the sides and roof, consistent with building code requirements. In addition, test data giving certified results of pull tests in soils representative of the area in which the anchors are to be used shall be submitted to the [PLANNING OFFICIAL]. Minimum load in direct pull shall be 5,400 pounds. Anchors shall be marked so that, after installation, the identification is in plain view for inspection.

5.13.3.3 Orientation

Manufactured homes that are narrower than 16 feet in width shall be oriented on the lot so that its long axis is parallel to the street.

5.13.4 Multifamily Dwellings

5.13.4.1 Applicability

Unless otherwise specified in this ordinance, this section applies to any of the following where located on a lot exceeding 10,000 square feet:

(A) Any townhouse or row house; and

(B) Any building that includes multifamily dwelling units.

For purposes of computing the number of dwelling units to determine applicability of the standards of this section, the number of existing or proposed dwelling units within any tract of land plus all existing or proposed multifamily dwellings on any adjacent property under common ownership shall be counted.

5.13.4.2 Entryways

For developments of 40 or more dwelling units, a divided ingress-egress driveway with a landscaped median for all entrances from public streets shall be provided. Median design shall conform to the standards in § 5.23 Street Design and Transportation of this chapter.

5.13.4.3 Common Open Space

Common open space areas shall be required in accordance with § 5.21 Parks/Open Space of this chapter. The [PLANNING OFFICIAL] may waive up to 50 percent of the open space requirement if all units within the development are located within 1,000 feet of a public park as measured along a public sidewalk. The open space requirements of this section shall not apply to multifamily residential developments that are second-floor units above first-floor commercial development, or to any residential developments in the "D" (Downtown) zoning district that are above the first floor. Open space provided pursuant to this requirement shall be accessible to all residents of the development and shall measure at least 30 feet across its narrowest dimension.

5.13.4.4 Pedestrian Facilities

Sidewalks shall be constructed within the interior of the development to link residential buildings with other destinations, such as, but not limited to, parking, adjoining streets, mailboxes, trash disposal, adjoining sidewalks or greenways, and on-site amenities, such as recreation areas. These interior sidewalks shall be constructed in accordance with the standards for sidewalks in § 5.23 Street Design and Transportation of this chapter. Sidewalks shall be provided adjacent to all public streets that provide access to the development.

5.13.4.5 Building Design

Building design for multifamily buildings shall:

- Provide interesting and aesthetically attractive multifamily developments;
- Avoid monotonous, "barracks"-style buildings;
- Ensure that multifamily buildings have a multi-faceted exterior form in which articulated façades are combined with window and door placements as well as other detailing; and
- Create an interesting and attractive architectural design.

These standards limit flat walls with minimal features.

5.13.4.6 Building Design Standards

The following standards shall apply to building design:

(A) Buildings shall not exceed 150 feet in length;

(B) Façades greater than 50 feet in length, measured horizontally, shall incorporate wall plane projections or recesses. Ground-floor façades that face public streets shall have arcades, windows, entry areas, awnings, or other such features for at least 60 percent of their horizontal length;

(C) Buildings shall be arranged so that they are aligned parallel to a sidewalk or around common open space, such as courtyards, greens, squares, or plazas; and

(D) Entryways shall face a street, sidewalk, or common area. Buildings shall not face the rear of other buildings on the same lot or parcel.

5.13.4.7 Utilities

All utility lines shall be located underground. Outdoor area lighting shall be provided for security. Such lighting shall be shielded to direct light downward and not into dwelling units on, or adjacent to, the multifamily site. Lighting shall be provided to illuminate the intersections of primary interior driveways and building entryways.

5.13.5 Commercial Buildings

Purpose and findings: These standards are designed to:

- Promote a quality, urban streetscape;
- Promote a pedestrian-friendly environment;
- Establish a variety of mixed uses in the core of the community;
- Provide an orderly development pattern;
- Maintain a supply of developable land while preserving the compact development;
- Improve traffic circulation and promote alternatives to automobile travel;
- Provide housing opportunities within walking distances of employment, service, and retail opportunities;
- Maintain an overall design theme;
- Preserve a human scale for new buildings;
- Provide economic development opportunities through clean industry, office, and commercial uses; and
- Provide for the daily needs and services of the community.

**Figure 5-2
Commercial Design Elements**

[Figure 5-2: Photograph of a commercial building with labels pointing to: Sidewalks & pedestrian connections, Building modules, Changes in building plane, Columns, towers, & architectural features, Texture & building materials, Landscaping]

These standards are not intended to restrict imagination, innovation, or variety. See Figure 5-2 for orientation of commercial design elements.

5.13.5.1 Applicability

Unless otherwise specified in this chapter, this section applies to any commercial building or structure.

5.13.5.2 Floor Area

In order to implement the goals and objectives of the comprehensive plan related to the impacts of large-scale development upon neighborhoods, the need for walkability and viable mixed-use communities to enhance the air quality, reduce traffic congestion, promote safety from traffic accidents, and enhance the land-use plans of the downtown and commercial corridors or centers, no commercial building or structure used for retail shall have a gross floor area (GFA) of 40,000 square feet or greater, or store or display lumber, or building materials outside of a completely enclosed building, except where located in a corridor commercial overlay zoning district, or downtown commercial district, where the GFA ratio may not exceed 60,000 gross square feet per building or structure and outside storage or display shall be subject to a special use permit.

Every commercial building used for retail or wholesale sales that exceeds 25,000 square feet shall obtain a special use permit prior to obtaining any development approval under the LDC. The special use permit shall require a written finding by the board of appeals that:

(1) The building intensity and use is consistent with the applicable comprehensive, area, or neighborhood plan goals, objectives, policies, and strategies;

(2) The building contains mixed uses of commercial, office, and residential;

(3) The building meets all of the other standards of the LDC, and particularly that of Chapter 2, Use Patterns, of the LDC; and

(4) The building will not create excessive on- or off-site traffic, environmental, aesthetic, storm drainage, fiscal, or noncompatibility impacts upon adjoining properties and neighborhoods.

The applicant for the special use permit shall provide to the board of appeals or legislative body a traffic fiscal impact report and an environmental impact assessment, along with the application for the special use permit. This documentation shall provide substantial competent evidence to support the findings in subsections (1) through (4), above.

5.13.5.3 Building Structure

(A) *Base, middle, and cap:* Buildings exceeding two stories shall incorporate a base, a middle, and a cap described as follows:

(1) The base shall include an entryway with transparent windows as set forth in the ground-floor design standards (§ 5.13.5.5 Ground-Floor Design of this chapter), and a molding or reveal placed between the first and second stories or over the second story. The molding or reveal shall have a depth of at least 2 inches and a height of at least 4 inches;

(2) The middle may include windows and/or balconies; and

(3) The cap shall include the area from the top floor to the roof of the building, and shall include a cornice or a roof overhang.

(B) *Alignment:* Windowsills, moldings, and cornices shall align with those of adjacent buildings. The bottom and top line defining the edge of the windows (the "windowsill alignment") shall vary not more than 2 feet from the alignment of surrounding buildings. If the adjoining buildings have a windowsill alignment that varies by more than 2 feet from one another, the proposed building shall align with one of the adjoining buildings.

5.13.5.4 Façade Size

"Façade size" refers to the length multiplied by the width of any façade that faces or is parallel to a public or private street. "Façade" means the exterior side of a building and includes the entire building walls, including wall faces, parapets, fascia, windows, doors, canopy, and visible roof structures of one complete elevation. The sum total of the façade areas on a lot may exceed the maximum façade size described in this section by dividing the buildings into two or more buildings, or into distinct "modules" that incorporate visible changes in the façade elevation through the use of wall plane projections, piers, columns, colonnades, arcades, or similar architectural features that create a distinct façade elevation (see Figure 5-2, above). Each module shall have separate windows and entryways. The modules for a single, continuous façade shall not exceed an average of 30 feet in width. No module shall exceed 50 feet in width (see Figure 5-3).

5.13.5.5 Ground-Floor Design

(A) All buildings subject to this section shall have their principal entrance opening to a street, square, plaza, or sidewalk. The principal entrance shall not open onto a parking lot. Pedestrian access from the public sidewalk, street right-of-way, or driveway to the principal structure shall be provided through an improved surface.

(B) The ground floor of the entryway shall align with the sidewalk elevation. Sunken terraces or stairways to a basement shall not constitute entryways for purposes of this section. It is not the intent of this section to preclude the use of below-grade entryways, provided, however, that such entryways shall not constitute a principal entryway and shall not be used to satisfy the distancing requirements of § 5.13.5.7 Windows and Entryways of this chapter.

5.13.5.6 Street Wall

Where a maximum front setback has been established, the front building wall or courtyard shall adjoin the sidewalk. The side setback shall be a minimum of 0 feet and a maximum of 10 feet.

**Figure 5-3
Form-Based Zoning**

Modules are useful in developing form-based zoning.

5.13.5.7 Windows and Entryways

(A) Windows above the ground floor shall have a minimum ratio of height to width of 2:1.

(B) The ground floors of all buildings shall be designed to encourage and to complement pedestrian-scale activity by the use of windows and doors arranged so that the uses are visible from and/or accessible to the street on at least 50 percent of the length of the first-floor street frontage. At least 60 percent nor more than 90 percent of the total surface area of the front elevation shall be in public entrances and windows (including retail display windows). Where windows are used, they shall be transparent.

(C) Solid walls shall not exceed 20 feet in length.

(D) All street-level retail uses with sidewalk frontage shall be furnished with an individual entrance and direct access to the sidewalk in addition to any other access that may be provided. This standard shall not apply to any lot with a street frontage of less than 24 feet.

(E) Doors shall be recessed into the face of the building to provide a sense of entry and to add variety to the streetscape. An entryway shall not be less than 1 square foot for each 1,000 square feet of floor area, and in all cases shall not be less than 15 square feet.

(F) The maximum setback requirements may be waived by the [PLANNING OFFICIAL] for an area not to exceed 90 percent of the frontage in order to accommodate courtyards.

(G) Canopies, awnings, and similar appurtenances may be constructed at the entrance to any building, subject to the criteria established in the Uniform Building Code.

5.13.5.8 Mechanical Equipment

Mechanical equipment, electrical meter and service components, and similar utility devices, whether ground level, wall mounted, or roof mounted, shall be screened from view at the front property line. Exterior screening materials shall be the same as the predominant exterior materials of the principal building. In cases where the front property line is higher than the roof line of the subject building, no screening shall be required for a line of sight exceeding 5 feet 6 inches above the finished elevation of the property at the front property line.

5.13.6 Civic Buildings

Civic buildings shall include columns, arcades, or colonnades in lieu of the ground-level design requirements of § 5.13 Building Design of this chapter.

5.14 FENCES AND WALLS

5.14.1 Design

5.14.1.1 Articulation

No fence or wall, or portion, shall exceed 100 horizontal feet in length unless one of the following architectural features visible from the paved surface of the street is provided as part of the fence:

(A) A column or pillar; or

(B) Articulation of the surface plane wall by incorporating plane projections or recesses having a depth of at least 1 foot and extending a horizontal distance of at least 3 feet and less than 20 feet.

5.14.1.2 Exception

§ 5.14.1.1 Articulation of this chapter does not apply to a fence or wall constructed of brick, masonry, or iron fencing that consists of at least 50 percent open voids. The square footage of the fence shall be measured by taking the total square footage of an area defined by the length of the fence and its average height. The percent of open voids shall then be derived by dividing the total square footage of the open voids by the total square footage of the area calculated above and multiplying this figure by 100. The fence's framing (the vertical posts supporting the fence from the ground and no more than three horizontal cross bars between the posts or brick or stone pillars) shall not be included in the calculation of the total square footage, provided that the framing posts and cross bars do not exceed a 4-inch width and the posts are spaced at least 8 feet apart.

5.14.2 Height

5.14.2.1 Front Yard

No fence or wall, other than the wall of a permitted structure, shall exceed a height of 4 feet in the front yard. No fence or wall shall obscure vision above a height of 3 feet.

5.14.2.2 Side or Rear Yard

(A) No fence or wall, other than the wall of a permitted structure, shall be erected or altered in any side or rear yard to exceed a height of 6 feet.

(B) The following exceptions apply to subsection (A), above:

(1) Subsection (A), above, does not apply where the supplemental use regulations in Chapter 7, Supplemental Use Regulations, of the LDC require a higher fence for screening or security purposes;

(2) A fence may be erected or altered up to a height of 8 feet where the fence abuts a collector or higher-order street, the ground-floor elevation of the principal dwelling on an abutting lot is at least 4 feet higher than the elevation at the abutting lot line (see Figure 5-4), the fence abuts a side or rear lot line that abuts a collector street or an arterial street (in which case streetscape planting shall be provided in accordance with § 5.32 Streetscape Landscaping of this chapter), or the fence is a sound wall or fence required by the State Department of Transportation. The additional fence height may be permitted by the [GOVERNING ENTITY] pursuant to a rezoning or conditional use permit (CUP).

5.14.2.3 Industrial Districts

Fence height restrictions do not apply in the "IL" (Industrial Light) or "IH" (Industrial Heavy) districts where:

(A) The lot does not abut a residential or commercial district; and

(B) The fence height and location do not adversely affect site distance at street and/or alley intersections.

5.14.3 Residential Subdivisions

The [LOCAL GOVERNMENT] finds that it is necessary for the public welfare to impose standards to improve and preserve the quality of fences in residential neighborhoods in order to avoid blighting influences on neighborhoods and public safety problems.

5.14.3.1 Applicability

This section applies to fences located along the perimeter of a tract or parcel subject to an application for subdivision approval and abutting a collector or arterial street.

5.14.3.2 Standards

(A) A fence may be constructed of permanent material, such as wood, chain link, stone, rock, concrete block, masonry brick, brick, decorative wrought iron, or other materials that are similar in durability.

(B) The following materials shall not be used for fencing subject to this section:

**Figure 5-4
Fence Height**

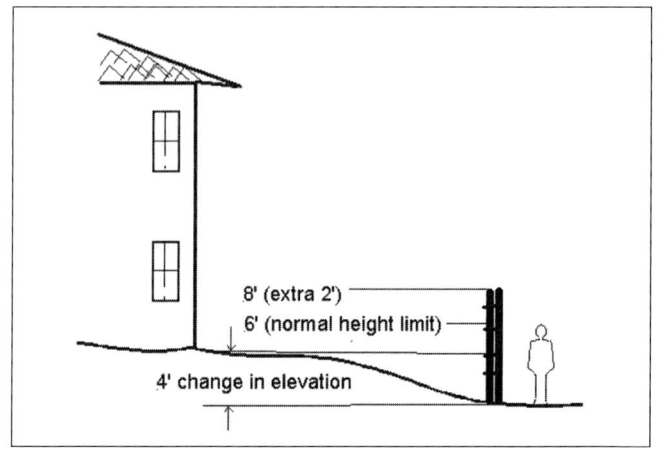

Additional height where home on adjacent lot is 4 feet higher.

(1) Cast-off, secondhand, or other items not originally intended to be used for constructing or maintaining a fence;

(2) Plywood less than 5/8 inches thick, plywood not of a grade approved by the code enforcement manager, particle board, paper, and visqueen plastic, plastic tarp, or similar material; and

(3) Barbed wire, razor wire, and other similar fencing materials capable of inflicting significant physical injury.

(C) A fence constructed of wooden boards shall include at least one of the following architectural or landscaping elements for every 50 lineal feet:

(1) A wall or column extending at least 12 inches vertically and 6 inches horizontally from the remainder of the fence;

(2) The fence, which shall be articulated by means of a recess or a projection extending at least 12 inches horizontally from the remainder of the fence; or

(3) Climbing vines, shrubs, or trees planted along the base of that portion of the wall or fence that fronts a public street. The remaining setback area between the fence and property line shall be landscaped with grass or other low ground cover. All plants shall be irrigated and maintained consistent with the provisions of this chapter. Only living vegetation may be used to meet these landscaping requirements.

(D) All fences shall be maintained by an HOA established consistent with the requirements of subsection (B), above, so as not to create a hazard, public nuisance, or blight in the surrounding neighborhood.

5.15 LIGHTING

Purpose and findings: These provisions are intended to control the use of outdoor, artificial illuminating devices emitting rays into the night sky that have a detrimental effect on the rural atmosphere and astronomical observations and that create glare. It is the intention of this section to:

- Encourage good lighting practices such that lighting systems are designed to conserve energy and money;
- Minimize glare;
- Protect the use and enjoyment of surrounding property; and
- Increase nighttime safety, utility, security, and productivity.

5.15.1 Applicability

5.15.1.1 Generally

(A) All outdoor, artificial illuminating devices shall be installed in conformance with the provisions of this section and the building code of the [LOCAL GOVERNMENT].

(B) This section does not prevent the use of any material or method of installation not specifically addressed. In considering any variance from the provisions of this section, the hearing officer shall take into consideration any state-of-the-art technology that is consistent with the intent of this section as new lighting technology develops that is useful in reducing light above the horizontal plane.

5.15.1.2 Exceptions

The following types of light fixtures shall be exempt from the provisions of this section:

(A) *Low-intensity luminaires:* Any luminaire with a lamp or lamps rated at a total of 1,800 lumens or less, and all flood or spot luminaires with a lamp or lamps rated at 900 lumens or less, may be used without restriction to light distribution or mounting height, except that if any spot or flood luminaire rated 900 lumens or less is aimed, directed, or focused to cause direct light from the luminaire to be directed toward residential buildings on adjacent or nearby land, or to create glare perceptible to persons operating motor vehicles on public ways, the luminaire shall be redirected or its light output controlled as necessary to eliminate such conditions.

(B) *Public street luminaires:* Luminaires used for public street illumination may be installed at a maximum height of 25 feet and may be positioned at that height up to the edge of any bordering property.

(C) *Emergency lighting:* All temporary emergency lighting needed by the police, the fire departments, or other emergency services, as well as all vehicular luminaires, shall be exempt from the requirements of this section.

(D) *Nonconforming fixtures:* All outdoor light fixtures installed prior to the adoption of the LDC and those equipped with a permanent automatic shut-off device may remain unchanged, except that the subject light fixtures shall not be operated between the hours of 11:00 PM and sunrise.

(E) *Fossil-fuel light:* This type of light is produced directly or indirectly by the combustion of natural gas or other utility-type fossil fuels.

(F) *Low-intensity fixtures:* Any outdoor lighting fixture that has a maximum candle power of less than 1,000 candelas is exempt from these provisions, if equipped with an automatic device that shuts off the fixture between the hours of 11:00 PM and sunrise.

5.15.2 Shielding and Filtration

(A) All nonexempt outdoor lighting fixtures shall be limited to the types of fixtures specified in Table 5-6 and shall have shielding and filtration as required by Table 5-6.

**Table 5-6
Shielding Requirements**

Fixture-Lamp Type	Shielded	Filtered
Low-pressure sodium[a]	No	None
High-pressure sodium	Fully	None
Metal halide	Fully[b, f]	Yes
Fluorescent	Fully[c, e]	Yes
Quartz[d]	Fully	No
Incandescent, greater than 150 watts	Fully	None
Incandescent, 150 watts or less	None	None
Fossil fuel	None	None
Glass tubes filled with neon, argon, and krypton	None	None

[a] *Preferred light source to minimize undesirable light emission into the night sky affecting astronomical observations.*
[b] *Metal halide lighting used primarily for display purposes shall not be used for security lighting after 11:00 PM. Metal halide lamps shall be installed only in enclosed luminaries.*
[c] *Outdoor advertising signs of the type constructed of translucent materials and wholly illuminated from within do not require shielding. Dark backgrounds with light lettering or symbols are preferred to minimize detrimental effects.*
[d] *For the purposes of the Land Development Code, quartz lamps shall not be considered an incandescent light source.*
[e] *Warm white and natural lamps are preferred to minimize detrimental effects.*
[f] *Metal halide fixture-lamp types shall be filtered. "Filtered" means any outdoor light fixture that has a glass, acrylic, or translucent enclosure of the light source (quartz glass does not meet this requirement).*

**Table 5-7
Illumination Standards**

Area/Activity	Lux	Foot Candles
Residential Zoning Districts		
Building exterior	50	5.0
Front, side, or rear yard (at property line)	10	1.0
Nonresidential Zoning Districts		
Adjoining another nonresidential zoning district along an arterial	20	2.0
Adjoining residential zoning district along arterial	10	1.0
Adjoining another nonresidential zoning district along arterial or collector street	13	1.2
Adjoining residential zoning district along arterial or collector street	6	0.6
Adjoining another nonresidential zoning district along local street	10	0.9
Adjoining residential zoning district along local street	4	0.4
Adjoining another nonresidential zoning district along property line	10	0.9
Adjoining residential zoning district along property line	2	0.2
Outdoor Events		
Adjoining nonresidential zoning district	1,000	100
Adjoining or within 1,000 feet of residential zoning district	100	10

(B) Light source locations shall be chosen to minimize the hazards of glare. The ratio of spacing to mounting height shall not exceed a 4:1 ratio.

(C) All poles or standards used to support outdoor lighting fixtures shall be anodized or otherwise coated to minimize glare from the light source.

5.15.3 Illumination

In order to minimize glare and hazardous conditions, illumination levels shall not exceed the levels set forth in Table 5-7 for any use permitted by this section. The maximum illumination shall be measured at grade at the property line of the site in accordance with § 5.15.8 Measurement of this chapter (see Figure 5-5).

5.15.4 Control of Glare—Luminaire Design Factors

(A) Any luminaire with a lamp or lamps rated at a total of more than 1,800 lumens, and all flood or spot luminaires with a lamp or lamps rated at a total of more than 900 lumens, shall not emit any direct light above a horizontal plane through the lowest direct light emitting part of the luminaire.

(B) Any luminaire with a lamp or lamps rated at a total of more than 1,800 lumens, and all flood or spot luminaires with a lamp or lamps rated at a total of more than 900 lumens, shall be mounted at a height not exceeding the value 3 + (D.3), where "D" is the distance in feet to the nearest property boundary. The maximum height of the luminaire shall not exceed 25 feet.

5.15.5 Prohibitions

5.15.5.1 Mercury-Vapor Fixtures and Lamps

The installation of any mercury-vapor fixture or lamp for use as outdoor lighting is prohibited.

5.15.5.2 Certain Other Fixtures and Lamps

The installation of any low-pressure sodium, high-pressure sodium, metal halide, fluorescent, quartz, or incandescent outdoor lighting fixture or lamp is prohibited unless it complies with the shielding and illu-

**Figure 5-5
Lighting Intensity**

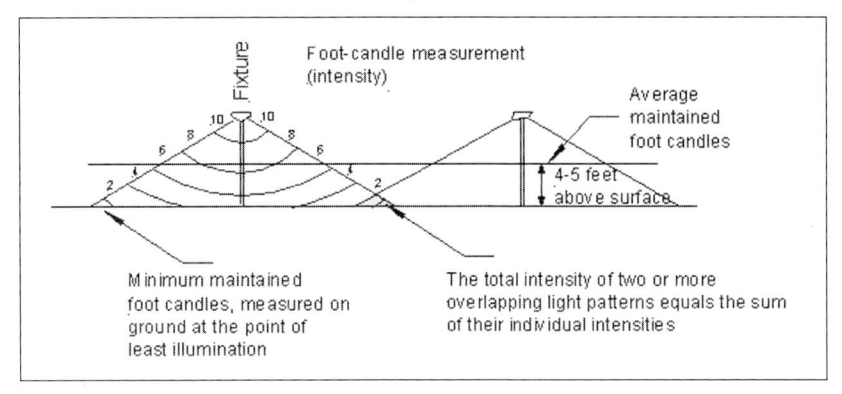

mination standards (§ 5.15.2 Shielding and Filtration and § 5.15.3 Illumination) of this chapter.

5.15.5.3 Laser Source Light

The use of laser source light or any similar high-intensity light for outdoor advertising, when projected above the horizontal, is prohibited.

5.15.5.4 Searchlights

The operation of searchlights for advertising purposes is prohibited between the hours of 11:00 PM and sunrise.

5.15.5.5 Recreational Facilities

No outdoor recreational facility, public or private, shall be illuminated by nonconforming means after 11:00 PM, unless otherwise permitted pursuant to a CUP, except to conclude specific recreational or sporting events or any other activity conducted at a ball park, outdoor amphitheater, arena, or similar facility in progress prior to 11:00 PM. All recreational outdoor lighting shall comply with height restrictions as specified in the building code. Outdoor lighting for open air arenas primarily used for rodeo and roping activities shall be permitted to a maximum height of 30 feet, provided that shielding and filtration requirements (§ 5.15.2 Shielding and Filtration and § 5.15.3 Illumination of this chapter) are met.

5.15.5.6 Outdoor Building or Landscaping Illumination

The unshielded outdoor illumination of any building, landscaping, signing, or other purpose is prohibited, except with incandescent fixtures of 150 watts or less, or low-pressure sodium fixtures.

5.15.6 Recreational Facilities

Any light source permitted by this section may be used for lighting of outdoor recreational facilities (public or private), such as, but not limited to, football fields, soccer fields, baseball fields, softball fields, tennis courts, auto racetracks, horse racetracks, or show arenas, consistent with the illumination standards specified in Table 5-7 provided that all of the following conditions are met:

(A) All fixtures used for event lighting shall be fully shielded, or shall be designed or provided with sharp cut-off capability, in order to minimize up light, spill light, and glare; and

(B) All events shall be scheduled in order to complete all activity before or as near to 10:30 PM as practical, but under no circumstances shall any illumination of the playing field, court, or track be permitted after 11:00 PM except to conclude a scheduled event that was in progress before 11:00 PM and circumstances prevented concluding before 11:00 PM.

5.15.7 Outdoor Display Lots

Any light source permitted by this section may be used for lighting of outdoor display lots, such as, but not limited to, automobile sales or rental, recreational vehicle sales, or building material sales, provided that all of the following conditions are met:

(A) All fixtures used for display lighting shall be fully shielded or be designed or provided with sharp cut-off capability, in order to minimize up light, spill light, and glare; and

(B) Display lot lighting shall be turned off within 30 minutes after the closing of business. The full illumination of the lot may be permitted after 11:00 PM pursuant to a temporary use permit. Any lighting used after that time shall be used as security lighting.

5.15.8 Measurement

5.15.8.1 Metering Equipment

Lighting levels are to be measured in foot candles with a direct reading, portable light meter. The meter typically has a color and cosine-corrected sensor with multiple scales and shall read within an accuracy of plus or minus 5 percent. It shall have been tested, calibrated, and certified by an independent, commercial photometric laboratory or the manufacturer within one year of its use.

5.15.8.2 Method of Measurement

The meter sensor shall be mounted not more than 6 inches above ground level in a horizontal position. Readings are taken by qualified personnel only after the cell has been exposed long enough to provide a constant reading. Measurements are made after dark with the light sources in question on, then with the same sources off. The difference between the two readings shall be compared to the maximum permitted illumination and property line at ground level. This procedure eliminates the effects of moonlight and other ambient light sources. Where light patterns overlap, their total intensity shall be the sum of their individual intensities.

5.16 HOMELAND SECURITY SITE-SPECIFIC VULNERABILITY ASSESSMENT

All applications for development approval for public, semipublic, and certain private facilities (e.g., power plants, electrical transmission facilities, dams, high-rise buildings, regional shopping facilities, industrial buildings, airports, bridges, chemical plants, convention centers, government buildings, hospitals, hotels, ports, railroads, rail yards, transportation terminals, transit station stops, schools, stadiums, multifamily apartment complexes, wastewater and water plants and facilities, and other uses identified through site- and threat-specific analyses) shall provide a site-specific vulnerability assessment incorporating the following minimum standards:

(A) The mission of the facility;

(B) Sensitive vulnerable areas;

(C) Types of activities and the site;

(D) Description of users of the facility;

(E) Site perimeter security (e.g., setbacks, unobstructed views, restricted access, and avoidance of unnecessary signage);

(F) Landscaping and external design (i.e., avoidance of high-speed access, restriction of entrance and parking accesses, use of secure concrete barriers, and incorporation of traffic patterns of pedestrians and vehicles in landscaping design); and

(G) Building design security measures (e.g., identification stations, facility entry checkpoints, vehicle inspection facilities, and surveillance equipment).

The [LOCAL GOVERNMENT] shall, within 90 days after adoption of the LDC, provide administrative regulations, checklists, and application forms necessary to carry out the provisions of this section. The administrative regulations shall provide for designation of the law enforcement officials, building inspectors, and architect/engineers required to approve plans and to carry out audits and inspections. The administrative regulations shall also provide for adoption of development approval fees to cover the costs of administering this section.

5.17 SUSTAINABILITY

These provisions are intended to promote sustainable development, which reduces the long-term operational costs of buildings and minimizes adverse effects on the environment, public works infrastructure, and occupant health and productivity. The following set of building practices is modeled on the "Green Building Rating System for New Construction & Major Renovations (LEED®-NC) Version 2.2" from the United States Green Building Council (USGBC). Categories include Sustainable Sites, Water Efficiency, Energy and Atmosphere, Materials and Resources, and Indoor Environmental Quality.

Commercial development consisting of new buildings, or major renovations to existing buildings, shall achieve a minimum score of 22 out of 64 possible points by employing a combination of the following building practices:

• Multifamily residential development consisting of new buildings, or major renovations to existing buildings, shall achieve a minimum score of 18 out of 52 possible points.

• All other residential development consisting of new buildings, or major renovations to existing buildings, shall achieve a minimum score of 17 out of 49 possible points.

Each [LOCAL GOVERNMENT] is encouraged to fit these criteria to its own climate, terrain, neighborhoods, environmentally sensitive areas, and cultural values, or to adopt the currently available Leadership in Energy and Environmental Design (LEED®) Rating System (see Table 5-8).

DIVISION 3: INFRASTRUCTURE STANDARDS

5.21 PARKS/OPEN SPACE

Parks and open space provide a valuable asset to the urban form of the [LOCAL GOVERNMENT], its historical development, and the general welfare of its residents. These standards ensure that parks and open space provide focal points for new communities. A central square or green, for example, may comprise a majority of the area required for dedication.

5.21.1 Applicability

(A) This section applies to any application for residential subdivision plat approval, unless exempt (refer to subsection (C), below).

(B) The location and extent of parks/open space or designation of a fee in lieu of park development (refer to § 5.21.4 Fee in Lieu of Park Development (Optional) of this chapter) shall be indicated on any preliminary plat or site plan.

(C) The provisions of this section do not apply to:

(1) A proposed subdivision located within an infill development zone; or

Table 5-8
Building Practices

Sustainable Sites	
Construction Activity Pollution Prevention: Implement a plan to prevent: (1) loss of soil during construction by runoff or wind erosion; (2) sedimentation of storm sewer or receiving streams; and (3) air pollution from dust or particulate matter.	1 point
Site Selection: Development is not located on: (1) prime farmland, defined by the United States Department of Agriculture; (2) previously undeveloped land at an elevation lower than 5 feet above the 100-year flood line, defined by the Federal Emergency Management Agency; (3) previously undeveloped land within 50 feet of a water body, defined by the Clean Water Act; (4) land that is habitat for threatened or endangered species, as defined by federal and state agencies; or (5) land that is within 100 feet of any wetlands, as defined by federal and state agencies.	1 point
Development Density and Community Connectivity: Development satisfies one or both of the following criteria: • Development is located on a previously developed site, within 1/2 mile of a residential zone or neighborhood with an average density of at least 7 units per acre. • Development is located on a previously developed site, within 1/2 mile of at least 10 compatible mixed uses, which include the following: (1) art gallery; (2) bank; (3) cellular telephone store; (4) community center; (5) convenience store; (6) cleaning and laundry; (7) day care; (8) fitness center; (9) gas station; (10) hardware store; (11) medical/dental; (12) outdoor café or Internet café; (13) pharmacy; (14) place of worship; (15) post office; (16) restaurant; (17) retail store; (18) supermarket; (19) theater; and (20) similar compatible mixed uses.	1-2 points
Brownfield Redevelopment: Development is located on a site defined as a brownfield by federal, state, or [LOCAL GOVERNMENT] agency.	1 point
Alternative Transportation: Development satisfies one or more of the following criteria: • **Public transportation access:** Development is located: (1) within 1/2 mile of a commuter rail, light rail, or subway station or (2) within 1/4 mile of a public bus line. • **Bicycle storage:** Provide secure bicycle racks and/or storage for 10% or more of all building occupants (commercial and multifamily only). • **Electric and hybrid vehicles:** Provide preferred parking for electric vehicles, hybrid vehicles, and other low-emitting or fuel-efficient vehicles achieving a minimum green score of 40 on the American Council for an Energy Efficient Economy annual vehicle rating guide, for 5% of the total vehicle parking capacity (commercial and multifamily only). • **Parking capacity:** Provide: (1) no new parking (all development) or (2) parking that does not exceed minimum local zoning requirements preferred parking for shared vehicle usage for 5% of the total vehicle parking capacity (commercial and multifamily only).	1-4 points

Site Development: Development satisfies one or both of the following criteria:
• Protect or restore habitat
  ○ On greenfield sites, limit all site disturbance to 40 feet beyond the building perimeter; 10 feet beyond surface walkways, patios, surface parking, and utilities less than 12 inches in diameter; 15 feet beyond primary roadway curbs and main utility branch trenches; and 25 feet beyond constructed areas with permeable surfaces.
  ○ On previously developed or graded sites, restore or protect a minimum of 50% of the site area (excluding the building footprint) with native or adapted vegetation.
• **Open space:** Provide vegetated open space that exceeds zoning requirements by 25%.
	1-2 points

Stormwater Design: Development satisfies one or both of the following criteria:
• **Quantity control**
  ○ If existing imperviousness is 50% or less, implement a stormwater management plan that (1) prevents the postdevelopment peak discharge rate and quantity from exceeding the predevelopment peak discharge rate and quantity, or (2) protects receiving stream channels from excessive erosion by implementing a stream channel protection strategy and quantity control strategies.
  ○ If existing imperviousness is greater than 50%, implement a stormwater management plan that decreases stormwater runoff by 25%.
  ○ Use bioswales instead of street curbing or piping.
• **Quality control:** Implement a stormwater management plan that reduces impervious cover, promotes infiltration, and captures and treats for reuse the stormwater runoff from 90% of the average annual rainfall.
	1-2 points

Table 5-8 (cont.)
Building Practices

Sustainable Sites (cont.)	

Heat Island Effect: Development satisfies one or both of the following criteria:
• **Nonroof:** Place at least 50% of parking spaces under cover that has a Solar Reflective Index (SRI) of at least 29, or provide any combination of the following strategies for 50% of the site hardscape (commercial and multifamily only):
  ○ Shade (within 5 years of occupancy).
  ○ Paving materials that have an SRI of at least 29.
  ○ Open grid pavement system.
• **Roof:** (1) Use roofing materials having an SRI of at least 78 for low-sloped roofs (slope ≤ 2:12) or 29 for steep-sloped roofs (slope > 2:12) for a minimum of 75% of the roof surface; (2) install a vegetated roof for at least 50% of the roof area; or (3) install a combination albedo-vegetated roof where (Area of SRI Roof / 0.75) + (Area of Vegetated Roof / 0.5) ≥ Total Roof Area.
	1-2 points

Light Pollution Reduction: Development restricts interior and exterior lighting as follows:
• **Interior lighting:** (1) the angle of maximum candela from each interior luminaire as located in the building shall intersect opaque building interior surfaces and not exit out through the windows (all development) or (2) nonemergency lighting is automatically controlled to turn off during nonbusiness hours (commercial only).
• **Exterior lighting**
  ○ In park and rural settings, design exterior lighting so that all site and building mounted luminaires produce a maximum initial illuminance value no greater than 0.01 horizontal and vertical foot candles at the site boundary and beyond.
  ○ In residential areas, design exterior lighting so that all site and building mounted luminaires produce a maximum initial illuminance value no greater than 0.10 horizontal and vertical foot candles at the site boundary and no greater than 0.01 horizontal foot candles 10 feet beyond the site boundary.
  ○ In commercial/industrial and high-density residential areas, design exterior lighting so that all site and building mounted luminaires produce a maximum initial illuminance value no greater than 0.20 horizontal and vertical foot candles at the site boundary and no greater than 0.01 horizontal foot candles 15 feet beyond the site boundary.
  ○ In major city centers and entertainment districts, design exterior lighting so that all site and building mounted luminaires produce a maximum initial illuminance value no greater than 0.60 horizontal and vertical foot candles at the site boundary and no greater than 0.01 horizontal foot candles 15 feet beyond the site boundary.
	1 point

Water Efficiency	
Water Efficient Landscaping: Development satisfies one or both of the following criteria: • **Reduce by 50%:** Reduce potable water consumption for irrigation by 50% from a calculated mid-summer baseline. • **No potable use or no irrigation:** Eliminate the use of potable water for landscape irrigation.	1-2 points
Innovative Wastewater Technologies: Either: (1) reduce potable water use for building sewage conveyance by 50% through the use of water-conserving fixtures or nonpotable water; or (2) treat 50% of wastewater on site to tertiary standards.	1 point
Water-Use Reduction: Development satisfies one or both of the following criteria: • **20% reduction:** Employ strategies to use 20% less water than the water-use baseline calculated for the building (not including irrigation). • **30% reduction:** Employ strategies to use 30% less water than the water-use baseline calculated for the building (not including irrigation).	1-2 points
Energy and Atmosphere	
Minimum Energy Performance: Design the building project to comply with both: (1) the mandatory provisions of American Society of Heating, Refrigerating and Air-Conditioning Engineers, Inc./Illuminating Engineering Society of North America (ASHRAE/IESNA) Standard 90.1-2004; and (2) the prescriptive requirements or performance requirements of ASHRAE/IESNA Standard 90.1-2004.	1 point
Fundamental Refrigerant Management: Zero use of chlorofluorocarbons (CFC)-based refrigerants in new base building heating, ventilation, air-conditioning, and refrigeration (HVAC&R) systems. When reusing existing base building HVAC equipment, complete a comprehensive CFC phase-out conversion prior to project completion.	1 point

Table 5-8 (cont.)
Building Practices

Energy and Atmosphere (cont.)	
Optimize Energy Performance: Using the Building Performance Rating Method in Appendix G of ASHRAE/IESNA Standard 90.1-2004, demonstrate an improvement in the proposed building performance rating compared to the baseline requirement by achieving one of the following energy cost savings percentages: 	New Buildings	Renovations	Points
---	---	---
10.5%	3.5%	1
14.0%	7.0%	2
17.5%	10.5%	3
21.0%	14.0%	4
24.5%	17.5%	5
28.0%	21.0%	6
31.5%	24.5%	7
35.0%	28.0%	8
38.5%	31.5%	9
42.0%	35.0%	10		1-10 points
On-Site Renewable Energy: Use on-site renewable energy systems (e.g., solar and wind systems) to offset building energy cost: | % Renewable Energy	Points
2.5%	1
7.5%	2
12.5%	3		1-3 points
Enhanced Refrigerant Management: Do not use refrigerants, or select refrigerants and base building HVAC&R systems that minimize or eliminate the emission of compounds that contribute to ozone depletion and global warming.	1 point
Green Power: Provide at least 35% of the building's electricity from renewable sources (e.g., solar and wind power) by engaging in at least a two-year renewable energy contract.	1 point
Materials and Resources	
Storage and Collection of Recyclables: Designate an area for the collection and storage of recyclables, including paper, corrugated cardboard, glass, plastics, and metals.	1 point
Building Reuse: Development satisfies one or more of the following criteria: • **Maintain 75% of existing walls, floors and roof:** Maintain at least 75% (based on surface area) of the existing building structure and envelope (excluding hazardous materials). • **Maintain 95% of existing walls, floors and roof:** Maintain at least 95% (based on surface area) of the existing building structure and envelope (excluding hazardous materials). • **Maintain 50% of interior nonstructural elements:** Maintain at least 50% of the existing interior nonstructural elements (e.g., interior walls, doors, floor coverings, and ceiling systems).	1-3 points
Construction Waste Management: Development satisfies one or both of the following criteria: • **Divert 50% from disposal:** Recycle and/or salvage at least 50% of nonhazardous construction and demolition debris. • **Divert 75% from disposal:** Recycle and/or salvage at least 75% of nonhazardous construction and demolition debris.	1-2 points
Materials Reuse: Development satisfies one or both of the following criteria: • **5%:** Use salvaged, refurbished, or reused materials, constituting at least 5% of the total value of materials for the project. • **10%:** Use salvaged, refurbished, or reused materials, constituting at least 10% of the total value of materials for the project.	1-2 points

Table 5-8 (cont.)
Building Practices

Materials and Resources (cont.)	
Recycled Content: Development satisfies one or both of the following criteria: • **10%:** Use materials with postconsumer + 1/2 preconsumer recycled content, constituting 10% of the total value of materials for the project. • **20%:** Use materials with postconsumer + 1/2 preconsumer recycled content, constituting 20% of the total value of materials for the project.	1-2 points
Regional Materials: Development satisfies one or both of the following criteria: • **10%:** Use building materials or products that have been extracted, processed, and manufactured regionally, constituting 10% of the total value of materials for the project. • **20%:** Use building materials or products that have been extracted, processed, and manufactured regionally, constituting 20% of the total value of materials for the project.	1-2 points
Rapidly Renewable Materials: Use building materials and products made from plants that are typically harvested within a 10-year cycle or shorter, constituting 2.5% of the total value of materials for the project.	1 point
Certified Wood: For a minimum of 50% of the project's wood building components, use wood-based materials and products that are certified in accordance with the Forest Stewardship Council's Principles and Criteria.	1 point
Indoor Environmental Quality (Commercial Only)	
Minimum Indoor Air Quality Performance: Meet the minimum requirements of Sections 4 through 7 of ASHRAE Standard 62.1-2004, Ventilation for Acceptable Indoor Air Quality.	1 point
Increased Ventilation: For mechanically ventilated spaces, increase breathing zone outdoor air ventilation rates to all occupied spaces by at least 30% above the minimum rates required by ASHRAE Standard 62.1-2004. For naturally ventilated spaces, design systems for occupied spaces to meet the recommendations set forth in the Carbon Trust "Good Practices Guide 237."	1 point
Low-Emitting Materials: Development satisfied one or more of the following criteria: • **Adhesives and sealants:** Adhesives, sealants, and sealant primers used on the interior of the building comply with the requirements set forth in South Coast Air Quality Management District Rule #1168. Aerosol adhesives used in the interior of the building comply with the requirements set forth in Green Seal Standard GS-36. • **Paints and coatings:** Architectural paints, coatings, and primers applied to interior ferrous metal substrates comply with the requirements set forth in Green Seal Standard GS-11. Anticorrosive and antirust paints applied to interior ferrous metal substrates comply with the requirements set forth in Green Seal Standard GC-03. Clear wood finishes, floor coatings, stains, and shellacs applied to interior elements comply with the requirements set forth in South Coast Air Quality Management District Rule #1113. • **Carpet systems:** All carpet installed in the building interior complies with the testing and product requirements of the Carpet and Rug Institute's Green Label Plus program. • **Composite wood and agrifiber products:** Composite wood and agrifiber products used on the interior of the building contain no added urea-formaldehyde resins.	1-4 points
Indoor Chemical and Pollutant Source Control: Employ permanent entryway systems to capture dirt and particulates from entering the building at all entryways that are directly connected to the outdoors. Where hazardous gases or chemicals may be present or used, exhaust each space sufficiently to create negative pressure with respect to adjacent spaces with the doors to the room closed. In mechanically ventilated buildings, provide occupied areas with air filtration media that provides a Minimum Efficiency Reporting Value of 13 or better.	1 point
Controllability of Systems: Development satisfied one or both of the following criteria: • **Lighting:** Provide individual lighting controls for at least 90% of the building occupants and lighting controls for all shared multioccupant spaces. • **Thermal comfort:** Provide individual comfort controls for at least 50% of the building occupants and comfort controls for all shared multioccupant spaces.	1-2 points
Thermal Comfort Design: HVAC systems and the building envelope meet the requirements set forth in ASHRAE Standard 55-2004.	1 point
Daylight and Views: Development satisfied one or both of the following criteria: • **Daylight 75% of spaces:** Achieve a minimum daylight illumination level of 25 foot candles in at least 75% of all regularly occupied areas. • **Views for 90% of spaces:** Achieve a direct line of sight to the outdoors for building occupants in 90% of all regularly occupied areas.	1-2 points

Table 5-9
Required Parks

(A) Zoning District(s) or Areas	(B) Required Parks/ Open Space
"IL" (Industrial Light) "IH" (Industrial Heavy)	Not applicable
"RP" (Resource Protection) "RE" (Residential Estate) "NS" (Neighborhood Suburban) "NU" (Neighborhood Urban) "MX" (Mixed Use) (residential uses) "NP" (Neighborhood Preservation)	900 square feet per dwelling unit
"O" (Office) "CN" (Commercial Neighborhood) "CG" (Commercial General) "CL" (Commercial Large-Scale) "MX" (Mixed Use) (nonresidential uses and mixed-use buildings)	450 square feet per 1,000 gross square feet for buildings exceeding 5,000 square feet
"D" (Downtown)	150 square feet per 1,000 gross square feet for buildings exceeding 15,000 square feet

(2) A proposed subdivision located within a planning area that has a surplus of neighborhood parks/open space, as designated in the [PARKS AND RECREATION MASTER PLAN], unless the surplus has been eliminated by the subsequent approval of residential dwelling units within the planning area, as measured by the "Required Parks/Open Space" standard established in Table 5-9, Column (B).

5.21.2 Required Parks/Open Space

Required parks/open space shall be reserved for any development in the zoning districts or areas as set forth in Table 5-9.

5.21.3 Categories of Parks/Open Space

The types of park or open space that may be provided to satisfy this chapter are described in Table 5-10. The minimum dimension, improvement, and maintenance requirements shall be consistent with Column (C) of Table 5-10. The applicant may choose among the types of parks or open space to include within the proposed development that is consistent with the overall minimum set-aside requirements of Table 5-10.

5.21.3.1 Exclusions

The following areas are not considered parks or open space pursuant to this section:

(A) Areas covered by buildings, parking lots, or other impervious surfaces accessible to automobiles;

(B) Utility easements, drainage easements, or street rights-of-way, unless such areas are usable for public recreational purposes and will not be permanently converted to a street or trench;

(C) Land underneath overhead utility lines, except where used for jogging trails, bicycle trails, or parking areas accessory to a park/open space;

(D) Streets; and

(E) Ponds or lakes exceeding 2,500 square feet, unless surrounded by an upland area with a minimum width of 25 feet.

5.21.3.2 Excess Capacity

Any excess capacity of a park or open space provided pursuant to this section may be credited toward the required dedication for another subdivision within a 1-mile radius or a benefit area for fees in lieu of park development, where:

(A) The subdivision for which the credit is applied is in the same ownership by the same applicant; and

(B) The park/open space areas are accessible to each subdivision.

5.21.4 Fee in Lieu of Park Development (Optional)

5.21.4.1 Applicability

In lieu of dedicating and improving park or open space lands as required by this section, the applicant may deposit with the [LOCAL GOVERNMENT] a cash payment in lieu of park development.

5.21.4.2 Amount

The [PLANNING OFFICIAL] shall determine the amount to be deposited, based on the following formula:

$C + (A \times V) = M$

where:

C = cost of park or open space improvements, as determined by the [PARKS/RECREATION DEPARTMENT];

A = the amount of land required for dedication as determined in § 5.21.2 Required Parks/Open Space of this chapter;

V = fair market value (per acre) of the property to be subdivided, as established by an appraisal; and

M = the number of dollars to be paid in lieu of dedication of land.

5.21.4.3 Fair Market Value

For purposes of computing fair market value of property, the subdivider may select one of the following fair market value determinations:

(A) The current fair market value of the land as shown on the records of the tax appraisal district if

Table 5-10
Park and Open Space Categories

(A) Park or Open Space Category	(B) Description	(C) Design and Maintenance Requirements
Natural areas and agricultural areas	Natural areas are areas established for the protection of natural attributes of local, regional, and statewide significance, which may be used in a sustainable manner for scientific research, education, aesthetic enjoyment, and appropriate use not detrimental to the primary purpose. These areas are resource- rather than user-based, but may provide some passive recreational activities, such as hiking, nature study, and picnicking.	Maintenance is limited to a minimum removal and avoidance of hazards, nuisances, or unhealthy conditions. Natural water courses shall be maintained as free flowing and devoid of debris. Stream channels shall be maintained so as not to alter floodplain levels. Land shall not be cleared except for trails.
Greenways	Greenways are areas connecting residences and recreational areas. Greenways are designed to incorporate natural settings, such as creeks and significant stands of trees within neighborhoods. Parkways and greenways differ from parks, plazas, and squares in that their detailing is natural (i.e., informally planted), except along rights-of-way, and may contain irregular topography.	A greenway shall have an average width of at least 50 feet. If the greenway consists of agricultural areas, the agricultural areas shall have a continuous area of at least 50 acres. The agricultural areas may be combined with adjacent agricultural lands provided, however, that the minimum width prescribed above shall be met on all portions of the agricultural greenbelt on the site. Land shall not be cleared except for trails.
Greenbelts	Greenbelts run along the perimeter of a proposed development and buffer a proposed development from surrounding incompatible uses or features, such as a highway corridor, industrial district, or agricultural areas. Greenbelts differ from other types of open spaces in that they are left natural and are not for recreational use.	The following uses are permitted within the greenbelt: • Critical areas; • Conservancy lots with a minimum lot size of 5 acres and a maximum impervious surface ratio of 5 percent; or • Linear parks improved with trails, benches, and/or playground equipment. Trails, benches, and playground equipment are not considered impervious surfaces for purposes of computing impervious surface. The greenbelt shall be an average of at least 100 feet in width and at least 50 feet at any point. A greenbelt shall be at least 300 feet in length. Land shall not be cleared except for trails.
Playgrounds	Playgrounds provide play areas for children as well as open shelter with benches for parents. Playgrounds may be built within squares and parks or may stand alone within a residential block.	Minimum size: 5,000 square feet Maximum size: 20,000 square feet Playing surfaces may be covered in sand, wood chips, or other equivalent material. Paths and walkways may be paved in concrete, crushed gravel, brick paver, or similar material, or partially paved.
Plazas	Plazas are areas for passive recreational use that are entirely bounded by streets and/or lanes. Plazas are intended for planned communities, such as planned developments, transit-oriented developments, traditional neighborhood developments, or nonresidential use patterns as defined in § 2.3 Neighborhood Center, § 2.4 Campus, and § 2.5 Commercial Retrofit in Chapter 2, Use Patterns, of the LDC.	Minimum width: 200 feet Minimum length: 300 feet Maximum width: 530 feet Maximum length: 800 feet The plaza shall be square or rectangular with a length of not less that 1-1/2 of its width. The plaza shall be bounded on all sides by streets, with streets originating in the middle of each side and two streets originating from each corner.

Table 5-10 (cont.)
Park and Open Space Categories

(A) Park or Open Space Category	(B) Description	(C) Design and Maintenance Requirements
Courtyard	A courtyard is an open area adjacent to, or part of, a building or facility and is surrounded by building frontages. Courtyards function as gathering places and may incorporate a variety of nonpermanent activities, such as vendors and display stands. Courtyards shall be credited toward parks and open space requirements only for nonresidential use patterns as defined in § 2.3 Neighborhood Center, § 2.4 Campus, and § 2.5 Commercial Retrofit in Chapter 2, Use Patterns, of the LDC, and shall be maintained in private ownership.	Minimum size: 2,000 square feet Maximum size: 30,000 square feet Courtyards shall be paved in brick or other type of paver or crushed stone. Courtyards shall be level, stepped, or gently sloping (less than 5% grade). At no time shall a courtyard's horizontal length or width be greater than three times the height of the surrounding building(s). Courtyards may be left unplanted or planted with trees along the edge of the courtyard space or the structure that the courtyard services. Tree spacing shall be a maximum of 25 feet on center. Parking is not permitted in a courtyard.
Forecourt	Forecourts are open space areas that act as buffers between residential and nonresidential buildings or streets. Forecourts shall be credited toward parks and open space requirements only for nonresidential use patterns as defined in § 2.3 Neighborhood Center, § 2.4 Campus, and § 2.5 Commercial Retrofit in Chapter 2, Use Patterns, of the LDC, and shall be maintained in private ownership.	Forecourts shall be entirely bounded by streets and shall be planted parallel to all street rights-of-way with one tree species.
Attached squares	Attached squares are areas for passive recreational use that are internal to a block.	Minimum size: 2,000 square feet Maximum size: 1 acre Squares shall be bounded by streets on a minimum of three sides or 75% of their perimeter. Squares may be bounded by buildings on a maximum of 60% of their perimeter (maximum of two sides). Squares shall be planted parallel to all rights-of-way with at least two tree species a minimum of 10 feet and a maximum of 50 feet on center. All internal tree plantings (if provided) shall be in geometrical layouts.
Detached square	Detached squares are bordered on all sides by streets. Detached squares provide a means to emphasize important places, intersections, or centers.	Minimum size: 200 square feet Maximum size: 1 acre Detached squares shall be bordered on four sides by a street or walkway. The geometric pattern of the square shall be a square or a rectangle with a length not exceeding twice the width.
Green	The green is an urban open space that is natural in its details. Like the square, it is small, civic, and surrounded by buildings. Unlike the square, it is informally planted and may have irregular topography.	Greens shall be landscaped with trees at the edges and open lawns at the center. Greens shall contain no structures other than benches, pavilions, and memorials. Trails or pedestrian pathways are optional.

Table 5-10 (cont.)
Park and Open Space Categories

(A) Park or Open Space Category	(B) Description	(C) Design and Maintenance Requirements
Park	Parks are designed for active recreational use. Parks create a central open space that services an entire neighborhood or group of neighborhoods, or incorporates physical features that are an asset to the community (e.g., lake or river frontage, high ground, or significant stands of trees). Parks may be combined with parkways and greenbelts.	Minimum size: 1 acre. Parks shall be bounded by streets on a minimum of 50% of their perimeter (subject to lot line configurations). Trees shall be planted parallel to all perimeter rights-of-way or at the edge of areas for active recreational use and any facilities that accompany such use. Tree spacing shall be a minimum of 15 feet to a maximum of 50 feet on center. Promenades and esplanades within a park may be formally planted with trees parallel to the walkway. Interior portions of parks may be kept free of tree plantings. Plantings in interior portions of parks may follow topographical lines.
Parkway	Parkways are open spaces designed to incorporate natural settings, such as creeks and significant stands of trees within neighborhoods. Parkways and greenways differ from parks, plazas, and squares in that their detailing is natural (i.e., informally planted) except along rights-of-way, and may contain irregular topography.	Parkways shall be entirely bounded by streets or pedestrian rights-of-way within developed areas. Parkways may be used for certain active recreational uses, such as walking, jogging, or bicycling. Trees shall be planted along all rights-of-way a minimum of 10 feet and a maximum of 50 feet on center. Interior areas shall remain natural or shall be planted with turf grass.
Community garden	Community gardens are areas where plants are raised and maintained by the homeowners' association, condominium association, or other established community association for scientific research, education, aesthetic enjoyment, and recreational purposes.	An irrigation system shall be installed in accordance with the landscaping standards. The area shall be maintained in a neat and clean condition and cleared of debris.

based upon an appraisal that occurred within two years prior to the application;

(B) The current fair market value of the land as determined by a qualified real estate appraiser at the subdivider's expense, if the [PLANNING OFFICIAL] certifies that the appraisal fairly reflects the land value;

(C) The current fair market value of the land as determined by a qualified real estate appraiser employed by the [LOCAL GOVERNMENT]; or

(D) The actual purchase price of the property as evidenced by a purchase money contract, or a closing statement within one year of the date of application.

5.21.4.4 Reductions

(A) The [LOCAL GOVERNMENT] shall reduce the land dedication component of the fee in lieu of parks or open space facilities by the amount of any reasonable costs for any land that has been dedicated to and accepted by the [DEVELOPING ACTIVITY] for park/open space facilities by the applicant within the proposed development, subject to the following:

(1) The reasonable costs of the park/open space facilities that have been dedicated shall reduce the fee in lieu of parks or open space due for only the same type of park facility;

(2) The unit costs used to calculate the reduction shall not exceed those assumed as the average costs of the park/open space facilities used to compute the fee in lieu of park development for the benefit area in which the property is located;

(3) No reduction shall be granted that exceeds the fee in lieu of park development due for the development; and

(4) Any reduction created by the dedication of park/open space facilities shall expire 10 years after the date that the offset was created.

(B) An applicant may apply for a reduction of fee in lieu of park development either at the time of approval of a subdivision plat or at the time of dedication by separate instrument. The applicant may appeal the determination of the [PLANNING OFFICIAL] of parks and recreation concerning the reduction to the [LOCAL GOVERNMENT].

(C) The amount of the reduction shall be prorated among the number of dwelling units approved for the development unless otherwise agreed to by the [GOVERNING ENTITY].

5.21.4.5 Timing

Fees in lieu of park and open space development shall be assessed at the time of plat approval and shall be paid at the time of plat recordation.

5.21.4.6 Earmarking

(A) All fees collected shall be used for the acquisition or development of land for a neighborhood park, or development or construction of improvements to existing unimproved parkland. The park development or improvement shall be located within 1 mile of the periphery of the proposed subdivision development, or within a park benefit district established by resolution of the [GOVERNING ENTITY]. However, if acquisition opportunities are not available, or existing parkland is already developed or improved within 1 mile of the proposed subdivision development, then areas within 2 miles of the periphery of the proposed subdivision development may be considered for the acquisition of neighborhood parkland and/or construction of improvements to existing parkland within such periphery.

(B) A special fund is established for the deposit of all fees in lieu of park development. The fund shall be known as the park acquisition and development fund. Within the fund, fees in lieu of park development paid shall be earmarked for expenditure on park improvements in a neighborhood park generally located within the distance described in subsection (A), above. All fees in lieu of park development paid must be expended within 10 years from the date of receipt for park facilities benefiting the residential subdivision or dwelling unit for which the fees are paid. Fees shall be considered expended if they are spent for acquisition or development, respectively, of neighborhood parks located within 1/2 to 1 mile of the subdivision for which the fees were paid within the 10-year period. If fees are not expended within such period, the then-current owner shall be entitled to a refund of the principal deposited by the applicant in such fund, together with accrued interest. The owner must request such refund in writing within 365 days of entitlement or such right shall be waived. Interest accruing to the parkland dedication fund and to the park development fund shall be expended on neighborhood parkland acquisition and for neighborhood park improvements, respectively.

5.21.5 Park and Open Space Characteristics

The standards provided below ensure that all designated parks and/or open space are usable and have suitable size, location, dimension, topography, character, and access.

5.21.5.1 Generally

The required park or open space areas shall be provided as common areas for the use of all residents/occupants of the proposed development. Land designated as a park or open space shall be maintained as a park or open space and may not be separately sold, subdivided, or developed except as provided in § 5.21.5.2 Designation through 5.21.5.10 Access of this chapter.

5.21.5.2 Designation

Any areas reserved as a park or open space shall be indicated on the application for development approval. A parks and open space provision and maintenance plan shall be submitted as a part of the application for development approval, including the project phasing schedule. This plan shall designate and indicate the boundaries of all proposed parks or open space required by this section and the type of park or open space provided.

Platted lots located within subdivisions and planned developments shall be located outside of the parks and open space areas. Parks and open space shall be placed in undivided preserves.

5.21.5.3 School Site Locations

Park sites shall be located, whenever possible, adjacent to and contiguous with school sites in order to make maximum use of common facilities and grounds. Land area dedicated to a school district shall be credited toward the minimum requirements of § 5.21.2 Required Parks/Open Space of this chapter if there is a joint use agreement between the [LOCAL GOVERNMENT] and the school district.

5.21.5.4 Distance from Lots

Parks and open space shall be not be further than 1/2 mile from any lot or, if the proposed development does not involve a subdivision or any principal building, this distance shall be measured from the entrance allowing people, bicycles, or equestrians to enter into the park or open space or to view the park or open space area. This distance shall be measured in a straight line, provided that the distance shall not be interrupted by an existing arterial street. The distance may be measured from a park or open space provided pursuant to this section or a public park or public open space area not provided by the applicant.

5.21.5.5 Parks or Open Space in Floodplains or Water Features

(A) Areas within a floodplain shall not exceed 50 percent of the area counted as parks or open space, except as provided by subsection (B), below. Water features exceeding 2,500 square feet shall not be considered as parks or open space unless permitted by subsection (B), below.

(B) The restriction on the maximum percentage of parks/open space in water features or floodplains (hereinafter "restricted areas") can be increased to 75 percent where:

(1) An area of a minimum 25 feet in width surrounding a restricted area is improved as a greenway;

(2) The structures or activities located with the restricted areas do not cause an increase in base flood elevations;

(3) The velocities during a 10-year flood event do not exceed 6 feet per second; and

(4) For parks/open space dedicated to the [LOCAL GOVERNMENT], at least 1 acre is located outside of the restricted area.

5.21.5.6 Percentage in Retention or Detention Areas

(A) Not more than 25 percent or 1 acre, whichever is less, of a retention area or detention basin required as part of the stormwater management standards (§ 5.22 Stormwater Management of this chapter) qualify as a park or open space area, subject to the requirements established in this section.

(B) 50 percent or more of the active and usable area shall be above the 25-year storm level and designed for multiple uses.

(C) Retention or detention areas used as park or open space shall be included as part of a greenbelt or a greenway. Retention or detention areas shall not be inundated in such a manner that they become unsuitable for their designated recreational purposes.

(D) Retention or detention areas shall be constructed of natural materials. Terracing, berming, and contouring is required in order to naturalize and enhance the aesthetics of the basin.

(E) Basin slopes shall not exceed a 3:1 slope.

5.21.5.7 Walls and Fences

Walls and fences, if used, shall not exceed 6 feet in height. This requirement does not apply to fences used in conjunction with athletic fields and tennis courts.

5.21.5.8 Buffers or Landscaped Areas

Any buffer or landscaped area provided pursuant to § 5.31 Buffers and Screening, § 5.34 Parking Lot Landscaping, and § 5.35 Entrance Landscaping of this chapter that meets the requirements of Table 5-10 for a particular category of parks or open space shall be credited toward the minimum parks and open space requirements of § 5.21.2 Required Parks/Open Space of this chapter.

5.21.5.9 Slopes

At least 50 percent of required dedicated park or open space land shall have slopes less than 7 percent.

5.21.5.10 Access

Parks and/or open space provided pursuant to this section shall have direct access to a public street or to a private street maintained by an HOA, condominium association, or apartment association.

5.21.6 Designation of Parks/Open Space

Areas designated as parks or open space shall not be subdivided but shall be shown as a "park" or "open space" on a plat. Land protected pursuant to this section that is intended to be used as a park shall be deeded as a park, regardless of ownership. In order to ensure that open space areas are maintained so that their use and enjoyment as parks and/or open space are not diminished or destroyed, parks and/or open space areas may be owned, preserved, and maintained by any mechanism or combination described in § 5.6 Operation and Maintenance of this chapter.

5.21.7 Development Phasing

This section establishes a procedure for enforcing the requirements for parks and open space through development phasing while providing flexibility in the development approval process. This procedure recognizes that there is usually a delay between the date when a subdivision plat is approved and when lots are built upon and occupied, thus creating a demand for parks and open space.

(A) In residential subdivisions that are to be platted in two or more phases, the required park or open space dedication must be provided in each phase of the subdivision except as provided in subsection (B), below.

(B) If a subdivision is proposed in phases, the applicant may plat the first 100 lots pursuant to the preliminary plat and defer the provision of parks and/or open space to future phases of the development. No further subdivision plat shall be approved unless and until parks or open space are provided in increments equal to the acreage required by § 5.21.2 Required Parks/Open Space of this chapter, subject to the phasing provisions of Table 5-11.

**Table 5-11
Development Phasing for
Parks and Open Space**

Number of Lots Per Phase	Acres of Parks or Open Space Required	Timing of Improvements
Phase 1: 1-100	Up to 1 (minimum size of 1 acre)	Phase 2
Phase 2: 101-300	Up to 2	Phase 3
Phase 3 through completion of development	As required by § 5.21.2 Required Parks/Open Space of this chapter	At time of platting

(C) If any phase of the subdivision is platted without providing the required parks or open space at the time of platting and no future subdivision phases are planned pursuant to the preliminary plat, the parks or open space required shall be provided within one year after recordation of the plat and shall be secured by deferment contract as provided in subsection (D), below.

(D) The [LOCAL GOVERNMENT] may authorize the developer to reserve parkland for dedication in subsequent phases of the subdivision by executing an enforceable contract with the [LOCAL GOVERNMENT]. The contract shall be approved as to form by the [LOCAL GOVERNMENT] attorney. In addition, the developer shall dedicate a reversionary public access easement on the final plat of the proposed development where necessary to provide effective public access, maintenance, and use of any parkland to be dedicated.

5.21.8 Connectivity

The [LOCAL GOVERNMENT] finds and determines that an interconnected system of parks, trails, greenways, and bikeways provides a greater public benefit than isolated parks with access exclusively by automobiles. Such areas can provide form to neighborhoods, a common public gathering space, and an opportunity to protect natural areas. Accordingly, this section provides incentives for developers to link parks and open space provided pursuant to this section with other public or private park and open space areas. It is not the intent of this section to require developers or landowners to provide a general public benefit but rather to create incentives for creativity in the design of parks and open space as well as creative opportunities to meet the requirements of this section.

(A) Greenbelts, greenways, or linear parks provided pursuant to this subsection shall be credited toward the minimum park and open space area requirements of § 5.21.2 Required Parks/Open Space of this chapter at a ratio of 1 acre for every 20,000 square feet provided, where:

(1) Such areas are aligned with a continuation of an area designated as a public greenway, linear park, or similar facility in a facilities plan officially adopted by the [LOCAL GOVERNMENT]; and

(2) Such areas include sidewalks, trails, or similar facilities that align with such facilities in an abutting tract or, where abutting tracts are unimproved, conform to the specifications set forth in the facilities plan.

(B) Parks or open space provided pursuant to this subsection shall be credited toward the minimum park and open space area requirements at a ratio of 1 acre for every 20,000 square feet provided, where:

(1) All lots within the proposed subdivision are within 1/4 mile of the park or open space; and

(2) The park or open space area abuts an area zoned "CN" (Commercial Neighborhood) or the area designated as a "center" in a TND.

5.22 STORMWATER MANAGEMENT

Purpose and findings: The purpose of this section is to provide adequate measures for the retention, detention, and distribution of stormwater in a manner that minimizes the possibility of adverse impacts on both water quantity and water quality during development.

5.22.1 Applicability

This section applies to any application for subdivision plat, site plan, or development approval except as otherwise provided by this chapter. A stormwater management plan shall be provided as set forth in Appendix B, Specifications for Documents to Be Submitted, of the LDC.

5.22.2 Regional Stormwater Management Program

The [LOCAL GOVERNMENT] has determined that regional stormwater management is preferable to site-specific stormwater mitigation. The regional stormwater management program (RSWMP) provides for the administration, planning, design, construction, and operational management of regional stormwater facilities (RSWFs).

Regional stormwater management uses a watershed-wide approach to analyze potential flooding problems, identify appropriate mitigation measures, and select site locations and design criteria for RSWFs. These RSWFs include, but are not limited to, regional detention and retention ponds, watershed protection, land purchase, waterway enlargement, channelization, and improved conveyance structures. The RSWMP allows developers to participate in the program rather than constructing the on-site detention controls required by § 5.22.5 System Criteria through § 5.22.18 Inlets and Openings of this chapter, where the resulting use of an RSWF will not produce a significantly adverse impact to other properties due to the increased run-off from the proposed development.

5.22.3 Options

Options available to developers to participate in the RSWMP include:

(A) Payment of a fee in lieu of on-site detention. The fee schedule is established by resolution of the [LOCAL GOVERNMENT];

(B) Construction of an RSWF to mitigate an existing flooding problem; and

(C) Construction or participation in the construction of an RSWF to mitigate increased stormwater run-off anticipated by ultimate development of the watershed.

5.22.4 Timing of Payment

The stormwater development fee in lieu of on-site detention must be paid prior to a plat being released for recordation by the [LOCAL GOVERNMENT] or the issuance of a development approval. The fee shall be determined in accordance with the resolution established pursuant to § 5.22.3 Options, subsection (A), above.

5.22.5 System Criteria

5.22.5.1 Design Conditions

All stormwater management facilities shall be designed for ultimate development. Three development conditions shall be analyzed for each development (see Table 5-12).

5.22.5.2 Design Storm Event

Facilities with drainage areas under 100 acres shall be designed for a 25-year storm. Facilities with drainage areas over 100 acres or areas within a designated floodplain shall be designed for a 100-year storm or a 25-year storm plus freeboard, if that elevation is higher. Detention facilities and streets are exceptions to the frequency criteria cited in this section. Detention facility outflows will be designed for 5-, 25-, and 100-year frequency storms.

5.22.5.3 Responsibility to Accept Stormwater

The owner or developer of property to be developed is responsible for the conveyance of all stormwater flowing through the property. This responsibility includes stormwater flowing onto the property by any other developed property as well as the drainage naturally flowing through the property by reason of topography.

Table 5-12
Stormwater Management Design Conditions

Condition	Design Parameters
Existing conditions	Current development conditions in the watershed and on site. Use as the baseline analysis for determining the impact of development.
Proposed conditions	Existing conditions with the proposed development added. Use to determine if the increased run-off from the proposed development results in an adverse impact to other properties.
Ultimate conditions	Ultimate development conditions within the watershed used to design the drainage facilities. May be used in lieu of proposed conditions to determine if the increased run-off from the ultimate watershed development results in an adverse impact to other properties.

Future upstream development shall be accounted for by assuming ultimate development when sizing drainage systems as specified in this section.

5.22.6 Level of Service

5.22.6.1 New Development

Peak stormwater run-off rates from all new development shall be less than or equal to the peak run-off rates from the site's predevelopment conditions for the 5-, 25-, and 100-year design storm events, except as provided in § 5.22.2 Regional Stormwater Management Program of this chapter.

5.22.6.2 Redevelopment

Peak stormwater run-off rates from an area of redevelopment due to zoning or replatting shall be less than or equal to the peak run-off rates produced by existing development conditions for the 5-, 25-, and 100-year design storm events, except as provided in § 5.22.2 Regional Stormwater Management Program of this chapter.

5.22.7 Method of Computing Run-off

5.22.7.1 Calculation Methods

(A) For drainage areas less than 640 acres, the basis for computing run-off shall be the rational formula. Hydraulic calculations shall be performed by using the United States Army Corps of Engineers' Hydrologic Engineering Center (HEC) "Water Surface Profiles" (HEC-2) or "River Analysis System" (HEC-RAS) computer models. Normal depth-channel calculations are permissible for constructed open channels with a uniform geometric cross section where:

(1) There is no potential for the water surface elevations to be controlled by backwater; and

(2) The channel is not in a Federal Emergency Management Agency floodplain.

(B) For drainage areas 640 acres or greater, the basis for computing run-off shall be a unit-hydrograph method, using the Soil Conservation Service Dimensionless Unit graph method as contained in the United States Army Corps of Engineers' HEC-1 "Flood Hydrograph Package." Antecedent moisture condition II shall be used in the run-off model. Design rainfall values listed in Table 5-13 shall be used for hydrograph calculations.

(C) Open channel hydraulic calculations shall be performed by using the United States Army Corps of Engineers' HEC-2 "Water Surface Profiles" or HEC-RAS "River Analysis System" computer models.

(D) Certain watersheds have hydrologic and hydraulic models that are available through and maintained by the [LOCAL GOVERNMENT]. Developments proposed within the limits of these watersheds must have

Chapter 5: Development Standards 207

**Table 5-13
Design Rainfall Values (Inches)**

Duration	Frequency					
	5 Year	10 Year	25 Year	50 Year	100 Year	500 Year
5 minute	0.58	0.64	0.73	0.8	0.87	1.03
15 minute	1.26	1.39	1.59	1.75	1.91	2.25
60 minute	2.53	2.9	3.43	3.84	4.25	5.2
2 hour	3.08	3.66	4.42	4.99	5.57	6.95
3 hour	3.57	4.23	5.04	5.64	6.23	7.6
6 hour	4.26	4.99	5.89	6.52	7.13	8.47
12 hour	4.68	5.55	6.58	7.32	8.05	9.68
24 hour	5.45	6.55	7.78	8.78	9.91	12.75

♦ *Note to reader*: This data should be revised to account for local conditions.

the models updated by the consultant to reflect changes in flow, channel configuration (including alterations to vegetation), and channel structures. The consultants' models must use the same computer program that was used in the existing model (e.g., HEC-RAS models will not be accepted where the original model used HEC-2). The updated models shall be submitted to the [DEPARTMENT] for incorporation into the master models. The [LOCAL GOVERNMENT] will periodically update the master models to reflect current watershed development conditions. The updated models will be made available for use and distribution as the latest existing condition models for the watershed.

5.22.7.2 Time of Concentration

Overland (sheet) flow, shallow concentrated flow, and channel flows shall be included in the calculation of time of concentration. The methods described in Table 5-14 shall be used to calculate time of concentration.

5.22.7.3 Run-off Coefficients

Minimum run-off coefficients (C value) for use in the rational formula are shown in Table 5-15 and Table 5-16, as appropriate.

5.22.7.4 Rainfall Intensity

Table 5-17 may be used to determine rainfall intensity.

5.22.7.5 Percent Impervious Cover

The percent impervious cover for land uses in the application are as shown in Table 5-18. In lieu of Table 5-18, the applicant may calculate run-off coefficients based on actual impervious cover, as shown on the preliminary plat or site plan.

5.22.7.6 Design Rainfall

A 24 hour rainfall distribution shall be applied for run-off calculations. Rainfall intensities as adopted for the [LOCAL GOVERNMENT] are given in Table 5-13 and shall be used for HEC-1 input. The lag value for a

**Table 5-14
Time-of-Concentration Calculation Methods**

Condition	Description	Calculation Method
Overland flow	Water moving over a plane surface	Maximum allowable time is 20 minutes. Minimum is 5 minutes. The overland flow time chart from *Design*[a] may be used to calculate overland flow times.
Shallow concentrated flow	Overland flow becomes shallow concentrated flow after a maximum of 300 feet	Use Manning's equation to estimate travel time for defined swales, bar ditches, and street sections. Figure 3-1 from TR-55[b] may be used where a geometric section has not been defined.
Channel flow	Flow water moving though a canal, flume, ditch, or other defined conduit	Use existing computer models where available or Manning's equation if data are not available. Nonfloodplain channel velocities for ultimate watershed development should not be less than 6 feet per second when estimating time of concentration.

[a] *Elwyn Seelye*, Design, Vol. I, Data Book for Civil Engineers, *3d ed. (New York: John Wiley & Sons, 1996).*
[b] *Soil Conservation Service, "Urban hydrology for small watersheds," Technical Release No. 55 (Washington, DC: United States Department of Agriculture, 1986).*

Table 5-15
Run-off Coefficients (C)—Percentage

Character of Area	Zoning District	Use Pattern	Slope Up to 1%	Slope Over 1% Up to 3%	Slope Over 3% Up to 5%	Slope Flow Over 5%
Business or commercial areas (90% or more impervious)	CG, CL, D, IL, IH	Transit-oriented development	95	96	97	97
Densely developed areas (80% to 90% impervious)	O, CN, PD, MX	Neighborhood center, campus	85	88	91	95
Closely built residential areas and school sites	NU	Traditional neighborhood development	75	77	80	84
Undeveloped areas—present land is undeveloped and ultimate land use is unknown			68	70	72	75
Large lot residential	RP, RE		55	57	62	64
Typical residential	NS	Conventional or conservation subdivision	65	67	69	72

CG = Commercial General; CL = Commercial Large-Scale; D = Downtown; IL = Industrial Light; IH = Industrial Heavy; O = Office; CN = Commercial Neighborhood; PD = Planned Development; MX = Mixed Use; NU = Neighborhood Urban; RP = Resource Protection; RE = Residential Estate; and NS = Neighborhood Suburban.

Table 5-16
Run-off Coefficients (C)—Percentage
(Areas That Will Not Be Developed)

Character of Area	Slope Up to 1%	Slope Over 1% Up to 3%	Slope Over 3% Up to 5%	Slope Flow Over 5%
Cultivated or range (grass cover < 50% of area)	44	47	53	55
Range (grass cover 50-75% of area)	37	41	49	53
Forest or range (grass cover > 75% of area)	35	39	47	52

Areas included within parks, greenbelts, or regulatory floodplains are considered undeveloped.

Table 5-17
Soil Conservation Service
Curve Number by Soil Type

Hydrologic Soil Group	Description	Soil Conservation Service Curve Number
A	Soils having a low run-off potential due to high infiltration rates. These soils consist primarily of deep, well-drained sand and gravels.	25
B	Soils having a moderately low run-off potential due to moderate infiltration rates. These soils consist primarily of moderately deep to deep, moderately well to well-drained soils with moderately fine to moderately coarse textures.	55
C	Soils having moderately high run-off potential due to slow infiltration rates. These soils consist primarily of soils in which a layer exists near the surface that impedes the downward movement of water or soils with moderately fine to fine texture.	70
D	Soils having a high run-off potential due to very slow infiltration rates. These soils consist primarily of clays with high swelling potential, soils with permanently high-water tables, soils with a claypan or clay layer at or near the surface, and shallow soils over nearly impervious parent material.	77

Table 5-18
Percent Impervious Cover by Land Use

Land-Use Category		Average Percent Impervious Cover
Residential	1/8-acre residential lots, or garden or townhouse apartments	65-85%
	1/4-acre residential lots	38%
	1/2-acre residential lots	25%
	1-acre residential lots	20%
Industrial		72-85%
Business or commercial		85-95%
Densely developed (apartments)		65-85%
Streets, roads, and parking areas		98%

Table 5-19
Channel Routing

Condition	Channel Routing Method
Overbank/channel storage is not significant	Use normal depth-channel routing.
Overbank/channel storage is significant	Use the Muskingum method where a hydraulic model is not available. Use Modified Puls Storage method where a hydraulic model is available to develop storage/out flow relationship.
Kinematic wave method	For channel reaches where inflow from overbank run-off or multiple point sources (e.g., storm sewer outfalls) is significant and where hydrograph attenuation is insignificant.

Table 5-20
Manning's Roughness Coefficient

Feature	Manning's "n" Value
Channel Description	
Concrete-lined channel	0.015
Grass-lined channel with regular maintenance	0.035
Grass-lined channel without recent maintenance	0.050
Vegetated channel with trees, little or no underbrush	0.055
Natural channel with trees, moderate underbrush	0.075
Natural channel with trees, dense underbrush	0.090
Natural channel with dense trees and dense underbrush	0.100
Overbank Description	
Pasture	0.035-0.055
Trees, little or no underbrush, scattered structures	0.060-0.075
Dense vegetation, multiple fences, and structures	0.075-0.090
Channel Description	
Earth channels	0.035
Concrete-lined channels	0.015
Reinforced concrete pipe	0.013
Concrete box culverts	0.013
Unpaved 1/2-inch corrugated metal pipe	0.024
Unpaved 1-inch corrugated metal pipe	0.027

subarea shall be calculated as 0.6 times the time of concentration.

5.22.7.7 Routing of Run-off

Routing of the run-off hydrograph through the channel from one subarea calculation point to the next in the HEC-1 shall be computed using one of the methods shown in Table 5-19.

5.22.7.8 Manning's Roughness Coefficient

(A) *Routing methods or hydraulic calculations:* Manning's roughness coefficients ("n" values) for use in routing methods or in hydraulic calculations shall be consistent with the values listed in Table 5-20.

(B) *Design:* Any other "n" value shall be based on generally accepted engineering principles.

5.22.8 Drainage Easements/Rights-of-Way

5.22.8.1 Applicability

Where a subdivision is traversed by a watercourse, drainageway, natural channel, or stream, an easement or right of way shall be indicated on the subdivision plat or site plan that conforms substantially to the limit of such watercourse, plus additional width required by the applicable stormwater management facility.

5.22.8.2 Natural Watercourses or Floodplains

Easements for natural watercourses shall be the 100-year floodplain or the 25-year plus freeboard. A driveable accessway shall be provided in floodplain easements for the length of the easement when regular maintenance of the floodplain is required.

5.22.8.3 Maintenance Access Right-of-Way

An unobstructed access right-of-way connecting the drainage easement with an alley or roadway parallel to or near the easement shall be provided at a minimum spacing of one access right-of-way at approximately 1,000-foot intervals. The access right-of-way shall be a minimum of 15 feet in width and shall be maintained clear of obstructions that limit maintenance vehicle access. If the flow line of the designed channel incorporates grade control structures or vehicular bridges that prevent maintenance equipment from accessing that portion of the channel, additional access points may be required. Channel design, earthen or concrete, shall have ramps in the side slopes near the access points that allow maintenance equipment to descend to the floor level of the channel. The maximum allowable ramp slope for vehicular access is 7:1.

5.22.8.4 Lot and Property Line Crossings

Where drainage easements cross lot and property lines, a statement shall be added to the plat that no fencing or structures that will interfere with drainage flow are permitted on or across such lines. Fencing may be allowed across drainage easements only in accordance with the following restrictions:
 (A) The bottom of the fence shall be a minimum of the flow depth plus freeboard above the design flow line of channel or drain; and
 (B) Fence posts located within the easement must be structurally designed to resist damage from the stormwater flows and impact from debris.

5.22.8.5 Interceptor Easements

Interceptor drainage easements and channels shall be provided where the drainage area to the back of platted lots exceeds the depth of two average residential lots. Interceptor drains shall be constructed prior to the issuance of development approvals on any lot that is affected by the intercepted natural drainage being intercepted.

5.22.8.6 Lower Elevation of Site

All developments shall provide for adequate drainage outfall at the lower end of the site into an existing street, alley, drainage, easements, or right-of-way, or to the centerline of an existing natural drain. Where the proposed street, storm sewer, or open channel does not discharge into a natural low area or into an existing drainage easement, then facilities and drainage easements of adequate width to contain the design discharge shall be constructed and dedicated to the centerline of an existing natural low area within the same watershed. However, where the natural low area lies within the developer's property, the developer will be required only to plat an easement to the centerline of the natural low area, provided that the easement is adequate to accommodate the facilities that will be built in conjunction with the future development of that property.

5.22.9 Site Design and Grading

A note must be placed on the plat for residential lots stating that finished floor elevations must be a minimum of 8 inches above final adjacent grade. A grading plan shall be prepared and submitted to the [DEPARTMENT] indicating typical lot grading for all lots in the subdivision. The grading plan shall use typical Federal Housing Administration lot grading types A-C and block grading types 1-5. No more than two average residential lots may drain onto another lot unless a drainage easement is dedicated to contain the run-off (see Figure 5-6).

5.22.10 Low-Impact Stormwater Management Design

5.22.10.1 Applicability

Applications for subdivision plat or site plan approval shall provide an analysis of low-impact development design practices to accommodate the stormwater level of service established in § 5.22.2 Regional Stormwater Management Program of this chapter. These practices shall be included as a condition of subdivision and site plan approval.

5.22.10.2 Generally

At least 20 percent of the stormwater design event established in § 5.22 Stormwater Management of this chapter shall be treated through low-impact, stormwater management, integrated management practices (IMPs) and design features that are consistent with the practices described in *Low-Impact Development Design Strategies: An Integrated Design Approach*[6] and *Low-Impact Development Hydrologic Analysis*,[7] which are incorporated by reference and are referred to as the "LID Manuals" (see Figure 5-7) and this section.

5.22.10.3 Integrated Management Practices

IMPs shall comply with the design standards described in Table 5-21.

5.22.10.4 Bioretention

The major components of a bioretention system shall include the following:
 (A) Pretreatment area (optional);
 (B) Ponding area;
 (C) Ground cover layer;
 (D) Planting soil;
 (E) In situ soil;
 (F) Plant material;
 (G) Inlet and outlet controls; and
 (H) Maintenance.

**Figure 5-6
Grading**

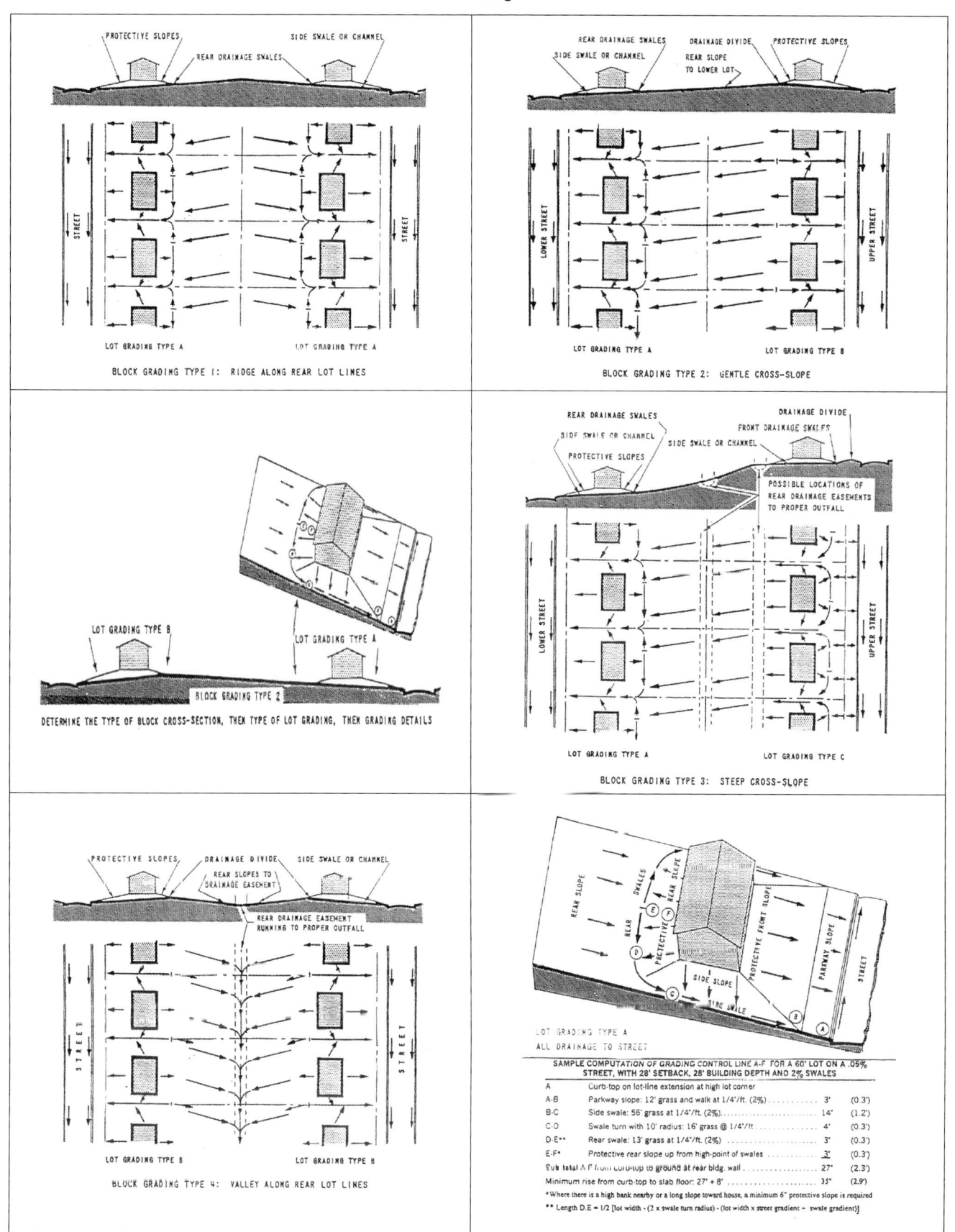

Figure 5-6 (cont.)
Grading

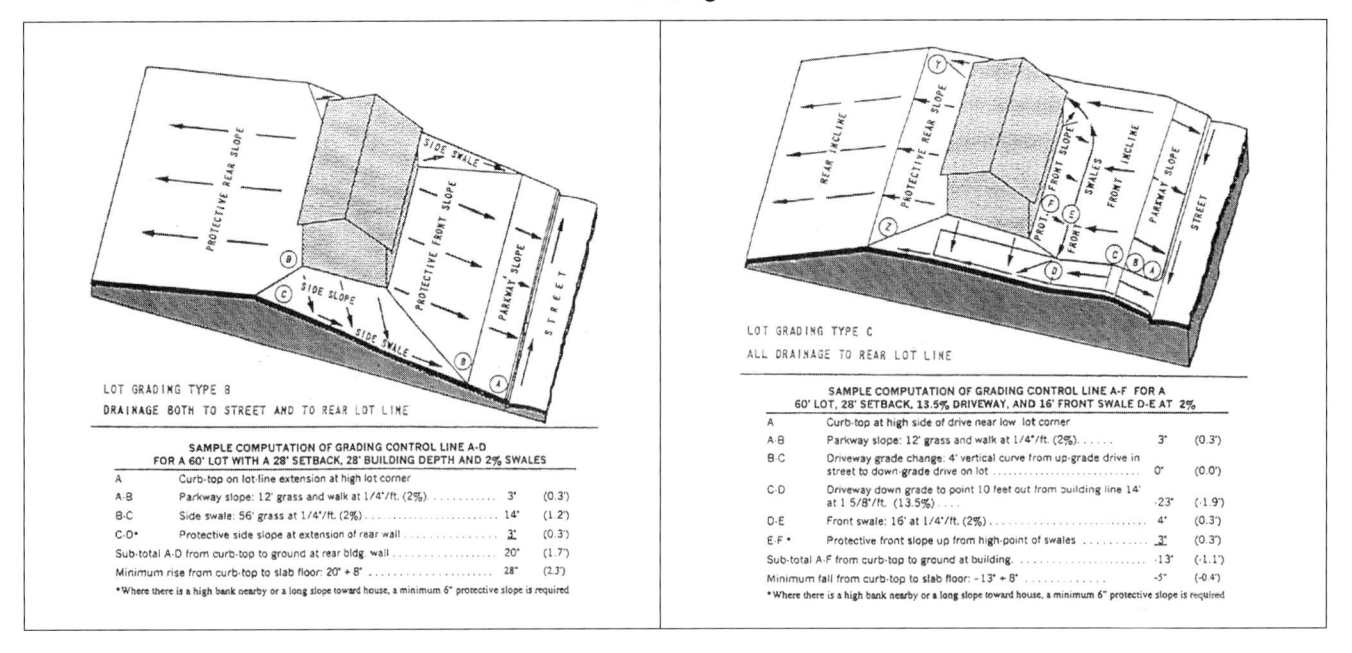

Figure 5-7
LID Manuals

Sources: Low-Impact Development Design Strategies: An Integrated Design Approach *(Washington, DC: United States Environmental Protection Agency, January 2000);* Low-Impact Development Hydrologic Analysis *(Washington, DC: United States Environmental Protection Agency, January 2000).*

Table 5-21
Integrated Management Practices

Design Factor	Bioretention	Dry Well	Filter/Buffer Strip	Grass Swales and Level Spreaders	Infiltration Trench
Space required	Minimum surface area range: 50-200 square feet. Minimum width: 5-10 feet. Minimum length: 10-20 feet. Minimum depth: 2-4 feet.	Minimum surface area range: 8-20 square feet. Minimum width: 2-4 feet. Minimum length: 4-8 feet. Minimum depth: 4-8 feet.	Minimum length: 15-20 feet.	Bottom width: 2 feet minimum, 6 feet maximum.	Minimum surface area range: 8-20 square feet. Minimum width: 2-4 feet. Minimum length: 4-8 feet.
Soils	Permeable soils with infiltration rates > 0.27 inches/hour shall be used. Soil limitations can be overcome with use of underdrains.	Permeable soils with infiltration rates > 0.27 inches/hour shall be used.	Permeable soils perform better, but soils not a limitation.	Permeable soils provide better hydrologic performance, but soils not a limitation. Selection of type of swale— grassed, infiltration, or wet—is influenced by soils.	Permeable soils with infiltration rates 0.52 inches/hour shall be used.
Slopes	Not a limitation, but a design consideration.	Not a limitation, but a design consideration. Must locate down gradient of building and foundations.	Not a limitation, but a design consideration.	Swale side slopes: 3:1 or flatter. Longitudinal slope: 1.0% minimum; maximum based on permissible velocities.	Not a limitation, but a design consideration. Must locate down gradient of buildings and foundations.
Water table/ bedrock	2- to 4-foot clearance above water table/bedrock recommended.	2- to 4-foot clearance above water table/bedrock recommended.	Generally not a constraint.	Generally not a constraint.	2- to 4-foot clearance.
Proximity to build foundations	Minimum distance of 10 feet down gradient from buildings and foundations recommended.	Minimum distance of 10 feet down gradient from buildings and foundations recommended.	Minimum distance of 10 feet down gradient from buildings and foundations recommended.	Minimum distance of 10 feet down gradient from buildings and foundations recommended.	Minimum distance of 10 feet down gradient from buildings and foundations recommended.
Maximum depth	2- to 4-foot depth depending on soil type.	6- to 10-foot depth depending on soil type.	Not applicable.	Not applicable.	6- to 10-foot depth depending on soil type.
Maintenance	Low requirement, property owner can include in normal site landscape maintenance.	Low requirement.	Low requirement, routine landscape maintenance.	Low requirement, routine landscape maintenance.	Moderate to high.

Table 5-22
Bioretention Design Components

Design Factor	Standard
Pretreatment area	Required where a significant volume of debris or suspended material is anticipated, such as parking lots and commercial areas. Grass buffer strip or vegetated swale are commonly used pretreatment devices.
Ponding area	Typically limited to a depth of 6 inches.
Ground cover area	3 inches of mature mulch recommended.
Planting soil	Depth = 4 feet. Soil mixtures include sand, loamy sand, and sandy loam. Clay content = 10%.
In situ soil	Infiltration rate = 0.5 inches/hour without underdrains. Infiltration rate = 0.5 inches/hour underdrain required.
Plant materials	Native species, minimum three species.
Inlet and outlet controls	Nonerosive flow velocities.
Maintenance	Routine landscape maintenance.
Hydrologic design	Determined by state or local agency.

Figure 5-8
Bioretention Facility

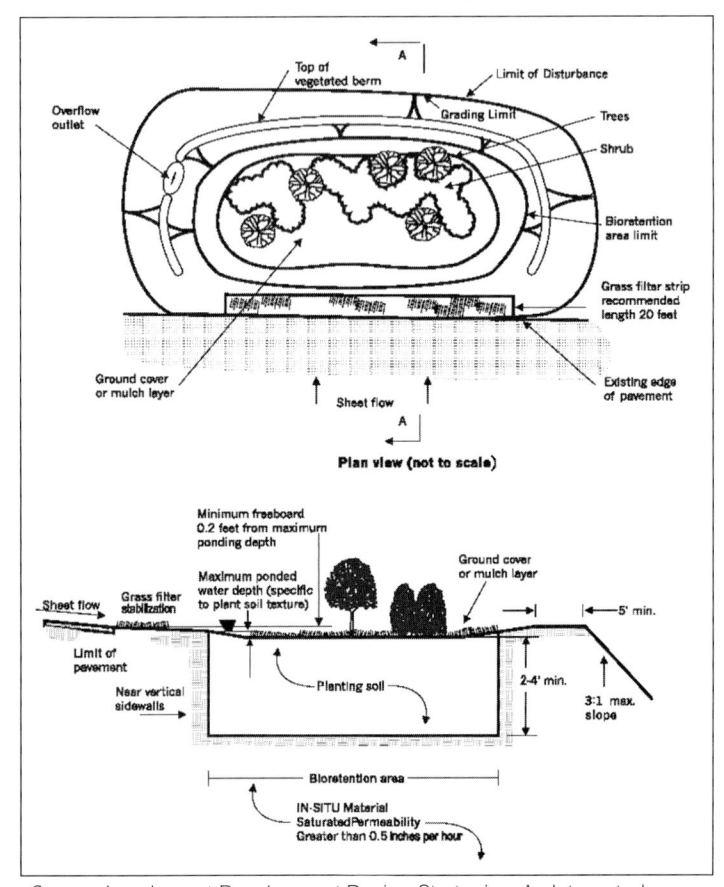

Source: Low-Impact Development Design Strategies: An Integrated Design Approach *(Washington, DC: United States Environmental Protection Agency, January 2000).*

Design of bioretention areas shall comply with Table 5-22 (see Figure 5-8).

5.22.11 Stormwater Detention

5.22.11.1 Applicability

This section applies to a proposed development that creates a net increase in impervious area of at least 4,000 square feet, and that elects not to participate or is not eligible to participate in the RSWMP.

5.22.11.2 Level of Service Standard

Stormwater detention shall mitigate peak flow rates to predevelopment or existing development conditions.

5.22.11.3 Maximum Outflow Rate

The maximum allowable outflow rate from the detention facility must be restricted to the flow rate from the undeveloped or existing development tract for the 5-, 25-, and 100-year frequency. The timing of the hydrograph released from the detention facility must be checked against the timing of the flow rate in the first open watercourse to prevent any increase in the peak flow rate in the receiving watercourse. For detention basins constructed in line on an existing watercourse, the creation of the basin shall not increase flood elevations in the channel upstream of the new development boundaries.

5.22.11.4 On-site Detention

On-site detention facilities must be privately owned and shall be maintained as required by § 5.6 Operation and Maintenance of this chapter. A maintenance schedule shall be approved by the [PLANNING OFFICIAL] prior to approval of construction plans.

5.22.12 Multiuse Facilities

The use of multiuse detention facilities to alleviate existing flooding problems, enhance and provide amenities for older neighborhoods, and support the revitalization of economically depressed areas is encouraged in public and private redevelopment initiatives. Multiuse facilities are stormwater management facilities that provide stormwater management functions and other benefits, such as water quality improvement, water recharge, open space, recreation, or habitat. Multiuse facilities are encouraged but not required by this section. Such facilities shall meet the standards set forth in § 5.22.2 Regional Stormwater Management Program of this chapter and shall not increase the rate or volume of erosion above, resulting from the use of a facility without multiple uses.

5.22.13 Location of Detention Facilities

Stormwater detention facilities (Figure 5-9) shall be located in topographically depressed areas.

**Figure 5-9
Sustainable Open Space**

This "rain garden" in Carpenter Village (Mooresville, North Carolina) drains 3 acres with underground rain storage and provides passive open space as part of a public green.

5.22.14 Streets for Stormwater Drainage

5.22.14.1 Generally

Streets shall be designed to avoid conflicts between stormwater conveyance, traffic, parking, pedestrian access, ADA requirements, and bicycle traffic.

5.22.14.2 Standards

(A) Streets draining a watershed greater than 100 acres must be designed for the 100-year frequency storm.

(B) Streets may be used for stormwater drainage only if the calculated stormwater flow does not exceed the flows outlined in Table 5-23 or the velocity does not exceed 10 feet per second.

(C) Where streets are not capable of carrying stormwaters, inlets or curb openings discharging to drainage channels or storm sewers shall be provided. Partial flow past the inlet will be allowed when the capacity of all downstream street systems can accommodate the flow.

(D) Street width shall not be widened beyond the width as determined by the street classification for drainage purposes.

(E) Stormwater conveyance on streets shall be designed to account for the cumulative impact of peak flows and run-off volumes on the system as it progresses downgrade.

(F) Curb cuts for driveways on all streets shall be designed for compatibility with the stormwater conveyance function of streets.

(G) Potential flooding problems or conflicts at the connection points where new or modified drainage systems (including streets and storm sewers) and the existing portions of the downstream street system and stormwater conveyance system shall be identified and resolved, either in the design of the new or modified drainage system or in modifications to the existing system.

(H) Dwelling units located on the downhill side of a T-intersection with a street or drainage channel discharging onto the intersection shall be sited in order to avoid obstruction of the drainage patterns.

5.22.14.3 All-Weather Crossings

Where streets cross existing or proposed watercourses, all-weather crossings are required. Culverts or bridges shall be adequate to allow passage of the design storm identified in § 5.22.2 Regional Stormwater Management Program of this chapter.

5.22.14.4 Standards by Street Classification

The stormwater capacity for streets shall conform to Table 5-23 and Table 5-24.

5.22.15 Drainage Channels and Watercourses

5.22.15.1 Applicability

This section addresses proposed improvements or modifications to drainage channels and watercourses required to convey stormwater run-off from or through the proposed development.

5.22.15.2 Standards

(A) Except as authorized by a development plan approved by the [PLANNING OFFICIAL], no person shall place any obstruction of any kind in any watercourse within the [LOCAL GOVERNMENT], except where specifically permitted by the LDC. The owner of any property within the [LOCAL GOVERNMENT], through which any watercourse may pass, shall keep the watercourse free from any obstruction not designated on a subdivision plat or site plan.

(B) Modifications to existing watercourses or newly created open channels may be designed as earth, sodded or as concrete-lined channels. Liners other than sod or concrete that enhance the aesthetics or habitat value of the watercourse and that reduce future maintenance requirements are permitted. Preliminary planning for the applicability of other channel liners shall be reviewed with the [PLANNING OFFICIAL] prior to the submittal of construction plans for approval.

(C) A maintenance schedule for any private channel shall be submitted to and approved by the [PLANNING OFFICIAL] prior to approval of construction plans. Maintenance requirements of concrete channels consist of desilting activities, prevention of vegetation

Table 5-23
Storm Drainage, Street Velocities, and Capacities

Slope %	Local W = 30 Feet Q cfs	V f/s	Subcollector W = 40 Feet Q cfs	V f/s	Collector W = 44 Feet Q cfs	V f/s	Secondary (with Median) Maximum Water Depth = 7 Inches W = 24 Feet Minimum and 29 Feet Maximum Q cfs	V f/s	Primary and Secondary (without Median) Maximum Water Depth = 7 Inches W = 24 Feet Minimum and 29 Feet Maximum Q cfs	V f/s
0.40	35.4	2.8	47.8	2.9	44.1	2.7	20.6	2.5	19.2	2.3
0.45	37.5	3.0	50.7	3.0	46.8	2.8	21.9	2.7	20.4	2.4
0.50	39.6	3.2	53.4	3.2	49.3	3.0	23.1	2.8	21.5	2.5
0.55	41.5	3.3	56.0	3.4	51.7	3.1	24.2	2.9	22.5	2.7
0.60	43.3	3.5	58.5	3.5	54.0	3.3	25.3	3.1	23.6	2.8
0.65	45.1	3.6	60.9	3.7	56.2	3.4	26.3	3.2	24.5	2.9
0.70	46.8	3.8	63.2	3.8	58.4	3.5	27.3	3.3	25.4	3.0
0.75	48.5	3.9	65.4	3.9	60.4	3.7	28.3	3.4	26.3	3.1
0.80	50.0	4.0	67.6	4.1	62.4	3.8	29.2	3.5	27.2	3.2
0.85	51.6	4.1	69.6	4.2	64.3	3.9	30.1	3.7	28.0	3.3
0.90	53.1	4.3	71.7	4.3	66.2	4.0	30.9	3.8	28.8	3.4
0.95	54.5	4.4	73.6	4.4	68.0	4.1	31.8	3.9	29.6	3.5
1.00	55.9	4.5	75.5	4.5	69.8	4.2	32.6	4.0	30.4	3.6
1.50	68.5	5.5	92.5	5.5	85.4	5.2	40.0	4.9	37.2	4.4
2.00	79.1	6.4	106.8	6.4	98.66	.0	46.1	5.6	43.0	5.1
2.50	88.5	7.1	119.4	7.2	110.3	6.7	51.6	6.3	48.1	5.7
3.00	96.9	7.8	130.8	7.8	120.8	7.3	56.5	6.9	52.7	6.2
3.50	104.7	8.4	141.3	8.5	130.5	7.9	61.0	7.4	56.9	6.7
4.00	111.9	9.0	151.1	9.1	139.5	8.5	65.2	7.9	60.8	7.2
4.50	118.7	9.5	160.2	9.6	148.0	9.0	69.2	8.4	64.5	7.6
5.00	125.1	10.0	168.9	10.0	156.0	9.5	72.9	8.9	68.0	8.0
5.50	116.0	10.0	153.0	10.0	163.6	9.9	76.5	9.3	71.3	8.4
6.00	108.0	10.0	143.0	10.0	157.0	10.0	79.9	9.7	74.5	8.8
6.50	102.0	10.0	134.0	10.0	148.0	10.0	81.0	10.0	77.5	9.1
7.00	96.0	10.0	127.0	10.0	140.0	10.0	76.0	10.0	80.4	9.5
7.50	91.0	10.0	120.0	10.0	132.0	10.0				
8.00	87.0	10.0	115.0	10.0	126.0	10.0				
8.50	83.0	10.0	110.0	10.0	120.0	10.0				
9.00	79.0	10.0	105.0	10.0	115.0	10.0				
9.5	76.0	10.0	101.0	10.0	111.0	10.0				
10	73.0	10.0	97.0	10.0	106.0	10.0				

Manning's "n" = 0.018. W = width of ponded water; Q cfs = design flow in cubic feet per second; V f/s = velocity feet per second.

◆ **Note to reader**: This table should be modified for local conditions.

**Table 5-24
Stormwater Management Capacity
by Street Classification**

Street Classification	Standard
Primary and secondary arterial streets or traditional neighborhood development (TND) boulevard/parkway	One lane in each direction on arterial streets shall remain passable with a flow depth not to exceed 0.30 feet during a 25-year storm event. The maximum depth of water in the street section shall not exceed 7 inches.
Collector streets or main streets with more than 34 feet of pavement width	A maximum flow depth to the top of curb on a subcollector and collector street is permitted during a 25-year storm event.
Local streets or TND avenues and main streets with less than 34 feet of pavement width	Five-year frequency design basis. A 25-year frequency storm must be contained within the street right-of-way.
Alleys or TND trails, alleys, and lanes	Alleys and TND trails, alleys, and lanes shall be designed for five-year frequency within the limits of the alley pavement/curbs and 25-year frequency within the right-of-way/easement to carry stormwater.

establishment in construction joints, and repair of concrete, as necessary. Maintenance of earthen channels includes regular observation and repair as necessary of erosion, scouring, and removal of silt deposits, as necessary to maintain design parameters. Applicants shall maintain newly planted channels until coverage is established throughout 85 percent of the area. This area shall include slopes, floor, and any attendant maintenance easement. New earthen channels shall be planted with drought-resistant, low-growth, native-species grasses, which will allow unobstructed passage of floodwaters. Johnsongrass, Giant Ragweed, and other invasive species are not permitted in channels.

These species shall include Common Bermuda, Coastal Bermuda, Buffalo Grass, Sideoats Grama, Seep Muhly, Little Bluestem, Indiangrass, or other species approved by the [ENGINEERING OFFICIAL] that meet the standards of this section. Mowing frequencies vary with the vegetation growth rates but is required when the grass exceeds the design roughness coefficient of the channel.

5.22.15.3 Velocity Criteria

Table 5-25 shall be used to determine the type of stormwater management facility that is used.

5.22.16 Concrete Channels

Concrete-lined channels shall not be used at velocities less than 6 feet per second unless a variance is granted pursuant to Chapter 4, Procedures, of the LDC.

5.22.17 Storm Sewers

(A) Storm sewers shall have sufficient capacity to accommodate full flow under the design discharge, pressure heads, and outfalls.

(B) No storm sewers shall be less than 24 inches in diameter.

(C) Storm sewer easements shall have a minimum width of 15 feet, or 6 feet on both sides of the extreme limits of the storm sewer, whichever is greater.

5.22.18 Inlets and Openings

(A) Where drop-curb openings are used to take stormwater off the streets and into drains, the length of the curb opening can be calculated as follows:

$L = Q \div Ch3/2$

where:

L = the length of drop-curb opening required in feet;

Q = amount of flow in cubic feet per second based on 25-year design frequency;

$C = 3.087$; and

h = head of weir in feet.

**Table 5-25
Velocity Control**

Velocity (Feet Per Second)	Type of Facility Required	Hydraulic Radius (Feet)	Correction Factor	Maximum Permissible Velocity (Feet Per Second)
1 to 6 (maximum average velocity = 6)	Vegetated earthen channel	0-1 1-3 3-5 5-8 8-10 Over 10	0.8 0.9 1.05 1.15 1.225 1.25	5 5.5 6.3 6.9 7.35 7.5
6 to 8	Concrete retards	Not applicable	Not applicable	Not applicable
> 8	Concrete lining or drop structures	Not applicable	Not applicable	Not applicable

(B) Gutter-line depressions are permitted where such depressions will not interfere with the flow of traffic.

(C) Where drop inlets are used, the [LOCAL GOVERNMENT] standard inlets with adequate reinforcing steel may be used as provided in [ENGINEERING SPECIFICATIONS].

(D) The flow of water through grate openings may be treated as the flow of water through a rectangular orifice. The following formula shall be used to determine grate capacity:

$Q = CA(2gh)^{1/2}$

where:

Q = discharge in cubic feet per second;
C = orifice coefficient of discharge (taken as 0.70);
A = net area of the openings in the grate in square feet;
g = acceleration due to gravity (32.2 feet/second^2); and
h = head on the grate in feet.

This formula gives the theoretical capacity of the grate inlet. Since grate inlets are subject to considerable clogging, capacity of the grate inlet will be taken as one-half of the value given by this formula.

(E) The capacity of curb opening inlets will depend on whether or not the opening is running partially full or is submerged. If the depth of flow at the curb opening inlet causes a partially full opening, capacity shall be determined by the following formula:

$Q = C_w L(h)^{3/2}$

where:

Q = the discharge of capacity in cubic feet per second;
C_w = the weir coefficient of discharge (3.087);
L = the length of curb opening in feet; and
h = the head or depth of water at the opening in feet.

(F) If the depth of flow at the curb opening fully submerges the opening, the orifice effect will develop and the formula used shall be identical to that given under grate inlets. The head ("h") on the curb opening orifice shall be taken as the depth from the top of the water surface to the center of the orifice or opening. One hundred percent efficiency is permitted for curb opening inlets.

5.23 STREET DESIGN AND TRANSPORTATION

Purpose and findings: These regulations are designed to:
- Ensure that the design of streets conforms to the recommendations of the comprehensive plan;
- Provide for the safety for both vehicular and pedestrian traffic;
- Provide for livable residential and commercial environments;
- Provide economy of land use, construction, and maintenance; and
- Provide safe and efficient access to property.

Unlike the situation in traditional subdivision regulations, one intent of this section is to permit narrower street widths while requiring greater connectivity in order to more efficiently disperse traffic, to protect pedestrians from high vehicular speeds, and to enhance the streetscape. The [LOCAL GOVERNMENT] further finds and determines that street layout and design can have a very significant influence on the total imperviousness and hydrology of a site. Alternative road layout can result in significantly reducing imperviousness, reducing stormwater run-off, protecting water quality, and providing cost savings for developers and home buyers.

5.23.1 Applicability

(A) This section applies to:

(1) Any application for subdivision plat approval;

(2) Any application for site plan approval if no subdivision plat is required; and

(3) Any ministerial development approval where required by subsection (B), below.

(B) The construction of standard curbs and sidewalks shall be a condition of the granting of a development approval, if:

(1) A new building or structure when curbing is in place or curb lines are established for a sidewalk; and

(2) A new or an additional driveway approach is required.

5.23.2 Classification

5.23.2.1 *Conventional*

Classification of an existing or proposed street not already identified on the major street plan, for the purpose of determining the appropriate design of a roadway or development, or for the purpose of determining the appropriateness of a location for a proposed use, shall be done by the [PLANNING OFFICIAL]. Pursuant to the major street plan, the classification system, as described in Table 5-26, is adopted.

5.23.2.2 *Factors*

In determining the classification of a street, factors to be considered include the following existing or proposed features:

(A) Facility geometrics, including the number and width of traffic lanes, turning lanes, and parking lanes;

(B) Access conditions, including any restrictions on access, the spacing of private accesses, and average lot frontages;

(C) Traffic characteristics, including average daily traffic, percentage of trucks, average operating speed, percentage of turning movements, origin-destination characteristics of the traffic, and peak-hour characteristics of traffic; and

(D) Adjacent land uses.

5.23.3 Geometric Design

Interior streets within the subdivision or development parcel shall conform to the standards described in Table 5-27.

**Table 5-26
Functional Street Classification System**

Classification	Definition	Average Daily Traffic Range	Subclassifications
Local street	As the lowest-order street, the access street usually carries no through traffic. With properly designed access streets without through traffic, travel distances from residences to collector streets are short, traffic speeds are low, lane capacity and design speed are not controlling design factors, and minor delays are inconsequential considerations. Drivers and residents expect and accept both brief delays and the need to decrease speed.	0-250	Local streets Rural streets Cul-de-sacs Alleys
Subcollector	The subcollector provides passage to access streets and conveys traffic to collectors. Like access streets, the subcollector provides frontage and access to residential lots but also carries some through traffic to lower-order (access) streets. The subcollector is a relatively low-volume street.	250-1,000	Avenue Main street
Collector	As the principal traffic artery within residential or commercial areas, the collector carries relatively high traffic volumes and conveys traffic from arterial streets to lower-order streets. Its function is to promote the free flow of traffic.	1,000-3,000	Boulevard Main street
Arterial	A high-volume street connects communities and activity centers, and connects communities to major state and interstate highways.	Over 3,000	Parkway Freeway Expressway

Source: United States Department of Housing and Urban Development, Proposed Model Land Development Standards and Accompanying State Enabling Legislation (Upper Marlboro, MD: National Association of Home Builders Research Center, June 1993), at 11; see also Institute of Transportation Engineers, "Guidelines for Residential Subdivision Street Design," ITE Publication No. RP-011C (Washington, DC: ITE, 1993), at 1; see also John D. Edwards, ed., Transportation Planning Handbook (Washington, DC: Institute of Transportation Engineers, 1999).

Row (A): Street Classifications

(1) Street types shall be indicated on the preliminary and final subdivision plats.

(2) Lane street types are permitted for a TND or transit-oriented development (TOD) if the abutting buildings are provided with:

(a) A National Fire Protection Agency (NFPA) 13D fire sprinkler system in the case of single-family dwelling units, single-family attached dwelling units, two family (duplex) dwelling units, and two-family attached dwelling units;

(b) An NFPA 13R fire sprinkler system for multi-family buildings; or

(c) An NFPA 13 fire sprinkler system for commercial buildings.

Row (B): Right-of-Way

Right-of-way width depends on the number of travel lanes and parking lanes provided. The dimensions are in feet and are a minimum width. The right-of-way includes all travel lanes, medians, sidewalks, and bike lanes.

Row (C): Travel Lanes

Row (C) refers to the number of travel lanes required. Travel lanes shall be a minimum of:

(1) 9 feet for lanes and local streets (traditional street design criteria);

(2) 10 feet in width for alleys, local roads, and rural streets;

(3) 11 feet in width for avenues, main streets, boulevards, and subcollectors; and

(4) 12 feet for all other streets.

Row (D): Parking Lanes

Row (D) refers to the minimum number of parking lanes. If two lanes are required, one parking lane shall be provided on each side of the street. Parking lanes shall be a minimum of 8 feet in width. For local streets and subcollectors, excluding rural streets, one parking lane may be included, in which case total required pavement width shall increase by an additional 8 feet.

Row (E): Pavement Width

Row (E) refers to the minimum width of the traveled way and any parking lanes, in feet, from the back of the curb (BOC) for curbed streets and to the edge of the pavement for all other streets. All streets shall be paved with a hard surface. Gravel or other loose surfacing material is not permitted.

Table 5-27
Street Geometric Design

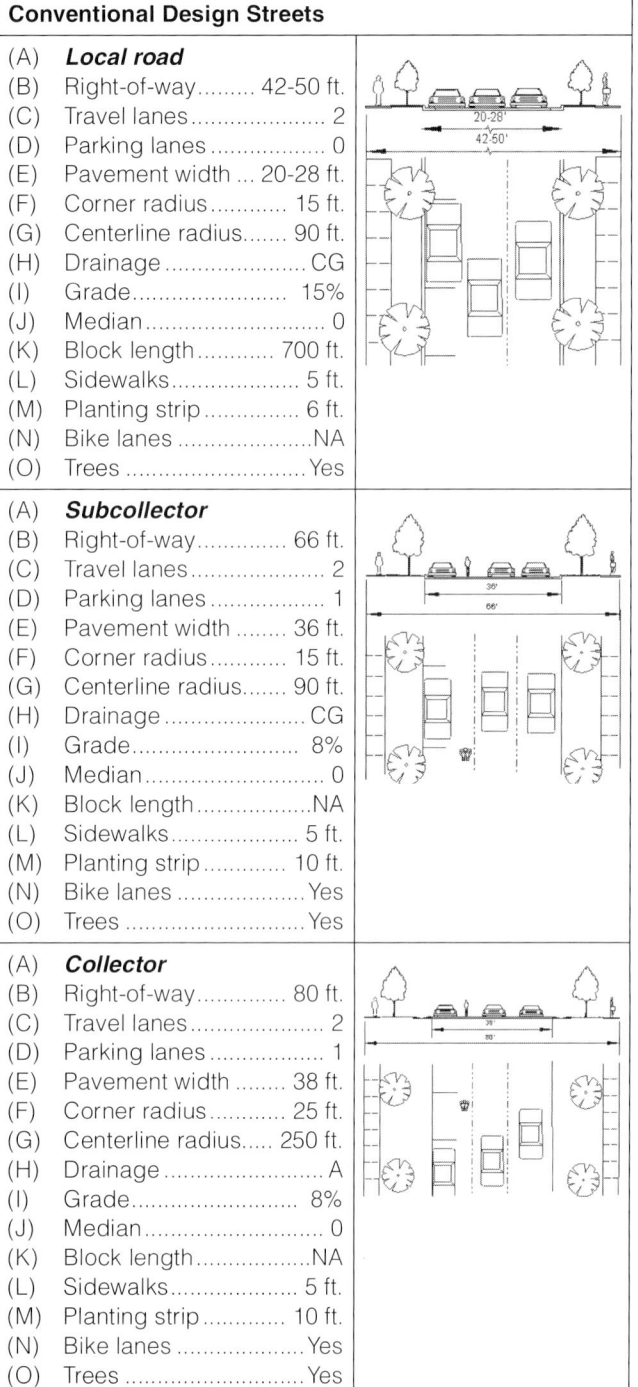

Conventional Design Streets
(A) *Local road*   (B) Right-of-way .... 42-50 ft.   (C) Travel lanes 2   (D) Parking lanes 0   (E) Pavement width ... 20-28 ft.   (F) Corner radius .... 15 ft.   (G) Centerline radius .... 90 ft.   (H) Drainage .... CG   (I) Grade .... 15%   (J) Median 0   (K) Block length .... 700 ft.   (L) Sidewalks .... 5 ft.   (M) Planting strip .... 6 ft.   (N) Bike lanes .... NA   (O) Trees .... Yes
(A) *Subcollector*   (B) Right-of-way .... 66 ft.   (C) Travel lanes 2   (D) Parking lanes 1   (E) Pavement width .... 36 ft.   (F) Corner radius .... 15 ft.   (G) Centerline radius .... 90 ft.   (H) Drainage .... CG   (I) Grade .... 8%   (J) Median 0   (K) Block length .... NA   (L) Sidewalks .... 5 ft.   (M) Planting strip .... 10 ft.   (N) Bike lanes .... Yes   (O) Trees .... Yes
(A) *Collector*   (B) Right-of-way .... 80 ft.   (C) Travel lanes 2   (D) Parking lanes 1   (E) Pavement width .... 38 ft.   (F) Corner radius .... 25 ft.   (G) Centerline radius ..... 250 ft.   (H) Drainage .... A   (I) Grade .... 8%   (J) Median 0   (K) Block length .... NA   (L) Sidewalks .... 5 ft.   (M) Planting strip .... 10 ft.   (N) Bike lanes .... Yes   (O) Trees .... Yes

Table 5-27 (cont.)
Street Geometric Design

(A) *Arterial*   (B) Right-of-way .... 70-118 ft.   (C) Travel lanes 2   (D) Parking lanes 0   (E) Pavement width .... 24-72 ft.   (F) Corner radius .... 25 ft.   (G) Centerline radius ..... 250 ft.   (H) Drainage .... SH   (I) Grade .... 8%   (J) Median 0   (K) Block length .... NA   (L) Sidewalks .... NA   (M) Planting strip .... 10 ft.   (N) Bike lanes .... Yes   (O) Trees .... Yes
Community Design Streets
(A) *Alley*   (B) Right-of-way .... 20 ft.   (C) Travel lanes 1   (D) Parking lanes 0   (E) Pavement width .... 10 ft.   (F) Corner radius .... 10 ft.   (G) Centerline radius .... 50 ft.   (H) Drainage .... NA   (I) Grade .... 10%   (J) Median 0   (K) Block length .... 400 ft.   (L) Sidewalks .... NA   (M) Planting strip .... NA   (N) Bike lanes .... NA   (O) Trees .... NA
(A) *Lane*   (B) Right-of-way .... 38 ft.   (C) Travel lanes 2   (D) Parking lanes 0   (E) Pavement width .... 18 ft.   (F) Corner radius .... 10 ft.   (G) Centerline radius .... 90 ft.   (H) Drainage .... CG   (I) Grade .... 10%   (J) Median 0   (K) Block length .... 150 ft.   (L) Sidewalks .... 5 ft.   (M) Planting strip .... 5 ft.   (N) Bike lanes .... NA   (O) Trees .... NA

Table 5-27 (cont.)
Street Geometric Design

	Local street	
(A)	**Local street**	
(B)	Right-of-way	48-56 ft.
(C)	Travel lanes	2
(D)	Parking lanes	1
(E)	Pavement width	26-34 ft.
(F)	Corner radius	10 ft.
(G)	Centerline radius	90 ft.
(H)	Drainage	CG
(I)	Grade	12%
(J)	Median	0
(K)	Block length	300 ft.
(L)	Sidewalks	5 ft.
(M)	Planting strip	6 ft.
(N)	Bike lanes	NA
(O)	Trees	Yes

(A)	**Rural street**	
(B)	Right-of-way	38 ft.
(C)	Travel lanes	2
(D)	Parking lanes	0
(E)	Pavement width	20 ft.
(F)	Corner radius	15 ft.
(G)	Centerline radius	90 ft.
(H)	Drainage	SW
(I)	Grade	15%
(J)	Median	0
(K)	Block length	NA
(L)	Sidewalks	NA
(M)	Planting strip	NA
(N)	Bike lanes	NA
(O)	Trees	Yes

	Avenue	
(A)	**Avenue**	
(B)	Right-of-way	59-118 ft.
(C)	Travel lanes	2
(D)	Parking lanes	0-2
(E)	Pavement width	22-50 ft.
(F)	Corner radius	15 ft.
(G)	Centerline radius	250 ft.
(H)	Drainage	CG
(I)	Grade	8%
(J)	Median	0
(K)	Block length	NA
(L)	Sidewalks	6-20 ft.
(M)	Planting strip	10 ft.
(N)	Bike lanes	Yes
(O)	Trees	Yes

Table 5-27 (cont.)
Street Geometric Design

	Main street	
(A)	**Main street**	
(B)	Right-of-way	68-130 ft.
(C)	Travel lanes	2-4
(D)	Parking lanes	2
(E)	Pavement width	48-70 ft.
(F)	Corner radius	15 ft.
(G)	Centerline radius	600 ft.
(H)	Drainage	CG
(I)	Grade	8%
(J)	Median	0
(K)	Block length	300 ft.
(L)	Sidewalks	10 ft.
(M)	Planting strip	NA
(N)	Bike lanes	Yes
(O)	Trees	Yes

	Boulevard	
(A)	**Boulevard**	
(B)	Right-of-way	90-168 ft.
(C)	Travel lanes	4-6
(D)	Parking lanes	0-2
(E)	Pavement width	44-94 ft.
(F)	Corner radius	25 ft.
(G)	Centerline radius	500 ft.
(H)	Drainage	A
(I)	Grade	8%
(J)	Median	14
(K)	Block length	1,000 ft.
(L)	Sidewalks	6-20 ft.
(M)	Planting strip	10 ft.
(N)	Bike lanes	Yes
(O)	Trees	Yes

NA = the standard does not apply. For rules of interpretation, see subsections "Row (A): Street Classifications" through "Row (O): Trees," of this chapter. Where a number is stated as a range, the street may include any dimension or number within the range at the discretion of the applicant. The methodology for calculating the geometric design factors shall conform to the [ENGINEERING SPECIFICATIONS] and AASHTO Green Book: A Policy on Geometric Design of Highways and Streets, 5th ed. (Washington, DC: American Association of State and Highway Transportation Officials, 2004), unless a different standard is prescribed in this section.

Row (F): Corner Radius

Row (F) refers to the minimum radius, in feet, of the curb located at the street intersection of a block corner.

Row (G): Centerline Radius

Row (G) refers to the radius, in feet, described by the radius of the circle formed by a curve that is tangent to the centerline of the road.

Row (H): Drainage

In Row (H), "CG" means curb and gutter; "A" means any combination of curb and gutter, swales, and shoulders; "SW" means swales; and "SH" means shoulders. All curbed streets shall be built in accordance with the [ENGINEERING SPECIFICATIONS] for vertical curb and gutter construction. Gutters shall be at least 2 feet in width, while gutters for lanes and street medians shall be at least 1 foot. For rural streets, the [PLANNING OFFICIAL] may waive the requirement for curb and gutter where buildings or structures are located on only one side of the street, and the lots or parcels abutting the opposite side of the street are reserved for parks or open space. For a promenade, the curb and gutter may be installed on one or both sides of the facility.

Row (I): Grade

Row (I) refers to the maximum slope of a street, in percent. Street and alley grades shall conform to the terrain. No street or alley grade shall be less than 0.5 percent if curb and gutter are provided. The minimum cross-slope of a road shall be 2 percent and the maximum shall be 4 percent.

Row (J): Median

(1) *Width:* Where median widths are specified in Row (J), a median of at least the designated width shall be provided.

(2) *Entrance roads:* Entrance roads shall include a median that complies with these requirements. Islands and medians shall be a minimum of 75 square feet in size.

(3) *Visibility:* Structures, permanent materials, or plantings within the island shall not obscure the visibility of cars entering a cross street for a distance of 20 feet back from the curb face of the cross street, unless a larger setback is needed due to inadequate sight distance created by horizontal or vertical curve alignment.

(4) *Planting materials:* Large to medium trees shall be planted within the median. The minimum median width for tree planting is 18 feet. Where left turn lanes are provided, the minimum width is 8 feet.

(5) *Spacing:* One medium tree shall be planted every 50 feet and shall be a minimum of 6 feet from the BOC. Where left turn lanes and/or crossovers are provided, the planting shall begin 15 feet from the nose of the turning island. Preservation of existing trees and understory vegetation may be used to meet this requirement.

Row (K): Block Length

Row (K) is the maximum block length, in feet.

Row (L): Sidewalks

Row (L) refers to the minimum and maximum width, in feet, of sidewalks. For parkways, the sidewalks shall take the form of multiuse greenways, which may meander at a distance of between 6 to 15 feet from the paved section of the roadway (see § 5.23.10 Pavement Design of this chapter for sidewalk design requirements). Roads and small roads may include sidewalks on only one side of the pavement section. Sidewalks shall be provided on both sides of the pavement section for all other streets.

Row (M): Planting Strip

Row (M) refers to the minimum width, in feet, of the planting strip, located between the curb and sidewalk parallel with the street. For main streets, grated tree wells shall be used in lieu of planting strips.

Row (N): Bike Lanes

Row (N) indicates whether bike lanes are required. Bike lanes may be included as individual bike lanes reserved for bicyclists, combined with trails, or striped as part of the street system. Bike lanes shall conform to the geometric design criteria as shown in Table 5-28.

Bike lanes shall connect to and align with the [LOCAL GOVERNMENT] bike lane plan and bike lanes on abutting property. Dimensional standards for bike route signage shall comply with the *Manual on Uniform Traffic Control Devices* (MUTCD).[8] Bike paths shall be paved with a minimum 2-inch thick asphaltic concrete top course placed on a 6-inch thick select granular subbase. The right-of-way outside of the paved lane shall be graded to provide clearance from trees, poles, walls, fences, guardrails, or other lateral obstructions.

Row (O): Trees

Column (O) indicates whether street trees are required. Street tree planting areas shall be a minimum of 4 feet. Street trees shall be located within the right-of-way on both sides of and parallel to the street. If sidewalks are used, street trees shall be located between the sidewalk and curb.

5.23.4 Connectivity

Purpose and findings: The [LOCAL GOVERNMENT] finds that discontinuous street systems are inefficient. Channel traffic onto relatively few points of the transportation network causes undue congestion. A well-connected street network spreads traffic efficiently, provides

Table 5-28
Bike Lane Geometric Design Criteria

Criteria	Bike Paths	Bike Lanes and Bike Routes
Overhead clearance (minimum, feet)	7.2	7.2
Right-of-way width (minimum, feet)	14	—
Lane width (minimum, feet) • Included in street lanes with curbs and no on-street parking (bike lane only, measured from curb face) • Street lanes with on-street parking (minimum, feet, combined bike lane and parking stall)	10	5 14
Stopping sight distance (minimum, feet)	250	—
Centerline radius	300	—

A dash ("—") means "not applicable."

Figure 5-10
Subdivision Connectivity

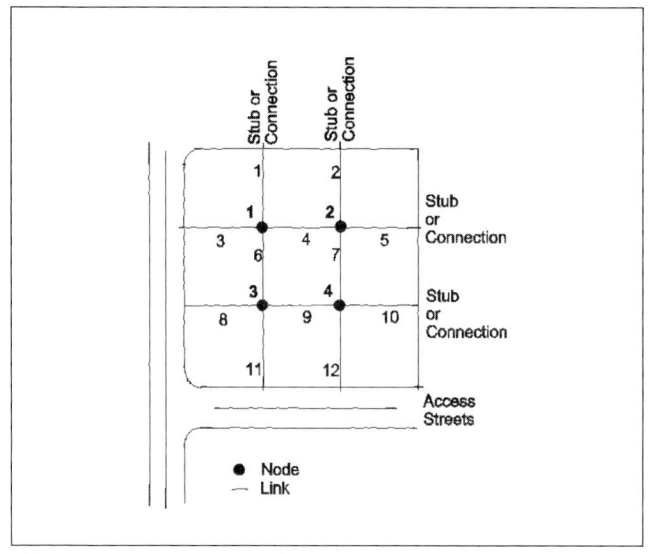

Maintaining connectivity from subdivision to subdivision in lieu of cul-de-sacs to create secondary road capacity.

greater opportunities for access by service and emergency vehicles, and furthers pedestrian mobility by increasing the number of destinations that can be reached by walking. Accordingly, this section provides for both external and internal connectivity. External connectivity is promoted by requiring developers to connect to the existing street network. Internal connectivity is promoted by requiring a connectivity index for internal streets. The [LOCAL GOVERNMENT] acknowledges that there is a market for cul-de-sacs and streets with few connections. The connectivity index preserves the opportunity to provide cul-de-sacs while maintaining the integrity of the network as a whole.

5.23.4.1 Connectivity Index for Internal Streets

The streets within any proposed subdivision shall provide a connectivity index of at least 1.20. A use pattern established by Chapter 2, Use Patterns, of the LDC may require a higher ratio. The connectivity ratio is computed by dividing the number of street links by the number of nodes within the subdivision. For purposes of this section, the intersection of a local street within the proposed subdivision with an arterial or collector street providing access to a proposed subdivision is not considered a node in computing the connectivity ratio. The connectivity ratio does not apply to minor subdivisions.

5.23.4.2 Projecting Streets

Where abutting areas are not subdivided, the arrangement of streets in the subdivision shall connect the streets to the unsubdivided areas. Parcels shall be arranged to allow the opening of future streets and logical further subdivision. Where streets change design in alignment and width, the street design shall provide a transition sufficient to ensure safe and efficient traffic flow. This section is not intended to require local streets to project into floodplains, bluffs, or other natural features or existing development that has not made accommodations for connection (see Figure 5-10).

5.23.4.3 Reserve Strips Prohibited

There shall be no reserve strips controlling access to land dedicated or intended to be dedicated to public use.

5.23.4.4 Half-streets

In the case of collector or local streets, no new half-street rights-of-way shall be platted. Where the proposed subdivision abuts an existing half-street, the other half of the street shall be platted.

5.23.4.5 Dead-end Streets

Dead-end streets are prohibited except as stubs to permit future expansion.

5.23.4.6 Nonaccess Easement

Where the connectivity index required in § 5.23.4.1 Connectivity Index for Internal Streets of this chapter is not reduced, a vehicular nonaccess easement is permitted to control ingress and egress to vehicular traffic.

5.23.4.7 Secondary Access

At least one access point into a single-family residential subdivision shall be provided for every 2,640 feet (1/2 mile) of frontage. Where a single-family residential subdivision exceeds 125 units, a secondary access will be required.

5.23.5 Cul-de-Sacs

The [LOCAL GOVERNMENT] finds and determines that the use of cul-de-sacs and dead-end streets is inconsistent with the public policy of preserving an interconnected street system. Cul-de-sacs and dead-end streets do not promote street connectivity, and create inefficiencies in the distribution of traffic and water as well as inefficiencies and increased municipal expenses in the delivery of public services. In limited situations, cul-de-sacs can be used to avoid disturbing sensitive environmental features. In addition, there is a strong market demand for cul-de-sac lots in many communities. Accordingly, this section restricts the use of cul-de-sacs to appropriate situations and establishes standards for development that utilize cul-de-sac streets.

5.23.5.1 Applicability

A cul-de-sac is a street, or a system of streets, having only one end open to traffic and the other end being permanently terminated and a vehicular turn-around provided. However, in situations where cul-de-sacs are permitted, they shall comply with this section. This section does not apply to a conservation subdivision use pattern. Cul-de-sacs are not permitted for the TND or TOD use patterns.

5.23.5.2 Generally

An applicant seeking a modification from this section shall demonstrate that the strict application of § 5.23.5.1 Applicability of this chapter will produce unnecessary hardship as the result of extreme topographic conditions. For purposes of this section, the following shall be considered "extreme topographic conditions":

(A) Slopes exceeding 20 percent;

(B) Marshes, wetlands, rivers, lakes, streams, or ponds; and

(C) Areas within a critical area protected by *Division 5: Environmental Protection of Critical Areas* of this chapter.

5.23.5.3 Right-of-Way and Pavement Design

(A) Cul-de-sacs and dead-end streets shall terminate in circular rights-of-way having a minimum pavement width radius of 45 feet for residential uses and 60 feet for commercial/industrial uses.

(B) In no event shall the cul-de-sac exceed the lengths established in Column (B) of Table 5-29.

5.23.5.4 Access Restriction

The site plan or subdivision plat shall show a stub connecting the cul-de-sac to adjoining areas or parcels where future roadways are delineated in the thoroughfare plan or a recorded subdivision or site plan. The

Table 5-29
Cul-de-sac Length (Maximum)

(A) Zoning District	(B) Maximum Cul-de-sac/Dead-End Street Length (Feet)
"RP" (Resource Protection) "RE" (Residential Estate)	600
"NS" (Neighborhood Suburban) "PD" (Planned Development)	150
"NU" (Neighborhood Urban)	75
"O" (Office) "CN" (Commercial Neighborhood) "CG" (Commercial General) "CL" (Commercial Large-Scale) "D" (Downtown) "IL" (Industrial Light) "IH" (Industrial Heavy) "MX" (Mixed Use)	50

stub shall be improved as a pedestrian walkway, trail, or bikeway.

5.23.5.5 Landscaping

At least 40 percent of the bulb of the cul-de-sac shall be landscaped in accordance with the standards set forth in the standards for subdivision entrance landscaping (§ 5.35 Entrance Landscaping of this chapter). For cul-de-sacs with a radius exceeding 80 feet, at least 25 square feet of the area within the turnaround area shall be landscaped (see Figure 5-11).

5.23.6 Street Intersections

Streets shall intersect at an angle of at least 75 degrees or more than 110 degrees. The centerline offset of intersections shall be at least 175 feet.

5.23.7 Street Names and Signage

5.23.7.1 Generally

Names of new streets shall not duplicate the names of existing streets unless the new street continues or aligns with an existing street. All new street names shall be submitted to and approved by the U.S. Postal Service.

5.23.7.2 Street Name Signs

Street name signs shall be installed at all intersections within and abutting the subdivision. Such signs shall be manufactured and installed by the subdivider in accordance with specifications of, and subject to plan reviews and inspections by, the [ENGINEERING OFFICIAL]. Street name signs shall not be accepted by the [LOCAL GOVERNMENT] until the street has been accepted for maintenance by the [LOCAL GOVERN-

**Figure 5-11
Cul-de-sac Landscaping**

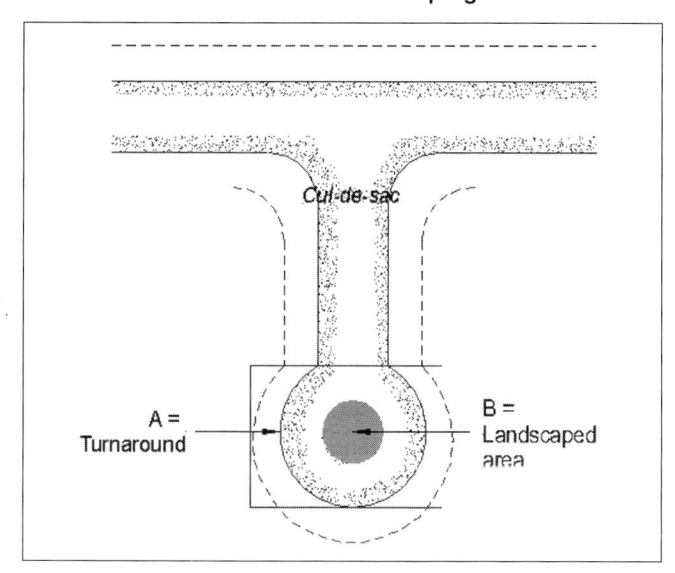

A = Turnaround
B = Landscaped area

MENT], unless approved by the [PLANNING OFFICIAL] in order to provide mail service.

5.23.7.3 Warning and Regulatory Traffic Signs

Within the [LOCAL GOVERNMENT] limits, warning and regulatory traffic signs shall be installed within and shall abut the subdivision in accordance with the MUTCD.[9]

5.23.8 Street Lights

Street lights shall be provided in all subdivisions within the [LOCAL GOVERNMENT]. Street lights shall conform to the [ENGINEERING SPECIFICATIONS].

5.23.9 Private Streets

5.23.9.1 Applicability

Private streets are permitted within Planned Development ("PD") districts.

5.23.9.2 Private Street Geometric Design

The design standards and construction specifications of private streets shall be the same as for public streets.

5.23.9.3 Certification

Upon completion of construction, the [PLANNING OFFICIAL] shall be provided with a written certification signed by a professional engineer, certifying that the private streets and sidewalks were designed and installed as required by this section.

5.23.9.4 Maintenance

Private streets and sidewalks shall be owned and maintained by an HOA, a community association, or other legal entity established for this purpose.

5.23.10 Pavement Design

5.23.10.1 Pavement Structure

The design of pavement structures shall conform to the *Guide for Design of Pavement Structures*.[10] The pavement design report shall be prepared and signed by, or shall be under the supervision of, a professional engineer.

5.23.10.2 Length of Service Life

Pavement shall be designed for a 20-year service life.

5.23.10.3 Serviceability

The "serviceability" of a pavement is defined as the pavement's ride quality and its ability to serve the type of traffic (e.g., automobiles and trucks) that uses the facility. The initial serviceability index (p0) for flexible pavements shall be 4.2; for rigid pavements, it shall be 4.5. The minimum terminal serviceability index (Pt) for local streets shall be 2.0; for collectors and arterials, it shall be 2.5. A standard deviation (S0) for flexible pavement shall be 0.45; for rigid pavement, it shall be 0.35.

5.23.10.4 Roadbed Soil

A soil investigation must be performed for the design of pavement structures. The number of borings and locations shall be sufficient to accurately determine the stratum along the route. Any existing soil information that is available either from the [LOCAL GOVERNMENT] or from private sources will be evaluated and, if determined to be applicable and valid, will be allowed in place of new soil tests.

Roadbed soil having a plasticity index (PI) greater than 20 shall be treated with lime to reduce the PI below 20. Application rate of lime shall be determined based on laboratory testing. In no case shall the lime be less than 15 pounds per square yard for 6 inches of lime-treated subgrade. Lime-treated subgrade will be included as a "structural layer" within the pavement design calculations. Proposals for stabilization alternatives in place of the use of lime will be considered upon submittal of an engineering report verifying adequate stabilization of the highly plastic soil.

Where the roadbed is in a rock excavation, a "structural layer" within the pavement design calculations can be used that is equivalent to a structural layer for lime-stabilized subgrade. If a roadbed structural layer is used in the pavement calculation for rock subgrade, an engineering report will be provided to public works addressing the consistency of the subgrade prior to base placement.

5.23.10.5 Pavement Layer Material

The combination of the following materials are permitted for the pavement structure:

(A) Lime treatment for subgrade;
(B) Flexible base;
(C) Prime coat;
(D) Tack coat;
(E) Hot-mix asphaltic concrete pavement;
(F) Asphalt-treated base;
(G) Reinforced concrete; and
(H) Base reinforcement (Geogrids).

5.23.10.6 Minimum Layer Thickness (Compacted)

If the following components are utilized in proposed pavement sections, the minimum thickness for the components shall be the following:

(A) Hot-mix asphaltic concrete pavement shall not be less than 1-1/2 inches thick for surface course;
(B) Hot-mix asphaltic concrete pavement shall not be less than 2-1/2 inches thick for a leveling-up course;
(C) Asphalt-treated base shall not be less than 4 inches thick;
(D) Flexible base shall not be less than 6 inches thick; and
(E) Lime treatment for subgrade shall not be less than 6 inches thick.

5.23.11 Sidewalks

5.23.11.1 Applicability

Sidewalks are required on both sides of all internal streets and the subdivision side of all adjacent or perimeter streets, except as specified in § 5.23.11.2 Sidewalk Exceptions of this chapter. Reverse frontage lots shall have sidewalks provided on both street frontages.

5.23.11.2 Sidewalk Exceptions

The planning commission may waive all or part of the sidewalk requirements in the following situations:

(A) When the [PLANNING OFFICIAL] determines that the sidewalks will interfere with or disrupt drainage;
(B) When the [PLANNING OFFICIAL] determines that public construction that requires sidewalk replacement will take place on the street within three years; and
(C) In single- or two-family residential subdivisions with a density less than one dwelling unit per acre.

5.23.11.3 Location

The field inspector may approve changes in the sidewalk location for a maximum linear distance of 200 feet without amending the street plan or utility layout provided if the plans are annotated with a note stating that intent. During the plat review process, reviewing agencies may designate areas where prior approval of the agency is necessary for any alteration to the sidewalk location. No other changes are permitted without the approval of all agencies that approved the original utility layout.

5.23.11.4 Continuity

Sidewalks shall align vertically and horizontally with abutting sidewalks. Sidewalks shall not be installed in such a manner that they conflict with or are obstructed by power lines, telephone poles, fire hydrants, traffic/street signs, mailboxes, trees, buildings, barriers, light poles, or any other structure. The grades of sidewalks shall be such that changes of grades greater than 10 percent are not encountered within blocks. When there is an existing or anticipated obstruction, the sidewalk shall be installed around the object and shall provide the required sidewalk width. When utility layouts are required as part of a plat, the location and extent of sidewalks within the subdivision shall be shown on the utility layout and shall be subject to the approval of the [PLANNING OFFICIAL] and the utility agencies.

5.23.12 Access and Driveways

5.23.12.1 Applicability

This section applies to all driveways. A lot that is a part of an approved plat, which does not otherwise limit access, which was approved by the [LOCAL GOVERNMENT] and filed for record as of the effective date of this section, and which does not have sufficient frontage to meet the driveway approach spacing requirements in this section, is allowed one driveway approach.

5.23.12.2 Single-Family Residential Subdivisions

(A) Lots occupied by single-family dwelling units shall not front on a collector or arterial street except as provided in subsections (B) or (C), below. Access points that permit vehicular access lots subject to this subsection are prohibited.

(B) Subsection (A), above, does not apply if:

(1) The lot is at least 1 acre in size; and

(2) The lot includes a permanent vehicular turn-around to prevent backing onto the collector or arterial street. This restriction shall be noted on the plat.

(C) If conditions are such that vehicular access to such lots cannot be provided other than from the collector or arterial street, the [PLANNING OFFICIAL] may permit the creation of a marginal access street or easement to serve two or more lots. The marginal access street or easement shall be designed to permit entry to the thoroughfare without requiring a motorist to execute a backing maneuver. Marginal access streets or easements shall be included on the subdivision plat.

**Figure 5-12
Cross Access**

Separate access

Cross access

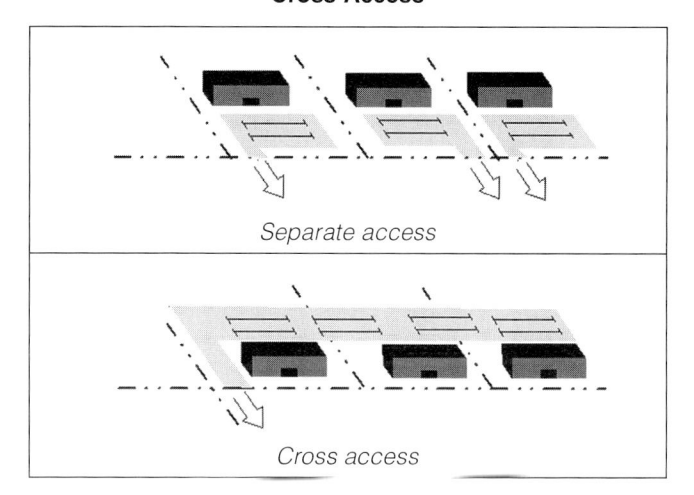

5.23.12.3 Nonresidential, Multifamily, or Mixed-Use Developments

Lots in all other zoning districts, or lots that are not used for single-family or duplex dwellings, are permitted vehicular access from a collector or higher-order street subject to this section. The number of access points shall not exceed one for every 200 feet of frontage.

5.23.12.4 Cross Access

All lots in commercial or mixed-use zoning districts that front an arterial or collector street shall provide an access connection to abutting parking areas that is at least 36 feet in width. The applicant may grant a common access easement across the lot or recorded deed covenant providing common access across the lot with adjacent lot or lots as mitigation pursuant to Chapter 6, Adequate Public Facilities, of the LDC (see Figure 5-12).

5.23.12.5 Location of Access Points

The location of access points shall be based on the following criteria:

(A) The access point shall not conflict with vehicle turning movements; and

(B) The access point shall be located at least 50 feet from an intersection.

On collector or higher-order streets in a commercial zoning district, the driveway approaches shall be located by a distance of at least 90 percent of the frontage length, or 125 feet, whichever distance is less.

5.23.12.6 Alignment

(A) Access points shall align with opposing driveway approaches, if any, or shall be offset by at least 150 feet. The [PLANNING OFFICIAL] may waive this requirement if the applicant provides a cross access as provided in § 5.23.12.4 Cross Access of this chapter.

(B) Access points shall align with the existing median opening. No cuts through the left turn reservoir of a median are permitted.

5.23.12.7 Driveway Throat or Vehicle Storage Length

For purposes of this section, "throat length" means the length extending from the entry into the site to the first left turn conflict or intersection with a parking aisle. "Vehicle storage length" means the length of a driveway, service lane, bay, or other passageway for motor vehicles that is designed to minimize queuing onto surrounding streets. Throat length shall be designed in accordance with the anticipated storage length for entering and exiting vehicles to prevent vehicles from backing into the flow of traffic on the public street or causing unsafe conflicts with on-site circulation. Throat length and vehicle storage length shall conform to Table 5-30 unless approved by the [PLANNING OFFICIAL]. These measures apply to the principal access to the property and not to driveways where access is restricted to one driving lane or to loading or service entries.

5.23.12.8 Parking Approaches

Parking aisles shall be located a minimum of 20 feet from the intersection of the driveway approach and the thoroughfare.

5.23.12.9 Driveway Approaches

Driveway approach materials may be asphalt, concrete, or other materials as provided in the [ENGINEERING SPECIFICATIONS].

5.23.13 Gated Subdivision Streets

Gated streets are subject to the following and § 5.23.9 Private Streets of this chapter.

5.23.13.1 Pavement Management

The applicant shall include with the HOA documents a forecast and schedule of street maintenance costs prepared by a professional engineer. A maintenance account with seed money shall be established by the developer to enable the HOA to meet the maintenance schedule until the HOA is self-sufficient. Any HOA requesting that the [LOCAL GOVERNMENT] acquire their private streets shall produce documentation that the maintenance schedule set forth in the HOA's original pavement management plan as part of the HOA documents has been followed.

5.23.13.2 Fire Lanes

The HOA documents shall require the HOAs to identify and enforce a no-parking restriction in fire lanes throughout the community.

**Table 5-30
Minimum Driveway Throat Lengths**

Land Use	Throat Length or Vehicle Storage Length
Shopping centers > 200,000 gross land area (GLA)	Throat length: 200 feet
Developments < 200,000 GLA not otherwise enumerated in this table	Throat length: 75 feet
Unsignalized driveways not otherwise enumerated in this table	Throat length: 40 feet minimum
Residential subdivision entryway (private, gated entries)	The entryway shall provide for vehicle turnaround capability based on the single-unit design vehicle as provided in the AASHTO Green Book.[†] The minimum entryway vehicle storage length is 40 feet.
Single-lane drive-in banks	Sufficient to accommodate minimum queue of six vehicles
Drive-in banks with more than one lane	Sufficient to accommodate minimum queue of four vehicles per service lane
Single-lane drive-through car washes	Sufficient to accommodate minimum queue of 12 vehicles
Automatic or self-serve car washes with more than one bay	Vehicle storage of 60 feet per bay
Fast-food restaurants with drive-in window service	Sufficient to accommodate minimum queue of eight vehicles per service lane
Gasoline service stations with pump islands perpendicular to the pavement edge	Minimum 35 feet between pump islands and right-of-way

[†] AASHTO Green Book: A Policy on Geometric Design of Highways and Streets, *5th ed.* (Washington, DC: American Association of State and Highway Transportation Officials, 2004).

5.23.13.3 Master Key Security System

A master key security system shall be provided on all gates. The security system shall include the following:
 (A) A gate override in case of power failure; and
 (B) A master key provided to the fire department, the school district, and the police department.

5.23.13.4 Queuing

At gated entrances where traffic can queue into public streets, the gates-and-entrances design must provide for sufficient storage capacity such that no queuing vehicles will queue into the public street. The entryway, including the paved surface area lying between the street providing access to the subdivision and the gates, shall include a turning radius of at least 40 feet.

5.23.14 Traffic Calming

5.23.14.1 Applicability

This section applies to local streets. Streets exceeding 300 feet in length shall include an approved traffic calming feature. The distance between traffic calming features shall not exceed the block length standards established in *Division 2: Design Standards* of this chapter.

5.23.14.2 Traffic Control Calming Features

The following provisions describe and establish standards for permitted traffic calming devices where traffic calming measures are permitted as part of the roadway design elements in § 5.23.14.1 Applicability of this chapter. The descriptions below are described in the document entitled *Traffic Calming: State of the Practice*.[11] Traffic calming options for local streets are noted in Table 5-31.

5.23.14.3 Maintenance

Maintenance of landscaping associated with traffic calming features shall be the sole responsibility of the HOA.

5.24 UTILITIES

This section provides for design and construction policies and standards for utility and transportation infrastructure, capital improvements projects, public facilities, and development projects that reinforce neighborhood centers and provide diverse, pedestrian-friendly neighborhoods. It encourages utility and telephone line locations to be in the rear of property, underground, or otherwise give aesthetic and economic consideration to alternative locations.

5.24.1 Applicability

This section applies to all persons, and political subdivisions of the state, designing or installing or causing to be designed or installed the following:
 (A) Sanitary sewers;
 (B) Storm sewers;
 (C) Water transmission or distribution lines;
 (D) Electric power lines that provide incentive and encourage the use of solar and other renewable energy sources;
 (E) Telephone lines;
 (F) Natural gas lines;
 (G) Cable television lines; and
 (H) Rain water capture systems.

Table 5-31
Approved Traffic Control Devices and Description

Device	Description
Neckdowns/flares/street narrowing/ intersection throating:	Neckdowns are curb extensions at intersections that reduce roadway width curb to curb. They are sometimes called slow points, nubs, bulbouts, knuckles, or intersection narrowing. These traffic control measures reduce the width of a section of roadway in a gradual manner. They shorten crossing distances for pedestrians and draw attention to pedestrians via raised peninsulas. By tightening curb radii at the corner, the pedestrian crossing distance is reduced and the speeds of turning vehicles are reduced. The effect of this measure is to reduce speed and discourage nonlocal traffic. Motorists react to this measure with slower speed because of a concern of a limited travel path.
Roundabouts/traffic circles:	These are raised circular structures constructed at a three- or four-way intersection. Their objectives are to slow speeding and reduce the number and severity of vehicular accidents. This measure is most suitable for wide intersections and may accommodate all sizes of vehicles by applying appropriate engineering designs.
Speed humps:	These are raised pavement features constructed across the width of the street. The speed hump shall be 3 inches high and 12 feet long from the leading edge to the trailing edge. This feature discourages motorists from speeding and encourages them to obey the posted speed limit. When speed humps are constructed, advisory signs shall be installed to notify motorists of the speed hump and an appropriate advisory travel speed
Median islands:	These are raised, circular landscaped areas located within nonintersection, midblock locations. Median islands channelize traffic and separate opposing flows. Traffic must slow down to maneuver around a median island. Median islands offer landscaping opportunities and maintenance responsibility. Median islands can be used to protect existing trees.
"T" intersections:	These are located at grade intersections where one of the intersecting street links is perpendicular to the other two. Traffic must slow down to negotiate the turning maneuvers in a "T" intersection. This roadway feature is very common. Motorists are familiar with T intersections.

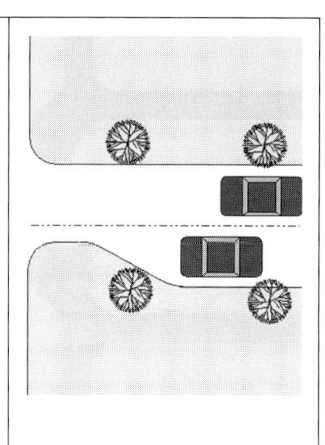

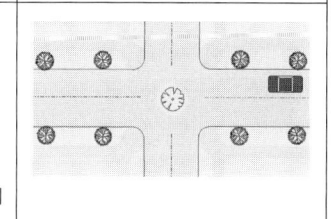

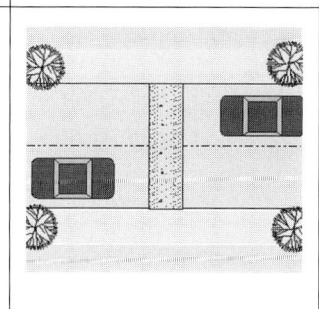

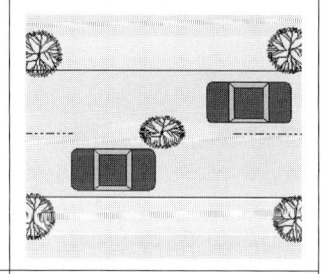

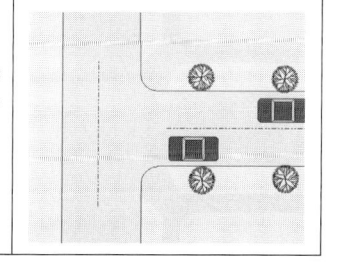

5.24.2 Generally

Easements shall be provided for the utilities set forth in § 5.24.1 Applicability of this chapter. Easement widths shall comply with the [ENGINEERING SPECIFICATIONS].

5.24.3 Central Water and Sewer Required

The proposed development shall connect to the [NAME OF CENTRAL WATER/SEWER SYSTEM], except as provided in § 5.15.4 Control of Glare— Luminaire Design Factors or § 5.15.5 Prohibitions of this chapter.

5.24.4 Private Water System

A water supply and distribution system is not required for subdivisions that meet all of the following conditions:

(A) The subdivision is located outside the service area included within the [WATER/SEWER MASTER PLAN];

(B) Each lot has a minimum size of 2 acres;

(C) A potable groundwater supply that meets the [STATE OR LOCAL HEALTH DEPARTMENT] drinking water standards underlies each lot, and such water is available in sufficient quantity to furnish the domestic water needs of the improvements to be constructed on the individual lots within the subdivision; and

(D) A rain water capture, storage, and treatment facility that meets sustainability criteria in § 5.53 Sustainability of this chapter is approved and installed.

(E) The plat of the subdivision is annotated with the following note:

> I certify to the best of my knowledge that at the time of planning commission approval, a potable groundwater supply that meets the current standards as established by the [STATE OR LOCAL HEALTH DEPARTMENT] for drinking water underlies each lot, and such water is of sufficient quantity to supply the domestic needs of the improvements to be constructed on the individual lots within the subdivision. Each individual property owner is responsible for the construction of an individual water well that is in compliance with the rules and regulations of the [STATE OR LOCAL HEALTH DEPARTMENT].
>
> Professional Engineer
>
> Sworn and subscribed before me this the _____ day of _____ [YEAR].
>
> Notary Public

5.24.5 Private Wastewater System

Connection to a central sanitary sewer system is not required for a subdivision that complies with the following conditions:

(A) The subdivision is located outside the service area included within the [WATER/SEWER MASTER PLAN];

(B) Connection to a central sanitary sewer system will require unreasonable expenditure when compared with other methods of sewage disposal. Such cost estimates shall be prepared by a professional engineer and shall be approved by the [PUBLIC WORKS OFFICIAL]; and

(C) The [STATE OR LOCAL HEALTH DEPARTMENT] approves the nonsite sewage disposal system.

5.24.6 Easements

5.24.6.1 Generally

Easements are permitted for a specific purpose when requested by a particular utility. Such specific use easements shall be a part of a lot or lots unless designated to be converted into a public street right-of-way. Easements may be designated to be converted into a public street right-of-way on a subsequent plat without vacating and replatting. Such easement shall be annotated with the following note:

> Easement to expire upon incorporation into a platted public street right-of-way.

5.24.6.2 Use of Easements

If the owner of the property upon which a utility easement is located desires to use it for lawn purposes, fencing across the easement is permitted if gates along the side lot lines are provided. The gates shall be 16 feet wide (two 8-foot gates) and shall be capable of being opened and closed at all times. The gates shall remain unlocked at all times. The property owner is responsible for the maintenance of the unused easement area even though it may be located beyond the rear fence of the property.

5.24.6.3 Maintenance

The property owner shall maintain the utility easement. The property owner shall keep the area clear of any structure, debris, vegetation, trees, shrubs, or landscaping, except that lawn grass that is regularly mowed is permitted.

5.24.6.4 Curb Exposure

Normal curb exposure shall be maintained where utility easements intersect streets.

5.24.6.5 Connection of Easements

Where utility easements are not straight within each block, or if they do not connect on a straight course with the utility easements of abutting blocks, an additional easement shall be provided for the placing of guy wires on lot division lines in order to support poles set on curving or deviating rights-of-way or alleys.

5.24.6.6 Structures Within Easements

No portion of a structure shall be placed within an easement, except for fences, as provided in § 5.14 Fences and Walls of this chapter.

5.24.6.7 Overhang Easements

Alleys shall include overhang easements for electric and telephone lines of at least 4 feet on each side of the alley strip with a minimum height of 18 feet.

DIVISION 4: GREENSPACE (LANDSCAPING, TREE PRESERVATION, SCREENING, AND ENVIRONMENTAL PROTECTION) STANDARDS

Purpose and findings: These landscaping, street tree, screening, and buffer requirements are designed to:
- Protect the health, safety, and general welfare of the public;
- Enhance property values;
- Improve the appearance of the community through preservation of natural resources, trees, and native plants; and
- Maintain the ecological balance of the area.

These minimum requirements will:
- Safeguard and enhance property values;
- Protect public and private investment;
- Encourage preservation of existing trees and other significant vegetation;
- Encourage proper selection, installation, and maintenance of plant materials that result in the conservation of natural resources, including water;
- Reduce the negative environmental effects of development while protecting and enhancing the value of developed properties and the surrounding area;
- Reduce soil erosion and increase infiltration in permeable land areas essential to stormwater management and aquifer recharge;
- Mitigate air, dust, noise, heat, chemical pollution and glare, and other adverse environmental effects of development;
- Reduce the "heat-island" effect of impervious surfaces, such as parking lots, by cooling and shading the surface area and breaking up large expanses of pavement;
- Establish a landscape theme, including street trees and streetscape designs, to be used throughout the [LOCAL GOVERNMENT] to promote the overall character and identity of the community;
- Address the design of entryways into the [LOCAL GOVERNMENT] to express the community's values;
- Preserve existing native vegetation as an integral part of the wildlife habitats, and incorporate native plants and ecosystems into landscape design;
- Promote innovative and cost-conscious approaches to the design, installation, and maintenance of landscaping while encouraging xeriscape planting techniques and water and energy conservation;
- Screen unsightly equipment or materials from the view of persons on public streets or abutting properties and buffering from uncomplimentary land uses;
- Maintain and increase property values by requiring site-appropriate landscaping to be incorporated into development that is designed and installed by a qualified landscape professional;
- Promote walkable, pedestrian-scale streetscapes, traditional neighborhoods, and compact centers by exempting uses that relate to each other functionally and visually from certain requirements of this section;
- Promote water conservation through rain water capture, treatment, and storage, and efficient landscape and irrigation design; and
- Promote and protect the health, safety, and welfare of the public by creating an urban environment that is aesthetically pleasing and that promotes economic development through an enhanced quality of life.

5.30 GREENSPACE AREAS, GENERALLY

5.30.1 Applicability

5.30.1.1 Generally

Greenspace areas include buffers (§ 5.31 Buffers and Screening), streetscape landscaping (§ 5.32 Streetscape Landscaping), building landscaping (§ 5.33 Building Landscaping), parking lot landscaping (§ 5.34 Parking Lot Landscaping), entrance landscaping (§ 5.35 Entrance Landscaping), house-lot landscaping (§ 5.36 House-Lot Landscaping), and tree save areas (§ 5.37 Tree Preservation and Tree Save Areas) of this chapter. This division applies to the applications described in Table 5-32.

5.30.1.2 Expansion

When a building or parking lot is enlarged, the requirements of this division apply on an incremental basis. This means that landscaping is required in the same proportion that the enlarged building area or off-street parking area has to the existing development (e.g., a 10 percent increase requires 10 percent of the required landscaping).

5.30.1.3 Exemptions

This section does not apply to the following situations:
(A) Residential uses located within a residential zoning district;
(B) Agricultural uses;
(C) The reconstruction of an existing building of which 50 percent or less of the floor area was destroyed or ruined by flooding, fire, wind storm, or act of God. This exemption shall apply only where reconstruction of that building will not result in an increase in building size or paving area of the parking facilities to be provided;
(D) Interior finish work or remodeling in a portion of a building unless the work results in an increase in the

**Table 5-32
Applicability of General Standards**

Type of Development	Buffer [a]	Streetscape Landscaping [b]	Building Landscaping [c]	Parking Lot Landscaping [d]	Entrance Landscaping [e]	House-Lot Landscaping [f]	Tree Save Areas [g]
Commercial zoning districts/commercial subdivisions	✓	✓	✓	✓			✓
Use patterns		✓	✓	✓			✓
Residential subdivisions		✓			✓		✓
Planned developments	✓	✓	✓	✓	✓		✓
Multifamily dwelling units	✓	✓	✓	✓	✓		✓
Single-family or duplex lots						✓	

[a] § 5.31 Buffers and Screening of this chapter.
[b] § 5.32 Streetscape Landscaping of this chapter.
[c] § 5.33 Building Landscaping of this chapter.
[d] § 5.34 Parking Lot Landscaping of this chapter.
[e] § 5.35 Entrance Landscaping of this chapter.
[f] § 5.36 House-Lot Landscaping of this chapter.
[g] § 5.37 Tree Preservation and Tree Save Areas of this chapter.

paving area of the parking facilities within the street yard or in an enlargement of the exterior dimensions of an existing building;

(E) Any use, building, or structure for which only a change of use is requested and which requires no structural modifications that increase its volume or scale;

(F) Single-family dwellings located on an existing lot of record;

(G) Buildings within the street yard of another building; and

(H) A building located within the street yard of another building, which shall be considered as a separate building site unless it has previously been included within an approved greenspace plan.

5.30.2 Interpretation of Terms

Where necessary to interpret the precise meaning of technical landscaping terms used in this division, reference shall be made to the *American Standard for Nursery Stock*.[12]

5.30.3 Greenspace Plan

Applications subject to this division shall include a greenspace plan bearing the seal of a registered landscape architect (see Appendix B, Specifications for Documents to Be Submitted, of the LDC for contents). The greenspace plan shall be approved as part of the underlying application.

5.30.4 Acceptable Landscape Materials

(A) No artificial plant materials shall be used to satisfy the requirements of this section.

(B) Plant materials required by this section shall comply with the minimum size requirements of Table 5-33 at the time of installation. Plant height shall be measured from the average grade level of the immediate planting area to the top horizontal plane of the shrub at planting; for single-trunk trees, the measurement shall be taken at 6 inches above grade level; for multitrunk trees, the tree shall be measured from the average grade level of the immediate planting area.

(C) Planting areas shall consist of permeable surface areas only. The permeable surface areas for shrubs may be included within permeable surface areas required for trees.

(D) In satisfying the requirements of this section, the use of 4 inches of organic mulch material shall be provided at the time of planting.

(E) Each large tree, small tree, or large shrub shall be planted at least 30 inches from the edge of any paved surface.

**Table 5-33
Minimum Greenspace Planting Specifications**

Landscape Feature	Minimum Caliper at the Time of Planting	Minimum Height at the Time of Planting	Minimum Planting Area
Trees	1-1/2 inches for single-trunk trees	Not applicable except for multitrunk trees, in which case the tree shall be a minimum of 6 feet in height at the time of planting	100 square feet
Small trees	1-1/2 inches for single-trunk trees	6 feet for multitrunk trees	25 square feet
Large shrubs	Not applicable	2 feet	9 square feet
Small to medium shrubs	Not applicable	1 foot	8 square feet

5.30.5 Protection of Plant Areas

5.30.5.1 Generally

Plant areas must be protected from vehicular traffic through the use of concrete curbs, wheel stops, or other permanent barriers.

5.30.5.2 Maintenance

Required plants shall be maintained in a healthy condition at all times. The property owner shall provide weeding, mowing of grass, irrigation, fertilization, prevention of pests, pruning, and other maintenance of all plantings as needed. Any plant that dies shall be replaced with another living plant that is comparable to the existing plant materials or plant materials specified in the approved greenspace plan within 90 days after notification by the [LOCAL GOVERNMENT]. The [PLANNING OFFICIAL] may extend this time period up to an additional 90 days due to weather considerations. If the plants have not been replaced after appropriate notification and/or extension, the property owner, or his/her designee or leasee, shall be in violation of this chapter.

5.30.5.3 Utility Lines

Any damage to utility lines resulting from the negligence of the property owner or his/her agents or employees in the installation and maintenance of required landscaping in a utility easement is the responsibility of the property owner. If a public utility disturbs plants within a utility easement, it shall preserve the plants and return them to their prior locations after the utility work. The property owner shall replace all required plants that die.

5.30.5.4 Irrigation

Landscaped areas shall be irrigated with a system that is suitable for the type of plantings installed. Where an irrigation system is required, the irrigation system shall comply with the requirements of [STATE LANDSCAPE IRRIGATION STANDARDS]. No irrigation is required for a Type N buffer if no additional planting is required. The [PLANNING OFFICIAL] may waive the irrigation requirements if no additional planting is required to meet this criteria.

5.31 BUFFERS AND SCREENING

This section:
- Provides landscaped separation between residential and nonresidential uses where appropriate;
- Screens from view certain land uses that may create visual clutter and distraction; and
- Provides for increases in the width and opacity of the buffer yard as the land-use intensity of the new or expanded development increases.

5.31.1 Applicability

5.31.1.1 Generally

This section applies to any of the following, except where exempted by § 5.31.1.2 Exemptions of this chapter:

(A) The construction or erection of any new building or structure for which a development approval is required;

(B) Any enlargement exceeding 1,000 square feet or 10 percent in area, whichever is greater, of the exterior dimensions of an existing building for which a development approval is required; and

(C) Any construction of a new parking lot or expansion of an existing parking lot within the street yard by more than 2,000 square feet or 10 percent in area, whichever is greater.

5.31.1.2 Exemptions

This section does not apply to the following situations:

(A) Single-family dwelling units on existing lots of record;

(B) Agricultural uses;

(C) Commercial uses that abut other commercial uses of the same zoning classification;

(D) Interior finish work or remodeling in a portion of a building unless the work results in an increase in the paving area of the parking facilities within the street yard or in an enlargement of the exterior dimensions of an existing building;

(E) Any use, building, or structure for which only a change of use is requested, and which use does not increase the existing building square footage; and

(F) Contiguous commercial parcels or land areas under common ownership.

5.31.1.3 Reduction in Required Buffer Yards

The buffer yard requirements shall be reduced where:

(A) A buffer yard exists on an abutting property, and the net buffer yard satisfies the minimum buffer yard requirements of this section; or

(B) The abutting property owners have provided a written agreement restricting the use of an established or proposed buffer yard to the uses provided for in this section.

5.31.2 Required Buffer Yards

5.31.2.1 Applicability

Table 5-34 shows when a buffer yard is required for an abutting zoning district. Uses in the "abutting zoning district" are not required to provide the buffer yard. The applicant shall install the type of buffer yard indicated in Table 5-34.

**Table 5-34
Required Buffer Yards**

Zoning District	RP, RE	NS	NU	CN, O	CG, CL	D	IL, IH	Major Arterial	Minor Arterial	Collector
RP, RE	—	—	—	—	—	—	—	—	—	—
NS	—	—	—	—	—	—	—	—	—	—
NU	—	—	—	—	—	—	—	A	—	—
CN, O	C	B	—	—	—	—	E	B	A	A
CG, CL	C	B	—	A	—	—	E	B	A	A
D	—	—	—	—	—	—	—	—	—	—
IL, IH	E	E	E	E	D	—	—	C	C	B

RP = Resource Protection; RE = Residential Estate; NS = Neighborhood Suburban; NU = Neighborhood Urban; CN = Commercial Neighborhood; O = Office; CG = Commercial General; CL = Commercial Large-Scale; D = Downtown; IL = Industrial Light; and IH = Industrial Heavy. A dash ("—") means that the buffer yard is not required. For A, B, C, D, and E, see buffer yard-type designations as shown in Table 5-35.

5.31.2.2 Description of Buffer Yards

There are six types of buffer yards. Table 5-35 illustrates a typical buffer yard and shows the minimum width and number of trees and/or plants required for each 100 lineal feet for each buffer yard. Each buffer yard type provides several plant material options. The applicant may either plant new trees or plants or preserve existing trees or plants within the required buffer that meet the requirements of this section.

5.31.2.3 Canopy Trees

Canopy trees required for Type D and E buffers shall be large shade trees that reach a mature height of at least 60 feet. Where existing or proposed overhead electric lines conflict with tree canopies, understory trees may substitute for canopy trees.

5.31.2.4 Shrubs

At a minimum, 50 percent of the shrubs for Type D and E buffers shall be evergreen.

5.31.3 Natural Buffer Yards

5.31.3.1 Applicability

In order to encourage the preservation of natural vegetation, the applicant may substitute a Type N buffer consistent with Table 5-35 for any category required. Natural areas with native vegetation may be used to meet any of the above buffer yard requirements if the criteria of Table 5-35 are met.

5.31.3.2 Buffer Yard Width Reduction

The width of a buffer yard shall be reduced by 20 percent when the criteria of § 5.31.3.1 Applicability of this chapter are met, provided that the minimum width shall be at least 10 feet.

5.31.3.3 Equivalent Planting Units

The number of equivalent planting units (EPUs) for purposes of applying a Type N buffer (§ 5.31.2.2 Description of Buffer Yards, Table 5-35 of this chapter) shall be calculated based on the following ratios:

(A) Canopy trees = 1 EPU;
(B) Understory = 0.5 EPU;
(C) Large shrubs = 0.25 EPU;
(D) Medium shrubs = 0.1 EPU; and
(E) Small shrubs = 0.05 EPU.

Each buffer Type A through Type E (see § 5.31.2.2 Description of Buffer Yards, Table 5-35 of this chapter) shall be assigned the number of EPUs as described in Table 5-36.

◆ *Note to reader:* Adjust this note to conform to local conditions.

5.31.4 Location of Buffer Yard

(A) A buffer yard required by this section shall be provided along the side or rear lot lines of abutting uses; and

(B) Buffer yards are not required along the front property line.

5.31.5 Permitted Uses Within the Buffer Yard

No active recreation area, storage of materials, parking, or structures, except for necessary utility boxes and equipment, shall be located within the buffer yard. The buffer yard may be included in the required building setback. Buffer yards may be used as greenways as defined in the parks/open space standards (§ 5.21 Parks/Open Space of this chapter).

5.31.6 Size and Type of Plant Materials

Trees shall measure a minimum of 1-1/2 inch caliper when measured 6 inches above grade. Shrubs shall reach a mature height within five growing seasons. In no case shall required shrubs measure less than the height required by Table 5-33 at the time of planting, when measured from the grade to the top horizontal plane of the shrub. Plant materials shall be selected from the approved plant list. Substitutions are permitted based on the recommendation of the qualified landscape professional preparing the plan. In addition, if a listed species is infested by fungi, disease, or pests, a substitution may be recommended.

◆ *Note to reader:* It is recommended that the [LOCAL GOVERNMENT] develop a list of trees and shrubs that

Table 5-35
Minimum Plant Materials Required for Each Buffer Yard Type

Buffer Yard Type		Minimum Width (Feet)	Trees - Canopy	Trees - Understory	Shrubs - Large	Shrubs - Medium	Shrubs - Small	Fence (F), Berm (B), or Wall (W)
A	Option 1	10	2	2	—	—	16	—
A	Option 2	10	2	2	—	8	—	—
B	Option 1	15	5	5	8	12	—	—
B	Option 2	5	2	2	6	8	6	—
C	Option 1	15	2	4	9	8	—	F or W
C	Option 2	15	2	3	10	10	—	F or W
D	Option 1	25	2	4	9	8	—	F or W
D	Option 2	25	2	3	10	10	—	B
E	Option 1	30	2	4	14	4	4	F or W
E	Option 2	30	2	3	12	8	4	B
N		20% reduction with minimum of 10 feet	Any combination of trees or shrubs is acceptable where: • The existing vegetation provides at least the number of equivalent planting units required by this table; or • The existing vegetation provides complete visual screening from the abutting property.					—

A dash ("—") means "not applicable."

Table 5-36
Buffer Yard Density

Buffer Type	Equivalent Planting Units
A	2.3
B	5.2
C	10.8
D	10.8
E	11.7

satisfies these requirements based on local conditions. This list should be attached to the LDC as an appendix.

5.31.7 Fences and Walls

(A) Fences or walls shall be a minimum height of 6 feet when used in Type D, E, and F buffer yards.

(B) No fence or wall is required if an existing fence or wall on an abutting property meets the requirements of this section.

(C) The fence or wall shall be solid and 100 percent opaque, except where otherwise required. Fence material shall be a minimum of 1/2 inches thick and shall be made of wood, precast concrete, metal, or wrought iron with an abutting hedge that provides an opaque barrier. Corrugated and galvanized steel or metal sheets are not permitted.

(D) Walls may be concrete, concrete block with stucco finish, masonry, stone, or a combination of these materials. The support posts shall be placed on and faced toward the inside of the developing property so that the surface of the wall or fence is smooth on the abutting property side.

5.31.8 Berms

Berms shall have a slope not greater than the slope created in 3 horizontal feet with a 1-foot vertical rise. The surface of the berm that is not planted with trees and shrubs shall be covered with grass, perennial ground cover, vines, and woody and herbaceous perennials, with mulch. Grass or other coverings shall be maintained in conformance with applicable [LOCAL GOVERNMENT] codes.

5.31.9 Screening

Off-street loading spaces, refuse and outdoor storage areas, antennas, satellite dishes, and mechanical equipment within the street yard shall be screened from all public streets. The screening shall be a minimum of 6 feet in height or a height sufficient to obscure the area or equipment requiring the screening, whichever is less. The screening may be provided by plants, a solid screen fence or wall, or a combination of walls and plants. The height of plants shall be based on reaching their size at maturity within five growing seasons.

5.31.10 Utilities

Utility companies shall provide a plant buffer within the street yard of electrical substations, water pumping/storage sites, and wastewater treatment plants. The buffer shall comply with the requirements for a Type E buffer as described in Table 5-35.

5.32 STREETSCAPE LANDSCAPING

5.32.1 Applicability

5.32.1.1 Generally

In addition to developments subject to § 5.30.1 Applicability of this chapter, the following are subject to the streetscape planting standards:

(A) All developments with five or more parking spaces; and

(B) All developments requiring subdivision review.

5.32.1.2 Exemptions

(A) Streetscape planting standards do not apply to any street classification unless street trees are required by the street improvement standards (§ 5.23 Street Design and Transportation of this chapter).

(B) If existing site conditions and/or existing development of the property render the planting of street trees impracticable, the applicant may submit a waiver or modification request in accordance with § 5.3 Variances of this chapter.

5.32.2 Street Trees

5.32.2.1 Applicability

This section applies to any street classification that requires trees (see § 5.23.3 Geometric Design and Table 5-27 of this chapter).

5.32.2.2 Planting Materials

(A) Where no existing or proposed overhead utility lines exist, street trees shall be large trees. If existing or proposed overhead utility lines exist along the right-of-way that are greater than 35 feet in height, then the trees shall be medium trees. If existing or proposed overhead utility lines exist along the right-of-way that are lower than 35 feet in height, then the trees shall be small trees.

(B) Preservation of existing trees to meet this requirement is permissible and recommended. A 15-foot existing vegetation buffer along the right-of-way line is required for this option. Waivers for spacing and alignment may be given in order for existing trees to meet street tree requirements.

5.32.2.3 Location

The street trees shall be planted:

(A) Within a planting strip required by § 5.23.3 Geometric Design of this chapter; and

(B) A minimum of 3 feet from the BOC.

5.32.2.4 Spacing

(A) Large trees shall be planted at a minimum ratio of one for every 50 feet.

(B) Medium trees or small trees shall be planted at a minimum ratio of one for every 30 feet.

(C) The spacing requirements are measured as an average of the street frontage along the particular street. In no instance shall the distance between street trees exceed 100 feet on center. Street trees shall be planted in an even, linear spacing. If shifts to the linear spacing not exceeding 10 feet are required due to the location of existing infrastructure, development, or required sight distance, these shifts may be approved by the [ENGINEERING OFFICIAL].

5.33 BUILDING LANDSCAPING

5.33.1 Applicability

This section applies to any commercial or multifamily building that:

(A) Has a building footprint that exceeds 1,000 square feet; and

(B) Is set back at least 20 feet from the front or side property line.

5.33.2 Standards

(A) A minimum of one small or medium shrub is required for each linear foot, and one understory tree is required for each 30 feet of exterior building perimeter.

(B) Building landscaping may be comprised of shrubs or ornamental plants in any combination, provided that at least 50 percent of the total required materials are shrubs.

(C) Building landscaping may be planted in groupings so long as at least the minimum number of required plants is provided.

(D) Building landscaping shall abut the building and shall be used or installed in such a manner as to screen mechanical equipment attached to or adjacent to the building, provide direction to and enhance entrances, and enhance walkways and provide visual breaks along blank building façades. Building landscaping is required on all building sides except those sides facing an alley, openings for overhead or loading-area doors, motor vehicle bays or entrances to the building, or the perimeter of attached or detached canopies.

5.34 PARKING LOT LANDSCAPING

5.34.1 Applicability

Shading is required for parking lots that are located within the street yard and any parking areas (excluding driveways or garages) in residential districts. Canopy trees, as identified on the approved plant list, shall provide shade for a minimum of 25 percent of a parking lot. Small or large trees may be used. A "parking lot" does not include an area used exclusively for the display of motor vehicles for sale as part of an automobile dealership.

5.34.2 Calculation of Shaded Area

(A) Table 5-37 provides the calculation for each of the three sizes of trees as required to create the minimum shade coverage.

(B) The minimum shade coverage shall be determined in accordance with the following formula:

$A \times B = C$

where:

A = percent of site requiring coverage (25 percent);

B = square feet of parking lot area (10,000 square feet); and

C = total number of square feet needed for shade.

Example:

0.20 x 10,000 = 2,000

Large tree = 1,200 square feet of shade (2,000/1,200 square feet = 1 tree)

Small tree = 550 square feet of shade (2,000/550 square feet = 3 trees)

5.34.3 Design

Trees shall be planted within an island at least 9 feet wide by 18 feet deep.

5.35 ENTRANCE LANDSCAPING

5.35.1 Applicability

Proposed developments subject to this requirement shall provide landscaping along or within any street providing access to the subdivision or a multifamily development. This section applies only to streets or driveways internal to the subdivision or proposed development.

Table 5-37
Parking Lot Shading

Category	Standard
Large trees	1,200 square feet per one tree
Medium trees	550 square feet per one tree
Small trees	No small trees shall be counted for canopy requirements

Table 5-38
Entrance Landscaping Standards

Standard	Illustration
Streets or driveways with only two lanes shall provide greenspace at the intersection of the external access street and the internal street or driveway leading into the proposed development.	
Streets or driveways exceeding two lanes or 36 feet shall provide greenspace and shall provide a landscaped median in addition to the greenspace area required above. The landscaped median shall have a minimum width of 8 feet.	
Streets or driveways separated by a distance of at least 40 feet may provide an open space area that conforms to *Division 2: Design Standards* of this chapter in lieu of the greenspace areas described above. Such area shall lie between the streets or driveway entrances. Parks or playgrounds shall not be used pursuant to this section where the external access road exceeds four lanes in width or has a posted speed limit exceeding 35 miles per hour.	

5.35.2 Standards

Subdivisions with 100 or more lots must comply with Table 5-38.

5.36 HOUSE-LOT LANDSCAPING

5.36.1 Applicability

This section applies to any application for approval of a single-family or duplex dwelling unit on a lot of record.

5.36.2 Generally

(A) House-lot landscaping must be located between the principal structure and the street.

(B) At least 20 percent of the calculation area of a site must have canopy cover either by preservation or by installation. The "calculation area" means the total area of the lot or parcel less the building footprint.

(C) If preservation is used, trees must have a protective device around the tree as required by § 5.36 House-Lot Landscaping of this chapter.

5.36.3 Installation Standards

If the canopy cover is accomplished by installation, the following factors shall be used to calculate tree canopy:

(A) A canopy credit of 400 square feet applies to large trees.

(B) A canopy credit of 200 square feet applies to small trees.

(C) The formula for calculating tree planting for canopy coverage required by ordinance is as follows:

(A x B) ÷ C = D

where:

A = percentage of site requiring coverage, as set forth in § 5.36.2 Generally, subsection (B), of this chapter;

B = calculation area, as set forth in § 5.36.2 Generally, subsection (B), of this chapter;

C = total number of square feet of new canopy provided as stated in subsections (A) and (B), above; and

D = number of trees to be provided (by square feet of canopy).

(D) When using varying sizes of trees, the total square footage of new canopy provided must equal the required percentage of the site calculation area. Combinations of large and small trees may be utilized to achieve the required coverage.

5.36.4 Greenspace Plan Not Required

A greenspace plan is not required for an application subject to this section.

5.37 TREE PRESERVATION AND TREE SAVE AREAS

5.37.1 Applicability

(A) This section applies to any application for development approval except as otherwise provided in this section. This section applies to all developers and/or owners of real property involved with the erection, repair, alteration, or removal of any building or structure as well as grading in anticipation of such development.

(B) This section does not apply to the harvesting of trees. For purposes of this section, "harvesting" means cutting or clearing trees for purposes relating to forestry, as defined by state law. "Harvesting" does not

Table 5-39
Preservation Ratios

(A) Area	(B) Preservation Ratio (Percent of Tree Protection Zone Category)
All areas within a riparian buffer (see § 5.40 Riparian Buffers of this chapter) or any "RP" (Resource Protection) district	75%
Lots within any commercial or industrial zoning district	20%
Lots within any neighborhood zoning district, traditional neighborhood development use pattern, or "PD" (Planned Development) district	35%
Lots within the "D" (Downtown) district	Exempt

include the clearing of land for purposes of development, even where the trees are sold for purposes of creating lumber or for related purposes.

(C) This section does not apply to the issuance of a development approval for a single-family residence on an existing platted lot of record.

5.37.2 Tree Protection Zone

For purposes of this section, a "tree protection zone" is established for any lot or parcel that has a woodland coverage of at least 50 percent. The tree protection zone includes all woodland areas within the required setbacks and outside of the designated building envelopes. The percentage of protected trees that must be preserved within the tree protection zone is established in Column (B) of Table 5-39.

5.37.3 Protected Trees

For purposes of this section, a "protected tree" means any large tree that is equal to or larger than 8-inch diameter breast height (DBH).

5.37.4 Preservation Standards

No grading, demolition, trenching, or other activity that may adversely affect trees in this zone may proceed prior to approval and issuance of necessary development approvals by the [LOCAL GOVERNMENT]. No person shall perform construction work (including the operation or storage of equipment or materials) within the drip line of any tree or shrub having its trunk on any public street or public property without first obtaining a development approval from the [PLANNING OFFICIAL] and complying with the requirements as described in § 5.37.4.1 Protective Barriers through § 5.37.4.4 Replacement of this chapter.

5.37.4.1 Protective Barriers

The applicant shall erect protective barriers as follows:
(A) Protective barriers shall be installed around each protected tree or group of protected trees that are designated for protection.
(B) Barriers shall not be supported by the plants they are protecting but shall be self-supporting.
(C) Protective barriers shall be a minimum of 4 feet high and constructed of a durable material that will last until construction is completed.
(D) Protective barriers shall be installed at least 1 foot from the drip line or 1 foot from the trunk of the tree for each 1 inch of tree caliper.

5.37.4.2 Irreparable Damage

Where the [PLANNING OFFICIAL] determines that irreparable damage has occurred to a tree within a tree protection zone, the tree shall be removed and replaced and protective fencing shall be installed as provided in § 5.37.4.1 Protective Barriers of this chapter.

5.37.4.3 Compaction

Where compaction might occur due to traffic or materials storage, the tree protection zone must first be mulched with a minimum 4 inch layer of processed pine bark or wood chips or a 6-inch layer of pine straw.

5.37.4.4 Replacement

When trees designated or planted in accordance with this section die or are removed for any reason, they must be replaced during the next suitable planting season in a manner, quantity, and size approved by the [PLANNING OFFICIAL].

5.37.5 Tree Survey Required

(A) Applications for development approvals and zoning clearance development approvals on all property subject to this section shall provide a tree survey as part of the greenspace plan.
(B) The tree survey shall include all trees of 8-inch DBH and larger within the tree protection zone and all trees over 1-inch caliper and 6 feet in height on the public right-of-way. Stands of species may be indicated by groups with the average tree DBH.
(C) The tree survey shall be prepared by:
   (1) A landscape architect, a surveyor, a professional engineer, or a certified arborist retained by the applicant; or
   (2) Upon mutual agreement between the [PLANNING OFFICIAL] and the applicant, a landscape architect, a surveyor, a professional engineer, or a certified arborist retained by the [LOCAL GOVERNMENT] at the expense of the applicant.
(D) The tree survey shall be reviewed by the [PLANNING OFFICIAL] as part of the normal process for

**Table 5-40
Definition of Stream Corridor Zones**

(A) Corridor Zone	Applicability (B) Perennial Stream	(C) Intermittent Stream	(D) Perennial Water Body	(E) Location and Required Width of Zone
Stream side	✓	✓	✓	50 feet from stream bank
Managed use	✓			50 feet from outer edge of stream side zone
Upland	✓			50 feet from managed use zone, or out to resource conservation district elevation, whichever is greater
Total corridor area	150	50	50	150 feet minimum from each side of stream bank

✓ = the corridor zone applies to the particular stream classification. The terms "perennial stream," "intermittent stream," and "perennial water body" are defined in Appendix A, Definitions and Rules of Interpretation, of the LDC.

approving the application. The [PLANNING OFFICIAL] may refer the tree survey to a certified arborist or other qualified official for his/her review and comments.

DIVISION 5: ENVIRONMENTAL PROTECTION OF CRITICAL AREAS

5.40 RIPARIAN BUFFERS

5.40.1 Applicability

This section applies to any development approval including but not limited to a subdivision plat or site plan.

5.40.2 Riparian Corridors

Riparian corridors are established in Table 5-40 (see Figure 5-13). These distances shall be measured as the horizontal, linear distance from the stream bank. There shall be three zones to stream corridors, with dimensions as shown in Table 5-40.

**Figure 5-13
Riparian Buffers**

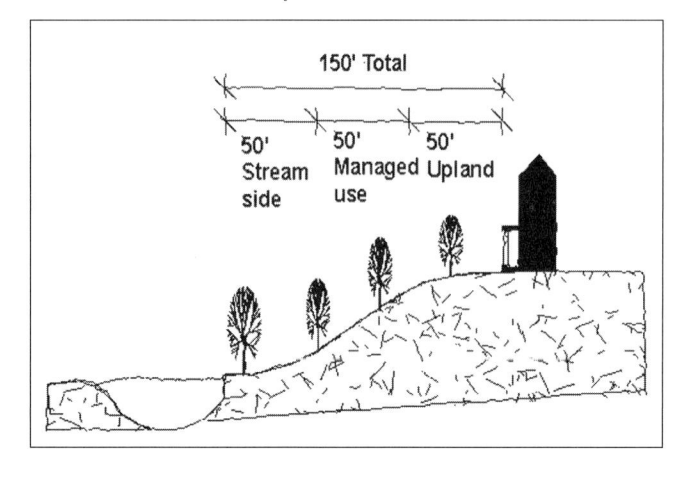

5.40.3 Permitted Uses and Activities in Riparian Buffers

Provided they are permitted within the applicable zoning district, the uses permitted in Column (A) of Table 5-41 are permitted within the applicable corridor zone as defined in Table 5-40. Such uses are restricted to the corridor zones indicated in Columns (B), (C), and/or (D) of Table 5-41.

5.40.4 Dimensional Regulations

In lieu of the dimensional regulations generally applicable to the zoning district, the standards in Table 5-42 shall apply to each riparian corridor zone. These standards do not apply to public greenways or necessary public utilities.

5.40.5 Development Standards in Riparian Buffers

The following standards and criteria shall apply to any portion of a development or, as appropriate, to any land disturbance, within the riparian buffers:

(A) No stormwater discharge is permitted directly off an impervious surface into a stream channel.

(B) Streets and driveways shall be located, as much as practicable, parallel to the flow of waters. Where a street, driveway, or utility line necessarily must cross a watercourse, such crossing shall be located and designed to allow convenient access by wildlife through and beyond such crossing, and shall be designed to safely convey floodwaters to the same extent as before construction of said crossings.

(C) Streets and bridges shall be spaced at an average interval of at least 400 feet within the proposed development, and not closer than 200 feet from streets on contiguous property. This distance shall be measured from the edge of the paved surface.

**Table 5-41
Permitted Uses Within
Riparian Buffer Corridor Zones**

(A) Use	(B) Stream Side Zone	(C) Managed Use Zone	(D) Upland Zone
Trails, greenways, open space, parks, and other similar public recreational uses and private recreational uses that do not require the use of fertilizers, pesticides, or extensive use of fences or walls	P	P	P
Outdoor horticulture, forestry, wildlife sanctuary, and other similar agricultural and related uses not enumerated elsewhere in this table that do not require land-disturbing activities, or use of pesticides or extensive use of fences or walls	P	P	P
Pastures or plant nurseries that do not require land-disturbing activities or use of pesticides, or extensive use of fences or walls	N	P	P
Gardens, play areas, and other similar uses that do not require the use of pesticides for routine maintenance	N	P	P
Lawns, golf course fairways, play fields, and other areas that may require the use of fertilizers or pesticides	N	N	P
Archery ranges, picnic structures, playground equipment, and other similar public and private recreational uses that do not require the use of fertilizers, pesticides, or extensive use of fences or walls	N	P	P
Public utility and storm drainage facilities where there is a practical necessity to their location within the resource conservation district (RCD)	P	P	P
Streets, bridges, and other similar transportation facilities where there is a practical necessity to their location within the RCD	C	C	C
Sidewalks	P	P	P
Accessory land-disturbing activities ordinarily associated with a single- or two-family dwelling, such as utility service lines, gardens, and similar uses	N	P	P
Public maintenance of streets, bridges, other similar transportation facilities and/or public utility and storm drainage facilities	P	P	P
Detention/retention basin and associated infrastructure	N	P	P
Lakes, ponds, and associated infrastructure, such as dams, spillways, riser pipes, and stilling basins, which are located outside of the regulatory floodplain	C	C	C
Stream and riparian area restoration and maintenance	P	P	P

P = the activity is permitted as of right; N = the activity is prohibited; and C = the activity is permitted only upon approval of a conditional use permit or a subdivision application.

**Table 5-42
Dimensional Regulations in Riparian Buffer Zones**

(A) Dimensional Requirement	(B) Stream Side Zone	(C) Managed Use Zone	(D) Upland Zone
Floor area ratio	.01	.019	Same as underlying zoning district
Impervious surface ratio (unsewered areas)	.06	.12	.12
Impervious surface ratio (sewered areas)	.10	.20	.20
Disturbed area ratio	.20	.40	.40

(D) Water supply, sanitary sewer, and on-site waste disposal systems shall be designed to:

(1) Prevent the infiltration of flood waters into the system;

(2) Prevent discharges from the system or systems into flood waters; and

(3) Avoid impairment during flooding to minimize flood damage. Finished floor elevations to be served by sanitary sewer shall be at or above the rim elevation of the nearest upstream manhole cover. Sanitary sewer manholes must be provided with locking, watertight manhole covers, or be elevated to a height sufficient to prevent submersion or infiltration by floodwaters. All sewer and sewer outfall lines shall use gravity flow to a point outside the riparian buffers.

(4) Promote rain water capture, treatment, and storage to promote recycling and reuse of water, including use of vegetated swales, rain gardens, rain barrels and cisterns, and permeable paving techniques.

(E) Electrical, heating, ventilation, plumbing, gas, air conditioning, and other service/utility facilities shall be designed and/or located in order to prevent water from entering or accumulating within the components during conditions of flooding during the base flood discharge.

5.41 STEEP SLOPES

This section minimizes the grading and site disturbance of steep slopes by restricting impervious surfaces and land disturbance in such areas and by requiring special construction techniques in steeply sloped areas in order to:

- Protect water bodies (streams and lakes) and wetlands from the effects of erosion on water quality and water body integrity;

- Protect the plant and animal habitat of steep slopes from the effects of land disturbance; and

- Preserve the natural beauty and economic value of hillsides.

5.41.1 Applicability

This section applies to any subdivision plat or site plan application.

5.41.2 Measurement of Slope

"Slope" means the ratio of elevation change to horizontal distance, expressed as a percentage. Slope is computed by dividing the vertical distance ("rise") by the horizontal distance ("run") and multiplying the ratio by 100. For purposes of this section, a slope shall include only those areas of a size 400 square feet or greater. Four different categories of slopes are established in this section and described in Table 5-43. The construction and development restrictions are established in Table 5-43 for each category of slope.

5.41.3 Contents of Application

(A) The following information shall be provided for any application proposing development on a lot or parcel that includes a slope of at least 10 percent:

(1) A slope and topographic map based on a certified boundary survey depicting contours at an interval of 5 feet or less. The map shall indicate, through crosshatching or separate colors, all areas within each slope category described in Table 5-43. Slope determinations shall be made upon areas with a size of 400 square feet or greater in the categories described in Table 5-43.

(2) An analysis of the direction, rate, and volume of stormwater run-off leaving each area within a slope category described in Table 5-43.

(3) The location of any existing swales, streams, or other watercourses.

Table 5-43
Slope Construction Restrictions

Slope Category	Illustration	Development Restrictions
Less than 10%	1.6' rise / 20' run = 8% slope	No additional building restrictions pursuant to this section.
10% to 15%	2.0' rise / 20' run = 10% slope	Site preparation techniques shall be utilized that minimize grading and site disturbance.
Greater than 15%, less than 25%	3.0' rise / 20' run = 15% slope	Building and site preparation may occur upon demonstration of specialized site design techniques and approaches as described in § 5.41.4 Construction Techniques of this chapter.
25% or higher	5.0' rise / 20' run = 25% slope	Generally unsuitable for development. Land disturbance shall not exceed 25% of the area containing 25% or greater slopes unless a variance is granted by the board of adjustment. For disturbed areas, building and site preparation shall utilize specialized site design techniques and approaches as described in § 5.41.4 Construction Techniques of this chapter.

(B) The following information shall be provided for any application proposing development on a lot or parcel that includes a slope greater than 15 percent:

(1) A detailed site analysis of soil conditions;

(2) A detailed site analysis of hydrology;

(3) A detailed site analysis of bedrock conditions; and

(4) A detailed site analysis of any other engineering and environmental considerations as may be required by the [PLANNING OFFICIAL] in order to determine whether the proposed development will create a threat to the public health, safety, and general welfare or cause land subsidence, erosion, or increases in the rate of volume of stormwater entering adjoining properties.

5.41.4 Construction Techniques

Construction activities on slopes greater than 15 percent shall comply with the following:

(A) Exposed soil that is not under continuous construction shall be revegetated with temporary or permanent vegetation so that the soil is not left exposed following issuance of a certificate of occupancy. If irrigation is not provided, then the exposed soil shall be planted with species that can survive without irrigation. Vegetative cover or alternative cover (e.g., rock or masonry) shall be maintained in perpetuity.

(B) Cut-and-fill slopes shall not exceed three (horizontal) to one (vertical) (3:1) ratio. A qualified soils engineer or geologist shall certify that the slope will remain stable under foreseeable conditions. The certification must delineate any specific stabilization measures deemed necessary by the soils engineer or geologist.

5.42 WETLANDS

This section provides flexible regulations that encourage the preservation of wetland areas. The [LOCAL GOVERNMENT] finds that wetlands provide the following public benefits:

• Wildlife, migratory birds, and resident species;
• Commercial and sport fisheries;
• Scientific and research values;
• Flood moderation and flood impact mitigation by slowing stormwater run-off;
• Surface and groundwater quality and quantity enhancement by removing sediment, nitrogen, phosphorus, and other pollutants from surface water;
• Habitats for fish and wildlife, including waterfowl and rare or endangered species, thereby promoting habitat and species diversity;
• Groundwater recharge, which can occur in wetlands and which will assist in ensuring that groundwater is available for the future;
• Outdoor recreation, including enhancement of scenic waterways and recreational uses for hunting, fishing, hiking, etc., which not only add to the quality of life but also have a significant economic impact on the [LOCAL GOVERNMENT], region, and state; and
• Timber and food production in properly managed wetlands, which can provide wood products, plants, and animals for human and livestock consumption.

5.42.1 Applicability

This section applies to any subdivision plat or site plan application.

5.42.2 Generally

Applications for subdivision or site plan approval shall include a true copy of any dredge or fill development approval requested or issued pursuant to § 404 of the Federal Water Pollution Control Act, 33 U.S.C. § 1344, or any other action requiring wetland mitigation. The applicant shall notify the [PLANNING OFFICIAL] of any changes or conditions to the application that are issued prior to final plat approval.

5.42.3 Exemption

(A) The planning commission may waive or reduce the wetlands protection or mitigation requirements established in this section if it finds that:

(1) The wetland area does not contribute to the public benefits listed or the specific subsection due to its size or the lack of hydrological connections to other water resources;

(2) Strict compliance with this section denies the applicant substantially all economic use of his/her property;

(3) Strict compliance with this section is inconsistent with an adopted comprehensive plan policy; or

(4) The applicant has mitigated the impacts on any affected wetlands on site through the purchase of wetland mitigation bank credits from the [STATE COMMISSION].

(B) If the applicant receives an exemption pursuant to subsection (A), above, the purchase, mitigation, or restoration requirements of the [STATE COMMISSION] shall be included as a condition of subdivision or site plan approval.

5.42.4 Standards

5.42.4.1 Buffer

A minimum 30-foot buffer shall be established around any wetland exceeding 3,000 square feet of contiguous wetland area.

5.42.4.2 Encroachment

No impervious surface, road and utility line, or water-dependent use (e.g., docks or bridges) may encroach into a wetland or wetland buffer unless the planning commission finds the following prior to approval that:

(A) The use or activity proposed and its attendant impacts cannot be reasonably avoided;

**Table 5-44
Outdoor Storage Categories**

Category	Description
Class 1	• The storage of passenger vehicles incidental to a residential use. • The incidental storage of materials on construction sites.
Class 2	• The storage of live plants on lots or parcels of at least 1 acre. • The storage of goods incidental to the on-site sale of feed, grain, fertilizers, pesticides, and similar goods, or the provision of agricultural services. • The display, except along a property line of a lot zoned for a residential use, of the following merchandise outdoors: artwork or pottery; flowers or plants; food products; handcrafted goods; and recreational equipment, including roller skates, bicycles, windsurf boards, and watercraft.
Class 3	• Storage of automobiles, noncommercial trucks, motorcycles, motor homes, recreational vehicles, or boats for sale incidental to the use of a lot or parcel as a car dealer, a bus, a truck, a mobile home, a large vehicle dealer, or a mini-warehouse. • Storage incidental to monument retail sales, including the retail sale of monuments for placement on graves; and the sale, storage, and delivery of headstones, footstones, markers, statues, obelisks, cornerstones, and ledgers.
Class 4	• The display of merchandise other than that described in Class 2, above, outdoors during business hours where screened from view off premises.
Class 5	• The storage of sports equipment, watercraft, watercraft motors, trailers, motorcycles, or motor homes. • The storage of materials or equipment related to research services, excluding bulk warehousing or permanent storage of hazardous or toxic substances. • The storage, sale, dismantling, or other processing of used or waste materials that are not intended for reuse in their original forms. This use includes automotive wrecking yards, junkyards and automobile graveyards, and paper salvage yards. • The long-term storage of vehicles, including the storage of vehicles towed from private parking areas and impound yards but excluding dismantling or salvage. For purposes of this subsection, "long-term" means a period of at least 14 days. • Storage incidental to the use of a site for the eradication or control of rodents, insects, or other pests on sites other than where the service is rendered. • Storage of materials or equipment, including monument or stone yards, grain elevators, and open storage yards. • Storage incidental to the maintenance, repair, vehicular or equipment servicing, equipment service centers, commercial services, contracting, or industrial activities, or similar activities. • Storage incidental to the use of a site for manufacture, predominantly from previously prepared materials, of finished products or parts, including processing, fabrication, assembly, treatment, and packaging of products. • Storage incidental to offices or administrative, clerical, or public contact services, together with incidental storage and maintenance of necessary vehicles.

(B) The least damaging route and methodology have been selected and that which is being proposed is the best practicable alternative available;

(C) Reasonable and acceptable impact mitigation measures have been incorporated where necessary and appropriate to minimize wetland loss or degradation;

(D) The overall impact of encroaching into wetland or buffer areas is necessary for the productive use of adjoining buildable land, and this impact outweighs the public benefits gained by preventing the encroachment;

(E) No significant impact on the aquatic habitat of rare or endangered species, as listed by the [STATE] or federal government, will result; and

(F) Erosion and sedimentation control methods are incorporated that will avoid any degradation in the water quality of the affected wetland.

DIVISION 6: PARKING AND STORAGE STANDARDS

5.50 OUTDOOR STORAGE

5.50.1 Applicability

This section applies to the keeping, in an unroofed area, any goods, junk, material, or merchandise in the same place for more than 24 hours. For purposes of this section, "outdoor storage" is divided into the categories described in Table 5-44.

**Table 5-45
Outdoor Storage Standards**

(A) Standard	(B) Class 1	(C) Class 2	(D) Class 3	(E) Class 4	(F) Class 5
Storage areas are restricted to the rear yard or, for passenger vehicles, to a garage or driveway.	✓				
Storage areas shall be located in the rear yard unless they are completely screened from view by the natural topography or by a Type B buffer (see § 5.31 Buffers and Screening of this chapter) or, in the "IL" (Industrial Light) or "IH" (Industrial Heavy) districts, a fence which complies with § 5.14 Fences and Walls of this chapter.				✓	✓
No storage of vehicles (other than noncommercial, off-street parking) or storage or display of any merchandise or materials of any kind is permitted in any front yard, side yard, or rear yard as required by this chapter, which abuts any residential district unless a Type C buffer (see § 5.31 Buffers and Screening of this chapter) is provided.		✓	✓	✓	✓
Outdoor storage areas shall be screened from the street view and adjacent residence, office, and commercial districts to a height commensurate with the location and height of the proposed storage. Outdoor storage areas shall be screened from the public street view to a height of at least 6 feet.				✓	✓
The storage area shall not exceed 20 percent of the site.	✓		✓		
The storage area shall not exceed 50 percent of the site.		✓		✓	

✓ = the standard applies to the outdoor storage classification indicated in the column.

5.50.2 Standards

Standards for outdoor storage are based upon the classification of the storage activities as set forth in Table 5-45.

5.51 PARKING

This section sets minimum standards for off-street requirements for new construction and expansion of or changes to existing uses. The purpose of this section is to ensure that uses have a minimum level of off-street parking to avoid congestion on surrounding streets while avoiding excessive parking, discouraging pedestrian access, driving up the cost of development, and inviting excessive levels of traffic congestion, which creates increases in flooding and nonpoint source pollution. On-street parking is also encouraged in some locations in order to provide a buffer between pedestrians and vehicular traffic.

5.51.1 Parking Ratios

5.51.1.1 Generally

(A) *Applicability:* The minimum parking ratio standards apply to all zoning districts except the "D" (Downtown) zoning district. The minimum parking ratios do not apply to the TND or TOD use patterns.

(B) *Uses not identified:* The [PLANNING OFFICIAL] shall determine the parking requirement for uses that do not correspond to the categories listed in Table 5-46. In such instances, the applicant shall provide adequate information by which the proposal can be reviewed, which includes but may not necessarily be limited to the following:

(1) Type of uses;
(2) Number of employees;
(3) Building design capacity;
(4) Square feet of sales area and service area;
(5) Parking spaces proposed on site;
(6) Parking spaces provided elsewhere; and
(7) Hours of operation.

(C) *Multiple uses:* Where the application identifies accessory or multiple uses within a structure or multiple structures, the minimum standards shall apply to each use or structure. This does not apply to § 5.51.2 Shared Parking of this chapter.

(D) *Fractional measurements:* When units or measurements determining the number of required off-street parking spaces result in a fractional space, then such fraction equal or greater than one-half shall require a full off-street parking space.

(E) *Floor area measurement:* Floor area and GFA are synonymous for purposes of this chapter (see "gross floor area," as defined in Appendix A, Definitions and Rules of Interpretation, of the LDC).

(F) *On-street parking:* The minimum number of required off-street parking spaces shall be reduced by the number of on-street parking spaces abutting the property lines of the lot or parcel.

5.51.1.2 Minimum Parking Ratios

Table 5-46 establishes the minimum numbers of parking spaces required for the uses indicated. For the purposes of parking calculations, the gross area of any parking garage within a building shall not be included within the GFA of the building. Parking requirements may be met by one or more of a combination of the following methods:

(A) *Providing on-site parking spaces:* Only spaces that are designed consistent with this section are counted toward the minimum parking required. Spaces at gasoline pumps and bays for auto repair/service are not counted toward the minimum parking required. No part of a parking or loading space required for any building to comply with this chapter shall be included as part of a parking or loading space required for another building.

(B) *Making payments in lieu of parking spaces that shall be contributed to a parking fund specifically set aside to provide public parking within 1/4 mile of the exterior boundaries of the proposed development:* The amount of the payment for each space shall be established by a resolution of the [GOVERNING ENTITY] and shall be reasonable and based on the actual or estimated cost to provide such spaces. No development approvals shall be issued until complete payment has been received by the [LOCAL GOVERNMENT].

(C) *Providing off-site parking spaces in a shared parking facility:* Shared parking facilities must conform to § 5.51.2 Shared Parking of this chapter.

5.51.1.3 Maximum Parking Ratios

(A) Table 5-46 indicates the maximum number of parking spaces established for the use or structure. If a maximum parking space ratio applies, the number of parking spaces shall not exceed the maximum number permitted.

(B) The maximum spaces allowed do not include accessible spaces required by the building code.

5.51.2 Shared Parking

5.51.2.1 Generally

Parking spaces required under this section may be provided cooperatively for two or more uses in a development or for two or more individual uses, subject to the requirements of this section.

5.51.2.2 Cooperative Parking

Off-street parking requirements of a given use may be met with off-site, off-street parking facilities of another use when, and if, all of the following conditions are met:

(A) The off-site, off-street parking facilities are within 300 feet of the property;

(B) The parking demands of the individual uses, as determined by the administrator based upon minimum off-street parking requirements, are such that the total parking demand of all the uses at any one time is less than the total parking stalls required;

(C) A written agreement between the owners and lessees is executed for a minimum of 20 years, approved by the [PLANNING OFFICIAL] as provided in subsection (D), below. The application shall be recorded and a copy maintained in the project file. Should the lease expire or otherwise terminate, the use for which the off-site parking was provided shall be considered nonconforming and any and all approvals, including CUPs, shall be subject to revocation. Continuation or expansion of the use shall be prohibited unless the use is brought into compliance with the parking regulations of this division;

(D) An application for approval of a cooperative parking plan shall be filed with the [PLANNING OFFICIAL] by the owner of the entire land area to be included within the cooperative parking plan, the owner or owners of all structures then existing on such land area, and all parties having a legal interest in such land area and structures. Sufficient evidence to establish the status of applicants as owners of parties in interest shall be provided. The application shall include plans showing the location of the uses or structures for which off-street parking facilities are required, the location of the off-street parking facilities, and the schedule of times used by those sharing parking in common; and

(E) Pursuant to the same procedure and subject to the same limitations and requirements by which the cooperative parking plan was approved and registered, any such plan may be amended or withdrawn, either partially or completely, if all land and structures remaining under such plan comply with all the conditions and limitations of the plan, and all land and structures withdrawn from such plan comply with the regulations of this division.

5.51.2.3 Shared Parking

Developments that contain a mix of uses on the same parcel, as set forth in Table 5-47, may reduce the amount of required parking in accordance with the following methodology:

(A) Determine the minimum parking requirements in accordance with Table 5-47 for each land use as if it were a separate use;

(B) Multiply each amount by the corresponding percentages for each of the five time periods set forth in Columns (B) through (F) of Table 5-47;

(C) Calculate the total for each time period; and

(D) Select the total with the highest value as the required minimum number of parking spaces.

**Table 5-46
Parking Ratios**

Use/Activity	Minimum Vehicle Spaces	Maximum Vehicle Spaces	Minimum Bicycle Spaces
Residential buildings			
Single-family detached dwellings	—	—	—
Single-family attached dwellings	—	—	—
Duplex structures	1 per DU	1.9 per DU	0.5 per DU
Zero lot line or row houses	1 per DU	1.9 per DU	0.5 per DU
Accessory dwelling units	—	—	—
Accessory apartments	—	—	—
Townhouses	1 per DU	1.9 per DU	0.5 per DU
Manufactured housing, residential design	—	—	—
Manufactured housing, other	—	—	—
Multifamily dwellings	1 per DU	1.9 per DU	0.5 per DU
Retirement housing services	1 per three DUs	1.5 per DU	—
Congregate living services	1 per three DUs	1.5 per DU	—
Assisted living services	0.3 per room	1 per room	—
Life care or continuing care services	0.3 per room	1 per room	—
Skilled nursing services	0.3 per room	1 per room	—
Community home	0.3 per room	1 per room	
Barracks	0.3 per room	1 per room	—
College fraternities	1 per 2 beds	1 per bed	0.5 per DU
Dormitories	1 per 2 beds	1 per bed	0.5 per DU
Single-room occupancy units	0.3 per room	1 per room	—
Temporary structures, tents, etc., for shelter	0.3 per room	1 per room	—
Other structurally converted buildings	0.3 per room	1 per room	—
Hotels, motels, or other accommodation services			
Bed-and-breakfast inn	1 per guest room plus 2 spaces for owner's portion	—	—
Rooming and boarding house	1 per guest room plus 2 spaces for owner's portion	—	—
Hotel, motel, or tourist court	0.8 per room plus 1 per 800 sf of public meeting area and restaurant space	1 per room plus 1 per 400 sf of public meeting area and restaurant space	—
Commercial buildings			
Commercial center	1 per 300 sf GFA	1 per 200 sf GFA	1 per 10 vehicle spaces
Shop or store building with drive through facility	1 per 250 sf GFA	1 per 140 sf GFA	—
Restaurant, with incidental consumption of alcoholic beverages	1 per 75 sf GFA	1 per 50 sf GFA	1 per 20 vehicle spaces
Stand-alone store or shop building	1 per 300 sf GFA	1 per 200 sf GFA	1 per 10 vehicle spaces
Department store building	1 per 300 sf GFA	1 per 200 sf GFA	1 per 10 vehicle spaces

Table 5-46 (cont.)
Parking Ratios

Use/Activity	Minimum Vehicle Spaces	Maximum Vehicle Spaces	Minimum Bicycle Spaces
Commercial buildings (cont.)			
Warehouse discount store/superstore	1 per 300 sf GFA	1 per 200 sf GFA	1 per 10 vehicle spaces
Market shops, including open markets	1 per 100 sf gross public sales area	1.5 per 100 sf gross sales area	—
Gasoline station	1 per 375 sf GFA, including service bays, wash tunnels, and retail areas	1 per 500 sf GFA, including service bays, wash tunnels, and retail areas	—
Automobile repair and service structures	1 per 375 sf GFA, including service bays, wash tunnels, and retail areas	1 per 500 sf GFA, including service bays, wash tunnels, and retail areas	—
Car dealer	1 per 375 sf GFA of sales and service building	1.5 per 375 sf GFA of sales and service building	—
Bus, truck, mobile homes, or large vehicle dealers	1 per 375 sf GFA of sales and service building	1.5 per 375 sf GFA of sales and service building	—
Bicycle, motorcycle, all-terrain vehicle dealers	1 per 375 sf GFA of sales and service building	1.5 per 375 sf GFA of sales and service building	—
Boat or marine craft dealer	1 per 375 sf GFA of sales and service building	1.5 per 375 sf GFA of sales and service building	—
Parts, accessories, or tires	1 per 375 sf GFA, including service bays, wash tunnels, and retail areas	1 per 500 sf GFA, including service bays, wash tunnels, and retail areas	—
Gasoline service	1 per 375 sf GFA, including service bays, wash tunnels, and retail areas	1 per 500 sf GFA, including service bays, wash tunnels, and retail areas	—
Lumberyard and building materials	1 per 375 sf GFA of sales and service building	1.5 per 375 sf GFA of sales and service building	—
Outdoor resale business	1 per 375 sf GFA of sales and service building	1.5 per 375 sf GFA of sales and service building	—
Pawnshops	1 per 300 GFA	1 per 150 sf GFA	1 per 20 vehicle spaces
Beer, wine, and liquor store (off-premises consumption of alcohol)	1 per 300 sf GFA	1 per 200 sf GFA	1 per 10 vehicle spaces
Neighborhood shopping center (convenience with one or more anchors)	1 per 300 sf GFA	1 per 200 sf GFA	1 per 10 vehicle spaces
Community shopping center (general merchandise with two or more anchors)	1 per 300 sf GFA	1 per 200 sf GFA	1 per 10 vehicle spaces
Regional shopping center (enclosed mall with two or more anchors)	1 per 300 sf GFA	1 per 200 sf GFA	1 per 10 vehicle spaces

Table 5-46 (cont.)
Parking Ratios

Use/Activity	Minimum Vehicle Spaces	Maximum Vehicle Spaces	Minimum Bicycle Spaces
Commercial buildings (cont.)			
Superregional center (similar to regional but has three or more anchors)	1 per 300 sf GFA	1 per 200 sf GFA	1 per 10 vehicle spaces
Fashion/specialty center (higher-end, fashion-oriented stores)	1 per 300 sf GFA	1 per 200 sf GFA	1 per 10 vehicle spaces
Power center (category-dominated anchors with few small tenants)	1 per 300 sf GFA	1 per 200 sf GFA	1 per 10 vehicle spaces
Theme or festival center (leisure, tourist-oriented, restaurants)	1 per 300 sf GFA	1 per 200 sf GFA	1 per 10 vehicle spaces
Outlet or discount center (manufacturer outlet stores)	1 per 300 sf GFA	1 per 200 sf GFA	1 per 10 vehicle spaces
Convenience stores or centers	6 per 1,000 sf GFA	10 per 1,000 sf GFA	1 per 10 vehicle spaces
Car care center	1 per 375 sf GFA, including service bays, wash tunnels, and retail areas	1 per 500 sf GFA, including service bays, wash tunnels, and retail areas	—
Car washes	1 per 375 sf GFA, including service bays, wash tunnels, and retail areas	1 per 500 sf GFA, including service bays, wash tunnels, and retail areas	—
Office or bank building, stand-alone (without drive-through)	1 per 250 sf GFA	1 per 140 sf GFA	—
Office building with drive-through facility	1 per 1,500 sf GFA plus required stacking spaces for drive-through facilities	5 per 1,000 sf GFA	1 per 10 vehicle spaces
Office or store building with residence on top	1 per 1,000 sf GFA	1 per 200 sf GFA	1 per 10 vehicle spaces
Office building over storefronts	1 per 1,000 sf GFA	1 per 200 sf GFA	1 per 10 vehicle spaces
Research-and-development services (scientific, medical, and technology)	1 per 1,000 sf GFA	1 per 200 sf GFA	1 per 10 vehicle spaces
Car rental and leasing	1 per 1,000 sf GFA	1 per 200 sf GFA	—
Leasing trucks, trailers, recreational vehicles, etc.	1 per 1,000 sf GFA	1 per 200 sf GFA	—
Services to buildings and dwellings (pest control, janitorial, landscaping, carpet/upholstery cleaning, parking, and crating)	1 per 1,000 sf GFA	1 per 200 sf GFA	—
Bars, taverns, nightclubs	1 per 2 seats	1 per 1.5 seats	1 per 10 vehicle spaces
Camps, camping, and related establishments	1 per 6 camp sites, plus 4 per laundry and shower facility	—	—
Tattoo parlors	1 per 300 sf GFA	1 per 200 sf GFA	1 per 10 vehicle spaces
Industrial buildings and structures			
Light industrial structures and facilities (not enumerated below)	1 per 300 sf GFA	1 per 1,500 sf GFA	—

Table 5-46 (cont.)
Parking Ratios

Use/Activity	Minimum Vehicle Spaces	Maximum Vehicle Spaces	Minimum Bicycle Spaces
Industrial buildings and structures (cont.)			
Loft building	1 per 300 sf GFA	1 per 1,500 sf GFA	—
Mill-type factory structures	1 per 300 sf GFA	1 per 1,500 sf GFA	—
Manufacturing plants	1 per 300 sf GFA	1 per 1,500 sf GFA	—
Industrial parks	1 per 300 sf GFA	1 per 1,500 sf GFA	—
Laboratory or specialized industrial facility	1 per 300 sf GFA	1 per 1,500 sf GFA	—
Assembly and construction-type plants	1 per 300 sf GFA	1 per 1,500 sf GFA	—
Process plants (metals, chemicals, etc.)	1 per 300 sf GFA	1 per 1,500 sf GFA	—
Construction-related businesses	1 per 1,000 sf GFA	1 per 200 sf GFA	—
Automotive wrecking and salvage yard/junkyard	1 per employee	—	—
Demolition business	1 per employee	—	—
Recycling business	1 per employee	—	—
Warehouse or storage facility			
Mini-warehouse	4 spaces plus 2 for manager's quarters	—	—
High-rise mini-warehouse	4 spaces plus 2 for manager's quarters	—	—
Warehouse structure	1 per 600 sf GFA	1 per 350 sf GFA	—
Produce warehouse	1 per 600 sf GFA	1 per 350 sf GFA	—
Refrigerated warehouse or cold storage	1 per 600 sf GFA	1 per 350 sf GFA	—
Large area distribution or transit warehouse	1 per 600 sf GFA	1 per 350 sf GFA	—
Wholesale trade—durable goods	1 per 600 sf GFA	1 per 350 sf GFA	—
Wholesale trade—nondurable goods	1 per 600 sf GFA	1 per 350 sf GFA	—
Warehouse and storage services	1 per 600 sf GFA	1 per 350 sf GFA	—
Tank farms	1 per 600 sf GFA	1 per 350 sf GFA	—
Public assembly structures			
Performance theater	1 per 6 seats	1 per 4 seats	1 per 20 vehicle spaces
Movie theater	1 per 6 seats	1 per 4 seats	1 per 20 vehicle spaces
Amphitheater	1 per 6 seats or 1 per 30 sf of GFA if no permanent seats	1 per 4 seats or 1 per 50 sf of GFA if no permanent seats	1 per 20 vehicle spaces
Drive-in theaters	—	—	1 per 20 vehicle spaces
Indoor games facility	5 per 1,000 sf GFA	6 per 1,000 sf GFA	1 per 10 vehicle spaces
Amusement, sports, or recreation establishment (not specifically enumerated)	1 per 6 seats or 1 per 30 sf of GFA if no permanent seats	1 per 4 seats or 1 per 50 sf of GFA if no permanent seats	1 per 20 vehicle spaces
Amusement or theme park	1 per 600 sf outdoor recreation area	1 per 500 sf outdoor recreation area	
Arcade	1 per game table, video game, amusement device	—	1 per 10 vehicle spaces

Table 5-46 (cont.)
Parking Ratios

Use/Activity	Minimum Vehicle Spaces	Maximum Vehicle Spaces	Minimum Bicycle Spaces
Public assembly structures (cont.)			
Miniature golf establishment	1 per hole	2 per hole	—
Fitness, recreational sports, gym, or athletic club	1.5 per 1,000 sf GFA	10 per 1,000 sf GFA	1 per 10 vehicle spaces
Bowling, billiards, pool, etc.	2 per lane	4 per lane	1 per 10 vehicle spaces
Skating rinks	5 per 1,000 sf GFA	7 per 1,000 sf GFA	1 per 10 vehicle spaces
Sports stadium or arena	1 per 6 seats or 1 per 30 sf of GFA if no permanent seats	1 per 4 seats or 1 per 50 sf of GFA	1 per 20 vehicle spaces
Racetrack	1 per 6 seats or 1 per 30 sf of GFA if no permanent seats	1 per 4 seats or 1 per 50 sf of GFA	1 per 20 vehicle spaces
Exhibition, convention, or conference structure	1 per 6 seats or 1 per 30 sf of GFA if no permanent seats	1 per 4 seats or 1 per 50 sf of GFA	1 per 20 vehicle spaces
Churches, temples, synagogues, mosques, and other religious facilities	1 per 8 seats	1 per 1.5 seats	1 per 20 vehicle spaces
Covered or partially covered atriums and public enclosures	—	—	—
Passenger terminal, mixed mode	—	—	—
Active open space/athletic fields/golf courses	—	6 per hole (golf courses)	—
Passive open space	—	—	—
Institutional or community facilities			
Hospital building	1 per 400 sf GFA	1 per 100 sf GFA	1 per 20 vehicle spaces
Medical clinic building	1 per 400 sf GFA	1 per 100 sf GFA	1 per 20 vehicle spaces
Social assistance, welfare, and charitable services (not otherwise enumerated)	1 per 250 sf GFA	1 per 200 sf GFA	1 per 20 vehicle spaces
Child and youth services	1 per 375 sf GFA	1.5 per 375 sf GFA	—
Child care institution (basic)	1 per 375 sf GFA	1.5 per 375 sf GFA	—
Child care institution (specialized)	1 per 375 sf GFA	1.5 per 375 sf GFA	—
Day care center	1 per 375 sf GFA	1.5 per 375 sf GFA	—
Community food services	1 per 250 sf GFA	1 per 200 sf GFA	1 per 20 vehicle spaces
Emergency and relief services	1 per 250 sf GFA	1 per 200 sf GFA	1 per 20 vehicle spaces
Other family services	1 per 250 sf GFA	1 per 200 sf GFA	1 per 20 vehicle spaces
Services for elderly and disabled	1 per 250 sf GFA	1 per 200 sf GFA	1 per 20 vehicle spaces
Animal hospitals	1 per employee	—	—
School or university buildings (privately owned)	1 per classroom	2 per classroom	1 per 10 students

Table 5-46 (cont.)
Parking Ratios

Use/Activity	Minimum Vehicle Spaces	Maximum Vehicle Spaces	Minimum Bicycle Spaces
Institutional or community facilities (cont.)			
Grade school (privately owned)	1 per classroom	2 per classroom	1 per 10 students
College or university facility (privately owned)	1 per 4 students	1 per 2 students	1 per 5 vehicle spaces
Trade or specialty school facility (privately owned)	1 per 200 sf	1 per 150 sf	1 per 10 students
Library building	1 per 300 sf GFA	1 per 125 sf GFA	1 per 20 vehicle spaces
Museum, exhibition, or similar facility	1 per 1,000 sf GFA	1.5 per 1,000 sf GFA	2 per 1,000 sf
Exhibitions and art galleries	1 per 1,000 sf GFA	1.5 per 1,000 sf GFA	2 per 1,000 sf
Planetarium	1 per 1,000 sf GFA	1.5 per 1,000 sf GFA	2 per 1,000 sf
Aquarium	1 per 1,000 sf GFA	1.5 per 1,000 sf GFA	2 per 1,000 sf
Outdoor facility, no major structure	1 per 1,000 sf GFA	1.5 per 1,000 sf GFA	2 per 1,000 sf
Zoological parks	1 per 1,000 sf GFA	1.5 per 1,000 sf GFA	2 per 1,000 sf
Public safety-related facility	1 per employee + 1 per each 3 volunteer personnel on normal shift + 1 per 200 sf usable office space	—	3% of number of parking spaces
Fire and rescue station	1 per employee + 1 per each 3 volunteer personnel on normal shift + 1 per 200 sf usable office space	—	3% of number of parking spaces
Police station	1 per employee + 1 per each 3 volunteer personnel on normal shift + 1 per 200 sf usable office space	—	3% of number of parking spaces
Emergency operation center	1 per employee	—	—
Correctional or rehabilitation facility	1 per employee on maximum shift, 1 per service vehicle	1 per employee on maximum shift, 1 per service vehicle	
Cemetery, monument, tombstone, or mausoleum	—	—	—
Funeral homes	1 per 4 seats	1 per 2 seats	—
Cremation facilities	1 per 4 seats	1 per 2 seats	—
Public administration	1 per 300 sf GFA	1 per 125 sf GFA	1 per 20 vehicle spaces
Post offices	1 per employee	—	—
Space research and technology	1 per employee	—	—
Clubs or lodges	1 per 3 persons	—	1 per 20 vehicle spaces
Transportation-related facilities			
Automobile parking facilities	—	—	—
Surface parking, open	—	—	—
Surface parking, covered	—	—	—
Multistoried parking structure with ramps	—	—	—

Table 5-46 (cont.)
Parking Ratios

Use/Activity	Minimum Vehicle Spaces	Maximum Vehicle Spaces	Minimum Bicycle Spaces
Transportation-related facilities (cont.)			
Underground parking structure with ramps	—	—	—
Rooftop parking facility	—	—	—
Bus terminal	1 per employee plus spaces required to satisfy projected peak parking needs	—	—
Bus stop shelter	—	—	—
Bus or truck maintenance facility	—	—	—
Truck and freight transportation services	—	—	—
Road, ground passenger, and transit transportation	1 per employee plus spaces required to satisfy projected peak parking needs		
Local transit systems, including mixed mode	1 per employee plus spaces required to satisfy projected peak parking needs	—	—
Local transit systems—commuter rail	1 per employee plus spaces required to satisfy projected peak parking needs	—	—
Local transit systems—bus, special needs, and other motor vehicles	1 per employee plus spaces required to satisfy projected peak parking needs	—	—
Interurban, charter bus, and other similar establishments	1 per employee plus spaces required to satisfy projected peak parking needs	—	—
Taxi and limousine service	—	—	—
School and employee bus transportation	—	—	—
Towing and other road services	—	—	—
Space transportation	—	—	—
Pipeline transportation	—	—	—
Postal transportation services	—	—	—
Courier and messenger services	—	—	—
Air and space transportation facility	—	—	—
Airport terminal	1 per 4 seating accommodations for waiting passengers plus 1 per each 2 employees	—	—
Runway	—	—	—
Airport maintenance and hangar facility	—	—	—
Airport control tower	—	—	—

Table 5-46 (cont.)
Parking Ratios

Use/Activity	Minimum Vehicle Spaces	Maximum Vehicle Spaces	Minimum Bicycle Spaces
Transportation-related facilities (cont.)			
Heliport facility	1 per 4 seating accommodations for waiting passengers plus 1 per each 2 employees	—	—
Glideport, seaport, stolport, ultralight, or baloonport facility	—	—	—
Railroad facility	1 per employee	—	—
Utility and other nonbuilding structures			
Utility structures on right-of-way	1 per employee	—	—
Water supply-related facility	1 per employee	—	—
Water supply pump station	1 per employee	—	—
Dam	1 per employee	—	—
Levee	1 per employee	—	—
Culvert	1 per employee	—	—
Water tank (elevated, at grade, underground)	1 per employee	—	—
Wells	1 per employee	—	—
Water treatment and purification facility	1 per employee	—	—
Water reservoir	1 per employee	—	—
Irrigation facilities	1 per employee	—	—
Wastewater storage or pumping station facility; lift stations	1 per employee	—	—
Solid waste landfill facility	1 per employee	—	—
Incinerator, composting, or similar facility	1 per employee	—	—
Hazardous waste collection	1 per employee	—	—
Hazardous waste treatment and disposal	1 per employee	—	—
Solid waste collection	1 per employee	—	—
Solid waste combustor or incinerator	1 per employee	—	—
Waste treatment and disposal	1 per employee	—	—
Septic tank and related services	1 per employee	—	—
Hazardous waste storage facility	1 per employee	—	—
Sewer treatment plant	1 per employee	—	—
Gas or electric power generation facility	1 per employee	—	—
Communication towers	1 per service employee	—	—
Radio, television, or wireless transmitter	1 per service employee	—	—

Table 5-46 (cont.)
Parking Ratios

Use/Activity	Minimum Vehicle Spaces	Maximum Vehicle Spaces	Minimum Bicycle Spaces
Utility and other nonbuilding structures (cont.)			
Weather stations or transmitters	1 per service employee	—	—
Environmental monitoring station (air, soil, etc.)	1 per employee	—	—
Sign or billboard	—	—	—
Highway rest stops and welcome centers	—	—	—
Roadside stand, pushcarts, etc.	—	—	—
Kiosks	—	—	—
Playground equipment	—	—	—
Fountain, sculpture, or other aesthetic structure	—	—	—
Outdoor stage, bandstand, or similar structure	—	—	—
Agriculture, forestry, fishing, and hunting			
Grain silos and other storage structure for grains and agricultural products	1 per 300 sf GFA	1 per 1,500 sf GFA	—
Animal production, including slaughter	1 per 300 sf GFA	1 per 1,500 sf GFA	—
Livestock pens or hog houses	1 per 300 sf GFA	1 per 1,500 sf GFA	—
Hatcheries and poultry houses	1 per 300 sf GFA	1 per 1,500 sf GFA	—
Greenhouse/nurseries	1 per 375 sf GFA of sales and service building	1.5 per 375 sf GFA of sales and service building	—
Stables and other equine-related facilities	1 per 300 sf GFA	1 per 1,500 sf GFA	—
Kennels and other canine-related facilities	1 per 300 sf GFA	1 per 1,500 sf GFA	—
Apiary and other related structures	1 per 300 sf GFA	1 per 1,500 sf GFA	—
Crop production	—	—	—
Forestry and logging	—	—	—
Fishing, hunting, and trapping, including game preserves and retreats	—	—	—
Support functions for agriculture and forestry	—	—	—
Mining and extraction establishments			
Oil and natural gas	1 per employee plus 1 per facility vehicle	—	—
Metals (iron, copper, etc.)	1 per employee plus 1 per facility vehicle	—	—
Coal	1 per employee plus 1 per facility vehicle	—	—
Nonmetallic mining	1 per employee plus 1 per facility vehicle	—	—
Quarrying and stone cutting	1 per employee plus 1 per facility vehicle	—	—

DU = dwelling unit; sf = square feet; and GFA = gross floor area. A dash ("—") means that the standard is not applicable.

Table 5-47
Shared Parking Standards

(A) Land Use	Weekday		Weekend		(F) Nighttime (Midnight–6 AM)
	(B) Daytime (9 AM–4 PM)	(C) Evening (6 PM–midnight)	(D) Daytime (9 AM–4 PM)	(E) Evenings (6 PM–midnight)	
Office/industrial	100%	10%	19%	5%	5%
Retail	60%	90%	100%	70%	5%
Hotel	75%	100%	75%	100%	75%
Restaurant	50%	100%	100%	100%	10%
Entertainment/commercial	40%	100%	80%	100%	10%

Table 5-48
Minimum Stall Length and Aisle Width (Feet)

(A) Parking Angle (Degrees)	(B) Stall Depth		(C) Aisle Width	
	Car-to-Wall Stalls	Interlocking Stalls	One-Way Operation	Two-Way Operation
30	17	13	12	19
45	19	16	12	19
60	20	18	16	20
75	20	19	22	22
90	18	18	25	25

Stall depth = the projected vehicle length from the wall measured perpendicular to the aisle; and aisle width = traveled path through a parking facility that provides access to one or two parking vehicles.

Reference: Weant and Levinson, 1990.

Figure 5-14
Parking Space and Stall Dimensions

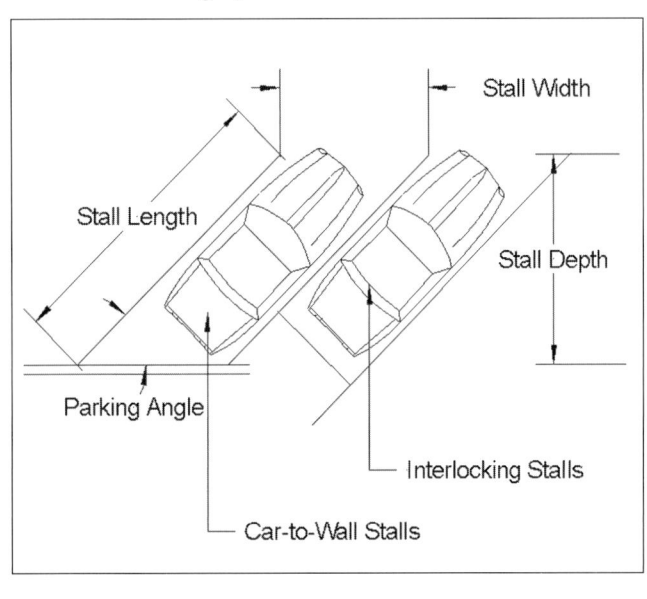

5.51.3 Dimensions

5.51.3.1 Generally

Off-street parking spaces shall have a width of 9 feet. Stall depth shall have the minimum established in Table 5-48 (see Figure 5-14), exclusive of access or maneuvering area, ramps, and other appurtenances. The minimum width of access aisles internal to a parking lot or structure shall be as prescribed in Table 5-48.

5.51.3.2 Compact Vehicles

Up to 30 percent of the required parking spaces may be designated for use by compact vehicles with minimum dimensions of 8 feet in width and 16 feet in length. Compact vehicle parking areas shall be identified by individually marking each parking space surface with lettering a minimum of 6 inches in size.

5.51.3.3 Turnarounds

All parking areas containing three or more parking spaces shall include a turnaround that is designed and located so that vehicles can enter and exit the parking area without backing onto a public right-of-way.

5.51.4 Location

5.51.4.1 Generally

Except as otherwise permitted under a cooperative parking plan, off-street parking facilities shall be located on the lots on which the use or structure for which they are provided is located.

5.51.4.2 Rear Parking

(A) For purposes of this section, "rear parking" means that parking areas are located between the principal building and the rear lot line or an alley, or interior to a block.

(B) All parking areas in the following districts shall be rear parking: "NU" (Neighborhood Urban), "CN" (Commercial Neighborhood), "D" (Downtown), and "MX" (Mixed Use).

**Figure 5-15
Utilizing Effective Parking**

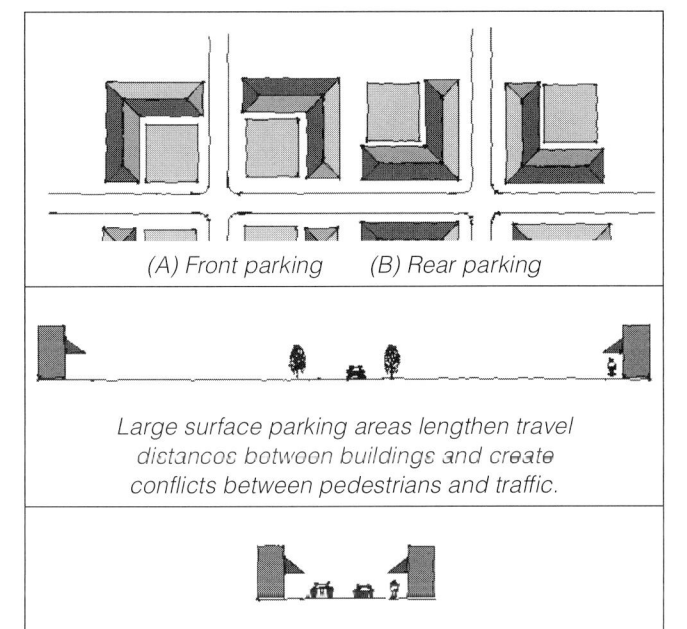

(A) Front parking   (B) Rear parking

Large surface parking areas lengthen travel distances between buildings and create conflicts between pedestrians and traffic.

Rear parking and small front setbacks minimize walking distances between buildings and conflicts between pedestrians and vehicles.

Source: Mike Greenberg, The Poetics of Cities: Designing Neighborhoods that Work *(Columbus: Ohio State University Press, 1995), at 198.*

(C) All parking areas for the TND and TOD use patterns shall be rear parking.

(D) Parking to the rear of the principal use or principal building is encouraged in all other zoning districts or use patterns.

(E) Rear parking areas that are screened from the view of public streets by the principal buildings are exempt from the parking lot screening requirements of the landscaping standards (§ 5.34 Parking Lot Landscaping) of this chapter (see Figure 5-15).

5.51.5 Construction and Maintenance

Off-street parking facilities shall be constructed, maintained, and operated in accordance with the specifications described in § 5.51.5.1 Pavement through § 5.51.5.6 Pervious Pavement of this chapter.

5.51.5.1 Pavement

Parking and loading service areas shall be paved with asphalt, bituminous, or concrete material to minimize nuisance from dust. Parking and loading areas shall be graded and drained in order to dispose of all surface water. All driveways and parking areas for such vehicles shall be constructed with rock, gravel, concrete, brick, asphalt, turf block, or other surfaces of comparable durability.

5.51.5.2 Drainage and Surfacing

Areas shall be properly graded for drainage; surfaced with concrete, asphaltic concrete, or asphalt; and maintained in good condition free of weeds, dust, trash, and debris.

5.51.5.3 Wheel Guards

Boundary or perimeter areas shall be provided with wheel guards, bumper guards, or continuous curbing so located that no part of parked vehicles will extend beyond the property line of the parking area. One wheel stop shall be placed at the end of each parking space.

5.51.5.4 Protective Screen Fencing

Areas shall be provided with protective screen fencing so that occupants of adjacent structures are not unreasonably disturbed by the movement of vehicles either during the day or at night.

5.51.5.5 Lighting

Facilities shall be arranged so that the source of light is concealed from public view and from adjacent residential properties and does not interfere with traffic.

5.51.5.6 Pervious Pavement

Vehicle parking spaces may exceed the maximum number of spaces permitted if the additional spaces are designed as pervious pavement. Pervious pavement shall comply with the following conditions:

(A) Pervious pavement shall be located only on soils having a permeability rating of moderate rapid to very rapid (see definition of "permeability" in Appendix A, Definitions and Rules of Interpretation, of the LDC);

(B) Pervious pavement shall not be located in soils with an apparent or perched high water table or a depth to bedrock of less than 10 feet, as set forth in the county soil survey;

(C) Pervious pavement shall not be located on any slope exceeding 10 percent over 20 feet; and

(D) The pervious pavement area shall be vacuum swept and washed with a high-pressure hose at least four times per year.

5.51.6 Bicycle Parking

5.51.6.1 Generally

Bicycle parking spaces shall be required for all nonresidential uses and structures. One bicycle parking space shall be required for each 20 parking spaces.

5.51.6.2 Design

Bicycle spaces may be provided through spaces or bicycle storage racks. Bicycle spaces shall be at least 2 feet 6 inches in width and 6 feet in length, with a minimum overhead vertical clearance of 7 feet. Racks and other fixtures used to provide for nonresidential uses must be securely affixed to the ground and allow for the bicycle to be locked and chained. The design of bicycle racks and fixtures shall be included in final site plans and approved by the public works or transportation department, and shall be separately marked.

5.51.6.3 Location

Where bicycle spaces are required by § 5.51.6.1 Generally of this chapter, the spaces may be indoors or outdoors and shall be located within 50 feet of the primary entrance. The spaces shall not be located behind any wall, shrubbery, or other visual obstruction lying between the principal building and the bicycle spaces. If required bicycle spaces are not visible from the street, signs must be posted indicating their location. Areas used for required bicycle parking shall be paved, drained, and well lighted. Spaces within offices and commercial facilities or located on balconies or within residential dwelling units shall not be counted toward required parking.

5.52 LOADING

5.52.1 General Requirements

(A) Truck loading facilities are required in all zones other than the "D" (Downtown) district for structures containing uses devoted to businesses, industry, manufacturing, storage, warehousing, processing, offices, professional buildings, hotels, multiple-family dwellings, hospitals, airports, railroad terminals, and any buildings of a commercial nature.

(B) If a structure is enlarged, expanded, or changed, it shall not be used, occupied, or operated unless it has at least the amount of off-street truck loading facilities that would apply if the increment were a separate structure.

5.52.2 Responsibility

The provision for and maintenance of the off-street truck loading facilities shall be the joint and several responsibility of the operator and owner of the land upon which the structure requiring the facilities is located.

5.52.3 Types and Location

There shall be two sizes of off-street truck loading spaces designated: "large" and "small." Each large space shall have an overhead clearance of at least 14 feet, shall be at least 12 feet wide, and shall be at least 50 feet long, exclusive of access or maneuvering area, platform, and other appurtenances. Each small space shall have an overhead clearance of at least 10 feet, shall be at least 8 feet wide, and shall be at least 20 feet long, exclusive of access or maneuvering area, platform, and other appurtenances.

5.52.4 Location

Off-street truck loading facilities shall be located on the same lot on which the structure for which they are provided is located. However, loading facilities that are available under a cooperative arrangement (refer to § 5.52.5.5 Combined Facilities of this chapter) may be located on another site not more than 300 feet from the structure for which they are provided. Service entrances and service yards shall be located only in the rear or side yard. Service yards shall be screened from adjacent residentially zoned or used property by the installation of a buffer yard, as set forth in the greenspace standards (§ 5.30 Greenspace Areas, Generally of this chapter).

5.52.5 Construction and Maintenance

Off-street truck loading facilities shall be constructed, maintained, and operated in accordance with the specifications described in § 5.52.5.1 Drainage and Surfacing through § 5.52.5.5 Combined Facilities of this chapter.

5.52.5.1 Drainage and Surfacing

Areas shall be properly graded for drainage; surfaced with concrete, asphaltic concrete, or asphalt; and maintained in good condition free of weeds, dust, trash, and debris.

5.52.5.2 Protective Screen Fencing

Areas shall be provided with protective screen fencing such that occupants of adjacent structures are not unreasonably disturbed by the movement of vehicles either during the day or at night.

5.52.5.3 Lighting

Lighting facilities shall be so arranged that they neither unreasonably disturb occupants of adjacent residential properties nor interfere with traffic.

5.52.5.4 Entrances and Exits

Areas shall be provided with entrances and exits so located as to minimize traffic congestion.

5.52.5.5 Combined Facilities

Requirements for the provision of off-street truck loading facilities with respect to two or more structures may be satisfied by the permanent allocation of the requisite number of spaces for each use in a common truck loading facility. The total number of spaces designated in a common truck loading facility shall be at least the sum of the individual requirements unless the [PLANNING OFFICIAL] determines that a lesser number of spaces will be adequate. In determining the number of revised spaces, the [PLANNING OFFICIAL] shall consider the respective times of usage of the truck loading facilities by the individual users and the character of the merchandise.

Table 5-49
Minimum Truck Loading Spaces

Square Feet of Gross Floor Area in Structure	Required Number of Spaces
0 up to and including 12,500	1 (small)
12,501 up to and including 25,000	2 (small)
25,001 up to and including 40,000	1 (large)
40,001 up to and including 100,000	2 (large)
For each additional 80,000 over 100,000	1 (large)

Table 5-50
LEED® Building Rating System Maximum and Required Points

Category	LEED Maximum Points	Points Required by This Ordinance
Sustainable Sites	[___]	[___]
Water Efficiency	[___]	[___]
Energy & Atmosphere	[___]	[___]
Materials & Resources	[___]	[___]
Indoor Environmental Quality	[___]	[___]
Innovation & Design Process	[___]	[___]

5.52.6 Minimum Requirements and Area

The minimum truck loading spaces shall be provided in all districts for structures containing the uses enumerated in Table 5-49.

5.52.7 Waiver

The [PLANNING OFFICIAL] is authorized to waive the off-street loading requirements for structures that are required to provide and maintain fewer than five off-street parking spaces, or any other structure if the design and the proposed use of the structure shows no need of off-street loading.

5.53 SUSTAINABILITY

The [LOCAL GOVERNMENT] recognizes that the design and construction of buildings can have adverse effects on the local environment, public works infrastructure, and employee health and productivity. The purpose of this section is to minimize these effects by providing specific criteria for sustainable development.

5.53.1 Generally

The construction of new buildings and major additions and renovations to existing buildings must meet the minimum requirements for certification under the LEED Green Building Rating System, as described below.

5.53.2 Site Design

Site design must achieve a minimum score of [___] points under the LEED Neighborhood Rating System.

5.53.3 Building Design

New construction must achieve a score of at least 60 points under the LEED Building Rating System. The minimum required points under each category shall be as defined in Table 5-50.

◆ *Note to reader:* The minimum point score is a policy issue. The point score should be determined by the [LOCAL GOVERNMENT] and inserted in § 5.53.1 Generally and 5.53.2 Site Design of this chapter.

COMMENTARY

This chapter addresses the substantive standards for granting development approvals. These include:
- Dimensional standards, including minimum lot size, height restrictions, and setbacks;
- Lot layout standards for new subdivisions;
- On-site infrastructure improvement requirements for streets, water, sewer, and other utilities;
- Off-site infrastructure requirements, primarily for streets and drainage;
- Park and open space improvement requirements;
- Landscaping and tree preservation requirements;
- Wetland, habitat, and protection of environmentally sensitive areas; and
- Sustainability requirements.

INTRODUCTION

This chapter consolidates the standards that are used to judge applications for development approval. This format provides a convenient reference for the specific criteria that applicants need to gain approval. These sections of the LDC that impose conditions on development approval and design standards may very well be the most important aspect of the process.

The right to require installation and construction of improvements prior to development approval is premised on two considerations:

(1) Protecting the health, safety, and welfare of the occupants of the development and its neighbors; and

(2) Reducing the financial burden on hard-pressed local governments by requiring the developer to make the initial installation of capital improvements reasonably required by development, after which point the local government assumes responsibility for maintenance and repair.[13]

STANDARDS NOT COVERED

The LDC does not include several types of standards covered in many development codes.

FLOODPLAINS

Model floodplain standards are not included in the LDC. Most states promulgate their own model floodplain regulations.[14]

GENERAL REQUIREMENTS

There generally are three types of requirements on which subdivision approval is conditioned:

(1) There is a prohibition against any subdivision activity in areas where soil, subsoil, or flooding conditions would create dangers to health or safety if development were allowed.[15] Here, coordination with the zoning ordinance and map is required to defeat a claim of a right to subdivide because the zoning regulations permit the intended use of property;

(2) The proposed subdivision should be consistent with the comprehensive plan for the area.[16] This often includes reservation of space within the subdivision for planned parks, schools, public roads, and other improvements. The subdivision should be designed to avoid overburdening area facilities—facilities that often are located outside the subdivision itself [17]; and

(3) The proposed subdivision should be coordinated with general neighborhood streets, drainage facilities, and open spaces.[18]

Enabling legislation generally sets the parameters within which requirements may be imposed by a local government. The Standard City Planning Enabling Act[19] defined these parameters as follows:

"Such regulations may provide for the proper arrangement of streets in relation to other existing or planned streets and to the master plan, for adequate and convenient open spaces; for traffic, utilities, access of fire-fighting apparatus, recreation, light, and air; and for the avoidance of congestion of population, including the minimum width and area of lots."[20]

The American Law Institute's Model Land Development Code (ALI Code) provides even greater flexibility. Subdivision control is exercised as part of a comprehensive set of development regulations, not under a separate procedure.[21]

In granting a special development approval, the land development agency may attach special conditions to the approval of the subdivision.[22] These conditions may concern any matter subject to regulation under the ALI Code, including means for:

- Minimizing any adverse impact of the development upon other land, including the hours of use and operation, and the type and intensity of activities that may be conducted[23];
- Controlling the timing and sequence of development, including when it must be commenced and completed;
- Controlling the duration of use of the development and the period of time within which any structure must be removed;
- Assuring that the development is maintained properly in the future;
- Designating the exact location and nature of the development; and
- Establishing more detailed records by submission of drawings, maps, plats, or specifications.

COMMENTARY, WAIVERS, AND VARIANCES

The LDC establishes a waiver of procedure for development standards. These procedures are distinguishable from zoning variances as they do not require unnecessary hardship. Unlike zoning variances, the waiver may be approved by an administrative official rather than the zoning board of adjustment. Most local ordinances do include a waiver of various procedures for subdivision plats that is similar to the zoning hardship standard, but which is approved by the planning board or legislative body rather than the zoning board of adjustment.[24] This affords the applicant and local government flexibility to address exceptional situations. In addition, the waiver requires compliance with the comprehensive plan. This, coupled with review by the planning official rather than an engineering official, ensures that the waiver proceeding is consistent with local planning policies.

Local governments should be careful to ensure that any type of waiver procedure, whether using the LDC language or an alternative procedure, complies with the particular requirements of state law. Under some statutes, the planning commission may waive subdivision standards but not zoning standards. In *York v. Town of Ogunquit*,[25] the planning board waived five standards as part of a plat approval: a 32-foot road width requirement, a 6 percent road grade requirement, a cul-de-sac dead-end street design requirement, a two street connections requirement, and a 5-foot sidewalk width requirement. The town subdivision regulations contained the following waiver authority:

"12.1. Where the Planning Board finds that extraordinary and necessary hardships may result from strict compliance with these standards or where there are special circumstances of a particular Plan, it may vary these standards so that substantial justice may be done and the public interest secure; provided that such variations will not have the effect of nullifying the intent and purpose of the Official Map, the Comprehensive Plan, or the Zoning Ordinance, where such exist.

"12.2. Where the Planning Board finds that, due to special circumstances of a particular Plan, the provision of certain required improvements is not requisite in the interest of public health, safety, and general welfare, or is inappropriate because of inadequacy or lack of connecting facilities adjacent or in proximity to the proposed subdivision, it may waive such requirements, subject to appropriate conditions."[26]

The court found that, under a general grant of ordinance authority granted by the statutes, the town could delegate the authority to waive subdivision standards to the planning board. However, the planning board was not empowered to waive compliance with zoning standards.[27] Because the street width requirement was found in the zoning as well as in the subdivision regulations, the court invalidated that waiver and remanded the case for either a finding of compliance with the street width requirement (requiring a revision to the plat), or a proceeding by the board of adjustment to vary the street width.

Engineering officials often press for authority to grant waivers from the standards established in this chapter. Engineering officials should be involved in reviewing waivers from street stormwater standards. However, it is important that the planning official either be involved in the waiver process or, as in the draft LDC, granted final authority to approve or deny the waiver.

Engineering officials are typically not conversant with the comprehensive plan and could grant waivers that obviate plan policies, such as encouraging pedestrian-friendly streets or the infiltration of stormwater run-off. While engineering considerations are important, they should not be allowed to override the comprehensive plan. In addition, the standards in this chapter relate to many issues not within the purview of most engineering officials' jurisdiction, such as lot design, parks and open space design, and building design. For this reason, the draft LDC assigns the authority to grant waivers from this chapter to the planning official.

ARCHITECTURE AND BUILDING DESIGN

With the exception of historic uses, many zoning ordinances do not comprehensively address the issue of urban design. When design is addressed, many ordinances rely heavily on words such as "compatible to" and "in harmony with," which are highly subjective terms and difficult to administer. The design standards should use numerical minimums and maximums in order to balance certainty to applicants with design flexibility.

To encourage pedestrian-oriented or new urbanist design, the most important standard is to include restrictions on blank walls adjoining sidewalks (see Figure 5-16). The LDC avoids the excessively fussy

**Figure 5-16
Fenestration**

Fenestration encourages pedestrian activity (right), while blank walls discourage it (left).

design standards found in many ordinances and instead focuses on basic principles. This streamlined set of rules addresses:

- Building orientation to the street;
- Entry features;
- Blank walls/garages; and
- Bulk and mass.

It does not address paint colors or similar specifics. Focusing on general design principles allows for creative approaches, adaptations suited to modern conditions, less regulation, and more efficient and productive use of staff time.

Design controls have importance beyond aesthetics. The controls established in the LDC are intended to improve street-building relationships, thereby reducing traffic congestion, encouraging walkability, and satisfying secondary public health concerns. It is important that written findings relate design controls to purposes other than appearance. While most states permit aesthetic-based regulations, some statutes continue to require other justifications.[28]

If the state does not enable design controls, incentive zoning can be used to encourage design features that may not be mandated unilaterally. Cities in Virginia use "incentive zoning" to encourage, rather than to mandate, better design. As defined in the state statute, "incentive zoning" means "the use of bonuses in the form of increased project density or other benefits to a developer in return for the developer providing certain features or amenities desired by the locality within the development."[29] By granting density bonuses, regulatory relief, development approval streamlining, and the ability to establish sites in locations not otherwise permitted in the zoning district, local governments can induce developers to provide a higher degree of design amenities.

Many corporate franchises rely on trade dress to sell their product. Customers often count on seeing a franchise's distinctive colors and familiar building design to remind them of that franchise's food, products, and services. This commitment to sameness, however, ignores the unique qualities and characteristics of communities, and the garish colors of some corporate franchises can change the feel of a community. This can be detrimental to a community's tourism revenues, property values, and community spirit.

Communities that want to control building design have, among others, the option to:

- *Require initial review of building elevations by the planning department before submitting the plan to the planning commission.* This is an informal process that does not have the effect of law. Planners do not necessarily have a background in building design or the time to review elevations. However, it ensures that the franchiser makes some attempt to work on design before the plan is submitted.

- *Establish a design review overlay zone.* This targets design review and standards to areas with particular issues, while avoiding areas that do not need the added layer of a design review process. Traditional corporate franchise design might not have a negative impact in some areas.

- *Establish a design review board.* This provides for professional review of building elevations. Administrative and elected officials avoid wasting time with preliminary design sketches; however, it adds a layer to the development approval process. Design review ordinances usually require the appointment of engineering and architectural professionals.

- *Expand the powers and duties of historic district commissions to include a more formal design review element.* This includes design guidelines and professional qualifications of members and avoids creating another board. At the same time, it neglects design review outside historic districts. If the concern is for the historic districts alone, then there is no need for another board.

- *Establish clear design standards without a formal review process.* This ensures a level of compliance without engaging a sometimes lengthy and unpredictable process. However, the clarity of the standards provides less room for direction and is therefore less predictable. The LDC uses this approach because these standards are the most difficult to write. We believe that communities will benefit from the guidance provided by these standards.

The LDC addresses residential—as well as commercial—corridor design. One technique is to restrict "snout houses" by eliminating residential façades dominated by garages. Other techniques include requiring a minimum percentage of commercial and residential front façades to include windows and entryways. Some studies show that such regulations promote community life, reduce vehicular traffic by favoring pedestrian activity, and reduce crime by putting "eyes on the street" (see Figure 5-17).[30]

**Figure 5-17
Snout-Featured Housing**

Eliminating the garage and front driveways as the principal design feature of housing is a key to form-based zoning.

Other observers have criticized such standards as impeding housing choice and failing to promote community and pedestrian friendliness.[31] Other critics claim that front garages are simply an honest way to respond to a transportation system dominated by cars.[32] In some cities, builders have claimed that such regulations increase housing costs but have provided no evidence to support the claim.[33] The standards presented in the LDC are adapted from cities, such as Portland, Oregon, that have tackled the politically sensitive issue of residential design.

ADDITIONAL GROSS FLOOR AREA AND FLOOR AREA RATIO LIMITATIONS

RETAIL AND WHOLESALE COMMERCIAL BUILDINGS

The "bigger-is-better" mantra has been challenged recently due to a growing concern that auto dependent living, which favors large-scale commercial development, is destroying quality of design; decreasing the viability of mixed-use and walkable neighborhoods; and increasing noise, air pollution, public safety and health risks, traffic congestion, and traffic accidents.

The LDC limits the size of commercial buildings to 40,000 square feet GFA, except in the "CG" (Commercial General) and "D" (Downtown) districts, where the limit is 60,000 square feet. It also requires a special use permit for all wholesale or retail commercial buildings over 25,000 square feet GFA with accompanying fiscal, environmental, and traffic assessments.

The requirement of an environmental impact assessment was upheld in *In re Wal-Mart Stores, Inc*.[34] Size limitations have been upheld where they are intended to limit commercial uses to those needed to serve area residents, to prevent traffic congestion and noise, and to preserve the residential and commercial neighborhood or small-town character of a city.[35] The use of ad-hoc design review alone has been held to be arbitrary, at least where the standards are too broad.[36] Local governments should also consider the antitrust and anti-competitive implications of protecting existing stores and businesses.[37]

If an overlay zone imposes the restrictions, the underlying zoning districts must be adjusted for GFA and FAR to make them uniform with overlay provisions.[38] The point in the process is also significant. Reserving design review to the development approval stage, which is a ministerial function, has been held inappropriate where the local government had previously approved a traffic study, sanitary sewer plan, drainage plan, and subdivision map, and the state had issued a stormwater development approval.[39] If done properly with appropriate studies consistent with comprehensive plan goals, objectives, and policies, a local government can reasonably decide what type of store it will permit.[40]

ENVIRONMENTAL ISSUES

This section establishes regulations for environmentally sensitive lands, such as riparian corridors, steep slopes, and wetlands. These regulations encourage either the preservation of sensitive areas in their natural state or development practices that do not impair the resource. These areas are important for their biological productivity and economic, aesthetic, and safety values.

There is some overlap in these regulations with state and federal regulations. The riparian and wetland regulations overlap in some areas with the floodplain management requirements of the Federal Emergency Management Agency[41] and the Corps of Engineers wetlands permitting program.[42] There is no parallel state or federal program for the control of development on steep slopes.

The riparian corridor standards are based on the three-phased stream-buffer architecture developed by the Center for Watershed Protection (CWP).[43] This increases regulatory protections through use and clearing restrictions with decreasing distance to the protected stream. This is an effective and flexible approach to regulation. Readers interested in more detail on watershed protection should consult the excellent and thorough research available through the CWP.[44]

Steep slope regulations are designed to protect the public from the dangers posed by stormwater run-off, sedimentation, and landslide resulting from inappropriate development on hillsides. The three major approaches to steep slope regulation are as follows:

(1) Slope-density regulations that decrease allowable density as slopes increase;

(2) Overlay regulations that assign uses and densities based on environmental limitations; and

(3) Discretionary approaches that use case-by-case discretion to control development on steep slopes.[45]

Because of the concerns with vague language presented in Chapter 1, General Provisions, of the LDC, the discretionary approach is rejected in the LDC. The LDC standards combine slope-density approaches with a flexible approach to encourage the sensitive development of sloped terrain. Instead of simply banning development in steeply sloped areas, the regulations require increased protections as slopes increase. This is a flexible approach, which can also avoid potential successful takings and due process challenges to steep slope regulations.

Courts have upheld restrictions on the development of steep slopes as a legitimate exercise of local police powers.[46] However, restrictions that encompass so much of a tract that it effectively prohibits all development can lead to successful takings challenges.[47] While courts are likely to defer to a local government's determination about the intensity of development permitted on slopes, the regulations should be examined to ensure that they are related to the goals of the ordinance.

In *Ginsburg Development Corp. v. Town Bd. of Town of Cortlandt*,[48] the town established an "Environmental Density Formula" that deducted environmentally sensitive areas from the gross acreage of cluster subdivisions. Two alternative methods of calculation were included, with the most restrictive used to establish permitted density. The first formula reduced total area by 25 percent before dividing square footage by minimum lot size. The second formula deducted the following from the GLA:

- 100 percent of all land within wetlands, 100-year floodplains, water bodies, and watercourses;
- 100 percent of all land with slopes of 40 percent or more; and
- 50 percent of all land with slopes of at least 25 percent and less than 40 percent.

The formula originally applied only to clustered, rather than conventional, subdivisions. Concerned about the impact of development on the environment, the town amended the formula to exclude all land on slopes exceeding 20 degrees in calculating lot counts in conventional as well as clustered subdivisions. The court noted that neither the original nor the revised ordinance prohibits construction on steep slopes, but instead "merely reduces the number of units in a subdivision that a developer would have otherwise been able to build."[49] Noting that the town had not adequately justified the relationship of the regulation to the environment, as well as related issues such as affordable housing and community character, the court annulled the town's negative declaration under the State Environmental Quality Review Act.

GRADING

Grading is generally necessary to develop streets and buildings that meet building codes, ensure safe engineering, and provide sufficient lots to generate a reasonable return on the developer's investment. The extent of grading is typically driven by economics. Developments in areas with low land costs and low densities typically avoid the expense of unnecessary grading. By contrast, developments in areas with higher market demands and higher land costs are typically graded more extensively in order to accommodate higher lot yields.[50]

Historically, grading is designed to achieve uniform patterns and coverage of an area. A site is flattened and vegetation is removed, which produces higher lot yields, but can also scar the landscape. This degree of grading can destabilize soils and increase stormwater run-off. Landform grading, which creates patterns that occur naturally and avoids the monotonous and potentially destructive effects of man-made grading, is a more contemporary approach to grading.[51]

Landform grading is a method of contour grading that manufactures slopes with curves and varying slope ratios in order to simulate the appearance of the surrounding natural terrain. Landform grading preserves wildlife habitat and wetland areas, reduces the costs that poor grading creates (e.g., unstable soils and stormwater run-off), and preserves unique natural features and aesthetic qualities. Landform grading complements efforts to preserve the natural grading and vegetation on a site by requiring the developer to recreate as much of the natural terrain as had to be moved, or grade it in such a manner as to give the site the effect of natural terrain. Native vegetation is planted to preserve the grading and the aesthetic effect after the land has been landform-graded.

Landform grading is applied to all types of construction. Instead of roads and built structures cutting through the natural terrain, roads and built structures can be molded or placed in areas to fit the natural features of the land. This type of grading is especially applicable in hilly environments.

INFRASTRUCTURE (STREET DESIGN, STORMWATER MANAGEMENT, UTILITIES, AND CONCURRENCY)

Improvement design issues are addressed in a jurisdiction's engineering manual. The engineering manual should be formally adopted in order to have a legally binding effect. While most professional engineers like to revise engineering manuals informally, they become a de facto development standard and should therefore be revised only by ordinance. This allows the governing bodies and applicants to fully debate issues that will affect the cost and viability of development.

With regard to water and wastewater, engineering manuals typically address pipe materials, pipe installation, jointing, cleanliness, valves, hydrants, service connections, reaction support, provisions for future connections, and testing. The LDC can prescribe where central water is required and where wells or community water systems are permitted.

Many local governments require that electric transmission lines be placed underground in order to minimize hazards and electrocution potential from falling wires, to facilitate passage on streets and sidewalks, and to promote aesthetic considerations.[52] However, the courts are split over the validity of local undergrounding requirements. Accordingly, an enforceable private agreement between electric utility providers and the landowner that provides for underground utilities might be considered as a submission requirement for subdivision or site plan approval.

GREENSPACE AND LANDSCAPING

Most modern zoning or development ordinances have landscaping standards. Buffer and landscaping requirements mitigate environmental site conditions, minimize conflicts between incompatible uses, and soften the visual impacts of parking areas and intensive uses. They also consume land area and can create physical barriers between uses that would otherwise be accessible by foot. In addition, they add to development costs, although long-term savings from stormwater management, and energy savings through shading of building and parking areas, can offset some of these costs. Accordingly, if buffers are to respond to a comprehensive plan mandate to create compact, walkable communities, they should be limited in scope to situations involving uses that are truly incompatible.

It is important to ensure that landscaping is maintained after it is installed. The LDC suggests a cross-reference to state regulations. Some states have detailed irrigation standards that are familiar to landscaping professionals and that can be incorporated by reference into the local codes. For example, the Texas Commission on Environmental Quality publishes detailed irrigation regulations[53] that address local regulation, local inspection, water conservation, backflow prevention, spacing, water pressure, wind derating, precipitation rate, piping, and wiring.

Buffers and setbacks are the primary methods for regulating use-to-use impacts. The effect of buffers on adjacent land uses is determined by the width and composition of the buffer and the land uses that it separates. For example, a shopping center adjacent to a single-family residential subdivision would require a wider and more heavily vegetated buffer than would the separation of larger from smaller dwelling units. A "setback" is a minimum distance between two land uses, such as a building and a street, while a "buffer" provides additional requirements for vegetation, fencing, and other barriers to noise, lighting, and other nuisances. In environmentally sensitive areas, buffers can also be used to filter nutrients and other pollutants entering streams, wetlands, and other sensitive lands.

The two major issues associated with buffer requirements are:

(1) Establishing the appropriate buffer width; and
(2) Establishing permissible use and activity regulations within the buffer.

Buffers can be either fixed or floating. A "fixed" buffer is an established requirement applicable to mapped or identified areas, while a "floating" buffer varies in accordance with the presence of physical features, such as adjacent sloping areas, poorly drained soils, and vegetative cover. While fixed buffers are easier to administer, floating buffers can be used to protect the full range of environmental resources that the community wishes to preserve.

Within the buffer area, regulations vary from the total prohibition of all uses, of planting and landscaping requirements, and to authorize approval for innocuous activities. The latter may include narrow footpaths or walkways and driveways. Buffers should be based upon use-to-use impact. Thus, a minimal buffer is needed to separate single-family from multifamily uses, while a much larger buffer is needed to separate single-family from industrial uses.

Ensuring adequate landscaping accomplishes more than aesthetic goals. By preserving trees and native understory, degradation of air and water quality will be abated, animal wildlife is preserved, and nuisance effects resulting from noise and glare generated by adjacent land uses are diminished. A general performance standard that accounts for landscaping and bulk attributable to natural land features can serve as a unifying framework for the administration of the more detailed landscaping standards.

Plant lists are important for proper administration. A list of nuisance-type trees, shrubs, and ground covers (i.e., prohibited landscaping materials) should be included. Plant lists should be broken down into categories with simple diagrams. For instance, group large trees together and label as "Type A" trees, and understory or small to medium trees should be labeled as "Type B." When a matrix indicates the type of trees to use, the ordinance can simply cite the tree type.

Parking lot landscaping is important because it improves the aesthetics and reduces the effect of weather elements on paving and parking areas. Consideration should be given to the hardiness of the chosen species. If salt is used to melt ice, the salt will have an impact on the health of the materials. Diagrams of parking lot landscape layouts and components should be used.

Inspection is important to ensure that landscaping is properly installed and maintained. It is assumed that the planner or the planning official checks the landscaping and buffering against the plan to ensure that the developer followed the approved plan. There should be a statement in the ordinance assigning responsibility for inspection and requiring that each item be checked against the approved landscaping plan to ensure completion. A maintenance bond requirement of 150 percent for up to five years should be adopted as a condition of development approval.

In terms of opacity of the buffer or screen required, a good approach is to include a standard for determining when and how a screen is judged to be effective. A standard of opacity of 90 percent is the target.

Irrigation requirements in arid areas is appropriate and cost efficient. A watering system ensures that plants receive adequate, consistent water, which avoids costly replacement. Areas that receive regular precipitation may omit irrigation requirements.

LIGHTING

Ordinances restricting lighting levels are becoming increasingly popular, with concerns ranging from the effect of lighting levels on the peace and tranquility of residential areas to environmental concerns, such as light pollution, ability to view stars and planets at night, and energy conservation. Lighting standards can range from detailed "dark-sky" ordinances, which proscribe maximum illumination levels, to simple height and shielding requirements.

A number of states have published model lighting ordinances, and at least one state (Arizona) expressly authorizes them.[54] While most ordinances proscribe maximum lighting levels for particular uses, the International Dark-Sky Association (IDA) model code provides an approach that limits lumens per acre.[55] According to the IDA, this approach is easier to use and provides flexibility because the lighting designer can decide how to allocate the lighting limits. The IDA cautions that proscribing maximum pole heights can simply result in more lighting poles, thereby defeating the purpose of controlling light pollution. Lighting levels should vary by development tier. In low-density residential locations, strict illumination levels should apply; in more intense areas, such as downtown areas, higher lighting levels are acceptable.

HOMELAND SECURITY SITE-SPECIFIC VULNERABILITY ASSESSMENT

Local government officials, police, fire, emergency personnel, architects, professional engineers, developers, and building owners must take proactive homeland security steps, including the review of certain site plans for building and on-site design.[56] Vulnerability assessments should be coordinated with the Department of Transportation, the United States Environmental Protection Agency (US EPA), the Department of Health and Human Services, and the Centers for Disease Control to prevent chemical, biological, and radioactive attacks.[57] Among building and land design features are:
- Identification stations;
- Facility entry checkpoints;
- Inspection facilities;
- Surveillance equipment;
- Access controls;
- Architectural site design; and
- Internal site design (e.g., lobbies, stairways, emergency stairs, mail-room design, isolation of loading and storage areas, protection of computer systems control and mechanical rooms, emergency generators, and fuel tanks).[58]

Applications seeking development approval for public, semipublic, and intensive private facilities (e.g., power plants, electrical transmission facilities, dams, high-rise buildings, regional shopping facilities, industrial buildings, airports, bridges, chemical plants, convention centers, government buildings, hospitals, hotels, ports, railroads, rail yards, transportation terminals, transit station stops, schools, stadiums, multifamily apartment complexes, wastewater and water plants and facilities, and other uses identified through site- and threat-specific analysis) should provide a site-specific vulnerability assessment identifying the following elements:
- The purpose of the facility;
- Sensitive or vulnerable areas;
- Types of activities at the site;
- A description of users of the facility;
- Site perimeter security (setbacks, unobstructed views, restricted access, and avoidance of unnecessary signage);
- Landscaping and external design (avoidance of high-speed access, restriction of entrance and parking accesses, use of secure concrete barriers, and incorporation of traffic patterns of pedestrians and vehicles in landscaping design); and
- Building design security measures (identification stations, facility entry checkpoints, vehicle inspection facilities, and surveillance equipment).[59]

Concerns that post-September 11, 2001, construction would be dominated by brute concrete bunkers, creating ugly cities, are ill founded. The designers of new public and private buildings are turning to glass façades. Learning from the lessons of Hurricane Andrew in 1992, the Oklahoma City terrorist act in 1995, and the World Trade Center terrorist act in 2001, designers and architects have designed glass curtain walls that can perform protectively and resiliently against blasts by holding panes in place and controlling flying debris.[60]

The local government shall, within 90 days after adoption of the LDC, provide administrative regulations, checklists, and application forms necessary to carry out the provisions of this section. The administrative regulations shall provide for designation of the law enforcement officials, building inspectors, and architect/professional engineers required to approve plans and carry out audits and inspections. The administrative regulations shall also provide for adoption of development approval fees to cover the costs of administering this section.[61]

The constraints placed on local budgets by additional security measures are of particular concern to local governments. Local governments and developers need to adopt new strategies to address these challenges by:
- Building within the constraints of existing infrastructure;
- Promoting mixed-use projects that combine investment in facilities;
- Quantifying the public benefits of projects that require public money;
- Leveraging federal and state resources devoted to security and terrorism protection[62]; and
- Carefully reviewing insurance policies to ensure that "acts of terrorism" are included in coverages and are excluded from exemptions for "force majeure" in contracts and project insurance.[63]

LOT DIMENSIONS, SETBACK, AND DENSITY STANDARDS

LOTTING STANDARDS

Lot dimensions affect the density and intensity of development, the public's ability to provide services, and the sizing of public facilities and utilities such as roads, water lines, and sewer lines. The following types of lots might be permitted in some situations to encourage innovative design and promote affordable housing:

- *Zero lot line lots:* These are lots in which the homes are sited on the lot line, either adjoining or on opposite sides.[64]
- *Z lots and angled Z lots:* These lots provide for a portion of opposite sides of the lot to be placed on the lot line. An angled Z lot tilts the lot 30 to 45 degrees to alternate side- and front-loaded garages.[65]
- *Wide-shallow lots:* These lots are more wide than deep, which provides comparable density to other small lot types while maintaining a front façade similar to conventional single-family detached homes.[66]
- *Zipper lots:* These lots feature a rear lot line that jogs back to vary the depth of the rear yard and to concentrate usable open space on the side of the lot.[67]

The zoning district regulations in Chapter 3, Zoning, of the LDC are generally flexible enough to accommodate these and other lot layouts.

FLAG LOTS

"Flag lots" are lots that do not meet minimum frontage requirements and where access is typically derived from a narrow right-of-way or driveway (referred to as the "stem" or "flagpole" portion of the lot).[68] Flag lots provide design flexibility and the ability to develop remote areas while maintaining rural character. They were originally designed to provide access to landlocked parcels.[69] Flag lots have also been used at the end of cul-de-sacs or dead-end streets in order to avoid street extensions. However, flag lots require homeowners to maintain extra driveway lengths, pose access constraints for emergency vehicles, and create compatibility issues where "pipestem" dwellings appear to be located in the rear yards of adjacent residences.[70] Flag lots with excessively long driveways can become de facto private roadways, especially where the lots are subdivided. This inhibits emergency access and increases public service costs.

The following additional standards have been used in some jurisdictions to prevent the abuse of flag lots:

- Easements may be prohibited as a means of access and the flagpole may be required to be under the same ownership as the flag portion of the lot.
- A numerical and/or percentage restriction on the number of flag lots may be provided. A restriction on the number of rear lots served by a common flagpole or driveway may also be provided. Conversely, flag lots may be restricted to minor subdivisions or where necessary to eliminate direct access to arterials and thoroughfares. A paved turnaround may be required for emergency access.
- Flag lots that increase the number of lots with direct access to a collector or arterial road may be restricted.
- Land divisions with two or more flag lots may be prohibited. As an alternative, private street standards may apply to partitions exceeding a designated number of flag lots.
- Nonresidential or multifamily development may be prohibited on flag lots.
- Landscaped buffers shall be required on the perimeter of the flag portion of the lot, or between the flag portion and the lot from which it was divided.

A "regularity" formula should be required to prevent excessively deep lots. An example of a regularity formula is as follows:

$r = 16A/p^2$

where:

r = regularity factor;
A = land area (in square feet); and
p = perimeter (in feet).

A complete legal description may be required to avoid confusion as to lot boundaries. Resubdivision of a flag lot may be prohibited in order to avoid the proliferation of dwellings on roads not built to public standards.

PARKING

Minimum parking requirements were historically designed to reduce street congestion and to avoid spillover parking on streets in residential neighborhoods. An unintended side effect of such requirements was the rise of excessively sized surface parking areas. These areas inhibit walkability by spreading uses apart, forcing pedestrians to compete with cars to reach retail and employment destinations, and making vehicular travel more convenient than foot travel. They create "urban heat islands" as the summer sun hits the pavement, increasing air conditioning costs as well as health problems. Stormwater management systems needed to capture run-off from parking areas further consumes land, spreading uses even farther apart and creating barriers to pedestrian access.

Most local governments seek to avoid parking shortages by requiring developers to provide a minimum amount of parking as a condition of zoning approval. However, municipal zoning codes do not address issues relating to an oversupply of parking. Only recently have local governments begun to address the problems that too much parking creates by limiting the number of parking spaces that developers can provide for their projects. Minimum parking requirements address problems associated with an undersupply of parking.

Minimum parking requirements require developers to provide at least a certain number of off-street parking spaces. Historically, these requirements were developed in the 1950s to address a lack of parking spaces that was making urban areas less economically competitive and attractive to residents, businesses, and their customers. Minimum parking requirements were implemented to ensure that there was parking within a reasonable distance of a driver's final destination.[71]

In addition to creating a more competitive urban environment, minimum parking requirements are thought to guard against parking spillover into residential neighborhoods. When there are not enough parking spaces at a certain destination, drivers park in the next convenient area. When the next convenient area is a residential neighborhood, local residents are left without a convenient place to park when they come home, and local elected officials are then given a highly contentious political issue.[72]

While minimum parking requirements alleviate some problems, it is increasingly recognized that they can create others. Minimum parking requirements are generally designed to satisfy peak demand for free parking.[73] They are not designed to accurately reflect the need for parking nor are they intended to optimize land usage.[74] Thus, minimum parking requirements can create an oversupply of parking spaces, which creates the following problems:

- *Parking has been described as a "fertility drug for cars."*[75] As more parking is provided, more cars take advantage of it.[76] As the number of cars increase, so do road congestion and traffic jams. In response, local governments must pay for the increased wear and tear on the roads, more sophisticated and expensive traffic control mechanisms at intersections, and eventually the widening of roads for drivers who wish to maintain their current degree of access within urban areas.[77]

- *The amount of parking affects public transportation.* As parking availability increases, fewer people use public transportation. Several reports even indicate that mass transit improvements will not increase ridership unless the parking supply is reduced.[78]

- *As the number of cars increase and mass transit use decreases, air quality decreases.* Decreased air quality creates and/or aggravates health problems for urban residents. Individuals who suffer from pulmonary diseases, such as asthma and bronchitis, suffer as the increased number of cars decrease air quality.[79]

- *Parking pavement creates environmental problems.* The impervious surfaces of parking lots do not allow water to be absorbed into the ground, which creates problems with stormwater run-off and water quality.[80] Parking lots with large, black tarmac surfaces attract heat and increase the ambient temperature in urban areas on hot summer days. Parking lots replace more productive types of urban land uses, including office buildings, shopping centers, or residential developments, causing urban space to be less dense.[81] Lower-density urban areas act as an impediment to current trends in pedestrian-friendly neighborhood design and in turn facilitate greater car dependency.[82]

- *Other negative fiscal consequences of parking lots.* Federal laws, including the Clean Air Act and the Transportation Equity Act for the 21st Century, are also forcing local governments to address the problems.[83] Increased taxes and poor environmental and driving conditions combine to create an incentive for businesses to invest in locations on the urban fringe instead of in the urban core.[84]

Failure to address the oversupply of parking creates many of the same problems that minimum parking requirements were supposed to solve (e.g., sprawl, poor economic environment, and loss of investment). To avoid these problems, a balance between an oversupply of parking and an undersupply of parking must be found. A balance is struck when there are sufficient parking spaces to accommodate recurrent peak parking demand but do not undercut current transit ridership nor a city's financial ability to meet other public needs and obligations. The underlying goal is reasonable and balanced land-use management, which creates travel choices that sustain local economies and their environments.[85]

Local governments in the U.S. have begun to supplement minimum parking requirements with maximum parking requirements in an attempt to achieve balanced land-use management. Maximum parking requirements limit the number of parking spaces a developer can provide.

Large cities (e.g., San Antonio, Texas; Seattle, Washington; San Francisco, California; and Portland, Oregon) have maximum parking requirements. Portland has one of the most sophisticated maximum parking requirement ordinances in the country. Portland's maximum parking requirements vary within a jurisdiction, depending on the characteristics of different districts and the distance of a land use from mass transit. Other cities, such as San Francisco and Seattle, apply maximum parking limits only to office buildings.[86]

Smaller local governments (e.g., Cambridge, Massachusetts; Redmond, Washington; Queen Creek, Arizona; and Concord, North Carolina) are also implementing maximum parking requirements. States and regional governments are beginning to support or implement maximum parking requirements. The State of Washington recently advised its local governments to consider implementing maximum parking requirements.[87] Regional councils in the Portland metropolitan area and in southwest Washington have also recommended that local governments adopt maximum parking requirements.[88]

The United Kingdom, which has a statutory system of urban planning, recently enacted a policy requiring every local government (counties, cities, and regional councils) to implement maximum parking requirements for retail stores, stadiums, office buildings, cinemas, and conference centers that reach sizes above relevant thresholds (e.g., 30,000 square feet). The central government also authorizes the application of maximum parking requirements to other land uses, depending on particular needs. Except in rare circumstances, minimum parking requirements have been abolished in favor of permitting developers to provide as many parking spaces as they think is fitting for the particular development.[89]

Maximum parking requirements work in the same way that minimum parking requirements do. Depending on the proposed land use (e.g., office building, golf course, or apartment building), there is a particular ratio of parking spaces allocated to the land use. For example, an office building might be limited to 2.5 parking spots per 1,000 square feet of gross leasable area. The numerical limits set by local governments for particular land uses usually come from either the parking generation manual published by the Institute of Transportation Engineers (ITE)[90] and/or from limits other local governments have instituted.[91] Determining the ratios for minimum and maximum parking requirements requires proper planning.[92]

CALCULATING MINIMUM AND MAXIMUM PARKING REQUIREMENTS

When local governments create minimum and maximum parking requirements, they are predicting parking demand. "Parking demand" is defined as the accumulation of vehicles parked at a given time as a result of activity at a given site. Parking demand is an outgrowth of a local government's political and economic environment and a local government's history.[93] There is no universal standard for parking demand.[94] Parking demand varies among and within local governments for a variety of reasons, including a local government's development patterns, financial resources, investment climate, street traffic, and mass transit use.[95]

Local governments cannot afford to be cavalier with maximum parking requirements.[96] The negative implications of an oversupply of parking can be more noticeable to the general public than an undersupply of parking. For instance, a driver is not as likely to associate poor air quality and congested roads with an oversupply of parking, but they will quickly associate not being able to find a parking spot with an undersupply of parking. Similarly, a business owner is not as likely to associate increased taxes for road construction with an oversupply of parking as they will associate a lack of parking spaces for customers with an undersupply of parking. Pressures may also come from lenders and developers who feel that only insufficient parking will harm their long-term investment in a building[97] (see Table 5-51).

Table 5-51
10 Questions for a Local Government to Consider When Creating a Parking Policy

1. What are the community's planning policies?
2. What is the best distribution of parking facilities with regard to intensity, parking needs, transit services, and roadway capacity?
3. Do parking requirements differ by area?
4. What opportunities exist for shared parking?
5. Can parking serve as a catalyst for desired development?
6. How does parking affect location and design of transportation improvements?
7. Should parking be provided for all users, or rationed?
8. Who develops, finances, and operates parking facilities?
9. What public-private arrangements are feasible developing, financing, and operating parking?
10. Should parking lead or follow development?

Source: Weant and Levinson, 1990.

ADJUSTING TO MAXIMUM PARKING STANDARDS

Precautions can be taken to avoid creating an undersupply of parking. As with any parking policy, a local government should diligently examine parking demand to understand the characteristics that create the unique parking demand for the area.[98] The parking generation manual from the ITE[99] and the parking requirements of other local governments can be used to reference parking requirement ratios, but should not be followed blindly.[100]

A local government can also hedge against creating an undersupply of parking with maximum parking requirements by using Transportation Demand Management (TDM).[101] "TDM" is the term used to describe strategies that result in the efficient use of transportation infrastructure.[102] The term also pertains to creating incentives for drivers to seek other methods of transportation.[103] Maximum parking requirements themselves are considered a TDM strategy.[104] Other TDM strategies include in-lieu parking fees, shared parking, centralized parking, parking freezes, subsidies for transit, cash-out programs, transit improvements, pedestrian and bicycle amenities, vehicle trip reductions, parking brokerages, and parking pricing.[105] The business community in Portland, Oregon, would not accept maximum parking requirements until Portland made a greater commitment to mass transit.[106]

TDM recognizes that travel patterns will change as parking conditions change, especially among individuals who drive to work.[107] As TDM strategies are implemented, people who live in the suburbs tend to shift

**Figure 5-18
Surface Parking**

**Figure 5-19
Rear Parking**

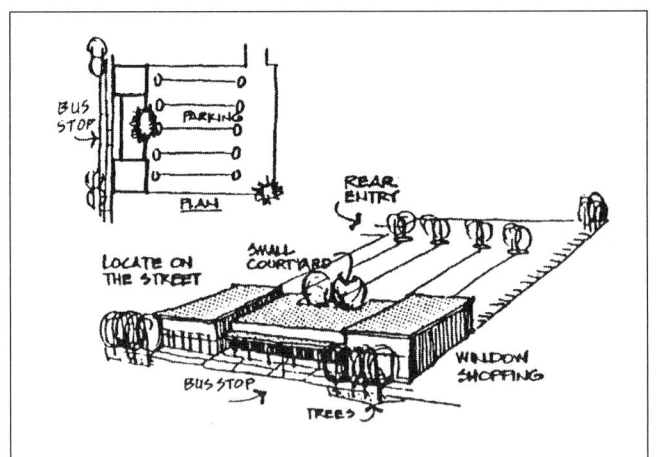

Source: Snohomish County Transportation Authority, "A Guide to Land Use and Public Transportation," United States Department of Transportation Report DOT-T-90-13 (1989).

more to ridesharing, telecommuting, and cycling, while people who live in urban areas shift primarily to transit and walking.[108] TDM builds flexibility into the rigidity of parking requirements and lessens the burden placed on maximum parking requirements to reduce the oversupply of parking.[109]

MAXIMUM PARKING STANDARDS

After a generation of minimum parking requirements, and given the current oversupply of parking in many regions, it might be easy to think that developers want to build as many parking spaces as possible, but this is not true. It cannot be assumed that developers will meet the parking demand for their projects.[110] Certain land uses may fail to provide an adequate parking supply.[111] Parking is costly to construct and developers are forced to pass on the cost of construction to the individuals who purchase or lease their buildings. The cost of providing parking, especially if underground or in parking structures, can increase the rent of office space by as much as 67 percent over asphalt paved parking lots.[112] Developers can actually benefit financially by not providing enough parking spaces for some projects.[113]

This disincentive shows that developers will not uniformly oppose maximum parking requirements. The disincentive to provide parking, however, is a factor that cautions against eliminating minimum parking requirements in favor of relying solely on maximum parking requirements. The goal is to find a balance between an undersupply and an oversupply of parking. While the United Kingdom did away with minimum parking requirements, it should be remembered that the United Kingdom's system of mass transportation and the development patterns of many of their cit-

ies are vastly different than cities in the U.S. In addition, the goals that the United Kingdom is trying to achieve with its parking policy might not be the same goals that local governments in the U.S. are trying to achieve.

Once a decision is made to implement maximum parking requirements, the local government should consider supplementing maximum parking limits with other TDM strategies in order to achieve a flexible parking policy tailored to the unique characteristics of the area. If implemented correctly, maximum parking requirements can achieve the goal of reasonable and balanced land-use management, which creates travel choices that sustain local economies and their environments (see Figure 5-18).

LOCATION OF PARKING AREAS

The location of parking significantly affects building-street relationships. Permitting on-street parking on local streets and collector roads is often cited as a way to accommodate parking needs while keeping traffic speeds low. Rear parking requirements are an emerging feature of design-oriented urban codes. Conventional surface parking located in front of buildings requires pedestrians to walk long distances to reach building entrances from the street. Rear parking permits the buildings to form a street wall along sidewalks and shortens sidewalk-to-building walking distances (see Figure 5-19).

PARKING RATIOS

A jurisdiction should establish minimum and maximum parking requirements based on a national standard, such as the parking generation manual published by the ITE.[114] A maximum parking requirement might apply exclusively to surface parking lots. Zoning incentives might be considered for nonresidential uses that utilize structured or underground parking rather than surface parking, with ground-floor retail and fenestration requirements to foster pedestrian activity at the street level.

The dimensions of parking stalls and aisles mediate traffic circulation, public safety, and design issues. Numeric standards should be established for stalls, parking angles, and aisle dimensions. The standards established in the LDC are based on commonly used nationally recognized standards.[115] Many jurisdictions require parking spaces to be paved in order to avoid dust and the deterioration of abutting street surfaces. The LDC suggests, in addition to paved surfaces, pervious pavements that infiltrate stormwater. This minimizes the amount of stormwater typically flowing from a paved parking area, and complements the infiltration policies established in § 5.22 Stormwater Management of this chapter. The standards are based on national technical and engineering sources.[116]

The legality of off-street parking requirements is uniformly accepted,[117] particularly with regard to minimum required spaces.[118] Other types of regulations include pavement specifications, parking space dimensions, landscaping, and lighting.

In recent years, traffic congestion has been tied to the availability of abundant, free parking, especially in large office and retail centers,[119] which also acts as a barrier to pedestrian activity. Some jurisdictions have established both maximum and minimum parking requirements. Others have also required rear parking in order to minimize the appearance of a "sea of asphalt," using buildings as a street buffer for parking areas. Shared parking standards have also been established in some jurisdictions, which reduce the parking requirements for multiple uses that have different peak parking utilization.

Parking requirements should be integrated with the use classifications in the zoning districts. A separate matrix of parking requirements for each permitted and conditional use minimizes the need for interpretation by the planning official (see Table 3-4, Use Matrix, in Chapter 3, Zoning, of the LDC).

In order to permit shared parking surfaces for mixed-use development, the jurisdiction should examine peak parking demand times for each type of new development. Shared use of parking spaces encourages mixed-use development and greater efficiency by providing incentives for more compact and efficient land use.[120]

Peak parking demand times fall into five general categories[121]:

(1) Weekday-daytime [9 AM–4 PM]
(2) Weekday-evening [6 PM–midnight]
(3) Weekend-daytime [9 AM–4 PM]
(4) Weekend-evening [6 PM–midnight]
(5) Nighttime [midnight–6 AM]

By breaking down mixed-use development into these five categories, shared parking can provide significant savings of impervious surface expansion.[122] Interior landscaping and parking island requirements should be included with the landscaping regulations in order to avoid heat islands and to improve the appearance of parking areas.

Many of the parking requirements are tied to factors (e.g., the number of seats, the number of employees, and the number of patients), and other factors that may vary through the life cycle of a building. From the public sector's perspective, this increases the need to track and monitor the requirements applicable to changes in land use for a given building. To the extent possible, parking requirements should be tied to square footage, which is easier to track and monitor from the application.[123]

A summary of peak parking demands and parking generation measured by square feet of gross leasable area is in Weant and Levinson's *Parking*.[124] Table 5-46 contains parking ratios for general types of use based on square footage. This approach makes great sense because the number of employees that will occupy a proposed building is often unknown.[125] This approach provides more uniform standards, which simplify compliance for developers.

Minimum and maximum parking requirements should be included in order to avoid the drainage problems and blighting effect of large expanses of impervious surfaces. A maximum parking requirement might apply exclusively to surface parking lots. Zoning incentives might be considered for nonresidential uses that utilize structured parking rather than surface parking, with ground-floor retail and fenestration requirements to foster pedestrian activity at the street level.

PARKS AND OPEN SPACE

In providing for parks and open space, several considerations are important. First, parks can spur economic development and neighborhood revitalization.[126] Second, recent U.S. Supreme Court precedent requires proportionality between infrastructure exactions and the needs generated by development, which places a higher scrutiny burden of proof on local governments to justify the magnitude of the exactions.[127] Using voluntary development agreements or voluntary dedications on greenway rights-of-way exempts the proffers from constitutional analysis.[128]

The design of parks and open space is as critical, if not more critical, than the sheer amount of space provided. The amount of open space provided may vary with the size and type of development. A jurisdiction should consider locational and design standards so that park and recreational facilities are able to serve as usable and functional space. Too many ordinances require only a minimum amount of open space, ignor-

**Figure 5-20
Effective Use of Open Space**

Open space surrounded by buildings and residences can provide form and function to a neighborhood or commercial activity center.

ing the more critical issues of design, location, and maintenance. This can result in parks and recreation facilities built on leftover spaces with poor public access. As with buildings, parks have a local design vernacular that can be reflected in the ordinance.

The LDC applies parks and open space set-aside requirements to all new residential and commercial development applications. Projects without adequate on-site space are required to pay a fee in lieu of the open space set-aside. The set-aside is based on the number of dwelling units or nonresidential floor space, as required by the constitutional rough proportionality standard.

Maintenance and ownership issues are also critical for several reasons:

• Parks must be maintained so that they do not become a blighting influence on surrounding neighborhoods;

• Maintenance avoids potentially expensive municipal obligations; and

• The LDC's ownership options could strengthen the regulations in the event of a constitutional challenge, as applicants have the option to own and maintain the parks themselves. Applicants would have the option to offer dedication to a jurisdiction or to maintain the open space through an HOA (see Figure 5-20).

The LDC also establishes locational standards so that park and recreational facilities are able to serve as usable and functional space. This ensures that parks are within a reasonable walking distance of residents. Public works officials sometimes suggest that numerous small parks are more costly to maintain than larger ones. However, larger parks typically define automobile access and can be more difficult to integrate with urban public usage.

The LDC's parks standards synchronize with urban form issues. Infill lots or subdivisions within walking distance of existing parks are exempt from the parks and open space standards. This incentivizes urban infill. The exemption furthers the legitimate public policy of underutilized capacity when taking into account the need for facilities generated by development in existing built-up areas.

STORMWATER MANAGEMENT

Stormwater management should be considered comprehensively, both at its source and at its destination. Reducing impervious surfaces minimizes stormwater generation. At the treatment end, engineered approaches (curbs and gutter, concrete drainageways, and detention or retention basins) are coming into disfavor for several reasons:

• Impervious surfaces designed to discharge stormwater from a site as quickly as possible impede infiltration of rainfall. Because infiltration captures rainfall, this has the effect of actually increasing the volume and rate of stormwater while impeding groundwater recharge and requiring that additional supplies of water be obtained than would otherwise be necessary;

• An engineered approach can have an adverse effect on environmental quality. Rainfall on concrete surfaces loses the opportunity for filtration of contaminants provided by natural soils and vegetation, and increased pavement can create urban heat islands and disrupt natural ecosystems;

• Engineered approaches, such as detention or retention basins, consume large land areas, which minimize redevelopment opportunities, segregate buildings and uses, and reduce land values. These approaches are inconsistent with the goal of promoting a compact, walkable community; and

• Basins are considered unsightly, even by some professionals who design them (see Figure 5-21).

Land-use tools to control stormwater run-off include the following options[129]:

• *Limit impervious surfaces through impervious surface ratios.* This limits run-off by limiting hard surfaces that generate run-off. However, this can reduce land densities and intensities by limiting site coverage and can induce sprawl by requiring more open space land in relation to buildings and separating buildings. An impervious surface ratio works best in areas where development is less intense and a jurisdiction seeks to maintain lower densities for policy reasons.

• *Establish a sensitive areas protection ordinance for wetlands, floodplains, steep slopes, and other areas that intercept and impede rainfall.* Limit impervious surfaces and site design and establish variable width buffers. This reduces development in areas that most effectively han-

**Figure 5-21
Sustainable Water Retention**

Bioretention facilities or "rain gardens" provide an alternative to basins and can double as open space.

dle stormwater run-off. Development in these areas produces run-off and destroys natural features that effectively retain it. However, there is often a perception that this restricts property rights and can result in takings issues if an entire site is sensitive and little or no beneficial economic use is allowed. Procedures for identifying these areas must be developed unless they are mapped in advance. Variances and ratios that vary by site size can minimize property rights issues as well as using cluster zoning and transfers of development rights

• *Establish conservation subdivision design options, which eliminate minimum lot size and require a higher percentage (e.g., 50 percent or above).* Only density is controlled. This creates design flexibility to avoid development of sensitive areas and preserves development potential. Eliminating minimum lot size could be controversial. The regulations are viable as an option for developers; however, the market has been slow to respond in many areas. A conservation design option is described in § 2.2 Conservation Subdivision in Chapter 2, Use Patterns, of the LDC.

• *Establish lower minimum street widths and parking space requirements.* Limit residential street right-of-way widths to the minimum needed to accommodate the travelway, the sidewalk, and open channels. This allows developers to directly limit paved surfaces. Concerns that are typically expressed by solid waste and fire protection officials for wider streets for access to fire fighting vehicles and dumpsters have been ameliorated by modern redesign or vehicles.

• *Establish maximum parking ratios (parking caps).* This requires developers to directly limit paved surfaces.

This is discussed under the section entitled "Parking," above.

• *Reduce the length of residential streets by permitting alternative layouts that increase the number of homes served per unit length.* This directly limits paved surfaces. It may contradict the goal of increasing connectivity if the decreased length results in cul-de-sacs. These conflicts are resolved in the ordinance language.

• *Allow vegetated open channels and swales in the street right-of-way to convey and treat stormwater run-off where density, topography, soils, and slope permit.* This minimizes and cleanses run-off to a greater extent than curb and gutter. Vegetated channels will consume more land than curb and gutter but as an incentive may be credited against open space requirements. In the past, professional engineers preferred the greater control over flows provided by curb and gutter. This approach has changed because the need for water in arid areas creates great cost incentives for rain storage.

• *Relax side yard setbacks and allow narrower frontages to reduce total road length.* This minimizes the length of roadways and therefore minimizes impervious surfaces. There may be resistance from neighborhoods that favor lower densities. These approaches are recommended because they are consistent with the new urbanist principles of the LDC and promote effective stormwater management.

• *Relax front setback requirements to minimize driveway lengths.* This minimizes the length of driveways and therefore minimizes impervious surfaces.

• *Use flexible design standards for residential subdivision sidewalks.* Allow sidewalks on only one side of the street and provide common walkways linking pedestrian areas. This minimizes impervious surfaces from sidewalk areas and reduces development costs. However, it can contradict pedestrian connectivity goals. Conflicts can be resolved by restricting the option to areas that the community wants to develop less intensively.

• *Allow alternative driveway surfaces and shared driveways that connect two or more units.* This minimizes impervious areas as well as discharges from areas that are graded. Maintenance of shared driveways must be assured. Maintenance should be required for approval of these options.

• *Direct rooftop run-off to pervious areas (e.g., yards, open channels, or vegetated areas) and avoid routing rooftop run-off to the roadway and the stormwater conveyance system (known as "low-impact design").* This directs stormwater to areas where infiltration is possible, thereby minimizing and slowing flows while protecting water quality and supply for rain storage.

STREET DESIGN

Street design has a profound impact on the built environment and utilization for various modes of travel. Most local street design standards are driven by service

**Figure 5-22
Narrowing Streets**

Narrow streets provide opportunities for sidewalks and street trees.

**Figure 5-23
Adaptable Fire Service Delivery**

Fire trucks, as shown here in Charleston, South Carolina, can be adapted to serve narrow streets with tight turning radii.

access, resulting in wide streets that are suitable primarily for automobiles. Wide streets and large turning radii produce faster vehicle speeds and require longer pedestrian crossings. Reducing street widths, curb radii, and street lengths creates a more pedestrian-friendly environment. The street design standards could be updated to encourage landscaped medians and to address the location of street trees and sidewalks.

STREET WIDTHS

Narrow streets have gained in popularity in recent years because of the neighborhoods in which narrow streets are frequently found. A TND (see Chapter 2, Use Patterns, of the LDC) considers the needs of pedestrians as well as cars. The needs of pedestrians are frequently overlooked in modern subdivision designs where there are no amenities within walking distance, no sidewalks, and where wide roads promote high speeds within the subdivision. TND promotes mixed-use development so that residents do not have to drive to amenities, but requires a pedestrian-friendly environment be created that slows traffic (see Figure 5-22).

Narrower streets slow traffic, minimize pavement, and provide a more inviting streetscape for pedestrians. Fire officials and other service providers request wider streets in order to accommodate truck access. Shorter blocks with hydrants, where a narrow street takes access to a wider collector street, could provide a partial solution. These concerns can be met by investing in smaller fire trucks with tighter turning radii. Fire departments will also support narrow streets where buildings and dwelling units are sprinklered (see Figure 5-23).

Concern has been expressed over the ability of emergency vehicles, school buses, solid waste collection equipment, utility company vehicles, and fire department equipment to access structures that access narrow streets with short turning radii and narrow service alleys. Options for addressing the concerns of public works officials in this regard include the following:

• *Require that equipment be available with a turning radius and wheel base that will function within the proposed street design criteria.* This has the advantage of providing accessibility to structures that will allow the traditional neighborhood design where desired. However, it involves some capital expense for the local jurisdiction, and alleys will be an added maintenance expense to the local jurisdiction for pavement and drainage structures.

• *Use existing equipment.* This requires that all utilities in the development would have to place service and distribution lines underground to facilitate a clear corner for turning and a clear overhead for hydraulic lifting and dumping equipment in the service alleys. The tight turning radii can be addressed with additional traffic operational provisions and utility facility placement standards. The jurisdiction can control on-street parking at street intersections and alley entrances and exits. Parking would be prohibited within the path of the necessary turning radius on all four corners of street and alley intersections. These parking distance restrictions can be calculated based on the wheel base and turning radius of the appropriate vehicle in each jurisdiction. The issue can also be addressed by requiring one-way traffic in alleys and prohibiting unattended vehicles in alleys. Outside the alley, the utility company may use overhead wiring to clear-span the curb line points of curve and tangency with any pole placement. This, combined with the on-street parking limits at intersections, will provide a large turning radius and a safety factor area behind the curb, which could be encroached if necessary by emergency vehicles. This approach limits additional capital expenses for the local jurisdiction but increases the development cost and capital outlay for utility companies. In addition, the authority to require underground utilities is uncertain.

Narrow streets also raise a concern of snow removal during heavy snow events. Generally, local governments only have a few heavy snow events a year but, when they do, the challenge arises as to where to put the cars during plowing and where to put the snow. A combination of regulatory measures and streetscape designs can solve the problems with snow removal. Even if the problem is not completely cured, many residents of TNDs usually expect the residual inconveniences as part of the cost of living in TNDs.

CONNECTIVITY

As in most cities, public works and transit officials struggle with the inefficiencies of providing services to subdivisions with few entry points, numerous cul-de-sacs, geomorphic roadway networks, and few interconnections. Some jurisdictions have responded with bans or strict restrictions on cul-de-sacs. Builders often counter that there is a market for cul-de-sacs, which is perceived to provide a high degree of privacy. As an alternative to outright restrictions on cul-de-sacs, a jurisdiction might consider a "connectivity ratio," which divides roadway links by nodes or link ends. A connectivity ratio of 1:4 has been identified by one transportation expert as providing a high ratio of connectivity without destroying the opportunity to provide cul-de-sacs.[130]

A continuing issue that has proven controversial is the lack of connectivity between subdivisions. The conventional subdivision pattern features curvilinear streets, few access points, and the liberal use of cul-de-sacs. The benefits of cul-de-sacs and curvilinear streets include the perception of market acceptability, reduced traffic on local roads, and, in some cases, the ability to respect the natural contours of the land. However, this development pattern has the following disadvantages:

• Response times for emergency services, such as fire and police protection, are increased, which creates serious health and safety issues;

• Homes that require emergency services can be difficult to find;

• Travel distances between residences and employment and retail destinations are significant because there are fewer alternative travel routes;

• Public transportation is impeded because walking distances to transit stops increase and buses cannot feasibly navigate each subdivision; and

• State requirements may discourage school bus service that requires children to walk long distances to a bus stop. Long cul-de-sacs, which are difficult to navigate by large school buses, may require walking distances that exceed the state recommendations.

Residential neighborhoods are often concerned about the effect of connectivity on local street traffic. Traversable barriers and traffic calming devices (e.g., pavement undulations, speed bumps, rumble strips, traffic circles, and raised intersections) may be used to reduce through traffic onto neighborhood streets.[131] Restrictions might also be included that prevent cars from parking in front of openings. Another tool to address the street connectivity issue is to combine official mapping powers with planning. A collector street plan could collect traffic generated by a neighborhood and move it to a thoroughfare or from one neighborhood to another as needed. Proposed developments would then be required to align with the collector street plan.[132]

CUL-DE-SACS

Cul-de-sacs are dead-end streets with a turnaround at the end for vehicles. Cul-de-sacs have the advantage of providing privacy and low local traffic volumes for the cul-de-sac residents. However, they are widely criticized because they inhibit street connectivity, complicate the service access (e.g., for fire trucks, garbage trucks, and school buses), and constrain public transportation.

The LDC encourages alternatives to cul-de-sacs. Loop lanes (see Figure 5-24) and "eyebrow" configurations (see Figure 5-25) provide a comparable measure of privacy while maintaining the connectivity of the street network. This layout is common in many new subdivisions.

The following options should be considered in order to address cul-de-sacs:

• *Cul-de-sacs may be banned, restricted, or limited to a specified number or percentage of road segments in a subdivision.* Banning cul-de-sacs would be extremely controversial; however, cul-de-sacs may be limited to areas

**Figure 5-24
Loop Lanes**

Loop lanes provide a safe, efficient alternative to cul-de-sacs.

**Figure 5-25
Eyebrow Road Configurations**

"Eyebrow" road configuration.

with topographical constraints, such as watersheds and steep slopes.

• *Planting areas may be required in the center of cul-de-sacs,* allowing adequate provision for fire and waste collection trucks. Turnaround diameters of 70 feet are considered sufficient for chassis sizes of 28-1/2 to 35 feet, while diameters exceeding 80 feet are considered wasteful.[133] Recommended turnaround radii typically range from 35 to 40 feet.[134]

**Table 5-52
Street-Drainage Elements**

Option	Advantages	Disadvantages
Vertical (barrier) curbs	• Provides a physical barrier to prevent cars from encroaching onto sidewalks. • Supports pavement, thereby decreasing life-cycle maintenance costs.	• More expensive to install. • Minimizes design flexibility during construction. • Does not permit infiltration of stormwater, thereby decreasing natural filtration and rain storage.
Mountable (rolled) curbs	• Less expensive to install. • Increases design flexibility because driveway location need not be determined prior to curb installation.	• Lower stormwater conveyance capacity. • Not recommended for grades exceeding 8%.
Natural swales or ditches	• Least expensive alternative up front. • Most effective for pollution control because it permits natural filtration, rain storage, and impedance of stormwater flows.	• Potentially most expensive to maintain. • Ditching can attract garbage. Culverts can become clogged, thereby flooding lots and roads.

• *Length restrictions can range from 400 to 1,500 feet in many jurisdictions.* Many jurisdictions have length restrictions as low as 400 feet.[135] Cul-de-sac lengths are typically restricted because, as lengths increase, circulation becomes indirect, service deliveries are longer, and emergency access is more complicated.[136]

• *Cul-de-sac length may be tied to traffic.* This is a function of the number of houses. A maximum of 200 trips per day or 20 to 30 homes, depending upon frontage, is the typical standard.[137]

• *Require loop lanes, eyebrow configurations, or similar alternatives.* Loop streets may be encouraged as an alternative to cul-de-sacs in order to provide privacy and to encompass groups of lots in odd corners.

• *Pedestrian and vehicle access may be required at the end of cul-de-sacs.* For example, "grass-crete," or concrete with grass planted in cells, has been used to permit emergency access.[138]

CURB AND GUTTER

Curbs serve six primary purposes:
(1) To provide lateral support for pavement edges;
(2) To prevent water from seeping under the pavement;
(3) To contain pavement base materials;
(4) To provide rigid channels for stormwater run-off;
(5) To provide a defined edge between the street and adjacent lots and open space; and
(6) To discourage off-street parking onto unpaved areas.[139]

The options described in Table 5-52 are for curbing requirements.[140]

Asphalt curbing is often discouraged because it tends to disintegrate quickly.[141] Belgian block or granite curbs might also be permitted in order to enhance appearance.

The US EPA's Phase II National Pollutant Discharge Elimination System regulations[142] approach stormwater issues in different ways than under the Phase I program (e.g., they encourage the use of sustainable natural drainage structures, bioretention, infiltration, and natural erosion control features; they discourage the use of lined channels, piping, and guttering). In some states, best management practices have been developed that utilize natural structures and features for stormwater management and control. Environmental agencies are increasingly encouraging "bioretention" and infiltration through vegetated berms and swales instead of constructing concrete stormwater drainage infrastructure.[143]

DRIVEWAYS

Some local governments establish standards for driveways, such as:
• Intersection angle with pubic roads (typically 90);
• Minimum length;
• Centerline radii;

- Minimum width;
- Maximum height and aesthetic requirements (e.g., texturing, coloring and landscaping) for retaining walls;
- Incentives for common driveways, including maintenance agreement requirements;
- Maximum grade (e.g., 15 to 25 percent or 8 percent within public right-of-way);
- Turnout and turnaround requirements;
- Transition requirements;
- Maximum approach requirements;
- Culvert standards; and
- Surfacing standards.

Some jurisdictions require driveways serving a threshold number of dwelling units to be treated as a private road.[144] Surfacing may be required in urban areas or areas exceeding a specified grade (e.g., 12 percent), with compacted crushed rock or other semi- or pervious pavements permitted where surfacing is not required.

Several other factors should be considered with regard to driveways:

- *Access management:* Driveways increase points of conflict with a street, thereby lowering street capacity.[145] While this may be considered desirable on local streets, access management policies should be considered for driveways abutting collector and arterial streets. Loop roads may be considered for small developments abutting arterial streets in order to minimize frequent driveway accesses.
- *Width:* The Urban Land Institute recommends a minimum width of 10 to 12 feet with a minimum 5-foot transition radius at the curb.[146] A 10- to 15-foot width is recommended for parking lots and other high-volume driveways.
- *Impervious surfaces:* Public policy calls for minimizing impervious surfaces in some environmentally constrained areas, such as watersheds. Limits on impervious surfaces facilitate stormwater management and create a sense of openness. Wider and longer driveways are inconsistent with these policies.
- *Urban versus rural standards:* Unpaved driveways are appropriate for lots in rural areas, which are above a threshold minimum lot size.

TRAFFIC CALMING

The purpose of this section, along with § 5.11.3 Length (block lengths) of this chapter, is to protect the public health, safety, and general welfare by ensuring that speeds on local streets are suitable for their intended purpose. Long blocks, wide street cross sections, and uninterrupted traffic flows can encourage speeding on local streets. Traffic calming slows traffic on local streets while allowing flexibility in design and offering applicants the choice of treatment that works best for the streets in a proposed development.

ACCESS MANAGEMENT

Access controls are imposed in order to minimize curb cuts. Access controls restrict the amount, spacing, and location of curb cuts. Cross access easements between businesses may be accepted as mitigation for concurrency requirements in order to minimize the proliferation of separate curb cuts (see Chapter 6, Adequate Public Facilities, of the LDC). Jurisdictions can create incentives for landowners to establish cross access arrangements through land-use regulations to avoid private purpose condemnation.

The throat lengths in the access management standards are designed to provide adequate stacking space within driveways for general land-use intensities. This helps prevent vehicles from stacking into the thoroughfare as they attempt to access the site. High-traffic generators, such as large shopping plazas, need much greater throat length than smaller developments or those with unsignalized driveways. These standards refer to the primary access drive.

Access spacing requirements provide adequate left turn storage capacity in advance of each driveway approach and to avoid the overlap of left turn lanes. A waiver provision is included for shared access between different property owners or users in order to minimize spacing requirements. No cuts through the left turn reservoir of a median are permitted in order to provide left turn movements for driveway approaches accessing major thoroughfares.

TREE PRESERVATION

A tree preservation ordinance typically restricts the removal of trees exceeding a specified DBH, either throughout the entire site or within designated setbacks. Some ordinances require only a designated percentage of protected or larger "heritage" trees to be protected. Most require construction practices, such as fencing around the tree's drip line, in order to avoid impacting the root system.

Most tree protection ordinances suffer from two key problems:

(1) They fail to distinguish valuable or slow-growing species from those that can withstand construction impacts well, or that provide fewer ecological or stormwater management or other benefits. The result is a "one-size-fits-all" approach, which restricts development around mature specimens that are approaching the end of their life cycle; and

(2) Few ordinances effectively protect clusters of trees, focusing instead on large specimens that attract media attention but provide fewer stormwater management or shading benefits. Regulations that require a percentage of the site's canopy to be designated as "tree save areas" provide flexibility while protecting forested areas.

These approaches have been lauded by building as well as environmental interests, while individual tree protection ordinances tend to be controversial.

The following policy issues should be considered when developing a tree preservation ordinance:

• *Scope:* Many jurisdictions exempt single-family residential building sites from the tree preservation ordinance. This option reduces development costs and minimizes the staff burdens that will be produced when individual development approvals need to be inspected for compliance with the tree preservation ordinance. Conversely, this could be seen as weakening the ordinance if grading and other construction practices are permitted to destroy existing trees.

• *Encouragement of innovative development:* Exempt cluster development or other development options with high, open space, set-aside requirements. This has the advantage of allowing subdividers to preserve interconnected stands of trees and to provide functional greenbelts, as opposed to isolated patches of trees on individual lots.

• *Addressing of urban situations:* Substitute a street tree planting requirement for tree preservation. For residential subdivisions, street trees can shade street pavement and provide a sense of community. Credits and incentives may be provided for incorporating existing trees into the streetscape.

• *Procedures:* Enforce tree preservation requirements for residential subdivisions at the subdivision plat, rather than at the development approval, stage of the development approval process. This approach would tie plat approval to the delineation of protected or heritage trees, or significant stands of trees, coupled with plat conditions that require the preservation of protected or heritage trees. A site inventory of trees by species, health, size, and age could be provided.[147] The "tree banking" concept can also provide developers with the flexibility to save, plant, and transplant trees of various sizes.[148] Flexible concepts, such as tree banking, are not easily accommodated on small sites.

• *Environmental linkage:* The ordinance can be strengthened by designating higher protection thresholds in areas where trees provide critical stormwater management, erosion control, or shading benefits, such as stream buffers, floodplains, and steep slopes.

SUSTAINABILITY

The USGBC has created the LEED Green Building Rating System™ in 1994 to establish a "consensus-based national standard" for defining, measuring, and certifying green building practices.[149] Although other such metrics have been created,[150] the LEED system is widely heralded as the "gold standard"[151] for sustainable development.[152] For an historical overview of sustainability, please refer to the section entitled "Introduction" under the heading "Sustainability."

The LEED system currently covers three broad project categories:

(1) New commercial construction and major renovation[153];

(2) Existing buildings[154]; and

(3) Commercial interiors.[155]

Pilot programs are underway for three additional categories:

(1) Core and shell development[156];

(2) Homes[157]; and

(3) Neighborhood development.[158]

Each category provides a checklist of green building practices, each with a point value, which must be tallied to determine a project's rating. The practices are listed under six headings:

(1) Sustainable sites;

(2) Water efficiency;

(3) Energy and atmosphere;

(4) Materials and resources;

(5) Indoor environmental quality; and

(6) Innovation and design process.

Using new commercial construction as an example, a project could earn one point for reducing water use by 20 percent, up to three points for on-site renewable energy, one point for using recycled building materials, and one point for increased ventilation.[159] Using this à la carte approach, each project must earn at least 26 points' worth of green building practices in order to qualify for LEED certification. A LEED Silver rating requires 33 points; Gold requires 39 points; and Platinum requires 52 points.[160] The LDC only requires minimum certification. Silver, Gold, or Platinum could earn proportionally greater incentives.

As the sustainable development movement has gained momentum, local governments across the country have incorporated green building mandates and incentives into their land-use laws.[161] Many have simply adopted the LEED system, requiring certain projects to meet specific LEED certification levels.[162] Others, using the LEED system as a baseline, have tailored the checklists to meet local[163] or regional[164] needs. Still others have developed their own flexible green development guidelines[165] or have chosen to emphasize specific green building practices.[166]

The types of projects covered by sustainable development requirements also vary by locality. Many communities have adopted measures requiring municipal or publicly financed projects to conform to green building standards. Typically, these requirements apply to all new construction, additions, or renovations,[167] or are triggered by project size or cost.[168] Some localities have imposed green building requirements on private commercial projects as well.[169] Others have gone so far as to mandate compliance for private residential projects,[170] although most communities have only issued hortatory green building guidelines for residential projects.

Finally, communities taking a voluntary approach toward green building have offered land-use incentives to encourage sustainable development. Most commonly, these seem to come in the form of a density bonus, allowing developers to exceed zoning code limitations by a specified percentage. For example, the County of Arlington, Virginia, offers projects that meet the minimum requirements for LEED certification the possibility of "additional density between .15 and .35 FAR and/or additional height up to 3 stories."[171] Arlington also established a unique "Green Building Fund," to which developers must contribute $.03 per square foot for each project that does not meet LEED certification requirements.[172] In lieu of or in addition to a density bonus, other communities promise an expedited plan review for projects that satisfy green building requirements. The City of Scottsdale, Arizona, offers a "fast track plan review service," giving green building projects "building permits in half the time as regular projects."[173]

NOTES

1. 42 U.S.C Subsection 12181 et seq., Pub. L 101-336 and implementing regulations at 28 C.F.R. parts 35 and 36.
2. *Americans with Disabilities Act, ADA Title III Technical Assistance Manual* (covering public accommodations and commercial facilities) (Washington, DC: United States Department of Justice), available on-line at www.usdoj.gov/crt/ada/taman3.html.
3. *Americans with Disabilities Act, Title II Technical Assistance Manual* (covering state and local government programs and services) (Washington, DC: United States Department of Justice), available on-line at www.usdoj.gov/crt/ada/taman2.html.
4. *Fair Housing Accessibility Guidelines* (Washington, DC: United States Department of Housing and Urban Development), available on-line at www.hud.gov/fhefhag.html; see also United States Department of Housing and Urban Development's Homes & Communities Web site at www.hud.gov/offices/fheo/disabilities/fhefhag.cfm.
5. The local government should identify the appropriate standard and insert a cross-reference. There are several national standards and a number of state standards for the installation of manufactured homes. DRM International, *A Review of Manufactured Housing Installation Standards and Instructions* (Washington, DC: U.S. Department of Housing and Urban Development, Office of Policy Development and Research, September 2003), available on-line at www.huduser.org/Publications/PDF/Report_DRM.pdf.
6. *Low-Impact Development Design Strategies: An Integrated Design Approach* (Washington, DC: United States Environmental Protection Agency, January 2000).
7. *Low-Impact Development Hydrologic Analysis* (Washington, DC: United States Environmental Protection Agency, January 2000).
8. *Manual on Uniform Traffic Control Devices* (MUTCD), 2003 ed. (Washington, DC: Federal Highway Administration, United States Department of Transportation, November 2004) (see http://mutcd.fhwa.dot.gov/kno-2003r1.htm).
9. Note 8 (MUTCD), supra.
10. *Guide for Design of Pavement Structures*, AASHTO GDPS-4 (Washington, DC: American Association of State Highway and Transportation Officials, 1993).
11. Reid Ewing, *Traffic Calming: State of the Practice* (Washington, DC: Institute of Transportation Engineers and the Federal Highway Administration, 1999).
12. *American Standard for Nursery Stock* (Washington, DC: American Nursery & Landscape Association (formerly the American Association of Nurserymen), 2004).
13. E.C. Yokley, *Yokley's Law of Subdivisions*, 2d ed. (Charlottesville, VA: Michie Co., 1981), § 58, at 273.
14. See, e.g., California (www.fpm.water.ca.gov/june%2099.html); Maine (www.state.me.us/spo/flood/docs/origpdf/pdf/chapter1.pdf); Minnesota (files.dnr.state.mn.us/waters/watermgmt_section/floodplain/no_map_ord_60.3_a_MN.pdf); North Carolina (www.dem.dcc.state.nc.us/mitigation/NFIP_instructions.htm); and Wisconsin (www.dnr.state.wi.us/org/water/wm/dsfm/flood/communities.htm).
15. See *Pearson Kent Corp. v. Bear*, 271 N.E.2d 218 (N.Y. 1971) (off-site roads); *Just v. Marinette County*, 201 N.W.2d 761 (Wis. 1972) (wetlands); *Eschette v. City of New Orleans*, 245 So.2d 383 (La. 1971) (drainage); *Rodrigues v. State*, 472 P.2d 509 (Haw. 1970) (sewers); *Frustuck v. City of Fairfax*, 28 Cal Rptr. 357 (Ct. App. 1963) (access roads).
16. Standard City Planning Enabling Act (SCPEA) § 14 (United States Department of Commerce, 1928); Nelson, "The Master Plan and Subdivision Controls," 16 *Me. L. Rev.* 107 (1964).
17. *Pearson-Kent Corp. v. Bear*, 271 N.E.2d 218 (N.Y. 1971); *Smith v. Morris Tp.*, 244 A.2d 145 (N.J. Super. Ct. App. Div. 1968); *Wheeler v. City of Berkeley*, 485 S.W.2d 707 (Mo. Ct. App. 1972).
18. William I. Goodman and Eric C. Freund, eds., *Principles and Practice of Urban Planning, Land Subdivision* (Washington, DC: International City Managers' Association, 1968).
19. See Note 16 (SCPEA), supra, at § 14.
20. Id.
21. American Law Institute, Model Land Development Code (ALI Code) § 2-203, "Division of Land into Parcels" (Proposed Official Draft No. 1, 1974): "If a development ordinance does not permit a division of land into parcels as general development, the Land Development Agency shall grant a special development permission for the division of land into parcels if it finds that each parcel resulting from the division can reasonably be developed under the general or special development provisions of the development ordinance." As the notes to the ALI Code suggest, modern subdivision control ordinances will be contained within a comprehensive set of development regulations, not under any separate procedure for land subdivision.
22. Note 21 (ALI Code), supra, at § 2-103(2).
23. Compare the approach of performance standards described in Luther McDougal III, "Performance

Standards: A Viable Alternative to Euclidean Zoning," 47 *Tul. L. Rev.* 255 (1973).

24. Kenneth H. Young, *Anderson's American Law of Zoning*, 4th ed. (Deerfield, IL: Clark Boardman Callaghan, 1996), § 25.48.
25. 769 A.2d 172, 2001 ME 53 (Me. 2001).
26. Id., 769 A.2d 172, 178.
27. Id., 769 A.2d at 178 (citing *Perkins v. Town of Ogunquit*, 1998 ME 42, 709 A.2d 106 (1998)).
28. *Board of Supervisors v. Rowe*, 216 Va. 128, 216 S.E.2d 199 (1975).
29. Virginia Code § 15.2-2201; see also § 15.2-2286.A.10 (grant of authority for incentive zoning).
30. Steve Abel, "In defense of Portland's new housing-design standards," *Oregon Live* (Aug. 3, 1999). For studies showing reductions in vehicular traffic resulting from smart growth designs, see Reid Ewing, *Pedestrian- and Transit-Friendly Design* (Tallahassee: Florida Department of Transportation, March 1996), at 8-9; Robert Cervero and Kara Kockelman, *Travel Demand and the 3Ds: Density, Diversity, and Design*, Transportation Research D, Vol. 2, No. 3 (1997); Anne V. Moudon et al., "Effects of Site Design on Pedestrian Travel in Mixed-Use, Medium-Density Environments," Report No. WA-RD 432.1 (Washington, DC: Transportation Research Board, May 1997); *Pedestrian Facilities Guidebook: Incorporating Pedestrians Into Washington's Transportation System* (Olympia: Washington State Department of Transportation, September 1997); 1000 Friends of Oregon, *Making Land Use Transportation Air Quality Connections, The Pedestrian Environment*, Vol. 4A (December 1993), available on-line at http://ntl.bts.gov/DOCS/tped.html; Randall Crane, "Cars and Drivers in the New Suburbs: Linking Access to Travel in Neotraditional Planning," 62 *JAPA* 51 (Winter 1996); Robert Cervero, "Land-Use Mixing and Suburban Mobility," 42 *Transportation Quarterly* 3 (1988); Colorado/Wyoming Section Technical Committee, "Trip Generation for Mixed Use Developments," 57 *ITE Journal* (1987), 27-32; Walter Kulash et al., "Traditional Neighborhood Development: Will the Traffic Work?" 21 *Development* (July/August 1990); Lloyd W. Bookout, "Neotraditional Town Planning: Cars, Pedestrians, and Transit," *Urban Land* (February 1992), at 10, 15; B. Friedman, S.P. Gordon, and J.B. Peers, "Effect of Neotraditional Neighborhood Design on Travel Characteristics," *Transportation Research Record* 1466: 63-70 (1993); Susan L. Handy, "Regional Versus Local Accessibility: Neo-Traditional Development and Its Implications for Non-work Travel," *Built Environment*, Vol. 18, No. 4 (1992), 253-267; John Holtzclaw, *Explaining Urban Density and Transit Impacts on Auto Use* (presentation to the State of California Energy Resources Conservation and Development Commission by the Natural Resources Defense Council and the Sierra Club, April 19, 1990); Ryuichi Kitamura, P. Mokhtarian and L. Laidet, *A Micro-Analysis of Land Use and Travel in Five Neighborhoods in the San Francisco Bay Area* (Institute of Transportation Studies, University of California at Davis, November 1994). For studies relating to crime, see Judith C. Feins, Ph.D., Joel C. Epstein, Esq., and Rebecca Widom, *Solving Crime Problems in Residential Neighborhoods: Comprehensive Changes in Design, Management, and Use* (United States Department of Justice, Office of Justice Programs, National Institute of Justice, April 1997); Jane Jacobs, *The Death and Life of Great American Cities* (New York: Vintage Books, 1992).
31. Randall O'Toole [Thoreau Institute], "Is New Urbanism Creeping Socialism?," *Austin Review* (October 1, 2000); Naomi Kaufman Price, "Confessions of a happy 'snout-house' owner," *The Oregonian* (July 26, 1999).
32. Alex Marshall, *How Cities Work: Suburbs, Sprawl, and the Roads Not Taken* (Austin: University of Texas Press, 2000).
33. Gordon Oliver, "Portland City Council may turn up its nose at 'snout' houses; Rules to reduce the dominance of garages in new homes are expected to pass this week," *The Oregonian* (July 20, 1999); Gordon Oliver, "Behind 'snout house' snub lie varied views," *The Oregonian* (July 22, 1999).
34. 702 A.2d 397 (Vt. 1997). See also William E. Roper and Elizabeth Humstone, "WalMart in Vermont—The Case Against Sprawl," 22 *Vt. L. Rev.* 755 (1998).
35. *Loreto Development Company, Inc. v. Village of Chardon*, 695 N.E.2d 1151 (Ohio App. 1996); *C&K Real Estate, L.L.C. v. Guilford Planning and Zoning Commission*, 2003 WL 213 84646 (Conn. Super. 2003).
36. *Friends of Davis v. City of Davis*, 83 Cal. App. 4th 1004, 1013 (2003), noting "the broad and standardless construction of the City's design review ordinance urged by plaintiff would confer on the City Planning Department virtually unrestrained power to decide who may or may not do business in the City."
37. *Great Atlantic and Pacific Tea Company v. Town of East Hampton*, 997 F.Supp. 340 (E.D.N.Y. 1998).
38. *Jochimek v. Superior Court, Maricopa County*, 819 P.2d 487 (Ariz. 1991) (40-foot height limit in an overlay zoning district void for lack of uniformity where underlying commercial zone allowed 100-foot height). Most courts read uniformity to be more flexible. *ASP Assocs. v. City of Raleigh*, 258 S.E.2d 444 (N.C. 1979).
39. *Wal-Mart Stores, Inc. v. County of Clark*, 125 F.Supp.2d 240 (D.Nev. 1999).
40. *Manalapan Realty, L.P. v. Township Committee of Manalapan Township*, 639 A.2d 318 (N.J. 1994).
41. 44 C.F.R. § 60.3.
42. Section 404 of the Federal Water Pollution Control Act Amendments of 1972, 33 U.S.C. 1334.
43. "The Architecture of Urban Stream Buffers," in Thomas R. Schueler and Heather K. Holland, *The Practice of Watershed Protection* (Ellicott City, MI: Center for Watershed Protection, 2000); *Riparian Buffer Strategies for Urban Watersheds* (Washington, DC: Metropolitan Washington Council of Governments, December 1995).
44. See the Center for Watershed Protection Web site at www.cwp.org.
45. Charles Thurow, William Toner, and Duncan Erley, "Performance Controls for Sensitive Lands: A Practical Guide for Local Administrators," Planning Advisory Service Report No. 307/308 (Chicago: American Planning Association, July 1975), at 67, 73.
46. *Sellon v. City of Manitou Springs*, 745 P.2d 229 (Colo. 1987); *Patterson Materials Corp. v. Zagata*, 237 A.D.2d 365, 655 N.Y.S.2d 72, 1997 N.Y. Slip Op. 02209 (N.Y.A.D. 2

Dept. 1997); *Girton v. City of Seattle,* 97 Wash. App. 360, 983 P.2d 1135 (Wash. App. 1999), *rev. denied*, 140 Wash.2d 1007, 999 P.2d 1259 (Wash. 2000); *cf. Pomona Pointe Associates, Ltd. v. Incorporated Village of Pomona*, 185 Misc.2d 131, 712 N.Y.S.2d 275, 2000 N.Y. Slip Op. 20342 (N.Y.Sup. 2000).

47. *Corrigan v. City of Scottsdale*, 149 Ariz. 538, 720 P.2d 513, 55 USLW 2051, 16 *Envtl. L. Rep. News & Analysis* 20, 985 (Ariz.), *cert. denied*, 479 U.S. 986, 107 S.Ct. 577, 93 L.Ed.2d 580 (1986).
48. 150 Misc.2d 24, 565 N.Y.S.2d 371 (N.Y.Sup. 1990).
49. Id., 150 Misc.2d 24, 26, 565 N.Y.S.2d 371, 372.
50. *Land Development Manual* (Washington, DC: National Association of Home Builders, 1969).
51. J. William Thompson, Kim Sorvig, and Craig D. Farnsworth, *Sustainable Landscape Construction: A Guide to Green Building Outdoors* (Washington, DC: Island Press, 2000), at 70-71.
52. Edward H. Ziegler, Jr., et al., *Rathkopf's The Law of Zoning and Planning, Vol. 7* (St. Paul, MN: West Group, 2004), § 40.03[4].
53. 30 Texas Administrative Code Chapter 344, §§ 344.72-344.77, available on-line at http://info.sos.state.tx.us/pls/pub.
54. Arizona Revised Statutes §§ 49-1101 through 49-1106, available on-line at www.azleg.state.az.us/ArizonaRevisedStatutes.asp?Title=49; see also discussion in New Hampshire Office of State Planning (Summer 2001).
55. *Outdoor Lighting Code Handbook,* Version 1.14 (Tucson: International Dark-Sky Association, December 2000/September 2002), available on-line at www.darksky.org/handbook/lc-hb-v1-14.html.
56. Patti Gallagher and Alex Krieger, "Security with Dignity," *Urban Land* (March 2003), 73.
57. See "Guidance for Protecting Building Environments from Airborne Chemical, Biological, or Radiological Attacks," Centers for Disease Control, Natural Institute for Occupational Safety and Health, DHHS (NIOSH), Pub. No. 2002-139 (May 2002). Vulnerability assessments are required by the Bio-Terrorism Act of 2002 (PL. 107-188) for drinking water systems.
58. Randall Atlas, *Designing Against Terror: Site Security Planning and Design Criteria* (Miami: Atlas Safety & Security Design, Inc., published in Architectural Graphics Standards, 1999); Barbara Nadel, "Better Safe: Planning Secure Environments," *Area Development: Site and Facility Planning* (May 2001).
59. For a comprehensive set of recommendations, see Rufus C. Young, Jr. and Dwight H. Merriam, "Homeland Security Begins at Home: Local Planning and Regulatory Review to Improve Security," *Land Use L. & Zon. Dig.* (November 2003), at 4.
60. David W. Dunlap, "Even in an Age of Urban Terrorism, Architects Sheathe Towers in Glass: New Designs Provide Security Behind Walls of Windows," *The New York Times* (Sept. 6, 2004), at A-15, col. 1.
61. See Note 59 (Young/Merriam), supra, at 3.
62. See Maureen McAvey, "The Price of Security and the Competition for Scarce Resources," in Deborah L. Myerson, ed., *ULI on the Future 2002: Cities Post-9/11* (Washington, DC: Urban Land Institute, 2002).
63. John M. Becket, "Combatting Terrorism: If Terrorism Reigns Will Torts Follow," 9 *Wid. L. Symp. J.* 485 (2003).
64. Sidney O. Dewberry and John S. Matusik, *Land Development Handbook: Planning, Engineering, and Surveying* (New York: McGraw-Hill, 1996), at 188.
65. Id., at 188-89.
66. Id., at 189.
67. James W. Wentling and Lloyd W. Bookout, eds., *Density by Design* (Washington, DC: Urban Land Institute, 1988), at 53.
68. Harvey S. Moskowitz and Carl G. Lindbloom, *The New Illustrated Book of Development Definitions* (New Brunswick, NJ: Center for Urban Policy Research, 1993), at 163.
69. Note 64 (Dewberry/Matusik), supra, at 187.
70. Id.
71. Kenneth J. Dueker et al., "Strategies to Attract Auto Users to Public Transportation," Transit Cooperative Research Program, TCRP Report 40 (Washington, DC: National Academy Press, 1998), available on-line at http://gulliver.trb.org/publications/tcrp/tcrp_rpt_40.pdf.
72. Donald Shoup, "Cashing Out Employer Paid Parking," Report No. FTA-CA-11-0035092-1 (Washington, DC: United States Department of Transportation, 1992); Victoria Transport Policy Institute, *Online TDM Encyclopedia* (Victoria, BC: VTPI, 2002), available on-line at www.vtpi.org/tdm.
73. United States Environmental Protection Agency, Urban and Economic Development Division, *Parking Alternatives: Making Way for Urban Infill and Brownfield Redevelopment* (Washington, DC: US EPA, 1999), available on-line at smartgrowth.org/pdf/PRKGDE04.pdf; Note 72 (Shoup), supra; Note 72 (VTPI), supra.
74. R. A. Weant and H.S. Levinson, *Parking* (Westport, CT: Eno Foundation for Transportation, Inc., 1990).
75. Tamim Raad, "Creating Regional Parking Policies." Paper presented at Moving Beyond Planning: A Conference on Transportation Demand Management, available on-line at www.best.bc.ca/resources/conference/pdf/regionalparkingpolicies.pdf.
76. Note 72 (Shoup), supra; Note 72 (VTPI), supra; Note 30 (Cervero, 1988), supra.
77. Note 71 (Dueker), supra.
78. Department of Environment, Transportation and the Regions, *Planning Policy Guidance 13: Transport* (London: DETR, 2001).
79. United States Environmental Protection Agency, Urban and Economic Development Division, *Parking Alternatives: Making Way for Urban Infill and Brownfield Redevelopment* (Washington, DC: US EPA, 1999), available on-line at smartgrowth.org/pdf/PRKGDE04.pdf; Note 72 (Shoup), supra; Note 72 (VTPI), supra.
80. Note 79 (US EPA), supra.
81. Richard W. Willson, "Suburban Parking Requirements: A Tacit Policy for Automobile Use and Sprawl," *JAPA* 61 (1995), 29-56.
82. Note 81 (Willson), supra; Note 79 (US EPA), supra.
83. Note 71 (Dueker), supra.
84. Note 79 (US EPA), supra; Note 78 (DETR), supra.

85. Note 74 (Weant/Levinson), supra; Note 78 (DETR), supra.
86. Note 72 (VTPI), supra.
87. Washington State Department of Transportation, *CTR Task Force Guidelines* (Seattle: Washington State Department of Transportation, 2002), available on-line at www.wsdot.wa.gov/tdm/tripreduction/CTRguide.
88. Metro Council, *Metro 2040 Land-Use Code Workbook: A Guide for Updating Local Land Use Codes* (Portland, OR: Metro Council, 1998); see also *Livable Communities Workbook*, available on-line at www.metro-region.org/article.cfm?articleid=436; Southwest Washington Regional Transportation Council, "Executive Summary: Transportation Futures Committee Report" (Vancouver, WA: Southwest Washington Regional Transportation Council, December 1996), available on-line at www.rtc.wa.gov/studies/archive/tfc/execsum.htm.
89. Note 78 (DETR), supra; East Midlands Regional Local Government Association. Statement of EMRLGA in Respect of Matter 5.4. (East Midlands, UK: East Midlands Regional Local Government Association, 2000), available on-line at www.emrlga.gov.uk/docs/5.4.pdf.
90. Institute of Transportation Engineers, *Parking Generation* (Washington, DC: ITE, 1987).
91. Donald C. Shoup, *The Trouble with Minimum Parking Requirements* (Los Angeles: Department of Urban Planning, School of Public Policy and Social Research, University of California, Los Angeles, 2002), available on-line at www.vtpi.org/shoup.pdf.
92. Note 91 (Shoup), supra; Urban Land Institute, *The Dimensions of Parking*, 3d ed. (Washington, DC: ULI, 1993); Note 74 (Weant/Levinson), supra.
93. Note 74 (Weant/Levinson), supra.
94. Note 92 (ULI), supra.
95. Note 74 (Weant/Levinson), supra.
96. Note 91 (Shoup), supra; Note 92 (ULI), supra; Note 74 (Weant/Levinson), supra.
97. Note 79 (US EPA), supra.
98. Note 74 (Weant/Levinson), supra.
99. Note 90 (ITE), supra.
100. Note 91 (Shoup), supra; Note 92 (ULI), supra; Note 74 (Weant/Levinson), supra.
101. Note 79 (US EPA), supra; British Chamber of Commerce, "Response to the Department of the Environment, Transport & the Regions Planning Policy Guidance Note 13 (Transport)," *News and Policy*, January 2000, available on-line at www.britishchambers.org.uk/newsandpolicy/transport/ppg13.htm.
102. Note 72 (VTPI), supra.
103. Note 71 (Dueker), supra.
104. Note 79 (US EPA), supra; Note 72 (VTPI), supra.
105. Note 79 (US EPA), supra; Note 72 (Shoup), supra; Note 72 (VTPI), supra.
106. Note 79 (US EPA), supra.
107. Note 71 (Dueker), supra.
108. Note 72 (VTPI), supra.
109. Thomas P. Smith, "Flexible Parking Requirements," Planning Advisory Service Report No. 377 (Chicago: American Planning Association, August 1983); Note 79 (US EPA), supra.
110. Note 79 (US EPA), supra.
111. Note 74 (Weant/Levinson), supra.
112. Note 91 (Shoup), supra.
113. Note 71 (Dueker), supra.
114. Note 90 (ITE), supra.
115. Note 74 (Weant/Levinson), supra.
116. Water Environment Federation and American Society of Civil Engineers, *Design and Construction of Urban Stormwater Management Systems*, Urban Runoff Quality Management (WEF Manual of Practice FD-20 and ASCE Manual and Report on Engineering Practice No. 77) (1992), at 496-97; Note 64 (Dewberry/Matusik), supra, at 629; E.Z. Bean, W.F. Hunt, and D.A. Bidelspach, "A Monitoring Field Study of Permeable Pavement Sites in North Carolina," available on-line at www.bae.ncsu.edu/topic/permeable-pavement/SWFWMD.pdf; United States Environmental Protection Agency, *Porous Pavement Phase I Design and Operational Criteria* (Washington, DC: US EPA, Aug. 1980).
117. Edward H. Ziegler, Jr., et al., *Rathkopf's The Law of Zoning and Planning*, Vol. 7 (St. Paul, MN: West Group, 2004), § 58.01[1]; Note 74 (Weant/Levinson), supra, at 42-43.
118. Note 92 (ULI), supra, at 47.
119. Robert H. Freilich and S. Mark White, "Transportation Congestion and Growth Management: Comprehensive Approaches to Resolving America's Major Quality of Life Crisis," 24 *Loy. L.A. L. Rev.* 915, 935 (June 1991).
120. Thomas P. Smith, "Flexible Parking Requirements," Planning Advisory Service Report No. 377 (Chicago: American Planning Association, August 1983), at 5, 8.
121. Id., at 6.
122. Id., at 7.
123. Note 74 (Weant/Levinson), supra, at 311-12.
124. Id.
125. Note 120 (Smith), supra, at 20.
126. Mary Eysenbach, "Learning from City Parks," *Planning* 24 (October 2003).
127. *Dolan v. City of Tigard*, 512 U.S. 374, 114 S.Ct. 2309, 129 L.Ed.2d 304 (1994).
128. See *Leroy Land Dev. v. Tahoe Regional Planning Agency*, 939 F.2d 696 (9th Cir. 1991); Daniel J. Curtin, Jr. and Cecile T. Talbert, *Curtin's California Land Use and Planning Law* (Point Arena, CA: Solano Press, 2006).
129. Most of these approaches are based upon the recommendations found in the Center for Watershed Protection, *Better Site Design: A Handbook for Changing Development Rules in Your Community* (Ellicott City, MD: CWP, 1998).
130. Reid Ewing et al., *Best Development Practices: Doing the Right Thing and Making Money at the Same Time* (Tallahassee: Florida Department of Community Affairs, January 1997).
131. Wolfgang Homburger et al., *Residential Street Design and Traffic Control* (Washington, DC: Institute of Transportation Engineers, 1989), at 104, 107.
132. *Batch v. Town of Chapel Hill*, 326 N.C. 1, 387 S.E.2d 665 (1990) (upholding against taking challenge requirement that new subdivision align with a collector street plan).
133. Bucks County Planning Commission, *Performance Streets: A Concept and Model Standards for Residential Streets* (Doylestown, PA: BCPC, April 1980), at 12.
134. Id.

135. Joseph De Chiara, Julius Panero, and Martin Zelnik, *Time-Saver Standards for Housing and Residential Development*, 2d ed. (New York: McGraw-Hill, 1995), at 88.
136. Kevin Lynch and Gary Hack, *Site Planning* (Cambridge, MA: MIT Press, 1984), at 215.
137. American Society of Civil Engineers, *Residential Streets*, 2d ed., co-authored with National Association of Home Builders and Urban Land Institute (Washington, DC: ULI, 1990), at 9.
138. Note 131 (Homburger), supra, at 102.
139. Urban Land Institute, *Residential Development Handbook*, 2d ed. (Washington, DC: ULI, 1990), at 218.
140. Note 137 (ULI), supra; David Listokin and Carole Walker, *The Subdivision and Site Plan Handbook* (New Brunswick, NJ: Center for Urban Policy Research, 1989), at 313-16.
141. Note 140 (Listokin/Walker), supra, at 316.
142. 40 C.F.R. Parts 9, 122, 123, and 124; 64 Fed. Reg. 68722 (Dec. 8, 1999).
143. The North Carolina Department of Transportation's *Best Management Practices for Protection of Surface Waters* (Raleigh: NCDOT, June 1991) encourages infiltration and filtration of run-off over grassed shoulder slopes and shallow, flat slope ditches. The North Carolina Department of Environment, Health and Natural Resources assumes a 35 percent reduction in total suspended solids through the use of grassed swales as an alternative to conventional curb-and-gutter systems. *Stormwater Best Management Practices* (Raleigh: NCDEHNR, Nov. 1995), at 1, 68-72.
144. E.g., Marin County, California, Code § 24.04.260.
145. Note 137 (ULI), supra.
146. Id.
147. Jack Petit, Debra Bassert, and Cheryl Kollin, *Building Greener Neighborhoods: Trees as Part of the Plan*, 2d ed. (Washington, DC: American Forests and National Association of Home Builders, 1998), at 48.
148. Id.
149. United States Green Building Council, *LEED®: Leadership in Energy and Environmental Design*, available on-line at www.usgbc.org/DisplayPage.aspx?CategoryID=19.
150. Capital E et al., *The Costs and Financial Benefits of Green Buildings: A Report to California's Sustainable Building Task Force* (October 2003), at 3, available on-line at www.cap-e.com/ewebeditpro/items/O59F3259.pdf (listing international standards such as the British Research Establishment Environmental Assessment Method and the Hong Kong Building Environmental Assessment Method, as well as state standards such as New York's High Performance Building Guidelines).
151. Jason Scully, *Sustainable Development and Green Building* (Washington, DC: Urban Land Institute, 2004), at 6, available on-line at www.uli.org/AM/TemplateRedirect.cfm?template-/CM/ContentDisplay.cfm&ContentID-11057.
152. See Note 150 (Capital E), supra, at 4 (commenting that "LEED has rapidly become the largest and most widely recognized green building design and certification program in the US, and probably in the world").
153. United States Green Building Council, *LEED for New Construction*, available on-line at www.usgbc.org/DisplayPage.aspx?CMSPageID=220.
154. United States Green Building Council, *LEED for Existing Buildings*, available on-line at www.usgbc.org/DisplayPage.aspx?CMSPageID=221.
155. United States Green Building Council, *LEED Rating System for Commercial Interiors*, available on-line at www.usgbc.org/DisplayPage.aspx?CMSPageID=145.
156. United States Green Building Council, *LEED Green Building Rating System for Core and Shell Development (LEED-CS)*, available on-line at www.usgbc.org/DisplayPage.aspx?CMSPageID=146.
157. United States Green Building Council, *LEED for Homes*, available on-line at www.usgbc.org/DisplayPage.aspx?CMSPageID=147.
158. United States Green Building Council, *LEED for Neighborhood Development*, available on-line at www.usgbc.org/DisplayPage.aspx?CMSPageID=148.
159. United States Green Building Council, *LEED-NC Version 2.2 Registered Project Checklist* (2005), available on-line at https://www.usgbc.org/FileHandling/show_general_file.asp?DocumentID=1096.
160. Id.
161. See "Building Green: Onus or Bonus?, Green Buildings Matrix," *Zoning Practice* (Chicago: American Planning Association, April 2005) (summarizing the green building requirements and incentive programs for 37 U.S. cities and counties), available on-line at www.planning.org/zoningpractice/pdf/ZPApr05Matrix.pdf.
162. See, e.g., Pleasanton, California, Ordinance 1873 (December 3, 2002) (requiring city-sponsored and commercial construction projects of a certain size to meet the minimum requirements for LEED certification), available on-line at www.ci.pleasanton.ca.us/pdf/greenbldg.pdf; Scottsdale, Arizona, Resolution 6644 (2005) (requiring all new city buildings to achieve a LEED Gold rating), available on-line at www.scottsdaleaz.gov/greenbuilding/LEED/LEED_ResNo6644.pdf.
163. The City of Scottsdale, Arizona, has tailored its commercial green building checklist to meet the needs of its desert climate. City of Scottsdale, *Commercial Green Building Checklist: New Construction and Major Renovation* (2004) (giving points for, among other things, the preservation of "natural desert features . . . [such as] washers, boulders, [and] vegetation," the use of a "low heat absorbing and low reflective . . . [parking lot] surface," and the installation of "a desert adapted 'green' . . . roof"), available on-line at www.scottsdaleaz.gov/greenbuilding/CommGBChecklist.pdf.
164. See, e.g., City of Portland Office of Sustainable Development, *City of Portland Supplement to the LEED Rating System* (2002), 3 (explaining that Portland's supplement to the LEED system was developed "to identify both local and state codes that go beyond LEED requirements and additional green building strategies that are regionally significant"), available on-line at www.portlandonline.com/shared/cfm/image.cfm?id=119695.

165. See, e.g., City of Austin, Texas, Green Building Program® (describing the Austin Green Building Program), available on-line at www.austinenergy.com/Energy%20Efficiency/Programs/Green%20Building/index.htm; City of Austin, Texas, *Green by Design: 7 Steps to Green Building* (detailing the cradle-to-grave green building process for home builders and renovators), available at www.austinenergy.com/energy%20efficiency/programs/Green%20Building/Resources/7steps.pdf.

166. See, e.g., Minneapolis, Minnesota, Zoning Code art. II, § 549.220(12) (2005) (offering land-use incentives to any project whose plan demonstrates a 35 percent increase in energy efficiency over the state's energy code).

167. See, e.g., Town of Arlington, Massachusetts, Building Regulations Bylaw Article 16, § 4 (requiring new town buildings and major renovations and additions to achieve a LEED Silver rating), available on-line at www.town.arlington.ma.us/Public_Documents/ArlingtonMA_TownBylaws/title1; Scottsdale, Arizona, Resolution 6644 (2005) (requiring new, occupied city buildings to achieve a LEED Gold rating), available on-line at www.scottsdaleaz.gov/greenbuilding/LEED/LEED_ResNo6644.pdf.

168. See, e.g., Atlanta, Georgia, Ordinance 03-O-1693 (December 9, 2003) (requiring new city buildings and renovations to achieve a LEED Silver rating where the project size is at least 5,000 square feet or the cost exceeds $2 million), available on-line at www.atlantaga.gov/client_resources/forms/energy%20conservation/adopted%20ordinance.pdf; Note 164 (*Portland Supplement*), supra, at 3 (describing requirements in Portland, Oregon, that new city buildings and renovations, as well as publicly financed buildings over 10,000 square feet, meet the minimum requirements for LEED certification).

169. See, e.g., Calabasas, California, Ordinance 2003 185 (January 7, 2004), available on-line at www.cityofcalabasas.com/pdf/green-building-ordinance.pdf (requiring new commercial buildings and renovations over 500 square feet to meet the minimum requirements for LEED certification, and those over 5,000 square feet to achieve a LEED Silver rating); Pleasanton, California, Ordinance 1873 (December 3, 2002) ("The green building practices referenced in this Chapter are designed . . . to encourage resource conservation; to reduce the waste generated by construction projects; to increase energy efficiency; and to promote the health and productivity of residents, workers, and visitors to the city."), available on-line at www.ci.pleasanton.ca.us/pdf/greenbldg.pdf (requiring new commercial buildings and renovations over 20,000 square feet to meet the minimum requirements for LEED certification).

170. See, e.g., Boulder, Colorado, Boulder Revised Code § 10-5.5 (requiring new residential construction, additions, and renovations to achieve a certain number of "Green Points," calculated according to project size), available on-line at www.bouldercolorado.gov/index.php?option=com_content&task=view&id=1619&Itemid=807.

171. County of Arlington, Virginia, *Green Building Incentive Program*, available on-line at www.arlingtonva.us/Departments/EnvironmentalServices/epo/EnvironmentalServicesEpoIncentiveProgram.aspx; see also Town of Acton, Maine, *Town of Acton Zoning Bylaw* § 5.5B.2.2(d) (2004) (allowing projects that meet the minimum requirements for LEED certification to increase their floor area ratio by .05), available on-line at http://doc.acton-ma.gov/dsweb/Get/Document-8222.

172. County of Arlington, Virginia, *Green Building* (noting that the fund "is used to provide education and outreach to developers and the community on green building issues"), available on-line at www.arlingtonva.us/Departments/EnvironmentalServices/epo/EnvironmentalServicesEpoGreenBuildings.aspx.

173. City of Scottsdale, Arizona, *Green Building Program: Program Incentives*, available on-line at www.scottsdaleaz.gov/greenbuilding/Incentives.asp; see also City of Issaquah, Washington, *Sustainable Building Incentives* (describing a similar service for commercial and residential green projects in Issaquah), available on-line at www.ci.issaquah.wa.us/Page.asp?NavID=327.

CHAPTER

6

Adequate Public Facilities

6.0 PURPOSE AND FINDINGS

An adequate public facilities ordinance (APFO) ties development approvals to the availability of infrastructure capacity measured by adopted levels of service (LOSs) in the comprehensive plan or in the APFO. An APFO accommodates anticipated growth by providing a rational system for expanding improvements while ensuring that the level of growth does not exceed a jurisdiction's ability to accommodate it.

An APFO differs markedly from exactions and impact fees. APFOs are regulatory measures that are used to deny development applications or to time and sequence development approval based on availability of infrastructure on an adopted, funded, and prioritized capital improvements program (CIP). Impact fees and exactions are conditions for financing off-site infrastructure attached to development approvals. APFOs provide the opportunity to enhance certainty in the development approval process. With an APFO, the applicant and the local government know the standards before applications are filed. The APFOs provide the opportunity to structure infrastructure mitigation requirements in a flexible manner. Providing cross access easements, a higher degree of street connectivity, and mixed uses can be factored into the traffic impact analyses (TIAs) to reduce development impact on the roadway network and thus create greater capacity.

APFOs must be reasonable and flexible in order to work efficiently. A "one-size-fits-all" LOS would have the unintended consequence of encouraging sprawl because uncongested roads tend to lie at greenfields at the periphery of the urbanized area. This situation is remedied by providing a lower LOS, or an exemption, for: (1) downtowns and mature, built-up areas; or (2) where the infrastructure network is fixed, infill opportunities and alternative transportation modes such as transit and pedestrian access exist.

An APFO raises numerous policy issues, which by themselves could comprise a separate report.[1] A summary of the issues is as follows:

• *Adequate public facilities:* These include water, sewer, stormwater management, police and fire protection solid waste, parks and recreation, schools, and transportation. Providers should include capital improvement districts, utilities, and local, regional, state, or federal jurisdictions. An APFO transportation LOS includes roads of the jurisdiction and state and federal highway passing through or adjacent to the jurisdiction. The same is true with an APFO based upon school facilities located in a separate school district.

• *Undesirable effects associated with timing or mitigating new development proposals:* These must be tempered or mitigated. Roads-based APFOs could require an unacceptable widening of roads. These can be addressed by designating the types of mitigation that will be accepted.

• *Establishing LOSs:* These must be established at levels that protect public health, safety, and welfare while not unreasonably restricting growth. Infill, corridors, and downtown areas could be exempt from the APFO in order to encourage development and to recognize the availability of existing facilities.

- *Development approvals:* An APFO could be triggered at early stages of the development approval process (plan amendments, rezoning, or discretionary decisions). This provides developers with knowledge of the requirements of the APFO, allowing structuring of proposals before significant expenditures have been committed to a project. APFOs can also be triggered late in the development approval process. This approach more efficiently uses staff and planning commission time because only those projects that will proceed to development are reviewed. However, it may also produce unanticipated delays in development after the applicant has committed substantial resources to the project.
- *Impact areas defining LOS:* For water, sewer, or piped facilities, the impact area consists of the fixed service area. For open-ended facilities, where demand is not physically restricted to a geographic area, the designation is a policy decision (e.g., roads and parks). An intersection or a park can be used by anyone inside or outside a jurisdiction but demand typically declines with distance from the facility. APFOs either provide a designated distance, a demarcation line (e.g., a designated park or traffic influenced areas), or a procedure for evaluating demand (e.g., evaluating all street links for which the development creates at least 5 percent of the roadway impact). Some road ordinances require a TIA only to the first intersection.
- *Existing facilities:* When determining whether adequate capacity exists, we count both existing facilities and those included in the CIP. Most programs count facilities within a third or fourth year of the CIP for various reasons (e.g., it takes several years for many developments to become fully occupied, thereby creating some lag time between development approval and the demand for facilities; and counting only existing facilities could unreasonably restrict growth).
- *Reservation of capacity—pipeline development:* When a development is approved and gains vested rights, the amount of capacity it utilizes must be debited against available capacity for future projects. This pipeline development reservation of capacity must be strictly limited to two to four years. Where an APFO is tested early in the process, the development is still in the formative stages and could fail due to financing problems or a changing market. In many communities, only a small percentage of rezoning or preliminary plats actually proceed to construction. In this event, approved projects should be counted toward available capacity only for a three- to four-year window and not a permanent reservation of capacity. Jurisdictions should implement a development approval tracking system.
- *Application of APFOs:* If the LOS is not met, development of approval can either be denied or the development can be given the option of timing and sequencing the project so that future stages of the proposal are not approved until the facilities are available.

Developers can also be given the option to voluntarily advance capacity through a development agreement if they wish to proceed at a faster pace. Constitutional requirements of proportionality do not apply to voluntary development agreements.

6.1 ADEQUATE PUBLIC FACILITIES

This section shall be known and may be cited as the "Adequate Public Facilities Ordinance" or "APFO."

6.2 APPLICABILITY

This section applies to any application for development approval as set forth in Column (B) of Table 6-1. This section applies as a condition to preliminary plat and site development plan approvals where no subdivision is required. Development applications subject to this section shall be accepted, approved, granted, or issued only where the application provides sufficient information to determine whether the capacity of public facilities is adequate to support the proposed development. This section does not apply to any use, development, project, structure, fence, sign, or activity that does not result in a new equivalent residential unit.

6.3 PROCEDURES FOR THE PROCESSING OF APPLICATIONS FOR DEVELOPMENT APPROVAL

6.3.1 Determination

After an application for development approval is filed, the [PLANNING OFFICIAL] shall prepare a staff report along with a recommendation to the approving agency. Upon receipt of the staff report, the approving agency shall determine that:

(A) The application shall be approved where public facilities and services are available at the adopted LOS;

(B) The application shall be denied where public facilities and services are not available at the adopted LOS; or

(C) The application shall be approved subject to phasing of development until all public facilities are available for the year the CIP shows that facilities will be built and adequate if public facilities in the impact area are not adequate to meet the adopted LOS for the entire proposed development, consistent with the requirements of Table 6-1.

6.3.2 Comprehensive Plan and Zoning Amendments

Comprehensive plan or zoning amendments that may create a range of potential impacts shall be reviewed as if the greatest impact results. The review of adequacy of public facilities for the application for a rezoning shall compare the capacity of public facilities to the maximum projected demand that may result from the proposed rezoning based upon the maximum density of the affected area pursuant to the amendment. Noth-

Table 6-1
Adopted Level of Service Standards

(A) Facility	(B) Applicability	(C) Level of Service	(D) Impact Area	(E) Year Planned Capacity Will Be Available
Streets—Downtown tier	Not applicable	Not applicable	Not applicable	Not applicable
Streets—Tier 1, Tier 2, Tier 3	All applications	LOS "C"	Traffic impact area is 1/2 mile	First year of CIP
Streets—Tier 4	All applications	LOS "B"	Traffic impact area is 1/2 mile	First year of CIP
Fire protection	All applications	ISO Rating not exceeding [LOCAL STANDARD]	City limits	First year of CIP
Water	All applications	[LOCAL STANDARD]	City water service area	First year of CIP
Sewer	All applications	[LOCAL STANDARD]	City sewer service area	First year of CIP
Community parks	All applications	See § 5.21 Parks/Open Space in Chapter 5, Development Standards, of the LDC	City limits	Third year of CIP
Stormwater management	All applications	See § 5.22 Stormwater Management in Chapter 5, Development Standards, of the LDC	Drainage basin	First year of CIP or on site

LOS = level of service; CIP = capital improvements program; and ISO = International Standards Organization.

ing in this section authorizes a development approval that would otherwise be inconsistent with the comprehensive plan.

6.4 DETERMINATION OF ADEQUACY OF PUBLIC FACILITIES

6.4.1 Scope

A determination of adequacy of public facilities for a development proposal finds that:

(A) Public facilities are available at the time of issuance of the determination; and

(B) Public facilities are deemed to be available at all subsequent stages of the development approval process up to the date of expiration of the development approval. Future availability of facilities shall be assured through a development agreement between the applicant and the [LOCAL GOVERNMENT], in which case the public facilities will be considered to be available for the duration of said development agreement.

6.4.2 Duration

A determination that public facilities are adequate is valid until the earlier of one of the following:

(A) The expiration of the development approval; or

(B) If no expiration period is provided in the development approval, the determination expires unless construction commences within one year after approval of the application. For a preliminary plat, the determination expires unless construction commences on at least one lot within two years after approval of the preliminary plat, and on at least 25 percent of the lots within three years after approval of the preliminary plat.

6.5 ADVANCEMENT OF CAPACITY

6.5.1 Advancement of Public Facilities

In order to avoid undue hardship, the applicant may propose to construct or to secure funding for the public facilities necessary to provide capacity to accommodate the proposed development at the adopted LOS and at the time that the impact of the development will occur as an alternative to the deferral of development or development approvals, consistent with the requirements of this chapter.

6.5.2 Standards

No advancement of capacity for public facilities needed to avoid a deterioration in the adopted LOSs shall be accepted by the approving agency unless:

(A) The proposed public facility is a prioritized and funded capital improvement shown in the adopted CIP; or

(B) Appropriate conditions are included to ensure that the applicant will obtain any necessary approvals for construction of the public facilities from any agency other than the [LOCAL GOVERNMENT].

6.5.3 Construction Commitment

The commitment for construction or advancement of public facilities prior to the development approval shall be included as a condition of the development approval. The commitment shall contain, at a minimum, the following:

(A) For planned capital improvements, either a finding that the planned capital improvement is included within the CIP for the year in which construction of the project is scheduled or the applicant commits to advancing the facilities;

(B) An estimate of the total financial resources needed to construct or expand the proposed public facilities, and a description of the incremental cost involved;

(C) A schedule for commencement and completion of construction of the planned capital improvement with specific target dates for multiphase or large-scale capital improvements projects;

(D) A statement that the planned capital improvement is consistent with the comprehensive plan and the [LOCAL GOVERNMENT]'s CIP;

(E) A statement that the planned capital improvement is consistent with any ordinances relating to the construction and design of the public facility; and

(F) If the planned capital improvement proffered by the applicant will provide capacity exceeding the demand generated by the proposed development, but is needed to meet past deficiencies reflected in the overall capacity needed for the project, reimbursement shall be offered to the applicant for the pro rata cost of the excess capacity for the year in which the capital facility would have been built as shown in the prioritized CIP.

6.5.4 Partial Construction or Funding

The construction or funding of only a portion of a public facility needed to meet the adopted LOS shall be approved only where:

(A) The public facility will be able to provide the capacity needed to meet the adopted LOS, and will be fully usable and operational, due to the characteristics of the facility; or

(B) The construction or funding of the balance of the public facility that is needed to meet the adopted LOS will be accomplished from other sources.

6.6 METHODOLOGY

6.6.1 Generally

No determination as to compliance with this section shall be recommended by the [PLANNING OFFICIAL] or rendered by the approving agency unless public facilities within the impact areas set forth in Column (D) of Table 6-1 are:

(A) Adequate, as measured by the adopted LOS (refer to Column (C) of Table 6-1); and

(B) Available (refer to Column (E) of Table 6-1).

6.6.2 Level of Service Standards

Compliance with LOS standards shall be measured for each public facility set forth in Column (A) of Table 6-1 in accordance with the corresponding standards set forth in Column (C) of Table 6-1. The LOS for each application for development approval shall be measured within the impact area set forth in Column (D) of Table 6-1 for each corresponding facility in Column (A). Column (E) of Table 6-1 indicates whether planned capacity may be included in determining whether the improvements are available. Rules for interpretation of Table 6-1 are in § A-1 Rules of Interpretation in Appendix A, Definitions and Rules of Interpretation, of the Land Development Code (LDC).

6.6.3 Adequacy of Public Facilities

Public facilities shall be adequate if it is demonstrated that they have available capacity to accommodate the demand generated by the proposed development as well as committed pipeline development approvals in accordance with the following calculation methodology:

(A) Calculate total capacity by adding together the total capacity of each public facility.

(B) Calculate available capacity by subtracting from the total capacity the sum of:

(1) The demand for each public facility created by existing development;

(2) The demand for each public facility created by the anticipated completion of committed pipeline development; and

(3) The demand for each public facility created by the anticipated completion of the proposed development under consideration for determination.

6.6.4 Transportation Analysis

6.6.4.1 Measurement

The procedure for calculating LOS is set forth in the *Highway Capacity Manual 2000*.[2] The impact of the proposed development shall be measured by average daily trips and peak-hour trips based upon the Institute of Transportation Engineers' *Trip Generation*.[3]

6.6.4.2 Mitigation

The applicant may propose mitigation measures, or a combination of measures, as described in this section, as an alternative to denial of the application. These measures shall be included as a condition for approval of the application. Mitigation measures may include:

(A) Phases so that no development approval is issued before streets or other transportation facilities needed to achieve the LOS standard are constructed;

(B) Measures that allow the transportation network to function more efficiently by adding sufficient capacity to the off-site street system. Such mitigation measures may include, but are not limited to, pavement widening, turn lanes, median islands, access controls, or traffic signalization; and

(C) Transportation congestion management measures that allow the transportation network to function more efficiently by adding sufficient capacity to the off-site street system.

6.6.4.3 Exemptions

The [LOCAL GOVERNMENT] finds and determines that downtown and urban core built-up areas consist of: (1) interconnected street systems, mixed uses, and the availability of pedestrian facilities that result in fewer trips than conventional subdivisions; (2) compact development patterns that produce fewer and shorter trips than conventional developments; and (3) established traffic patterns and infrastructure within the urban core—constitute a strong public policy to exempt the downtown area built-up areas and adjacent urban core from APFO requirements. The [LOCAL GOVERNMENT] further finds that there is a strong public policy to encourage infill development and little opportunity to expand transportation capacity in many infill areas without destroying the historic built environment.

Accordingly, the following are exempt from the provisions of this section:

(A) Applications for development approval within the "D" (Downtown) district;

(B) Any traditional neighborhood development (TND) or transit-oriented development (TOD);

(C) Infill development where public transit is available within a 1/4-mile distance, or broad-based retail commercial is within walking distance; and

(D) Mixed-use development with a 2:3 ratio of jobs-housing balance.

6.6.5 Fire, Police, and Emergency Services

Needed fire flow shall be determined in accordance with the Insurance Services Office, "Fire Suppression Rating Schedule" (June 1980 edition). In determining the impact of the proposed development on fire, police, and emergency service LOS, the approving agency shall primarily take into consideration response times, and the number and location of available apparatus and fire, police, and emergency service stations. For purposes of this section, the placement of fire hydrants, the size of water lines, and the distance between buildings shall not be considered in determining the capacity of fire protection improvements.

6.6.6 Water

(A) Development approval applications shall be analyzed with respect to the availability of adequate potable water, and shall be determined pursuant to the following information:

(1) System capacity;

(2) Capacity of wellfield, or other source of raw water supply;

(3) Historical average flow of potable water;

(4) Historical peak flow of potable water;

(5) Number of hook-ups and the estimated potable water demand per hook-up; and

(6) Number of hook-ups for which contractual commitments have been made.

(B) The determination of the [PLANNING OFFICIAL] shall provide substantial evidence that the project is within its service area and that it has the capacity to serve the project as proposed. If the ability of a provider to serve a proposed development is contingent upon planned facility expansion in accordance with a CIP, details regarding such planned improvements shall be submitted.

6.6.7 Sewer

(A) Applications shall be analyzed with respect to the availability of adequate sanitary sewer capacity, and shall be determined pursuant to the following information:

(1) System capacity;

(2) Historical average daily flow of treated sewage;

(3) Historical peak flow of treated sewage;

(4) Number of hook-ups and estimated sewer demand per hook-up; and

(5) Number of hook-ups for which contractual commitments have been made.

(B) The applicant shall provide documentation to the [PLANNING OFFICIAL] indicating that the project meets the service area LOS and has the capacity to serve the project. If the ability of a provider to serve a proposed development is contingent upon planned facility expansion in accordance with a CIP, details regarding such planned improvements shall be submitted.

6.6.8 Community Parks

In determining compliance with the LOS standard for community parks, an inventory of the number of community parks shall be maintained in the CIP. The distance of a proposed development from a community park shall not be considered for purposes of determining compliance with the adopted LOS. The [PLANNING OFFICIAL] shall forward the application to the Parks and Recreation Department for review and comments. The approving agency shall consider the comments and recommendations of the Parks and Recreation Department but shall retain ultimate discretion to determine whether community parks are adequate for purposes of this section.

6.7 CAPITAL IMPROVEMENTS PROGRAM

The CIP is the mechanism by which the [LOCAL GOVERNMENT] provides new public facilities and expansion of the capacity of public facilities, which are needed to accommodate existing and anticipated future population and employment. Through the CIP, the [LOCAL GOVERNMENT] intends to use all reasonable means to provide the public facilities and services needed to accommodate new growth and development consistent with the availability of revenue sources, and contributions for capital improvements provided by state or federal sources or applicants, taking into account physical, environmental, and topographical constraints on the expansion of the capacity of public facilities.

The CIP shall:

(A) Prioritize the need for public facilities subject to this section;

(B) Estimate the cost of improvements for deficiencies or repairs for which the [LOCAL GOVERNMENT] has fiscal responsibility;

(C) Analyze the fiscal capability of the [LOCAL GOVERNMENT] to finance and construct improvements;

(D) Establish financial policies to provide for the funding of improvements from grants, development exactions and impact fees, dedications of land, taxes, assessments, rates, and charges; and

(E) Schedule the funding, prioritization, and construction of improvements in a manner necessary to ensure that capital improvements are provided when required based on needs identified in the comprehensive plan.

6.7.1 Capital Improvements Data Requirements

The CIP shall be based upon:

(A) Public facility needs as identified in the comprehensive plan. Where the comprehensive plan does not identify a need for public facilities within a given category, public facility needs shall be determined on the basis of project population and employment growth as set forth in the comprehensive plan;

(B) The geographic service area and location of major system components for each public facility shall be identified; and

(C) Existing revenue sources and funding mechanisms available for capital improvements financing shall be inventoried for each public facility.

6.7.2 Capital Improvements Analysis Requirements

The CIP shall be based upon the following analyses:

(A) Current local practices that guide the timing, phasing, priority, and location of construction, extension, or increases in capacity of each public facility;

(B) The fiscal implications of existing deficiencies and future needs for each type of public facility. This analysis shall be based on the needed improvements, as identified by applying the LOS within each impact area, and shall address the relative priority of need among facility types;

(C) The costs of needed capital improvements for mitigation of existing deficiencies, replacement, and new growth needs;

(D) The basis of cost estimates; and

(E) An assessment of the service provider's ability to finance capital improvements based upon anticipated population and revenues, including:

(1) Forecasting of revenues and expenditures for five years;

(2) Projections of debt service obligations for currently outstanding bond issues;

(3) Projection of ad valorem tax base, assessment ratio, and ad valorem tax rate;

(4) Projections of other tax bases and other revenue sources, such as development agreement financing, dedications, impact fees, and service charges;

(5) Projection of operating cost considerations; and

(6) Projection of debt capacity.

6.7.3 Requirements for Capital Improvements Implementation

The CIP shall contain:

(A) The five-year schedule of year-by-year capital improvements that the [LOCAL GOVERNMENT] has accepted to reduce existing deficiencies, to remain abreast of replacements, and to meet future demand;

(B) Project description and general location; and

(C) A list of projected costs and revenue sources by type of public facility for the five-year period (see Table 6-2 and Table 6-3).

Table 6-2
Equivalent Residential Units for Transportation (Per Day)

Land Use	Variable	Trip Generation Rate	Equivalent Residential Unit
Residential single-family	Dwelling unit	9.55	1.00
General light industrial	1,000 sf	6.97	0.73
Industrial park	1,000 sf	6.97	0.73
Manufacturing	1,000 sf	3.85	0.40
Warehousing	1,000 sf	4.88	0.51
Mini-warehouse	1,000 sf	2.61	0.27
Apartments (post-1973)	Dwelling unit	6.28	0.66
Low-rise apartment	Dwelling unit	6.59	0.69
High-rise apartment	Dwelling unit	4.2	0.44
Condominium/townhouse	Dwelling unit	5.86	0.61
High-rise condominium	Dwelling unit	4.18	0.44
Mobile homes	Dwelling unit	4.81	0.50
Hotel	Room	5.10.7	0.91
Elementary school	1,000 sf	10.72	1.12
High school	1,000 sf	10.9	1.14
Church	1,000 sf	9.32	0.98
Day care center	1,000 sf	79.26	5.10.30
Hospital	1,000 sf	16.78	1.76
General office (<10,000 sf)	1,000 sf	24.6	2.58
General office (10,000 to 25,000 sf)	1,000 sf	19.72	2.06
General office (25,000 to 50,000 sf)	1,000 sf	16.58	1.74
General office (50,000 to 100,000 sf)	1,000 sf	14.03	1.47
General office (100,000 to 200,000 sf)	1,000 sf	11.85	1.24
General office (200,000 to 300,000 sf)	1,000 sf	10.77	1.13
General office (300,000 to 400,000 sf)	1,000 sf	9.96	1.04

Table 6-2 (cont.)
Equivalent Residential Units for Transportation (Per Day)

Land Use	Variable	Trip Generation Rate	Equivalent Residential Unit
General office (400,000 to 500,000 sf)	1,000 sf	9.45	0.99
General office (600,000 to 700,000 sf)	1,000 sf	9.05	0.95
General office (700,000 to 800,000 sf)	1,000 sf	5.10.75	0.92
General office (> 800,000 sf)	1,000 sf	5.10.46	0.89
Corporate headquarters	1,000 sf	6.27	0.66
Single-tenant office	1,000 sf	11.5	1.20
Office park	1,000 sf	11.42	1.20
Research and development center	1,000 sf	7.7	0.81
Business park	1,000 sf	14.37	1.50
Building materials store	1,000 sf	30.56	3.20
Specialty retail	1,000 sf	40.67	4.26
Discount store	1,000 sf	70.13	7.34
Hardware store	1,000 sf	51.29	5.37
Nursery	1,000 sf	36.08	3.78
Shopping center (<10,000 sf GLA)	1,000 sf	167.59	17.55
Shopping center (10,000 to 50,000 sf GLA)	1,000 sf	91.65	9.60
Shopping center (50,000 to 100,000 sf GLA)	1,000 sf	70.67	7.40
Shopping center (100,000 to 200,000 sf GLA)	1,000 sf	54.5	5.71
Shopping center (200,000 to 300,000 sf GLA)	1,000 sf	46.81	4.90
Shopping center (300,000 to 400,000 sf GLA)	1,000 sf	42.02	4.40
Shopping center (400,000 to 500,000 sf GLA)	1,000 sf	35.10.65	4.05

Table 6-2 (cont.)
Equivalent Residential Units for Transportation (Per Day)

Land Use	Variable	Trip Generation Rate	Equivalent Residential Unit
Shopping center (500,000 to 600,000 sf GLA)	1,000 sf	36.35	3.81
Shopping center (600,000 to 800,000 sf GLA)	1,000 sf	33.88	3.55
Shopping center (800,000 to 1,000,000 sf GLA)	1,000 sf	32.09	3.36
Shopping center (1,000,000 to 1,200,000 sf GLA)	1,000 sf	30.69	3.21
Shopping center (1,200,000 to 1,400,000 sf GLA)	1,000 sf	29.56	3.10

Table 6-2 (cont.)
Equivalent Residential Units for Transportation (Per Day)

Land Use	Variable	Trip Generation Rate	Equivalent Residential Unit
Shopping center (1,400,000 to 1,600,000 sf GLA)	1,000 sf	25.10.61	3.00
Quality restaurant	1,000 sf	96.51	10.11
Sit-down restaurant	1,000 sf	205.36	21.50
Fast food without drive-through	1,000 sf	786.22	82.33
Fast food with drive-through	1,000 sf	632.12	66.19
New car sales	1,000 sf	47.91	5.02
Convenience market	1,000 sf	737.99	77.28
Furniture store	1,000 sf	4.34	0.45

sf = square feet; GLA = gross land area; > = more than; and < = less than.

Table 6-3
Equivalent Residential Units for Law Enforcement or Parks/Open Space

Principal Building Activity	Square Feet Per Employee	Employees Per 1,000 Square Feet	Equivalent Residential Units (Square Footage Needed to Equal One Residential Dwelling Unit)
Education	767	1.30	1,764
Food sales	984	1.02	2,263
Food service	578	1.73	1,329
Health care	520	1.92	1,196
Lodging	1,317	0.76	3,029
Mercantile and service (commercial)	945	1.06	2,174
Office	387	2.58	890
Public assembly	1,317	0.76	3,029
Public order and safety	746	1.34	1,716
Religious worship	726	1.38	1,671
Warehouse and storage	1,730	0.58	3,979
Other	544	1.84	1,251

No equivalent residential unit applies to fire protection or community parks.

Source: United States Department of Energy, Energy Information Administration, A Look at Commercial Buildings in 1995: Characteristics, Energy Consumption, and Energy Expenditures *(Washington, DC: US DOE, EIA, October 1998).*

COMMENTARY

This chapter consolidates "adequate public facilities" or "concurrency" requirements. While growth is essential to the continual health of a community, development places strains on community infrastructure, including roads, water, sewer, drainage, schools, fire, police, emergency service, parks and recreation, libraries, and community facilities. This requires the community to turn toward higher taxes or lower LOSs to accommodate new population and construction. Communities have to make choices about the timing and phasing of growth in accordance with service provider CIPs and who bears the responsibility for financing public facilities.[4]

Impact fees requiring developers to pay for infrastructure generated by new development cannot require payment for past deficiencies.[5] One of the issues relating to new development in the community is the timing and phasing of development. Some communities used large lot holding zones,[6] and others use urban growth boundaries[7] and development approval limits,[8] to control development while infrastructure capacity is increased.

Unlike direct controls, the impact of each project vis-à-vis existing facilities and services under an APFO is not measured only for each development but is measured against projected development within the respective service areas.

Timing and phasing of development approval to the availability of adequate public facilities began with the seminal growth management Ramapo Plan.[9] *Ramapo* eliminated the need to use holding zones or large lot zoning, which has been invalidated under the rationale that cities cannot "stand in the way" of natural forces of growth.[10]

Courts have also recognized that holding zones have potential exclusionary effects. The use of large lot zoning or holding zones has been invalidated by reason of excluding the creation of affordable housing for low- or moderate-income housing.[11] Courts have been more solicitous of attempts to control growth in resort or environmentally sensitive areas where growth pressures have been induced by upscale, second-home developments as opposed to suburban residential areas with primary residences.[12]

A better method for ensuring adequate facilities to serve new developments is through the use of subdivision regulations. Subdivision approval can impose adequate facilities requirements on a project-specific basis.[13] Approval is often contingent on the provision of off-site improvements, such as intersection upgrades, parks, and open space. These off-site requirements have been upheld pursuant to enabling legislation authorizing the use of subdivision controls to avoid "premature subdivision."[14] Many of these controls are employed on a case-by-case basis, lacking a systematic focus. First-generation direct controls were often based on broad standards, requiring a finding that facilities are "existing," "planned," or "reasonably expected to expand in a manner adequate to support future residents."[15]

UTILITY EXTENSIONS

The extension of utilities is also a critical aspect of growth control. As the public services moratoria cases indicate, denying utility extensions is one way for a local government to control urban sprawl on an interim basis. It can also be used as a long-term control. The local government's comprehensive plan should include processes and rules governing utility extension by the local government or by independent public or private utility districts or providers. If the comprehensive plan controls the location and timing of utilities, a local government can restrict utility service extensions where such extensions would be inconsistent with the plan. In *Dateline Builders, Inc. v. City of Santa Rosa*,[16] the court upheld a city's decision not to extend sewer connections to a development beyond the city's corporate boundaries but within its utility boundaries. The proposed development was in an agricultural area and was inconsistent with the city and county general plans.

A public utility has a duty to provide service to all inhabitants within its service area. If a local government's provision of water or sewer is viewed under public utility law, services may be denied for a utility-related reason. While a local government cannot be required to extend utility services beyond its borders, if it does so and "stakes out" a service area, courts may require that it impartially serve all inhabitants reasonably within reach of its supply system. One way a local government may avoid this rule is to extend services by contract.[17]

Service refusal to new users may be based on a utility-related reason. The court in *Mayor & City Council of Cumberland v. Powles*[18] noted that a water shortage or financial crisis would justify refusal.[19]

FISCAL IMPACT ANALYSIS

In addition to an APFO, a local government can provide for fiscal impact analysis in its regulations. Fiscal impact analysis has been approved by the courts in the following situations:

• Rezonings: *Bell v. City of Bridgeport*[20]; *Guest v. King George County*[21]
• Tax increment finance: *Torres v. City of Yorba Linda*[22]
• Zoning initiatives: *In re Advisory Opinion*[23]
• Administrative regulations: *In re Department of Health*[24]
• Public facility siting: *West Charter Area School District v. Collegium Charter School*[25]

- Urban service area boundary location: *Theobald v. Board of County Commissioners*[26]

Fiscal impact assessments conducted at the rezoning approval stage will allow the local government to identify not only the capital costs of supplying infrastructure, but also the positive or negative costs resulting from service costs, operation, maintenance, and administration.[27]

Interim development controls and moratoria may be used to regulate growth while the community devises plans to increase infrastructure capacity.[28] Service moratoria enacted in response to shortfalls in specific utility or municipal services have been upheld.[29] Interim controls have been upheld where they were enacted in response to environmental or public safety concerns and were limited in duration, and where the local government developed comprehensive studies leading to permanent controls.[30] While effectively halting growth during their pendency, they must not become comprehensive or permanent systems. The interim regulation must be implemented by a master plan and regulations within a reasonable period of time[31] in order to avoid a taking.[32] When lifted, the community loses the power to control or to stage growth affected by the moratorium, unless a permanent growth management system was prepared during the moratorium.

The traditional approach of using land-use controls to address public facility concerns often does not tie development approval to a CIP. Traditional land-use controls must be limited to type, location, and density of development, and cannot deal with timing. Instead, jurisdictions react to congestion issues with hastily drawn moratoria in response to specific development proposals. The section entitled "Adequate Public Facilities Ordinances," below, describes how an APFO and other concurrency regulations better implement the traditional forms of land-use control employed by most jurisdictions.

ADEQUATE PUBLIC FACILITIES ORDINANCES

APFOs and other concurrency requirements control the timing of new development by linking development approval to the timing and priorities of the CIP. Requiring facilities adequacy for new development has two primary advantages over indirect controls:

(1) Development cannot proceed where, because of its location, adequate public facilities are not yet available at the adopted LOS to serve it; and

(2) Concurrency, unlike indirect controls, addresses the timing of development in order to prevent overtaxing existing facilities (see Figure 6-1).

Concurrency regulations and APFOs condition development on the adequacy of public facilities based on adopted LOS, regardless of location, and subject all development proposals to adequacy evaluation. The use of a systematic approach to control growth by tying development approvals to the adequacy of facilities was pioneered by the Town of Ramapo, New York. The Ramapo system used an ordinal point scale to evaluate development proposals, and required all residential projects to obtain a special use permit, the issuance of which was conditioned on the adequacy of sewers, drainage facilities, parks/recreation, roads, and firehouses, as shown in a prioritized three-phase, six-year CIP (totaling 18 years), demonstrating the town's commitment to provide facilities in a timed and sequential manner.

In the landmark decision of *Golden v. Planning Board of the Town of Ramapo*,[33] the New York Court of Appeals (the highest court in New York State) upheld the system and rejected a challenge to the ordinance as an unconstitutional exercise of the town's police powers. This decision:

"[R]epresent[ed] the first time that any court in the United States ha[d] upheld the concept of restricting development in metropolitan areas through comprehensive planning, coupled with an exercise of the zoning power without compensation."[34]

By combining the police powers with planning efforts and capital budgeting, *Ramapo* was the first systematic attempt to employ direct controls relating the adequacy of public facilities to development approvals. The *Ramapo* concept has since been refined in larger areas to incorporate a tier system where regulations become increasingly stringent from urban core to outlying exurban areas.[35] Under the San Diego tier system, growth is actively encouraged in "urbanizing areas," including the downtown and central city. Development in "planned urbanizing areas" is staged through a Ramapo system of capital improvements planning with an APFO, special use permits, official mapping, and other innovative land-use controls. "Future urbanizing areas" are held in

**Figure 6-1
Synchronizing Growth with
Adequate Public Facilities**

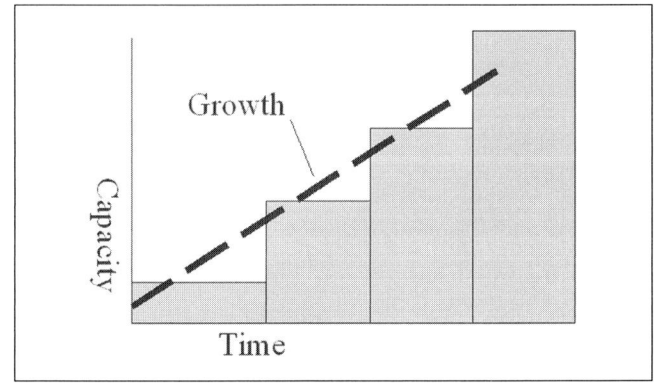

Timing and sequencing of growth with adequate public facilities was the fundamental growth management principle introduced by Ramapo.

reserve and redesignated as "planned urbanizing" as land in the planned urbanizing area is developed.[36]

Relying on the concepts in *Ramapo*, an APFO[37] regulates land use to ensure that necessary public facilities and services are available and adequate to support new development, based on adopted LOS standards, at the time that the impacts of new development occur.[38] An APFO does not necessarily control a development's location (as do zoning districts or the tier system in *Ramapo*) or building design or layout (as do architectural design standards).[39] If infrastructure capacity is limited, an APFO might require an applicant to delay construction of part of a development using timing and phasing,[40] or to deny the development application.

An APFO is generally implemented by local governments through all the land-use regulatory processes for development approval coupled with public facilities and service provision through the CIP.

Most communities tie some development approvals to infrastructure capacity on an ad-hoc basis using traditional land use controls (such as conditional zoning and subdivision approval conditions) to regulate traffic congestion under an APFO. When a specific development proposal will create intolerable congestion or burden the existing public facilities, the local government denies the rezoning request or development approval. This stands in contrast with the traditional approach, which does not tie development approval to the availability of specified facilities or LOS standards for facilities in the vicinity of the project, nor does it involve affirmative steps to identify those facilities needed to serve new growth at the adopted LOS standards. Rezonings and subdivision plats are routinely denied in many communities based on "traffic congestion" or other capacity shortfalls. The APFO simply expands and refines concepts already enforced by many local governments by integrating them with comprehensive plan policies and CIPs, thereby providing certainty and predictability for the private development community and service providers.

An APFO augments the comprehensive plan—often incorporating goals and policies regarding the adequacy of public facilities and services—and land development regulations. While comprehensive plans often reference the need for adequate public facilities as a development approval condition, those plans fail to further the objectives of an APFO because:

• No LOS standards are included by which "adequacy" can be measured;

• No present measurements of facility capacity are included to determine whether capacity is "available" to serve a proposed development; and

• No formal mechanism for adequate public facilities review is included as a systemic part of the development review and approval process.[41]

The APFO in the LDC furthers the goal of promoting smart growth through proper regulation of land use and the built environment. While concurrency regulations are often criticized by smart growth advocates based on a perception that they encourage sprawling, low-density development patterns, these ordinances actually prevent sprawl and encourage the creation of more compact mixed-use environments. Some of these criticisms focus on the possibility of developers in jurisdictions with concurrency regulations seeking locations in remote greenfield conversion areas where facilities are relatively uncongested, or seeking to develop in other jurisdictions without concurrency requirements.[42] Opponents criticize the focus on streets and other automobile-related infrastructure instead of transit and pedestrian requirements,[43] which encourage service providers to widen roads and expand roadway capacity in response to growth demands, thereby creating further automobile dependence and sprawling development patterns.[44]

It is also argued that concurrency requirements drive up housing costs and reduce affordable housing options by preventing development and slowing growth.[45] The LDC APFO addresses these concerns and criticisms. Specifically, the LDC APFO provisions link the availability of key public facilities and services with the type, amount, location, density, rate, and timing of new development. It manages the location of new growth and development so that it does not outpace the ability of service providers to accommodate the development at established LOS standards.

The model APFO coordinates public facility and service capacity with the demands created by new development, encourages redevelopment, and promotes infill development by increasing limits on sprawl and leap-frog developments by the LOS standards adopted to future urbanizing areas. The APFO promotes and encourages development types, styles, and sustainable features that efficiently use infrastructure and capacity, such as TND and TOD. The LOS standards and the adequate capacity requirements of the APFO allow a local government to prevent new development from causing a reduction in the LOSs to existing residents while still providing the necessary infrastructure for new residents.

The major structural components of the LDC APFO[46] include the following:

• *The areas and subareas of the community within which the APFO will apply*: APFO regulations may or may not be appropriate for every area of a community, depending on the present service capacity of each area and subarea and the community's long-range planning goals. Florida permits exemption from APFOs in redevelopment, infill areas, and downtown areas.[47]

• *The public facilities and services that will be included in the APFO*: In many jurisdictions, the APFO only applies to roadways and intersections, though the ordinances can be expanded to include water; schools; stormwater management; pedestrian and public transit facilities; fire, police, and emergency services; parks and recreation; and other community infrastructure needs. Communities may include facilities funded and constructed in the jurisdiction by utilities, improvement districts, and state and federal agencies.

• *The LOS standard for each public facility or service to be included in the APFO:* An LOS standard measures the capacity and performance characteristics of each facility included in a concurrency ordinance. It governs the rate and intensity of development approvals, the quality of infrastructure, and the capital investment needed to correct existing deficiencies and accommodate new growth.

• *Current and projected public facility and service capacities:* The ordinance designates the current LOS standards and plan for future capacities as identified in a CIP.

• *The type of development approval and land uses to which the APFO will apply:* The ordinance describes the type of development approvals to which the APFO regulations apply. The APFO should not exempt small developments as they cumulatively create major impacts on public facility needs. To alleviate extensive costs for small development, the local government could do its own study in such a case.

• *The development approvals to which the APFO will apply:* Concurrency regulations should not apply to minor construction that does not affect public facilities, such as signs, pools, fences, and sheds. Enlargement of structures that create additional need for capital facilities and services shall comply with the APFO.

• *The step in the development approval process when adequacy of public facilities will be determined:* The local government must establish the stage or stages in the development approval process at which a determination can be made as to whether facilities are adequate to accommodate the impacts of development.

• *The effect of failing to meet an LOS standard:* Development approvals may be denied if they fail to meet APFO standards. The ordinance shall define criteria for determining whether projects will be denied or conditioned and specify appropriate mitigation measures.

• *The conditions and mitigation requirements that may be attached to APFO approval:* Developers whose projects are denied approvals under the APFO regulations can be authorized to advance those facilities through a development agreement in order to meet the APFO and/or to mitigate the impacts of the project. The APFO should include criteria to evaluate the proposed mitigation measures and to formulate regulations governing the reservation of capacity as facilities are advanced. Credits for advancement should be given in the year in the CIP when the facility being advanced was to be financed through impact fees or other revenues.

THE RESERVATION OF FACILITY CAPACITY

When developments are approved or exempted, the capacity for public facilities created by those developments is debited against available facility capacity for future applicants. The ordinance should indicate the duration for which the capacity can be debited and address other issues of facility capacity.

MITIGATION

APFOs differ from impact fees. Impact fees cannot be collected for past deficiencies. Deficiencies are taken into account when utilizing APFO LOS analysis. Where public facilities are currently operating below the adopted LOS standards (deficiencies), development may be denied or approved subject to timing and phasing. Developers may be allowed to proceed by advancing the facility deficiencies needed to attain the LOS standards and to accommodate the marginal impacts of the development. The alternative requires awaiting the provision of those facilities as scheduled in the CIP. Provisions allowing developers to advance public facilities and services subject to reimbursement alleviate the hardship of delay and have been approved by courts in several states.[48]

MULTIPLE FACILITIES

Some commentators have suggested allowing developers to advance facility capacity only where deficiencies exist in more than one, or a specified number of, facilities. The rationale for such a requirement is unclear, although a case could probably be made that it enhances administrative convenience. The better policy is to allow developers to advance facility capacity regardless of how many facilities are deficient. If developers have the financial wherewithal to provide funding for such facilities, there is little reason to deny this option. The advancement policy provides scarce money for infrastructure deficiencies and allows developers to proceed more quickly with project approval.

However, developers will have to advance money for all facilities that are deficient to obtain expedited approval. In other words, if both water and sewer facilities are deficient, and the developer provides the necessary facilities to meet the LOS standard for water but not for sewer, development approvals will still be deferred until sewer facilities are available at the adopted LOS standards. If the facilities are scheduled in the CIP, the policy decision that those facilities will be constructed has already been made. Therefore, there would be no reason to prohibit the expedited construction of those facilities.

REIMBURSEMENT FOR PROVIDING EXCESS CAPACITY

Where water and sewer mains must be oversized to accommodate future demands, developers should be reimbursed for providing capacity in excess of what is warranted by the size and scale of the proposed development. The correction of existing deficiencies will also, by definition, exceed the marginal impacts created by the proposed development.

While most jurisdictions provide reimbursement for oversized facilities, few address the issue of reimbursement for correcting existing deficiencies. Embodying the developers' and local governments' obligations in a development agreement can authorize reimbursement.[49] The local government can provide mechanisms for reimbursing developers for the use of the additional capacity by charging subsequent projects within the impact area for their proportional cost. Impact fees, user fees, assessments, or utility fees for the use of such facilities would then be transferred to the developer as they are collected.

ENFORCEMENT

Under the LDC APFO, the following conditions apply where public facilities are insufficient to accommodate the impacts of a proposed development:

• Development approvals may be deferred pending the availability of public facilities and services at the adopted LOS standards;

• The applicant may agree to reduce the density or intensity of the proposed development within the parameters of available facility capacity; or

• The developer may agree to provide those facilities needed to attain the adopted LOS standards, provided that those facilities will be available when the impacts of the development occur.

With the exception of drainage facilities, which may affect the degree of impervious coverage, the deferral of development approval or provision of public facilities can be addressed through appropriate mitigation conditions rather than requiring reapplication.

When facilities are found to be adequate before a final development order is issued, it must be determined whether this finding "reserves" that capacity for the development or whether a new finding must be secured at a later stage in the development approval process. If planned facilities are included in the earlier finding, it must be specified whether the reservation remains valid in the event that the facilities do not proceed to construction. Reservations of capacity must be integrated with development monitoring procedures in order to prevent the over allocation of capacity. Procedures also should be developed to prevent the "hoarding" of capacity by approved, but unbuilt, projects through a "use it or lose-it" procedure if the project does not meet threshold benchmarks within three or four years.

Where the developer provides excess capacity, it must be determined whether the excess capacity may then be allocated to other projects. Where facilities are currently operating with deficiencies below the adopted LOS standards, the local government has three options:

(1) For state roadways defined as "backlogged facilities," the local government may allow development to proceed if the development will not degrade the existing LOS. This concept is known as "equal mitigation" and would be satisfied by the construction of facilities or payment of an in-lieu fee sufficient to accommodate the full impacts of the development. "Backlogged facilities" are defined as those facilities operating below the required LOS for which capacity improvements are not scheduled in the CIP.

(2) On state or county roads, the local government may deny or defer development until the facilities are operating at the adopted LOS. Thus, development would be delayed until the necessary improvements are scheduled in the CIP. A developer correcting the roadway deficiencies cannot proceed at an earlier date than anticipated in the CIP. This protects against a shifting of priorities of the CIP.

(3) The local government could deny or defer development as provided in subsection (2), above, but add an additional provision allowing the developer to provide those facilities necessary to allow those facilities to operate at the adopted LOS standards. This is known as the "mitigation" or "abatement" of existing deficiencies. If the developer provides facilities in addition to those necessitated by the impacts created by the proposed development, the developer would be entitled to reimbursement, but the reimbursement is delayed to the date the facility was scheduled to be built in the CIP.

If the concurrency review results in a determination that public facilities and services are not currently adequate to support the development at the adopted LOS standards, the LDC provides that the conditional approval must satisfy the following standards:

• The necessary facilities and services will be in place when the final development approval is issued;

• The development approval is subject to the condition that the necessary facilities and services will be in place when the impacts of the development occur;

• Final development approvals may be deferred or phased until public facilities and services needed to meet the LOS standards are available;

The developer may be allowed to reduce the demand on public facilities for the development through the following:

• A reduction in the density or intensity of the development;

• The use of transportation systems management for traffic;

• An increase in retention drainage.; or

• Meeting new urbanism standards.

CONDITIONS

If public facilities are not available at the adopted LOS standards, the concurrency review committee should allow the applicant to agree to one of the conditions set forth above. Conditions are generally utilized early in the development approval process where the requirements of concurrency cannot be immediately satisfied. If the concurrency approval is conditional, a condition should be attached to the final development approval requiring a reexamination of the availability and capacity of public facilities serving the development.

DEVELOPMENT AGREEMENTS

Development agreements may be used by local governments to ensure that the necessary public facilities will be provided by the developer. Unlike impact fees, development agreements can provide for meeting past deficiencies as well as new growth related to facilities.[50] The development agreement becomes the basic tool for carrying out APFOs.[51]

COMPONENTS OF AN ADEQUATE PUBLIC FACILITIES ORDINANCE

The LDC sets forth the LOS standards governing the amount and timing of growth and development that will be permitted, as well as the level of public/private investment needed in order to achieve and maintain those standards. In Florida, where concurrency has been part of the state's growth management legislation for two decades, "level of service" is defined as follows:

> "'Level of service' means an indicator of the extent or degree of service provided by, or proposed to be provided by a facility, based on and related to the operational characteristics of the facility. Level of service shall indicate the capacity per unit of demand for each public facility."[52]

Transportation engineers use a traditional academic rating system of "A" to "F" for streets based upon traffic volumes compared to the rated capacity of the street.[53] For water or sewer service, LOS may be stated as average or peak gallons per capita per day of demand. Whatever measurement the jurisdiction uses, it should be tied to units or increments of demand created by new development, tied to the existing and committed capacity of the system.

As a means of measuring performance, an LOS standard considers both the capacity of a public facility and the current and potential demand placed on the public facility from existing development, approved but unbuilt developments ("pipeline"), and projected future growth. By comparing demand to capacity, the community determines how much of the capacity of a given facility may be allocated to development within a designated area upon project approval.[54]

Once the applicable LOS standard has been identified for purposes of issuing development orders and initiating capital investment and budgeting strategies, the local government must decide when the LOS standard must be attained in order for development to proceed. A critical policy issue is the duration of the "lag time" that the local government will tolerate between the construction and occupancy of development units and the actual on-ground availability of the public facilities needed to serve the development. The question of when public facilities must be available and how they will be guaranteed is referred to as the "minimum requirements" for concurrency.

The minimum requirements issue is distinguishable from the LOS that must be attained when those facilities are available. While the adopted LOS standard could affect the community's policy decision regarding the minimum requirements imposed for concurrency—and vice versa—the standards are distinguishable. The former refers to the capacity and/or quality of the public facilities, while the latter refers to when the facilities must be available and, if not presently available, how provision of the public facilities will be guaranteed to be provided at the time of actual development.[55]

Once a community adopts LOS standards, difficulties might occur if existing public facilities are determined to be insufficient to accommodate the impacts of a proposed development. Where that is the case, a community has four options:

(1) Development approval may be deferred pending the availability of public facilities and services at the adopted LOS standard;

(2) The applicant may agree to reduce the density or intensity of the proposed development within the parameters of available facility capacity;

(3) The applicant may agree to a phasing schedule; or

(4) The developer may agree to advance those public facilities needed (or a payment to construct those facilities) to attain the adopted LOS standards, provided that they will be available when the impacts of the development occur. The deferral of development approval or the provision of public facilities by the developer can be addressed through appropriate conditions, including the date when reimbursement will be provided.

A prerequisite to allocating available capacity is determining how much capacity is available and how much capacity is used by specific types of development. Most communities allocate capacity on a first-come, first-served basis as development applications are processed. However, where available capacity is constricted, the community might consider prioritizing allocations of capacity to those projects that adhere to the comprehensive plan or that should be granted preferential treatment to meet estoppel and vested rights, or to avoid constitutional deprivations.

Preferential allocation might be achieved through a set-aside. Under a set-aside system, a percentage of available capacity is reserved for certain types or categories of development. In Montgomery County, Maryland, projects defined as "affordable housing" may be approved where the available capacity threshold in the applicable impact area has been exceeded. This approval is conditioned on review of the projects for impacts on localized facilities, such as nearby intersections and roadway links.[56]

A similar policy is authorized by New Jersey's Council on Affordable Housing, which administers that state's housing policies for local governments.[57] In addition, the program in Montgomery County, Maryland, allocates capacity to residential and nonresidential projects within each impact area so as to maintain a favorable ratio between jobs and housing. This is accomplished by computing a separate development threshold within each area for employment and housing.[58]

Preferential allocation might also be achieved through a "point system," which enables the reviewing agency to balance concurrency review with other public policies, and which could include a "weighting system" on the capacity and availability of public facilities for purposes of concurrency review.[59] The community could assign point scores for the availability of a specified amount of capacity for each public facility and/or for the achievement of other public policies, such as the provision of affordable housing. Thus, a project that would create a deficiency in one public facility, such as transportation, could receive approval if a compensating point score is achieved for other public facilities and/or for the provision of other public benefits. Care must be taken, however, to assure that minimum standards are met.[60] A similar system is used for Leadership in Energy and Environmental Design certification of sustainable projects (see § 5.17 Sustainability in Chapter 5, Development Standards, of the LDC).

The community may vary the LOS standards for each public facility by geographic area, over time, or by development type. LOS standards may vary by geographic area in order to allow flexibility in the achievement of other public objectives, such as promoting infill, corridor center, downtown, or TOD. LOS standards may also be varied by geographic area where substantial deficiencies exist or where environmental or other constraints prevent facility expansion (sometimes referred to as "backlogged" or "constrained" facilities). LOS standards may be "tiered" over time in order to avoid the effect of an immediate, high LOS standard on growth and development in the jurisdiction. To achieve this result, LOS standards can be set in increasing steps to govern concurrency review for a specified period of time following the adoption of the APFO, with a higher standard taking effect at a specified future date.

A differential LOS standard is one which varies according to the location of development, the type of development, or other policy considerations. Typically, higher LOS standards are established in rural areas to discourage sprawl development. LOS standards can be adjusted to encourage infill development, redevelopment, brownfields, the production of affordable housing, or important public projects. The LOS standards adjustments must be justified, supported by data and analysis, and bear a rational relationship to a legitimate public purpose, as discussed further in the section entitled "Legal Issues," below.

Ramapo used a point system that based the adequacy of public facilities upon the distance from specified capital improvements. To arrive at a point score for each type of facility, overlay maps were prepared depicting the level of infrastructure capacity by location.[61] An ordinal scale was used, assigning a maximum of five points each to sewer, drainage, parks, schools, and roads, and three points to firehouses. For parks, roads, and firehouses, points were assigned on the basis of the project's distance from existing facilities.

Later systems have expanded upon the Ramapo Plan by tying development approvals to LOS standards. LOS standards measure the ratio of public facility capacity to the need for the facility.[62] This deceptively simple concept incorporates several features missing from the point system:

- The LOS standards take into account all demand for the facilities, including existing demand as well as the additional population added by new development proposals. By contrast, the point system only accounts for those facilities available to the project under review;
- An adopted LOS standard reflects a policy decision concerning the appropriate equilibrium between population and public facilities that may be applied to new development in standard setting and development approval review, and to the public sector in the capital budgeting process; and
- LOS standards provide a convenient benchmark for monitoring growth management systems.

While "points" are generally used to evaluate individual projects in relation to nearby (if any) facilities, the LOS standards relate capital improvements to community-wide population and development. LOS standards are more flexible than a rigid point system. Because LOS standards are performance oriented, developers can mitigate the effects of their projects through project design, roadway exactions, or other solutions, such as the provision of transit facilities, which would alleviate the demand for roads.

LEGAL ISSUES

Implementation of APFOs requires enabling legislation and adherence to constitutional principles regarding takings, equal protection, and due process. This section addresses those issues generally, though each state will have specific statutory and case law that will direct particular ordinances.

ENABLING LEGISLATION

Local land-use authority is typically derived from enabling legislation.[63] Enabling legislation is a state statute that establishes local authority to exercise a certain power (e.g., zoning) and then describes the conditions by which the power may be exercised (e.g., notification, hearings, and applicability).

Enabling legislation is the threshold issue for APFOs because local governments are creatures of the state, and the authority to adopt local land-use legislation must be granted by the state.[64] Only Maryland has specific APFO enabling legislation,[65] while Florida,[66] Vermont,[67] and Washington[68] mandate concurrency at the state level by prohibiting new development that would adversely affect specified facilities or fail to meet adopted LOS standards. New Hampshire's legislation allows development timing ordinances, subject to preparation of a master plan and CIP. [69]

Authority for APFOs is more frequently found through purposes language in the Standard State Zoning Enabling Act (SZEA). In *Golden v. Planning Board of the Town of Ramapo*,[70] the seminal case that paved the way for concurrency, the court found the requisite statutory authority for a tiered growth plan. The Town of Ramapo adopted a master plan, comprehensive zoning ordinance, and CIP spanning a period of 18 years.[71] The town's zoning act was based on the SZEA. The town also adopted amendments, for the purpose of limiting urban sprawl, requiring that residential development could only proceed "according to the provision of adequate municipal facilities and services, with the assurance that any concomitant restraint upon property use is to be of a 'temporary' nature . . ."[72]

The standards for development approval issuance were based on the availability of five essential facilities:

(1) Public sanitary sewers or approved alternative;
(2) Drainage facilities;
(3) Improved public parks or recreation facilities, including public schools;
(4) Major, secondary, or collector roads; and
(5) Firehouses.[73]

The system was based on an elaborate point system, whereby each public facility was allotted certain point values, and a developer had to earn a certain number of points to be granted a development approval.

The court held that Ramapo had the authority in the language of the Purposes of Zoning provision in the SZEA: ". . . to facilitate the adequate provision of transportation, water, sewerage, schools, parks and other public requirements,"[74] holding:

"The power to restrict and regulate conferred under Section 261 includes within its grant, by way of necessary implication, the authority to direct the growth of population for purposes indicated, within the confines of the township. It is the matrix of land-use restrictions, common to each of the enumerated powers and sanctioned goals, a necessary concomitant to the municipalities' recognized authority to determine the lines along which local development shall proceed, though it may divert from its natural course."[75]

Nor did the court find that the ordinance was exclusionary, stating "the present amendments seek, by implementation of sequential development and timed growth, to provide a balanced cohesive community dedicated to the efficient utilization of land."[76] Finally, the court found that implementation of the plan did not constitute a taking because, while the restrictions upon property in *Ramapo* were substantial, they were not absolute.[77] The takings issue will be considered further (see the section entitled, "Takings," below).

Other communities have followed *Ramapo*, finding authority for concurrency regulations through state statutes that confer the police power to zone.[78] Other states have statutory restrictions that limit interim or moratorium types of concurrency standards.

In *Toll Bros., Inc. v. West Windsor Township*,[79] the Township of West Windsor passed an ordinance in response to rapid growth, adopting a 50-year program to increase road capacity and other capital improvements. In conjunction with the program, it passed "timed growth controls" to control the rate of growth and defer development until the necessary road improvements were complete. Because of the delay on development of their property, the Toll brothers sued the township, seeking to invalidate the growth controls. They claimed that the growth controls were a moratorium on development, which violated a state statute prohibiting moratoria on development except in cases of imminent public health risks. The court upheld the challenge, finding that the ordinance was in violation of state law. In *Toll Bros.*, however, the following provisions of the Ramapo Plan to ameliorate takings were absent: a funded CIP; definitive authority to develop within a one- to 18-year time frame; allowing limited development by clustering units at urban densities; authorizing development of the balance of the land at the time that concurrency is met; advancement of facilities; and interim taxing at agricultural value by voluntary "development easements" from the property owner.[80]

CONSTITUTIONAL CHALLENGES TO ADEQUATE PUBLIC FACILITIES ORDINANCES

TAKINGS

The "Public Use and Just Compensation Clause" within the Fifth Amendment to the U.S. Constitution provides that private property shall not be taken for public use without just compensation. Most states have parallel "just compensation," "takings," or "damages" clauses in their state constitutions.[81]

Concurrency regulations are often litigated as facial or as applied regulatory takings because they may postpone the economic use of property until adequate public facilities are available.[82] Concurrency regulations are similar to interim development controls because they place temporary, as opposed to permanent, timing and phasing restrictions on growth.[83]

In *First English Evangelical Lutheran Church v. County of Los Angeles*,[84] the U.S. Supreme Court considered a case with a five-year interim development control on development, due to severe flooding in a canyon, until permanent regulations could be adopted. The court held that temporary takings would be compensable under the principles of *Penn Central Transportation Co. v. City of New York*[85] if the regulation effected a permanent taking that lasted for a temporary period of time.[86] Concurrency regulations will not effect a permanent taking if they are tied to the availability of adequate public facilities based upon a prioritized CIP that the local government is funding in good faith.[87] In *Wincamp Partnership v. Anne Arundel County*,[88] both the state statute and the ordinance prohibited the issuance of development approvals without adequate sewer capacity. A local government decision not to allocate funds immediately to expand capacity was upheld because the local government was following a prioritized CIP.[89]

A local government's ability to apply temporary restrictions was further upheld by the Supreme Court in *Tahoe Sierra Preservation Council v. Tahoe Regional Planning Agency*.[90] The Court held that a 32-month total moratorium on development did not constitute a per se taking.[91] The Court first rejected the landowners' assertion that *First English* and *Lucas* stand for the proposition that whenever the government imposes a deprivation of all economically viable use of property, no matter how briefly it effects a per se *Lucas* taking.[92] The Court noted that those cases did not address temporary takings as would be effected by a concurrency regulation.

The Court found that a local government could indeed institute a moratorium without effecting a taking, finding it necessary to protect the decision-making process. The Court cited an important interest in fostering informed planning decisions by regulatory agencies. The Court noted that "otherwise, the financial constraints of compensating property owners during a moratorium may force officials to rush through the planning process or to abandon the practice altogether."[93] The Court also noted the importance of protecting the decision-making process in the context of regional planning.[94]

A number of state courts have affirmed a local government's authority to use temporary regulations for planning purposes. In *Woodbury Place Partners v. City of Woodbury*,[95] the court affirmed the principle that all use of a property may be denied for a temporary period of time without effecting a taking. In *W.R. Grace & Co. v. Cambridge*,[96] the court held that a two-year moratorium that deprived a landowner of value for a temporary period is not a per se taking of property requiring compensation because the deprivation is not permanent. Even though there was an economic impact on the landowner's property as a result of a moratorium imposed by a zoning amendment, it was insufficient to constitute compensable regulatory taking under the Fifth Amendment because the landowner continued to realize return on the investment property; continued to use various production, research, and development facilities located on the property throughout the interim period; and had already voluntarily delayed developing the property for a period of approximately seven years.[97]

An APFO might be challenged as an economic taking where development is deferred pending the availability of facilities to meet LOS standards.[98] Since the property is only provisionally burdened, the landowner may argue that the regulations are a "temporary taking."[99] The critical issue is the amount of time that a property can be burdened before a taking is deemed to have occurred.

If development approval is denied or deferred because of the unavailability of public facility capacity, the community must show that the public facilities forming the basis for the concurrency determination will be provided within a "reasonable" period of time. A 10-year period has been upheld if based on planning studies and a prioritized CIP adopted in good faith.[100] In *Golden*,[101] the court approved a concurrency ordinance based upon a staged, 18-year CIP that would have deferred some development approvals for the duration of the plan. Slowing the rate of growth over a decade based upon a lack of adequate public facilities has been upheld.[102]

SUBSTANTIVE DUE PROCESS

Substantive due process requires that land-use regulations have a reasonable relationship to the protection of public health, safety, and welfare.[103] The requirement has two prongs:

(1) That the land-use regulations address a legitimate public purpose; and

(2) That the method of achieving that goal is closely related to that purpose.

Like the standard for the rational basis test, courts are generally very deferential to local governments, such that only egregious acts will lead to a violation of substantive due process rights.[104] This deference derives from the longstanding recognition of the legitimacy of growth management and planning controls by the Supreme Court.[105] Similarly, in *Village of Belle Terre v. Boraas*, the Court stated, "The police power is not confined to the elimination of filth, stench, and unhealthy places. It is ample to lay out zones where family values, youth values, and the blessings of quiet seclusion, and clean air make the area a sanctuary for people."[106]

This approach was confirmed in *Sylvia Development Corp. v. Calvert County*,[107] where a developer alleged due process and equal protection violations arising out of the denial of the application to increase the density of a proposed development under the county's transfer zone district program. The court upheld the county's denial of the application, which was in part based on an adequate public facilities requirement and on findings that the proposed subdivision could not be served by adequate road facilities for traffic or water supplies for fire fighters. The court found no egregious behavior on the part of the commission, noting that the decision was supportable on a rational basis.[108]

Planning Studies and Capital Improvements Programs

A key underpinning to an effective and legally defensible concurrency management system is proper planning supported by detailed studies:

"The importance of a sound factual presentation is apparent in the urban context as well. The town of Ramapo, on the outskirts of the New York Metropolitan area, successfully defended a growth control ordinance before New York's highest court with success due in no small part to a thorough presentation of their case. ***

"The town was able to present a vast array of planning data in their defense. In its statement of the facts in *Golden v. Planning Board of the Town of Ramapo*, . . . the Court of Appeals pointed to the Town Master Plan, whose 'preparation included a four volume study of the existing land uses, public facilities, transportation, industry and commerce, housing needs, and projected population trends . . . Additional sewage district and drainage studies were undertaken which culminated in the adoption of a Capital Budget . . .' Thus, not only could the town rely upon a large number of formal municipal actions, adoption of a Master Plan, a Capital Budget, zoning and subdivision ordinances and the like, but they could also document each with thorough and detailed planning studies."[109]

In *Stoney-Brook Development Corporation v. Town of Fremont*,[110] the New Hampshire Supreme Court held a growth control ordinance invalid because it failed to follow the requirement that assessments of community development needs must be carefully studied.[111]

Good Faith Implementation

As with interim development ordinances, the actions of local governments or counties in enacting APFOs must be rational and made in good faith.[112] In *Wincamp Partnership v. Anne Arundel County*,[113] both the state statute and local ordinance prohibited issuance of development approvals without adequate sewer capacity. A county decision not to allocate funds to expand capacity to allow immediate development of plaintiff's land was upheld because the county was attempting to meet problems in good faith, had no improper motive, and used a rational approach in establishing priorities for extending hook-ups. Compare that case with *Charles v. Diamond*.[114]

RIGHT TO TRAVEL

Of particular importance to concurrency regulations, the Supreme Court has recognized the fundamental right to travel freely among the states under the Due Process clause.[115] A government regulation that restricts the right to travel freely among the states, and to relocate to another state, might be struck down as a substantive due process violation. A right-to-travel challenge to an APFO typically alleges interference with one's ability to relocate. These arguments generally fail because APFOs allow developers to advance necessary infrastructure.[116]

FUNDAMENTAL LIBERTY INTEREST

Federal courts have created an enormous hurdle for substantive due process claims. They must demonstrate that the restriction "shocks the conscience of the court."[117] Freedom from delay in receiving development approvals is not among these fundamental liberty interests.[118] A substantive due process claim of a non-fundamental liberty interest must be dismissed; such a claimant can only look to the Equal Protection clause or Takings clause.[119]

EQUAL PROTECTION CLAUSE

The Fourteenth Amendment to the U.S. Constitution provides that states cannot deny persons the equal protection of the laws. This provision applies to legislative classifications and distinctions. Legislative classifications are typically upheld where they are rationally related to a legitimate government interest. This standard is very deferential. If a fundamental right or a suspect class is the basis of a classification, then the court will apply strict scrutiny, upholding a regulation only if the regulation is based upon a compelling state interest met by the least restrictive means.[120]

In land-use matters free of race or other discriminations, a court will apply the rational basis test and uphold the regulation if it bears a rational relationship to a legitimate public purpose.[121] The rational basis test is an extremely deferential standard for local governments. Most decisions have found that developers are not a suspect class, nor have courts found that land development is a fundamental right.[122] Nonetheless, the ordinance must still bear a rational relationship to the purpose, so communities must take care to conduct careful studies that justify the adopted LOS standards and their effect on the physical geography of a community.

Claims brought under the Equal Protection clause have a major advantage over substantive due process claims: no property interest need be shown. Nevertheless, courts apply the same rational basis scrutiny as in substantive due process cases.[123] Only in cases involving a totally unreasonable, hostile animus will such claims be forthcoming.[124] Such claims have almost universally be denied,[125] and long-term, area-wide, adequate public facilities regulations leave little room for individual discrimination.[126]

CONCLUSION

Concurrency ordinances are an effective means to manage the timing and phasing of public services and infrastructure in a community, and will guarantee that all new residents receive services. They are more advantageous than other traditional land-use controls because they directly control the level of population and employment growth, which represents a major component of infrastructure demand. Concurrency ordinances are also more popular than some traditional land-use controls because they necessitate exact standards against which proposed development can be measured, thereby reducing the likelihood of a successful legal challenge.

Moreover, APFOs can serve as a springboard for other innovative land-use controls, such as traffic demand management ordinances, transfer of development rights, and negotiated exactions and impact fees, and may be used to meet other comprehensive planning goals relating to urban development patterns and affordable housing. While they will not stop growth, downzone property, deter economic development, or raise housing prices, they are not a catch all solution to growth management. They are one tool in the planning toolbox to help a community meet their expectation of growth and their visions for the future.

NOTES

1. See S. Mark White, "Adequate Public Facilities Ordinances and Transportation Management," Planning Advisory Service Report No. 465 (Chicago: American Planning Association, 1996).
2. Transportation Research Board, *Highway Capacity Manual 2000* (Washington, DC: TRB, 2000).
3. Institute of Transportation Engineers, *Trip Generation*, 7th ed. (Washington, DC: ITE, 2003).
4. See "Hard Choices," summary report of the National Infrastructure Study, Joint Economic Committee of Congress, 98th Cong., 2nd Sess. (1984) (deficiencies exceed $400 billion). By 2003, deficiencies exceeded $1.6 trillion just for transportation needs. Robert H. Freilich, David L. Callies, and Thomas E. Roberts, *Callies, Freilich and Roberts Cases and Material on Land Use*, 4th ed. (Minneapolis: West, 2004), 231.
5. *Marblehead v. City of San Clemente*, 277 Cal.Rptr. 550 (Cal. App. 1991).
6. David J. Brower, D.W. Owens, R. Rosenberg, I. Botvinick, and M. Mandel, *Urban Growth Management Through Development Timing* (New York: Praeger, 1976), 51-63; Michael E. Gleeson et al. "Urban Growth Management Systems: An Evaluation of Policy-Related Research," Planning Advisory Service Report Nos. 309/310 (Chicago: American Planning Association, August 1975), 12-13 (describing creation of rural zones in unserviced areas supplemented with a subdivision regulation mandating the availability of drainage facilities in Brooklyn Park, Minnesota).
7. Urban growth boundaries generally couple urban service areas beyond which utilities will not be extended with land-use controls prohibiting urban-scale development beyond the urban growth boundary. Morgan and Shonkwiler, "Urban Development and Statewide Planning: Challenges of the 1980's," 61 *Or. L. Rev.* 351, 456-65 (1982); *1000 Friends of Oregon v. LCDC*, 301 Or. 447, 724 P.2d 268 (1986); *Kilausa Neighborhood Ass'n v. Land Use Comm'n*, 751 P.2d 1031 (HI 1988).
8. See, e.g., *Construction Industry Association v. City of Petaluma*, 522 F.2d 897 (9th Cir. 1975), *cert. denied*, 424 U.S. 934 (1976).
9. *Golden v. Planning Board of the Town of Ramapo*, 30 N.Y.2d 359, 334 N.Y.S.2d 138, 285 N.E.2d 291, *appeal dismissed*, 409 U.S. 1003 (1972).
10. *National Land & Investment v. Kohn*, 419 Pa. 504, 215 A.2d 597 (1965); *In re Concord Township Appeal (Kit-Mar Builders)*, 268 A.2d 765 (Pa. 1970); see also Richard Cutler, "Legal and Illegal Methods for Controlling Community Growth on the Urban Fringe," *Wis. L. Rev.* 370 (1961).
11. *Associated Home Builders v. City of Livermore*, 135 Cal.Rptr. 41, 52, 55, 557 P.2d 473, 18 Cal.3d 582 (1976) (distinguishing between large lot zoning, which favors the wealthy, with even-handed adequate public facilities requirements).
12. See, e.g., *Steel Hill Development, Inc. v. Town of Sanbornton*, 469 F.2d 956 (1st Cir. 1972); see also *Sturges v. Town of Chilmark*, 402 N.E.2d 1346 (Mass. 1980) (upholding rate-of-growth ordinance).
13. *Garipay v. Town of Hanover*, 116 N.H. 34, 351 A.2d 64 (1976); *Pearson Kent Corp. v. Bear*, 271 N.E.2d 218 (N.Y. 1971); or rezoning, *Freundshuh v. City of Blaine*, 385 N.W.2d 6 (Minn. App. 1986); *Larsen v. County of Washington*, 387 N.W.2d 902 (Minn. App. 1986); *Board of Supervisors v. Allman*, 215 Va. 434, 211 S.E.2d 48 (1975); *Board of Supervisors v. Williams*, 216 Va. 49, 216 S.E.2d 33 (1975).
14. See, e.g., *Garipay v. Town of Hanover*, 116 N.H. 34, 351 A.2d 64 (1976).
15. See, e.g., *Matter of Joseph v. Town Board of Town of Clarkstown*, 24 Misc.2d 366, 198 N.Y.S.2d 695 (Supreme Ct. 1960).
16. 194 Cal.Rptr. 258 (Cal. App. 1983).
17. *City of Milwaukee v. Public Service Commission*, 5 N.W.2d 800 (Wis. 1942) (utility need not service outside city limits because service provided in the past to limited area had been done so under contract), with *City of Milwaukee v. Public Service Commission*, 66 N.W.2d 716 (Wis. 1954). See Biggs, "No Drop, No Flush, No Growth: How Cities Can Control Growth Beyond Their Boundaries by Refusing to Extend Utility Services," 22 *Urb. Law.* 285 (1990).
18. 258 A.2d 410 (Md. 1969).
19. See also *Reid Development Corp. v. Parsippany-Troy Hills Township*, 107 A.2d 20 (N.J. App. Div. 1954) (utility extension as growth control allowed so long as reasonable utility-related reasons alleged). Such reasons include: limited financial resources, *Rose v. Plymouth Town*, 173 P.2d 285 (Utah 1946); insufficient facilities or shortage of capacity, *Swanson v. Marin Municipal Water District*, 128 Cal.Rptr. 485 (Cal. App. 1976); and environmental concerns, *Cappture Realty Corp. v. Board of Adjustment*, 313 A.2d 624 (N.J. Super. Law Div. 1973), *aff'd.*, 336 A.2d 30 (N.J. Super. App. Div. 1975); *Robinson v. City of Boulder*, 547 P.2d 228 (Colo. 1976) (land-use policies); see generally Stuart A. Deutsch, "Capital Improvement Controls as Land Use Devices," 9 *Envtl. Law.* 61 (1978); *Swanson v. Marin Municipal Water District*, 128 Cal.Rptr. 485 (Cal. App. 1976) (recognizing a continuing obligation on the part of the district to "exert every reasonable effort to augment its available water supply in order to meet increasing demands"). See Dennis J. Herman, Note,

"Sometimes There's Nothing Left to Give: The Justification for Denying Water Service to New Consumers to Control Growth," 44 *Stan. L. Rev.* 429 (1992).

20. 1997 WL 133447 (Conn. Super 1997).
21. 42 Va. Civ. 348 (1997).
22. 13 Cal. App. 2d 1035 (1992).
23. 644 So.2d 486 (Fla. 1994).
24. 681 A.2d 484 (Md. 1996).
25. 760 A.2d 452 (Pa. Commw. 2000).
26. 644 P.2d 942 (Colo. 1982).
27. R.W. Burchell, W.R. Dolphin and C.C. Galley, *The Costs and Benefits of Alternative Growth Patterns: The Impact Assessment of the New Jersey State Plan* (New Brunswick, NJ: Center for Urban Policy Research, Rutgers University, 2000).
28. See Robert Freilich, "Development Timing, Moratoria, and Controlling Growth," 1974 Institute on Planning, Zoning and Eminent Domain, 147, 151-57; e.g., *Tisei v. Town of Ogunquit*, 491 A.2d 564 (Me. 1985).
29. E.g., *Smoke Rise, Inc. v. Washington Suburban Sanitary Commission*, 400 F.Supp. 1369 (D.Md. 1975) (upholding sewer connection moratoria adopted by regional sewer authority in response to system inadequacies).
30. *First English Evangelical Lutheran Church v. County of Los Angeles*, 210 Cal. App. 3d 1353, 258 Cal.Rptr. 893 (Cal. App. 1989), *cert. denied*, 493 U.S. 1056 (1990) (upholding construction ban on floodplain); *Tahoe-Sierra Preservation Council v. Tahoe Regional Planning Agency*, 535 U.S.302 (2002) (31-month interim ordinance restricting run-off into Lake Tahoe while study underway); *Woodbury Place Partners v. City of Woodbury*, 492 N.W.2d 258 (Minn. App. 1992) (24-month interim control during study for location of freeway interchange).
31. *Conway v. Town of Stratham*, 414 A.2d 539 (N.H. 1980).
32. Note 30 (*Tahoe-Sierra*), supra, at note 21.
33. Note 9 (*Golden*), supra.
34. See John R. Nolon, "Golden and Its Emanations: The Surprising Origins of Smart Growth," 35 *Urb. Law.* 15 (2003).
35. (Ramapo Plan). See Thomas G. Pelham, "From the Ramapo Plan to Florida's Statewide Concurrency System: Ramapo's Influence on Infrastructure Planning," 35 *Urb. Law.* 113 (Winter 2003).
36. The system was upheld in two landmark cases argued by Dr. Freilich as the land-use consultant for the San Diego General Plan. *J.W. Jones & Co. v. City of San Diego*, 157 Cal. App. 3d 745 (1984) and *City of Del Mar v. City of San Diego*, 133 Cal. App. 3d 401 (1983).
37. An adequate public facilities ordinance is commonly referred to as a "concurrency" regulation. Fla. Stat. Ann. § 163.177 (10)(h); Wash. Stat. Ann. § 36.70A.70(6)(e) (2001). Both terms are used interchangeably in this article.
38. See Wests Fla. Stat. Ann. § 163 3177 (10)(h) ("Public facilities and services needed to support development shall be concurrent with the impacts of such development."). See also Note 35 (Pelham), supra.
39. S. Mark White, "Adequate Public Facilities Ordinances and Transportation Management," Planning Advisory Service Report No. 465 (Chicago: American Planning Association, 1996).
40. See *Wincamp Partnership v. Anne Arunde County*, 458 F. Supp. 1009 (D. Md. 1978); *In re Petition of Dolington Group*, 839 A.2d 1021 (Pa. 2003).
41. See, e.g., Albuquerque/Bernalillo County Planning Division, Albuquerque/Bernalillo Comprehensive Plan Policies II.B.2.a.4 (phase Planned Communities in Reserve Area with respect to capital improvements program (CIP)), II.B.4.a.7 and b.3 (use CIP to implement development objectives and guide development through facilities plans in Semi-Urban Area); II.D.1.d (review zoning requests for compliance with "service level performance standards"), II.D.4.c.2 (amend land development regulations to provide "service levels and performance standards for streets and intersections") (1988).
42. State of Florida, "Final Report of the Transportation and Land Use Study Committee" (Jan. 15, 1999), at 20, available on-line at www.dot.state.fl.us/planning/publications/landusestudy.pdf.
43. Id.
44. See, e.g., Note 39 (White), supra; Robert H. Freilich and S. Mark White, "Transportation Congestion and Growth Management: Comprehensive Approaches to Resolving America's Major Quality of Life Crisis," 24 *Loy. L.A. L. Rev.* 917 (1991).
45. Note 39 (White), supra, at 31.
46. The LDC commentary does not discuss every component of an adequate public facilities ordinance. For a more detailed discussion of the components of a concurrency ordinance, see Note 39 (White), supra.
47. Note 35 (Pelham), supra.
48. Note 9 (*Golden*), supra.
49. See, e.g., *Leroy Land Development v. Tahoe Regional Planning Agency*, 939 F.2d 696 (9th Cir. 1991) (environmental mitigation measures embodied in settlement agreement cannot be challenged on takings grounds).
50. David L. Callies, Daniel J. Curtin, and Julie A. Tappendorf, *Bargaining for Development: A Handbook on Development Agreements, Annexation Agreements, Land Development Conditions, Vested Rights and the Provision of Public Facilities* (Washington, DC: Environmental Law Institute, 2003); *Leroy Land Development v. Tahoe Regional Planning Agency*, 939 F.2d 6961 (9th Cir. 1991) (proportionality standards not applicable to voluntary agreement).
51. See *Beaver Meadows v. Larimer County*, 709 P.2d 928 (Colo. 1985) (requiring developer to pay for off-site roads as condition of approval invalid where not roughly proportional, but county could have denied development based on lack of road adequate public facilities and required developer to voluntarily advance deficient facilities through a development agreement).
52. Fla. Admin. Code r. 9J-5.003(62) (2001).
53. Note 44 (Freilich/White), supra, at 942-43; see also Washington State, R.C.W.A. § 36.70.
54. The adequate public facilities ordinance in Palm Beach County, Florida, provides that new development approvals shall not cause the county's total mass transit capacity to fall below "that which can accommodate 0.75 percent of the total County transportation trips." See Note 39 (White), supra, at 20.
55. See, e.g., *Annapolis Market Place, L.L.C. v. Parker*, 802 A.2d 1029 (Md. 2002). Landowner's neighbors sought judicial

review of county board of appeals decision to permit rezoning from residential to commercial district. The Court of Appeals held that: (1) adequate facilities are not "programmed for construction" when the developer agrees to construct them at rezoning; (2) the developer's agreement thus does not satisfy county ordinance that prohibits rezoning without finding that facilities, infrastructure systems, and schools adequate to serve uses allowed by the new zoning classification are either in existence or programmed for construction; and (3) county board of appeals failed to make adequate findings.

56. Note 44 (Freilich/White), supra, at 943; Note 39 (White), supra, at 24, 31, 33-34.
57. N.J. Admin. Code § 5:92-8.6(c) provides: "Notwithstanding the prohibitive cost of adequate public facilities and infrastructure at the time a local government petitions for substantive certification, the local government shall reserve and set aside new infrastructure capacity, when it becomes available for low and moderate income housing on a priority basis."
58. See Douglas Porter, ed., "Performance Standards in Growth Management," Planning Advisory Service Report No. 461 (Chicago: American Planning Association, January 1996) (excellent description of adequate public facilities ordinances in Maryland).
59. See Robert H. Freilich, *From Sprawl to Smart Growth: Successful Legal, Planning, and Environmental Systems* (Chicago: American Bar Association, 1999).
60. See, e.g., a related practice in Austin, Texas, which uses a smart growth criteria matrix that assigns points to proposed developments based on achieving objectives, such as mixed use, streetscape treatment, transit-oriented development, etc. City of Austin, "About the Smart Growth Criteria Matrix" (2000), available on-line at www.ci.austin.tx.us/smartgrowth/smartmatrix.htm.
61. Manuel E. Emanuel, "Ramapo's Managed Growth Program: After Five Years Experience," 4 *Planning Notebook*, No. 5 (1974, reprinted in 3 *Management and Control of Growth*, Scott ed., Washington, DC: National Science Foundation, 1975), 302.
62. Montgomery County Planning Department, "Fourth Annual Growth Policy Report: Carrying Capacity and Adequate Public Facilities" (Silver Spring MD: Maryland National Capital Park and Planning Commission, 1977), 1-5 (ratio of public facilities and services to population); Fla. Admin. Code § 9J-5.003(41) (1988) (capacity per unit of demand).
63. 8 McQuillin Municipal Corporations § 25.37 (3d ed., 2000). Some local governments derive land-use authority directly from a state constitution or a municipal charter, but enabling legislation is the most common source of authority.
64. See Edward H. Ziegler, Jr., *Rathkopf's The Law of Zoning and Planning*, Vol. 1C, Chapter 2, 3d ed. (St. Paul, MN: West Group, 2004).
65. Md. Ann. Code Art 66B, § 10.01 (1978); Md. Health-Envt. Code Ann. § 9.512(b)(1) (1987 and Supp. 1989) (wastewater facilities).
66. Fla. Sta. Ann. § 163.3177 (10) (h), 163.03202(2)(g), 163.3180 (West Supp. 1989).
67. Vt. Stat. Ann. Tit. 10 § 6086(a)(1)(J) (2000).
68. Wash. Stat. Ann. § 36.70A.70(6)(e) (2001).
69. N.H. Rev. Stat. Ann. § 674:22 (1986 and Supp. 1988).
70. Note 9 (*Golden*), supra, 285 N.E.2d at 294.
71. Id. at 294.
72. Id. at 295.
73. Id. at 295.
74. § 261 of the New York Town laws granted local governments authority to zone for purpose of promoting the health, safety, and general welfare of the community, and § 263 of the New York Town Law required that such regulations be made in accordance with a comprehensive plan and designed, among other things, to "facilitate the adequate provision of transportation, water, sewerage, schools, parks and other public requirements." See Robert H. Freilich, *From Sprawl to Smart Growth* (Chicago: American Bar Association, 1999), 58 (quoting New York Town Law § 261 (McKinney 1965)).
75. Note 9 (*Golden*), supra, 285 N.E.2d at 297.
76. Id. at 302.
77. Id. at 304.
78. See, e.g., *Schenck v. City of Hudson*, 997 F.Supp. 902, 905 (N.D.Ohio 1998) ("Under its police power, Defendant City of Hudson has the right to maintain its character and to grow at a slower pace to allow orderly provision of services, including infrastructure service levels."); compare *Halle Development, Inc. v. Anne Arundel County*, 808 A.2d 1280 (Md. 2002).
79. 712 A.2d 266 (N.J.Super.A.D. 1998).
80. See Note 9 (*Golden*), supra, 285 N.E.2d at 297.
81. Timothy J. Dowling, "Reflections on Urban Sprawl, Smart Growth, and the Fifth Amendment," 148 *U. Pa. L. Rev.* 873 (2000).
82. Note 35 (Pelham), supra.
83. H. Glen Boggs and Robert C. Apgar, "Concurrency and Growth Management: A Lawyer's Primer," 7 *J. Land Use and Envt'l L.* 1 (1991).
84. 482 U.S. 304 (1987); on remand, the California Court held that there was no taking because the restriction was reasonable in duration. 258 Cal.Rptr. 893, 906 (Cal. App. 1989).
85. 438 U.S. 104 (1978).
86. Robert H. Freilich, "Time, Space, and Value in Inverse Condemnation: A Unified theory for Partial Takings Analysis," 24 *U. Haw. L. Rev.* 589 (2002).
87. Note 9 (*Golden*), supra, at 304. "Without a doubt restrictions upon the property—are substantial in nature and duration. They are not, however, absolute. The amendments contemplate a definite term (not to exceed 18 years) and during that time the Town is committed to the construction and installation of improvements. . . . While even the best of plans may not always be realized—we must assume the Town will put its best effort forward in implementing the physical and fiscal timetable. . . . There will be ample opportunity to undo the restrictions upon default." See *Charles v. Diamond*, 392 N.Y.S.2d 594 (Ct. App. 1977) (remanding for evaluation of "good faith" in light of a 10-year delay).
88. 458 F.Supp. 1009 (D. Md. 1978); Malcolm D. Rivkin, "Sewer Moratoria as a Growth Control Technique," in Randall W. Scott, David J. Brower, and Dallas D. Miner, eds., 2 *Management Control of Growth* 473 (1975); *Belle Harbor Realty Co. v. Kerr*, 364 N.Y.S.2d (Ct. App. 1974);

Swanson v. Marin Municipal Water District, 128 Cal.Rptr 485 (Cal. App. 1976) (a moratorium on new water service was reasonable in light of threatened water shortages, but recognizing a continuing obligation on the part of the district to "extend every reasonable effort to augment its available water supply to meet increasing demand"); *C.F. Cappture Realty Co. v. Board of Adjustment*, 313 A.2d 624 (N.J. Super. 1973) aff'd., 336 A.2d 30 (N.J. App. 1975).

89. See also *Associated Homebuilders v. City of Livermore*, 135 Cal.Rptr. 41 (Cal. 1976) (upholding concurrency regulations against charges of exclusionary zoning).
90. 535 U.S. 302, 122 S.Ct. 1465 (2002).
91. *Lucas v. South Carolina Coastal Comm'n*, 438 U.S. 104 (1994). This establishes a per se take if the regulation takes 100 percent of value permanently. If not permanent or 100 percent of value, then partial ad hoc taking analysis is conducted under *Penn Central Terminal Co. v. City of New York*, 438 U.S. 104 (1978).
92. 535 U.S. at 328-331.
93. 535 U.S. at 337-339.
94. 535 U.S. at 341.
95. 492 N.W.2d 258 (Minn. App. 1992), *cert. denied*, 113 S.Ct. 2929 (1993).
96. 56 Mass. App. Ct. 559 (Mass. App. 2002).
97. See also *Williams v. City of Central*, 907 P.2d 701 (Colo. App. 1995) (10-month moratorium on special use permits, while city studied impact of its growing gaming district, did not constitute categorical compensable taking of development approval applicant's property; even if all economically viable uses were temporarily barred, moratorium was intended to be temporary and delay was not extraordinary); *Santa Fe Village Venture v. Albuquerque*, 914 F.Supp. 478, 483 (D.N.M. 1995) (30-month moratorium on development of lands within the Petroglyph National Monument was not a taking); see also *Long Beach Equities, Inc. v. County of Ventura*, 282 Cal.Rptr. 877 (Cal. App. 2. Dist., 1991) (growth control tier system preventing urban development on agricultural land is not total and unreasonable in purpose, duration, or scope, and restrictions it places on development are not compensable).
98. Note 39 (White), supra, at 10.
99. Id.
100. *Sturges v. Town of Chilmark*, 402 N.E.2d 1346 (Mass. 1980).
101. Note 9 (*Golden*), supra.
102. *B. Schenck v. City of Hudson*, 114 F.3d 590 (6th Cir. 1997); *Boulder Buildings Group v. City of Boulder*, 759 P.2d 752 (Colo. App. 1988); *Williamson v. Pitkin County*, 872 P.2d 1263 (Colo. App. 1993).
103. Daniel R. Mandelker, *Land Use Law*, 4th ed. (Albany, NY: Lexis Law Publishing, 1997), § 2.39.
104. See *Licari v. Ferruzzi*, 22 F.3d 344 (1st Cir. 1994); *Chesterfield Development Corp. v. City of Chesterfield*, 963 F.2d 1102 (8th Cir.); *Creative Environments, Inc. v. Estabrook*, 680 F.2d 822 (1st Cir. 1982), *cert. denied*, 459 U.S. 989 (1982); *PFZ Properties, Inc. v. Rodriquez*, 928 F.2d 28 (1st Cir. 1991), *cert. dismissed as improvidently granted*, 112 S.Ct. 1151 (1992).
105. *Agins v. City of Tiburon*, 447 U.S. 255 (1980) (regulation of sprawl and urbanization is a valid public purpose); *Norbeck Village Joint Venture v. Montgomery County*, 254 A.2d 700 (Md. 1969) (control of urban sprawl a public purpose).
106. 416 U.S. 1, 9 (1974).
107. 842 F.Supp. 183 (D.Md. 1994).
108. Id. at 189.
109. See Fred P. Bosselman, David Callies, and John Banta, *The Taking Issue* (Washington, DC: Council on Environmental Quality, 1973), at 290.
110. 474 A.2d 561 (N.H. 1984).
111. *Rancourt v. Town of Barnstead*, 523 A.2d 55 (N.H. 1986) (lack of capital improvements program convinced court adequate public facilities ordinance not based on scientific data).
112. Note 9 (*Golden*), supra.
113. 458 F.Supp. 1009 (D.Md. 1978).
114. 392 N.Y.S.2d 594 (N.Y. 1977) (remanding case to the trial court for determination of whether a 10-year delay by the local government in making remedial municipal improvements was unreasonable and dilatory; during the delay, all development was barred). See also *Medical Services, Inc. v. City of Savage*, 487 N.W.2d 263 (Minn. App. 1992) (bad faith reaction to development application).
115. See *Zobel v. Williams*, 457 U.S. 55 (1982); *Saenz v. Roe*, 526 U.S. 489 (1999).
116. See, e.g., *Construction Industry Association v. City of Petaluma*, 522 F.2d 897 (9th Cir. 1975) *cert. denied*, 424 U.S. 934 (1976).
117. *County of Sacramento v. Lewis*, 523 U.S. 833, 834 (1998).
118. *City of Cuyahoga Falls v. Buckeye Community Hope Foundation*, 538 U.S. 188 (2003).
119. *Graham v. Connor*, 490 U.S. 386, 395 (1989) (precludes use of substantive due process under the Fourteenth Amendment when a more specific constitutional provision, such as the Fifth Amendment takings clause, applies).
120. S. Mark White, "Development Fees and Exemptions for Affordable Housing: Tailoring Regulations to Achieve Multiple Public Objectives," 6 *Fla. J. Land Use & Envtl. L.* 25, 32 (1990).
121. See *Village of Euclid v. Ambler Realty*, 272 U.S. 365 (1926).
122. *Russ Building Partnership v. City of San Francisco*, 199 Cal. App. 3d 1506 (App. 1987) (citing *Candid Enterprises, Inc. v. Grossmont Union High School Dist.*, 39 Cal.3d 878 (1985); *Loup-Miller Const. Co. v. City and County of Denver*, 676 P.2d 1170 (Colo. 1984)).
123. *Bryan v. City of Madison, Miss.* 213 F.3d 267 (5th Cir. 2000), *cert. denied* 531 U.S. 1145 (2001).
124. *Village of Willowbrook v. Olech*, 528 U.S. 562 (2000).
125. Paul D. Wilson, "What Hath Olech Wrought? The Equal Protection Clause in Recent Land Use Damages Litigation," 33 *Urb. Law.* 729 (2001); for a rare successful Olech claim, see *Cruz v. Town of Cicero*, 275 F.3d 579 (7th Cir. 2001).
126. *Tri-County Paving, Inc. v. Ashe County*, 281 F.3d 430 (4th Cir. 2002) (similar treatment).

CHAPTER

7

Supplemental Use Regulations

7.0 PURPOSE AND FINDINGS

This chapter establishes additional standards, exceptions to standards, or alternative standards (e.g., screening, landscaping, and/or design standards) for particular uses. The purpose of this chapter is to:

- Provide supplemental standards for individual uses in order to protect surrounding property values and uses;
- Protect the public health, safety, and general welfare; and
- Implement the comprehensive plan.

This chapter provides supplemental regulations for certain uses, structures, and facilities. These regulations are in addition to the other applicable standards of this chapter. In some cases, the establishment of these standards streamlines the permitting process by permitting the use as of right in certain districts subject to the supplemental regulations rather than a case-by-case consideration for a conditional use permit (CUP). In other instances, the supplemental regulations do not streamline the process but address the unique development challenges of certain uses and structures whether permitted as of right or as a conditional use.

7.1 GENERALLY

7.1.1 Compliance Mandatory

No supplemental use may be initiated, established, or maintained unless it complies with the standards set forth for such use in this chapter.

7.1.2 Regulations Supplement Other Code Regulations

The regulations of this chapter shall supplement the requirements of the base applicable and overlay zoning district regulations and the other applicable standards of this chapter. These standards are in addition to, and do not replace, the other standards for development set forth in other chapters of the Land Development Code (LDC) unless otherwise provided. To the extent that there is a conflict between a standard in another chapter of the LDC and a standard in this chapter, the standard in this chapter governs unless otherwise indicated.

7.2 ACCESSORY USES AND STRUCTURES

7.2.1 Applicability

(A) This section applies to any subordinate use of a building or other structure, or use of land that is:

(1) Conducted on the same lot as the principal use to which it is related; and

(2) Clearly incidental to, and customarily found in connection with, the principal use or structure.

(B) Where a principal use or structure is permitted, such use shall include accessory uses and structures subject to this section.

7.2.2 Establishment

(A) Accessory buildings or uses shall not be constructed or established on a lot until construction of the principal structure is completed or the principal use is established.

(B) In no instance shall an accessory building or use be established on a vacant lot.

(C) Accessory buildings shall not be used for dwelling purposes except where permitted in the use matrix (§ 3.11 Use Regulations and Table 3-4, Use Matrix, in Chapter 3, Zoning, of the LDC).

7.2.3 Dimensional and Density Standards

(A) The location of accessory uses and structures is subject to § 5.10 Lots in Chapter 5, Development Standards, of the LDC.

(B) For residential lots not exceeding 2 acres, detached accessory buildings shall not be located in the front yard. Detached accessory buildings may be located in the required rear yard.

(C) For residential lots exceeding 2 acres, detached accessory buildings may be located in the front yard.

(D) The location of permitted, nonresidential accessory structures is governed by the same dimensional regulations as set forth for the principal use or principal structure or structures.

(E) The maximum lot coverage of all accessory structures shall not exceed 50 percent of the total area of the side and rear yards, provided that, in residential districts, the total floor area does not exceed a maximum of 2,500 square feet.

(F) Accessory uses and structures shall not exceed 60 percent of the gross floor area (GFA) of the principal use.

(G) Within nonresidential districts, accessory structures, except for carports, are prohibited within the side and rear yards of lots adjacent to a neighborhood district. The total floor area of all accessory structures shall not exceed 2,500 square feet.

7.2.4 General Requirements

(A) Accessory uses shall not include the conduct of trade unless permitted in conjunction with a permitted use.

(B) Accessory uses shall be located on the same lot as the principal use for which they serve.

7.2.5 Height

Accessory buildings (see Table 7-1) shall not exceed:

(A) The height regulations of the applicable zoning district; or

(B) 15 feet in height, where the accessory structure is located within a yard.

7.3 ACCESSORY DWELLING UNITS

Purpose and findings: Affordable housing and neighborhood stability are important public objectives in the [LOCAL GOVERNMENT]. In recent years, accessory dwellings have become an important method to permit

Table 7-1
Accessory Uses

(A) Accessory Use	(B) Zoning Districts
Accessory dwellings	See Table 3-4, Use Matrix, in Chapter 3, Zoning, of the LDC.
Fencing and walls	All zoning districts
Garages or carports (noncommercial)	All zoning districts
Home occupations (subject to § 7.30 Home Occupations of this chapter)	All residential zoning districts
Mailboxes	All zoning districts
Off-street parking and driveways	All zoning districts
Wireless telecommunications antennas or tower (subject to § 7.92 Wireless Communications Facilities of this chapter)	All zoning districts
Other telecommunications antennas or tower	See Table 3-4, Use Matrix, in Chapter 3, Zoning, of the LDC.
Satellite dishes (subject to § 7.80 Satellite Dish Antennas of this chapter)	All zoning districts
Signs (see [LOCAL GOVERNMENT CODE])	All zoning districts
Storage buildings (residential)	All zoning districts
Swimming pools	All residential zoning districts
Stables/private	"RP" (Resource Protection) and "RE" (Residential Estate) districts
Tennis courts	All zoning districts
Any other building or use that the [PLANNING OFFICIAL] determines is customarily incidental to the permitted principal use or principal building	All zoning districts

families to remain in their homes by securing rental income, while at the same time providing affordable housing for the elderly, single-person households, students, and other types of households. Accessory dwellings are also known as "carriage houses," "granny flats," or "ECHO homes" (an acronym for "elder cottage housing opportunities").

This section allows accessory dwelling units to provide the opportunity to develop small dwellings designed, in particular, to meet the special housing needs of single persons and couples of modest income. This section allows and encourages the more efficient use of the existing housing stock to preserve historic structures and to provide an incentive for their maintenance. Design standards are established to ensure that accessory dwelling units are located, designed, constructed, landscaped, and decorated in such a manner that, to the maximum extent feasible, the appearance of the principal building remains as a single-family detached dwelling. It is also the intent of these regulations to assure that the single-family character of the property will be maintained and that the accessory dwelling unit remains subordinate to the primary living quarters.

7.3.1 Accessory Dwelling Units in Detached Buildings

7.3.1.1 Applicability

This section applies to any accessory dwelling unit that is located in a building that is not attached to the principal dwelling (see Figure 7-1).

7.3.1.2 Number Permitted

Only one accessory dwelling unit is permitted per lot. An accessory dwelling unit shall not contain more than two bedrooms.

**Figure 7-1
Accessory Dwelling Units**

Providing housing opportunities for extended families living together is a fundamental principle of traditional neighborhood development.

7.3.1.3 Location

Separate detached garages and separate accessory units are not permitted on the same lot. Accessory units may be created as a second story within detached garages if the height of the accessory unit and/or garage does not exceed the height of the principal structure on the lot.

7.3.1.4 Scale

(A) The GFA of an accessory dwelling unit shall not exceed 50 percent of the principal building's floor area. The building footprint of the accessory dwelling unit shall not exceed 40 percent of the building footprint of the principal residence. The "building footprint" shall include patios but shall not include porches.

(B) The accessory dwelling shall not exceed 800 square feet of GFA in the "NU" (Neighborhood Urban) or "NS" (Neighborhood Suburban) zoning districts, or 1,200 square feet in the "RE" (Residential Estate) zoning district. This restriction applies only to that portion of a structure that constitutes living area for an accessory dwelling.

7.3.1.5 Building Design

(A) In order to maintain the architectural design, style, appearance, and character of the main building as a single-family residence, the accessory dwelling unit shall have a roof pitch, siding, and window proportions identical to that of the principal dwelling.

(B) An accessory dwelling shall not exceed two stories or the height of the principal dwelling unit, whichever is less.

(C) No exterior stairway to the second floor is permitted at the front or side of the building.

7.3.1.6 Occupancy

(A) The total number of occupants in the accessory dwelling unit shall comply with the occupancy standards of the building code.

(B) The property owner must occupy either the principal dwelling or the accessory dwelling as the permanent residence. The property owner shall not receive rent for the principal dwelling. For purposes of this section, "property owner" means the title holder and/or contract purchaser of the lot, and "owner occupancy" means that a property owner, as reflected in the title records, makes his/her legal residence at the site, as evidenced by voter registration, vehicle registration, or similar means.

(C) The property owner shall sign an affidavit before a notary public affirming that the owner occupies either the principal dwelling or the accessory dwelling. The applicant shall provide a covenant suitable for recording with the recorder of deeds providing notice to future owners or long-term lessors of the subject lot that the existence of the accessory dwelling unit is predicated upon the occupancy of either the accessory dwelling or the principal dwelling by the person to whom the certificate of occupancy has been issued. The covenant shall also require any owner of the property to notify a prospective buyer of the limitations of this section, and to provide for the removal of improvements added to convert the premises to an accessory dwelling and the restoration of the site to a single-family dwelling in the event that any condition of approval is violated.

7.3.1.7 *Parking*

The number and design of parking spaces are established in § 5.51 Parking in Chapter 5, Development Standards, of the LDC. Parking spaces shall be located in the rear yard and behind the principal building.

7.3.1.8 *Utilities*

The accessory dwelling shall be connected to the central water and sewer system of the principal dwelling.

7.3.2 Accessory Apartments

(A) This section applies to any accessory apartment. The provisions of § 7.31 Housing Facilities for Older Persons of this chapter pertaining to occupancy and parking apply to accessory apartments.

(B) The GFA of the accessory apartment shall not exceed 35 percent of the total floor area of the principal dwelling unit.

(C) Occupancy of the accessory apartment shall not exceed one person per 400 square feet of GFA.

7.4 AUTO-ORIENTED DEVELOPMENT

Purpose and findings: The "AOD" (Auto-oriented District) permits a number of lawful uses that are inherently dependent on automobile access. Typical lot layouts include large front parking or vehicular storage areas, gasoline canopies, and buildings or lot layouts that are inconsistent with the scale of a neighborhood or a traditional neighborhood. Use and building forms in this district have few precedents for compact or pedestrian-friendly site layout. However, these types of building forms have occupied the corner of many corridors in the [LOCAL GOVERNMENT], creating an auto-dependent building form.

It is the intent of this district to accommodate these building forms with site layouts that reflect market-driven design practices. It is also recognized that these uses, properly located and in proper amounts, fulfill the public and market needs for automobiles, automobile maintenance, and services that depend on automobile access. However, it is the [LOCAL GOVERNMENT]'s desire to control the amount, spacing, and design of such uses through the rezoning process.

This section establishes [LOCAL GOVERNMENT] policies for controlling the location of these uses, and development standards to provide for vehicular circulation and better design practices. These standards encourage such development to occur along major transportation arteries where sites are adequate for an integrated design of automotive services and where such development most adequately serves the needs of the community's residents without creating excessive strip development.

7.4.1 Applicability

This section applies to any lot or parcel designated as "AOD" (Auto-oriented District) on the zoning map. The "AOD" includes permissions, standards, and requirements in addition to those contained in the underlying zoning district. This section affects the "AOD" overlay zoning district only. Issues not specifically addressed in this "AOD" overlay zoning district are governed by the remaining provisions of the LDC (see Figure 7-2).

7.4.2 Permitted Uses

The uses described in Table 7-2 are permitted as of right in an "AOD."

7.4.3 General Standards

As part of an application for a rezoning to an "AOD" (Auto-oriented District), the applicant may submit a development agreement for approval by the [LOCAL GOVERNMENT]. The development agreement may include the following in addition to the requirements of Chapter 4, Procedures, of the LDC:

(A) Building design and architectural standards consistent with the regulations established in § 7.4.4 Automobile Service and Repair of this chapter;

(B) The location, width, planting materials, and planting density for proposed landscaping;

Figure 7-2
Architectural Design

The gas station pump canopy matches the style of the principal building.

**Table 7-2
Permitted Uses for "AOD" (Auto-oriented District)**

Use	LBCS Function Code	LBCS Structure Code	NAICS Code
Garage, service, and repair	2110	2280	811
Car wash		2593	811192
Drive-in window or drive-through facilities, not otherwise listed in the use matrix (see Table 3-4, Use Matrix, and § 3.3 Official Zoning Map in Chapter 3, Zoning, of the LDC)	2110	2210	
Gas stations	2116	2270	44719
Joint or multiple use with service station or gas station			
Large vehicle retail/leasing, indoor or outdoor	2112 2331 2332		441210 5321
Self-service storage mini-warehouse		2710-2720	

LBCS = Land-Based Classification Standards; and NAICS = North American Industry Classification System.

(C) The location and dimensions of parking areas, storage areas, gasoline pump islands, and drive-through lanes; and

(D) Any restriction on uses, lot design, and building scale otherwise permitted in the underlying zoning district and this district.

7.4.4 Automobile Service and Repair

(A) This section applies to any automobile service and repair establishment in the "AOD" (Auto-oriented District).

(B) All automobile servicing and repair activities must either be:

(1) Carried on within an enclosed building; or

(2) Screened with one of the following along any property line that abuts a residential zoning district:

(a) A minimum of 6-foot high masonry or decorative wood fence; or

(b) In lieu of subsection (a), above, a minimum Type B buffer as provided in § 5.31 Buffers and Screening in Chapter 5, Development Standards, of the LDC.

(C) Automobile repair bays shall not face a local, collector, or arterial street, but may face an alley or rear lot line.

(D) The following activities and equipment are permitted only in the rear yard and at least 50 feet from a residential zoning district:

(1) Storage of vehicle parts and refuse;

(2) Temporary storage of vehicles during repair and pending delivery to the customer; and

(3) Vacuuming and cleaning.

(E) The following activities and equipment are permitted only within an enclosed building:

(1) Lubrication equipment;

(2) Motor vehicle washing equipment; and

(3) Hydraulic hoists and pits.

(F) Outside storage or parking of any disabled, wrecked, or partially dismantled vehicle is not permitted for a period exceeding 10 days during any 30-day period.

(G) No building, structure, canopy, gasoline pump, or storage tank shall be located within 25 feet of a residential zoning district.

(H) Body work and painting shall be conducted within fully enclosed buildings. All motorized vehicles not in safe operating condition shall be kept in fully enclosed buildings.

7.4.5 Car Washes

(A) This section applies to any car wash established as a permanent use. This section does not apply to temporary car-washing activities sponsored by schools, churches, or other nonprofit organizations or groups in order to raise money for designated events, and that occur not longer than three continuous days.

(B) All car-washing activities must either be:

(1) Carried on within an enclosed building; or

(2) Screened with one of the following along any property line that abuts a residential zoning district:

(a) A minimum of 6-foot high masonry or decorative wood fence; or

(b) In lieu of subsection (a), above, a minimum Type B buffer as provided in § 5.31 Buffers and Screening in Chapter 5, Development Standards, of the LDC.

(C) Vacuuming equipment is permitted only in the rear yard and at least 50 feet from a residential zoning district.

7.4.6 Service Stations, Gas Stations, and Related Uses

7.4.6.1 Applicability

This section applies to any of the following uses:

(A) Gas station;

(B) Garage;

(C) Service and repair;

(D) Joint or multiple use with filling or service station; and

(E) Service station.

7.4.6.2 Definitions

For purposes of this section:

(A) A "canopy" means any structural protective cover that is not enclosed on any of its four sides and is provided for a service area designated for the dispensing or installation of gasoline, oil, antifreeze, headlights, wiper blades, and similar products.

(B) A "fuel pump" means any device that dispenses automotive fuel and/or kerosene. A fuel pump may contain multiple hoses or be capable of serving more than one fueling position simultaneously.

(C) A "pump island" means a concrete platform measuring a minimum of 6 inches in height from the paved surface on which fuel pumps are located.

7.4.6.3 Generally

(A) All accessory service and repair operations shall occur within buildings enclosed by a roof and a wall on all sides.

(B) Principal buildings shall be oriented to the street.

(C) Service bay doors shall not face any neighborhood district or use.

(D) Display of products, cars, or trailers shall be at least 25 feet from the street or avenue property line.

(E) Curb lowerings shall not begin closer than 20 feet to the intersecting street right-of-way. Curb lowerings may not begin closer than 6 feet to abutting property lines or alleys. Maximum driveway width shall be 32 feet at the curb line.

(F) A masonry wall shall be constructed and maintained along all property lines abutting a neighborhood zoning district. The minimum and maximum height of the wall is described in Table 7-3.

(G) In order to address potential traffic, noise, or other nuisance impacts, the hours of operation for sales, deliveries, and services for uses that are not located on a major street are limited from 8:00 AM to 9:00 PM.

(H) All fuel pumps and pump islands shall be set back a minimum distance of at least 15 feet from any right-of-way line or property line. Fuel pumps and canopied areas shall be located between the principal building and the rear lot line and not between the building and the street.

7.4.6.4 Dimensional Standards

The maximum floor area ratio (FAR) shall be 0.3. The building setback and height requirements shall be as established in the underlying zoning district.

7.4.6.5 Accessory Uses

A service station may include the following accessory uses:

(A) Sales and servicing of spark plugs, batteries, and distributors;

(B) Tire repair and servicing, but not recapping;

(C) Replacement of mufflers and tail pipes, water hoses, fan belts, brake fluids, light bulbs, floor mats, seat covers, wiper blades, windshield wipers, and replacement of grease retainers and wheel bearings;

(D) Radiator cleaning and flushing;

(E) Washing and polishing, without specialized mechanical equipment;

(F) Greasing and lubrication;

(G) Exchanging fuel oil pumps and installing;

(H) Minor servicing and replacing of carburetors;

(I) Emergency wiring repairs;

(J) Adjustment and repair of brakes and alignment of wheels and headlights;

(K) Minor adjustment of engines, not involving removal of the head and/or crank case, or racing the motor;

(L) Accessory commercial, not to exceed 25 percent of the total floor area, which includes all areas under a canopy or roof and all pump areas of the principal use to which it is accessory; and

(M) The sale of cut flowers.

7.4.6.6 Canopies

(A) Canopies (see Figure 7-3) shall not exceed 16 feet in height or the height of the principal building, whichever is less.

(B) Canopies shall be architecturally integrated with the principal building and all other accessory struc-

Table 7-3
Height Accessory Structures

Location	Minimum Height	Maximum Height
Front 25 feet (i.e., an area extending from the property line intersecting the neighborhood district or abutting alley to a point 25 feet interior to the lot)	3 feet	5 feet
Balance of property line abutting neighborhood zoning district	5 feet	10 feet

Figure 7-3
Form-Based Zoning

Form-based zoning provides the design features required in obtaining development approval.

tures on the site through the use of the same or compatible materials, colors, and roof pitch.

(C) Any lighting fixtures or sources of light that are a part of the underside of the canopy shall be recessed into the underside of the canopy so as not to protrude below the canopy ceiling surface more than 2 inches.

(D) Permitted materials for exterior building façades or canopies include brick, stone stucco, and any other material if consistent with an architectural style set forth in this chapter, if the principal building conforms to that style. The following materials are not permitted:

(1) Cinder block;
(2) Unfinished poured concrete,
(3) Unfaced concrete block;
(4) Plastic; or
(5) Vinyl.

7.4.6.7 Trailers and Operable Vehicle Display

The display and storage of trailers, operable motor vehicles, and car-top carriers for rental purposes only are permitted as an accessory use in an "AOD" (Auto-oriented District) subject to the following limitations:

(A) Where the service station premises is located within an area less than 10,000 square feet, the maximum number of items that may be displayed or stored is six, of which no more than three items can be operable motor vehicles;

(B) Where the service station premises is located within an area of 10,000 to 20,000 square feet, the maximum number of items that may be displayed or stored is 10, of which no more than five items can be operable motor vehicles;

(C) Where the service station premises is located within an area of over 20,000 square feet, the maximum number of items that may be displayed or stored is 10, of which no more than seven items can be operable motor vehicles; and

(D) No vehicle or equipment shall be parked or placed within the setback area along the street.

7.5 COMMERCIAL BUILDINGS

7.5.1 Applicability

(A) Unless otherwise specified in this chapter, this section applies to any commercial building or structure.

(B) This section applies to any commercial building or structure located in the "MX" (Mixed Use) district or a traditional neighborhood development (TND) or transit-oriented development (TOD) use pattern.

(C) This section does not apply to any of the following:
(1) Car wash;
(2) Car, boat, or marine craft dealers;
(3) Flea markets (out of doors);
(4) Lumberyard and building material sales with outside storage, wholesale or retail;
(5) Lumberyard and building material sales within enclosed buildings only, wholesale or retail;
(6) Photography studio;
(7) Rentals; and
(8) Vehicle repair and service.

7.5.2 Big-Box Development

This section implements the goals and objectives of the comprehensive plan prohibiting excessive impacts of large-scale development upon downtown, commercial corridors or centers, and neighborhoods, which depend upon walkability and viable mixed-use development to enhance their air quality, reduce traffic congestion, promote safety from traffic accidents, and enhance their land-use plans.

7.5.2.1 Large-Scale Commercial Retail Development

(A) A commercial building or structure used for retail or wholesale sales, in whole or in part, shall not:
(1) Exceed a GFA of 40,000 square feet; or
(2) Store or display lumber, or building materials outside of a completely enclosed building.

(B) In a "CG" (Commercial General) or "D" (Downtown) district, the gross FAR may not exceed 60,000 gross square feet per building or structure, but the provision of subsection (A)(2), above, shall still apply.

(C) Every commercial building used for retail or wholesale sales, in whole or in part, that exceeds 25,000 square feet shall obtain a CUP prior to obtaining any development approval under the LDC. The application for the CUP shall include a traffic assessment, a fiscal impact assessment, and an environmental impact assessment, along with the application for the CUP.

7.5.3 Building Structure

7.5.3.1 Base, Middle, and Cap

Buildings exceeding two stories shall incorporate a base, a middle, and a cap described as follows:

(A) The base shall include an entryway with transparent windows as set forth in the ground-floor design standards (see § 7.5.4 Ground-Floor Design of this chapter) and a molding or reveal placed between the first and second stories or over the second story. The molding or reveal shall have a depth of at least 2 inches and a height of at least 4 inches;

(B) The middle may include windows and/or balconies; and

(C) The cap shall include the area from the top floor to the roof of the building and a cornice or roof overhang.

7.5.3.2 Alignment

Windowsills, moldings, and cornices shall align with those of adjacent buildings. The bottom and top line defining the edge of the windows (the "windowsill alignment") shall vary not more than 2 feet from the alignment of surrounding buildings. If the adjoining buildings have windowsill alignments that vary by more than 2 feet from one another, the proposed building shall align with one of the adjoining buildings.

7.5.4 Ground-Floor Design

(A) All buildings subject to this section shall have their principal entrance opening to a street, square, plaza, or sidewalk. The principal entrance shall not open onto a parking lot. Pedestrian access from the public sidewalk, street right-of-way, or driveway to the principal structure shall be provided through an improved surface.

(B) The ground floor of the entryway shall align with the sidewalk elevation. Sunken terraces or stairways to a basement shall not constitute entryways for purposes of this section. It is not the intent of this section to preclude the use of below-grade entryways, provided that such entryways shall not constitute a principal entryway and shall not be used to satisfy the distancing requirements of § 7.5.5 Street Wall Standards of this chapter.

7.5.5 Street Wall Standards

Where a maximum front setback has been established, the front building wall or courtyard shall adjoin the sidewalk. The side setback shall be a minimum of 0 feet and a maximum of 10 feet.

7.5.6 Windows and Entryways

(A) Windows above the ground floor shall have a ratio of height to width of at least 2:1.

(B) The uses on the ground floor shall be visible from and/or accessible to the street through the use of windows and doors on at least 50 percent of the length of the first-floor street frontage. At least 60 percent or more than 90 percent of the total surface area of the front elevation shall be in public entrances and windows (including retail display windows). Where windows are used, they shall be transparent.

(C) Solid walls shall not exceed 20 feet in length.

(D) All street-level retail uses with sidewalk frontage shall be furnished with an individual entrance and direct access to the sidewalk in addition to any other access that may be provided. This standard shall not apply to any lot with a street frontage of less than 24 feet.

(E) Doors shall be recessed into the face of the building to provide a sense of entry and to add variety to the streetscape. An entryway shall not be less than 1 square foot for each 1,000 square feet of floor area, and in all cases shall not be less than 15 square feet.

(F) The maximum setback requirements may be waived by the [PLANNING OFFICIAL] for an area not to exceed 90 percent of the frontage in order to accommodate courtyards.

(G) Canopies, awnings, and similar appurtenances may be constructed at the entrance to any building, subject to the criteria established in the building code.

7.5.7 Pedestrian-oriented Uses

In order to stimulate pedestrian activity, the first floor (street level) of any new building abutting a major arterial roadway, minor arterial roadway, or major collector roadway shall devote at least 50 percent of the net first-floor area to retail uses. Residential dwellings shall be permitted above or below the first floor of any building with commercial and/or retail uses.

7.5.8 Mechanical Equipment

Mechanical equipment, electrical meter and service components, and similar utility devices—whether ground level, wall mounted, or roof mounted—shall be screened from view at the front property line. Exterior screening materials shall be the same as the predominant exterior materials of the principal building. In cases where the front property line is higher than the roof line of the subject building, no screening shall be required for a line of sight exceeding 5 feet 6 inches above the finished elevation of the property at the front property line.

7.20 EXTRACTIVE USE

This section applies to specific, intensive land-use activities that have unique impacts both on and off site. The regulations and approval processes established by this section ensure their short- and long-term compatibility with the on- and off-site environment and adjacent properties and neighborhoods.

Purpose and findings: The specific purpose and intent of these provisions are to:

• Protect the health, safety, and welfare of the citizens of the [LOCAL GOVERNMENT];

• Preserve the quality of life, economy, infrastructure, environment, natural resources, and natural landscapes;

• Protect the environment of the [LOCAL GOVERNMENT] and protect its residents from the harmful or hazardous effects of, or nuisances resulting from, substantial land alteration activities, quarrying, and sand or gravel excavation, including, but not limited to, degradation of air quality, stormwater run-off, ground and subsurface water quality, visual quality, erosion of soils, adverse noise and vibration, explosive hazards, adverse traffic and road conditions, and any adverse effects of processing materials;

• Protect the scenic quality of the [LOCAL GOVERNMENT], its natural landscapes, environment, wildlife, and wildlife habitat, and protect its residents from significant adverse effects of excavation activities;

• Ensure the compatibility of the proposed excavation activities with existing development and development anticipated in the future pursuant to the [LOCAL GOVERNMENT]'s adopted comprehensive plan;

• Assure that the required reclamation of affected areas that are disturbed by excavation activities is sufficient to provide for short- and long-term development meeting all environmental, infrastructure, and aesthetic needs of the [LOCAL GOVERNMENT] and of surrounding properties and neighborhoods;

• Assure that necessary off-site maintenance and improvements to public roads or utilities required as a result of the on-site effects of excavation activities and the off-site effects of traffic and damage to properties are adequately and fully funded and implemented;

• Provide for a fair and efficient system for the engineering, planning, environmental regulation, and monitoring of excavation activities, both on and off site;

• Protect the long-term usefulness of adjacent properties for the permitted purposes as identified in the [LOCAL GOVERNMENT]'s adopted comprehensive plan;

• Protect the tax base of the community;

• Protect the use and enjoyment of adjacent properties;

• Ensure the reasonable use of the limestone, sand, gravel, and other mineral resources excavated or extracted from the site or the excavation activities;

• Establish regulations and performance standards for the excavation, processing, use, and transport of earth materials, mined materials, quarried materials, and unconsolidated sediments in such a manner as to ensure maximum protection to surrounding properties and to the physical environment through proper siting of activities and structure, and through the use of time of operation, buffering, setbacks, visual screening, height limitations, proper access routing, and appropriate noise, vibration, air quality, and water quality controls;

• Ensure that all permitted excavation activities are compatible with the [LOCAL GOVERNMENT], regional, state, and federal water quality plans and stormwater management plans and adopted drainage or stormwater policies; and

• Ensure that all permitted excavation activities are compatible with all current and applicable neighborhood plans, area or regional plans, public facility and utility plans, [LOCAL GOVERNMENT] policies, and the [LOCAL GOVERNMENT]'s budget and capital improvements program.

7.20.1 Applicability

7.20.1.1 Generally

This section applies to quarries, sand, or gravel excavation, and substantial land alteration activities. This section constitutes the standards for development in the "EU" (Extractive Use) zoning district. The permitted uses in the "EU" district are the following, subject to the standards established in this section:

(A) Quarries;
(B) Sand and gravel extraction; and
(C) Substantial land alteration.

7.20.1.2 Substantial Land Alteration

(A) "Substantial land alteration" is a development activity that meets or exceeds any of the following thresholds:

(1) Land-disturbing activities designed to occur for more than three months;

(2) The removal from a site of more than 100 cubic yards of earth material per acre (gross) and less than 1,000 cubic yards of material per acre;

(3) Results at any time during or following excavation in an exposed bedrock slope steeper than 2:1 and less than 3:1;

(4) A movement of 100 cubic yards or more of earth that involves a change in natural or preexisting grades of 5 or more vertical feet for any portion of a parcel; or

(5) Any movement of earth on the entire parcel in excess of 1,000 cubic yards.

(B) A substantial land alteration activity is permitted as a conditional use in all zoning districts subject to all of the requirements of this section, including performance standards, site location criteria, exterior storage regulations, and reclamation standards as set forth in Table 7-4. A substantial land alteration shall require a grading development approval to be issued in addition to obtaining a conditional use approval. If the substantial land alteration involves a quarry, sand, or gravel excavation, it shall require a development order approving an "EU" (Extractive Use) district.

7.20.1.3 Quarry Excavation

Quarry excavation is a development activity that constitutes a substantial land alteration and includes any of the additional following characteristics:

(A) Activities principally designed to mine, extract, or remove limestone, minerals, or bedrock materials for commercial purposes;

(B) Activities resulting at any time during or following excavation in an exposed bedrock slope steeper than 3:1;

(C) Activities resulting from one or several cuts made as part of the activity at any time following excavation in an exposed rock face that is in excess of 5 feet in height;

(D) Removal from a site of more than 1,000 cubic yards of earth material per acre of land being excavated or 10,000 cubic yards of earth for the entire site, or

(E) An excavation activity utilizing a crusher.

A quarry is only permitted in an "EU" (Extractive Use) overlay zoning district. Operation of a quarry shall require a rezoning to an "EU" overlay zoning dis-

**Table 7-4
Quarry, Sand, and Gravel Excavation and
Land Alteration Separation Distances**

Required Minimum Distance from Adjacent Property Zoned	(A) Separation Distance (Without Buffer) (Feet)			(B) Separation Distance (With Buffer) (Feet)			(C) Sand and Gravel Excavation When the Proposed Activity Will Not Exceed 24 Months (Feet)			(D) Temporary Excavation or Land Alteration With Buffer (Feet)		
	Residential	Commercial	Industrial	Residential	Commercial	Industrial	Residential	Commercial	Industrial	Residential	Commercial	Industrial
Excavation area with an elevation change of greater than 10 feet	500	100	50	250	50	50	200	50	50	100	50	50
To vegetated stockpiles	500	100	50	250	50	50	200	50	50	100	50	50
To any nonvegetated stockpiles or loading points	750	200	50	300	100	50	400	100	50	200	100	50
To any crushing or processing												
• Quarries	1,000	500	100	1,000	500	100						
• Sand and gravel excavation/land alteration	1,000	500	100	1,000	200	100	750	250	100	300	100	100
To any blasting—from a developed property	1,000	500	400									
• Quarries, sand, and gravel excavation				1,000	500	400						
• Land alteration				1,000	400	400	750	400	400	750	250	400

trict with detailed site and grading plans pursuant to this section and Table 7-4.

7.20.1.4 Sand or Gravel Excavation

Sand or gravel excavation is a development activity constituting excavation of unconsolidated sediments that constitutes a substantial land alteration and includes any of the following characteristics:

(A) Activities principally designed to mine, extract, or remove unconsolidated sediments for commercial purposes;

(B) Removal from the site of more than 1,000 cubic yards of unconsolidated sediments per acre of land being excavated or more than 2,500 cubic yards from a single site; or

(C) A substantial land alteration designed to occur for more than three months.

Sand or gravel excavation activities shall be permitted only in an "EU" (Extractive Use) overlay zoning district. Sand or gravel excavation shall obtain a rezoning to a sand or gravel overlay zoning district with a detailed site and grading plan pursuant to a CUP process and standards and the site location criteria, exterior storage regulations, and reclamation standards as set forth in Table 7-4.

7.20.1.5 Definitions

For purposes of this section, "site" means all contiguous or noncontiguous land holdings in the same ownership.

7.20.1.6 Exempt Activities

Except as required for a reclamation plan, which may be imposed on any of the following activities as part of any development approval or development order, this section does not apply to the following activities:

(A) The land area included within 15 feet or as reasonably defined by the [PLANNING OFFICIAL] to allow soil stabilization of the identified boundaries of a building submitted for a development approval;

(B) Stormwater management facilities or other public infrastructure approved by the [LOCAL GOVERNMENT];

(C) Excavations or blasting for wells, tunnels, or utilities that have received all necessary governmental approvals;

(D) Refuse disposal sites controlled by other applicable [LOCAL GOVERNMENT], state, or federal regulations;

(E) Ongoing cemetery (burial) operations; and

(F) Development activity pursuant to this section for which a development approval has been issued by the [LOCAL GOVERNMENT], has resulted in the review of the proposed cut-and-fill work, and has made the findings established in § 7.20.3 Separation Distances of this chapter.

7.20.2 Development Approvals and Orders

7.20.2.1 Other Required Development Approvals

(A) *Generally:* Excavation activities include a broad range of land disturbance activities, which may require a grading development approval and may require other local, state, and federal development approvals. It is the sole responsibility of the applicant to secure any development approvals required by other governmental entities for the proposed use. The [LOCAL GOVERNMENT] may, at its sole discretion, require that the applicant obtain all other required development approvals prior to applying for the required CUP, and to require the applicant to submit evidence of such other development approvals to the [LOCAL GOVERNMENT] as part of the CUP application.

(B) *Subdivision plats:* Applicants are not required to apply for subdivision approval for "excavation activities" located on a single parcel of land unless the activity constitutes a subdivision or platting of two or more parcels.

7.20.2.2 "EU" (Extractive Use) Overlay Zoning District

All excavation activities defined as quarry excavation or sand or gravel excavation pursuant to § 7.20.1 Applicability of this chapter shall apply for and obtain a zoning amendment to an "EU" (Extractive Use) zoning district. All development in the "EU" zoning district is subject to the standards and procedures established in this section. The standards and procedures of this section constitute the standards for development in the "EU" district.

7.20.2.3 Conditional Use Permit

All excavation activities as defined in this section shall be considered "conditional uses" in all of the zoning districts in which they are listed, and requests for approval of such activities shall be processed pursuant to § 4.23 Conditional Use Permits in Chapter 4, Procedures, of the LDC.

7.20.2.4 Required Plans and Information

An application for rezoning to an "EU" (Extractive Use) district and a CUP shall include a complete application for a land alteration development approval (see § B-4 Land Alteration Development Approval in Appendix B, Specifications for Documents to Be Submitted, of the LDC).

7.20.2.5 Project Site Expansion or Modification

(A) Changes to the CUP for the "excavation activity" on the site shall be applied for and reviewed in accordance with § 4.23 Conditional Use Permits in Chapter 4, Procedures, of the LDC.

(B) Changes other than changes to the phasing plan shall be reviewed and approved in accordance with the process by which the original CUP was approved.

(C) An expansion of the site on which an "excavation activity" has previously been approved will require a complete review of the proposed new (expanded) site, as if an original application was being made, as well as a review of the relationship and coordination of activities between the original site and the expanded portion of the site. Of principal concern during this review shall be the additional and cumulative impacts that will be caused by the combined operations on factors such as the environment, traffic, safety, noise, air pollution, neighborhoods, and adjacent land uses.

(D) Contraction of the site on which the "excavation activity" has been approved will require a review in order to:

(1) Evaluate how the loss of a portion of the site will affect buffers, land-use compatibility, noise, reclamation, and reuse of the site and related factors; and

(2) Determine what will be done on the excised portion of the site (e.g., if another land use is proposed, a complete, original review may be required).

7.20.2.6 Transfer of Development Approvals

(A) No transfer of a CUP by the original applicant to another party nor a transfer of any other development approval issued by the [LOCAL GOVERNMENT] that was necessary to authorize or allow the "excavation activity" shall be permitted unless the [LOCAL GOVERNMENT] is notified at least 90 days prior to such transfer and has an opportunity to assure that:

(1) All conditions, standards, and requirements imposed on the original applicant will continue to be met; and

(2) All security instruments remain in full effect and, if also transferred, the new CUP holder agrees to comply in full and has the necessary financial security to hold the [LOCAL GOVERNMENT] harmless.

(B) If the subject property is sold, the CUP and all of the conditions, standards, and requirements run with the land, and the new property owner is fully bound as if he/she were the original owner.

(C) When an operator succeeds to the interest of another on an uncompleted site, the [PLANNING OFFICIAL] shall release the first operator of the responsibilities imposed by the development approval only if:

(1) Both operators are in full compliance with the requirements and standards of this ordinance and all development approvals;

(2) The new operator assumes all responsibilities of the former operator, including operations, maintenance, and reclamation, and provides a written, wit-

nessed, notarized document asserting, inter alia, that reclamation of the entire site will be completed as planned; and

(3) The new operator provides the [LOCAL GOVERNMENT] with all appropriate financial assurances, approved by the [LOCAL GOVERNMENT] attorney, to ensure completion of the project.

7.20.2.7 Extension of Development Approval

(A) Requests for CUP extensions must be submitted in writing to the planning department at least three months prior to the expiration date of the existing development approval.

(B) The [GOVERNING ENTITY] may grant a CUP extension for not more than one-half the duration of the original CUP approval.

(C) No development approval extension shall be granted unless the project is in full compliance with the terms of the existing development approval or a compliance plan and schedule have been submitted and approved by the [GOVERNING ENTITY]. If there have been any notices of default issued by the [LOCAL GOVERNMENT], these shall be reviewed and may be taken into consideration by the [GOVERNING ENTITY] on the extension request.

(D) A CUP extension may include conditions to address conflicts with adjacent properties or other circumstances unforeseen at the time of original development approval.

(E) The extension of the CUP shall not be unreasonably denied, provided that the conditional use permittee has complied with all of the conditions of the CUP and the standards and requirements for "excavation activities" and has not been issued a notice of default nor cited for a violation of the [LOCAL GOVERNMENT] code or state or federal regulations.

7.20.2.8 Required Findings

The [GOVERNING ENTITY] shall approve an overlay zoning district or a CUP authorizing an excavation activity only if all of the following findings with respect to the proposed activity are made:

(A) The activity will not result in a danger to life or property due to:

(1) Steep or unstable slopes;

(2) Unsafe access to the property;

(3) Excessive traffic; or

(4) Proximity to existing or planned residential areas, parks, and roadways;

(B) Visual, noise, dust, and/or excessive on- or off-site environmental impacts on public parks, roadways, and residential areas can be adequately mitigated by the applicant and a fully detailed plan is submitted by the applicant to demonstrate the mitigation methods to be used, the cost of such mitigation, the source of funds for such mitigation, and adequate legal assurance that all such mitigation activities are carried out;

(C) The use of trucks and heavy equipment will not adversely impact the safety and maintenance or cause excessive congestion of public roads providing access to the site, or such impacts will be mitigated;

(D) The proposed use will not adversely affect air quality or groundwater or surface water quality;

(E) The proposed use will not adversely affect scenic quality or natural landscapes, environment, wildlife and wildlife habitat or, if such effects are anticipated to occur, the reclamation plan provides for adequate restoration of the site following completion of the excavation activity;

(F) The activity will be compatible with existing development and development anticipated in the future, including other uses as shown in the comprehensive plan, including, but not limited to, patterns of land use, recreational uses, existing or planned development, public facilities, open space resources, and other natural resources;

(G) The activity will not unduly affect buffers and screening year-round from unsightly features of the excavation operation;

(H) The activity will not result in the disturbance of a natural community;

(I) The reclamation plan provides adequate and appropriate restoration and stabilization of cut-and-fill areas;

(J) The excavation activity will not result in negative impacts on drainage patterns or stormwater management facilities;

(K) The proposed activity will minimize impacts on wetlands and other natural features affecting groundwater or surface water quality;

(L) The intensity and anticipated duration of the proposed excavation activity is appropriate for the size and location of the activity;

(M) Permanent and interim erosion and sediment control plans have been approved by the [LOCAL GOVERNMENT];

(N) Surety has been provided that guarantees the site will be fully restored, after completion of the excavating activity, to a safe condition, and one that permits reuse of the site in a manner compatible with the comprehensive plan, neighborhood plans, specific plans, and applicable [LOCAL GOVERNMENT] policies; and

(O) A schedule of appropriate tipping and host fees has been established and included in the development order approving the CUP.

7.20.3 Separation Distances

7.20.3.1 Generally

Required minimum distance of specific on-site activities for quarries, sand, or gravel excavation (when the proposed activity will exceed 24 months) or substantial land alteration (when the proposed activity will exceed 24 months) from adjacent property zoned residential, commercial, and industrial shall be as shown in Column (A) of Table 7-4. In lieu of Column (A) of Table 7-4, if a Type E buffer is installed consistent with § 5.31 Buffers and Screening in Chapter 5, Development Standards, of the LDC, the required distance of specific on-site activities from adjacent property zoned residential, commercial, and industrial shall be as shown in Column (B) of Table 7-4.

7.20.3.2 Short-Term Activities

Required minimum distance of specific on-site activities for sand or gravel excavation or substantial land alteration (when the proposed activity will not exceed 24 months) from adjacent property zoned residential, commercial, and industrial shall be as shown in Column (C) of Table 7-4. In lieu of Column (C) of Table 7-4, if a Type E buffer is installed consistent with § 5.31 Buffers and Screening in Chapter 5, Development Standards, of the LDC, the required distance of specific on-site activities from adjacent property zoned residential, commercial, and industrial shall be as shown in Column (C) of Table 7-4.

7.20.3.3 Sound Barrier

If a sound barrier is constructed that is capable of reducing sound levels at the nearest residential lot line to a level meeting the performance standards of the [LOCAL GOVERNMENT NOISE ORDINANCE], the required distance from residential zones for crushing, processing, and blasting may be reduced to 500 feet.

7.20.3.4 Required Buffer Yards

(A) During the excavation activity, a minimum buffer yard of 100 feet shall be maintained adjacent to all property boundaries and all existing rights-of-way and any proposed rights-of-way for roadways included in the comprehensive plan or for which a major street plan has been prepared. Upon completion of the excavation activity, the buffer yard may be discontinued and the buffer yard land area may be used for development purposes.

(B) If the duration of an excavation activity will not exceed 24 months from the date of approval of an overlay zoning district or issuance of a CUP to the date of completion of all activities, buffer yard plantings shall not be required. In all other cases, buffer yard plantings are required to be installed within the first planting season.

(C) No excavation shall occur within the buffer yard and no storage of equipment or materials may be located within the buffer yard.

(D) A vegetated earthen berm for erosion control purposes pursuant to the required stormwater run-off, erosion, and sedimentation control plan may be placed in the buffer yard, where approved.

(E) An excavation activity shall have a minimum Type E buffer as required by § 5.31 Buffers and Screening in Chapter 5, Development Standards, of the LDC within the 50-foot buffer yard. The reviewing agency may require additional screening, including berms, to protect the adjacent property owners from the visual and operational impacts of the excavation activity.

(F) An excavation activity may be conducted closer than 50 feet from an adjacent platted or planned road right-of-way as identified on a major street plan, only if approved by the [LOCAL GOVERNMENT] engineer and by the appropriate road authority.

7.20.4 Quarries

7.20.4.1 Operation/Performance Standards

The following minimum operation/performance standards apply to quarries unless otherwise specified:

(A) Any topsoil removed from the surface and retained on the site shall be removed carefully and stockpiled in a manner to prevent erosion for reapplication to disturbed areas during reclamation.

(B) Hours of operation for quarries shall be limited to the hours of 7 AM to 10 PM for operational activities, including blasting, excavation, processing, and hauling. Hours and days of operation may be restricted by the reviewing agency for operations within 1,000 feet of any residential uses or that rely on residential roadways for access.

(C) To the extent possible, designated truck routes shall be used for all hauling as well as for all access to the site. All other routes and access shall be approved by the [LOCAL GOVERNMENT] engineer prior to CUP approval.

(D) Stormwater run-off, erosion, and sedimentation shall be controlled by a plan submitted to the [LOCAL GOVERNMENT] by the applicant and approved by the [LOCAL GOVERNMENT] engineer, pursuant to Chapter 5, Development Standards, of the LDC. The plan shall address the compatibility of the proposed use with any adopted [LOCAL GOVERNMENT] drainage or stormwater plans applicable to the area.

(E) The applicant shall provide signs on the property and along haul routes where deemed necessary to promote the safety and general welfare of the neighborhood and general area. Required signs may include, but shall not be limited to, "No Trespassing," "Trucks Hauling," "Blasting," and "Danger." Other signs may be required if necessary.

(F) Operations shall maintain compliance with local and state standards for noise, dust, and vibration. All equipment and machinery shall be operated and maintained in such a manner as to minimize dust, noise, and vibration. Access roads shall be maintained in a dust-free condition by surfacing or other treatment on a regular basis as may be specified by the [LOCAL GOVERNMENT] engineer. A water truck for the purposes of dust control may be required on site.

(G) Adequate dust control methods shall be implemented. Roadways adjacent to the property shall be swept and cleaned on a regular basis and when directed by the [LOCAL GOVERNMENT] engineer as being necessary.

(H) A performance bond or other financial security in an amount satisfactory to the [LOCAL GOVERNMENT] engineer, and in a form approved by the [LOCAL GOVERNMENT] attorney, shall be secured from the applicant to ensure that all standards are fully met during operation and to ensure that proper reclamation of the site is completed in a timely manner.

(I) A 6-foot continuous security fence shall be provided around the entire perimeter of the property on which the quarrying activity will take place. Additional fencing requirements may be imposed on portions of the site abutting residentially zoned or planned areas, parks, playgrounds, sidewalks, trails, schools, churches, and other public facilities and gathering places.

(J) Where a stockpile is visible from an arterial roadway or residential district, the height of a stockpile may be limited by the reviewing agency to the lowest height that is economically feasible on the site. In no case shall the height of a stockpile exceed 50 feet for permanent stockpiles and 75 feet for temporary stockpiles unless the reviewing agency finds that the stockpile would not be visible from an arterial roadway or residential district.

(K) Any lighting or signage, other than security signage, on the property shall meet the standards for the zoning district in which the activity is located.

(L) A blasting plan shall be submitted to the [GOVERNING ENTITY], public works, and planning departments with proof of insurance in an amount and form as approved by the [LOCAL GOVERNMENT] attorney. Such activity shall be conducted only by licensed, insured individuals or entities and shall be in conformance with all applicable federal, state, and local regulations.

(M) No quarry activity shall be conducted in such a manner as to permanently lower the water table of surrounding properties, except in quaternary deposits, nor shall such excavation activity cause the drainage of a wetland without the applicant first obtaining an approved wetland replacement plan.

(N) A weight scale may be required to be located at the site and, if necessary, other restrictions may be imposed if roadways adjacent to the site and operations are not suitable for heavy truck traffic. A record of all truck load weights exiting the site must be maintained for at least two years as evidence of weight limit compliance, and such records shall be available for inspection by the [LOCAL GOVERNMENT] engineer.

(O) Where applicable, no excavation shall occur within 100 feet of a protected water body, unless otherwise permitted by the [STATE ENVIRONMENTAL AGENCY]. Where excavation occurs on more than one side of a protected water body, a setback of 50 feet may be maintained on one side when a setback of 200 feet or more is maintained on the other, if approved by [STATE ENVIRONMENTAL AGENCY] and the [LOCAL GOVERNMENT] engineer.

7.20.4.2 Reclamation

See § 7.20.7 Reclamation Standards of this chapter.

7.20.4.3 Postreclamation Land Use

(A) If the owner proposes to construct structures on the site as part of the postreclamation land-use activities, all of such uses shall be specified.

(B) The owner shall submit all necessary documentation for such proposed uses, including, but not limited to, a site plan, an application for rezoning, an application for a development approval, or other required documentation necessary for approval of the proposed use on the reclaimed site.

(C) Where a development is proposed as part of a postreclamation plan, all applicable development approvals are required by the LDC.

7.20.5 Sand or Gravel Excavation

7.20.5.1 Operation/Performance Standards

The following minimum operation/performance standards apply to sand and gravel excavation activities unless otherwise specified:

(A) Any topsoil removed from the surface and retained on the site shall be removed carefully and stockpiled in a manner to prevent erosion for reapplication to disturbed areas during reclamation.

(B) Hours of operation shall be limited to the hours of 7 AM to 10 PM for operational activities, including blasting, excavation, dredging, processing, and hauling. Hours and days of operation may be restricted by the reviewing agency for operations within 1,000 feet of any residential areas or that rely on residential roadways for access.

(C) To the extent possible, designated truck routes shall be used for all hauling as well as for all access to the site. All other routes and access shall be approved by the [LOCAL GOVERNMENT] engineer prior to CUP approval. The plan shall address the compatibility of the proposed use with the [LOCAL GOVERNMENT] stormwater management plan or adopted [LOCAL GOVERNMENT] drainage or stormwater policies applicable to the area.

(D) Stormwater run-off, erosion, and sedimentation shall be controlled by a plan submitted to the [LOCAL GOVERNMENT] by the applicant and approved by the

[LOCAL GOVERNMENT] engineer. The plan shall address the compatibility of the proposed use with any required governmental entity water quality plan and the [LOCAL GOVERNMENT] stormwater management plan or adopted [LOCAL GOVERNMENT] drainage or stormwater policies applicable to the area.

(E) The applicant shall provide signs on the property and along haul routes where deemed necessary to promote the safety and general welfare of the neighborhood and general area. Required signs may include, but shall not be limited to, "No Trespassing," "Danger—No Swimming," and "Trucks Hauling." Other signs may be required if necessary.

(F) Activities shall be phased to identify the sequence of operation. A new phase shall not begin until at least 50 percent of an active/current phase is reclaimed as per the reclamation plan and the [LOCAL GOVERNMENT] has verified the completion of the reclamation of the phase to the extent that it can be reclaimed.

(G) Operations shall maintain compliance with local and state standards for noise, dust, and vibration. All equipment and machinery shall be operated and maintained in such a manner as to minimize dust, noise, and vibration. Access roads shall be maintained in a dust-free condition by surfacing or other treatment on a regular basis as may be specified by the [LOCAL GOVERNMENT] engineer. A water truck for the purpose of dust control may be required on site.

(H) Adequate dust control methods shall be implemented. Roadways adjacent to the property shall be swept and cleaned on a regular basis and when directed by the [LOCAL GOVERNMENT] engineer as being necessary.

(I) A performance bond or other financial security in an amount satisfactory to the [LOCAL GOVERNMENT] engineer and in a form approved by the [LOCAL GOVERNMENT] attorney shall be secured from the applicant to ensure that all applicable standards are fully met during operation and to ensure that proper reclamation of the site is completed in a timely manner.

(J) A 6-foot continuous security fence shall be provided around the entire perimeter of the property on which the sand or gravel excavation activity will take place. Additional fencing requirements may be imposed on portions of the site abutting residentially zoned or planned areas, parks, playgrounds, sidewalks, trails, schools, churches, and other public facilities and gathering places.

(K) Where a stockpile is visible from an arterial roadway or residential district, the height of a stockpile may be limited by the reviewing agency. In any case, the height of a stockpile may not exceed 50 feet for permanent stockpiles and 75 feet for temporary stockpiles in a nonresidential district.

(L) Any lighting or signage, other than security signage, on the property shall meet the standards for the zoning district in which the activity is located.

(M) No excavation operation shall be conducted in such a manner as to permanently lower the water table of surrounding properties, except in quaternary deposits, nor shall such excavation activity cause the drainage of a wetland without the applicant first obtaining an approved wetland replacement plan.

(N) A weight scale may be required to be located at the site and, if necessary, other restrictions may be imposed if roadways adjacent to the site and operations are not suitable for heavy truck traffic. A record of all truck load weights exiting the site must be maintained for at least two years as evidence of weight limit compliance, and such records shall be available for inspection by the [LOCAL GOVERNMENT] engineer or the agents of other applicable road authorities.

(O) Where applicable, no excavation shall occur within 100 feet of a protected water body unless otherwise permitted by the [STATE ENVIRONMENTAL AGENCY]. Where excavation occurs on more than one side of a protected water body, a setback of 50 feet may be maintained on one side when a setback of 200 feet or more is maintained on the other, if approved by the [STATE ENVIRONMENTAL AGENCY] and the [LOCAL GOVERNMENT] engineer.

7.20.5.2 Reclamation Standards

See § 7.20.7 Reclamation Standards of this chapter.

7.20.6 Land Alteration

The following minimum operation/performance standards shall apply to all other substantial land alteration activities unless otherwise specified:

(A) Any topsoil removed from the surface and retained on the site shall be removed carefully and stockpiled in a manner to prevent erosion for reapplication to disturbed areas during reclamation.

(B) Hours of operation shall be limited to the hours of 7 AM to 10 PM for operational activities, including blasting, dredging, excavation, processing, and hauling. Hours and days of operation may be restricted by the reviewing agency for operations within 1,000 feet of any residential areas or that rely on residential roadways for access.

(C) To the extent possible, designated truck routes shall be used for all hauling as well as for all access to the site. All other routes and access shall be approved by the [LOCAL GOVERNMENT] engineer.

(D) Stormwater run-off, erosion, and sedimentation shall be controlled by a plan submitted to the [LOCAL GOVERNMENT] by the applicant and approved by the [LOCAL GOVERNMENT] engineer. The plan shall address the compatibility of the proposed use with the county water quality plan and the [LOCAL GOVERN-

MENT] stormwater management plan or adopted [LOCAL GOVERNMENT] drainage or stormwater policies applicable to the area.

(E) The applicant shall provide signs on the property and along haul routes where deemed necessary to promote the safety and general welfare of the neighborhood and general area. Required signs may include, but shall not be limited to, "No Trespassing," "Trucks Hauling," "Danger," and "Blasting." Other signs may be required if necessary.

(F) Activities shall be phased to identify the sequence of operation. A new phase shall not begin until at least 50 percent of an active/current phase is reclaimed as per the reclamation plan and the [LOCAL GOVERNMENT] has verified the completion of the reclamation of the phase to the extent that it can be reclaimed.

(G) Operations shall maintain compliance with local and state standards for noise, dust, and vibration. All equipment and machinery shall be operated and maintained in such a manner as to minimize dust, noise, and vibration. Access roads shall be maintained in a dust-free condition by surfacing or other treatment on a regular basis and as may be specified by the [LOCAL GOVERNMENT] engineer. A water truck for the purposes of dust control may be required on site.

(H) Adequate dust control methods shall be implemented. Roadways adjacent to the property shall be swept and cleaned on a regular basis and when directed by the [LOCAL GOVERNMENT] engineer as being necessary.

(I) A performance bond or other financial security in an amount satisfactory to the [LOCAL GOVERNMENT] engineer and in a form approved by the [LOCAL GOVERNMENT] attorney shall be secured from the applicant to ensure that all applicable standards are fully met during operation and to ensure that proper reclamation of the site is completed in a timely manner.

(J) A 6-foot continuous security fence shall be provided around the entire perimeter of the property on which the substantial land alteration activity will take place. Additional fencing requirements may be imposed on portions of the site abutting residentially zoned or planned areas, parks, playgrounds, sidewalks, trails, schools, churches, and other public facilities and gathering places.

(K) Where a stockpile is visible from an arterial roadway or residential district, the height of a stockpile may be limited by the reviewing agency. In any case, the height of a stockpile may not exceed 50 feet for permanent stockpiles and 75 feet for temporary stockpiles in a nonresidential district.

(L) Any lighting or signage, other than security signage, on the property shall meet the standards for the zoning district in which the activity is located.

(M) A blasting plan shall be submitted to the [LOCAL GOVERNMENT] fire, public works, and planning departments with proof of insurance in an amount as approved by the [LOCAL GOVERNMENT] engineer and in a form as approved by the [LOCAL GOVERNMENT] attorney. Such activity shall be conducted only by licensed, insured individuals or entities and shall be in conformance with all applicable federal, state, and local regulations.

(N) No excavation operation shall be conducted in such a manner as to permanently lower the water table of surrounding properties, except in quaternary deposits, nor shall such excavation activity cause the drainage of a wetland without the applicant first obtaining an approved wetland replacement plan.

(O) A weight scale may be required to be located at the site, and, if necessary, other restrictions may be imposed if roadways adjacent to the operations are not suitable for heavy truck traffic. A record of all truck load weights exiting the site must be maintained for at least two years as evidence of weight limit compliance, and such records shall be available for inspection by the [LOCAL GOVERNMENT] engineer.

(P) Where applicable, no excavation shall occur within 100 feet of a protected water body unless otherwise permitted by the [STATE ENVIRONMENTAL AGENCY]. Where excavation occurs on more than one side of a protected water body, a setback of 50 feet may be maintained on one side when a setback of 200 feet or more is maintained on the other, if approved by the [STATE ENVIRONMENTAL AGENCY] and the [LOCAL GOVERNMENT] engineer.

(Q) A traffic analysis may be required by the [LOCAL GOVERNMENT] engineer to determine the impacts of the truck traffic generated by the land alteration activity on the traffic safety and service levels of area roads and intersections in the vicinity of the site.

7.20.7 Reclamation Standards

The minimum reclamation standards in § 7.20.7.1 Topsoil through § 7.20.7.10 Postreclamation Land Use of this chapter shall apply to quarries unless otherwise specified.

7.20.7.1 Topsoil

Topsoil capable of sustaining vegetative growth shall be provided and evenly spread on all disturbed areas.

7.20.7.2 Timing

(A) Disturbed areas shall be stabilized and seeded at the earliest possible time or as specified, and any development approvals issued for the proposed use shall establish a schedule for stabilization and temporary and permanent seeding for the site.

(B) For quarries and sand and gravel excavation, seeding and planting shall occur during the appropriate seasons and times of year in accordance with published regulations, standards, or guidelines for this climate and region issued by the [STATE ENVIRONMENTAL AGENCY].

(C) For sand and gravel excavation, progressive reclamation practices shall be utilized to continue to reclaim and stabilize disturbed areas prior to moving to a new phase.

7.20.7.3 Drainage

Any alteration of the natural drainage system or public waters or jurisdictional wetlands shall not adversely affect any other adjacent properties or public facilities.

7.20.7.4 Erosion Control

(A) Erosion control shall conform with the § 5.22 Stormwater Management in Chapter 5, Development Standards, of the LDC and this section.

(B) Silt fences, bale checks, sediment basins, and other similar structures and methods that require ongoing maintenance do not satisfy the requirements of this section for long-term reclamation. The intent of final reclamation is to leave the site in a maintenance-free and stable condition.

(C) Seeding shall be done in accordance with National Resources Conservation Service technical standards.

(D) All exposed area shall be seeded and stabilized with an appropriate seeding mixture in order to prevent erosion. Sodding or other erosion control methods or materials approved by the [LOCAL GOVERNMENT] engineer may be required for highly erodible areas or in areas where seed growth cannot be established in a reasonable time period.

(E) All equipment, stockpiles, debris, signs, silt fences, and other erosion control structures shall be removed from the site after completion of the activity.

(F) Adjacent roadways shall be swept and cleared of loose or foreign materials resulting from the reclamation operation.

(G) Erosion control measures shall be kept in place until permanent vegetation has been established on site and erosion is controlled.

7.20.7.5 Water Bodies—Shaping and Enhancement

For sand and gravel excavation:

(A) Where water bodies are created in commercial and residential zones, only free-form and natural-form water bodies will be allowed. All water bodies shall include variation in shoreline and depth and shall include curvilinear shorelines.

(B) Where practical, the minimum size of water bodies fed by groundwater and not connected to streams shall be 5 acres with a minimum average depth of 24 to 30 feet. Shallow water bodies may be considered where the applicant can provide evidence that such water body will not result in poor water quality and that it will not result in a nuisance to the area.

7.20.7.6 Slope

For sand and gravel excavation:

(A) No site shall exceed 3 feet horizontal to 1 foot vertical incline over a distance of 30 feet. This angle of repose shall be modified to a flatter angle, but not a steeper angle, if it is shown that the site will be unstable at a 3:1 ratio or that vegetation cannot be established on the 3:1 slope. This provision may be waived or modified by the reviewing agency upon the recommendation of the [LOCAL GOVERNMENT] engineer.

(B) For all locations where water bodies are created, the slope of the bottom of the lake from water's edge shall not exceed 4:1 for a distance of 20 feet from the water's edge and shall not exceed a depth of 10 feet beyond that point for a distance of 20 feet. The slope above the water's edge shall not exceed 3:1 for a distance of 20 feet from the water's edge.

7.20.7.7 Revegetation

In addition to required seeding, the reclaimed site shall be landscaped. The applicant shall have the flexibility to arrange plant material to best suit the ultimate proposed use and design of the property, provided that:

(A) At least eight deciduous and eight evergreen trees from the [LOCAL GOVERNMENT]'s approved plant list are planted for each disturbed acre; and

(B) At least 25 percent of required trees are planted within 30 feet of the perimeter of the site.

7.20.7.8 Cleanup and Maintenance

(A) All equipment, stockpiles, debris, signs, silt fences, and other erosion control structures shall be removed from the site after completion of the activity.

(B) Adjacent roadways shall be swept and cleared of loose or foreign materials resulting from the reclamation operation.

(C) A permanent 6-foot security fence shall be provided along the perimeter of the entire site to protect adjacent residentially zoned or planned areas, parks, playgrounds, sidewalks, trails, schools, churches, and other public facilities and gathering places.

7.20.7.9 Final Reclamation

Final reclamation of each phase of the operation shall be completed within six months of completion of each phase of the operation. Extensions may be granted by the [PLANNING OFFICIAL] not exceeding six months. No development approvals shall be issued on the property prior to completion of reclamation of the site.

7.20.7.10 Postreclamation Land Use

(A) If the owner proposes to construct structures on the site as part of the postreclamation land-use activities, all such uses shall be specified.

(B) The owner shall submit all necessary documentation for such proposed uses, including, but not limited to, a site plan, an application for rezoning, an application for a development approval, or other required documentation necessary for development approval of the proposed use on the reclaimed site.

7.20.8 Financial Assurances

(A) Financial assurances shall be required in an amount as determined by the [LOCAL GOVERNMENT] engineer, but in no event to be less than $10,000, and in a form approved by the [LOCAL GOVERNMENT] attorney and the finance director, prior to commencement of any substantial land alteration, quarry, or sand or gravel excavation activity.

(B) Financial assurances may be in the form of surety bonds, irrevocable letters of credit, or cash bonds. Other alternatives providing adequate assurance may be considered by the [LOCAL GOVERNMENT] attorney and the finance director and, if approved by them, may be recommended to the [GOVERNING ENTITY].

(C) Failure to stabilize the site, failure to make necessary corrections and improvements to roadways caused by the excavation activity, failure to reclaim the property as specified in the approved reclamation plan, and other inconsistencies between the approved operations and reclamation plans and actual activities shall, at the discretion of the [GOVERNING ENTITY], be cause for the [LOCAL GOVERNMENT] to redeem the financial assurance to make the necessary corrections.

7.20.9 Inspection and Monitoring

7.20.9.1 Annual Inspection and Report

(A) At the discretion of the [PLANNING OFFICIAL], not less frequently than once per year, the appropriate [LOCAL GOVERNMENT] officials may undertake and conduct a detailed inspection of the site, using the required plans and information; the appropriate standards for the activity; the development approvals, with or without conditions and other relevant information; and commitments to the compliance checklist.

(B) Based on the annual inspection and the compliance checklist, the [LOCAL GOVERNMENT] may identify any and all violations of the terms and conditions of the plans and development approvals.

(C) In addition to the annual inspection, the [LOCAL GOVERNMENT] may make "spot" inspections at any time during the year, and multiple times as may be deemed appropriate utilizing the compliance checklist, and shall report such findings to the appropriate [LOCAL GOVERNMENT] officials.

(D) The [PLANNING OFFICIAL] may prepare a "Project Compliance Sheet" for each quarry, sand, or gravel excavation, and substantial land alteration activity as defined herein, and may compile the individual "Project Compliance Sheet" into an annual report for presentation to the [LOCAL GOVERNMENT] administrator.

7.20.9.2 Monitoring

(A) At the discretion of the [PLANNING OFFICIAL], the [LOCAL GOVERNMENT] may, in addition to site inspections, monitor the issuance of the development approvals for the above-described "excavation activities" on a broader level, considering such issues as:

(1) The concentration of such activities and the effect of such concentration on particular neighborhoods and areas of the [LOCAL GOVERNMENT];

(2) The effect of such activities on the transportation system and the provision of other required public facilities and services;

(3) The effect of numerous "excavation activities" on air and water quality and the environment;

(4) The effect of such activities on the land values of adjacent and nearby properties;

(5) The extra expenses incurred by the [LOCAL GOVERNMENT] relative to the operation and/or reclamation of such activities;

(6) The actual usability of the sites after reclamation;

(7) The average duration of "excavation activities"; and

(8) The average time it takes to fully reclaim a site and make it available for an alternative use.

(B) Based on the information collected, the [PLANNING OFFICIAL] may prepare an annual monitoring report for review by the [PLANNING OFFICIAL] and, at the [PLANNING OFFICIAL]'s discretion, by the hearing officer.

7.21 GROUP HOMES

Purpose and findings: This section is designed to protect the rights of handicapped and disabled persons subject to the federal Fair Housing Act (FHA) and to accommodate housing for persons protected by the FHA by establishing uniform and reasonable standards for the siting of group homes and criteria that protect the character of existing neighborhoods.

7.21.1 Applicability

This section applies to all group homes. For purposes of this section, a "group home" means a residential facility in which more than eight handicapped persons unrelated by blood, marriage, adoption, or guardianship reside with one or more resident counselors or other staff persons. A "handicapped person" means a person with a significant temporary or permanent physical, emotional, or mental disability, including, but not limited to, mental retardation, cerebral palsy, epilepsy, autism, hearing and sight impairments, emotional disturbances, and orthopedic impairments, but not including mentally ill persons.

7.21.2 Fair Housing Act Protections

The [PLANNING OFFICIAL] may render an interpretation that any other facility, which is protected by the federal FHA, 42 U.S.C. § 3601 et seq., but not expressly enumerated in § 7.21.1 Applicability of this chapter, is subject to the protections provided by this section. The [PLANNING OFFICIAL] may waive any provision of this section upon determination that the waiver is necessary to afford handicapped persons equal opportunity to use and enjoy a dwelling.

7.21.3 Location

Group homes are permitted as of right in all residential zoning districts, all commercial zoning districts, and other zones as specified in the LDC. Pursuant to the requirements of the federal FHA and applicable case law, the LDC does not require CUPs or any other form of discretionary development approval for group homes. A variance is required to the extent that the group home seeks a variance from the standards that apply to other uses in the base zoning district.

7.21.4 Standards

The standards applicable to group homes are the same as for single-family dwelling units located within the base district. Evidence of any license, certification, or registration required for the group home by a state or federal agency, or a copy of all materials submitted for an application for any such license, shall be provided.

7.30 HOME OCCUPATIONS

Purpose and findings: This section—

• Establishes criteria for operation of home occupations in dwelling units within residential districts;

• Permits and regulates the conduct of home occupations as an accessory use in a dwelling unit, whether owner- or renter-occupied;

• Ensures that such home occupations are compatible with, and do not have a deleterious effect on, adjacent and nearby residential properties and uses;

• Ensures that public and private services, such as streets, sewers, or water or utility systems, are not burdened by the home occupation to the extent that usage exceeds that normally associated with residential use;

• Allows residents of the community to use their residences as places to enhance or fulfill personal economic goals, under certain specified standards, conditions, and criteria;

• Enables the fair and consistent enforcement of these home occupation regulations; and

• Promotes and protects the public health, safety, and general welfare.

7.30.1 Applicability

(A) This section applies to any occupation, profession, or business activity customarily conducted entirely within a dwelling unit and carried on by a member of the family residing in the dwelling unit, and which occupation or profession is clearly incidental and subordinate to the use of the dwelling unit for dwelling purposes and does not change the character of the dwelling unit. A home occupation is an accessory use to a dwelling unit.

(B) No home occupation, except as otherwise provided in this section, may be initiated, established, or maintained in the unit except in conformance with the regulations and performance standards set forth in this section. A home occupation shall be incidental and secondary to the use of a dwelling unit for residential purposes.

7.30.2 Exempt Home Occupations

The activities listed in subsections (A) through (D), below, are not subject to this section, provided that all persons engaged in such activities reside on the premises:

(A) Artists, sculptors, and composers not selling their artistic product to the public on the premises;

(B) Craft work, such as jewelry-making and pottery, with no sales permitted on the premises;

(C) Home offices with no client visits to the home permitted; and

(D) Telephone answering and message services.

7.30.3 Permitted Home Occupations

(A) The home occupations permitted in subsection (B), below, are allowed in a residential setting because they do not compromise the residential character of an area, do not generate conspicuous traffic, do not visually call unusual attention to the home, and do not generate noise of a nonresidential level. A home occupation is permitted as an accessory use in the districts shown in the use matrix (Table 3-4, Use Matrix, in Chapter 3, Zoning, of the LDC) and in the planned development, TND, and "MX" (Mixed Use) districts.

(B) The following home occupations are permitted subject to the standards established in this section:

(1) Accounting, tax preparation, bookkeeping, and payroll services (North American Industry Classification System (NAICS) 5412;

(2) Land-Based Classification Standards (LBCS) Function 2412;

(3) Baking and cooking (NAICS 3118; LBCS 2151);

(4) Catering (NAICS 72232; LBCS 2560);

(5) Child care (NAICS 6244; LBCS 6562);

(6) Computer repair training (NAICS 611519);

(7) Computer systems design and related services (NAICS 5415);

(8) Computer training (NAICS 61142; LBCS Function 6143);

(9) Drafting services (NAICS 54134);

(10) Engineering, architecture, and landscape architecture (NAICS 5413; LBCS 2413);

(11) Financial planning and investment services (NAICS 52393; LBCS 2250);

(12) Fine arts studio (creation of individual works only, no mass production) (NAICS 7115, 7121);

(13) Hair salon, barbering, hairdressing, and other personal care services (NAICS 8121);

(14) Information and data processing services (NAICS 51421; LBCS Function 4240) (includes Standard Industrial Classification (SIC) 7374 computer processing and data preparation and processing services, and SIC 7379 computer-related services, National Electrical Code (NEC)) (CD or DVD conversion and recertification);

(15) Insurance sales (NAICS 52421; LBCS 2240);

(16) Interior decoration (no studio permitted) (NAICS 54141; LBCS 2414);

(17) Legal services (NAICS 5411; LBCS Function 2411);

(18) Mail order business (order taking only, no stock in trade) (NAICS 4541);

(19) Musical instruction, voice, or instrument (NAICS 61161);

(20) Musical instrument tuning and repair (NAICS 811211, 81149, 4511);

(21) Offices for professional, scientific, or technical services (NAICS 54; LBCS 2400) or administrative services (NAICS 5611; LBCS 2420);

(22) Photographic services (NAICS 54192);

(23) Professional services, including the practice of law (NAICS 54);

(24) Real estate services and appraisal (NAICS 531);

(25) Tailoring (e.g., dressmaking and alterations) services (NAICS 81149; 3152);

(26) Teaching of crafts and incidental sale of supplies to students (NAICS 61161); and

(27) Tutoring (NAICS 611691).

7.30.4 Prohibited Home Occupations

The following uses are not permitted as home occupations in residential zoning districts, except where permitted in § 7.30.7 Unsafe Home Occupations of this chapter:

(A) Medical/dental office;
(B) Motor vehicle and engine repair;
(C) Furniture refinishing;
(D) Gymnastic facilities;
(E) Recording studios;
(F) Outdoor recreation activities;
(G) Medical/cosmetic facilities for animals, including animal care or boarding facilities;
(H) Machine shop/metal working;
(I) Retail sales;
(J) Commercial food preparation;
(K) Contractors shops;
(L) Mortuaries;
(M) Medical procedures;
(N) Body piercing and/or painting, tattoos, or any type of physical therapy or psychotherapy; or
(O) Any other use not allowed in accordance with § 7.30 Home Occupations of this chapter.

7.30.5 Performance Standards

Home occupations shall comply with the performance standards set forth in Table 7-5.

7.30.6 Rural Home Occupations

7.30.6.1 Permitted Home Occupations

The following home occupations are permitted in the "RP" (Resource Protection) and "RE" (Residential Estate) zoning districts in addition to those specified in § 7.30.3 Permitted Home Occupations of this chapter:

(A) Auto repair work (LBCS Structure 2280);
(B) Contractor and trade shops, indoor operations only, including electrical, plumbing, and mechanical (LBCS Function 7210);
(C) Machine welding shops (NAICS 23899);
(D) Office machinery and equipment rental and leasing (NAICS 53242) (includes SIC 7377 computer rental and leasing); and
(E) Computer and office machine repair and maintenance (NAICS 811212).

7.30.6.2 Performance Standards

All home occupations permitted in § 7.30.6.1 Permitted Home Occupations of this chapter shall comply with the criteria of Table 7-5 consistent with this section. In the event of an inconsistency between Table 7-5 and this section, this section controls.

7.30.6.3 Outdoor Storage

Outdoor storage shall comply with the following standards:

(A) Storage shall be limited to materials related to the business and shall not involve any hazardous materials;
(B) Outdoor storage areas shall comply with § 5.50 Outdoor Storage in Chapter 5, Development Standards, of the LDC and shall not occupy an area of land exceeding 80 square feet;
(C) Materials shall not be stacked to a height exceeding 4 feet and shall not be visible from the public right-of-way or an adjacent lot or parcel zoned or occupied for residential use. Any screening required to comply with this subsection shall use wood or masonry fencing or a vegetative hedge;
(D) The rural home occupation shall not create any smoke, odors, dust, or noise at a level discernible at any of its lot lines; and

Table 7-5
Home Occupation Performance Standards By Zoning District

Performance Standards	RP, RE	All Other Districts
The use shall be clearly incidental and secondary to residential occupancy.	✓	✓
The use shall be conducted entirely within the interior of the residence.	✓	✓
No more than one nonresident employee shall be permitted.	✓	✓
Not more than six clients per day (limit one visit per day per each client) are permitted to visit home occupation. Hours for visits shall be between 8:00 AM and 8:00 PM.	✓	✓
Not more than 25% of the gross floor area of the principal dwelling structure shall be utilized for the home occupation.	✓	✓
Music, art, craft, or similar lessons are permitted (12 or fewer clients per day).	✓	✓
Child care (maximum of six or fewer children) is permitted.	✓	✓
Public facilities and utilities shall be adequate to safely accommodate equipment used for home occupation.	✓	✓
Storage of goods and materials shall be inside and shall not include flammable, combustible, or explosive materials.	✓	✓
Parking shall be provided only in the driveway.	✓	✓
Outside storage of heavy equipment or material shall be prohibited.		✓
No truck or van with a payload rating of more than 1 ton shall be parked on the site or in front of the site on a regular basis.		✓
Mechanized equipment shall be used only in a completely enclosed building.		✓
Electronically amplified sounds shall not be audible from adjacent properties or public streets.	✓	✓
No generation of dust, odors, noise, vibration, or electrical interference or fluctuation shall be perceptible beyond the property line.	✓	✓
Deliveries and pickups shall be those normally associated with residential services, shall not block traffic circulation, and shall occur only between 8:00 AM and 8:00 PM, Monday through Saturday.	✓	✓
Accessory buildings shall not be used for home occupation purposes.		✓
Signage shall: (1) be limited to one sign of 4 square feet in area; (2) be mounted flush against the wall of principal dwelling unit; and (3) not be illuminated.	✓	✓

RP = Resource Protection; RE = Residential Estate; and ✓ = the performance standard applies in the applicable district.

(E) The minimum lot size shall be 2 acres. In no event shall a home occupation be established on a lot that is nonconforming as to the minimum lot size.

7.30.6.4 Accessory Buildings

Where a home occupation is conducted in an accessory building, such accessory building shall not exceed the lesser of the following:

(A) The square footage of the footprint of the dwelling; or

(B) 2,000 square feet.

7.30.6.5 Employees

Nonresident employees may work in the home occupation as follows:

(A) *Up to 1,000 square feet of floor area:* one nonresident employee; and

(B) *1,000 square feet and over of floor area:* two nonresident employees.

For the purpose of this subsection, "floor area" refers to the GFA of the entire dwelling unit and not the floor area devoted to the home occupation.

7.30.7 Unsafe Home Occupations

If any home occupation has become dangerous or unsafe; presents a safety hazard to the public, pedestrians on public sidewalks, or motorists on a public right-of-way; or presents a safety hazard to adjacent or nearby properties, residents, or businesses, the [PLANNING OFFICIAL] shall issue an order to the dwelling owner and/or tenant on the property on which the home occupation is being undertaken, directing that the home occupation immediately be made safe or be terminated. The property owner and/or tenant shall take the necessary corrective steps or measures but, in the event of a failure to do so by the owner and/or tenant, after notice and a reasonable period of time, the [PLANNING OFFICIAL] may take any and all available enforcement actions to render the home occupation and dwelling safe. Costs incurred by the [PLANNING OFFICIAL], if forced to take enforcement actions, shall be borne by the property owner and shall be treated as a zoning violation.

7.31 HOUSING FACILITIES FOR OLDER PERSONS

7.31.1 Applicability

"Housing Facility for Older Persons" (HFOP) means any apartment that complies with the provisions of 24 C.F.R. §§ 100.304-100.307.

7.31.2 Uses

An HFOP is permitted as of right in any "NS" (Neighborhood Suburban) or "NU" (Neighborhood Urban) zoning district subject to the requirements of this section.

7.31.3 Federal Restrictions

Prior to issuance of an application for development approval authorizing construction or establishment of an HFOP, the applicant shall provide to the [PLANNING OFFICIAL]:

(A) A copy of the policies and procedures required by 24 C.F.R. § 100.306; and

(B) A copy of the verification of occupancy required by 24 C.F.R. § 100.307.

7.31.4 "NS" (Neighborhood Suburban) Districts

An HFOP permitted within "NS" (Neighborhood Suburban) zoning districts shall comply with the following:

(A) The building shall not exceed two stories in height;

(B) The building shall conform to the setback standards generally applicable within the zoning district;

(C) The building shall comply with the minimum and maximum parking standards applicable to multifamily dwellings; and

(D) The proposed development shall comply with all applicable standards of Chapter 5, Development Standards, of the LDC.

7.32 INCLUSIONARY ZONING/ AFFORDABLE DWELLING UNITS

Purpose and findings: The purpose of this section is to:
• Provide affordable shelter for all residents of the [LOCAL GOVERNMENT];
• Address housing needs;
• Promote a full range of housing choices; and
• Encourage the construction and continued existence of very low- to low-income housing by providing for optional increases in density in order to reduce land costs for such affordable housing.

7.32.1 Applicability

7.32.1.1 Generally

This section applies to any application for development approval, as set forth in § 7.32.1.2 Qualifying Applications of this chapter, which include affordable dwelling units with the maximum ratio specified in Column (B) of Table 7-6. For purposes of this section, an "affordable dwelling unit" means any dwelling unit required to provide only low-income or very low-income housing.

7.32.1.2 Qualifying Applications

The provisions of this section apply to a site, or a portion of a site, which is the subject of an application for a development approval.

7.32.2 Architectural Design and Character

Affordable dwelling units shall comply with the residential urban design criteria of § 5.13 Building Design in Chapter 5, Development Standards, of the LDC.

7.32.3 Density Bonus and Set-Aside Requirements

(A) A qualifying application (as defined in § 7.32.1 Applicability of this chapter) may be approved with an increase in the density of the site as set forth in Table 7-6. The applicant shall consent to a voluntary and enforceable condition in which the specified percentage of the developable density of the site, as specified in Column (B) of Table 7-6, is reserved as affordable dwelling units.

(B) Table 7-6 shall be construed as follows:

(1) Determine the category of housing as set forth in Column (A) of Table 7-6.

(2) Determine the required set-aside for the application category by referring to Column (B) Table 7-6. For purposes of this subsection, the number of required affordable dwelling units is determined by multiplying the total number of dwelling units permissible on the site as set forth in Table 7-6 by the percentage prescribed in Column (B) of Table 7-6.

(3) Determine the density increase that may be awarded by referring to Column (C) in Table 7-6. For

Table 7-6
Affordable Dwelling Unit Set-Aside Requirements

(A) Application Category	(B) Set-Aside	(C) Density Bonus
Low-income housing	10%	20%
Very low-income housing	5%	10%

purposes of this subsection, the additional density that may be awarded is determined by multiplying the total number of dwelling units permissible for the site as set forth in Table 7-6 by the percentage prescribed in Column (C) of Table 7-6. The [LOCAL GOVERNMENT] shall not require the additional dwelling units to be restricted as to income.

(4) In some instances, developers will not be able to provide the number of dwelling units permissible after applying Table 7-6. In such cases, the applicant may reduce the number of affordable dwelling units. However, the number of affordable dwelling units provided in such cases must at least equal the ratio to the additional units that result from dividing Column (B) of Table 7-6 by Column (C) of Table 7-6 and multiplying the dividend by the number of affordable dwelling units required.

7.32.4 Project Phasing

No qualifying application shall be approved unless the applicant consents to a condition that development approvals for nonaffordable dwelling units (hereinafter "market rate units") shall be issued as follows:

(A) Development approvals may be issued for the first 50 percent of the market rate units prior to the construction and offering for sale or rental of any affordable dwelling unit.

(B) No development approvals may be issued for the next 25 percent of the market rate units (i.e., from 51 percent up to 75 percent of the approved market rate units) prior to the construction and offering for sale or rental of at least 25 percent of the approved affordable dwelling units.

(C) No development approvals may be issued for the next 15 percent of the market rate units (i.e., from 76 percent up to 90 percent of the approved market rate units) prior to the construction and offering for sale or rental of at least 75 percent of the approved affordable dwelling units.

(D) No development approvals may be issued for the remainder of the market rate units (i.e., from 91 percent to 100 percent of the approved market rate units) prior to the construction and offering for sale or rental of 100 percent of the approved affordable dwelling units.

7.32.5 Enforcement

The [LOCAL GOVERNMENT] or its designee may enforce compliance with the standards of this section and may impose penalties for noncompliance as set forth in Chapter 4, Procedures, of the LDC.

7.32.6 Administration

(A) Affordable dwelling units shall be offered for sale or rent exclusively to persons, households, or families who meet the income criteria for "low-income housing" or "very low-income housing" (hereinafter "target households") as defined in Appendix A, Definitions and Rules of Interpretation, of the LDC.

(B) This section may be administered by the [HOUSING OFFICIAL]. The [LOCAL GOVERNMENT] shall have an exclusive right to purchase any units offered for sale to target households but not purchased or rented within a time period mutually agreed upon between the applicant and the [HOUSING OFFICIAL].

(C) Affordable dwelling unit sales prices throughout the [LOCAL GOVERNMENT] shall be established by the [HOUSING OFFICIAL] initially and shall be adjusted semiannually, based on a determination of all ordinary, necessary, and reasonable costs required to construct the prototype affordable dwelling units by private industry, and other information, including the area's current general market and economic condition. Sales prices may not include the cost of land, on-site sales commissions, and marketing expenses, but may include, among other costs, builder-paid permanent mortgage placement costs and buy-down fees and closing costs except for prepaid expenses required at settlement.

(D) Affordable dwelling unit rental prices shall be established by the [HOUSING OFFICIAL] initially and shall be adjusted semiannually, based on a determination of all ordinary, necessary, and reasonable costs required to construct and market the required number of affordable dwelling rental units by private industry in the area, and other information, such as the area's current general market and economic conditions.

(E) Prices for re-sales and re-rentals shall be controlled by the [HOUSING OFFICIAL] for a period of 50 years after the initial sale or rental transaction for each affordable dwelling unit.

(F) The sales or re-sales price for an affordable dwelling unit shall be established, taking into consideration as one factor alleged economic loss sustained by the owner as a result of providing the required affordable dwelling units. "Economic loss" for sales units results when the owner fails to recoup the cost of construction and certain allowances as may be determined by the [HOUSING OFFICIAL] for the affordable dwelling units, exclusive of the cost of land acquisition and costs voluntarily incurred but not authorized by this section.

7.40 JUNKYARDS AND AUTOMOBILE GRAVEYARDS

Purpose and findings: This section establishes regulations for junkyards and automobile graveyards to insure that neighborhoods and economic development opportunities are protected, consistent with state law.

7.40.1 Applicability

This section applies to any junkyard or automobile graveyard.

7.40.2 Conditional Use Permit

(A) Junkyards and automobile graveyards shall be located at least 500 feet from any dwelling unit or residential zoning district.

(B) Any new automobile graveyard or junkyard and substantial intensification of an existing junkyard or automobile graveyard requires approval of a CUP.

7.40.3 Standards for Conditional Use Permit

7.40.3.1 New Facilities

A new junkyard or automobile graveyard may be established only in an "IH" (Industrial Heavy) zoning district.

7.40.3.2 Definition

A new junkyard or automobile graveyard shall mean any facility, structure, or land-use storage of used scrap salvage materials, including but not limited to shredding, milling, grinding, baling, or packing equipment for the handling of scrap, salvage materials, or used materials.

7.40.3.3 Standards

(A) No material shall be placed in any automobile graveyard or junkyard in such a manner that it is capable of being transferred out of the automobile graveyard or junkyard by wind, water, or other natural causes. The loose storage of paper and the spilling of flammable or other liquids into streams or sewers are prohibited.

(B) All materials shall be stored in such a manner as to prevent the breeding or harboring of rats, insects, or other vermin. Where necessary, this shall be accomplished by enclosure in containers, raising of materials above the ground, separation of types of materials, prevention of the collection of stagnant water, extermination procedures, or other means. Professional monthly exterminating services are required, and a log indicating the dates and findings of such professional services shall be maintained on the premises.

(C) A junkyard or automobile graveyard shall include a Type E buffer yard (see § 5.31 Buffers and Screening in Chapter 5, Development Standards, of the LDC) along all property lines abutting a public street or any zoning district other than "IH" (Industrial Heavy).

(D) All other standards for CUPs contained in § 4.23 Conditional Use Permits in Chapter 4, Procedures, of the LDC.

7.40.3.4 Substantial Intensification of an Existing Junkyard or Automobile Graveyard

(A) Substantial intensification means any of the following:

(1) Any geographic expansion of the facility;

(2) The addition of any shredding, milling, grinding, baling, or packing equipment for the handling of scrap or salvage materials, or the replacement of any existing shredding, milling, grinding, baling, or packing equipment for the handling of scrap and salvage materials; and

(3) The replacement of any existing shredding, milling, grinding, baling, or packing equipment for the handling of scrap and salvage materials, which results in an increase of greater than 10 percent in the rated compression capacity, shear force capacity, or other appropriate power or capacity measurement approved by the [PLANNING OFFICIAL] for the piece of equipment being replaced.

(B) A substantial alteration of a junkyard or automobile graveyard shall be subject to a CUP and all of the standards contained in § 7.40.3 Standards for Conditional Use Permit of this chapter.

7.50 MANUFACTURED HOME LAND-LEASE COMMUNITIES

Purpose and findings: Manufactured homes provide a viable and affordable housing option for a segment of the [LOCAL GOVERNMENT]'s population. This housing option is provided in areas predominately of agricultural and forest use with minimal requirements consistent with the state code. This option is also provided under certain design criteria in more residentially developed areas where they will not conflict with developments planned for site-built dwellings.

The purpose of this section is to:

• Achieve orderly development of manufactured home and recreational vehicle parks;

• Promote and develop the use of land to assure the best possible community environment in accordance with the comprehensive plan of the [LOCAL GOVERNMENT]; and

• Protect and promote the health, safety, and general welfare.

The specific purposes of these restrictions are to:

• Accommodate an important source of affordable housing for the community;

• Protect neighborhood character;

• Obtain sufficient distances between the manufactured home stand on its lot and obstructions on adjoining land to assure privacy, adequate natural light and air, and convenient access to the unit; and

• Provide for circulation around the unit for such uses of the yard spaces as are considered essential to the manufactured home.

7.50.1 Applicability

This section applies to manufactured home land-lease communities, as defined in Appendix A, Definitions and Rules of Interpretation, of the LDC.

7.50.2 Density

A manufactured home land-lease community shall not exceed a density of seven units per gross acre. This restriction supersedes the density restrictions of the underlying zoning district.

7.50.3 Standards

7.50.3.1 Buffer

A minimum Type A buffer shall be installed along the boundary of the development site and any abutting lot or parcel zoned "RE" (Residential Estate), "RP" (Resource Protection), "NS" (Neighborhood Suburban), "NU" (Neighborhood Urban), "PD" (Planned Development), or "MX" (Mixed Use) district.

7.50.3.2 Parks and Open Space

See § 5.21 Parks/Open Space in Chapter 5, Development Standards, of the LDC.

7.50.3.3 Yards and Building Separation

(A) *Determination of yards:* Yard width shall be measured from the required manufactured home stand to the individual manufactured home lot line. At every point, it shall be at least equal to the required minimum. Patios, carports, and individual storage lockers shall be disregarded in determining yard widths.

(B) *Yard requirements:* Manufactured home stands shall be separated from each manufactured home site line a distance of at least 10 feet on the entry side and 5 feet on all other sides. Detached accessory structures shall be located no nearer than 3 feet from any required site line. In no case shall the accessory structure occupy more than 30 percent of the required yard area of the entry side. Accessory structures attached to a manufactured home shall be construed to be a part of that structure and shall adhere to the yard requirements of same.

(C) *Yards abutting common areas:* The distance from any manufactured home stand to a street right-of-way shall be 8 feet minimum.

7.50.4 Streets

7.50.4.1 Generally

Streets shall be provided within manufactured home land-lease communities to provide convenient circulation by means of local streets and properly located collector streets. Streets within a manufactured home land-lease community shall be private streets and shall be maintained by the manufactured home land-lease community owner or licensee.

7.50.4.2 Design Standards and Construction Specifications

The street system shall comply with the standards for private streets as specified in the transportation standards in § 5.23 Street Design and Transportation in Chapter 5, Development Standards, of the LDC.

7.50.4.3 Driveways

The minimum width of driveways to manufactured home stands and other facilities shall be 12 feet, plus any extra width necessary for maneuvering a manufactured home on a curve.

7.50.5 Infrastructure and Utilities

7.50.5.1 Stormwater Management

Provision for the collection and disposal of surface and subsurface water to protect buildings and manufactured home stands, and to provide safe and convenient use of streets, lot areas, and other improvements, shall be required in all manufactured home land-lease communities in accordance with the stormwater management standards of § 5.22 Stormwater Management in Chapter 5, Development Standards, of the LDC.

7.50.5.2 Water Supply

Every manufactured home land-lease community shall be provided by the park licensee with an ample supply of water under pressure and approved by the [HEALTH OFFICIAL]. Individual water lines from service outlets to manufactured homes shall comply with the utilities standards (§ 7.91 Utilities of this chapter).

7.50.5.3 Sewage Disposal

All the sewer lines shall be connected to the public sewage system or a private sewage disposal system approved by the [HEALTH OFFICIAL]. Individual sewage drains from manufactured homes to the park service connections shall comply with the utilities standards (§ 7.91 Utilities of this chapter).

7.50.5.4 Electrical Power Lines

Electrical facilities shall comply with the rules and regulations regarding placement, installation, operation, and maintenance of electrical facilities as included in, but not limited to, the NEC and the National Electrical Safety Code.

7.50.5.5 Fire Hydrants

Standard fire hydrants, in workable condition, shall be located within 500 feet of each manufactured home. All such fire hydrants shall be connected to at least a 6-inch diameter water line.

**Figure 7-4
Vertical Mixed Use**

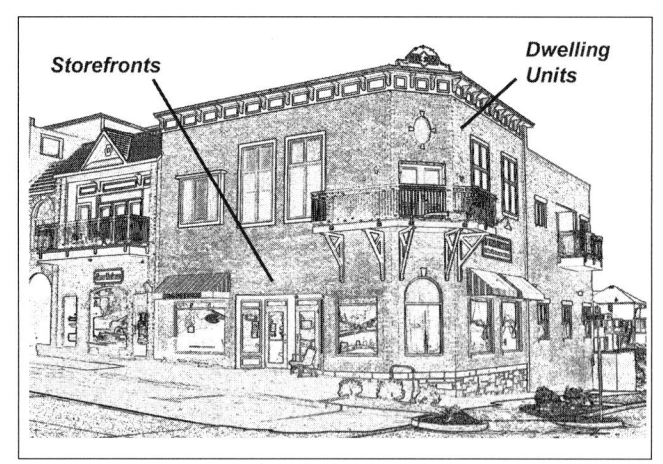

Vertical mixed-use building in the Village of Cherry Hill (Columbia, Missouri).

7.51 MIXED-USE BUILDINGS AND LIVE-WORK UNITS

Purpose and findings: This section establishes standards including, but not limited to, special height and intensity for innovative, mixed-use developments, and provides flexible parking standards to recognize internal vehicular trip capture from mixed uses. This section clarifies the applicable use, parking, and open space standards established by the LDC and applies to mixed-use buildings.

7.51.1 Location of Uses and Density

Mixed-use buildings or live-work units (see Figure 7-4) are subject to the criteria described in Table 7-7.

7.51.2 Mix of Uses

The mix of uses and density of mixed-use buildings or live-work units shall not exceed that which is described in Table 7-8 at locations where the building is listed as a permitted use in the applicable zoning district.

7.51.3 Parking

In order to encourage mixed-use buildings, and to protect the character of residential neighborhoods, the standards as defined in § 7.51.3.1 Number of Spaces through § 7.51.3.3 Adaptive Reuse of this chapter apply to parking for mixed-use buildings.

7.51.3.1 Number of Spaces

The number of parking spaces to which mixed-use buildings are subject is described in Table 7-9. Where indicated by Column (D) of Table 7-9, the applicant may reduce the minimum parking spaces required by Column (D) of Table 7-9 by using the shared parking formula established in § 5.51.2 Shared Parking in Chapter 5, Development Standards, of the LDC.

7.51.3.2 Location of Spaces

Parking spaces shall be located to the rear of the principal building or in a midblock location.

7.51.3.3 Adaptive Reuse

The standards established in § 5.51 Parking in Chapter 5, Development Standards, of the LDC for maximum parking ratios and location of parking do not apply to existing parking areas for mixed-use buildings that are established in an existing commercial building.

**Table 7-7
Mixed-Use Buildings and Live-Work Units**

(A) Development Standards	(B) Mixed-Use Building	(C) Live-Work Units
Locational criteria	Where permitted by the zoning district In any adaptive reuse project	Where permitted by the use matrix (Table 3-4, Use Matrix, in Chapter 3, Zoning, of the LDC) in any adaptive reuse project
Permitted density or intensity	No density restrictions apply. The building is subject to the setback and dimensional requirements of the applicable zoning district.	The building is subject to the setback and dimensional requirements of the dimensional matrix (Table 3-6, Dimensional Standards, in Chapter 3, Zoning, of the LDC) for the applicable zoning district.
Distribution of uses: • Uses permitted on first floor	By floor: • Retail, office, industrial	By floor: • Commercial, office, or residential. Residential uses may be located to the rear of the principal building.
• Uses permitted on second floor	• Residential, retail, office, industrial	• Residential only
• Uses permitted above second floor	Residential, office	Residential only

7.60 OUTDOOR DISPLAY AREAS

7.60.1 Applicability

This section applies to the display of retail goods in parking areas, sidewalks, and other locations outside of an enclosed building. This section does not apply to farmers' markets or produce stands where permitted by the applicable zoning district.

7.60.2 Permitted

(A) Outdoor display of retail goods, wares, and merchandise are permitted accessory uses in the "CG" (Commercial General) and "CL" (Commercial Large-Scale) districts if expressly permitted pursuant to a site plan. No such outdoor display is permitted unless the site plan shows the location, area, and boundaries of the outdoor display.

(B) Retail goods may be displayed on public or private sidewalks in the "CN" (Commercial Neighborhood) and "D" (Downtown) zoning districts, on any lot that abuts a TND main street or in the TOD, or on any designated "A" street, where:

(1) The goods are located entirely under an awning or canopy that complies with the [LOCAL GOVERNMENT] code of ordinances. If no awning or canopy is present, the goods may be displayed on an area abutting and not more than 3 feet from the storefront; and

Table 7-8
Mixed-Use Buildings—Ratio of Uses

Zoning Districts	Density (Dwelling Units Per Gross Acre)	Ratio of Residential Floor Space to Non-residential Floor Space (Square Footage)
"CN" (Commercial Neighborhood) "CG" (Commercial General) "D" (Downtown)	Up to 18	1:1
"CN" (Commercial Neighborhood) "CG" (Commercial General) "D" (Downtown)	24 to 49	2:1
"CG" (Commercial General) (no ratio applies in "D" (Downtown) district)	50 or more	4:1

Table 7-9
Mixed-Use Buildings—Parking Adjustments

(A) Zoning District	(B) Minimum Number of Spaces[a]	(C) Maximum Number of Spaces[a]	(D) Shared Parking[b]
"RP" (Resource Protection) "RE" (Residential Estate) "NS" (Neighborhood Suburban)	Minimum required by § 5.51.1 Parking Ratios in Chapter 5, Development Standards, of the LDC	Maximum permitted by § 5.51.1 Parking Ratios in Chapter 5, Development Standards, of the LDC	Yes
"NU" (Neighborhood Urban) "O" (Office) "CN" (Commercial Neighborhood) "CG" (Commercial General) "CL" (Commercial Large-Scale) "D" (Downtown) "IL" (Industrial Light) "IH" (Industrial Heavy) "PD" (Planned Development)	50% of minimum	Maximum permitted by § 5.51.1 Parking Ratios in Chapter 5, Development Standards, of the LDC	Yes
"MX" (Mixed Use) Traditional neighborhood development or neighborhood commercial use pattern	50% of minimum	Maximum permitted by § 5.51.1 Parking Ratios in Chapter 5, Development Standards, of the LDC	Yes
Transit-oriented development use pattern	No minimum parking requirements apply	75% of maximum permitted by § 5.51.1 Parking Ratios in Chapter 5, Development Standards, of the LDC	Yes

[a] See § 5.51.1 Parking Ratios in Chapter 5, Development Standards, of the LDC.
[b] See § 5.51.2 Shared Parking in Chapter 5, Development Standards, of the LDC.

(2) The display shall conform to the [LOCAL GOVERNMENT] streets and right-of-way management ordinances.

(C) Such outdoor display must be customarily incidental to a principal use in the district in which the outdoor display is permitted. Only the business or entity occupying the principal use or structure shall sell merchandise in the outdoor display areas.

(D) Such outdoor display is permitted in any yard, subject to a minimum setback of 20 feet from an adjoining property line.

(E) Outdoor display shall be screened from view along any property line abutting a residential zoning district by a minimum Type C buffer that conforms to § 5.31.2 Required Buffer Yards in Chapter 5, Development Standards, of the LDC. To the extent that buildings on the premises are located in order to screen views from adjacent streets and properties, such buildings may be considered to be part of the required screening in lieu of landscaping, fences, walls, and enclosures.

(F) The height of displayed merchandise shall not exceed the height of any fence or wall in the buffer or 6 feet, whichever is less.

(G) All outdoor displays must be located on the same lot as the principal use.

(H) Areas used for such display shall be furnished with an all-weather hard surface of a material such as bituminous or Portland concrete cement.

(I) Merchandise shall not be placed or located where it will interfere with pedestrian or building access or egress, required vehicular parking and handicapped parking, aisles, access or egress, loading space parking or access, public or private utilities, services or drainage systems, fire lanes, alarms, hydrants, standpipes, or other fire protection equipment, or emergency access or egress.

(J) Outdoor display areas shall not be located on any parking spaces needed to comply with the minimum parking ratios of § 5.51 Parking in Chapter 5, Development Standards, of the LDC. Outdoor display areas shall be considered part of the floor area of the principal use or structure for purposes of computing the minimum number of parking spaces required.

7.61 OUTDOOR STORAGE

Purpose and findings: This section establishes regulations for permanent storage areas that are in "IL" (Industrial Light) and "IH" (Industrial Heavy) zoning districts. Storage incidental to construction activities is permitted in all zoning districts.

7.61.1 Applicability

This section applies to commercial outdoor storage (with the exception of salvage operations and yards as defined and regulated by this ordinance), including contractors' yards, building supply sales, coal sales and storage, scrap metal storage, and paper and rag storage.

7.61.2 Standards

Storage yards shall be enclosed by a:

(A) Nonclimbable fence or wall at least 6 feet in height; or

(B) Type D landscaped buffer strip, as described in § 5.31.2 Required Buffer Yards in Chapter 5, Development Standards, of the LDC.

7.70 RESIDENTIAL DWELLING UNITS

Purpose and findings: These criteria are not intended to restrict imagination, innovation, or variety, but rather to assist in focusing design principles, which can result in creative solutions that will develop a satisfactory visual appearance, preserve taxable values, and promote the public health, safety, and general welfare. This section establishes design standards to permit appropriate densities while avoiding impacts on neighborhoods.

These standards:

• Coordinate diverse housing types so that they are compatible with other types of housing;

• Avoid long, unbroken lines of row housing;

• Encourage housing layouts that make efficient, economical, comfortable, and convenient use of land and open space;

• Provide a physical and visual connection between the living area of the residence and the street;

• Enhance public safety by allowing people to survey their neighborhood from inside their residences, places of work, or shopping areas;

• Provide a more pleasant pedestrian environment by preventing large expanses of blank façades along streets;

• Ensure that the location and amount of the living area of the residence, as seen from the street, is more prominent than the garage;

• Prevent garages from obscuring the main entrance from the street and ensure that the main entrance for pedestrians, rather than automobiles, is the prominent entrance;

• Provide for a more pleasant pedestrian environment by preventing garages and vehicle areas from dominating the views of the neighborhood from the sidewalk;

• Enhance public safety by preventing garages from blocking views of the street from inside the residence;

• Supplement the zoning regulations applied to site-built, modular, and manufactured homes with additional standards and procedures, which will promote a satisfactory living environment for residents of single-family homes and which will permit a mix of homes and other types of housing;

• Permit greater diversity in the types of housing communities;

- Ensure that all new single-family dwellings are compatible with other forms of housing;
- Ensure the provision of single-family housing opportunities for persons or families of low or moderate income by providing for design standards that ensure compatibility among various types of housing units as an alternative to exclusionary zoning practices;
- Provide interesting and aesthetically attractive multifamily developments while avoiding monotonous, "barracks"-style buildings;
- Ensure that multifamily buildings have a multifaceted exterior form in which articulated façades are combined with window and door placements, as well as other detailing, to create an interesting and attractive architectural design and limit flat walls with minimal features; and
- Provide for zero lot line (ZLL) developments in which houses are shifted to one side of the lot, thereby providing for greater usable yard space on each lot, providing greater flexibility in site development standards, and maintaining a single-family detached character of a neighborhood.

In order to provide design flexibility and to encourage the production of affordable housing, this section allows attached dwelling units without adherence to the minimum lot area and internal yard requirements provided for in the zoning district. The impervious surface ratio and recreation area of the district apply to the total subdivision and not to each lot within the subdivision. Common open space is distributed in order to provide readily available amenities and visual relief to the entire development.

7.70.1 Applicability

(A) This section applies to any of the following:

(1) Any single-family detached dwelling unit;

(2) Any single-family attached or two-family dwelling unit (duplex);

(3) Any townhouse or row house;

(4) Any cottage house;

(5) Any triplex, quadraplex, apartment, or other multifamily dwelling unit; and

(6) Any zero lot line dwelling.

(B) This section does not apply to dwelling units that are included in a mixed-use building, or accessory dwelling units, which are regulated separately in this chapter (see § 7.51 Mixed-Use Buildings and Live-Work Units of this chapter).

(C) This section applies to manufactured homes located on platted lots of record or in a subdivision. This section does not apply to manufactured home land-lease communities, which are regulated separately by this chapter (see § 7.50 Manufactured Home Land-Lease Communities of this chapter).

(D) Nothing in this section prevents the creation of a subdivided lot for individual dwelling units within a building that includes attached dwellings.

7.70.2 General Criteria

7.70.2.1 Applicability

The combination of design elements, as described in Table 7-10, is required for any dwelling unit subject to this section.

7.70.2.2 Scale

No single-family dwelling unit, duplex, or triplex shall exceed 8,000 square feet in size, nor exceed a FAR of .60. The total area of all dwellings and accessory structures shall not exceed a FAR of .75.

7.70.2.3 Main Entrance

(A) *Location of main entrance*

(1) A building must include a front porch or stoop at all main entrances that face a street. The porch or stoop shall adjoin the main entrance and the main entrance shall be accessible from the porch.

(2) The main entrance of each principal building must face the street. On corner lots, the main entrance may face either of the streets or be oriented to the corner. With buildings that have more than one main entrance, only one entrance must meet this requirement.

(B) *Porches:* Porches used to satisfy the design criteria shall comply with the following:

Table 7-10
Applicability of Design Regulations

Dwelling Unit Feature	RE, RP	NS, NU	D, TND, PD
Main entrance[a]	M	M	M
Garage[b]	O	M	M
Roof[c]	O	O	O
Foundation[d]	O	O	O
Exterior finish materials[e]	O	O	O
Windows and entryways[f]	O	O	M

[a] § 7.70.2.3 Main Entrance of this chapter.
[b] § 7.70.2.4 Garage of this chapter.
[c] § 7.70.2.5 Roofs of this chapter.
[d] § 7.70.2.6 Foundation of this chapter.
[e] § 7.70.2.7 Exterior Finish Materials of this chapter.
[f] § 7.70.2.8 Windows and Entryways of this chapter.

RE = Residential Estate; RP = Resource Protection; NS = Neighborhood Suburban; NU = Neighborhood Urban; D = Downtown; TND = traditional neighborhood development; PD = Planned Development; M = the standard is mandatory; and O = the standard is optional.

(1) Porches shall be covered by a solid roof. The roof shall not be located more than 12 feet above the floor of the porch. If the roof of a required porch is developed as a deck or balcony, it may be flat.

(2) The porch shall have minimum dimensions of 6 feet by 6 feet. For single-family detached dwelling units, the covered area provided by the porch must be at least 48 square feet and a minimum of 8 feet wide. If the main entrance is for more than one dwelling unit, the covered area provided by the porch must be at least 63 square feet and a minimum of 9 feet wide.

(C) *Covered balconies:* The covered area provided by the balcony must be at least 48 square feet, a minimum of 8 feet wide, and no more than 15 feet above grade. The covered balcony must be accessible from the interior living space of the house.

(D) *Openings between porch floor and ground:* Openings of more than 1 foot between the porch floor and the ground must be covered with a solid material or lattice.

7.70.2.4 Garage

(A) *Generally:* A garage wall may not be closer to the street lot line than the front façade elevation.

(B) *Detached garages:* These standards encourage detached garages as an alternative to front-loaded attached garages.

(1) Detached garages are permitted in any zoning district. Detached garages shall be located in the rear yard. The footprint for the garage structure shall not exceed 24 feet by 24 feet. The garage walls shall not exceed 15 feet in height or the height of the principal structure, whichever is less.

(2) A detached garage that is nonconforming due to its location in a setback may be rebuilt on its existing foundation if it was originally constructed legally. An addition may be made to these types of garages if the addition complies with the standards of this section, or if the combined size of the existing foundation and any additions is no larger than 12 feet wide by 18 feet deep. The garage walls may be up to 10 feet high.

(C) *Street-facing garage walls*

(1) *Applicability:* This section applies to garages that are accessory to single-family detached dwelling units, manufactured homes, duplexes, or triplexes. This section does not apply to development on flag lots or development on lots that slope up or down from the street with an average slope of 20 percent.

(2) *Maximum length and size:* The length of that portion of a garage wall facing the street shall not exceed 30 percent of the length of the street-facing building façade. Garage doors may not exceed 75 square feet in area. No more than two individual garage doors are permitted. On corner lots, only one street-facing garage wall must meet this standard. Where the street-facing façade of the building is less than 24 feet long, the garage wall facing the street may be up to 12 feet long if there is one of the following:

(a) Interior living area above the garage; or

(b) A covered balcony above the garage that is at least the same length as the street-facing garage wall, at least 6 feet deep, and accessible from the interior living area of the dwelling unit.

(3) *Street lot line setbacks:* A garage wall that faces a street shall be located at least 20 feet behind the plane of the front façade. A street-facing garage wall may adjoin the front façade or be located within the area described in this subsection, where:

(a) The street-facing garage wall does not exceed 30 percent of the length of the building façade; and

(b) The interior living area is located above the garage. The living area must be set back no more than 4 feet from the street-facing garage wall or shall include a covered balcony above the garage that is at least the same length as the street-facing garage wall, at least 6 feet deep, and accessible from the interior living area of the dwelling unit.

(4) *Street-facing garage walls prohibited in "D" (Downtown) district or TND:* Garage walls facing the street or extending beyond the front elevation of a dwelling unit are prohibited in the "D" (Downtown) district or a TND use pattern or district.

7.70.2.5 Roofs

(A) *Slope:* Principal structures must have a roof that is sloped, with a pitch that is no flatter than six units of horizontal run to 12 units of horizontal rise.

(B) *Architectural features:* The roof of a principal structure shall include the following architectural details:

(1) At least one dormer facing the street. If only one dormer is included, it shall be at least 5 feet wide and shall be centered horizontally between each end of the front elevation. If more than one dormer is provided, a dormer at least 4 feet wide must be provided on each side of the front elevation; or

(2) A gabled end, or a gabled end of a roof projection, facing the street.

(C) *Roof eaves:* Roof eaves must project from the building wall at least 12 inches, measured horizontally, on at least the front and side elevations.

7.70.2.6 Foundation

The ground level of the first floor, including the lowest elevation of any point of the front façade, shall be elevated at least 3 feet from the horizontal surface of the street or sidewalk. Plain concrete block or plain concrete may be used as foundation material if the foundation material is not visible more than 3 feet above the finished grade level adjacent to the foundation wall.

7.70.2.7 Exterior Finish Materials

(A) Plain concrete block, plain concrete, and corrugated metal are not permitted as exterior finish material. Composite boards manufactured from wood or other products, such as hardboard or hardiplank, may be used when the board product is less than 6 inches wide.

(B) Where wood products are used for siding, the siding must be shingles or horizontal siding. Shakes are not permitted.

(C) Where horizontal siding is used, it must be shiplap or clapboard siding composed of boards with a reveal of 3 to 6 inches, or vinyl or aluminum siding that is in a clapboard or shiplap pattern where the boards in the pattern are 6 inches or less in width.

7.70.2.8 Windows and Entryways

(A) At least 15 percent of the area of a street-facing façade must include windows or main entryways.

(B) All street-facing windows must comply with the requirements of this subsection. Windows in rooms with a finished floor height 4 feet or more below grade are exempt from this standard.

(C) Windows on the upper floors shall be vertically oriented, except as provided in subsection (D), below. Windows may be horizontally oriented if they are grouped as provided in subsection (D), below, or if there is a band of individual lites across the top of the horizontal window. The individual lites must be vertically oriented and cover at least 20 percent of the total height of the window.

(D) Windows on the first floor shall be vertically oriented or grouped to provide a horizontal opening. If only two windows are grouped, both must be vertically oriented. Where more than two sizes are grouped, the windows on the outer edges of the grouping must be vertically oriented.

(E) In determining whether a window is vertically oriented as provided in this subsection, the area of the window that includes the panes, mullions, and transoms shall be included, and embellishments, such as shutters, shall be excluded (see Figure 7-5).

7.70.3 Single-Family Dwelling Units

§ 7.4.2 Permitted Uses of this chapter applies to any single-family detached dwelling units. Single-family detached dwellings subject to this section must comply with at least two of the optional standards as set forth in Table 7-10.

7.70.4 Attached Dwellings, Generally

7.70.4.1 Applicability

This section applies to any attached dwelling unit. An "attached dwelling unit" means any duplex, townhouse, or row house.

**Figure 7-5
Window Treatments**

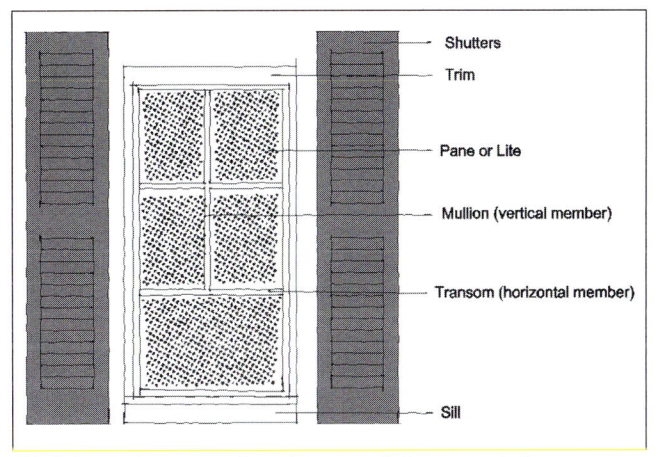

Nothing is too insignificant for good design palettes, although multiple alternatives can be offered.

7.70.4.2 Zoning Dimensional Standards

(A) The minimum lot size regulations apply to a building that contains multiple attached dwelling units but not to each individual dwelling unit.

(B) The side yard regulations of the applicable zoning district do not apply to an attached dwelling unit. However, this section establishes setback requirements where the building abuts single-family residential zoning districts.

7.70.4.3 Building Design

(A) Attached dwellings subject to this section must comply with at least two of the optional standards as set forth in Table 7-10.

(B) Each dwelling unit shall have a ground-floor entrance that faces a public street or common open space.

7.70.5 Two-Family Dwellings (Duplexes)

Duplexes shall conform to § 7.70.5.1 Subdivision through § 7.70.5.3 Lot Design of this chapter.

7.70.5.1 Subdivision

A lot that includes two attached dwelling units may be subdivided or resubdivided through the common wall into separate fee simple lots for each dwelling unit subject to the following requirements:

(A) The two-family dwelling or duplex lot shall be vacated and replatted as provided in Chapter 4, Procedures, of the LDC.

(B) Each single-family lot resulting from the subdivision shall have a minimum lot area of 4,000 square feet and shall be at least 40 feet wide, except in the case of a planned development, TND, or TOD.

(C) Separate utility meters shall be provided to each newly created lot. Separate water and wastewater

**Figure 7-6
Human Versus Auto Design**

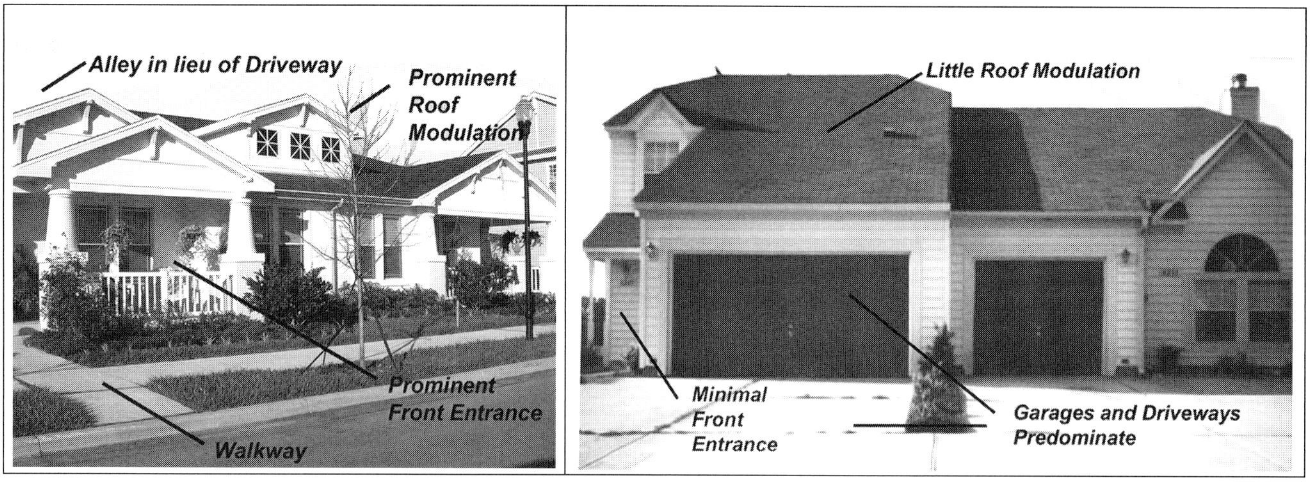

Providing rear alleys enables the home to present itself to the street, which promotes sociability and walkability.

service lines shall be provided to each newly created lot and shall not traverse any other lot. Where common gas and electrical lines are provided to two single-family lots, easements approved by the [SERVICE PROVIDER] shall be provided.

7.70.5.2 Building Design

(A) Garages shall either be detached or shall face the side or rear lot line.

(B) Duplexes shall include at least two of the following architectural elements:

(1) Dormers;

(2) Front porches;

(3) Bay windows;

(4) Balconies; and

(5) Roof details, including chimneys or roof overhangs of at least 16 inches (measured horizontally).

7.70.5.3 Lot Design

(A) Driveways or other paved surfaces shall not comprise more than 50 percent of the front yard. Applicants are encouraged to provide the principal vehicular access from an alley.

(B) Driveways that enter more than one garage shall be separated by a grass or landscaped strip extending at least 75 percent of the length of the driveway and at least 3 feet in width (see Figure 7-6).

7.70.6 Townhouses or Row Houses

Townhouses or row houses shall conform to § 7.70.6.1 Building Design through § 7.70.6.4 Parking of this chapter.

7.70.6.1 Building Design

No more than 10 dwelling units shall be contiguous. No contiguous group of townhouse dwellings shall exceed 150 feet in length.

7.70.6.2 Lot Design

(A) Minimum frontage and lot width for the portion of the lot on which each unit is to be constructed shall be 15 feet. This dimension supersedes any lot width or frontage dimension required by the applicable zoning district.

(B) Interior dwelling units are not subject to the side setback requirements of the zoning district.

(C) Where a lot containing a townhouse or row house abuts a lot containing a single-family detached dwelling unit located in a residential zoning district, the abutting yard shall have a minimum width of 10 feet.

(D) A rear yard is not required when a townhouse/row house lot abuts an alley or driveway having a minimum right-of-way width of 12 feet that is used to provide ingress and egress to the lot. If the lot does not have alley access, a 12-foot rear yard setback is required.

7.70.6.3 Open Area

If the dwelling units do not abut the front lot line, at least 200 square feet of contiguous open area shall be provided behind the front setback. The "contiguous open area" may consist of lawns, landscaped areas, a sidewalk, or a parkway. "Contiguous open area" does not include parking, driveways, or other impervious surfaces other than sidewalks or walkways from the front entrance to the street or parking areas.

7.70.6.4 Parking

Off-street parking facilities may be grouped in bays, either adjacent to streets or in the interior of the lot.

**Figure 7-7
Townhouses**

Good design makes density attractive and unique.

Off-street parking areas shall not be located in the front yard (see Figure 7-7).

7.70.7 Multifamily Housing

Multifamily dwelling units shall conform to § 7.70.7.1 Entryways through § 7.70.7.6 Utilities of this chapter.

7.70.7.1 Entryways

For developments of 40 or more dwelling units, a divided ingress-egress driveway with a landscaped median for all entrances from public streets shall be provided. Median design shall conform to the standards in § 5.23 Street Design and Transportation in Chapter 5, Development Standards, of the LDC.

7.70.7.2 Common Open Space

(A) Common open space areas are required in accordance with § 5.21 Parks/Open Space in Chapter 5, Development Standards, of the LDC. Common open space areas are not required in the "D" (Downtown) district or in a TOD.

(B) The [PLANNING OFFICIAL] may waive up to 50 percent of the open space requirement if all units within the development are located within 1,000 feet of a public park as measured along a public sidewalk. Open space provided pursuant to this requirement shall be accessible to all residents of the development and shall measure at least 30 feet across its narrowest dimension.

7.70.7.3 Private Open Space

Each dwelling unit shall have appurtenant private open space, such as a private porch, a deck, a balcony, a patio, an atrium, or other outdoor private area. The private open space shall be contiguous with the unit in a single area. The private open space shall have the dimensions as described in Table 7-11.

7.70.7.4 Pedestrian Facilities

Sidewalks shall be constructed within the interior of the development to link residential buildings with other destinations, such as, but not limited to, parking, adjoining streets, mailboxes, trash disposal, adjoining sidewalks or greenways, and on-site amenities, such as recreation areas. These interior sidewalks shall be constructed in accordance with the standards for sidewalks in § 5.23 Street Design and Transportation in Chapter 5, Development Standards, of the LDC. Sidewalks shall be provided adjacent to all public streets that provide access to the development.

7.70.7.5 Building Design

The following standards shall apply to building design:

(A) *Building size*

(1) Multifamily buildings shall not exceed 100 feet in length, or 30 percent of the length of the blockface, whichever is less.

(2) A multifamily building or part of a multifamily building that is located within 200 feet of an "NS" (Neighborhood Suburban) district or a single-family dwelling unit in an "NU" (Neighborhood Urban) district shall not exceed the maximum primary or secondary height permitted by that district (see Figure 7-8).

**Table 7-11
Private Open Space**

Number of Dwelling Units in Multifamily Building	Minimum Area (Percent of Dwelling Unit Floor Area)	Minimum Area (Square Feet)	Minimum Depth (Feet)
4 to 6	15%	100	6
6 to 20	10%	60	6
20 or more	10%	48	6

**Figure 7-8
Multifamily Transitional Standards**

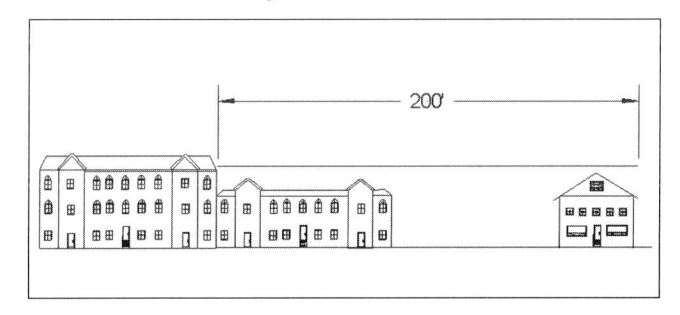

(B) *Orientation:* Multifamily buildings shall be oriented as follows:

(1) For lots not exceeding 30,000 square feet, all multifamily buildings shall be oriented to the street.

(2) For lots that are at least 30,000 square feet, at least 80 percent of the ground area between the front lot line and the maximum setback, excluding required driveways and access points, shall be occupied by multifamily dwelling units that are oriented to the street. The remaining area may include driveways and required access points, or courtyards or similar open spaces.

(C) *Fenestration:* Windows, porches, balconies, and entryways shall comprise at least 30 percent of the length of the front elevation on each floor.

(D) *Articulation/modulation:* Buildings that contain multifamily dwellings shall be articulated as follows:

(1) Multifamily buildings on multiple lots with an average frontage of less than 50 feet in width shall be articulated at intervals consistent with the existing lot lines or the lot lines of the opposing block.

(2) Multifamily buildings on a single or on multiple lots with at least 50 feet of frontage shall be articulated at intervals of not more than 50 feet.

(3) Multifamily buildings that face single-family homes shall be articulated at intervals consistent with the existing lot lines or the lot lines of the opposing block.

(4) The articulation of buildings pursuant to this section shall include at least two of the following:

  (a) Horizontal projections or offsets, such as towers or turrets, which extend at least 5 feet from the front elevation and the height of the building up to the eaves. Projections or offsets shall be at least 3 feet in depth and 8 feet in width;

  (b) Projecting entryways, such as stoops, balconies, porticoes, bay windows, arcades, or porches;

  (c) Changes in roof elevations, roof dormers, hips, or gables; or

  (d) Open balconies that project at least 6 feet from the front building plane (see Figure 7-9).

Figure 7-9
Compatible Multifamily and Single-Family Massing

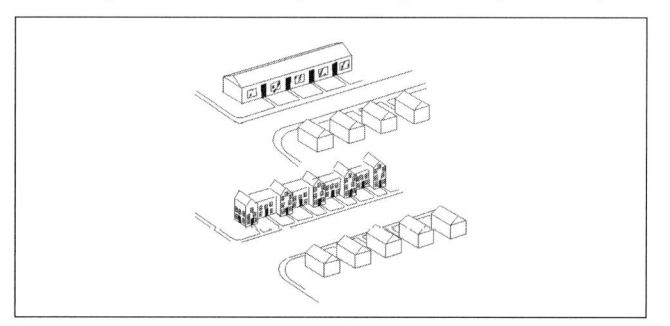

7.70.7.6 Utilities

All utility lines shall be located underground. Outdoor area lighting shall be provided for security. Such lighting shall be shielded to direct light downward and not into dwelling units on or adjacent to the multifamily site. Lighting shall be provided to illuminate the intersections of primary interior driveways and building entryways.

7.70.8 Manufactured Homes

Manufactured homes shall conform to the requirements of § 7.4.2 Permitted Uses and to the standards and criteria defined in § 7.70.8.1 Zoning Standards through § 7.70.8.3 Orientation of this chapter.

7.70.8.1 Zoning Standards

Any manufactured home on an individual lot shall conform to the same building setback standards, side and rear yard requirements, standards for enclosures, access, vehicle parking, and square footage standards and requirements to which a conventional, single-family residential dwelling on the same lot is subject.

7.70.8.2 Foundation

The dwelling shall be attached to a permanent foundation system in compliance with the International Conference of Building Officials, *Guidelines for Manufactured Housing Installation,*[1] as may be amended, and the following requirements:

(A) All wheels, hitches, axles, transporting lights, and removable towing apparatus shall be permanently removed prior to installation of the dwelling unit.

(B) The foundation shall be excavated and shall have continuous skirting or backfill, leaving no uncovered open areas excepting vents and crawl spaces. The foundation shall either not be located above grade or shall include masonry skirting.

(C) All manufactured homes shall be anchored to the ground by means of anchors attached both to the frame and with straps extending over the top and completely surrounding the sides and roof, consistent with building code requirements. In addition, test data giving certified results of pull tests in soils representative of the area in which the anchors are to be used shall be submitted to the [PLANNING OFFICIAL]. Minimum load in direct pull shall be 5,400 pounds. Anchors shall be marked so that, after installation, the identification is in plain view for inspection.

7.70.8.3 Orientation

Manufactured homes that are narrower than 16 feet in width shall be oriented on the lot so that its long axis is parallel to the street.

7.70.9 Cottage Housing Developments

The following regulations apply to cottages and cottage housing developments (CHDs). For purposes of this subsection, a "cottage" means a single-family detached dwelling that meets the requirements of this section, and a "cottage housing development" means a lot, parcel, or contiguous development site on which one or more cottages are located.

7.70.9.1 Density

The permitted density in CHDs is described in Table 7-12.

7.70.9.2 Building Design

(A) The height of dwelling units in a CHD shall not exceed 18 feet or one and one-half stories.

(B) The building footprint of a cottage shall not exceed 1,700 square feet.

(C) The maximum first floor or principal floor area for an individual principal structure in a CHD shall not exceed 800 square feet.

(D) The total floor area of each cottage shall not exceed either one and one-half times the area of the principal floor area, or 975 square feet, whichever is less.

(E) The ridge of pitched roofs with a minimum slope of 6:12 may extend up to 25 feet. All parts of the roof above 18 feet shall be pitched (see Figure 7-10).

7.70.9.3 Lot Coverage

The maximum lot coverage permitted for principal and accessory structures in a CHD shall not exceed 40 percent.

7.70.9.4 Required Open Space

(A) In lieu of the requirements of § 5.21.2 Required Parks/Open Space in Chapter 5, Development Standards, of the LDC, a minimum of 400 square feet per unit of common open space per dwelling unit is required. A fee pursuant to § 5.21.4 Fee in Lieu of Park Development (Optional) in Chapter 5, Development Standards, of the LDC shall not be paid in lieu of this open space.

(B) Each dwelling shall have a principal entryway that opens to the common open space.

(C) All of the cottage units shall be within 60 feet walking distance of the common open space.

(4) The common open space shall have cottages abutting at least two sides.

(5) The open space shall in all other respects conform to the parks and open space standards (*Division 3: Infrastructure Standards* and § 5.21 Parks/Open Space in Chapter 5, Development Standards, of the LDC).

Table 7-12
Attached Dwelling Unit Dimensional Standards

Zoning District	Lot or Parcel Square Footage Per Unit	Dwelling Units Per Acre
"NU" (Neighborhood Urban)	3,300	11
"NS" (Neighborhood Suburban)	4,800	9

7.70.9.5 Parking

(A) The amount of parking spaces shall be as provided in Chapter 5, Development Standards, of the LDC.

(B) Parking may be in or under a structure or outside a structure, provided that:

(1) The parking is screened from direct street view by one or more street façades, by garage doors, or by a fence and landscaping.

(2) Parking between structures is only allowed when it is located to the rear of the principal structure and is served by an alley or private driveway.

(3) Parking may not be located in the front yard or common open space.

(4) Parking may be located between any structure and the rear lot line of the lot or between any structure and a side lot line that is not a street side lot line (see Figure 7-11).

7.70.10 Zero Lot Line

ZLL developments shall conform to the requirements of § 7.4.2 Permitted Uses and to the standards and criteria in § 7.70.10.1 Applicability through § 7.70.10.2 Building Design of this chapter.

Figure 7-10
Cottages

Minimum roof pitch for cottage housing.

**Figure 7-11
Smaller Homes Promote Usable Open Space**

Cottages open onto common open space.

7.70.10.1 Applicability

This section applies to a ZLL development. A "zero lot line development" is any subdivision or site plan in which a single-family detached dwelling unit is sited on a lot in such a manner that one or more of the building's sides rests directly on or immediately adjacent to the lot line.

7.70.10.2 Building Design

(A) The eaves on the side of a house with a reduced setback may project a maximum of 18 inches over the adjacent property line. In this case, an easement for the eave projection shall be recorded on the deed for the lot where the projection occurs.

(B) An easement to allow for maintenance or repair is required when the eaves or side wall of a house are within 4 feet of the adjacent property line. The easement on the adjacent property shall provide at least 5 feet of unobstructed space between the furthermost projection of the structure and be wide enough to allow 5 feet between the eaves or side wall and the edge of the easement.

(C) If the side wall of the house is on the property line, or within 3 feet of the property line, windows or other openings that allow for visibility into the side yard of the adjacent lot are not permitted. Windows that do not allow visibility into the side yard of the adjacent lot, such as a clerestory window or a translucent window, are permitted.

(D) In no case shall the reduced setbacks result in a distance of less than 10 feet between residential structures.

(E) The reduced setbacks shall be denoted on the preliminary subdivision plat and final plat.

7.80 SATELLITE DISH ANTENNAS

7.80.1 Applicability

This section applies to any satellite dish antenna except as follows:

(A) An antenna that is used to receive direct broadcast satellite service, including direct-to-home satellite service, or to receive or transmit fixed wireless signals via satellite, and is 1 meter (3.28 feet) or less in diameter;

(B) An antenna that is:

(1) Used to receive video programming services via multipoint distribution services, including multichannel multipoint distribution services, instructional television fixed services, and local multipoint distribution services, or to receive or transmit fixed wireless signals other than via satellite; and

(2) 1 meter (3.28 feet) or less in diameter or diagonal measurement;

(C) An antenna that is used to receive television broadcast signals;

(D) A mast supporting an antenna described in (A) through (C), above;

(E) A satellite earth station antenna that is 2 meters (6.56 feet) or less in diameter and is located or proposed to be located in any commercial or industrial zoning district;

(F) A satellite earth station antenna that is 1 meter (3.28 feet) or less in diameter in any area, regardless of land use or zoning category.[2]

7.80.2 Location

A satellite dish antenna shall not be located or mounted:

(A) In the required front or side yards in any residential or commercial district; or

(B) On the roof or wall of a building that faces a public right-of-way.

7.80.3 Zoning Certificate

A satellite dish antenna in excess of the dimensions prescribed in § 7.81.1 Applicability of this chapter requires a basic development plan approval.

7.80.4 Screening

Without restricting its operation, a satellite dish antenna located on the ground shall be screened from view from public streets and from adjacent properties.

7.80.5 Height

A satellite dish antenna located on the building roof shall be governed by the regulations for the maximum height of structures of the applicable district.

7.81 SELF-STORAGE FACILITY

Purpose and findings: This section establishes standards to permit the establishment of self-storage facilities, along with standards designed to protect surrounding neighborhoods and to implement the comprehensive plan. This section establishes screening, landscaping, and design standards for self-storage facilities.

7.81.1 Applicability

This section applies to any self-storage facility. A "self-storage facility" is any building or group of buildings that is composed of contiguous individual rooms, which are rented to the public for the storage of personal property and which have independent access and locks under the control of the tenant. This section constitutes the standards for development in the "SSF" (Self-storage Facility) zoning district. Self-storage facilities are the only permitted use in the "SSF" district, subject to the standards established in this section.

7.81.2 Procedures

(A) No self-service storage unit is permitted until the following development approvals and development orders are approved by the reviewing agency:

   (1) The lot or parcel shall be rezoned to the "SSF" (Self-storage Facility) zoning district; and

   (2) A plan of development shall be submitted to the [PLANNING OFFICIAL] indicating location of buildings, lot area, number of storage units, type and size of signs, height of buildings, parking layout with points of ingress and egress, and location and type of visual screening and landscaping being proposed.

(B) An application for rezoning, site plan approval, and any CUP required by § 7.81.2 Procedures of this chapter may be processed concurrently. No site plan shall authorize development or the establishment of a self-storage unit until a rezoning to the "SSF" (Self-storage Facility) zoning district is approved. If the [LOCAL GOVERNMENT] denies an application for rezoning to an "SSF" zoning district, any site plan purporting to authorize the establishment of a self-storage facility shall be null and void.

7.81.3 Standards

(A) The lot size shall be between a minimum of 2 acres and a maximum of 5 acres.

(B) The total area covered by buildings shall not exceed 50 percent of the site.

(C) The maximum height of the building or buildings permitted as of right is 20 feet or one story. Additional height up to four stories is permitted

(D) No outside storage is permitted.

(E) The storage of hazardous, toxic, or explosive substances, including, but not limited to, but excluding the storage of hazardous waste, industrial solid waste, medical waste, municipal solid waste, septage, or used oil, is prohibited.

(F) No business activity other than the rental of storage units shall be conducted on the premises.

(G) One dwelling unit is permitted on the same lot for use as a caretaker dwelling.

(H) A minimum Type B buffer as provided in § 5.31 Buffers and Screening in Chapter 5, Development Standards, of the LDC shall be provided:

   (1) Along the front property line; and

   (2) Along any property line that abuts a residential zoning district.

7.82 SOLID WASTE FACILITIES

7.82.1 Applicability

This section applies to any of the following, which are referred to collectively as "solid waste facilities":

(A) Any "sanitary landfill," which means a facility for disposal of solid waste on land in a sanitary manner in accordance with the rules concerning sanitary landfills adopted under this chapter.

(B) Any "solid waste convenience center," which means a facility that accepts only bagged residential waste and specified recyclable goods. Solid waste convenience centers are permitted in the zones indicated only if:

   (1) The waste does not include waste generated by construction and demolition activities, yard waste, liquid waste, or hazardous waste;

   (2) The facility is enclosed by a buffer (as defined by § 5.30 Greenspace Areas, Generally in Chapter 5, Development Standards, of the LDC) that completely screens from view the operational activity; and

   (3) The facility is aesthetically landscaped to further assure that the facility becomes a more-than-acceptable neighbor for the area in which the facility is designed, constructed, and operated.

(C) "Solid waste transfer station," which means a place or facility where waste materials are taken from smaller collection vehicles (e.g., compactor trucks) and placed in larger transportation vehicles (e.g., over-the-road tractors utilizing trailers that are top-loaded) for movement to designated disposal areas (usually landfills). The stations are usually served by a fleet of over-the-road semitractors and transfer trailers, as well as specialized on-site loading and trailer staging equipment. Solid waste transfer stations may accept only residential; commercial; institutional; and industrial, nonhazardous, solid municipal waste. Solid waste transfer stations are permitted only if the waste taken to the transfer station is stored and transferred entirely within covered buildings.

7.82.2 Standards for Sanitary Landfills

(A) No CUP or, if no CUP is required, zoning clearance development approval, shall be issued for a solid waste facility until all applicable development approvals have been issued by the [STATE ENVIRONMENTAL DEPARTMENT].

(B) A Type D buffer, as provided in § 5.31 Buffers and Screening in Chapter 5, Development Standards, of the LDC, shall be established along street frontages and property boundaries that border residential zoning districts and residential uses. Trees shall be of such height when planted that they shall reach a height of 10 feet in two years.

(C) Only one ground sign per entrance to the storage yard is permitted. Such sign shall not exceed 9 square feet in area. If lighted, such sign may include indirect lighting or nonflashing illumination. Such sign shall be located on the same lot or parcel as the solid waste facility.

(D) New solid waste disposal facilities are prohibited in the 100-year floodplain.

(E) Ingress to and egress from solid waste facilities shall be permitted by roads to serve only the solid waste facilities. Such roads shall be designed and constructed consistent with § 5.23 Street Design and Transportation in Chapter 5, Development Standards, of the LDC, except that sidewalks and street trees are not required. Street design shall allow a weight limit of 19,000 pounds per axle and shall intersect directly with a federal or state maintained road. Approach and departure traffic routes for a solid waste facility shall not be permitted through local streets or any other system of streets primarily intended to provide access to residences in a neighborhood.

(F) A nonclimbable security fence at least 7 feet in height shall be installed around all portions of solid waste facilities directly involved in the storage, handling, and disposal of solid waste.

(G) All buildings or structures used for the storage, treatment, processing, recycling, collection, recovery, or disposal of solid waste shall be located at least 500 feet from any exterior property line when such property line abuts a residential zoning district.

(H) The hours of operation shall be limited from 7:00 AM to 7:00 PM, except that the hours of operation may be extended when the planning department certifies that sanitation conditions require an extension of operating hours.

(I) Municipal solid waste landfills shall be covered in accordance with the [STATE ENVIRONMENTAL REGULATIONS].

(J) Exterior lighting shall not cause illumination in excess of 1 foot candle at any property line, except that internally illuminated signs at the entrance to the landfill may exceed this standard where necessary.

7.82.3 Submittal Requirements

An application for development approval shall include the information submitted to the Department of Environment and Natural Resources for the permitting of a solid waste management facility.

7.90 TEMPORARY USES

7.90.1 Applicability

Authorized temporary commercial uses, including permitted locations, duration, and number per year, and whether a zoning development approval is required, are as set forth in Table 7-13.

7.90.2 Construction Dumpsters

In all districts, the following requirements shall apply:

(A) No construction dumpster may impede pedestrian or vehicular access to and from adjoining properties or otherwise create an unsafe condition for pedestrian and vehicular traffic;

(B) Every construction dumpster shall clearly identify the owner of such dumpster and telephone number and shall be clearly labeled for the purpose of containment of construction materials only; and

(C) Every construction dumpster shall be routinely emptied so it does not create an unsightly or dangerous condition on the property resulting from the deposit, existence, and accumulation of construction materials.

7.90.3 Construction-Related Uses

Temporary buildings, structures, or construction dumpsters are permitted in any district in connection with and on the site of building and land development or redevelopment, including, but not limited to, grading, paving, installation of utilities, and building construction, and such buildings or structures may include offices, construction trailers or construction dumpsters, storage buildings, and signs.

7.90.4 Public Assembly

Temporary buildings, structures, or tents, other than those used in conjunction with [LOCAL GOVERNMENT] functions, those proposed to be used for a period of three business days or less, or those proposed to be used as accessory structures in areas zoned for commercial and industrial uses may be used for public assembly (including carnivals, circuses, and similar events) in any district subject to issuance of a zoning clearance development approval, provided that:

(A) No such building, structure, or tent shall be permitted to remain on site for a consecutive period exceeding one week;

(B) Sufficient space for parking shall be provided on the site to meet the anticipated needs;

Table 7-13
Temporary Uses

Activity	Zoning Districts Where Permitted	Duration	Maximum Number Per Year for Lot or Parcel	Zoning Development Approval Required?
Auctions	Any district	3 days	1	No
Christmas tree sales	RP, commercial or industrial districts	60 days	1	Yes
Office in a model home	Any district	Six months, renewable by the [PLANNING OFFICIAL] for additional periods of not more than six months each	Not applicable	Yes
Fireworks stand	RP, CG	30 days	1	Yes
Outdoor retail sales	CG, CL	10 days	4	Yes, unless expressly shown on development plan
Produce stand or farmers' market (not applicable to permanent farmers' markets in "D" (Downtown) district)	RP	90 days	Not applicable	No
Public assembly, including carnival, circus, festival, show, exhibit, outdoor dance, community fair, concert, or other enterprise of a similar nature	CG, D, IL, IH	1 week	Not applicable	Yes
Yard/garage sales	Any residential district	2 consecutive days, limited to the daylight hours	2, with an interval of at least 3 months between sales	No

RP = Resource Protection; CG = Commercial General; CL = Commercial Large-Scale; IL = Industrial Light; and IH = Industrial Heavy.

(C) Adequate provision shall be made for utility services;

(D) Such facility shall not be used between the hours of 10:00 PM and 10:00 AM; and

(E) No exterior amplifiers, speakers, or other similar equipment shall be permitted outside of the temporary building, structure, or tent.

7.90.5 Yard/Garage Sales

Limited temporary outdoor sales are permitted in residential zoning districts. Yard/garage sales are a permitted use in all residential zoning districts. Items purchased elsewhere expressly for resale at a yard/garage sale are prohibited. Goods intended for sale shall not be stored or displayed in the front or side yards of a dwelling except on the day or days of the sale. Commercial outdoor sales activities are prohibited. For purposes of this section, a "yard/garage sale" means a public sale at a dwelling at which personal items belonging to the residents of the dwelling are sold.

7.91 UTILITIES

7.91.1 Applicability

Notwithstanding other provisions of this chapter, the zoning standards of Chapter 3, Zoning, of the LDC do not apply to the following:

(A) The location of utility lines, poles, and related facilities, other than plants or substations;

(B) The location of necessary drainage lakes, canals, or subgrade facilities that are part of the community drainage system; or

(C) Private borrow pit operations, which, after completion, are to be taken over and owned by the [LOCAL GOVERNMENT] as part of the community drainage system, and are not exempt from any special exception requirement.

7.91.2 Utility Stations and Plants

7.91.2.1 Applicability

This section applies to electric and gas substations, repeater huts, sewage treatment plants, control houses, pressure regulator stations, buildings to house pumps and lift stations, and similar structures.

7.91.2.2 Standards

(A) Structures shall conform to all dimensional and other requirements, except lot area requirements, of the zoning district in which the structures are located.

(B) The design of structures shall conform as closely as possible to the character of the area or neighborhood in which it is located, so that the use and value of adjacent properties will not be adversely affected.

(C) Fences that are not easily climbed and other safety devices shall be installed and maintained around electric and gas substations and sewage treatment plants in order to make the facilities inaccessible to the general public.

(D) A Type D buffer yard shall be installed and maintained in accordance with § 5.31 Buffers and Screening in Chapter 5, Development Standards, of the LDC.

7.92 WIRELESS COMMUNICATIONS FACILITIES

Purpose and findings: The purpose and intent of this section is to:
 • Promote the health, safety, and general welfare of the public by regulating the siting of wireless communications facilities;
 • Minimize the impacts of wireless communications facilities on surrounding areas by establishing standards for location, structural integrity, and compatibility;
 • Encourage the location and collocation of wireless communications equipment on existing structures, thereby minimizing visual, aesthetic, and public safety impacts and effects upon the natural environment and wildlife, and reducing the need for additional antenna supporting structures;
 • Accommodate the growing need and demand for wireless communications services;
 • Encourage coordination between providers of wireless communications services in the [LOCAL GOVERNMENT];
 • Protect the character, scale, stability, and aesthetic quality of the residential districts of the [LOCAL GOVERNMENT] by imposing certain reasonable restrictions on the placement of certain amateur radio facilities;
 • Respond to the policies embodied in the Telecommunications Act of 1996 in such a manner as to not unreasonably discriminate between providers of functionally equivalent personal wireless service or to prohibit or have the effect of prohibiting personal wireless service in the [LOCAL GOVERNMENT];
 • Establish predictable and balanced regulations governing the construction and location of wireless communications facilities within the confines of permissible local regulation;
 • Establish review procedures to ensure that applications for wireless communications facilities are reviewed and acted upon within a reasonable period of time;
 • Provide for the removal of discontinued antenna supporting structures; and
 • Provide for the replacement or removal of nonconforming antenna supporting structures.

7.92.1 Applicability

(A) Except as provided in subsection (B), below, this division will apply to the installation, construction, or modification of the following wireless communications facilities:

(1) Existing and proposed antenna supporting structures;

(2) Replacement antenna supporting structures;

(3) Broadcast antenna supporting structures;

(4) Collocated and combined antennas on existing antenna supporting structures;

(5) Roof-mounted antenna supporting structures;

(6) Surface-mounted antennas;

(7) Stealth wireless communications facilities; and

(8) Amateur radio antennas with an overall height of greater than 50 feet.

(B) The following items are exempt from the provisions of this section:

(1) Amateur radio antenna with an overall height of 50 feet or less; however, any such structure may be developed only in accordance with the provisions of § 7.80 Satellite Dish Antennas of this chapter;

(2) Satellite earth stations; however, satellite earth stations may be developed only in accordance with § 7.80 Satellite Dish Antennas of this chapter;

(3) Regular maintenance of any existing wireless communications facility that does not include the placement of a new wireless communications facility;

(4) Any existing or proposed antenna supporting structure with an overall height of 35 feet or less, except that those proposed within an outer island's future land-use district are not exempt from the provisions of this division;

(5) Any wireless communications facility erected as a temporary use and that receives a temporary use permit pursuant to the provisions of § 7.90 Temporary Uses of this chapter;

(6) Any wireless communications facility that is not visible from the exterior of the building or structure in which it is mounted; and

(7) Wireless communications facilities erected upon the declaration of a state of emergency by a federal, state, or [LOCAL GOVERNMENT]. However, no wireless communications facility will be exempt pursuant to this paragraph unless a written determination of public necessity for the facility is made by the [PUBLIC SAFETY OFFICIAL] and submitted to the [PLANNING OFFICIAL]. No wireless communications facility will be exempt from the provisions of this division beyond the duration of the state of emergency, and such facility must be removed or approved pursuant to this division within 90 days of the termination of the state of emergency.

7.92.2 Development Review and Permitted Uses

(A) Except as provided in subsections (B) through (D), below, no wireless communications facility is permitted except in accordance with the development review process as indicated in Table 7-14, based on the applicable zoning district and height of the proposed facility. Regardless of the development review process required, the applicant must comply with all applicable submission, procedural, and substantive provisions of the LDC.

(B) Broadcast antenna supporting structures are only permitted within the "RP" (Resource Protection) zoning district. However, broadcast studios are not allowed in the "RP" district.

(C) All collocations and roof- and surface-mounted facilities are subject to administrative approval as set forth in § 7.92.3 Development Review Process of this chapter.

(D) Within the outer island future land-use districts, wireless communications facilities will be allowed only as a CUP.

7.92.3 Development Review Process

7.92.3.1 Administrative Approval

Where, pursuant to § 7.92.2 Development Review and Permitted Uses of this chapter, administrative review is required, the application will be reviewed for compliance with this chapter by the [PLANNING OFFICIAL], who will render a final decision of approval, denial, or approval with conditions. Within 30 days of the [PLANNING OFFICIAL]'s decision, appeal may be made to the hearing officer pursuant to Chapter 4, Procedures, of the LDC.

When circumstances so warrant, the [PLANNING OFFICIAL] may determine that administrative approval is not appropriate and that the applicant must instead apply for a CUP. Such circumstances may include the complexity of technical issues involved, previous denials of similar wireless communications facilities in the vicinity of the one proposed, significant public opposition to the proposed facility, the presence of environmentally sensitive lands on or near the proposed facility, and similar circumstances.

7.92.3.2 Conditional Use Permit

Where, pursuant to § 7.92.2 Development Review and Permitted Uses of this chapter, a CUP is required, the application will be reviewed as provided in Chapter 4, Procedures, of the LDC and this section. If the CUP is not approved, approved with conditions, or denied within 30 days after the submittal of a complete application, the application shall be deemed approved. The applicant may agree to an extension of this time limit. Within 30 days of the decision, an appeal may be made to the hearing officer.

Table 7-14
Telecommunications Facility Height and Procedures

Zoning Districts	36 to 50 Feet	51 to 75 Feet	76 to 100 Feet	100 or More Feet
"RP" (Resource Protection) "RE" (Residential Estate)	Zoning certificate	Conditional use permit (CUP)	CUP	CUP
"AO" (Airport Overlay)	Zoning certificate	Zoning certificate	CUP	Prohibited
"CN" (Commercial Neighborhood) "CG" (Commercial General) "CL" (Commercial Large-Scale) "D" (Downtown)	Zoning certificate	Zoning certificate	CUP	Prohibited
"IL" (Industrial Light) "IH" (Industrial Heavy)	Zoning certificate	Zoning certificate	CUP	CUP
"NS" (Neighborhood Suburban) "NU" (Neighborhood Urban) "PD" (Planned Development) "MX" (Mixed Use)	Zoning certificate	CUP	CUP	Prohibited

Table 7-15
Telecommunications Facility
Submittal Requirements

Antenna Supporting	Collocations	Roof-Mounted	Surface-Mounted	Stealth Facilities	Required Submissions
✓	✓	✓	✓	✓	A complete application on a form provided by the department
✓	✓	✓	✓	✓	A signed statement from the facility's owner or owner's agent stating that the radio frequency emissions comply with Federal Communications Commission (FCC) standards for such emissions [†]
✓	✓	✓	✓	✓	Proof that the proposed wireless communications facility has been designed to withstand sustained winds of 110 mph and a 15-second wind gust of 130 mph
✓	—	✓	—	✓	Proof that the proposed antenna supporting structure has been designed so that, in the event of structural failure, the facility will collapse within the boundaries of the lot on which it is located
✓	—	—	—	✓	A license (and for broadcast structures, a construction development approval) issued by the FCC to transmit radio signals in the [LOCAL GOVERNMENT]
✓	✓	—	—	—	The name, address, and telephone contact information for the owner of any proposed or existing antenna supporting structure, and a statement that such information will be updated annually or upon a change of ownership after the application is approved
✓	—	✓	—	✓	A statement of the height above sea level of the highest point of the proposed facility
✓	✓	—	—	✓	A stamped or sealed structural analysis of the proposed wireless communications facility prepared by a professional engineer, indicating the proposed and future loading capacity of the facility
✓	—	—	—	✓	One original and two copies of a survey of the lot completed by a registered land surveyor that shows all existing uses, structures, and improvements
✓	—	—	—	✓	Photo-simulated postconstruction renderings of the proposed wireless communications facility, equipment enclosures, and ancillary appurtenances as they would look after construction from locations to be determined by the participants during the required preapplication conference
✓	—	✓	—	✓	Proof of Federal Aviation Administration compliance with Subpart C of the Federal Aviation Regulations Part 77, "Objects Affecting Navigable Airspace"
✓	—	✓	✓	✓	Shared use plan
✓	—	—	—	✓	If required by the United States Fish and Wildlife Service, a letter indicating that the proposed antenna supporting structure and appurtenances are in compliance with all applicable federal rules and regulations
✓	✓	✓	✓	✓	Existing wireless communications facilities to which the proposed facility will be a hand-off candidate, including latitude, longitude, and power levels of each
✓	✓	✓	✓	✓	A graphical representation, and an accompanying statement, of the coverage area planned for the cell to be served by the proposed facility
✓	✓	✓	✓	✓	A graphical representation, and an accompanying statement, of the search area used to locate the proposed facility
✓	✓	✓	✓	✓	A radio frequency plot indicating the coverage of existing wireless communications sites, and that of the proposed site sufficient to demonstrate geographic search area, coverage prediction, and design radius
✓	—	✓	—	✓	A statement by a qualified professional engineer specifying the design structural failure modes of the proposed facility
✓	✓	✓	✓	✓	Antenna heights and power levels of the proposed facility and all other facilities on the subject property

[†] *The letter of consent will be issued unless the airport authority documents air obstruction hazards that would be created by the proposed facility.*

7.92.3.3 Final Decision

Any decision by the [GOVERNING ENTITY] to deny an application for a proposed wireless communications facility must be in writing and supported by substantial evidence contained in a written record.

7.92.4 Submission Requirements

(A) In addition to the submissions required for a zoning certificate, the requirements as indicated in Table 7-15 must be provided with an application for any wireless communications facility. The application must be signed by the property owner, the applicant, and a provider who will be placing antennas on the proposed wireless communications facility.

(B) The [PLANNING OFFICIAL] may modify the submission requirements where it is determined that certain information is not required or useful in determining compliance with the provisions of the LDC. A decision to modify certain submission requirements must be in writing and made a part of the application file.

(C) If the property owner is not a provider, the application must include a copy of an executed lease agreement between the applicant or property owner and a provider, or, where no lease agreement has been executed, an affidavit signed by a carrier attesting to an intent to place antennas on the wireless communications facility if the application is approved.

7.92.5 Standards

The standards for the establishment of all proposed wireless communications facilities are as indicated by type of facility in § 7.92.6 Antenna Supporting Structures through § 7.92.10 Stealth Wireless Communications Facilities of this chapter. Where overall height requirements set forth in § 7.92 Wireless Communications Facilities of this chapter conflict with those set forth in the applicable zoning district, those set forth in § 7.92 Wireless Communications Facilities of this chapter govern.

7.92.6 Antenna Supporting Structures

7.92.6.1 Setbacks

(A) Antenna supporting structures, equipment enclosures, and ancillary appurtenances must meet the minimum setback requirements for the zoning district in which they are proposed.

(B) Antenna supporting structures must be set back a distance equal to their overall height from the lot line of any lot that contains a residential use or that is within a residential zoning district; however, guy-wire anchors need only comply with the provisions of subsection (A), above.

(C) If more than one of the above setback requirements applies to an antenna supporting structure, the more restrictive requirement will govern.

In accordance with the development review process set forth in § 7.92.3 Development Review Process of this chapter, setback requirements for replacement antenna supporting structures may be reduced by an amount not to exceed 50 percent of that required by this chapter, but in no case may a replacement structure be placed any closer to a lot line than the antenna supporting structure it is replacing. No waiver will be granted pursuant to this paragraph unless the applicant demonstrates that the existing structure cannot be replaced in compliance with this chapter without a waiver.

7.92.6.2 Height

(A) The overall height of any antenna supporting structure may not exceed 149 feet, except as provided in subsections (B)(1) and (B)(2), below.

(B) Proposed broadcast antenna supporting structures that have received a construction development approval from the Federal Communications Commission may be constructed in accordance with the following:

(1) AM broadcast antenna supporting structures may not exceed 250 feet in overall height; and

(2) Except as provided in subsection (1), above, the overall height of a broadcast antenna supporting structure may not exceed 500 feet.

(C) Within the outer island's future land-use districts, no antenna supporting structure may exceed 35 feet in overall height.

7.92.6.3 Construction

Antenna supporting structures must have a monopole-type construction only, except as follows:

(A) Broadcast structures with an overall height of greater than 200 feet may have a lattice-type construction;

(B) Amateur radio antennas may have a monopole-, lattice-, or guyed-type construction; and

(C) AM broadcast antenna supporting structures may have a monopole or lattice-type construction.

7.92.6.4 Location and Placement

Within the density reduction/groundwater resource future land-use districts, wireless communications facilities will be allowed only on existing utility poles within a right-of-way or ingress/egress or access easement.

7.92.6.5 Lighting

(A) No lights, signals, or other illumination will be permitted on any antenna supporting structure or ancillary appurtenances unless the applicant demonstrates that lighting is required by the Federal Aviation Administration (FAA) or the Federal Communications Commission (FCC).

(B) Site lighting may be placed in association with an approved equipment enclosure but must be shielded to prevent light trespass. Site lighting must remain unlit except when authorized personnel are present.

7.92.6.6 Intensity Requirements

The floor area for a wireless communications facility will be calculated based on the total square footage of all equipment enclosures associated with the facility.

7.92.6.7 Accommodation of Future Collocations

(A) Antenna supporting structures must be designed to accommodate future collocations. The exact amount of additional equipment to be accommodated will be agreed upon during the preapplication conference.

(B) As a condition of approval under this chapter, the applicant must submit a shared use plan that commits the owner of the proposed antenna supporting structure to accommodate future collocations where reasonable and feasible in light of the criteria set forth in this section.

7.92.6.8 Proliferation Minimized

(A) *Generally:* No antenna supporting structure will be permitted unless the applicant demonstrates that the proposed antenna cannot be accommodated on an existing building or structure or by construction of a stealth facility.

(B) *Letters of coordination:* The applicant must provide documentation that the following notice was mailed, via certified mail, to all providers or, where applicable, to owners of existing antenna supporting structures, and that the applicant was unable to secure a lease agreement with a provider to allow the placement of the proposed antennas on an existing structure or building within the geographic search area:

> Pursuant to the requirements of the Land Development Code, [NAME OF APPLICANT] is providing you with notice of our intent to meet with the [DEPARTMENT] in a preapplication conference to discuss the location of a free-standing wireless communications facility to be located at [LOCATION]. We plan to construct an antenna supporting structure of [NUMBER OF] feet in height for the purpose of providing [TYPE OF WIRELESS SERVICE]. Please inform the [GOVERNING ENTITY] and us if either of the following applies:
>
> (A) You intend to place additional wireless communications facilities within 2 miles of our proposed facility; or
>
> (B) You know of an existing building or structure that might accommodate the antennas associated with our proposed facility.
>
> Please provide us with this information within 10 days following the receipt of this letter.
>
> Sincerely,
> [APPLICANT, WIRELESS PROVIDER]

The department will maintain a list of known service providers and owners. Letters of coordination must be mailed at least 15 days prior to the preapplication conference required by this section and must request a response from the recipient within 10 days of receipt.

(C) *Siting priorities:* In order to justify the construction of an antenna supporting structure, the applicant must demonstrate that higher-ranking alternatives in the following hierarchy, beginning with subsection (1), below, do not constitute feasible alternatives. Such demonstration must be made by submission of a statement of position, qualifications, and experience by a licensed radio frequency engineer. with the following facilities:

(1) Collocated or combined antennas;
(2) Surface-mounted antennas;
(3) Roof-mounted antenna supporting facility; and
(4) Stealth wireless communications facility.

(D) *Additional evidence:* As appropriate, the following evidence may also be submitted to demonstrate compliance with this section:

(1) That no existing wireless communications facility within the geographic search area meets the applicant's radio frequency engineering or height requirements;

(2) That no building or structure within the geographic search area has sufficient structural strength to support the applicant's proposed antennas; or

(3) That there are other limiting factors that render collocated, surface-mounted, roof-mounted, or stealth facilities unsuitable or unreasonable.

7.92.6.9 Color

Antenna supporting structures and ancillary appurtenances, including transmission lines, must maintain a galvanized grey finish or other contextual or compatible color as determined by the [LOCAL GOVERNMENT], except as otherwise required by the FAA or the FCC.

7.92.6.10 Fencing

A fence of at least 8 feet in height from finished grade must be installed in order to enclose the base of the antenna supporting structure and associated equipment enclosures. Access to the antenna supporting structure must be controlled by a locked gate. The fence must be constructed in accordance with § 5.14 Fences and Walls in Chapter 5, Development Standards, of the LDC, except that barbed wire construction will be allowed at the discretion of the applicant.

7.92.6.11 Landscaping

(A) A landscaped buffer of at least 10 feet in width must be planted along the entire exterior perimeter of the fence or wall as required by § 7.92.6.9 Color of this chapter. Where the proposed antenna supporting structure will be located adjacent to a residential or public recreational use, or a lot within a residential zoning district, a landscaped buffer of at least 15 feet must be planted.

(B) A buffer required by this section must contain at least one row of native vegetation and form a continuous hedge at least 3 feet in height at planting and maintained at 6 feet.

7.92.6.12 Signage

(A) No signs may be placed on antenna supporting structures, ancillary appurtenances, equipment enclosures, or on any fence or wall required by this section.

(B) If high voltage is necessary for the operation of proposed wireless communications facilities, "High Voltage—Danger" and "No Trespass" warning signs not greater than 1 square foot in area must be permanently attached to the fence or wall at intervals of at least 40 feet and upon the access gate.

(C) A sign not greater than 1 square foot in area must be attached to the access gate that indicates the following information:

(1) Federal registration number, if applicable;
(2) Name of owner or contact person; and
(3) Emergency contact number.

7.92.6.13 Private Aircraft and Helicopter Landing Facilities

Antenna supporting structures proposed within a designated notification height boundary of a private aircraft or helicopter landing facility, as specified on the Airspace Notification Map, will be limited to the height specified, based on the proposed facility's distance from the runway or landing facility.

7.92.6.14 Visual Impacts Minimized

(A) *Generally:* Antennas must be configured on antenna supporting structures in a manner that is consistent with the character of the surrounding community and that minimizes adverse visual impacts on adjacent properties.

(B) *Antenna-type priorities:* In order to justify the use of an antenna type lower in the hierarchy in subsection (1), below, the applicant must adequately demonstrate that higher-ranked alternatives in the following hierarchy, beginning with subsection (1), below, cannot be used. Such demonstration must be made by submission of a statement of position, qualifications, and experience by a licensed radio frequency engineer familiar with the following features:

(1) Flush-mounted;
(2) Panel;
(3) Whip; and
(4) Dish.

7.92.6.15 District Impacts Minimized

(A) *Generally:* Antenna supporting structures must be located in a manner that is consistent with the [LOCAL GOVERNMENT]'s interest in land-use compatibility, with and between zoning districts, as set forth in Chapter 6, Adequate Public Facilities, of the LDC.

(B) *Zoning district priorities:* In order to justify locating a proposed antenna supporting structure within a zoning district lower in the hierarchy in subsection (1), below, the applicant must adequately demonstrate that siting alternatives within higher-ranked districts, beginning with subsection (1), below, are not reasonable or feasible. Such demonstration must be made by submission of a statement of position, qualifications, and experience by a licensed radio frequency engineer.

(1) Industrial;
(2) Commercial;
(3) Residential; and
(4) Airport overlay.

7.92.6.16 Preapplication Conference

(A) Prior to submitting an application for an antenna supporting structure, the applicant must request in writing a preapplication conference with the [PLANNING OFFICIAL]. The purpose of the preapplication conference is to acquaint the participants with the applicable requirements of this chapter, as well as any preliminary concerns of the department. This provision is not applicable to replacement antenna supporting structures.

(B) Among the matters to be addressed at the preapplication conference are:

(1) The ability of the proposed antenna supporting structure to accommodate future collocations;
(2) Alternative locations or facility configurations that may result in reduced impacts on adjacent properties and the surrounding community;
(3) Compatible colors for the proposed facility;
(4) The vantage points from which required photo-simulated, postconstruction renderings must be oriented;
(5) The need for any variance or deviation from the provisions of this chapter; and
(6) The expected date of application submission and a preliminary schedule for development review.

(C) The applicant's written request for a preapplication conference must include the following information with regard to the proposed facility:

(1) Location;
(2) Overall height;
(3) Number of antennas proposed, including those of other providers;
(4) Type or types of wireless communications to be provided; and
(5) Proof that the letters of coordination were mailed as required by § 7.92.6.7 Accommodation of Future Collocations of this chapter.

7.92.7 Collocations

(A) *Height:* Collocations may not increase the overall height of an antenna supporting structure.

(B) *Visual impact minimized:* Collocations will be approved only in accordance with the visual impact requirements and hierarchy set forth at § 7.92.6.13 Private Aircraft and Helicopter Landing Facilities of this chapter.

(C) *Color:* All collocated antennas and ancillary appurtenances must maintain a galvanized grey finish or other contextual color that is compatible with the environment or the building to which they are attached.

7.92.8 Roof-Mounted Antenna Supporting Structure

(A) *Location and placement:* Roof-mounted antennas may be placed only on commercial, institutional, industrial, and multifamily buildings at least 35 feet in height.

(B) *Height*

(1) The roof-mounted antenna, attachment device, equipment enclosure, and/or any ancillary appurtenance may not extend above the roof line of the building upon which it is attached by more than 20 feet.

(2) Roof-mounted wireless structures with an overall height of greater than 50 feet are considered antenna supporting structures subject to § 7.92.5 Standards of this chapter.

(C) *Construction:* Roof-mounted structures must have a monopole-type construction.

(D) *Visual impact minimized:* Roof-mounted structures will be approved only in accordance with the visual impact requirements and hierarchy set forth at § 7.92.6.13 Private Aircraft and Helicopter Landing Facilities of this chapter.

(E) *Color:* Roof-mounted structures, ancillary appurtenances, and equipment enclosures must maintain a galvanized grey finish or other contextual color that is compatible with the environment or the building to which they are attached.

(F) *Signage:* No signs may be placed on any roof-mounted structure, ancillary appurtenances, or equipment enclosures.

(G) *Screening and placement*

(1) Roof-mounted structures must be screened by a parapet or other device in order to minimize their visual impact as measured from the lot line of the subject property. Roof-mounted facilities must be placed as near the center of the roof as possible.

(2) Transmission lines placed on the exterior of a building must be camouflaged or otherwise shielded within an appropriate material that is the same color as, or a color consistent with, the building to which they are attached.

(H) *Private aircraft and helicopter landing facilities:* Roof-mounted antenna supporting structures proposed within a designated notification height boundary of a private aircraft or helicopter landing facility, as specified on the Airspace Notification Map, will be limited to the height specified, based on the proposed facility's distance from the runway or landing facility.

7.92.9 Surface-Mounted Antennas

(A) *Color:* Surface-mounted antennas and associated ancillary appurtenances must maintain a color that is the same as the surface to which they are attached, unless another color is more compatible within the context of the proposed facility and the surrounding environment.

(B) *Screening and placement*

(1) Surface-mounted antennas must be placed no less than 15 feet from the ground and, where proposed for placement on a building, must be placed so that no portion of the antenna is less than 3 feet below the roof line.

(2) Transmission lines must be camouflaged or otherwise shielded within an appropriate material that is the same color as, or a color consistent with, the building or structure to which they are attached.

(C) *Visual impact minimized:* Surface-mounted antennas will be approved only in accordance with the visual impact requirements and hierarchy set forth at § 7.92.6.13 Private Aircraft and Helicopter Landing Facilities of this chapter.

7.92.10 Stealth Wireless Communications Facilities

(A) *Setbacks*

(1) Stealth wireless communications facilities, ancillary appurtenances, and equipment enclosures must meet the minimum setback requirements for the zoning district in which they are proposed.

(2) In accordance with the development review process set forth in § 7.92.3 Development Review Process of this chapter, setback requirements for stealth facilities may be reduced if it is determined that such a waiver is necessary to reduce the visual impact or enhance the compatibility of the proposed facility on adjacent properties and the surrounding community.

(B) *Height:* The overall height of a proposed stealth facility must be limited to that which is consistent with the scale and aesthetic qualities of the proposed facility, and to that which blends and is consistent with the character of the surrounding community. However, in no case may the overall height of any stealth facility exceed 149 feet.

(C) *Aesthetics:* No stealth facility may have antennas or ancillary equipment that is readily identifiable from the public domain as wireless communications equipment. Stealth facilities must be designed so they are reasonably consistent with the surrounding built or natural environment. In order to determine compliance with this requirement, the [LOCAL GOVERNMENT] will consider the following criteria:

(1) Overall height;

(2) The compatibility of the proposed facility with surrounding built and nature features;

(3) Scale;

(4) Color;

(5) The extent to which the proposed facility blends with the surrounding environment;

(6) The extent to which the proposed facility has been designed to reasonably replicate a nonwireless facility (e.g., a silo, flagpole, or tree); and

(7) The extent to which the proposed facility is not readily identifiable as a wireless communications facility.

(D) *Private aircraft and helicopter landing facilities:* Stealth wireless communications facilities proposed within a designated notification height boundary of a private aircraft or helicopter landing facility, as specified on the Airspace Notification Map, will be limited to the height specified, based on the proposed facility's distance from the runway or landing facility.

7.92.11 Expert Review

(A) Due to the complexity of the methodology or analysis required to review an application for a wireless communications facility, the [PLANNING OFFICIAL] may require a technical review by a third-party expert, the costs of which are to be borne by the applicant.

(B) The expert review may address the following:

(1) The accuracy and completeness of submissions;

(2) The applicability of analysis techniques and methodologies;

(3) The validity of conclusions reached;

(4) Whether the proposed wireless communications facility complies with the applicable approval criteria set forth in this chapter; and

(5) Other matters deemed by the [PLANNING OFFICIAL] to be relevant in determining whether a proposed wireless communications facility complies with the provisions of this division.

(C) Based on the results of the expert review, the [PLANNING OFFICIAL] may require changes to the applicant's application or required submissions.

(D) The applicant must reimburse the [LOCAL GOVERNMENT] within 10 working days of the date of receipt of an invoice for expenses associated with the third-party expert's review of the application. Failure by the applicant to make reimbursement pursuant to this section will abate the pending application until payment in full is received by the [LOCAL GOVERNMENT].

7.92.12 Discontinuance

(A) *Notice of discontinuance:* In the event that all legally approved use of an antenna supporting structure or antenna has been discontinued for a period of 180 days, the [PLANNING OFFICIAL] may make a preliminary determination of discontinuance. In making such a determination, the [PLANNING OFFICIAL] may request documentation and/or affidavits from the property owner regarding the structure's usage, including evidence that use of the structure is imminent. Failure on the part of a property owner to provide updated contact information for the owner of the antenna supporting structure for four consecutive years will be presumptive evidence of discontinuance. At such time as the [PLANNING OFFICIAL] reasonably determines that an antenna supporting structure or antenna has been discontinued, the [PLANNING OFFICIAL] will provide the property owner with a written notice of discontinuance by certified mail.

(B) *Declaration of discontinuance:* Failure on the part of the property owner to respond to the notice of discontinuance within 90 days, or to adequately demonstrate that the structure is not discontinued, will be evidence of discontinuance. Based on the foregoing, or on any other relevant evidence before the [PLANNING OFFICIAL], the [PLANNING OFFICIAL] may make a final determination of discontinuance, whereupon a declaration of discontinuance will be issued to the property owner by certified mail.

(C) *Removal of facility:* Within 120 days of a declaration of discontinuance, the property owner must either:

(1) Reactivate the use of the structure as a wireless communications facility or transfer ownership of the structure to another owner who will make such use of the facility; or

(2) Dismantle and remove the facility.

If the facility remains discontinued upon the expiration of 120 days, the [LOCAL GOVERNMENT] may enter upon the property and remove the facility, with all costs to be borne by the property owner.

7.92.13 Nonconforming Antenna Supporting Structures

Within 10 years of its effective date, antenna supporting structures made nonconforming by implementation of this ordinance must comply with the provisions of this chapter or must be removed. However, the [GOVERNING ENTITY] may extend the time period for compliance or removal where the property owner demonstrates that the requirements of this section impose an unreasonable burden on the ability of a provider to provide personal wireless services or to otherwise comply with federal regulations.

7.92.14 Variances—Additional Criteria

No variance will be granted to the provisions of this division unless the hearing officer makes one of the following findings of fact:

(A) That failure to grant the variance would prohibit or have the effect of prohibiting the provision of personal wireless services;

(B) That failure to grant the variance would unreasonably discriminate among providers of functionally equivalent personal wireless services;

(C) That the variance will obviate the need for additional antenna supporting structures;

(D) That the variance is necessary to ensure adequate public safety and emergency management communications; or

(E) That the variance is the minimum necessary in order for the applicant to provide broadcast services pursuant to an FCC-issued construction development approval.

7.92.15 Signs

Insert the [LOCAL GOVERNMENT] code provisions.

7.92.16 Satellite Antennas

Insert your city's code provisions.

7.92.17 Adult-oriented Uses

Insert your city's code provisions.

7.92.18 Flood Controls

Insert your city's code provisions.

7.92.19 Affordable Dwelling Units/ Inclusionary Zoning

Insert your city's code provisions (see § 7.32 Inclusionary Zoning/ Affordable Dwelling Units in this chapter).

COMMENTARY

Many uses, by their nature, pose special compatibility or health and safety problems if permitted on an unrestricted basis. Accordingly, most zoning ordinances prescribe special standards for such uses. These uses fall into several categories. The first category are those uses that create special neighborhood compatibility or environmental problems. The second category are those uses with special needs that require different dimensional requirements than what is normally required in the district (see Figure 7-12). Some codes place supplemental use regulations in a separate chapter, while others include them with zoning. They are left with zoning in the LDC because they relate primarily to the use of zoning powers. However, either approach is valid.

The number of uses that could be included in this section of the LDC is nearly infinite, each of which could be the subject of an entirely separate code. The LDC includes a number of uses that are found in most land-use regulations or that are representative of typical local land-use issues. In the interest of brevity, some uses are not included in this chapter but are found in the supplemental use regulations of many zoning ordinances. These include:

- *Adult uses:* The regulation of adult uses raises serious First Amendment issues. These regulations require specific findings of the "secondary impacts" of adult businesses, including reductions in property values and crime. Clear nondiscretionary standards are required. The permitting procedures must expressly indicate a date certain for issuance of any development approvals. Since these factors are quite excessively detailed, they are omitted from the LDC.

**Figure 7-12
Design Standards**

Appropriate design standards can minimize use conflicts, as with this body shop near Fort Sam Houston (San Antonio, Texas).

- *Flood controls:* Flood controls trigger important federal regulations and insurance requirements under the aegis of the Federal Emergency Management Agency (FEMA). Standardized flood control provisions are available from FEMA.
- *Signs:* Sign regulations also trigger First Amendment requirements. Some communities regulate signs in their zoning ordinances, while others include them in other chapters or articles of the local code or as a separate chapter of their land development regulations. Readers interested in more detail on sign regulations, including model ordinances, can consult several excellent publications by the American Planning Association (APA).[3] Since these publications are dated and the law is in a continuous state of flux, future editions of the LDC may include sign regulations.
- *Affordable dwelling units/inclusionary zoning:* There is growing interest in the use of land-use regulations to encourage or require developers to provide affordable housing. This important topic is covered adequately in other publications[4] and is not addressed here.
- *Religious land uses:* These include churches, synagogues, parish houses, Sunday school buildings, and convents. For legal reasons, the LDC treats these uses as it would any other commercial or institutional use (see "Religious Institutions," below).
- *Satellite antennas:* The FCC has established limited federal preemption of satellite dishes. There are two sets of regulations. The first covers dishes 1 meter or less in diameter along with supporting masts, and the second addresses dishes 1 to 2 meters. There are no federal regulations to date governing dishes exceeding 2 meters.[5] Readers can consult the FCC's model ordinance. Readers interested in supplemental use regulations that are not included in the LDC can refer to past issues of the APA's *Zoning News, Zoning Practice,* or Planning Advisory Service Reports for examples of regulatory issues and local ordinance language.

ACCESSORY USES

Most zoning regulations permit uses that are "customarily incidental" to principal uses on the same property in zoning district regulations.[6] While most courts have upheld this standard, a few have ruled it excessively vague and have demanded greater specificity as to the types of uses that are considered incidental to principal uses.[7] The LDC adds more specificity than is usually found in local accessory use regulations without attempting to recite every conceivable use that could be established.

The LDC does not attempt to enumerate every type of accessory use. Some zoning regulations address commercial vehicles, cargo containers (such as the popular "Portable on Demand Storage" units), and similar items in residential neighborhoods. The LDC leaves the regulation of these types of issues to local property maintenance codes, reserving the planning department functions for true development code issues.

ACCESSORY DWELLING UNITS

Accessory apartments, or "granny flats," are generally excluded from single-family residential districts.[8] Several states, however, authorize the establishment of accessory uses in single-family districts as a mechanism to encourage the production of affordable housing.[9] For instance, the New Jersey Council on Affordable Housing regulations authorize local governments to zone for accessory apartment units.[10] Local governments that participate in the substantive certification program may fulfill a limited portion of their regional fair share obligations through accessory apartments. California authorizes local governments to designate areas in single- and multifamily residential zones in which accessory dwelling units may be permitted.[11]

While local governments may condition accessory units on the adequacy of water, sewer, and roadway facilities, they are not subject to residential growth control programs. Local governments may develop standards pertaining to parking, height, setback, lot coverage, architectural review, and maximum unit size in the accessory unit ordinance. Accessory units must be approved in accordance with statutory standards if an ordinance has not been adopted. Special use permits, CUPs, or variances may also be granted for accessory units intended for occupancy by up to two adults who are 55 years of age or older. The accessory housing portion of the LDC focuses on the design and placement of the dwelling unit.

Through contextual design and proper placement, accessory dwellings can be integrated into most residential areas, including single-family areas. This allows for a greater variety of housing choices, more family living options, and a possible source of income.

EXCAVATION ACTIVITIES AND SUBSTANTIAL LAND ALTERATION

This section of the LDC imposes site location, environmental, and discretionary review criteria for extractive uses. Some states have approved site location ordinances that are not based on zoning authority.[12]

AUTO-ORIENTED DEVELOPMENT

America's dependence on vehicular travel has contributed to a proliferation of gas stations in many cities. The gas station has evolved from small-scale, neighborhood serving uses to a wide variety of ancillary uses,[13] including:

• Car care centers, which provide automobile repair, muffler installation, brake repair, oil change, tune-up, and car wash facilities; and

• Convenience stores, where groceries are sold as well as gasoline.

In fact, "Gasoline Stations with Convenience Stores" and "Other Gasoline Stations" have separate NAICS classifications.

Street corners that were formerly occupied by storefronts are now the domain of canopies, gasoline pumps, parking, and other uses incidental to gasoline and service stations. While concerns originally arose from the environmental and safety impacts of gasoline pumps, many cities now recognize their impact on urban form and design as well. While gasoline stations are a necessary use, many local governments want to control their location and design in order to blend them more effectively into urban and suburban locations.

There are several approaches to controlling auto-oriented development:

• *Districting:* Auto-dependent uses are sometimes excluded from "main street" or neighborhood locations, such as neighborhood commercial districts.

• *Spacing controls:* Zoning ordinances can establish distancing requirements for auto-dependent uses, dispersing them to avoid inundating certain neighborhoods with a use that generates heavy traffic and may be perceived as undesirable.

• *Design controls:* Cities have struggled with ways to improve the appearance of filling stations by encouraging the use of monument rather than free-standing signage, by requiring landscaping, and by controlling building design.

In an unusual case, the City of Kansas City, Missouri, applied a "Main Street Special Review District" to a gasoline station.[14] This was an overlay zoning district that included, among other requirements, a 10-foot build-to line. The application of the district regulations would have required the gasoline station to place its pumps to the rear of the site. The applicant sued, claiming that the overlay zoning district was confiscatory. The court sided with the landowner, claiming that a gas station could not effectively operate with its pumps to the rear of the site. Because gasoline stations were permitted as of right in the underlying district, the court incomprehensibly found that this effectively destroyed a use permitted by right. Rules of construction require a court to read all parts of the ordinance harmoniously, including the base and overlay zoning districts. There were also numerous other uses that could have been made of the property, which eliminates any possibility of a taking.[15] The case is an aberration and should not deter communities that permit auto-dependent uses to demonstrate community-based design standards.

The LDC addresses auto-dependent uses in a flexible manner that demands better design. First, the uses are placed in a floating zone that requires legislative review. This ensures maximum discretion in the review of these uses. Second, the floating zone requires a development agreement that incorporates infrastructure obligations as well as design considerations. Third, the ordinance establishes reasonable design standards found in many new stations, such as architecturally compatible canopies, landscaping, and monument signage. Finally, these uses are restricted to designated "B" streets in TNDs and other use patterns.

LARGE-SCALE COMMERCIAL DEVELOPMENT

The term "big box" refers to large-scale retail stores, such as Wal-Mart and The Home Depot. The typical building form is a large, stand-alone building surrounded by a substantial hard surface parking area. These "superstores" are marketed as a central location for consumers to meet all of their needs in one convenient location. They often sell groceries, pharmaceuticals, clothing, and household goods—all under one roof. These stores tend to generate negative externalities such as traffic, stormwater run-off, elimination of neighborhood retail, and a perceived blighting influence on surrounding residential neighborhoods. They do not depend on pedestrian access as do more traditional "corner stores" or main street storefronts with smaller footprint buildings.

Big-box stores are a major factor in producing urban sprawl. Because of their massive size and need for parking space, these stores usually are situated on large parcels of land far removed from urban centers where greenfield land is less expensive.[16] Customers have to drive farther to get to them, which contributes to traffic, air pollution, and increased fuel consumption.[17] The concentration of cars going in and out of parking lots also leads to traffic congestion on arterials.[18]

Studies suggest that big-box stores contribute to sprawl by drawing business away from urban stores, leading to the physical and economic deterioration of urban retail centers.[19] As one author wrote, a new superstore can hit local businesses "with the force of 100 new businesses opening at once."[20] Big-box stores, such as Wal-Mart, often pay low wages,[21] resist unionization,[22] and increase the trade deficit by using their market leverage to lower supply cost by manufactured goods in foreign countries.[23] Small business competitors are often forced into niche markets, or out of business altogether, and local workers are left with lower-paying jobs.[24]

Similar to other forces of sprawl, big-box development strains local infrastructure. The location and design of stores require local governments to commit general revenues, which in many situations have reduced or eliminated by tax revenue subsidies or super tax increment financing, in order to provide water, electricity, gas, sewers, roads and highways, schools, and emergency services to outlying areas.[25] The resulting impact on public finances is increased as big-box development spurs secondary commercial and residential growth in these areas.[26]

Finally, the negative impacts of vacant big-box stores vacated when tax subsidies end can be just as significant as those remaining in operation. One group estimated that "of the five billion square feet of retail space in the country, fully half a billion sits empty."[27] When big-box stores close down or relocate, they leave behind large, empty buildings that lower surrounding property values and create blight.[28] Many of these "buildings are unsuitable for much besides big-box retailing," and take months or even years to sell or lease, if at all.[29] In extreme cases, buildings remain vacant despite interested buyers or tenants because the owners have limited their use in an "effort to stave off competition from other discounters."[30]

Local governments throughout the country, recognizing the land-use issues created by big-box stores, have responded with zoning ordinances designed to curtail or regulate their development. These ordinances either ban all buildings over a certain size, require a special or conditional use, or subject them to design and environmental review procedures. Courts almost consistently have upheld these ordinances, allowing local legislatures to rein in the negative externalities discussed above.

In *Loreto Development Co. v. Village of Chardon*,[31] the Ohio Court of Appeals upheld an ordinance restricting stores exceeding 10,000 square feet.[32] Loreto, seeking to build a 98,000-square-foot Wal-Mart, challenged the ordinance's constitutionality, claiming that it "bore no rational relationship to the public health, safety, or general welfare" and "deprived [Loreto] of the economically feasible use of its land."[33] With regard to the former claim, the town found that the ordinance would serve legitimate governmental interests, such as preventing traffic congestion and preserving the area's small town character.[34] The court held that it was at least fairly debatable that the ordinance was rationally related to those interests.[35] Turning to Loreto's second claim, the court noted, "The fact that the existing zoning is not in tune with the modern trend or that it does not allow the most profitable retail development ... will not invalidate the existing zoning."[36] In order to effect a regulatory taking, an ordinance must be so restrictive that it "denies an owner of all uses of the property except those which are highly unlikely or practically impossible under the circumstances."[37]

In some states, conditions on large-scale retail development are imposed by statewide planning provisions. In *In re Wal-Mart Stores, Inc.*,[38] the Vermont Supreme Court affirmed an order of the state's environmental board, denying Wal-Mart's application for a development approval where it did not satisfy the environmental review criteria of Act 250. Act 250 allows the board to consider, inter alia, the ability of local governments to provide educational, municipal, and governmental services in light of the project.[39]

The court held that the board may consider the project's impact on market competition, reasoning that a "municipality's ability to pay for these services depends on its tax base, that is, the appraised value of property in the municipality ... To the extent that a project's impact on existing retail stores negatively affects appraised property values, such impact is a factor that relates to the public health, safety, and welfare."[40] The court also affirmed the board's right to require secondary growth studies from Wal-Mart, in order to facilitate the board's assessment of the "financial capacity of the town and region to accommodate growth" and provide "educational, municipal, and governmental services."[41]

Courts also have upheld big-box ordinances against claims that absolute floor area restrictions are exclusionary. In *Home Depot U.S.A., Inc. v. City of Portland*,[42] the zoning amendment banned large-scale retail stores exceeding 60,000 square feet, where previously they had been allowed as a conditional use. The city found that the restriction would protect jobs and prevent "negative impacts on traffic and land value."[43] The Home Depot's challenge centered on state and city comprehensive plans requiring the city to provide for "a variety of industrial and commercial uses," which The Home Depot read to require provision of, or at least consideration of, sites for large-scale retail use.[44] The court disagreed, stating that local governments need not "make land available for every specific kind of economically productive use that anyone wishes to conduct (let alone ... in a particular zone ...)."[45]

In *Montgomery Crossing Associates v. Township of Lower Gwynedd*,[46] the Pennsylvania Commonwealth Court further discussed why absolute floor area restrictions are not exclusionary. A developer from The Home Depot challenged an ordinance as de jure and de facto exclusionary because it restricted retail buildings to 6,500 square feet.[47] The court held that the size limitation did not amount to a de jure exclusion because it did not specifically prohibit any commercial use.[48] Furthermore, the fact that "Home Depot ... may not find it profitable to open a hardware store in less than 50,000 square feet" did not give rise to a de facto exclusion either.[49] A de facto exclusion under such circumstances would exist only if "a small hardware store could not have been constructed within the space limitation."[50] Emphasizing its point, the court stated that towns are "not required to zone for every business model. ... [I]f an ordinance provides for a particular use, ... it will not be held exclusionary because it limits that use to a particular size building."[51]

GROUP HOMES

Group homes for the handicapped are protected by the federal FHA. The FHA, as enacted in 1968, originally prohibited discrimination on the basis of race, color, religion, sex, familial status, or national origin.[52] It was amended in 1988 to protect persons with handicaps and to protect against "familial status" discrimination, or discrimination against parents or other custodial persons domiciled with children under the age of 18.[53] It does not prohibit discrimination on the basis of age or geography,[54] although discrimination on the basis of familial status has cast some doubt on the continuation of age-restrictive zoning practices in some communities. A "handicap," as defined in the FHA, includes a physical or mental impairment that "substantially limits one or more of such person's major life activities."[55] The definition does not apply to the "current, illegal use of or addiction to a controlled substance."[56]

Communities have used three major tools to regulate group homes:

(1) *Discretionary review:* This technique requires special/conditional use permits or special exceptions for group homes for the handicapped. Depending on how it is employed, this technique has encountered serious difficulty in both constitutional and FHA challenges. In *City of Cleburne, Texas v. Cleburne Living Center*,[57] a special use permit requirement failed the lenient "rational basis" test for equal protection challenges. Some courts have also found that discretionary review requirements that are targeted to group homes for the handicapped violate the FHA.

(2) *Occupancy restrictions:* Restrictions on the number of unrelated occupants of a dwelling unit are a common feature of local zoning ordinances and are within the police power of local governments. The FHA exempts "any reasonable local, State, or Federal restrictions regarding the maximum number of occupants permitted to occupy a dwelling."[58] The U.S. Supreme Court has ruled that this exemption applies to absolute occupancy restrictions, such as those based on square footage imposed by building codes, but not to family composition rules found in most single-family residential use restrictions.[59] In other words, zoning regulations that impose a blanket restriction on the number of unrelated persons who may occupy a unit, with no restrictions on the number of related persons, are subject to the antidiscrimination rules of the FHA.

(3) *Spacing requirements:* Some local governments have imposed spacing requirements between group homes. The stated purposes of these regulations are typically:

(a) To prevent the "ghettoization" of group homes by avoiding their concentration in certain neighborhoods; and

(b) To encourage the deinstitutionalization of handicapped persons by dispersing group home facilities. As is discussed below, this technique has received mixed results in the courts.

Some courts have upheld occupancy[60] and spacing[61] restrictions that are targeted to group homes. The trend in the case law since these cases is that zoning restrictions should be uniformly applied to handicapped residences and single-family dwelling units.[62] Accordingly, the LDC accommodates group homes as follows:

• The LDC acknowledges that group homes are subject to the same requirements that apply to other forms of housing. It does not impose a different regulation on group homes than those applicable to similar residential uses, but rather acknowledges that residential uses are to be treated uniformly.

• Group homes are exempt from the occupancy restrictions of § 5.13 Building Design in Chapter 5, Development Standards, of the LDC.

• The planning official may waive uniformly applicable standards of the LDC that would have the effect of prohibiting the accommodation of housing for handicapped persons. This is important because the exemption can be granted "behind the counter" without an expensive and unpredictable public hearing process. The planning official may consult with the local government attorney to ensure that the exemption is truly needed to accommodate housing for the handicapped.

• The group home procedure is patterned after amendments to the state enabling legislation for group homes in the State of New Jersey.[63] The New Jersey legislation formerly permitted local governments to deny CUPs for group homes that were located within 1,500 feet of an existing residence or shelter, or if the total number of persons residing in the group home exceeded 50 persons or 0.5 percent of the municipal population, whichever was greater. These provisions were invalidated by the federal courts because they imposed restrictions on the housing of handicapped persons that were not imposed on the housing of others.[64] The statute was amended to end disparate treatment of the handicapped.

HOME OCCUPATIONS

Most zoning ordinances allow persons to establish businesses in their residence subject to certain standards. Typical standards include floor area restrictions, limits on the number of employees, limitations on nonresidents, bans or size restrictions on signage, and restrictions on storage and sales.[65] Many communities permit home occupations as of right, subject to standards designated in the ordinance. If no alteration of the appearance of the dwelling is permitted, and these other standards are in place, it is not clear why special exception review is needed.

HOUSING FOR OLDER PERSONS/SENIOR HOUSING

While many older Americans are physically able to remain in their own homes, those with limited income and diminishing strength and health have difficulty coping with the cost and design of housing. Aspects of a house, such as stairs, that were once taken for granted

Table 7-16
Senior Housing

Type of Senior Housing	Description
Small houses	Includes ranch-style housing and manufactured homes
Accessory apartments	Independent dwelling units developed in connection with existing single-family homes as part of the existing space or through an accessory building
Retirement communities	A group of homes for sale or rent primarily for elderly persons, which commonly include supportive services and recreational activities
Continuing care retirement communities	Membership in a community that offers continuing care (e.g., medical and security)
Elder cottage housing	Small, self-contained, portable housing units that can be placed in the rear or side yards of single-family houses
Shared housing	Long-term arrangement where two unrelated persons share a housing unit with common areas (e.g., kitchen/living area) but have their own bedrooms
Congregate senior housing	Provides individual living areas but has shared common uses, such as dining and social activities (like a college dorm setup)
Adult foster homes	Licensed family-oriented homes providing room and board
Assisted living	Care facility providing necessary daily care of seniors (usually for those with physical or mental handicaps)
Nursing homes	Total patient care around the clock for residents

become a daily challenge. Mortgage payments can become unmanageable on a fixed income during retirement. These life changes require many older persons to seek out specific types of senior housing.

Planning for senior housing, or "elder housing," allows seniors to remain in the community where they have lived for many years (see Table 7-16). This preserves the connections a senior has developed within a community. Seniors can visit their favorite restaurants, parks, or shopping centers; contribute to organizations of which they have been a part; and continue to play a part in the lives of friends and family in the community. With friends and family nearby, seniors can rely on someone they know to help with basic tasks and can avoid or lower the costs of assistants or nurses. Integrating seniors into the fabric of a community also gives the community a perspective of age. The fabric of a community is enhanced when people of all ages are exposed to and learn from each other.

**Figure 7-13
Jobs-Housing Balance**

Live-work units in Vermillion, a community in Huntersville, North Carolina, reduce auto trips and arterial congestion.

It is important for a local government to consider the type of senior for which they are planning because there is no set type of senior housing. Seniors who are not dependent on someone else for assistance can live in communities that are formally arranged for seniors (e.g., in retirement communities where a group of homes are for sale or rent primarily for elderly persons, which commonly include supportive services and recreational activities) or ones that are simply convenient for seniors (e.g., a neighborhood with small houses, affordable houses, and conveniences located within a short distance). Seniors who are dependent on someone else for assistance require more formal arrangements, such as continuing care retirement communities and assisted living nursing homes, which assist seniors' transportation and personal care needs. When assisted living is no longer enough, nursing homes help seniors who require medical attention 24 hours a day.

MIXED-USE BUILDINGS AND LIVE-WORK UNITS

Live-work units are an emerging trend involving residential dwelling units combined with on-site working areas (see Figure 7-13). Unlike home occupations in which work spaces are integrated into living areas, live-work units are constructed with distinct areas for working and living. The traditional arrangement involves working and living areas on separate floors, with limited retail or artisan space on the ground floor and residences above. These types of spaces provide direct internal capture of work trips, thereby minimizing traffic congestion (see Table 7-17).

RELIGIOUS INSTITUTIONS

Religious institutions (e.g., churches, synagogues, and mosques) are not singled out for regulation by the LDC. Instead, they are subject to the uniform design standards applicable to other institutional uses in specific zoning districts. Religious institutions provide an important civic asset for traditional neighborhoods.[66] However, as with retail, religious institutions have increased in size and face greater demands for parking.

This has become a great concern for local planning officials throughout the nation.[67] Religious institutions have expanded beyond their traditional role of providing religious services on designated days, and now provide day care and other functions during the week. The increased activity levels, including parking demands, have created conflicts with residential neighborhoods. In urban neighborhoods, religious institutions sometimes demolish homes to create parking areas, which creates neighborhood compatibility issues and reduces housing supply. Preserving these neighborhood assets requires a delicate balance between the economic needs of growing congregations and neighborhood concerns over traffic, noise, and character.

In many conventional zoning regulations, religious institutions are permitted as of right in all residential districts. This may create a substantial impact on neighborhoods and should be reviewed more carefully. In some states, religious institutions cannot be restricted to nonresidential districts.[68] Local zoning regulations must also conform to the federal Religious Land Use and Institutionalized Persons Act of 2000 (RLUIPA).[69] Some states have enacted similar legislation.[70] The RLUIPA

**Table 7-17
Live-Work Regulatory Options**

Regulatory Alternative	Advantages	Disadvantages
Allow live-work units as of right in all residential districts with some locational criteria (e.g., fronting major streets)	Most streamlined approach to encourage establishment of live-work units	Might not be acceptable to some neighborhoods because of noise and traffic concerns
Allow live-work units as of right in some residential districts	Expands use of concept while protecting neighborhoods with special concerns	May require additional zoning districts
Allow live-work units as special use in all or some districts	Expands concept but with discretionary review	Discretionary review could inhibit use of concept or require lengthy delays
Establish design standards for live-work units	Protects neighborhoods from inappropriate levels of commercial activity	May be seen as an unnecessary regulatory burden

generally prohibits land-use regulations that impose a "substantial burden" on the religious exercise of a person, including a religious assembly or institution, unless the government demonstrates that the burden:

- Furthers a compelling government interest; and
- Is the least restrictive means of furthering that interest.[71]

The RLUIPA does not exempt religious institutions from uniformly applicable zoning restrictions.[72] Instead, the legislation targets discriminatory land-use practices. Specifically, local governments are prohibited from treating religious assemblies or institutions on less than equal terms with nonreligious assemblies or institutions,[73] and from imposing or implementing land-use regulations that discriminate against assemblies or institutions on the basis of religion or religious denomination.[74] Furthermore, governments shall not "impose or implement a land use regulation that … unreasonably limits religious assemblies, institutions, or structures within a jurisdiction."[75]

In order to avoid potential conflicts with the RLUIPA and the emerging body of RLUIPA case law, the LDC establishes the following provisions:

- Religious institutions are permitted in the same location and in the same manner as similar types of assemblies in the use matrix (Table 3-4, Use Matrix, in Chapter 3, Zoning, of the LDC). Many ordinances can cure RLUIPA issues by synchronizing restrictions. In *Civil Liberties for Urban Believers v. City of Chicago*,[76] the city successfully defended a zoning ordinance that required a special use permit for churches in designated districts. The city amended the ordinance in response to a religious freedom lawsuit to require a special use permit for all similar uses, such as "clubs and lodges," "meeting halls," and "recreation buildings and community centers" in those districts.[77] In addition, churches were permitted in all residential districts but the other uses were not. Further, the special use permit standard, which required applicants to demonstrate that the proposed use is "necessary for the public convenience at that location," was removed for churches.[78]
- Religious assemblies are not targeted for special treatment in the LDC. Instead, the regulations applicable to religious assemblies are those applicable to similar nonresidential uses in residential neighborhoods.
- The development approval process in Chapter 4, Procedures, of the LDC includes a waiver provision for the RLUIPA or other claims relating to constitutional, state, or federal law. The RLUIPA allows local governments to avoid violating the act by: (1) changing the regulation that substantially burdens religious exercise; (2) exempting the religious exercise from application of the regulation; (3) providing exemptions as a matter of policy for religious uses; or (4) employing any other means of eliminating the substantial burden imposed on the exercise of religion.[79]

In addition to these provisions, local governments should articulate the interests that support the regulations, scrutinize their regulations for compliance with the specific planning objectives, and develop a strong record that demonstrates compliance with RLUIPA mandates.

RESIDENTIAL DESIGN

Providing affordable housing does not require communities to relinquish design controls. Some housing design elements can deaden streetscapes with blank walls and garages, which discourage pedestrian activity, create auto-oriented neighborhoods, and diminish the aesthetic qualities of historic areas. One example is the "snout house," which features a front garage that protrudes closer to the street than the remainder of the unit, typically creating a series of garages along the street.

Portland, Oregon, has adopted regulations that ban snout houses.[80] Portland's regulations require a front door within 8 feet of the longest street-facing wall of a house, and restrict the width of garages to half of the house's front wall. Garages that take up less than 40 percent of the house's width can protrude 6 feet beyond the longest front wall. At least 15 percent of street-facing walls have to be windows or doors. The rules apply to most single-family houses, manufactured homes, duplexes, and row houses.

Residential design standards should include restricting the percentage of front yards in driveways and requiring garages to be set back from the front façade of a home. These regulations minimize street-deadening design features without regulating house design. Suffolk, Virginia, and San Antonio, Texas, have adopted these types of regulations.[81]

Some studies show that such regulations promote community life, reduce vehicular traffic by favoring pedestrian activity, and reduce crime by putting "eyes on the street."[82] Other observers have criticized such standards as impeding housing choice and failing to promote community and pedestrian friendliness.[83] Other critics claim that front garages are simply an honest way to respond to a transportation system dominated by cars.[84] In some cities, builders have claimed that such regulations increase housing costs but have provided no evidence to support the claim.[85]

MANUFACTURED HOUSING

The LDC recognizes that the economies of scale associated with the production of manufactured housing present a viable source of affordable single-family housing. However, local land-use regulations frequently discriminate against manufactured housing by confining them to parks, singling them out for special permitting procedures, or excluding them from most residential districts. The following types of discriminatory local regulations have been invalidated on constitutional grounds:

- Confinement of manufactured homes to parks[86];
- Exclusion of manufactured homes from all zoning districts[87]; and
- Confining manufactured homes to unreasonably small areas of land.[88]

In addition, at least 14 states now have legislation prohibiting discrimination against manufactured housing. An increasing number of jurisdictions now permit manufactured homes as of right in residential districts and outside of parks.[89] State antidiscrimination laws generally take the following forms:

- Broadly worded prohibitions of ordinances having the effect of excluding prefabricated housing, except on the same terms and conditions as conventional housing[90];
- Prohibition of discriminatory treatment while still preserving to local governments the right to impose zoning standards and procedural requirements (e.g., setback, minimum square footage, yard, parking, roofing/siding, and density) on the same terms as site-built housing[91];
- Mandates that manufactured homes must be allowed in all residential areas[92];
- Prohibition of complete exclusion of manufactured homes from a community[93]; and
- Active encouragement of local governments to utilize manufactured homes as a vehicle for providing affordable housing.[94]

The LDC provides regulations promoting the integration of manufactured homes into the built environment.

Communities should consider permitting manufactured housing on individual lots in residential districts, subject to design standards and permanent foundation requirements. Manufactured homes can be produced for approximately half the cost of site-built homes, and therefore provide a source of affordable single-family housing.[95] Some studies have indicated that the United States Department of Housing and Urban Development Code (the HUD Code, a national building code for manufactured homes) is at least as strict as local building codes and produces homes with quality similar to that of site-built homes.[96]

The HUD Code defines "modular" homes as those built in factories to local building code standards. By contrast, "mobile" homes typically do not comply with local building code standards. The term "mobile" is misleading because few manufactured homes are moved after placement on a lot.

Manufactured homes, while resisted by neighborhood activists, provide an affordable source of single-family shelter. Federal law prohibits local governments from imposing local building code standards that discriminate against homes built to HUD Code standards.[97] However, most cases have ruled that this restriction does not apply to local zoning, on the theory that zoning regulates location rather than building construction. Most states afford local governments wide discretion in the regulation of manufactured homes.[98]

WIRELESS COMMUNICATIONS

Cell towers may be regulated through zoning but are protected by federal law. Section 704(c)(7) of the Telecommunications Act (TCA) of 1996,[99] entitled "Preservation of local zoning authority," provides:

"(A) General authority

Except as provided in this paragraph, nothing in this chapter shall limit or affect the authority of a State or local government or instrumentality thereof over decisions regarding the placement, construction, and modification of personal wireless service facilities.

(B) Limitations

(i) The regulation of the placement, construction, and modification of personal wireless service facilities by any State or local government or instrumentality thereof—

(I) shall not unreasonably discriminate among providers of functionally equivalent services; and

(II) shall not prohibit or have the effect of prohibiting the provision of personal wireless services.

(ii) A State or local government or instrumentality thereof shall act on any request for authorization to place, construct, or modify personal wireless service facilities within a reasonable period of time after the request is duly filed with such government or instrumentality, taking into account the nature and scope of such request.

(iii) Any decision by a State or local government or instrumentality thereof to deny a request to place, construct, or modify personal wireless service facilities shall be in writing and supported by substantial evidence contained in a written record.

(iv) No State or local government or instrumentality thereof may regulate the placement, construction, and modification of personal wireless service facilities on the basis of the environmental effects of radio frequency emissions to the extent that such facilities comply with the Commission's regulations concerning such emissions."

Most courts have construed these regulations to require local governments to allow service providers to fill gaps in coverage. Most local governments conduct gap studies prior to developing comprehensive wireless zoning regulations to ensure that service gaps do not result, and to ensure compliance with other provisions of the TCA. To address the impacts of wireless facilities on property values and aesthetics, most courts have approved a number of techniques,[100] including:

- Selecting a less sensitive site;
- Reducing tower heights;
- Using preexisting structures; and
- Camouflaging the towers and/or antennas.

The TCA does not give providers carte blanche to construct any given number of towers at any location. "A local government may also reject an application that seeks permission to construct more towers than the minimum required to provide wireless telephone services in a given area. A denial of such a request is not a prohibition of personal wireless services as long as fewer towers would provide users in the given area with some ability to reach a cell site."[101]

Wireless communications towers have become controversial in recent years because of appearance and compatibility issues, as well as concerns over radio frequency emissions. In addition, the TCA has generated considerable litigation over the meaning of several new restrictions on local zoning authority. While the act affirms the authority of local governments to apply zoning restrictions to such facilities, it applies several important restrictions:

• Local governments cannot regulate such facilities on the basis of their environmental effects, to the extent that they comply with the FCC's emission regulations;

• Local governments must act on an application for approval within a reasonable period of time, given the nature and scope of the request; and

• The agency must issue findings of fact and conclusions of law relating to its decision on the application.

NOTES

1. International Conference of Building Officials, *Guidelines for Manufactured Housing Installation* (June 1983).
2. 47 C.F.R. § 1.4000; 47 C.F.R. § 25.104.
3. Eric Damian Kelly and Gary J. Raso, "Sign Regulation for Small and Midsize Communities: A Planners Guide and a Model Ordinance," Planning Advisory Service Report No. 419 (Chicago: American Planning Association, November 1989); Daniel R. Mandelker and William R. Ewald, *Street Graphics and the Law* (Chicago: American Planning Association, 1988).
4. See, e.g., S. Mark White, "Affordable Housing: Proactive and Reactive Planning Strategies," Planning Advisory Service Report No. 441 (Chicago: American Planning Association, 1992).
5. 47 C.F.R. §§ 1.4000, 25.104 (preemption of local zoning of earth stations); Patrick J. Rohan, *Zoning and Land Use Controls* (New York: M. Bender, 2003), § 10A.05; Harry B. Roth, "Regulating Satellite Dish Antennas," Planning Advisory Service Report No. 394 (Chicago: American Planning Association, 1986).
6. Note 5 (Rohan), supra, Vol. 7, § 40A.01.
7. Id., § 40A.02[3].
8. See, e.g., *Town of Highland Park v. Marshall*, 235 S.W.2d 658 (Tex. Civ. App. Dallas 1950, writ ref'd n.r.e.).
9. See, generally, *Solar v. Zoning Board of Appeals*, 33 Mass. App. Ct. 398, 600 N.E.2d 187 (1992). Martin Gellen, *Accessory Apartments in Single-Family Housing* (New Brunswick, NJ: Rutgers University, 1985); Dwight Merriam, "Accessory Apartments," *Zoning and Planning Law Report* (1983), 351; George W. Liebmann, "Suburban Zoning—Two Modest Proposals," *Real Property, Probate, and Trust Journal* (Spring 1990), 81; Rodney L. Cobb and Scott Dvorak, "Accessory Dwelling Units: Model State Act and Local Ordinance," Public Policy Institute (Washington, DC: American Association of Retired Persons, 2000), available on-line at www.aarp.org/research/legis-polit/legislation/aresearch-import-163-D17158.html.
10. N.J. Admin. Code § 5:92-16.1.
11. Cal. Gov't Code § 65852.2 (West Supp. 1991); *Wilson v. City of Laguna Beach*, 6 Cal. App. 4th 543, 7 Cal.Rptr.2d 848 (Cal. App. 4 Dist. 1992) (second-unit owners entitled to writ of mandate to compel compliance with statutory provisions governing accessory units).
12. N.R. Shortlidge and Mark White, "The Use of Zoning and Other Local Controls for Siting Solid and Hazardous Waste Facilities," *Natural Resources and Environment* (1993), 7:3-45; S. Mark White, "Regulation of Concentrated Animal Feeding Operations: The Legal Context," 52 *Land Use L. & Zon. Dig.*, 2, at 3 (February 2000).
13. John A. Jakle and Keith A. Sculle, *The Gas Station in America* (Baltimore: Johns Hopkins University Press, 1994), at 79-80.
14. *Dallen v. City of Kansas City*, 822 S.W.2d 429 (Mo. App. 1991).
15. The site is now used for a franchise pharmacy, with a front-loaded parking lot at the corner and a blank brick wall along the street.
16. See, e.g., *Anderson First Coalition v. City of Anderson*, 2005 Cal. App. LEXIS 1043, at *2 (June 30, 2005), where the proposed Wal-Mart Supercenter measured in at 184,000 square feet, situated on some 26 acres.
17. See, e.g., *Wal-Mart Stores, Inc. v. City of Turlock*, No. 345253, slip op. at 3 (Cal. Super. Ct., Dec. 7, 2004) (repeating the city's concern that "consumers are forced to take longer and more frequent trips to the regional commercial center").
18. See, e.g., *In re Wal-Mart Stores, Inc.*, 702 A.2d 397, 404 (Vt. 1997) (discussing the state environmental board's projection that a particular Wal-Mart development would cause unreasonable traffic congestion "outside compact urban areas").
19. See generally Benedict Sheehy, "Corporations and Social Costs: The Wal-Mart Case Study," 24 *J.L. & Com.* 1 (2004). Small businesses comprising urban retail centers contribute socially and economically to the community. They "tend to be highly involved in the community, create employment which pays sufficiently to sustain a reasonable standard of living, . . . are innovative . . . [and] promot[e] ideas of individual ability, responsibility and an entrepreneurial spirit." Id. at 35. However, when "[labor] opportunities [are shifted] from the downtown urban areas to suburban big-box retailers . . . detrimental community effects can be expected. These effects include decreased community involvement, decreased community building efforts, decreased small business, decreased [labor]

opportunities, and increased commercial vacancies." Id. at 35-36.
20. Al Norman, *Slam-Dunking Wal-Mart: How You Can Stop Superstore Sprawl in Your Hometown* (St. Johnsbury, VT: Raphel Marketing, 1999), 21.
21. See Note 19 (Sheehy), supra, at 37-40 (while Wal-Mart employees are paid at or above minimum wage, the company uses a "cap on hours worked . . . to avoid costs such as health insurance it may otherwise be forced to incur."). "[B]ecause of low wages, Wal-Mart employees must look elsewhere for supplemental income. Such supplemental income can come from the state, other part-time jobs, the underground economy, or illegal activities." Id. at 38-39.
22. Id. at 39 ("Wal-Mart has taken a defiantly anti-union stance. It maintains an active anti-union response team of 70 people ready to descend on any Wal-Mart where employees are considering unionizing. It attempts to inoculate employees against unions by threats rather than by providing competitive benefits.").
23. Id. at 36 ("The pressure Wal-Mart place on suppliers is enormous. Wal-Mart requires its suppliers to drop prices annually by as much as 5%.").
24. See, e.g., *Anderson First Coalition*, 2005 Cal. App. LEXIS 1043, at *19 ("[T]he key survival strategy for local merchants is to specialize in unique products and services. Local merchants need to create niches. . . .").
25. See text accompanying Notes 38-41, infra.
26. See text accompanying Note 41, infra.
27. Stacy Mitchell, "Abandoned Malls, Suburban Blight," *Miami Herald* (Dec. 20, 2000).
28. Eric M. Weiss, "'Big-Box' Stores Leave More Than a Void," *Washington Post* (Jan. 20, 2004), at B1 (commenting that "[e]mpty stores are sometimes a magnet for graffiti, dumped furniture and unsavory activity").
29. Note 27 (Mitchell), supra. See also Jennifer Liberto, "Empty Big Box Stores Piling Up in County," *St. Petersburg Times* (May 12, 2003) (stating that it "often take[s] real estate brokers at least six months to find tenants" for abandoned big boxes, in part because "[t]hey have a certain configuration they like to have, and they might not be able to do that in the places already built up").
30. Whitney Gould, "Don't Get Boxed in by Abandoned Big-Boxes," *Milwaukee Journal Sentinel* (July 4, 2004).
31. 695 N.E.2d 1151 (Ohio Ct. App. 1996).
32. Id. at 1152.
33. Id.
34. Id. at 1154.
35. Id. The court, stressing the appropriate level of legislative deference, stated that "the judicial judgment is not to be substituted for the legislative judgment in any case in which the issue or matter is fairly debatable." Id.
36. Id. at 1153.
37. Id.
38. 702 A.2d 397 (Vt. 1997).
39. Id. at 401.
40. Id.
41. Id. at 402.
42. 10 P.3d 316 (Or. Ct. App. 2000).
43. Id. at 317.
44. Id.
45. Id. at 317-18.
46. 758 A.2d 285 (Pa. Commw. Ct. 2000).
47. Id. at 286-87.
48. Id. at 288 ("In determining whether an ordinance creates a de jure exclusion, uncertainties in the interpretation of an ordinance are to be resolved in favor of a construction which renders the ordinance constitutional.").
49. Id. at 289.
50. Id.
51. Id.
52. 42 U.S.C.A. § 3604(a).
53. 42 U.S.C.A. § 3602(k).
54. *Caron v. City of Pawtucket*, 307 F.Supp.2d 364 (D.R.I. 2004); *Chiara v. Dizoglio*, 81 F.Supp.2d 242, 246 (D.Mass. 2000), aff'd., 6 Fed.Appx. 20, 2001 WL 288613 (1st Cir. 2001); *Keeney v. Kemper Nat. Ins. Companies*, 960 F.Supp. 617 (E.D.N.Y. 1997).
55. 42 U.S.C.A. § 3602(h).
56. Id.
57. 473 U.S. 432 (1985).
58. 42 U.S.C. § 3607(b)(1).
59. *City of Edmonds v. Oxford House, Inc.*, 514 U.S. 725 (1995).
60. *Oxford House-C v. City of St. Louis*, C.A.8 (Mo.) 1996, 77 F.3d 249, certiorari denied 117 S.Ct. 65, 519 U.S. 816, 136 L.Ed.2d 27.
61. *Familystyle of St. Paul, Inc. v. City of St. Paul*, 923 F.2d 91 (8th Cir. 1991) (upholding requirement that new group home be located at least 1/4 mile from an existing residential program); *Appeal of Lynch Community Homes, Inc.*, 554 A.2d 155, 123 Pa.Cmwlth. 278 (1989) (upholding 250-foot spacing requirement).
62. Daniel R. Mandelker, Jules B. Gerard, and E. Thomas Sullivan, *Federal Land Use Law: Limitations/Procedures/Remedies* (St. Paul, MN: West Group Zoning and Land Use Library, 1992), § 3.08 (criticizing *Familystyle* decision).
63. N.J.S.A. 40:55D-66.1 (community residences for developmentally disabled or persons with head injuries; community shelters for victims of domestic violence; residential districts; conditional use permits).
64. *ARC of New Jersey, Inc. v. State of New Jersey*, 950 F.Supp. 637 (D.N.J. 1996) and *Association for Advancement of the Mentally Handicapped, Inc. v. City of Elizabeth*, 876 F.Supp. 614 (D.N.J. 1994).
65. Charles Wunder, "Regulating Home-Based Businesses in the Twenty-First Century," Planning Advisory Service Report No. 499 (Chicago: American Planning Association, 2000); JoAnn Butler and Judith Getzels, "Home Occupation Ordinances," Planning Advisory Service Report No. 391 (Chicago: American Planning Association, 1995).
66. Congress for the New Urbanism, *Charter of the New Urbanism* (New York: McGraw-Hill, 2000), at 105-108, 161-68.
67. Jim Schwab, "Zoning and Big Box Religion," *Zoning News* (November 1996).
68. John Mixon, James L. Dougherty, Jr., and Brenda McDonald, *Texas Municipal Zoning Law*, 3d ed. (Albany, NY: Michie Publications, 1999), § 6.207.

69. 42 U.S.C. § 2000cc et seq.; E. Tyson Smith, "Do Unto Religious Uses As You Would Have Done Unto Nonreligious Uses: An Overview of the Religious Land Use and Institutionalized Persons Act of 2000," *Fla. Bar Envt'l & Land Use Law Section Reporter* (January 2002) (reprinted at www.eluls.org/reporter-jan2002/jan2002_smith.html).
70. See, e.g., Florida Religious Freedom Restoration Act of 1998, Florida Statutes § 761.01 et seq.; Illinois Religious Freedom Restoration Act, 775 ILCS 35/15 and 775 ILCS 35/20.
71. 42 U.S.C.A. § 2000cc(a)(1) (2002).
72. Note 69 (Smith), supra ("the legislative history behind RLUIPA states that the 'Act does not provide religious institutions with immunity from land use regulation . . .'").
73. 42 U.S.C.A. § 2000cc(b)(1).
74. 42 U.S.C.A. § 2000cc(b)(2).
75. 42 U.S.C.A. § 2000cc(b)(3).
76. 342 F.3d 752 (7th Cir. 2003), *cert. denied*, 124 S.Ct. 2816, 72 USLW 3644, 72 USLW 3740 (2004).
77. Id.
78. Id.
79. Note 69 (Smith), supra.
80. Portland City Code, § 33.218.100 (Standards for Primary and Attached Accessory Structures in Single-Dwelling Zones); Gordon Oliver, "Portland City Council may turn up its nose at 'snout' houses; Rules to reduce the dominance of garages in new homes are expected to pass this week," *The Oregonian* (July 20, 1999); Gordon Oliver, "Behind 'snout house' snub lie varied views," *The Oregonian* (July 22, 1999).
81. Suffolk, Virginia, Unified Development Ordinance, § 31-605(e); San Antonio, Texas, Unified Development Code, § 35-515(d).
82. Steve Abel, "In defense of Portland's new housing-design standards," *Oregon Live* (August 3, 1999). For studies showing reductions in vehicular traffic resulting from smart growth designs, see Reid Ewing, *Pedestrian- and Transit-Friendly Design* (Tallahassee: Florida Department of Transportation, March 1996), at 8-9; Robert Cervero and Kara Kockelman, "Travel Demand and the 3Ds: Density, Diversity, and Design," *Transportation Resource D*, Vol. 2, No. 3 (1997); Anne V. Moudon et al., "Effects of Site Design on Pedestrian Travel in Mixed-Use, Medium-Density Environments," Report No. WA-RD 432.1 (Washington, DC: Transportation Research Board, May 1997); Washington State Department of Transportation, *Pedestrian Facilities Guidebook: Incorporating Pedestrians Into Washington's Transportation System* (Olympia: WSDOT, September 1997); 1000 Friends of Oregon, "Making Land Use Transportation Air Quality Connections, The Pedestrian Environment," Vol. 4A (December 1993), available on-line at ntlbts.gov/DOCS/tped.html; Randall Crane, "Cars and Drivers in the New Suburbs: Linking Access to Travel in Neotraditional Planning," 62 *APA Journal* 51 (Winter 1996); Robert Cervero, "Land Use Mixing and Suburban Mobility," 42 *Transportation Quarterly* 3 (1988); Colorado/Wyoming Section Technical Committee, "Trip Generation for Mixed Use Developments," *ITE Journal* 57, 2 (1987), 27-32; Walter Kulash, Joe Anglin, and David Marks, "Traditional Neighborhood Development: Will the Traffic Work?," *Development* (July/August 1990); Lloyd W. Bookout, "Neotraditional Town Planning: Cars, Pedestrians & Transit," *Urban Land* (February 1992), at 10, 15; Bruce Friedman, Stephen Gordon and John Peers, "Effect of Neotraditional Neighborhood Design on Travel Characteristics," *Transportation Research Record* 1466: 63-70 (1993); Susan L. Handy, "Regional Versus Local Accessibility: Neo-traditional Development and Its Implications for Non-work Travel," *Built Environment*, Vol. 18, No. 4 (1992), 253-267; John Holtzclaw, "Explaining Urban Density and Transit Impacts on Auto Use," presented by the Natural Resources Defense Council and the Sierra Club to the State of California Energy Resources Conservation and Development Commission (April 19, 1990); Ryuichi Kitamura, Patricia L. Mokhtarian, and Laura Laidet, "A Micro-Analysis of Land Use and Travel in Five Neighborhoods in the San Francisco Bay Area," Institute of Transportation Studies, University of California at Davis (November 1994). For studies relating to crime, see Judith D. Feins, Ph.D., Joel C. Epstein, Esq., and Rebecca Widom, *Solving Crime Problems in Residential Neighborhoods: Comprehensive Changes in Design, Management, and Use* (Washington, DC: United States Department of Justice, Office of Justice Programs, National Institute of Justice, April 1997); Jane Jacobs, *The Death and Life of Great American Cities* (New York: Vintage Books, 1992).
83. Randall O'Toole [Thoreau Institute], "Is New Urbanism Creeping Socialism?," *Austin Review* (Oct. 1, 2000); Naomi Kaufman Price, "Confessions of a happy 'snout-house' owner," *The Oregonian* (July 26, 1999); Gary Hallberg, "A City Council outrage," *Oregon Live* (August 1, 1999).
84. Alex Marshall, *How Cities Work: Suburbs, Sprawl, and The Roads Not Taken* (Austin: University of Texas Press, 2000).
85. Gordon Oliver, "Behind 'snout house' snub lie varied views—Opinions on the City Council range from concern about state control to need for tougher standards," *The Oregonian* (July 22, 1999); Gordon Oliver, "Portland City Council may turn up its nose at 'snout' houses: Rules to reduce the dominance of garages in new homes are expected to pass this week," *The Oregonian* (July 20, 1999).
86. *Cannon v. Coweta County*, 389 S.E.2d 329 (Ga. 1990); *Robinson Township v. Knoll*, 410 Mich. 293, 302 N.W.2d 146 (1981) (violation of equal protection); *Luczynski v. Temple*, 203 N.J. Super. 377, 497 a.2d 211 (N.J. Super. Ct. Ch. Div. 1985); *Borough of Malvern v. Jackson*, 529 A.2d 96 (Pa. Commw. 1987); *Bourgeois v. Parish of St. Tammany*, 628 F.Supp. 159 (E.D. La. 1986); *Geiger v. Zoning Hearing Board*, 510 Pa. 231, 507 A.2d 361 (1986); compare *City of Brookside Village v. Comeau*, 633 S.W.2d 790 (Tex.), *cert. denied*, 459 U.S. 1087 (1974) (approving mobile home restrictions). See also *In re Shore*, 528 A.2d 1045 (Pa. Commw. 1987) (ordinance permitting manufactured homes on individual lots but excluding mobile home parks unconstitutional).
87. *Cannon v. Coweta County*, 389 S.E.2d 329 (1990) (exclusion of manufactured homes from entire community a violation of substantive due process);

88. *Environmental Communities of Pennsylvania v. North Coventry Township*, 49 Pa. Commw. 167, 412 A.2d 650 (1980) (limiting manufactured homes to 1.5 percent of township land exclusionary); *Nickola v. Township of Grand Blanc*, 394 Mich. 589, 232 N.W.2d 604 (1975) (confining manufactured homes to 10 percent of township land exclusionary and invalid).

Board of Supervisors of Upper Frederick Township v. Moland Development Co., 19 Pa.Commw. 207, 339 A.2d 141 (1975).

89. See Welford Sanders, "Regulating Manufactured Housing," Planning Advisory Service Report No. 398 (Chicago: American Planning Association, 1986).

90. Vt. Stat. Ann. tit. 24, § 4406(4)(A) (1975 & Supp. 1989).

91. Cal. Gov't. Code § 65852.3 (West 1983 & Supp. 1991); Iowa Code Ann. § 358A.30 (West 1983 & Supp. 1989); Minn. Stat. Ann. §§ 394.25, 462.357(1) (West Supp. 1989); see Kansas S.B. No. 23, § 19 (1991) ("residential design" manufactured homes must be permitted in residential areas, subject to architectural and design controls).

92. Colo. Rev. Stat. § 30-28-115 (1986); Iowa Code Ann. § 358A.30 (West 1983 & Supp. 1989); Me. Rev. Stat. Ann. tit. 30, § 4965 (West 1973 & Supp. 1986); N.J. Stat. Ann. § 40:55D-100 (West 1983 & Supp. 1987); or in designated residential areas, Fla. Stat. Ann. § 553.35; Minn. Stat. Ann. § 394.25; Or. Rev. Stat. § 197.295; N.H. Rev. Stat. § 674.32; N.M. Rev. Stat. § 3-21A-3(2)(A).

93. Neb. Stat. Ann. § 15-902 (1987); N.H. Rev. Stat. Ann. § 674.32 (1986); Tenn. Code Ann. § 13-24-201 (1987); see also Kansas S.B. No. 23, § 19 (1991).

94. 1989 Washington Laws, H.B. No. 2167, P. 1365 (encouraging revision of land-use regulations and development approval procedures, requiring needs assessment by certain counties and promulgation of the LDC).

95. S. Mark White, "State and Federal Planning Legislation and Manufactured Housing: New Opportunities for Affordable, Single-Family Shelter," 28 *Urb. Law.* 263 (1996).

96. Kate Warner and Robert Johnson, *Manufactured Housing Research Project* (Ann Arbor: University of Michigan, January 1993).

97. Note 95 (White), supra.

98. See, e.g., *Bibco Corp. v. City of Sumter*, 504 S.E.2d 112 (S.C. 1998) (upholding ordinance excluding mobile homes from some residential districts); *Town of Scranton v. Willoughby*, 306 S.C. 421, 412 S.E.2d 424 (1991) (upholding municipal ordinance excluding mobile homes from all areas except mobile home districts).

99. Pub. L. No. 104, 110 Stat. 56, codified at 47 U.S.C.§ 332(c)(7).

100. See *Sprint Spectrum L.P. v. Willoth*, 176 F.3d 630, 643 (2nd Cir. 1999).

101. Id.

CHAPTER

8

Nonconforming Uses/ Vested Rights

Purpose and findings: The purpose of this chapter is to protect the rights of property owners who have lawfully established, and continuously maintained in a lawful manner, a use prior to the adoption of this chapter or prior to any amendment to this chapter that otherwise renders such use unlawful. A nonconforming use or structure that was recognized prior to the adoption of this chapter shall continue to operate under the provision of law under which the nonconforming structure or use was recognized so long as the nonconforming use or structure is not in violation of such provision of law, the adoption of this chapter notwithstanding. Nothing in this chapter prohibits the voluntary compliance with any future ordinance, regulation, or incentive.

DIVISION 1: NONCONFORMITIES

8.10 GENERALLY

8.10.1 Applicability

This division applies to any nonconformity. There are four categories of nonconformities as defined in Table 8-1.

8.10.2 Continuation

On or after the effective date of the Land Development Code (LDC), a nonconformity that was lawfully operated, established, or commenced in accordance with the provisions of all ordinances, statutes, or regulations in effect at that time may continue subject to this division.

8.10.3 Abandonment

If a nonconformity is abandoned for 12 months, any future use of such premises shall be in conformity with the provisions of this chapter. Abandonment of a nonconformity shall terminate the right to continue the nonconformity.

8.11 NONCONFORMING USES

8.11.1 Applicability

This section applies to the continuation, enlargement, or expansion of a nonconforming use.

8.11.2 Continuance

The lawful use of any structure existing as of the effective date of this chapter may be continued, although such use does not conform to the provisions of this chapter. Such use may be extended throughout the structure, provided that no structural alterations or additions to the structure, except those made in conformance with law or ordinance.

Table 8-1
Nonconformities

Situation	Definition
Nonconforming uses (§ 8.11 Nonconforming Uses of this chapter)	A use that was lawfully established but that no longer complies with the use regulations applicable to the zoning district in which the property is located
Nonconforming site (§ 8.12 Nonconforming Sites of this chapter)	A lot, parcel, or development site that was lawfully established but that does not comply with the standards of Chapter 5, Development Standards, of the LDC
Nonconforming structure (§ 8.13 Nonconforming Structures of this chapter)	A structure that was lawfully erected but that no longer complies with all the regulations applicable to the zoning district in which the structure is located
Nonconforming lot (§ 8.14 Nonconforming Lots of this chapter)	A lot that fails to meet the requirements for area, height, yards, buffer, or other bulk standards and regulations, generally applicable in the district because of a change in the applicable zoning district regulations, annexation, condemnation of a portion of the lot, or other governmental action

Table 8-2
Change of Use

Use Permitted in:	Located in:	May be Changed to Use Permitted in:
"RP" (Resource Protection) "RE" (Residential Estate)	Less restricted residential district	Any greater restricted district
Any commercial or industrial use	Any residential district	Any residential use or a more restrictive business use as follows: • "IH" (Industrial Heavy) uses may be changed to any "IL" (Industrial Light) use; • "IL" uses may be changed to any "CL" (Commercial Large-Scale), "CG" (Commercial General), "CN" (Commercial Neighborhood), or "O" (Office) use; • "CL" uses may be changed to any "CG," "CN," or "O" use; • "CG" uses may be changed to any "CN" or "O" use; and • "O" uses may be changed to any "CN" use.
Any commercial district	More restricted commercial district	A greater restrictive commercial use as follows: • "IL" uses may be changed to any "CL," "CG," "CN," or "O" use; • "CL" uses may be changed to any "CG," "CN," or "O" use; • "CG" uses may be changed to any "CN" or "O" use; and • "O" uses may be changed to any "CN" use.
"IL" district	More restricted commercial district	"IL" district

8.11.3 Enlargement

A conforming structure in which a nonconforming use is operated shall not be enlarged or extended except as required by law or ordinance.

8.11.4 Conditions

The right of nonconforming uses to continue is subject to such regulations as to the maintenance of the premises and conditions of operation as may, in the judgment of the board of adjustment, be reasonably required for the protection of adjacent property.

8.11.5 Change of Use Regulations

8.11.5.1 Changes to Conforming Uses

Any nonconforming use may be changed to a use conforming with these regulations established for the district in which the nonconforming use is located, provided, however, that a nonconforming use so changed shall not in the future be changed back to a nonconforming use. A nonconforming use may be changed to another nonconforming use by order of the board of adjustment, provided that the new use is determined to be more consistent with the spirit of the LDC, the neighborhood, and the comprehensive plan.

8.11.5.2 Changes to Other Nonconforming Uses

Nonconforming uses may be changed to another nonconforming use only if provided for in Table 8-2. A nonconforming use that is changed to another nonconforming use shall not be changed back to the former nonconforming use.

8.11.5.3 Limitations on Changing Nonconforming Uses

All changes of nonconforming uses shall conform to all regulations established in Chapter 5, Development Standards, of the LDC. A nonconforming use shall not be changed to another nonconforming use that requires more off-street parking and loading space than the former nonconforming use unless additional adequate off-street parking and loading space is provided for the increment of the new nonconforming use as if the increment were a separate use. A nonconforming use shall not be changed to another nonconforming use unless the original nonconforming use was registered in conformance with this chapter.

8.12 NONCONFORMING SITES

Purpose and findings: The LDC establishes various site design standards in Chapter 5, Development Standards, of the LDC. Consequently, many development sites do not meet current requirements for such items as parking lot standards, landscaping, and other design specifications. This section requires that such nonconforming sites be brought into conformance with the site development standards prescribed by the LDC.

8.12.1 Applicability

This section applies to the continuation, enlargement, or expansion of a nonconforming site.

8.12.2 Authority to Continue

Any lawfully existing nonconforming site may be continued so long as it remains otherwise lawful subject to this section.

8.12.3 Nonconforming Site Categories

Lots, parcels, or sites devoted to the uses described in Column (A) of Table 8-3 shall have the time period established in Column (B) of Table 8-3 to either bring the site into conformance with the provisions of the ordinance or have a variance approved for the site. All owners of record of commercially zoned properties shall be notified by the building inspector by first class mail of this provision prior to the end of the nine-year period.

8.12.4 Extension

A conforming use located on a nonconforming site shall not be expanded until the site is brought into conformance with the provisions of this ordinance. However, single-family residential structures that are located

Table 8-3
Nonconforming Site Categories

(A) Site Category	(B) Conformance Period
Shopping centers	10 years
Commercial sites on parcels of at least 10 acres	10 years
Commercial sites on parcels of less than 10 acres	12 years
Multifamily developments	15 years

on a legally nonconforming site with respect to required yards, areas, or height may be structurally altered or enlarged, providing the portion of the structure that is altered or enlarged conforms with the provisions of this ordinance.

8.12.5 Relocations

No structure shall be relocated to a nonconforming site until the site is brought into conformance with the provisions of this ordinance.

8.12.6 Change in Use

No existing structure located on a nonconforming site shall be changed from one use classification to another use classification as listed in Chapter 6, Adequate Public Facilities, of the LDC until the site is brought into conformance with the provisions of this ordinance or a nonconforming site variance has been approved by the board of adjustment.

8.12.7 Abandonment

When the use of a nonconforming site has been abandoned for a period of 12 months, the site shall not be used, developed, or improved until it is brought into conformance with this chapter. The board of adjustment may grant a one-time, six-month extension period for the purpose of bringing the site into conformance with this chapter. Extension applications shall be filed in accordance with the procedures for site plan review in the LDC. For purposes of this ordinance, rental payments or lease payments and taxes shall not be considered as a continued use, and the disconnection of utilities shall constitute a means of establishing the commencement of the abandonment of the use of the development site.

8.12.8 Exception for Repairs Pursuant to Public Order

Nothing in this section shall be deemed to prevent the strengthening or restoration to a safe condition of a building or structure in accordance with an order of a public official who is charged with protecting the public safety and who declares such structure to be unsafe and orders it to restoration to a safe condition, provided that such restoration is not otherwise in violation of the various provisions of this section prohibiting the repair or restoration of partially damaged or destroyed buildings or structures.

8.13 NONCONFORMING STRUCTURES

8.13.1 Applicability

This section applies to the continuation, enlargement, or expansion of a nonconforming structure.

8.13.2 Continuance of Nonconforming Structures

Subject to all limitations in this section, and the provisions of § 8.12.8 Exception for Repairs Pursuant to Public Order of this chapter, any nonconforming structure may be occupied, operated, and maintained in a state of good repair, but no nonconforming structure shall be enlarged or extended.

8.13.3 Enlargement

A nonconforming structure in which only permitted uses are operated may be enlarged or extended if the enlargement or extension can be made in compliance with all of the provisions of this chapter established for structures in the district in which the nonconforming structure is located. Such enlargement shall also be subject to all other applicable [LOCAL GOVERNMENT] ordinances.

8.13.4 Termination of Nonconforming Structures

8.13.4.1 Damage to Structures

The right to operate and maintain any nonconforming structure shall terminate and shall cease to exist whenever the nonconforming structure is damaged in any manner and from any cause whatsoever, and the cost of repairing such damage exceeds 50 percent of the replacement cost of such structure on the date of such damage.

8.13.4.2 Obsolescence of Structure

The right to operate and maintain any nonconforming structure shall terminate and shall cease to exist whenever the nonconforming structure becomes obsolete or substandard under any applicable ordinance of the [LOCAL GOVERNMENT], and the cost of placing such structure in lawful compliance with the applicable ordinance exceeds 50 percent of the replacement cost of such structure on the date that the proper official of the [LOCAL GOVERNMENT] determines that such structure is obsolete or substandard.

8.13.4.3 Determination of Replacement Cost

In determining the replacement cost of any nonconforming structure, the cost of land or any factors other than the nonconforming structure itself shall not be included.

8.14 NONCONFORMING LOTS

8.14.1 Applicability

This section applies to the continuation, enlargement, or expansion of a nonconforming lot.

8.14.2 Generally

A substandard lot shall comply with the yard, buffer, setback, and bulk regulations of the zoning district that makes the lot conforming to the area of the lot. This section does not require the replatting or combination of platted lots under same ownership that is protected by state vested rights law.

8.14.3 Newly Annexed Territory

Conforming rights shall be granted to all properties in newly annexed areas in accordance with the provisions of this division. All applications for registration for nonconforming rights must be filed within 60 days of the effective date of annexation.

8.14.4 Incomplete Construction

Construction may be completed on any structure legally under construction upon annexation, provided that:

(A) The owner or his/her designated representative applies to the [PLANNING OFFICIAL] for a development approval to authorize further work on the structure, stating the proposed use of the structure and attaching the plans and specifications relating to the construction; and

(B) The construction is completed within two years of the effective date of annexation. Action on the development approvals shall be taken by the [PLANNING OFFICIAL] within 15 days from the date of application. The [PLANNING OFFICIAL] shall deny the development approval if he/she finds that the construction will not meet the requirements of the building, fire protection, or minimum housing codes and other applicable ordinances and codes of the [LOCAL GOVERNMENT]. If the development approval is refused, the construction work shall cease until necessary corrections are made.

8.14.5 Proposed Construction

Proposed construction may be completed upon a finding by the board of adjustment that sufficient evidence exists that a valid development approval was obtained from the [LOCAL GOVERNMENT] and was validly in place on the date of annexation. Within 15 days from the date of such filing, the [PLANNING OFFICIAL] shall present the evidence to the board of adjustment for its determination, unless the applicant agrees to a longer period. The applicant shall have 12 months from the date of the board of adjustment's favorable determination to secure all development approvals.

8.15 CERTIFICATE OF NONCONFORMING USE

8.15.1 Applicability

8.15.1.1 Generally

The owner of a nonconformity shall register such nonconformity by filing with the [PLANNING OFFICIAL] a registration statement.

8.15.1.2 Exemptions

Registration is not required for:
(A) Any use or structure that is made nonconforming by any governmental action other than annexation or rezoning;
(B) Any fence of legal height and construction that does not constitute a nonconforming use and does not require registration; and
(C) Any nonconforming lot.

8.15.2 Contents

Registration shall be made on behalf of the owner by any person, firm, corporation, or other entity that has a legal or equitable interest in the nonconformity. Registration statements shall require a disclosure of the complete ownership of the land and/or structure, and shall be in such form and require the furnishing of such information, photographs, and documentation as are needed to show that:
(A) The use was lawfully established prior to the effective date of the applicable regulations;
(B) The use has been continuously maintained since it was established; and
(C) The use has not been abandoned.

8.15.3 Denial of Registration

The [PLANNING OFFICIAL] shall deny any registration if it appears that the documents relied thereon are not valid, or that the documents produced do not show the existence of a lawful nonconformity in accordance with the criteria set forth in § 8.15.1.2 Exemptions, subsection (A). The applicant may appeal this determination to the board of adjustment.

8.15.4 Amendment

At any time after registration, upon application to the [PLANNING OFFICIAL] and with the written consent of the owner affected thereby, a registration statement may be amended to indicate changes in ownership. A copy of each registration statement shall be returned to the owner and a copy filed among the records of the department. The [PLANNING OFFICIAL] shall accept and file all tendered registration statements within the permitted time period, but the acceptance of such statements shall not constitute an authorization to operate an unlawful use. The filing of a false registration statement with the department shall constitute a violation of this chapter.

8.16 TERMINATION OF NONCONFORMITIES

8.16.1 Violation of Chapter

The violation of this chapter shall immediately terminate a nonconformity.

8.16.2 Specific Acts of Termination

Any of the following specific acts of termination shall immediately terminate a nonconformity:
(A) Changing a nonconformity to conform to this type of termination applies only to the nonconforming use existing prior to any change;
(B) Abandonment of a nonconformity for a period of 12 or more successive calendar months; or
(C) Failure to register a nonconformity as provided in § 8.15 Certificate of Nonconforming Use of this chapter.

8.16.3 Notice

Termination of nonconforming rights under this section shall provide for 30 days' notice and hearing before the board of adjustment.

8.16.4 Action of the Board of Adjustment

The board of adjustment may inquire into the existence of a nonconformity, fire or health hazards, and any other danger or nuisance to the public due to or created by any condition or use existing on the property. Upon written findings, the board may require the discontinuance of such use. The owner of the use under inquiry shall have at least 20 days' written notice prior to the day of the public hearing. Time allowed for discontinuance of such use shall be prescribed by the board at a subsequent public hearing, after having heard from the affected parties, based on the board's ruling as to a reasonable amortization period for the nonconforming use.

In prescribing said time period, the board shall consider the following factors:
(A) The owner's capital investment in structures, fixed equipment, and other assets (excluding inventory and other assets that may be feasibly transferred to another site) on the property before the time the use became nonconforming;
(B) Any costs that are directly attributable to the establishment of a compliance date, including demolition expenses, relocation expenses, termination of leases, and discharge of mortgages;
(C) Any return on investment since inception of the use, including net income and depreciation; and

(D) The anticipated annual recovery of investment, including net income and depreciation.

8.16.5 Destruction or Damage of Structure

The right to operate and maintain any nonconformity, except for a single-family dwelling unit, shall terminate and shall cease to exist whenever the structure or structures in which the nonconforming use is operated and maintained is damaged or destroyed from any cause whatsoever, and the cost of repairing such damage or destruction exceeds 50 percent of the replacement cost of such building or structure on the date of such damage or destruction. A nonconforming single-family dwelling unit that is destroyed or damaged more than 50 percent of the replacement cost may be rebuilt, provided that a development approval is issued within one year of the date of such damage or destruction. The [PLANNING OFFICIAL] shall require the submission of sufficient evidence to verify the date of damage or destruction.

8.17 EXPANSION OF NONCONFORMITY

8.17.1 Applicability

No nonconformity may expand unless a conditional use permit (CUP) has been granted as set forth in Chapter 4, Procedures, of the LDC.

8.17.2 Criteria for Conditional Use Permit

In addition to the criteria required to be met for a CUP, the following criteria shall apply to the issuance of a CUP for the expansion of a nonconformity:

(A) The termination of such nonconformity will result in unnecessary hardship;

(B) The continuation of the nonconformity will not be contrary to the public interest;

(C) The continuation of the nonconformity will not substantially or permanently injure the appropriate use of adjacent conforming property in the same district;

(D) The use will be in harmony with the spirit and purpose of these regulations and the comprehensive plan goals, objectives, and policies;

(E) The plight of the applicant for which the continuation of the nonconformity is sought is due to unique circumstances existing on the property and/or within the surrounding district;

(F) The continuation of the nonconformity will not substantially weaken the general purposes of this chapter or the regulations established in this chapter for the applicable zoning district;

(G) The continuation of the nonconformity will not adversely affect the public health, safety, and welfare; and

(H) The continuation of the nonconformity through a reasonable amortization period is appropriate.

8.17.3 Conditions Applicable

Any conditions attached to any rezoning, CUP, variance, use permitted by [LOCAL GOVERNMENT] review, or any other development approval or development order issued under any previously enacted zoning regulations, subdivision, or other land development regulations (LDRs) shall continue to apply to the proposed use and shall be enforceable as provided in Chapter 4, Procedures, of the LDC. Such conditions may be waived if an application is approved pursuant to this chapter whereby the applicant agrees to waive and abandon all rights secured under the regulations formerly in effect.

DIVISION 2: VESTED RIGHTS

8.20 COMMON LAW, STATUTORY, AND CONSENT AGREEMENT RIGHTS

8.20.1 Applicability

This section applies to any application for development approval in which the applicant claims an exemption from any provision of this chapter based on common law or statutory vested rights or estoppel.

8.20.1.1 Common Law Vested Rights

Common law vested rights shall be acknowledged by the [PLANNING OFFICIAL] after consultation with the [LOCAL GOVERNMENT] attorney if the applicant for common law vested rights does not demonstrate entitlement to statutory vested rights as provided in subsection (B), below. The applicant for common law vested rights must show compliance with the following criteria for the specific project to acquire such rights:

(A) In reliance upon lawfully issued development approval, the applicant makes a substantial financial commitment or assumes substantial financial obligations within the purview of the activities authorized by said development approval;

(B) The applicant has proceeded in good faith, has relied upon the issuance of the development approval, and such development approval has not lapsed or been revoked;

(C) The applicant has established any other factor that may establish estoppel under state or federal law; and

(D) The applicant has obtained a favorable vested rights determination.

8.21 VESTED RIGHTS DETERMINATION

8.21.1 Generally

Any applicant may apply for a vested rights determination, provided that the requirements of this section are satisfied. An application for a vested rights determination may be approved subject to compliance with a consent agreement.

8.21.2 Consent Agreement

At any time prior to a final decision relating to an application for a vested rights determination, the applicant and the [LOCAL GOVERNMENT] may enter into a voluntary consent agreement conferring vested rights.

8.21.3 Terms and Conditions

A consent agreement shall be executed by the [LOCAL GOVERNMENT] and the applicant and shall include the following terms and conditions:

(A) A legal description of the subject property and the names of the legal and equitable owners;

(B) The duration of the consent agreement and the conditions that will result in revocation;

(C) The uses permitted on the property, including population densities and/or building intensities and height, yards, floor area ratio, setbacks, and other bulk regulation requirements;

(D) A description of the public facilities that will service the proposed development, including who shall provide such facilities; the date that any new facilities, if needed, will be constructed; and a schedule to assure that public facilities are available concurrent with the impacts of the development;

(E) A description of any reservation or dedication of land for public purposes;

(F) A description of all development approvals or other local, state, or federal approvals needed for the proposed development;

(G) A finding that the proposed development is consistent with the comprehensive plan and the relevant provisions of this chapter;

(H) A description of any conditions, terms, restrictions, or other requirements determined to be necessary for the preservation and protection of the public health, safety, or welfare;

(I) A statement indicating that the omission of a limitation or restriction shall not relieve the applicant of the necessity of complying with all applicable local, state, and federal laws;

(J) A phasing plan indicating the anticipated commencement and completion date of all phases of the proposed development;

(K) Provisions for remedies in the event of default;

(L) A statement that the [LOCAL GOVERNMENT] attorney shall review progress pursuant to the consent agreement at least once every 12 months to determine if there has been demonstrated good faith compliance with the terms of the consent agreement; and

(M) Any other provisions consonant with law.

8.21.4 Failure to Comply with Consent Agreement

If the board of adjustment finds, on the basis of substantial competent evidence, that there has been a failure to comply with the terms of the consent agreement, the consent agreement may be revoked or modified by the board of adjustment after a public hearing, which has been noticed by publication and for which notice has been expressly provided to the applicant.

8.22 VESTED RIGHTS DETERMINATION PROCESS

8.22.1 Initiation

An application may be made to the planning board of adjustment for recognition of vested rights for a particular project by completion of a form provided by the [PLANNING OFFICIAL] that indicates which development approval or development approvals are being relied on by the applicant for establishment of vested rights. The applicant for a vested rights determination shall provide the [PLANNING OFFICIAL] with a completed application and two copies of any documents on which the applicant is relying to establish vested rights.

8.22.2 Review and Approval

After receiving an application for a vested rights determination, the board of adjustment, upon notice duly published and provided to all owners of land within 500 feet of the applicant's property, shall review the application and determine if the applicant shall provide additional information for consideration of the application within 20 working days.

After the application is completed, the board of adjustment shall hold a public hearing and, upon the evidence submitted and upon review of the application, if the board of adjustment finds that there is sufficient evidence to establish vested rights, the board of adjustment shall issue a certificate to the applicant recognizing vested rights for the project. The certificate shall set forth all terms and conditions required for the continuance of the vested rights being recognized.

8.22.3 Variance

An individual, or business entity, that requests a vested rights determination may at the same time request a variance from the time limit, required action, or term that otherwise would cause the vested rights to expire. An individual requesting a variance must file a written application to the board of adjustment, which may be filed concurrently with the application for a vested rights determination. The request for variance must identify the specific provisions for which a variance is being requested and the reasons the applicant feels will justify the granting of the variance.

The board of adjustment shall review the application for variance and shall determine whether the variance is granted, conditionally granted, or denied. In granting a variance, the board of adjustment must make written findings establishing that:

(A) The applicant will suffer undue hardship in the absence of a variance that is not the result of the applicant's own negligence;

(B) The applicant has been actively attempting to pursue and complete development of the project that is the subject of the vested rights; and

(C) Compliance with rules and regulations passed after the recognition of vested rights will cause a substantial economic hardship to the developer/property owner, which precludes the capability of completing the project in a reasonable and prudent manner.

8.22.4 Recordation

The [PLANNING OFFICIAL] shall create a catalogued file of all certificates issued pursuant to this provision, which will be available to the public for inspection during regular business hours. The file shall be reviewed annually to remove certificates more than 10 years old.

COMMENTARY

A nonconforming use of land is a use lawfully established prior to the enactment or amendment of a zoning ordinance and maintained after the effective date of the ordinance or amendment even though not in compliance with the provisions of the zoning ordinance then in effect.[1] These nonconforming uses may or may not be incompatible with the zoning district in which they are located.

Vested rights issues concern "[t]he point at which a developer-landowner has proceeded sufficiently far enough with a project, once legal but now contrary to the terms of applicable land-use controls, so that his right to proceed is 'vested.'"[2] Vested rights decisions place limitations on the ability to apply newly adopted land-use regulations to developments that are proceeding through the permitting process. If a vested right to initiate the use or complete construction is found to exist, the use or structure will generally be allowed to continue as a protected nonconforming use.[3]

Vested rights issues are generally addressed under two theoretically distinct doctrines: vested rights and equitable estoppel. "Vested rights" is a constitutional doctrine that addresses whether a landowner has acquired property rights that cannot be divested, without compensation, by a subsequent affirmative governmental action. A denial of a vested right will lead to a claim of inverse condemnation against the government. "Estoppel" is an equitable doctrine that focuses on whether a government, because of its actions and reliance by the property owner or developer, may repudiate prior development approvals.[4]

Many courts treat equitable estoppel and vested rights as interchangeable doctrines. In determining whether a property owner has vested rights, the courts will examine whether the property owner has relied on an action of government, such as the issuance of a development approval, to expend money, leading to a finding that it would be inequitable to allow the government to change its position in the face of such reliance, thus granting the property owner a vested right.

Vested rights issues generally arise when a zoning regulation has changed prior to the completion of construction of a building or structure and, as a result of such change, the building or structure no longer conforms to the zoning and, without a vested right, will not be permitted to be completed. The LDC resolves issues as to when a use is lawfully established (i.e., the point at which a vested right arises, the rights acquired by a property owner, and the extent to which land-use regulations enacted subsequent to actions by a property owner can operate to limit those rights).

NONCONFORMING USES

In all states, nonconforming structures and uses existing at the time of the effective date of a zoning ordinance or restriction may be continued as a vested right.[5] Nonconforming uses are not favored by the law because they are inconsistent with the local government's LDRs. Zoning restrictions are designed to decrease and to diminish nonconforming uses in the public interest.[6] The goal of nonconforming use regulation is the eventual elimination of the nonconforming use or structure.[7] Nevertheless, nonconforming uses are resistant to change and either continue as a virtual local monopoly or are abandoned, creating visual blight.

Under the LDC, nonconforming properties are not treated as harshly as in the past. The LDC recognizes that some uses and structures should eventually be discontinued or be brought into compliance, while others should be allowed to continue and, in certain instances, grow and expand. In further reevaluating the existence and the continuance of nonconforming uses, each local government should provide its own guidance with respect to concerns about particular nonconforming uses.

The LDC:

• Reflects the growing trend to allow nonconforming uses and structures to continue and expand by considering the effect on the neighborhoods, particularly positive effects of expanding restaurants on and stores with mixed-use areas[8];

• Incorporates language that allows a nonconforming use and structure to be expanded through discretionary (CUP) review; and

• Encourages redevelopment of underutilized parcels and nonconforming uses and parcels.

Most state enabling acts require local governments to include regulations that address uses and structures which were lawfully in use prior to adoption of the zoning ordinance but which do not comply with the use, area, or setback requirements of the current regulations. Policy issues for regulating nonconforming uses include the following provisions:

• A reasonable amortization period should be established for certain uses to be amortized; and

• Many states permit the local government to require a certificate of nonconforming use to be filed within a designated period of time after an amendment that renders the use nonconforming. If the certificate is not filed within the designated time period, the nonconforming use is lost. Most courts have upheld such provisions, even where amortization of a nonconforming use without compensation is considered invalid.

This regulation permits local governments to determine, after the period for filing a certificate has expired, whether a nonconforming use or vested rights claim is viable.[9] This allows the public sector to take legitimate vested rights claims into consideration when engaging in comprehensive land-use planning. Landowners receive the benefit of a written certification as to the legality of their use, which provides certainty as to future investments.

The LDC addresses nonconforming issues comprehensively, embracing the philosophy introduced in *A Unified Development Ordinance*.[10] This embraces several distinct philosophies:

• Nonconformities are treated comprehensively. While most codes apply only to nonconforming uses, this chapter addresses nonconformity as to standards and lots; and

• Nonconforming uses rarely disappear but instead tend to worsen because their ability to obtain financing disappears.

Accordingly, this chapter permits nonconformities to expand subject to discretionary review.

ESTABLISHMENT

The burden of proving the right to maintain a nonconforming use is on the party seeking to continue said use. It is that party who must prove the essential elements of the right to maintain the use, including prior existence of the use, and denial of such use will be sustained where the evidence in support of such prior use is insufficient or contradictory. In order to establish a nonconforming use, the applicant must prove and establish the elements set forth as follows:

• The establishment of the use before the effective date of changes in regulations that render the use nonconforming;

• The use was lawful when established;

• The use existed prior to the adoption of the regulations against which the nonconforming use is asserted; and

• The use has been lawfully continued from its inception.

REGULATION

Nonconformities are subject to future LDRs, provided that the nonconformity is not totally abrogated.[11]

TERMINATION

Abandonment

A landowner or occupant of a property, building, or structure who voluntarily, with an intent to abandon, or who commits an overt act of a substantial discontinuance, forfeits the vested right to continue a nonconformity.[12]

Governmental Action

Amortization Period for Certain Nonconformities

Any nonconforming fence over legal height, obstruction, sign, junkyard and automobile graveyard, billboard, landfill, or fenced outdoor commercial or industrial storage area shall be removed after a period of five years after the effective date of registration. The board of adjustment shall, after the five-year period has elapsed, provide notice and a hearing to the property owner affected and to all properties within 500 feet of the property affected, and shall determine whether an order of termination shall be issued. The board of adjustment may extend the amortization period at any time upon application of an affected property owner upon establishment that the amortization period deprives the owner of all or substantial economic use of the property, may order termination, or may request the local government to provide funds for zoning with compensation.

The local government, considering regulations for terminating nonconforming situations, should include the following techniques:

• Amortization;

• Registration of nonconforming uses, which many jurisdictions require. If the applicant fails to file the registration within a designated time period, the nonconforming use lapses. This does not amortize the uses but does require some administrative staffing to maintain the nonconforming use registry.[13] The trend of recent decisions is that failure to file a registration certificate terminates the use.[14] Registration is permitted in some states that do not permit amortization[15];

• Authorization of expansion of some nonconforming uses/structures subject to discretionary review criteria, such as a CUP; and

• Creation of regulatory trade-offs, such as elimination of some nonconforming features coupled with regulatory incentives, such as height or floor area bonuses.

To encourage compact and/or mixed-use development, not all nonconforming situations are bad. Some may be encouraged to continue and/or to expand, provided that they do not set a precedent for similar situations in the district. In addition, the existing distinction between nonconforming lots, structures, and uses is typical of a more advanced nonconforming use regulation, although the language may need to be rewritten for clarity and be revised to implement the comprehensive plan.

ZONING WITH COMPENSATION

The local government may, in any circumstance, when the board of adjustment has determined that the period of amortization has deprived an owner of a nonconformity of all or substantial economic use of the property that would amount to a taking of the property, request the local government to provide compensation for the loss in market value of the property occasioned by the regulation and continue the zoning and amortization period in place,[16] and may create a special assessment district to distribute the cost to the benefiting area.[17]

VESTED RIGHTS

"Vested rights" commonly refer to rights granted to applicants for development approval to proceed with a permitted, but not established, project following changes in a development code. The majority rule is that a landowner's right to develop land vests only at that point in time when there has been substantial construction or action in reliance upon a lawfully issued development approval.[18] There is no vested right to an existing zoning classification.[19] Some states have changed this rule by statute[20] or jurisdiction if the change in the law occurred after an application has been filed.[21] The *Growing Smart* ™*Legislative Guidebook*[22] offers a number of alternatives in § 8-501 for model vested rights legislation.

GOVERNMENTAL ACT OR OMISSION

A governmental act or omission is the key threshold requirement for establishing a vested rights claim. The more recent a governmental action, the better the applicant's position for vested rights.[23] Governmental actions are listed below in order of their relative strength, from the applicant's viewpoint, in asserting a vested rights claim.

Development Approval

Most jurisdictions agree that the issuance of a development approval vests land development rights of a landowner. In fact, some jurisdictions require issuance of the final development approval in the development approval process—typically, a development approval—in order to successfully assert a vested rights claim.[24] The minority view is that the right to a development approval vests at the time of application as long as the application is consistent with the building codes and ordinances then in effect.[25]

Plat Approval

Many courts will vest land development rights upon actions in reliance of preliminary or final plat approvals.[26] In jurisdictions where the receipt of a final discretionary approval vests development rights, approval of a preliminary subdivision plat is sufficient to vest development rights on the condition that it must be the last discretionary development approval needed.[27] Most jurisdictions require a landowner to make substantial expenditures on a subdivision before rights to complete the subdivision will vest,[28] although others confer vested rights when a complete application is filed.[29] Several states have enacted legislation to protect the property owner's right to continue development once a governing authority has approved a preliminary plat.[30]

In the subdivision approval context, plat approval vests a subdivider's rights to construct uses on the subdivided land. In *Youngblood v. Board of Supervisors*,[31] the California Supreme Court affirmed the approval of a final plat by the board of supervisors despite the fact that the plat was inconsistent with a comprehensive plan amendment that had been enacted after approval of the preliminary plat. Interpreting California's subdivision enabling legislation, the court held that:

> "Once the [preliminary plat] is approved, the developer often must expend substantial sums to comply with the conditions attached to that approval. These expenditures will result in the construction of improvements consistent with the proposed subdivision, but often inconsistent with alternative uses of the land. Consequently, it is only fair to the developer and to the public interest to require the government to render its discretionary decision whether and upon what condition to approve the proposed subdivision when it acts on the [preliminary plat]. Approval of the final [plat] thus becomes a ministerial act once the appropriate officials certify that it is in substantial compliance with the previously approved tentative map."[32]

While *Youngblood* seems to preclude the application of new development standards upon the approval of a preliminary subdivision plat, subsequent California decisions have indicated that the scope of that opinion is limited to subdivision conditions that could have been imposed at the preliminary approval stage and not to conditions beyond the ambit of subdivision control.[33] Subsequent California decisions uniformly distinguished *Youngblood* to hold that preliminary plat approval does not bar the imposition of other police power regulations that are related to subdivision regulation.

In *El Patio v. Permanent Rent Control Board of City of Santa Monica*,[34] tentative map approval was held not to confer a vested right to proceed with development notwithstanding subsequently adopted permitting requirements, so long as such requirements arise under authority other than the subdivision enabling legislation. The court held that development approvals had a reason for existence independent of the Subdivision Map Act, and therefore that no rights to commence construction arose until a development approval had been issued. Map approval conferred no such right.

Planned Development Plan Approval

The law regarding planned development plan approval is largely the same as preliminary subdivision plat approval.[35] Some states, such as Colorado and North Carolina, protect multiphased development plans if they meet designated statutory criteria.[36]

Special Use or Conditional Use Permit

A number of jurisdictions vest rights upon issuance of a special use permit if it is the last discretionary development approval issued. The conditional or special use permit must be validly issued in order to vest development rights.[37]

Site Plan Approval

Some states have equated site plan approval with issuance of a development approval.[38] In those states, a local government cannot deny a development approval application if a site plan is approved and the property owner has made substantial expenditures in reliance on the approval.[39]

Grading or Other Site Preparation

Many courts are unlikely to confer vested rights based on preliminary approvals, such as grading and other site preparation. Other states do not distinguish between building or CUPs and a grading development approval.[40]

Rezoning

A landowner has no vested right in a zoning classification unless the classification is passed or is created principally to frustrate a land development project. However, some states have found estoppel when a landowner exercises an option to purchase the property following rezonings or subdivision approval at the landowner's request.[41]

Detrimental Reliance

Estoppel requires detrimental reliance constituting a substantial or prejudicial change in position. Some jurisdictions require both substantial expenses and actual construction to invoke the doctrine.[42] No rule of thumb exists as to the amount of expenditures that will be deemed "substantial"; change in position is judged on a case-by-case basis.[43] Reliance expenditures include monies spent in preparation for development and construction. Reliance must also be justified. Developers are charged with knowledge of applicable regulations and cannot use mere misstatements of public officials to thwart the application of legislation.

Good Faith

Good faith on behalf of the applicant is often required by the courts.[44] Courts that apply this test may defeat a vested rights claim where the applicant rushes to begin a project in order to avoid a zoning change or prior to a pending election.[45] Good faith may also apply to government actions.[46] If a development approval is willfully withheld by a local government by deceptive conduct, a new intervening law will not apply[47] and an action for damages may lie.[48] While courts are loath to estop local governments in the exercise of their police powers, landowners have a right to expect fair dealing on the part of elected and appointed officials. Accordingly, some courts may find vested rights or estoppel in the face of a rezoning with knowledge that the purchase was contingent on the rezoning and the attempt to downzone to prevent development.[49]

Scope of Vested Rights

A determination that a landowner has vested rights requires a further analysis of what rights have vested. Especially in the context of large, multiphased development proposals, a landowner may have vested rights as to some phases or components of a development but not as to others. The scope of a landowner's rights is determined by the language of the development approval and, in the equitable estoppel context, other evidence of knowledge by town officials as to the developer's plans.[50]

Vested rights may also be thwarted by the presence of preexisting public rights. For example, the "public trust" doctrine subordinates the rights of riparian or littoral landowners to the paramount public right to free navigation.[51] The court in *Compass Lake Hills Development v. State Dept. of Community Affairs*,[52] stated:

"In determining whether rights have vested . . . the existence of a development plan is of critical importance. The plan shows what the developer intends to do with the land, and once the development is approved, what he is permitted to do. . . . Without a plan, neither the department nor the local government can determine what the developer has the right to do, nor can either determine later whether the vested plan is being carried out."

In *City Ice Delivery Co. v. Zoning Board of Adjustment for the County of Charleston*,[53] the plaintiff had obtained a development approval for a food store on its property—a use that later became a lawful nonconforming use when the zoning ordinance was amended. When the plaintiff later tried to install gasoline pumps and tanks, they were prevented by the county from doing so. The court, in upholding the county's position, ruled that county officials could not be charged with knowledge of the respondent's intentions where the plans submitted as the basis for the development approval made no reference to gasoline pumps, service islands, or electrical wiring necessary for such facilities.

In *Friarsgate, Inc. v. Town of Irmo*,[54] the court held that holding that "[a] contemplated use of property by a landowner on the date a zoning ordinance becomes effective to preclude such a use is not protected as a nonconforming use" to which rights may vest. In *Friarsgate*, a developer who had received a development approval for one building in a planned multibuilding condominium project, prior to adoption of a zoning ordinance that would have precluded such a use, did not have a vested right to the entire project.[55] Even though the entire project was planned prior to receiving the development approval on the first building, the court reasoned that the developer could have obtained development approvals for all 14 buildings in the development at the same time. The court characterized the failure to secure development approvals to the entire project as the product of market decisions rather than governmental conduct. As such, no rights had vested.

The most important limitations on the scope of vested rights are those conditions attached to previously issued development approvals. Such conditions define the parameters of what may be constructed and may allow the local government to impose additional conditions. In *Russ Building Partnership*,[56] the California Supreme Court specifically held that if a development approval contains conditions which clearly contemplate later legislation, no vested rights with regard to this contemplated legislation exists.[57]

Revocation or Divestment of Vested Rights

A vested development right is not an absolute one. The courts have allowed that the revocation of vested rights upon the finding of public necessity or evidence of a new peril to the health, safety, or welfare of a community may be sufficient to allow a revocation of a vested right.[58] There is no hard and fast rule as to what constitutes a sufficient finding of public necessity. Under the common law, state courts and the U.S. Supreme Court have supported the concept that vested rights may lapse through inaction by the property owner or by the sheer passage of time.[59] In *United States vs. Lock*,[60] the U.S. Supreme Court stated that:

"Even with respect to vested property rights, a legislature generally has the power to impose new regulatory constraints on the way in which those rights are used, or to condition their continued retention on performance of certain affirmative duties. As long as the constraint or duty imposed is a reasonable restriction designed to further legitimate legislative objectives, the legislature acts within its powers in imposing such new constraints or duties. See, e.g., Village of Euclid v. Ambler Realty Co., 272 U.S. 365 (1926); Turner v. New York, 168 U.S. 90, 94 (1897); Vance v. Vance, 108 U.S. 514, 517 (1883); Terry v. Anderson, 95 U.S. 628 (1877). [L]egislation readjusting rights and burdens is not unlawful solely because it upsets otherwise settled expectations." Usery v. Turner Elkhorn Mining Co., 428 U.S. 1, 16 (1976) (citations omitted).

The Ninth Circuit has noted that the law of vested rights is intended, in part, to avoid an indefinite freezing of local police powers, citing the leading California case.[61] In an outright rejection of the developer's arguments that its vested rights were permanent in nature, the court reasoned as follows:[62]

"In these circumstances, for [the developer] to argue that the expenditures it has made on Unit One and hotel in reliance on the 1969 permit entitle it to a vested right for Unit Two is for it to argue in effect that its right to develop Unit Two is vested forever. Yet such a permanent vesting is the evil that the Avco court said that it would not tolerate. It matters not that Unit Two may have been conceived of as a dependent part of a planned unitary development. The rationale for departing from the 'building permit' rule [which establishes that vested rights cannot be acquired until such time as a building permit is issued] as applied to such developments is that the preliminary development expenses are high and cannot be recouped if the government prohibits development before a sufficiently substantial portion of the project is completed. When, as in this case, the government does not interfere until well after the time the developer could have completed the entire project, the reason for recognizing a vested right evaporates."

This rationale parallels situations in which the courts allow local governments to "amortize" nonconforming uses in zoning districts by requiring landowners to demolish such uses after a particular period of time.

NOTES

1. *City of Sugar Creek v. Reese*, 969 S.W.2d 888 (Mo. App. 1998).
2. For a complete analysis of theories of vested rights, see David L. Callies, Daniel J. Curtin, and Julie A. Tappendorf, *Bargaining for Development: A Handbook on Development Agreements, Annexation Agreements, Land Development Conditions, Vested Rights and the Provision of Public Facilities* (Washington, DC: Environmental Law Institute, 2003).
3. See Edward H. Ziegler, Jr., et al., *Rathkopf's The Law of Zoning and Planning* (St. Paul, MN: West Group, 2004), § 70:2 at 70-3.
4. Patrick J. Rohan and Eric Damien Kelly, *Zoning and Land Use Controls*, Vol. 8, § 52.08(4)(b) (1997).
5. A local government may not zone to eliminate a nonconforming use. *Town of Lyons v. Bashor*, 867 P.2d 159 (Colo. App. 1993).
6. *Acton v. Jackson County*, 854 S.W.2d 447, 448 (Mo. App. W.D. 1993); *Suzuki v. City of Los Angeles*, 51 Cal.Rptr.2d 880 (Cal.App 1996) (elimination promotes "nuisance abatement").
7. See Daniel R. Mandelker, *Land Use Law*, 5th ed. (Newark, NJ: LexisNexis Matthew Bender, 2003), § 5.78.
8. *Nettleton v. Zoning Board of Adjustment*, 828 A.2d 1033 (Pa 2003) (addition of two stores to one-story building if setback not violated); *Domeisen v. Zoning Hearing Board*, 814 A.2d 851 (Pa. Commw. 2003) (expansion of flower business).
9. American Law Institute, *A Model Land Development Code: Complete Text and Commentary* (Philadelphia: American Law Institute, 1976), § 5-102 (limiting measures for elimination of nonconforming uses to well-established homogenous areas where the use would be anomalous).
10. Michael B. Brough, *A Unified Development Ordinance* (Chicago: American Planning Association, 1985), Article VIII.

11. *Suzuki v. City of Los Angeles*, 51 Cal.Rptr. 880 (Cal. App. 1996); *Mayor and City Council v. Dembo*, 719 A.2d 1007 (Md. App. 2001).

12. Abandonment usually means a voluntary act with the local government offering proof of intent to abandon, or an overt act of substantial discontinuance. *City of University Place v. McGuire*, 30 P.3d 453 (Wash. 2001); *City of Myrtle Beach v. Jual B. Corp.*, 543 S.E.2d 538 (S.C. 2001). Most courts today apply an objective test of an overt act of discontinuance without proof of intent. *Toys-R-Us v. Silva*, 676 N.E.2d 862 (N.Y. 1996) (substantial discontinuance upheld); *Latrobe Speedway, Inc. v. Zoning Hearing Board of Unity Township*, 553 Pa. 583, 592, 720 A.2d 127, 132 (1998) (discontinuance is evidence of intent to abandon and burden shifts to person challenging claim of abandonment).

13. The American Planning Association's *Growing Smart™ Legislative Guidebook: Model Statutes for Planning and the Management of Change* (Stuart Meck, FAICP, gen. ed.) (Chicago: APA, 2002), recommends registration of nonconforming uses. Registration has been upheld as advancing legitimate governmental purposes. *Board of Zoning Appeals v. Leisz*, 702 N.E.2d 1026 (Ind. 1998).

14. 3 *Board of Zoning Appeals v. Leisz*, 702 N.E.2d 1026 (Ind. 1998); *Board of Adjustment of City of San Antonio v. Nelson*, 577 S.W.2d 783 (Tex. Civ. App. San Antonio), writ refused n.r.e, 584 S.W.2d 701 (Tex. 1979); *Uncle v. New Jersey Pinelands Com'n*, 275 N.J.Super. 82, 645 A.2d 788 (N.J.Super.A.D. 1994); *County Com'rs of Carroll County v. Uhler*, 78 Md. App. 140, 552 A.2d 942 (Md. App.), *cert. denied*, 316 Md. 428, 559 A.2d 791 (Md. 1989); *Lichte v. Heidlage*, 536 S.W.2d 898 (Mo. App. 1976); *Schroeder v. Dane County Bd. of Adjustment*, 228 Wis.2d 324, 596 N.W.2d 472 (Wis. App. 1999), *rev. denied*, 228 Wis.2d 176, 602 N.W.2d 761 (Wis. 1999).

15. Compare Note 14 (*Lichte*), supra, with *Hoffmann v. Kinealy*, 389 S.W.2d 745 (Mo.1965) (amortization ruled unconstitutional under state law).

16. See *City of Kansas City v. Kindle*, 446 S.W.2d 807 (Mo. 1969).

17. *In re Coleman Highlands*, 777 S.W.2d 621, 624 (Mo. App. W. D. 1989).

18. Note 3 (Ziegler), supra, § 70:10 at 70-6 (2004), the leading case in the field is *Avco Community Developer v. South Coast Regional Commission*, 553 P.2d 546 (Cal. 1976).

19. *City of Kawai v. Pacific Life Ins. Co.*, 653 P.2d 766 (Haw. 1982).

20. For example, the common law in Texas does not provide vested rights even at late stages in the development approval process, such as preliminary subdivision plats. The Texas legislature passed HB 1704, which provides an opportunity for developers to obtain vesting upon the submission of an application for development approval. The law protects local governments by providing an opportunity to terminate dormant projects (Texas Local Government Code § 245.005). To some, the law strikes a balance between the needs of private developers to proceed with certainty to completion of a project without new unanticipated requirements, and the planning needs of local governments faced with antiquated subdivisions and approvals.

21. *Folsom Enterprises v. City of Scottsdale*, 620 F.Supp. 1372 (D. Ariz. 1985); *WMM Properties, Inc. v. Cobb County*, 339 S.E.2d 252 (Ga. 1986); *Pokoik v. Silsdorf*, 358 N.E.2d 874 (N.Y. 1976).

22. Stuart Meck, FAICP, gen. ed., *Growing Smart™ Legislative Guidebook: Model Statutes for Planning and the Management of Change* (Chicago: American Planning Association, 2002).

23. Patrick J. Rohan, *Zoning and Land Use Controls* (New York: M. Bender, 2003), at § 52D.02(1) at § 52D-5. Several cases have found estoppel when a city adopts zoning to frustrate a landowner entitled to a development approval under existing law under a valid application. *Lake Housing Bluff Partners v. City of South Milwaukee*, 525 N.W.2d 59 (Wis. App. 1994); *Interstate Power Company v. Nobles County*, 617 N.W.2d 556 (Minn. 2000); *Whitehead Oil Co. v. City of Lincoln*, 515 N.E.2d 390 (Neb. 1994) (downzoning after application is arbitrary and capricious).

24. Note 23 (Rohan), supra, at § 52D.02(2). "If a property owner has performed substantial work and incurred substantial liabilities in good faith reliance upon a permit issued by the government, he acquires a vested right to complete construction in accordance with the terms of the permit." *Avco Community Developers, Inc. v. South Coast Regional Commission*, 132 Cal.Rptr. 386, 389 (1976). The Court in *Avco* stated that the general rule that "a builder must comply with the laws which are in effect at the time a building permit is issued," include laws that are enacted after application for the development approval. Id. at 392-393. The Court noted that "plaintiffs had not cited a single California decision [in which] a property owner has been held to have acquired a vested right against future zoning without having first acquired a building permit to construct a specific type of building and having thereafter expended a considerable sum and reliance upon said permit. Such authority would appear nonexistent for the reason that the vested rights theory is predicated upon estoppel of the governing body. . . . Where no permit has been issued, it is difficult to conceive any basis for such estoppel." Id. at 391 (citing *Anderson v. City Council of City of Pleasant Hill*, 40 Cal.Rptr. 41, 47 (1964)).

25. Note 3 (Ziegler), supra, § 70:16 at 70-18. *The Villages L.L.C. v. Delaware Agricultural Lands Foundation*, 808 A.2d 753 (Del. 2002); *Western Land Equities v. City of Logan*, 617 P.2d 388 (Utah 1980).

26. *Board of Commissioners of South Whitehall Township, Lehigh County v. Toll Brothers*, 607 A.2d 824 (Pa. 1992) (local government may not apply a new ordinance increasing fee schedules to development for which it previously granted final subdivision plan approval); *Ramapo 287 Ltd. Partnership v. Village of Montebello*, 568 N.Y.S.2d 492, 494 (N.Y. App. Div. 1991); but see *In re Appeal of Taft Corners Assocs.*, 758 A.2d 804 (2000) and *P.W. Investments, Inc. v. City of Westminster*, 655 P.2d 1365 (Colo. 1982); *Lake City Corp. v. City of Mequon*, 544 N.W.2d 600 (Wis. 1996) (holding that plat that conformed to then existing ordinances must be approved, even if landowner was submitting plats on "dormant" project to "beat the clock" of new regulations).

27. Note 23 (Rohan), supra, § 52D.03(2) at 52D-16.1; *Villa at Greely, Inc. v. Hopper*, 917 P.2d 350 (Colo. App. 1996).

28. Note 23 (Rohan), supra, § 52D.03(2) at 52D-16; *North Georgia Mountain Cross of Blue Ridge v. City Network, Inc.*,

546 E.2d 850 (Ga. App. 2001) (purchase of land not sufficient).
29. *Adams v. Thurston County,* 855 P.2d 284 (Wash. 1993); *FM Properties v. City of Austin,* 93 F.3d 167 (5th Cir. 1996).
30. Note 23 (Rohan), supra, § 52D.03[2], citing New Jersey (three years), New Hampshire (four years), Pennsylvania (five years), and Washington (five years).
31. 22 Cal.3d 644, 150 Cal.Rptr. 242, 586 P.2d 556 (1978).
32. 150 Cal.Rptr. at 248; see also *City National Bank of Miami v. City of Coral Springs,* 475 So.2d 984, 985 (Fla. App. 4 Dist. 1985) ("It is elementary that once a party complied with all legal requirements for platting there is no discretion in government authority to refuse approval of the plat"), citing *Broward County v. Narco Realty, Inc.,* 359 So.2d 509 (Fla. 4th Dist. Ct. App. 1978).
33. See *FM Properties Operating Co. v. City of Austin,* 93 F.3d 167 (5th Cir. 1996) (vested rights at time of zoning application does not vest rights to subsequent separate subdivision under existing law).
34. 110 Cal. App. 3d 915, 168 Cal.Rptr. 276 (Cal. App. 2d 1980); see also *Scarborough, N.V. v. Santa Monica Rent Control Board,* 217 Cal.Rptr. 259, 703 P.2d 1153 (Cal., August 1985), *rev. dismissed, Scarborough, N.V. v. Santa Monica Rent Control Bd.,* 237 Cal.Rptr. 455, 737 P.2d (preliminary plat approval does not vest subdivider from condominium conversion development approval requirement); *People v. H&H Properties,* 154 Cal. App. 3d 894, 201 Cal.Rptr. 593, 697 P.2d 27 (1984) (final plat approval does not vest subdivider against application of rent control law); *Laguna Village,* 166 Cal. App. 3d 125, 212 Cal.Rptr. 267, 23 Ed. Law Rep. 948 (Cal. App. 1985), *review denied* (1985) (subdivision approval does not preclude imposition of school impact fees); *Billings v. California Coastal Commission,* 103 Cal. App. 3d 729, 163 Cal.Rptr. 288 (1980) (rejecting final discretionary approval test but holding that landowners were entitled to coastal development approval under arbitrary and capricious standard); *In re Appeal of Taft Corners Assocs.,* 758 A.2d 804 (2000) (right to complete development to the extent of building particular buildings may not vest).
35. *City of Suffolk v. Board of Zoning Appeals,* 580 S.E.2d 796 (Va. 2003) (quasi-judicial approval of a proposed development).
36. Colo. Rev. Stat. § 24-68-103; N.C.G.S. §§ 160A-385.1 (cities), 153A-344.1.
37. A Massachusetts law protects a holder of a special use permit from a zoning change if the permit was issued before notice of the zoning change was given. See Mass. Gen. Law, ch. 40A § 6; Va. Code Ann. § 15.2-2307.
38. Note 23 (Rohan), supra, § 52D.03[4].
39. *Village of Palatine v. LaSalle National Bank,* 445 N.E.2d 1277 (Ill. 1983).
40. *Juanita Bay Valley Community Ass'n. v. City of Kirkland,* 510 P.2d 1140 (Wash. 1973).
41. *Franklin County v. Leisure Properties,* 430 S.2d 475 (Fla. App. 1975) (rezoning); *Disabatino v. New Castle County,* 781 A.2d 687 (Del. 2001) (subdivision approval).
42. Note 23 (Rohan), supra, § 52.08(4)(b).
43. Richard B. Cunningham and David H. Kremer, "Vested Rights, Estoppel, and the Land Development Process," 29 Hastings L. J. 625, 651 (1978); *Daniels v. City of Goose Creek,* 431 S.E.2d 256 (S.C. App. 1993) (purchase of land not enough); *Robert Rieke Bldg. Co. v. City of Olathe,* 697 P.2d 72 (Kan. App. 1985) (preliminary expenses not enough).
44. Most courts allow revocation of illegally issued development approvals and even demolition of structures. *Parkview Assoc. v. City of New York,* 519 N.E.2d 1372 (N.Y. 1988); *Town of Lauderdale By-The-Sea v. Meretzky,* 773 So.2d 1245 (Fla. App. 2000).
45. See *Smith v. City of Clearwater,* 383 So.2d 681 (Fla. App. 1980) (bad faith found).
46. *Hill v. Zoning Hearing Board,* 626 A.2d 510 (Pa. 1993) (local government must act without unreasonable delay).
47. *Eiggie Int'l v. Town of Huntington,* 620 N.Y.S.2d 563 (N.Y. App. 1994).
48. *Mission Springs, Inc. v. City of Spokane,* 954 P.2d 250 (Wash. 1998).
49. Daniel R. Mandelker, *Land Use Law,* 5th ed. (Albany, NY: Lexis Law Publishing, 2003) at § 6.18.
50. In *Pardee Construction Co. v. City of Camarillo,* 690 P.2d 701 (Cal. 1984), a developer was vested to 1,000 units by a development agreement but was subjected to a later initiative restricting his annual development approvals to 50 per year because the development agreement was silent on timing and phasing.
51. *South Carolina Electric & Gas Company v. Hix,* 410 S.E.2d 582, 584 (S.C. App. 1991) (collecting issues).
52. 379 So.2d 376 (Fla. 1st Dist. Ct. App. 1979).
53. 203 S.E.2d 385 (S.C. 1974).
54. 339 S.E.2d 891 (S.C. App. 1986).
55. Id. at 895.
56. 750 P.2d 324 (Cal. 1988).
57. However, if the agreement is specific, then developer is vested to cost basis of fees despite subsequent ordinance. *City of North Las Vegas v. Pardee Construction Co.,* 21 P.3d 8 (Nev. 2001).
58. *Pendleton v. City of Columbia,* 40 S.E.2d 499 (S.C. 1946) (development approval for addition to single-family home that authorities suspected would be used as a duplex, contrary to the zoning ordinance, could not be revoked absent showing that proposed addition would adversely affect health, comfort, or safety of the surrounding neighborhood); *Pure Oil Division,* 173 S.E.2d at 143; *Belle Harbor Realty Corp. v. Kerr,* 35 N.Y.2d 507, 364 N.Y.S.2d 160, 323 N.E.2d 697 (1974) (revocation of development approval permissible under general police powers where sewer system operating over capacity and local government was taking steps to rectify the problem).
59. See *Pompano Beach v. Yardarm Restaurant,* 509 So.2d 1295 (Fla. App. 1987) (vested rights pursuant to issuance of special exception to height limit and development approvals lapsed where applicant delayed construction for 12 years); but see *Thompson v. Village of Tequesta,* 564 So.2d 457 (Fla. App. 4 Dist. 1989) (vested rights acquired pursuant to issuance of a variance could not be divested after 21-year period delay under terms of local ordinance).
60. 471 U.S. 84 (1985).
61. Note 24 (*Avco*), supra. *Lakeview Devel. Corp. v. City of South Lake Tahoe,* 915 F.2d 1290 (9th Cir. 1990).
62. 915 F.2d at 1298.

CHAPTER

9

Administrative Agencies

9.1 AUTHORITY

9.1.1 Generally

The [GOVERNING ENTITY] shall render final decisions pertaining to the enactment or development of the comprehensive plan, any neighborhood plan, and this chapter, except where authority for a final decision is delegated to another agency by this chapter. The [GOVERNING ENTITY] shall render final decisions pertaining to applications for development approval where such authority is assigned pursuant to this chapter.

9.1.2 Specific Power

The [GOVERNING ENTITY] shall have the following powers and duties:
  (A) To initiate, adopt, and amend a comprehensive plan;
  (B) To initiate amendments to the text and map of this chapter;
  (C) To hear, review, and adopt amendments to the text of this chapter after a recommendation of the planning commission;
  (D) To approve or deny or to amend and grant applications for development approval, excluding appeals and variances, which have been delegated to the board of adjustment;
  (E) To approve or deny or to amend and grant applications for conditional use permits or development agreements; and
  (F) To take such other action not expressly delegated exclusively to the [PLANNING OFFICIAL], the planning commission, or the board of adjustment as the [GOVERNING ENTITY] may deem desirable and necessary to implement the provisions of this chapter and the comprehensive plan.

9.2 PLANNING COMMISSION

The planning commission is established pursuant to the [STATUTE OR CHARTER].

9.2.1 Duties of Planning Commission

The duties of the planning commission are as follows:
  (A) To recommend the boundaries of original zoning districts and appropriate regulations for enforcement;
  (B) To hold public hearings and prepare a final report for the [GOVERNING ENTITY] on recommendations for change in zoning district boundaries or regulations in zoning districts; and
  (C) To perform such other functions as are necessary or required by state law or [LOCAL GOVERNMENT] ordinance.

9.2.2 Quorum, Majority Vote

A quorum shall consist of six members of the commission. The chairman shall be counted as any other member when establishing a quorum. Final action on any matter shall require a majority vote of six members, except when the commission has twice held a public hearing and considered a zoning application and is unable to reach a majority vote. In such instances, the commission may submit a report instead of a recommendation to the [GOVERNING ENTITY].

9.2.3 Conflict of Interest

A member shall not vote or participate as a member in any matter before the commission if the member has any interest in this matter, whether such interest is direct or indirect, financial, or otherwise. In any case, where the question of a member's interest is raised, the chairman shall rule on whether the member should be disqualified.

9.2.4 Recommendations

The commission shall take no final action on any matter before it without first obtaining a recommendation from the [PLANNING OFFICIAL] and reports from the other [LOCAL GOVERNMENT] departments concerned, as determined by the commission.

9.2.5 Robert's Rules of Order

Any question of order or procedure not covered by these rules shall be decided according to the latest edition of *Robert's Rules of Order*,[1] insofar as that may be applicable.

9.3 PLANNING DEPARTMENT AND ADMINISTRATION

The administrative official for the purposes of this chapter shall be the [PLANNING OFFICIAL] and his/her assistants, deputies, and department heads insofar as they may be charged by the [PLANNING OFFICIAL] and the provisions of this chapter with duties and responsibilities with reference thereto. The directors of planning, public works, and building inspections shall administer and enforce the provisions of this chapter. The [PLANNING OFFICIAL] shall serve as staff to the planning commission and the [GOVERNING ENTITY] except where otherwise provided by this chapter.

9.4 HEARING OFFICER (OPTIONAL PROVISION)

9.4.1 Establishment

For the purpose of adjudicating quasi-judicial land-use hearings, the [LOCAL GOVERNMENT] has established the position of hearing officer.[2]

9.4.2 Appointment and Removal

(A) The [GOVERNING ENTITY OR EXECUTIVE OFFICER] shall appoint one or more hearing officer(s) to conduct quasi-judicial hearings. Should the [GOVERNING ENTITY OR EXECUTIVE OFFICER] appoint more than one hearing officer, the terms of office shall be appropriately staggered and applications shall be equally assigned to hearing officers by a confidential rotation system.

(B) Each hearing officer shall be appointed for a definite term of office, not to exceed four years, and may be reappointed at the conclusion of any term.

(C) A hearing officer may be removed by the [GOVERNING ENTITY] only for cause. Cause for removal of a hearing officer shall include, but not be limited to, violations of these standards set forth in the [STATE] Code of Judicial Conduct, as adopted by the [STATE] Supreme Court.

9.4.3 Qualifications

(A) A hearing officer shall be appointed solely with regard to the qualifications for the duties of the office.

(B) A hearing officer shall have a degree in urban planning or related professional field, with at least three years of professional experience in planning; or shall have a degree in architecture, engineering, or law and shall have been licensed to practice in [STATE] for at least three years.

(C) A hearing officer shall not hold other appointive or elective office or position in government during his/her term.

(D) A hearing officer shall not be an employee of the [LOCAL GOVERNMENT].

9.4.4 Compensation

The hearing officer shall be compensated for his/her services from the general revenue funds of the [LOCAL GOVERNMENT]. The [GOVERNING ENTITY] shall set the compensation.

9.4.5 Powers and Duties

The hearing officer shall hear appeals and variances pursuant to *Division 6: Variances and Appeals* of Chapter 4, Procedures, of the Land Development Code (LDC). The hearing officer shall have all powers necessary to conduct the hearings assigned to the hearing officer by the LDC.

COMMENTARY

This chapter formally establishes agencies and officials necessary to implement the development approval process. To streamline ordinance length, this chapter may be omitted if another part of the local government's code establishes these agencies, or if the traditional agencies are required by state law or the local government charter.

This chapter, if utilized, must be carefully structured to conform to the specific appointment, jurisdictional, and procedural aspects of state law. Some state statutes or local charter provisions are sufficiently specific so that a sample cross-reference may suffice. The optional section on hearing officers is designed for those communities with extensive quasi-judicial hearings. Hearing officers are also useful in the local governments that have provided for vested rights determinations

NOTES

1. Henry M. Robert III et al., *Robert's Rules of Order*, 10th ed. (Cambridge, MA: Perseus Publishing, 2000).
2. Hearing officers are now used in a number of states—Maryland, Florida, Oregon, and Washington. Many other local governments use hearing officers through their charters or broad interpretation of the statutory zoning and planning laws. See *Almquist v. Town of Marshan*, 245 N.W.2d 819, 825 (Minn. 1976) ("We are of the view, however, that in the absence of explicit expression of a contrary purpose by the legislature, we are free to hold . . . that the Municipal Planning Act . . . provides municipalities in a single body of law with the necessary powers and a uniform procedure for adequately conducting and implementing municipal planning" (emphasis supplied) at p. 825. See also David L. Callies, Robert H. Freilich, and Thomas E. Roberts, *Cases and Materials on Land Use,* 4th ed. (Eagan, MN: West, 2004), at note 8, p. 503. ("In many communities throughout the country, the device of the hearing examiner empowered to convene quasi-judicial public hearings on variance applications, special use permits and rezonings of single parcels has alleviated much of the processing delay and inefficiency historically associated with such decisions when handled by the local government. The device originated in Maryland, modeled on the format of the federal hearing examiner's role in administrative agencies. The inefficient and often inequitable procedures and results of hearings before boards of zoning adjustment or city councils, combined with the additional procedural requirements imposed by cases such as *Fasano*, caused may communities to seek a better forum for assessing applications for zoning changes or variances. Hearing examiners can bring professionalism to land use administration. The replacement of the lay commission or council formerly utilized to hear actions for variances or special uses has been acclaimed by the proponents of hearing examiners as producing more consistent decisions, rendered free of political pressure, and with a more thorough examination of the facts and policy Discussions of the hearing examiner's role in land use planning and administration include R. Fishman, Housing For All Under Law, 287-303 (1978); Lauber, The Hearing Examiner in Zoning Administration, PAS Rept. No. 312, American Society of Planning Officials, 1975. See also ALI Model Land Development Code 176 (adopted May 21, 1975) (1976).").

CHAPTER

10

Legal Status

10.1 SEVERABILITY

It is the legislative intent that, in adopting this chapter, all of its provisions shall be liberally construed to protect and preserve the peace, health, safety, and general welfare of the [LOCAL GOVERNMENT]. It is the further legislative intent of the council that this chapter shall stand, notwithstanding the invalidity of any part, and that, should any provision of this chapter be held to be unconstitutional or invalid, such holding shall not be construed as affecting the validity of any of the remaining provisions.

10.2 CONFLICT WITH OTHER LAWS

When provisions of this chapter impose higher standards than are required in any other provision or regulation, provisions of this chapter shall govern. When the provisions of any other provision or regulation impose higher standards than are required by the provisions of this chapter, the provisions of that statute, ordinance, or regulation shall govern.

10.3 REPEAL OF EXISTING ZONING REGULATIONS

The existing zoning regulations entitled, "_____," as passed on _____ [DATE] and as subsequently amended, are repealed. The subdivision regulations contained in Chapter _____ of the Code of Ordinances, as passed on _____ [DATE] and as subsequently amended, are repealed. The adoption of this chapter, however, shall not affect nor prevent any pending or future prosecution of, or action to abate, an existing violation of prior regulations.

10.4 EFFECTIVE DATE

The Land Development Code shall become effective at the date specified by the enabling ordinance.

COMMENTARY

This chapter establishes legal language that must be included to formally interpret the code and to establish its legal status.

- § 10.1 Severability of this chapter establishes what happens in the event that part of the code is struck down by a court. The authors believe that the approaches taken in the code are legally defensible. However, the law varies from state to state and not every state permits all of the approaches used in the model code. In addition, state law can always be amended to remove authority to use regulatory approaches in effect today.
- § 10.2 Conflict with Other Laws of this chapter addresses what happens if there are conflicts between the code and other provisions of the local government code, state law, or state regulations. Conflicts can arise due to amendments to state law or the local code of ordinances after the code is adopted. This provision is consistent with the law in most states.
- § 10.3 Repeal of Existing Zoning Regulations of this chapter clarifies that the code repeals other codes previously in effect. Without this provision, applicants could be held to compliance with standards and prior regulations not addressed in the code. This section effectively "cleans the slate" and clarifies that applicants and administrators need only concern themselves with the current development code.
- § 10.4 Effective Date of this chapter addresses when the code becomes effective. State law on this issue differs widely. Some states provide that ordinances become effective on adoption, while others provide that ordinances only become effective after a designated waiting period (usually 10 to 30 days). Different rules are sometimes prescribed for zoning and land-use regulations than for other ordinances adopted by the local government. State law should be consulted before this provision is drafted.

Appendix A

Definitions and Rules of Interpretation

A-1 RULES OF INTERPRETATION

(A) Words, phrases, and terms defined in the Land Development Code (LDC) shall be given the defined meaning as set forth below. Words, phrases, and terms not defined in the LDC shall be given their usual and customary meanings except where the context clearly indicates a different meaning.

(B) The text of this appendix shall control captions, titles, and maps.

(C) The word "shall" is mandatory and not permissive; the word "may" is permissive and not mandatory.

(D) Words used in the singular include the plural; words used in the plural include the singular.

(E) Words used in the present tense include the future tense; words used in the future tense include the present tense.

(F) Within the LDC, sections prefaced "purpose and findings" are included. Each purpose statement is intended as an official statement of legislative finding or purpose. The "purpose and findings" statements are legislatively adopted, together with the formal text of the LDC. They are intended as a guide to the administration and interpretation of the LDC and shall be treated in the same manner as other aspects of legislative history. However, they are not binding standards.

(G) In their interpretation and application, the provisions of the LDC are considered minimal in nature. Whenever the provisions, standards, or requirements of any other applicable chapter of the LDC are higher or more restrictive, the latter shall control.

(H) In computing any period of time prescribed or allowed by this appendix, the day of the notice or final application, after which the designated period of time begins to run, is not to be included. Further, the last day is to be included unless it is not a working day, in which event the period runs until the next working day.

A-2 DEFINITIONS

Words with specific defined meanings are as follows:

Abandonment: The discontinuance of a nonconformity voluntarily for a period of 12 months with an intent to abandon, or the commission of an overt act of substantial discontinuance for a period of 12 months with or without voluntary intent.

Abut or abutting: Having property lines in common.

Accessory apartment: A dwelling unit located within the principal dwelling, which is accessory, supplementary, and secondary to the principal dwelling unit. May be constructed as an attached addition to the principal use or be occupied as an accessory to the principal use and is located within the same building as the principal dwelling unit.

Accessory detached dwelling unit: A dwelling unit that is accessory, supplementary, and secondary to the principal dwelling, which may be constructed as an addition to the principal structure or as an accessory to the principal structure. An accessory dwelling unit is detached from the principal dwelling.

Accessory dwelling: An accessory detached dwelling unit or an accessory apartment.

Accessory dwelling standards: See Chapter 7, Supplemental Use Regulations, of the LDC.

Accessory use or building: A subordinate use or building customarily incidental to and located on the same lot with the main use or building.

Accessory use regulations: See Chapter 7, Supplemental Use Regulations, of the LDC.

Addition: A completely new structure or new component to an existing structure.

Adequate public facility: A public facility or system of facilities that has sufficient available capacity to service the physical area and designated intensity and use of development at adopted specified levels of service. See *concurrency.*

Adjacent: Two properties, lots, or parcels are "adjacent" where they abut, or where they are separated by a roadway or street, right-of-way, or railroad line, or any stream, river, canal, lake, or other body of water.

Adopted level of service (LOS): The LOS standards adopted, as referenced in Chapter 6, Adequate Public Facilities, of the LDC for a particular public facility. All applications are evaluated for the purposes set forth in this ordinance in accordance with these adopted LOSs. The adopted LOS also provides a basis for the establishment or expansion of a public facility or service that is subject to Chapter 6.

Adverse effect: A negative change in the quality of the historical, architectural, archaeological, or cultural significance of a resource, or in the characteristics that qualify the resource as historically, architecturally, archaeologically, or culturally important.

Affordable housing: Housing that is affordable to very low-income, low-income, or moderate-income persons as defined by the Department of Housing and Urban Development regulation for the [LOCAL GOVERNMENT], and is maintained for occupancy exclusively for such very low-income, low-income, or moderate-income person or persons for a period of at least 30 years, through the use of a covenant or deed restriction, by a development agreement, or by transferring an interest to a state or municipal housing agency or nonprofit housing organization.

Affordable unit: A designated unit of affordable housing that is sold or rented to a household of very low, low, or moderate income.

Airport: Any area of land or water, whether of public or private ownership, designed and set aside for the landing and taking off of aircraft, including all contiguous property that is held or used for airport purposes.

Airport hazard: Any structure, tree, or use of land that obstructs the air space required for the flight of aircraft. The term "obstructs" includes any interference with or any situation that creates a hazard to the control of tracking and/or data acquisition in handling, taking off, or flight at any airport, or any installation or facility relating to flight and tracking and/or data acquisition of flight craft that is hazardous to or interferes with tracking and/or data acquisition pertaining to flight and flight vehicles.

Airport hazard area: Any area of land or water upon which an airport hazard might be established if not prevented as provided in this appendix, and for the purposes hereof, in that area underlying or within the lateral limits of the imaginary surfaces that are within the controlled area of these regulations.

Alley: A public or private right-of-way primarily designed to serve as secondary access to the side or rear of those properties whose principal frontage is on some other street.

Alteration: Generally, as applied to a building or structure, a change or rearrangement in the structural parts or an enlargement, whether by extending on a side or by increasing in height, or the moving from one location or position to another.

Americans with Disabilities Act: 42 U.S.C. Subsection 1281 et seq., Pub. L. 101-336 and implementing regulations at 28 C.F.R. parts 35 and 36.

Amortization: The required removal of a nonconformity after a stated period of time without compensation.

Ancillary appurtenances: Equipment associated with a wireless communications facility, including, but not limited to, antennas, attaching devices, transmission lines, and all other equipment mounted on or associated with a wireless communications facility. Does not include equipment enclosures.

Annexation: The addition of unincorporated territory to an incorporated area pursuant to [STATE ANNEXATION STATUTE].

Antenna: Any apparatus designed for the transmitting and/or receiving of electromagnetic waves for telephonic, radio, or television communications. This includes omni-directional (whip) antennas, sectorized (panel) antennas, microwave dish antennas, multibay or single bay (frequency modulation and television), yaggie, or parabolic (dish) antennas, but does not include satellite earth stations.

Antenna, dish: A parabolic, spherical, or elliptical antenna intended to receive wireless communications.

Antenna, flush-mounted: An antenna that is attached flush to an antenna supporting structure, without the use of side-arms or other extension devices.

Antenna, panel: A directional antenna designed to transmit and/or receive signals in a directional pattern that is less than 360 degrees and is not a flush-mounted or dish antenna.

Antenna supporting structure: A vertical projection, including a foundation, designed and primarily used to support one or more antennas or that constitutes an antenna itself. This does not include stealth wireless communications facilities, but does include roof-mounted, antenna supporting structures that extend above the roof lines by more than 20 feet, or that have an overall height of greater than 50 feet. In addition, this does not include utility equipment.

Antenna supporting structure, broadcast: An antenna supporting structure, including replacements, that contains antennas that transmit signals for radio and television communications.

Antenna supporting structure, replacement: The construction of an antenna supporting structure intended to replace an antenna supporting structure in existence at the time of application.

Antenna supporting structure, roof-mounted: An antenna supporting structure mounted on the roof of a building that extends above the roof line by 20 feet or less and that has an overall height of 50 feet or less.

Antenna, surface-mounted: An antenna that is attached to the surface or façade of a building or structure other than an antenna supporting structure.

Antenna, whip: A cylindrical, omnidirectional antenna designed to transmit and/or receive signals in a 360-degree pattern.

Antiquated subdivision: Any subdivision or partition of land into lots, parcels, or building sites that was recorded prior to the adoption of land development regulations by the [LOCAL GOVERNMENT] requiring governmental planning and regulatory approval pursuant to the state enabling act, and that has two or more vacant undeveloped lots, parcels, or building sites.

Antique: An object d'art or household furnishing that was not mass produced and was characteristic of a specific period in a specific country.

Apartment: See *dwelling, multifamily.*

Appeal: An appeal to the board of adjustment where it is alleged that there is an error in any order, requirement, decision, or determination made by an administrative official in the enforcement of the LDC.

Applicant: The owner of land proposed to be subdivided or its representative who shall have express written authority to act on behalf of the owner. Consent shall be required from the legal owner of the premises.

Application: Any application for a development order or a development approval.

Approach departure path: A path for flight in a plane leading outward and upward from the end of the take-off and landing area, under which adequate areas are located to permit a safe landing in the event of a malfunction.

Appurtenance: Any accessory or ancillary building, object, structure, fence, street furniture, fixture, vending machine, fountain, public artwork, or bicycle rack located on the grounds of an historic landmark, in an historic district, on public property, or in the public right-of-way.

Archaeology: The science or study of the material remains of past life or activities and the physical site, location, or context in which they are found, as delineated in the Archaeological Resources Protection Act of 1979, as amended.

Architect: A professional architect holding a valid registration by [APPLICABLE STATE AGENCY].

Area of benefit: An area of land that is designated by the planning commission as receiving benefits from or creating the need for the construction, acquisition, or improvement of a public facilities project.

Area of flood inundation: Sites that are subject to flooding as a result of water ponding in the controlled storage areas of dams and detention and retention ponds.

Area of shallow flooding: A Federal Emergency Management Agency-designated AO, AH, or VO zone on a community's Flood Insurance Rate Map with a 1 percent chance or greater annual chance of flooding to an average depth of 1 to 3 feet where a clearly defined channel does not exist, where the path of flooding is unpredictable, and where velocity flow may be evident. Such flooding is characterized by ponding or sheet flow.

Area of special flood hazard: The land in the floodplain within a community subject to a 1 percent or greater chance of flooding in any given year. The area is designated as a Federal Emergency Management Agency Zone A, AE, AH, AO, A1-99, VO, V1-30, VE, or V on the Flood Insurance Rate Maps. See *flood or flooding, floodplain,* and *100-year floodplain.*

Area-related facility: A capital improvement that is designated in the capital improvements program as serving new development and that is not a site-related facility. May include land dedication or construction of an oversized capital improvement, whether located off site or within or on the perimeter of the development site.

Average density: See *cluster zoning*

Balcony: A cantilevered platform that projects from the wall of a building above the first level and is surrounded by a rail, balustrade, or parapet that does not extend more than 42 inches above the platform surface.

Balustrade: A rail or row of posts that support the rail, as along the edge of a staircase.

Base density: The total permitted dwelling units computed by dividing the minimum lot size by the gross acreage for conventional subdivisions, or the maximum density applied to gross acreage for conservation subdivisions.

Base flood: The flood having a 1 percent chance of being equaled or exceeded in any given year (also called "100-year frequency flood").

Base flood elevation: The elevation for which there is a 1 percent chance in a given year that flood levels will equal or exceed it.

Basement: Any area of the building having its floor subgrade (below ground level) on all sides.

Base zoning district: Any of the zoning districts established pursuant to § 3.2 Establishment of Districts in Chapter 3, Zoning, of the LDC.

Best management practices: An effective integration of stormwater management systems, with appropriate combinations of landscape conservation, enhancement, structural controls, impervious cover, schedules of activities, prohibitions of practices, maintenance procedures, and other management practices that provide an optimum way to convey, store, and release run-off, in order to reduce peak discharge, remove pollutants, and enhance the environment.

Bicycle facility: Any bicycle path, bicycle trail, bicycle lane, or bicycle route.

Bicycle lane: A designated portion of a street pavement for the exclusive use of bicycles. Bicycle signs and pavement markings designate the presence and limits of a bicycle lane.

Bicycle path: A designated paved travelway intended for bicycle use, to the exclusion of routine motor vehicle use. Typically used by two-way bicycle traffic.

Bicycle route: A street that is used by motor vehicles and is designated by the presence of specific bicycle route signing, for use by bicycles.

Bicycle trail: See *bicycle path.*

Block: A tract of land bounded by streets, or by a combination of streets and public parks, cemeteries, railroad rights-of-way, shorelines of waterways, or boundary lines of local governments.

Boarding house: A building other than a hotel where lodging is provided for definite periods for compensation pursuant to previous arrangements.

Bond: Any form of a surety bond in an amount and form satisfactory to the [LOCAL GOVERNMENT] attorney. All bonds shall be approved by the [LOCAL GOVERNMENT] attorney whenever a bond is required by these regulations.

Boundary street: A public street that is adjacent to and that abuts one or more sides of the proposed site.

Broken-back curve: A curve consisting of two curves in the same direction joined by a short tangent.

Buffer yard: The required installation of landscaping and screening materials between zoning districts and certain uses.

Building: A structure designed, built, or occupied as a shelter or roofed enclosure for persons, animals, or property. For the purpose of this definition, "roof" shall include an awning or other similar coverings, whether or not they are permanent in nature. Without limiting the generality of the foregoing, the following shall be considered a "building": a house, a barn, a church, a hotel, a warehouse, or a similar structure, or an historically related complex, such as a courthouse and a jail or a house and a barn.

Building elevation: The view of any building or other structure from any one of four sides showing features, such as construction materials, design, height, dimensions, windows, doors, other architectural features, and the relationship of grade to floor level.

Building footprint: The horizontal area measured within the outside of the exterior walls of the ground floor of the main structure.

Building inspector or building official: See *[PLANNING OFFICIAL]*.

Building permit: See *development approval*.

Building setback line: See *setback line*.

Building site: The lot or portion of a lot that is designated on the development approval application and any existing buildings and appurtenant parking on the lot.

Bulk plant: A facility where flammable or combustible liquids are received by tank vessel, pipelines, tank car, or tank vehicle, and which are stored or blended in bulk for the purpose of distributing such liquids by tank vessel, pipeline, tank car, tank vehicle, portable tank, or container. See *terminal*.

Bus shelter: A roofed structure with at least three walls located on or adjacent to the right-of-way of a street, and which is designed and used primarily for the protection and convenience of bus passengers.

Business: See *school, business, or commercial trade*.

Business park: A master planned development with a common theme and name intended to be used primarily for office, showroom, service, warehouse, and/or distribution purposes.

Business services: Establishments primarily engaged in rendering services to business establishments on a fee or contract basis, such as advertising and mailing, building maintenance, employment services, management and consulting services, protective services, equipment rental and leasing, commercial research, development and testing, and photo finishing.

Busway: A bus route, as designated in the major thoroughfare plan, with an existing or projected peak-hour headway not exceeding 26 minutes.

Caliper: The minimum diameter of a tree measured 6 inches above the ground for trees up to and including 4 inches in diameter, and 12 inches above the ground for trees having a larger diameter.

Canopy: Any structural protective cover that is not enclosed on any of its four sides and is provided for a service area designated for the dispensing or installation of gasoline, oil, antifreeze, headlights, wiper blades, and similar products.

Canopy tree: Either a medium or large deciduous tree with a mature height of more than 25 feet at maturity.

Capacity: The maximum demand that can be accommodated by a public facility or service without exceeding the adopted level of service (LOS). For streets, "capacity" shall be measured by the maximum number of vehicles that can be accommodated by an intersection or street link, during the time period specified in Chapter 6, Adequate Public Facilities, of the LDC, under prevailing traffic and control conditions at that street's adopted LOS.

Capital improvement: A public facility with a life expectancy of three or more years, to be owned and operated by or on behalf of the [LOCAL GOVERNMENT].

Capital improvements budget: The list of recommended capital improvements to be constructed during the forthcoming five-year period.

Capital improvements plan: A plan setting forth, by category of public facilities, those capital improvements and that portion of their costs that are attributable to serving new development or resolving existing infrastructure deficiencies within designated service areas for such public facilities over a period of specified years (e.g., 10 to 20).

Carport: Space for the housing or storage of motor vehicles and enclosed on not more than two sides by walls.

Carrying capacity: A measure to determine environmental infrastructure or fiscal criteria upon which to ground developmental approval. Refers to the extent to which land in its natural or current state can be developed without degrading the environment's infrastructure, level of service, or fiscal impact.

Car wash, automatic: A structure where chairs, conveyors, blowers, steam cleaners, or other mechanical devices are used for the purpose of washing motor vehicles and where the operation is generally performed by an attendant.

Car wash, self-service: A structure where washing, drying, and polishing of vehicles is generally on a self-service basis without the use of chain conveyors, blowers, steam cleaning, or other mechanical devices.

Cemetery: Any site containing at least one burial, marked or previously marked, dedicated to and used or intended to be used for the permanent interment of the human dead, including perpetual care and nonperpetual care cemeteries.

Centerline (waterway): The centerline of the waterway refers to existing topographically defined channels. If not readily discernible, the centerline shall be determined by the "low flow line" whenever possible; otherwise, it shall be determined by the centerline of the two-year floodplain.

Central sewer system: A community sewer system, including collection and treatment facilities.

Central water system: A private water company formed by a developer to serve new subdivisions in an outlying area. Includes water treatment and distribution facilities.

Certificate of occupancy: A certificate indicating that the premises comply with all the provisions of the LDC and the building code. (Note: The certificate of occupancy is issued after approval of a development approval and construction has occurred pursuant to the development approval.)

Certify: Whenever these regulations require that an agency or official certify the existence of some fact or circumstance, the [GOVERNING ENTITY] by administrative rule may require that such certification be made in any manner, oral or written, which provides reasonable assurance of the accuracy of the certification.

Child care facility: A facility that provides care, training, education, custody, treatment, or supervision for a child who is not related by blood, marriage, or adoption to the owner or operator of the facility, for all or part of the 24-hour day, whether or not the facility is operated for profit or charges for the services it offers.

Child care institution (basic): A child care facility licensed by [STATE] that provides care for more than 12 children for 24 hours a day. Does not include a 24-hour a day program offered by a specialized child care institution.

Child care institution (specialized): A child care facility licensed by [STATE] that provides specialized care for more than 12 children for 24 hours a day. Includes residential treatment centers, emergency shelters, halfway houses, therapeutic camps, and institutions serving mentally retarded children.

Church: Any place of worship, including any church, synagogue, temple, mosque, or other building or facility, primarily engaged in religious worship. The term "church" does not include uses, such as schools, recreational facilities, day care or child care facilities, kindergartens, dormitories, or other facilities, for temporary or permanent residences, which are connected or related to the church or the principal buildings on the site, or are located on the same site, even if the curriculum or services offered as part of such use includes religious services and/or training.

Civic uses: Any of the following uses, as defined in the use matrix (Table 3-4, Use Matrix, in Chapter 3, Zoning, of the LDC) and which uses are found to provide focal points for community interaction and foster citizen participation in civic activities: churches, temples, synagogues, mosques, and other religious facilities; clubs or lodges; college or university facilities; day care centers; exhibitions and art galleries; grade schools; library buildings; meeting halls or clubhouses; movie theaters; museum, exhibition, or similar facilities; performance theaters; postal; public administration; school or university buildings; and trade or specialty school facilities.

Clear vision area: The triangular area adjacent to the intersection of any street within which no obstruction may be placed that blocks the sight lines for vehicular traffic.

Clinic, dental or medical: A building in which 10 or more physicians and/or dentists or their allied professional assistants carry on their profession; a building that contains one or more physicians, dentists, and their assistants, and a laboratory and/or an apothecary limited to the sale of pharmaceutical and medical supplies. Shall not include inpatient care or operating rooms for major surgery.

Close: A front space for buildings interior to the block that includes a roadway loop around a green area. An alternative to the cul-de-sac, as the focus is a greenspace rather than vehicular paving. Provides additional frontage for deep squares and organic blocks.

Club: A group of people organized for a common purpose to pursue common goals, interests, or activities. Usually characterized by certain membership qualifications, payment of fees and dues, regular meetings, a constitution, and by-laws.

Clubhouse: A building and related facilities used by a club, fraternal organization, or a membership organization.

Cluster: A group of cultural, historical, architectural, or archaeological resources with compatible buildings, objects, or structures geographically or thematically relating to and reinforcing one another through design, setting, materials, workmanship, congruency, and association.

Cluster zoning: A zoning technique where the maximum number of dwelling units on a site is determined by density levels instead of minimum lot size.

Collector street/road: See *street/road, collector.*

Collocation: A situation in which two or more providers place an antenna on a common antenna supporting structure, or the addition or replacement of antennas on an existing structure. Includes combined antennas but does not include roof- or surface-mounted wireless communications facilities, or the placement of any personal wireless service antenna on an amateur radio antenna within a residential district.

Combined antenna: An antenna designed and utilized to provide services by more than one provider.

Commercial driveway approach: A driveway that provides access to property on which an office, retail, or industrial use is located; a building having more than five dwelling units that is located on any driveway approach that accesses property primarily used for a nonresidential purpose.

Commercial/industrial developments: Any land area zoned or devoted primarily to commercial or industrial use, including areas zoned as "O" (Office), "CG" (Commercial General), "IL" (Industrial Light), or "IH" (Industrial Heavy).

Commercial living unit: A building that includes commercial uses on the first floor and residential dwelling units above the first floor.

Commercial property: A building, site, or structure whose use after rehabilitation or restoration (for ad valorem tax exemption) will be for other than residential use (i.e., for a single-family, duplex, or a three- or four-family dwelling).

Commercial trade: See *school, business, or commercial trade.*

Commercial urban design standards: See § 5.13.6 Civic Buildings in Chapter 5, Development Standards, of the LDC.

Committed development: A proposed development that has received final subdivision plat approval or, for a proposed development that does not involve the subdivision of land, an approved master site plan or minor site plan.

Common area: A parcel or parcels of land, or an area of water, or a combination of land and water, and/or developed facilities and complimentary structures and improvements, including, but not limited to, areas for vehicular and pedestrian access and recreational facilities within the site.

Comment element: That portion of condominium property that lies outside all owners' units and is owned, maintained, and operated by the condominium association.

Common ownership: Ownership by the same person, corporation, firm, entity, partnership, or unincorporated association, or ownership by different corporations, firms, partnerships, entities, or unincorporated associations, in which a stockbroker, partner, associate, or a member of his/her family owns an interest in each corporation, firm, partnership, entity, or unincorporated association.

Common worker: An individual who performs labor involving physical tasks that do not require a particular skill; training in a particular occupation, craft, or trade; or practical knowledge of the principles or processes of an art, science, craft, or trade.

Community improvement district: See *public facility service area.*

Completely enclosed structure: See *structure, completely enclosed.*

Comprehensive plan: A statutorily defined long-range plan intended to guide the growth and development of a [LOCAL GOVERNMENT] for a set period of time and which includes inventory, analytical sections, and elements leading to recommendations for the entire [LOCAL GOVERNMENT]'s land use, future economic development, housing, recreation, parks, open space, environment, libraries, utilities, public safety, fiscal integrity, transit, transportation, infrastructure, facilities, and community design, all related to the goals and objectives, policies, and strategies contained within the elements. A comprehensive plan, depending on a states's statutory definition, may be denominated as a "general plan" or "master plan."

Concentrated Animal Feeding Operation: See 40 C.F.R. Part 122.

Concurrency: A requirement that development applications demonstrate in which adequate public facilities be available at prescribed levels of service concurrent with the impact or occupancy of development units. See *adequate public facility*.

Conditional Letter of Map Revision: Will be submitted for Federal Emergency Management Agency approval for all proposed physical changes to the floodplain that will result in a change to the floodplain boundary.

Condominium: A unit available for sale in fee simple contained in a multioccupancy project subject to covenants, conditions, and restrictions placing control over the common facilities owned by the condominium. Condominium shall mean a condominium, cooperative, trust, partnership, or other similar association.

Connectivity standards: The standards for the connectivity of proposed streets, as set forth in the transportation standards (§ 5.23 Street Design and Transportation in Chapter 5, Development Standards, of the LDC).

Conservation easement: A nonpossessory interest of a holder in real property that imposes limitations or affirmative obligations designed to: retain or protect natural, scenic, or open space values of real property or assure its availability for agricultural, forest, recreational, or open space use; protect natural resources; maintain or enhance air or water quality; or preserve the historical, architectural, archeological, or cultural aspects of real property.

Construction: The act of adding an addition to an existing building or structure; the erection of a new principal or accessory building or structure on a lot or property; the addition of walks, driveways, or parking lots; or the addition of appurtenances to a building or structure.

Construction drawings: The maps or drawings and engineering specifications accompanying a final plat or final site plan and showing the specific location and design of public and private improvements to be completed as a condition of a development order.

Construction plan: The maps or drawings accompanying a subdivision plat and showing the specific location and design of improvements to be installed in the subdivision in accordance with the requirements of the planning commission as a condition of the approval of the plat.

Contiguous: Lots are contiguous when at least one boundary line of one lot touches a boundary line or lines of another lot.

Contractor: Any person doing work within the building trades or construction professions, either licensed or unlicensed.

Control joint: A continuous groove or vertical joint in a masonry wall or concrete slab that is designed to control cracking.

Controlled area, airport: That area within which the airport zoning regulations are effective, and which includes all airport hazard areas that are within the corporate limits of the [LOCAL GOVERNMENT] and the area outside the corporate limits of the [LOCAL GOVERNMENT], which is within a rectangle bounded by lines located 1.5 statute miles (7,920 feet) from the centerline and lines located 5 statute miles (25,400 feet) from each end of the paved surfaces of each of the runways.

Cooperative: An entire project that is under the common ownership of a board of directors with units leased and stock sold to individual cooperators.

Courtyard: A space, open and unobstructed to the sky, located at or above grade level on a lot, and bounded on three or more sides by the walls of a building.

Craftsman: A practitioner of a trade or handicraft, generally recognized by critics and peers as a professional of serious intent and recognized ability, who produces artwork.

Credit: The amount of the reduction of an impact fee, fees, rates, assessments, charges, or other monetary exaction for the same type of capital improvement for which the monetary exaction has been required.

Critical area: Any natural resource or environmentally sensitive area subject to the standards set forth in *Division 4: Greenspace (Landscaping, Tree Preservation, Screening, and Environmental Protection) Standards* in Chapter 5, Development Standards, of the LDC in order to protect the public health, safety, and general welfare.

Critical root zone: A circular region measured outward from a tree trunk, representing the essential area of the roots that must be maintained for the tree's survival; 1 foot of radial distance for every inch of tree diameter breast height with a minimum of 8 feet.

Crosswalk: That part of a street at an intersection included within the connections of the lateral lines of the sidewalks on opposite sides of the street (public, private, or safety lane) measured from the curbs, in the absence of curbs from the edges of the traversable roadway; any portion of a street (public, private, or safety lane) at an intersection or elsewhere distinctly indicated for pedestrian crossing by lines or other markings on the street surfaces.

Crown: The upper mass or head of a tree, shrub, or vine, including branches with foliage.

Cul-de-sac: A local street with only one outlet that terminates in a vehicular turnaround, having an appropriate terminal for the safe and convenient reversal of traffic movement.

Cultural facilities: Establishments, such as museums, art galleries, botanical and zoological gardens, and other facilities of an historic, an educational, or a cultural interest.

Cultural resources: Those resources that possess qualities of significance in American, state, or city history, architecture, archaeology, and culture present in districts, sites, structures, and objects that possess integrity of location, design, setting, materials, workmanship, congruency, and association.

Cumulative impact: The impact of a series of development projects taken together to measure the joint and several impacts on the level of service and capacity of a public facility.

Curtain wall: An exterior building wall that carries no roof or floor loads, and consists entirely or principally of metal or a combination of metal, glass, and other surfacing materials supported by a metal frame. A curtain wall that consists of glass has the appearance and function of a solid wall.

Cut-off angle: The angle formed by a line drawn from the direction of light rays at the light source and a line perpendicular to the ground from the light source, above which no light is emitted.

Day care center: A child care facility that provides care for more than 12 children under 14 years of age for less than 24 hours a day.

Deciduous: Plants that lose their leaves annually.

Deciduous tree: A tree that sheds or loses foliage at the end of the growing season.

Deck: A platform extending horizontally from the rear or side yard of the structure, located to the rear of the front building line of the lot and not within the front yard.

Dedication: The transfer of fee simple title to, or grant of an easement over lands and improvements from, property to the [LOCAL GOVERNMENT] subject to the conditions of a development order requiring such transfer and acceptance by the [GOVERNING ENTITY] of such transfer.

Degradation: Pollution of a representative sample of water that unreasonably reduces the quality of such water. The quality of a representative sample of water is unreasonably reduced when such water is rendered harmful, detrimental, or injurious to humans, animal life, vegetation, or property, or the public health, safety, or welfare, or impairs the usefulness or the public enjoyment of the water for any lawful or reasonable purpose.

Demolition: Any act or process that destroys or razes in whole or in part, or permanently impairs the structural integrity, or allows deterioration by neglect of a building or structure, wherever located, or a building, object, site, or structure, including interior spaces, located within an historic district, on public property, or on the public right-of-way.

Demolition business: A business that demolishes structures, including houses and other buildings, in order to salvage building materials, and that stores those materials before disposing of them.

Density: An objective measurement of the number of people or residential units allowed per unit of land, such as residents or employees per acre.

Density, gross: The number of dwelling units divided by the total land area subject to an application for development approval, stated as dwelling units per acre.

Density, maximum: The maximum number of dwelling units that may be constructed where indicated in this appendix, stated as gross density unless otherwise indicated.

Density, minimum: The minimum number of dwelling units that must be constructed where indicated in this appendix, stated as gross density unless otherwise indicated.

Density, net: The number of dwelling units divided by the net developable area. The "net developable area" means the land area of the site after deducting unbuildable areas, including road rights-of-way, open space, and environmentally sensitive areas, stated as dwelling units per net acre.

Design consideration/criteria: Guidelines that are set forth in this appendix by the Historic and Design Review Commission, or that are subsequently adopted by the [LOCAL GOVERNMENT], which preserve the historical, architectural, archaeological, or cultural character of an area or of a building, object, site, or structure; standards that set forth specific improvement requirements.

Design enhancements: Uniquely crafted and decorative artwork in a variety of media that are an integral part of eligible capital improvement projects, and are produced by professional craftspeople, or craftspeople in collaboration with an architect, landscape architect, or professional engineer. Works shall be permanent, functional, or nonfunctional.

Designer: The person or entity responsible for preparing site plans, subdivision plats, or building elevations that are part of an application.

Destination resort: Lodging accommodations and complementary recreational or entertainment facilities that are comprehensively planned and integrated in order to provide a variety of activities, services, and amenities that comprise a visitor attraction in and of themselves.

Detached structure: A structure having no party wall or common wall with another structure unless it is an accessory structure.

Detention: The temporary storage of stormwater run-off, which is used to control the peak discharge rates, and which provides gravity settling of pollutants.

Detention facility: A facility that provides temporary storage of stormwater run-off and controlled release of this run-off.

Detention time: The amount of time a parcel of water is actually present in a stormwater basin. Theoretical detention time for a run-off event is the average time a parcel of water resides in the basin over the period of release from the best management practice.

Developer: A person responsible for any undertaking that requires a development approval.

Development: Any man-made change in improved and unimproved real estate, including, but not limited to, buildings or other structures, mining, dredging, filling, grading, paving, diking, berming, excavation, drilling operations, or storage of equipment or materials.

Development agreement: Agreement between the [LOCAL GOVERNMENT] and the developer regarding the development and use of the property through which the [LOCAL GOVERNMENT] agrees to vest development use or intensity, or refrain from interfering with subsequent phases of development through new legislation, in exchange for the provision of public facilities or amenities by the developer in excess of those required under current community regulations.

Development approval: Any authorized action by an officer or agency of the [LOCAL GOVERNMENT] that approves, conditions, or denies a development of a parcel, tract, building, or structure, including any of the following: master site plan; zoning map amendment; concept plan; conditional zoning; conditional use permit; grading or other permit; certificate of occupancy; subdivision plat; certificate of appropriateness; site plan; sketch plan; landscape plan; tree preservation development approval; variance; appeal; and development plan.

Development order: The official ordinance, resolution, or decision of an officer or agency of the [LOCAL GOVERNMENT] with respect to the granting, granting with conditions, or denial of a development application.

Development plan: A proposal for development approval, including such drawings, documents, and other information necessary to illustrate completely the proposed development. Shall specifically include such information as required by this appendix.

Development standards: Standards and technical specifications for improvements to land required for development approval, including specifications for the placement, dimension, composition, and capacity of: streets and roadways; sidewalks and pedestrian and bicycle paths; signage for traffic control and other governmental purposes, including street name signs, and other traffic control devices on streets, roadways, and pedestrian and bicycle paths; lighting of streets, pedestrian, and bicycle paths; water mains and connections, including facilities and connections for the suppression of fires; sanitary sewer facilities, mains, and connections; utility lines and poles, conduits, and connections; off-street parking and access; landscaping and contouring of land, and other provisions for drainage, sedimentation, and erosion control; open space, parks, recreational facilities, and playgrounds; public elementary and secondary school sites; and storm drainage culvert facilities, including drains, conduits, and ditches.

Diameter breast height: The average cross-sectional measurement of the trunk of an existing tree at 4-1/2 feet above grade. If the tree is on a slope, it shall be measured from the high side of the slope. Newly planted trees shall be measured 6 inches above grade.

Diameter inches: See *diameter breast height*.

Disabled person: A person who has a physical or mental impairment, or both, that substantially limits one or more major life activities, including caring for oneself, performing manual tasks, walking, seeing, hearing, speaking, breathing, learning, or working.

Discontinuance: See *abandonment*.

Discretionary decision: Any development approval in which an official or official body of the [LOCAL GOVERNMENT] exercises legislative, administrative, or quasi-judicial authority involving the exercise of discretion and which is subject to a public hearing.

District: A geographically definable area, urban or rural, possessing a significant concentration, linkage, or continuity of buildings, objects, sites, or structures united by past events or aesthetically by plan or physical development, which may also comprise individual elements separated geographically but thematically linked by association or history.

Drainage system: All streets, gutters, inlets, swales, storm sewers, channels, streams, or other pathways, either naturally occurring or man-made, which carry and convey stormwater during rainfall events.

Drip line: A vertical line of a tree canopy or shrub branch extending from the outermost edge to the ground.

Drive-through use: An establishment that by design, physical facilities, service, or packaging procedures encourages or permits customers to receive services, to obtain goods, or to be entertained while remaining in their motor vehicles.

Driveway: Entrance to and exit from premises where it is possible to park completely off the street, and which is not open for vehicular traffic except by permission of the owner of such private property.

Driveway approach: A way or place, including paving and curb returns, between the street travel lanes and private property, which provides vehicular access between the roadway and such private property.

Driveway, front-loaded: A driveway that begins at, or abuts, the front property line of a lot or parcel.

Duplex: See *dwelling, two-family (duplex)*.

Dwelling: One or more rooms providing complete living facilities for one family, including kitchen facilities or equipment for cooking or provisions for same, and including a room or multiple rooms for living, sleeping, bathing, and eating. Also known as a "dwelling unit."

Dwelling, attached: Two or more dwelling units with common walls between the units.

Dwelling, four-family (quadraplex): A detached house with common walls between the units, designed for and occupied exclusively as the residence of not more than four families, each living as an independent housekeeping unit.

Dwelling, multifamily: A dwelling or group of dwellings on one lot containing separate living units for five or more families, but which may have joint services or facilities.

Dwelling, single-family: A single structure occupied exclusively by not more than one family.

Dwelling, single-family attached: Two or more dwelling units with common walls between the units.

Dwelling, single-family detached: A single-family dwelling that is not attached to any other dwelling by any means and is surrounded by open space or yards.

Dwelling, three-family (triplex): A detached house designed for and occupied exclusively as the residence of not more than three families, each living as an independent housekeeping unit.

Dwelling, two-family attached: Any two dwelling units with a common wall between the units, under single ownership, which may be attached by a common wall to the units.

Dwelling, two-family (duplex): A detached house designed for and occupied exclusively as the residence of not more than two families, each living as an independent housekeeping unit.

Dwelling unit: See *dwelling*.

Earth change: Excavating, grading, regrading, landfilling, berming, or diking of land.

Easement: Authorization by a property owner for another to use the owner's property for a specified purpose.

Easement, utility: An easement granted for installing and maintaining utilities across, over, or under land, together with the right to enter the land with machinery and other vehicles necessary for the maintenance of utilities.

Easement, vehicular nonaccess: An easement established on a lot for the purpose of prohibiting ingress and egress to vehicular traffic.

Economic return: A profit or capital appreciation from the use or ownership of a building, object, site, or structure that accrues from investment or labor.

Effect: A change in the quality of the historical, architectural, archaeological, or cultural significance of a resource, or in the characteristics that qualify the resource as historically important.

Elevated building: A nonbasement building built, in the case of a building in Federal Emergency Management Agency Zones A 1-30, AE, A, A99, AO, AH, B, C, X, and D, to have the top of the elevated floor, or in the case of a building in Zone V 1-30, VE, or V, to have the bottom of the lowest horizontal structure member of the elevated floor elevated above the ground level by means of pilings, columns (posts and piers), or shear walls parallel to the flow of the water, and adequately anchored so as not to impair the structural integrity of the building during a flood of up to the magnitude of the base flood. In the case of Zones A 1-30, AE, A, A99, AO, AH, B, C, X, and D, "elevated building" also includes a building elevated by means of fill or solid foundation perimeter walls with openings sufficient to facilitate the unimpeded movement of flood waters. In the case of Zone V 1-30, VE, or V, "elevated building" also includes a building otherwise meeting the definition of "elevated building," even though the lower area is enclosed by means of breakaway walls if the breakaway walls meet the standards of Section 60.3(e)(5) of the National Flood Insurance Program regulations.

Emergency, utility-related: A break or leak in an underground utility line or a disruption in a utility service.

Emergency vehicle: A vehicle of the police or fire departments or ambulances, and vehicles conveying an airport official or airport employee in response to any emergency call.

Table A-1
Equivalent Dwelling Units

Principal Building Activity	Square Feet Per Employee	Employees Per 1,000 Square Feet	Equivalent Dwelling Unit (Square Footage Needed to Equal One Residential Dwelling Unit)
Education	767	1.30	1764
Food sales	984	1.02	2263
Food service	578	1.73	1329
Health care	520	1.92	1196
Lodging	1317	0.76	3029
Mercantile and service (commercial)	945	1.06	2174
Office	387	2.58	890
Public assembly	1317	0.76	3029
Public order and safety	746	1.34	1716
Religious worship	726	1.38	1671
Warehouse and storage	1730	0.58	3979
Other	544	1.84	1251

Source: United States Department of Energy, Energy Information Administration, A Look at Commercial Buildings in 1995: Characteristics, Energy Consumption, and Energy Expenditures (Washington, DC: US DOE, EIA, October 1998).

Employment agency: An establishment whose business is to find jobs for people seeking them or to find people to fill jobs that are open.

Enclosure ratio: The ratio of building height to the distance between buildings facing across a street. The distance between buildings shall be measured from the front façade, including any porch, stoop, or other area integral to the building.

Engineer: See *professional engineer.*

Environmental impact assessment: A process to examine the adverse on- and off-site environmental impacts to the ecosystem by a development project.

Equipment enclosure: An enclosed structure, cabinet, or shelter used to contain radio or other equipment necessary for the transmission or reception of wireless communications signals, but not primarily to store equipment or to use as a habitable space.

Equivalent dwelling unit: The service unit used that is equal to 750 gallons per day of peak wastewater flow and 300 gallons per day of average wastewater flow. For purposes of applying parks and open space requirements to nonresidential uses, equivalent dwelling units shall be measured as described in Table A-1.

Escrow: A deposit of cash with the [LOCAL GOVERNMENT] or escrow agent to secure the promise to perform some act.

Estoppel: See *vested rights.*

Evergreen: Plants that retain their foliage throughout the year.

Evergreen screen: A dense vegetative screen that grows over 20 feet high at maturity and retains foliage year round; used for purposes of visual mitigation between zoning districts.

Evergreen tree: A tree that holds green leaves, either broadleaf or needle-shaped, throughout the year.[1]

Exaction: The requirement for development to dedicate a portion of land or a payment in lieu of land or facilities costs of public facilities as a condition of a development order.

Existing structure: A structure that is built and completed as of the effective date of this code.

Expenditure: A sum of money paid out in return for some benefit or to fulfill some obligation. Includes binding contractual commitments, whether by development agreement or otherwise, to make future expenditures as well as any other substantial change in position.

External buffer: A naturally vegetated area or a vegetated area along the exterior boundaries of an entire development processed in accordance with a multiphase or phased subdivision application, which is landscaped and maintained as open space in order to eliminate or minimize conflicts between such development and adjacent land uses.

Fabrication: The manufacturing, excluding the refining or other initial processing of basic raw materials, such as metal ores, lumber, or rubber. Relates to assembling, stamping, cutting, or otherwise shaping the processed materials into useful objects.

Façade: The exterior wall of a building exposed to public view or that wall viewed by persons not within the building.

Fair share: A properly balanced and well-ordered plan to meet the housing needs of the community and the region.

Family: One or more persons occupying a dwelling and living together as a separate housekeeping unit in one or more rooms with complete living facilities, including kitchen facilities or equipment for cooking or provisions for same, and including a room or rooms for living, sleeping, bathing, and eating.

Fenestration: Window treatment in a building or façade.

Filtration basin: Secondary treatment structures that follow sedimentation basins and release stormwater run-off through a filter media to remove additional pollutants.

Final subdivision plat: A map of a subdivision to be recorded after approval by the planning commission and any accompanying material as described in these regulations.

First flush: At least the first 1/2 inch of run-off from a storm event that flushes off and contains a disproportionately large loading of the accumulated pollutants from impervious and nonimpervious surfaces.

Fiscal impact analysis: The process of assessment of land development proposals as to the positive or negative impact they will have on the community's revenues and expenditures for public improvements, delivery of services, and net cash flow.

Flea market: See *outdoor resale business.*

Flexible zoning: Zoning that permits uses of land and density of buildings and structures different from those that are allowed as of right within the zoning district in which the land is situated. Flexible zoning applications shall include, but not be limited to, all special development approvals and special uses, planning developments, group housing projects, community unit projects, and average density or density zoning projects.

Flex space: A building designed to accommodate a combination of office, wholesale, and warehousing functions, the exact proportions of each use being subject to user needs over time. Flex-space buildings are typically located in business or industrial parks, which usually have a footprint exceeding 10,000 square feet, and which are usually designed with loading docks to the rear and parking in the front. The front façade is often treated with a higher quality of architectural finish than the rear and sides.

Flood fringe: That portion of the floodplain outside of the floodway.

Flood Insurance Rate Map: An official map of a community on which the Federal Emergency Management Agency has delineated both the areas of special flood hazards and the risk premium zones applicable to the community.

Flood Insurance Study: The official report provided by the Federal Emergency Management Agency, which contains flood profiles, water surface elevation, or the base flood, as well as the Flood Boundary Map.

Flood or flooding: A general and temporary condition of partial or complete inundation of normally dry land areas from the overflow of inland or tidal waters or the unusual and rapid accumulation of run-off of surface waters from any source.

Floodplain: Any land area susceptible to being inundated by water from any source. See *area of special flood hazard, flood or flooding,* and *100-year floodplain.*

Floodplain, 100-year: See *100-year floodplain.*

Floodway: A channel, river, or other watercourse and the adjacent land areas that must be reserved in order to discharge the base flood; the 100-year floodplain.

Floor area: The sum of the gross horizontal areas of all floors of a structure, including interior balconies and mezzanines, measured from the exterior face of exterior walls or from the centerline of a wall separating two structures. Shall include the area of roofed porches having more than one wall and of accessory structures on the same lot. Stairwells and elevator shafts shall be excluded.

Floor area ratio: The ratio of the total building floor area in square feet to the total land area in square feet, based upon a 1:0 ratio, constituting a one-story building or structure occupying 100 percent of the underlying land.

Foster family home: A child care facility certified or licensed by the [STATE] that provides care 24 hours a day for not more than six children.

Foster group home: A child care facility licensed by the [STATE] that provides care 24 hours a day for seven to 12 children.

Fraternal organization: A group of people formally organized for a common interest, usually for cultural, religious, or entertainment purposes, with regular meetings, rituals, and formal written membership requirements.

Frontage: That distance where a property line is common with a street right-of-way line.

Frontage street: Any street to be constructed by the developer or any existing street where development shall take place on both sides.

Front yard: An area extending the full width of a lot between the front lot line and the nearest principal structure.

Fuel pump: Any device that dispenses automotive fuel and/or kerosene. A fuel pump may contain multiple hoses or be capable of serving more than one fueling position simultaneously.

Functionally dependent use: A use that cannot perform its intended purpose unless it is located or carried out in close proximity to water. Includes only docking facilities, port facilities that are necessary for the loading and unloading of cargo or passengers, and ship building and ship repair facilities. Does not include long-term storage or related manufacturing facilities.

Gabion: A wire basket containing primarily stones deposited to provide protection against erosion.

Garage, private: A building or building appendage that is accessory to a main building, providing for the storage of automobiles and in which no occupation or business for profit is carried on, and enclosed on all four sides and pierced only by windows and customary doors.

Gated community: A residential area in which access to the subdivision streets is restricted by the use of a guard house or electronic arms, and in which residents may gain entry by using electronic cards, identification stickers, codes, or remote control devices.

General plan: See *comprehensive plan.*

Geographic search area: An area in which the proposed antenna must be located in order to provide the designed coverage or capacity. Must be based on radio frequency engineering considerations, including grids, frequency coor-

*dination, propagation analyses, and levels of service consistent with accepted engineering standards and practices.

Glare: The sensation produced by luminance within the visual field that is sufficiently greater than the luminance to which the eyes are adapted to cause annoyance, discomfort, or loss in visual performance and visibility.

Glide path: A ratio equation used for the purposes of limiting the overall height of vertical projections in the vicinity of private airports. The ratio limits each foot of height for a vertical projection based upon a horizontal distance measurement.

Grade: The slope of a road, street, or other public way specified in percentage terms.

Grading development approval: A development approval required when land disturbance or excavation exceeds 10 cubic feet but less than 100 cubic feet.

Gravel pit: See *sand or gravel pit.*

Greenspace: The land shown on an urban corridor site plan that may be improved or maintained in a natural state and that is reserved for preservation, recreation, or landscaping.

Gross acreage: The total acreage of a development.

Gross floor area: The aggregate floor area of an entire building or structure enclosed by and including the surrounding exterior walls.

Ground cover: A prostrate plant growing less than 2 feet in height at maturity that is used for ornamental purposes, alternatives to grasses, and erosion control on slopes.

Groundwater: Any water percolating below the surface of the ground.

Group day care home: A child care facility that provides care for seven to 12 children under 14 years of age for less than 24 hours a day.

Guyed: A style of antenna supporting structure consisting of a single truss assembly composed of sections with bracing incorporated. The sections are attached to each other, and the assembly is attached to a foundation and supported by a series of guy wires that are connected to anchors placed in the ground or on a building.

Habitable structure: A structure that has facilities to accommodate people for an overnight stay, including, but not limited to, residential homes, apartments, condominiums, hotels, motels, and manufactured homes, and which does not include recreational vehicles.

Habitable use: See *inhabitable use.*

Half story: An uppermost story usually lighted by dormer windows, in which a sloping roof replaces the upper part of the front wall, and habitable areas on the uppermost story do not exceed a floor area derived by multiplying the floor area of the ground floor by 50 percent.

Half-way house: See *transitional home.*

Head shop: Any retail establishment having a substantial or significant portion of its stock in trade in, or which has as its main purpose the offering for sale of, paraphernalia or items designed or marketed for use with illegal cannabis or drugs.

Headway: The amount of time between transit vehicles, including buses operating on a particular transit route.

Health department and health officer: The agency and person designated by the [GOVERNING ENTITY] to administer the health regulations of the [LOCAL GOVERNMENT].

Height, building: The vertical dimension measured from the average elevation of the finished lot grade at the front of the building to the highest point of the ceiling of the top story in the case of a flat roof; to the deck line of a mansard roof; and to the average height between the plate and ridge of a gable, hip, or gambrel roof.

Height limit: For purposes of the "AO" (Airport Overlay) district, the elevation in feet above mean sea level, the projection above which a proposed structure or tree is not permitted, except as otherwise provided in the LDC.

Heliport: That area used by helicopters or other steep gradient aircraft for take-offs and landings. Such area may include passenger, cargo, maintenance, and overhaul facilities, plus fueling service, storage space, tie-down area, hangars, and other accessory buildings and open spaces.

Helistop: That area used by helicopters or other steep gradient aircraft for the purpose of take-offs and landings. May be used for the pickup or discharge of passengers and cargo, storage space, and tie-down, but shall not include maintenance, overhaul, or fueling services and facilities.

Heritage tree: A tree, of any species, having a trunk size of 30 inches diameter breast height or larger.

High density: Those residential zoning districts in which the density is equal to or greater than one dwelling unit per 10,000 square feet.

Highest adjacent grade: The highest natural elevation of the ground surface, prior to construction, next to the proposed walls of a structure.

Highway, limited access: A freeway or expressway providing a trafficway for through traffic where owners or occupants of abutting property on lands and other persons have no legal right to access to or from same, except at such points and in such manner as may be determined by the public authority having jurisdiction over the trafficway.

Historic district: An area, urban or rural, defined as an historic district by the [LOCAL GOVERNMENT], state or federal authority, and which may contain, within definable geographic boundaries, one or more buildings, objects, sites, or structures designated as exceptional or significant historic landmarks or clusters, as defined herein, including their accessory buildings, fences, and other appurtenances, and natural resources having historical, architectural, archaeological, and cultural significance, and which may have within its boundaries other buildings, objects, sites, or structures, which, while not of such historical, architectural, archaeological, or cultural significance as to be designated landmarks, nevertheless contribute to the overall visual setting of or characteristics of the landmark or landmarks located within the district.

Historic tree: A tree that has been officially found by the [LOCAL GOVERNMENT] to be of a character (e.g., age, size, species, or historic association) and/or to have had a role in local, state, or federal historical events that warrant its protection.

Home occupation: Any activity carried out for gain by a resident conducted as an accessory use in the resident's dwelling unit.

Homeowners' association: See *property owners' association.*

Horizontal zone: An area longitudinally centered on the perimeter of a private airport's runway that extends outward from the edge of the primary surface a distance equivalent to 1 statute mile.

Horticulturist: A qualified professional who has studied the science or art of cultivating plants especially for ornamental use.

Hospital: An institution providing health services, primarily for inpatients, and medical or surgical care of the sick or injured, including as an integral part of the institution such related facilities as laboratories, outpatient departments, training facilities, central service facilities, and staff offices.

Hotel: A building containing rooms intended or designed to be used or that are used, rented, or hired out to be occupied or that are occupied for sleeping purposes by guests, and where only a general kitchen and dining room are provided within the building or in an accessory building.

Household: Any person or persons who reside or intend to reside in the same housing unit.

Housing Facility for Older Persons: Any apartment that complies with the provisions of 24 C.F.R. §§ 100.304-100.307.

Housing unit: A dwelling unit as defined in the [APPROPRIATE STATE OR LOCAL CODE SECTION].

HUD Code manufactured home: A structure, constructed on or after June 15, 1976, according to the rules of the United States Department of Housing and Urban Development (HUD), transportable in one or more sections, which, in the traveling mode, is 8 body feet or more in width or 40 body feet or more in length, or, when erected on site, is 320 or more square feet, and which is built on a permanent chassis and designed to be used as a dwelling with or without a permanent foundation when connected to the required utilities, and which includes plumbing, heating, air conditioning, and electrical systems.

Impact analysis: See *fiscal impact analysis* and *environmental impact assessment.*

Impact area: The area within which a proposed development is presumed to create a demand for public services and/or facilities and is evaluated for compliance pursuant to Chapter 6, Adequate Public Facilities, of the LDC; that area in which the capacity of public facilities will be aggregated and compared to the demand created by existing development, committed development, and the proposed development. The impact areas for specific public facilities are defined in Chapter 6.

Impact fee: A charge or assessment imposed by the [LOCAL GOVERNMENT] against new development in order to generate revenue for funding the costs of capital improvements or facility expansions necessitated by and attributable to the new development.

Impervious cover: Roads, parking areas, buildings, pools, patios, sheds, driveways, private sidewalks, and other impermeable construction covering the natural land surface, including, but not limited to, all streets and pavement within the subdivision. "Percent impervious cover" is calculated as the area of impervious cover within a lot, tract, or parcel or within the total site being developed divided by the total area within the perimeter of such lot, tract, parcel, or development. Vegetated water quality basins, vegetated swales, other vegetated conveyances for overland drainage, and public sidewalks shall not be calculated as impervious cover.

Improvement: Any one or more of the following that is required by a development order or legislation requiring financing of capital facilities, the need for which is generated by a development project: streets, roadways, and bicycle paths; sidewalks and pedestrian paths; signage for traffic control and other governmental purposes, including street name, signs, and other traffic control devices on streets, roadways, and pedestrian and bicycle paths; lighting of streets and pedestrian and bicycle paths; water mains and connections, including facilities and connections for the suppression of fires; sanitary sewers and storm drainage sewer mains and connections; utility lines and poles, conduits, and connections; off-street parking and access; landscaping and contouring of land and other provisions for drainage, sedimentation, and erosion control; open space, parks, recreation facilities, and playgrounds; and public elementary and secondary school sites.

Improvement guarantee: A security instrument, including, but not limited to, a bond, a letter of credit, or other sufficient surety, accepted by a [LOCAL GOVERNMENT] to ensure that all public and nonpublic improvements required as a condition of approval of a development project will be completed in compliance with the plans and specifications of the development approved in the development order.

Individual sewage disposal system: A septic tank, seepage tile sewage disposal system, or any other approved sewage treatment device.

Infill development: Development designed to occupy scattered or vacant parcels of land that remain after the majority of development has occurred in an area.

Infrastructure: Any physical system or facility that provides essential services, such as transportation, utilities, energy, telecommunications, waste disposal, parklands, sports, buildings, housing facilities, and the management and use of resources regarding same. Includes drainage systems, irrigation systems, sidewalks, roadways, sewer systems, water systems, driveways, trails, parking lots, and other physical systems or facilities as generally described above that may not be specifically enumerated in this definition.

Infrastructure expenses: Those expenses that shall include engineering costs, impact fees, platting fees (including the amount of bond, trust agreement, or irrevocable letter of credit posted with the [LOCAL GOVERNMENT] to assure compliance with platting requirements), as well as necessary development costs actually paid (if such costs actually paid exceed or are necessary but are not included infrastructure costs covered by the bond, trust agreement, or irrevocable letter of credit), including off-site infrastructure costs that are necessary for plat approval of a specific parcel of real property. A property owner or developer shall be allowed to include as infrastructure expenses costs incurred by voluntary compliance with development ordinances, including, by way of example but not limitation, tree survey costs.

Inhabitable use: A use that involves the construction or placement of permanent or temporary dwelling units.

Institution for children or the aged: An establishment providing residence and care for children or the aged.

Intensity: The number of square feet of development per acre by land-use type with respect to nonresidential land uses.

Intermediate construction phase: On land development projects with multiple phases of construction, there may be several intermediate construction phases that precede the final construction phase. The final construction phase is completed in the build-out year.

Intermediate floodplain: Any channel, creek, stream, branch, or watercourse for surface water drainage that drains an area greater than 320 acres but less than 640 acres.

Intermittent stream: A stream in which surface water is absent during a portion of the year, as shown on the most recent 7.5-minute topographic quadrangle published by the United States Geologic Survey as confirmed by field verification.

Intersection: The area embraced within the prolongation or connection of the lateral curb lines, or, if none, then the lateral boundary lines of two or more roadways, including a public street, a private street, a commercial driveway, a residential driveway, a driveway approach, or an alley that join one another at, or approximately at, right angles, or the area within which vehicles traveling upon different roadways joining at any other angle may come into conflict.

Intrusion: A building, object, site, or structure that detracts from the historical significance of a district or cluster because of its incompatibility with the sense of time and place and historical development of a district or cluster; because of its incompatibility of scale, materials, texture, or color; whose integrity has been irretrievably lost; or whose physical deterioration or damage makes it infeasible to rehabilitate.

Inventory: A systematic listing of cultural, historical, architectural, or archaeological resources prepared by a city, state, or federal government or a recognized local historical authority, following standards set forth by federal, state, and city regulations for evaluation of cultural properties.

Junk: Any worn-out, cast-off, or discarded article or material that is ready for destruction or has been collected or stored for salvage or conversion to some use. Does not include any article or material that, unaltered or unchanged and without further reconditioning, can be used for its original purpose as readily as when new.

Junkyard: Any premises where junk, articles, or materials, including junked, wrecked, or inoperable vehicles, that are ready for destruction or that have been collected are stored for salvage or conversion to some use. Also known as "salvage yard."

Kennel: Any lot or premises on which domestic or wild animals are kept, boarded, or raised for sale.

Kindergarten: See *nursery school.*

Laboratory: A building or part of a building devoted to the testing and analysis of any product or animal. No manufacturing is conducted on the premises except for experimental or testing purposes.

Land development regulations: All ordinances including zoning, subdivision, official mapping, capital improvements programming, building, housing, safety, and environmental codes that relate to land use.

Landscape architect: A landscape architect licensed by the [STATE AGENCY].

Landscape planting area: An area that accommodates the installation of trees, shrubs, and ground covering consistent with the standards of *Division 4: Greenspace (Landscaping, Tree Preservation, Screening, and Environmental Protection) Standards* in Chapter 5, Development Standards, of the LDC.

Landscaping: The process or product of installing plants for purposes of screening or softening the appearance of a site, including grading, installation of plant materials, and seeding of turf or ground cover.

Land-use assumptions: A description of changes in projected wastewater demand contained in the land-use assumptions plan.

Land-use category: A classification of uses as set forth in the use matrix (Table 3-4, Use Matrix, in Chapter 3, Zoning, of the LDC).

Large shrub: Any plant, deciduous, or evergreen, that is generally multistemmed and reaches a height of 6 feet or more upon maturity.

Large tree: A tree of a species that normally reaches a height of 30 feet or more upon maturity.

Lattice: A style of antenna supporting structure, not supported by guy wires, which consists of vertical and horizontal supports with multiple legs and cross-bracing and metal-crossed strips or bars to support antennas.

Lattice antenna structure: A steel lattice, self-supporting structure with no guy-wire support, so designed to support fixtures that hold one or more antennas and related equipment for wireless communications transmission.

Lease: See *sale or lease.*

LEED® Building Rating System: The document entitled "Green Building Rating System for New Construction & Major Renovations (LEED®-NC) Version 2.2" (October 2005), published by the United States Green Building Council, which document is hereby incorporated by this reference.

LEED® Neighborhood Rating System: The document entitled "LEED for Neighborhood Developments Rating System—Preliminary Draft" (September 6, 2005), published by the United States Green Building Council, which document is hereby incorporated by this reference.

Levee: A man-made structure, usually an earthen embankment, designed and constructed in accordance with sound engineering practices, to contain, control, or divert the flow of water in order to provide protection from temporary flooding.

Levee system: A flood protection system that consists of a levee or levees and associated structures, such as closure and drainage devices, which are constructed and operated in accordance with sound engineering practices.

Level of service: An indicator of the extent or degree of service provided by, or proposed to be provided by, a facility based upon and related to the operational characteristics of the facility. Indicates the capacity per unit of demand for each public facility, including the cumulative impacts or capacity of a series of development projects taken together to measure the joint and several impacts.

Light rail line: A public rail transit line that usually operates at grade level and that provides high-capacity, regional-level transit service. Does not include low-capacity, district level, or excursion rail transit service, such as a vintage trolley line. Designed to share a street right-of-way, although it may also use a separate right-of-way.

Link: See *street link.*

Linkage: A system by which a developer who creates a need for affordable or workforce housing is required to build housing on or off site, or make a payment in lieu of such construction, or dedicate land for construction of such housing by public or nonprofit entities.

Live-work unit: A building in which offices, studios, or other commercial uses are located on the first floor and a dwelling unit is located above the first floor.

[LOCAL GOVERNMENT]: The [CITY/COUNTY], which is established by state statute or home rule to adopt land development regulations.

[LOCAL GOVERNMENT] attorney: The licensed attorney designated by the [GOVERNING ENTITY] to furnish legal assistance for the administration, interpretation, enforcement, and implementation of these regulations.

[LOCAL GOVERNMENT] engineer: The licensed professional engineer designated by the [GOVERNING ENTITY] to furnish engineering assistance for the administration of these regulations.

Lodge: The place where members of a club or fraternal organization hold their meetings.

Lot: A tract, plot, or portion of a subdivision or other parcel of land intended as a unit for the purpose, whether immediate or future, of transfer of ownership, or possession, or for building development. See *tract.*

Lot, corner: A lot or parcel of land abutting upon two or more streets at their intersection, or upon two parts of the same street forming an interior angle of less than 135 degrees.

Lot depth: The mean horizontal distance between the front and rear lot lines.

Lot design standards: See *Division 2: Design Standards,* § 5.10 Lots, in Chapter 5, Development Standards, of the LDC.

Lot improvement: Any building, structure, place, work of art, or physical object situated on a lot.

Lot, reversed corner: A corner lot, the rear of which abuts upon the side of another lot whether across an alley or not.

Lot width: The width of a lot at the front setback line.

Low density: Those residential zoning districts in which the density is equal to or less than one dwelling unit per 40,000 square feet.

Lowest floor: The lowest floor of the lowest enclosed area (including the basement). An unfinished or flood-resistant enclosure, usable solely for parking of vehicles, building access, or storage in an area other than a basement area, is not considered a building's lowest floor, provided that such enclosure is not built in order to render the structure in violation of the applicable nonelevation design requirement of Section 60.3 of the National Flood Insurance Program regulations.

Low-income housing: A household composed of one or more persons with a combined annual net income for all adult members that does not exceed the qualifying limit for a lower-income family of a size equivalent to the number of persons residing in such household, as set forth in the [APPROPRIATE STATE OR LOCAL CODE SECTION].

Lux: The standard unit of illuminance. One lux is equal to 1 lumen per square meter.

Maintenance easement: An easement granted by the owner of a lot adjacent to a zero lot line development, exclusively for the purpose of allowing the occupant of a residence on the lot line access to the adjoining property in order to maintain that portion of his/her dwelling situated on the property line.

Maintenance guarantee: Any security instrument required by a [LOCAL GOVERNMENT] to ensure that public or non-public improvements will be operated, maintained, and repaired for a period of time following construction of the improvement as specified in a development order.

Major arterial: A street that connects two or more subregions; provides secondary connections outside cities; complements freeway in high-volume corridors, as designated in the [COMPREHENSIVE PLAN TRANSPORTATION ELEMENT OR THOROUGHFARE PLAN].

Major bus boarding location: The right-of-way of any street link or series of street links in which at least four bus shelters are located within a distance of 1 mile.

Major floodplain: Any channel, creek, stream, branch, or watercourse for surface water drainage that drains 640 acres or more.

Major subdivision: All subdivisions not classified as minor subdivisions, including, but not limited to, subdivisions of four or more lots, or any size subdivision requiring any new street or extension of the [LOCAL GOVERNMENT] facilities or the creation of any public improvements. Includes the resubdivision amendment or modification of a major subdivision, or series of related minor subdivisions on contiguous land that cumulatively amount to the creation of four or more lots.

Major thoroughfare: Street routes as set forth in the major thoroughfare plan, and as may from time to time be amended, which are devoted to moving large volumes of traffic over long distances.

Major thoroughfare plan: The major thoroughfare plan as adopted by the [LOCAL GOVERNMENT].

Manufactured home: A United States Department of Housing and Urban Development Code (HUD Code) manufactured home. For purposes of the floodplain ordinance, a "manufactured home" means a structure transportable in one or more sections, which is built on a permanent chassis and is designed for use with or without a permanent foundation when connected to the required utilities. Does not include a "recreational vehicle." Also known as "manufactured housing."

Manufactured home land-lease community: A parcel in which individual spaces are leased for the purpose of installing, placing, or occupying a manufactured home.

Manufactured home park: A plot or tract of land separated into two or more spaces or lots, which are rented or leased or offered for rent or lease to persons for the installation of manufactured homes for use and occupancy as residences, provided that the lease or rental agreement is for a term of less than 60 months and contains no purchase option.

Manufactured home site: A plot of ground within a manufactured home park that is designed for and designated as the location for only one manufactured home and customary accessory uses.

Manufactured home stand: That part of a manufactured home site that has been reserved for the placement of the manufactured home, appurtenant structures, or additions.

Manufactured housing: See *manufactured home.*

Manufacturing: Operations required in the mechanical, biological, or chemical transformation of materials or substances into new products, including the assembling of component parts; the manufacture of products; and the blending of materials, such as lubricating oils, plastics, resins, or liquors. Covers all mechanical, biological, or chemical transformations, whether the new product is finished or semifinished as raw materials in some other process.

Marginal access: The type of street used to provide direct access to abutting properties and protection from through traffic.

Mass: The size, height, symmetry, and overall proportion of a structure in relation to the original style and/or to surrounding structures.

Mass transit: The transportation of passengers and hand-carried packages or baggage of a passenger by a surface, overhead, or underground means of transportation, or a combination of those means, including motorbus, trolley coach, rail, and suspended overhead rail transportation. Does not include taxicab transportation.

Mean sea level: For purposes of the National Flood Insurance Program, the National Geodetic Vertical Datum of 1929 or other datum to which base flood elevations shown on a community's Flood Insurance Rate Map are referenced.

Medium density: Those residential zoning districts in which the density is between 10,000 and 40,000 square feet per dwelling unit.

Medium tree: A tree of a species that normally reaches a height exceeding 15 feet but less than 30 feet upon maturity

Membership organization: An organization operating on a membership basis with preestablished formal membership requirements and with the intent to promote the interests of its members. Includes trade associations, professional organizations, unions, and similar political and religious organizations

Mental impairment: See *physical or mental impairment.*

Ministerial decision: A decision on a development approval application rendered by an administrative official that does not require legislative, administrative, or quasi-judicial discretion and is not subject to a public hearing.

Miniwarehouse: A storage enterprise dealing with the reception of goods of residential or commercial orientation that lie dormant over extended periods of time. Separate storage units are rented to individual customers who are entitled to exclusive and independent access to their respective units.

Minor floodplain: Any channel, creek, stream, branch, or watercourse for surface water drainage that drains an area greater than 100 acres but less than 320 acres.

Minor subdivision: Any subdivision containing not more than three lots fronting on an existing street, not including any new street, the extension of municipal facilities, or the creation of public improvements, and not adversely affecting the remainder of the comprehensive plan, official map, or zoning regulations. A series of related minor subdivisions on contiguous land cumulatively totaling four or more lots shall be construed to create a major subdivision.

Mitigation: A system by which a developer causing some adverse agricultural, environmental, or fiscal impact is required to counterbalance that impact by creating an equivalent benefit through dedication, payments, offsets, and alternative construction of self-imposed restrictions.

Mitigation tree: A tree used for the purpose of mitigating the destruction or removal of a protected or heritage tree pursuant to the requirements of *Division 4: Greenspace (Landscaping, Tree Preservation, Screening, and Environmental Protection) Standards* in Chapter 5, Development Standards, of the LDC. Must have a trunk size of at least 2-1/2 inches, measured at 6 inches above grade for single-trunk species trees, or 1-1/2 inches measured at 6 inches above grade for multitrunk species trees. In the case of multitrunked species trees, a tree will be qualified as a mitigation tree based on the measured diameter of the largest of the existing trunks at 6 inches together with one-half of the measured diameter of the remaining trunks at the same height.

Mixed-use building: A building that contains two or more of the following major use types: residential, office, or retail.

Mobile home: A manufactured home that does not conform to the United States Department of Housing and Urban Development Code (HUD Code) or the local building code.

Model home: A dwelling unit used initially for display purposes, which typifies the type of units that will be constructed in the subdivision and which will not be permanently occupied during its use as a model.

Molding: Any linear plane that deviates from a flat surface. On buildings, molding consists of strips of wood used to conceal joints and to provide a decorative finished appearance. No portion of a control joint shall be considered a molding.

Money in lieu of land: Payment of money into a municipally earmarked fund to provide for acquisition of facilities off site in place of dedicating land or providing such facility on site.

Monopole: A style of free-standing, antenna supporting structure, which is composed of a single shaft that is attached to a foundation. This type of antenna supporting structure is designed to support itself without the use of guy wires or other stabilization devices, and is mounted to a foundation that rests on or in the ground or on a building's roof.

Monopole antenna structure: A self-supporting, pole type structure with no guy-wire support, tapering from base to top, and so designed to support fixtures that hold one or more antennas and related equipment for wireless telecommunications transmission.

Motel: A building or group of detached, semidetached, or attached buildings on a lot containing guest dwellings, each of which has a separate outside entrance leading directly to rooms, with a garage or parking space conveniently located with each unit, and which is designed, used, or intended to be used primarily for the accommodation of automobile transients. Motels may include bed-and-breakfast inns or boarding houses if they meet the above-defined criteria.

Mulch: Nonliving organic and inorganic materials customarily used in landscape design to retard erosion, retain moisture, maintain even soil temperature, control weeds, and enrich the soil.

Multiple Resource Historic District: An area defined by the [LOCAL GOVERNMENT], state, or federal authority within a defined geographical area that identifies specific cultural resources having historic, architectural, cultural, or archaeological significance.

Multitrunk tree: A tree having two or more main trunks arising from the root collar or main trunk.

National Historic Preservation Act: 16 U.S.C. Part 470.

Natural state: The topography that exists at the time information is gathered for Flood Insurance Rate Maps or any subsequent approved revisions to those maps.

Neighborhood Park and Recreation Improvement Fund: A special fund established by the [LOCAL GOVERNMENT] to retain monies contributed by developers in accordance with the "money-in-lieu-of-land" provisions of these regulations.

Neighborhood unit: An area that includes residences, businesses, parks, schools, and other community facilities. Populations may range from 4,000 to 10,000, depending on the geographic area and boundaries, and which usually contains at least 1,500 housing units.

Net acreage: The gross acreage of a development site excluding those portions of a development dedicated to public use, such as street rights-of-way, drainage, and open space.

New development: Any new demand that increases the number of equivalent dwelling units, including, but not limited to, the subdivision and/or resubdivision of land; the construction, reconstruction, redevelopment, conversion, structural alteration, relocation, or enlargement of any structure; or any use or extension of the use of land, any of which increases the number of equivalent dwelling units.

Node: The terminus or intersection of two or more streets, including the head or bulb of a cul-de-sac.

Nonconforming lot, parcel, or use: A lot or parcel (subdivided or unsubdivded) that was lawfully established or commenced prior to the adoption or amendment of the [LOCAL GOVERNMENT]'s land development regulations and that fails to meet the current requirements for area, height, yards, setback, or use generally applicable in the district because of a change in the applicable zoning district regulations, annexation, condemnation of a portion of the lot, or other governmental action.

Nonconforming sign: A sign that was lawfully constructed or installed prior to the adoption or amendment of a [LOCAL GOVERNMENT]'s land development regulations, which was in compliance with any land development regulations then in effect but which does not presently comply with the land development regulations.

Nonconforming site: A lot, parcel, or development site that was lawfully established but that does not comply with the area, height, yards, setback, or other bulk standards of the LDC.

Nonconforming structure: A building or structure that was lawfully erected prior to the adoption or amendment of the [LOCAL GOVERNMENT]'s land development regulations but that no longer complies with all the regulations applicable to the zoning district in which the structure is located.

Nonconformity: Any nonconforming use, sign, lot, parcel, building, site, or structure.

Noncontributing: A building, object, site, or structure that neither adds to nor detracts from a sense of time and place or historical development of a district or cluster.

Nonliving materials: Plant materials used for landscaping, such as river rock, stone, bark, and similar materials.

Nonpublic improvement: Any improvement for which the owner of the property, a homeowners' association, or some other nongovernmental entity is presently responsible and which the [LOCAL GOVERNMENT] will not be assuming the responsibility for maintenance or operation.

Nonresidential subdivision: A subdivision whose intended use is other than residential, such as commercial or industrial.

Notice of noncompliance: A notice issued by the administrative assistant to the planning commission informing the applicant for approval of a major subdivision that the sketch plat is not in compliance with these regulations and that the applicant may not apply for preliminary plat approval.

Nursery: Land or greenhouses used to raise flowers, shrubs, trees, grass, and other plants for sale.

Nursery school: A child care facility offering a program for children between two and seven years of age for four hours or less per day.

Object: A material thing of functional, aesthetic, cultural, historical, archaeological, or scientific value that may be, by nature or design, movable yet related to a specific setting or environment.

Obstruction: Any structure, growth, or other object, including a mobile object, that exceeds a limiting height established by federal regulations or by the airport zoning regulations.

Occupancy: The presumed level of build-out as estimated by the property owner of the proposed development at the later of five years or build-out.

Office: A building used primarily for conducting the affairs of a business, profession, service, industry, government, or like activity, which may include ancillary services for office workers, such as a restaurant, coffee shop, or newspaper or candy stand.

Official map: A map established by law showing the streets, highways, parks, drainage systems, and setback lines laid out, adopted, and established by law. The official map shall be amended from time to time to show any amendments or additions resulting from the recording and filing of approved subdivision plats.

Official zoning map: The map of all zoning districts, including but not limited to overlay and "PD" (Planned Development) districts, that is on file with the [LOCAL GOVERNMENT], clerk, and the [PLANNING OFFICIAL]'s office.

Offset: The amount of the reduction of an impact fee designed to fairly reflect the value of area-related facilities or other oversized facilities pursuant to rules or administrative guidelines provided in the [LOCAL GOVERNMENT'S IMPACT FEE ORDINANCE OR REGULATIONS].

Off site: Any premises not located within the area of the property subject to development approval, whether or not in the common ownership of the applicant.

Off-site facility: Any structure, facility, equipment, or installation, the purpose and function of which is to receive wastewater from a development's internal collection system and to transport, treat, and ultimately discharge that wastewater to a receiving stream at a permanent location determined by the board.

Off-site mains: Sewer or water mains totally outside of a subdivision.

100-year floodplain: The land in the floodplain within a community subject to a 1 percent or greater chance of flooding in any given year, and the area designated as a Federal Emergency Management Agency Zone A, AE, AH, or AO on the Flood Insurance Rate Maps. See *area of special flood hazard, flood or flooding,* and *floodplain.*

100-year frequency flood: See *base flood.*

100-year frequency rainstorm: The rainstorm having an average statistical frequency of occurrence in the order of once in 100 years, although the rainstorm may actually occur in any year.

On site: Development, construction, installation of infrastructure, or any other activity that occurs on the site that is the subject of an application.

On-site facility: Any structure, facility, equipment, or installation that collects and transports wastewater generated from within a development to the off-site system at a designated point.

On-site mains: Sewer or water mains totally within a subdivision, including mains lying along one or more sides of a subdivision that serve such subdivision exclusively.

Opaque: Incapable of transmitting light.

Open space: An area that is intended to provide light and air, and is designed, depending upon the particular situation, for environmental, scenic, or recreational purposes. May include, but need not be limited to, lawns, decorative plantings, bikeways, walkways, outdoor recreation areas, wooded areas, greenways, and water courses. The computation of open space shall not include driveways, parking lots, or other surfaces designed or intended for motorized vehicular traffic, or to buildings. The term "open space" also includes any land, water, or submerged land that is provided for, preserved for, or used for park or recreational purposes; conservation of land or other natural resources; cultural, historic, or scenic purposes; assisting in the shaping of the character, direction, and timing of community development; or wetlands.

Order: See *development approval.*

Ordinance: Any legislative action, however denominated, of the [GOVERNING ENTITY] that has the force of law, including any amendment or repeal of any ordinance.

Ordinary repair and maintenance: Any work, the purpose and effect of which is to correct any deterioration or decay of or damage to a building, object, or structure, and to restore it as nearly as practicable to its condition prior to the deterioration, decay, or damage.

Outdoor resale business: A business that sells used merchandise, other than automobiles, logging equipment, or other agricultural equipment, and stores or displays the merchandise outdoors.

Outdoor storage: The keeping, in an unroofed area, of any goods, junk, material, or merchandise in the same place for more than 24 hours.

Overall height: The height of a wireless communications facility, which includes all antennas and other ancillary appurtenances.

Overland flow: Stormwater run-off that is not confined by any natural or man-made channel, such as a creek, drainage ditch, or storm sewer. Involves the movement of run-off in a thin layer (usually less than 1 inch in depth) over a wide surface, which begins when water ponded on the surface of the land becomes deep enough to overcome surface retention forces. Also known as "sheet flow."

Overlay zoning district: A district that is superimposed over one or more zoning districts or parts of districts and that imposes specified requirements in addition to those applicable in the underlying base zoning district.

Oversized vehicle: A motor vehicle, trailer, or boat that by itself, or together with other structure or structures or vehicle or vehicles attached to it, exceeds 24 feet in length, 8 feet in width, or 8 feet in height, exclusive of appurtenances, such as antennas, air conditioners, luggage racks, and mirrors.

Owned unit: A designated unit that is a condominium, stock cooperative, timeshare, or other legal or equitable instrumentality that creates a legal or equitable title in the property.

Owner: The record owners of the fee or a vendee in possession, including any person, group of persons, firm or firms, corporation or corporations, or any other legal entity having legal title to or sufficient proprietary interest in the land sought to be subdivided under the definition of same ownership.

Park: Land and facilities, such as playgrounds, fountains, or swimming pools, used or to be used as a park as defined in § 5.21 Parks/Open Space in Chapter 5, Development Standards, of the LDC, regardless of location, including the acquisition of such land, the construction of improvements, provision of pedestrian and vehicular access, and purchase of equipment for the facility.

Parking lot: An off-street, ground-level open area for the temporary storage of motor vehicles. Does not include an area used exclusively for the display of motor vehicles for sale as part of an automobile dealership.

Parking lot plantings: Plantings that shade and improve the appearance of large areas of pavement that are located within planting areas adjacent to parking areas.

Parking standards: See § 5.21 Parks/Open Space in Chapter 5, Development Standards, of the LDC.

Parking structure, commercial: An area or structure area used exclusively for the temporary storage of motor vehicles.

Parkway: The area located within a public right-of-way between the outer curb line and the adjacent property line.

Parkway tree: A tree 10 inches or larger, which is located within the parkway and which may be used for meeting tree preservation requirements and landscape requirements, but is not required to be counted in calculating the minimum tree preservation percentage.

Parolee: A convicted felon who has been approved for parole but who is to be housed in a short-term "transitional home" *prior to entering society with the privileges and conditions of a parolee.*

Pattern book: A visual presentation of the architectural styles of buildings, including the height of cornice lines, roof profiles, finish materials, windows, and ornamentation.

Pavement section: The portion of a municipal street that is improved, designed, or ordinarily used for vehicular travel. Does not include a curb, berm, or shoulder. Where curbs are laid, the portion between the face of curbs.

Pawnshop: A business that lends money on the security of pledged goods. May also purchase merchandise for resale from dealers and traders.

Peak-hour trips: The number of traffic units generated by and attracted to the proposed development during its heaviest hour of use, dependent on type of use.

Peak shaving: Controlling postdevelopment peak discharge rates to predevelopment levels by providing temporary detention in a best management practice.

Perennial stream: A stream that contains surface water throughout an average rainfall year, as shown on the most recent 7.5-minute topographic quadrangle published by the United States Geologic Survey, as confirmed by field verification.

Perennial water body: A lake, pond, or other water body (other than a stream) that contains surface water throughout an average rainfall year, as shown on the most recent 7.5-minute topographic quadrangle published by the United States Geologic Survey, as confirmed by field verification.

Performance standards: Regulation of development based on open space ratio, impervious surface ratio, density, and floor area ratio.

Perimeter street: A street adjoining the exterior boundaries of a subdivision plat or site plan.

Permanent foundation: A system of supports for a structure that supports its maximum design load, is constructed of concrete or masonry materials, and is placed at a sufficient depth below grade adequate to prevent frost damage.

Permanent residence: The residential address inhabited and maintained by the property owner, which is also listed with the United States Postal Service and with the [STATE BOARD] as the property owner's official residence.

Permeability: The capacity of a material to transmit a liquid, which is expressed in terms of hydraulic conductivity of water in centimeters-per-second units of measurement.

Permit: See *development approval*.

Person: Any natural person, corporation, partnership, joint venture, association (including homeowners' or neighborhood associations), trust, or any other entity recognized by law.

Personal services: Establishments primarily engaged in providing services involving the care of a person or his/her apparel, such as laundry cleaning and garment services, garment pressing, linen supply, diaper service, coin-operated laundries, dry cleaning plants, carpet and upholstery cleaning, photographic studios, beauty shops, barber shops, shoe repair, hat cleaning, funeral services, reducing salons and health clubs, and clothing rental.

Personal wireless service: Commercial mobile services (including cellular, personal communication services, specialized mobile radio, enhanced specialized mobile radio, and paging), unlicensed wireless services, and common carrier wireless exchange access services, as defined in the Telecommunications Act of 1996.

Pervious pavement: A pavement system with traditional strength characteristics but which allows rainfall to percolate through it rather than running off. A pervious pavement system uses either porous asphalt, pervious concrete, or plastic pavers interlaid in a running bond pattern and either pinned or interlocked in place. Porous asphalt consists of an open graded course aggregate held together by asphalt with sufficient interconnected voids to provide a high rate of permeability. Pervious concrete is a discontinuous mixture of Portland cement, coarse aggregate, admixtures, and water that allows for passage of run-off and air. Examples of permeable pavement systems include Grasspave2®, Gravelpave2®, Turfstone®, and UNI Eco-stone®.[2]

Phased construction project: Any land development project that is developed in greater than a single phase and that is identified by the issuance of development approvals.

Phased subdivision application: An application for subdivision approval submitted pursuant to a preliminary plat, or at the option of the subdivider, pursuant to a specific plan in which the applicant proposes to immediately subdivide the property but will develop in one or more individual phase or phases over a period of time. May include an application for approval of, or conversion to, horizontal or vertical condominiums, nonresidential development projects, planned developments, mixed-use projects, and residential developments.

Physical or mental impairment: Orthopedic, visual, speech, or hearing impairments; Alzheimer's disease; presterile dementia; cerebral palsy; epilepsy; muscular dystrophy; multiple sclerosis; cancer; heart disease; diabetes; mental retardation; autism; or emotional illness.

Pipeline development: A project that has received final development approval but construction has not commenced on the project.

Pitch: The slope of a roof as determined by the vertical rise in inches for every horizontal 12-inch length (called the "run"). Expressed with the rise mentioned first and the run mentioned second (e.g., a roof with a 4-inch rise for every horizontal foot has a 4:12 pitch).

Planned capital improvement: A capital improvement that does not presently exist but which is included within the capital improvements program, and is funded, constructed, or otherwise made available within the time period prescribed by Chapter 6, Adequate Public Facilities, of the LDC.

Planned development: A development constructed on a tract of minimum size under single ownership planned and developed as an integral unit and consisting of a combination of residential and/or nonresidential uses on the land.

Planning commission: The [LOCAL GOVERNMENT]'s planning commission established in accordance with law.

[PLANNING OFFICIAL]: The director of the department of planning or appointed designee, including the building official or building inspector where appropriate.

Plat: A complete and exact map representing a tract of land, showing the boundaries and location of individual lots, easements, and streets, which has been approved by the planning commission and recorded in the office of the county clerk. Includes a replat.

Police power: Inherent, delegated, or authorized legislative power for purposes of regulation to secure health, safety, and general welfare.

Pollutants: Any element, chemical, compound, organism, or material that alters the chemical, physical, biological, and/or radiological integrity of water.

Pollution: The alteration of the physical, thermal, chemical, or biological quality of, or the contamination of, any water.

Porch: A roofed area, which may be glazed or screened, attached to or part of and with direct access to or from a structure, and usually located on the front or side of the structure.

Preliminary plat: The preliminary drawing or drawings, described in these regulations, indicating the proposed manner or layout of the subdivision to be submitted to the planning commission for approval.

Primary arterial: A road intended to move through traffic to and from major attractors, such as central business districts, regional shopping centers, colleges and/or universities, military installations, major industrial areas, and similar traffic generators within the governmental unit; and/or as a route for traffic between communities or large areas and/or that carries high volumes of traffic.

Primary surface: The area extending a distance of 50 feet to both sides of the centerline of a private airport's runway, and running the distance of the runway.

Principal arterial: See *major arterial*.

Principal building: A building or structure or, where the context so indicates, a group of buildings or structures, in which the principal use of a lot or parcel is conducted. This includes any buildings that are attached to the principal structure by a covered structure. Also known as "principal structure."

Principal dwelling: A dwelling unit that constitutes the principal building or principal structure on a lot or parcel.

Principal structure: See *principal building*.

Principal use: The primary or main use of land or structures, as distinguished from a secondary or accessory use.

Private club: See *club*.

Process: The act of reviewing and providing a decision on an application. This includes providing notice to the applicant and interested parties, conducting a hearing, making recommendations, and rendering a decision.

Processing and warehousing: The storage of materials in a warehouse or terminal and where such materials may be combined, broken down, or aggregated for transshipment or storage purposes where the original material is not chemically or physically changed.

Professional engineer: An engineer licensed by the [STATE AGENCY].

Projected traffic: The traffic that is projected to exist on an existing or proposed street exclusive of site-generated traffic.

Property owner: The person, entity, corporation, or partnership in whose name a certificate of occupancy is issued; the current owner of the property if a certificate of occupancy is no longer valid; or, if the current owner cannot be contacted after due diligence, the lessee/occupant of the property who is in apparent control of such property.

Property owners' association: An association or organization, whether or not incorporated, which operates under and pursuant to recorded covenants or deed restrictions, through which each owner of a portion of a subdivision—whether a lot, parcel site, unit plot, condominium, or any other interest—is automatically a member as a condition of ownership, and each such member is subject to a charge or assessment for a prorated share of expense of the association, which may become a lien against the lot, parcel, unit, condominium, or other interest of the member.

Proportionate share: Bearing a reasonable relationship to the burden imposed by a development project upon the [LOCAL GOVERNMENT] to provide additional public services to a development; calculated using the same methodology used to determine an impact fee for such services, if any.

Proposed development: The uses, structures, and buildings contained in the application for development approval.

Protected tree: A tree designated as a protected tree pursuant to § 5.36.3 Installation Standards in Chapter 5, Development Standards, of the LDC.

Provider: A business, corporation, partnership, or other entity licensed by the Federal Communications Commission to provide wireless services in the [LOCAL GOVERNMENT].

Public art: Unique artwork in a variety of media that may be an integral part of eligible capital improvements projects, and produced by a professional artist, or an artist in collaboration with an architect, landscape architect, or professional engineer. Works may be permanent or temporary and functional or nonfunctional.

Public facilities project: Any and all public improvements, including, but not limited to: (1) water mains, pipes, conduits, tunnels, hydrants, and other necessary works and appliances for providing water service; (2) lines, conduits, and other necessary works and appliances for providing electric power service; (3) mains, pipes, and other necessary works and appliances for providing gas service; (4) poles, posts, wires, pipes, conduits, lamps, and other necessary works and appliances for lighting purposes; (5) pedestrian facilities, such as sidewalks, bikeways, crosswalks, steps, safety zones, platforms, seats, statuary, fountains, culverts, and bridges; (6) parks and parkways, recreation areas (including all structures, buildings, and other facilities necessary to make parks and parkways and recreation areas useful for the purposes for which they were intended); (7) sanitary sewers or instrumentalities of sanitation, together with the necessary outlets, cesspools, manholes, catch basins, flush tanks, septic tanks, disposal plants, connecting sewers, ditches, drains, conduits, tunnels, channels, or other appurtenances; (8) drains, tunnels, sewers, conduits, culverts and channels for drainage purposes, with necessary outlets, cesspools, manholes, catch basins, flush tanks, septic tanks, disposal plants, connecting sewers, ditches, drains, conduits, channels, and appurtenances; (9) stations, trucks, pumps, pipes, hydrants, and appliances for fire protection; (10) breakwaters, levees, bulkheads, groins and walls of rock, or other material to protect the streets, places, public ways, and other property from overflow by water, or to prevent beach erosion or to promote accretion to beaches; (11) works, systems, or facilities for the transportation of people, including rolling stock and other appurtenant equipment such as traffic signs, signals, lights, and lighting; (12) temporary and permanent school buildings; (13) police stations; (14) public works maintenance facilities; and (15) all other work auxiliary to any of the above that may be required to carry out that work, including, but not limited to, administrative, engineering, architectural, and legal work performed in connection with establishing, implementing, and monitoring public facilities projects; and acquisition of any and all property, easements, and rights-of-way that may be required to carry out the purposes of the project.

Public facility service area: Any area to which public facilities are extended or constructed and that obtain a benefit from the facilities.

Public hearing: A proceeding preceded by published notice and actual notice to certain persons and at which certain persons, including the applicant, may call witnesses and introduce evidence. In a quasi-judicial hearing, witnesses are sworn and are subject to cross-examination.

Public improvement: Any drainage ditch, roadway, parkway, bikeway, park, school site, drainageway, easement, open space, natural resource, sidewalk, pedestrian way, off-street parking area, lot improvement, or other facility or land for which the [LOCAL GOVERNMENT] may ultimately assume responsibility for maintenance and operation, or which may effect an improvement for which [LOCAL GOVERNMENT] responsibility is established.

Public meeting: A meeting of the [GOVERNING ENTITY], planning commission, the board of adjustment, or other administrative agency, preceded by notice, open to the public, and at which the public may, at the discretion of the body holding the public meeting, be heard.

Public property: Property that is owned by the [LOCAL GOVERNMENT] or any agency of the state or federal government.

Public right-of-way: A strip of land acquired by reservation, dedication, forced dedication, prescription, or condemnation, and used or intended to be used, wholly or in part, as a public street, alley, walkway, drain, or public utility line.

Public works official: The official designated by the [LOCAL GOVERNMENT] to manage the Department of Public Works or his/her designee.

Quadraplex: See *Dwelling, four-family (quadraplex)*.

Quarry: A tract of land used primarily for the extraction of limestone or other similar materials for processing, sale, or use for any purpose. Does not include exploration, excavation, or extraction of oil or natural gas, or excavation or grading necessary for the development of a lot or tract.

Radio frequency emissions: Any electromagnetic radiation or other communications signal emitted from an antenna or antenna-related equipment on the ground, antenna supporting structure, building, or other vertical projection.

Rear yard: An area extending the full width of a lot between the rear lot line and the nearest principal structure.

Reconstruction: The act or process of reassembling, reproducing, or replacing by new construction the form, detail, and appearance of property and its setting as it appeared at a particular period of time by means of the removal of later work, by the replacement of missing earlier work, or by the reuse of original materials.

Recreational vehicle: A vehicle that is built on a single chassis; 400 square feet or less when measured at the largest horizontal projections; designed to be self-propelled or permanently towable by a light duty truck; and designed primarily not for use as a permanent dwelling but as temporary living quarters for recreational, camping, travel, or seasonal use.

Recreation facility, neighborhood: Those recreational facilities operated on a nonprofit basis to include a swimming pool, wading pool, tennis courts, badminton courts, play areas, and clubhouse, all to be used exclusively by and for the benefit of dwelling owners, tenants, and their guests in certain defined adjoining areas.

Recycling business: A business that is: (1) primarily engaged in converting ferrous or nonferrous metals or other materials into raw material products having prepared grades and having an existing or potential economic value; or (2) using raw material products of that kind in the production of new products; or obtaining or storing ferrous or nonferrous metals or other materials for a purpose described by subsections (1) or (2), above.

Regional stormwater improvements: Regional detention and retention ponds, watershed protection, land purchase, waterway enlargement, channelization, and improved conveyance structures.

Registered engineer: A professional engineer properly licensed and registered in the state.

Registered family home: A child care facility that regularly provides care in the caretaker's own residence for not more than six children under 14 years of age, excluding the caretaker's own children, and that provides care after school hours for not more than six additional elementary school children, but where the total number of children, including the caretaker's own, does not exceed 12 children at any given time.

Registered land surveyor: A land surveyor properly licensed and registered in the state.

Regulatory flood: A flood having a 1 percent chance of being equaled or exceeded in any given year.

Regulatory floodplain: The land within the community subject to flooding during a 100-year frequency storm event, assuming that ultimate development has occurred throughout the watershed. The regulatory 100-year floodplain is limited to the reach of the stream that is designated as an area of special flood hazard on the Flood Insurance Rate Maps.

Rehab center: See *transitional home*.

Rehabilitation: The act or process of returning a building, object, site, or structure to a state of utility through repair, remodeling, or alteration, which makes possible an efficient contemporary use while preserving those portions or features of the building, object, site, or structure that are significant to its historical, architectural, and cultural values.

Relocation: Any change of the location of a building, object, or structure in its present setting or to another setting.

Rental unit: A designated unit that is not a condominium, stock cooperative, or community apartment.

Repetitive loss: Flood-related damages sustained by a structure on two separate occasions during a 10-year period for which the cost of repairs at the time of each such flood event, on the average, equals or exceeds 25 percent of the market value of the structure before the damage occurred.

Reservation: The designation of a portion of a property for a proposed right-of-way without dedication of the right-of-way to the agency providing the facility. Also called "reserve."

Reserve: See *reservation*.

Residential development: All areas devoted primarily to residential use.

Residential district or residential zoning district: Any of the following zoning districts: "RP" (Resource Protection), "NS" (Neighborhood Suburban), and "NU" (Neighborhood Urban).

Residential driveway approach: A driveway that provides access to property on which a single-family residence, duplex, or multifamily building containing five or fewer dwelling units is located.

Residential property: A building, site, or structure whose use after rehabilitation or restoration (for ad valorem tax exemption) will be for residential uses (i.e., for a single-family, duplex, three-, or four-family dwelling).

Residential streets: Street routes that provide access to local property owners and that connect property to the major thoroughfare or other collector street networks.

Residential structure: A single-family home, an apartment house, a townhouse, a condominium, or any type of dwelling unit.

Resource: A source or collection of buildings, objects, sites, structures, or areas that exemplify the cultural, social, economic, political, archaeological, or architectural history of the nation, state, or city.

Restoration: The act or process of accurately recovering the form and details of a building, object, site, or structure and its setting as it appeared at a particular period of time by means of the removal of later work or by the replacement of missing earlier work.

Restricted parking area: The area within the front yard of a lot within which the parking of oversized vehicles is regulated. Extends to a depth of 15 feet from the street curb or, if there is no curb, from the edge of the roadway whether paved or unpaved.

Restrictive covenant: A covenant creating restrictions applicable to development within a subdivision.

Resubdivision: Any change in a finally approved or recorded subdivision plat that affects any condition of the development order, any street layout on the map, any area that is reserved for public use, or any lot line. Any plat, map, or plan legally recorded prior to the adoption of any regulations controlling subdivisions shall not be valid and no development approval shall be issued on such map, plat, or plan until same has been approved through the resubdivision process.

Retail trade: Establishments engaged in selling goods or merchandise to the general public for personal or household consumption and rendering services incidental to the sale of such goods. Characteristics of retail trade establishments include the following: the establishment is usually a place of business and is engaged in activity to attract the general public to buy; the establishment buys and receives as well as sells merchandise; the establishment may process some of the products, but such processing is incidental or subordinate to the selling activities; and retail establishments sell to customers for their own personal or household use.

Retail use: Any use engaged in retail trade, including any use listed under the category "Commercial Buildings" in the use matrix (Table 3-4, Use Matrix, in Chapter 3, Zoning, of the LDC).

Reverse curve: A segment of a street at which two horizontal curves reverse direction.

Reviewing agency: Any agency of the [LOCAL GOVERNMENT] charged with the authority to render a decision approving, denying, or approving with conditions an application.

Rezoning: The redesignation of an area, lot, or parcel from one zoning district to another.

Right-of-way: Property that is publicly owned or upon which a governmental entity has an express or implied property interest (e.g., fee title or easement) held for a public purpose. Examples of such public purpose include, by way of example and not by limitation, a highway, a street, sidewalks, drainage facilities, a crosswalk, a railroad, a road, an electric transmission line, an oil or gas pipeline, a water main, a sanitary or storm sewer main, shade trees, or for any other special use. The usage of the term "right-of-way" for subdivision platting purposes means that every right-of-way established and shown on a final plat is separate and distinct from the lots or parcels adjoining the right-of-way, and is not included within the dimensions or areas of such lots or parcels. Rights-of-way involving maintenance by a public agency are dedicated to public use by the maker of the plat on which the right-of-way is established.

Roof line: In the case of a flat or pitched roof, the uppermost line of the roof of a building; in the case of a parapet, the uppermost height of the parapet.

Roof sign: A sign erected and constructed wholly on or above the roof of a building and supported by the roof structure.

Rooming house: See *boarding house*.

Root collar: An encircling structure of swollen tissue or a marked color change (from the tree bark) located at the highest part of the root system joining into the trunk of a tree at or slightly below the surrounding soil line.

Root protection area: An area in which limited construction may take place for the purposes of establishing sidewalks, driveways, utility connections, sodding, and landscaping within single-, two-, and three-family developments.

Root protection zone: An area with a radius of 1/2 foot for each inch of diameter breast height of a trunk or, if branching occurs at 4-1/2 inches, the diameter is measured at the point where the smallest diameter closest to the branching occurs. The zone need not be exactly centered around the tree or be circular in shape, but it must be positioned so that no disturbance occurs closer to the tree that lesser of one-half of the radius of the zone or within 5 feet of the tree. For any tree or groups of trees, the zone need not exceed 1,000 square feet in size. The radial root protection zones of trees may overlap one another so that the area of protection required for one tree may be shared by the area of protection required for another tree in order to minimize the total square footage of protected area where possible.

Runway: A defined area in an airport prepared for landing and taking off of aircraft along its length. Includes planned future paved runways and extensions of runways as shown on the official airport layout plan and on the Airport Hazard Zoning Maps of these regulations.

Rural tier: See *tier.*

Safety lane: A designated area on an approved plat that has a primary purpose of providing access for safety vehicles.

Sale or lease: Any immediate or future transfer of ownership, or any possessory interest in land, including contract of sale, lease, devise, intestate succession, or other transfer of an interest in a subdivision, whether by metes and bounds or lot and block description.

Salvage yard: See *junkyard.*

Same ownership: Ownership in whole or in part or separate parcels, tracts, or lots, whether contiguous or not, by any corporation, partnership, trust, business entity, or any individual owning any stock or legal or equitable interest in such corporation, partnership, trust, or business entity, or individually.

Sand or gravel pit: A tract of land used primarily for the extraction of soil, sand, gravel, clay, and other similar materials, other than oil or gas, which are processed and sold or used for commercial purposes. Does not include the excavation or grading necessary for the development of a lot or tract.

Sanitary landfill: A controlled area of land upon which solid waste is disposed of in accordance with standards, rules, or orders established by [STATE AGENCY].

Satellite dish antenna: A device incorporating a reflective surface that is solid, open mesh, or bar configured; is in the shape of a shallow dish, cone, or horn; and is to be used to transmit and/or receive electromagnetic waves between terrestrially and/or orbitally based uses.

Satellite earth station: Any device or antenna, including associated mounting devices or antenna supporting structures, used to transmit or receive signals from an orbiting satellite, including television broadcast signals; direct broadcast satellite services; multichannel, multipoint distribution services; fixed wireless communications signals; and any designated operations indicated in the Federal Communications Commission's Table of Allocations for satellite services.

Scale: The relationship of a building or structure to its surroundings with regard to its size, height, bulk, and/or intensity.

School: An institution or place for instruction or education, such as kindergarten; elementary, middle, or junior high school; high school; college; or university. See *school, business, or commercial trade.*

School, business, or commercial trade: A business organized to operate for a profit, offering instruction and training in a trade, a service, or an art.

School, public: A building or structure, including accessory buildings, grounds, or areas, owned and operated by a school or university, which is part of a school district or system organized pursuant to [STATE EDUCATIONAL STATUTES] and which is used for teaching, research, or the preservation of knowledge.

Screen or screening: Vegetation, fence, wall, berm, or a combination of any or all of these that partially or completely blocks the view of, and provides spatial separation of a portion or all of a site from, an adjacent property or right-of-way.

Secondary arterial: A road intended to collect and distribute traffic in a manner similar to primary arterials, except that these roads service minor traffic-generating areas, such as community commercial areas, primary and secondary educational facilities, hospitals, major recreational areas, churches, and offices, and are designed to carry traffic from collector streets to the system of primary arterials.

Security: The letter of credit or cash escrow provided by the applicant to secure its promises in the subdivision improvement agreement.

Sedimentation basins: Basins that remove pollutants by creating conditions under which suspended solids can settle out of the water column.

Sedimentation facilities: Facilities that include debris basins, sedimentation traps, berms, interceptor ditches, land terraces, hay bales, and vegetation ground cover.

Self-storage facility: Any building or group of buildings that is composed of contiguous individual rooms, which are rented to the public for the storage of personal property and which have independent access and locks under the control of the tenant.

Septic system: A system for the treatment of sewage or waterborne wastes from a dwelling or business establishment. The septic tank system consists of a watertight drain line from the house to a watertight septic tank, a distribution box, and an absorption field consisting of trench, gravel, and a disposal line.

Servant's quarters: An accessory building or portion of a main building located on the same lot as the principal building, occupied only by such persons and their families as are employed full time by occupants of the principal residence.

Service plan: A plan that identifies existing and future sewer, water, or utility capital improvements or expansions within designated service areas.

Setback: The distance between a building and the street line nearest to the building. Establishes the minimum required yard and governs the placement of structures and uses on the lot.

Setback line: The distance from which a building or structure is separated from a designated reference point, such as a property line.

Shade tree: A tree in a public place, a street, a special easement, or a right-of-way adjoining a street as provided in these regulations.

Shared use plan: A plan that includes the following: a signed statement from the antenna supporting structure owner agreeing to allow future collocations (including combined antennas) on the facility, where reasonable and structurally feasible, including those initiated by providers other than the applicant or provider signing the application; and a written evaluation of the feasibility of accommodating future collocations, which evaluation must address the following, as appropriate: structural capacity of the proposed antenna supporting structure; radio frequency limitations impacting the ability to accommodate collocations; geographical search area requirements; mechanical or electrical compatibility; any restrictions imposed upon the facility by the Federal Communications Commission that preclude future collocations; and additional relevant information as required by the [LOCAL GOVERNMENT].

Sheet flow: See *overland flow.*

Shop: A use devoted primarily to the sale of a service or a product or products.

Shopping mall: An integrated grouping of commercial activity, primarily of a retail and personal service nature, in a single building complex having the individual establishments joined by a common covered pedestrian mall.

Shrub, large: An upright plant growing to a mature height of more than 10 feet for use as a natural ornamentation or screening.

Shrub, medium: An upright plant growing to a mature height of 5 to 10 feet.

Shrub, small: An upright plant growing to a mature height of less than 5 feet.

Side street: A street intersecting another street with a higher street classification (e.g., a collector street adjoining an arterial street).

Sidewalk: The portion of a municipal street between the curb lines or lateral lines of a roadway and the adjacent property lines, which is improved and designed for or is ordinarily used for pedestrian travel.

Sidewalk café: An outdoor dining area that is located on a sidewalk and that contains removable tables, chairs, planters, or related appurtenances.

Side yard: An area extending the depth of a lot from the front yard to the rear yard between the side lot line and the nearest principal structure.

Sign: Any device, fixture, placard, or structure that uses any color, form, graphic, illumination, symbol, or writing to advertise, announce the purpose of, or identify the purpose of a person or entity, or to communicate information of any kind to the public.

Sign area: The entire advertising area of a sign excluding any framing, trim, or moulding, and the supporting structure.

Sign, billboard (off premise): Any outdoor sign, description, device, figure, painting, drawing, message, placard, poster, structure, or thing that directs the attention of the traveling public to a business, commercial product, commercial activity, or commercial service, which is conducted, sold, or offered at a location other than the premises on which the sign is located.

Significant stand of trees or shrubs: A clustering of at least three trees, of 2 1/2 inches of caliper or greater in size, and trunks spaced at no greater than 10-foot intervals.

Single-family dwelling: See *dwelling, single-family detached* or *dwelling, single-family.*

Single-family residential development: A development consisting of a parcel, a lot, or lots, containing only one dwelling unit. The dwelling unit may be detached or attached, a townhouse, a small lot, a home, a manufactured home, or a mobile home.

Site: The location of a significant event, a prehistoric or an historic occupation or activity, or a building, structure, or cluster, whether standing, ruined, or vanished, and where the location itself maintains historical, architectural, archaeological, or cultural value regardless of the value of any existing structure.

Site-generated traffic: Vehicular trips attracted to, or produced by, the proposed development site.

Site plan: A scaled drawing for a project that shows the proposed development of the lots, parcels, or tracts, including elevations, sections, architectural, landscape, engineering, and ecological drawings as is required for development approval of the project.

Sketch plat: A sketch preparatory to the preliminary plat (or final plat in the case of minor subdivisions) to enable the subdivider to save time and expense in reaching general agreement with the planning commission as to the form of the plat and the objectives of these regulations, and to indicate all roads, parks, rights-of-way, and public sites proposed for dedication to the [LOCAL GOVERNMENT].

Slope: The ratio of elevation change to horizontal distance, expressed as a percentage. Computed by dividing the vertical distance by the horizontal distance and multiplying the ratio by 100. For purposes of this appendix, a "slope" shall include only those areas with a horizontal distance of at least 50 feet.

Small animal breeder: Any person or establishment that breeds and/or engages in the feeding or care of more than 10 adult animals other than fish that do not normally exceed 5 pounds at maturity, including, but not limited to, white rats, gerbils, guinea pigs, prairie dogs, gophers, chipmunks, frogs, lizards, the smaller nonpoisonous varieties of snakes, and nonpoultry fowl, such as parakeets, parrots, doves, pigeons, cockatiels, and canaries.

Small tree: A tree of a species that normally reaches a height of less than 30 feet upon maturity.

Soils: Dirt, sand, and other similar earth matter; rocks and other solid or semisolid mass material, whether produced by man or by nature.

Solid waste: Any garbage; refuse; sludge from a waste treatment plant, water supply treatment plant, or air pollution control facility; and other discarded material, including solid, liquid, semisolid, or contained gaseous material resulting from industrial, municipal, commercial, mining, and agricultural operations, and from community and institutional activities. Does not include: solid or dissolved material in domestic sewage, solid or dissolved material in irrigation return flows, or industrial discharges subject to regulation by development approval issued pursuant to the [STATE WATER CODE]; soil, dirt, rock, sand, and other natural or man-made inert solid materials used to fill land if the object of the fill is to make the land suitable for the construction of surface improvements; or waste materials that result from activities associated with the exploration, development, or production of oil or gas.

Solid waste facility: All continuous land and structures, other appurtenances, and improvements on the land, used for processing, storing, or disposing of solid waste, or used for the purpose of processing, extracting, converting, or recovering energy or materials from solid waste. A facility may be publicly or privately owned and may consist of several processing, storage, or disposal operational units (e.g., one or more landfills, surface impoundments, or combinations of them).

Solid waste transfer station: A place or facility where waste materials are taken from smaller collection vehicles (e.g., compactor trucks) and placed in larger transportation vehicles (e.g., over-the-road tractors utilizing trailers that are top-loaded) for movement to designated disposal areas (usually landfills).

Special merit: A building, object, site, or structure having significant benefits to the [LOCAL GOVERNMENT] or to the community by virtue of exemplary architecture; specific features of land planning; or historic social, cultural, or other benefits having a high priority for community services.

Specific plan: A document encompassing a specific geographic area of the [LOCAL GOVERNMENT], which is prepared for the purpose of specifically implementing the [LOCAL GOVERNMENT] comprehensive plan by refining the policies of the comprehensive plan to a specific geographic area or containing specific recommendation as to the detailed policies and regulations applicable to a focused development scheme. A specific plan shall consist of goals, objectives, policies, and implementing strategies for capital improvements zoning; the level of service required for public facilities and services; physical and environmental conditions; housing and land-use characteristics of the area; and maps, diagrams, and other appropriate materials showing existing and future conditions.

Specified anatomical areas: Any showing of either the adult or minor human male or female genitals, anus or pubic area with less than a full opaque covering, or the showing of the post-puberty female areola with less than a full opaque covering.

Specified sexual activities: Acts of masturbation, sexual intercourse, homosexuality or lesbianism, sodomy, fellatio, sadomasochism, or physical contact with a person's own or another's specified anatomical areas.

Stabilization: The act or process of applying measures designed to reestablish a weather-resistant enclosure and the structural stability of an unsafe or deteriorated building, object, site, or structure while maintaining the essential form as it exists at present.

Stealth wireless communications facility: A wireless communications facility, ancillary appurtenance, or equipment enclosure that is not readily identifiable as such, and is designed to be camouflaged and aesthetically compatible with nearby uses. A stealth facility may have a secondary function, including, but not limited to, a church steeple, a bell tower, a spire, a clock tower, a cupola, a light standard, or a flagpole with a flag.

Steep slope: A slope exceeding 15 percent.

Store: A use devoted exclusively to the retail sale of commodity or commodities.

Stormwater drainage fees: A method or mix of methods for providing adequate, stable, and equitable funding for a comprehensive stormwater or drainage program. The financing mechanisms included in the method may include, but not be limited to, user fees, new development impact fees, or surcharges on other utility fees.

Stormwater run-off: That portion of the rainfall that is drained into the stormwater drainage system.

Story: That part of a building between the surface of a floor and the ceiling immediately above.

Streamflow: Water flowing in a natural channel, above ground.

Street: A right-of-way that provides a channel for vehicular circulation; is the principal means of vehicular access to abutting properties; and includes space for utilities, sidewalks, pedestrian walkways, and drainage. Any such right-of-way is included in this definition, regardless of whether or not it is developed. Includes any vehicular way that: is an existing state, county or municipal roadway; is shown upon a plat approved pursuant to law; or is approved by other official action; and includes the land between the street lines, whether improved or unimproved.

Street, arterial: A street use primarily for fast or heavy traffic and designated in the major thoroughfare plan as a primary arterial street, secondary arterial street, or expressway.

Street classification: See Table 5-26, Functional Street Classification System, § 5.23 Street Design and Transportation in Chapter 5, Development Standards, of the LDC.

Street, collector: See § 5.23.2 Classification in Chapter 5, Development Standards, of the LDC.

Street, cul-de-sac: A street with a single common ingress and egress and with a turnaround at the end.

Street, dead-end: A street with a single common ingress and egress.

Street, elbow: A turn in a minor street that includes extra pavement adequate for a turnaround.

Street, eyebrow: A paved area placed along the linear portion of a street that allows both unimpeded through and turn-around traffic movements.

Street, intersection: The area in which two or more streets cross at grade.

Street lawn: A planting area parallel to a public street designed to provide continuity of vegetation along the right-of-way, and that provides a transition from vehicular thoroughfares, pedestrian areas, or the built environment.

Street link: A section of a street on the major thoroughfare plan or a local street, which is defined by a node at each end or at one end. Stubs to adjacent property shall not be considered links.

Street, local: A street designed to provide vehicular access to abutting property and to discourage through traffic.

Street, private: Any street not dedicated to the public and to be maintained by a private entity.

Street right-of-way width: The distance between property lines measured at right angles to the centerline of the street.

Street/road, collector: A "collector," as defined in Table 5-26, Functional Street Classification System, in Chapter 5, Development Standards, of the LDC.

Streetscape: The general appearance of a block or group of blocks with respect to the structures, setbacks from public rights-of-way, open space, and the number and proportion of trees and other vegetation.

Street, stub: A temporary portion of a street not greater than one lot's length allowed as a future connection to an adjacent subdivision or phase.

Street tree: A tree planted along a street or roadway behind the right-of-way line or between a sidewalk and the edge of the paved surface of a roadway.

Structure: Anything constructed or a combination of materials that form a construction for use, occupancy, or ornamentation, whether installed on, above, or below the surface of land or water.[3]

Structure, completely enclosed: A structure that is enclosed on all sides by permanent walls.

Structured parking: The provision of parking in a building involving at least two levels.

Study area boundary: For purposes of the adequate public facilities standards, the boundary identified in Chapter 6, Adequate Public Facilities, of the LDC for a traffic impact analysis.

Subdivide: The act or process of creating a subdivision.

Subdivider: Any person who: having an interest in land, causes it, directly or indirectly, to be divided into a subdivision; directly or indirectly, sells, leases, or develops, or offers to sell, lease, or develop, or advertises to sell, lease, or develop, any interest, lot, parcel site, unit, or plat in a subdivision; engages directly or through an agent in the business of selling, leasing, developing, or offering for sale, lease, or development a subdivision or any interest, lot, parcel site, unit, or plat in a subdivision; or is directly or indirectly controlled by, or under direct or indirect common control with, any of the foregoing.

Subdivision: Any land, vacant or improved, which is divided or proposed to be divided into two or more lots, parcels, sites, units, plots, condominiums, tracts, or interests for the purpose of offer, sale, lease, or development, whether immediate or future, either on the installment plan or upon any and all other plans, terms, and conditions. Includes the division or development of residential and nonresidential zoned land, whether by deed, metes-and-bounds description, devise, intestacy, lease, map, plat, or other recorded instrument, resubdivision approval of antiquated plats, and condominium creation or conversion. Any land, vacant or improved, which is divided, or proposed to be divided, into two or more lots, parcels, sites, units, condominium units, tracts, plots, or interests for the purpose of offer, sale, lease, or development, whether immediate or future, either on the installment plan or upon any and all other plans, terms, and conditions. Subdivision includes the division or development of residential and nonresidential zoned land, whether by deed, partition, devise, intestacy, lease, map, plat, or any other recorded instrument. Subdivision includes resubdivision, approval of antiquated plats, condominium, cooperative, or time-share creation or conversion, judicial partition, or division into lots, parcels, or unit through probate, equitable proceedings, or any other judicial proceeding.

Subdivision agent: Any person who represents, or acts for or on behalf of, a subdivider or developer, in selling, leasing, or developing, or offering to sell, lease, or develop, any interest, lot, parcel, unit, site, or plat in a subdivision, except an attorney at law whose representation of another person consists solely of rendering legal services.

Subdivision improvement agreement: A contract entered into by the applicant and the planning commission on behalf of the [LOCAL GOVERNMENT], which the applicant promises to complete the required public improvements within the subdivision within a specified time period following final subdivision plat approval.

Subdivision, major: See *major subdivision.*

Subdivision, minor: See *minor subdivision.*

Subdivision plat: The final map or drawing, described in these regulations, on which the subdivider's plan of subdivision is presented to the planning commission for approval and which, if approved, may be submitted to the [LOCAL GOVERNMENT] clerk or recorder of deeds for filing.

Subject property: The property subject to an application for development approval.

Subsystem improvement: A capital improvement that is not a project improvement nor a system improvement, and which may include, but is not necessarily limited to, collector streets, lateral and collector sewer lines and pump stations serving a subdrainage basin, pocket and neighborhood parks, subarea water storage facilities and distribution lines, and subdrainage basin drainage improvements.

Suburban tier: See *tier.*

Swale: A low lying or depressed stretch of land without a defined channel or tributaries.

Symmetry: A balance of architectural components in a structure.

System improvement: The following capital improvements: arterial streets, wastewater treatment plants, pump stations and interceptor lines serving a drainage basin, community and regional parks, water supply, mains and storage facilities, and major drainage improvements serving a drainage basin.

Tavern: Any use in which the primary purpose is the sale of alcoholic beverages for on-premises consumption, which may or may not include dancing.

Temporary common worker employer: A person or agency that provides common worker employees to a third-party user, that maintains a central location where common workers assemble and are dispatched to work, and that is required to obtain a license from the [STATE DEPARTMENT].

Temporary improvement: Improvements built and maintained by a subdivider during construction of the subdivision and prior to release of the performance bond.

Terminal: A facility where flammable or combustible liquids are received by a tank vessel, pipelines, a tank car, or a tank vehicle, and which are stored or blended in bulk for the purpose of distributing such liquids by tank vessel, pipeline, tank car, tank vehicle, portable tank, or container. See *bulk plant.*

Tertiary containment: A method by which a third level of containment is provided for underground storage tanks by means of a wall or barrier installed around a double-walled tank and piping system (or approved alternative) in a manner designed to prevent a release of the regulated substance from migrating beyond the tertiary wall or barrier before the release can be detected if a failure in the secondary containment level occurs.

Tertiary protection: A method by which a third level of protection is provided for underground storage tank systems by means of either: a physical level to be installed around a double-walled tank and piping system, designed to prevent a release of the regulated substance from migrating into the environment, should such a release go undetected at the secondary containment level; or equivalent technology, which includes continuous electronic leak detection for the entire system at a centralized location with dedicated personnel, site-specific training, annual testing for system integrity, and reporting to the [WATER SYSTEM] any release from the primary system.

Thematic group: A finite group of resources related to one another in a clearly distinguishable way, by association with a single historic person, event, or developmental force, as one building type or use, as designed by a single architect, as a single archaeological site form, or as a particular set of archaeological research.

Tier: A geographical and functional basis for ordering of zoning districts based upon location within a rural, suburban, and urban setting.

Townhouse: A building that has single-family dwelling units erected in a row as a single building on adjoining lots, each being separated from the adjoining unit or units by a fire wall (to be constructed in accordance with city codes and ordinances), along the dividing lot line, and each such building being separated from any other building by space on all sides.

Tract: A lot. The term "tract" is used interchangeably with the term "lot," particularly in the context or subdivision, where a "tract" is subdivided into several lots, parcels, sites, units, plots, condominiums, tracts, or interests.

Traditional neighborhood development regulations: See § 2.6 Traditional Neighborhood Development in Chapter 2, Use Patterns, of the LDC.

Traffic impact report or analysis: A study performed by professional engineers with expertise in traffic engineering principles and practice, which reviews development of a specific property and analyzes how it integrates into the existing and proposed city street network and ongoing traffic study. The report or analysis utilizes data and conclusions developed in previous studies, and identifies improvements needed to mitigate the impact of traffic generated by a development on the street network system.

Transfer of development rights: The conveyance of development rights by deed, easement, or other legal instrument, authorized by ordinance or regulation, to another parcel of land and the recording of that conveyance.

Transitional home: A residential facility, differentiated from facilities that provide on-site, supervised lodging for individuals who are required to reside at the facility as a term of parole or who are under mandatory supervision. Also called "rehab center" or "half-way house."

Transit station: A building, structure, or area designed and located on a busway or a light rail line, used for the picking up and/or dropping off of passengers, embarking, or changing transportation modes. Facilities and improvements may include shelters, benches, signs, structures, and other improvements that provide security, weather protection, and access to nearby services.

Transparent: Capable of transmitting light in a manner that permits a person standing outside of a building to view shapes, tones, and objects inside a building. A tinted window is considered "transparent" if it meets this definition.

Transportation standards: See § 5.23 Street Design and Transportation in Chapter 5, Development Standards, of the LDC.

Tree: A perennial woody plant, with single or multiple trunks, with few if any branches on its lower part, and which at maturity will obtain a minimum 6-inch caliper.

Tree, ornamental: A small to medium tree, growing to a mature height of 15 to 40 feet.

Tree preservation development approval: An authorization by the city arborist authorizing specific work as it relates to protected and mitigation tree or trees.

Tree, shade: A large tree growing to a height of 40 feet or more at maturity.

Trip generation summary: A table summarizing the trip generation characteristics of the development for the entire day and the AM and PM peak periods, including the rates and units used to calculate the number of trips.

Triplex: See *dwelling, three-family (triplex)*.

Underground storage tank: Any one or a combination of underground storage tanks and any connecting underground pipes used to contain an accumulation of regulated substances, the volume of which, including the volume of the connecting underground pipes, is 10 percent or more below grade.

Underground storage tank system: An underground storage tank, all associated piping and ancillary equipment, spill and overfill prevention equipment, release detection equipment, corrosion protection system, secondary and tertiary containment equipment (as applicable), and all other related systems and equipment.

Understory: Assemblages of natural, low-level, woody, herbaceous, and ground cover species.

Unrated Resource: A building, object, site, or structure that appears on a federal, state, or city inventory or survey but has not been reviewed and rated by the Historic and Design Review Commission following criteria set forth this appendix.

Unreasonable economic hardship: An economic burden imposed upon the owner that is unduly excessive and which prevents a realization of a reasonable rate of return on the value of his/her property as an investment, applying the test utilized by the state case law relating to zoning variances in determining the existence of an unreasonable economic hardship.

Urban tier: See *tier*.

Use: The purpose for which a land or a structure is designed, arranged, or intended to be occupied or used, or for which it is occupied, maintained, rented, or leased.

Use matrix: The list of uses permitted as of right, prohibited, or permitted as a conditional use as set forth in Table 3-4, Use Matrix, in Chapter 3, Zoning, of the LDC.

Use-to-use relationship: Focusing on the unique aspects of established, newly developed and redeveloping neighborhoods, and commercial/industrial areas in order to achieve improved compatibility and fit of infill development projects and, at the same time, assist in the preservation and conservation of stable existing neighborhoods and commercial areas.

Utilities standards: See § 5.24 Utilities of Chapter 5, Development Standards, of the LDC.

Variance: Any of the following: a request to the planning commission for permission to vary or depart from a requirement of Chapter 4, Procedures, and Chapter 5, Development Standards, of the LDC where, due to special conditions, a literal enforcement of the requirement will result in an unnecessary hardship; or a request to the hearing officer for permission to vary or depart from a requirement of Chapter 3, Zoning, of the LDC where, due to special conditions, a literal enforcement of the requirement will result in an unnecessary hardship.

Verification: The confirmation by the Historic and Design Review Commission that restoration or rehabilitation work completed on an historically significant site in need of tax relief to encourage preservation was substantially completed.

Vertically oriented: Having a height equal to or exceeding at least one and one-half times the width.

Very low-income housing: A household composed of one or more persons with a combined annual net income for all adult members that does not exceed the qualifying limit for a very low-income family of a size equivalent to the number of persons residing in such household, as set forth in the [APPROPRIATE STATE OR LOCAL CODE SECTION].

Vested rights: Right to initiate or continue the use or occupancy of land or structures, or to continue construction of a structure or initiation of a use, where such use, occupancy of land, or construction is prohibited by a law or regulation in effect. Includes rights obtained under principles of estoppel.

Vine: A woody plant that spreads as it grows over the ground, walls, or trellises.

Violation: The failure of a site, building, or structure to comply with the LDC. A structure or other development without an approved development approval required by the LDC is presumed to be in violation until such time as that documentation is provided.

Vista: A view through or along a street, which, as a view corridor, frames, highlights, or accentuates a prominent building, object, site, structure, scene, or panorama, or patterns or rhythms of buildings, objects, sites, or structures.

Visually compatible: The relationship between the scale and design of buildings as defined in § 5.13 Building Design of Chapter 5, Development Standards, of the LDC.

Warehousing: See *processing and warehousing*.

Watercourse: A natural or man-made channel through which stormwater flows.

Watershed: The area drained by a given stream, river, watercourse, or other body of water.

Water surface elevation: The height, in relation to the National Geodetic Vertical Datum of 1929 (or other datum, where specified), of floods of various magnitudes and frequencies in the floodplains of coastal or riverine areas.

Wetland: Land that has a predominance of hydric soil; is inundated or saturated by surface or groundwater at a frequency and duration sufficient to support a prevalence of hydrophytic vegetation typically adapted for life in saturated soil conditions; and under normal circumstances supports a prevalence of that vegetation.

Wheelchair ramp: A sloping concrete pad constructed at crosswalks to assist mobility-impaired citizens using the sidewalks and crosswalks.

Wholesale trade: Establishments or places of business primarily engaged in selling merchandise to retailers; to industrial, commercial, institutional, or professional business users; to other wholesalers; or to those acting as agents or brokers and buying merchandise for, or selling merchandise to, such individuals or companies.

Window: An opening constructed in a wall, which admits light or air to an enclosure, is framed and spanned with glass, and which may be mounted to permit opening and closing.

Wireless communications: Any personal wireless service, radio and television broadcast services, and any other radio frequency signals, including amateur radio. Does not include signals transmitted to or from a satellite earth station.

Wireless communications facility: Any staffed or unstaffed facility used for the transmission and/or reception of wireless communications, usually consisting of an antenna or group of antennas, transmission lines, ancillary appurtenances, and equipment enclosures, and may include an antenna supporting structure. The following developments will be considered as a wireless communications facility: antenna supporting structures (including replacements and broadcast); collocated antennas; roof-mounted structures; surface-mounted antennas; stealth wireless communications facilities; and amateur radio facilities.

Wireless communications system: Antenna support structures for mobile and land-based telecommunication facilities. Whip antennas, panel antennas, microwave dishes and receive-only satellite dishes, cell enhancers, and related equipment for wireless transmission from a sender to one or more receivers, such as for mobile cellular telephones, mobile radio systems facilities, and commercial radio service. This facility is inclusive of the placement of the above-referenced equipment on a monopole tower, a steel lattice tower, and any self-supporting communications tower that does not utilize guy-wire support. This facility shall also allow as one of its components an unmanned equipment shelter.

Woodland: An area of contiguous wooded vegetation where trees are at a density of at least one 6-inch or greater caliper tree per 325 square feet of land and where the branches and leaves provide a continuous canopy. For purposes of submitting a site plan or preliminary plat, a "woodland" shall include areas with a continuous canopy of trees over an area of at least 20,000 square feet, and which may be delineated through an aerial photograph or a ground survey.

Xeric landscaping: A type of landscaping that conserves water and protects the environment by using site-appropriate plants, an efficient watering system, proper planning and design, soils analysis, practical use of turf, the use of mulches, and proper maintenance. Does not refer to the use of cactus and/or rock gardens in a landscape design.

Xeriscape: Landscaping with native plants that utilizes the existing environmental conditions to the best advantage, conserving water and protecting the native environment.

Yard: An area on a lot between the lot line and the nearest principal structure, unoccupied and unobstructed by any portion of a structure from the ground upward, except as otherwise provided in this appendix.

Zero lot line: The location of a building on a lot in such a manner that one or more of the building's sides rests directly on or immediately adjacent to the lot line.

Zero lot line development: Any subdivision or site plan in which a single-family detached dwelling unit is sited on a lot in such a manner that one or more of the building's sides rests directly on or immediately adjacent to the lot line.

Zoning map: See *official zoning map.*

NOTES

1. G. Hightshoe, *Native Trees, Shrubs, and Vines for Urban and Rural America* (New York; Van Nostrand Reinhold & Co., 1988), at 791.

2. See Watershed Management Institute, Inc., *Operation, Maintenance & Management of Stormwater Management Systems* (Washington, DC: United States Environmental Protection Agency Office of Water, 1997), at 2-32; Derek B. Booth and Jennifer Leavitt, "Field Evaluation of Permeable Pavement Systems for Improved Stormwater Management," 65 *JAPA* 314 (Summer 1999), at 314-325.

3. By this definition, all buildings are structures; however, not all structures are buildings. See Harvey S. Moskowitz and Carl G. Lindbloom, *The Latest Illustrated Book of Development Definitions,* New Expounded Edition (New Brunswick, NJ: Center for Urban Policy Research, 2004); Robert H. Freilich and Michael M. Shultz, *Model Subdivision Regulations*, 2d ed. (Chicago: American Planning Association, 1995).

Appendix B

Specifications for Documents to Be Submitted

B-1 GENERALLY

The purpose of this appendix is to streamline the development approval process by prescribing the information necessary for complete review of an application for development approval.

B-1.1 General Requirements

No application for development approval shall be considered complete, and the [PLANNING OFFICIAL] or any other agency or official of the [local government] shall not process any application for development approval, unless all of the information required by this appendix is included. The [PLANNING OFFICIAL] or any other agency or official of the [local government] shall not delay the processing of any application for development approval if it contains the information prescribed by this appendix.

B-1.2 Forms

The [PLANNING OFFICIAL] shall promulgate necessary forms for the administration, interpretation, and enforcement of the Land Development Code (LDC). The [PLANNING OFFICIAL] shall maintain such forms at the offices of the planning department. The forms shall require the information set forth in this appendix for any application for development approval.

B-1.3 Information Required

No application for development approval shall be accepted unless the following information and data required are included. The required information and data are set forth in Table B-1 and any specific regulations set forth in this appendix.

B-1.4 Certifications

Where this section requires a certification and/or signature by the applicant, a professional, or a public agency or official, the signature lines shall be provided in the lower right-hand corner of the plans, plats, or other required documents.

B-1.5 Digital Plat Requirements

B-1.5.1 Generally

(A) Plat information shall be provided to the [LOCAL GOVERNMENT] in two forms: hard-copy subdivision plat sheets and digital plat data. The purpose of the digital plat data requirement is to coordinate with the [LOCAL GOVERNMENT]'s geographic information systems program and is to be used for information only. Unlike the hard-copy subdivision plat, which represents a legal document, the digital plat data may be subjected to adjustment by the [LOCAL GOVERNMENT] and has no legal significance. However, the digital plat data may be used to assist [LOCAL GOVERNMENT] officials in analyzing, understanding, interpreting, and presenting the data.

(B) Digital data of subdivision plats will consist of graphical elements representing the hard-copy subdivision plat. The applicant shall provide digital data twice during the subdivision review process: initially, when the subdivision plat is submitted to the [PLANNING OFFICIAL] for plan review, and secondly, before the subdivision plat is approved by the planning commission. Additional digital submittals are required if changes occur between the second digital submittal and the recordation of the plat. The final digital submittal must reflect the graphical elements of the recorded plat.

(C) The initial digital data submittal shall include the subdivision boundary, as a minimum. The electronic medium shall bear a label similar to that of the final medium, as described in § B-1.5.6 Media Requirements and File Creation of this appendix, with the exception of the plat number.

(D) The final digital data may be submitted with the final subdivision plat documents to the planning department. The final digital data must be submitted before the subdivision plat is considered complete and ready for planning commission consideration.

(E) The digital data submittals are subject to review and approval as a condition to the subdivision plat review and approval process. The X-Y coordinates indicated with the initial submittal are subject to approval as provided in Chapter 4, Procedures, of the LDC. If an error is found to exist in the digital data that the [LOCAL GOVERNMENT] cannot correct, or if the digital data are otherwise unacceptable, the [LOCAL GOVERNMENT] will contact the submitting organization to have the digital data corrected.

(F) Both the digital and hard-copy files must contain all the elements consistent with accurately defining the geometry and global position of the proposed subdivision. In addition, the following two key data elements are also required on plat submittals:

**Table B-1
Summary of Application Requirements**

Material/Information	Rezoning	Conditional Use Permit	Site Plan	Preliminary Plat	Final Plat
General					
Proposed name of subdivision or development if not within a previously platted subdivision.			✓	✓	✓
Plan identification (ID) number assigned by planning department.	✓	✓	✓	✓	✓
Plat ID number assigned by planning department.					✓
An analysis prepared and signed by a member of the American Institute of Certified Planners indicating that the project complies with the minimum point score required by the Land Development Code (LDC) for the Leadership in Energy and Environmental Design (LEED®) Neighborhood Rating System.	✓	✓	✓	✓	✓
A Final LEED Review issued by the United States Green Building Council for the LEED Building Rating System, indicating the minimum score required by the LDC for all principal buildings on the site.		✓	✓	✓	✓
Ownership					
Name and address of owner of record, developer, and designer.	✓	✓	✓	✓	✓
Names of all adjacent property owners as shown on current tax records.	✓	✓	✓	✓	
Certificate of agency or power of attorney if other than owner.	✓	✓	✓	✓	✓
Names and lot numbers of adjacent plats.					✓
Signature blocks prepared for the dated signatures of the chairperson of the reviewing agency.			✓	✓	✓
Owner's certificate of consent, including a legal description of the boundaries of the proposed development and the dedication of public ways or spaces. This certificate shall be signed, dated, and notarized prior to recording the instrument.					✓
Proposed covenants on the property, if any, including a map and legal description of area affected.				✓	
Copies of maintenance agreements for any privately owned stormwater management facilities, parks or open space, and private streets.					✓
Property Survey and Topography					
Two points identified by State Plane Coordinates.			✓	✓	✓
Basis of bearings used and a north point.			✓	✓	✓
Boundary of the development and total acreage encompassed, described and mapped at a scale of at least 1 inch = 200 feet.	✓	✓	✓	✓	
Legal description and exhibit of the property at appropriate scale of at least 1 inch = 50 feet showing the boundary. Description may be related to the United States Geological Survey, state grid north, if two adjacent corners are shown.					✓
Topographic contour intervals of no greater than 10 feet.			✓	✓	
Existing topography with maximum contour interval of 2 feet. If existing ground is on a slope of less than 5 percent, then either 1-foot contours or spot elevation shall be provided.				✓	✓
All monuments erected and corners established in the field. The material of which the monuments, corners, or other points are made shall be noted by legend. Lot corners need not be shown.					✓
Sufficient data to determine readily and reproduce accurately on the ground the location, bearing, and length of every street and alley line, lot line, building line, easements required hereunder or of record in the [LOCAL GOVERNMENT] or ascertainable by physical inspection of the property, and boundary lines of reserved or dedicated areas. All linear dimensions shall be in feet and hundredths thereof. The maximum allowable error of linear closure shall not be in excess of 1:10,000. In closed traverses, the sum of the measured angles shall vary with the theoretical sum by a difference not greater than an average of 7.5 seconds per angle, or the sum of the total shall not differ from the theoretical sum by more than 90 seconds, whichever is smaller. The information shall be provided on tracing cloth or reproducible Mylar and in digital format in ArcInfo or ArcView software, or a computer file with a ".dfx" format, which is translatable to ArcView.					✓

Table B-1 (cont.)
Summary of Application Requirements

Material/Information	Rezoning	Conditional Use Permit	Site Plan	Preliminary Plat	Final Plat
Property Survey and Topography (cont.)					
Location of property lines, existing easements, burial grounds, railroad rights-of-way, and watercourses; location, width, and names of all existing or platted streets or other public ways within or immediately adjacent to the tract; and names of adjacent property owners or subdivision name when adjacent property is a platted subdivision from the latest certified assessment rolls.			✓		✓
Final location, arrangement, and dimensions of all proposed and existing lots.					✓
Lots numbered as approved by the [LOCAL GOVERNMENT].					✓
Planning					
Date of preparation.	✓	✓	✓	✓	✓
Graphic and written scale and north arrow.	✓	✓	✓	✓	✓
A location map at a scale of at least 1 inch = 2,000 feet, indicating the location and distance in relation to adjacent streets and all surrounding major thoroughfares. The location map is to be located in the top left-hand corner of the sheet.	✓	✓	✓	✓	✓
Total area of property.			✓	✓	✓
All existing easements or rights-of-way and street names, including those contiguous to the development area, their nature, width, and the volume and page number of their recording.			✓	✓	✓
All existing easements or rights-of-way with street names impacting the development area, their nature, and width.			✓	✓	
The location of all proposed uses/building forms or zoning classifications as applicable and the maximum allowable intensity (residential density or nonresidential floor area ratio (FAR)).	✓	✓	✓	✓	
The location and general nature of proposed uses/building forms and proposed intensity (residential density or nonresidential FAR).	✓	✓	✓	✓	
Notation of any restrictions required by the reviewing agency in accordance with the LDC.			✓	✓	✓
Notation of any restrictions required as part of the platting process in accordance with the LDC.			✓		✓
The location and dimensions of all proposed or existing lots.				✓	✓
A development phasing schedule, including the sequence for each phase; approximate size in area of each phase; and proposed phasing of construction of public improvements, recreation, and common open space areas.			✓	✓	
(Conservation subdivisions only.) A slope analysis of the proposed development site, showing slopes for the following percent of existing grades: 0-10%, 10-20%, 21-30%, 31-40%, and slopes exceeding 40%, including a tabulation of the number of acres in each slope percentage.			✓	✓	
A delineation of wetlands, floodplains, and other environmentally sensitive areas protected by *Division 4. Greenspace (Landscaping, Tree Preservation, Screening, and Environmental Protection) Standards* in Chapter 5, *Development Standards*, of the LDC. Conservation subdivisions and planned developments shall also delineate woodlands.			✓	✓	
Tabulation of the number of acres in the proposed development, showing the total number of lots, and area of open space for the site, including the following:					
• Square footage of all buildings and structures.			✓	✓	
• For nonresidential uses, multifamily dwellings, and any portion of a site located within a critical area, the approximate location and area of impervious cover.			✓	✓	
• Square footage of all paved or otherwise hard-surfaced streets, parking facilities, including curb and gutters, walks, loading areas, and asphalt or concrete aprons for solid waste containers, signs, or outdoor mechanical equipment.			✓	✓	

Table B-1 (cont.)
Summary of Application Requirements

Material/Information	Rezoning	Conditional Use Permit	Site Plan	Preliminary Plat	Final Plat
Planning (cont.)					
A final statement in tabular form that sets forth the following data, when such data are applicable to a given development plan:					
• Total number of dwelling units, by development phase.			✓	✓	
• Residential density and units per acre.			✓	✓	
• Total floor area and FAR for each type of use.			✓	✓	
• Total area in passive open space.			✓	✓	
• Total area in active developed recreational open space.			✓	✓	
• Total number of off-street parking and loading spaces.			✓	✓	
Infrastructure					
The location and widths of all proposed public and private streets within the development's boundaries.					✓
The approximate location and widths of all proposed public and private streets within the development's boundaries.			✓	✓	
The location of all entrances onto existing and/or proposed adjacent roadways, whether existing or proposed.			✓	✓	
The schematic location of all existing and proposed streets, as well as proposed access points.			✓	✓	
The schematic location of the pedestrian circulation system, including walkways and bicycle paths, where applicable.			✓	✓	
All street locations and dimensions, their names, numbers, and rights-of-way with profiles and cross sections of all proposed streets showing proposed cuts and fills.			✓	✓	
Street, alley, and cross walkway plans.			✓	✓	
Traffic impact analysis.			✓	✓	✓
The location, dimensions, type, and area of all parcels of land to be set aside for parks and open space, or for the use of residents of the proposed development.			✓	✓	✓
Location, sizes, elevations, and slopes of existing sewers, water mains, culverts, and other underground structures within or abutting the tract, and existing permanent building and utility poles on or abutting the site and utility rights-of-way.			✓	✓	
Location and size of existing water and sewer mains together with intended water sources and sewage disposal sites.			✓	✓	
Location of existing springs or public water supply.			✓	✓	
Utilities plan, including proposals for connection with existing water supply and sanitary sewage systems, or alternative means of providing water supply and sanitary waste treatment and disposal, and location of proposed water and sewer lines.			✓	✓	
Location of proposed fire hydrants.			✓	✓	
Stormwater management plan.		✓	✓	✓	
Design					
Layout showing required lot setbacks.		✓	✓	✓	✓
Off-street parking and loading areas and structures, including the number of spaces, dimensions of spaces and aisles, and landscaping for parking areas.		✓	✓	✓	
Tree preservation plan.			✓	✓	
The location, dimensions, and type of all walls, fences (other than fences on private residential lots), and landscaping.		✓	✓	✓	
Location and size in acres of school sites, as applicable.			✓	✓	

Table B-2
Layer and Level Element Types

Feature	Element Types
Subdivision boundary data	Lines and curves
Control points and ties to boundary text	Points and cells
Text†	Text
Primary lot line data	Lines and curves
Right-of-way centerline data	Lines and curves
Right-of-way data	Lines and curves
Easement data	Lines and curves

† Subdivision plat certification data are not required to be included in the digital plat data.

Table B-3
Digital Plat Submittal

Plat submitted from AutoCAD	xxxxx.DWG
Plat submitted from MicroStation	xxxxx.DGN
Plat submitted from other software products	xxxxx.DXF

(1) All new street names must have been approved by the United States Postal Service and shown on the hard-copy and digital plat submittals. The [LOCAL GOVERNMENT] will not accept unnamed street designations, such as Street "A."

(2) The plat must contain a lot number for each proposed lot. The [LOCAL GOVERNMENT] will not accept invalid block numbers, such as Block "D."

(G) Failure to provide approved street names and correct and unique block and lot numbers may result in significant delays as no plat will be approved until these key data are determined.

B-1.5.2 Data Layer/Level Requirements

Data shall be separated into the feature categories as defined in Table B-2, each residing on its own unique level or layer. Any layer name or level number is acceptable as long as each feature set is on its own individual layer or level.

B-1.5.3 Additional Digital Criteria

The following additional criteria will apply to data submitted digitally:

(A) Cells shall be fully expanded.

(B) Curves shall only be used to represent irregular boundaries.

(C) The subdivision outside of the boundary shall be transmitted as a closed figure. For example, the subdivision boundary is represented as one polyline rather than a series of lines, arcs, and curves. This will assure closure of the subdivision perimeter.

(D) Curvilinear boundaries, rather than lines or arcs, shall be represented by sufficient points to unambiguously define the boundary. Examples of curvilinear boundaries might include the centerline of a stream, a high-water mark, contour lines, and transition curves on railroads.

B-1.5.4 Formats for Graphical Data

Any of the following formats are allowed for digital plat data submitted to the [PLANNING OFFICIAL] or [ENGINEERING DEPARTMENT]:

◆ *Note to reader:* The LDC, as adopted in your community, should indicate which software is the graphics format used by the reviewing agency, and that no conversion is required when data are provided in this format. The regulations may provide that the software used to produce the files should be the most current or prior version of the product. It may also indicate that files produced using older versions of the software (e.g., over two releases old) will not be accepted.

• *DWG (AutoCAD) (Autodesk):* This file format is used by Autodesk with their AutoCAD product. This is the preferred way for AutoCAD users to transfer files to the [LOCAL GOVERNMENT].

• *DGN (MicroStation) (Bentley):* DGN files created on electronic media for delivery to the [LOCAL GOVERNMENT] will be created as ASCII files. No reference files will be attached to DGN files submitted to the [LOCAL GOVERNMENT].

• *DXF (generic):* DXF (Drawing Exchange File) is an exchange format developed by Autodesk for use with their AutoCAD product. This format is the preferred exchange format for organizations that use graphics software provided by vendors other than Bentley or Autodesk. Only the ASCII output file option will be accepted for this exchange format. A binary DXF output format option is available, but it will not be accepted as a valid exchange format.

B-1.5.5 File-Naming Conventions

The applicant shall submit one file for each plat that is submitted to the [LOCAL GOVERNMENT]. File-naming conventions will be used as described in Table B-3, with "xxxxx" representing the assigned plat number.

B-1.5.6 Media Requirements and File Creation

The [LOCAL GOVERNMENT] shall accept files on compact discs (CDs), digital video discs (DVDs), or Universal Serial Bus (USB) flash drives. Files shall be produced using Windows® output formats. WinZip® may be used to compress the files being submitted. CDs, DVDs, and USB flash drives shall be labeled with the following information: plat or plan identification number assigned by the planning department; subdivision name; number of files (sheets) on the CD, DVD, or USB flash drive; file creation date; company name; and contact name and phone number.

B-1.5.7 Fees for [LOCAL GOVERNMENT] Workstation Operator Services

If the submitting organization elects to submit the hard copy only, the [LOCAL GOVERNMENT] will produce digital data from the hard copy as part of the map-checking process, but will charge the submitting organization at the rate of $_____ per hour, up to an amount not exceeding $_____, for workstation operator services.

B-1.5.8 Use of Digital Data

The [LOCAL GOVERNMENT] staff may make minor corrections to the digital data if the file needs correcting due to minor differences between the hard-copy plats and the digital

Table B-4
Horizontal Control Points

Plat Size	Number of Points
20 acres or less	2 points
20+ to 50 acres	3 points
Greater than 50 acres	4 points

data, or if other minor errors, such as layering errors, are detected. In instances where differences exist, the information provided on the hard-copy plats will take precedence over the digital information. The digital information has no legal significance.

B-1.6 Control Points and Monumentation Guidelines

(A) Primary horizontal control points will be used when surveying each tract being subdivided. These primary horizontal control points must be established by using centimeter-grade accuracy Global Positioning System devices, procedures, and methods that meet the [STATE STANDARDS]. New primary horizontal control points must be established and monumented for each subdivision.

(B) Primary horizontal control points shall be tied to at least one National Geodetic Survey mark and the point will be identified as the datum point on both the hard-copy and digital plat submittals.

(C) The minimum number of required primary horizontal control points (reference corners) is based upon the overall plat size in acres as described in Table B-4.

(D) The plat must include the X-Y coordinates for each of the primary horizontal control points, and consistent and appropriate bearings between each of the primary horizontal control points. These primary horizontal control points will be provided in NAD83 United States survey feet, State Plane Coordinates for [STATE].

(E) All primary horizontal control points shall be permanently identified with monumentation set to [STATE BOARD OF LAND SURVEYOR]'s minimum standards.

B-1.7 Digital Requirements for Street and Drainage Construction Plan Submittals

B-1.7.1 Generally

(A) Street and drainage construction plan drawings shall be provided to the [LOCAL GOVERNMENT] as traditional hard-copy Mylar drawings and as drawing digital data. The purpose of the drawing digital data requirement is to allow for improved document storage, retrieval, and review within various [LOCAL GOVERNMENT] departments, and is to be used for information purposes only. Unlike the hard-copy documents that are signed and sealed legal documents, the drawing digital data will have no legal significance. However, the drawing digital data may be used to assist [LOCAL GOVERNMENT] employees in analyzing, understanding, interpreting, and presenting the data.

(B) Drawing digital data will consist of the graphical elements represented on the final hard-copy street and drainage construction plans submitted to the [LOCAL GOVERNMENT]. Signatures, seals, stamps, and other nongraphical drawing elements are not required as part of the drawing digital data submittal. The drawing digital data shall comply with § B-1.5 Digital Plat Requirements of this appendix unless a different requirement is provided in this section.

(C) Drawing digital data submittals, delivered to the [LOCAL GOVERNMENT] on electronic media, are required as a condition to the final approval of the street and drainage drawing set. If the [LOCAL GOVERNMENT] determines that an error is found to exist in the digital data, including the inability to read the media on which the drawing data are delivered, discrepancies between the hard-copy drawings and the digital data, or if the digital data are otherwise unacceptable, the [LOCAL GOVERNMENT] will contact the submitting organization to have the digital data corrected and/or redelivered to the [LOCAL GOVERNMENT] prior to public works approval of the final plat.

B-1.7.2 Standard Detail Sheets in a Digital Format

The [LOCAL GOVERNMENT]'s drainage and capital programs departments will provide standard details in a digital format to anyone requesting the files. The request must be in writing and indicate the preferred file format (MicroStation (DGN), AutoCad (DWG), or generic (DXF) format). These files may be e-mailed to the requestor, or provided on electronic media. Since the [LOCAL GOVERNMENT] does not use AutoCad, the requests for this format will be performed using the conversion software available within MicroStation, and is provided with no claims as to the requestor's ability to read or use the delivered files.

B-2 CITIZEN PARTICIPATION PLAN

Documentation of citizen participation shall include the following information:

(A) The residents, property owners, interested parties, political jurisdictions, and public agencies that may be affected by the application;

(B) How those interested in and potentially affected by an application were notified that an application has been made;

(C) How those interested and potentially affected parties were informed of the substance of the change, amendment, or development proposed by the application;

(D) How those affected or otherwise interested were provided an opportunity to discuss the applicant's proposal with the applicant and express any concerns, issues, or problems they may have with the proposal in advance of the public hearing;

(E) The applicant's schedule for continued citizen participation during the application processing stage and development; and

(F) How the applicant will keep the planning department informed on the status of their citizen participation efforts.

B-3 CONDITIONAL USE PERMIT

B-3.1 Number of Copies

The applicant shall provide 15 folded prints and digital files of the proposed conditional use. One 8-1/2 x 11-inch reduced copy of the plan shall also be provided.

B-3.2 Format

A site plan, with associated detail drawings, must be submitted when approval of the [LOCAL GOVERNMENT] is required pursuant to this appendix. The site plan shall be prepared to scale. The site plan scale must be drawn numerically and a graphic scale must be provided. The maximum scale acceptable for a site plan shall be 1 inch = 100 feet.

B-3.3 Contents

The application shall include the information required by Table B-1 of this appendix.

B-4 LAND ALTERATION DEVELOPMENT APPROVAL

B-4.1 Required Plans

All applicants for a conditional use permit (CUP) for an excavation activity shall submit the following plans:

(A) Site/grading plan;
(B) Permanent and interim erosion and sediment control plan;
(C) Traffic impact analysis (TIA);
(D) Operational plan;
(E) Reclamation plan;
(F) Phasing plan;
(G) Drainage plan;
(H) Completed wetland delineation; and
(I) Other plans and/or information as may be reasonably requested by staff, the planning commission, or the [LOCAL GOVERNMENT].

B-4.2 Assessment of Existing/Prealteration Conditions

The assessment shall be submitted at the time of submission of the CUP application, and shall include the following additional information:

(A) Soil types, including soil borings and soils report, depth of overburden, and area to be disturbed;
(B) Existing topography (at 2-foot contours) of the property and 200 feet beyond the property lines of the site; where there is an existing water body, 2-foot contours for a distance of 20 feet from the water's edge into the water body shall be included;
(C) Existing roads and rights-of-way, and proposed roads as identified in the comprehensive plan, including adopted street plan boundaries;
(D) An assessment of existing roadway conditions adjacent to the site and proposed to be used for hauling. This assessment is to be prepared in coordination with, and approved by, the [LOCAL GOVERNMENT] engineer;
(E) Existing land use, land cover, and structures, including fences and abandoned structures on the site and properties abutting the subject site, and identification of the distance to the nearest habitable dwelling;
(F) Boundaries of any previous excavations or excavation activities on the site or on adjacent properties;
(G) Wells, abandoned or active, on the subject property. Where blasting is proposed, all wells, abandoned or active, within 1/2 mile of the property; where open water bodies will be created, active or abandoned wells within 1/4 mile of the property;
(H) Location of any floodway, 100-year flood fringe, shoreland areas, and wetland delineation;
(I) The existence and location of any historic sites or native plant communities on the property;
(J) Existing water and/or sanitary sewer lines crossing the site and any existing water or sanitary sewer facilities on the site or on property adjacent to the site;
(K) Existing public facilities on the site or on property adjacent to the site;
(L) Any schools within 2,000 feet of the outer boundaries of any portion of the site;
(M) Existing land use on all adjacent properties and on properties within 1,000 feet of the site;
(N) If adjacent and nearby properties are undeveloped, the current zoning of such parcels and the land-use description of such parcels as shown on the adopted [LOCAL GOVERNMENT] comprehensive plan;
(O) Any adopted area or specific plans that include the site and surrounding areas;
(P) Any public facility or utility plans that indicate the probable future expenditure of public funds for facilities or utilities on or adjacent to the site;
(Q) Any proposed or future public improvements on the site or adjacent to the site as indicated in the [LOCAL GOVERNMENT]'s annual budget or current capital improvements program;
(R) Any traffic studies, including the site, areas adjacent to the site, or existing or future roads serving the site, or adjacent parcels, including traffic counts, levels of service, demand/capacity ratios, congestion, signalization, safety, and other relevant traffic information or analyses;
(S) The present use of the site, if any;
(T) Any previous uses of the site, including a description of the use and when the site was utilized for such use, and why the previous use was stopped, if known;
(U) Existing zoning of the site and any previous rezonings; and
(V) Other information as may be deemed relevant by the [LOCAL GOVERNMENT] staff, the planning commission, or the [GOVERNING ENTITY].

B-4.3 Grading Plan

A grading plan shall be submitted at the time of submission of the application for an amendment to an overlay zoning district or for a CUP application. The staff, the planning commission, and/or the [GOVERNING ENTITY] may recommend and the [GOVERNING ENTITY] may impose reasonable conditions to mitigate the potential impacts of extensive grading. The [GOVERNING ENTITY] shall consider the following factors in its review of the grading plan:

(A) Restoration and stabilization of cut-and-fill areas;
(B) Impact on drainage patterns and stormwater management facilities, as well as the consistency with the stormwater management plan or adopted drainage or stormwater policies;
(C) Potential impacts on sinkholes, wells, and other features affecting groundwater quality;
(D) Impact on wetlands and compliance with [STATE OR FEDERAL WETLANDS REGULATIONS];
(E) The duration of the proposed grading activity;
(F) The amount and type of material being removed from, or imported to, the site;
(G) Compliance with erosion and sediment control standards as set forth in [CITY/COUNTY CODE STANDARDS OR STATE STANDARDS];
(H) Adequate and appropriate surety, approved by the [LOCAL GOVERNMENT] engineer and [CITY/COUNTY]

attorney, provided to ensure that the site will be restored to a safe condition;

(I) Visual, noise, and dust impact upon public parks, major roadways, and residential areas;

(J) Impacts of trucks and heavy equipment on the safety and maintenance of roads providing access to the site and adjacent properties; and

(K) Compliance with the [LOCAL GOVERNMENT] building code and other state and federal requirements.

B-4.4 Operations Plan

An operations plan shall be submitted at the time of submission of the application for an amendment to an overlay zoning district or for a CUP application, and shall include the following information in the form of a site plan and an attached report. If the operations plan also shows grading, then the required scale for grading plans shall apply.

B-4.4.1 Site Plan

The site plan shall show:

(A) The area of the site to be disturbed or used as part of an excavation activity;

(B) The area of the site to be used for ancillary purposes, but not specifically the area to be disturbed (e.g., roads, buildings, structures, and storage areas);

(C) The area of the site to remain completely in open space, including proposed buffer yards and required buffer yards (refer to § 5.31 Buffers and Screening in Chapter 5, Development Standards, of the LDC);

(D) The location and types of buffering and screening to be used;

(E) The location of access roads, haul roads, storage areas, structures, buildings, crushers, and any other man-made structures;

(F) The location of storage areas, proposed stockpiles, processing, and loading areas, and any other areas or portions of the site not kept permanently in open space;

(G) A signage plan, both on site and immediately off site, if necessary;

(H) A traffic plan showing the movement of the trucks onto the site, within the site, and from the site. The off-site portion of this plan shall show the vehicle movement to the nearest arterial street, the identification of truck movement on collector and local streets, and the land uses along the routes, paying special attention to residential land uses, schools, churches, public parks, and other places where the public may gather; and

(I) Such other information as the [LOCAL GOVERNMENT] staff, the planning commission, or the [GOVERNING ENTITY] deems relevant and necessary.

B-4.4.2 Report

The report shall include a complete description of the following:

(A) All materials intended to be excavated, quarried, mined, or otherwise removed from the site;

(B) The method of removal of these materials, including the type of all equipment to be used;

(C) The nature, type, use, and hazards posed by any chemicals to be used or stored on the site or used in the excavation activity, processing, or other activity on the site;

(D) The nature, type, use, and hazards posed by any toxic materials of any kind to be used or stored on the site or used in the excavation activity, processing, or other activity on the site;

(E) The phases (and associated timetable) for excavation of the site;

(F) The method of removal and disposal of vegetation from the site, including the types of vegetation to be removed, plant communities to be removed or affected, and habitat loss;

(G) The amount of overburden to be removed and total per phase;

(H) The amount of mineral to be removed and total per phase;

(I) The method of land alteration activity and sequence of progression, including phasing and progressive reclamation and site stabilization;

(J) The proposed hours and days of operation on the site, including hauling and ancillary activities in addition to the excavation activity;

(K) A dust control plan;

(L) A noise control plan, including a map showing the decibel range at various distances from the site, in all directions from the site;

(M) A stormwater management plan in accordance with § B-12 Stormwater Management Plan of this appendix;

(N) A safety plan, including, but not limited to, the location and type of all site security and safety features, including signs, gates, and fences;

(O) An emergency evacuation plan;

(P) A lighting plan;

(Q) An emergency lighting plan;

(R) The quantity of material anticipated to be removed per day;

(S) The method of hauling the material to be removed, including the number and types of trucks to be used each day;

(T) A TIA in accordance with § B-15 Traffic Impact Analysis of this appendix, to the extent applicable;

(U) A description of any effects of the excavation activity off site;

(V) A maintenance schedule and plan for cleaning vehicles, equipment, and adjacent off-site public roadways;

(W) A description of the total anticipated duration (in months or years) of excavation activities on the site;

(X) A description of the anticipated extent of use of [LOCAL GOVERNMENT] sewer, water, gas, electricity, and other utilities on a monthly basis; and

(Y) The proximity of the nearest police and fire stations to the site and insurance of access for emergency vehicles.

The operations plan shall be consistent with, and fulfill all of the standards and requirements of, Chapter 7, Supplemental Use Regulations, of the LDC.

B-4.5 Reclamation Plan

The reclamation plan shall be submitted at the time of submission of the CUP application, and shall include the information as described in § B-4.5.1 Final Site Plan (Reclaimed Land) and § B-4.5.2 Report of this appendix in the form of a final site plan and an attached report. The scale of the overall reclamation plan must comply with the submittal requirements for CUPs. However, if the reclamation plan also shows grading, then the required scale for grading plans apply.

B-4.5.1 Final Site Plan (Reclaimed Land)

The final site plan shall clearly and effectively show:

(A) The area of the site reclaimed;

(B) The condition of the site after all excavation activities have been completed and after the applicant has undertaken and completed full reclamation of the site in accordance with state statutes and regulations;

(C) If reclamation is proposed to be done in phases, a final postreclamation site plan shall be submitted for the reclaimed portion of the site after the completion of each phase;

(D) A grading plan, including finished grades of all disturbed areas at 2-foot interval contours. Where a water body is created, 2-foot contours to the bottom of the water body;

(E) The proposed use of the reclaimed area of the site, including any structures proposed to be built on the site as part of, or subsequent to, reclamation;

(F) The grade of the reclaimed area and of the entire site;

(G) Public services that need to be provided to the proposed use of the reclaimed area, including the size of water and sewer lines, and the demand for other public facilities and services;

(H) The compatibility of the proposed use with adjacent properties, with the existing zoning in the area, and with the neighborhood as a whole;

(I) The buffering or screening of the site after reclamation;

(J) The elimination of haul roads, storage facilities, and other site features no longer needed after the excavation activity has been completed;

(K) A new access at a location to be approved by the [ENGINEERING DEPARTMENT] and internal/external roadway system for the site, based on its proposed use after reclamation;

(L) The demolition of any buildings on the site;

(M) A vegetation plan for the site after reclamation;

(N) The timetable for development of the site for the proposed use; and

(O) A noise assessment of the proposed use, at a level of detail to be determined by the [LOCAL GOVERNMENT] engineer.

B-4.5.2 Report

The report shall include:

(A) Phasing and schedule of reclamation;

(B) Methods and process of reclamation;

(C) Erosion control plan;

(D) Planting/revegetation plan, including number and size of plants to be used and placement;

(E) Maintenance and replacement plan for monitoring and ensuring survival of reclamation efforts;

(F) Conformance with future roadways and ultimate land use as reflected in the [LOCAL GOVERNMENT]'s comprehensive plans for land use, transportation, stormwater management (or adopted drainage or stormwater policies), and the Olmsted County Water Quality Plan;

(G) Lighting and/or signage plan;

(H) Schedule for the removal of stockpiles, unneeded signage, or lighting, or erosion control devices when excavation or substantial land alteration activities are complete;

(I) Where open water bodies are created:

(1) The normal depth of water bodies at 2-foot interval contours; and

(2) Cross-section views of the reclaimed area showing grading of shoreline, depth of lake, subsurface lake shoreline grading, anticipated design normal pool elevation, anticipated two-year storm event lake-level bounce elevation, depth of soil cover on reclaimed areas, and floodplain elevations;

(J) Maintenance plan;

(K) Where surface alternatives are proposed, above the water table, method of stabilization of the disturbed areas;

(L) A narrative report examining possible hydrogeologic effects on any existing or proposed bodies of surface water and wetlands, and on groundwater, including public and private wells. The report shall also include a description of the controls needed to assure compliance with federal, state, and local surface water quality, erosion control, sediment control, stormwater management, and other standards applicable to surface waters;

(M) A description of any proposed uses to be conducted on the site; and

(N) A description of any proposed structures to be built on the site, including the size, scale, height, building footprint, and location of such structures, and a description, including all other requirements necessary for site plan approval and development approval issuance.

B-5 LANDSCAPE PLANS

B-5.1 Number of Copies

A landscape plan shall consist of two sets of plans with the information required below.

B-5.2 Format

The landscape plan shall delineate the treatment of materials used for open space, landscaped buffers, and common ownership. A landscape plan shall be drawn to scale with sufficient clarity to indicate the location, nature, and extent of the work proposed, and show in detail that it conforms to the requirements of this section. The plan shall be submitted on sheets of a size not to exceed 30 x 42 inches. A plan that cannot be drawn in its entirety on a single sheet shall be drawn with appropriate match lines on two or more sheets.

B-5.3 Contents

The landscape plan shall include the following information:

(A) Project name, street address, legal description, date, scale, and north arrow, and the names, addresses, and telephone numbers of both the property owner and the person preparing the plan;

(B) A vicinity map, the location of lot lines, and the dimensions of the building site and the street yard;

(C) Approximate centerlines of existing water courses and the location of the 100-year floodplain;

(D) Approximate location of significant drainage features;

(E) Location and width of existing and proposed streets and alleys, utility easements, driveways, and sidewalks on or adjacent to the lot;

(F) Identification, location, and dimensions of required plant materials for screening, and off-street parking and loading spaces within the street yard;

(G) Description of plant materials shown on the plan, including names (common and botanical), quantities, container or caliper sizes at installation, heights, spread, and spacing. The plan may designate alternative species or reference species listed in a [LOCAL GOVERNMENT]-prepared landscape manual;

(H) Description of proposed irrigation systems, as set forth in subsection (K), below;

(I) Tabulation of points earned by the plan. In calculating points, plant materials may be used to satisfy a maximum of two mandatory and/or elective requirements;

(J) If points for the preservation of existing trees and/or understory are requested, the information specified in subsections (1) through (4), below, shall also be included on the landscape plan;

(1) Trees and understory to be preserved and for which credit is being requested;

(2) Delineation of proposed limit of clearance and establishment of protection zones, which shall extend to just outside the root protection zone of trees and outside the understory area to be preserved;

(3) Tree and understory preservation specifications; and

(4) Specification of ground plane treatment as either turf or ground cover. If a combination of both is utilized, the limit of each shall be indicated;

(K) Delineation of irrigation installations with the following information:

(1) Name of project and address;

(2) North compass indication;

(3) Prevailing wind direction;

(4) Graphic and written scale;

(5) Date of design;

(6) State of licensed irrigator seal with number clearly visible as required by state law;

(7) Clear, consistent symbols for system component legend;

(8) Backflow prevention unit installed per code requirements;

(9) Symbol, operating pressure (pounds per square inch), flow rate (gallons per minute), and radius of coverage for sprinkler/emitter legend;

(10) Symbol of other major components;

(11) Installation details and specifications, which shall describe and/or illustrate all materials used and the method for installing them. These may be brief statements shown on the plan or included in a supplemental document and must be site- and project-specific;

(12) Point of connection, which shall indicate location and size of meter;

(13) Static pressure and design pressure; and

(14) Pressure loss calculation, which shall be available for review.

B-5.4 Certification

A landscape plan shall be prepared by a registered landscape architect.

B-9 NONCONFORMING USE CERTIFICATION

B-9.1 Number of Copies

To establish nonconforming rights, the owner or his/her designated representative must file three copies of the required documents with the [PLANNING OFFICIAL].

B-9.2 Format

The applicant shall provide a site plan, including an 8-1/2 x 11-inch reduction of the plan on vellum or equivalent material, and narrative material as required. The site plan shall indicate proposed and existing uses as well as the appropriate zoning designation.

B-9.3 Contents

As a minimum, the documentation shall include:

(A) Evidence of financial investment;

(B) Affidavit of ownership;

(C) Narrative explanation of the proposed project and its status; and

(D) Any development approvals previously approved by the [LOCAL GOVERNMENT], including the type of development approval, date of approval, approving agency, and scope of approval, including all uses, buildings, structures, or other activities authorized by the development approval.

B-10 PLAT VACATION AND RESUBDIVISION

B-10.1 Number of Copies

The [PLANNING OFFICIAL] may require the applicant to submit the original vacating declaration and up to 12 copies with respective department/agency request for reviews, and two legible 8-1/2 x 11-inch reduced copies of the plat being vacated attached. In addition, the submittal shall include two full-sized copies of the original plat folded prints together with the required processing fee. A vacating declaration processing fee and copies as listed above are not required in connection with the processing of a resubdivision plat.

B-10.2 Format

All filed plat copies shall clearly delineate the area to be vacated.

B-10.3 Contents

The applicant shall include the names and addresses of all owners of lots within the subdivision and their signed written consent.

B-10.4 Certification

The resubdivision plat shall be annotated generally as follows:

> The area being resubdivided in this plat had been previously platted on plat no. _____ known as _____ subdivision, which is recorded in volume _____, page _____, County Plat and Deed Records, and was vacated through a vacating declaration being recorded on the same date as this resubdivision plat.

B-11 REZONING

No application for a rezoning shall be certified as complete unless the following information is provided:

(A) The name, address, and telephone number of the owner of the property for which the rezoning is requested and, if different, the applicant. The application shall state whether the applicant is the owner or leasee, optionee, or licensee of the property proposed to be rezoned. If the applicant is different than the owner, the application shall contain the following statement with the names of the owner of the property and the applicant, and signed by the owner of the property:

I, _____, the owner of the property to be considered, give _____ permission to submit this application.

(B) The location of property where change is requested, described according to the subdivision plat filed with the recorder of deeds or the [LOCAL GOVERNMENT] tax rolls, including the parcel identification number. This information shall include all applicable lot and block numbers. If the property is not part of a subdivision, the application shall include a metes-and-bounds description along with an exhibit of the property in digital form, if available. If only a portion of a lot or parcel is to be reclassified, the application shall include a legal description, by metes and bounds, of the land to be reclassified.

(C) Address of subject property, if applicable.

(D) The total acreage proposed to be rezoned for each zoning district requested.

(E) The book and page number where the deed to the property is recorded in the county clerk's office, along with a description of any deed restrictions that prohibit the proposed use.

(F) If more than one district is being requested, areas to be zoned shall be indicated in accordance with the petition. A separate sheet shall be attached with a legal description of each area to be considered.

(G) A dimensioned map of the property referred to in the application, and all street, lots, and parcels of land within 200 feet of the property, based upon information provided by the planning department.

(H) A typed list of the owners (together with their addresses) of all property within 200 feet of said property and a description of the property owners.

(I) If available, a map indicating the location, dimensions, and uses of existing and proposed structures, easements, water sources, fences, curb cuts, and street and alley right-of-way lines on and within 1 foot of the property proposed for rezoning. This information may be submitted on a separate map.

(J) A statement of the reasons for seeking the rezoning.

(K) A TIA or worksheet, if required by this appendix.

B-12 STORMWATER MANAGEMENT PLAN

B-12.1 Number of Copies

The applicant shall provide two blue- or black-line copies of the plat together with two construction drawings.

B-12.2 Format

(A) Plats shall be drawn in India ink on Mylar on sheets 18 inches wide and 24 inches long, with a margin of 2-1/2 inches on the left side of the sheet, and appropriate margins on the other three sides. Plats shall be drawn at a scale of 100 feet = 1 inch unless a smaller scale is approved by the [PLANNING OFFICIAL]. Plats that include 1/2 acre or less in area shall be drawn at a scale of 50 feet = 1 inch.

(B) Where more than one sheet is necessary to accommodate the entire area to be subdivided, an index sheet showing the entire subdivision at an appropriate scale shall be attached to the plat.

B-12.3 Contents

To standardize the review process and minimize the time for approval by the [LOCAL GOVERNMENT] during review of the plat and construction drawings for a subdivision, a complete submittal regarding the analysis of existing drainage conditions and the design of modifications or new drainage facilities is necessary. The owner of the property to be developed is required by the [ENGINEERING OFFICIAL] to provide, at the owner's expense and as a condition of construction plan approval, a stormwater management report for the total development area to be ultimately constructed. The stormwater management report shall contain all of the necessary support data, methodologies used in calculations, and conclusions.

A checklist (see § B-12.5 HEC-2 Submittal Checklist of this appendix) will be used by the [LOCAL GOVERNMENT] reviewer as a guide during the evaluation of all stormwater management reports submitted to the [LOCAL GOVERNMENT]. The purpose of the checklist is to expedite the review process for both the professional engineer and the [LOCAL GOVERNMENT], and to aid the professional engineer in the preparation of reports for the [LOCAL GOVERNMENT]'s review. The stormwater management report shall be submitted to the [ENGINEERING OFFICIAL] prior to approval of any construction plans.

B-12.4 Report

The stormwater management plan shall include two copies of a written report, which include the following information, as applicable:

(A) A vicinity map of the site and affected reach of the outfall channel.

(B) A detailed map of the area and the outfall channel with all pertinent physiographic information.

(C) A watershed map showing the existing and proposed drainage area boundary along with all subarea delineations and all areas of existing and proposed development.

(D) United States Geological Survey (USGS) quadrangle map showing overall drainage areas, run-off coefficients, time of concentration, intensity, and quantities.

(E) Subdivision master drainage plan with overall interior drainage area of subdivision showing drainage area, time of concentration run-off coefficients, intensities, quantities for the street and alley flows, and channel and underground system design.

(F) Subdivision plat showing interior drainage areas, time of concentration, run-off coefficients, intensities, quantities for street and alley flows, and channel and underground system design.

(G) Discharge calculations specifying methodology and key assumptions used, including a table of discharges at key locations.

(H) Hydraulic calculations specifying methodology used, assumptions, and values of the design parameters.

(I) Profiles of the affected channels, including water surface elevations for the specified design frequencies; all existing and proposed bridge, culvert, and pipeline crossings; the location of all tributary and drainage confluences; and the location of all hydraulic structures.

(J) Detention basin design calculations, including those used for design of the control structure.

(K) Right-of-way and easement requirements and a map showing locations of all rights-of-way and easements.

(L) A soils report that addresses erosion and slope stability of new or altered channels and detention facilities.

(M) Digital files of all existing and proposed condition United States Army Corps of Engineers Hydrologic Engineering Center (HEC) models HEC-1 and HEC-2 used in analysis.

(N) Information for preparation of an HEC-2 model as provided in § B-12.4 Report of this appendix.

(O) The following drainage calculations:
   (1) Open channel design;
   (2) Underground systems;
   (3) Box culverts;
   (4) Pipe culverts;
   (5) Hydraulic jump;
   (6) Super elevation in channel bends;
   (7) Retard spacing;
   (8) Backwater curves with cross sections;
   (9) Drawdown curves with cross sections;
   (10) Energy dissipators;
   (11) Hydraulic grade lines of pipes;
   (12) Inlets on grades;
   (13) Inlets in sump;
   (14) Drop-curb openings;
   (15) Sidewalk culverts;
   (16) Regulatory floodway conveyance calculations with cross sections;
   (17) Weir structures;
   (18) Orifice formulas;
   (19) Grade to drain channels;
   (20) Upstream pickup and flared section;
   (21) Downstream backwater control and flare to match downstream condition;
   (22) Required free board;
   (23) Improper "N" value;
   (24) Improper velocity used;
   (25) Improper easement width;
   (26) Access road on each sodded channel;
   (27) Improper run-off coefficient used;
   (28) Improper time of concentration used;
   (29) Improper quantities used;
   (30) Steel calculations for box culvert; and
   (31) Street quantities for 5-year (30-foot street) and 25-year (greater than 44-foot street) frequency showing that street capacities are correct based on Chapter 5, Development Standards, of the LDC;

(P) Subdivision plat showing:
   (1) All interior drainage easements;
   (2) Outfall drainage easements;
   (3) USGS contour map and all other necessary drainage information;
   (4) Outfall drainage easements to the centerline of existing natural low;
   (5) Finished fill contours; and
   (6) Interceptor drainage easements.

(Q) Typical details for the following elements:
   (1) Box culvert with headwalls or wingwalls;
   (2) Pipe culverts with headwalls or wingwalls;
   (3) Culvert headwalls shown with proper safety measures;
   (4) Drop-curb openings;
   (5) Inlets on grade;
   (6) Inlets on sump;
   (7) Drop structures;
   (8) Retards;
   (9) Sidewalks over drains;
   (10) Guard-post installations;
   (11) Guard rail on structures;
   (12) Header curb;
   (13) Energy dissipators;
   (14) Junction boxes;
   (15) Concrete-lined channels with free board;
   (16) Earth-sodded channels with free board;
   (17) Other concrete structures;
   (18) Grade to drain sections;
   (19) Transition sections;
   (20) Fencing for vertical wall channels greater than 2 feet deep; and
   (21) Side slope.

(R) Street plans and profiles;

(S) Drainage plan and profile, including the following:
   (1) Proposed flowline slopes with grades and elevations shown every 50 feet in profile;
   (2) Proposed top-of-channel profile;
   (3) Existing ground right and left profile at property line;
   (4) Finished fill profiles;
   (5) Locations and size of culverts;
   (6) Drop structures;
   (7) Retards;
   (8) Grade to drain profiles;
   (9) Flowline elevations at every 50-foot station and at each structure and change in grade;
   (10) Junction boxes;
   (11) Channel plan views;
   (12) Channel sections;
   (13) Pipes with hydraulic grade lines on profile;
   (14) Cross sections of existing natural channels or lows, which are not to be improved but are left in natural state and dedicated to high water calculated;
   (15) Angles, bearings, and distances for structures and channels;
   (16) Lot grading-layout drains; and
   (17) Culvert structural details.

(T) Unit and storm hydrographs for major streams (over 2,000 acres);

(U) Drainage easements to the centerline of natural low area;

(V) Cost estimate; and

(W) Professional engineer's seal.

B-12.5 HEC-2 Submittal Checklist

The applicant shall include the following information in the preparation of HEC-2 studies and reports and to expedite the [LOCAL GOVERNMENT]'s review procedure. Any information required for a floodplain development approval supersedes the requirements of this section in the regulatory floodplain.

(A) Certification of a professional engineer certified to practice in [STATE], including the name of the submitter and professional engineer registration number;

(B) Electronic media with all input files;

(C) Copy of condensed printouts;

(D) Project description and history;

(E) Location;
(F) Scope and objective of analysis;
(G) Previous and related studies that may affect the analysis;
(H) Methodology;
(I) Sources of discharges;
(J) Bridge routines;
(K) Base or effective models (mention source);
(L) Revised base model;
(M) Proposed model;
(N) Summary, conclusions, and recommendations;
(O) Water surface elevation impacts;
(P) Information in tabular format, including:
   (1) Water surface comparison table at each cross section;
   (2) Floodway table;
   (3) Cross-section numbering table (if stationing changes);
   (4) Vicinity map;
   (5) Plan view of project reach;
   (6) Water surface profiles for design storm;
   (7) Channel cross sections showing limits of drainage easements and property lines;
   (8) Bridge cross sections;
   (9) Plan view of bridge; and
   (10) Photographs (if available);
(Q) Survey and/or certified "as-built" information for all revisions to base model; and
(R) Sample calculations.

B-13 STREET PLANS

B-13.1 Number of Copies

The applicant shall provide three sets of construction plans and two sets of the pavement design report.

B-13.2 Format

(A) Construction plans shall be 24 x 36 inches, with a margin of 2-1/2 inches on the left side of the sheet and appropriate margins on the other three sides. Construction plans shall be drawn at a scale of 50 feet = 1 inch.

(B) Where more than one sheet is necessary to accommodate the entire area to be subdivided, an index sheet showing the entire subdivision at an appropriate scale shall be attached to the plat.

B-13.3 Contents

The plans and profiles for street, alley, cross walkway, and drainage easement improvements submitted shall include the following information:
(A) Typical sections showing:
   (1) The proposed pavement width, type, thickness, and crown;
   (2) The proposed curb and gutter type, and the location in relation to centerline and exposure;
   (3) The proposed parkway grading slopes;
   (4) The proposed locations and type of wheelchair ramps;
   (5) The location of traffic signal conduit; and
   (6) Construction details of all drainage, including dimensions, reinforcing, and components, such as grates and manhole covers. The information shall be given for each different type of street and alley in the subdivision.
(B) Street specifications and property boundaries showing:
   (1) Alignment of each street, alley, cross walkway, and drainage easement showing a beginning and an ending station;
   (2) Each deflection angle of the centerline and the station of the point of intersection;
   (3) The station of the point of curvature and the point of tangency of each curve;
   (4) The station and angle of intersection of each intersection with another street, alley, or drainage easement;
   (5) The station and radius of each curb return;
   (6) The location of adjacent right-of-way lines;
   (7) The location and limits of sidewalks and curbs of each street;
   (8) The location of each drainage structure;
   (9) The location and size of all storm sewers; and
   (10) The length, width, and thickness of the cement-stabilized base.
(C) Stormwater management facility information including:
   (1) The top of curb grade at each curb end, each 50-foot station, and each end of each curb return;
   (2) The centerline grade at each end and at each 50-foot station of alleys and drainage ditches;
   (3) The gradient of each tangent grade and the location and length of each vertical curve;
   (4) The direction of storm drainage flow at each intersection;
   (5) The flow-line elevations of each drainage structure; and
   (6) The flow-line elevation of each storm sewer at each point of change of grade, at each end, and at the intervening gradients. The profiles of streets, alleys, and drainage ditches shall show the natural ground at adjacent property lines and the proposed centerline.
(D) Scale, north arrow, date, and plat number of the associated plat. Plans and profiles shall be drawn to scales of 50 feet = 1 inch horizontally and 5 feet = 1 inch vertically, unless different scales are approved by the [ENGINEERING OFFICIAL].
(E) All street and alley plans and profiles shall bear the seal of a professional engineer.

B-14 SUBDIVISION PLAT APPLICATIONS

B-14.1 Number of Copies

The [PLANNING OFFICIAL] may require the applicant to submit up to 40 blue- or black-line folded copies of the final plat, one legible 8-1/2 x 11-inch reduced copy, and an original and reproducible matte film of the plat.

B-14.2 Format

(A) Plats shall be drawn in ink on Mylar on sheets 18 inches wide and 24 inches long, with a margin of 2-1/2 inches on the left side of the sheet and appropriate margins on the other three sides. Plats shall be drawn at a scale of 100 feet = 1 inch unless the [PLANNING OFFICIAL] approves a smaller scale. Plats that include 1/2 acre or less in area shall be drawn at a scale of 50 feet = 1 inch.

(B) Where more than one sheet is necessary to accommodate the entire area to be subdivided, an index sheet showing the entire subdivision at an appropriate scale shall be attached to the plat.

B-14.3 Contents

The plat applications shall include the following:

(A) All of the information required by Table B-1 of this appendix.
(B) A performance agreement.
(C) The plat number issued by the planning department in the upper right corner, scale, north arrow, and date.
(D) The name of the subdivider and the name of the record owner of the land involved.
(E) The location of the subdivision with respect to a corner of the survey or tract, or an original corner of the original survey of which it is a part, giving the dimensions of the subdivision.
(F) The primary control points, approved by the [ENGINEERING OFFICIAL], or descriptions and ties to such control points, to which all dimensions, angles, bearings, new [LOCAL GOVERNMENT] block number or county block number, and similar data on the plat shall be referred, and four points on the perimeter of the subdivision, identified by coordinates that relate to the State Plane Coordinate system.
(G) The tract boundary lines, the exact location and width of all existing or recorded streets, easements, and other rights-of-way intersecting the boundary or streets, easements, and other rights-of-way forming the boundary of the tract being subdivided, and property lines of residential lots and other sites with accurate dimensions, bearing or deflecting angles and radii, area, and central angles of all curves.
(H) Final contour data to show drainage of the site of the proposed subdivision. If the average grade of the site is 5 percent or less, the maximum contour interval to be used shall be 2 feet. If the average grade exceeds 5 percent, the maximum contour interval may be increased to 5 feet.
(I) The name and width of each public and private street or other right-of-way in or adjacent to the subdivision. The right-of-way width on all streets and safety lanes shall be displayed by an overall dimension. The dimensions of the division of the right-of-way on public streets between the centerline of the right-of-way and respective adjacent property line shall be shown. Private streets and safety lanes shall also be designated as such.
(J) The name of the subdivision (no more than 35 characters), legal description of the property, and a number to identify each lot or site.
(K) Location, dimensions, and purpose of any easement or reservation and location of any high-pressure oil, gas, or gasoline lines. Easements that are designated to be converted into public street rights-of-way on a subsequent plat shall be annotated with the following note:

"Easement to expire upon incorporation into platted public street right-of-way."

(L) Front and side setback lines adjacent to streets, where required.
(M) The [LOCAL GOVERNMENT] limits line and the extraterritorial jurisdiction line if either traverses the subdivision.
(N) The location map indicating the location of the plat in relation to adjacent streets and at least two major thoroughfares in the vicinity.
(O) The county clerk's certificate of authentication as required by the applicable county.
(P) If part of the plat is within a regulatory floodplain, two copies of all data, as specified by the latest requirements of the Federal Emergency Management Agency, to apply for a conditional Letter of Map Revision and payment of the associated fees, when the proposed plat shall cause a change in the alignment, width, or elevation of a 100-year floodplain identified on a Flood Insurance Rate Map.

B-15 TRAFFIC IMPACT ANALYSIS

B-15.1 Applicability

The TIA shall be signed and sealed by a professional engineer, registered to practice in [STATE].

B-15.2 Contents

The following information shall be provided in the following format:
(A) Traffic analysis map.
(B) Land use, site, and study area boundaries, as defined, with a map.
(C) Existing and proposed site uses.
(D) Where land use is a basis for estimating projected traffic volumes, existing and proposed land uses on both sides of boundary streets for all parcels within the study area (provide map).
(E) Existing and proposed roadways and intersections of boundary streets within the study area of the subject property, including traffic conditions (provide map).
(F) All major driveways and intersecting streets adjacent to the property will be illustrated in detail sufficient to serve the purposes of illustrating traffic function. This may include showing lane widths, traffic islands, medians, sidewalks, curbs, traffic control devices (e.g., traffic signs, signals, and pavement markings), and a general description of the existing pavement condition.
(G) Photographs of adjacent streets of the development and an aerial photograph showing the study area.
(H) Trip generation and design-hour volumes (provide table).
(I) A trip generation summary table listing each type of land use, the building size assumed, the average trip generation rates used (e.g., total daily traffic and AM/PM peaks), and the resultant total trips generated.
(J) Generated vehicular trip estimates may be discounted in recognition of other reasonable and applicable modes (e.g., transit, pedestrian, and bicycles). Trip generation estimates may also be discounted through the recognition of pass-by trips and internal site trip satisfaction.
(K) Proposed trip generation calculations for commercial properties shall be based on proposed floor area.
(L) Trip distribution (provide figure by site exit).
(M) Estimates of percentage distribution of trips by turning movements from the proposed development.
(N) Trip assignment (provide figure by site entrance and boundary street).
(O) Direction of approach of site-attracted traffic via the area's street system.
(P) Existing and projected traffic volumes (provide figure for each item).
(Q) "Existing traffic volumes" are the numbers of vehicles on the streets within the impact area during the time periods listed in subsections (1) through (8), below, immediately prior to the beginning of construction of the land development project. "Projected traffic volumes" are the numbers of vehicles, excluding the site-generated traffic, on the streets of

interest during the time periods listed in subsections (1) through (8), below, in the build-out year.

(1) AM peak-hour site traffic (including turning movements).

(2) PM peak-hour site traffic (including turning movements).

(3) AM peak-hour total traffic, including site-generated traffic and projected traffic (including turning movements).

(4) PM peak-hour total traffic, including site-generated traffic and projected traffic (including turning movements).

(5) For special situations where peak traffic typically occurs at nontraditional times (e.g., major sporting venues and large, specialty Christmas stores), any other peak hour necessary for complete analysis, including turning movements.

(6) Total daily existing traffic for street system in study area.

(7) Total daily existing traffic for street system in study area and new site traffic.

(8) Total daily existing traffic for street system in study area plus new site traffic and projected traffic from build-out of study area land uses.

(R) Capacity analysis (the applicant shall provide analysis sheets in appendices).

(S) A capacity analysis shall be conducted for all public street intersections and junctions of major driveways with public streets that are significantly impacted (within the study area boundary as defined in the LDC).

(T) Capacity analysis will follow the principles established in the latest edition of the *Highway Capacity Manual 2000*,[1] unless otherwise directed by the [ENGINEERING OFFICIAL]. Capacity will be reported in quantitative terms as expressed in the *Highway Capacity Manual 2000* and in terms of traffic level of service.

(U) Capacity analysis will include traffic queuing estimates for all critical applications where the length of queues is a design parameter (e.g., auxiliary turn lanes and traffic gates).

(V) Study area boundaries, consistent with the impact areas required by Chapter 6, Adequate Public Facilities, of the LDC.

B-16 TREE PRESERVATION PLAN

B-16.1 Number of Copies

The applicant shall submit three sets of tree preservation plans, surveys, and/or drawings with the information required below.

B-16.2 Format

All tree preservation plans, surveys, and/or drawings shall be submitted in the form required by the [LOCAL GOVERNMENT] arborist, and shall contain and provide tree protection notes, details, and specifications clearly indicating the trees that will remain and the trees that are to be removed.

B-16.3 Contents

A tree survey shall be prepared for the subject area/property under one of the following criteria, dependent on type of development:

(A) For contiguously developed lots located inside the [LOCAL GOVERNMENT] limits, the developer or property owner must provide a tree survey of the area contained in the front and rear yard setbacks, as established in the lot layout standards (§ 5.10 Lots in Chapter 5, Development Standards, of the LDC) of the lots that are to be made ready for construction. The tree survey is not required to include the area located within easements;

(B) For individually developed lots located inside the [LOCAL GOVERNMENT] limits, the developer or property owner must provide a tree survey of the area contained in the front, rear, and side yard setbacks, as established in the lot layout standards (§ 5.10 Lots in Chapter 5, Development Standards, of the LDC) of the lots that are to be made ready for construction. However, the tree survey is not required to include the area located within easements;

(C) The location and size in diameter inches of each protected and/or heritage tree (and significant stands at the discretion of the applicant) located in the front, rear, and side yard setbacks (as applicable) of each lot or contiguous lots for which a tree removal development approval is requested (and parkway trees as defined);

(D) The existing and/or proposed topographical information, easements, rights-of-way, setbacks, parkways, and property lines;

(E) The location and size of each existing or proposed tree or groups of trees that will be relied on by the applicant for mitigation;

(F) A summary table indicating the total number, diameter inches, and species of protected trees and protected trees to be removed within the surveyed area, and the total number and caliper inches of mitigation trees to be planted or alternative mitigation trees to be saved and maintained;

(G) Location of all existing and proposed structures, utilities, paved areas, and sidewalks, to the extent such information is available;

(H) Tree protection notes, details, and specifications; and

(I) Written statement by the applicant explaining the purpose for the requested tree removal.

B-17 VESTED RIGHTS DETERMINATION

An application for a vested rights determination shall be made by the applicant on a form established for such purpose and provided by the [LOCAL GOVERNMENT], which shall contain at least the following information:

(A) Name and address of applicant;

(B) Project description and name of subdivision or development, if applicable;

(C) Location of development;

(D) Total land area, in square feet;

(E) Total area of impervious surface, in square feet;

(F) Number of residential dwelling units, by type;

(G) Type and amount of nonresidential square footage;

(H) Phases of the development, if applicable;

(I) Verified or certified copies of all development approvals, contracts, appraisals, reports, correspondence, letters, or other documents or materials upon which the applicant's claim for vested rights or equitable estoppel is based;

(J) Sworn statement, in a form prescribed by the [LOCAL GOVERNMENT], and signed by the applicant; and

(K) Legal description of the property.

In addition to the required processing as set forth in subsections (A) through (K), above, an application for consent agreement approval shall include, but shall not be limited to, the following:

(A) A timing and phasing plan for the proposed development;

(B) A plan for the provision of public facilities and services to the proposed development, by phase;

(C) The conditions under which the proposed development will be authorized to proceed; and

(D) The conditions under which development approvals will lapse or may be revoked.

A document shall be considered "verified" or "certified," whether an original or a copy, if it is signed by the official with decision-making authority for the development approval application.

B-18 SITE PLAN CHECKLIST

See Table B-1, above.

NOTE

1. Transportation Research Board, *Highway Capacity Manual 2000* (Washington, DC: TRB, 2000).

Table of Cases

*In page references containing an "n" (e.g., "379n6"),
the number before the "n" is the page number and the number after the "n" is the note number.*

A

Acton v. Jackson County, 379n6
Adams v. Thurston County, 381n29
Advisory Opinion, In re, 293
Agins v. City of Tiburon, 306n105
Akin v. South Middleton Township Zoning Hearing Board, 38n16
Almquist v. Town of Marshan, 385n2
A Local & Regional Monitor v. City of Los Angeles, 117n39
Amcare 2 Partners v. Zoning Hearing Board, 37n13
American Nat'l Bank & Trust Co. v. Arlington Heights, 116n17
Anderson First Coalition v. City of Anderson, 363n16, 364n24
Anderson v. City Council of City of Pleasant Hill, 380n24
Annapolis, City of, v. Waterman, 175n73
Annapolis Market Place, L.L.C. v. Parker, 305n
Annbar Assocs. v. West Side Redevelopment Corp., 65n38, 175n79
ARC of New Jersey, Inc. v. State of New Jersey, 364n64
Askew v. Cross Key Waterways, 23n34
A-S-P Associates v. City of Raleigh, 38n20
Associated Home Builders of Greater East Bay, Inc. v. City of Walnut Creek, 25n70
Associated Home Builders v. City of Livermore, 303n11, 306n89
Association for Advancement of the Mentally Handicapped, Inc. v. City of Elizabeth, 364n64
Association of Rural Residents v. Kitsap County, 175n57
Avco Community Developers, Inc. v. South Coast Regional Commission, 175n55, 380n18, 380n24
Ayres v. City of Los Angeles, 25n69

B

Batch v. Town of Chapel Hill, 282n132
Beaver Meadows v. Larimer County, 304n51
Beck Development Co., Inc. v. Southern Pacific Transportation Co., 174n46
Belgrade Shores, Inc., In re, 27n97
Bell v. City of Bridgeport, 293
Belle Harbor Realty Co. v. Kerr, 305n88, 381n58
Belle Terre, Village of, v. Boraas, 38n15, 301
Benchmark Land Company v. City of Battle Ground, 175n63
Bensalem Township v. Blank, 174n43

Bibco Corp. v. City of Sumter, 366n98
Billings v. California Coastal Commission, 381n34
Black v. City of Waukesha, 25n70
Blades v. City of Raleigh, 116n17
Bloom v. Planning Board of Brookline, 173n16
Board of Adjustment of City of San Antonio v. Nelson, 380n14
Board of Commissioners of South Whitehall Township, Lehigh County v. Toll Brothers, 380n26
Board of County Commissioners of Larimer County v. Conder & Sommervold, 24n63
Board of County Commissioners v. O'Dell, 173n26
Board of County Commissioners v. Sommerudd, 174n37
Board of County Comm'rs v. Gaster, 24n63
Board of Supervisors of Upper Frederick Township v. Moland Development Co., 366n87
Board of Supervisors v. Allman, 303n13
Board of Supervisors v. Rowe, 280n28
Board of Supervisors v. West Chestnut Realty Corp., 175n53
Board of Supervisors v. Williams, 303n13
Board of Zoning Appeals v. Leisz, 380n13,14
Boulder Buildings Group v. City of Boulder, 306n102
Bourgeois v. Parish of St. Tammany, 365n86
Bove v. Donna-Hanna Coke Corporation, 21n13
Braddock, Borough of, v. Allegheny County Planning Dept., 173n20
Brookside Village, City of, v. Comeau, 365n86
Brous v. Smith, 24n68
Broward County v. Narco Realty, Inc., 381n32
Bryan v. City of Madison, Miss., 306n123
Buckingham Developers Inc., Appeal of, 116n25, 116n32, 117n39
Burnt Fork Citizen's Coalition v. Ravalli County BCC, 37n11
Bussieve v. Roberge, 37n10

C

Candid Enterprises, Inc. v. Grossmont Union High School Dist., 306n122
Cannon v. Coweta County, 365n86, 365n87
Canter v. Planning Bd. of Westborough, 25n73
Cappture Realty Co. v. Board of Adjustment, 303n19, 306n88
Carmel Valley View, Ltd. v. Maggini, 174n48
Caron v. City of Pawtucket, 364n54

Carroll County, County Com'rs of, v. Uhler, 380n14
Charles v. Diamond, 302
Cherry Hills Village, Town of, v. Shafroth, 173n24
Chesterfield Development Corp. v. City of Chesterfield, 306n104
Chiara v. Dizoglio, 364n54
Chicago v. Handler, 38n24
Chrismon v. Guilford County, 116n18
Citizens Against Lewis & Clark Landfill v. Pottawattamie County Bd. of Adj., 173n14
City Ice Delivery Co. v. Zoning Board of Adjustment for the County of Charleston, 378
City National Bank of Miami v. City of Coral Springs, 381n32
City of West Hollywood v. Beverly Towers, Inc., 174n30
Civil Liberties for Urban Believers v. City of Chicago, 361
C&K Real Estate, L.L.C. v. Guilford Planning and Zoning Commission, 280n35
Clark v. Sunset Hills Memorial Park, 173n19
Clayton v. Village of Oak Park, 29n153, 65n46
Cleburne, Texas, City of, v. Cleburne Living Center, 358
Coffey v. Maryland National Capital Park and Planning Comm'n, 174n37
Cohen v. Town of Henniker, 174n31
Coleman Highlands, In re, 380n17
College Station, City of, v. Turtle Rock Corp., 25n70
Commercial Builders v. City of Sacramento, 27n93
Commonwealth Properties, Inc. v. Washington County, 175n54
Compass Lake Hills Development v. State Dept. of Community Affairs, 378
Concord Township (Kit-Mar Builders), In re Appeal, 303n10
Construction Industry Association v. City of Petaluma, 303n8, 306n116
Contractors & Builders Association of Pinellas County v. City of Dunedin, 25n75
Conway v. Town of Stratham, 304n31
Coots v. J.A. Tobin Construction Co., 37n3
Corcoran v. Planning Bd. of Sudbury, 173n29
Corrigan v. City of Scottsdale, 281n47
Coscan Washington, Inc. v. Maryland-National Capital Park & Planning Comm'n, 117n43
Coulter v. City of Rawlins, 25n70, 25n75
Creative Environments, Inc. v. Estabrook, 306n104
Crowder v. Vandendeale, 24n60
Cruz v. Town of Cicero, 306n125
Cunningham v. Board of Aldermen of City of Overland, 37n7
Cuyahoga Falls, City of, v. Buckeye Community Hope Foundation, 306n118
Cyclone Sand & Gravel v. ZBA of the City of Ames, 116n16

D

Dallen v. City of Kansas City, 60–61, 64n36, 363n14
Dateline Builders, Inc. v. City of Santa Rosa, 293
Del Mar, City of, v. City of San Diego, 304n36
Department of Health, In re, 293
Diamond Multimedia Systems, Inc. v. Superior Court, 26n79
W.S. Dickey Clay Mfg. Co. v. Ferguson Investment Co., 175n68
Disabatino v. New Castle County, 381n41
Divan Builders, Inc. v. Planning Bd,. of the Township of Wayne, 27n92

Diversified Properties, Inc. v. Town of Hopkinton Planning Bd., 25n76, 26n89
Dolan v. City of Tigard, 171, 282n127
Domeisen v. Zoning Hearing Board, 379n8
D.S. Alamo Assocs. v. Commissioner of Finance, 65n38
Dube v. Senter, 173n24
Duffcon Concrete Products, Inc. v. Borough of Cresskill, 22n32
DuFour v. Montgomery County, 116n38

E

Edmonds, City of, v. Oxford House, Inc., 364n59
Eiggie Int'l v. Town of Huntington, 381n47
El Patio v. Permanent Rent Control Board of City of Santa Monica, 377
Environmental Communities of Pennsylvania v. North Coventry Township, 366n88
Eschete v. City of New Orleans, 25n73
Euclid, Village of, v. Ambler Realty, 22n15, 100, 115n2, 306n121, 379

F

Familystyle of St. Paul, Inc. v. City of St. Paul, 364n61
Fasano v. Washington County Comm'n, 27n94
First English Evangelical Lutheran Church v. County of Los Angeles, 300–301, 304n30
Fleming v. Moore Bros. Realty Co., 37n12
Florida Realty, Inc. v. Kirkpatrick, 24n60
FM Properties Operating Co. v. City of Austin, 381n33
Folsom Enterprises v. City of Scottsdale, 380n21
Foxcroft Townhome Owners Association v. Hoffman Rossner Corp., 24n60
Frankland v. City of Lake Oswego, 174n44
Franklin County v. Leisure Properties, 381n41
Fred F. French Inv. Co. v. City of New York, 116n37
Freundshuh v. City of Blaine, 303n13
Friarsgate, Inc. v. Town of Irmo, 378–379
Friends of Davis v. City of Davis, 280n36, 280n37
Fulling v. Palumbo, 171

G

Garipay v. Town of Hanover, 25n73, 174n40, 303n13, 303n14
Geiger v. Zoning Hearing Board, 365n86
Gerard v. San Juan County, 173n29
Giger v. City of Omaha, 115n11
Ginsburg Development Corp. v. Town Bd. of Town of Cortlandt, 117n41, 264
Girton v. City of Seattle, 281n46
Giuliano v. Town of Edgertown, 174n37
Glassboro, Borough of, v. Vallorosi, 38n15
Godorov v. Board of Comm'rs, 26n82
Golden v. Planning Board of the Town of Ramapo, 4–5, 6, 23n35, 23n42, 25n74, 25n76, 293, 294, 295, 300, 302, 303n9, 303n33, 304n48, 305n70, 305n75, 305n80, 305n87, 306n101, 306n112
Goldman v. Crowther, 22n19
Goldstein v. Planning Board of Lincoln Park, 173n16
Goodman v. Board of Commissioners of the Township of Whitehall, 25n68, 174n39
Gorieb v. Fox, 116n21
Graham v. Connor, 306n119

Graves v. Bloomfield Planning Board, 173n28
Green v. Bourbon County Joint Planning Comm'n, 173n19
Griffin Development Co. v. City of Oxnard, 174n30
E. Grossman & Sons, Inc. v. Rocha, 26n88
Guest v. King George County, 293

H
Hale v. First Nat'l Bank of Mt. Prospect, 27n97
Halle Development, Inc. v. Anne Arundel County, 305n78
Hensler v. City of Glendale, 170
Heritage Park Development Corp. v. Town of Southbridge, 175n56
Higdon v. Campbell County Fiscal Court, 173n17
Highland Park, Town of, v. Marshall, 363n8
Hill v. Zoning Hearing Board, 381n46
Hock v. Board of Sup'rs of Mount Pleasant Township, 115n3
Hoepker v. City of Madison Plan Commission, 173n20
Hoffmann v. Kincaly, 380n15
Hollywood, City of, v. Hollywood, Inc., 116n32, 117n39
Hollywood, Inc. v. Broward County, 25n75
Home Depot U.S.A., Inc. v. City of Portland, 358
Howard County v. JJM, Inc., 27n98
Hrenchuk v. Planning Bd. of Walpole, 25n73
Hunter v. City of Pittsburgh, 22n31
Hurrle v. County of Sherburne, 175n65

I
Interstate Power Company v. Nobles County, 380n23
Isabelle v. Town of Newbury, 26n89

J
Jenad, Inc. v. Village of Scarsdale, 25n70
Jochimek v. Superior Court, Maricopa County, 280n38
J.W. Jones & Co. v. City of San Diego, 304n36
Jones v. Zoning Hearing Board of Town of McCandless, 117n42
Jordan v. Village of Menomonee Falls, 26n83
Joseph, Matter of, v. Town Board of Town of Clarkstown, 303n15
Juanita Bay Valley Community Ass'n. v. City of Kirkland, 381n40
Just v. Marinette County, 25n73, 27n91

K
Kamhi v. Yorktown, 25n69
Kansas City, City of, v. Kindle, 380n16
Kansas City, City of, v. Taylor, 37n9
Kass v. Lewin, 173n28
Kawai, City of, v. Pacific Life Ins. Co., 380n19
Keeney v. Kemper Nat. Ins. Companies, 364n54
Kessler v. Town of Shelter Island Planning Bd., 26n88
Keystone Bituminous Coal Assoc. v. DeBenedictus, 116n33
Kilausa Neighborhood Ass'n v. Land Use Comm'n, 303n7
Kiska v. Skrensky, 173n21
Kosinski v. Lawlor, 115n3
Kozesnik v. Township of Montgomery, 22n26
Krughoff v. City of Naperville, 25n70

L
Laguna Village, 381n34

Lake City Corp. v. City of Mequon, 174n36, 380n26
Lake Housing Bluff Partners v. City of South Milwaukee, 380n23
Lake Intervale Homes, Inc. v. Parsippany-Troy Hills, 24n67
Lakeview Devel. Corp. v. City of South Lake Tahoe, 381n61
Lampton v. Pinaire, 175n85
Land County v. Oregon Bldgs., Inc., 25n73
Landmark Land Co. v. City and County of Denver, 38n19
L.A. Ray Realty v. Town of Cumberland, 38n22
Larsen v. County of Washington, 303n13
Latrobe Speedway, Inc. v. Zoning Hearing Board of Unity Township, 380n12
Lauderdale By-The-Sea, Town of, v. Meretzky, 381n44
Legion Manor, Inc. v. Township of Wayne, 175n69
Leroy Land Dev. v. Tahoe Regional Planning Agency, 282n128, 304n49
Licari v. Ferruzzi, 306n104
Lichte v. Heidlage, 380n14
Lincoln Trust Co., v. Williams Bldg. Corp., 22n18
Long Beach Equities, Inc. v. County of Ventura, 306n97
Loreto Development Co. v. Village of Chardon, 280n35, 357
Loup-Miller Const. Co. v. City and County of Denver, 306n122
Lowe, In re, 174n33
Lucas v. South Carolina Coastal Council, 3, 306n91
Luczynski v. Temple, 365n86
Lynch Community Homes, Inc., Appeal of, 364n61
Lyons, Town of, v. Bashor, 379n5

M
Malvern, Borough of, v. Jackson, 365n86
Manalapan Realty, L.P. v. Township Committee of the Township of Manalapan, 38n18, 280n40
Mansfield & Swett, Inc. v. West Orange, 24n64
Maplewood Village Tenants Ass'n v. Maplewood Village, 174n31
Marblehead v. City of San Clemente, 303n5
Marshall v. Salt Lake City, 101
Marx v. Zoning Bd. of Appeals of Vil. of Mill Neck, 24n61
Maselli v. Orange County, 175n71
Matlack v. Burlington County Freeholders Board, 116n32, 117n39
Matthew v. Smith, 64n2
Mayor & City Council of Cumberland v. Powles, 293
Mayor and City Council v. Dembo, 380n11
McDonald's Corp., In re, 25n68, 174n39
Medical Services, Inc. v. City of Savage, 306n114
Metropolitan Homes, Inc. v. Town Plan & Zoning Commission, 174n49
Metzdorf v. Borough of Rumson, 173n21
Miles v. Foley, 170
Miller v. City of Port Angeles, 24n66, 27n94, 174n39
Milwaukee, City of, v. Public Service Commission, 303n17
Mission Springs, Inc. v. City of Spokane, 381n48
Montgomery Crossing Associates v. Township of Lower Gwynedd, 358
Myrtle Beach, City of, v. Jual B. Corp., 380n12

N
National Land & Investment v. Kohn, 303n10
National Realty Corp. v. City of Virginia Beach, 175n61

Nettleton v. Zoning Board of Adjustment, 379n8
New Jersey Builders Assn. v. Nernards Township, 24n68
New Jersey Builders Ass'n v. Mayor, 26n90
Nickola v. Township of Grand Blanc, 366n88
Noble v. Chairman of Menahem Township, 26n86
Norbeck Village Joint Venture v. Montgomery County, 306n105
Norco Constr., Inc. v. King County, 27n98
Norsco Enterprises v. City of Fremont, 26n83, 174n30
North Georgia Mountain Cross of Blue Ridge v. City Network, Inc., 380n28
North Landers Corp. v Planning Bd., 25n73
North Las Vegas, City of, v. Pardee Construction Co., 381n57
Novi v. City of Pacifica, 35, 38n17
Nunziato v. Planning Bd. of Edgewater, 25n69

O
Ohio Mall Contractors, Inc. v. Dickinson, 174n33
Ojavan v. California Coastal Comm'n, 26n81
Olivieri v. Planning Board, 173n28
Olympia, City of, v. Bd. of Comm'r, 28n151
Olympia, City of, v. Drebick, 28n151
1000 Friends of Oregon v. LCDC, 303n7
Orrin Dressler, Inc. v. Burr Ridge, 173n29
Oxford House-C v. City of St. Louis, 364n60

P
Paladac Realty Trust v. Rockland Planning Comm'n, 174n43
Palatine, Village of, v. LaSalle National Bank, 381n39
Palm Beach County v. Wright, 20n3
Palm Beach Polo, Inc. v. Village of Wellington, 28n151
Pardee Construction Co. v. City of Camarillo, 381n50
Parks v. Watson, 24n68
Parkview Assoc. v. City of New York, 38n24, 381n44
Pasaro Builders, Inc. v. Township of Piscataway, 173n23
Patterson Materials Corp. v. Zagata, 280n46
Pearson Kent Corp. v. Bear, 25n73, 26n89, 279n17, 303n13
Pendleton v. City of Columbia, 381n58
Pendoley v. Ferreira, 21n14
Penn-Central Transportation Co. v. City of New York, 23n58, 116n30, 117n39, 301, 306n91
Pennobscot v. Board of County Commissioners, 37n10, 173n15, 173n30
Pennsylvania Coal Co. v. Mahon, 116n28
People v. H&H Properties, 381n34
Perkins v. Town of Ogunquit, 280n27
Petition of Dolington Group, In re, 304n40
Petrone v. Town of Foster, 174n42
PFZ Properties, Inc. v. Rodriquez, 306n104
Pharr, City of, v. Tippitt, 115n8
Pierro v. Baxendale, 38n14
P.O.K. RSA, Inc. v. Village of New Paltz, 174n33
Pokoik v. Silsdorf, 380n21
Pomona Pointe Associates, Ltd. v. Incorporated Village of Pomona, 281n46
Pompano Beach v. Yardarm Restaurant, 381n59
Powell v. Taylor, 22n16
Prudential Co-op. Realty Co. v. City of Youngstown, 171
PSI Energy, Inc. v. Indiana Office of Utility Consumer Counsel, 173n14
Pure Oil Division, 381n58

Purser v. Mecklenburg County, 115n11
P.W. Investments, Inc. v. City of Westminster, 380n26

R
Ramapo 287 Ltd. Partnership v. Village of Montebello, 380n26
Rancourt v. Town of Barnstead, 306n111
Reid Development Corp. v. Parsippany-Troy Hills Township, 303n19
River Birch Assoc. v. City of Raleigh, 25n69
R.J.P. Builders, Inc. v. Township of Woolwich, 172n2
Robert Rieke Bldg. Co. v. City of Olathe, 381n43
Robinson Township v. Knoll, 365n86
Robinson v. City of Boulder, 25n76, 303n19
Ronning v. Thompson, 37n11, 173n15, 173n16, 174n30, 174n31
Rose v. Plymouth Town, 303n19
Rosen v. Village of Downers Grove, 25n69
Rouse/Chamberlain, Inc. v. Board of Supervisors of Charlestown Township, 25n73
Rumson Estates, Inc. v. Mayor and Council of the Borough of Fair Haven, 37n10
Russ Building Partnership v. City of San Francisco, 306n122, 379

S
Sacramento, County of, v. Lewis, 306n117
Salamar Builders Corp. v. Tuttle, 25n73, 26n89
Salem, Town of, v. Kenosha County, 27n91
Samperi v. Planning and Zoning Commission, 24n63, 174n37
San Francisco, City and County of, v. Municipal Court, 65n48
Santa Fe Village Venture v. Albuquerque, 306n97
S.A.V.E. v. City of Bothell, 22n25
Save Centennial Valley Ass'n. v. Schultz, 24n63, 174n37
Sayewich, Estate of, In re, 173n21
Scarborough, N.V. v. Santa Monica Rent Control Board, 381n34
Schenck v. City of Hudson, 305n78, 306n102
Schroeder v. Dane County Bd. of Adjustment, 380n14
Schultheis v. Board of Supervisors, 24n63, 174n37
Scranton, Town of, v. Willoughby, 366n98
Scrutton v. County of Sacramento, 116n18
Sellon v. City of Manitou Springs, 280n46
Serpa v. County of Washoe, 174n40
Seventh Street LLC v. Baldwin County Planning and Zoning Commission, 28n151
Shelter Creek Development Corp. v. City of Oxnard, 174n30
Sherman-Colonial Realty Corp. v. Goldsmith, 175n77
Shorb v. Barkley, 26n87
Shore, In re, 365n86
Simplex Technologies v. Town of Newington, 64n2
Smith v. City of Clearwater, 381n45
Smith v. Township Comm., 26n89
Smoke Rise, Inc. v. Washington Suburban Sanitary Commission, 304n29
Soderling v. City of Santa Monica, 174n30
Solar v. Zoning Board of Appeals, 363n9
South Carolina Electric & Gas Company v. Hix, 381n51
Southern Burlington County N.A.A.C.P. v. Township of Mount Laurel, 22n25
Southern Coop. Dev. Fund v. Driggers, 25n68
S&P Enterprises v. City of Memphis, 175n61
Sprint Spectrum L.P. v. Willoth, 366n100

Steel Hill Development, Inc. v. Town of Sanbornton, 303n12
Stillwater Condominium Association v. Town of Salem, 174n31
Stoney-Brook Development Corporation v. Town of Fremont, 302
Sturges v. Town of Chilmark, 303n12, 306n100
Sudarsky v. City of New York, 25n69
Suffolk, City of, v. Board of Zoning Appeals, 381n35
Sugar Creek, City of, v. Reese, 379n1
Sun Prairie, Town of, v. Storms, 174n36
Sussex Woodlands, Inc. v. Mayor and Council of West Milford, 175n61
Suzuki v. City of Los Angeles, 379n6, 380n11
Swanson v. Marin Municipal Water District, 303n19, 306n88
Sylvia Development Corp. v. Calvert County, 301

T

Taft Corners Assocs., In re Appeal of, 380n26, 381n34
Tahoe-Sierra Preservation Council v. Tahoe Regional Planning Agency, 301, 304n30, 304n32
Tanner Cos. v. Insurance Marketing Services, Inc., 175n67
Terry v. Anderson, 379
Teter v. Clark County, 175n61
Theobald v. Board of County Commissioners, 294
The Villages L.L.C. v. Delaware Agricultural Lands Foundation, 380n25
Thompson v. Village of Toquerta, 381n59
Tisei v. Town of Ogunquit, 304n28
Toll Bros., Inc. v. West Windsor Township, 300
Toothaker v. Planning Board of Billerica, 175n77
Torres v. City of Yorba Linda, 293
Toys-R-Us v. Silva, 380n12
Traymore Associates v. Board of Supervisors of Northhampton, 26n89
Tri-County Paving, Inc. v. Ashe County, 306n126
Turner v. New York, 379
Turnpike Woods, Inc. v. Town of Stony Point, 170
232511 Investments, Ltd., In re, 28n151

U

Udell v. Haas, 22n26
Uncle v. New Jersey Pinelands Com'n, 380n14
United Parcel Service v. People's Counsel for Baltimore County, 38n25
United States v. Lock, 379

University Place, City of, v. McGuire, 380n12
Usery v. Turner Elkhorn Mining Co., 175n72, 379

V

Vance v. Vance, 379
Villa at Greely, Inc. v. Hopper, 380n27
Vinyard v. St. Louis County, 173n18
Von Der Heide v. Zoning Board of Appeals, 38n14

W

Wal-Mart Stores, Inc., In re, 263, 357, 363n18
Wal-Mart Stores, Inc. v. City of Turlock, 363n17
Wal-Mart Stores, Inc. v. County of Clark, 280n39
West Charter Area School District v. Collegium Charter School, 293
West Montgomery County Citizens Association v. Maryland National Capital Park & Planning Comm'n, 116n25
West Park Ave., Inc. v. Ocean Township, 175n61
Western Land Equities v. City of Logan, 380n25
Whitehead Oil Co. v. City of Lincoln, 380n23
Williams v. City of Central, 306n97
Williamson v. Pitkin County, 306n102
Willowbrook, Village of, v. Olech, 306n124
Wilson v. City of Laguna Beach, 363n11
Wincamp Partnership v. Anne Arundel County, 301, 302, 304n40
Windham, Town of, v. Lawrence Savings Bank, 173n20
WMM Properties, Inc. v. Cobb County, 380n21
Wolf Pen Preservation Association v. Louisville and Jefferson County Planning Commission, 24n68–25n68, 174n38
Wood v. City of Madison, 174n35, 174n36
Woodbury Place Partners v. City of Woodbury, 301, 304n30
Woodhouse v. Board of Commissioners of Town of Nag's Head, 115n5
W.R. Grace & Co. v. Cambridge, 301
Wright Dev., Inc. v. City of Wellsville, 25n73

Y

York v. Town of Ogunquit, 261
Young v. Flathead County, 174n33
Youngblood v. Board of Supervisors of San Diego County, 170, 175n51, 377

Z

Zobel v. Williams, 306n115

Subject Index

A

Abandonment of nonconforming use, 367, 369, 376
Access management development standards, 277
Accessibility, 8, 178
Accessory dwellings, 50, 57, 308–310, 356
Accessory uses (A) in use matrix, 78, 80. *See also* Supplemental use regulations
    supplemental use regulations, 307–308, 355–356
Adequate public facilities ordinance (APFO). *See also* Public facilities
    in application processing procedure, 286–287
    components of, 295–296, 298–299
    conditional approval under, 297–298
    constitutional challenges to, 300–302
    defined, 285
    enforcing, 297
    legislation allowing, 299–300
    role of, 294–296
Adjacency, in subdivision design, 8
Administrative agencies, 383–385
Adult use regulations, 355
Agricultural preserves, development rights in, 112
Agriculture, in use matrix, 78–79
Aircraft facility use regulations, 351
Airport Overlay (AO) zoning district, 94–96
Alabama, subdivision in, 169
Alleys, 11, 13, 180, 220. *See also* Streets/roads
Amendments, 162. *See also specific Code topic*
American Law Institute Model Land Development Code, 260
Americans with Disabilities Act (ADA), 178
Amortization period, 376
Annexation, 70, 158, 370
Antennas
    for satellites, 342, 355
    for wireless communication, 349–352, 353, 362–363
Antimerger legislation, 171–172
Antiquated subdivisions, 171
"Antisocial values" use, 2–3
Apartments. *See also* Housing
    as accessory dwellings, 310, 356
    in commercial retrofit, 47
    conversion of, 169
    density improvement with, 110
    as senior housing, 359
Appeals, 162. *See also specific Code topic*
Applicability, 162. *See also specific Code topic*

Application procedures, 119–175. *See also* Approvals; Development standards
    completeness review, 120–125
    cost of, 170–171
    development agreement procedures, 155–159
    development approval categories, 120
    document specifications, 417–432
        conditional use permits, 422–425
        general requirements, 417, 421–422
        landscape plans, 425–426
        nonconforming use, 426
        plat vacation and resubdivision, 426
        public involvement, 422
        requirements grid, 418–420
        rezoning, 426–427
        site plan checklist, 432
        stormwater management, 427–429
        street plans, 429
        subdivision plat specifications, 429–430
        traffic impact analysis, 430–431
        tree preservation plan, 431
        vested rights determination, 431–432
    elements of, 119, 120, 161–162, 166–167
    enforcement, violations, and penalties, 159–160
    public involvement
        documentation of, 422
        neighborhood participation, 129–130, 165–166
        notice provisions, 126–127
        public hearing, 127
    quasi-judicial and legislative approvals, 127–129, 163
    role of, 161
    subdivision rules (*see* Subdivisions)
    subsequent applications, 162
    variances and appeals
        general, 152–153
        to hearing officer, 153–154
        post-appeal, 154–155
        summary, 172
    wireless communication facilities, 349
    zoning versus comprehensive plan, 133–135, 162–163
        (*see also* Zoning)
Approvals. *See also* Application procedures
    of Airport Overlay district, 94, 96
    certificate of occupancy, 132
    criteria, 162, 167
    development, 131

grading and land disturbance, 131
requirement for, 119, 120
revocation of, 128–129
scope of, 167
streamlining, 163–165
of traditional neighborhood development, 49, 58
zoning certificates, 131–132
Architecture. *See* Building design; Landscaping/screening
Arizona
green buildings, 13–14
growth management, 5
LEED® program, 279
lighting ordinances, 266
parking standards, 268
subdivision, 7, 171
Arlington, Virginia, LEED® program in, 279
"As of right" use permit, 67
Asia, subdivision in, 171
Atmosphere, LEED® rating system, 196–197
Attached homes, 337–340. *See also* Housing
Auto graveyard use regulations, 329–330
Auto-oriented District (AOD) zoning, 69, 310–313, 356–357

B

Baltimore County, Maryland, development approval in, 35, 37
Base zoning district, 70–92
determining, 20
dimensional regulations, 80, 81
role of, 67
summary, 101, 105–107
in tier system, 68, 69
types of, 68 (*see also specific*)
use matrix, 71–79, 103–105
use regulations, 70, 79–81
Beaux Arts movement, 2
Bicycle parking development standards, 247–255, 257–258
Big-box stores. *See* Commercial buildings
Binding codes, 17
Block design, 41, 59–60, 183. *See also* Streets/roads
Bonds, 149, 150, 171, 324
Boston, Massachusetts, planning history of, 2
Boundaries, zoning, 69–70
Brownfields, in LEED® rating system, 195
Buffers. *See also* Greenspace; Landscaping/screening
in campus-style development, 46
development standards, 233–236, 240–242, 263
setbacks versus, 265
supplementary use regulations, 316, 318–319, 331
in traditional neighborhood development, 59
for wetlands preservation, 243
Building design. *See also* Dimensional standards; Housing; Lot design; Scale
development standards, 183–189, 261–263
civic buildings, 189
commercial buildings, 187–189, 198, 263
height, 183
landscaping, 237
manufactured homes, 186
multifamily dwellings, 186, 187
single-family dwellings, 184–186
nonconforming structures, 368, 370
supplemental use regulations
accessory dwelling units, 308–310, 356
affordable housing, 328
auto-oriented development, 310–313
commercial development, 313–314, 357–358
residential dwelling units, 335–341, 342, 361
use patterns and
campus-style development, 46
commercial retrofit, 47
traditional neighborhood development, 51, 59
transit-oriented development, 53–54
by zoning district
Airport Overlay, 94, 95
Commercial Neighborhood, 85
Downtown, 88
incentives for, 98
Mixed Use, 92
Neighborhood Preservation, 93–94
Office, 84
Planned Development, 90
Building envelope, 84, 109–110, 115
Building volume ratio (BVR), 113, 115
Burnham, Daniel, 2

C

Calabasas, California, sustainable development in, 14
California
accessory apartments, 356
code drafting leniency, 35
environmental controls, 4, 13, 14
growth management, 5
hybrid development, 11, 13
land-use policy, 15
new urbanist development, 13
nonconventional zoning, 105
Ramapo system, 294–295
subdivision, 7, 170, 171
transit-oriented development, 57
vested rights, 377, 379
Calthorpe, Peter, 9
Cambridge, Massachusetts, parking in, 268
Campus-style development, 45–46
Capacity, reimbursement for excess, 296–297
Capacity allocation, 298–299. *See also* Adequate public facilities ordinance (APFO); Public facilities
Capital improvements program (CIP), 285, 286, 289–292, 302. *See also* Adequate public facilities ordinance (APFO); Public facilities
Carriage houses. *See* Accessory dwellings
Carrying capacity, 114
Cary, North Carolina, new urbanist development in, 13
Cashier's check, in subdivision agreements, 149–150
Centers, in traditional neighborhood development, 49, 59
Centers for Disease Control, 266
Certificate of nonconforming use, 371
Certificate of occupancy, 132
Chapel Hill, North Carolina
joint planning, 17
new urbanist development, 13
Charleston, South Carolina, zoning in, 105
Charlotte, North Carolina, joint planning in, 17
Charrette, 165

Chicago, Illinois, church regulations in, 361
Chula Vista, California, hybrid development in, 11, 13
Citation, in land development code, 32
Citizen participation plan, 422. *See also* Public involvement
"City beautiful" movement, 2
Civic building development standards, 189
Civic uses, in traditional neighborhood development, 11
Civil Rights Act of 1964, 4
Clean Air Act, 268
Clean Water Act of 1977, 4
Cleburne, Texas, group home in, 358
Coastal Zone Management Act of 1972, 4
Collocation use regulations, 352
Colorado
    growth management, 5
    state controls, 4
    subdivision, 7, 168, 171
    vested rights, 377
Commercial buildings. *See also* Building design
    big-box stores, 357, 358
    development standards, 187–189, 198, 263
    supplemental use regulations, 313–314, 357–358
    in use matrix, 71–73
Commercial General (CG) zoning district
    dimensional standards, 80, 86
    summary, 85–86
    in tier system, 68
    in use matrix, 71–79
Commercial Large-Scale (CL) zoning district
    dimensional standards, 80, 87
    summary, 86–87
    in tier system, 68
    in use matrix, 71–79
Commercial Neighborhood (CN) zoning district
    dimensional standards, 80
    summary, 84–85
    in tier system, 68
    in use matrix, 71–79
Commercial retrofit use pattern, 46–48
Common areas and facilities, 40, 91–92
Common law vested rights, 372. *See also* Vested rights
Community facilities, 75–76. *See also* Public facilities
Completeness review, 162, 164, 166
Comprehensive Environmental Response, Compensation, and Liability Act of 1980, 4
Comprehensive plan
    preparing or amending, 132–133
    public facility adequacy and, 286–287, 295
    role of, 33
    subdivision control in, 169
    substitute provision for, 31–32
    zoning inconsistent with, 133–135, 162–163
Concord, North Carolina, parking in, 268
Concurrency regulations, 295. *See also* Adequate public facilities ordinance (APFO)
Conditional use permit (CUP). *See also* Variances
    application requirements, 418–420, 422–425
    approval of, 105
    nonconforming use, 372
    procedures, 137–139
    supplemental use regulations, 317, 330, 347
    in vested rights claim, 377–378

Conditional uses (C), 71–79, 80. *See also* Special use district
Conditional zoning district, 69, 135–137. *See also* Zoning
Condominiums, 169, 179. *See also* Housing
Connectivity ratio, 223, 275. *See also* Streets/roads
Consent agreement rights, 373. *See also* Vested rights
Conservation area standards, 42–43
Conservation subdivisions, 39–43
Consolidated commission approach, 17
Construction plans, 147–148
Construction-related use regulations, 344
Continuance of nonconforming use, 367. *See also* Nonconforming use
Contract zoning, 105
Conventional subdivisions, 40, 57
Conventional zoning, 1, 102. *See also* Zoning
Cornell University, 59
Corps of Engineers, 263
Courtyards, 40, 41, 110
Critical areas, development rights in, 112
Cross-referencing, in writing code, 33–34
Cul-de-sacs. *See* Streets/roads
Curbs. *See* Streets/roads

D

Decision, formal, 162, 166. *See also* Application procedures
Deemed-approved statutes, 170
Density. *See also* Floor area ratio (FAR)
    in Planned Development district, 90
    supplemental use regulations, 308, 331, 332, 341
    in traditional neighborhood development, 11, 49, 50, 59
    in transit-oriented development, 53, 62–63
    zoning by, 110
Density bonus. *See also* Incentives
    for affordable housing, 328–329
    in flexible zoning, 19, 96–99, 102–103
    in transfer of development rights, 111
Design regulations, 35. *See also* Building design; Development standards; Lot design
Detrimental reliance, 378
Development agreements, 70, 155–159, 286, 298
Development approvals, 131, 286, 317–318, 377
Development constraints, 135–136
Development review, 164, 165, 347–349
Development rights transfer, 97, 99, 110–113
Development standards, 177–284. *See also* Application procedures
    administrative exceptions, 177
    Americans with Disabilities Act in, 178
    design, 179–194 (*see also* Building design; Lot design)
        blocks, 183
        fences/walls, 190–191
        homeland security assessment, 194, 266
        lighting, 191–194, 265–266
        sustainability, 194, 195–198, 278–279
    environmental, 240–244, 263–264
    greenspace (*see* Landscaping/screening)
    infrastructure, 199–231 (*see also* Stormwater management; Streets/roads)
    parks/open space, 194, 199–205, 271–272
    utilities, 228, 230–231
    operation and maintenance, 178–179
    parking and storage, 244–259 (*see also* Parking)

loading areas, 258–259
outdoor storage, 244–245
standard specifications, 177–178
variances, 177
waivers, 260–261
Dimensional standards, 80–84, 86–90, 308. *See also* Building design; Lot design
Discretionary review, 165, 167. *See also* Public hearings
Discretionary uses, 105
Douglas Commission, 6
Downtown (D) zoning district
dimensional standards, 80, 88
summary, 87–88
in tier system, 68
in use matrix, 71–79
Drafting of code. *See* Language
Driveways. *See also* Streets/roads
in conservation subdivisions, 40
development standards
restrictions, 180, 182
summary, 276–277
throat length, 227, 228
Duplexes, 337–338. *See also* Housing
Dwelling units. *See* Housing

E

Easements
maintaining, 179
in Planned Development district, 91
for stormwater management, 209–210
for utilities, 230–231
Edge areas, 11
Elder cottage housing opportunities (ECHO homes). *See* Accessory dwellings; Senior housing regulations
Emergency Planning and Community RIght-to-Know Act of 1986, 4
Emergency services adequacy, 289
Employment center area design, 11
Enabling legislation on public facility adequacy, 299–300
Endangered Species Act of 1973, 4
Energy, LEED® rating system, 196–197
Energy Policy and Conservation Act of 1975, 4
Enforcement of procedures, 159–160
England, development influence from, 2
Enlargement of nonconforming use, 368, 370. *See also* Nonconforming use
"Environmental Density Formula," 264
Environmental protection. *See also* Landscaping/screening; Leadership in Energy and Environmental Design (LEED®)
in commercial retrofit, 48
in conservation subdivision use pattern, 39–43
in conventional versus traditional neighborhood development, 12
development standards, 240–244, 263–264
driving increase affecting, 58
extraction activity regulations, 322–324
in stormwater management design, 210, 212–214
subdivision degrading, 7–8
in transit-oriented development, 54
Equal mitigation concept, 297

Equal protection clause, 302
Escrow account, 150
Estoppel, 375. *See also* Vested rights
Euclidean zoning. *See* Conventional zoning
Europe, subdivision in, 171
Exaction, versus adequate public facilities ordinance, 285
Expansion of nonconforming use, 372. *See also* Nonconforming use
Expert reviews, 353
Extractive Use (EU) zoning district, 314–324
in floating zone matrix, 69
supplemental use regulations
development approvals and orders, 317–318
exemptions to, 316–317
financial assurances, 324
inspections and monitoring, 324
land alteration, 321–322
quarries, 315–316, 319–320
reclamation standards, 322–324
regulation of, 356
sand/gravel, 316, 320–321
separation distances, 316, 318–319
Eyebrow homes, 40

F

Fair Housing Act, 4, 178, 324, 325
Fair Housing Administration (FHA), 358
Federal Emergency Management Agency (FEMA), 42, 263, 355
Federal Highway Beautification Act of 1965, 4
Federal Land Policy and Management Act of 1976, 4
Federal Securities Act of 1934, 4
Federal Trade Commission Act of 1914, 4
Federal Uniform Relocation Assistance and Real Property Acquisitions Act of 1970, 4
Fences/walls. *See also* Landscaping/screening
development standards, 190–191, 204, 236, 258
wireless communication facility, 350
Fire department adequacy, 289
Fiscal impact analysis, 293–294
Fishing, in use matrix, 78–79
Flexible zoning. *See also* Zoning
density bonus in, 96–99, 102–103
role of, 67, 102–103
transfer of development rights in, 97, 99, 110–113
Floating zones, 69, 101
Flood control use regulations, 355
Floodplains, 260
Floor area ratio (FAR). *See also* Density
building envelope versus, 109–110
development standards, 263
in flexible zoning, 102–103
intensity ratio, 113
wireless communication facility, 350
Florida
concurrency regulations, 298
greyfield development, 62
growth management, 4, 5, 14
land-use policy, 15
legislation in, 172, 300
neighborhood participation, 165
new urbanist development, 13

official map, 20n3
state controls, 3
subdivision, 7, 171, 172
Forestry, in use matrix, 78–79
Form-based zoning, 102. *See also* Zoning
Forms. *See* Application procedures
Franchise design, 262
Front porches, 51

G

Gaithersburg, Maryland, new urbanist development in, 13
Garage sale regulations, 345
Garages, 185, 262–263, 336. *See also* Building design
Garbage collection, 91
Gas station design, 60–61, 311–312
General district. *See* Base zoning district
General Mining Act of 1872, 4
General plan. *See* Comprehensive plan
Georgia
    land-use policy, 15
    planning history, 2
    smart growth legislation, 5
    state controls, 4
Germany, development influence from, 2
Good faith, 302, 378
Grading and land disturbance, 131, 378, 423–424
Grading, development standards, 264
Granny flats. *See* Accessory dwellings
Graphics/matrices, 33–34
Gravel excavation. *See* Quarry use regulations
Green building. *See* Leadership in Energy and Environmental Design (LEED®)
Greenbelts, 59. *See also* Buffers
Greenfields, 13. *See also* Parks/open space
Greenspace, 232, 264–265. *See also* Buffers; Environmental protection; Landscaping/screening; Trees
Greyfield redevelopment, 47, 62, 63
Gross floor area (GFA), 263
Group home regulations, 324–325, 358–359
Growth management, 1, 4–5. *See also* Smart growth
Gutters. *See* Stormwater management; Streets/roads

H

Hawaii
    smart growth legislation, 5
    state controls, 3
Health, sprawl impacting, 58–59
Hearing officers, 128, 153–154, 384. *See also* Application procedures; Public hearings
Heat island effect, 196
Hillsborough County, Florida, neighborhood participation in, 165
The Home Depot, 358
Home occupation use regulations, 325–328, 359
Homeland security, 194, 266
Homeowner's Association (HOA), 178–179
Hoover, Herbert, 3
Hotels, 71
Housing. *See also* Manufactured homes; Single-family dwellings
    affordable (*see* Inclusionary zoning)
    in conventional versus traditional neighborhood development, 12
    design of (*see* Building design)
    in Planned Development district, 90
    supplemental use regulations, 334–342
        attached units, 337–340
        cottage housing developments, 341
        design elements, 335–337, 361
        manufactured homes, 330–331, 340, 361–362
        for older people, 328, 359–360
        single-family, 337
        zero lot line developments, 335, 341–342
    in use matrix, 71
Housing and Community Development Act of 1974, 4
Houston, Texas, land-use control in, 2–3
Huntersville, North Carolina, live-work units in, 360
Hunting, in use matrix, 78–79
Hybrid development, 10

I

Illinois church regulations, 361
Impact fees, versus adequate public facilities ordinances, 285, 293, 296
Impervious surface intensity ratio, 113. *See also* Parking
Improvements, development standards for, 179
Incentives. *See also* Density bonus
    affordable housing, 96, 98–99, 355
    better design, 262
    concept overview, 16
    greyfield redevelopment, 47
    infill development, 62
Inclusionary zoning
    incentives, 96, 98–99, 355
    supplemental use regulations, 328–329
Industrial buildings, in use matrix, 73–74. *See also* Commercial buildings
Industrial Heavy (IH) zoning district
    dimensional standards, 80, 89, 90
    fences and walls in, 190
    summary, 88–89
    in tier system, 68
    in use matrix, 71–79
Industrial Light (IL) zoning district
    dimensional standards, 80, 89
    fences and walls in, 190
    summary, 88
    in tier system, 68
    in use matrix, 71–79
Infill development, 62
Infrastructure. *See* Adequate public facilities ordinance (APFO); Public facilities; *specific infrastructure element*
Initiation, 162. *See also specific Code topic*
Inspections, 148, 324
Institute of Transportation Engineers (ITE), 269
Institutional facilities, in use matrix, 75–76
Intensity, 109–110, 113–115. *See also* Density
Intergovernmental agreement (IGA), 17
International Dark-Sky Association (IDA), 266
Interstate Land Sales Full Disclosure Act of 1968, 4, 7

J

Joint commission approach, 17
Joint planning areas (JPA), 17
Joint venture subdivision development, 8
Judicial review. *See* Quasi-judicial development approval
Junkyards use regulations, 329–330

K

Kansas City, Missouri
    gas station design, 356
    zoning, 3, 105
Kitsap County, Washington, subdivision in, 170

L

Land-Based Classification Standards (LBCS), 103–105
Land Development Code (LDC)
    agencies/officials needed for, 383–385
    guidelines for writing, 33–37
    how to use, 14–20, 31–32
    legal status of, 387–388
    role of, 1, 33
    rules of interpretation, 389
Land disturbance. *See* Grading and land disturbance
Land-use control, 1–3, 8
Land-use intensity (LUI) ratios, 114–115
Landfills, 343–344
Landscaping/screening. *See also* Buffers; Environmental protection; Fences/walls; Lot design; Trees
    development standards, 231–240
        acceptable materials, 197–198, 232, 265
        building landscaping, 237, 264–265
        cul-de-sacs, 224, 225
        entrance landscaping, 237–238
        goal of, 231
        house-lot landscaping, 238
        LEED® rating system, 196
        lighting, 193
        parking lot landscaping, 237
        parks/open areas, 204
        plant area protection, 233
        streetscape landscaping, 236–237
        tree preservation, 238–240, 277–278
        written plan for, 232
    document requirements, 425–426
    supplemental use regulations, 342, 350–351
    use patterns and
        campus-style development, 46
        commercial retrofit, 48
        conservation subdivisions, 43
        neighborhood centers, 44
        traditional neighborhood development, 52
        transit-oriented development, 54
Language
    Code terminology listing, 389–416
    for readability, 15–16
    technical writing principles, 33–37
Laws of the Indies, 1–2
Leadership in Energy and Environmental Design (LEED®). *See also* Environmental protection
    building practices point system, 194, 195–198, 259
    summary, 278–279
    trend in, 13, 14
Legal status of Land Development Code, 387–388
Legislative development approval, 120, 163
Legislative hearings, 128
Letter of credit, 149, 324
Letter of map revision, 42, 430
Levels of service (LOS), 285, 286, 287, 288, 298. *See also* Adequate public facilities ordinance (APFO); Public facilities
Lighting
    development standards, 191–194
    in LEED® rating system, 196
    loading areas, 258
    parking areas, 257
    summary, 265–266
    wireless communication facilities, 349–350
Livability space intensity ratio, 113
Live-work units, 332, 333. *See also* Mixed use development
Loading area development standards, 258–259
Local Government Antitrust Act of 1984, 4
Lot design. *See also* Building design; Landscaping/screening; Setbacks
    development standards, 179–183, 181–182 (*see also* Setbacks)
        frontage, 179–180
        size reduction, 183
        stormwater management, 210, 211–212
        summary, 267
    supplemental use regulations, 338, 340, 341
    use patterns and
        campus-style development, 45–46
        commercial retrofit, 47
        conservation subdivisions, 40, 41
        neighborhood centers, 44
        traditional neighborhood development, 50–51, 60–61
        transit-oriented development, 53
    by zoning district, 90, 92, 108–109

M

Maine
    smart growth legislation, 5
    state controls, 4
Maintenance bond, 150, 171
Major subdivision, 168
Manning's roughness coefficients, 209
Manufactured homes
    supplemental use regulations, 330–331, 340, 361–362
    zoning and design, 186
Mariemont, Ohio, zoning in, 105
Maryland
    capacity allocation, 298, 299
    development approval, 35, 37
    gas station design, 61
    legislation in, 5, 300
    new urbanist development, 13
    state controls, 4
Massachusetts
    parking, 268
    planning history, 2
Master plan. *See* Comprehensive plan

Master planned development, 70. *See also* Planned Development (PD) zoning district
Master site plan, 92
Matrices. *See* Graphics/matrices
Mecklenburg County, North Carolina, joint planning in, 17
Memoranda of Understanding (MOU), 17
Mid-America Regional Council, 9
Mining, in use matrix, 79. *See also* Extractive Use (EU) zoning district
Ministerial development approval, 120
Minneapolis-St. Paul, Minnesota
　growth management, 5
　zoning, 3
Minor subdivision, 168–169
Missouri
　gas station design, 356
　zoning, 3, 105
Mixed residential areas, 11
Mixed use development
　in neighborhood design, 11
　reducing vehicle trips, 57
　segregation of use versus, 3
　supplemental use regulations, 332, 333, 360
　in tier system, 68
Mixed Use (MX) zoning district, 92
Model Land Development Code (ALI Code), 260
Model ordinance approach, 16–17
Monitoring. *See* Inspections
Montgomery County, Maryland, capacity allocation in, 298, 299
Motels, 71
Multifamily dwellings, 41, 187. *See also* Building design; Housing
Multijurisdictional codes, 16–17

N

National Association of Home Builders, 13
National Commission on Urban Problems, 6
National Environmental Policy Act of 1969, 4
National Historic Preservation Act of 1966, 4
Neighborhood, commercial. *See* Commercial Neighborhood (CN) zoning district
Neighborhood centers, 11, 43–45, 56
Neighborhood cluster streets, 41
Neighborhood meetings, 49, 164. *See also* Public hearings
Neighborhood participation, 129–130, 165–166
Neighborhood Preservation (NP) zoning district, 92–94
Neighborhood registration, 129
Neighborhood Suburban (NS) zoning district
　dimensional standards, 80, 83
　summary, 82
　in tier system, 68
　in use matrix, 71–79
Neighborhood Urban (NU) zoning district
　dimensional standards, 80, 83
　summary, 82–83
　in tier system, 68
　in use matrix, 71–79
Neotraditional development, 8, 11. *See also* New Urbanism
Nevada growth management, 5
New Hampshire enabling legislation, 300

New Jersey
　accessory apartments, 356
　capacity allocation, 298–299
　group homes, 359
　smart growth legislation, 5
　state controls, 3, 4
　subdivision ruling, 7–8
　transfer of development rights, 112
New Mexico subdivisions, 7, 171
New urbanism
　conventional subdivisions versus, 56, 57
　design in, 10–13
　reasons for using, 1
　traditional neighborhood development in, 8–9 (*see also* Traditional neighborhood development (TND))
　transit-oriented development in, 5, 9–10 (*see also* Transit-oriented development (TOD))
New York
　Central Park design in, 2
　environmental controls, 4
　Ramapo landmark decision, 4–5, 6, 293, 294, 295, 300, 302
　well pollution ruling, 7
Nodal zoning, 101–102
Noise ordinances, 319
Nonbinding codes, 16–17
Nonconforming lots, 368, 370–371
Nonconforming sites, 368, 369–370
Nonconforming structures, 368, 370
Nonconforming use. *See also* Vested rights
　categories of, 367, 368
　certificate of, 371
　changes to, 368–369
　continuation of, 367
　defined, 375
　document requirements, 426
　enlargement of, 368
　establishing right to, 376
　expansion of, 372
　loss compensation for, 376
　lots, 368, 370–371
　regulation summary, 375–376
　sites, 368, 369–370
　structures, 368, 370
　termination of, 371–372, 376
North American Industry Classification System (NAICS), 79–81, 103, 104
North Carolina
　joint planning, 17
　live-work units, 360
　new urbanist development, 13
　parking, 268
　vested rights, 377
Notice requirements, 126–128
Nuisance law, 2–3

O

Office (O) zoning district
　dimensional standards, 80, 84
　summary, 83–84
　in tier system, 68
　in use matrix, 71–79
Office of Interstate Land Sales Registration (OILSR), 7

Official map, 20n3, 69
Ohio
    big-box stores, 357
    zoning, 105
Olmstead, Frederick Law, 2
Open space. See Parks/open space
Operations plan, 424
Orange County, North Carolina, joint planning in, 17
Oregon
    big-box development, 358
    land-use policy, 3, 5, 15
    parking, 268, 269
    residential design regulations, 361
    subdivision, 172
    transit-oriented development, 57
Orientation, 12, 186, 340. See also Building design; Lot design
Orlando, Florida, new urbanist development in, 13
Outdoor display/sales, 84, 86, 87, 333–334
Outdoor storage, 244–245, 334
Overlay zoning district
    defined, 18–19
    role of, 67
    summary, 101, 107–108
    types of, 69, 92–96
Oversized facilities approvals, 171

P

Paper subdivisions, 171
Parking. See also Streets/roads; Transportation
    in conventional versus traditional neighborhood development, 12
    development standards, 245–258, 267–271
        for bicycles, 247–255, 257–258
        construction/maintenance, 257
        dimensions, 256
        landscaping, 237, 265
        location, 256–257, 270
        optimum amount of, 267–270
        ratios, 245–246, 247–255, 270–271
        shared, 246, 256, 271
    supplemental use requirements
        accessory dwelling units, 310
        mixed-use buildings, 332, 333
        multifamily dwellings, 338–339, 341
    use patterns and
        campus-style development, 46
        commercial retrofit, 48
        conservation subdivisions, 41, 43
        neighborhood centers, 44, 45
        traditional neighborhood development, 52, 58, 61
        transit-oriented development, 54, 63
    by zoning district, 84, 85, 91, 113
Parks/open space
    adequate amount of, 289, 292
    development standards, 199–205
        categories, 199, 200–202
        characteristics, 203–204
        connectivity, 205
        designation, 204
        by district type, 194, 199
        fee in lieu of parks, 199, 202–203
        phasing, 204–205
    summary, 271–272
    supplemental use regulations, 331, 338, 339, 341
    in traditional neighborhood development, 11
    use patterns and
        campus-style development, 46
        commercial retrofit, 48
        neighborhood centers, 44–45
        traditional neighborhood development, 49, 51–52
        transit-oriented development, 54
    by zoning district, 91, 96, 98, 113
Patio homes, 40
Payment bond, 171
Pedestrian access
    campus-style development, 46
    commercial retrofit, 47
    conservation subdivisions, 41, 42
    dangers of, 59
    neighborhood centers, 44
    traditional neighborhood development, 11, 58, 60, 274
    transit-oriented development, 53–54
Pedestrian-oriented development, 314, 339
Penalties for code violations, 159
Pennsylvania
    big-box development, 358
    performance zoning, 113
    planning history, 2
Performance bond, 149, 171
Performance standards, 113–115. See also Density
Performance zoning, 113. See also Zoning
Permitted uses (P), 71–79, 80
Phasing of projects, 166, 204–205, 329
Philadelphia, Pennsylvania, planning history in, 2
Planned Development (PD) zoning district
    defined, 19
    negative aspects of, 55
    summary, 89–92, 101, 108
    in tier system, 68
Planning commission, 133–134, 383–384
Planning department, 384
Plats
    approving and amending, 151–152, 377
    document requirements
        digital, 417, 421–422
        summary, 418–420
        vacation and subdivision, 172, 426, 429–430
    final, 145–147, 418–420
    preliminary, 143–145, 166, 418–420
    sketch, 142
Point system of capacity allocation, 299
Police department adequacy, 289
Pollution, from increased driving, 58. See also Environmental protection
Portland, Oregon
    big-box development, 358
    parking, 268, 269
    residential design regulations, 361
    transit-oriented development, 57
Postal Reorganization Act of 1969, 4
Preapplication conference, 121, 351
Premature subdivision, 7, 171, 293
Procedures. See Application procedures
Prohibited uses, 71–79, 80

Public assembly structures, 74–75, 344–345
Public facilities, 285–306
　adequacy of, 287–289 (*see also* Adequate public facilities ordinance (APFO))
　advancing capacity of, 287–288, 296, 302 (*see also* Capital improvements program (CIP))
　deficiencies in multiple, 296
　developers providing excess, 296–297
　development agreements, 298
　tracking capacity of, 296
　use patterns and, 47, 50, 54
　utilities extensions, 293–294
　variance requests, 155
Public hearings, 127–128, 163, 164–165
Public involvement
　documentation of, 422
　neighborhood participation, 129–130, 165–166
　notice provisions, 126–127
　public hearings, 127–128, 163, 164–165
Puerto Rico development rights, 112

Q
Quadrangle homes, 41
Quarry use regulations, 315–316, 319–320
Quasi-judicial development approval, 120, 163, 170
Quasi-judicial public hearings, 127–128
Queen Creek, Arizona, parking in, 268

R
Ramapo, New York, landmark decision, 4–5, 6, 293, 294, 295, 300, 302
Ramapo Plan
　history of, 4–5
　point scale, 294–295, 299
　role of, 293
Reclamation plan, 322–324, 424–425
Recording procedures, 162. *See also* Application procedures
Recreation space intensity ratio, 113
Redmond, Washington, parking in, 268
Regional stormwater management program (RSWMP), 205, 214. *See also* Stormwater management
Religious Land Use and Institutional Property Act of 2000 (RLUIPA), 4, 360–361
Religious land use regulations, 355, 360–361
Reservation of capacity, 286, 296
Residential buildings, in use matrix, 71. *See also* Housing
Residential Estate (RE) zoning district
　annexed territory, 70
　dimensional standards, 80, 82
　summary, 81–82
　in tier system, 68
　in use matrix, 71–79
Resource Conservation and Recovery Act of 1976, 4
Resource Protection (RP) zoning district, 68, 71–79, 80, 81
Restrictive covenants, 2–3
Retrofit use pattern, 46–48
Rezoning. *See also* Zoning
　documentation requirements, 418–420, 426–427
　procedures for, 167–168
　vested rights and, 378
Rhode Island
　smart growth legislation, 5
　state controls, 4
Right-of-way
　development standards, 210, 219, 220–221, 224
　zoning for, 99
Right-to-travel challenges, 302
Riparian buffers, 240–242, 263. *See also* Buffers
Roads. *See* Streets/roads
Rural tier, 68

S
Sacramento, California
　new urbanism, 13
　transit-oriented development, 57
Safe Drinking Water Act of 1996, 4
Sampling of construction materials, 177–178
San Antonio, Texas
　design in, 2, 361
　parking, 268
San Diego, California
　growth management, 5
　Ramapo system, 294–295
　transit-oriented development, 57
San Francisco, California
　nonconventional zoning, 105
　parking, 268
Sand excavation. *See* Quarry use regulations
Santa Fe, New Mexico, design of, 2
Satellite antenna use regulations, 342, 355
Savannah, Georgia, planning history, 2
Scale. *See also* Building design; Building envelope
　supplemental use regulations, 309, 335
　by zoning district, 84, 85, 86, 87
Scope of approval, 162, 167. *See also* Application procedures
Scottsdale, Arizona
　green buildings, 13–14
　LEED® program, 279
Screening. *See* Landscaping/screening
Seaside, Florida, new urbanist development in, 13
Seattle, Washington, parking in, 268
Segregation of use, 3
Self-storage Facility (SSF) zoning district, 69, 343
Senior housing regulations, 328, 359–360
Separation distances. *See* Buffers
Septic systems. *See* Utilities
Service entrances/service yards, 85
Set-aside systems, 298, 328–329
Setbacks. *See also* Lot design
　antenna supporting structures, 349
　buffers versus, 265
　in campus-style development, 46
　development standards for, 180, 181–182
　in Planned Development district, 90–91
Sewer, 289, 298, 331. *See also* Utilities
Sidewalks, 147, 182, 226. *See also* Pedestrian access; Streets/roads
Signs, use regulations for, 351, 354, 355
Single-family dwellings. *See also* Building design
　in conservation subdivisions, 40, 41
　development standards, 184–186
　supplemental use regulations, 337

in traditional neighborhood development, 51, 59
Site plan
  checklist, 432
  document requirements, 424
  master, 92
  procedures, 140–141
  requirements summary, 418–420
  in vested rights claim, 378
Slope construction, 242–243, 263–264
Smart growth, 4–5, 13. *See also* Growth management, New urbanism
Solid waste facility use regulations, 343–344
South Carolina
  nonconventional zoning, 105
  state controls, 4
Special assessment districts, 179, 376
Special district, 19
Special use district, 101, 377–378
Spot zoning, 101–102
Sprawl
  components of, 8
  development codes identifying, 13
  health impacted by, 58–59
  history of, 5, 6
St. Paul, Minnesota. *See* Minneapolis-St. Paul, Minnesota
Standard City Planning Enabling Act (SPEA), 3, 5–6, 260
Standard State Zoning Enabling Act (SZEA), 3, 33, 300
State Environmental Quality Review Act, 264
Statutory vested rights, 372. *See also* Vested rights
Stealth wireless communication facilities, 352–353
Storage
  for home occupations, 326–327
  outdoor, 244–245, 334
  self-storage facilities, 69, 343
Stormwater management. *See also* Water
  in commercial retrofit, 47
  in conservation subdivisions, 42
  in construction plans, 147
  development standards for, 205–218
    drainage channels/watercourses, 215, 217
    drainage easements, 209–210
    LEED® rating system, 195
    level of service, 206
    low-impact design, 210, 212–214
    payments, 206
    regional program for, 205
    runoff computation, 206–209
    site design/grading, 210, 211–212
    storm sewers, 217
    stormwater detention, 214–215
    street design, 215, 216, 217–218, 276
    summary, 264, 272–273
    system criteria, 206
  document requirements, 427–429
  manufactured home communities, 331
Streets/roads. *See also* Block design; Driveways; Transportation
  in conventional development, 12
  development standards for, 218–228, 273–277
    access/driveways, 226–227, 276–277
    classification, 218, 219
    connectivity, 222–224, 275
    cul-de-sacs, 224, 225, 275–276
    gated subdivisions, 227–228
    geometric design, 218, 219–222, 274–275
    intersections, 224
    lighting, 225
    names and signage, 224–225
    pavement design, 225–226, 276
    private, 225
    sidewalks, 147, 182, 226
    stormwater management, 215, 216, 217–218, 276
    traffic calming, 228, 229, 277
  document requirements, 429
  manufactured home communities, 331
  in Planned Development district, 91
  subdivision requirements for, 7
  in traditional neighborhood development, 11, 12, 59–60
Subdivisions
  application procedures, 141–152
    applicability and general rules, 141–142
    classification, 142
    construction plans, 147–148
    dedication/acceptance, 151
    improvement agreements, 149–150
    plats, 142–147, 151–152, 166
    summary, 168–172
    variances, 150–151
  conventional design of, 8
  defined, 168
  duplexes in, 337–338
  plat application requirements, 429–430
  premature, 7, 171, 293
  regulation history, 5–8
Substantive due process, 301–302
Suburban tier, 68
Suffolk, Virginia, residential design regulations in, 361
Sullivan, Louis, 2
Sunset period, 164
Supplemental use regulations, 307–366. *See also* Zoning
  accessory uses, 307–308, 355–356
  affordable housing, 328–329
  auto-oriented development, 69, 310–313, 356–357
  commercial buildings, 313–314, 357–358
  extractive uses (*see* Extractive Use (EU) zoning district)
  group homes, 324–325, 358–359
  home occupations, 325–328, 359
  junkyards/auto graveyards, 329–330
  mixed-use/live-work buildings, 332, 333, 360
  outdoor display areas, 333–334
  outdoor storage, 334
  religious institutions, 4, 355, 360–361
  residential dwelling units (*see* Housing)
  role of, 67
  satellite dish antennas, 342, 355
  self-storage facilities, 69, 343
  solid waste facilities, 343–344
  temporary uses, 316, 344–345
  utilities, 345–346
  wireless communication (*see* Wireless communication facilities)
Surety bond, 150, 324
Sustainability. *See* Leadership in Energy and Environmental Design (LEED®)

Subject Index 449

T
"T model" design, 62
Takings litigation, 300–301
Technical writing principles, 33–37. *See also* Language
Telecommunications Act of 1996, 4, 362–363
Temporary improvements, 150
Temporary uses, 316, 344–345
Tennessee smart growth legislation, 5
Termination of nonconforming use, 370, 371, 376. *See also* Nonconforming use
Testing of construction materials, 177–178
Texas
    design regulations, 2, 361
    group home, 358
    irrigation regulations, 265
    land-use control, 2–3
    parking, 268
    subdivisions, 7, 171
Tier system, 68, 69. *See also* Growth management
Time limits in application process, 121
Title VIII of the Civil Rights Act of 1968. *See* Fair Housing Act
TOD core (TOD-C), 52–53. *See also* Transit-oriented development (TOD)
TOD periphery (TOD-P), 52–53. *See also* Transit-oriented development (TOD)
Townhouses, 41, 338–339. *See also* Housing
Toxic Substances Control Act of 1976, 4
Traditional neighborhood development (TND)
    concept overview, 8–9 (*see also* New Urbanism)
    development rights transfer in, 112–113
    use patterns, 48–52, 56–61, 274
Traditional tier, 68
Traffic calming, 228, 229, 277
Traffic impact analysis (TIA), 122–125, 285, 430–431
Transfer of development rights (TDR), 97, 99, 110–113
Transit-oriented development (TOD)
    concept overview, 9–10
    development rights transfer in, 112–113
    growth management with, 5
    traditional neighborhood development versus, 57
    use patterns, 52–54, 62–63
Transportation. *See also* Streets/roads
    adequate facilities for, 288, 291–292, 297, 298
    traffic impact analyses, 122–125, 285, 430–431
    in transit-oriented development (*see* Transit-oriented development (TOD))
    in use matrix, 76–77
    use patterns and, 41–42, 46, 47, 51
Transportation corridors, 112
Transportation Demand Management (TDM), 269–270
Transportation Equity Act for the 21st Century, 4, 268
Trees. *See also* Landscaping/screening
    in Airport Overlay district, 94
    in commercial retrofit, 48
    development standards, 236–240, 277–278
    preservation documentation requirements, 431
Trust agreement, 149
Truth in Lending Act of 1968, 4

U
Unitary view, 33

United Kingdom, parking in, 268–269, 270
United Parcel Service (UPS), 35, 37
United States Green Building Council (USGBC), 13–14, 194, 278. *See also* Leadership in Energy and Environmental Design (LEED®)
Urban Land Institute, 58, 277
"Urban vestibule" design, 62
U.S. Department of Agriculture Natural Resources Conservation Service, 42
U.S. Department of Health and Human Services, 266
U.S. Department of Housing and Urban Development (HUD), 362
U.S. Department of Transportation, 266
U.S. Environmental Protection Agency (EPA), 266, 276
U.S. Federal Housing Administration, 114
Use matrix, 71–79, 103–105
Use patterns
    campus-style, 45–46
    commercial retrofit, 46–48, 62
    conservation subdivision, 39–43
    defined, 39
    implementing, 55–56
    infill, 62
    neighborhood center, 43–45, 56
    role of, 55
    in traditional neighborhood development, 11, 48–52, 56–61, 274
    in transit-oriented development, 52–54, 62–63
Utah, subdivision in, 168
Utilities
    in commercial retrofit, 48
    in conservation subdivisions, 42
    in construction plans, 147
    development standards
        easements, 230–231
        landscaping, 233
        multifamily dwellings, 187
        overview, 228
        underground, 264
    extension of, 293 (*see also* Adequate public facilities ordinance (APFO); Public facilities)
    supplemental use regulations, 310, 331, 340, 345–346
    by zoning district, 77, 78, 91, 96

V
Variances. *See also specific Code topic*
    Airport Overlay district, 94
    application process, 150–154, 172
    conditional zoning, 136–137
    development approvals, 177, 260–261
    drawbacks to seeking, 55
    supplemental use, 353
    vested rights and, 373
    wireless communication facilities, 353–354
Vehicle access. *See* Driveways; Parking; Streets/roads; Transportation
Vehicle miles traveled (VMT), 57, 58, 60
Vermont
    big-box stores, 357–358
    legislation in, 3, 5, 300
    subdivision, 169

Vested rights. *See also* Nonconforming use
    claiming, 377–378
    defined, 375, 377
    determination of, 372–374, 431–432
    estoppel versus, 375
  revocation/divestment of, 379
  scope of, 378–379
  in subdivision approval, 170
"Vestibule and liner" design, 62
Violations of code procedures, 159–160
Virginia
  incentive zoning, 262
  LEED® program, 279
  residential design regulations, 361
Vision statement, 31
Vistas, 49–50

W

Wal-Mart, 357–358
Walkability, 11, 58. *See also* Pedestrian access
Walkways. *See* Sidewalks
Walls. *See* Fences/walls
Washington State
  land-use policy, 15
  legislation in, 4, 5, 300
  parking, 268
  subdivision, 170
Water. *See also* Stormwater management
  LEED® rating system, 196
  manufactured home communities, 331
  public facilities for, 289, 298
  riparian buffers, 240–242, 263 (*see also* Buffers)
  subdivision affecting, 7–8
Weighting system of capacity allocation, 299
Wetland development standards, 243–244. *See also* Environmental protection
Wide-shallow lots, 41, 267
Wireless communication facilities, 346–354
  antenna structures, 349–352, 353, 362–363
  development review process, 347–349
  discontinuances and variances, 353–354
  expert review, 353
  standards, 349
  stealth locations, 352–353
  submission requirements, 349
Wisconsin
  smart growth legislation, 5
  water protection, 7
Writing development code. *See* Language

Y

Yard sale regulations, 345

Z

"Z" lot homes, 40, 267
Zero lot line (ZLL) developments, 84, 267, 335, 341–342
Zipper lots, 267
Zoning, 67–117. *See also* Rezoning; Special assessment districts; Supplemental use regulations
  for affordable housing (*see* Inclusionary zoning)
  application procedures (*see also* Conditional use permit (CUP))
    code amendments, 133–135, 162–163
    conditional zoning, 135–137
    plans and plan amendments, 132–133
    site plans, 140–141
    summary, 167–168
    in vested rights claim, 378
  building envelope, 115
  contract and conditional, 69, 105
  conventional versus form-based, 102
  density, 110 (*see also* Density)
  district boundaries, 69–70, 101
  district types, 67, 68–69, 100, 101 (*see also specific*)
  floating, 69
  "form-based," 57
  history of, 3
  incentive (*see* Incentives)
  intensity, 109–110, 113–115
  introduction to, 67–70
  lot standards, 108–109
  for manufactured homes, 186
  of newly annexed territory, 70
  official map, 69
  performance, 113
  procedures (*see* Application procedures)
  public facility adequacy and, 286–287
  repeal of, 387, 388
  role of, 100
  spot versus nodal, 101–102
Zoning certificates, 131–132

Bibliography

Adler, Jerry, "Bye-Bye, Suburban Dream," *Newsweek* (May 15, 1995), 40-53.

Alexander, Christopher, *A Pattern Language* (New York: Oxford University Press, 1977).

———, *The Timeless Way of Building* (New York: Oxford University Press, 1979).

American Planning Association, "The Principles of Smart Development," Planning Advisory Service Report No. 479 (Chicago: APA, 1998).

American Society of Civil Engineers, *Residential Streets*, 2d ed., co-authored with National Association of Home Builders and Urban Land Institute (Washington, DC: ULI, 1990).

American Society of Planning Officials, *Local Capital Improvements and Development Management: Case Study Method and Procedures* (Chicago: ASPO, November 1977).

Arendt, Randall G., "Rural Design Manual for Conservation and Development," *Zoning News* (October 1988), 2.

———, *Rural By Design* (Chicago: American Planning Association, 1994).

———, *Growing Greener: Putting Conservation into Local Plans and Ordinances* (Washington, DC: Island Press, 1999).

Atash, Farhad, "Redesigning Suburbia for Walking and Transit: The Emerging Concepts," 120 *J. Urb. Plng. & Devt.* 48-57 (March 1994).

Avin, Uri P., *Chewing the Cud with a PUD—Lessons from Howard County and Columbia New Town*, in Southwest Legal Foundation Institute on Planning, Zoning & Eminent Domain (1993).

———, "Design Innovation in the Urbs, Burbs and Exurbs," National Continuing Education Seminars (Madison: University of Wisconsin, 1996).

Bailey, Richard, "Mall Over: A retail hybrid helps to revitalize an inner suburban ring in Chattanooga, Tennessee," *Urban Land* (July 1998) 46-49, 84-85.

Bair, Jr., Frederick H., "Intensity Zoning: Regulating Townhouses, Apartments, and Planned Developments," Planning Advisory Service Report No. 314 (Chicago: American Planning Association, February 1976).

Bechtel, Robert, *Environment and Behavior: An Introduction* (Thousand Oaks, CA: Sage Publications, 1997).

Beimborn, E. and H. Rabinowitz, *Guidelines for Transit Sensitive Suburban Land Use Design* (Milwaukee: Center for Urban Transportation Studies, University of Wisconsin-Milwaukee, 1991).

Bishop, Kirk R., "Designing Urban Corridors," Planning Advisory Service Report No. 418 (Chicago: American Planning Association, September 1989).

Bookout, Lloyd W., "Neotraditional Town Planning: A New Vision for the Suburbs?" *Urban Land* (January 1992), 20-26.

———, "Neotraditional Town Planning: Cars, Pedestrians, and Transit," *Urban Land* (February 1992), 10-15.

———, "Neotraditional Town Planning: Bucking Conventional Codes and Standards," *Urban Land* (April 1992), 18-25.

———, "Neotraditional Town Planning: The Test of the Marketplace," *Urban Land* (June 1992), 12-17.

———, "Neotraditional Town Planning: Toward a Blending of Design Approaches," *Urban Land* (August 1992), 14-19.

Bosselman, Fred, "Time and the Regulatory Process: Recent Decisions," 1 Land Use Institute: Planning, Regulation, Litigation, Eminent Domain, and Compensation 1 (ALI-ABA Course of Study Materials, 1986).

British Department for Communities and Local Government, Planning Policy Guidance 13: Transport, available on-line at www.communities.gov.uk/index.asp?id=1144015.

Bucks County Planning Commission, *Performance Streets: A Concept and Model Standards for Residential Streets* (Doylestown, PA: BCPC, 1980).

Burby, Raymond J., Peter J. May, and Robert C. Paterson, "Improving Compliance with Regulations: Choices and Outcomes for Local Government," *JAPA* 64:3 (Summer 1998), at 324-334.

Burden, Dan, *Street Design Guidelines for Healthy Neighborhoods* (Sacramento, CA: Local Government Commission, January 1999).

Butler, JoAnn and Judith Getzels, "Home Occupation Ordinances," Planning Advisory Service Report No. 391 (Chicago: American Planning Association, October 1985).

Callies, David L. and Robert H. Freilich, *Cases and Materials on Land Use* (Minneapolis: West Publishing Co., 1986), 837.

Calthorpe, P. et al., *Design for Efficient Suburban Activity Centers* (Washington, DC: United States Department of Transportation and Federal Transit Administration, March 1997).

Calthorpe, Peter, *The Next American Metropolis: Ecology, Community, and the American Dream* (New York: Princeton Architectural Press, 1993).

Carlisle & White, "Administrative and Legislative Techniques for Resolving Vested Rights and Condemnation Issues," in Julius Sackman, *Nichols' The Law of Eminent Domain* (New York: M. Bender, 1993), Chapter 25.

Center for Urban Forest Research, "Air Quality and Parking Lot Shade," (United States Department of Agriculture Forest Service, Pacific Southwest Research Station).

Cervero, Robert, *Suburban Gridlock* (New Brunswick, NJ: Center for Urban Policy Research, 1986).

———, *America's Suburban Centers: The Land-Use Transportation Link* (Boston: Unwin-Hyman, 1989).

Childs, Mark, *Parking Spaces: A Design, Implementation, and Use Manual For Architects, Planners, and Engineers* (New York: McGraw-Hill, 1999).

City of Virginia Beach Department of Planning/Comprehensive Planning, *Crime Prevention Through Environmental Design: General Guidelines For Designing Safer Communities* (Virginia Beach, VA: City of Virginia Beach, Jan. 20, 2000).

Congress for the New Urbanism, *Charter of the New Urbanism* (New York: McGraw-Hill, 2000).

———, Local Government Commission, Surface Transportation Policy Project, *Civilizing Downtown Highways: Putting New Urbanism to Work on California's Highways* (San Francisco: Congress for the New Urbanism, 2002).

Craighead, Paul, ed., *The Hidden Design in Land Use Ordinances* (Portland: University of Southern Maine, 1991).

De Chiara, Joseph, Julius Panero, and Martin Zelnik, *Time-Saver Standards for Housing and Residential Development,* 2d ed. (New York: McGraw-Hill, 1995).

Department of Environment, Transportation and the Regions, *Planning Policy Guidance 13: Transport* (London: DETR, 2001).

Dewberry and Davis, *Land Development Handbook: Planning, Engineering, and Surveying* (New York: McGraw-Hill, 1996).

Dock, Frederick, William Morrish, and Carol Swenson, "Design/Development Principles for Livable Suburban Arterial Roadways," Minnesota Department of Transportation and University of Minnesota Design Center for the American Landscape, Report No. 2001-17 (June 2001).

Dover, Kohl & Partners, *Alternative Methods of Land Development Regulation*. Prepared for the Town of Fort Myers Beach, Florida, by Victor Dover, AICP, Sept. 2, 1996) (posted at www.spikowski.com/victor_dover.htm).

Duany, Andres and Elizabeth Plater-Zyberk, *Towns and Town-Making Principles*, 2d ed. (Cambridge, MA: Harvard University Graduate School of Design, 1992).

Duany, Andres, Elizabeth Plater-Zyberk, and Richard Shearer, "Zoning for Traditional Neighborhoods," *Land Development* (Fall 1992), 20-26.

Duany, Andres et al., *Suburban Nation: The Rise of Sprawl and the Decline of the American Dream* (New York: North Point Press, 2000).

East Midlands Regional Local Government Association. Statement of EMRLGA in Respect of Matter 5.4. (East Midlands, UK: East Midlands Regional Local Government Association, 2000), available on-line at www.emrlga.gov.uk/docs/5.4.pdf.

Ewing, Reid, "The Evolution of New Community Planning Concepts," *Urban Land* (June 1990), 13-17.

———, *Developing Successful New Communities* (Washington, DC: Urban Land Institute, 1991).

———, *Pedestrian- and Transit-Friendly Design* (Tallahassee: Florida Department of Transportation, March 1996).

Ewing, Reid et al., *Best Development Practices: Doing the Right Thing and Making Money at the Same Time* (Tallahassee: Florida Department of Community Affairs, January 1997).

Ferguson, Erik, "Office Development, Parking Management, and Travel Behavior: The Case of Midtown Atlanta," *Journal of Transportation Statistics* (May 1999).

Freedman, Jonathan, *Crowding and Behavior* (New York: Viking Press, 1975).

Freilich, Robert H., "A Growth Management Program for San Diego." Report to the San Diego City Council and Planning Commission (July 8, 1976).

Freilich, R. and J. Ragsdale, "Timing and Sequential Controls—The Essential Basis for Effective Regional Planning: An Analysis of the New Directions for Land Use Control in the Minneapolis-St. Paul Metropolitan Region," 58 *Minn. L. Rev.* 1009 (1974).

Freilich, R.H. and S.P. Chinn, "Transportation Corridors: Shaping and Financing Urbanization Through Integration of Eminent Domain," Zoning and Growth Management Techniques, 55 *UMKC L. Rev.* 153, 206-07 (1987).

Freilich, Robert H. and Eric O. Stuhler, *The Land Use Awakening: Zoning Law in the Seventies* (Washington, DC: American Bar Association, 1981).

Freilich, Robert H. and S. Mark White, "Transportation Congestion and Growth Management: Comprehensive Approaches to Resolving America's Major Quality of Life Crisis," 24 *Loy. L.A. L. Rev.* 915, 935 (June 1991).

Freilich, Robert H., Elizabeth A. Garvin, and S. Mark White, "Economic and Growth Management Objectives: How to Marry the Two Using Regional Transit," 16 *U. Puget Sound L. Rev.* 949 (1993).

Freilich, R. and M. Leitner, *County Growth Management Regulation: A Guide for Zoning and Subdivision Administration*, C. Forrest, ed. (Urbana-Champaign: University of Illinois, 1979).

Freilich, Robert H. and Michael M. Schultz, *Model Subdivision Regulations,* 2d ed. (Chicago: American Planning Association, 1995).

Gibbs, Robert, "Main Street Retail," *New Urban Publications* (2001).

Gleeson, Michael E. et al. "Urban Growth Management Systems: An Evaluation of Policy-Related Research," Planning Advisory Service Report Nos. 309/310 (Chicago: American Planning Association, August 1975).

Hanke, R., "Planned Unit Development and Land Use Intensity," 114 *U. Pa. L. Rev.* 15 (1965).

Hershey, S. S. and C. Garmise, *Streamlining local regulations: A handbook for reducing housing and development costs* (Washington, DC: U. S. Department of Housing and Urban

Development/Government Printing Office (HUD-1114-PA), 1983/87).

Homburger, Wolfgang et al., *Residential Street Design and Traffic Control* (Englewood Cliffs, NJ: Prentice Hall, 1989).

Institute of Transportation Engineers, *Guidelines for Residential Subdivision Street Design*, ITE Publication No. RP-011C (Washington, DC: ITE, 1993).

International Dark-Sky Association, *Outdoor Lighting Code Handbook*, Version 1.13 (Tucson: IDSA, December 2000/January 2002).

Jakle, John A. and Keith A. Sculle, *The Gas Station in America* (Baltimore: Johns Hopkins University Press, 1994).

Jarvis, Frederick D., *Site Planning and Community Design for Great Neighborhoods* (Washington, DC: Home Builder Press, National Association of Home Builders, August 1993).

Johnson, R.A., S.I. Schwartz, and S. Tracy, "Growth Phasing and Resistance to Infill Development in Sacramento County," 54 *JAPA* 434 (1984).

Kaplan, Sam Hall, "The Holy Grid: A Skeptic's View," *Planning* (November 1990), 10-11.

Kelbaugh, Doug, ed., *The Pedestrian Pocket Book: A New Suburban Design Strategy* (New York: Princeton Architectural Press, 1989).

Kelly, Eric D. and Gary J. Raso, "Sign Regulation for Small and Midsize Communities," Planning Advisory Service Report No. 419 (Chicago: American Planning Association, 1989).

Kendig, Lane et al., *Performance Zoning* (Chicago: American Planning Association, 1980).

Kendig, Lane, "New Standards for Nonresidential Uses," Planning Advisory Service Report No. 405 (Chicago: American Planning Association, December 1987).

Knack, Ruth Eckdish, "Repent, Ye Sinners, Repent," *Planning* (August 1989), 4-8.

Kulash, Walter, Joe Anglin, and David Marks, "Traditional Neighborhood Development: Will the Traffic Work?," *Development* (July/August 1990), 21-23.

Langdon, Philip, "A Good Place to Live," *The Atlantic Monthly* (March 1988), 39.

———, "Pumping Up Suburban Downtowns," *Planning* (July 1990), 22-28.

———, "How Portland Does It: A City that Protects its Thriving, Civil Core," *Urban Design* (November 1992), 134-141.

LeCraw, Charles S., Jr. and Wilbur S. Smith, *Zoning Applied to Parking* (Saugatuck, CN: Eno Foundation for Highway Traffic Control, Inc., 1947).

Listokin, David and Carole Walker, *The Subdivision and Site Plan Handbook* (New Brunswick, NJ: Center for Urban Policy Research, 1989).

Loughlin, Peter J., *Land Use Planning and Zoning*, 3d ed. (New York: Lexis Publishing, New Hampshire Practice Series, 2000).

Lynch, Kevin and Gary Hack, *Site Planning* (Cambridge, MA: MIT Press, 1984).

Mandelker, Daniel R. and William R. Ewald, Jr., *Street Graphics and the Law* (Chicago: American Planning Association, 1988).

Marshall, Alex, *How Cities Work: Suburbs, Sprawl, and the Roads Not Taken* (Austin: University of Texas Press, 2000).

McHarg, Ian L., *Design with Nature* (Garden City, NY: Natural History Press, 1969).

Meck, Stuart, FAICP, gen. ed., *Growing Smart™ Legislative Guidebook: Model Statutes for Planning and the Management of Change* (Chicago: American Planning Association, 2002).

Metro Council, *Metro 2040 Land-Use Code Workbook: A Guide for Updating Local Land Use Codes* (now called *Livable Communities Workbook*) (Portland, OR: Metro Council, 1998), available on-line at www.metro-region.org/article.cfm?ArticleID=436.

Millard-Ball, Adam, "Putting on Their Parking Caps," *Planning* (April 2002).

Miller, Catherine G., *Carscape: A Parking Handbook* (Columbus, IN: published for the Irwin-Sweeney-Miller Foundation by Washington Street Press, 1988).

Morgan and Shonkwiler, "Urban Development and Statewide Planning: Challenges of the 1980's," 61 *Or. L. Rev.* 351 (1982).

Moskowitz, Harvey S. and Carl G. Lindbloom, *The New Illustrated Book of Development Definitions* (New Brunswick, NJ: Center for Urban Policy Research, 1993).

Mott, Seward H., *Commercial Parking In Residential Areas: A Transitional Use Under Zoning* (Washington, DC: Urban Land Institute, 1948).

Nashua Regional Planning Commission, *Non-Residential Development: Community Character Guidelines* (Nashua, NH: NRPC, August 2000).

National Association of Home Builders, *Land Development Manual* (Washington, DC: NAHB, 1969).

———, *Smart Growth: Building Better Places to Live, Work and Play* (Washington, DC: NAHB, 1999).

National Crime Prevention Council, *Designing Safer Communities: A Crime Prevention Through Environmental Design Handbook* (Washington, DC: NCPC, 1997).

Nelessen, Anton C., *Visions for a New American Dream*, 2d ed. (Chicago: American Planning Association, 1994).

New Hampshire Office of State Planning, *Outdoor Lighting*, Technical Bulletin 16 (Summer 2001).

"New Traditionalism in Suburban Design," *Zoning News* (June 1989), 1-2.

New Urban Publications, Inc., *New Urbanism: Comprehensive Report and Best Practices Guide*, 2d ed. (Ithica, NY: New Urban Publications, 2001).

Newman, Oscar, *Defensible Space: Crime Prevention through Urban Design* (New York: Collins Books, 1973).

Okamoto, Paul, "Designing the Ecological Suburb? The Neotraditionalists: Peter Calthorpe and Andres Duany/Elizabeth Plater-Zyberk," *The Urban Ecologist* (Fall 1991), 7, 14-15.

Oregon Department of Transportation, *Main Street . . . When a Highway Runs Through It: A Handbook for Oregon Communities and the Supporting Workshop Series* (Salem: ODT, November 1999).

Patton, Phil, "In Seaside, Florida, the Forward Thing is to Look Backward," *Smithsonian* (January 1991), 82-93.

Pennsylvania Department of Community Affairs, "Reducing Barriers to Affordable Housing," Planning Series No. 10, (Harrisburg: PDCA, January 1991).

Porter, Douglas R., Patrick L. Phillips and Terry J. Lassar, *Flexible Zoning: How it Works* (Washington, DC: Urban Land Institute, 1988).

PWC Global Strategic Real Estate Research Group, *Greyfield Regional Mall Study* (San Francisco: Congress for the New Urbanism, January 2001).

Raad, Tamim, "Creating Regional Parking Policies." Paper presented at "Moving Beyond Planning: A Conference on Transportation Demand Management" (2002), available on-line at www.best.bc.ca/resources/conference/pdf/regionalparkingpolicies.pdf.

Sanders, Welford and David Mosena, "Changing Development Standards for Affordable Housing," Planning Advisory Service Report No. 371 (Chicago: American Planning Association, October 1982).

Sanders, Welford, Judith Getzels, David Mosena, and JoAnn Butler, "Affordable Single-Family Housing: A Review of Development Standards," Planning Advisory Service Report No. 385 (Chicago: American Planning Association, August 1984).

Schneider, Devon M., David R. Godschalk, and Norman Axler, "The Carrying Capacity Concept as a Planning Tool," Planning Advisory Service Report No. 338 (Chicago: American Planning Association, December 1978).

Schwab, Jim, "When Cities and Counties Cooperate," *Zoning News* (November 1993).

Scott, K.I., J.R. Simpson, and E.G. McPherson, "Effects of Tree Cover on Parking Lot Microclimate and Vehicle Emissions," 25 *Journal of Aboriculture*, No. 3, at 129-142 (1999);

Shoup, Donald, "Cashing Out Employer-Paid Parking," Report No. FTA-CA-11-0035092-1 (Washington, DC: United States Department of Transportation, 1992).

Shoup, Donald C., *The Trouble with Minimum Parking Requirements* (Los Angeles: Department of Urban Planning, School of Public Policy and Social Research, University of California, Los Angeles, 2002), available on-line at www.vtpi.org/shoup.pdf.

Slater, David C. and Marya Morris, "A Critical Look at Neotraditional Town Planning," Planning Advisory Service Memo (Chicago: American Planning Association, November 1990), 1-3.

Smith, Thomas P., "Flexible Parking Requirements," Planning Advisory Service Report No. 377 (Chicago: American Planning Association, August 1983).

Snohomish County Transportation Authority, *A Guide to Land Use and Public Transportation for Snohomish County, Washington, Vol. I* (Lynwood, WA: SCTA, 1989).

———, *A Guide to Land Use and Public Transportation—Volume II: Applying the Concepts* (Lynwood, WA: SCTA, 1993).

Southwest Washington Regional Transportation Council, "Executive Summary: Transportation Futures Committee Report" (Vancouver, WA: SWRTC, December 1996), available on-line at www.rtc.wa.gov/studies/archive/tfc/execsum.htm.

Spielberg, Frank, "The Traditional Neighborhood Development: How Will Traffic Engineers Respond?" *ITE Journal* (1989).

Sucher, David, *City Comforts: How to Build an Urban Village* (Seattle: City Comforts Press, 1994).

Sutro, Suzanne, "Reinventing the Village: Planning, Zoning, and Design Strategies," Planning Advisory Service Report No. 430 (Chicago: American Planning Association, December 1990).

Thompson, J. William and Kim Sorvig, *Sustainable Landscape Construction: A Guide to Green Building Outdoors* (Washington, DC: Island Press, 2000).

Tolles, Bryant F., Jr., and Carolyn K. Tolles, *New Hampshire Architecture: An Illustrated Guide* (Hanover: University Press of New England, 1979).

Transit Cooperative Research Program, "Strategies to Attract Auto Users to Public Transportation," TCRP Report 40 (Washington, DC: National Academy Press, 1998), available on-line at gulliver.trb.org/publications/tcrp/tcrp_rpt_40.pdf.

United States Department of Housing and Urban Development, *Affordable Housing: Guidelines for State and Local Government* (Washington, DC: Office of Policy Development & Research, November 1991).

———, *Proposed Model Land Development Standards and Accompanying State Enabling Legislation* (Upper Marlboro, MD: National Association of Home Builders Research Center, June 1993).

United States Environmental Protection Agency, Urban and Economic Development Division, *Parking Alternatives: Making Way for Urban Infill and Brownfield Redevelopment* (Washington, DC: US EPA, 1999), available on-line at smartgrowth.org/pdf/PRKGDE04.pdf.

Untermann, Richard K. and Anne Vernez Moudon, "Designing Pedestrian-Friendly Commercial Streets," *Urban Design and Preservation Quarterly*, Vol. 13, No. 3 (Fall 1990), 7-10.

Urban Land Institute, "Thirteen Perspectives on Regulatory Simplification," Research Report No. 29 (Washington, DC: ULI, 1979).

———, *The Dimensions of Parking*, 3d ed. (Washington, DC: ULI, 1993).

Victoria Transport Policy Institute, *Online TDM Encyclopedia* (Victoria, BC: VTPI, 2002), available on-line at www.vtpi.org/tdm.

Vranicar, John, Welford Sanders, and David Mosena, *Streamlining Land Use Regulation: A Guidebook for Local Governments* (Chicago: American Planning Association, November 1980).

Washington State Department of Community, Trade, and Economic Development, *Working Together: A Guide to Intergovernmental Coordination Under the Growth Management Act* (Olympia: WSDCTED, 1992).

Washington State Department of Transportation, *CTR Task Force Guidelines* (Seattle: WSDT, 2002), available on-line at www.wsdot.wa.gov/tdm/tripreduction/CTRguide.

Weant, Robert A. and Herbert S. Levinson, *Parking* (Westport, CN: Eno Transportation Foundation, 1990).

Wentling, James W. and Lloyd W. Bookout, eds., *Density by Design* (Washington, DC: Urban Land Institute, 1988).

White, S. Mark, "Affordable Housing: Proactive and Reactive Planning Strategies," Planning Advisory Service Report No. 441 (Chicago: American Planning Association, December 1992).

———, "Adequate Public Facilities Ordinances and Transportation Management," Planning Advisory Service Report No. 465 (Chicago: American Planning Association, 1996).

———, "State and Federal Planning Legislation and Manufactured Housing," 28 *Urb. Law.* 263 (1996).

———, "The Zoning and Real Estate Implications of Transit-Oriented Development," National Research Council, Transportation Research Board, TCRP Report No. 12 (January 1999).

White, S. Mark and Dawn Jourdan, "Neotraditional Development: A Legal Analysis," 49 *Land Use L. & Zon. Dig.* 3 (August 1997).

Williams, Kristine M., "Neotraditional Town Planning," *Planning & Zoning News* (January 1991), 10-18.

Willson, Richard W., "Suburban Parking Requirements: A Tacit Policy for Automobile Use and Sprawl," *JAPA* 61 (1995), 29-56.

Winburn IV, William A., "The Development Realities of Traditional Town Design," *Urban Land* (August 1992), 20-21, 47.

Witheford, David K., *Zoning, Parking, and Traffic* (Westport: CN: Eno Foundation for Transportation, 1972).

Wood, Joseph S., "'Build, Therefore, Your Own World': The New England Village as Settlement Ideal," *Annals of the Association of American Geographers* 81(1) (1991), 32-50.

Zelinka, Al and Dean Brennan, *Safescape: Creating Safer, More Livable Communities Through Planning and Design* (Chicago: American Planning Association, 2001).

Ziegler, Jr., Edward H. et al., *Rathkopf's The Law of Zoning and Planning* (St. Paul, MN: West Group, 2004).

TECHNICAL WRITING

Bremer, Michael, "Untechnical writing: how to write about technical subjects and products so anyone can understand" (Concord, CA: UnTechnical Press, 1999) [KCPL 808.066/B83u; ISBN: 0966994906].

Nanney, Rodney C., "Is it Time for a New Zoning Ordinance," *Florida Planning* (December 2001), at 7.

Perry, Carol Rosenblum, "The fine art of technical writing: key points to help you think your way through writing scientific or technical publications, theses, term papers, & business reports" (Hillsboro, OR: Blue Heron Publishing, 1991) [KCPL 808.02/P46f; ISBN: 093608524X].

Rubens, Philip (gen. ed.), "Science and technical writing: a manual of style" (New York: H. Holt, 1992) [KCPL 808.066/S416; ISBN: 080501831X].

Sides, Charles H., "How to write & present technical information" (Phoenix: Oryx Press, 1999) [KCPL 808.066/S568h; ISBN: 1573561339].

Slatkin, Elizabeth, "How to write a manual" (Berkeley, CA: Ten Speed Press, 1991) [KCPL 808.066/S631h; ISBN: 0898154308].

About the Authors

ROBERT H. FREILICH

Robert H. Freilich is a partner in the law firm of Miller Barondess, LLP, Los Angeles, California, where he currently represents government entities, major developers, and investment firms on building new towns and master planned communities and land-use and takings litigation. Previously, he was the founder of Freilich, Leitner & Carlisle, Kansas City, Missouri. Dr. Freilich is at the forefront of zoning, subdivision, land-use litigation, the preparation of comprehensive and growth management plans, and development codes for state, county, and local governments. During his distinguished career, he has represented more than 250 cities, states, and counties from San Diego to Baltimore and Seattle-Tacoma to the Florida Keys, as well as private developers in master planned communities and joint public-private projects. He is a leading figure in the growth management and smart growth movements in the United States, having designed and argued the seminal case of *Golden v. Planning Board of the Town of Ramapo,* in the New York Court of Appeals and the United States Supreme Court, establishing the constitutionality of growth management in the U.S.

Dr. Freilich is the national editor of *The Urban Lawyer,* the national quarterly journal on state and local government of the American Bar Association; director of the Annual Planning and Zoning Institutes and past chair of the Advisory Board, Municipal Legal Studies Center of the American Center For National and International Law; past chair of the Planning and Law Division of the American Planning Association; a member of the Federalism Committee of the International Municipal Lawyers Association; a member of the Advisory Board of the Land Use and Environment Law Review; and a member of the American Institute of Certified Planners and the Urban Land Institute.

Dr. Freilich is a coauthor (with David L. Callies and Thomas E. Roberts) of the leading casebook in the field, *Cases and Materials on Land Use* (St. Paul, MN: West-Thomsen, American Casebook Series, 2004); *From Sprawl to Smart Growth: Successful Legal, Planning and Environmental Systems* (Chicago: American Bar Association, 1999); *The Model Subdivision Regulations; Planning and Law,* 2d ed. (with Shultz) (Chicago: American Planning Association, 1995); *After Lucas: Land Use Regulation and the Taking of Property Without Compensation* (Chicago: American Bar Association, 1995); and *Exactions, Impact Fees and Dedication: Shaping Land Use Development and the Funding of Infrastructure in the Dolan Era* (with David W. Bushek) (Chicago: American Bar Association, 1995).

Dr. Freilich received his A.B. degree from the University of Chicago, holds a Juris Doctor from Yale Law School, and M.I.A., LL.M., and J.S.D. degrees from Columbia University. In 1968, he became Hulen Professor of Law in Urban Affairs at the University of Missouri-Kansas City School of Law. He has served as Visiting Professor of Law at Harvard Law School (1984-1985), the London School of Economics (1974-1975), and the University of Miami School of Law (1996-1997).

S. MARK WHITE

Mark White is a partner with White & Smith, LLC, a national planning and law firm with offices in Kansas City, Missouri, and Baltimore-Washington. Mr. White is recognized as an expert in zoning and subdivision law, land-use and takings litigation, housing, development of comprehensive growth management plans, and implementation systems. He has represented clients at every level including city, state, and local governments, as well as major private developers, many of whom are involved in environmental permitting proceedings and takings litigation.

Mr. White received his Bachelor of Arts degree, magna cum laude, in history and political science, from Bethany College in Lindborg, Kansas, and holds a Juris Doctor and Master of Regional Planning from the University of North Carolina at Chapel Hill. While in law school, Mr. White was a research editor for the *North Carolina Journal of International Law and Commercial Regulation,* and worked at the Department of City and Regional Planning as a research assistant in the Center of Urban and Regional Studies.

Mr. White is a former president of the board of directors of the nonprofit community development group, Westside Housing Organization, and is a member of the North Carolina and Missouri Bars, the American Institute of Certified Planners, and the American Planning Association. In addition, he has published a variety of notable articles, including "Unified Development Codes," *Municipal Lawyer* (Washington, DC: International Municipal Lawyer Association, August 2006); "Classifying and Defining Uses and Building Forms: Land-Use Coding for Zoning Regulations" (*Zoning News,* September 2005); "Adequate Public Facilities Ordinances and Transportation Management," Planning Advisory Service Report Number 465 (Chicago: American Planning Association, August 1996); "State and Federal Planning Legislation and Manufactured Housing: New Opportunities for Affordable, Single-Family Shelter" (*Urb. Law.* 28: 263 (1996); "The Interaction of Land Use Planning and Transportation Management: Lessons from the American Experience" (with Robert H. Freilich) (Amsterdam, the Netherlands: Elsevier, *Transport Policy,* Vol. 1, Issue 2, 1994), 101-115; and "Affordable Housing: Proactive and Reactive Planning Strategies," Planning Advisory Service Report Number 441 (Chicago: American Planning Association, December 1992).

Mr. White was a reviewer or contributor for the following publications: *Planning and Urban Design Standards* (Chicago: American Planning Association, 2006); Congress for the New Urbanism, "Codifying the New Urbanism," Planning Advisory Service Report Number 526 (Chicago: American Planning Association, 2004); and Susan Handy, Robert G. Paterson, and Kent Butler, "Planning for Street Connectivity: Getting from Here to There," Planning Advisory Service Report Number 515 (Chicago: American Planning Association, 2003).

Mr. White is also a frequent speaker at the national meetings of the American Planning Association, the Southwestern Legal Foundation, and various other professional organizations.

Mr. White's emphasis is on the development and drafting of effective land development regulations for local governments, including facilitation, code drafting, form-based codes, and smart growth strategies. Representative clients include San Antonio, Texas; Frederick, Maryland; Prince Georges County, Maryland; Metro Council (Minneapolis-St. Paul); Chapel Hill, North Carolina; Hillsborough County (Tampa), Florida; Charlotte-Mecklenburg County, North Carolina; St. Petersburg, Florida; Suffolk, Virginia; Roanoke, Virginia; Nashua, New Hampshire; Albuquerque-Bernalillo County, New Mexico; Summit County, Utah; and San Diego, California.